America's Fastest Growing Jobs

Details on the Best Jobs at All Levels of Education and Training

Fifth Edition

J. Michael Farr

rica's Fastest Growing Jobs

Best Jobs at All Levels of Education and Training
Fifth Edition

© 1999 by JIST Works, Inc.

Some other books by J. Michael Farr:

- *The Very Quick Job Search*
- *America's Top Resumes for America's Top Jobs®*
- *The Quick Resume & Cover Letter Book*
- *How to Get a Job Now!*
- *The Quick Interview & Salary Negotiation Book*
- *Getting the Job You Really Want*

Other books in the America's Top Jobs® series:

- *America's Top Jobs® for College Graduates*
- *America's Top Federal Jobs*
- *America's Top Medical, Education & Human Services Jobs*
- *America's Top Military Careers*
- *America's Top Office, Management, Sales & Professional Jobs*
- *America's Top Jobs® for People Without a Four-Year Degree*
- *America's Top 300 Jobs*
- *Career Guide to America's Top Industries*

Several pages at the back of this book present some of our many career-related products. Please look there for additional resource materials and for ordering information.

These and other books from JIST can be ordered from your bo   e or distributor.

Cover design by Michael Nolan

Published by JIST Works, Inc.
720 N. Park Avenue
Indianapolis, IN 46202-3490
Phone: 317-264-3720   Fax: 317-264-3709   E-mail: jistworks@aol.com
World Wide Web Address: http://www.jist.com

Printed in the United States of America
03 02 01 00 99   5 4 3 2 1

Preface

Relax, You Don't Have to Read This Whole Book! This is a big book, but you really don't need to read it all. I've organized it into easy-to-use sections so you can browse just the information you want. To get started, simply scan the Table of Contents, where you'll find brief explanations of the major sections plus a list of the jobs described in Section 1.

Who Should Use This Book?

This is more than just a book of job descriptions. It's tailor-made for people in a variety of situations:

- **Those exploring career options:** The descriptions in this book give a wealth of information on many of the most desirable jobs in the labor market.

- **Anyone considering more education or training:** The information here can help you avoid costly mistakes in choosing a career or additional training or education—and increase your chances of planning a bright future.

- **Job seekers:** This book will help you identify new job targets, prepare for interviews, and write targeted resumes. And the advice in Section 2 has been proven to cut job search time in half!

- **Counselors:** This is a valuable source of information on jobs and trends.

I've made some changes in this edition of *America's Fastest Growing Jobs;* other features I've kept from earlier editions. I think this is the best edition yet—of course. Here are the major features:

I simplified the introduction to encourage more people to actually read it. It is shorter now and makes for a quick and easy read.

I increased the number of job descriptions, from 101 in the last edition to 138 here. This book includes 114 jobs projected to have average or higher growth rates, *plus* the 100 jobs projected to create the largest number of openings. Since many jobs were on both lists, I ended up with 138 descriptions in Section 1.

Once again, I have included substantial advice on career planning and job seeking in Section 2.

The appendices have updated information on 500 major occupations and all major industries.

The bibliography of career and job search resources is a new feature I hope you will find useful. It includes Internet sites that provide information on careers and education.

The occupational descriptions come from the good people at the U.S. Department of Labor, as published in the most recent edition of the *Occupational Outlook Handbook*. The *OOH* is the best source of career information available anywhere, and the descriptions include the latest data on earnings and other details. Information in the appendices comes from a variety of other Department of Labor publications. The appendices contain some of the most accurate and up-to-date information on the market today.

I hope you learn some interesting things from this book.

Regards,

Mike Farr

Table of Contents

Summary of Major Sections

Introduction: This short introduction explains the job descriptions and gives tips on using the book for career exploration and job seeking. *Begins on page 1.*

Section One. The Job Descriptions: This is the major section of the book, with thorough descriptions of the 138 fastest growing jobs in the United States. Each description gives information on working conditions, skills required, projections for growth, training or education needed, typical earnings, and other information. *Begins on page 17.*

Section Two. Career Planning and Job Search Advice: This brief but powerful section gives results-oriented career planning and job search techniques, including tips on exploring career options, defining your ideal job, writing resumes, getting interviews, answering problem questions, surviving unemployment and much more. *Begins on page 321.*

Appendix A: Tomorrow's Jobs: Important Labor Market Trends Through the Year 2006. This article provides an excellent review of important trends in the labor market, including occupations and industries that are growing and declining, the fastest growing jobs, the importance of education, and fast-growth jobs with high pay. *Begins on page 353.*

Appendix B: Details on the Top 500 Jobs. This includes a brief overview of major trends and a chart with details on 500 major occupations—including data on earnings, employment growth, education required, unemployment rates, and more. *Begins on page 375.*

Appendix C: Employment Trends Within Major Industries. This introduction to trends in major industries will help you make good employment decisions. *Begins on page 407.*

Bibliography of Useful Career Resources and Internet Sites. Reviews hundreds of career-related books, software, and Internet sites. *Begins on page 417.*

Descriptions of America's Fastest Growing Jobs

Introduction

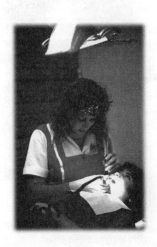

This book is about improving your life, not just choosing a job. The right kind of job has an enormous impact on your life.

Today's labor market is more competitive than ever, and earning good pay is not as easy as it once was. More training typically is required to get better jobs now–and good career planning and job seeking skills are essential for long-term career success.

This book will help. It describes the jobs with the highest projected growth rates, the highest earnings for different levels of education, and the highest number of openings. Tables in the following pages will help you identify these jobs.

Clearly, jobs that require more training or education pay off. For example, high school graduates working in jobs that require at least some training make an average of $7,500 more a year than those working in jobs requiring no training. That is a lot of money, and, over the years, the earnings difference will have a big impact on your lifestyle. Those with four-year college degrees earn, on average, substantially more than those without. But averages can be misleading. Some jobs (including self-employment) pay quite well, even for those without advanced degrees. This book will help you identify those jobs.

But money isn't everything. The time you spend planning your career can pay off in more than just higher earnings. Being satisfied with your work and with your life often is more important than how much you earn. This book will help you explore a variety of options to find the work best suited to you.

Should You Consider Only Rapidly Growing Jobs?

With major labor market changes projected for the coming years, it might seem wise to consider only those jobs that are growing most rapidly. Rapidly growing jobs often offer better-than-average opportunities for employment and job security. For this reason, you should certainly pay attention to jobs that are projected to grow rapidly. But there will always be some openings for new people even in slower-growing or declining jobs. Some of these slower-growing job fields are quite large and have many openings because people retire or leave the field.

So my advice to you is this: *Consider jobs that interest you*, even if they are not among the fastest growing ones. The more you know about your options, the better decisions you will make. In the appendices, you will find information on all major jobs in the U.S. labor market, including those that are growing slower than average or even declining. And Section 2 gives career planning and job search advice you should consider.

Four Important Labor Market Trends

Our economy has changed in dramatic ways, with profound effects on how we work and live. Here are four labor market trends you *must* consider in your career plans.

1. Education and Earnings Are Related

It should come as no surprise that people with higher levels of education and training have higher average earnings. The data that follow are from the Department of Labor's Bulletin #2502, published in February of 1998. It reflects a new way of measuring earnings based on the education or training typically required for employment. High school graduates with no technical training and high school dropouts typically hold jobs that require on-the-job training or experience. I used the earnings of these jobs to calculate the premium in earnings for those with additional education.

	Average Annual Earnings	Premium over High School Graduates
Professional degree	$55,111	166%
Ph.D.	$44,162	113%
Master's degree	$35,559	71%
Bachelor's degree plus experience	$40,982	98%
Bachelor's degree	$35,768	72%
Associate degree	$33,317	61%
On-the-job training or experience	$20,699	
Average for all workers	$25,183	

The average earnings difference between a college graduate and someone with a high school education is more than $15,000 a year—enough to buy a nice car, or even a month's vacation for two to Europe. Over a lifetime, this earnings difference has an enormous impact.

And what is more, jobs that require a four-year college degree are projected to grow about twice as fast as jobs that do not. Note, however, that many rapidly growing and good-paying jobs do not require a four-year college degree. Many of the jobs listed here don't require such a degree, but most of the better-paying jobs do require training beyond high school or substantial work experience.

2. Computer Knowledge Is Increasingly Important

As you look over the list (later in this introduction) of the most rapidly growing jobs, you will notice that many require computer or technical skills. Even jobs that don't appear to be "technical" now require computer literacy. Managers, for example, typically are expected to understand and use computer software for things like spreadsheets, word-processing, and databases. Most clerical workers cannot find employment without appropriate computer skills. Factory workers, auto mechanics, and many others need technical training to handle increasingly complex jobs. Those who do not have these skills often have a more difficult time finding good jobs.

3. Ongoing Education and Training Are Essential

It used to be that school and work were separate activities; most people did not go back to school once they began working. But with rapid changes in technology, most people must continue to learn throughout their work lives. Jobs are being continually upgraded, and many of today's jobs cannot be handled with skills learned only five years ago. What this means is that you should plan on upgrading your job skills throughout your working life. This may include taking formal courses, doing after-work reading, on-the-job training, and pursuing other forms of adult education. Continual upgrading of your work-related skills is no longer optional for most jobs, and you ignore it at your peril.

4. Good Career Planning Is Critical

Most people spend more time watching TV during the week than they spend on career planning in an entire year. Yet most people will change jobs many times during their work lives; today's workers are projected to make major career changes five to seven times.

The information on occupations in this book will help in your career planning. Section 2 has career planning and job seeking advice, and the appendices give information on major labor market trends. I urge you to read these and other career planning materials, because career planning and job seeking skills are adult survival skills in this new economy.

Section 1: The Job Descriptions

This is the main part of the book, offering brief descriptions for the 138 fastest growing jobs in the United States, at all different levels of education and earnings.

One way to explore your career options is to scan the Table of Contents and check the jobs that seem interesting. If you are interested in medical jobs, for example, go through the list and identify those you want to learn more about. You may see other jobs that look interesting as well, and you should consider them, too. Then read the descriptions for the jobs you checked and identify those that most interest you.

Later in the introduction you'll find several tables listing jobs in a variety of useful ways. For example, one lists all the jobs in this book by percentage of projected increase in employment. Another lists jobs with fast growth and high pay by levels of education and training. These tables also can help you identify jobs you want to explore in more detail.

The appendices also provide useful information. One lists 500 major jobs, grouped into clusters of similar jobs, and gives summary information on each. This is useful for identifying related jobs that might interest you. Other appendices present trends in major industries and occupational groups.

What Each Job Description Provides

Each job description presents similar information and uses a standard format. Most are only one to two pages long, and each is packed with useful information, including:

- **Job Title:** This is the job title used by the *Occupational Outlook Handbook*, a book published by the Department of Labor.

- ***Dictionary of Occupational Titles* Codes:** The numbers in parentheses that appear just below each job title are from the *Dictionary of Occupational Titles (D.O.T.)*, Fourth Edition, a U.S. Department of Labor publication. *D.O.T.* numbers are used by state employment service offices to classify applicants and job openings. They are included because some career information centers and libraries use them for filing occupational information. The Department of Labor has recently replaced the *D.O.T.* with the *O*NET*–the *Occupational Information Network*. JIST publishes *The O*NET Dictionary of Occupational Titles*™, which provides descriptions for each *O*NET* occupation as well as other information related to the new *O*NET* system. See the back pages of this book for additional details.

- **Significant Points:** This section provides highlights of key occupational characteristics for each job.

- **Nature of the Work:** Here you will find a variety of information including:
  - What workers do, the equipment they use, and how closely they are supervised
  - How the duties of workers vary by industry, establishment, and size of firm
  - How the responsibilities of entry-level workers differ from those of experienced, supervisory, or self-employed workers
  - How technological innovations are affecting what workers do and how they do it
  - Emerging specialties

- **Working Conditions:** This section describes typical working and environmental conditions for workers in that occupation, including:
  - Typical hours worked
  - The workplace environment
  - Susceptibility to injury, illness, and job-related stress
  - Necessary protective clothing and safety equipment
  - Physical activities required
  - Extent of travel required

- **Employment:** Here you will find information on who is working in the occupation and where they are employed, including:
  - The number of people working in the job
  - Key industries employing workers in the occupation
  - Geographic distribution of jobs
  - The proportion of part-time (fewer than 35 hours a week) and self-employed workers in the occupation

- **Training, Other Qualifications, and Advancement:** What kind of training will you need to perform a job? Where can you receive that training? What is the typical route of advancement? Those and other questions are answered here. This section includes information on:
  - Most significant sources of training, typical length of training, and training preferred by employers
  - Whether workers acquire skills through previous work experience, informal on-the-job training, formal training (including apprenticeships), the Armed Forces, home study, or hobbies and other activities
  - Formal educational requirements (high school, postsecondary vocational or technical training, college, or graduate or professional education)
  - Desirable skills, aptitudes, and personal characteristics
  - Certification, examination, or licensing required for entry into the field, advancement, or independent practice
  - Continuing education or skill improvement requirements
  - Advancement opportunities

- **Job Outlook:** Where will the occupation be in the future? This valuable section gives projections, including:
  - Forces that will result in growth or decline in the number of jobs
  - Relative number of job openings an occupation provides (Large occupations with high turnover rates generally provide the most job openings-reflecting the need to replace workers who transfer to other occupations or stop working.)
  - Degree of competition for jobs (Is there a surplus or shortage of job seekers compared to the number of openings? Do opportunities vary by industry, size of firm, or geographic location? Even in overcrowded fields, job openings exist, and good students or well-qualified individuals should not be deterred from undertaking training or seeking entry.)
  - Susceptibility to layoffs due to imports, slowdowns in economic activity, technological advancements, or budget cuts

- **Earnings:** Here's an issue that's on everyone's mind: How much money will you make? This section includes:
  - Typical earnings of workers in the occupation
  - How earnings vary with experience, location, and tenure
  - Whether workers are compensated through annual salaries, hourly wages, commissions, piece rates, tips, or bonuses
  - Earnings of wage and salary workers compared to self-employed persons
  - Benefits, including health insurance, pensions, paid vacation and sick leave, family leave, child care or elder care, employee assistance programs, summers off, sabbaticals, tuition for dependents, discounted airfare or merchandise, stock options, profit-sharing plans, savings plans, and expense accounts

- **Related Occupations:** This section can point you to other jobs involving similar aptitudes, interests, education, and training.

■ **Sources of Additional Information:** So you've found a job that looks interesting. How can you find out more? This section includes:

● Addresses for associations, government agencies, unions, and other organizations that provide useful occupational information. In some cases, toll-free phone numbers, Internet homepage addresses, fax numbers, and electronic mail addresses are included.

● Free or inexpensive publications offering more information, some of which are available in libraries, school career centers, and guidance offices.

Key Phrases Used in the Descriptions

The Department of Labor's Office of Employment Projections uses some key phrases to describe projected changes in employment and the relationship between the supply of and demand for workers in a particular occupation. But how do you interpret those phrases?

If the statement reads:	Employment is projected to:
Grow much faster than average	increase 36 percent or more
Grow faster than average	increase 21 to 35 percent
Grow about as fast as average	increase 10 to 20 percent
Grow more slowly than average or little or no change	decrease 0 to 9 percent
Decline	decrease 1 percent or more

If the statement reads:	Job openings compared to job seekers may be:
Very good to excellent opportunities	More numerous
Good or favorable opportunities	In rough balance
May face keen competition or can expect keen competition	Fewer

---

Section 2: Career Planning and Job Search Advice

I know that most people who read this book do so because they want to improve themselves or because they need to find a job. For the past 20 years, I have been interested in helping people find better jobs in less time. So I have included advice on career planning and job seeking in this book. Section 2 is short, but it gives you the basics you need to plan your career and reduce the time it takes to get a job.

Many people resist completing the activities in this section, but consider this: Often, it is not the best person who gets the job, but the best job seeker. Those who do their homework often get jobs over those with better credentials. People who have spent time planning their careers and who know how to conduct effective job searches have some distinct advantages over those who don't, including these:

1. **They get more interviews.** In fact, they get interviews for jobs that are never advertised.

2. **They do better in interviews.** They know how to present their skills and they can answer problem questions. This can mean the difference between getting a job offer or sitting at home.

So please spend some time reading Section 2 and completing the activities. It *can* make a difference.

The Appendices

The appendices provide some very helpful information. I encourage you to explore them—and to read those that interest you. All the content came from publications from the U.S. Department of Labor.

Appendix A reprints an article titled *Tomorrow's Jobs: Important Labor Market Trends Through the Year 2006,* which highlights many important trends in employment and includes information on the fastest growing jobs, jobs with high pay at various levels of education, and other details.

Appendix B gives growth projections on 500 jobs. It is not a fun read, I admit, but it lets you browse a list of jobs that cover about 90 percent of the workforce. This is a much bigger list of titles than I can cover in this book, and reviewing it might help you identify new and surprising possibilities. Information on these jobs is available from various sources listed at the end of Section 2.

Appendix C reviews trends within major industries. Often, you can use skills or training you already have in a variety of industries you may not have considered. This appendix provides a good review of major trends with an emphasis on helping you make good employment decisions. This information can help you seek jobs in industries that offer higher pay or that are growing fast.

The Bibliography

I've included a list of books and other resources on career planning, job seeking, and related topics. It includes many resources you can find in a library and on the Internet.

Keep in mind that this is simply a beginning in your search for information. What matters most is that you include elements of meaning and fun into your career and life plans. Otherwise, why bother?

Tips on Using the Job Descriptions

The information in this book came from government sources. It is the most up-to-date and accurate information of its kind available anywhere. The job descriptions in Section 1 are well-written and contain a lot of useful information. What follow are some tips for four groups of people who can best use this book.

Tips for Exploring Career, Education, or Training Alternatives

This book is an excellent resource for anyone exploring career, education, or training alternatives. Many people take career interest tests to identify their career options; this book can perform a similar function. If you do not have a good idea of what you want to do in your career—or if you are considering additional training or education but don't know what sort you should pursue—there are several ways this book can help.

Review the List of Jobs

First of all, trust yourself. Many studies indicate that your interests are your best guide to career options. Begin by looking over the list of occupations in the Table of Contents. If others will be using this book, please don't mark in it. Instead, make a photocopy of the Table of Contents, then check each job title that sounds interesting to you. Look at all the clusters, since you may identify job possibilities you have previously overlooked.

The next step is to read the job descriptions that most interest you. A quick review often will eliminate one or more of these jobs based on earnings, education required, or other considerations. Once you have identified the three or four jobs that are most interesting, research each one more thoroughly before making any important decisions.

Consider Additional Training or Education

Too often people pursue training or education without knowing much about the jobs related to that training. Reviewing the descriptions in this book is one way to learn more about an occupation before you enroll in an education or training program. If you are currently a student, the job descriptions can also help you decide on a major course of study or tell you about the jobs for which your studies are preparing you.

Don't eliminate a job that interests you too quickly. If a job requires more education or training than you have, there are many ways you can pursue the training you need.

Tips for Experienced Workers and Career Changers

If you have significant work experience, training, or education, don't abandon them too quickly. Many skills you have used in previous jobs or other settings can be used in related jobs. Many people have changed careers after finding that the skills they already have can be used in new careers.

This book can help you explore career options in several ways. First, carefully review descriptions for jobs you have held in the past. On a separate sheet of paper, write the words used in these descriptions to describe the skills needed in those jobs. Then do the same with the jobs that interest you now. You will quickly see skills used in previous jobs that are needed in the jobs that interest you for the future. These transferable skills can form the basis for your new career.

You can also identify skills you have developed or used in nonwork activities, such as leisure, hobbies, family responsibilities, volunteer work, school, military, and extracurricular activities.

You can even use the job descriptions if you want to stay with your current employer. For example, you may identify jobs within your organization that offer more rewarding work, higher pay, or other advantages. After reading the descriptions, you may find you can transfer to another job rather than leave the organization.

Tips for Job Seekers

The descriptions in this book can give you an edge in finding job openings and getting job offers. Here are some of the ways you can use the job descriptions in your job search:

1. **Identify related job targets.** If you are like most people, you are limiting your search to a small number of jobs you think you are qualified for. But this approach eliminates many jobs that you could do and could enjoy. You need to broaden your search to include more job possibilities.

   Go through the entire list of jobs in the Table of Contents and check any that require skills similar to those you have. Look over all the jobs; often, doing so will identify one or more job targets you have overlooked before.

   The job descriptions can also point out jobs that are related to those that interest you now but that have higher levels of responsibility or compensation. While you may not consider yourself qualified for such jobs now, you should think about seeking jobs that are above your previous levels but within your ability to handle.

   Most people are not aware of the specialized jobs that are related to their training or experience. This book lists only major job titles, but the descriptions include cross-references to more specialized jobs that are directly related. The *D.O.T.* numbers at the beginning of each description cross-reference to more than 7,000 job titles. You can find descriptions of these jobs in the *Dictionary of Occupational Titles* or in other materials that use the *D.O.T.* system.

   The appendices also give information on occupations and industries. Appendix B lists earnings, education required, projected growth, and other details for 500 major jobs.

2. **Prepare for an interview.** The job descriptions contain information that can help you prepare for interviews. Before an interview, you should carefully review the description for the job so you can emphasize your key skills. You should also review descriptions for jobs you have held in the past and identify skills that are needed in the new job.

3. **Negotiate pay.** The job descriptions will tell you what pay range to expect and give many other details about the job and trends that are affecting it. (Note that local pay and other details can differ substantially from the national averages provided here.)

Tips for Employers and Business People

Employers, human resource personnel, and other business people can use the information in this book in a variety of ways: You can use the job descriptions to write your company job descriptions, establish pay ranges, and set criteria for new employees. Reading the descriptions will also help you conduct effective interviews by creating a list of key skills needed by new hires.

Tips for Counselors, Instructors, and Other Career Specialists

The information in this book is widely used by career counselors, vocational rehabilitation professionals, instructors, program managers, and many others who want accurate and reliable career information.

Sources of Information Used in This Book

The best source of data on labor market trends is the U.S. Department of Labor; their information is as reliable as it gets. The information in this book on career planning and job search is mine, although it has been influenced by many people over the years.

One thing to note is that the data in this book was collected and reported at different times. I have included some very recent data (the job descriptions, for example, were first available in 1998) and some based on earlier information. In all cases, I have tried to find the most recent information available and have included previously published data because of its value.

The Tables

One of the things I do in creating this book is research data on growth for major jobs in the labor market. All of this information is available from government sources, but often it needs to be reorganized. Doing this is an essential step in choosing the job descriptions for this book.

For example, Table 1 lists 111 jobs projected to have average or higher-than-average growth. But many occupations with lower growth rates will actually generate more job openings. Table 2 lists the 100 jobs projected to create the highest numbers of openings. As you will see, some jobs are listed in both tables, but the second includes many jobs that are not among the fastest growing. Descriptions for all jobs on these lists are included in Section 1.

You'll also find tables listing high-growth jobs listed by different levels of education and high-growth jobs with high earnings. You'll find descriptions for most of these jobs in Section 1 as well.

As you review the tables, check jobs that interest you. Then look them up in the Table of Contents and find their descriptions in Section 1; descriptions for most (but not all) will be included there.

Table 1. The 111 Fastest Growing Jobs

In Table 1 you will note that 6 of the 10 fastest growing jobs are in the medical area. The medical field is projected to continue to grow rapidly.

Note also that 9 of the 10 fastest growing jobs require technical training beyond high school. Only the occupation "Homemaker-home health aides" can be learned in a few months. While jobs opportunities at all levels of education and training are listed in Table 1, many of the better paying jobs require education or training beyond high school.

Table 1[1]

Occupation	Percentage Growth	Number Employed	New Openings
Computer scientists, computer engineers, and systems analysts	108	933,000	1,004,000
Physical therapy assistants and aides	79	84,000	66,000
Homemaker-home health aides	79	697,000	550,000
Medical assistants	74	225,000	166,000
Physical therapists	71	115,000	81,000

Occupation	Percentage Growth	Number Employed	New Openings
Occupational therapy assistants and aides	69	16,000	11,000
Paralegals	68	113,000	76,000
Occupational therapists	66	57,000	38,000
Special education teachers	59	407,000	241,000
Services sales representatives	57	694,000	39,300
Social and human services assistants	55	178,000	98,000
Speech-language pathologists and audiologists	51	87,000	44,000
Health information technicians	51	87,000	44,000
Dental hygienists	48	133,000	64,000
Physician assistants	47	64,000	30,000
Respiratory therapists	46	82,000	37,000
Emergency medical technicians	45	150,000	67,000
Engineering, science, and computer systems managers	45	343,000	155,000
Engineering, science, and computer systems managers	45	343,000	155,000
Dental assistants	38	202,000	77,000
Securities and financial services sales representatives	38	263,000	100,000
Teacher aides	38	981,000	370,000
Computer and office machine repairers	37	141,000	53,000
Flight attendants	35	132,000	46,000
Restaurant and food service managers	34	493,000	166,000
Musicians	33	274,000	92,000
Surgical technologists	32	49,000	15,000
Correctional officers	32	320,000	103,000
Social workers	32	585,000	188,000
Preschool teachers and child-care workers	32	1,172,000	379,000
Receptionists	30	1,074,000	318,000
Radiologic technologists	29	174,000	50,000
Electrical and electronics engineers	29	367,000	105,000
Marketing, advertising, and public relations managers	29	482,000	138,000
Dancers and choreographers	28	23,000	6,500
Library technicians	28	78,000	22,000
Loan officers and counselors	28	209,000	59,000
Visual artists	28	276,000	78,000
Health services managers	28	329,000	93,000
Chiropractors	27	44,000	12,000
Public relations specialists	27	110,000	30,000
Designers	26	342,000	89,000

Occupation	Percentage Growth	Number Employed	New Openings
Biological and medical scientists	25	118,000	29,000
Adjusters, investigators, and collectors	25	1,340,000	335,000
Electroneurodiagnostic technologists	24	6,500	1,500
Actors, directors, and producers	24	105,000	25,000
Travel agents	24	142,000	34,000
Nursing aides and psychiatric aides	24	1,415,000	342,000
Veterinarians	23	58,000	13,000
Water and wastewater treatment plant operators	23	98,000	23,000
Veterinary assistants and nonfarm animal caretakers	23	163,000	37,000
Counter and rental clerks	23	374,000	84,000
Computer programmers	23	568,000	129,000
Guards	23	955,000	221,000
Information clerks	23	1,591,000	366,000
Recreation workers	22	233,000	52,000
Adult education teachers	22	559,000	123,000
Landscape architects	21	17,000	3,500
Recreational therapists	21	38,000	8,000
Hotel and motel desk clerks	21	144,000	30,000
Management analysts and consultants	21	244,000	52,000
Writers and editors	21	286,000	61,000
Physicians	21	560,000	118,000
Licensed practical nurses	21	699,000	148,000
Registered nurses	21	1,971,000	411,000
Agricultural scientists	20	24,000	4,800
Architects	20	94,000	18,000
Bus drivers	20	592,000	117,000
Landscaping, groundskeeping, nursery, greenhouse, and lawn service occupations	20	925,000	180,000
Economists and marketing research analysts	19	51,000	9,400
Insulation workers	19	65,000	13,000
Counselors	19	175,000	33,000
College and university faculty	19	864,000	162,000
Clerical supervisors and managers	19	1,369,000	262,000
Dietitians and nutritionists	18	58,000	11,000
Private detectives and investigators	18	58,000	11,000
Chemists	18	91,000	17,000
Civil engineers	18	196,000	35,000
Construction managers	18	249,000	45,000
Human resources specialists and managers	18	544,000	97,000
Financial managers	18	800,000	146,000

Occupation	Percentage Growth	Number Employed	New Openings
General maintenance mechanics	18	1,362,000	246,000
Engineers	18	1,382,000	250,000
Foresters and conservation scientists	17	37,000	6,400
Photographers and camera operators	17	154,000	26,000
Heating, air-conditioning, and refrigeration technicians	17	256,000	44,000
Lawyers and judges	17	699,000	120,000
Cashiers	17	3,146,000	530,000
Chefs, cooks, and other kitchen workers	17	3,402,000	583,000
Property managers	16	271,000	44
Employment interviewers	16	87,000	14,000
Cost estimators	16	188,000	29,000
Mechanical engineers	16	228,000	36,000
School teachers— kindergarten, elementary, and secondary	16	3,053,000	483,000
Archivists and curators	15	20,000	2,900
Geologists and geophysicists	15	47,000	6,900
Broadcast technicians	15	46,000	6,900
Chemical engineers	15	49,000	7,400
Library assistants and bookmobile drivers	15	125,000	19,000
Clinical laboratory technologists and technicians	15	285,000	42,000
Painters and paperhangers	15	444,000	66,000
Truck drivers	15	3,050,000	442,000
General managers and top executives	15	3,210,000	467,000
Dispensing opticians	14	67,000	9,400
Construction and building inspectors	14	66,000	10,000
Brokerage clerks and statement clerks	14	102,000	14,000
Aircraft pilots	14	110,000	15,000
Industrial engineers	14	115,000	16,000
Bricklayers and stonemasons	14	142,000	19,000
Line installers and cable splicers	14	309,000	44,000
Manufacturers' and wholesale sales representatives	14	1,557,000	211,000
Handlers, equipment cleaners, helpers, and laborers	14	4,975,000	679,000

1. The occupations listed here are those in the current edition of the *Occupational Outlook Handbook*, published by the U.S. Department of Labor. Another DOL pub-

lication gives detailed growth projections, and I sorted this data by the percentage increase in employment growth projected for each of these jobs. Overall employment is projected to increase by 14% by the year 2006. I included all jobs projected to grow 14% or more.

These are the jobs projected to have average or above-average growth through the year 2006. The first column shows the projected increase in employment. The second shows how many people are currently employed in that job. And the third shows how many new positions are projected in that occupation by 2006.

Table 2. 100 Jobs Projected to Have the Most Openings

Occupations that employ large numbers of people, such as cashiers or retail sales workers, will generate large numbers of new openings, even though they are not growing rapidly. The 100 occupations in Table 2 are those projected to create the highest number of new openings. While many of the jobs in Table 2 are listed in Table 1, their "place" on the lists may be quite different.

More of the jobs in Table 2's top 10 do not require a college degree or technical training. Some of them also do not pay well, though several do. For example, some truck drivers and retail sales workers have above-average earnings. Two of the top 10 occupations in Table 2 are also among the top 10 occupations from Table 1: "computer scientists, computer engineers, and systems analysts" and "homemaker-home health aides." Section 1 gives descriptions for each of the occupations in Table 2.

Table 2²

Occupation	Percentage Growth	Number Employed	New Openings
Computer scientists, computer engineers, and systems analysts	1,004,000	933,000	108
Handlers, equipment cleaners, helpers, and laborers	679,000	4,975,000	14
Chefs, cooks, and other kitchen workers	583,000	3,402,000	17
Homemaker-home health aides	550,000	697,000	79
Cashiers	530,000	3,146,000	17
Food and beverage service workers	530,000	4,766,000	11
Retail sales workers	499,000	4,522,000	11
School teachers— kindergarten, elementary, and secondary	483,000	3,053,000	16
General managers and top executives	467,000	3,210,000	15
Truck drivers	442,000	3,050,000	15
Registered nurses	411,000	1,971,000	21
Preschool teachers and child-care workers	379,000	1,172,000	32
Teacher aides	370,000	981,000	38
Information clerks	366,000	1,591,000	23
Nursing aides and psychiatric aides	342,000	1,415,000	24

Occupation	Percentage Growth	Number Employed	New Openings
Adjusters, investigators, and collectors	335,000	1,340,000	25
Receptionists	318,000	1,074,000	30
Clerical supervisors and managers	262,000	1,369,000	19
Engineers	250,000	1,382,000	18
General maintenance mechanics	246,000	1,362,000	18
Special education teachers	241,000	407,000	59
Material recording, scheduling, dispatching, and distributing occupations	224,000	3,633,000	6
Guards	221,000	955,000	23
General office clerks	215,000	3,111,000	7
Manufacturers' and wholesale sales representatives	211,000	1,557,000	14
Social workers	188,000	585,000	32
Landscaping, grounds-keeping, nursery, greenhouse, and lawn service occupations	180,000	925,000	20
Medical assistants	166,000	225,000	74
Restaurant and food service managers	166,000	493,000	34
College and university faculty	162,000	864,000	19
Engineering, science, and computer systems managers	155,000	343,000	45
Licensed practical nurses	148,000	699,000	21
Financial managers	146,000	800,000	18
Marketing, advertising, and public relations managers	138,000	482,000	29
Janitors and cleaners and cleaning supervisors	135,000	3,242,000	4
Computer programmers	129,000	568,000	23
Accountants and auditors	125,000	1,002,000	12
Adult education teachers	123,000	559,000	22
Lawyers and judges	120,000	699,000	17
Physicians	118,000	560,000	21
Bus drivers	117,000	592,000	20
Material moving equipment operators	114,000	1,097,000	10
Electrical and electronics engineers	105,000	367,000	29
Correctional officers	103,000	320,000	32
Securities and financial services sales representatives	100,000	263,000	38

Occupation	Percentage Growth	Number Employed	New Openings
Social and human services assistants	98,000	178,000	55
Human resources specialists and managers	97,000	544,000	18
Automotive mechanics	96,000	775,000	12
Health services managers	93,000	329,000	28
Musicians	92,000	274,000	33
Police, detectives, and special agents	90,000	704,000	13
Designers	89,000	342,000	26
Counter and rental clerks	84,000	374,000	23
Traffic, shipping, and receiving clerks	83,000	759,000	11
Physical therapists	81,000	115,000	71
Visual artists	78,000	276,000	28
Dental assistants	77,000	202,000	38
Paralegals	76,000	113,000	68
Barbers and cosmetologists	72,000	701,000	10
Retail sales worker managers and supervisors	71,000	929,000	8
Engineering technicians	70,000	698,000	10
Emergency medical technicians	67,000	150,000	45
Physical therapy assistants and aides	66,000	84,000	79
Painters and paperhangers	66,000	444,000	15
Dental hygienists	64,000	133,000	48
Writers and editors	61,000	286,000	21
Carpenters	60,000	996,000	6
Loan officers and counselors	59,000	209,000	28
Billing clerks and billing machine operators	54,000	437,000	12
Stock clerks	54,000	1,844,000	3
Computer and office machine repairers	53,000	141,000	37
Recreation workers	52,000	233,000	22
Management analysts and consultants	52,000	244,000	21
Electricians	52,000	575,000	9
Metalworking and plastics-working machine operators	51,000	1,512,000	3
Radiologic technologists	50,000	174,000	29
Blue-collar worker supervisors	48,000	1,899,000	3
Flight attendants	46,000	132,000	35
Construction managers	45,000	249,000	18
Education administrators	45,000	386,000	12
Speech-language pathologists and audiologists	44,000	87,000	51

Occupation	Percentage Growth	Number Employed	New Openings
Health information technicians	44,000	87,000	51
Heating, air-conditioning, and refrigeration technicians	44,000	256,000	17
Line installers and cable splicers	44,000	309,000	14
Clinical laboratory technologists and technicians	42,000	285,000	15
Postal clerks and mail carriers	41,000	629,000	7
Services sales representatives	39,300	694,000	57
Occupational therapists	38,000	57,000	66
Respiratory therapists	37,000	82,000	46
Veterinary assistants and nonfarm animal caretakers	37,000	163,000	23
Mechanical engineers	36,000	228,000	16
Civil engineers	35,000	196,000	18
Travel agents	34,000	142,000	24
Counselors	33,000	175,000	19
Administrative services managers	33,000	291,000	11
Real estate agents, brokers, and appraisers	32,000	408,000	8
Electronic equipment repairers	32,000	386,000	8
Welders, cutters, and welding machine operators	32,000	453,000	7
Purchasers and buyers	32,000	639,000	5
Physician assistants	30,000	64,000	47

2. This table was constructed from the same source as Table 1.1 sorted the occupations by the number of new openings projected, from highest to lowest, then selected the top 100.

Table 3. Occupations That Are Rapidly Declining

While this book focuses on occupations that are growing, it's interesting to look at jobs that are declining. Table 3 lists 50 major occupations with the lowest rates of projected growth. Many of these jobs are being eliminated as the result of changes in technology: Drafters, secretaries, bank tellers, record clerks, and tool and die makers are a few examples. Others are declining because of changes in the culture (e.g., the reduced demand for private household workers), changes in regulations (e.g., telephone installers and repairers), foreign competition (e.g., shoe and leather workers and repairers), and other factors.

As in the past, demand for some jobs increases as the demand for others decreases. This constant change in the economy will continue. But even jobs that are declining will have new openings as workers leave the field for a variety of reasons. Those who look

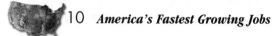

persistently will find opportunities for these jobs, though at lower levels than for more rapidly growing occupations.

Table 3

Occupation	Percentage Increase or Decline	Number (in Thousands)
Woodworking occupations	2	7,600
Drafters	2	7,000
Government chief executives and legislators	2	2,100
Funeral directors	2	700
Actuaries	2	300
Secretaries	1	25,000
Bank tellers	1	4,600
Precision assemblers	1	2,800
Loan clerks and credit authorizers, checkers, and clerks	1	3,400
Personnel clerks	1	1,800
Forestry and logging occupations	1	1,300
Dental laboratory technicians	1	300
Statisticians	1	100
Record clerks	0	16,000
Machinists and tool programmers	0	-1,600
Upholsterers	0	300
Air traffic controllers	0	0
Ophthalmic laboratory technicians	0	100
Surveyors and mapping scientists	-1	-1,400
Radio and television announcers and newscasters	-1	-300
Millwrights	-2	-1,700
Jewelers	-2	-500
Physicists and astronomers	-2	-300
Industrial production managers	-3	-5,200
Reservation and transportation ticket agents and travel clerks	-3	-4,500
Reporters and correspondents	-3	-1,900
Boilermakers	-3	-600
Inspectors, testers, and graders	-4	-24,000
Water transportation occupations	-4	-2,000
Bookkeeping, accounting, and auditing clerks	-5	-102,000
Rail transportation occupations	-5	-3,800
Payroll and time-keeping clerks	-6	-9,600
Stationary engineers	-6	-1,600
Typists, word processors, and data entry keyers	-7	-74,000
Tool and die makers	-7	-9,400
Vending machine servicers and repairers	-7	-1,300
Farmer and farm managers	-9	-118,000
Telephone operators	-9	-30,000
Mining engineers	-13	-400
Textile machinery operators	-14	-38,000
Petroleum engineers	-14	-1,900

Occupation	Percentage Increase or Decline	Number (in Thousands)
Private household workers	-15	-121,000
Apparel workers	-16	-133,000
Farm equipment mechanics	-16	-7,000
Prepress workers	-17	-27,000
Electronic home entertainment equipment repairers	-19	-6,200
Shoe and leather workers and repairers	-20	-4,300
Fishers, hunters, and trappers	-21	-9,600
Computer operators	-32	-94,000
Telephone installers and repairers	-74	-27,000

Table 4. Employment Growth and Earnings by Education[3]

Table 4 outlines the clear upward trend in earnings as education and training requirements increase. showing the percentage of the workforce who have the education or training at various levels as well as the projected increase in employment increases for each. The column presenting the number increase is in thousands of jobs.

Table 4[3]

	Percentage of the Workforce	Number (in Thousands)	Percentage Increase	Weekly Earnings
First professional degree	1.3	308	18	1,057
Doctoral degree	.8	193	19	847
Master's degree	1.0	206	15	682
Bachelor's degree or higher plus experience	7	1,597	17.8	786
Bachelor's degree	13.1	4,017	25.4	686
Associate degree	3.3	915	22.2	444
Work experience in a related occupation	7.4	1211	12.2	534
Long-term, on-the-job training	7.9	879	8	487
Moderate-term, on-the-job training	12.1	1368	8.7	434
Short-term, on-the-job training	40.2	7183	13.4	342
Totals	100	18,574	14	483

3. This information was published in the Department of Labor's *Monthly Labor Review*, (vol. 120, no. 11). It is based on 1996 employment figures and projections through the year 2006. These were the most recent figures available, since DOL data tends to lag two years.

Table 5. Occupations with the Highest Earnings

The 20 occupations with the highest earnings (shown in Table 5) all require at least a bachelor's degree. Many are in the engineering and health fields. Some of the jobs on this list are projected to decline in terms of numbers employed, although all are projected to have very low rates of unemployment.

Table 5

	Number Increase	Percentage Change
Systems analysts	519.6	103
Computer engineers	235.3	109
Marketing, advertising, and public relations managers	137.6	29
Lawyers	118.4	19
Physicians	117.5	21
Electrical and electronics engineers	104.8	29
Mechanical engineers	36	16
Pharmacists	21.6	13
Aircraft pilots and flight engineers	15.2	14
Dentists	13.2	8
Chiropractors	11.8	27
Chemical engineers	7.4	15
Optometrists	4.8	12
Aeronautical and astrological engineers	4.1	8
Judges, magistrates, and other judicial workers	1.7	2
Metallurgists and metallurgical, ceramic, and materials engineers	1.2	7
Podiatrists	1.2	10
Nuclear engineers	.7	5
Mining engineers, including mine safety engineers	-0.4	-13
Petroleum engineers	-1.9	-14

Table 6. Occupations with Fast Growth, High Earnings, and Low Unemployment

Of all the jobs with higher-than-average employment growth, above-average earnings, and below-average unemployment rates, the 25 listed in Table 6 have the largest number of projected openings. This combination of factors make these jobs among the most desirable. The jobs listed in Table 6 are projected to account for 27 percent of total job growth—and 18 require at least a bachelor's degree.

Table 6[4]

	Number of Openings (in Thousands)
Systems analysts	519.6
General managers and top executives	567.0
Registered nurses	410.8
Secondary school teachers	312.1
Clerical supervisors and managers	261.5
Computer database administrators, support specialists, and all other computer scientists	249.2
Maintenance repairers	245.8
Special education teachers	240.7
Computer engineers	235.3
Social workers	187.6
Food service and lodging managers	167.7
College and university faculty	162.3
Engineering, math, and natural scientists	155.1
Licensed practical nurses	148.4
Financial managers	146.4
Marketing, advertising, and public relations managers	137.6
Computer programmers	129.2
Instructors and coaches, sports and physical education	123.4
Lawyers	118.4
Physicians	117.5
Electrical and electronics engineers	104.8
Correction officers	103.3
Securities and financial services sales workers	99.6
Physical therapists	81.1
Artists and commercial artists	78.2

4. This information comes from the Department of Labor's *Occupational Outlook Quarterly* (vol. 41, no. 4).

Table 7. Best Opportunities for Self-Employment

Many occupations provide opportunities for self-employment. About 11 percent of all working people are self-employed, a sizable portion of the U.S. workforce. Table 7 lists occupations that meet some interesting criteria: Each is projected to have fast growth and low unemployment, and at least 20 percent of all workers in each are self-employed or family workers. While people are self-employed in all kinds of jobs, the biggest opportunities are in those fields requiring creativity, artistic ability, or design skills. All but one of the jobs in Table 7 typically require a bachelor's degree.

Table 7

	Projected Employment Growth
Food service and lodging managers	167.7
Lawyers	118.4
Securities and financial services sales workers	99.6
Artists and commercial artists	78.2
Designers, except interior designers	71.8
Writers and editors, including technical writers	60.7
Management analysts	51.7
Adult education instructors (nonvocational)	51.1
Property and real estate managers	44.3
Photographers	23.2

	Projected Employment Growth
Architects, except landscape and marine	18.5
Interior designers	17.3
Veterinarians and veterinarian inspectors	13.2
Chiropractors	11.8
Economists	9.4
Recreational therapists	8.0
Locksmiths and safe repairers	3.7
Landscape architects	3.5
Camera and photographic equipment repairers	4.4

Table 8. Jobs with Fast Growth, High Pay, and Low Unemployment, Organized by Education or Training Required[5]

Ask people what makes for a "good job," and many will list three criteria: faster-than-average projected employment growth, above-average earnings, and lower-than-average unemployment rates.

Relatively few occupations meet all three measures; the ones that do are arranged in Table 8 by the education or training typically required. Some jobs meet the criteria at all levels of education and training, although most require education or technical training beyond high school or significant on-the-job training.

Table 8[5]

First Professional Degree	
Lawyers and physicians account for more than 75% of all new jobs in this group.	
Lawyers	118.4
Physicians	117.5
Veterinarians and veterinary inspectors	13.1
Chiropractors	11.8

Doctoral Degree	
College and university faculty account for 84% of the projected job growth in this group.	
College and university faculty	162.3
Biological scientists	20.7
Medical scientists	8.8

Master's Degree	
Speech-language pathologists and audiologists	44.2
Counselors	20.7
Curators, archivists, museum technicians, and restorers	2.9

Work Experience Plus a Bachelor's Degree	
General managers and top executives account for 29 percent of the projected new jobs in this group. It is also projected to be the third largest of all occupations in numbers of new jobs created.	
General managers and top executives	467
Engineering, science, and computer systems managers	155.1
Financial managers	146.4
Marketing, advertising, and public relations managers	137.6
Artists and commercial artists	78.2
Management analysts	51.7
Personnel, training, and labor relations managers	38.4
Communication, transportation, and utilities operations managers	22.7

Bachelor's Degree	
A number of computer-related occupations are included in this list and are projected to be among the fastest growing of all.	
Systems analysts	519.6
Secondary school teachers	312.1
Computer database administrators, support specialists, and all other computer scientists	249.2
Special education teachers	240.7
Computer engineers	235.3
Social workers	187.6
Computer programmers	129.2
Electrical and electronics engineers	104.8
Securities and financial services sales workers	99.6
Physical therapists	81.1
Residential counselors	74.3
Designers, except interior designers	71.8
Writers and editors, including technical writers	60.7
Personnel, training, and labor relations specialists	58.8
Loan officers and counselors	58.7
Construction managers	44.9
Property and real estate managers	44.3
Clinical laboratory technologists and technicians	42.5
Occupational therapists	37.9
Mechanical engineers	36.0

Associate Degree	
Health occupations account for two-thirds of the projected job growth among occupations that require an associate degree. Much of this growth is due to the large increase in demand for registered nurses.	
Registered nurses	410.8
Paralegals	76.4
Dental hygienists	64
Radiologic technologists and technicians	50.3
Medical records technicians	44.5
Electrical and electronic technicians and technologists	43.1
Respiratory therapists	37.5

Postsecondary Vocational Training	
Only 4 of the 28 occupations typically requiring postsecondary vocational training meet the criteria here.	
Licensed practical nurses	148.4
Data processing equipment repairers	41.7
Aircraft mechanics	15.8
Broadcast technicians	6.9

Work Experience in a Related Occupation

Two occupations account for one-third of projected growth in these jobs: clerical supervisor and food service and lodging manager.

Clerical supervisors and managers	261.5
Food service and lodging managers	167.7
Vocational education teachers and instructors	71.6
Adult education instructors	51.1
Construction and building inspectors	9.6

Long-Term, on-the-Job Training (One Year or More)

Correction and police officers account for more than one-fifth of projected job growth in this group.

Correction officers	103.3
Police patrol officers	73.3
Flight attendants	46.3
Heat, air-conditioning, and refrigeration mechanics and installers	43.5
Telephone and cable TV line installers and repairers	41.0
Insurance adjusters, examiners, and investigators	38.0
Water and liquid waste treatment plant and system operators	22.8
Office machine and cash register servicers	11.0

Moderate-Term on-the-Job Training (1 to 12 Months)

Only 7 of the 119 jobs in this group are projected to grow faster than average and have above-average earnings and below-average unemployment rates.

Sports and physical education instructors and coaches	123.4
Insurance claims clerks	31.2
Photographers	23.2
Bicycle repairers	4.3
Locksmiths and safe repairers	3.7
Camera and photographic equipment repairers	3.4
Camera operators–television, motion picture, and video	2.9

Short-Term on-the-Job Training (One Month or Less)

Only four jobs in this group meet the criteria for this list. Since this group contains occupations that employ large numbers of people, the jobs listed here account for less than 5 percent of the new jobs projected for this group.

Maintenance repairers	245.8
Customer service representatives, utilities	54.9
Library technical assistants	21.8
Correspondence clerks	9.5

5. The numbers in column 2 refer to the projected number of openings in each occupation, in thousands.

Table 9. The 20 Fastest Growing Industries

Table 9 lists the 20 industries projected to have the highest growth rates through 2006. All are in the services sector rather than in manufacturing. While most people think about *occupations* in career planning, the *industry* in which you work can have a dramatic affect on your earnings and satisfaction. Appendix C provides additional information on trends in major industries, and I encourage you to read it.

Table 9

Industry	Percentage Growth Through 2006
Computer and data processing services	108
Home health care services	90
Automotive services, except repair	80
Water supply and sanitary services	66
Management and public relations	60
Residential care	59
Freight transportation arrangement	56
Personnel supply services	53
Individual and miscellaneous social services	50
Offices of physicians, including osteopaths	46
Medical service and health insurance	40
School buses	38
Public warehousing and storage	38
Nursing and personal care facilities	37
Security and commodity brokers and dealers	36
Producers, orchestras, and entertainers	35
Offices and clinics of dentists	34
Mortgage bankers and brokers	34
Motion picture production and distribution	33
Passenger transportation arrangement	30

Table 10. The 20 Fastest Growing Jobs Requiring a College Degree

Table 10 lists the fastest growing jobs typically requiring a four-year college degree. Note that some of these jobs (such as construction manager) can be held by a person without a four-year degree. But new entrants will find it difficult to obtain these jobs without a degree.

Table 10[6]

Computer engineers and scientists
Systems analysts
Physical therapists
Teachers, special education
Operations research analysts
Occupational therapists
Teachers, preschool and kindergarten
Speech-language pathologists and audiologists
Psychologists
Construction managers
Management analysts
Recreational therapists
Social workers
Recreation workers
Podiatrists
Teachers, secondary schools
Teachers and instructors, vocational education and training (see Adult education teachers)
Instructors and coaches, sports and physical training
Personnel training and labor relations specialists
Marketing, advertising, and public relations managers

6. The information in Table 10 came from a Department of Labor publication covering projections through 2005. I used this information in the previous edition

of this book, and, while there may be few changes in data to be released later this year, the trends tend to change slowly. Most rapidly growing occupations will remain that way, though their relative rate of growth may change. This table uses different job titles from those in other tables. In a few instances, I used the title most closely related to the titles in the other tables. The table also includes jobs that are not among the 250 listed in the *OOH*; and these descriptions are not included in Section 1 for this reason.

Table 11. The 20 Fastest Growing Jobs Requiring Some Postsecondary Training

Table 11 lists jobs that don't require a four-year college degree but do require formal training, education after high school, or substantial on-the-job experience. Some of these jobs pay well, so it's not entirely true that you have to have a four-year college degree to earn a higher-than-average salary.

Table 11[7]

Chefs, cooks, and other kitchen workers
Computer and office machine repairers
Dental hygienists
Electroneurodiagnostic technologists
Food service and lodging managers (see Food service
   managers and Hotel managers and assistants)
Insurance adjusters, examiners, and investigators
   (see Adjusters, investigators and collectors)
Legal secretaries (see Secretaries)
Licensed practical nurses
Medical assistants
Medical records technicians
Medical secretaries (see Secretaries)
Nuclear medicine technologists
Occupation therapy assistants and aides
Paralegals
Pharmacy assistants (no description provided,
   as it is not among the largest 250 occupations)
Physical and corrective therapy assistants and aides
   (see Physical therapy assistants and aids)
Producers, directors, actors, and entertainers
   (see Actors, directors, and producers)
Radiologic technologists and technicians
Respiratory therapists
Surgical technologists

7. See note 6 for Table 10.

Table 12. The 20 Fastest Growing Jobs Requiring High School Education or Less

Table 12 lists the fastest growing jobs that don't require education beyond high school. Some have very high projected growth rates and some (like detectives) pay fairly well, although those often require substantial on-the-job experience. You should also realize (should you be pondering this list for good jobs you can get without going to school) that high school grads often have to compete with those who have more education. For example, many detectives have college degrees, and college graduates often are given preference in hiring or promotion. I'm not saying you can't get ahead without an education, just that it is very competitive for some jobs if you don't have the best credentials.

Table 12[8]

Amusement and recreation attendants (no description provided,
   since this is not among the 250 largest occupations)
Baggage porters and bellhops (no description provided,
   since this is not among the 250 largest occupations)
Bakers, bread and pastry
   (see Chefs, cooks, and other kitchen workers)
Bicycle repairers (no description provided, since this is not
   among the 250 largest occupations)
Preschool teachers and child-care workers
Correctional officers
Detectives except public (see Private detectives and
   investigators and Police detectives and special agents)
Electronic pagination systems workers (no description provided,
   since this is not among the 250 largest occupations)
Flight attendants
Guards
Homemaker-home health aides
Human service workers
Laundry and dry-cleaning machine operators and tenders
   except pressing (no description provided, since this is not
   among the 250 largest occupations)
Manicurists (see Barbers and cosmetologists)
Nursery workers (no description provided, since this is not
   among the 250 largest occupations)
Nursing aides, orderlies, and attendants
   (see Nursing aides and psychiatric aides)
Paving, surfacing, and tamping equipment operators
Personal and home health care aides (see Private household
   workers and Homemaker-home health aides)
Subway and streetcar operators
   (see Rail transportation workers)
Travel agents

8. See note 6 for Table 10.

Table 13. High-Wage Jobs That Don't Require a College Degree

Table 13 lists occupations in which significant percentages of workers do not have college degrees and earnings average over $700 a week. New entrants into some of these jobs often are required to have a degree, but many now employed in these fields were hired before the requirements were standard.

Table 13[9]

	Percentage Not Having a Degree
Accountants and auditors	28
Administrators and officials, public administration (see Government chief executives and legislators)	42
Assemblers (see Precision assemblers)	96
Automobile mechanics	96
Bus, truck, and stationary engine mechanics (see Diesel mechanics)	98
Carpenters	93

	Percentage Not Having a Degree
Computer operators (see Computer and peripheral equipment operators)	82
Computer programmers	40
Computer scientists and system analysts	31
Correctional officers	91
Designers	53
Electrical and electronic engineers	26
Electrical and electronic equipment repairers, except telephone (see Electronic equipment repairers)	87
Electrical and electronic technicians (see Engineering technicians)	83
Electrical power installers and repairers (see Line installers and cable splicers)	96
Electricians	95
Engineering technicians	75
Financial managers	42
Fire-fighting occupations	90
Food service managers	78
Health technologists and technicians (various descriptions refer to this general category)	79
Industrial machinery repairers	96
Insurance sales occupations (see Insurance agents and brokers)	55
Investigators and adjusters, insurance and other (see Adjusters, investigators, and collectors)	75
Machine operators and tenders, except precision (see Metalworking and plastics-working machine operators)	96

	Percentage Not Having a Degree
Machinists and precision metalworking occupations (see Machinists and tool programmers)	96
Managers and administrators (many descriptions fall under this general category)	57
Manufacturers' and wholesale sales representatives	56
Marketing, advertising, and public relations managers	41
Personnel, training, and labor relations specialists and managers	47
Plumbers and pipefitters	96
Police and detectives	75
Postal clerk and mail carriers	89
Property and real estate managers	65
Purchasers and buyers	66
Rail transportation workers	??
Real estate agents, brokers, and appraisers	54
Registered nurses	51
Sales occupations, (various descriptions)	53
Secretaries	90
Stationary engineers and other plant and system operators	91
Supervisors, various occupations (such as police and fire fighting; mechanics and repairers; construction; production; administrative support; and sales)	??
Telephone installers and repairers	95
Truck drivers	96
Welders, cutters, and welding machine operators	98

9. See note 6 for Table 10.

Table 14. Earnings of Workers at Various Education Levels

The average earnings for all workers, at all levels of education, is about $25,000 a year. Those with four-year college degrees earn more, on average. But averages can be misleading, and some people with less than a four-year degree do quite well. Table 14 shows how much workers at various education levels earn, compared with the average for all workers and the average for those with four-year degrees. As you can see, many people without four-year degrees have relatively high earnings.

Table 14

Education Level	All Workers	College Graduates
Less than high school	19.4%	6.8%
High school	37	14.5

Occupational Group	Percentage Growth	High School	1 to 3 Years of College	4+ Years of College	Median Weekly Earnings
Executives, administrators and managers	26	25	27	48	652
Professional specialty	37	9	19	72	596
Technicians and related support	32	26	45	29	489
Marketing and sales	21	46	32	22	346
Administrative support and clerical	13	50	37	13	341

Occupational Group	Percentage Growth	Educational Attainment			Median Weekly Earnings
		High School	1 to 3 Years of College	4+ Years of College	
Service workers	33	68	26	6	232
Agriculture, forestry, fishing, and related	4	75	17	8	258
Precision production, craft, and repair	13	68	26	6	470
Operators, fabricators, and laborers	10	80	17	3	331
Averages	22	50	27	23	406

Occupational Group	Percentage Not Having a Degree	Number Employed (in Thousands)
Accountants and auditors	313	28
Administrators and officials, public administration	215	42
Assemblers	845	96
Automobile mechanics	480	96
Bus, truck, and stationary engine mechanics	274	98
Carpenters	606	93
Computer operators	367	82
Computer programmers	197	40
Computer system analysts and scientists	190	31
Correctional institution officers	261	91
Designers	154	53
Electrical and electronic engineers	121	26
Electrical and electronic equipment repairers, except telephone	271	87
Electrical and electronic technicians	212	83
Electrical power installers and repairers	101	96
Electricians	475	95
Financial managers	203	42
Fire-fighting occupations	155	90
Health technologists and technicians	808	79
Industrial, mechanical, and all other engineers	274	27
Industrial machinery repairers	487	96
Insurance sales occupations	200	55
Investigators and adjusters, insurance and other	673	75
Machine operators and tenders, except precision	3,667	96
Machinists and precision metalworkingoccupations	669	96
Mail carriers and postal clerks	513	89
Managers, marketing, advertising, and public relations	181	41
Managers, properties and real estate	201	65

Occupational Group	Percentage Not Having a Degree	Number Employed (in Thousands)
Managers, food service and lodging establishments	469	78
Managers and administrators not elsewhere classified	2,065	57
Other financial officers	249	43
Personnel, training, and labor relations specialists	164	47
Plumbers, pipefitters, and steamfitters	287	96
Police and detectives	353	75
Purchasing agents and buyers	260	66
Rail transportation occupations	95	94
Real estate sales occupations	168	54
Registered nurses	656	51
Sales occupations, other business services	190	53
Sales representatives, mining and manufacturing and wholesale	635	56
Science and engineering technicians	287	75
Secretaries	2,326	90
Stationary engineers and other plant and system operators	230	91
Supervisors, police and fire fighting	92	71
Supervisors, mechanics and repairers	181	89
Supervisors, construction occupations	419	88
Supervisors, production occupations	1,010	87
Supervisors, administrative support occupations	519	73
Supervisors and proprietors, sales occupations	1,658	72
Telephone and telephone line installers and repairers	211	95
Truck drivers	2,000	96
Welders and cutters	438	98
All other occupations	26,021	70

Section One

DESCRIPTIONS FOR THE FASTEST GROWING JOBS

This is the major section of this book. It contains descriptions for 138 major occupations, arranged in alphabetic order. Refer to the Table of Contents for a list of the jobs and the page numbers where their descriptions begin.

The introduction to this book provides additional information on what each description contains along with other details. If you are not the sort of person to read introductions, the descriptions in this section are easy to understand and well written, so feel free to jump right in and begin reading those that interest you.

A good way to identify job descriptions you want to explore is to use the Table of Contents as a checklist. If you are interested in technical jobs, for example, you can go through the list and quickly identify those you want to learn more about. If you look at all the titles, you will identify other jobs that "might" be interesting, and you should consider these as well. The Introduction to this book provides lists of jobs in a variety of ways that may interest you. For example, one list puts them in order of highest percentage growth, another lists jobs with high earnings, and another organizes jobs by education and training required.

Of course, there is more to selecting and learning about career options than simply reading job descriptions. For this reason, I suggest that you read Section Two, which provides advice on planning your career and on getting a good job.

The Appendices also provide lots of useful information to help you consider your options and to make good decisions. For example, the Appendix A article titled "Tomorrow's Jobs–Important Labor Market Trends Through the Year 2006" provides a list of rapidly growing jobs as well as trends in all major occupational groups. Other appendices provide information on industry growth, educational options, earnings, and other details on 500 major jobs and more. The Bibliography also provides lots of additional sources of information on career planning, education and training options, job seeking, using the Internet, and related topics.

When reading the descriptions, keep in mind that they present information that is the average for the country. Conditions in your area and with specific employers may be quite different than the average. For example, average pay may be higher or lower, and the same jobs are often in great demand in one location at the same time they are hard to obtain in another. People just entering a job will also typically earn considerably less than the "average" pay for a more experienced worker. These are just several examples of how the typical situation may not fit your own.

Accountants and Auditors

(D.O.T. 160 through .167-042, -054, .267-014)

Significant Points

✓ *Most jobs require at least a bachelor's degree in accounting or a related field.*

✓ *Professional recognition through certification or licensure, a master's degree, familiarity with accounting and auditing computer software, or specialized expertise provide an advantage in the job market.*

✓ *Competition will remain keen for the most prestigious jobs—those with major accounting and business firms.*

Nature of the Work

Accountants and auditors prepare, analyze, and verify financial reports and taxes, and monitor information systems that furnish this information to managers in business, industry, and government.

The major fields of accounting are public, management, and government accounting, and internal auditing. Public accountants have their own businesses or work for public accounting firms. They perform a broad range of accounting, auditing, tax, and consulting activities for their clients, who may be corporations, governments, nonprofit organizations, or individuals. Management accountants—also called industrial, corporate, or private accountants—record and analyze the financial information of the companies for which they work. Other responsibilities include budgeting, performance evaluation, cost management, and asset management. They are usually part of executive teams involved in strategic planning or new product development. Internal auditors verify the accuracy of their organization's records and check for mismanagement, waste, or fraud. Government accountants and auditors maintain and examine the records of government agencies, and audit private businesses and individuals whose activities are subject to government regulations or taxation.

Within each field, accountants often concentrate on one aspect of accounting. For example, many public accountants concentrate on tax matters, such as preparing individual income tax returns and advising companies of the tax advantages and disadvantages of certain business decisions. Others concentrate on consulting and offer advice on matters such as compensation or employee health care benefits; the design of accounting and data processing systems; and controls to safeguard assets. Some specialize in forensic accounting—investigating and interpreting bankruptcies and other complex financial transactions. Still others work primarily in auditing—examining a client's financial statements and reporting to investors and authorities that they have been prepared and reported correctly. However, accounting firms are performing less auditing relative to consulting services, which are more profitable.

Increasing numbers of accounting graduates are working in private corporations. Management accountants analyze and interpret the financial information corporate executives need to make sound business decisions. They also prepare financial reports for nonmanagement groups, including stockholders, creditors, regula-

tory agencies, and tax authorities. Within accounting departments, they may work in financial analysis, planning and budgeting, cost accounting, and other areas.

Internal auditing is increasingly important. As computer systems make information more timely, top management can base its decisions on actual data, rather than personal observation. Internal auditors examine and evaluate their firms' financial and information systems, management procedures, and internal controls to ensure that records are accurate and controls are adequate to protect against fraud and waste. They also review company operations—evaluating their efficiency, effectiveness, and compliance with corporate policies and procedures, laws, and government regulations. There are many types of highly specialized auditors, such as electronic data processing, environmental, engineering, legal, insurance premium, bank, and health care auditors.

Accountants employed by federal, state, and local governments see that revenues are received and expenditures are made in accordance with laws and regulations. Many persons with an accounting background work for the federal government as Internal Revenue Service agents or in financial management, financial institution examination, and budget analysis and administration.

Computers are widely used in accounting and auditing. With the aid of special software packages, accountants summarize transactions in standard formats for financial records, or organize data in special formats for financial analysis. These accounting packages greatly reduce the amount of tedious manual work associated with data and records; some packages require few specialized computer skills, while others require formal training. Personal and laptop computers enable accountants and auditors in all fields to use their clients' computer system and to extract information from large mainframe computers. Internal auditors may recommend controls for their organization's computer system to ensure the reliability of the system and the integrity of the data. A growing number of accountants and auditors have extensive computer skills and specialize in correcting problems with software or developing software to meet unique data needs.

Working Conditions

Accountants and auditors work in a normal office setting. Self-employed accountants may be able to do part of their work at home. Accountants and auditors employed by public accounting firms and government agencies may travel frequently to perform audits at clients' places of business, branches of their firm, or government facilities.

Most accountants and auditors generally work a standard 40-hour week, but many work longer, particularly if they are self-employed and free to take on the work of as many clients as they choose. Tax specialists often work long hours during the tax season.

Employment

Accountants and auditors held over a million jobs in 1996. They worked throughout private industry and government, but about one-third worked on salary for accounting, auditing, and bookkeeping firms, or were self-employed.

Many accountants and auditors were unlicensed management accountants, internal auditors, or government accountants and auditors. However, many are state-licensed Certified Public Accountants (CPAs), Public Accountants (PAs), Registered Public Accountants (RPAs), and Accounting Practitioners (APs).

Most accountants and auditors work in urban areas, in which public accounting firms and central or regional offices of businesses are concentrated.

Many individuals with backgrounds in accounting and auditing are full-time college and university faculty; others teach part time while working as self-employed accountants, or as salaried accountants for private industry or government.

Training, Other Qualifications, and Advancement

Most accountant and internal auditor positions require at least a bachelor's degree in accounting or a related field. Based on recommendations made by the American Institute of Certified Public Accountants, a small number of states currently require CPA candidates to complete 150 semester hours of college coursework–an additional 30 hours beyond the usual four-year bachelor's degree–and many more states are expected to introduce this requirement in the future. Most schools have altered their curricula accordingly, and prospective accounting majors should carefully research accounting curricula and the requirements for any states in which they hope to become licensed before enrolling. Some employers prefer applicants with a master's degree in accounting, or a master's degree in business administration with a concentration in accounting. Most employers also prefer applicants who are familiar with computers and their applications in accounting and internal auditing.

For beginning accounting and auditing positions in the federal government, four years of college (including 24 semester hours in accounting or auditing) or an equivalent combination of education and experience is required.

Previous experience in accounting or auditing can help an applicant get a job. Many colleges offer students an opportunity to gain experience through summer or part-time internship programs conducted by public accounting or business firms. Such training is advantageous in gaining permanent employment in the field.

Professional recognition through certification or licensure provides a distinct advantage in the job market. All CPAs must have a certificate and the partners in their firm must have a license issued by a state board of accountancy. The vast majority of states require CPA candidates to be college graduates, but a few states substitute a certain number of years of public accounting experience for the educational requirement. As indicated earlier, a growing number of states require 150 hours of coursework; the composition of the additional 30 hours is unspecified by most states.

All states use the four-part Uniform CPA Examination prepared by the American Institute of Certified Public Accountants. The two-day CPA examination is rigorous, and only about one-quarter of those who take it each year pass each part they attempt. Candidates are not required to pass all four parts at once, although most states require candidates to pass at least two parts for partial credit. Many states require all sections of the test to be passed within a certain period of time. Most states also require applicants for a CPA certificate to have some accounting experience.

The designations PA or RPA are also recognized by most states, and several states continue to issue these licenses. With the growth in the number of CPAs, however, the majority of states are phasing out non-CPA designations–PA, RPA, and AP–by not issuing any more

new licenses. Accountants who hold PA or RPA designations have similar legal rights, duties, and obligations as CPAs, but their qualifications for licensure are less stringent. The AP designation requires less formal training and covers a more limited scope of practice than the CPA.

Nearly all states require CPAs and other public accountants to complete a certain number of hours of continuing professional education before their licenses can be renewed. The professional associations representing accountants sponsor numerous courses, seminars, group study programs, and other forms of continuing education.

Professional societies bestow other forms of credentials on a voluntary basis. Voluntary certification can attest to professional competence in a specialized field of accounting and auditing. It can also certify that a recognized level of professional competence has been achieved by accountants and auditors who acquired some skills on the job, without the formal education or public accounting work experience needed to meet the rigorous standards required to take the CPA examination. Employers are increasingly seeking applicants with these credentials.

The Institute of Management Accountants (IMA) confers the Certified Management Accountant (CMA) designation upon applicants who complete a bachelor's degree, although a minimum score on specified graduate school entrance exams can be substituted for a bachelor's degree; pass a four-part examination; agree to meet continuing education requirements; comply with standards of professional conduct; and have at least two years' work in management accounting. The CMA program is administered through the Institute of Certified Management Accountants, an affiliate of the IMA.

The Institute of Internal Auditors confers the designation Certified Internal Auditor (CIA) to graduates from accredited colleges and universities who have completed two years' work in internal auditing, and who have passed a four-part examination. The Information Systems Audit and Control Association confers the designation Certified Information Systems Auditor (CISA) upon candidates who pass an examination, and who have five years of experience in auditing electronic data processing systems. However, auditing or data processing experience and college education may be substituted for up to three years. The Accreditation Council for Accountancy and Taxation, a satellite organization of the National Society of Public Accountants, confers three designations–Accredited in Accountancy (AA), Accredited Tax Advisor (ATA), and Accredited Tax Preparer (ATP). Candidates for the AA must pass an exam, while candidates for the ATA and ATP must complete the required coursework and pass an exam. Other organizations, such as the National Association of Certified Fraud Examiners and the Bank Administration Institute, confer specialized auditing designations. It is not uncommon for a practitioner to hold multiple licenses and designations. For instance, an internal auditor might be a CPA, CIA, and CISA.

Persons planning a career in accounting should have an aptitude for mathematics; be able to analyze, compare, and interpret facts and figures quickly; and make sound judgments based on this knowledge. They must be able to clearly communicate the results of their work, orally and in writing, to clients and management.

Accountants and auditors must be good at working with people as well as with business systems and computers. Accuracy and the ability to handle responsibility with limited supervision are important. Perhaps most important, because millions of financial statement users rely on their services, accountants and auditors should have high standards of integrity.

Capable accountants and auditors should advance rapidly; those having inadequate academic preparation may be assigned routine jobs and find promotion difficult. Many graduates of junior colleges and business and correspondence schools, as well as bookkeepers and accounting clerks who meet the education and experience requirements set by their employers, can obtain junior accounting positions and advance to more responsible positions by demonstrating their accounting skills on the job.

Beginning public accountants usually start by assisting with work for several clients. They may advance to positions with more responsibility in one or two years, and to senior positions within another few years. Those who excel may become supervisors, managers, partners, open their own public accounting firms, or transfer to executive positions in management accounting or internal auditing in private firms.

Beginning management accountants often start as cost accountants, junior internal auditors, or as trainees for other accounting positions. As they rise through the organization, they may advance to accounting manager, chief cost accountant, budget director, or manager of internal auditing. Some become controllers, treasurers, financial vice presidents, chief financial officers, or corporation presidents. Many senior corporation executives have a background in accounting, internal auditing, or finance.

There is a large degree of mobility among public accountants, management accountants, and internal auditors. Practitioners often shift into management accounting or internal auditing from public accounting, or between internal auditing and management accounting. However, it is less common for accountants and auditors to move from either management accounting or internal auditing into public accounting.

Job Outlook

Accountants and auditors who have earned professional recognition through certification or licensure should have the best job prospects. For example, CPAs should continue to enjoy a wide range of job opportunities, especially as more states enact the 150-hour requirement, making it more difficult to obtain this certification. Similarly, CMAs should be in demand as their management advice is increasingly sought. Applicants with a master's degree in accounting, or a master's degree in business administration with a concentration in accounting, may also have an advantage in the job market. Familiarity with accounting and auditing computer software, or expertise in specialized areas such as international business, specific industries, or current legislation, may also be helpful in landing certain accounting and auditing jobs. In addition, employers increasingly seek well rounded applicants with strong interpersonal and communication skills. Regardless of one's qualifications, however, competition will remain keen for the most prestigious jobs—those with major accounting and business firms.

Employment of accountants and auditors is expected to grow about as fast as the average for all occupations through the year 2006. The need to replace accountants and auditors who retire or transfer to other occupations will produce thousands of additional job openings annually, reflecting the large size of this occupation.

As the economy grows, the number of business establishments increases, requiring more accountants and auditors to set up their books, prepare their taxes, and provide management advice. As these businesses grow, the volume and complexity of information developed by accountants and auditors on costs, expenditures, and taxes will increase as well. More complex requirements for accountants and auditors also arise from changes in legislation related to taxes, financial reporting standards, business investments, mergers, and other financial matters. In addition, businesses will increasingly need quick, accurate, and individually tailored financial information due to the demands of growing international competition.

The changing role of accountants and auditors also will spur job growth. Accountants will perform less auditing work due to potential liability and relatively low profits, and less tax work due to growing competition from tax preparation firms, but they will offer more management and consulting services in response to market demand. Accountants will continue to take on a greater advisory role as they develop more sophisticated and flexible accounting systems, and focus more on analyzing operations rather than just providing financial data. Internal auditors will be increasingly needed to discover and eliminate waste and fraud.

Earnings

According to a salary survey conducted by the National Association of Colleges and Employers, bachelor's degree candidates in accounting received starting offers averaging $29,400 a year in 1996; master's degree candidates in accounting, $33,000.

According to a survey of workplaces in 160 metropolitan areas, accountants with limited experience had median earnings of $26,000 in 1995, with the middle half earning between $23,300 and $29,400. The most experienced accountants had median earnings of $87,400, with the middle half earning between $77,600 and $98,000. Public accountants—employed by public accounting firms—with limited experience had median earnings of $29,400, with the middle half earning between $28,200 and $32,000. The most experienced public accountants had median earnings of $48,700, with the middle half earning between $44,500 and $54,000. Many owners and partners of firms earned considerably more.

According to a salary survey conducted by Robert Half International, a staffing services firm specializing in accounting and finance, accountants and auditors with up to one year of experience earned between $25,000 and $39,400 in 1997. Those with one to three years of experience earned between $27,000 and $46,600. Senior accountants and auditors earned between $34,300 and $57,800; managers earned between $40,000 and $81,900; and directors of accounting and auditing earned between $54,800 and $109,800 a year. The variation in salaries reflects differences in size of firm, location, level of education, and professional credentials.

In the federal government, the starting annual salary for junior accountants and auditors was about $19,500 in 1997. Candidates who had a superior academic record might start at $24,200, while applicants with a master's degree or two years of professional experience might begin at $29,600. Beginning salaries were slightly higher in selected areas where the prevailing local pay level was higher. Accountants employed by the federal government in nonsupervisory,

supervisory, and managerial positions averaged about $54,000 a year in 1997; auditors averaged $57,900.

Related Occupations

Accountants and auditors design internal control systems and analyze financial data. Others for whom training in accounting is invaluable include appraisers, budget officers, loan officers, financial analysts and managers, bank officers, actuaries, underwriters, tax collectors and revenue agents, FBI special agents, securities sales representatives, and purchasing agents.

Sources of Additional Information

Information about careers in certified public accounting and about CPA standards and examinations may be obtained from:

- ❏ American Institute of Certified Public Accountants, Harborside Financial Center, 201 Plaza III, Jersey City, NJ 07311-3881. Homepage: http://www.aicpa.org

Information on careers in management accounting and the CMA designation may be obtained from:

- ❏ Institute of Management Accountants, 10 Paragon Dr., Montvale, NJ. Homepage: http://www.imanet.org

Information on the Accredited in Accountancy/Accredited Business Accountant, Accredited Tax Advisor, or Accredited Tax Preparer designations may be obtained from:

- ❏ National Society of Accountants and the Accreditation Council for Accountancy and Taxation, 1010 North Fairfax St., Alexandria, VA 22314. Homepage: http://www.nspa.org

Information on careers in internal auditing and the CIA designation may be obtained from:

- ❏ The Institute of Internal Auditors, 249 Maitland Ave., Altamonte Springs, FL 32701-4201. Homepage: http://www.theiia.org

Information on careers in information systems auditing and the CISA designation may be obtained from:

- ❏ The Information Systems Audit and Control Association, 3701 Algonquin Rd., Suite 1010, Rolling Meadows, IL 60008. Homepage: http://www.isaca.org

For information on accredited programs in accounting and business, contact:

- ❏ American Assembly of Collegiate Schools of Business, 605 Old Ballas Rd., Suite 220, St. Louis, MO 63141. Homepage: http://www.aacsb.edu

Actors, Directors, and Producers

(D.O.T. 139.167; 150 except .027-014; 159.041, .044, .047, .067, .117, .167-010 through -022, .267, .341, .344-010, -014, .347 except -010, .367, .647 except -018; 184.117-010, .162, .167-014, -022, -034; 187.167-174, -178, -182; 961.364, .667-014; 962.162-010, .167-014)

Significant Points

- ✓ *Aspiring actors face frequent rejections when auditioning for work and long periods of unemployment between jobs; competition for roles is extremely keen because the glamour associated with this profession attracts large numbers of individuals.*

- ✓ *While formal training is helpful, experience and talent are more critical for success.*

Nature of the Work

Actors, directors, and producers include stage and screen actors; narrators; magicians; clowns; comedians; impersonators; acrobats; jugglers; equestrians; amusement park entertainers; stunt, rodeo, and aquatic performers; casting, stage, news, sports, and public service directors; production, stage, and artist and repertoire managers; and producers and their assistants. This statement focuses on actors, directors, and producers.

Actors, directors, and producers express ideas and create images, based on a script, in theaters, film, television, and radio. They make the words come alive for their audiences.

Actors entertain and communicate with people through their interpretation of dramatic roles. However, only a few actors ever achieve recognition as stars–whether on stage, in motion pictures, or on television. A somewhat larger number are well-known, experienced performers, who frequently are cast in supporting roles. Most actors struggle for a toehold in the profession and pick up parts wherever they can. Although actors often prefer a certain type of role, experience is so critical to success in this field that even established actors continue to accept small roles, including commercials and product endorsements. Other actors work as extras, who have small parts with no lines to deliver; still others work for theater companies, teaching acting courses to the public.

Directors interpret plays or scripts. In addition, they audition and select cast members, conduct rehearsals, and direct the work of the cast and crew. Directors use their knowledge of acting, voice, and movement to achieve the best possible performance and usually approve the scenery, costumes, choreography, and music.

Producers are entrepreneurs. They select plays or scripts, arrange financing, and decide on the size and content of the production and its budget. They hire directors, principal members of the cast, and key production staff members, and negotiate contracts with artistic personnel, often in accordance with collective bargaining agreements. Producers also coordinate the activities of writers, directors, managers, and other personnel. Producers must have a working knowledge of new technologies as they relate to creating special effects.

Working Conditions

Acting demands patience and total commitment, because there are often rejections when auditioning for work and long periods of unemployment between jobs. Actors typically work long, irregular hours, sometimes under adverse weather conditions that may exist on location, and must travel when shows are on the road. Coupled with the heat of stage or studio lights and heavy costumes, these factors require stamina. Evening work is a regular part of a stage actor's life as several performances are often held on one day. Flawless performances require tedious memorizing of lines and repetitive rehearsals. On television, actors must deliver a good performance with very little preparation.

Actors working on Broadway productions often work long hours during rehearsals. However, once the show opens, they have more regular hours, working about 30 hours a week.

Directors and producers often work under stress as they try to meet schedules, stay within budgets, and resolve personnel problems while putting together a production. Directors must be aware of union rules and how they effect production schedules. For example, actors must be paid a minimum salary and can work no more than a set number of hours, depending on their contract.

Employment

In 1996, actors, directors, and producers held an average of about 105,000 jobs in motion pictures, stage plays, television, and radio. Many others were between jobs, so that the total number of people actually employed as actors, directors, and producers over the year was higher. In winter, most employment opportunities on stage are in New York and other large cities, many of which have established professional regional theaters. In summer, stock companies in suburban and resort areas also provide employment. Cruise lines and amusement parks also provide opportunities. In addition, many cities have small nonprofit professional companies such as "little theaters," repertory companies, and dinner theaters, which provide opportunities for local amateur talent as well as for professional entertainers. Normally, casts are selected in New York City for shows that go on the road.

Employment in motion pictures and films for television is centered in Hollywood and New York City. However, studios are also located in Florida, Seattle, and other parts of the country. In addition, many films are shot on location and may employ local professionals and nonprofessionals as day players and extras if the union contract allows. In television, opportunities are at the network entertainment centers in New York, Los Angeles, and Atlanta, and at local television stations around the country.

Training, Other Qualifications, and Advancement

For experience, aspiring actors and directors should take part in high school and college plays, or work with little theaters and other acting groups. Most actors and directors try to work their way up to major productions, although few succeed, due to the intense competition.

Formal dramatic training or acting experience is generally necessary, although some people enter the field without it. Most people take college courses in theater, arts, drama, and dramatic literature. Many experienced actors get additional formal training to learn new skills and improve old ones. Training can be obtained at dramatic arts schools in New York and Los Angeles, and at colleges and universities throughout the country offering bachelor's or higher degrees in dramatic and theater arts. College drama curriculums usually include courses in liberal arts, stage speech and movement, directing, play writing, play production, design, and history of the drama, as well as practical courses in acting.

The best way to start is to use local opportunities and build on them. Local and regional theater experience may help in obtaining work in New York or Los Angeles. Modeling experience may also be helpful. Actors need talent, creative ability, and training that will enable them to portray different characters. Training in singing and dancing is especially useful for stage work. Actors must have poise, stage presence, the capability to affect an audience, plus the ability to follow directions. Physical appearance is often a deciding factor in being selected for particular roles.

Many professional actors rely on agents or managers to find work, negotiate contracts, and plan their careers. Agents generally earn a percentage of an actor's contract. Other actors rely solely on attending open auditions for parts. Trade publications list the time,

date, and location of these auditions–referred to as "cattle calls" in this industry.

To become a movie extra, one must usually be listed by a casting agency, such as Central Casting, a no-fee agency that supplies all extras to the major movie studios in Hollywood. Applicants are accepted only when the number of persons of a particular type on the list–for example, athletic young women, old men, or small children–is below the foreseeable need. In recent years, only a very small proportion of the applicants have succeeded in being listed.

There are no specific training requirements for directors and producers. However, talent, experience, and business acumen are very important. Directors and producers come from different backgrounds. Actors, writers, film editors, and business managers often enter these fields. Producers often start in the industry working behind the scenes with successful directors. Additionally, formal training in directing and producing is available at some colleges and universities.

As actors', directors', and producers' reputations grow, they are able to work on larger productions or in more prestigious theaters. Actors may also advance to lead or specialized roles. A few actors move into acting-related jobs, as drama coaches or directors of stage, television, radio, or motion picture productions. Some teach drama in colleges and universities. Many actors find that they must take a second job to support themselves.

The length of a performer's working life depends largely on training, skill, versatility, and perseverance. Some actors, directors, and producers continue working throughout their lives; however, many leave the occupation after a short time because they cannot find enough work to make a living.

Job Outlook

The glamour of actor, director, and producer jobs attracts a large number of people; this supply of potential workers, coupled with the lack of formal entry requirements, will continue to produce keen competition for these jobs. Only the most talented will find regular employment.

Employment of actors, directors, and producers is expected to grow faster than the average for all occupations through the year 2006. Rising foreign demand for American productions, combined with a growing domestic market–fueled by the growth of cable television, satellite television, home movie rentals, and television syndications–should stimulate demand for actors and other production personnel. Growth of opportunities in recorded media should be accompanied by increasing jobs in live productions. Growing numbers of people who enjoy live theatrical entertainment for excitement and aesthetics will attend stage productions. Touring productions of Broadway plays and other large shows are providing new opportunities for actors and directors. However, employment may be somewhat affected by government funding for the arts–a decline in funding could dampen future employment growth. Workers leaving the field will continue to create most job openings.

Earnings

Minimum salaries, hours of work, and other conditions of employment are covered in collective bargaining agreements between producers of shows and unions representing workers in this field. The Actors' Equity Association represents stage actors; the Screen

Actors Guild and the Screen Extras Guild cover actors in motion pictures, including television, commercials, and films; and the American Federation of Television and Radio Artists (AFTRA) represents television and radio performers. Most stage directors belong to the Society of Stage Directors and Choreographers, and film and television directors belong to the Directors Guild of America. Of course, any actor or director may negotiate for a salary higher than the minimum.

According to Actors Equity Association, minimum weekly salary for actors in Broadway stage productions was $1,040 per week in 1997. Those in small "off-Broadway" theaters received minimums ranging from $400 to $625 a week, depending on the seating capacity of the theater. Smaller regional theaters pay $375 to $600 per week. For shows on the road, actors receive about $100 per day more for living expenses. However, less than 15 percent of dues-paying members work during any given week. In 1996, less than half worked on a stage production. Average earnings for those able to find employment were $13,700 in 1996.

According to the Screen Actors Guild, motion picture and television actors with speaking parts earned a minimum daily rate of $559, or $1,942 for a five-day week, in 1997. Actors also receive contributions to their health and pension plans and additional compensation for reruns and foreign telecasts.

Earnings from acting are low, because employment is so erratic. The Screen Actors Guild also reports that the average income its members earn from acting is less than $5,000 a year. Therefore, most actors must supplement their incomes by holding jobs in other fields.

Some well-known actors have salary rates well above the minimums, and the salaries of the few top stars are many times the figures cited, creating the false impression that all actors are highly paid.

Many actors who work more than a set number of weeks per year are covered by a union health, welfare, and pension fund, including hospitalization insurance, to which employers contribute. Under some employment conditions, Actors' Equity and AFTRA members have paid vacations and sick leave.

Earnings of stage directors vary greatly. According to the Society of Stage Directors and Choreographers, summer theaters offer compensation, including "royalties" (based on the number of performances), usually ranging from $2,500 to $8,000 for a three- to four-week run of a production. Directing a production at a dinner theater will usually pay less than a summer theater but has more potential for royalties. Regional theaters may hire directors for longer periods of time, increasing compensation accordingly. The highest paid directors work on Broadway productions, typically earning $80,000 plus royalties.

Producers seldom get a set fee; instead, they get a percentage of a show's earnings or ticket sales.

Related Occupations

People who work in occupations requiring acting skills include dancers, choreographers, disc jockeys, drama teachers or coaches, and radio and television announcers. Others working in occupations related to acting are playwrights, scriptwriters, stage managers, costume designers, makeup artists, hair stylists, lighting designers, and set designers. Workers in occupations involved with the business aspects of theater productions include managing directors, company managers, booking managers, publicists, and agents for actors, directors, and playwrights.

Sources of Additional Information

Information about opportunities in regional theaters may be obtained from:

❏ Theatre Communications Group, Inc., 355 Lexington Ave., New York, NY 10017.

A directory of theatrical programs may be purchased from:

❏ National Association of Schools of Theater, 11250 Roger Bacon Dr., Suite 21, Reston, VA 22090.

For general information on actors, directors, and producers, contact:

❏ Screen Actors Guild, 5757 Wilshire Blvd., Los Angeles CA 90036-3600.

❏ Association of Independent Video and Filmmakers, 304 Hudson Street, 6th Floor, New York, NY 10013.

❏ American Federation of Television and Radio Artists–Screen Actors Guild, 4340 East-West Hwy., Suite 204, Bethesda, MD 20814-4411.

Adjusters, Investigators, and Collectors

(D.O.T. 168.267-014 and -038; 191.167-022; 195.267-010; 203.382-014; 205.367-018, -034 and -046; 209.382-014 and .687-018; 219.362-042, and -050, .367-014, and .482-014; 241.217, .267-014, -018, -030, and -034, .357, .362, .367-010, -014, -022, and -034, and .387; and 249.367-030)

Significant Points

✓ *A high school education is sufficient to qualify for most positions, but a bachelor's degree is preferred for most claim representative positions.*

✓ *Projected employment change varies widely by occupation—for example, adjustment clerks are expected to grow much faster than average as businesses emphasize good customer relations, while policy processing clerks decline as their duties are increasingly computerized and assumed by other workers.*

Nature of the Work

Organizations must deal smoothly and efficiently with a variety of problems to maintain good relations with their customers. Handling complaints, interpreting and explaining policies or regulations, resolving billing disputes, collecting delinquent accounts, and determining eligibility for governmental assistance are just a few examples. Organizations like insurance companies, department stores, banks, and government social services agencies employ adjusters, investigators, and collectors to act as intermediaries with the public in these situations. The following is a discussion of occupations that comprise this group of workers.

Claim Representatives. Claim representatives at insurance companies investigate claims, negotiate settlements, and authorize payments to claimants. When a policyholder files a claim for damage or a loss, the claim adjuster, claim examiner, or claim investigator must initially determine whether the customer's insurance policy covers the loss and the amount of the loss covered.

Minor claims filed by automobile or homeowner policyholders are frequently handled by "inside adjusters" or "telephone adjusters." These workers contact claimants by telephone or by mail to get information on repair costs, medical expenses, or other details the company requires. Many companies centralize this operation in a drive-in claims center, where the cost of repair is determined and a check is issued immediately.

More complex cases are referred to an "independent adjuster" or "insurance company adjuster." Claim adjusters plan and schedule the work required to process a claim. They investigate claims by interviewing the claimant and witnesses, consulting police and hospital records, and inspecting property damage to determine the extent of the company's liability. They make photographs, take written or taped statements, and maintain computer files of information obtained from witnesses, and then prepare reports of their findings. When the policyholder's claim is legitimate, the claim adjuster negotiates with the claimant and settles the claim. When claims are contested, adjusters may testify in court.

Some adjusters work with multiple lines of insurance. Others specialize in claims associated with fire damage, marine loss, automotive damage, product liability, or workers' compensation. Material damage adjusters inspect automobile damage and use the latest computerized estimating equipment to prepare estimates of the damage.

In life and health insurance companies, the counterpart of the claim adjuster is the claim examiner. In property and casualty insurance companies, the claim examiner may supervise claim adjusters. In both cases, they investigate questionable claims or authorize payment for those exceeding a designated amount. Larger claims are referred to senior examiners. Examiners may check claim applications for completeness and accuracy, interview medical specialists, consult policy files to verify information on a claim, or calculate benefit payments. They also maintain records of settled claims and prepare reports to be submitted to their company's data processing department.

Claim representatives are making greater use of computers to keep records of clients and actions taken in various claims. Most have computer terminals on their desks, and many use portable laptop computers to enter or access information when they are on assignment outside the office.

Insurance Processing Clerks. Policy processing clerks use computers to process new insurance policies, modifications to existing policies, and claims. They begin the new policy process by reviewing the insurance application to ensure that all the questions have been answered. After an application has been reviewed by underwriters and the company determines that it will issue a policy, a policy processing clerk prepares the necessary forms and informs the insurance sales agent of an application's processing status. Policy processing clerks also update existing policies–such as a change in beneficiary, amount of coverage, or type of insurance–and recalculate premiums. They mail correspondence notices regarding changes to the sales agent and to the policyholder. Policy processing clerks maintain computer files for each policyholder, including policies that are to be reinstated or canceled.

Claim clerks, also called claim interviewers, obtain information from policyholders regarding claims. Claims may concern various types of loss, such as fire damage, personal injury, or an automobile accident. They prepare reports and review insurance claim forms and related documents for completeness. They call or write the insured or other party involved for missing information to update claim files. They may transmit routine claims for payment or advise the claim supervisor if further investigation is needed.

Like policy processing clerks, claim clerks use computers extensively in their work. Most spend a large part of their time creating and updating records at a personal computer or terminal.

Adjustment Clerks. Adjustment clerks investigate and resolve customers' complaints about merchandise, service, billing, or credit rating. They may work for banks, department stores, utility companies, and other large organizations selling products and services to the public. Sometimes they are referred to as customer service representatives, customer complaint clerks, or adjustment correspondents.

Adjustment clerks examine all pertinent information to determine if a customer's complaint is valid. In a department store, this may mean checking sales slips or warranties, as well as the merchandise in question. In a bank, it could mean reviewing records and videotapes of automated teller machine transactions. In a utility company, they review meter books, microfilm, computer printouts, and machine accounting records. Regardless of the setting, these clerks get information–in person, by telephone, or through written correspondence–from all parties involved.

After an investigation and evaluation of the facts, adjustment clerks report their findings, adjustments, and recommendations. These may include exchanging merchandise, refunding money, crediting customers' accounts, or adjusting customers' bills. Adjustment clerks ensure that the appropriate changes are set in motion and follow up on the recommendations to ensure customer satisfaction. To prevent similar complaints in the future, they may recommend to management improvements in product, packaging, shipping methods, service, or billing methods and procedures. Adjustment clerks keep records of all relevant matters, using them to prepare reports for their supervisors.

Adjustment clerks also respond to inquiries from customers. Clerks frequently can answer these inquiries with a form letter, but other times they must compose a letter themselves. Upon request, adjustment clerks issue duplicate or additional credit cards for banks and department stores.

Bill and Account Collectors. Bill and account collectors, sometimes called collection correspondents, are responsible for ensuring customers pay their overdue accounts. Some are employed by third-party collection agencies, while others, known as "in-house collectors," work directly for the original creditors, like department stores, hospitals, or banks.

Many companies automatically notify customers by mail if their account is overdue. When customers do not respond, collectors are called on to locate and notify them of the delinquent account, usually over the telephone, sometimes by letter. When customers move without leaving a forwarding address, collectors may check with the post office, telephone companies, credit bureaus, or former neighbors to obtain their new address. This is called "skip-tracing."

Once collectors find the debtor, they inform them of the overdue account and solicit payment. If necessary, they review the terms of the sale, service, or credit contract with the customer. Collectors may attempt to learn the cause of the delay in payment. Where feasible, they offer the customer advice and counsel on how to pay off the debts, such as by taking out a bill consolidation loan. However, the collector's objective is always to ensure that the customer first pays the debt in question.

If customers agree to pay, collectors note that for the record and check later to verify that the payment was indeed made. Collectors may have authority to grant an extension of time if customers ask for one. If customers fail to respond at all, collectors prepare a statement to that effect for the credit department of the establishment. In more extreme cases, collectors may initiate repossession proceedings or service disconnections, or hand the account over to an attorney for legal action.

Most collectors handle other administrative functions for the accounts assigned to them. This may include recording changes of addresses, and purging the records of the deceased. Bill and account collectors keep records of the amounts collected and the status of the accounts. Some fill out daily reports to keep their supervisors apprised of their progress. In some organizations, inside collectors receive payments and post the amounts to the customers' account. In most operations, however, the posting and receiving are done by other clerical workers. Collectors employed by collection agencies do not receive payments; rather, their primary responsibility is to get customers to pay their obligation.

Collectors use computers and a variety of automated systems to keep track of overdue accounts. Typically, collectors work at video display terminals that are linked to computers. In sophisticated predicted dialer systems, the computer dials the telephone automatically and the collector speaks only when a connection has been made. Such systems eliminate time spent calling busy or nonanswering numbers. Many collectors use regular telephones; some wear headsets like those used by telephone operators. Occasionally, supervisors may listen in on collectors' conversations with customers to evaluate their job performance.

Welfare Eligibility Workers and Interviewers. Welfare eligibility workers and interviewers—sometimes referred to as intake workers, eligibility determination workers, eligibility specialists, family investment counselors, or income maintenance specialists—determine who can receive welfare and other types of social assistance. They interview and investigate applicants and recipients; based on the personal and financial information they obtain and the rules and regulations of each program, they initiate procedures to grant, modify, deny, or terminate individuals' eligibility for various aid programs. This information is recorded and evaluated to determine the amounts of the grants.

Welfare eligibility workers and interviewers work with various public assistance programs. The best-known are Aid to Families with Dependent Children, Medicaid, Food Stamps, and the Work Incentive Program. Depending on local circumstances, there may be other programs, such as those for public housing, refugee assistance, and fuel assistance.

Many welfare eligibility workers and interviewers specialize in an area such as housing, but most are responsible for several areas. They may assist social workers by informing them of pertinent information they have gathered during their interviews with applicants. In some areas, particularly rural ones, eligibility workers may also perform other welfare duties.

These workers often provide information to applicants and current recipients. For example, they may explain and interpret eligibility rules and regulations or identify other resources available in the community for financial or social welfare assistance. More experienced workers may help train new workers. In addition, they may be assigned to special units whose responsibility is to detect fraud.

An increasing number of jurisdictions are using computers to increase worker productivity and to reduce the incidence of welfare fraud. In these settings, welfare eligibility workers and interviewers sit in front of computer terminals when they interview applicants and recipients. Welfare eligibility workers then enter the information provided. In the most advanced systems, the computer terminal prompts them with a variety of questions to ask during an interview.

Although these workers usually interview applicants and recipients who visit their offices, they may make occasional home visits, especially if the applicant or recipient is elderly or disabled. They may also check with employers or other references to verify answers and get further information.

The authority of welfare eligibility workers and interviewers varies from one jurisdiction to another. In some places, these workers are authorized to decide on an applicant's eligibility, subject to review by their supervisor. In other places, however, they can only make recommendations to their supervisors, who in turn make the ultimate decision.

Working Conditions

Most claim examiners have desk jobs that require no unusual physical activity. They typically work a standard five-day, 40-hour week. Claim examiners may work longer hours during peak periods or when quarterly and annual statements are prepared. Sometimes they travel to obtain information by personal interview.

Many claim adjusters work outside the office, visiting and inspecting damaged buildings, for example. Occasionally, experienced adjusters are away from home for days when they travel to the scene of a disaster—such as a tornado, hurricane, or flood—to work with local adjusters and government officials. Some adjusters are on emergency call in the case of such incidents. Material damage adjusters work at local claim centers where policyholders take their cars for estimates of damage.

Adjusters generally have the flexibility to arrange their work schedule to accommodate evening and weekend appointments with clients. Some report to the office every morning to get their assignments while others simply call from home and spend their days traveling to claim sites. This enables some adjusters to work independently.

Most insurance processing clerks work 40 hours a week in an office. Much of the work is routine and requires remaining at work stations for extended periods of time. Because most insurance information is stored in computers, many of these workers sit at video display terminals and enter or access information while the customer is on the phone. Because most companies provide 24-hour claim service to their policyholders, some claim clerks work evenings and weekends. Many claim clerks work part-time.

Adjustment clerks, bill and account collectors, and welfare eligibility workers and interviewers work in offices, usually during regular business hours. Some work part-time. Many bill and account collectors work as temporaries for collection agencies. From their offices, they deal with customers, clients, or applicants, either by telephone or in person. Dealing with upset or angry clients is often part of the daily routine in these jobs, making the work stressful at times.

Some welfare eligibility workers and interviewers may be hired on a seasonal basis to help administer a specific program. For example, some states hire these workers for the winter to help run emergency fuel-assistance programs.

Employment

Adjusters, investigators, and collectors held about 1.3 million jobs in 1996. The following tabulation shows the percent distribution of employment by detailed occupation in 1996.

Adjustment clerks	30
Bill and account collectors	20
Insurance policy processing clerks	14
Insurance adjusters, examiners, and investigators	12
Insurance claims clerks	9
Welfare eligibility workers and interviewers	8
Claims examiners, property and casualty insurance	4
All other adjusters and investigators	3

Insurance companies employ the vast majority of claim adjusters, examiners, investigators, property and casualty insurance claim examiners, policy processing clerks, and claim clerks. The remainder are employed by real estate firms and government agencies.

Nearly two out of ten adjustment clerks are employed by department stores, grocery stores, or catalog and mail order houses. Manufacturing firms, banks and other financial institutions, and telephone companies are other major employers of these workers.

About one in six bill and account collectors works for a credit reporting and collection agency. Many others work in banks, department stores, and other institutions that extend credit.

Around nine of every ten welfare eligibility workers and interviewers work for state or local government agencies. In many states, these workers are employed exclusively by the state government. In the remainder, they are employed by the county or municipal government. Most of those not employed by government work for private social service agencies.

Training, Other Qualifications, and Advancement

Training and entry requirements vary widely for adjuster, investigator, and collector jobs. A high school education is sufficient to qualify for most insurance processing clerk , adjustment clerk, and bill and account collector positions, while a bachelor's degree is preferred for most claim representative positions. While some college education is preferred for positions as adjuster or welfare eligibility worker or interviewer, many people qualify for these positions on the strength of related prior work experience. Because a significant and growing proportion of adjusters, investigators, and collectors use computers, word processing skills are recommended. Employers view experience with computers as an asset.

Claim Representatives. Most companies prefer to hire college graduates for claim representative positions. Entry-level workers may be hired without college course work if they have specialized experience. For example, people with knowledge of automobile mechan-

ics or body repair may qualify as material damage adjusters and those with extensive clerical experience might be hired as inside adjusters. Both adjusters and examiners should be observant and enjoy working with details.

No specific college major is recommended as the best preparation for these occupations. Although courses in insurance, economics, or other business subjects are helpful, a degree in almost any field is adequate. An adjuster who has a business or an accounting background might specialize in claims of financial loss due to strikes, breakdowns in equipment, or damage to merchandise. College training in engineering is helpful in adjusting industrial claims, such as damage from fires and other accidents. A legal background is most helpful to those handling workers' compensation and product liability cases. Knowledge of computer applications is extremely important.

Many states require adjusters to be licensed. Applicants usually must comply with one or more of the following: Pass a licensing examination covering the fundamentals of adjusting; complete an approved course in insurance or loss adjusting; furnish character references; be at least 20 or 21 years of age and a resident of the state; and file a surety bond.

Because they often work closely with claimants, witnesses, and other insurance professionals, claim representatives must be able to communicate effectively with others. Some companies require applicants to pass a battery of written aptitude tests designed to measure communication, analytical, and general mathematical skills. Examiners must understand federal and state insurance laws and regulations.

Some large insurance companies provide on-the-job training and home-study courses for entry-level claim adjusters and examiners. For example, material damage adjusters would learn about automobile body construction, analysis of collision data, and repair cost estimation, including computerized estimating equipment. They also learn how to deal with customers.

Workers may receive their training through courses offered by the Insurance Institute of America , a nonprofit organization offering educational programs and professional certification to persons in the property-liability insurance industry. The Insurance Institute of America offers an Associate in Claims designation upon successful completion of four essay examinations. Adjusters can prepare for the examination by independent home study or through company or public classes. The Institute also offers a certificate upon successful completion of the Introduction to Claims program and an examination.

The International Claim Association offers a program on life and health insurance claim administration. Completion of the six-examination program leads to the professional designation, Associate, Life and Health Claims.

The Life Office Management Association (LOMA) offers a comprehensive ten-course life and health insurance educational program that leads to the professional designation, Fellow, Life Management Institute (FLMI). LOMA also offers the Master Fellow Program that is designed specifically to meet the continuing education needs of life and health insurance professionals. Students can prepare for FLMI exams through independent home study or through insurance company or FLMI Society classes.

Beginning adjusters and examiners work on small claims under the supervision of an experienced worker. As they learn more about claim investigation and settlement, they are assigned larger, more complex claims. Trainees are promoted as they demonstrate competence in handling assignments and as they progress in their course work. Because of the complexity of insurance regulations and claim procedures, workers who lack formal academic training tend to advance more slowly than those with additional education. Employees who demonstrate competence in claim work or administrative skills may be promoted to department supervisor in a field office or to a managerial position in the home office. Other claim examiners are promoted to investigators, whose role is to detect fraud.

Insurance Processing Clerks. High school graduation is considered adequate preparation for most insurance processing clerk positions. Courses in typing and word processing, and business arithmetic are desirable. Employers view favorably previous office experience and familiarity with computers. Most new workers begin as file clerks and move into insurance processing positions as they demonstrate their ability. However, people with considerable clerical experience may begin processing insurance policies immediately.

A few experienced insurance processing clerks may be promoted to a clerical supervisor position. Advancement to a claim representative or an underwriting technician position is possible for clerks who demonstrate potential, have college course work, or have taken specialized courses in insurance. Many companies offer home-study courses for their employees so they can acquire the knowledge necessary to advance.

Adjustment Clerks. Many employers do not require any formal education for adjustment clerk positions. Instead, they look for people who can read and write well and who possess good communication and interpersonal skills. Word processing ability is also viewed favorably.

Adjustment clerk is an entry-level position in some, but not all, organizations. Depending on their assignment, new adjustment clerks may receive training on the job from a supervisor or an experienced coworker, or they may enter a formal training course offered by the organization. Training covers such topics as how to use computers, what standard forms to use, whom to contact in other departments of the organization, and how to deal with customers. Some employers provide more advanced training for experienced adjustment clerks. This training may be offered in-house or from trade associations or local colleges.

Bill and Account Collectors. While high school graduation sometimes is required by employers when they hire bill and account collectors, formal education beyond high school is not stressed. Previous work experience as a collector is particularly valuable. Experience in the field of telemarketing or as a telephone operator also is helpful, as is knowledge of the billing process. Employers seek individuals who speak well and who are persistent and detail-oriented.

Employers normally provide training to new bill and account collectors. This training, which may last up to a couple of months, is usually conducted in a classroom or on the job. Although not required by law, many employers also require their collectors to get certified through the American Collectors Association (ACA). ACA seminars concentrate on current state and federal compliance laws.

Since most states recognize these credentials, ACA-certified collectors have greater career mobility. In training seminars, employers use videotapes, computer programs, role-playing, and hands-on experience. Novice collectors learn about skip-tracing, billing procedures, and most importantly, communications and negotiating. Learning to use the firm's computer and telephone systems is also an integral part of their training.

Successful bill and account collectors may become supervisors. Some even start their own collection agencies.

Welfare Eligibility Workers and Interviewers. Hiring requirements for welfare eligibility workers and interviewers vary widely. Depending on the jurisdiction, applicants may need a high school diploma, associate degree, or bachelor's degree. Work experience in a closely related field–such as employment interviewing, social work, or insurance claims–may also qualify one for this job. In parts of the country with a high concentration of non-English speaking people, fluency in a foreign language may be an advantage.

Because they deal with people who are in difficult economic circumstances, welfare eligibility workers and interviewers should be compassionate and empathetic. Attention to detail is important because there are many procedures and regulations that must be observed.

After they are hired, eligibility workers are given training, sometimes in a formal classroom setting, other times in a more informal manner. They are taught the policies, procedures, and program regulations that they are expected to use to determine eligibility. If a formal training program is selected, it generally is followed by on-the-job training provided by the supervisor.

Advancement to the job of social worker is possible, although additional formal education, such as a bachelor's or master's degree, usually is needed.

Job Outlook

Overall employment of adjusters, investigators, and collectors is expected to grow faster than the average for all occupations over the 1996-2006 period. Most job openings, however, will result from the need to replace workers who transfer to other occupations or leave the labor force.

Growth rates will vary considerably by occupation. Employment of insurance claim examiners is expected to grow faster than the average as the increasing volume of insurance results in more insurance claims. As people accumulate assets and take on family responsibilities, the need for insurance–including life, health, home, and automobile–will increase. Also, new or expanding businesses will need protection for new plants and equipment and for insurance covering their employees' health and safety. Opportunities should be particularly good for claim representatives who specialize in complex business insurance such as marine cargo, workers' compensation, and product and pollution liability.

Employment of adjustment clerks is expected to grow much faster than average as business establishments place an increased emphasis on maintaining good customer relations. An important aspect of good customer service is resolving customers' complaints in a friendly and timely fashion. Because much of their work involves direct communication with customers, demand for adjustment clerks is expected to keep pace with growth in the number of customers.

Bill and account collector jobs also are expected to grow much faster than average as the level of consumer debt rises. As the economy expands, firms will strive to increase the efficiency of their debt collection to keep losses at a minimum. Contrary to the pattern in most occupations, employment of bill and account collectors tends to rise during recessions, reflecting the difficulty that many people have in meeting their financial obligations.

Overall employment of insurance claims and policy processing occupations is expected to grow about as fast as the average for all occupations. Within this group, employment of adjusters and claim clerks will increase faster than average because their work requires much interpersonal contact, which cannot be automated. However, employment of policy processing clerks will decline as their duties are increasingly computerized and assumed by other workers.

Employment of welfare eligibility workers and interviewers is expected to decline as many people move from welfare to work, and as state and local governments attempt to curb the growth in their expenditures for public assistance.

Earnings

Earnings of adjusters, investigators, and collectors vary significantly. For adjusters and investigators, the median weekly earnings in 1996 were $440. The middle 50 percent earned between about $340 and $590 a week. Adjusters are also furnished a company car or are reimbursed for use of their own vehicle for business purposes.

Specific information on earnings of insurance processing clerks is not available. However, median weekly earnings for records clerks, a category that includes policy processing clerks, were $390 in 1996. Interviewers, whose work is similar to that of claim clerks, also had median weekly earnings of $390.

Median weekly earnings of full-time bill and account collectors were $410 in 1996; the middle 50 percent earned between $330 and $510 a week. Ten percent earned less than $280 and 10 percent earned more than $660. Some bill and account collectors receive a base salary and work on commission beyond that.

Median weekly earnings of full-time welfare eligibility workers and interviewers were about $450 in 1996; the middle 50 percent earned between $360 and $590 a week. The lowest 10 percent earned less than $290 and the top 10 percent earned more than $670.

Welfare eligibility workers and interviewers are twice as likely to belong to unions than workers in all occupations. In 1996, about 26 percent of all welfare eligibility workers and interviewers were union members, compared to 13 for all occupations. The two principal unions representing these workers are the American Federation of State, County, and Municipal Employees, and the Service Employees International Union.

Related Occupations

Insurance adjusters and examiners investigate, analyze, and determine the validity of their firm's liability concerning personal, casualty, or property loss or damages, and settle with claimants. Workers in other occupations that require similar skills include cost estimators, budget analysts, and private investigators.

The work of insurance processing clerks and adjustment clerks is similar to that of other workers who compile, review, or maintain records—including title searchers and coding, contract, auditing, and reservation clerks.

The work of bill and account collectors is related to that of customer service representatives, telemarketers, telephone interviewers, and other workers who deal with the public over the telephone.

The work of welfare eligibility workers is similar to that of social and human service assistants, financial aid counselors, loan and credit counselors, probation officers, and other workers who interview customers or clients.

Sources of Additional Information

General information about a career as a claim representative or an insurance processing clerk is available from the home offices of many life and property and liability insurance companies.

Information about career opportunities in these occupations may be obtained from:

- ❑ Insurance Information Institute, 110 William St., New York, NY 10038.
- ❑ Alliance of American Insurers, 1501 Woodfield Rd., Suite 400 West, Schaumburg, IL 60173-4980.

Information about licensing requirements for claim adjusters may be obtained from the department of insurance in each state.

For information about the designation, Associate in Claims (AIC), or the Introduction to Claims program, contact:

- ❑ Insurance Institute of America, 720 Providence Rd., P.O. Box 3016, Malvern, PA 19355-0716.

Information on the Associate, Life and Health Claims, and the Fellow, Life Management Institute designations can be obtained from:

- ❑ Life Office Management Association, 2300 Windy Ridge Pkwy., Atlanta, GA 30327-4308.

Career information on bill and account collectors is available from:

- ❑ American Collectors Association, Inc., P.O. Box 39106, Minneapolis, MN 55439-0106. Homepage: http//www.collector.com/ consumer/careers.html

Employment information on welfare eligibility workers and interviewers is available at social service offices of municipal, county, and state governments.

Administrative Services Managers

(D.O.T. 163.167-026; 169.167-034; 188.117-122, .167-106)

Significant Points

- ✓ *Many advance to these jobs by acquiring work experience in various administrative positions.*
- ✓ *Keen competition is expected due to low turnover and an ample supply of competent, experienced workers seeking managerial jobs.*

Nature of the Work

Administrative services managers are employed throughout the American economy, and their range of duties is broad. They coordinate and direct support services, which may include: secretarial and reception; administration; payroll; conference planning and travel; information and data processing; mail; facilities management; materials scheduling and distribution; printing and reproduction;

records management; telecommunications management; personal property procurement, supply, and disposal; security; and parking.

In small organizations, a single administrative services manager may oversee all support services. In larger ones, however, first-line administrative services managers report to mid-level supervisors who, in turn, report to proprietors or top-level managers.

First-line administrative services managers directly oversee a staff that performs various support services. Mid-level managers develop departmental plans, set goals and deadlines, develop procedures to improve productivity and customer service, and define the responsibilities of supervisory-level managers. They are often involved in the hiring and dismissal of employees, but generally have no role in the formulation of personnel policy.

As the size of the firm increases, administrative services managers are more likely to specialize in one or more support activities. For example, some administrative services managers work primarily as facilities managers, office managers, property managers, or unclaimed property officers. In many cases, the duties of these administrative services managers are quite similar to those of other managers and supervisors.

Administrative services managers who specialize in facilities management or planning may oversee the purchase, sale, or lease of facilities; redesign work areas to be more efficient and user-friendly; ensure that facilities comply with government regulations; and supervise maintenance, grounds, and custodial staffs. In some firms, they are called facilities managers.

Some mid-level administrative services managers oversee first-line supervisors from various departments, including the clerical staff. In small firms, however, clerical supervisors perform this function.

Property management is divided into the following functions: Management and use of personal property such as office supplies, administrative services management, and real property management. Personal property managers acquire, distribute, and store supplies, and may sell or dispose of surplus property. Other property managers are engaged solely in surplus property disposal, which involves the resale of scraps, rejects, and surplus or unneeded supplies and machinery. This is an increasingly important source of revenue for many commercial organizations. In government, surplus property officers may receive surplus from various departments and agencies, and then sell or dispose of it to the public or other agencies.

Some administrative services managers oversee unclaimed property disposal. In government, this activity may entail auctioning off unclaimed liquid assets such as stocks, bonds, the contents of safe deposit boxes, or personal property such as motor vehicles, after attempts to locate their rightful owners have failed.

Working Conditions

Administrative services managers generally work in comfortable offices. In smaller organizations, they may work alongside the people they supervise and the office may be crowded and noisy.

The work of administrative services managers can be stressful, as they attempt to schedule work to meet deadlines. Although the 40-hour week is standard, uncompensated overtime is often required to resolve problems. Managers involved in personal property procurement, use, and disposal may travel extensively between their home office, branch offices, vendors' offices, and property sales sites. Facilities managers who are responsible for the design of work spaces may spend time at construction sites and may travel between different facilities while monitoring the work of maintenance, grounds, and custodial staffs.

Employment

Administrative services managers held about 291,000 jobs in 1996. Over half worked in service industries, including management, business, social, and health services organizations. Others were found in virtually every other industry.

Training, Other Qualifications, and Advancement

Many administrative services managers advance through the ranks in their organization, acquiring work experience in various administrative positions before assuming first-line supervisory duties. All managers who oversee departmental supervisors should be familiar with office procedures and equipment. Facilities managers may have a background in architecture, engineering, construction, interior design, or real estate, in addition to managerial experience. Managers of personal property acquisition and disposal need experience in purchasing and sales, and knowledge of a wide variety of supplies, machinery, and equipment. Managers concerned with supply, inventory, and distribution must be experienced in receiving, warehousing, packaging, shipping, transportation, and related operations. Managers of unclaimed property often have experience in insurance claims analysis and records management.

Educational requirements for these managers vary widely, depending on the size and complexity of the organization. In small organizations, experience may be the only requirement needed to enter a position as office manager. When an opening in administrative services management occurs, the office manager may be promoted to the position based on past performance. In large organizations, however, administrative services managers are normally hired from outside, and each position has formal requirements concerning education and experience. For first-line administrative services managers of secretarial, mail room, and related support activities, many employers prefer an associate degree in business or management, although a high school diploma may suffice when combined with appropriate experience. For managers of audiovisual, graphics, and other technical activities, postsecondary technical school training is preferred. For managers of highly complex services, a bachelor's degree in business, human resources, or finance is often required. The curriculum should include courses in office technology, accounting, business mathematics, computer applications, human resources, and business law. Similarly, facilities managers may need a bachelor's degree in engineering, architecture, or business administration, although some have an associate degree in a technical specialty. Some administrative services managers have advanced degrees. Whatever the manager's educational background, it must be accompanied by related work experience reflecting demonstrated ability.

Persons interested in becoming administrative services managers should have good communication skills and be able to establish effective working relationships with many different people, ranging from managers, supervisors, and professionals, to clerks and blue-collar workers. They should be analytical, detail oriented, flexible, and decisive. The ability to coordinate several activities at once and quickly analyze and resolve specific problems is important. Ability to work under pressure and cope with deadlines is also important.

Advancement in small organizations is normally achieved by moving to other management positions or to a larger organization. Advancement is easier in large firms employing several levels of administrative services managers. Attainment of the Certified Administrative Manager (CAM) designation, through work experience and successful completion of examinations offered by the Institute of Certified Professional Managers, can increase one's advancement potential. A bachelor's degree enhances a first-level manager's opportunities to advance to a mid-level management position, such as director of administrative services, and eventually to a top-level management position, such as executive vice president for administrative services. Those with the required capital and experience can establish their own management consulting firm.

Job Outlook

Employment of administrative services managers is expected to grow about as fast as the average for all occupations through the year 2006. Like other managerial occupations, this occupation is characterized by low turnover. These factors, coupled with the ample supply of competent, experienced workers seeking managerial jobs, should result in keen competition for administrative services management positions in the coming years.

Many firms are increasingly contracting out administrative services positions and otherwise streamlining these functions in an effort to cut costs. Corporate restructuring has reduced the number of administrative services manager positions in recent years, and this trend is expected to continue.

As it becomes more common for firms and governments at all levels to contract out administrative services, demand for administrative services managers will increase in the management services, management consulting, and facilities support services firms providing these services.

Earnings

Earnings of administrative services managers vary greatly depending on their employer, specialty, and geographic area in which they work. According to a 1996 survey conducted by the AMS Foundation, building services/facilities managers earned about $53,800 a year in 1996; office/administrative services managers earned about $41,400; and records managers about $37,900.

In the federal government, facilities managers in nonsupervisory, supervisory, and managerial positions averaged $49,140 a year in early 1997; miscellaneous administrative and program officers, $53,330; industrial property managers, $47,930; property disposal specialists, $43,460; administrative officers $49,070, and support services administrators, $39,700.

Related Occupations

Administrative services managers direct and coordinate support services and oversee the purchase, use, and disposal of personal property. Occupations with similar functions include administrative assistants, appraisers, buyers, clerical supervisors, contract specialists, cost estimators, procurement services managers, property and real estate managers, purchasing managers, and personnel managers.

Sources of Additional Information

For information about careers in facilities management, contact:

❑ International Facility Management Association, 1 East Greenway Plaza, Suite 1100, Houston, TX 77046-0194 Homepage: Http://www.IFMA.org

For information about the certified administrative manager designation, contact:

❑ Institute of Certified Professional Managers, James Madison University, College of Business, Harrisonburg, VA 22807.

For information about compensation of administrative managers, contact:

❑ AMS Foundation, 350 W. Jackson Boulevard, Suite 360, Chicago, IL 60661.

Adult Education Teachers

(*D.O.T.* 075.127-010; 090.222, .227-018; 097.221, .227; 099.223, .224-014, .227-014, -018, -026, -030, -038; 149.021; 150.027-014; 151.027-014; 152.021; 153.227-014; 159.227; 166.221, .227; 239.227; 375.227; 522.264; 621.221; 683.222; 689.324; 715.221; 740.221; 788.222; 789.222; 919.223; and 955.222)

Significant Points

✓ *About half work part-time; many also hold other jobs— often involving work related to the subject they teach.*

✓ *A graduate degree may be required to teach nonvocational courses, whereas practical experience is often all that is needed to teach vocational courses.*

✓ *Rising demand for adult education courses for career advancement, skills upgrading, or personal enrichment and enjoyment will spur faster-than-average employment growth; opportunities should be best for part-time positions.*

Nature of the Work

Adult education teachers work in four main areas—adult vocational-technical education, adult remedial education, adult continuing education, and prebaccalaureate training. Adult vocational-technical education teachers provide instruction for occupations that do not require a college degree, such as welder, dental hygienist, automated systems manager, x-ray technician, auto mechanic, and cosmetologist. Other instructors help people update their job skills or adapt to technological advances. For example, an adult education teacher may train students how to use new computer software programs. Adult remedial education teachers provide instruction in basic education courses for school dropouts or others who need to upgrade their skills to find a job. Adult continuing education teachers teach courses which students take for personal enrichment, such as cooking, dancing, writing, exercise and physical fitness, photography, and finance. Some adult education teachers in junior or community colleges prepare students for a four-year degree program, teaching classes for credit that can be applied toward that degree.

Adult education teachers may lecture in classrooms or work in an industry or laboratory setting to give students hands-on experience. Increasingly, adult vocational-technical education teachers integrate academic and vocational curriculums so that students obtain a variety of skills that can be applied to the real world. For example, an electronics student may be required to take courses in principles of mathematics and science in conjunction with hands-on electronics skills. Generally, teachers demonstrate techniques, have students apply them, and critique the students' work. For example, welding instructors show students various welding techniques, including the use of tools and equipment, watch them use the techniques, and have them repeat procedures until specific standards required by the trade are met.

Increasingly, minimum standards of proficiency are being established for students in various vocational-technical fields. Adult education teachers must be aware of new standards and develop lesson plans to ensure that students meet basic criteria. Also, adult education teachers and community colleges are assuming a greater role in students' transition from school to work, by helping establish internships and providing information about prospective employers.

Businesses also are increasingly providing their employees with work-related training to keep up with changing technology. Training is often provided through contractors, professional associations, or community colleges.

Adult education teachers who instruct in adult basic education programs may work with students who do not speak English; teach adults reading, writing, and mathematics up to the 8th-grade level; or teach adults through the 12th-grade level in preparation for the General Educational Development tests (GED). The GED offers the equivalent of a high school diploma. These teachers may refer students for counseling or job placement. Because many people who need adult basic education are reluctant to seek it, teachers also may recruit participants.

Adult education teachers also prepare lessons and assignments, grade papers and do related paperwork, attend faculty and professional meetings, and stay abreast of developments in their field.

Working Conditions

Since adult education teachers work with adult students, they do not encounter some of the behavioral or social problems sometimes found when teaching younger students. The adults are there by choice, are highly motivated, and bring years of experience to the classroom—attributes that can make teaching these students rewarding and satisfying. However, teachers in adult basic education deal with students at different levels of development who may lack effective study skills and self-confidence, and who may require more attention and patience than other students.

About one out of two adult education teachers work part-time. To accommodate students who may have job or family responsibilities, many institutions offer courses at night or on weekends, which range from two- to four-hour workshops and one-day mini-sessions to semester-long courses. Some adult education teachers have several part-time teaching assignments or work a full-time job in addition to their part-time teaching job, leading to long hours and a hectic schedule.

Although most adult education teachers work in a classroom setting, some are consultants to a business and teach classes at the job site.

Employment

Adult education teachers held about 559,000 jobs in 1996. Many adult education teachers are self-employed.

Adult education teachers are employed by public school systems; community and junior colleges; universities; businesses that provide formal education and training for their employees; automotive repair, bar-tending, business, computer, electronics, medical technology, and similar schools and institutes; dance studios; health clubs; job training centers; community organizations; labor unions; and religious organizations.

Training, Other Qualifications, and Advancement

Training requirements vary by state and by subject. In general, teachers need work or other experience in their field, and a license or certificate in fields where these usually are required for full professional status. In some cases, particularly at educational institutions, a master's or doctoral degree is required to teach nonvocational courses which can be applied toward a four-year degree program. Many vocational teachers in junior or community colleges do not have a master's or doctoral degree but draw on their work experience and knowledge, bringing practical experience to the classroom. For general adult education classes that are taken for interest or enjoyment, an acceptable portfolio of work is required. For example, to secure a job teaching a photography course, an applicant would need to show examples of previous work.

Most states and the District of Columbia require adult basic education teachers and adult literacy instructors to have a bachelor's degree from an approved teacher training program, and some require teacher certification.

Adult education teachers update their skills through continuing education to maintain certification—requirements vary among institutions. Teachers may take part in seminars, conferences, or graduate courses in adult education or training and development, or may return to work in business or industry for a limited time. Businesses are playing a growing role in adult education, forming consortiums with training institutions and junior colleges and providing input to curriculum development. Adult education teachers maintain an ongoing dialogue with businesses to determine the most current skills required in the workplace.

Adult education teachers should communicate and relate well with students, enjoy working with them, and be able to motivate them. Adult basic education instructors, in particular, must be patient, understanding, and supportive to make students comfortable, develop trust, and help them better understand concepts.

Some teachers advance to administrative positions in departments of education, colleges and universities, and corporate training departments. These positions often require advanced degrees, such as a doctorate in adult and continuing education.

Job Outlook

Employment of adult education teachers is expected to grow faster than the average for all occupations through the year 2006 period as the demand for adult education programs continues to rise. Opportunities should be best for part-time positions, especially in fields such as computer technology, automotive mechanics, and medical technology, which offer very attractive, and often higher-paying, job opportunities outside of teaching.

An estimated four out of ten adults participated in some form of adult education in 1995. Participation in continuing education grows as the educational attainment of the population increases. Both employers and employees are realizing that life-long learning is important for success. To keep abreast of changes in their fields and advances in technology, an increasing number of adults are taking courses–often subsidized or funded entirely by employers–for career advancement or to upgrade their skills. Also, an increasing number of adults are participating in classes for personal enrichment and enjoyment. Enrollment in adult basic education and literacy programs is increasing because of changes in immigration policy that require basic competency in English and civics. And, more employers are demanding higher levels of basic academic skills–reading, writing, and arithmetic–which is increasing enrollment in remedial education and GED preparation classes.

Employment growth of adult vocational-technical education teachers will result from the need to train young adults for entry-level jobs. Experienced workers who want to switch fields or whose jobs have been eliminated due to changing technology or business reorganization also require training. Businesses are finding it essential to provide training to their workers to remain productive and globally competitive. Cooperation between businesses and educational institutions continues to increase to insure that students are taught the skills employers desire. This should result in greater demand for adult education teachers, particularly at community and junior colleges. Since adult education programs receive state and federal funding, employment growth may be affected by government budgets.

Additional job openings for adult education teachers will stem from the need to replace persons who leave the occupation. Many teach part-time and move into and out of the occupation for other jobs, family responsibilities, or to retire.

Earnings

In 1996, salaried adult education teachers who usually worked full-time had median earnings around $31,300 a year. The middle 50 percent earned between $19,200 and $44,800. The lowest 10 percent earned about $13,100, while the top 10 percent earned more than $56,600. Earnings varied widely by subject, academic credentials, experience, and region of the country. Part-time instructors generally are paid hourly wages and do not receive benefits or pay for preparation time outside of class.

Related Occupations

Adult education teaching requires a wide variety of skills and aptitudes, including the ability to influence, motivate, train, and teach; organizational, administrative, and communication skills; and creativity. Workers in other occupations that require these aptitudes include other teachers, counselors, school administrators, public relations specialists, employee development specialists, and social workers.

Sources of Additional Information

Information on adult basic education programs and teacher certification requirements is available from state departments of education and local school districts.

For information about adult vocational-technical education teaching positions, contact state departments of vocational-technical education.

For information on adult continuing education teaching positions, contact departments of local government, state adult education departments, schools, colleges and universities, religious organizations, and a wide range of businesses that provide formal training for their employees.

General information on adult education is available from:
❑ American Association for Adult and Continuing Education, 1200 19th St. NW, Suite 300, Washington, DC 20036.
❑ American Vocational Association, 1410 King St., Alexandria, VA 22314.
❑ ERIC Clearinghouse on Adult, Career, and Vocational Education, 1900 Kenny Rd., Columbus, OH 43210-1090.

Agricultural Scientists

(D.O.T. 040.061-010, -014, -018, -038, -042, and -058; 041.061-014, -018, -046, and -082; and 041.081)

Significant Points

✓ *A large proportion, about 30 percent, work for federal, state, and local governments.*

✓ *A bachelor's degree in agricultural science is sufficient for some jobs in applied research; a master's or doctoral degree is required for basic research.*

✓ *Those with advanced degrees have the best prospects; however, competition may be keen for some basic research jobs if federal and state funding for these positions is cut.*

Nature of the Work

The work agricultural scientists do plays an important part in maintaining and increasing the nation's agricultural productivity. Agricultural scientists study farm crops and animals and develop ways of improving their quantity and quality. They look for ways to improve crop yield and quality with less labor, control pests and weeds more safely and effectively, and conserve soil and water. They research methods of converting raw agricultural commodities into attractive and healthy food products for consumers.

Agricultural science is closely related to biological science, and agricultural scientists use the principles of biology, chemistry, physics, mathematics, and other sciences to solve problems in agriculture. They often work with biological scientists on basic biological research and in applying to agriculture the advances in knowledge brought about by biotechnology.

Many agricultural scientists work in basic or applied research and development. Others manage or administer research and development programs or manage marketing or production operations in companies that produce food products or agricultural chemicals, supplies, and machinery. Some agricultural scientists are consultants to business firms, private clients, or to government.

Depending on the agricultural scientist's area of specialization, the nature of the work performed varies.

Food science. Food scientists or technologists are usually employed in the food processing industry, universities, or the federal government, and help meet consumer demand for food products that are healthful, safe, palatable, and convenient. To do this, they use their knowledge of chemistry, microbiology, and other sciences to develop new or better ways of preserving, processing, packaging, storing, and delivering foods. Some engage in basic research, discovering new food sources; analyzing food content to determine levels of vitamins, fat, sugar, or protein; or searching for substitutes for harmful or undesirable additives, such as nitrites. Many food technologists work in product development. Others enforce government regulations, inspecting food processing areas and ensuring that sanitation, safety, quality, and waste management standards are met.

Plant science. Agronomy, crop science, entomology, and plant breeding are included in plant science. Scientists in these disciplines study plants and their growth in soils, helping producers of food, feed, and fiber crops to continue to feed a growing population while conserving natural resources and maintaining the environment. Agronomists and crop scientists not only help increase productivity, but also study ways to improve the nutritional value of crops and the quality of seed. Some crop scientists study the breeding, physiology, and management of crops and use genetic engineering to develop crops resistant to pests and drought. Entomologists conduct research to develop new technologies to control or eliminate pests in infested areas and prevent the spread of harmful pests to new areas, and which are compatible with the environment. They also do research or engage in oversight activities aimed at halting the spread of insect-borne disease.

Soil science. These workers study the chemical, physical, biological, and mineralogical composition of soils as they relate to plant or crop growth. They study the responses of various soil types to fertilizers, tillage practices, and crop rotation. Many soil scientists who work for the federal government conduct soil surveys, classifying and mapping soils. They provide information and recommendations to farmers and other landowners regarding the best use of land and how to avoid or correct problems such as erosion. They may also consult with engineers and other technical personnel working on construction projects about the effects of, and solutions to, soil problems. Since soil science is closely related to environmental science, persons trained in soil science also apply their knowledge to ensure environmental quality and effective land use.

Animal science. Developing better, more efficient ways of producing and processing meat, poultry, eggs, and milk is the work of animal scientists. Dairy scientists, poultry scientists, animal breeders, and other related scientists study the genetics, nutrition, reproduction, growth, and development of domestic farm animals. Some animal scientists inspect and grade livestock food products, purchase livestock, or work in technical sales or marketing. As extension agents or consultants, animal scientists advise agricultural producers on how to upgrade animal housing facilities properly, lower mortality rates, or increase production of animal products, such as milk or eggs.

Working Conditions

Agricultural scientists involved in management or basic research tend to work regular hours in offices and laboratories. The working environment for those engaged in applied research or product development varies, depending on the discipline of agricultural science and the type of employer. For example, food scientists in private industry may work in test kitchens while investigating new processing techniques. Animal scientists working for federal, state, or university research stations may spend part of their time at dairies, farrowing houses, feedlots, farm animal facilities, or outdoors conducting research associated with livestock. Soil and crop scientists also spend time outdoors conducting research on farms agricultural research stations. Entomologists work in laboratories, insectories, or agricultural research stations, and may also spend time outdoors studying or collecting insects in their natural habitat.

Employment

Agricultural scientists held about 24,000 jobs in 1996. In addition, several thousand persons held agricultural science faculty positions in colleges and universities.

About 30 percent of all nonfaculty agricultural scientists work for federal, state, or local governments. Nearly one out of five worked for the federal government in 1996, mostly in the Department of Agriculture. In addition, large numbers worked for state governments at state agricultural colleges or agricultural research stations. Some worked for agricultural service companies; others worked for commercial research and development laboratories, seed companies, pharmaceutical companies, wholesale distributors, and food products companies. About 2,000 agricultural scientists were self-employed in 1996, mainly as consultants.

Training, Other Qualifications, and Advancement

Training requirements for agricultural scientists depend on their specialty and the type of work they perform. A bachelor's degree in agricultural science is sufficient for some jobs in applied research or for assisting in basic research, but a master's or doctoral degree is required for basic research. A Ph.D. degree in agricultural science is usually needed for college teaching and for advancement to administrative research positions. Degrees in related sciences such as biology, chemistry, or physics or in related engineering specialties also may qualify persons for some agricultural science jobs.

All states have a land-grant college which offers agricultural science degrees. Many other colleges and universities also offer agricultural science degrees or some agricultural science courses. However, not every school offers all specialties. A typical undergraduate agricultural science curriculum includes communications, economics, business, and physical and life sciences courses, in addition to a wide variety of technical agricultural science courses. For prospective animal scientists, these technical agricultural science courses might include animal breeding, reproductive physiology, nutrition, and meats and muscle biology; students preparing as food scientists take courses such as food chemistry, food analysis, food microbiology, and food processing operations; and those preparing as crop or soil scientists take courses in plant pathology, soil chemistry, entomology, plant physiology, and biochemistry, among others. Advanced degree programs include classroom and fieldwork, laboratory research, and a thesis or dissertation based on independent research.

Agricultural scientists should be able to work independently or as part of a team and be able to communicate clearly and concisely,

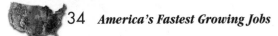

both orally and in writing. Most agricultural scientists also need an understanding of basic business principles.

The American Society of Agronomy offers certification in agronomy, crop science, soil science, soil classification, horticulture, plant pathology, and weed science. To become certified, applicants must meet certain examination, education, and professional work experience standards.

Agricultural scientists who have advanced degrees usually begin in research or teaching. With experience, they may advance to jobs such as supervisors of research programs or managers of other agriculture-related activities.

Job Outlook

Employment of agricultural scientists is expected to grow about as fast as the average for all occupations through the year 2006. Additionally, the need to replace agricultural scientists who retire or otherwise leave the occupation permanently will account for many more job openings than projected growth.

Past agricultural research has resulted in the development of higher-yielding crops, crops with better resistance to pests and plant pathogens, and chemically-based fertilizers and pesticides. Further research is necessary as insects and diseases continue to adapt to pesticides, and as soil fertility and water quality deteriorate. Agricultural scientists will be needed to balance increased agricultural output with protection and preservation of the soil, water, and ecosystems. They will practice "sustainable agriculture" by developing and implementing plans to manage pests, crops, soil fertility and erosion, and animal waste in ways that reduce the use of harmful chemicals and do little damage to the natural environment. Products developed using biotechnology methods will assist in these challenges. Also, an expanding population and a public increasingly focused on diet, health, and food safety, will result in growing opportunities for agricultural scientists to work in food science and technology.

Generally speaking, those with advanced degrees will be in the best position to enter jobs as agricultural scientists. However, competition may be keen for teaching positions in colleges or universities and for some basic research jobs, even for doctoral holders. Federal and state budget cuts may limit funding for these positions through the year 2006.

Bachelor's degree holders can work in some applied research and product development positions, but usually only in certain subfields, such as food science and technology. Also, the federal government hires bachelor's degree holders to work as soil scientists. Despite the more limited opportunities for those with only a bachelor's degree to obtain jobs as agricultural scientists, a bachelor's degree in agricultural science is useful for managerial jobs in businesses that deal with ranchers and farmers, such as feed, fertilizer, seed, and farm equipment manufacturers; retailers or wholesalers; and farm credit institutions. Four-year degrees may also help persons enter occupations such as farmer or farm or ranch manager, cooperative extension service agent, agricultural products inspector, or purchasing or sales agent for agricultural commodity or farm supply companies.

Earnings

According to the National Association of Colleges and Employers, beginning salary offers in 1997 for graduates with a bachelor's

degree in animal science averaged about $24,900 a year, and for graduates in plant science, $24,000.

The median salary for full-time food scientists or technologists was $55,200, according to a 1995 salary survey by the Institute of Food Technologists.

Average federal salaries for employees in nonsupervisory, supervisory, and managerial positions in certain agricultural science specialties in 1997 were as follows: Animal science, $65,500; agronomy, $52,000; soil science, $49,400; horticulture, $50,400; and entomology, $62,200.

Related Occupations

The work of agricultural scientists is closely related to that of biologists and other natural scientists such as chemists, foresters, and conservation scientists. It is also related to agricultural production occupations such as farmer and farm manager and cooperative extension service agent. Certain specialties of agricultural science are also related to other occupations. For example, the work of animal scientists is related to that of veterinarians; horticulturists, to landscape architects; and soil scientists, to soil conservationists.

Sources of Additional Information

Information on careers in agricultural science is available from:
❑ American Society of Agronomy, Crop Science Society of America, Soil Science Society of America, 677 S. Segoe Rd., Madison, WI 53711-1086.
❑ Food and Agricultural Careers for Tomorrow, Purdue University, 1140 Agricultural Administration Bldg., West Lafayette, IN 47907-1140.

For information on careers in food technology, write to:
❑ Institute of Food Technologists, Suite 300, 221 N. LaSalle St., Chicago IL 60601.

For information on careers in entomology, contact:
❑ Entomological Society of America, 9301 Annapolis Rd., Lanham, MD 20706. Attn: Public Relations Coordinator.

Information on acquiring a job as an agricultural scientist with the federal government may be obtained from the Office of Personnel Management through a telephone-based system. Consult your telephone directory under U.S. government for a local number, or call (912) 757-3000 (TDD 912-744-2299). That number is not toll-free and charges may result. Information also is available from their Internet site: http://www.usajobs.opm.gov

Aircraft Pilots

(D.O.T. 196, except .163 and .167-014 and 621.261-018)

Significant Points

Competition is expected for jobs because aircraft pilots have very high earnings, especially those employed by airlines.

Pilots usually start with smaller commuter and regional airlines to acquire the experience needed to qualify for higher paying jobs with national airlines.

Most pilots have traditionally learned to fly in the military, but growing numbers are entering from civilian FAA certified pilot training schools.

Nature of the Work

Pilots are highly trained professionals who fly airplanes and helicopters to carry out a wide variety of tasks. Although most pilots transport passengers and cargo, others are involved in more unusual tasks, such as dusting crops, spreading seed for reforestation, testing aircraft, directing fire fighting efforts, tracking criminals, monitoring traffic, and rescuing and evacuating injured persons.

Except on small aircraft, two pilots usually make up the cockpit crew. Generally, the most experienced pilot, the captain, is in command and supervises all other crew members. The pilot and copilot split flying and other duties, such as communicating with air traffic controllers and monitoring the instruments. Some large aircraft still have a third pilot in the cockpit–the flight engineer–who assists the other pilots by monitoring and operating many of the instruments and systems, making minor inflight repairs, and watching for other aircraft. New technology can perform many flight tasks, however, and virtually all new aircraft now fly with only two pilots, who rely more heavily on computerized controls. Flight engineer jobs will be completely eliminated in the future.

Before departure, pilots plan their flights carefully. They thoroughly check their aircraft to make sure that the engines, controls, instruments, and other systems are functioning properly. They also make sure that baggage or cargo has been loaded correctly. They confer with flight dispatchers and aviation weather forecasters to find out about weather conditions en route and at their destination. Based on this information, they choose a route, altitude, and speed that should provide the fastest, safest, and smoothest flight. When flying under instrument flight rules–procedures governing the operation of the aircraft when there is poor visibility–the pilot in command, or the company dispatcher, normally files an instrument flight plan with air traffic control so that the flight can be coordinated with other air traffic.

Takeoff and landing are the most difficult parts of the flight and require close coordination between the pilot and first officer. For example, as the plane accelerates for takeoff, the pilot concentrates on the runway while the first officer scans the instrument panel. To calculate the speed they must attain to become airborne, pilots consider the altitude of the airport, outside temperature, weight of the plane, and the speed and direction of the wind. The moment the plane reaches takeoff speed, the first officer informs the pilot, who then pulls back on the controls to raise the nose of the plane.

Unless the weather is bad, the actual flight is relatively easy. Airplane pilots, with the assistance of autopilot and the flight management computer, steer the plane along their planned route and are monitored by the air traffic control stations they pass along the way. They regularly scan the instrument panel to check their fuel supply, the condition of their engines, and the air-conditioning, hydraulic, and other systems. Pilots may request a change in altitude or route if circumstances dictate. For example, if the ride is rougher than expected, they may ask air traffic control if pilots flying at other altitudes have reported better conditions. If so, they may request a change. This procedure also may be used to find a stronger tailwind or a weaker headwind to save fuel and increase speed.

In contrast, helicopters are used for short trips at relatively low altitude, so pilots must be constantly on the lookout for trees, bridges, power lines, transmission towers, and other dangerous obstacles.

Regardless of the type of aircraft, all pilots must monitor warning devices designed to help detect sudden shifts in wind conditions that can cause crashes.

If visibility is poor, pilots must rely completely on their instruments. Using the altimeter readings, they know how high above ground they are and whether or not they can fly safely over mountains and other obstacles. Special navigation radios give pilots precise information which, with the help of special maps, tell them their exact position. Other very sophisticated equipment provides directions to a point just above the end of a runway and enables pilots to land completely "blind."

Once on the ground, pilots must complete records on their flight for their organization and the Federal Aviation Administration (FAA).

The number of nonflying duties that pilots have depends on the employment setting. Airline pilots have the services of large support staffs, and consequently, perform few nonflying duties. Pilots employed by other organizations such as charter operators or businesses have many other duties. They may load the aircraft, handle all passenger luggage to ensure a balanced load, and supervise refueling; other nonflying responsibilities include keeping records, scheduling flights, arranging for major maintenance, and performing minor aircraft maintenance and repair work.

Some pilots are instructors. They teach their students the principles of flight in ground-school classes and demonstrate how to operate aircraft in dual-controlled planes and helicopters. A few specially trained pilots are "examiners" or "check pilots." They periodically fly with other pilots or pilot's license applicants to make sure that they are proficient.

Working Conditions

By law, airline pilots cannot fly more than 100 hours a month or more than 1,000 hours a year. Most airline pilots fly an average of 75 hours a month and work an additional 75 hours a month performing nonflying duties. Fifty percent of all pilots work more than 40 hours a week. Most spend a considerable amount of time away from home because the majority of flights involve overnight layovers. When pilots are away from home, the airlines provide hotel accommodations, transportation between the hotel and airport, and an allowance for meals and other expenses. Airlines operate flights at all hours of the day and night, so work schedules often are irregular. Flight assignments are based on seniority.

Those pilots not employed by the airlines often have irregular schedules as well; they may fly 30 hours one month and 90 hours the next. Because these pilots frequently have many nonflying responsibilities, they have much less free time than airline pilots. Except for business pilots, most do not remain away from home overnight. They may work odd hours. Flight instructors may have irregular and seasonal work schedules depending on their students' available time and the weather and often give lessons at night or on weekends.

Airline pilots, especially those on international routes, often suffer jet lag–fatigue caused by many hours of flying through different time zones. The work of test pilots, who check the flight performance of new and experimental planes, may be dangerous. Pilots who are crop dusters may be exposed to toxic chemicals and seldom have the benefit of a regular landing strip. Helicopter pilots involved in police work may be subject to personal injury.

Although flying does not involve much physical effort, the mental stress of being responsible for a safe flight, no matter what the weather, can be tiring. Particularly during takeoff and landing, pilots must be alert and quick to react if something goes wrong.

Employment

Civilian pilots held about 110,000 jobs in 1996. Three-fifths worked for airlines. Many others worked as flight instructors at local airports or for large businesses that fly company cargo and executives in their own airplanes or helicopters. Some pilots flew small planes for air taxi companies, usually to or from lightly traveled airports not served by the airlines. Others worked for a variety of businesses performing tasks such as crop dusting, inspecting pipelines, or conducting sightseeing trips. Federal, state, and local governments also employed pilots. A few pilots were self-employed.

The employment of airplane pilots is not distributed like the population. Pilots are more concentrated in the states of California, Texas, Georgia, Washington, Nevada, Hawaii, and Alaska, which have a higher amount of flying activity relative to their population.

Training, Other Qualifications, and Advancement

All pilots who are paid to transport passengers or cargo must have a commercial pilot's license with an instrument rating issued by the FAA. Helicopter pilots must hold a commercial pilot's certificate with a helicopter rating. To qualify for these licenses, applicants must be at least 18 years old and have at least 250 hours of flight experience. The time can be reduced through participation in certain flight school curricula approved by the FAA. They also must pass a strict physical examination to make sure that they are in good health and have 20/20 vision with or without glasses, good hearing, and no physical handicaps that could impair their performance. Applicants must pass a written test that includes questions on the principles of safe flight, navigation techniques, and FAA regulations. They also must demonstrate their flying ability to FAA or designated examiners.

To fly in periods of low visibility, pilots must be rated by the FAA to fly by instruments. Pilots may qualify for this rating by having a total of 105 hours of flight experience, including 40 hours of experience in flying by instruments; they also must pass a written examination on procedures and FAA regulations covering instrument flying and demonstrate to an examiner their ability to fly by instruments.

Airline pilots must fulfill additional requirements. Those hired as flight engineers must pass FAA written and flight examinations to earn a flight engineer's license. Captains and first officers must have an airline transport pilot's license. Applicants for this license must be at least 23 years old and have a minimum of 1,500 hours of flying experience, including night and instrument flying. Usually they also have one or more advanced ratings, such as multi-engine aircraft or aircraft type ratings dependent upon the requirements of their particular flying jobs. Because pilots must be able to make quick decisions and accurate judgments under pressure, many airline companies reject applicants who do not pass required psychological and aptitude tests.

All licenses are valid as long as a pilot can pass the periodic physical examinations and tests of flying skills required by government and company regulations.

The Armed Forces have always been an important source of trained pilots for civilian jobs. Military pilots gain valuable experience on jet aircraft and helicopters, and persons with this experience are generally preferred for civilian pilot jobs. This primarily reflects the extensive flying time military pilots receive. Persons without armed forces training also become pilots by attending flight schools. The FAA has certified about 600 civilian flying schools, including some colleges and universities that offer degree credit for pilot training. Over the projected period, federal budget reductions are expected to reduce military pilot training. As a result, FAA certified schools will train a larger share of pilots than in the past.

Although some small airlines will hire high school graduates, most airlines require at least two years of college and prefer to hire college graduates; almost 90 percent of all pilots have completed some college. In fact, most entrants to this occupation have a college degree. If the number of college educated applicants continues to increases, employers may make a college degree an educational requirement.

Depending on the type of aircraft in use, new airline pilots start as first officers or flight engineers. Although some airlines favor applicants who already have a flight engineer's license, they may provide flight engineer training for those who have only the commercial license. Many pilots begin with smaller regional or commuter airlines where they obtain vital experience flying passengers on scheduled flights into busy airports in all weather conditions. These jobs are often a steppingstone to higher paying jobs with the bigger national airlines.

Initial training for pilots includes a week of company indoctrination, three to six weeks of ground school and simulator training, and 25 hours of initial operating experience, including a check-ride with an FAA aviation safety inspector. Once trained and "on the line" pilots are required to attend recurrent training and simulator checks periodically throughout their employment. Recurrent training is required twice a year.

Organizations other than airlines generally require less flying experience. However, a commercial pilot's license is a minimum requirement, and employers prefer applicants who have experience in the type of craft they will be flying. New employees usually start as first officers, or fly less sophisticated equipment. Test pilots often are required to have an engineering degree.

Advancement for all pilots generally is limited to other flying jobs. Many pilots start as flight instructors, building up their flying hours while they earn money teaching. As they become more experienced, these pilots occasionally fly charter planes or perhaps get jobs with small air transportation firms, such as air taxi companies. Some advance to business flying jobs. A small number get flight engineer jobs with the airlines.

In the airlines, advancement usually depends on seniority provisions of union contracts. After one to five years, flight engineers advance according to seniority to first officer and, after 5 to 15 years, to captain. Seniority also determines which pilots get the more desirable routes. In a nonairline job, a first officer may advance to pilot and, in large companies, to chief pilot or director of aviation in charge of aircraft scheduling, maintenance, and flight procedures.

Job Outlook

Pilots are expected to face considerable competition for jobs through the year 2006 because the number of applicants for new positions is expected to exceed the number of job openings. Competition will be especially keen early in the projection period due to a temporary increase in the pool of qualified pilots seeking jobs. Mergers and bankruptcies during the recent restructuring of the industry caused a large number of airline pilots to lose their jobs. Also, federal budget reductions resulted in many pilots leaving the Armed Forces. These and other qualified pilots seek jobs in this occupation because it offers very high earnings, glamour, prestige, and free or low cost travel benefits. As time passes, some pilots will fail to maintain their qualifications and the number of applicants competing for each opening should decline. Factors affecting demand, however, are not expected to ease that competition.

Relatively few jobs will be created from rising demand for pilots as employment is expected to increase about as fast as average for all occupations through the year 2006. The expected growth in airline passenger and cargo traffic will create a need for more airliners, pilots, and flight instructors. However, computerized flight management systems on new aircraft will eliminate the need for flight engineers on those planes, thus restricting the growth of pilot employment. In addition, the trend toward using larger planes in the airline industry will increase pilot productivity. Future business travel could also be adversely affected by advances in teleconferencing and facsimile mail and the elimination of many middle management positions in corporate downsizing. Employment of business pilots is expected to grow more slowly than in the past as more businesses opt to fly with regional and smaller airlines serving their area rather than buy and operate their own aircraft. On the other hand, helicopter pilots are expected to grow more rapidly as the demand expands for the type of services helicopters can offer.

Job openings resulting from the need to replace pilots who retire or leave the occupation traditionally have been very low. Aircraft pilots understandably have an extremely strong attachment to their occupation because it requires a substantial investment in specialized training that is not transferable to other fields and it generally offers very high earnings. However, many of the pilots who were hired in the late 1960s during the last major industry boom are approaching the age for mandatory retirement, so during the projected period, retirements of pilots are expected to increase and generate several thousand job openings each year.

Pilots who have logged the greatest number of flying hours in the more sophisticated equipment generally have the best prospects. This is the reason military pilots usually have an advantage over other applicants. Job seekers with the most FAA licenses will also have a competitive advantage. Opportunities for pilots in the regional commuter airlines and international service are expected to be more favorable as these segments are expected to grow faster than other segments of the industry.

Employment of pilots is sensitive to cyclical swings in the economy. During recessions, when a decline in the demand for air travel forces airlines to curtail the number of flights, airlines may temporarily furlough some pilots. Commercial and corporate flying, flight instruction, and testing of new aircraft also decline during recessions, adversely affecting pilots employed in those areas.

Earnings

Earnings of airline pilots are among the highest in the nation. According to the Future Aviation Professionals of America (FAPA), the 1996 average starting salary for airline pilots ranged from about $15,000 at the smaller turboprop airlines to $26,2900 at the larger major airlines. Average earnings for experienced pilots with six years of experience ranged from $28,100 at the turboprop airlines to almost $76,8000 at the largest airlines. Some senior captains on the largest aircraft earned as much as $200,000 a year. Earnings depend on factors such as the type, size, and maximum speed of the plane, and the number of hours and miles flown. Extra pay may be given for night and international flights. Generally, pilots working outside the airlines earn lower salaries. Usually, pilots who fly jet aircraft earn higher salaries than non-jet pilots.

Data from the Future Aviation Professionals of America for 1996 show that commercial helicopter pilots averaged from $33,700 to $59,900 a year. Average pay for corporate helicopter pilots ranged from $47,900 to $72,500. Some helicopter pilots earned over $100,000 a year.

Airline pilots generally are eligible for life and health insurance plans financed by the airlines. They also receive retirement benefits and if they fail the FAA physical examination at some point in their careers, they get disability payments. In addition, pilots receive an expense allowance, or per diem, for every hour they are away from home. Per diem can represent up to $500 each month in addition to their salary. Some airlines also provide allowances to pilots for purchasing and cleaning their uniforms. As an additional benefit, pilots and their immediate families usually are entitled to free or reduced fare transportation on their own and other airlines.

Most airline pilots are members of unions. Most airline pilots are members of the Airline Pilots Association, International, but those employed by one major airline are members of the Allied Pilots Association. Some flight engineers are members of the Flight Engineers' International Association.

Related Occupations

Although they are not in the cockpit, air traffic controllers and dispatchers also play an important role in making sure flights are safe and on schedule, and participate in many of the decisions pilots must make.

Sources of Additional Information

Information about job opportunities, salaries for a particular airline and the qualifications required may be obtained by writing to the personnel manager of the airline.

For information on airline pilots, contact:

❑ Airline Pilots Association, 1625 Massachusetts Ave. NW, Washington, DC 20036.

❑ Air Transport Association of America, 1301 Pennsylvania Ave. NW, Suite 1110, Washington, DC 20006.

For information on helicopter pilots, contact:

❑ Helicopter Association International, 1619 Duke St., Alexandria, VA 22314.

For a copy of List of Certificated Pilot Schools, write to:

❑ Superintendent of Documents, U.S. Government Printing Office, Washington, DC 20402.

For information about job opportunities in companies other than airlines, consult the classified section of aviation trade magazines and apply to companies that operate aircraft at local airports.

Architects

(D.O.T. 001.061-010 and .167-010)

Significant Points

- ✓ *Nearly 30 percent—over three times the proportion for all professionals—are self-employed, practicing as partners in architecture firms or on their own.*
- ✓ *Licensure requirements include a professional degree in architecture, a period of practical training or internship, and passage of all sections of the Architect Registration Examination.*
- ✓ *Prospective architects may face competition, especially for jobs in the most prestigious firms; those who complete at least one summer internship while in school and know computer-aided design and drafting technology may have a distinct advantage in the job market.*

Nature of the Work

Architects design buildings and other structures. The design of a building involves far more than its appearance. Buildings must also be functional, safe, and economical, and must suit the needs of the people who use them. Architects take all these things into consideration when they design buildings and other structures.

Architects provide a wide variety of professional services to individuals and organizations planning a construction project. They may be involved in all phases of development, from the initial discussion of general ideas with the client through the entire life of the facility. Their duties require a number of skills—design, engineering, managerial, communication, and supervisory.

The architect and client first discuss the purposes, requirements, and budget of a project. In some cases, architects provide various predesign services—conducting feasibility and environmental impact studies, selecting a site, or specifying the requirements the design must meet. For example, they may determine space requirements by researching the number and type of potential users of a building. The architect then prepares drawings and a report presenting ideas for the client to review.

After the initial proposals are discussed and accepted, architects develop final construction plans. These plans show the building's appearance and details for its construction. Accompanying these are drawings of the structural system; air-conditioning, heating, and ventilating systems; electrical systems; plumbing; and possibly site and landscape plans. They also specify the building materials and, in some cases, the interior furnishings. In developing designs, architects follow building codes, zoning laws, fire regulations, and other ordinances, such as those requiring easy access by disabled persons. Throughout the planning stage, they make necessary changes. Although they have traditionally used pencil and paper to produce design and construction drawings, architects are increasingly turning to computer-aided design and drafting (CADD) technology for these important tasks.

Architects may also assist the client in obtaining construction bids, selecting a contractor, and negotiating the construction contract. As construction proceeds, they may visit the building site to ensure the contractor is following the design, adhering to the schedule, using the specified materials, and meeting quality work standards. The job is not complete until all construction is finished, required tests are made, and construction costs are paid. Sometimes, architects also provide postconstruction services, such as facilities management. They advise on energy efficiency measures, evaluate how well the building design adapts to the needs of occupants, and make necessary improvements.

Architects design a wide variety of buildings, such as office and apartment buildings, schools, churches, factories, hospitals, houses, and airport terminals. They also design multibuilding complexes such as urban centers, college campuses, industrial parks, and entire communities. In addition to designing buildings, they may advise on the selection of building sites, prepare cost analysis and land-use studies, and do long-range planning for land development.

Architects sometimes specialize in one phase of work. Some specialize in the design of one type of building—for example, hospitals, schools, or housing. Others focus on planning and predesign services or construction management, and do little design work. They often work with engineers, urban planners, interior designers, landscape architects, and others.

During a training period leading up to licensure as architects, entry-level workers are called intern-architects. This training period gives them practical work experience while they prepare for the Architect Registration Examination (ARE). Typical duties may include preparing construction drawings on CADD, or assisting in the design of one part of a project.

Working Conditions

Architects generally work in a comfortable environment. Most of their time is spent in offices advising clients, developing reports and drawings, and working with other architects and engineers. However, they often visit construction sites to review the progress of projects.

Architects may occasionally be under great stress, working nights and weekends to meet deadlines. In 1996, about two out of five architects worked more than 40 hours a week, in contrast to one in four workers in all occupations combined.

Employment

Architects held about 94,000 jobs in 1996. The majority of jobs were in architecture firms—most of which employ fewer than five workers. A few worked for builders, real estate developers, and for government agencies responsible for housing, planning, or community development, such as the U.S. Departments of Defense and Interior, and the General Services Administration. Nearly three in ten architects is self-employed, practicing as partners in architecture firms or on their own.

Training, Other Qualifications, and Advancement

All states and the District of Columbia require individuals to be licensed (registered) before they may call themselves architects or contract to provide architectural services. Many architecture school graduates work in the field even though they are not licensed. However, a licensed architect is required to take legal responsibility for all work. Licensure requirements include a professional degree in architecture, a period of practical training or internship, and passage of all sections of the ARE.

In many states, the professional degree in architecture must be from one of the 105 schools of architecture with programs accredited by the National Architectural Accrediting Board (NAAB). However, state architectural registration boards set their own standards, so graduation from a non-NAAB-accredited program may meet the education requirement for licensure in some states. There are several types of professional degrees in architecture. The majority of all architecture degrees are from five-year Bachelor of Architecture programs, intended for students entering from high school or with no previous architecture training. Some schools offer a two-year Master of Architecture program for students with a preprofessional undergraduate degree in architecture or a related area, or a three- or four-year Master of Architecture program for students with a degree in another discipline. In addition, there are many combinations and variations of these degree programs.

The choice of degree type depends upon each individual's preference and educational background. Prospective architecture students should carefully consider the available options before committing to a program. For example, although the five-year Bachelor of Architecture program offers the fastest route to the professional degree, courses are specialized and, if the student does not complete the program, moving to a nonarchitecture program may be difficult. A typical program includes courses in architectural history and theory, building design, professional practice, math, physical sciences, and liberal arts. Central to most architecture programs is the design studio, where students put into practice the skills and concepts learned in the classroom. During the final semester of many programs, students devote their studio time to creating an architectural project from beginning to end, culminating in a three-dimensional model of their design.

Many architecture schools also offer graduate education for those who already have a bachelor's or master's degree in architecture or other areas. Although graduate education beyond the professional degree is not required for practicing architects, it is normally required for research, teaching, and certain specialties.

Architects must be able to visually communicate their ideas to clients. Artistic and drawing ability is very helpful in doing this, but not essential. More important is a visual orientation and the ability to conceptualize and understand spatial relationships. Good communication skills, the ability to work independently or as part of a team, and creativity are important qualities for anyone interested in becoming an architect. Computer literacy is also required as most firms use computers for specifications writing, two- and three-dimensional drafting, and financial management. A knowledge of computer-aided design and drafting (CADD) is helpful and will become more important as architecture firms continue to adopt this technology.

All state architectural registration boards require a training period before candidates may sit for the ARE and become licensed. Many states have adopted the training standards established by the Intern Development Program, a branch of the American Institute of Architects and the National Council of Architectural Registration Boards. These standards stipulate broad and diversified training under the supervision of a licensed architect over a three-year pe-

riod. New graduates usually begin as intern-architects in architecture firms, where they assist in preparing architectural documents or drawings. They may also do research on building codes and materials, or write specifications for building materials, installation criteria, the quality of finishes, and other related details. Graduates with degrees in architecture also enter related fields such as graphic, interior, or industrial design; urban planning; real estate development; civil engineering; or construction management. In such cases, an architectural license, and thus the internship period, is not required.

After completing the internship period, intern-architects are eligible to sit for the ARE. The examination tests candidates on a broad body of architectural knowledge, and is given in sections throughout the year. Candidates who pass the ARE and meet all standards established by their state board are licensed to practice in that state.

After becoming licensed and gaining experience, architects take on increasingly responsible duties, eventually managing entire projects. In large firms, architects may advance to supervisory or managerial positions. Some architects become partners in established firms; others set up their own practice.

Several states require continuing education to maintain licensure, and many more states are expected to adopt mandatory continuing education. Requirements vary by state, but usually involve the completion of a certain number of credits every year or two through seminars, workshops, formal university classes, conferences, self-study courses, or other sources.

Job Outlook

Despite projected average employment growth coupled with job openings stemming from the need to replace architects who retire or leave the labor force for other reasons, prospective architects may face competition, especially if the number of architecture degrees awarded remain at, or above, current levels. Many individuals are attracted to this occupation, and the number of applicants often exceeds the number of available jobs, especially in the most prestigious firms. Prospective architects who complete at least one summer internship—either paid or unpaid—while in school and know CADD technology, may have a distinct advantage in getting an intern-architect position after graduation.

Because construction—particularly office and retail—is sensitive to cyclical changes in the economy, architects will face particularly strong competition for jobs or clients during recessions, and layoffs may occur. Those involved in the design of institutional buildings such as schools, hospitals, nursing homes, and correctional facilities, will be less affected by fluctuations in the economy.

Even in times of overall good job opportunities, however, there may be areas of the country with poor opportunities. Architects who are licensed to practice in one state must meet the licensing requirements of other states before practicing . These requirements are becoming more standardized, however, facilitating movement to other states.

Employment of architects is strongly tied to the level of local construction, particularly nonresidential structures such as office buildings, shopping centers, schools, and healthcare facilities. The boom in nonresidential construction during the 1980s resulted in high vacancy rates and a slowdown in this type of construction during the first half of the 1990s. Although this sector of the construction industry is beginning to recover, slower labor force growth, rapid increases in telecommuting and flexiplace work, and the earlier overbuilding are expected to continue to suppress demand for new office space between 1996 and 2006. Nevertheless, employment of architects is expected to grow about as fast as the average for all occupations during this period.

As the stock of buildings ages, demand for remodeling and repair work should grow considerably. The needed renovation and rehabilitation of old buildings, particularly in urban areas where space for new buildings is becoming limited, is expected to provide many job opportunities for architects. In addition, demographic trends and changes in health care delivery are influencing the demand for certain institutional structures, and should also provide more jobs for architects in the future. For example, increases in the school-age population will result in new school construction and additions to existing schools. And, growth is expected in the number of adult care centers, assisted-living facilities, and community health clinics, all of which are preferable, less costly alternatives to hospitals and nursing homes.

Earnings

According to The American Institute of Architects, the median compensation, including bonuses, for intern-architects in architecture firms was $27,000 in 1996. Licensed architects with three to five of years experience had median earnings of $33,000; licensed architects with eight to ten years of experience, but who were not managers or principals of a firm, earned $45,000. Principals or partners of firms earned $75-100,000 in 1996, although partners in some large practices earned considerably more. Similar to other industries, small architecture firms (fewer than five employees) are less likely than larger firms to provide employee benefits.

Earnings of partners in established architecture firms may fluctuate due to changing business conditions. Some architects may have difficulty establishing their own practices, and may go through a period when their expenses are greater than their income, requiring substantial financial resources.

Related Occupations

Architects design and construct buildings and related structures. Others who engage in similar work are landscape architects, building contractors, civil engineers, urban planners, interior designers, industrial designers, and graphic designers.

Sources of Additional Information

Information about education and careers in architecture can be obtained from:

❑ Careers in Architecture Program, The American Institute of Architects, 1735 New York Ave. NW, Washington, DC 20006. Homepage: http://www.aiaonline.com

❑ Society of American Registered Architects, Nathan Kolodny Consultants, Suite 2A, 100 Pinewood Rd., Hartsdale, NY 10530.

Archivists and Curators

(D.O.T. 099.167-030; 101; 102 except .261-014 and .367-010; 109.067-014, .267-010, .281, .361, .364; 979.361)

Significant Points

✓ *Employment generally requires graduate education and substantial work experience.*

✓ *Competition for jobs is expected to be keen as qualified applicants outnumber job openings.*

Nature of the Work

Archivists, curators, museum and archives technicians, and conservators search for, acquire, appraise, analyze, describe, arrange, catalogue, restore, preserve, exhibit, maintain, and store items of lasting value so that they can be used by researchers or for exhibitions, publications, broadcasting, and other educational programs. Depending on the occupation, these items may consist of historical documents, audiovisual materials, institutional records, works of art, coins, stamps, minerals, clothing, maps, living and preserved plants and animals, buildings, computer records, or historic sites.

Archivists and curators plan and oversee the arrangement, cataloguing, and exhibition of collections and, along with technicians and conservators, maintain collections. Archivists and curators may coordinate educational and public outreach programs, such as tours, workshops, lectures, and classes, and may work with the boards of institutions to administer plans and policies. They also may conduct research on topics or items relevant to their collections. Although some duties of archivists and curators are similar, the types of items they deal with differ. Curators usually handle objects found in cultural, biological, or historical collections, such as sculptures, textiles, and paintings, while archivists mainly handle valuable records, documents, or objects that are retained because they originally accompanied and relate specifically to the document.

Archivists determine what portion of the vast amount of records maintained by various organizations, such as government agencies, corporations, or educational institutions, or by families and individuals, should be made part of permanent historical holdings, and which of these records should be put on exhibit. They maintain records in their original arrangement according to the creator's organizational scheme, and describe records to facilitate retrieval. Records may be saved on any medium, including paper, film, videotape, audiotape, electronic disk, or computer. They also may be copied onto some other format to protect the original from repeated handling, and to make them more accessible to researchers who use the records. As computers and various storage media evolve, archivists must keep abreast of technological advances in electronic information storage.

Archives may be part of a library, museum, or historical society, or may exist as a distinct archival unit within an organization or company. Archivists consider any medium containing recorded information as documents, including letters, books, and other paper documents, photographs, blueprints, audiovisual materials, and computer records. Any document which reflects organizational transactions, hierarchy, or procedures can be considered a record. Archivists often specialize in an area of history or technology so they can better determine what records in that area qualify for retention and should become part of the archives. Archivists also may work with specialized forms of records, such as manuscripts, electronic records, photographs, cartographic records, motion pictures, and sound recordings.

Computers are increasingly used to generate and maintain archival records. Professional standards for use of computers in handling archival records are still evolving. However, use of computers is expected to transform many aspects of archival collections as computer capabilities, including multimedia and worldwide web use, expand and allow more records to be stored electronically.

Curators oversee collections in museums, zoos, aquariums, botanic gardens, nature centers, and historic sites. They acquire items through purchases, gifts, field exploration, intermuseum exchanges, or, in the case of some plants and animals, reproduction. Curators also plan and prepare exhibits. In natural history museums, curators collect and observe specimens in their natural habitat. Their work involves describing and classifying species, while specially trained collection managers and technicians provide hands-on care of natural history collections. Most curators use computer databases to catalogue and organize their collections. Many also use the Internet to make information available to other curators and the public. Increasingly, curators are expected to participate in grant writing and fund raising to support their projects.

Most curators specialize in a specific field, such as botany, art, paleontology, or history. Those working in large institutions may be highly specialized. A large natural history museum, for example, would employ specialists in birds, fishes, insects, and mollusks. Some curators maintain the collection, others do research, and others perform administrative tasks. Registrars, for example, keep track of and move objects in the collection. In small institutions, with only one or a few curators, one curator may be responsible for multiple tasks, from maintaining collections to directing the affairs of museums.

Conservators manage, care for, preserve, treat, and document works of art, artifacts, and specimens. This may require substantial historical, scientific, and archaeological research. They use x rays, chemical testing, microscopes, special lights, and other laboratory equipment and techniques to examine objects and determine their condition, the need for treatment or restoration, and the appropriate method for preservation. They then document their findings and treat items to minimize deterioration or restore items to their original state. Conservators usually specialize in a particular material or group of objects, such as documents and books, paintings, decorative arts, textiles, metals, or architectural material.

Museum directors formulate policies, plan budgets, and raise funds for their museums. They coordinate activities of their staff to establish and maintain collections. As their role has evolved, museum directors increasingly need business backgrounds in addition to an understanding and empathy for the subject matter of their collections.

Museum technicians assist curators and conservators by performing various preparatory and maintenance tasks on museum items. Some museum technicians may also assist curators with research. Archives technicians help archivists organize, maintain, and provide access to historical documentary materials.

Working Conditions

The working conditions of archivists and curators vary. Some spend most of their time working with the public, providing reference assistance and educational services. Others perform research or process records, which often means working alone or in offices with only a few people. Those who restore and install exhibits or work with bulky, heavy record containers may climb, stretch, or lift. Those in zoos, botanical gardens, and other outdoor museums or historic sites frequently walk great distances.

Curators who work in large institutions may travel extensively to evaluate potential additions to the collection, organize exhibitions, and conduct research in their area of expertise. However, in small institutions, travel for curators is rare.

Employment

Archivists and curators held about 20,000 jobs in 1996. About a quarter were employed in museums, botanical gardens, and zoos, and approximately two in ten worked in educational services, mainly in college and university libraries. About four in ten worked in federal, state, and local government. Most federal archivists work for the National Archives and Records Administration; others manage military archives in the Department of Defense. Most federal government curators work at the Smithsonian Institution, in the military museums of the Department of Defense, and in archaeological and other museums managed by the Department of Interior. All state governments have archival or historical records sections employing archivists. State and local governments have numerous historical museums, parks, libraries, and zoos employing curators.

Some large corporations have archives or records centers, employing archivists to manage the growing volume of records created or maintained as required by law or necessary to the firms' operations. Religious and fraternal organizations, professional associations, conservation organizations, major private collectors, and research firms also employ archivists and curators.

Conservators may work under contract to treat particular items, rather than as a regular employee of a museum or other institution. These conservators may work on their own as private contractors, or as an employee of a conservation laboratory or regional conservation center which contracts their services to museums.

Training, Other Qualifications, and Advancement

Employment as an archivist, conservator, or curator generally requires graduate education and substantial work experience. Many archivists and curators work in archives or museums while completing their formal education, to gain the hands-on experience that many employers seek when hiring.

Employers generally look for archivists with undergraduate and graduate degrees in history or library science, with courses in archival science. Some positions may require knowledge of the discipline related to the collection, such as business or medicine. An increasing number of archivists have a double master's degree in history and library science. There are currently no programs offering a bachelor's or master's degree in archival science. However, approximately 65 colleges and universities offer courses or practical training in archival science as part of history, library science, or another discipline. The Academy of Certified Archivists offers voluntary certification for archivists. Certification requires the applicant to have experience in the field and to pass an examination offered by the Academy.

Archivists need research and analytical ability to understand the content of documents and the context in which they were created, and to decipher deteriorated or poor quality printed matter, handwritten manuscripts, or photographs and films. A background in preservation management is often required of archivists since they are responsible for taking proper care of their records. Archivists also must be able to organize large amounts of information and write clear instructions for its retrieval and use. In addition, computer skills and the ability to work with electronic records and databases are increasingly important.

Many archives are very small, including one-person shops, with limited promotion opportunities. Archivists typically advance by transferring to a larger unit with supervisory positions. A doctorate in history, library science, or a related field may be needed for some advanced positions, such as director of a state archives.

In most museums, a master's degree in an appropriate discipline of the museum's specialty—for example, art, history, or archaeology—or museum studies is required for employment as a curator. Many employers prefer a doctoral degree, particularly for curators in natural history or science museums. Earning two graduate degrees—in museum studies (museology) and a specialized subject—gives a candidate a distinct advantage in this competitive job market. In small museums, curatorial positions may be available to individuals with a bachelor's degree. For some positions, an internship of full-time museum work supplemented by courses in museum practices is needed.

Curatorial positions often require knowledge in a number of fields. For historic and artistic conservation, courses in chemistry, physics, and art are desirable. Since curators—particularly those in small museums—may have administrative and managerial responsibilities, courses in business administration, public relations, marketing, and fundraising also are recommended. Similar to archivists, curators need computer skills and the ability to work with electronic databases. Curators also need to be familiar with digital imaging, scanning technology, and copyright infringement, since many are responsible for posting information on the Internet.

Curators must be flexible because of their wide variety of duties. They need an aesthetic sense to design and present exhibits and, in small museums, manual dexterity to erect exhibits or restore objects. Leadership ability and business skills are important for museum directors, while marketing skills are valuable for increasing museum attendance and fundraising.

In large museums, curators may advance through several levels of responsibility, eventually to museum director. Curators in smaller museums often advance to larger ones. Individual research and publications are important for advancement in larger institutions.

Museum technicians generally need a bachelor's degree in an appropriate discipline of the museum's specialty, museum studies training, or previous museum work experience, particularly in exhibit design. Similarly, archives technicians generally need a bachelor's degree in library science or history, or relevant work experience. Technician positions often serve as a stepping stone for individuals interested in archival and curatorial work. With the exception of small museums, a master's degree is needed for advancement.

When hiring conservators, employers look for a master's degree in conservation, or in a closely related field, and substantial experience. There are only a few graduate programs in museum conservation techniques in the United States. Competition for entry to these programs is keen; to qualify, a student must have a back-

ground in chemistry, archaeology or studio art, and art history, as well as work experience. For some programs, knowledge of a foreign language is also helpful. Conservation apprenticeships or internships as an undergraduate can also enhance one's admission prospects. Graduate programs last two to four years; the latter years include internship training. A few individuals enter conservation through apprenticeships with museums, nonprofit organizations, and conservators in private practice. Apprenticeships should be supplemented with courses in chemistry, studio art, and history. Apprenticeship training, although accepted, generally is a more difficult route into the conservation profession.

Relatively few schools grant a bachelor's degree in museum studies. More common are undergraduate minors or tracks of study that are part of an undergraduate degree in a related field, such as art history, history, or archaeology. Students interested in further study may obtain a master's degree in museum studies. Colleges and universities throughout the country offer master's degrees in museum studies. However, many employers feel that, while museum studies are helpful, a thorough knowledge of the museum's specialty and museum work experience are more important.

Continuing education, which enables archivists, curators, conservators, and museum technicians to keep up with developments in the field, is available through meetings, conferences, and workshops sponsored by archival, historical, and museum associations. Some larger organizations, such as the National Archives, offer such training in-house.

Job Outlook

Competition for jobs as archivists and curators is expected to be keen as qualified applicants outnumber job openings. Graduates with highly specialized training, such as master's degrees in both library science and history, with a concentration in archives or records management, and extensive computer skills should have the best opportunities for jobs as archivists. A job as a curator is attractive to many people, and many applicants have the necessary training and subject knowledge; yet there are only a few openings. Consequently, candidates may have to work part-time, as an intern, or even as a volunteer assistant curator or research associate after completing their formal education. Substantial work experience in collection management, exhibit design, or restoration, as well as database management skills, will be necessary for permanent status. Job opportunities for curators should be best in art and history museums, since these are the largest employers in the museum industry.

The job outlook for conservators may be more favorable, particularly for graduates of conservation programs. However, competition is stiff for the limited number of openings in these programs, and applicants need a technical background. Students who qualify and successfully complete the program, have knowledge of a foreign language, and are willing to relocate, will have an advantage over less qualified candidates in obtaining a position.

Employment of archivists and curators is expected to increase about as fast as the average for all occupations through the year 2006. Jobs are expected to grow as public and private organizations put more emphasis on establishing archives and organizing records and information, and as public interest in science, art, history, and technology increases. However, museums and other cultural institutions are often subject to funding cuts during recessions or periods of budget tightening, reducing demand for archivists and curators during these times. Although the rate of turnover among archivists and curators is relatively low, the need to replace workers who leave the occupation or stop working will create some additional job openings.

Earnings

Earnings of archivists and curators vary considerably by type and size of employer, and often by specialty. Average salaries in the federal government, for example, are generally higher than those in religious organizations. Salaries of curators in large, well-funded museums may be several times higher than those in small ones.

The average annual salary for all museum curators in the federal government in nonsupervisory, supervisory, and managerial positions was about $55,000 in 1997. Archivists averaged $53,600; museum specialists and technicians, $36,300; and archives technicians, $31,200.

According to a survey by the Association of Art Museum Directors, median salaries for selected workers in larger art museums in 1996 were as follows:

Director	$103,000
Curator	50,000
Senior conservator	48,500
Curatorial assistant	22,600

Related Occupations

Archivists' and curators' skills in preserving, organizing, and displaying objects or information of historical interest are shared by anthropologists, arborists, archaeologists, artifacts conservators, botanists, ethnologists, folklorists, genealogists, historians, horticulturists, information specialists, librarians, paintings restorers, records managers, and zoologists.

Sources of Additional Information

For information on archivists and on schools offering courses in archival studies, contact:

❑ Society of American Archivists, 600 South Federal St., Suite 504, Chicago, IL 60605.

For general information about careers as a curator and schools offering courses in museum studies, contact:

❑ American Association of Museums, 1575 I St. NW, Suite 400, Washington, DC 20005.

For information about conservation and preservation careers and education programs, contact:

❑ American Institute for Conservation of Historic and Artistic Works, 1717 K St. NW, Suite 301, Washington, DC 20006.

Automotive Mechanics

(D.O.T. 620.261-010, -012, -030, and -034; .281-010, -026, -034, -038, -062, -066, and -070; .381-010 and -022; .682; .684-018 and -022; 706.381-046; 806.361-026 and .684-038; 807.664 and .684-022; 825.381-014)

Significant Points

✓ *Automotive mechanics will be among the occupations with the most job openings.*

✓ *Opportunities are expected to be good for persons who complete formal automotive training programs.*

✓ *Knowledge of basic electronics is becoming essential for mechanics because computers are increasingly being used in components throughout the vehicle.*

Nature of the Work

Automotive mechanics, often called automotive service technicians, inspect, maintain, or repair automobiles and light trucks with gasoline engines, such as vans and pickups. (Mechanics who work on diesel-powered trucks, buses, and equipment are discussed in the statement on diesel mechanics. Motorcycle mechanics—who repair and service motorcycles, motor scooters, mopeds, and occasionally small all-terrain vehicles—are discussed in the statement on motorcycle, boat, and small-engine mechanics.)

Anyone whose car or light truck has broken down knows the importance of the mechanic's job. The ability to diagnose the source of the problem quickly and accurately, one of the mechanic's most valuable skills, requires good reasoning ability and a thorough knowledge of automobiles. Many mechanics consider diagnosing hard-to-find troubles one of their most challenging and satisfying duties.

When mechanical or electrical troubles occur, mechanics first get a description of the symptoms from the owner or, if they work in a large shop, the repair service estimator who wrote the repair order. To locate the problem, the mechanic may have to test drive the vehicle or use a variety of testing equipment, such as on-board and hand-held diagnostic computers and compression gauges. Mechanics make adjustments or repairs once the cause of the problem is found. If a part is damaged, worn beyond repair, or not repairable at a reasonable cost, it is replaced, usually after consultation with the vehicle's owner.

During routine service, mechanics inspect and lubricate engines and other components. They also repair or replace parts before they cause breakdowns. Mechanics usually follow a checklist to ensure they examine all important parts. Belts, hoses, plugs, brake and fuel systems, and other potentially troublesome items are among those closely watched.

Mechanics use a variety of tools in their work. They use power tools such as pneumatic wrenches to remove bolts quickly, machine tools like lathes and grinding machines to rebuild brakes, welding and flame-cutting equipment to remove and repair exhaust systems, and jacks and hoists to lift cars and engines. They also use common hand tools like screwdrivers, pliers, and wrenches to work on small parts and in hard-to-reach places.

In the most modern shops of automobile dealers, service technicians use electronic service equipment, such as infrared engine analyzers and computerized diagnostic devices. These devices diagnose problems and make precision adjustments with precise calculations downloaded from large databases. The computerized systems have the capacity to automatically update technical manuals and allow technicians unlimited access to manufacturers' service information, technical service bulletins, and other computerized information databases to keep current on trouble spots and new procedures

Automotive mechanics in larger shops have increasingly become specialized. For example, automatic transmission mechanics work on gear trains, couplings, hydraulic pumps, and other parts of automatic transmissions. Extensive training and experience in electronics is needed for the complex components and technology used in new vehicles. Tune-up mechanics adjust the ignition timing and valves, and adjust or replace spark plugs and other parts to ensure efficient engine performance. They often use electronic test equipment to locate and adjust malfunctions in fuel, ignition, and emissions control systems.

Automotive air-conditioning mechanics install and repair air conditioners and service components such as compressors, condensers, and controls. They require special training in federal and state regulations governing the handling and disposal of refrigerants. Front-end mechanics align and balance wheels and repair steering mechanisms and suspension systems. They frequently use special alignment equipment and wheel-balancing machines. Brake repairers adjust brakes, replace brake linings and pads, and make other repairs on brake systems. Some mechanics specialize in both brake and front-end work.

Automotive-radiator mechanics clean radiators with caustic solutions, locate and solder leaks, and install new radiator cores or complete replacement radiators. They also may repair heaters and air-conditioners, and solder leaks in gasoline tanks.

Working Conditions

Most automotive mechanics work a standard 40-hour week, but many self-employed mechanics work longer hours. To satisfy customer service needs, many mechanics provide evening and weekend service. Generally, mechanics work indoors in well ventilated and lighted repair shops. However, some shops are drafty and noisy. Mechanics frequently work with dirty and greasy parts, and in awkward positions. They often lift heavy parts and tools. Minor cuts, burns, and bruises are common, but serious accidents are avoided when the shop is kept clean and orderly and safety practices are observed. Some problems can be fixed with simple computerized adjustments avoiding the need to get dirty.

Employment

Automotive mechanics held about 775,000 jobs in 1996. The majority worked for retail and wholesale automotive dealers and independent automotive repair shops, and gasoline service stations. Others found employment in automotive service facilities at department, automotive, and home supply stores. A small number maintained automobile fleets for taxicab and automobile leasing companies; federal, state, and local governments; and other organizations. Motor vehicle manufacturers employed some mechanics to test, adjust, and repair cars at the end of assembly lines. About 20 percent of automotive mechanics were self-employed.

Training, Other Qualifications, and Advancement

Automotive technology is rapidly increasing in sophistication and most training authorities strongly recommend that persons seeking automotive mechanic jobs complete a formal training program after graduating from high school. However, some automotive mechanics still learn the trade solely by assisting and working with experienced mechanics.

Many high schools, community colleges, and public and private vocational and technical schools offer automotive mechanic training programs. Postsecondary programs generally provide more thor-ough career preparation than high school programs. High school programs, while an asset, vary greatly in quality. Some high school programs offer only an introduction to automotive technology and service for the future consumer or hobbyist, while others aim to equip graduates with enough skills to get a job as a mechanic's helper or trainee mechanic after graduation.

Postsecondary automotive mechanic training programs vary greatly in format, but generally provide intensive career preparation through a combination of classroom instruction and hands-on practice. Some trade and technical school programs provide concentrated training for six months to a year, depending on how many hours the student must attend each week. Community college programs normally spread the training out over two years, supplement the automotive training with instruction in English, basic mathematics, computers, and other subjects, and award an associate degree or certificate.

The various automobile manufacturers and their participating dealers sponsor two-year associate degree programs at 213 postsecondary schools across the nation. The manufacturers provide ASE certified instruction, service equipment and current model cars on which students practice new skills, and learn the latest automotive technology. Curriculums are updated frequently to reflect changing technology and equipment. Students in these programs typically spend alternate 6- to 12-week periods attending classes full-time and working full-time in the service departments of sponsoring dealers. While working in the dealerships, they are assigned an experienced mechanic to relate experiences and provide hands-on instruction. Also, some sponsoring dealers provide students with financial assistance for tuition or the purchase of tools.

The National Automotive Technicians Education Foundation (NATEF), an affiliate of the National Institute for Automotive Service Excellence (ASE), certifies automobile mechanic, collision specialist, and diesel and medium/heavy truck mechanic training programs offered by high schools, postsecondary trade schools, technical institutes, and community colleges. While NATEF certification is voluntary, certification does signify that the program meets uniform standards for instructional facilities, equipment, staff credentials, and curriculum. In early 1996, 1,245 high school and postsecondary automotive mechanic training programs had been certified by NATEF, of which 1,033 trained automobile service technicians, 174 collision specialists, and 38 diesel and medium/heavy truck specialists.

There are more computers aboard a car today than aboard the first spaceship. A new car today has from 10 to 15 on-board computers operating everything from the engine to the radio. As a result, knowledge of electronics has grown increasingly important for automotive mechanics. Engine controls and dashboard instruments were among the first components to use electronics, but now electronics are used in brakes, transmissions, steering systems, and a variety of other components. In the past, a specialist usually handled any problems involving electrical systems or electronics. But electronics are now commonplace, so all automotive mechanics must be familiar with at least the basic principles of electronics to recognize when an electronic malfunction may be responsible for a problem. In addition, automotive mechanics must be able to test and replace electronic components.

For trainee mechanic jobs, employers look for people with strong communication and analytical skills. Quality mathematics and computer skills are needed to study technical manuals to keep abreast of new technology. People who have a desire to learn new service and repair procedures and specifications are excellent candidates for trainee mechanic jobs. Trainees also must possess mechanical aptitude and knowledge of how automobiles work. Most employers regard the successful completion of a vocational training program in automotive mechanics at a postsecondary institution as the best preparation for trainee positions. Experience working on motor vehicles in the Armed Forces or as a hobby is also valuable. Because of the complexity of new vehicles, completion of high school is required by a growing number of employers. Courses in automotive repair, electronics, physics, chemistry, English, computers, and mathematics provide a good educational background for a career as an automotive mechanic.

Beginners usually start as trainee mechanics, helpers, lubrication workers, or gasoline service station attendants and gradually acquire and practice their skills by working with experienced mechanics. Beginners perform many routine service tasks and make simple repairs with a few months' experience. It usually takes two to five years of experience to acquire adequate proficiency to become a journey-level service mechanic and quickly perform the more difficult types of routine service and repairs. However, graduates of the better postsecondary mechanic training programs are often able to earn promotion to the journey level after only a few months on the job. An additional one to two years experience familiarizes the mechanic with all types of repairs. Difficult specialties, such as transmission repair, require another year or two of training and experience. In contrast, automotive radiator mechanics and brake specialists, who do not need an all-round knowledge of automotive repair, may learn their jobs in considerably less time.

In the past, many persons have become automotive mechanics through three- or four-year formal apprenticeship programs. However, more employers now look for persons who have completed formal automotive training programs to reduce the amount of time invested in training a prospective mechanic.

The most important possessions of mechanics are their hand tools. Mechanics usually provide their own tools and many experienced mechanics have thousands of dollars invested in them. Employers typically furnish expensive power tools, engine analyzers, and other diagnostic equipment, but hand tools are accumulated with experience.

Employers increasingly send experienced automotive mechanics to manufacturer training centers to learn to repair new models or to receive special training in the repair of components such as electronic fuel injection or air-conditioners. Motor vehicle dealers may also send promising beginners to manufacturer sponsored mechanic training programs. Factory representatives come to many shops to conduct short training sessions. This additional training is typically furnished by the employer to maintain or upgrade employee skills and increase their value to the dealership.

The standard achievement for automotive mechanics is voluntary certification by Automotive Service Excellence (ASE). Certification in one or more of eight different service areas, such as electrical systems, engine repair, brake systems, suspension and steering, and heating and air conditioning is awarded to mechanics. To be certified as a master automotive mechanic, mechanics must be certified in all eight areas. For certification in each area, mechanics must have at least two years of experience and pass a written examination. Completion of an automotive mechanic program in high school, vocational or trade school, or community or junior college may be substituted for one year of experience. Mechanics must retake the examination at least every five years to maintain their certification.

Experienced mechanics who have leadership ability may advance to shop supervisor or service manager. Mechanics who work well with customers may become automotive repair service estimators. Some with sufficient funds open independent repair shops.

Job Outlook

Job opportunities in this occupation are expected to be good for persons who complete automotive training programs in high school, vocational and technical schools, or community colleges. Persons whose training includes basic electronics skills should have the best opportunities. Persons without formal mechanic training are likely to face competition for entry level jobs. Mechanic careers are attractive to many because they afford the opportunity for good pay and the satisfaction of highly skilled work with one's hands.

Employment opportunities for automotive mechanics are expected to increase about as fast as the average for all occupations through the year 2006. Employment growth will continue to be concentrated in automobile dealerships, independent automotive repair shops, and specialty car care chains. Employment of automotive mechanics in gasoline service stations will continue to decline as fewer stations offer repair services.

The number of mechanics will increase because expansion of the driving age population will increase the number of motor vehicles on the road. The growing complexity of automotive technology necessitates that cars be serviced by skilled workers, contributing to the growth in demand for highly trained mechanics. With more young people entering the job market not interested in mechanic and repairer careers, automotive mechanics presents an excellent opportunity for bright, motivated people who have a technical background and desire to make a good living.

More job openings for automotive mechanics are expected than for most other occupations as experienced workers transfer to related occupations, retire, or stop working for other reasons. This large occupation needs a substantial number of entrants each year to replace the many mechanics who leave the occupation.

Most persons who enter the occupation can expect steady work because changes in economic conditions have little effect on the automotive repair business. During a downturn, however, some employers may be more reluctant to hire inexperienced workers.

Earnings

Median weekly earnings of automotive mechanics who were wage and salary workers were $478 in 1996. The middle 50 percent earned between $333 and $667 a week. The lowest paid 10 percent earned less than $250 a week, and the top 10 percent earned more than $850 a week.

Many experienced mechanics employed by automotive dealers and independent repair shops receive a commission related to the labor cost charged to the customer. Under this method, weekly earnings depend on the amount of work completed by the mechanic.

Employers frequently guarantee commissioned mechanics a minimum weekly salary. Many master mechanics earn from $70,000 to $100,000 annually.

Some mechanics are members of labor unions. The unions include the International Association of Machinists and Aerospace Workers; the International Union, United Automobile, Aerospace and Agricultural Implement Workers of America; the Sheet Metal Workers' International Association; and the International Brotherhood of Teamsters.

Related Occupations

Other workers who repair and service motor vehicles include diesel truck and bus mechanics, motorcycle mechanics, and automotive body repairers, painters, customizers, and repair service estimators.

Sources of Additional Information

For more details about work opportunities, contact local automotive dealers and repair shops, or the local office of the state employment service. The state employment service also may have information about training programs.

A list of certified automotive mechanic training programs may be obtained from:

❑ National Automotive Technicians Education Foundation, 13505 Dulles Technology Dr., Herndon, VA 22071-3415.

Information on automobile manufacturer sponsored two-year associate degree programs in automotive service technology may be obtained from:

❑ Ford ASSET Program, Ford Customer Service Division, Fairlane Business Park III, 1555 Fairlane Dr., Allen Park, MI 48101. Phone (800) 272-7218.

❑ Chrysler Dealer Apprenticeship Program, National C.A.P. Coordinator, CIMS 423-21-06, 26001 Lawrence Ave., Center Line, MI 48015. Phone (800) 626-1523.

❑ General Motors Automotive Service Educational Program, National College Coordinator, General Motors Service Technology Group, MC 480-204-001, 30501 Van Dyke Ave., Warren, MI 48090. Phone (800) 828-6860.

Information on how to become a certified automotive mechanic is available from:

❑ ASE, 13505 Dulles Technology Dr., Herndon, VA 22071-3415.

For general information about the work of automotive mechanics, write:

❑ Automotive Service Association, Inc., 1901 Airport Freeway, Bedford, TX 76021-5732.

❑ Automotive Service Industry Association, 25 Northwest Point, Elk Grove Village, IL 60007-1035.

❑ National Automobile Dealers Association, 8400 Westpark Dr., McLean, VA 22102

For a directory of accredited private trade and technical schools that offer programs in automotive technician training, write:

❑ Accrediting Commission of Career Schools and Colleges of Technology, 2101 Wilson Blvd., Suite 302, Arlington, VA 22201.

For a list of public automotive mechanic training programs, contact:

❑ Vocational Industrial Clubs of America, P.O. Box 3000, 1401 James Monroe Hwy, Leesburg, VA 22075.

Barbers and Cosmetologists

(D.O.T. 330; 331; 332; 333; 339.361, .371)

Significant Points

✓ *The proportion who are self-employed is very high, as is the proportion who work part-time.*

✓ *All barbers and cosmetologists must be licensed.*

✓ *Cosmetologists will account for virtually all employment growth; employment of barbers is expected to decline.*

Nature of the Work

Looking your best has never been easy. It requires the perfect hairstyle, exquisite nails, a neatly trimmed beard, or the proper make-up to accent your coloring. More and more, it also requires the services of barbers and cosmetologists. As people increasingly demand styles that are better suited to their individual characteristics, they must choose from a vast array of cosmetic products and rely on these workers to help them make sense of the different options. Although tastes and fashions change from year to year, the basic job of barbers and cosmetologists has remained the same–helping people to look their best.

Barbers cut, trim, shampoo, and style hair. Many people still go to a barber for just a haircut, but an increasing number seek more personalized hairstyling services, such as perms or coloring. In addition to these services, barbers may fit hairpieces, provide hair and scalp treatments, shave male customers, or give facial massages. Barbers in most states are licensed to perform all the duties of cosmetologists except skin care and nail treatment, but a growing number of barbers are trained to perform these services as well.

Cosmetologists primarily shampoo, cut, and style hair, but they also perform a number of other services. These workers, who are often called hairstylists, may advise patrons on how to care for their hair, straighten or permanent wave a customer's hair, or lighten or darken hair color. In addition, most cosmetologists are trained to give manicures, pedicures, and scalp and facial treatments; provide makeup analysis for women; and clean and style wigs and hairpieces. Cosmetologists generally are licensed to provide all of the services that barbers do except shaving men.

A growing number of workers in cosmetology offer specialized services. The largest and fastest growing of these is manicurists, who work exclusively on nails and provide manicures, pedicures, and nail extensions to clients. Another group of specialists are estheticians, who cleanse and beautify the skin by giving facials, full-body treatments, head and neck massages, and offer hair-removal through waxing. Electrologists, on the other hand, use an electrolysis machine to remove hair. Finally, shampooers specialize in shampooing and conditioning patrons' hair in some larger salons.

In addition to their work with customers, barbers and cosmetologists are expected to keep their work area clean and their hairdressing implements sanitized. They may make appointments and keep records of hair color and permanent wave formulas used by their regular patrons. A growing number also actively sell hair products and other cosmetic supplies. Barbers and cosmetologists who operate their own salons have managerial duties that include hiring, supervising, and firing workers, as well as keeping records and ordering supplies.

Working Conditions

Barbers and cosmetologists generally work in clean, pleasant surroundings with good lighting and ventilation. Good health and stamina are important because these workers usually have to be on their feet for most of their shift. Prolonged exposure to some hair and nail chemicals may be hazardous and cause irritation, so special care must be taken when working with these chemicals.

Most full-time barbers and cosmetologists work 40 hours a week, but longer hours are common in this occupation, especially among self-employed workers. Work schedules may include evenings and weekends, when beauty and barber shops and salons are busiest. Although weekends and lunch periods are generally very busy, barbers and cosmetologists are able to take breaks during less popular times. Nearly half of all cosmetologists are part-time workers, double the rate for barbers and for all other workers in the economy.

Employment

Barbers and cosmetologists held 701,000 jobs in 1996. Employment in these occupations is distributed as follows:

Hairdressers, hairstylists, and cosmetologists	586,000
Barbers	59,000
Manicurists	43,000
Shampooers	13,000

Most of these workers are employed in beauty salons, barber shops, or department stores, and a few are employed by hospitals, hotels, and prisons. Nearly every town has a barber shop or beauty salon, but employment in this occupation is concentrated in the most populous cities and states. Hairstylists usually work in cities and suburbs, where the greatest demand for their services exists. Stylists who set fashion trends with their hairstyles usually work in New York City, Los Angeles, and other centers of fashion and the performing arts.

Approximately three of every four barbers and two in five cosmetologists are self-employed. Many self-employed barbers and cosmetologists own the salon in which they work, but a growing share of these workers leases the booth or chair where they work from the salon's owner.

Training, Other Qualifications, and Advancement

Although all states require barbers and cosmetologists to be licensed, the qualifications necessary to obtain a license vary. Generally, a person must have graduated from a state-licensed barber or cosmetology school, pass a physical examination, and be at least 16 years old. Some states require graduation from high school while others require as little as an eighth grade education. In a few states, completion of an apprenticeship can substitute for graduation from a school, but very few barbers or cosmetologists learn their skills in this way. Applicants for a license usually are required to pass a written test and demonstrate an ability to perform basic barbering or cosmetology services.

Some states have reciprocity agreements that allow licensed barbers and cosmetologists to practice in a different state without additional formal training. Other states do not recognize training or licenses obtained in another state; consequently, persons who wish to become a barber or a cosmetologist should review the laws of the state in which they want to work before entering a training program.

Public and private vocational schools offer daytime or evening classes in barbering and cosmetology. Full-time programs in barbering and cosmetology usually last six to twelve months, but training for manicurists, estheticians, and electrologists requires significantly less time. An apprenticeship program can last from one to two years. Formal training programs include classroom study, demonstrations, and practical work. Students study the basic services—haircutting, shaving, facial massaging, and hair and scalp treatments—and, under supervision, practice on customers in school "clinics." Most schools also teach unisex hairstyling and chemical styling. Students attend lectures on barber services, the use and care of instruments, sanitation and hygiene, basic anatomy, and recognition of certain skin ailments. Instruction also is provided in sales and general business practices. There are also advanced courses for experienced barbers in hairstyling, coloring, and the sale and service of hairpieces. Most schools teach hairstyling of men's as well as women's hair.

After graduating from a training program, students can take the state licensing examination. The examination consists of a written test and, in some cases, a practical test of cosmetology skills. A few states include an oral examination in which the applicant is asked to explain the procedures he or she is following while taking the practical test. In many states, cosmetology training may be credited towards a barbering license, and vice versa. A few states have even combined the two licenses into one hair styling license. In most states, a separate examination is given for people who want only a manicurist, esthetician, or electrolysis license.

For many cosmetologists, formal training and a license are only the first steps in a career that requires years of continuing education. Because hairstyles are constantly changing, barbers and cosmetologists must keep abreast of the latest fashions and beauty techniques. They do this by attending training in salons, at cosmetology schools, or at product shows. These shows offer workshops and demonstrations of the latest techniques and expose cosmetologists to a wide range of products that they can recommend to clients, an important skill as retail sales become a more important part of the beauty salon industry.

Successful barbers or cosmetologists usually have finger dexterity and a sense of form and artistry. They should enjoy dealing with the public and be willing and able to follow patrons' instructions. Some cosmetology schools consider people skills to be such an integral part of the job that they require course work in this area. Business skills are important for those who plan to operate their own salons, and the ability to be an effective salesperson is becoming vital for nearly all barbers and cosmetologists.

During their first months on the job, new workers are given relatively simple tasks or are assigned the simpler hairstyling patterns. Once they have demonstrated their skills, they are gradually permitted to perform the more complicated tasks such as giving

shaves, coloring hair, or applying a permanent. As they continue to work in the field, more training is generally required to learn the techniques used in each salon and to build on the basics learned in cosmetology school.

Advancement usually takes the form of higher earnings as barbers and cosmetologists gain experience and build a steady clientele. Some barbers and cosmetologists manage large salons or open their own after several years of experience. Others teach in barber or cosmetology schools. Other options include becoming sales representatives for cosmetics firms, opening businesses as beauty or fashion consultants, or working as examiners for state licensing boards.

Job Outlook

Overall employment of barbers and cosmetologists is expected to grow about as fast as the average for all occupations through the year 2006. Increasing population, incomes, and demand for cosmetology services will stimulate job growth. In addition, numerous job openings will stem from rapid turnover in salons and the large size of the occupation. The extent of competition for jobs and customers may be greater at the higher paying, prestigious salons, however, as applicants vie with a large pool of licensed and experienced cosmetologists. The number of part-time and self-employed, booth-renting cosmetologists should continue to grow, creating a dynamic labor market with many opportunities for people to enter the field, particularly workers who are licensed to provide a broad range of cosmetology services.

Different employment trends are expected among barbers and cosmetologists. Cosmetologists will account for virtually all of the employment growth, reflecting the continuing shift in consumer preferences to more personalized services in unisex establishments. Demand for manicurists and for cosmetologists who are trained in nail care will be particularly strong. In addition, cosmetologists who are trained to provide specialized services such as skin care and manicurists who learn new skills like air brushing should be able to attract more clients. Employment of barbers is expected to decline slightly, but in spite of this decline, a couple of thousand job openings will arise annually for new barber licensees as older barbers retire.

Earnings

Barbers and cosmetologists receive income either from commissions or wages and tips. Their median weekly income in 1996 was $290, significantly lower than the $490 for all workers. A number of factors determine the total income for barbers and cosmetologists, including the size and location of the shop, the number of hours worked, customers' tipping habits, and the competition from other barber shops and salons. A cosmetologist's or barber's initiative and ability to attract and hold regular customers are also key factors in determining their earnings. Earnings for entry-level workers are generally lower, ranging from the minimum wage to considerably more in prestigious or exceptionally busy salons.

Related Occupations

Other workers whose main activity consists of improving a patron's personal appearance include beauty consultants and make-up and wig specialists. Other related workers are employed in the cosmetology industry as instructors, beauty supply distributors, and salon managers.

Sources of Additional Information

A list of licensed training schools and licensing requirements for cosmetologists can be obtained from:
- ❑ National Accrediting Commission of Cosmetology Arts and Sciences, 901 North Stuart St., Suite 900, Arlington, VA 22203-1816.

Information about a career in cosmetology is available from:
- ❑ National Cosmetology Association, 3510 Olive St., St. Louis, MO 63017.

For details on state licensing requirements and approved barber or cosmetology schools, contact the state board of barber examiners or the state board of cosmetology in your state capital.

Billing Clerks and Billing Machine Operators

(D.O.T. 184.387-010; 210.382-022, -026, -066; 211.482-014, -018; 214.267-010, .362-010, -014, -022, -026, -038, -042, .382-014, -018, -030, .387-010, -014, -018, .462-010, .467-010, -014; 214.482-010, -014, -018, -022, .587-010; 216.382-022, -034, -050, -054; 217.382-010; 241.267-026; and 249.367-034)

Significant Points

- ✓ *Most billing clerk and billing machine operator jobs require only a high school diploma, but earnings are low.*
- ✓ *Turnover in this occupation will result in numerous job opportunities.*
- ✓ *Job growth is projected for billing clerks.*

Nature of the Work

Billing clerks keep the records, calculate the charges, and maintain the files of payments made for goods or services. Billing machine operators run the machines that generate the bills, statements, and invoices.

Billing clerks review purchase orders, bills of lading, sales tickets, hospital records, or charge slips to calculate the total amount due from a customer. In accounting, law, consulting, and similar firms, billing clerks calculate client fees based on the actual time required to perform the task. They keep track of the accumulated hours and dollar amounts to charge to each job, the type of job performed for a customer, and the percentage of work completed. In hospitals, calculating the charges for an individual's hospital stay may require a letter to an insurance company, whereas a clerk computing trucking rates for machine parts may consult a rate book. After billing clerks review all necessary information, they compute the charges using calculators or computers. They then prepare the itemized statements, bills, or invoices–depending on the organization's needs–used for billing and record keeping purposes. In one organization, the clerk might prepare a simple bill that only contains the amount due and the date and type of service; in another, the clerk would produce a detailed invoice that includes the codes for all goods and services provided. This latter form might list the items sold, credit terms, date of shipment or dates services were provided, a salesperson's or doctor's identification, if necessary, and the sales total.

Once all the information has been entered, billing machine operators then run off the bill that will be sent to the customer. In a growing number of firms, billing machines are being replaced by computers and specialized billing software that allow clerks to calculate charges and prepare bills in one step. Computer packages prompt clerks to enter data from hand-written forms and manipulate the necessary entries of quantities, labor, and rates to be charged. Billing clerks verify the entry of information and check for errors before the bill is printed by the computer. After the bills are printed, billing clerks check them again for accuracy.

Working Conditions

Billing clerks and billing machine operators typically are employed in an office environment. Most work alongside their organization's other clerical workers, but some work in centralized units away from the front office. They may have to sit for extended periods of time.

As the majority of Billing clerks use computers as part of their daily routine, these workers may experience eye and muscle strain, backaches, headaches, and repetitive motion injuries.

Most billing clerks and billing machine operators work regular business hours. Billing clerks in hotels, restaurants, and stores may work overtime during peak holiday and vacation seasons.

Employment

In 1996, billing clerks held about 335,000 jobs, and billing machine operators held about 102,000. About one of every ten billing clerks and billing machine operators were employed by banks and other financial institutions, insurance companies, and other organizations providing business and health services. About two of every ten employees was found in wholesale and retail establishments, and a significant number worked in manufacturing, transportation, communications, and utilities. Approximately two in ten billing clerks and billing machine operators worked part-time in 1996.

Training, Other Qualifications, and Advancement

Most billing clerk and billing machine operator jobs are entry-level, with most employers requiring applicants to have at least a high school diploma or its equivalent. A higher level of education is usually favored over a high school diploma, but is not generally required. Most employers prefer workers who are computer-literate. Knowledge of word processing and spreadsheet software is especially valuable, as are experience working in an office and good interpersonal skills.

High schools, business schools, and community colleges teach those office skills needed by billing clerks and billing machine operators. Business education programs typically include courses in typing (keyboarding), word processing, shorthand, business communications, records management, and office systems and procedures.

Some entrants into the billing clerk field are college graduates with degrees in business, finance, or liberal arts. Although a degree is rarely required, many graduates accept entry-level clerical positions to get into a particular company, with the hope of being promoted to professional or managerial jobs. Workers with college degrees are likely to start at higher salaries and advance more easily than those without degrees.

Once hired, billing clerks and billing machine operators generally receive on-the-job training. Under the guidance of a supervisor or other senior worker, new employees learn company procedures. Some formal classroom training may also be necessary, such as training in specific computer software.

Billing clerks and billing machine operators must be careful, orderly, and detail-oriented, in order to avoid making errors and to be able to recognize errors made by others. They must also be honest, discreet, and trustworthy, because they frequently come in contact with confidential material. Additionally, billing clerks should have a strong aptitude for numbers.

Billing clerks and billing machine operators usually advance by taking on more duties in the same occupation for higher pay. Others advance by transferring to closely related occupations or by moving into other clerical jobs, such as secretary. With appropriate experience and education, some clerks may become accountants.

Job Outlook

Job openings for persons seeking work as billing clerks or billing machine operators are expected to be numerous through the year 2006. Despite the lack of employment growth, many job openings will occur as these workers transfer to other occupations or leave the labor force. Turnover in this occupation is relatively high, characteristic of an entry-level occupation requiring only a high school diploma.

Employment of billing clerks is expected to grow about as fast as the average for all occupations through the year 2006. A growing economy and a greater demand for billing services will result in more business transactions; rising worker productivity stemming from the increasing use of computers to manage account information will not keep employment from rising. More complex billing applications will increasingly require workers with greater technical expertise.

Employment of billing machine operators, on the other hand, is expected to decline through the year 2006 as billing machines are replaced by more advanced machines and computers which enable billing clerks to perform the jobs formerly done by billing machine operators. In some organizations, productivity gains from billing software will increasingly allow accounting clerks to take over the responsibilities of billing clerks and billing machine operators.

Earnings

Salaries of billing clerks and billing machine operators vary by region of the country, size of city, and type and size of establishment. The level of industry or technical expertise required and the complexity and uniqueness of a clerk's responsibilities may also affect earnings. Median earnings of full-time billing clerks in 1996 were $20,600.

Related Occupations

Today, most billing clerks enter data into a computer system and perform basic analysis of the data. Other clerical workers who enter and manipulate data include bank tellers, statistical clerks, receiving clerks, medical record clerks, hotel and motel clerks, credit clerks, and reservation and transportation ticket agents.

Sources of Additional Information

State employment service offices can provide information about job openings for billing clerks and billing machine operators.

Biological and Medical Scientists

(D.O.T. 022.081-010; 041.061, except -014, -018, -046, and -082; 041.067-010; 041.261-010)

Significant Points

✓ *For biological scientists, a Ph.D. degree is generally required for independent research; a master's degree is sufficient for some jobs in applied research or product development; a bachelor's degree is adequate for some nonresearch jobs.*

✓ *For medical scientists, the Ph.D. degree in a biological science is required; some need a medical degree.*

✓ *Doctoral degree holders face considerable competition for independent research positions; those with a bachelor's or master's degree in biological science can expect better opportunities for nonresearch positions.*

Nature of the Work

Biological and medical scientists study living organisms and their relationship to their environment. Most specialize in some area of biology such as zoology (the study of animals) or microbiology (the study of microscopic organisms).

Many biological scientists and virtually all medical scientists work in research and development. Some conduct basic research to advance knowledge of living organisms, including viruses, bacteria, and other infectious agents. Past research has resulted in the development of vaccines, medicines, and treatments for cancer and other diseases. Basic biological and medical research continues to provide the building blocks necessary to develop solutions to human health problems and to preserve and repair the natural environment. Biological and medical scientists may work independently in private industry, university, or government laboratories, often exploring new areas of research or expanding on specialized research started in graduate school. Those who are not wage and salary workers in private industry typically submit grant proposals to obtain funding for their projects. Colleges and universities, private industry, and federal government agencies, such as the National Institutes of Health and the National Science Foundation, contribute to the support of scientists whose research proposals are determined to be financially feasible and have the potential to advance new ideas or processes.

Biological and medical scientists who work in applied research or product development use knowledge provided by basic research to develop new drugs and medical treatments, increase crop yields, and protect and clean up the environment. They usually have less autonomy than basic researchers to choose the emphasis of their research, relying instead on market-driven directions based on the firm's products and goals. Biological and medical scientists doing applied research and product development in private industry may be required to express their research plans or results to nonscientists who are in a position to veto or approve their ideas, and they must understand the business impact of their work. Scientists are increasingly working as part of teams, interacting with engineers, scientists of other disciplines, business managers, and technicians. They may also work with customers or suppliers, and manage budgets.

Biological and medical scientists who conduct research usually work in laboratories and use electron microscopes, computers, thermal cyclers, or a wide variety of other equipment. Some conduct experiments using laboratory animals or greenhouse plants. For some biological scientists, a good deal of research is performed outside of laboratories. For example, a botanist may do research in tropical rain forests to see what plants grow there, or an ecologist may study how a forest area recovers after a fire.

Some biological and medical scientists work in managerial or administrative positions, usually after spending some time doing research and learning about the firm, agency, or project. They may plan and administer programs for testing foods and drugs, for example, or direct activities at zoos or botanical gardens. Some biological scientists work as consultants to business firms or to government, while others test and inspect foods, drugs, and other products.

In the 1980s, swift advances in basic biological knowledge related to genetics and molecules spurred growth in the field of biotechnology. Biological and medical scientists using this technology manipulate the genetic material of animals or plants, attempting to make organisms more productive or resistant to disease. Research using biotechnology techniques, such as recombining DNA, has led to the discovery of important drugs, including human insulin and growth hormone. Many other substances not previously available in large quantities are starting to be produced by biotechnological means; some may be useful in treating cancer and other diseases. Today, many biological and medical scientists are involved in biotechnology, including those who work on the Human Genome project, isolating, identifying, and sequencing human genes. This work continues to lead to the discovery of the genes associated with specific diseases and inherited traits, such as certain types of cancer or obesity. These advances in biotechnology have opened up research opportunities in almost all areas of biology, including commercial applications in agriculture, environmental remediation, and the food and chemical industries.

Most biological scientists who come under the broad category of biologist are further classified by the type of organism they study or by the specific activity they perform, although recent advances in the understanding of basic life processes at the molecular and cellular levels have blurred some traditional classifications.

Aquatic biologists study plants and animals living in water. Marine biologists study salt water organisms and limnologists study fresh water organisms. Marine biologists are sometimes erroneously called oceanographers, but oceanography is the study of the physical characteristics of oceans and the ocean floor.

Biochemists study the chemical composition of living things. They try to understand the complex chemical combinations and reactions involved in metabolism, reproduction, growth, and heredity. Much of the work in biotechnology is done by biochemists and molecular biologists because this technology involves understanding the complex chemistry of life.

Botanists study plants and their environment. Some study all aspects of plant life; others specialize in areas such as identification and classification of plants, the structure and function of plant parts, the biochemistry of plant processes, the causes and cures of plant diseases, and the geological record of plants.

Microbiologists investigate the growth and characteristics of microscopic organisms such as bacteria, algae, or fungi. Medical microbiologists study the relationship between organisms and disease or the effect of antibiotics on microorganisms. Other microbiologists may specialize in environmental, food, agricultural, or industrial microbiology, virology (the study of viruses), or immunology (the study of mechanisms that fight infections). Many microbiologists use biotechnology to advance knowledge of cell reproduction and human disease.

Physiologists study life functions of plants and animals, both in the whole organism and at the cellular or molecular level, under normal and abnormal conditions. Physiologists may specialize in functions such as growth, reproduction, photosynthesis, respiration, or movement, or in the physiology of a certain area or system of the organism.

Zoologists study animals—their origin, behavior, diseases, and life processes. Some experiment with live animals in controlled or natural surroundings while others dissect dead animals to study their structure. Zoologists are usually identified by the animal group studied—ornithologists (birds), mammalogists (mammals), herpetologists (reptiles), and ichthyologists (fish).

Ecologists study the relationship among organisms and between organisms and their environments and the effects of influences such as population size, pollutants, rainfall, temperature, and altitude.

Biological scientists who do biomedical research are usually called medical scientists. Medical scientists working on basic research into normal biological systems often do so to understand the causes of and to discover treatment for disease and other health problems. Medical scientists may try to identify the kinds of changes in a cell, chromosome, or even gene that signal the development of medical problems, such as different types of cancer. After identifying structures of or changes in organisms that provide clues to health problems, medical scientists may then work on the treatment of problems. For example, a medical scientist involved in cancer research might try to formulate a combination of drugs which will lessen the effects of the disease. Medical scientists who have a medical degree might then administer the drugs to patients in clinical trials, monitor their reactions, and observe the results. (Medical scientists who do not have a medical degree normally collaborate with a medical doctor who deals directly with patients.) The medical scientist might then return to the laboratory to examine the results and, if necessary, adjust the dosage levels to reduce negative side effects or to try to induce even better results. In addition to using basic research to develop treatments for health problems, medical scientists attempt to discover ways to prevent health problems from developing, such as affirming the link between smoking and increased risk of lung cancer, or alcoholism and liver disease.

Working Conditions

Biological and medical scientists generally work regular hours in offices or laboratories and usually are not exposed to unsafe or unhealthy conditions. Those who work with dangerous organisms or toxic substances in the laboratory must follow strict safety procedures to avoid contamination. Medical scientists also spend time working in clinics and hospitals administering drugs and treatments to patients in clinical trials. Many biological scientists such as botanists, ecologists, and zoologists take field trips which involve strenuous physical activity and primitive living conditions.

Biological and medical scientists who depend on grant money to support their research may be under pressure to meet deadlines and conform to rigid grant-writing specifications when preparing proposals to seek new or extended funding.

Employment

Biological and medical scientists held about 118,000 jobs in 1996. Almost one in four biological scientists were employed by federal, state, and local governments. Federal biological scientists worked mainly in the U.S. Departments of Agriculture, the Interior, and Defense, and in the National Institutes of Health. Most of the rest worked in the drug industry, which includes pharmaceutical and biotechnology establishments; hospitals; or research and testing laboratories. About one in five medical scientists worked in state government, with most of the remainder found in research and testing laboratories, educational institutions, the drug industry, and hospitals.

In addition, many biological and medical scientists held biology faculty positions in colleges and universities.

Training, Other Qualifications, and Advancement

For biological scientists, the Ph.D. degree generally is required for independent research and for advancement to administrative positions. A master's degree is sufficient for some jobs in applied research or product development and for jobs in management, inspection, sales, and service. The bachelor's degree is adequate for some nonresearch jobs. Some graduates with a bachelor's degree start as biological scientists in testing and inspection, or get jobs related to biological science such as technical sales or service representatives. In some cases, graduates with a bachelor's degree are able to work in a laboratory environment on their own projects, but this is unusual. Some may work as research assistants. Others become biological technicians, medical laboratory technologists or, with courses in education, high school biology teachers. Many with a bachelor's degree in biology enter medical, dental, veterinary, or other health profession schools. Some enter a wide range of occupations with little or no connection to biology.

Most colleges and universities offer bachelor's degrees in biological science and many offer advanced degrees. Curriculums for advanced degrees often emphasize a subfield such as microbiology or botany, but not all universities offer all curriculums. Advanced degree programs include classroom and field work, laboratory research, and a thesis or dissertation. Biological scientists who have advanced degrees often take temporary postdoctoral research positions which provide specialized research experience. In private industry, some may become managers or administrators within biology; others leave biology for nontechnical managerial, administrative, or sales jobs.

Biological scientists should be able to work independently or as part of a team and be able to communicate clearly and concisely, both orally and in writing. Those in private industry, especially those who aspire to management or administrative positions, should possess strong business and communication skills and be familiar with regulatory issues and marketing and management techniques. Those doing field research in remote areas must have physical stamina.

The Ph.D. degree in a biological science is the minimum education required for prospective medical scientists because the work of medical scientists is almost entirely research oriented. A Ph.D. degree qualifies one to do research on basic life processes or on particular medical problems or diseases, and to analyze and interpret the results of experiments on patients. Medical scientists who administer drug or gene therapy to human patients, or who otherwise interact medically with patients–such as drawing blood, excising tissue, or performing other invasive procedures–must have a medical degree. It is particularly helpful for medical scientists to earn both Ph.D. and medical degrees.

In addition to the formal education, medical scientists are usually expected to spend several years in a postdoctoral position before they are offered permanent jobs. Postdoctoral work provides valuable laboratory experience, including experience in specific processes and techniques, such as gene splicing, which are transferable to other research projects. In some institutions, the postdoctoral position can lead to a permanent position.

Job Outlook

Despite prospects of faster-than-average job growth over the 1996-2006 period, biological and medical scientists can expect to face considerable competition for coveted basic research positions. Much research and development, including many areas of medical research, is funded by the federal government. Recent budget tightening has led to smaller increases in research and development expenditures, further limiting the dollar amount of each grant and slowing the growth of the number of grants awarded to researchers. At the same time, the number of newly trained scientists has continued to increase at a steady rate, so both new and established scientists have experienced greater difficulty winning and renewing research grants. If the number of advanced degrees awarded continues to grow unabated, this competitive scenario is likely to persist. Additionally, applied research positions in private industry may become more difficult if more scientists seek jobs in private industry than in the past due to the competitive job market for college and university faculty.

Opportunities for those with a bachelor's or master's degree in biological science are expected to be better. The number of science-related jobs in sales, marketing, and research management, for which non-Ph.D.s generally qualify, are expected to be more plentiful than independent research positions. They may also fill positions as science or engineering technicians or health technologists and technicians. Some become high school biology teachers, while those with a doctorate in biological science may become college and university faculty.

Biological and medical scientists enjoyed very rapid gains in employment between the mid-1980s and mid-1990s, in part reflecting increased staffing requirements in new biotechnology companies. Employment growth should slow as increases in the number of new biotechnology firms slows and existing firms merge or are absorbed into larger ones. However, much of the basic biological research done in recent years has resulted in new knowledge, including

the isolation and identification of new genes. Biological and medical scientists will be needed to take this knowledge to the next stage, which is the understanding of how certain genes function within an entire organism so that gene therapies can be developed to treat diseases. Even pharmaceutical and other firms not solely engaged in biotechnology are expected to increasingly use biotechnology techniques, spurring employment increases for biological and medical scientists. In addition, efforts to discover new and improved ways to clean up and preserve the environment will continue to add to growth. More biological scientists will be needed to determine the environmental impact of industry and government actions and to prevent or correct environmental problems. Expected expansion in research related to health issues–such as AIDS, cancer, and Alzheimer's disease–should also result in growth.

Biological and medical scientists are less likely to lose their jobs during recessions than those in many other occupations because many are employed on long-term research projects. However, a recession could further influence the amount of money allocated to new research and development efforts, particularly in areas of risky or innovative research. A recession could also limit the possibility of extension or renewal of existing projects.

Earnings

According to the National Association of Colleges and Employers, beginning salary offers in private industry in 1997 averaged $25,400 a year for bachelor's degree recipients in biological science; about $26,900 for master's degree recipients; and about $52,400 for doctoral degree recipients.

Median annual earnings for biological and life scientists were about $36,300 in 1996; the middle 50 percent earned between $28,400 and $50,900. Ten percent earned less than $22,000, and 10 percent earned over $66,000. For medical scientists, median annual earnings were about $34,300; the middle 50 percent earned between $25,200 and $52,200. Ten percent earned less than $18,700, and 10 percent earned over $74,000.

In the federal government in 1997, general biological scientists in nonsupervisory, supervisory, and managerial positions earned an average salary of $52,100; microbiologists, $58,700; ecologists, $52,700; physiologists, $65,900; and geneticists, $62,700.

Related Occupations

Many other occupations deal with living organisms and require a level of training similar to that of biological and medical scientists. These include the conservation occupations of forester, range manager, and soil conservationist; animal breeders, horticulturists, soil scientists, and most other agricultural scientists. Many health occupations are also related to those in the biological sciences, such as medical doctors, dentists, and veterinarians.

Sources of Additional Information

For information on careers in the biological sciences, contact:
❑ American Institute of Biological Sciences, Suite 200, 1444 I St. NW, Washington, DC 20005. Homepage: http://www.aibs.org

For information on careers in physiology, contact:
❑ American Physiological Society, Education Office, 9650 Rockville Pike, Bethesda, MD 20814. Homepage: http://www.faseb.org/aps

For information on careers in biotechnology, contact:

❑ Biotechnology Industry Organization, 1625 K St. NW, Suite 1100, Washington, DC 20006.

For information on careers in biochemistry, contact:

❑ American Society for Biochemistry and Molecular Biology, 9650 Rockville Pike, Bethesda, MD 20814.

For information on careers in biophysics, contact:

❑ Biophysical Society, 9650 Rockville Pike, Room 0512, Bethesda, MD 20814.

For information on careers in botany, contact:

❑ Botanical Society of America, Business Office, 1735 Neil Ave., Columbus, OH 43210-1293. Homepage: http://www.botany.org

For information on careers in microbiology, contact:

❑ American Society for Microbiology, Office of Education and Training–Career Information, 1325 Massachusetts Ave. NW, Washington, DC 20005. Homepage: http://www.asmusa.org

Information on acquiring a job as a biological or medical scientist with the federal government may be obtained from the Office of Personnel Management through a telephone-based system. Consult your telephone directory under U.S. government for a local number or call (912) 757-3000 (TDD 912 744-2299). That number is not toll-free and charges may result. Information also is available from their Internet site: http://www.usajobs.opm.gov

Blue-Collar Worker Supervisors

(*D.O.T.* codes are too numerous to list.)

Significant Points

✓ *Although many workers still rise through the ranks with high school diplomas, employers increasingly seek applicants with postsecondary training.*

✓ *Employment in manufacturing is expected to decline, reflecting the increasing use of computers, the implementation of self-directed work teams, and corporate downsizing; employment in construction and most other nonmanufacturing industries is expected to rise along with employment of the workers they supervise.*

✓ *Supervisors in the highly cyclical construction industry may be laid off when construction activity declines.*

Nature of the Work

For the millions of workers who assemble manufactured goods, service electronics equipment, work in construction, load trucks, or perform thousands of other activities, a blue-collar worker supervisor is the boss. In addition to *the boss,* blue-collar worker supervisors go by many other titles. The most common are *first-line supervisor* or *foreman/forewoman*, but titles vary according to the industry in which these workers are employed. For example, in the textile industry, these supervisors may be referred to as *second hands*; on ships, they may be called *boatswains*. In the construction industry, they can be referred to as *superintendents, crew chiefs,* or *foremen/forewomen*, depending on the type and size of their employer. *Toolpushers* or *gang pushers* are common terms used to describe blue-collar supervisors in the oil-drilling business.

Although the responsibilities of blue-collar worker supervisors are as varied as the titles they hold, their primary task is to ensure that workers, equipment, and materials are used properly to maxi-

mize productivity. To accomplish this, they perform many duties. Supervisors make sure machinery is set up correctly, schedule or perform repairs and maintenance work, create work schedules, keep production and employee records, monitor employees, and ensure that work is done correctly and on time. In addition, they organize workers' activities, make necessary adjustments to ensure that work continues uninterrupted, train new workers, and ensure the existence of a safe working environment.

The means by which supervisors perform these duties have changed dramatically in recent years as companies have restructured their operations for maximum efficiency. Supervisors now use computers to schedule work flow, monitor the quality of workers' output, keep track of materials used, update the inventory control system, and perform other supervisory tasks. In addition, new management philosophies that emphasize fewer levels of management and greater employee power in decision making have altered the role of these supervisors. In the past, supervisors exercised their authority to direct the efforts of blue-collar workers; increasingly, supervisors are assuming the role of a facilitator for groups of workers, aiding in group decision making and conflict resolution.

Because they serve as the main conduit of information between management and blue-collar workers, supervisors have many interpersonal tasks related to their job. They inform workers about company plans and policies; recommend good performers for wage increases, awards, or promotions; and deal with poor performers by outlining expectations, counseling workers in proper methods, issuing warnings, or recommending disciplinary action. They also meet on a regular basis with their managers, reporting any problems and discussing possible solutions. Supervisors may often meet among themselves to discuss goals, company operations, and performance. In companies with labor unions, supervisors must follow all provisions of labor-management contracts.

Working Conditions

Blue-collar worker supervisors work in a wide range of settings based on the industry in which they are employed. Many supervisors work on the shop floor. This can be tiring if they are on their feet most of their shift, working near loud and dangerous machinery. Other supervisors, such as those in construction and oil exploration and production, sometimes work outdoors in severe weather conditions.

Supervisors may be on the job before other workers arrive and often stay after others leave. Some supervisors work in plants that operate around the clock, so they may work any one of three shifts, as well as weekends and holidays. In some cases, supervisors work all three shifts on a rotating basis; in others, shift assignments are made on the basis of seniority.

Because organizational restructuring and downsizing have required many blue-collar worker supervisors to oversee more workers and departments in recent years, longer hours and added responsibilities have increased on-the- job stress for many supervisors.

Employment

Blue-collar worker supervisors held about 1.9 million jobs in 1996. Although salaried supervisors are found in almost all industries, two of every five work in manufacturing. Other industries employing blue-collar worker supervisors include wholesale and retail trade, public utilities, repair shops, transportation, and government. The vast majority of the 188,000 self-employed workers in this occupation are employed in construction.

Training, Other Qualifications, and Advancement

When choosing supervisors, employers generally look for experience, job knowledge, organizational skills, and leadership qualities. Employers also emphasize the ability to motivate employees, maintain high morale, and command respect. In addition, well-rounded applicants who are able to deal with different situations and a diverse work force are desired. Communication and interpersonal skills are also extremely important attributes in this occupation.

Completion of high school is often the minimum educational requirement to become a blue-collar worker supervisor, but workers generally receive training in human resources, computer software, and management before they advance to these positions. Although many workers still rise through the ranks with high school diplomas, employers increasingly seek applicants with postsecondary technical degrees. In high-technology industries, such as aerospace and electronics, employers may require a bachelor's degree or technical school training. Large companies usually offer better opportunities for promotion to blue-collar worker supervisor positions than do smaller companies.

In most manufacturing companies, a degree in business or engineering, combined with in-house training, is needed to advance from supervisor to department head or production manager. In the construction industry, supervisors increasingly need a degree in construction management or engineering if they expect to advance to project manager, operations manager, or general superintendent. Some use their skills and experience to start their own construction contracting firms. Supervisors in repair shops may open their own businesses.

Job Outlook

Employment of blue-collar worker supervisors is expected to grow more slowly than average through the year 2006. As the number of workers in the economy increases, so will the need to supervise these workers. In addition to growth, many openings will arise from the need to replace workers who transfer to other occupations or leave the labor force.

Projected job growth varies by industry. In manufacturing, employment of supervisors is expected to decline slightly as each supervisor is expected to oversee more workers. This trend reflects the increasing use of computers to meet supervisory responsibilities, such as production analysis and scheduling; greater involvement of production workers in decision making and the formation of self-directed work teams; and corporate downsizing. These developments are not as prevalent in construction and most other nonmanufacturing industries, where the employment of blue-collar worker supervisors is expected to rise along with employment of the workers they supervise.

Because of their skill and seniority, blue-collar worker supervisors often are protected from layoffs during a recession. However, some supervisors in the highly cyclical construction industry may be laid off when construction activity declines.

Earnings

Median weekly earnings for blue-collar worker supervisors were about $640 in 1996. The middle 50 percent earned between $480 and $820. The lowest 10 percent earned less than $350, while the highest 10 percent earned over $1,020. Most supervisors earn significantly more than the workers they supervise. While most blue-collar workers are paid by the hour, the majority of supervisors receive an annual salary. Some supervisors receive extra pay when they work overtime.

Related Occupations

Other workers with supervisory duties include those who supervise professional, technical, sales, clerical, and service workers. Some of these are retail store or department managers, sales managers, clerical supervisors, bank officers, head tellers, hotel managers, postmasters, head cooks, head nurses, and surveyors.

Sources of Additional Information

For information on educational programs for blue-collar worker supervisors, contact:

❑ American Management Association, 1601 Broadway, New York, NY 10019.

❑ National Management Association, 2210 Arbor Blvd., Dayton, OH 45439.

❑ American Institute of Constructors, 466 94th Ave. North, St. Petersburg, FL 33702.

Bricklayers and Stonemasons

(D.O.T. 779.684-058; 861.361-010 and -014, .381-010 through -042, except -034, .684-010 and -014; and 899.364-010)

Significant Points

✓ *Opportunities should be very good because job openings are expected to grow faster than the number of workers being trained.*

✓ *Work is often outdoors, requires lifting heavy bricks and blocks, and sometimes involves working on scaffolds.*

✓ *Nearly one out of every four bricklayers and stonemasons is self-employed.*

Nature of the Work

Bricklayers and stonemasons work in closely related trades producing attractive, durable surfaces and structures. The work they perform varies in complexity, from laying a simple masonry walkway to installing the ornate exterior of a high-rise building. Bricklayers build walls, floors, partitions, fireplaces, chimneys, and other structures with brick, precast masonry panels, concrete block, and other masonry materials. Some specialize in installing firebrick linings in industrial furnaces. Stonemasons build stone walls, as well as set stone exteriors and floors. They work with two types of stone—natural cut, such as marble, granite, and limestone, and artificial stone made from concrete, marble chips, or other masonry materials. Stonemasons usually work on structures such as houses of worship, hotels, and office buildings.

In building a wall, bricklayers create the corners of the structure first. Due to the necessary precision, these corner leads are very time consuming to construct erect and require the skills of the most experienced bricklayers on the job. After the corner leads are complete, less experienced bricklayers fill in the wall between the corners, using a line from corner to corner to guide each course or layer of brick. Because of the expense associated with building corner leads, an increasing number of bricklayers are using corner poles, also called masonry guides, that enable them to build the entire wall at the same time. They fasten the corner posts or poles in a plumb position to define the wall line, and stretch a line between them. The line serves as a guide for each course of brick. Bricklayers then spread a bed of mortar (a cement, sand, and water mixture) with a trowel (a flat, bladed metal tool with a handle), place the brick on the mortar bed, and then press and tap it into place. As blueprints specify, they either cut brick with a hammer and chisel, or saw them to fit around windows, doors, and other openings. Mortar joints are finished with jointing tools for a sealed, neat, and uniform appearance. Although bricklayers generally use steel supports, or "lintels," at window and door openings, they sometimes build brick arches that support and enhance the beauty of the brickwork.

Bricklayers are assisted by hod carriers, or helpers, who bring bricks and other materials to them while working, mix mortar, and set up and move the scaffolding.

Stonemasons often work from a set of drawings in which each stone has been numbered for identification. Helpers may locate and bring the prenumbered stones to the masons. A derrick operator using a hoist, may be needed to lift large pieces into place.

When building a stone wall, masons set the first course of stones into a shallow bed of mortar. They align the stones with wedges, plumblines, and levels, and adjust them into position with a hard rubber mallet. Masons build the wall by alternating layers of mortar and courses of stone. As the work progresses, they remove the wedges and fill the joints between stones and use a pointed metal tool, called a "tuck pointer," to smooth the mortar to an attractive finish. To hold large stones in place, stonemasons attach brackets to the stone and weld or bolt them to anchors in the wall. Finally, masons wash the stone with a cleansing solution to remove stains and dry mortar.

When setting stone floors, which often consist of large and heavy pieces of stone, masons first use a trowel to spread a layer of damp mortar over the surface to be covered. Using crowbars and hard rubber mallets for aligning and leveling, they then set the stone in the mortar bed. To finish, workers fill the joints and wash the stone slabs.

Masons use a special hammer and chisel to cut stone. They cut it along the grain to make various shapes and sizes. Valuable pieces often are cut with a saw that has a diamond blade. Some masons specialize in setting marble which, in many respects, is similar to setting large pieces of stone. Bricklayers and stonemasons also repair imperfections and cracks, or replace broken or missing masonry units in walls and floors.

Most nonresidential buildings are now built with prefabricated panels made of concrete block, brick veneer, stone, granite, marble, tile, or glass. In the past, bricklayers performed mostly interior work, such as block partition walls and elevator shafts. Now they must be more versatile and work with many materials. For example, brick-

layers now install lighter-weight insulated panels used in new skyscraper construction.

Refractory masons are bricklayers who specialize in installing firebrick and refractory tile in high-temperature boilers, furnaces, cupolas, ladles, and soaking pits in industrial establishments. Most work in steel mills, where molten materials flow on refractory beds from furnaces to rolling machines.

Working Conditions

Bricklayers and stonemasons usually work outdoors. They stand, kneel, and bend for long periods and often have to lift heavy materials. Common hazards include injuries from tools and falls from scaffolds, but these can be avoided when proper safety practices are followed.

Employment

Bricklayers and stonemasons held about 142,00 jobs in 1996. The vast majority were bricklayers. Workers in these crafts are employed primarily by special trade, building, or general contractors. They work throughout the country but, like the general population, are concentrated in metropolitan areas.

Nearly one-fourth of all bricklayers and stonemasons were self-employed. Many of the self-employed specialize in contracting on small jobs such as patios, walkways, and fireplaces.

Training, Other Qualifications, and Advancement

Most bricklayers and stonemasons pick up their skills informally, observing and learning from experienced workers. Many receive training in vocational education schools. The best way to learn these skills, however, is through an apprenticeship program, which generally provides the most thorough training.

Individuals who learn the trade on the job usually start as helpers, laborers, or mason tenders. They carry materials, move scaffolds, and mix mortar. When the opportunity arises, they are taught to spread mortar, lay brick and block, or set stone. As they gain experience, they make the transition to full-fledged craft workers. The learning period generally lasts much longer than an apprenticeship program, however.

Apprenticeships for bricklayers and stonemasons are usually sponsored by local contractors or by local union-management committees. The apprenticeship program requires three years of on-the-job training in addition to a minimum 144 hours of classroom instruction each year in subjects such as blueprint reading, mathematics, layout work, and sketching.

Apprentices often start by working with laborers, carrying materials, mixing mortar, and building scaffolds. This period generally lasts about a month and familiarizes them with job routines and materials. Next, they learn to lay, align, and join brick and block. Apprentices also learn to work with stone and concrete. This enables them to be certified to work with more than one masonry material.

Applicants for apprenticeships must be at least 17 years old and in good physical condition. A high school education is preferable, and courses in mathematics, mechanical drawing, and shop are helpful. The International Masonry Institute, a division of the International Union of Bricklayers and Allied Craftsmen, operates training centers in several large cities that help job seekers develop the skills needed to successfully complete the formal apprenticeship program.

Bricklayers who work in nonresidential construction usually work for large contractors and receive well-rounded training in all phases of brick/stone work, usually through apprenticeship. Those who work in residential construction usually work primarily for small contractors and specialize in only one or two aspects of the job.

Experienced workers can advance to supervisory positions or become estimators. They also can open contracting businesses of their own.

Job Outlook

Job opportunities for skilled bricklayers and stonemasons are expected to be good as the growth in demand outpaces the supply of workers trained in this craft. Employment of bricklayers and stonemasons is expected to grow about as fast as the average for all occupations through the year 2006, and additional openings will result from the need to replace bricklayers and stonemasons who retire, transfer to other occupations, or leave the trades for other reasons. However, the pool of young workers available to enter training programs will also be increasing slowly, and many in that group are reluctant to seek training for jobs that may be strenuous and have uncomfortable working conditions.

Population and business growth will create a need for new factories, schools, hospitals, offices, and other structures, increasing the demand for bricklayers and stonemasons. Also stimulating demand, will be the need to restore a growing stock of old masonry buildings, as well as the increasing use of brick for decorative work on building fronts and in lobbies and foyers. Brick exteriors should continue to be very popular as the trend continues toward more durable exterior materials requiring less maintenance. Employment of bricklayers who specialize in refractory repair will decline, along with employment in other occupations in the primary metal industries.

Employment of bricklayers and stonemasons, like that of many other construction workers, is sensitive to changes in the economy. When the level of construction activity falls, workers in these trades can experience periods of unemployment.

Earnings

Median weekly earnings for bricklayers and stonemasons were about $484 in 1996. The middle 50 percent earned between $345 and $624 weekly. The highest 10 percent earned more than $926 weekly; the lowest 10 percent earned less than $247. Earnings for workers in these trades may be reduced on occasion, because poor weather and downturns in construction activity limit the time they can work.

In each trade, apprentices or helpers usually start at about 50 percent of the wage rate paid to experienced workers. This increases as they gain experience.

Some bricklayers and stonemasons are members of the International Union of Bricklayers and Allied Craftsmen.

Related Occupations

Bricklayers and stonemasons combine a thorough knowledge of brick, concrete block, stone, and marble with manual skill to erect very attractive yet highly durable structures. Workers in other occupations with similar skills include concrete masons, plasterers, terrazzo workers, and tilesetters.

Sources of Additional Information

For details about apprenticeships or other work opportunities in these trades, contact local bricklaying, stonemasonry, or marble setting contractors; a local of the union listed above; a local joint union-management apprenticeship committee; or the nearest office of the state employment service or state apprenticeship agency.

For general information about the work of either bricklayers or stonemasons, contact:

❑ International Union of Bricklayers and Allied Craftsmen, International Masonry Institute Apprenticeship and Training, 823 15th St. NW, Suite 1001, Washington, DC 20005.

Information about the work of bricklayers also may be obtained from:

❑ Associated General Contractors of America, Inc., 1957 E St. NW, Washington, DC 20006.
❑ Brick Institute of America, 11490 Commerce Park Dr., Reston, VA 22091-1525.
❑ Home Builders Institute, National Association of Home Builders, 1201 15th St. NW, Washington, DC 20005.
❑ National Concrete Masonry Association, 2302 Horse Pen Rd., Herndon, VA 22071.

Broadcast Technicians

(D.O.T. 193.167-014, .262-018, and -038; 194.062, .122, .262-010, -014, -018, -022, .282, .362, and .382-014, -018, 962.167-010, and .382-010)

Significant Points

✓ *Competition is expected for the better paying jobs at radio and television stations serving large cities.*

✓ *Beginners need formal training in broadcast technology to obtain their first job at a smaller station.*

✓ *Evening, weekend, and holiday work is common.*

Nature of the Work

Broadcast technicians install, test, repair, set up, and operate the electronic equipment used to record and transmit radio and television programs. They work with television cameras, microphones, tape recorders, light and sound effects, transmitters, antennas, and other equipment. Some broadcast technicians develop movie sound tracks in motion picture production studios.

In the control room of a radio or television broadcasting studio, these technicians operate equipment that regulates the signal strength, clarity, and range of sounds and colors of recordings or broadcasts. They also operate control panels to select the source of the material. Technicians may switch from one camera or studio to another, from film to live programming, or from network to local programs. By means of hand signals and, in television, telephone headsets, they give technical directions to other studio personnel.

Broadcast technicians in small stations perform a variety of duties. In large stations and at the networks, technicians are more specialized, although job assignments may change from day to day. The terms "operator," "engineer," and "technician" often are used interchangeably to describe these jobs. Transmitter operators monitor and log outgoing signals and operate transmitters. Maintenance technicians set up, adjust, service, and repair electronic broadcasting equipment. Audio control engineers regulate sound pickup, transmission, and switching of television pictures while, video control engineers regulate their quality, brightness, and contrast. Recording engineers operate and maintain video and sound recording equipment. They may operate equipment designed to produce special effects, such as the illusions of a bolt of lightning or a police siren. Field technicians set up and operate broadcasting portable field transmission equipment outside the studio.

Television news coverage requires so much electronic equipment, and the technology is changing so fast, that many stations assign technicians exclusively to news. Chief engineers, transmission engineers, and broadcast field supervisors supervise the technicians who operate and maintain broadcasting equipment.

Technicians in the motion picture industry are called sound mixers or rerecording mixers. Mixers produce the sound track of a movie, using a process called dubbing. They sit at sound consoles facing the screen and fade in and fade out each sound and regulate its volume. Each technician is responsible for certain sounds. Technicians follow a script that tells at precisely what moment, as the film runs through the projector, each of the sounds must be faded in and out. All the sounds for each shot are thus blended on a master sound track.

Working Conditions

Broadcast technicians generally work indoors in pleasant surroundings. However, those who broadcast from disaster areas or crime scenes may work under unfavorable conditions. Technicians doing maintenance may climb poles or antenna towers, while those setting up equipment do heavy lifting.

Technicians in large stations and the networks usually work a 40-hour week, but may occasionally work overtime, under great pressure to meet broadcast deadlines. Technicians in small stations routinely work more than 40 hours a week. Evening, weekend, and holiday work is usual, because most stations are on the air 18 to 24 hours a day, seven days a week.

Those who work on motion pictures may be on a tight schedule to finish according to contract agreements.

Employment

Broadcast technicians held about 46,000 jobs in 1996. About seven out of ten broadcast technicians were in radio and television broadcasting. Almost two in ten worked in the motion picture industry. About 8 percent worked for cable and other pay television services. A few were self-employed. Television stations employ, on average, many more technicians than do radio stations. Some broadcast technicians are employed in other industries, producing employee communications, sales, and training programs. Technician jobs in television are located in virtually all cities, while jobs in radio are also found in many small towns. The highest paying and most specialized jobs are concentrated in New York City, Los Angeles, Chicago, and Washington, DC—the originating centers for most of network programs. Motion picture production jobs are concentrated in Los Angeles and New York City.

Training, Other Qualifications, and Advancement

The best way to prepare for a broadcast technician job in radio or television is to obtain technical school, community college, or college training in broadcast technology or in engineering or electronics. This is particularly true for those who hope to advance to supervisory positions or jobs at large stations or the networks. On the other hand, there is no formal training for jobs in the motion picture industry. People are hired as apprentice editorial assistants and work their way up to more skilled jobs. Employers in the motion picture industry usually hire freelance technicians on a picture-by-picture basis. Reputation, determination, and luck are important in getting jobs.

Beginners learn skills on the job from experienced technicians and supervisors. They generally begin their careers in small stations and, once experienced, move on to larger ones. Large stations generally only hire technicians with experience. Many employers pay tuition and expenses for courses or seminars to help technicians keep abreast of developments in the field.

The federal Communications Commission no longer requires the licensing of broadcast technicians, as the Telecommunications Act of 1996 eliminated this licensing requirement. Certification by the Society of Broadcast Engineers is a mark of competence and experience. The certificate is issued to experienced technicians who pass an examination. By offering the Radio Operator and the Television Operator levels of certification, the Society of Broadcast Engineers has filled the void left by the elimination of the FCC license.

Prospective technicians should take high school courses in math, physics, and electronics. Building electronic equipment from hobby kits and operating a "ham," or amateur radio, are good experience, as is work in college radio and television stations.

Broadcast technicians must have manual dexterity and an aptitude for working with electrical, electronic, and mechanical systems and equipment.

Experienced technicians may become supervisory technicians or chief engineers. A college degree in engineering is needed to become chief engineer at a large TV station.

Job Outlook

People seeking beginning jobs as radio and television broadcast technicians are expected to face strong competition in major metropolitan areas, where the number of qualified job seekers greatly exceeds the number of openings. There, stations seek highly experienced personnel. Prospects for entry level positions generally are better in small cities and towns for people with appropriate training.

The overall employment of broadcast technicians is expected to grow about as fast as the average through the year 2006. Growth in the number of new radio and television stations and an increase in the number of programming hours should require additional technicians. However, employment growth in radio and television broadcasting may be tempered somewhat because of laborsaving technical advances, such as computer-controlled programming and remote control of transmitters.

Employment in the cable industry should grow because of new products coming to market, such as cable modems, which deliver high speed Internet access to PCs, and digital set-top boxes, which transmit better sound and pictures, allowing cable operators to offer many more channels than in the past. These new products should cause traditional cable subscribers to sign up for additional services. Also, employment in the cable industry should grow, as today's young people establish their own households, for they are more accustomed to the idea of paying for TV than their parents.

Employment in the motion picture industry will grow faster than the average for all occupations. Job prospects are expected to remain competitive, because of the large number of people attracted to this relatively small field.

Virtually all job openings will result from the need to replace experienced technicians who leave the occupation. Turnover is relatively high for broadcast technicians. Many leave the occupation for electronic jobs in other areas, such as computer technology or commercial and industrial repair.

Earnings

Television stations usually pay higher salaries than radio stations; commercial broadcasting usually pays more than educational broadcasting; and stations in large markets pay more than those in small ones.

According to a survey conducted by the National Association of Broadcasters and the Broadcast Cable Financial Management Association, average earnings for technicians at radio stations were $30,251 a year in 1996. For chief engineer, average earnings were $46,602; and salaries ranged from $34,714 in the smallest markets to $46,602 in the largest markets. In television, average earnings for operator technicians were $24,260 a year and salaries ranged from $16,422 to $45,158; for technical directors, average earnings were $25,962 a year and the range was $18,444 to $44,531; for maintenance technicians, average earnings were $32,533 a year and the range was $24,210 to $50,235; and for chief engineers, the average earnings were $53,655 a year and salaries ranged from $38,178 in the smallest markets to $91,051 in the largest.

Earnings in the motion picture industry depend on skill and reputation and, based on limited information, range from $20,000 to $100,000 a year.

Related Occupations

Broadcast technicians need the electronics training and hand coordination necessary to operate technical equipment, and they generally complete specialized postsecondary programs. Others with similar jobs and training include drafters, engineering and science technicians, surveyors, air traffic controllers, radiologic technologists, respiratory therapy workers, cardiovascular technologists and technicians, electroneurodiagnostic technicians, and clinical laboratory technologists and technicians.

Sources of Additional Information

For information on careers for broadcast technicians, write to:
❑ National Association of Broadcasters Employment Clearing-house, 1771 N St. NW, Washington, DC 20036.

For a list of schools that offer programs or courses in broadcasting, contact:
❑ Broadcast Education Association, National Association of Broadcasters, 1771 N St. NW, Washington, DC 20036.

For information on certification, contact:
❑ Society of Broadcast Engineers, 8445 Keystone Crossing, Suite 140, Indianapolis, IN 46240.

For information on careers in the motion picture and televi-

sion industry, contact:
❑ Society of Motion Picture and Television Engineers (SMPTE), 595 W. Hartsdale Ave., White Plains, NY 10607.

Brokerage Clerks and Statement Clerks

(D.O.T. 214.362-046; 216.362-046, .382-046, .482-034; 219.362-018, -054, .482-010)

Significant Points

✓ *Most brokerage clerk and statement clerk jobs require only a high school diploma, but earnings are low.*

✓ *Turnover in this occupation will result in numerous job opportunities.*

✓ *Little or no change is expected in employment of brokerage clerks and statement clerks, reflecting the spread of computers and other office automation.*

Nature of the Work

Brokerage clerks and statement clerks work behind the scenes to produce records associated with financial transactions.

Brokerage clerks, who work in the operations areas of securities firms, perform many duties to facilitate the sale and purchase of stocks, bonds, commodities, and other kinds of investments. These clerks produce the necessary records of all transactions that occur in their area of the business.

Job titles depend upon the type of work performed. *Purchase-and-sale clerks* match orders to buy with orders to sell. They balance and verify stock trades by comparing the records of the selling firm to those of the buying firm. *Dividend clerks* ensure timely payments of stock or cash dividends to clients of a particular brokerage firm. *Transfer clerks* execute customer requests for changes to security registration and examine stock certificates for adherence to banking regulations. *Receive-and-deliver clerks* facilitate the receipt and delivery of securities among firms and institutions. *Margin clerks* post accounts and monitor activity in customers' accounts. Their job is to ensure that customers make their payments and stay within legal boundaries concerning stock purchases.

A significant and growing number of brokerage clerks use custom-designed software programs to process transactions, allowing transactions to be processed more quickly than if they were done manually. Currently, only a few customized accounts are handled manually.

Statement clerks assemble, verify, and send individual and commercial bank statements every month.

In most banks, statement clerks, sometimes called *statement operators,* run sophisticated, high-speed machines. These machines fold the computer-printed statement, collate it if it is more than one page, insert the statement and canceled checks into an envelope, seal it, and weigh it for postage. Statement clerks load the machine with the statements, canceled checks, and envelopes. They then monitor the equipment and correct minor problems. For serious problems, they call repair personnel.

In banks that do not have such machines, statement clerks perform all operations manually. They may also be responsible for verifying signatures and checking for missing information on checks, placing canceled checks into trays, and retrieving them to send with the statements.

In a growing number of banks, only the statement is printed and sent to the account holder. The canceled checks are not returned; this is known as check truncation.

Statement clerks are employed primarily by large banks. In smaller banks, their function is usually handled by a teller or a bookkeeping clerk who performs other duties during the rest of the month. Some small banks send their statement information to larger banks for processing, printing, and mailing.

Working Conditions

Brokerage clerks and statement clerks typically are employed in an office environment. Most work alongside their organization's other clerical workers, but some work in centralized units away from the front office. They may have to sit for extended periods of time.

As the majority of brokerage clerks and statement clerks use computers as part of their daily routine, these workers may experience eye and muscle strain, backaches, headaches, and repetitive motion injuries.

Most brokerage clerks and statement clerks work regular business hours. Brokerage clerks may also have to work overtime, if there is a high volume of activity in the stock or bond markets.

Employment

Brokerage clerks held about 76,000 jobs in 1996, and statement clerks held about 25,000 jobs. Brokerage clerks worked in firms involved in the sales of securities and commodities. Almost all statement clerks were employed by banking institutions.

Training, Other Qualifications, and Advancement

Most brokerage clerk jobs are entry-level, with most employers requiring applicants to have at least a high school diploma or its equivalent. A higher level of education is usually favored over a high school diploma, but is not generally required. However, brokerage firms increasingly seek college graduates for brokerage clerk jobs. Most employers prefer workers who are computer-literate. Knowledge of word processing and spreadsheet software is especially valuable, as are experience working in an office and good interpersonal skills.

High schools, business schools, and community colleges teach those office skills needed by brokerage clerks. Business education programs typically include courses in typing (keyboarding), word processing, shorthand, business communications, records management, and office systems and procedures.

Some entrants into the brokerage clerk field are college graduates with degrees in business, finance, or liberal arts. Although a degree is rarely required, many graduates accept entry-level clerical positions to get into a particular company or to enter the finance field, with the hope of being promoted to professional or managerial jobs. Some brokerage firms have a set plan of advancement that tracks college graduates from entry-level clerk jobs into managerial positions. Workers with college degrees are likely to start at higher salaries and advance more easily than those without degrees.

Once hired, brokerage clerks generally receive on-the-job training. Under the guidance of a supervisor or other senior worker, new employees learn company procedures. Some formal classroom training may also be necessary, such as training in specific computer software.

Brokerage clerks must be careful, orderly, and detail-oriented, in order to avoid making errors and to be able to recognize errors made by others. These workers must also be honest, discreet, and trustworthy, because they frequently come in contact with confidential material.

Brokerage clerks usually advance by taking on more duties in the same occupation for higher pay. Others advance transferring to closely related occupations. With appropriate experience and education, some brokerage clerks may become securities sales representatives.

Job Outlook

Employment of brokerage clerks is expected to grow about as fast as the average for all occupations through the year 2006. Employment of statement clerks is projected to decline. Nevertheless, some jobs will become available each year to replace brokerage and statement clerks who transfer to other occupations or leave the labor force.

Similar to other record clerks, employment will be adversely affected by automation and changes in business practices. For example, computers now calculate the dividends due on stocks, something done for decades by brokerage clerks with adding machines and calculators. However, brokerage clerks are still needed to enter data into the computer and to process information. In the past, the record of security ownership was a piece of paper—a stock certificate. Today, most securities are stored in computer form and traded using electronic data interchange. Although less paper changes hands, clerks continue to enter and verify all transactions.

Automated statement processing will grow as the increased volume of transactions justifies the cost of the necessary equipment, and this will dampen demand for statement clerks. In addition, the further spread of check truncation is expected to hold down employment of statement clerks. The use of automatic teller machines and other electronic money transfers should increase as well, resulting in significantly fewer checks being written and processed.

Earnings

Salaries of brokerage clerks and statement clerks vary by region of the country, size of city, and type and size of establishment. The level of industry or technical expertise required and the complexity and uniqueness of a clerk's responsibilities may also affect earnings. Median earnings of full-time brokerage clerks and statement clerks in 1996 were $20,700.

Related Occupations

Today, most brokerage clerks and statement clerks enter data into a computer system and perform basic analysis of the data. Other clerical workers who enter and manipulate data include bank tellers, statistical clerks, receiving clerks, medical record clerks, hotel and motel clerks, credit clerks, and reservation and transportation ticket agents.

Sources of Additional Information

State employment service offices can provide information about job openings for brokerage clerks and statement clerks.

Bus Drivers

(D.O.T. 913.363, .463-010, and .663-014 and -018)

Significant Points

✓ *Opportunities should be good, particularly for school bus driver jobs.*

✓ *Many full-time transit, inter-city, and motorcoach bus driver jobs offer relatively high earnings but have few prerequisite training requirements.*

Nature of the Work

Bus drivers provide transportation for millions of Americans every day. Inter-city bus drivers transport people between regions of a state or of the country; local transit bus drivers, within a metropolitan area or county; motorcoach drivers, on charter excursions and tours; and school bus drivers, to and from schools and related events. All drivers follow time schedules and routes over highways and city and suburban streets, to provide passengers with an alternative to the automobile and other forms of transportation.

Inter-city bus drivers and local transit bus drivers report to their assigned terminal or garage, where they receive tickets or transfers and prepare trip report forms. School bus drivers do not always have to report to an assigned terminal or garage. In some cases, school bus drivers often have the choice of taking their bus home, or parking it in a more convenient area. Before beginning their routes, drivers check their vehicle's tires, brakes, windshield wipers, lights, oil, fuel, and water supply. Drivers also verify that the bus has safety equipment, such as fire extinguishers, first aid kits, and emergency reflectors in case of an emergency.

Drivers pick up and drop off passengers at bus stops, stations, or, in the case of students, at regularly scheduled neighborhood locations. Inter-city and local transit bus drivers collect fares; answer questions about schedules, routes, and transfer points; and sometimes announce stops. School bus drivers do not collect fares. Instead, they prepare weekly reports with the number of students, trips or runs, work hours, miles, and the amount of fuel consumption. Their supervisors set time schedules and routes for the day or week. School bus drivers also must maintain order on their bus and enforce school safety standards by allowing only students to board.

Bus drivers' days are run by the clock, as they must adhere to strict time schedules. Drivers must operate vehicles safely, especially when traffic is heavier than normal. However, they cannot let light traffic put them ahead of schedule so that they miss passengers.

Bus drivers must be alert to prevent accidents, especially in heavy traffic or in bad weather, and to avoid sudden stops or swerves which jar passengers. School bus drivers must exercise particular caution when children are getting on or off the bus. They must know and reinforce the same set of rules used elsewhere in the school system.

Bus routes vary. Local transit bus drivers may make several trips each day over the same city and suburban streets, stopping as frequently as every few blocks. School bus drivers also drive the same routes each day, stopping to pick up pupils in the morning and return them to their homes in the afternoon. School bus drivers

may also transport students and teachers on field trips or to sporting events. Inter-city bus drivers may make only a single one-way trip to a distant city or a round trip each day, stopping at towns just a few miles apart or only at large cities hundreds of miles apart.

Motorcoach drivers transport passengers on charter trips and sightseeing tours. Drivers routinely interact with customers and tour guides to make the trip as comfortable and informative as possible. They are directly responsible for keeping to strict schedules, adhering to the guidelines of the tours' itinerary, and the overall success of the trip. Trips frequently last more than one day, and if they are assigned to an extended tour, they may be away for a week or more.

Local transit bus drivers submit daily trip reports with a record of tickets and fares received, trips made, and significant delays in schedule, and report mechanical problems. All bus drivers must be able to fill out accident reports when necessary. Inter-city drivers who drive across state or national boundaries must comply with U.S. Department of Transportation regulations. These include completing vehicle inspection reports and recording distances traveled and the periods of time they spend driving, performing other duties, and off duty.

Working Conditions

Driving a bus through heavy traffic while dealing with passengers is not physically strenuous, but it can be stressful and fatiguing. On the other hand, many drivers enjoy the opportunity to work without direct supervision, with full responsibility for the bus and passengers.

Inter-city bus drivers may work nights, weekends, and holidays and often spend nights away from home, where they stay at hotels at company expense. Senior drivers with regular routes have regular weekly work schedules, but others do not have regular schedules and must be prepared to report for work on short notice. They report for work only when called for a charter assignment or to drive extra buses on a regular route. Inter-city bus travel and charter work tend to be seasonal. From May through August, drivers may work the maximum number of hours per week that regulations allow. During winter, junior drivers may work infrequently, except for busy holiday travel periods, and may be furloughed for periods of time.

School bus drivers work only when school is in session. Many work 20 hours a week or less, driving one or two routes in the morning and afternoon. Drivers taking field or athletic trips or who also have midday kindergarten routes may work more hours a week.

Regular local transit bus drivers usually have a five-day workweek; Saturdays and Sundays are considered regular workdays. Some drivers work evenings and after midnight. To accommodate commuters, many work "split shifts," for example, 6 A.M. to 10 A.M. and 3 P.M. to 7 P.M., with time off in-between.

Tour and charter bus drivers may work any day and all hours of the day, including weekends and holidays. Their hours are dictated by the charter trips booked and the schedule and the prearranged itinerary of tours. However, like all bus drivers, their weekly hours must be consistent with the Department of Transportation's rules and regulations concerning hours of service. For example, a long-distance driver cannot work more than 60 hours in any seven-day period and drivers must rest eight hours for every ten hours of driving.

Employment

Bus drivers held about 592,000 jobs in 1996. More than a third worked part time. Nearly three out of four drivers worked for school systems or companies providing school bus services under contract, as shown in the accompanying chart. Most of the remainder worked for private and local government transit systems; some also worked for inter-city and charter bus lines.

Training, Other Qualifications, and Advancement

Bus driver qualifications and standards are established by state and federal regulations. All drivers must comply with federal regulations and any state regulations that exceed federal requirements. Federal regulations require drivers who operate vehicles designed to transport 16 or more passengers to hold a commercial driver's license (CDL) from the state in which they live.

To qualify for a commercial driver's license, applicants must pass a written test on rules and regulations and then demonstrate they can operate a bus safely. A national data bank permanently records all driving violations incurred by persons who hold commercial licenses. A state may not issue a commercial driver's license to a driver who already has a license suspended or revoked in another state. Trainees must be accompanied by a driver with a CDL until they get their own CDL. Information on how to apply for a commercial driver's license may be obtained from state motor vehicle administrations.

While many states allow those who are 18 years and older to drive buses within state borders, the U.S. Department of Transportation establishes minimum qualifications for bus drivers engaged in interstate commerce. Federal Motor Carrier Safety Regulations require that drivers must be at least 21 years old and pass a physical examination once every two years. The main physical requirements include good hearing, 20/40 vision with or without glasses or corrective lenses, and a 70 degree field of vision in each eye. Drivers must not be color blind. Drivers must be able to hear a forced whisper in one ear at not less than five feet, with or without a hearing aide. Drivers must have normal use of arms and legs and normal blood pressure. Drivers may not use any controlled substances, unless prescribed by a licensed physician. Persons with epilepsy or diabetes controlled by insulin are not permitted to be interstate bus drivers. Federal regulations also require employers to test their drivers for alcohol and drug use as a condition of employment, and require periodic random tests while on duty. In addition, a driver must not have been convicted of a felony involving the use of a motor vehicle; a crime involving drugs; driving under the influence of drugs or alcohol; or hit-and-run driving which resulted in injury or death. All drivers must be able to read and speak English well enough to read road signs, prepare reports, and communicate with law enforcement officers and the public. In addition, drivers must take a written examination on the Motor Carrier Safety Regulations of the U.S. Department of Transportation.

Many employers prefer high school graduates and require a written test of ability to follow complex bus schedules. Many inter-city and public transit bus companies prefer applicants who are at least 24 years of age; some require several years of bus or truck driving experience. In some states, school bus drivers must pass a background investigation to uncover any criminal record or history of mental problems.

Because bus drivers deal with passengers, they must be courteous. They need an even temperament and emotional stability because driving in heavy, fast-moving, or stop-and-go traffic and dealing with passengers can be stressful. Drivers must have strong communication skills and be able to coordinate and manage large groups of people.

Most inter-city bus companies and local transit systems give driver trainees two to eight weeks of classroom and behind-the-wheel instruction. In the classroom, trainees learn U.S. Department of Transportation and company work rules, safety regulations, state and municipal driving regulations, and safe driving practices. They also learn to read schedules, determine fares, keep records, and deal courteously with passengers.

School bus drivers are also required to obtain a commercial driver's license from the state in which they live. Many persons who enter school bus driving have never driven any vehicle larger than an automobile. They receive between one and four weeks of driving instruction plus classroom training on state and local laws, regulations, and policies of operating school buses; safe driving practices; driver-pupil relations; first aid; disabled student special needs; and emergency evacuation procedures. School bus drivers must also be aware of school systems rules for discipline and conduct for bus drivers and the students they transport.

During training, bus drivers practice driving on set courses. They practice turns and zigzag maneuvers, backing up, and driving in narrow lanes. Then they drive in light traffic and, eventually, on congested highways and city streets. They also make trial runs, without passengers, to improve their driving skills and learn the routes. Local transit trainees memorize and drive each of the runs operating out of their assigned garage. New drivers begin with a "break-in" period. They make regularly scheduled trips with passengers, accompanied by an experienced driver who gives helpful tips, answers questions, and evaluates the new driver's performance.

New inter-city and local transit drivers are usually placed on an "extra" list to drive charter runs, extra buses on regular runs, and special runs (for example, during morning and evening rush hours and to sports events). They also substitute for regular drivers who are ill or on vacation. New drivers remain on the extra list, and may work only part time, perhaps for several years, until they have enough seniority to receive a regular run.

Senior drivers may bid for runs they prefer, such as those with more work hours, lighter traffic, weekends off, or, in the case of inter-city bus drivers, higher earnings or fewer workdays per week.

Opportunities for promotion are generally limited. However, experienced drivers may become supervisors or dispatchers, assigning buses to drivers, checking whether drivers are on schedule, rerouting buses to avoid blocked streets or other problems, and dispatching extra vehicles and service crews to scenes of accidents and breakdowns. In transit agencies with rail systems, drivers may become train operators or station attendants. A few drivers become managers. Promotion in publicly owned bus systems is often by competitive civil service examination. Some motorcoach drivers purchase their own equipment and go in to business for themselves.

Job Outlook

Persons seeking jobs as bus drivers over the 1996-2006 period should encounter good opportunities. Many employers are having difficulty finding qualified candidates to fill vacancies left by departing employees. Opportunities should be best for individuals with good driving records who are willing to start on a part-time or irregular schedule, as well as for those seeking jobs as school bus drivers in metropolitan areas that are growing rapidly. Those seeking higher paying inter-city and public transit bus driver positions may encounter competition.

Employment of bus drivers is expected to increase about as fast as average for all occupations through the year 2006, primarily to meet the transportation needs of a growing school-age population. Thousands of additional job openings are expected to occur each year because of the need to replace workers who take jobs in other occupations, retire, or leave the occupation for other reasons.

School bus driving jobs should be easiest to acquire because most of these positions are part time and often have a high turnover rate. The number of school bus drivers is expected to increase as a result of growth in elementary and secondary school enrollments. In addition, as more of the nation's population is concentrated in suburban areas–where students generally ride school buses–and less in the central cities–where transportation is not provided for most pupils–more school bus drivers will be needed.

Employment of local transit and inter-city drivers will grow as bus ridership increases. Local and inter-city bus travel is expected to increase as the population and labor force grow and incomes rise, but more individual travelers will opt to travel by airplane or automobile rather than by bus. Most growth in inter-city drivers will probably be in group charter travel, rather than scheduled inter-city bus services. There may continue to be competition for local transit and inter-city bus driver jobs in some areas because many of these positions offer relatively high wages and attractive benefits. The most competitive positions will be those offering regular hours and steady driving routes.

Full-time bus drivers are rarely laid off during recessions. However, hours of part-time local transit and inter-city bus drivers may be reduced if bus ridership decreases, because fewer extra buses would be needed. Seasonal layoffs are common. Many inter-city bus drivers with little seniority, for example, are furloughed during the winter when regular schedule and charter business falls off; school bus drivers seldom work during the summer or school holidays.

Earnings

Median weekly earnings of bus drivers who worked full time were $400 in 1996. The middle 50 percent earned between about $293 and $588 a week. The lowest 10 percent earned less than $233 a week, while the highest 10 percent earned more than $760 a week.

According to the American Public Transit Association, in early 1997 local transit bus drivers in metropolitan areas with more than 2 million inhabitants were paid an average hourly wage rate of $17.06 by companies with over 1,000 employees, and $15.43 by those with fewer than 1,000 employees. In smaller metropolitan areas, they had an average hourly wage rate of $14.04 in areas with between 250,000 and 500,000 residents, and $11.76 in areas with populations below 50,000. Generally, drivers can reach the top rate in three or four years.

According to a survey by the Educational Research Service, the average rate for school bus drivers employed by public school sys-

tems was $11.50 an hour during the 1996-97 school year. Lowest hourly rates averaged $9.93 while highest hourly rate averaged $13.06.

The fringe benefits bus drivers receive from their employers vary greatly. Most inter-city and local transit bus drivers receive paid health and life insurance, sick leave, and free bus rides on any of the regular routes of their line or system. Drivers who work full time also get as much as four weeks of vacation annually. Most local transit bus drivers are also covered by dental insurance and pension plans. School bus drivers receive sick leave, and many are covered by health and life insurance and pension plans. Because they generally do not work when school is not in session, they do not get vacation leave. In a number of states, local transit and school bus drivers who are employed by local governments are covered by a statewide public employee pension system.

Most inter-city and many local transit bus drivers are members of the Amalgamated Transit Union. Local transit bus drivers in New York and several other large cities belong to the Transport Workers Union of America. Some drivers belong to the United Transportation Union and the International Brotherhood of Teamsters.

Related Occupations

Other workers who drive vehicles on highways and city streets are taxi drivers, truck drivers, and chauffeurs.

Sources of Additional Information

For further information on employment opportunities, contact local transit systems, inter-city bus lines, school systems, or the local offices of the state employment service.

General information on bus driving is available from:
- ❏ American Bus Association, 1100 New York Ave. NW, Suite 1050, Washington, DC 20005.

General information on school bus driving is available from:
- ❏ National School Transportation Association, P.O. Box 2639, Springfield, VA 22152.

General information on local transit bus driving is available from:
- ❏ American Public Transit Association, 1201 New York Ave. NW, Suite 400, Washington, DC 20005.

General information on motorcoach driving is available from:
- ❏ United Motorcoach Association, 113 S. West St., 4th Floor, Alexandria, VA 22314. Phone 1-800-424-8262.

Carpenters

(D.O.T. 806.281-058; 860.281-010 through .664-010 and .684-101 and -014; 863.684-010; 869.361-018, .381-010, -034, .684-018, -034, -042, and -058; and 962.281-010)

Significant Points

- ✓ *The largest construction trade in 1996 with 996,000 workers, nearly one-third of whom were self-employed.*
- ✓ *Although employment is expected to grow slowly, job opportunities should be excellent because high turnover rates create many job openings.*
- ✓ *Carpenters with skills in all aspects of carpentry work the most steadily because they have the versatility to perform whatever types of jobs that may be available.*

Nature of the Work

Carpenters are involved in many different kinds of construction activity. They cut, fit, and assemble wood and other materials in the construction of buildings, highways, bridges, docks, industrial plants, boats, and many other structures. Their duties vary by type of employer. A carpenter employed by a special trade contractor, for example, may specialize in one or two activities, such as setting forms for concrete construction or erecting scaffolding. However, a carpenter employed by a general building contractor may perform many tasks, such as framing walls and partitions, putting in doors and windows, hanging kitchen cabinets, and installing paneling and tile ceilings.

Local building codes often dictate where certain materials can be used, and carpenters must know these requirements. Each carpentry task is somewhat different, but most involve the same basic steps. Working from blueprints or instructions from supervisors, carpenters first do the layout—measuring, marking, and arranging materials. They then cut and shape wood, plastic, ceiling tile, fiberglass, or drywall using hand and power tools, such as chisels, planes, saws, drills, and sanders, and then join the materials with nails, screws, staples, or adhesives. In the final step, they check the accuracy of their work with levels, rules, plumb bobs, and framing squares and make any necessary adjustments. When working with prefabricated components, such as stairs or wall panels, the carpenter's task is somewhat simpler because it does not require as much layout work or the cutting and assembly of as many pieces. These components are designed for easy and fast installation and generally can be installed in a single operation.

Carpenters employed outside the construction industry perform a variety of installation and maintenance work. They may replace panes of glass, ceiling tiles, and doors, as well as repair desks, cabinets, and other furniture. Depending on the employer, they may install partitions, doors, and windows; change locks; and repair broken furniture. In manufacturing firms, carpenters may assist in moving or installing machinery.

Working Conditions

As in other building trades, carpentry work is sometimes strenuous. Prolonged standing, climbing, bending, and kneeling are often necessary. Carpenters risk injury from slips or falls, working with sharp or rough materials, and using of sharp tools and power equipment. Many carpenters work outdoors.

Some carpenters change employers each time they finish a construction job. Others alternate between working for a contractor and working as contractors themselves on small jobs.

Employment

Carpenters, the largest group of building trades workers, held about 996,000 jobs in 1996. Four of every five worked for contractors who build, remodel, or repair buildings and other structures. Most of the remainder worked for manufacturing firms, government agencies, wholesale and retail establishments, and schools. Nearly one-third were self-employed.

Carpenters are employed throughout the country in almost every community.

Training, Other Qualifications, and Advancement

Carpenters learn their trade through on-the-job training and through formal training programs. Some pick up skills informally by working under the supervision of experienced workers. Many acquire skills through vocational education. Others participate in employer training programs or apprenticeships.

Most employers recommend an apprenticeship as the best way to learn carpentry. Because the number of apprenticeship programs is limited, however, only a small proportion of carpenters learn their trade through these programs. Apprenticeship programs are administered by local joint union-management committees of the United Brotherhood of Carpenters and Joiners of America, the Associated General Contractors, Inc., or the National Association of Home Builders. Training programs are administered by local chapters of the Associated Builders and Contractors and by local chapters of the Associated General Contractors, Inc. These programs combine on-the-job training with related classroom instruction. Apprenticeship applicants must generally be at least 17 years old and meet local requirements. For example, some union locals test an applicant's aptitude for carpentry. The length of the program, usually about three to four years, varies with the apprentice's skill.

On the job, apprentices learn elementary structural design and become familiar with common carpentry jobs such as layout, form building, rough framing, and outside and inside finishing. They also learn to use the tools, machines, equipment, and materials of the trade. Apprentices receive classroom instruction in safety, first aid, blueprint reading, and freehand sketching, basic mathematics, and different carpentry techniques. Both in the classroom and on the job, they learn the relationship between carpentry and the other building trades.

Informal on-the-job training is usually less thorough than an apprenticeship. The degree of training and supervision often depends on the size of the employing firm. A small contractor specializing in home-building may only provide training in rough framing. In contrast, a large general contractor may provide training in several carpentry skills. Although specialization is becoming increasingly common, it is important to try to acquire skills in all aspects of carpentry and to have the flexibility to perform any kind of work. Carpenters with a well-rounded background can switch from residential building to commercial construction to remodeling jobs, depending on demand.

A high school education is desirable, including courses in carpentry, shop, mechanical drawing, and general mathematics. Manual dexterity, eye-hand coordination, physical fitness, and a good sense of balance are important. The ability to solve arithmetic problems quickly and accurately is also helpful. Employers and apprenticeship committees generally view favorably, training and work experience obtained in the Armed Services and the Job Corps.

Carpenters may advance to carpentry supervisors or general construction supervisors. Carpenters usually have greater opportunities than most other construction workers to become general construction supervisors, because they are exposed to the entire construction process. Some carpenters become independent contractors. To advance, carpenters should be able to estimate the nature and quantity of materials needed to properly complete a job. They must also be able to estimate, with accuracy, how long a job should take to complete, and its cost.

Job Outlook

Job opportunities for carpenters are expected to be plentiful through the year 2006, due primarily to extensive replacement needs. Thousands of job openings will become available each year as carpenters transfer to other occupations or leave the labor force. The total number of job openings for carpenters is usually greater than for other craft occupations, because the occupation is large and the turnover rate is high. Because there are no strict training requirements for entry, many people with limited skills take jobs as carpenters but eventually leave the occupation because they dislike the work or cannot find steady employment.

Increased demand for carpenters will create additional job openings. Employment is expected to increase more slowly than the average for all occupations through the year 2006. Construction activity should increase slowly in response to demand for new housing and commercial and industrial plants, and the need to renovate and modernize existing structures. Opportunities for frame carpenters will be particularly good. The demand for carpenters will be offset somewhat by expected productivity gains resulting from the increasing use of prefabricated components, such as prehung doors and windows and prefabricated wall panels and stairs, that can be installed much more quickly. Prefabricated walls, partitions, and stairs can be quickly lifted into place in one operation; beams, and in some cases entire roof assemblies, can be lifted into place using a crane. As prefabricated components become more standardized, their use will increase. In addition, stronger adhesives reducing the time needed to join materials and lightweight cordless pneumatic and combustion tools such as nailers and drills, as well as sanders with electronic speed controls, will make carpenters more efficient and reduce fatigue.

Although employment of carpenters is expected to grow over the long run, people entering the occupation should expect to experience periods of unemployment. This results from the short-term nature of many construction projects, and the cyclical nature of the construction industry. Building activity depends on many factors—interest rates, availability of mortgage funds, government spending, and business investment—that vary with the state of the economy. During economic downturns, the number of job openings for carpenters declines. The introduction of new and improved tools, equipment, techniques, and materials has vastly increased carpenters' versatility. Therefore, carpenters with all-round skills will have better opportunities than those who can only do relatively simple, routine tasks.

Job opportunities for carpenters also vary by geographic area. Construction activity parallels the movement of people and businesses and reflects differences in local economic conditions. Therefore, the number of job opportunities and apprenticeship opportunities in a given year may vary widely from area to area.

Earnings

Median weekly earnings of carpenters, excluding the self-employed, were $476 in 1996. The middle 50 percent earned between $345 and $660 per week. Weekly earnings for the top 10 percent of all carpenters were more than $874; the lowest 10 percent earned less than $267.

Earnings may be reduced on occasion because carpenters lose work time in bad weather and during recessions when jobs are unavailable.

Many carpenters are members of the United Brotherhood of Carpenters and Joiners of America.

Related Occupations

Carpenters are skilled construction workers. Workers in other skilled construction occupations include bricklayers, concrete masons, electricians, pipefitters, plasterers, plumbers, stonemasons, and terrazzo workers.

Sources of Additional Information

For information about carpentry apprenticeships or other work opportunities in this trade, contact local carpentry contractors, locals of the union mentioned above, local joint union-contractor apprenticeship committees, or the nearest office of the state employment service or state apprenticeship agency.

For general information about carpentry, contact:

❑ Associated Builders and Contractors, 1300 North 17th Street, Rosslyn, VA 22209.

❑ Associated General Contractors of America, Inc., 1957 E St. NW, Washington, DC 20006.

❑ Home Builders Institute, National Association of Home Builders, 1201 15th St. NW, Washington, DC 20005.

❑ United Brotherhood of Carpenters and Joiners of America, 101 Constitution Ave. NW, Washington, DC 20001.

Cashiers

(D.O.T. 209.567-014; 211.362-010, .367, .462, .467, .482-010; 249.467; and 294.567)

Significant Points

✓ *Good employment opportunities are expected due to the large number who leave this occupation each year.*

✓ *The occupation offers plentiful opportunities for part-time work.*

Nature of the Work

Supermarkets, department stores, gasoline service stations, movie theaters, restaurants, and many other businesses employ cashiers to register the sale of their merchandise. Most cashiers total bills, receive money, make change, fill out charge forms, and give receipts.

Although specific job duties vary by employer, cashiers are usually assigned to a register at the beginning of their shifts and given drawers containing "banks" of money. They must count their banks to ensure that they contain the correct amount of money and that there are adequate supplies of change. At the end of their shifts, they once again count the drawers' contents and compare the totals with sales data. An occasional shortage of small amounts may be overlooked, but in many establishments, repeated shortages are grounds for dismissal.

In addition to counting the contents of their drawers at the end of their shifts, cashiers usually separate charge forms, return slips, coupons, and any other noncash items.

Cashiers also handle returns and exchanges and must ensure that merchandise is in good condition and determine where and when it was purchased and what type of payment was used.

After entering charges for all items and subtracting the value of any coupons or special discounts, cashiers total the bill and take payment. Acceptable forms of payment usually include cash, personal check, charge, and increasingly, debit cards. Cashiers must know the store's policies and procedures for accepting each type of payment the store accepts. For checks and charges, they may have to request additional identification from the customer or call in for an authorization. When the sale is complete, cashiers issue a receipt to the customer and return the appropriate change. They may also wrap or bag the purchase.

Cashiers traditionally have totaled customers' purchases using cash registers—manually entering the price of each product bought. However, most establishments are now using more sophisticated equipment, such as scanners and computers. In a store with scanners, a cashier passes a product's Universal Product Code over the scanning device, which transmits the code number to a computer. The computer identifies the item and its price. In other establishments, cashiers manually enter codes into computers, and descriptions of the items and their prices appear on the screen.

Depending on the type of establishment, cashiers may have other duties as well. In many supermarkets, for example, cashiers weigh produce and bulk food as well as return unwanted items to the shelves. In convenience stores, cashiers may be required to know how to use a variety of machines, other than cash registers, and how to furnish money orders. Operating ticket-dispensing machines and answering customers' questions are common duties for cashiers who work at movie theaters and ticket agencies. Counter and rental clerks perform many similar duties.

Working Conditions

More than one-half of all cashiers are on part-time schedules. Hours of work often vary depending on the needs of the employer. Generally, cashiers are expected to work weekends, evenings, and holidays to accommodate customers' needs. However, because of this, many employers offer flexible schedules. For example, full-time workers who work on weekends may receive time off during the week. Because the holiday season is the busiest time for most retailers, many employers restrict the use of vacation time from Thanksgiving through the beginning of January.

Most cashiers work indoors, usually standing in booths or behind counters. In addition, they are often unable to leave their workstations without supervisory approval because they are responsible for large sums of money. The work of cashiers can be very repetitious but improvements in workstation design are being made to combat problems caused by repetitive motion.

Employment

Cashiers held about 3,146,000 jobs in 1996. Although employed in nearly every industry, nearly one-third of all jobs were in supermarkets and other food stores. Department stores, gasoline service stations, drug stores, and other retail establishments also employed large numbers of these workers. Because cashiers are needed in businesses and organizations of all types and sizes, job opportunities are found throughout the country.

Training, Other Qualifications, and Advancement

Cashier jobs tend to be entry-level positions requiring little or no previous work experience. Although there are no specific educational requirements, employers filling full-time jobs often prefer applicants with high school diplomas.

Nearly all cashiers are trained on the job. In small firms, beginners are often trained by an experienced worker. The first day is usually spent observing the operation and becoming familiar with the store's equipment, policies, and procedures. After this, trainees are assigned to a register—frequently under the supervision of a more experienced worker. In larger firms, before being placed at cash registers, trainees first spend several days in classes. Topics typically covered include a description of the industry and the company, instruction on the store's policies, procedures, and equipment operation, and security.

Training for experienced workers is not common, except when new equipment is introduced or when procedures change. In these cases, training is given on the job, by the employer or a representative of the equipment manufacturer.

Persons who want to become cashiers should be able to do repetitious work accurately. They also need basic arithmetic skills and good manual dexterity; and, because they deal constantly with the public, cashiers should be neat in appearance and able to deal tactfully and pleasantly with customers. In addition, some firms seek persons who have operated specialized equipment or who have business experience, such as typing, selling, or handling money.

Advancement opportunities for cashiers vary. For those working part time, promotion may be to a full-time position. Others advance to head cashier or cash office clerk. In addition, this job offers a good opportunity to learn an employer's business and can serve as a steppingstone to a more responsible position.

Job Outlook

As in the past, employment opportunities for cashiers are expected to continue to be good, because of the many job openings created each year due to the need to replace the large number of workers who transfer to other occupations or leave the labor force. Additional openings will be created by growth in employment of cashiers.

Cashier employment is expected to increase about as fast as the average for all occupations through the year 2006 due to expanding demand for goods and services by a growing population. Traditionally, workers under the age of 25 have filled many of the openings in this occupation—in 1996, about half of all cashiers were 24 years of age or younger. Recently, some establishments have begun hiring elderly and disabled persons as well to fill some of their job openings. Opportunities for part-time work are expected to continue to be excellent.

Earnings

Cashiers have earnings ranging from the minimum wage, to several times that amount. Wages tend to be higher in areas where there is intense competition for workers. In establishments covered by federal law, those beginning at the minimum wage earned $5.15 an hour in 1997. In some states, the minimum wage in many establishments is governed by state law, and where state minimums are higher, the establishment must pay at least that amount.

In 1996, median weekly earnings for full-time cashiers were $247. The middle 50 percent earned between $198 and $328; 10 percent earned below $165; and 10 percent earned above $486.

Benefits for full-time cashiers tend to be better than for those working part time. Cashiers often receive health and life insurance and paid vacations. In addition, those working in retail establishments often receive discounts on purchases, and cashiers in restaurants may receive free or low-cost meals. Some employers also offer employee stock option plans.

Related Occupations

Cashiers accept payment for the purchase of goods and services. Other workers with similar duties include food counter clerks, bank tellers, counter and rental clerks, postal service clerks, and sales clerks.

Sources of Additional Information

General information on retailing is available from:

❏ National Retail Federation, 325 7th St. NW, Suite 1000, Washington, DC 20004. Homepage: http://www.nrf.com

❏ Food Marketing Institute, 800 Connecticut Ave. NW, Washington, DC 20006.

For information about employment opportunities as a cashier, contact:

❏ National Association of Convenience Stores, 1605 King St., Alexandria, VA 22314-2792.

❏ Service Station Dealers of America, 9420 Annapolis Rd., Suite 307, Lanham, MD 20706.

❏ International Mass Retail Association, 1700 N. Moore St., Suite 2250, Arlington, VA 22209-1998.

❏ United Food and Commercial Workers International Union, Education Office, 1775 K St. NW, Washington, DC 20006-1502.

Chefs, Cooks, and Other Kitchen Workers

(D.O.T. 311.674-014; 313 except .131; 315.361, .371, and .381; 316.661 and .684-014; 317; 318.687; and 319.484)

Significant Points

✓ *About 40 percent of cooks and 60 percent of other kitchen and food preparation workers were on part-time schedules, approximately two and three times the proportion for all workers throughout the economy.*

✓ *Many young people work in these occupations—over 20 percent of food preparation workers are 16 to 19 years old.*

✓ *Job openings are expected to be plentiful through the year 2006, reflecting substantial turnover—characteristic of occupations attractive to people seeking a short-term source of income rather than a career.*

Nature of the Work

A reputation for serving good food is essential to any restaurant or hotel, whether it prides itself on exotic cuisine or hamburgers. Chefs, cooks, and other kitchen workers are largely responsible for the reputation a restaurant acquires. Some restaurants offer a varied menu featuring meals that are time-consuming and difficult to prepare, requiring highly skilled employees. Other restaurants emphasize fast service, offering hamburgers and other food that can be prepared in advance or in a few minutes by a fast-food or short-order cook, with limited cooking skills.

Chefs and cooks are responsible for preparing meals that are pleasing to the palate and the eye. Chefs are the most highly skilled and trained of all kitchen workers. Although the terms chef and cook are still used interchangeably, cooks are less skilled. Due to their skillful preparation of traditional dishes and refreshing twists in creating new ones, many chefs have earned fame for both themselves and the establishments where they work.

Institutional chefs and cooks work in the kitchens of schools, industrial cafeterias, hospitals, and other institutions. For each meal, they prepare a small selection, but large quantity, of entrees, vegetables, and desserts. Restaurant chefs and cooks generally prepare a wide selection of dishes for each meal, cooking most orders individually. Whether in institutions or restaurants, chefs and cooks measure, mix, and cook ingredients according to recipes. In the course of their work they use a variety of pots, pans, cutlery, and other equipment, including ovens, broilers, grills, slicers, grinders, and blenders. They are often responsible for directing the work of other kitchen workers, estimating food requirements, and ordering food supplies. Some chefs and cooks also assist in planning meals and developing menus.

Bread and pastry bakers, called pastry chefs in some kitchens, produce baked goods for restaurants, institutions, and retail bakery shops. Unlike bakers who work in large, automated industrial bakeries, bread and pastry bakers need only to supply the customers who visit their establishment. They bake small quantities of breads, rolls, pastries, pies, and cakes, doing most of the work by hand. They measure and mix ingredients, shape and bake the dough, and apply fillings and decorations.

Short-order cooks prepare foods to order in restaurants and coffee shops that emphasize fast service. They grill and garnish hamburgers, prepare sandwiches, fry eggs, and cook French fries, often working on several orders at the same time. Prior to busy periods, short-order cooks slice meats and cheeses and prepare coleslaw or potato salad. During slow periods, they may clean the grill, food preparation surfaces, counters, and floors.

Specialty fast-food cooks prepare a limited selection of menu items in fast-food restaurants. They cook and package batches of food, such as hamburgers and fried chicken, which are prepared to order or kept warm until sold.

Some workers are employed in coffee houses which may also serve pastries or other snacks. These workers operate specialized equipment such as cappuccino and espresso machines. Some food products are made on the premises, while others are delivered daily.

Other kitchen workers, under the direction of chefs and cooks, perform tasks requiring less skill. They weigh and measure ingredients, fetch pots and pans, and stir and strain soups and sauces. These workers also clean, peel, and slice potatoes, other vegetables, and fruits and make salads. They may cut and grind meats, poultry, and seafood in preparation for cooking. And their responsibilities also include cleaning work areas, equipment, utensils, dishes, and silverware.

The number and types of workers employed in kitchens depends on the type of establishment. For example, fast-food outlets offer only a few items, which are prepared by fast-food cooks. Small, full-service restaurants offering casual dining often feature a limited number of easy-to-prepare items, supplemented by short-order specialties and ready-made desserts. Typically, one cook prepares all the food with the help of a short-order cook and one or two other kitchen workers.

Large eating places tend to have varied menus and employ kitchen workers who prepare much more of the food they serve from scratch. Kitchen staffs often include several chefs and cooks, sometimes called assistant or apprentice chefs and cooks; a bread and pastry baker; and many less-skilled kitchen workers. Each chef or cook usually has a special assignment and often a special job title—vegetable, fry, or sauce cook, for example. Executive chefs coordinate the work of the kitchen staff and often direct the preparation of certain foods. They decide the size of servings, sometimes plan menus, and buy food supplies. They often adjust their menu in response to changes in dietary standards or food consumption.

Working Conditions

Many restaurant and institutional kitchens have modern equipment, convenient work areas, and air-conditioning; but in older and smaller eating places, the kitchens often are not as well equipped. Working conditions depend on the type and quantity of food being prepared and the local laws governing food service operations. Workers generally must withstand the pressure and strain of working in close quarters, standing for hours at a time, lifting heavy pots and kettles, and working near hot ovens and grills. Job hazards include slips and falls, cuts, and burns, but injuries are seldom serious.

Work hours in restaurants may include early mornings, late evenings, holidays, and weekends, while hours in factory and school cafeterias may be more regular. Over four out of ten cooks and six out of ten other kitchen and food preparation workers were on part-time schedules, compared to one out of four workers throughout the economy. The wide range in dining hours creates work opportunities attractive to homemakers, students, and other individuals seeking supplemental income. For example, well over 20 percent of food preparation workers are 16 to 19 years old. Kitchen workers employed by public and private schools may work during the school year only, usually for nine or ten months. Similarly, establishments at vacation resorts generally only offer seasonal employment.

Employment

Chefs, cooks, and other kitchen workers held more than 3.4 million jobs in 1996. Short-order and fast-food cooks held 804,000 of the jobs; restaurant cooks, 727,000; institutional cooks, 435,000; bread and pastry bakers, 182,000; and other kitchen workers, 1,252,000.

About three-fifths of all chefs, cooks, and other kitchen workers were employed in restaurants and other retail eating and drinking places. One-fifth worked in institutions such as schools, universities, hospitals, and nursing homes. The remainder were employed by grocery stores, hotels, and many other organizations.

Training, Other Qualifications, and Advancement

Most kitchen workers start as fast-food or short-order cooks, or in another low-skilled kitchen position. These positions require little education or training and most skills are learned on the job. After acquiring some basic food handling, preparation, and cooking skills, these workers may be able to advance to an assistant cook or short-order cook position. To achieve the level of skill required of an executive chef or cook in a fine restaurant, many years of training and experience are necessary. Although a high school diploma is not required for beginning jobs, it is recommended for those planning a career as a cook or chef. High school or vocational school courses in business arithmetic and business administration are particularly helpful. Large corporations in the food service and entertainment industries also offer paid internships and summer jobs, which can provide valuable experience.

Many school districts, in cooperation with state departments of education, provide on-the-job training and sometimes summer workshops for cafeteria kitchen workers with aspirations of becoming cooks. Employees who have participated in these training programs are often selected for jobs as cooks.

An increasing number of chefs and cooks obtain their training through high school, post-high school vocational programs, or two- or four-year colleges. Chefs and cooks also may be trained in apprenticeship programs offered by professional culinary institutes, industry associations, and trade unions. An example is the three-year apprenticeship program administered by local chapters of the American Culinary Federation in cooperation with local employers and junior colleges or vocational education institutions. In addition, some large hotels and restaurants operate their own training programs for cooks and chefs.

People who have had courses in commercial food preparation may be able to start in a cook or chef job without having to spend time in a lower-skilled kitchen job. Their education may give them an advantage, when looking for jobs in better restaurants and hotels, where hiring standards often are high. Although some vocational programs in high schools offer this kind of training, employers usually prefer training given by trade schools, vocational centers, colleges, professional associations, or trade unions. Postsecondary courses range from a few months to two years or more, and are open in some cases only to high school graduates. The Armed Forces are also a good source of training and experience.

Although curricula may vary, students usually spend most of their time learning to prepare food through actual practice. They learn to bake, broil, and otherwise prepare food, and to use and care for kitchen equipment. Training programs often include courses in menu planning, determination of portion size, food cost control, purchasing food supplies in quantity, selection and storage of food, and use of leftover food to minimize waste. Students also learn hotel and restaurant sanitation and public health rules for handling food. Training in supervisory and management skills sometimes is emphasized in courses offered by private vocational schools, professional associations, and university programs.

Culinary courses are offered by 700 schools across the nation. The American Culinary Federation accredited about 100 programs in 1996. Accreditation is an indication that a culinary program meets recognized standards regarding course content, facilities, and quality of instruction. The American Culinary Federation has been accrediting culinary programs for a relatively short time; many programs have yet to seek accreditation.

Certification provides valuable formal recognition of the skills of a chef or cook. The American Culinary Federation certifies chefs and cooks at the levels of cook, working chef, executive chef, and master chef. It also certifies pastry professionals and culinary educators. Certification standards are based primarily on experience and formal training.

Important qualifications for chefs, cooks, and other kitchen workers include the ability to work as part of a team, possessing a keen sense of taste and smell, and personal cleanliness. Most states require health certificates indicating workers are free from communicable diseases.

Advancement opportunities for chefs and cooks are better than for most other food and beverage preparation and service occupations. Many acquire high-paying positions and new cooking skills by moving from one job to another. Besides culinary skills, advancement also depends on ability to supervise less-skilled workers and limit food costs, by minimizing waste and accurately anticipating the amount of perishable supplies needed. Some cooks and chefs gradually advance to executive chef positions or supervisory or management positions, particularly in hotels, clubs, or larger, more elegant restaurants. Some eventually go into business as caterers or restaurant owners, while others become instructors in vocational programs in high schools, community colleges, or other academic institutions.

Job Outlook

Job openings for chefs, cooks, and other kitchen workers are expected to be plentiful through the year 2006. While job growth will create new positions, the overwhelming majority of job openings will stem from replacement needs. There is substantial turnover in many of these jobs because of the minimal educational and training requirements. The occupation also offers many part-time positions, attractive to people seeking a short-term source of income rather than a career. Many workers who leave these jobs transfer to other occupations, while others stop working to assume household responsibilities or to attend school full-time.

Overall employment of chefs, cooks, and other kitchen workers is expected to increase about as fast as the average for all occupations through the year 2006. Employment growth will be spurred by increases in population, household income, and leisure time that will allow people to dine out and take vacations more often. In addition, as the number of two-income households grows, more families may find dining out a convenience.

Projected employment varies by specialty, however. As the number of families grows and as the more affluent, 55-and-older population increases rapidly, demand will grow for restaurants that offer table service and more varied menus—requiring more higher-skilled cooks and chefs. The popularity of fresh baked breads and pastries should ensure continued rapid growth in the employment of bakers. Employment of short-order and specialty fast-food cooks, most of whom work in fast-food restaurants, is also expected to increase in response to growth of the 16- to 24-year-old population and the continuing fast-pace lifestyle of many Americans. Employment of institutional and cafeteria chefs and cooks, on the other hand, will grow more slowly than other types of cooks. Their employment will not keep pace with the rapid growth in the educational and health services industries—where their employment is concentrated. Many high schools and hospitals are trying to make "institutional food" more attractive to students, staff, visitors, and patients. While some

establishments employ more highly trained chefs and cooks to prepare more appealing meals, many contract out their food services. Many of the contracted companies emphasize fast food and employ short-order and fast-food cooks, instead of institutional and cafeteria cooks.

Earnings

Wages of chefs, cooks, and other kitchen workers depend greatly on the part of the country and the type of establishment in which they are employed. Wages generally are highest in elegant restaurants and hotels, where many executive chefs earn over $38,000 annually, according to a survey conducted by the National Restaurant Association. Median hourly earnings of cooks were less than $7.00 in 1995, with most earning between $6.00 and $8.00. Assistant cooks had median hourly earnings of $6.25, with most earning between $5.50 and $7.00.

The same survey indicated that short-order cooks had median hourly earnings of $6.50 in 1995; most earned between $5.50 and $7.25. Median hourly earnings of bread and pastry bakers were $6.50; most earned between $6.00 and $7.75. Salad preparation workers generally earned less, with median hourly earnings of $5.50; most earned between $5.25 and $6.50.

Some employers provide employees with uniforms and free meals, but federal law permits employers to deduct from their employees' wages the cost or fair value of any meals or lodging provided, and some employers do so. Chefs, cooks, and other kitchen workers who work full-time often receive typical benefits, but part-time workers generally do not.

In some large hotels and restaurants, kitchen workers belong to unions. The principal unions are the Hotel Employees and Restaurant Employees International Union and the Service Employees International Union.

Related Occupations

Workers who perform tasks similar to those of chefs, cooks, and other kitchen workers include butchers and meat cutters, cannery workers, and industrial bakers.

Sources of Additional Information

Information about job opportunities may be obtained from local employers and local offices of the state employment service.

Career information about chefs, cooks, and other kitchen workers, as well as a directory of two- and four-year colleges that offer courses or programs that prepare persons for food service careers, is available from:

❏ The National Restaurant Association, 1200 17th St. NW, Washington, DC 20036-3097.

For information on the American Culinary Federation's apprenticeship and certification programs for cooks, as well as a list of accredited culinary programs, send a self addressed, stamped envelope to:

❏ American Culinary Federation, P.O. Box 3466, St. Augustine, FL 32085.

For general information on hospitality careers, write to:

❏ Council on Hotel, Restaurant, and Institutional Education, 1200 17th St. NW, Washington, DC 20036-3097.

For general career information and a directory of accredited private career and technical schools offering programs in the culinary arts, write to:

❑ Accrediting Commission of Career Schools and Colleges of Technology, 2101 Wilson Blvd., Suite 302, Arlington, VA 22201.

Chemical Engineers

(D.O.T. 008.061)

Significant Points

✓ *A bachelor's degree in chemical engineering is almost always required for beginning jobs. Good employment opportunities are expected for new graduates.*

✓ *Starting salaries for chemical engineers are significantly higher than those of bachelor's degree graduates in other fields.*

✓ *Knowledge of technological advances must be acquired through continued study and education.*

Nature of the Work

Chemical engineers apply the principles of chemistry and engineering to solve problems involving the production or use of chemicals. They design equipment and develop processes for large scale chemical manufacturing, plan and test methods of manufacturing the products and treating the by-products, and supervise production. Chemical engineers also work in industries other than chemical manufacturing such as electronics or photographic equipment. Because the knowledge and duties of chemical engineers cut across many fields, they apply principles of chemistry, physics, mathematics, and mechanical and electrical engineering in their work. They frequently specialize in a particular operation such as oxidation or polymerization. Others specialize in a particular area such as pollution control or the production of specific products such as automotive plastics or chlorine bleach. Chemical engineers are increasingly using computer technology to optimize all phases of production, and therefore need to understand how to apply computer skills to process analysis, computer control systems, and statistical quality control.

Working Conditions

Most chemical engineers work in office buildings, laboratories, or industrial plants. Some chemical engineers travel extensively to plants or worksites.

Most chemical engineers work a standard 40-hour week. At times, deadlines or design standards may bring extra pressure to a job. When this happens, chemical engineers may work long hours and experience considerable stress.

Employment

Chemical engineers held over 49,000 jobs in 1996. Manufacturing industries employed two-thirds of all employees, primarily in the chemical, petroleum refining, paper, and related industries. Most of the rest worked for engineering services, research and testing services, or consulting firms that design chemical plants. Still others worked on a contract basis, for government agencies or as independent consultants.

Training, Other Qualifications, and Advancement

A bachelor's degree in engineering is usually required for beginning engineering jobs. College graduates with a degree in a physical science or mathematics may occasionally qualify for some engineering jobs, especially in engineering specialties in high demand. Most engineering degrees are granted in electrical, mechanical, or civil engineering. However, engineers trained in one branch may work in related branches; for example, many aerospace engineers have training in mechanical engineering. This flexibility allows employers to meet staffing needs in new technologies and specialties in which engineers are in short supply. It also allows engineers to shift to fields with better employment prospects, or to ones that match their interests more closely.

In addition to the standard engineering degree, many colleges offer degrees in engineering technology, which are offered as either two- or four-year programs. These programs prepare students for practical design and production work rather than for jobs that require more theoretical, scientific and mathematical knowledge. Graduates of four-year technology programs may get jobs similar to those obtained by graduates with a bachelor's degree in engineering. Some employers regard them as having skills between those of a technician and an engineer.

Graduate training is essential for engineering faculty positions, but is not required for the majority of entry-level engineering jobs. Many engineers obtain graduate degrees in engineering or business administration to learn new technology, broaden their education, and enhance promotion opportunities. Many high-level executives in government and industry began their careers as engineers.

About 320 colleges and universities offer bachelor's degree programs in engineering that are accredited by the Accreditation Board for Engineering and Technology (ABET), and about 250 colleges offer accredited bachelor's degree programs in engineering technology. ABET accreditation is based on an examination of an engineering program's faculty, curricular content, facilities, and admissions standards. Although most institutions offer programs in the major branches of engineering, only a few offer some of the smaller specialties. Also, programs of the same title may vary in content. For example, some emphasize industrial practices, preparing students for a job in industry, while others are more theoretical and are better for students preparing to take graduate work. Therefore, students should investigate curricula and check accreditations carefully before selecting a college. Admissions requirements for undergraduate engineering schools include a solid background in mathematics (algebra, geometry, trigonometry, and calculus), sciences (biology, chemistry, and physics), and courses in English, social studies, humanities, and computers.

Bachelor's degree programs in engineering are typically designed to last four years, but many students find that it takes between four and five years to complete their studies. In a typical four-year college curriculum, the first two years are spent studying mathematics, basic sciences, introductory engineering, humanities, and social sciences. In the last two years, most courses are in engineering, usually with a concentration in one branch. For example, the last two years of an aerospace program might include courses such as fluid mechanics, heat transfer, applied aerodynamics, analytical mechanics, flight vehicle design, trajectory dynamics, and aerospace propulsion systems. Some programs offer a general engineering curriculum; students then specialize in graduate school or on the job.

Some engineering schools and two-year colleges have agreements whereby the two-year college provides the initial engineering education and the engineering school automatically admits students for their last two years. In addition, a few engineering schools have arrangements whereby a student spends three years in a liberal arts college studying pre-engineering subjects and two years in the engineering school, and receives a bachelor's degree from each. Some colleges and universities offer five-year master's degree programs. Some five- or even six-year cooperative plans combine classroom study and practical work, permitting students to gain valuable experience and finance part of their education.

All 50 states and the District of Columbia require registration for engineers whose work may affect life, health, or property, or who offer their services to the public. Registration generally requires a degree from an ABET-accredited engineering program, four years of relevant work experience, and passing a state examination. Some states will not register people with degrees in engineering technology. Engineers may be registered in several states.

Engineers should be creative, inquisitive, analytical, and detail-oriented. They should be able to work as part of a team and be able to communicate well, both orally and in writing.

Beginning engineering graduates usually work under the supervision of experienced engineers and, in larger companies, may also receive formal classroom or seminar-type training. As they gain knowledge and experience, they are assigned more difficult projects with greater independence to develop designs, solve problems, and make decisions. Engineers may advance to become technical specialists or to supervise a staff or team of engineers and technicians. Some eventually become engineering managers or enter other managerial, management support, or sales jobs.

Job Outlook

Although employment in the chemical manufacturing industry is projected to grow slowly through 2006, employment of chemical engineers should increase about as fast as the average for all occupations as chemical companies research and develop new chemicals and more efficient processes to increase output of existing chemicals. Much of the projected growth in employment, however, will be in nonmanufacturing industries, especially service industries. Chemical engineering graduates may face competition for jobs as the number of openings is projected to be lower than the number of graduates. Areas relating to the production of specialty chemicals, pharmaceuticals, and plastics materials may provide better opportunities than other portions of the chemical industry.

Earnings

Starting salaries for chemical engineers with the bachelor's degree are significantly higher than starting salaries of bachelor's degree graduates in other fields. According to the National Association of Colleges and Employers, starting salaries for those with the bachelor's degree in 1996 were about $42,817 in 1996.

The median annual salary for all chemical engineers who worked full-time in 1996 was $52,600.

The average annual salary for engineers in the federal government in nonsupervisory, supervisory, and managerial positions was $61,950 in 1997.

Related Occupations

Chemical engineers apply the principles of physical science and mathematics in their work. Other workers who use scientific and mathematical principles include engineering, science, and computer systems managers; physical, life, and computer scientists; mathematicians; engineering and science technicians; and architects.

Sources of Additional Information

High school students interested in obtaining general information on a variety of engineering disciplines should contact the Junior Engineering Technical Society by sending a self-addressed business-size envelope with six first-class stamps affixed, to:

❑ JETS-Guidance, at 1420 King St., Suite 405, Alexandria, VA 22314-2794. Homepage: http://www.asee.org/jets

High school students interested in obtaining information on ABET accredited engineering programs should contact:

❑ The Accreditation Board for Engineering and Technology, Inc., at 111 Market Place, Suite 1050, Baltimore, MD 21202-4012. Homepage: http://www.abet.ba.md.us

Non-high school students and those wanting more detailed information should contact:

❑ American Institute of Chemical Engineers, 345 East 47th St., New York, NY 10017-2395.

❑ American Chemical Society, Department of Career Services, 1155 16th St. NW, Washington, DC 20036.

Chemists

(D.O.T. 022.061-010, -014, and .137-010)

Significant Points

✓ *A bachelor's degree in chemistry or a related discipline is usually the minimum educational requirement; however, many research jobs require a Ph.D. degree.*

✓ *Job growth will be concentrated in drug manufacturing and research, development, and testing services firms.*

Nature of the Work

Everything in our physical environment, whether naturally occurring or of human design, is composed of chemicals. Chemists search for and put to practical use new knowledge about chemicals. Chemical research has led to the discovery and development of new and improved synthetic fibers, paints, adhesives, drugs, cosmetics, electronic components, lubricants, and thousands of other products. Chemists also develop processes which save energy and reduce pollution, such as improved oil refining and petrochemical processing methods. Research on the chemistry of living things spurs advances in medicine, agriculture, food processing, and other fields.

Chemists can apply their knowledge of chemistry to various purposes. Many work in research and development (R&D). In basic research, chemists investigate the properties, composition, and structure of matter and the laws that govern the combination of elements and reactions of substances. In applied research and development, they create new products and processes or improve existing ones, often using knowledge gained from basic research. For example, synthetic rubber and plastics resulted from research on small molecules uniting to form large ones, a process called polymerization. R&D chemists use computers and a wide variety of sophisticated laboratory instrumentation. They also spend time documenting and analyzing the results of their work and writing formal reports.

Chemists also work in production and quality control in chemical manufacturing plants. They prepare instructions for plant workers which specify ingredients, mixing times, and temperatures for each stage in the process. They also monitor automated processes to ensure proper product yield, and they test samples of raw materials or finished products to ensure they meet industry and government standards, including the regulations governing pollution. Chemists also record and report on test results, and improve existing or develop new test methods.

Chemists often specialize in a subfield. Analytical chemists determine the structure, composition, and nature of substances by examining and identifying the various elements or compounds that make up a substance. They study the relations and interactions of the parts and develop analytical techniques. They also identify the presence and concentration of chemical pollutants in air, water, and soil. Organic chemists study the chemistry of the vast number of carbon compounds which make up all living things. Many commercial products, such as drugs, plastics, and elastomers (elastic substances similar to rubber), have been developed by organic chemists who synthesize elements or simple compounds to create new compounds or substances that have different properties and applications. Inorganic chemists study compounds consisting mainly of elements other than carbon, such as those in electronic components. Physical chemists study the physical characteristics of atoms and molecules and investigate how chemical reactions work. Their research may result in new and better energy sources.

Working Conditions

Chemists usually work regular hours in offices and laboratories. Research chemists spend much time in laboratories, but also work in offices when they do theoretical research or plan, record, and report on their lab research. Although some laboratories are small, others are large and may incorporate prototype chemical manufacturing facilities as well as advanced equipment. Chemists may also do some of their work in a chemical plant or outdoors—while gathering water samples to test for pollutants, for example. Some chemists are exposed to health or safety hazards when handling certain chemicals, but there is little risk if proper procedures are followed.

Employment

Chemists held about 91,000 jobs in 1996. Nearly half of chemists are employed in manufacturing firms—mostly in the chemical manufacturing industry, which includes firms that produce plastics and synthetic materials, drugs, soaps and cleaners, paints, industrial organic chemicals, and other miscellaneous chemical products. Chemists also work for state and local governments, and for federal agencies. Health and Human Services, which includes the Food and Drug Administration, the National Institutes of Health, and the Center for Disease Control, is the major federal employer of chemists. The Departments of Defense and Agriculture, and the Environmental Protection Agency, also employ chemists. Other chemists work for research, development, and testing services. In addition, thousands of persons held chemistry faculty positions in colleges and universities.

Chemists are employed in all parts of the country, but they are mainly concentrated in large industrial areas.

Training, Other Qualifications, and Advancement

A bachelor's degree in chemistry or a related discipline is usually the minimum educational requirement for entry-level chemist jobs. However, many research jobs require a Ph.D.

Many colleges and universities offer a bachelor's degree program in chemistry, about 620 of which are approved by the American Chemical Society (ACS). Several hundred colleges and universities also offer advanced degree programs in chemistry; around 320 master's programs, and about 190 doctoral programs are ACS-approved.

Students planning careers as chemists should enjoy studying science and mathematics, and should like working with their hands building scientific apparatus and performing experiments. Perseverance, curiosity, and the ability to concentrate on detail and to work independently are essential. In addition to required courses in analytical, inorganic, organic, and physical chemistry, undergraduate chemistry majors usually study biological sciences, mathematics, and physics. Those who are interested in the environmental field should take courses in environmental studies and become familiar with current legislation and regulations. Computer courses are essential, as employers increasingly prefer job applicants who are able to apply computer skills to modeling and simulation tasks and operate computerized laboratory equipment.

Because research and development chemists are increasingly expected to work on interdisciplinary teams, some understanding of other disciplines, including business and marketing or economics, is desirable, along with leadership ability and good oral and written communication skills. Experience, either in academic laboratories or through internships or co-op programs in industry, also is useful. Some employers of research chemists, particularly in the pharmaceutical industry, prefer to hire individuals with several years of postdoctoral experience.

Graduate students typically specialize in a subfield of chemistry, such as analytical chemistry or polymer chemistry, depending on their interests and the kind of work they wish to do. For example, those interested in doing drug research in the pharmaceutical industry usually develop a strong background in synthetic organic chemistry. However, students normally need not specialize at the undergraduate level. In fact, undergraduates who are broadly trained have more flexibility when job hunting or changing jobs than if they narrowly define their interests. Most employers provide new bachelor's degree chemists with additional training or education.

In government or industry, beginning chemists with a bachelor's degree work in quality control, analytical testing, or assist senior chemists in research and development laboratories. Many employers prefer chemists with a Ph.D. or at least a master's degree to lead basic and applied research. A Ph.D. is also often preferred for advancement to many administrative positions.

Job Outlook

Employment of chemists is expected to grow about as fast as the average for all occupations through the year 2006. Job growth will be concentrated in drug manufacturing and research, development, and testing services firms. The chemical industry, the major employer of chemists, should face continued demand for goods such as new and better pharmaceuticals and personal care products, as well as more specialty chemicals designed to address specific problems or applications. To meet these demands, chemical firms will continue to devote money to research and development–through in-house teams or outside contractors–spurring employment growth of chemists.

Within the chemical industry, job opportunities are expected to be most plentiful in pharmaceutical and biotechnology firms. Stronger competition among drug companies and an aging population are contributing to the need for innovative and improved drugs discovered through scientific research. Chemical firms that develop and manufacture personal products such as toiletries and cosmetics also must continually innovate and develop new and better products to remain competitive. Additionally, as the population grows and becomes better informed, the demand for different or improved grooming products–including vegetable-based products, products with milder formulas, treatments for aging skin, and products that have been developed using more benign chemical processes than in the past–will remain strong, spurring the need for chemists.

In the remaining segments of the chemical industry, employment growth is expected to be much slower than in drug manufacturing, and in some cases, may decline as companies downsize and turn to outside contractors to provide specialized services. Nevertheless, some job openings will result from the need to replace chemists who retire or otherwise leave the labor force. Quality control will continue to be an important issue in the chemical and other industries that use chemicals in their manufacturing processes. Chemists will also be needed to develop and improve the technologies and processes used to produce chemicals for all purposes, and to monitor and measure air and water pollutants to ensure compliance with local, state, and federal environmental regulations.

Outside the chemical industry, firms that provide research, development, and testing services are expected to be the source of numerous job opportunities between 1996 and 2006. Chemical companies, including drug manufacturers, are increasingly turning to these services to perform specialized research and other work formerly done by in-house chemists. Chemists will also be needed to work in research and testing firms that focus on environmental testing and cleanup.

During periods of economic recession, layoffs of chemists may occur–especially in the industrial chemicals industry. This industry provides many of the raw materials to the auto manufacturing and construction industries, both of which are vulnerable to temporary slowdowns during recessions.

Earnings

A survey by the American Chemical Society reports that the median salary of all their members with a bachelor's degree was $49,400 a year in 1997; with a master's degree, $56,200; and with a Ph.D., $71,000. Median salaries were highest for those working in private industry; those in academia earned the least. According to an ACS survey of recent graduates, inexperienced chemistry graduates with a bachelor's degree earned a median starting salary of $25,000 in 1996; with a master's degree, $31,100; and with a Ph.D.,

$45,000. Among bachelor's degree graduates, those who had completed internships or had other work experience while in school commanded the highest starting salaries.

In 1997, chemists in nonsupervisory, supervisory, and managerial positions in the federal government earned an average salary of $60,000.

Related Occupations

The work of chemical engineers, agricultural scientists, biological scientists, and chemical technicians is closely related to the work done by chemists. The work of other physical and life science occupations, such as physicists and medical scientists, may also be similar to that of chemists.

Sources of Additional Information

General information on career opportunities and earnings for chemists is available from:

❑ American Chemical Society, Education Division, 1155 16th St. NW, Washington, DC 20036.

Information on acquiring a job as a chemist with the federal government may be obtained from the Office of Personnel Management through a telephone-based system. Consult your telephone directory under U.S. government for a local number, or call (912) 757-3000 (TDD 912-744-2299). That number is not toll-free and charges may result. Information also is available from their Internet site: HYPERLINK http://www..usajobs

Chiropractors

(D.O.T. 079.101-010)

Significant Points

✓ *Employment of chiropractors is expected to increase rapidly and job prospects should be good.*

✓ *Chiropractic treatment of back, neck, extremities, and other joint damage has become more accepted as a result of recent research and changing attitudes.*

✓ *In chiropractic, as in other types of independent practice, earnings are relatively low in the beginning, and increase as the practice grows.*

Nature of the Work

Chiropractors, also known as doctors of chiropractic or chiropractic physicians, diagnose and treat patients whose health problems are associated with the body's muscular, nervous, and skeletal systems, especially the spine. Chiropractors believe interference with these systems impairs normal functions and lowers resistance to disease. They also hold that spinal or vertebral dysfunction alters many important body functions by affecting the nervous system, and that skeletal imbalance through joint or articular dysfunction, especially in the spine, can cause pain.

The chiropractic approach to health care is holistic, stressing the patient's overall well-being. It recognizes that many factors affect health, including exercise, diet, rest, environment, and heredity. Chiropractors use natural, drugless, nonsurgical health treatments, and rely on the body's inherent recuperative abilities. They also recommend lifestyle changes–in eating, exercise, and sleeping habits, for example—to their patients. When appropriate, chiropractors consult with and refer patients to other health practitioners.

Like other health practitioners, chiropractors follow a standard routine to secure the information needed for diagnosis and treatment: They take the patient's medical history, conduct physical, neurological, and orthopedic examinations, and may order laboratory tests. X rays and other diagnostic images are important tools because of the emphasis on the spine and its proper function. Chiropractors also employ a postural and spinal analysis common to chiropractic diagnosis.

In cases in which difficulties can be traced to involvement of musculoskeletal structures, chiropractors manually manipulate or adjust the spinal column. Many chiropractors also use water, light, massage, ultrasound, electric, and heat therapy and may apply supports such as straps, tapes, and braces. They may also counsel patients about wellness concepts such as nutrition, exercise, lifestyle changes, and stress management, but do not prescribe drugs or perform surgery.

Some chiropractors specialize in sports injuries, neurology, orthopedics, nutrition, internal disorders, or diagnostic imaging.

Many chiropractors are solo or group practitioners who also have the administrative responsibilities of running a practice. In larger offices, chiropractors delegate these tasks to office managers and chiropractic assistants. Chiropractors in private practice are responsible for developing a patient base, hiring employees, and keeping records.

Working Conditions

Chiropractors work in clean, comfortable offices. The average workweek is about 42 hours, although longer hours are not uncommon. Solo practitioners set their own hours, but may work evenings or weekends to accommodate patients.

Chiropractors who take x rays employ appropriate precautions against the dangers of repeated exposure to radiation.

Employment

Chiropractors held about 44,000 jobs in 1996. About 70 percent of active chiropractors are in solo practice. The remainder are in group practice or work for other chiropractors. A small number teach, conduct research at chiropractic institutions, or work in hospitals and clinics.

Many chiropractors are located in small communities. There are geographic imbalances in the distribution of chiropractors, in part because many establish practices close to chiropractic institutions.

Training, Other Qualifications, and Advancement

All states and the District of Columbia regulate the practice of chiropractic and grant licenses to chiropractors who meet educational requirements and pass a state board examination. Chiropractors can only practice in states where they are licensed. Some states have agreements that permit chiropractors licensed in one state to obtain a license in another without further examination.

Most state licensing boards require completion of a four-year chiropractic college course following at least two years of undergraduate education, although a few states require a bachelor's degree. All state boards recognize academic training in chiropractic programs and institutions accredited by the Council on Chiropractic Education.

For licensure, most state boards recognize either all or part of the four-part test administered by the National Board of Chiropractic Examiners. State examinations may supplement the National Board tests, depending on state requirements.

To maintain licensure, almost all states require completion of a specified number of hours of continuing education each year. Continuing education programs are offered by accredited chiropractic programs and institutions, and chiropractic associations. Special councils within some chiropractic associations also offer programs leading to clinical specialty certification, called "diplomate" certification, in areas such as orthopedics, neurology, sports injuries, occupational and industrial health, nutrition, diagnostic imaging, thermography, and internal disorders.

In 1997, there were 16 chiropractic programs and institutions in the United States accredited by the Council on Chiropractic Education. All required applicants to have at least 60 semester hours of undergraduate study leading toward a bachelor's degree, including courses in English, the social sciences or humanities, organic and inorganic chemistry, biology, physics, and psychology. Many applicants have a bachelor's degree, which may eventually become the minimum entry requirement. Several chiropractic colleges offer prechiropractic study, as well as a bachelor's degree program.

During the first two years, most chiropractic programs emphasize classroom and laboratory work in basic science subjects such as anatomy, physiology, public health, microbiology, pathology, and biochemistry. The last two years stress courses in manipulation and spinal adjustments, and provide clinical experience in physical and laboratory diagnosis, neurology, orthopedics, geriatrics, physiotherapy, and nutrition. Chiropractic programs and institutions grant the degree of Doctor of Chiropractic (DC).

Chiropractic requires keen observation to detect physical abnormalities. It also takes considerable hand dexterity to perform manipulations, but not unusual strength or endurance. Chiropractors should be able to work independently and handle responsibility. As in other health-related occupations, empathy, understanding, and the desire to help others are good qualities for dealing effectively with patients.

Newly licensed chiropractors can set up a new practice, purchase an established one, or enter into partnership with an established practitioner. They may also take a salaried position with an established chiropractor, a group practice, or a health care facility.

Job Outlook

Job prospects are expected to be good for persons who enter the practice of chiropractic. Employment of chiropractors is expected to grow faster than the average for all occupations through the year 2006 as consumer demand for alternative medicine grows. Chiropractors emphasize the importance of healthy lifestyles and do not prescribe drugs or perform surgery. As a result, chiropractic care is appealing to many health-conscious Americans. Chiropractic treatment of back, neck, extremities, and other joint damage has become more accepted as a result of recent research and changing attitudes. The rapidly expanding older population, with their increased likelihood of mechanical and structural problems, will also increase demand.

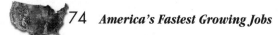

Demand for chiropractic treatment is also related to the ability of patients to pay, either directly or through health insurance. Although more insurance plans now cover chiropractic services, details of such coverage vary among plans. Increasingly, chiropractors must educate communities about the benefits of chiropractic care, in order to establish a successful practice.

In this occupation, replacement needs arise almost entirely from retirements. Chiropractors generally remain in the occupation until they retire; few transfer to other occupations. Establishing a new practice will be easiest in areas with a low concentration of chiropractors.

Earnings

In 1995, median income for chiropractors was about $80,000, after expenses, according to the American Chiropractic Association. In chiropractic, as in other types of independent practice, earnings are relatively low in the beginning, and increase as the practice grows. In 1995, the lowest 10 percent of chiropractors had median net incomes of $30,000 or less, and the highest 10 percent earned $170,000 or more. Earnings are also influenced by the characteristics and qualifications of the practitioner, and geographic location. Self-employed chiropractors must provide for their own health insurance and retirement.

Related Occupations

Chiropractors treat and work to prevent bodily disorders and injuries. So do physicians, dentists, optometrists, podiatrists, veterinarians, occupational therapists, and physical therapists.

Sources of Additional Information

General information on chiropractic as a career is available from:

❏ American Chiropractic Association, 1701 Clarendon Blvd., Arlington, VA 22209.

❏ International Chiropractors Association, 1110 North Glebe Rd., Suite 1000, Arlington, VA 22201.

❏ World Chiropractic Alliance, 2950 N. Dobson Rd., Suite 1, Chandler, AZ 85224-1802.

For a list of chiropractic programs and institutions, as well as general information on chiropractic education, contact:

❏ Council on Chiropractic Education, 7975 North Hayden Rd., Suite A-210, Scottsdale, AZ 85258.

For information on state education and licensure requirements, contact:

❏ Federation of Chiropractic Licensing Boards, 901 54th Ave., Suite 101, Greeley, CO 80634.

For information on requirements for admission to a specific chiropractic college, as well as scholarship and loan information, contact the admissions office of the individual college.

Civil Engineers

(D.O.T. 005.061 except-042, .167-014 and -018; and 019.167-018)

Significant Points

✓ *A bachelor's degree in civil engineering is almost always required for beginning jobs. Good employment opportunities are expected for new graduates.*

✓ *Starting salaries for civil engineers are significantly higher than those of bachelor's degree graduates in other fields.*

✓ *Knowledge of technological advances must be acquired through continued study and education.*

Nature of the Work

Civil engineers work in the oldest branch of engineering, designing and supervising the construction of roads, buildings, airports, tunnels, bridges, and water supply and sewage systems. Major specialties within civil engineering are structural, water resources, environmental, construction, transportation, and geotechnical engineering.

Many civil engineers hold supervisory or administrative positions, ranging from supervisor of a construction site to city engineer. Others may work in design, construction, research, and teaching.

Working Conditions

Most civil engineers work in office buildings, laboratories, or industrial plants. Some civil engineers travel extensively to plants or worksites.

Most civil engineers work a standard 40-hour week. At times, deadlines or design standards may bring extra pressure to a job. When this happens, civil engineers may work long hours and experience considerable stress.

Employment

Civil engineers held about 196,000 jobs in 1996. Almost 47 percent were in firms providing engineering consulting services, primarily developing designs for new construction projects. Another 39 percent of the jobs were in federal, state, and local government agencies. The construction industry, public utilities, transportation, and manufacturing industries accounted for most of the rest. About 13,000 civil engineers were self-employed, many as consultants.

Civil engineers usually work near major industrial and commercial centers, often at construction sites. Some projects are situated in remote areas or in foreign countries. In some jobs, civil engineers move from place to place to work on different projects.

Training, Other Qualifications, and Advancement

A bachelor's degree in engineering is usually required for beginning engineering jobs. College graduates with a degree in a physical science or mathematics may occasionally qualify for some engineering jobs, especially in engineering specialties in high demand. Most engineering degrees are granted in electrical, mechanical, or civil engineering. However, engineers trained in one branch may work in related branches; for example, many aerospace engineers have training in mechanical engineering. This flexibility allows employers to meet staffing needs in new technologies and specialties in which engineers are in short supply. It also allows engineers to shift to fields with better employment prospects, or to ones that match their interests more closely.

In addition to the standard engineering degree, many colleges offer degrees in engineering technology, which are offered as either two- or four-year programs. These programs prepare students for practical design and production work rather than for jobs that require more theoretical, scientific and mathematical knowledge. Graduates of four-year technology programs may get jobs similar to those obtained by graduates with a bachelor's degree in engineering. Some employers regard them as having skills between those of a technician and an engineer.

Graduate training is essential for engineering faculty positions, but is not required for the majority of entry-level engineering jobs. Many engineers obtain graduate degrees in engineering or business administration to learn new technology, broaden their education, and enhance promotion opportunities. Many high-level executives in government and industry began their careers as engineers.

About 320 colleges and universities offer bachelor's degree programs in engineering that are accredited by the Accreditation Board for Engineering and Technology (ABET), and about 250 colleges offer accredited bachelor's degree programs in engineering technology. ABET accreditation is based on an examination of an engineering program's faculty, curricular content, facilities, and admissions standards. Although most institutions offer programs in the major branches of engineering, only a few offer some of the smaller specialties. Also, programs of the same title may vary in content. For example, some emphasize industrial practices, preparing students for a job in industry, while others are more theoretical and are better for students preparing to take graduate work. Therefore, students should investigate curricula and check accreditations carefully before selecting a college. Admissions requirements for undergraduate engineering schools include a solid background in mathematics (algebra, geometry, trigonometry, and calculus), sciences (biology, chemistry, and physics), and courses in English, social studies, humanities, and computers.

Bachelor's degree programs in engineering are typically designed to last four years, but many students find that it takes between four and five years to complete their studies. In a typical four-year college curriculum, the first two years are spent studying mathematics, basic sciences, introductory engineering, humanities, and social sciences. In the last two years, most courses are in engineering, usually with a concentration in one branch. For example, the last two years of an aerospace program might include courses such as fluid mechanics, heat transfer, applied aerodynamics, analytical mechanics, flight vehicle design, trajectory dynamics, and aerospace propulsion systems. Some programs offer a general engineering curriculum; students then specialize in graduate school or on the job.

Some engineering schools and two-year colleges have agreements whereby the two-year college provides the initial engineering education and the engineering school automatically admits students for their last two years. In addition, a few engineering schools have arrangements whereby a student spends three years in a liberal arts college studying pre-engineering subjects and two years in the engineering school, and receives a bachelor's degree from each. Some colleges and universities offer five-year master's degree programs. Some five- or even six-year cooperative plans combine classroom study and practical work, permitting students to gain valuable experience and finance part of their education.

All 50 states and the District of Columbia require registration for engineers whose work may affect life, health, or property, or who offer their services to the public. Registration generally requires a degree from an ABET-accredited engineering program, four years of relevant work experience, and passing a state examination.

Some states will not register people with degrees in engineering technology. Engineers may be registered in several states.

Engineers should be creative, inquisitive, analytical, and detail-oriented. They should be able to work as part of a team and be able to communicate well, both orally and in writing.

Beginning engineering graduates usually work under the supervision of experienced engineers and, in larger companies, may also receive formal classroom or seminar-type training. As they gain knowledge and experience, they are assigned more difficult projects with greater independence to develop designs, solve problems, and make decisions. Engineers may advance to become technical specialists or to supervise a staff or team of engineers and technicians. Some eventually become engineering managers or enter other managerial, management support, or sales jobs.

Job Outlook

Employment of civil engineers is expected to increase about as fast as the average for all occupations through the year 2006. Graduates of civil engineering programs should find favorable opportunities. Spurred by general population growth and an expanding economy, more civil engineers will be needed to design and construct higher capacity transportation, water supply, and pollution control systems; large buildings and building complexes; and to repair or replace existing roads, bridges, and other public structures. Most job openings, however, will result from the need to replace civil engineers who transfer to other occupations or leave the labor force.

Because construction and related industries—including those providing design services—employ many civil engineers, employment opportunities will vary by geographic area and may decrease during economic slowdowns, when construction is often curtailed.

Earnings

Starting salaries for civil engineers with the bachelor's degree are significantly higher than starting salaries of bachelor's degree graduates in other fields. According to the National Association of Colleges and Employers, starting salaries for those with the bachelor's degree were about $33,119 in 1996.

The median annual salary for all civil engineers who worked full-time in 1996 was $46,000.

The average annual salary for engineers in the federal government in nonsupervisory, supervisory, and managerial positions was $61,950 in 1997.

Related Occupations

Civil engineers apply the principles of physical science and mathematics in their work. Other workers who use scientific and mathematical principles include engineering, science, and computer systems managers; physical, life, and computer scientists; mathematicians; engineering and science technicians; and architects.

Sources of Additional Information

High school students interested in obtaining general information on a variety of engineering disciplines should contact the Junior Engineering Technical Society by sending a self-addressed business-size envelope with six first-class stamps affixed, to:

❑ JETS-Guidance, at 1420 King St., Suite 405, Alexandria, VA 22314-2794. Homepage: http://www.asee.org/jets

High school students interested in obtaining information on ABET accredited engineering programs should contact:

❑ The Accreditation Board for Engineering and Technology, Inc., at 111 Market Place, Suite 1050, Baltimore, MD 21202-4012. Homepage: http://www.abet.ba.md.us

Non-high school students and those wanting more detailed information should contact:

❑ American Society of Civil Engineers, 1801 Alexander Bell Drive, Reston, VA 20191-4400.

Clerical Supervisors and Managers

(*D.O.T.* codes are too numerous to list.)

Significant Points

✓ *Most jobs are filled by promoting individuals from within the organization, very often from the ranks of clerks they subsequently supervise.*

✓ *While office automation will cause employment in some clerical occupations to slow or even decline, supervisors will be more likely to retain their jobs because of their relatively higher skills and longer tenure.*

Nature of the Work

All organizations need timely and effective clerical and administrative support to operate efficiently. Coordinating this support is the responsibility of clerical supervisors and managers. They can be found in nearly every sector of the economy, working in fields as varied as office management or customer services.

Although some functions may vary considerably, many duties are common to all clerical supervisors and managers. Supervisors perform administrative tasks to ensure that their staffs can work efficiently. For example, equipment and machinery used in their departments must be in good working order. If the computer system goes down or a photocopier malfunctions, they must try to correct the problem or alert repair personnel. They also request new equipment or supplies for their department when necessary.

Planning and supervising the work of their staff is another key function of this job. To do this effectively, the supervisor must know the strengths and weaknesses of each member of the staff, as well as the required level of quality and time allotted to each job. They must make allowances for unexpected absences and other disruptions, and adjust assignments or perform the work themselves if the situation requires it.

After allocating work assignments and issuing deadlines, clerical supervisors oversee the work to ensure that it is proceeding on schedule and meets established quality standards. This may involve reviewing each person's work on a computer, as in the case of accounting clerks, or, in the case of cashiers, listening to how they deal with customers. When supervising long-term projects, the supervisor may establish regular meetings with staff members to discuss their progress.

Clerical supervisors also evaluate each worker's performance. If a worker has done a good job, the supervisor records it in the employee's personnel file and may recommend a promotion or other award. Alternatively, if a worker is performing poorly, the supervisor discusses the problem with the employee to determine the cause

and helps the worker improve his or her performance. This might entail sending the employee to a training course or arranging personal counseling. If the situation does not improve, the supervisor may recommend a transfer, demotion, or dismissal.

Clerical supervisors and managers generally interview and evaluate prospective clerical employees. When new workers arrive on the job, supervisors greet them and provide orientation to acquaint them with the organization and its operating routines. Some may be actively involved in recruiting new workers by performing functions such as making presentations at high schools and business colleges. They may also serve as the primary liaisons between their offices and the general public through direct contact and helping to prepare promotional information.

Supervisors also help train new employees in organization and office procedures. They may teach them how to use the telephone system and operate office equipment. Because much clerical work is computerized, they must also teach new employees to use the organization's computer system. When new office equipment or updated computer software is introduced, supervisors retrain experienced employees in using it efficiently. If this is not possible, they may arrange for special outside training for their employees.

Clerical supervisors often act as liaisons between the clerical staff and the professional, technical, and managerial staff. This may involve implementing new company policies or restructuring the workflow in their departments. They must also keep their superiors informed of their progress, and abreast of any potential problems. Often this communication takes the form of research projects and progress reports. Because they have access to information such as their department's performance records, they may compile and present these data for use in planning or designing new policies.

Clerical supervisors may be called upon to resolve interpersonal conflicts among the staff. In organizations covered by union contracts, supervisors must know the provisions of labor-management agreements and run their departments accordingly. They may meet with union representatives to discuss work problems or grievances.

Working Conditions

Clerical supervisors and managers are employed in a wide variety of work settings, but most work in offices that are clean, well-lit, and generally comfortable.

Most work a standard 40-hour week. Because some organizations operate around the clock, however, clerical supervisors may have to work nights, weekends, and holidays. In some cases, supervisors rotate among the three shifts. In others, shifts are assigned on the basis of seniority.

Employment

Clerical supervisors and managers held nearly 1.4 million jobs in 1996. Although jobs for clerical supervisors are found in practically every industry, the largest number are found in organizations with a large clerical work force, such as government agencies, retail establishments, wholesalers, business service firms, banks, and insurance companies. Due to the need in most organizations for continuity of supervision, few clerical supervisors and managers work on a temporary or part-time basis.

Training, Other Qualifications, and Advancement

Most firms fill clerical supervisory and managerial positions by promoting individuals within their organization from the clerical ranks. To be eligible for promotion to a supervisory position, clerical or administrative support workers must prove they are capable of handling additional responsibilities. When evaluating candidates, superiors look for strong teamwork skills, determination, loyalty, poise, and confidence. They also look for more specific supervisory attributes, such as the ability to organize and coordinate work efficiently, set priorities, and motivate others. Increasingly, supervisors need a broad base of office skills coupled with personal flexibility to adapt to changes in organizational structure and move among departments when necessary.

In addition, supervisors must pay close attention to detail in order to identify and correct errors made by subordinates. Good working knowledge of the organization's computer system is also an advantage. Many employers require postsecondary training—in some cases, an associate or even a bachelor's degree.

A clerk with potential supervisory abilities may be given occasional supervisory assignments. To prepare for full-time supervisory duties, he or she may attend in-house training or take courses in time management or interpersonal relations, for example, at a local community college or vocational school.

Some clerical supervisors are hired from outside the organization for positions with more managerial duties. These positions may serve as entry-level training for potential higher-level managers. New college graduates may rotate through departments of an organization at this level to learn the work of the entire organization.

Job Outlook

Like other supervisory occupations, applicants for clerical supervisor or manager jobs will encounter competition because the number of applicants is expected to exceed the number of job openings. Employment of clerical supervisors and managers is expected to grow about as fast as the average for all occupations through the year 2006. Most job openings, however, will stem from the need to replace workers who transfer to other occupations or leave this large occupation for other reasons.

Employment of clerical supervisors is affected by the demand for clerical workers, which is determined by the volume of clerical work and the development of office automation. More managers will be needed to coordinate the increasing amount of clerical work. With the spread of office automation, however, this work can be accomplished with fewer clerical workers. As office automation causes employment in some clerical occupations to slow or even decline, supervisors may have smaller staffs and perform more professional tasks. In other cases, fewer supervisors will be needed. In most cases though, the relatively higher skills and longer tenure of clerical supervisors and managers places them among the clerical workers most likely to retain their jobs.

Earnings

Median annual earnings of full-time clerical supervisors were about $28,900 in 1996; the middle 50 percent earned between $21,500 and $38,900 a year. The lowest paid 10 percent earned less than $16,300, while the highest paid 10 percent earned more than $50,600. Employers in major metropolitan areas tend to pay higher salaries than those in rural areas.

Clerical supervisors generally receive typical benefits. Some clerical supervisors in the private sector may receive additional compensation in the form of bonuses and stock options.

Related Occupations

Clerical supervisors and managers must understand and sometimes perform the work of the people whom they oversee, including accounting clerks, cashiers, bank tellers, and telephone operators. Their supervisory and administrative duties are similar to those of other managers.

Sources of Additional Information

State employment service offices can provide information about earnings, hours, and employment opportunities in this and other clerical jobs.

Clinical Laboratory Technologists and Technicians

(D.O.T. 078.221-010, .261-010, -014, -026, -030, and -038, .281-010, .381-014, .687-010, and 559.361-010)

Significant Points

- ✓ *Medical and clinical laboratory technologists usually have a bachelor's degree with a major in medical technology or in one of the life sciences; medical and clinical laboratory technicians typically need either an associate degree or a certificate.*
- ✓ *Competition for jobs has increased and individuals may now have to look longer to find employment than in the past.*

Nature of the Work

Clinical laboratory testing plays a crucial role in the detection, diagnosis, and treatment of disease. Clinical laboratory technologists and technicians, also known as medical technologists and technicians, perform most of these tests.

Clinical laboratory personnel examine and analyze body fluids, tissues, and cells. They look for bacteria, parasites, or other micro-organisms; analyze the chemical content of fluids; match blood for transfusions, and test for drug levels in the blood to show how a patient is responding to treatment. They also prepare specimens for examination, count cells, and look for abnormal cells. They use automated equipment and instruments that perform a number of tests simultaneously, as well as microscopes, cell counters, and other kinds of sophisticated laboratory equipment to perform tests. Then they analyze the results and relay them to physicians.

The complexity of tests performed, the level of judgment needed, and the amount of responsibility workers assume depend largely on the amount of education and experience they have.

Medical and clinical laboratory technologists generally have a bachelor's degree in medical technology or in one of the life sciences, or have a combination of formal training and work experience. They perform complex chemical, biological, hematological, immunologic, microscopic, and bacteriological tests. Technologists microscopically examine blood, tissue, and other body substances. They make cultures of body fluid or tissue samples to determine the presence of bacteria, fungi, parasites, or other micro-organisms. They analyze samples for chemical content or reaction and determine blood glucose or cholesterol levels. They also type and cross-match blood samples for transfusions.

Medical and clinical laboratory technologists may evaluate test results, develop and modify procedures, and establish and monitor programs to insure the accuracy of tests. Some medical and clinical laboratory technologists supervise medical and clinical laboratory technicians.

Technologists in small laboratories perform many types of tests, while those in large laboratories generally specialize. Technologists who prepare specimens and analyze the chemical and hormonal contents of body fluids are clinical chemistry technologists. Those who examine and identify bacteria and other micro-organisms are microbiology technologists. Blood bank technologists collect, type, and prepare blood and its components for transfusions. Immunology technologists examine elements and responses of the human immune system to foreign bodies. Cytotechnologists, prepare slides of body cells and microscopically examine these cells for abnormalities which may signal the beginning of a cancerous growth.

Medical and clinical laboratory technicians perform less complex tests and laboratory procedures than technologists. Technicians may prepare specimens and operate automatic analyzers, for example, or they may perform manual tests following detailed instructions. Like technologists, they may work in several areas of the clinical laboratory or specialize in just one. Histology technicians cut and stain tissue specimens for microscopic examination by pathologists, and phlebotomists draw and test blood. They usually work under the supervision of medical and clinical laboratory technologists or laboratory managers.

Working Conditions

Hours and other working conditions vary according to the size and type of employment setting. In large hospitals or in independent laboratories that operate continuously, personnel usually work the day, evening, or night shift, and may work weekends and holidays. Laboratory personnel in small facilities may work on rotating shifts rather than on a regular shift. In some facilities, laboratory personnel are on call, available in case of an emergency, several nights a week or on weekends.

Clinical laboratory personnel are trained to work with infectious specimens. When proper methods of infection control and sterilization are followed, few hazards exist.

Laboratories generally are well lighted and clean; however, specimens, solutions, and reagents used in the laboratory sometimes produce odors. Laboratory workers may spend a great deal of time on their feet.

Employment

Clinical laboratory technologists and technicians held about 285,000 jobs in 1996. More than half worked in hospitals. Most others worked in medical laboratories and offices and clinics of physicians. Some worked in blood banks, research and testing laboratories, and in the federal government–at Department of Veterans Affairs hospitals and U.S. Public Health Service facilities. About one

laboratory worker in six worked part-time.

Training, Other Qualifications, and Advancement

The usual requirement for an entry level position as a medical or clinical laboratory technologist is a bachelor's degree with a major in medical technology or in one of the life sciences. Universities and hospitals offer medical technology programs. It is also possible to qualify through a combination of on-the-job and specialized training.

Bachelor's degree programs in medical technology include courses in chemistry, biological sciences, microbiology, and mathematics, and specialized courses devoted to knowledge and skills used in the clinical laboratory. Many programs also offer or require courses in management, business, and computer applications.

Master's degrees in medical technology and related clinical laboratory sciences provide training for specialized areas of laboratory work or teaching, administration, or research.

The Clinical Laboratory Improvement Act (CLIA) requires technologists who perform certain highly complex tests to have at least an associate degree.

Medical and clinical laboratory technicians generally have either an associate degree from a community or junior college, or a certificate from a hospital, vocational or technical school, or from one of the Armed Forces. A few technicians learn on the job.

Nationally recognized accrediting agencies in the clinical laboratory science include the National Accrediting Agency for Clinical Laboratory Sciences, and the Accrediting Bureau of Health Education Schools (ABHES). National Accrediting Agency for Clinical Laboratory Sciences fully accredits 621, and approves 72 programs that provide education for medical and clinical laboratory technologists, cytotechnologists, histologic technicians, specialists in blood bank technology, and medical and clinical laboratory technicians. ABHES accredits training programs for medical and clinical laboratory technicians.

Some states require laboratory personnel to be licensed or registered. Information on licensure is available from state departments of health or boards of occupational licensing. Certification is a voluntary process by which a nongovernmental organization such as a professional society or certifying agency, grants recognition to an individual whose professional competence meets prescribed standards. Widely accepted by employers in the health industry, certification is a prerequisite for most jobs and often is necessary for advancement. Agencies that certify medical and clinical laboratory technologists and technicians include the Board of Registry of the American Society of Clinical Pathologists, the American Medical Technologists, the American Society for Clinical Laboratory Science, and the Credentialing Commission of the International Society for Clinical Laboratory Technology. These agencies have different requirements for certification and different organizational sponsors.

Clinical laboratory personnel need analytical judgment and the ability to work under pressure. Close attention to detail is essential because small differences or changes in test substances or numerical readouts can be crucial for patient care. Manual dexterity and normal color vision are highly desirable. With the widespread use of automated laboratory equipment, computer skills are important. In addition, technologists in particular are expected to be good at problem solving.

Technologists may advance to supervisory positions in laboratory work or become chief medical or clinical laboratory technologists or laboratory managers in hospitals. Manufacturers of home diagnostic testing kits and laboratory equipment and supplies seek experienced technologists to work in product development, marketing, and sales. Graduate education in medical technology, one of the biological sciences, chemistry, management, or education usually speeds advancement. A doctorate is sometimes needed to become a laboratory director. However, federal regulation allows directors of moderate complexity laboratories to have either a master's degree or a bachelor's degree combined with the appropriate amount of training and experience. Technicians can become technologists through additional education and experience.

Job Outlook

Employment of clinical laboratory workers is expected to grow about as fast as the average for all occupations through the year 2006 as the volume of laboratory tests increases with population growth and the development of new types of tests. Hospitals and independent laboratories have recently undergone considerable consolidation and restructuring that has boosted productivity and allowed the same number of personnel to perform more tests than previously possible. As a result, competition for jobs has increased and individuals may now have to look longer to find employment than in the past.

Technological advances will continue to have two opposing effects on employment through 2006. New, more powerful diagnostic tests will encourage more testing and spur employment. However, advances in laboratory automation and simpler tests, which make it possible for each worker to perform more tests, should slow growth. Research and development efforts are targeted at simplifying routine testing procedures so that nonlaboratory personnel, physicians and patients in particular, can perform tests now done in laboratories. Also, robots may prepare specimens, a job done now by technologists and technicians.

Although significant, growth will not be the only source of opportunities. As in most occupations, many openings will result from the need to replace workers who transfer to other occupations, retire, or stop working for some other reason.

Earnings

Median weekly earnings of full-time, salaried clinical laboratory technologists and technicians were $520 in 1996. Half earned between $403 and $706. The lowest 10 percent earned less than $298 and the top 10 percent more than $852.

According to a Hay Group survey of acute care hospitals, the median annual base salary of full-time laboratory technicians was $26,500 in January 1997. The middle 50 percent earned between $23,700 and $29,500. Full-time salaried staff medical laboratory technologists earned about $35,100; the middle 50 percent earned between $32,500 and $37,900.

The average annual salary for medical technologists employed by the federal government was $40,680 in early 1997. Medical technicians earned an average of $26,130.

Related Occupations

Clinical laboratory technologists and technicians analyze body fluids, tissue, and other substances using a variety of tests. Similar or related procedures are performed by analytical, water purification, and other chemists; science technicians; crime laboratory analysts; food testers; and veterinary laboratory technicians.

Sources of Additional Information

Career and certification information is available from:
- American Society of Clinical Pathologists, Board of Registry, P.O. Box 12277, Chicago, IL 60612.
- American Medical Technologists, 710 Higgins Rd., Park Ridge, IL 60068.
- American Society of Cytopathology, 400 West 9th St., Suite 201, Wilmington, DE 19801.
- American Society for Clinical Laboratory Science, 7910 Woodmont Ave., Suite 530, Bethesda, MD 20814.
- International Society for Clinical Laboratory Technology, 917 Locust St., Suite 1100, St. Louis, MO 63101-1413.

For more career information, write to:
- American Association of Blood Banks, 8101 Glenbrook Rd., Bethesda, MD 20814-2749.

For a list of accredited and approved educational programs for clinical laboratory personnel, write to:
- National Accrediting Agency for Clinical Laboratory Sciences, 8410 W. Bryn Mawr Ave., Suite 670, Chicago, IL 60631.

For a list of training programs for medical and clinical laboratory technicians accredited by the Accrediting Bureau of Health Education Schools, write to:
- Secretary-ABHES, 2700 S. Quincy St., Suite 210, Arlington,, VA 22206.

For information about a career as a medical and clinical laboratory technician and schools offering training, contact:
- National Association of Health Career Schools, 750 First St. NE., Suite 940, Washington, DC 20002. FAX: (202) 842-1565 E-mail: NAHCS@aol.com

College and University Faculty

(D.O.T. 090.227-010)

Significant Points

- ✓ *A Ph.D. is generally required for full-time positions in four-year colleges and universities; in two-year institutions, master's degree holders may qualify.*
- ✓ *Applicants for full-time college faculty positions face keen competition because many colleges and universities, in an effort to cut costs, will hire more part-time faculty.*
- ✓ *Job prospects will continue to be better in certain fields—computer science, engineering, and business, for example—that offer attractive nonacademic job opportunities and attract fewer applicants for academic positions.*

Nature of the Work

College and university faculty teach and advise nearly 15 million full- and part-time college students and perform a significant part of our nation's research. They also study and meet with colleagues to keep up with developments in their field and consult with government, business, nonprofit, and community organizations.

Faculty generally are organized into departments or divisions, based on subject or field. They usually teach several different courses in their department—algebra, calculus, and statistics, for example. They may instruct undergraduate or graduate students, or both. College and university faculty may give lectures to several hundred students in large halls, lead small seminars, or supervise students in laboratories. They prepare lectures, exercises, and laboratory experiments, grade exams and papers, and advise and work with students individually. In universities, they also counsel, advise, teach, and supervise graduate student teaching and research. College faculty work with an increasingly varied student population made up of growing shares of part-time, older, and culturally and racially diverse students.

Faculty keep abreast of developments in their field by reading current literature, talking with colleagues, and participating in professional conferences. They also do their own research to expand knowledge in their field. They experiment, collect and analyze data, and examine original documents, literature, and other source material. From this, they develop hypotheses, arrive at conclusions, and publish their findings in scholarly journals, books, and electronic media.

College and university faculty increasingly use technology in all areas of their work. In the classroom, they may use computers—including the Internet; electronic mail; software programs, such as statistical packages; and CD-ROMs—as teaching aids. Some professors teach "satellite" courses that are broadcast to students at off-campus sites through closed-circuit or cable television. Faculty also use computers to do their own research, participate in discussion groups in their field, or publicize their professional research papers.

Most faculty members serve on academic or administrative committees which deal with the policies of their institution, departmental matters, academic issues, curricula, budgets, equipment purchases, and hiring. Some work with student as well as community organizations. Department chairpersons are faculty members who usually teach some courses but generally have heavier administrative responsibilities.

The proportion of time spent on research, teaching, administrative, and other duties varies by individual circumstance and type of institution. Faculty members at universities generally spend a significant part of their time doing research; those in four-year colleges, somewhat less; and those in two-year colleges, relatively little. However, the teaching load usually is heavier in two-year colleges and somewhat lower at four-year institutions. Full professors at all types of institutions usually spend a larger portion of their time conducting research than assistant professors, instructors, and lecturers.

Working Conditions

College faculty generally have flexible schedules. They must be present for classes, usually 12 to 16 hours a week, and for faculty and committee meetings. Most establish regular office hours for student consultations, usually three to six hours per week. Otherwise, faculty are free to decide when and where they will work, and how much time to devote to course preparation, grading papers and exams, study, research, graduate student supervision, and other activities. Initial adjustment to these responsibilities can be challenging as new faculty adapt to switching roles from student to teacher. This adjustment may be even more difficult as class size grows in response to faculty and budget cutbacks, increasing an instructor's workload. Also, many institutions are increasing their reliance on part-time faculty, who generally have limited administrative and student advising duties, which leaves the declining number of full-time faculty with a heavier workload.

Some faculty members work staggered hours and teach classes at night and on weekends. This is particularly true for faculty who teach at two-year community colleges or institutions with large enrollments of older students with full-time jobs or family responsibilities on weekdays. Most faculty are employed on a nine-month contract, which allows them the time to teach, do research, travel, or pursue nonacademic interests during the summer and school holidays. Most colleges and universities have funds to support faculty research or other professional development needs, including travel to conferences and research sites.

Faculty may experience a conflict between their responsibilities to teach students and the pressure to do research and publish their findings. This may be a particular problem for young faculty seeking advancement in four-year research universities. Increasing emphasis on undergraduate teaching performance in tenure decisions may alleviate some of this pressure, however.

Part-time faculty generally spend little time on campus, because they usually don't have an office. In addition, they may teach at more than one college, requiring travel between their various places of employment, earning the name "gypsy faculty." Part-time faculty are usually not eligible for tenure. Dealing with this lack of job security can be stressful.

Employment

College and university faculty held about 864,000 jobs in 1996, mostly in public institutions.

About four out of ten college and university faculty worked part-time in 1996. Some part-timers, known as "adjunct faculty," have primary jobs outside of academia—in government, private industry, or in nonprofit research—and teach "on the side." Others seek full-time jobs but are unable to obtain them due to intense competition for available openings. Some work part-time in more than one institution.

Training, Other Qualifications, and Advancement

Most college and university faculty are in four academic ranks: Professor, associate professor, assistant professor, and instructor. These positions are usually considered to be tenure-track positions. A small number of faculty, called lecturers, usually are not on the tenure track.

Most faculty members are hired as instructors or assistant professors. Four-year colleges and universities generally only consider doctoral degree holders for full-time, tenure-track positions, but may hire master's degree holders or doctoral candidates for certain disciplines, such as the arts, or for part-time and temporary jobs. In two-year colleges, master's degree holders often qualify for full-time positions. However, with increasing competition for available jobs, institutions can be more selective in their hiring practices. Master's degree holders may find it increasingly difficult to obtain employment as they are passed over in favor of candidates holding a Ph.D.

Doctoral programs, including time spent completing a master's degree and a dissertation, take an average of six to eight years of full-time study beyond the bachelor's degree. Some programs, such as the humanities, take longer to complete; others, such as engineering, generally are shorter. Candidates usually specialize in a subfield of a discipline–for example, organic chemistry, counseling psychology, or European history–but also take courses covering the entire discipline. Programs include 20 or more increasingly specialized courses and seminars plus comprehensive examinations on all major areas of the field. Candidates also must complete a dissertation–a written report on original research in the candidate's major field of study. The dissertation sets forth an original hypothesis or proposes a model and tests it. Students in the natural sciences and engineering usually do laboratory work; in the humanities, they study original documents and other published material. The dissertation, done under the guidance of one or more faculty advisors, usually takes one or two years of full-time work.

In some fields, particularly the natural sciences, some students spend an additional two years on postdoctoral research and study before taking a faculty position. Some Ph.D.s extend or take new postdoctoral appointments if they are unable to find a faculty job. Most of these appointments offer a nominal salary.

A major step in the traditional academic career is attaining tenure. New tenure-track faculty are usually hired as instructors or assistant professors, and must serve a certain period (usually seven years) under term contracts. At the end of the contract period, their record of teaching, research, and overall contribution to the institution is reviewed; tenure is granted if the review is favorable. According to the American Association of University Professors, in 1995-96 about 65 percent of all full-time faculty held tenure while 88 percent were in tenure-track positions. Those denied tenure usually must leave the institution. Tenured professors cannot be fired without just cause and due process. Tenure protects the faculty's academic freedom–the ability to teach and conduct research without fear of being fired for advocating unpopular ideas. It also gives both faculty and institutions the stability needed for effective research and teaching, and provides financial security for faculty. Some institutions have adopted post-tenure review policies to encourage ongoing evaluation of tenured faculty.

The number of tenure-track positions is expected to decline as institutions rely more heavily on less costly part-time faculty who do not hold tenure-track positions. Consequently, increased reliance on part-time faculty is expected to shrink the total pool of faculty who hold tenure. Some institutions have placed caps on the percentage of faculty who can be tenured. Other institutions offer prospective faculty limited term contracts–typically two-, three-, or five-year, full-time contracts–in an effort to adapt to changes in the budget and the size of the student body. These contracts may be terminated or extended at the end of the period. Institutions are not obligated to grant tenure to these contract holders.

Some faculty–based on teaching experience, research, publication, and service on campus committees and task forces–move into administrative and managerial positions, such as departmental chairperson, dean, and president. At four-year institutions, such advancement requires a doctoral degree. At two-year colleges, a doctorate is helpful but not generally required, except for advancement to some top administrative positions.

College faculty should have inquiring and analytical minds, and a strong desire to pursue and disseminate knowledge. They must be able to communicate clearly and logically, both orally and in writing. They should be able to establish rapport with students and, as models for them, be dedicated to the principles of academic integrity and intellectual honesty. Additionally, they must be self-motivated and able to work in an environment where they receive little direct supervision.

Job Outlook

Employment of college and university faculty is expected to increase about as fast as the average for all occupations through the year 2006 as enrollments in higher education increase. Many additional openings will arise as faculty members retire. Faculty retirements should increase significantly from the late 1990s through 2006 as a large number of faculty who entered the profession during the 1950s and 1960s reach retirement age. Most faculty members likely to retire are full-time tenured professors. However, in an effort to cut costs, some institutions are expected to either leave these positions vacant or hire part-time, non-tenured faculty as replacements. Prospective job applicants should be prepared to face keen competition for available jobs as growing numbers of Ph.D. graduates, including foreign-born Ph.D.s, vie for fewer full-time openings. As more and more Ph.D.s compete for openings, master's degree holders may find competition for jobs even more intense.

Enrollments in institutions of higher education increased in the mid-1980s through the early 1990s despite a decline in the traditional college-age (18-to-24) population. This resulted from a higher proportion of 18- to 24-year-olds attending college, along with a growing number of part-time, female, and older students. Between 1996 and 2006, the traditional college-age population will begin to grow again, spurred by the leading edge of the baby-boom "echo" generation (children of the baby-boomers) reaching college age. College enrollment is projected to rise from 14 million in 1996 to 16 million in 2006, an increase of 14 percent.

In the past two decades, keen competition for faculty jobs forced some applicants to accept part-time or short-term academic appointments that offered little hope of tenure, and others to seek nonacademic positions. This trend of hiring adjunct or part-time faculty is likely to continue due to financial difficulties faced by colleges and universities. Many colleges, faced with reduced state funding for higher education, have increased the hiring of part-time faculty to save money on pay and benefits. Public two-year colleges employ a significantly higher number of part-time faculty as a percentage of their total staff than public four-year colleges and universities, but all institutions have increased their part-time hiring. With uncertainty over future funding, many colleges and universities are continuing to cut costs by eliminating some academic programs, increasing class size, and closely monitoring all expenses.

Once enrollments and retirements start increasing at a faster pace in the late 1990s, opportunities for college faculty may begin to improve somewhat. Growing numbers of students will necessitate hiring more faculty to teach. At the same time, many faculty will be retiring, opening up even more positions. Job prospects will continue to be better in certain fields—business, engineering, health science, and computer science, for example—that offer attractive nonacademic job opportunities and attract fewer applicants for academic positions.

Employment of college faculty is affected by the nonacademic job market. Excellent job prospects in a field—for example, computer science from the late 1970s to the mid-1980s—cause more students to enroll, increasing faculty needs in that field. On the other hand, poor job prospects in a field, such as history in recent years, discourages students and reduces demand for faculty.

Earnings

Earnings vary according to faculty rank and type of institution, geographic area, and field. According to a 1995-96 survey by the American Association of University Professors, salaries for full-time faculty averaged $51,000. By rank, the average for professors was $65,400; associate professors, $48,300; assistant professors, $40,100; instructors, $30,800; and lecturers, $33,700. Faculty in four-year institutions earn higher salaries, on the average, than those in two-year schools. Average salaries for faculty in public institutions—$50,400—were lower in 1995-96 than those for private independent institutions—$57,500—but higher than those for religion-affiliated private institutions—$45,200. In fields with high-paying nonacademic alternatives—notably medicine and law but also engineering and business, among others—earnings exceed these averages. In others—such as the humanities and education—they are lower.

Most faculty members have significant earnings in addition to their base salary, from consulting, teaching additional courses, research, writing for publication, or other employment, both during the academic year and the summer.

Most college and university faculty enjoy some unique benefits, including access to campus facilities, tuition waivers for dependents, housing and travel allowances, and paid sabbatical leaves. Part-time faculty have fewer benefits than full-time faculty, and usually do not receive health insurance, retirement benefits, or sabbatical leave.

Related Occupations

College and university faculty function both as teachers and researchers. They communicate information and ideas. Related occupations include elementary and secondary school teachers, librarians, writers, consultants, lobbyists, trainers and employee development specialists, and policy analysts. Faculty research activities often are similar to those of scientists, as well as managers and administrators in industry, government, and nonprofit research organizations.

Sources of Additional Information

Professional societies generally provide information on academic and nonacademic employment opportunities in their fields.

Special publications on higher education, available in libraries, such as *The Chronicle of Higher Education*, list specific employment opportunities for faculty.

Computer and Office Machine Repairers

(D.O.T. 633.261-014, .281; 706.381-010 and -030)

Significant Points

✓ *Most employers prefer to hire persons who have completed one- or two-year formal training programs in electronics.*

✓ *Overall employment of computer and office machine repairers should increase rapidly.*

Nature of the Work

Computer and office machine repairers install equipment, do preventive maintenance, and correct problems. Computer repairers work on computers (mainframes, minis, and micros), peripheral equipment, and word processing systems, while office machine repairers work on photocopiers, cash registers, mail processing equipment, fax machines, and typewriters. Some repairers service both computer and office equipment. They also make cable and wiring connections when installing equipment, and work closely with electricians who install the wiring.

Even with preventive maintenance, computers and other machines break down. Repairers run diagnostic programs to locate malfunctions. Although some of the most modern and sophisticated computers have a self-diagnosing capacity that identifies problems, computer repairers must know enough about systems software to determine if the malfunction is in the hardware or in the software.

Working Conditions

Some computer and office machine repairers work shifts, including weekends and holidays, to service equipment in computer centers, manufacturing plants, hospitals, and telephone companies operating round the clock. Shifts are generally assigned on the basis of seniority. Repairers may also be on call at any time to handle equipment failure.

Computer and office machine repairers generally work in clean, well-lighted, air-conditioned surroundings. However, some may be exposed to heat, grease, and noise on factory floors. Some may occasionally have to work in cramped spaces.

The work of most computer and office machine repairers involves lifting, reaching, stooping, crouching, and crawling. Adherence to safety precautions is essential to guard against work hazards such as minor burns and electrical shock.

Employment

Computer and office machine repairers held about 141,000 jobs in 1996. Approximately 80,000 worked mainly on computer equipment, and the other 61,000 repaired mainly office machines. About three of every five were employed by wholesalers of computers and other office equipment, including the wholesaling divisions of equipment manufacturers, and by firms that provide maintenance services for a fee. Others worked for retail establishments and some with organizations that serviced their own equipment.

Repairers work throughout the country, even in relatively small communities. Most repairers, however, work in large cities, where computer and office equipment is concentrated.

Training, Other Qualifications, and Advancement

Most employers prefer applicants with formal training in electronics. Electronic training is offered by public post secondary vocational-technical schools, private vocational schools and technical institutes, junior and community colleges, and some high schools and correspondence schools. Programs take one to two years. The military services also offer formal training and work experience.

Training includes general courses in mathematics, physics, electricity, electronics, schematic reading, and troubleshooting. Students also choose courses which prepare them for a specialty, such as computers, commercial and industrial equipment, or home entertainment equipment. A few repairers complete formal apprenticeship programs sponsored jointly by employers and local chapters of the International Brotherhood of Electrical Workers.

Applicants for entry-level jobs may have to pass tests measuring mechanical aptitude, knowledge of electricity or electronics, manual dexterity, and general intelligence. Newly hired repairers, even those with formal training, usually receive some training from their employer. They may study electronics and circuit theory and math. They also get hands-on experience with equipment, doing basic maintenance and using diagnostic programs to locate malfunctions. Training may be in a classroom or it may be self-instruction, consisting of videotapes, programmed computer software, or workbooks that allow trainees to learn at their own pace.

Experienced computer and office machine repairers attend training sessions and read manuals to keep up with design changes and revised service procedures. Many also take advanced training in a particular system or type of repair.

Good eyesight and color vision are needed to inspect and work on small, delicate parts and good hearing to detect malfunctions revealed by sound. Because field repairers usually handle jobs alone, they must be able to work without close supervision. For those who have frequent contact with customers, a pleasant personality, neat appearance, and good communications skills are important. Computer and office machine repairers must also be trustworthy, because they may be exposed to money and other valuables in places such as banks and securities offices, and some employers require that they be bonded. A security clearance may be required for those who repair equipment or service machines in areas in which people are engaged in activities related to national security.

The International Society of Certified Electronics Technicians and the Electronics Technicians Association each administer a voluntary certification program. In both, an electronics repairer with four years of experience may become a Certified Electronics Technician. Certification, which is by examination, is offered in computer, radio-TV, industrial and commercial equipment, audio, avionics, wireless communications, video distribution, satellite, and radar systems repair. An Associate Level Test, covering basic electronics, is offered for students or repairers with less than four years of experience. An A+ certification is now desired for computer technicians. This certification is awarded by the Computing Technology Industry Association (CompTIA) and requires knowledge of specific products manufactured by the vendor.

Experienced computer and office machine repairers with advanced training may become specialists or troubleshooters who help other repairers diagnose difficult problems, or work with engineers in designing equipment and developing maintenance procedures.

Because of their familiarity with equipment, computer and office machine repairers are particularly well qualified to become manufacturers' sales workers. Workers with leadership ability also may become maintenance supervisors or service managers. Some experienced workers open their own repair services or shops, or become wholesalers or retailers of electronic equipment.

Job Outlook

Employment of computer and office machine repairers is expected to grow much faster than the average for all occupations through the year 2006. However, employment of repairers will grow less rapidly than the anticipated increase in the amount of equipment because of the improved reliability of computer and office machines and ease of repair. Applicants for computer repairer positions will have the most favorable job prospects.

Employment of those who repair computers is expected to grow much faster than the average for all occupations. Demand for computer repairers will increase as the amount of computer equipment increases–organizations throughout the economy should continue to automate in search of greater productivity and improved service. The development of new computer applications and lower computer prices will also spur demand. More repairers will be needed to install new equipment coming on the market and upgrade existing systems.

Employment of those who repair office machines is expected to grow about as fast the average for all occupations. Slower growth in the amount of non-computer-based office equipment will somewhat dampen the demand for these repairers.

Earnings

In 1996, median weekly earnings of full-time computer and office machine repairers were $582.

According to a survey of workplaces in 160 metropolitan areas, beginning maintenance electronics technicians had median earnings of $11.50 an hour in 1995, with the middle half earning between $10.50 and $13.25 an hour. The most experienced repairers had median earnings of $20.13 an hour, with the middle half earning between $18.24 and $22.12 an hour.

Related Occupations

Workers in other occupations who repair and maintain the circuits and mechanical parts of electronic equipment include appliance and power tool repairers, automotive electricians, broadcast technicians, electronic organ technicians, and vending machine repairers. Electronics engineering technicians may also repair electronic equipment as part of their duties.

Sources of Additional Information

For career, and certification information, contact:
- ❏ The International Society of Certified Electronics Technicians, 2708 West Berry St., Fort Worth, TX 76109.

For certification, career, and placement information, contact:
- ❏ Electronics Technicians Association, 602 North Jackson, Greencastle, IN 46135.

For information on electronic equipment repairers in the telephone industry, write to:
- ❏ Communications Workers of America, Department of Apprenticeships, Benefits, and Employment, 501 3rd St. NW, Washington, DC 20001.

Computer Programmers

(D.O.T. 030.162-010, -018, -022, and .167-010)

Significant Points

✓ *The level of education and quality of training required by employers has been rising due to the increasing complexity of programming tasks.*

✓ *A growing number of computer programmers are employed on a temporary or contract basis.*

Nature of the Work

Computer programmers write, test, and maintain the detailed instructions–called *programs* or *software*–that list in a logical order the steps computers must execute to perform their functions. Programmers often are categorized as technicians, distinct from the higher level of theoretical expertise characteristic of computer scientists, computer engineers, and systems analysts. However, many technical innovations in programming–advanced computing technologies and sophisticated new languages and programming tools– have redefined the role of a programmer and elevated much of the programming work done today. It is becoming much more difficult to distinguish different computer specialists–including programmers–since job titles shift so rapidly, reflecting new areas of specialization or changes in technology. Job titles and descriptions also may vary depending on the organization. In this statement, "computer programmer" refers to individuals whose main job function is programming; this group has a wide range of responsibilities and educational backgrounds.

Computer programs tell the computer what to do, such as which information to identify and access, how to process it, and what equipment to use. Programs vary widely depending upon the type of information to be accessed or generated. For example, the instructions involved in updating financial records are very different from those required to duplicate conditions on board an aircraft for pilots training in a flight simulator. Although simple programs can be written in a few hours, programs that use complex mathematical formulas, whose solutions can only be approximated, or that draw data from many existing systems, require more than a year of work. In most cases, several programmers work together as a team under a senior programmer's supervision.

Programmers write specific programs by breaking down each step into a logical series of instructions the computer can follow. They then code these instructions in a conventional programming language, such as C and FORTRAN,; an artificial intelligence language, such as LISP or Prolog; o or one of the more advanced function-oriented or object-oriented languages, such as UML, Java, C++, Visual Basic, or Ada. Programmers usually know more thaen one programming language and since many languages are alike, they can often learn new languages relatively easily. In practice, programmers are often referred to by the language they know or the type of environment they generally work in such as mainframe programmer, object-oriented programmer, or Internet or World Wide Web programmer. In many large organizations, programmers follow descriptions that have been prepared by software engineers or systems analysts. These descriptions list the input required, the steps the computer must follow to process data, and the desired arrangement of the output.

Many programmers are involved in updating, repairing, modifying and expanding existing programs. When making changes to a section of code, called a "routine," programmers need to make other users aware of the task the routine is to perform. They do this by inserting comments in the coded instructions so others can understand the program. Innovations such as Computer-Aided Software Engineering (CASE) tools enable a programmer to concentrate on writing the unique parts of the program because the tools automate various pieces of the program being built. CASE tools generate whole sections of code automatically, rather than line by line. This also yields more reliable and consistent programs and increases programmers' productivity by eliminating some of the routine steps.

Programmers test a program by running it to ensure the instructions are correct and it produces the desired information. If errors do occur, the programmer must make the appropriate change and recheck the program until it produces the correct results, a process called *debugging*. Programmers working in a mainframe environment may still prepare instructions for a computer operator who will run the program. They may also contribute to a user's manual for the program.

Programmers often are grouped into two broad types: Applications programmers and systems programmers. Applications programmers usually are oriented toward business, engineering, or science. They write software to handle specific jobs within an organization, such as a program used in an inventory control system. They may also work alone to revise existing packaged software. Systems programmers, on the other hand, maintain and control the use of computer systems software. These workers make changes in the sets of instructions that determine how the network, workstations, and central processing unit of the system handles the various jobs they have been given and how they communicate with peripheral equipment, such as terminals, printers, and disk drives. Because of their knowledge of the entire computer system, systems programmers often help applications programmers determine the source of problems that may occur with their programs.

In some organizations, particularly smaller ones, workers more commonly referred to as programmer-analysts are responsible for both the systems analysis and the actual programming work. Advanced programming languages and new object-oriented programming capabilities are increasing the efficiency and productivity of both programmers and users. The transition from a mainframe environment to a primarily PC-based environment has blurred the once rigid distinction between the programmer and the user. Increasingly, adept users are taking over many of the tasks previously performed by programmers. For example, the growing use of packaged software, like spreadsheet and data base management software packages, allows users to write simple programs to access data and perform calculations.

Programmers in software development companies may work directly with experts from various fields to create software–either programs designed for specific clients or packaged software for general use–ranging from games and educational software to programs for desktop publishing, financial planning, and spreadsheets. Much of this type of programming is in the preparation of packaged software, which comprises one of the most rapidly growing segments of the computer services industry.

Working Conditions

Programmers generally work in offices in comfortable surroundings. Although they usually work about 40 hours a week, programmers may work longer hours or weekends in order to meet deadlines or fix critical problems that occur during off hours. Given the technology available, telecommuting is becoming more common for a wider range of computer professionals—including computer programmers. Programmers can access a system directly, but from remote locations, to make corrections or fix problems.

Like other workers who spend long periods of time in front of a computer terminal typing at a keyboard, they are susceptible to eyestrain, back discomfort, and hand and wrist problems such as carpal tunnel syndrome or cumulative trauma disorder.

Employment

Computer programmers held about 568,000 jobs in 1996. Programmers are employed in almost every industry, but the largest concentration is in the computer and data processing services industry which includes firms that write and sell software. Large numbers of programmers can also be found working for firms that provide engineering and management services, manufacturers of computer and office equipment, financial institutions, insurance carriers, educational institutions, and government agencies.

A growing number of computer programmers are employed on a temporary or contract basis or work as independent consultants as companies demand expertise with newer programming languages or more specialized areas of application. Rather than hiring programmers as permanent employees and then laying them off after a job is completed, employers can contract with temporary help agencies, consulting firms, or directly with programmers themselves. A marketing firm, for example, may only require the services of several programmers to write and "debug" the software necessary to get a new database management system running. This practice also enables companies to bring in people with a specific set of skills, usually in one of the latest technologies as it applies to their business needs. Bringing in an independent contractor or consultant with a certain level of experience in a new or advanced programming language, for example, enables an establishment to complete a particular job without having to retrain existing workers. Such jobs may last anywhere from several weeks to a year or longer. There were 20,000 self-employed computer programmers in 1996 and this number is expected to increase.

Training, Other Qualifications, and Advancement

While there are many training paths available for programmers, mainly because employers' needs are so varied, the level of education and quality of training employers seek have been rising due to the growth in the number of qualified applicants and the increasing complexity of some programming tasks. Bachelor's degrees are now commonly required, although some programmers qualify with two-year degrees or certificates. College graduates who are interested in changing careers or developing an area of expertise also may return to a two-year community college or technical school for additional training. In the absence of a degree, substantial specialized experience or expertise may be needed. Even with a degree, employers appear to be placing more emphasis on previous experience for all types of programmers.

Table 1. Percent distribution of highest level of school completed or degree received, computer programmers, 1996

	Percentage
High school graduate or equivalent or less	10.0
Some college, no degree	20.9
Associate degree	9.6
Bachelor's degree	45.2
Graduate degree	14.2

The majority of computer programmers—almost 60 percent—had a bachelor's degree or higher in 1996 (see Table 1). Of these, some hold a B.A. or B.S. in computer science, mathematics, or information systems while others have taken special courses in computer programming to supplement their study in fields such as accounting, inventory control, or other business areas. As the level of education and training required by employers continues to rise, this percentage should increase in the future.

Skills needed vary from job to job and the demand for various skills is generally driven by changes in technology. Employers using computers for scientific or engineering applications generally prefer college graduates who have degrees in computer or information science, mathematics, engineering, or the physical sciences. Graduate degrees in related fields may be required for some jobs. Employers who use computers for business applications prefer to hire people who have had college courses in management information systems (MIS) and business, and who possess strong programming skills. Although knowledge of traditional languages such as FORTRAN, COBOL, or C is still important, increasing emphasis is placed on more advanced object-oriented languages and tools such as CASE tools, C++, Visual C++, Ada, Smalltalk, Visual Basic, PowerBuilder, and Java as well as 4th and 5th generation languages, graphic user interface (GUI) and systems programming. General business skills and experience related to the operations of the firm are preferred by employers as well.

Most systems programmers hold a four-year degree in computer science. Extensive knowledge of a variety of operating systems is essential. This includes being able to configure the operating system to work with different types of hardware, and adapting the operating system to best meet the needs of the particular organization. They must also be able to work with database systems such as DB2, Oracle, or Sybase, for example.

When hiring programmers, employers look for people with the necessary programming skills who can think logically and pay close attention to detail. The job calls for patience, persistence, and the ability to work on exacting analytical work, especially under pressure. Ingenuity and imagination are also particularly important when programmers design solutions and test their work for potential failures. The ability to work with abstract concepts and do technical analysis is especially important for systems programmers because they work with the software that controls the computer's operation. Since programmers are expected to work in teams and interact directly with users, employers want programmers who are able to communicate with non-technical personnel.

Beginning programmers may work alone on simple assignments after some initial instruction, or on a team with more experienced programmers. Either way, beginning programmers generally must work under close supervision. Because technology changes so rapidly, programmers must continuously update their training by taking courses sponsored by their employer or software vendors.

For skilled workers who keep up to date with the latest technology, the prospects for advancement are good. In large organizations, they may be promoted to lead programmer and be given supervisory responsibilities. Some applications programmers may move into systems programming after they gain experience and take courses in systems software. With general business experience, programmers may become programmer-analysts or systems analysts, or be promoted to a managerial position. Other programmers, with specialized knowledge and experience with a language or operating system, may work in research and development areas such as multimedia or Internet technology. As employers increasingly contract out programming jobs, more opportunities should arise for experienced programmers with expertise in a specific area to work as consultants.

Technical or professional certification is becoming more common as a way for employers to ensure a level of competency or quality in all areas. Many product vendors offer certification or may even require certification of technicians and professionals who work with their products. The number of voluntary certificate or certification programs is also growing and this type of certification is available through organizations such as the Institute for Certification of Computing Professionals (ICCP). ICCP confers the designation Certified Computing Professional (CCP) to those who have at least four years of experience or two years of experience and a college degree. To qualify, individuals must pass a core examination plus exams in two specialty areas, or an exam in one specialty area and two computing languages. Those with little or no experience may be tested for certification as an Associate Computer Professional (ACP). Certification is not mandatory, but it may give a jobseeker a competitive advantage.

Job Outlook

Employment of programmers is expected to grow faster than the average through the year 2006. Jobs for both systems and applications programmers should remain plentiful in data processing service firms, software houses, and computer consulting businesses. These types of establishments are part of one of the fastest growing industries—computer and data processing services, which is projected to be the fastest growing industry. As companies attempt to control costs and keep up with changing technology, they will maintain a need for programmers to assist in conversions to new languages and from one system to the next. In addition, numerous a majority of the job openings for programmers will should still result from the need to replace programmers who move to other occupations or leave the labor force replacement needs. Most programmers who leave transfer to other occupations, such as manager or systems analyst.

Despite numerous openings, however, the consolidation and centralization of systems and applications should continue to mod-

erate growth, as will developments in packaged software, advanced programming languages and tools, and the growing ability of users to design, write, and implement more of their own programs to meet their changing needs. As the level of technological innovation and sophistication increases, programmers should continue to face increasing competition from programming businesses overseas where more of the routine work can be outsourced at a lower cost.

As programming tasks become more complex and increasingly sophisticated skills and experience are demanded by employers, graduates of two-year programs, and people with less than a two-year degree or its equivalent in work experience, should face stronger competition for programming jobs. Competition for entry-level positions, however, can even affects applicants with a bachelor's degree. Although demand fluctuates as employer's needs change with technology, prospects should be best for college graduates with knowledge of and experience working with a variety of programming languages and tools, particularly C++ and other object oriented languages—such as Smalltalk, Visual Basic, Ada, and Java—as well as newer, domain-specific languages that apply to computer networking, data base management, and Internet applications. In order to remain competitive, college graduates should keep up to date with the latest skills and technologies.

Many employers prefer to hire applicants with previous experience in the field. Employers are increasingly interested in programmers who can combine areas of technical expertise or who are adaptable and able to learn and incorporate new skills. Therefore, individuals who want to become programmers can enhance their chances of doing so by combining the appropriate formal training with practical work experience. Students should try to gain experience by participating in a college work-study program, or undertaking an internship. Students also can greatly improve their employment prospects by taking courses such as accounting, management, engineering, or science—allied fields in which applications programmers are in demand.

With the expansion of client/server environments, employers will continue to look for programmers with strong technical skills who understand their business and its programming needs. Businesses also look for programmers who develop a technical specialization in areas such as client/server programming, multimedia technology, graphic user interface (GUI), and fourth- and fifth-generation programming tools. Programmers will be creating and maintaining expert systems and embedding these technologies in more and more products. Other areas of progress include data communications and the business application of Internet technologies. Networking computers so they can communicate with each other is necessary to achieve the greater efficiency organizations require to remain competitive. Demand for programmers with strong object-oriented programming capabilities and experience should arise from the expansion of Intranets, extranets and World Wide Web applications.

Earnings

Median earnings of programmers who worked full-time in 1996 were about $40,100 a year. The middle 50 percent earned between $30,700 and $52,000 a year. The lowest 10 percent earned less than $22,700; the highest 10 percent earned more than $65,200. Starting salary offers for graduates with a bachelor's degree in the area of computer programming averaged about $35,167 a year in private industry in 1997, according to the National Association of Colleges and Employers. Programmers working in the West and Northeast earned somewhat more than those working in the South and Midwest. On average, systems programmers earn more than applications programmers.

A survey of workplaces in 160 metropolitan areas reported that beginning programmers had median annual earnings of about $27,000 in 1995. Experienced mid-level programmers with some supervisory responsibilities had median annual earnings of about $40,000. Median annual earnings for programmers at the supervisory or team leader level were about $55,000.

According to Robert Half International, Inc., starting salaries ranged from $32,500 to $39,000 for programmers and $47,500 to $60,000 for systems programmers in large establishments in 1997. Starting salaries for programmers in small establishments ranged from $28,000 to $37,000.

In the federal government, the entrance salary for programmers with a college degree or qualifying experience was about $19,520 a year in early 1997; for those with a superior academic record, $24,180.

Related Occupations

Programmers must pay great attention to detail as they write and debug programs. Other professional workers who must be detail-oriented include computer scientists, computer engineers, and systems analysts, statisticians, mathematicians, engineers, financial analysts, accountants, auditors, actuaries, and operations research analysts.

Sources of Additional Information

State employment service offices can provide information about job openings for computer programmers. Also check with your city's chamber of commerce for information on the area's largest employers.

For information about certification as a computing professional, contact:

❑ Institute for Certification of Computing Professionals (ICCP), 2200 East Devon Ave., Suite 268, Des Plaines, IL 60018. Homepage: http://www.iccp.org

Further information about computer careers is available from:

❑ The Association for Computing (ACM), 1515 Broadway, New York, NY 10036.

❑ IEEE Computer Society, Headquarters Office, 1730 Massachusetts Ave., NW, Washington, DC 20036-1992.

Computer Scientists, Computer Engineers, and Systems Analysts

(D.O.T. 030.062-010, .162-014, .167-014; 031; 032; 033; 039; and 109.067-010)

Significant Points

✓ *Expected to be the top three fastest growing occupations and among the top twenty in the number of new jobs as computer applications continue to expand throughout the economy.*

✓ *A bachelor's degree is virtually a prerequisite for most employers. Relevant work experience also is very important. For some of the more complex jobs, persons with graduate degrees are preferred.*

Nature of the Work

The rapid spread of computers has generated a need for highly trained workers to design and develop new hardware and software systems and to incorporate technological advances into new or existing systems. The *OOH* refers to this group of professionals as computer scientists, computer engineers, and systems analysts, but in reality this group includes a wide range of professional computer-related occupations. Job titles used to describe this broad category of workers evolve rapidly, reflecting new areas of specialization or changes in technology as well as the preferences and practices of employers. Although many narrow specializations exist, the professional specialty group is commonly referred to as computer scientists, computer engineers, and systems analysts.

The title computer scientist can be applied to a wide range computer professionals who generally design computers and the software that runs them, develop information technologies, and develop and adapt principles for applying computers to new uses. Computer scientists perform many of the same duties as other computer professionals throughout a normal workday, but their jobs are distinguished by the higher level of theoretical expertise and innovation they apply to complex problems and the creation or application of new technology.

Computer scientists can work as theorists, researchers, or inventors. Those employed by academic institutions work in areas ranging from complexity theory, to hardware, to programming language design. Some work on multi-discipline projects, such as developing and advancing uses of virtual reality in robotics. Their counterparts in private industry work in areas such as applying theory, developing specialized languages or information technologies, or designing programming tools, knowledge-based systems, or even computer games.

Computer engineers also work with the hardware and software aspects of systems design and development. Whereas computer scientists emphasize the application of theory, computer engineers emphasize the building of prototypes, although there is much crossover. Computer engineers generally apply the theories and principles of science and mathematics to the design of hardware, software, networks, and processes to solve technical problems. They often work as part of a team that designs new computing devices or computer-related equipment, systems, or software. Computer hardware engineers generally design, develop, test, and supervise the manufacture of computer hardware—for example, chips or device controllers. Software engineers, on the other hand, are involved in the design and development of software systems for control and automation of manufacturing, business, and management processes. Software engineers or software developers also may design and develop both packaged and systems software or be involved in creating custom software applications for clients. These professionals also possess strong programming skills, but they are more concerned with analyzing and solving programming problems than with simply writing the code for the programs.

Far more numerous, systems analysts use their knowledge and skills to solve computer problems and enable computer technology to meet the individual needs of an organization. They study business, scientific, or engineering data processing problems and design new solutions using computers. This process may include planning and developing new computer systems or devising ways to apply existing systems' resources to additional operations. Systems analysts may design entirely new systems, including both hardware and software, or add a single new software application to harness more of the computer's power. They work to help an organization realize the maximum benefit from its investment in equipment, personnel, and business processes. Most systems analysts generally work with a specific type of system depending on the type of organization they work for–for example, business, accounting or financial systems, or scientific and engineering systems. Companies generally seek business systems analysts who specialize in the type of systems they use.

Analysts begin an assignment by discussing the systems problem with managers and users to determine its exact nature. Much time is devoted to clearly defining the goals of the system and understanding the individual steps used to achieve them so that the problem can be broken down into separate programmable procedures. Analysts then use techniques such as structured analysis, data modeling, information engineering, mathematical model building, sampling, and cost accounting to plan the system. Analysts must specify the inputs to be accessed by the system, design the processing steps, and format the output to meet the users' needs. Once the design has been developed, systems analysts prepare charts and diagrams that describe it in terms that managers and other users can understand. They may prepare cost-benefit and return-on-investment analyses to help management decide whether implementing the proposed system will be financially feasible.

When a system is accepted, analysts determine what computer hardware and software will be needed to set it up. They coordinate tests and observe initial use of the system to ensure it performs as planned. They prepare specifications, work diagrams, and structure charts for computer programmers to follow and then work with them to "debug," or eliminate errors from the system.

In some organizations a single worker called a programmer-analyst is responsible for both systems analysis and programming. As this becomes more commonplace, these analysts will increasingly work with Computer Aided Software Engineering (CASE) tools and object-oriented programming languages, as well as client/server applications development, and multimedia and Internet technology.

One obstacle associated with expanding computer use is the inability of different computer systems to communicate with each other. Because maintaining up-to-date information–accounting records, sales figures, or budget projections, for example–is important in modern organizations, systems analysts may be instructed to make the computer systems in each department compatible so that information can be shared. Many systems analysts are involved with "networking" or connecting all the computers in an individual office, department, or establishment. A primary goal of networking is to allow users to retrieve data from a mainframe computer or a server and use it on their machine. This connection also allows data to be entered into the mainframe from a personal computer. Analysts must design the hardware and software to allow free exchange of data, custom applications, and the computer power to process it all. They study the seemingly incompatible pieces and create ways to link them so users can access information from any part of the system. Networks come in many variations and network systems and data communications analysts design, test, and evaluate systems such as Local Area Networks (LAN), Wide Area Networks (WAN), Internet, and Intranet and other data communications systems. These analysts perform network modeling, analysis and planning, and even research and recommend necessary hardware and software.

Other computer professionals include database administrators and computer support specialists. Database administrators work with database management systems software, coordinating changes to, testing, and implementing computer databases. Since they also may be responsible for design implementation and system security, database administrators plan and coordinate security measures. Computer support specialists provide assistance and advice to users. They interpret problems and provide technical support for hardware, software, and systems. Support specialists may work within an organization or directly for a computer or software vendor. Increasingly, these technical professionals work for help-desk or support services firms, providing customer support on a contract basis to clients as more of this type of work is outsourced.

Many others specialize in analysis, application, or design of a particular system or piece of the system. Network or systems administrators, for example, may install, configure, and support an organizations systems or portion of a system. Telecommunications specialists generally are involved with the interfacing of computer and communications equipment. Computer security specialists are responsible for planning, coordinating, and implementing an organizations' information security measures. These and other growing specialty occupations reflect the increasing emphasis on client-server applications, the growth of the Internet, the expansion of World Wide Web applications and Intranets, and the demand for more end-user support. An example of this is the growing number of job titles relating to the Internet and World Wide Web such as Internet and Web developers, or Webmasters.

Working Conditions

Computer scientists, computer engineers, and systems analysts normally work in offices or laboratories in comfortable surroundings. They usually work about 40 hours a week–the same as many other professional or office workers. However, evening or weekend work may be necessary to meet deadlines or solve specific problems. Given the technology available today, telecommuting is becoming more common for computer professionals. More work, including technical support, can be done from remote locations using modems, laptops, electronic mail, and even through the Internet. It is now possible for technical personnel, such as computer support specialists, to tap into a customer's computer remotely to identify and fix problems.

Like other workers who spend long periods of time in front of a computer terminal typing on a keyboard, computer scientists, engineers, and systems analysts are susceptible to eye strain, back discomfort, and hand and wrist problems such as carpal tunnel syndrome or cumulative trauma disorder.

Employment

Computer scientists, computer engineers, and systems analysts held about 933,000 jobs in 1996, including about 58,000 who were self-employed. About 216,000 were computer engineers, about 506,000 were computer systems analysts, and about 212,000 were database administrators, computer support specialists, and all other computer scientists.

Although they are employed in most industries, the greatest concentration is in the computer and data processing services industry. This industry includes firms providing nearly every service related to commercial computer use on a contract basis. Services include customized computer programming services and applications and systems software design; the design, development, and production of prepackaged computer software; systems integration, networking, and reengineering services; data processing and preparation services; information retrieval services including on-line data bases and Internet services; on-site computer facilities management; the development and management of data bases; and a variety of specialized consulting services. Many others work for government agencies, manufacturers of computer and related electronic equipment, insurance companies, financial institutions, and universities.

A growing number of computer professionals are employed on a temporary or contract basis—many of whom are self-employed, working independently as contractors or self-employed consultants. For example, a company installing a new computer system may need the services of several systems analysts just to get the system running. Because not all of them would be needed once the system is functioning, the company might contract directly with the systems analysts themselves or with a temporary help agency or consulting firm. Such jobs may last from several months up to two years or more. This growing practice enables companies to bring in people with the exact skills they need to complete a particular project, rather than having to spend time or money training or retraining existing workers. Often, experienced consultants then train a company's in-house staff as a project develops.

Training, Other Qualifications, and Advancement

While there is no universally accepted way to prepare for a job as a computer professional because employers' preferences depend on the work to be done, a bachelor's degree is virtually a prerequisite for most employers. Relevant work experience also is very important. For some of the more complex jobs, persons with graduate degrees are preferred.

Computer hardware engineers generally require a bachelor's degree in computer engineering or electrical engineering, whereas software engineers are more likely to need a degree in computer science. For systems analyst or even database administrator positions, many employers seek applicants who have a bachelor's degree in computer science, information science, computer information systems, or data processing. Computer support specialists may also need a bachelor's degree in a computer-related field, as well as significant experience working with computers, including programming skills. Generally, a Ph.D., or at least a master's degree in computer science or engineering, is required for computer scientist jobs in research laboratories or academic institutions.

Many people develop advanced computer skills in other occupations in which they work extensively with computers, and then transfer into computer occupations. For example, an accountant may become a systems analyst or computer support specialist specializing in accounting systems development, or an individual may move into a systems analyst job after working as a computer programmer.

Regardless of college major, employers generally look for people who are familiar with programming languages and have broad knowledge of and experience with computer systems and technologies, strong problem-solving and analysis skills, and good interpersonal skills. Courses in computer programming or systems design offer good preparation for a job in this field. For jobs in a business environment, employers usually want systems analysts to have a background in business management or a closely related field, while a background in the physical sciences, applied mathematics, or engineering is preferred for work in scientifically oriented organizations. Since employers generally look for experience, entry-level employees enhance their employment opportunities by participating in internship or co-op programs offered through their schools. A related background in the industry in which the job is located, such as financial services, banking, or accounting, can also give an applicant an edge.

Computer scientists, computer engineers, and systems analysts must be able to think logically and have good communication skills. They often deal with a number of tasks simultaneously; the ability to concentrate and pay close attention to detail is important. Although many computer specialists sometimes work independently, they often work in teams on large projects. They must be able to communicate effectively with computer personnel, such as programmers and managers, as well as with users or other staff who may have no technical computer background.

Systems analysts may be promoted to senior or lead systems analysts with experience. Those who show leadership ability also can advance to management positions, such as manager of information systems or chief information officer.

Computer engineers and scientists employed in industry may eventually advance into managerial or project leadership positions. Those employed in academic institutions can become heads of research departments or published authorities in their field. Computer professionals with several years of experience and considerable expertise in a particular subject area or application may find lucrative opportunities as independent consultants or choose to start their own computer consulting firms.

Technological advances come so rapidly in the computer field that continuous study is necessary to keep skills up to date. Continuing education is usually offered by employers, hardware and software vendors, colleges and universities, or private training institutions. Additional training may come from professional development seminars offered by professional computing societies.

As technology becomes more sophisticated and complex, a higher level of skill and expertise is demanded by employers in all areas. Technical or professional certification is becoming a more common way to ensure employers of a level of competency or quality in a prospective employee. Many product vendors offer and may even require professionals who work with their products to be certified. Voluntary certification is also available through organizations such as the Institute for Certification of Computing Professionals (ICCP). ICCP offers the designation Certified Computing Professional (CCP) to those who have at least four years of work experience as a computer professional, or at least two years experience and a college degree. Candidates must pass a core examination testing general knowledge, plus exams in two specialty areas, or in one specialty area and two computer programming languages. The Quality Assurance Institute (QAI) awards the designation Certified Quality Analyst (CQA) to those who meet education and experience requirements, pass an exam, and endorse a code of ethics. Neither designation is mandatory, but professional certification may provide a job seeker a competitive advantage.

Job Outlook

Computer scientists, computer engineers, and systems analysts are expected to be the three fastest growing occupations through the year 2006. Employment of computing professionals is expected to increase much faster than average as technology becomes more sophisticated and organizations continue to adopt and integrate these technologies, making for plentiful job openings. Growth will be driven by very rapid growth in the computer and data processing services industry, which is projected to be the fastest growing industry. In addition, thousands of job openings will result annually from the need to replace workers who move into managerial positions or other occupations or who leave the labor force.

Nevertheless, computer scientists, computer engineers, and systems analysts will need to continually upgrade their technical expertise and improve their ability to interact with users as the sophistication and complexity of technology advances. As more computing power is made available to the individual user and users develop more sophisticated knowledge of computers, they become more aware of the machine's potential and better able to suggest how computers could be used to increase their own productivity and that of the organization. Increasingly, users are able to design and implement more of their own applications and programs. The result is a growing demand for computer support specialists, help desk personnel, and technical consultants.

The demand for *networking* to facilitate the sharing of information, the expansion of client/server environments, and the need for specialists to use their knowledge and skills in a problem solving capacity will be a major factor in the rising demand for systems analysts. Falling prices of computer hardware and software should continue to induce more businesses to expand computerized operations and integrate new technologies. In order to maintain a competitive edge and operate more cost effectively, firms will continue to demand computer professionals who are knowledgeable about the latest technologies and able to apply them to meet the needs of businesses.

New growth areas generally arise from the development of new technologies. Therefore, it is important for computer professionals at all levels to keep their skills up to date. The expanding integration of Internet technologies by businesses, for example, has resulted in a rising demand for a variety of skilled professionals who can develop and support Internet, Intranet, and World Wide Web applications. Growth in these areas is also expected to create demand for computer scientists, computer engineers, and systems analysts knowledgeable about network, data and communications security.

Since employers look for the most qualified applicants possessing a high level of technical expertise, individuals with an advanced degree in computer science, management information systems (MIS), computer engineering, or an MBA with a concentration in information systems should enjoy very favorable employment prospects. College graduates with a bachelor's degree in computer science, computer engineering, information science, or information systems should also enjoy favorable prospects, very particularly if they have supplemented their formal education with some level of practical experience. College graduates with non-computer science majors who have had courses in computer programming, systems analysis, and other data processing areas, as well as training or experience in an applied field, should also be able to find jobs as computer professionals. Those who are familiar with client/server environments, CASE tools and object-oriented programming, Internet, Intranet, and multimedia technology will have an even greater advantage, as will individuals with significant networking, database, and systems experience. Employers will continue to seek computer professionals who can combine strong programming and traditional systems analysis skills with good interpersonal and business skills.

Earnings

Median annual earnings of computer systems analysts and scientists who worked full-time in 1996 were about $46,300. The middle 50 percent earned between $34,000 and $59,900. The lowest 10 percent earned less than $24,800 and the highest tenth, more than $76,200. Computer scientists with advanced degrees generally earn more than systems analysts.

Starting salaries for computer scientists or computer engineers with a bachelor's degree can be significantly higher than starting salaries of bachelor's degree graduates in many other fields. According to the National Association of Colleges and Employers, starting salary offers for graduates with a bachelor's degree in computer engineering averaged about $39,722 a year in 1997; those with a master's degree, $44,734 a year; and those with a Ph.D., $63,367. Starting offers for graduates with a bachelor's degree in computer science averaged about $36,597 a year; in information sciences, about $35,407 a year; and in systems analysis, about $43,800 a year in 1997. Offers for those with the bachelor's degree vary by functional area for all types of employers, as shown in the following tabulation.

Computer programming	$35,167
Information systems	34,689
Systems analysis and design	36,261
Software design and development	39,190
Hardware design and development	41,237

Offers for graduates with a master's degree in computer science in 1997 averaged $45,853 a year; and those with a Ph.D. in computer and information sciences, $61,306.

According to Robert Half International, Inc., starting salaries in 1997 for systems analysts employed by large establishments employing more than 50 staff members ranged from $46,000 to $57,500. Salaries for those employed in small establishments ranged from

$38,000 to $48,000. Salaries for programmer-analysts ranged from $39,000 to $50,000 in large establishments andto $33,500 to $43,000 in small establishments. Starting salaries ranged from $54,000 to $67,500 for data base administrators, from $36,000 to $55,000 for network administrators, from $25,000 to $36,500 for help desk support technicians, and from $49,000 to $67,500 for software development specialists.

In the federal government, the entrance salary for systems analysts who are recent college graduates with a bachelor's degree was about $19,520 a year in early 1997; for those with a superior academic record, $24,180. The average annual salary for computer engineers in employed by the federal government in nonsupervisory, supervisory, and managerial positions was $62,900 in early 1997.

Related Occupations

Other workers who use research, logic, and creativity to solve business problems are computer programmers, financial analysts, urban planners, engineers, mathematicians, statisticians, operations research analysts, management analysts, and actuaries.

Sources of Additional Information

Further information about computer careers is available from:
❑ Association for Computing (ACM), 1515 Broadway, New York, NY 10036.
❑ IEEE Computer Society, Headquarters Office, 1730 Massachusetts Ave., NW, Washington, DC 20036-1992.

Information about the designation Certified Computing Professional is available from:
❑ Institute for Certification of Computing Professionals (ICCP), 2200 East Devon Ave., Suite 268, Des Plaines, IL 60018. Homepage: http://www.iccp.org

Information about the designation Certified Quality Analyst is available from:
❑ Quality Assurance Institute, 7575 Dr. Phillips Blvd., Suite 350, Orlando, FL 32819.

Construction and Building Inspectors

(*D.O.T.* 168.167-030, -034, -038, -046, and -050; .267-010, -102; 182.267; 850.387, .467)

Significant Points

✓ *Over 50 percent are employed by local governments, primarily municipal or county building departments.*

✓ *Construction and building inspectors tend to be older, more experienced workers who have spent years working in other related occupations.*

Nature of the Work

Construction and building inspectors examine the construction, alteration, or repair of buildings, highways and streets, sewer and water systems, dams, bridges, and other structures to ensure compliance with building codes and ordinances, zoning regulations, and contract specifications. Throughout the country, building codes and standards are the primary means by which building construction is regulated to assure the health and safety of the general public. Inspectors make an initial inspection during the first phase of construction, and follow-up inspections throughout the construction

project to monitor compliance with regulations. However, no inspection is ever exactly the same. In areas where certain types of severe weather or natural disasters are more common, inspectors monitor compliance with additional safety regulations designed to protect structures and occupants in these events.

Building inspectors inspect the structural quality and general safety of buildings. Some specialize—for example, in structural steel or reinforced concrete structures. Before construction begins, plan examiners determine whether the plans for the building or other structure comply with building code regulations, and if they are suited to the engineering and environmental demands of the building site. Inspectors visit the work site before the foundation is poured to inspect the soil condition and positioning and depth of the footings. Later, they return to the site to inspect the foundation after it has been completed. The size and type of structure and the rate of completion determine the number of other site visits they must make. Upon completion of the entire project, they make a final comprehensive inspection.

In addition to structural characteristics, a primary concern of building inspectors is fire safety. They inspect structure's fire sprinklers, alarms, and smoke control systems, as well as fire doors and exits. Inspectors assess the type of construction, building contents, adequacy of fire protection equipment, and risks posed by adjoining buildings.

There are many types of inspections and inspectors. Electrical inspectors examine the installation of electrical systems and equipment to ensure they function properly and comply with electrical codes and standards. They visit work sites to inspect new and existing sound and security systems, wiring, lighting, motors, and generating equipment. They also inspect the installation of the electrical wiring for heating and air-conditioning systems, appliances, and other components.

Elevator inspectors examine lifting and conveying devices such as elevators, escalators, moving sidewalks, lifts and hoists, inclined railways, ski lifts, and amusement rides.

Mechanical inspectors inspect the installation of the mechanical components of commercial kitchen appliances, heating and air-conditioning equipment, gasoline and butane tanks, gas and oil piping, and gas-fired and oil-fired appliances. Some specialize in boilers or ventilating equipment as well.

Plumbing inspectors examine plumbing systems, including private disposal systems, water supply and distribution systems, plumbing fixtures and traps, and drain, waste, and vent lines.

Public works inspectors ensure that federal, state, and local government construction of water and sewer systems, highways, streets, bridges, and dams conforms to detailed contract specifications. They inspect excavation and fill operations, the placement of forms for concrete, concrete mixing and pouring, asphalt paving, and grading operations. They record the work and materials used so contract payments can be calculated. Public works inspectors may specialize in highways, structural steel, reinforced concrete, or ditches. Others specialize in dredging operations required for bridges and dams or for harbors.

Home inspectors generally conduct inspections of newly built or previously owned homes. Increasingly, prospective home buyers hire home inspectors to inspect and report the condition of a home's major systems, components, and structure. They are typically hired either immediately prior to a purchase offer on a home, or as a contingency to a sales contract. In addition to structural quality, home inspectors must be able to inspect all home systems and features, from plumbing, electrical, and heating or cooling systems to roofing.

Specification inspectors are employed by the owner of a building or structure under construction to ensure work is done according to design specifications. They represent the owners' interests, not the general public. These inspectors may also be utilized by insurance companies or financial institutions.

Details concerning construction projects, building and occupancy permits, and other documentation are generally stored on computers so they can easily be retrieved and kept accurate and up to date. For example, inspectors may use laptop computers to record their findings while inspecting a site. Most inspectors use computers to help them monitor the status of construction inspection activities and keep track of issued permits.

Although inspections are primarily visual, most inspectors, except home inspectors, may use tape measures, survey instruments, metering devices, and test equipment such as concrete strength measurers. They keep a log of their work, take photographs, file reports, and, if necessary, act on their findings. For example, construction inspectors notify the construction contractor, superintendent, or supervisor when they discover a code or ordinance violation or something that does not comply with the contract specifications or approved plans. If the problem is not corrected within a reasonable or specified period of time, government inspectors have authority to issue a "stop-work" order.

Many inspectors also investigate construction or alterations being done without proper permits. Inspectors who are employees of municipalities enforce laws pertaining to the proper design, construction, and use of buildings. They direct violators of permit laws to obtain permits and submit to inspection.

Working Conditions

Construction and building inspectors usually work alone. However, several may be assigned to large, complex projects, particularly because inspectors tend to specialize in different areas of construction. Though they spend considerable time inspecting construction work sites, inspectors may spend much of their time in a field office reviewing blueprints, answering letters or telephone calls, writing reports, and scheduling inspections.

Inspection sites are dirty and may be cluttered with tools, materials, or debris. Inspectors may have to climb ladders or many flights of stairs, or may have to crawl around in tight spaces. Although their work is not generally considered hazardous, inspectors, like other construction workers, wear hard hats and adhere to other safety requirements while at a construction site.

Inspectors normally work regular hours. However, if an accident occurs at a construction site, inspectors must respond immediately and may work additional hours to complete their report.

Employment

Construction and building inspectors held about 66,000 jobs in 1996. Over 50 percent worked for local governments, primarily municipal or county building departments. Employment of local government inspectors is concentrated in cities and in suburban areas undergoing rapid growth. Local governments employ large inspection staffs, including many plan examiners or inspectors who specialize in structural steel, reinforced concrete, boiler, electrical, and elevator inspection.

Another 19 percent of all construction and building inspectors worked for engineering and architectural services firms, conducting inspections for a fee or on a contract basis. Most of the remaining inspectors were employed by the federal and state governments. Many construction inspectors employed by the federal government work for the U.S. Army Corps of Engineers. Other federal employers include the Tennessee Valley Authority and the Departments of Agriculture, Housing and Urban Development, and Interior.

Training, Other Qualifications, and Advancement

Although requirements vary considerably depending upon where one is employed, individuals who want to become construction and building inspectors should have a thorough knowledge of construction materials and practices in either a general area, such as structural or heavy construction, or in a specialized area, such as electrical or plumbing systems, reinforced concrete, or structural steel. Construction or building inspectors need several years of experience as a manager, supervisor, or craft worker before becoming inspectors. Many previously worked as carpenters, electricians, plumbers, or pipefitters.

Because inspectors need to posses the right mix of technical knowledge, experience and education, employers prefer to hire inspectors who have formal training, as well as experience. Most require at least a high school diploma or equivalent even for those with considerable experience. More often, employers look for persons who have studied engineering or architecture, or who have a degree from a community or junior college, with courses in construction technology, drafting, mathematics, and building inspection. Many community colleges offer certificate or associate degree programs in building inspection technology. Courses in blueprint reading, algebra, geometry, and English are also useful.

Construction and building inspectors must be in good physical condition in order to walk and climb about construction sites. They must also have a driver's license. In addition, federal, state, and many local governments may require that inspectors pass a civil service examination.

Construction and building inspectors usually receive much of their training on the job, although they must often learn building codes and standards on their own. Working with an experienced inspector, they learn about inspection techniques; codes, ordinances, and regulations; contract specifications; and record keeping and reporting duties. They may begin by inspecting less complex types of construction, such as residential buildings, and then progress to more difficult assignments. An engineering or architectural degree is often required for advancement to supervisory positions.

Because they advise builders and the general public on building codes, construction practices, and technical developments, construction and building inspectors must keep abreast of changes in these areas. Continuing education is imperative in this ever-changing field. Many employers provide formal training programs to broaden inspectors' knowledge of construction materials, practices, and techniques. Inspectors who work for small agencies or firms that do not conduct training programs can expand their knowledge and upgrade their skills by attending state-sponsored training programs, by taking college or correspondence courses, or by attending seminars sponsored by various related organizations such as model code organizations.

Most states and cities require some type of certification for employment and, even if not required, certification can enhance an inspector's opportunities for employment and advancement to more responsible positions. To become certified, inspectors with substantial experience and education must pass stringent examinations on code requirements, construction techniques, and materials. The three major model code organizations offer voluntary certification as do other professional membership associations. In most cases, there are no education or experience prerequisites, and certification consist of passing an examination in a designated field. Many categories of certification are awarded for inspectors and plan examiners in a variety of disciplines, including the designation *CBO*, Certified Building Official.

Job Outlook

Employment of construction and building inspectors is expected to grow as fast as the average for all occupations through the year 2006. Growing concern for public safety and improvements in the quality of construction should continue to stimulate demand for construction and building inspectors. Despite the expected employment growth, most job openings will arise from the need to replace inspectors who transfer to other occupations or leave the labor force. Construction and building inspectors tend to be older, more experienced workers who have spent years working in other occupations.

Opportunities should be best for highly experienced supervisors and craft workers who have some college education, engineering or architectural training, or who are certified as inspectors or plan examiners. Thorough knowledge of construction practices and skills in areas such as reading and evaluating blueprints and plans are essential. However, inspectors are involved in all phases of construction, including maintenance and repair work, and are therefore less likely to lose jobs during recessionary periods when new construction slows. As the population grows and the volume of real estate transactions increases, greater emphasis on home inspections should result in rapid growth in employment of home inspectors. In addition, there should be good opportunities in engineering, architectural and management services firms due to the tendency of governments—particularly the federal and state—to contract out inspection work, as well as expected growth in private inspection services.

Earnings

The median annual salary of construction and building inspectors was about $33,700 in 1996. The middle 50 percent earned between $26,500 and $45,800. The lowest 10 percent earned less than $21,600 and the highest 10 percent earned more than $55,800 a year. Generally, building inspectors, including plan examiners, earn the highest salaries. Salaries in large metropolitan areas are substantially higher than those in small local jurisdictions.

Related Occupations

Construction and building inspectors combine a knowledge of construction principles and law with an ability to coordinate data, diagnose problems, and communicate with people. Workers in other occupations using a similar combination of skills include engineers, drafters, estimators, industrial engineering technicians, surveyors, architects, and construction managers.

Sources of Additional Information

Information about certification and a career as a construction or building inspector is available from the following model code organizations:

❑ International Conference of Building Officials, 5360 Workman Mill Rd., Whittier, CA 90601-2298. Homepage: http://www.icbo.org
❑ Building Officials and Code Administrators International, Inc., 4051 West Flossmoor Rd., Country Club Hills, IL 60478. Homepage: http://www.bocai.org
❑ Southern Building Code Congress International, Inc., 900 Montclair Rd., Birmingham, AL 35213.

Information about a career as a home inspector is available from:

❑ American Society of Home Inspectors, Inc., 85 West Algonquin Rd., Arlington Heights, IL 60005. Homepage: http://www.ashi.com

For information about a career as a state or local government construction or building inspector, contact your state or local employment service.

Construction Managers

(*D.O.T.* 182.167-010, -018, -026, -030, and -034)

Significant Points

✓ *Construction managers make decisions regarding daily construction activities at the job site.*

✓ *Good employment opportunities are expected because the increasing complexity of construction projects should increase demand for management level personnel.*

✓ *More and more employers—particularly, large construction firms—seek to hire individuals who combine industry work experience with a bachelor's degree in construction or building science or construction management.*

Nature of the Work

Construction managers plan and direct construction projects. They may hold a variety of job titles, such as construction superintendent, general superintendent, project engineer, project manager, general construction manager, or executive construction manager. Construction managers may be owners or salaried employees of a construction management or contracting firm, or may work under contract or as a salaried employee of the owner, developer, contractor, or management firm overseeing the construction project. The *OOH* uses the term "construction manager" to describe all salaried or self-employed managers of construction who oversee construction supervisors and workers.

In contrast with the *OOH* definition, the term "construction manager" is used more narrowly within the construction industry to denote a management firm, or an individual employed by such a firm, involved in management oversight of a construction project. Under this narrower definition, construction managers generally act as representatives of the owner or developer with other participants throughout the life of a project. Although they generally play no direct role in the actual construction of a structure, they typically schedule and coordinate all design and construction processes including the selection, hiring, and oversight of specialty subcontractors.

Managers and other professionals who work in the construction industry, such as general managers, project engineers, cost estimators, and others, are increasingly referred to as constructors. This term refers to a broad group of professionals in construction who, through education and experience, are capable of managing, coordinating, and supervising the construction process from conceptual development through final construction on a timely and economical basis. Given designs for buildings, roads, bridges, or other projects, constructors oversee the organization, scheduling, and implementation of the project to execute those designs. They are responsible for coordinating and managing people, materials, and equipment; budgets, schedules, and contracts; and the safety of employees and the general public.

On large projects, construction managers may work for a general contractor—the firm with overall responsibility for all activities. There they oversee the completion of all construction in accordance with the engineer or architect's drawings and specifications and prevailing building codes. They arrange for subcontractors to perform specialized craft work or other specified construction work. On small projects, such as remodeling a home, a self-employed construction manager or skilled trades worker who directs and oversees employees is often referred to as the construction "contractor."

Large construction projects, such as an office building or industrial complex, are too complicated for one person to manage. These projects are divided into many segments: Site preparation, including land clearing and earth moving; sewage systems; landscaping and road construction; building construction, including excavation and laying foundations, erection of structural framework, floors, walls, and roofs; and building systems, including fire protection, electrical, plumbing, air-conditioning, and heating. Construction managers may work as part of a team or be in charge of one or more of these activities.

Construction managers evaluate various construction methods and determine the most cost-effective plan and schedule. They determine the appropriate construction methods and schedule all required construction site activities into logical, specific steps, budgeting the time required to meet established deadlines. This may require sophisticated estimating and scheduling techniques, and use of computers with specialized software. This also involves the selection and coordination of subcontractors hired to complete specific pieces of the project—which could include everything from structural metalworking and plumbing, to painting and carpet installation. Construction managers determine the labor requirements and, in some cases, supervise or monitor the hiring and dismissal of workers. They oversee the performance of all trade contractors and are responsible for ensuring all work is completed on schedule.

Managers direct and monitor the progress of construction activities, at times through other construction supervisors. This includes the delivery and use of materials, tools, and equipment; the quality of construction, worker productivity, and safety. They are responsible for obtaining all necessary permits and licenses and, depending upon the contractual arrangements, direct or monitor compliance with building and safety codes and other regulations. They may have several subordinates, such as assistant managers or superintendents, field engineers, or crew supervisors, reporting to them.

Construction managers regularly review engineering and architectural drawings and specifications to monitor progress and ensure compliance with plans and specifications. They track and control construction costs to avoid cost overruns. Based upon direct observation and reports by subordinate supervisors, managers may prepare daily reports of progress and requirements for labor, material, and machinery and equipment at the construction site. They meet regularly with owners, subcontractors, architects, and other design professionals to monitor and coordinate all phases of the construction project.

Working Conditions

Construction managers work out of a main office from which the overall construction project is monitored or out of a field office at the construction site. Management decisions regarding daily construction activities are usually made at the job site. Managers usually travel when the construction site is in another state or when they are responsible for activities at two or more sites. Management of overseas construction projects usually entails temporary residence in another country.

Construction managers must be on call to deal with delays, bad weather, or emergencies at the site. Most work more than a standard 40-hour week because construction may proceed around-the-clock. This type of work schedule can go on for days, even weeks, to meet special project deadlines, especially if there are delays.

Although the work generally is not considered dangerous, construction managers must be careful while touring construction sites. Managers must be able to establish priorities and assign duties. They need to observe job conditions and to be alert to changes and potential problems, particularly involving safety on the job site and adherence to regulations.

Employment

Construction managers held about 249,000 jobs in 1996. Around 40,000 were self-employed. Over 85 percent were employed in the construction industry, primarily by specialty trade contractors—for example, plumbing, heating and air-conditioning, and electrical contractors—and general building contractors. Others were employed by engineering, architectural, surveying, and construction management services firms, as well as local governments, educational institutions, and real estate developers.

Training, Other Qualifications, and Advancement

Persons interested in becoming a construction manager need a solid background in building science, business, and management, as well as related work experience within the construction industry. They need to be able to understand contracts, plans, and specifications, and to be knowledgeable about construction methods, materials, and regulations. Familiarity with computers and software programs for job costing, scheduling, and estimating is increasingly important.

Traditionally, persons advanced to construction management positions after having substantial experience as construction craft workers–for example, as carpenters, masons, plumbers, or electricians–or after having worked as construction supervisors or as owners of independent specialty contracting firms overseeing workers in one or more construction trades. However, more and more employers–particularly, large construction firms–seek to hire individuals who combine industry work experience with a bachelor's degree in construction or building science or construction management.

Construction managers should be adaptable and be able to work effectively in a fast-paced environment. They should be decisive and able to work well under pressure, particularly when faced with unexpected occurrences or delays. The ability to coordinate several major activities at once, while analyzing and resolving specific problems, is essential, as is understanding engineering, architectural, and other construction drawings. Good oral and written communication skills are also important. Managers must be able to establish a good working relationship with many different people including owners, other managers, design professionals, supervisors, and craft workers.

Advancement opportunities for construction managers vary depending upon the size and type of company for which they work. Within large firms, managers may eventually become top-level managers or executives. Highly experienced individuals may become independent consultants; some serve as expert witnesses in court or as arbitrators in disputes. Those with the required capital may establish their own construction management services or general contracting firm.

In 1996, over 100 colleges and universities offered four-year degree programs in construction management or construction science. These programs include courses in project control and development, site planning, design, construction methods, construction materials, value analysis, cost estimating, scheduling, contract administration, accounting, business and financial management, building codes and standards, inspection procedures, engineering and architectural sciences, mathematics, statistics, and information technology. Graduates from four-year degree programs are usually hired as assistants to project managers, field engineers, schedulers, or cost estimators. An increasing number of graduates in related fields–engineering or architecture, for example–also enter construction management, often after having had substantial experience on construction projects or after completing graduate studies in construction management or building science.

Around 30 colleges and universities offer a master's degree program in construction management or construction science, and at least two offer a Ph.D. in the field. Master's degree recipients, especially those with work experience in construction, typically become construction managers in very large construction or construction management companies. Often, individuals who hold a bachelor's degree in an unrelated field seek a master's degree in order to work in the construction industry. Doctoral degree recipients generally become college professors or work in an area of research.

Many individuals also attend training and educational programs sponsored by industry associations, often in collaboration with postsecondary institutions. A number of two-year colleges throughout the country offer construction management or construction technology programs.

Both the American Institute of Constructors (AIC) and the Construction Management Association of America (CMA) have established voluntary certification programs for construction professionals. Both programs' requirements combine written examinations with verification of professional experience. AIC awards the designations Associate Constructor (AC) and Certified Professional Constructor (CPC) to candidates who meet the requirements and pass appropriate construction examinations. CMA awards the designation Certified Construction Manager (CCM) to practitioners who meet the requirements, complete a professional construction management "capstone" course, and pass a technical examination. Although certification is not required to work in the construction industry, voluntary certification can be valuable because it provides evidence of competence and experience.

Job Outlook

Employment of construction managers is expected to increase as fast as the average for all occupations through the year 2006, as the level of construction activity and complexity of construction projects continues to grow. Prospects in construction management, engineering and architectural services, and construction contracting firms should be particularly favorable for persons with a bachelor's degree or higher in construction science, construction management, or construction engineering who have worked in construction. Employers prefer applicants with previous construction work experience who can combine a strong background in building technology with proven supervisory or managerial skills. In addition, many job openings should result annually from the need to replace workers who transfer to other occupations or leave the labor force.

The increasing complexity of construction projects should increase demand for management level personnel within the construction industry, as sophisticated technology and the proliferation of laws setting standards for buildings and construction materials, worker safety, energy efficiency, and environmental protection have further complicated the construction process. Advances in building materials and construction methods and the growing number of multipurpose buildings, electronically operated "smart" buildings, and energy-efficient structures will further add to the demand for more construction managers. However, employment of construction managers can be sensitive to the short-term nature of many construction projects and cyclical fluctuations in construction activity.

Earnings

Earnings of salaried construction managers and incomes of self-employed independent construction contractors vary depending upon the size and nature of the construction project, its geographic location, and economic conditions. According to a 1997 salary survey by the National Association of Colleges and Employers, bachelor's degree candidates with degrees in the field of construction management received offers averaging $28,060 a year. Bachelor's degree candidates with degrees in the field of construction science received offers averaging $31,949 a year. Based on the limited information available, the average salary for experienced construction managers in 1996 ranged from around $40,000 to $100,000 annually. Many salaried construction managers receive benefits such as bonuses, use of company motor vehicles, paid vacations, and life and health insurance.

Related Occupations

Construction managers participate in the conceptual development of a construction project and oversee its organization, scheduling, and implementation. Occupations in which similar functions are performed include architects, civil engineers, construction supervisors, cost engineers, cost estimators, developers, electrical engineers, industrial engineers, landscape architects, and mechanical engineers.

Sources of Additional Information

For information about career opportunities in the construction industry contact:

❑ Associated Builders and Contractors, 1300 North 17th St., Rosslyn, VA 22209. Homepage: http://www.abc.org

❑ Associated General Contractors of America, 1957 E St. NW, Washington, DC 20006-5199. Homepage: http://www.agc.org

For information about constructor certification and professional career opportunities in the construction industry, contact:

❑ American Institute of Constructors, 466 94th Ave. North, St. Petersburg, FL 33702. E-mail address: aicnatl@aol.com Homepage: http://www.aicnet.org

For information about construction management and construction manager certification contact:

❑ Construction Management Association of America, 7918 Jones Branch Dr., Suite 540, McLean, VA 22102. Homepage: http://www.access.digex.net/~cmaa

Information on accredited construction science and management programs and accreditation requirements is available from:

❑ American Council for Construction Education, 1300 Hudson Lane, Suite 3, Monroe, LA 71201-6054. E-mail address: acce@iamerica.net

Correctional Officers

(D.O.T. 372.367-014, .567-014, .667-018, and .677; and 375.367-010)

Significant Points

✓ *Job opportunities are expected to be plentiful due to much faster than average employment growth coupled with high turnover.*

✓ *Most jobs are in large regional jails or prisons located in rural areas.*

✓ *The work can be stressful because of concerns about personal safety.*

Nature of the Work

Correctional officers are responsible for overseeing individuals who have been arrested, are awaiting trial or other hearing, or who have been convicted of a crime and sentenced to serve time in a jail, reformatory, or penitentiary. They maintain security and observe inmate conduct and behavior to prevent disturbances and escapes.

Correctional officers' duties differ with the setting in which they are performed. The majority of the approximately 3,300 jails in the United States are operated by county governments, with about three-quarters of all jails under the jurisdiction of an elected sheriff. Duty in jails differs from that in prisons in a number of important ways. For instance, the jail population changes constantly. The American jail system processes more than 22 million people a year, with about half a million inmates in jail at any given time. Approximately one million inmates are incarcerated in federal and state prisons. The prison population by contrast is far more stable.

Many correctional officers are employed by police and sheriffs departments in county and municipal jails or precinct station houses. These officers often have no law enforcement responsibilities outside the jail. Others are employed by large regional jails or state and federal prisons where job duties are specialized. A relatively small number supervise aliens being held by the Immigration and Naturalization Service before being released or deported. Regardless of the setting, correctional officers maintain order within the institution, enforce rules and regulations, and may supplement whatever counseling inmates receive.

To make sure inmates are orderly and obey rules, correctional officers monitor inmates' activities, including working, exercising, eating, and showering. They assign and supervise inmates' work assignments. Sometimes it is necessary for them to search inmates and their living quarters for weapons or drugs, to settle disputes between inmates, and to enforce discipline. Correctional officers cannot show favoritism and must report any inmate who violates the rules. A few officers in prison settings hold security positions in towers, where they are equipped with high-powered rifles. In both jail and prison facilities with direct supervision cell blocks, officers are unarmed—they are locked in a cell-block alone, or with another officer, among the 50 to 100 inmates who reside there. The officers enforce regulations primarily through their interpersonal communications skills, although they may have inmates who do not obey their orders transferred to facilities with less desirable living arrangements and fewer privileges.

Correctional officers periodically inspect the facilities. They may, for example, check cells and other areas of the institution for unsanitary conditions, weapons, drugs, fire hazards, and any evidence of infractions of rules. In addition, they routinely inspect locks, window bars, grille doors, and gates for signs of tampering.

Correctional officers report orally and in writing on inmate conduct and on the quality and quantity of work done by inmates. Officers also report disturbances, violations of rules, and any unusual occurrences. They usually keep a daily record of their activities. In the most high security facilities where the most dangerous inmates are housed, correctional officers can monitor the activities of prisoners from a centralized control center with the aid of closed circuit television cameras and a computer tracking system. In such an environment, the inmates may not see anyone but officers for days or weeks at a time and only rarely leave their cells.

Depending on the offender's security classification within the institution, correctional officers may have to escort inmates to and from cells and other areas and accompany them to see authorized visitors. Officers may also escort prisoners between the institution and courtrooms, medical facilities, and other destinations. Officers inspect mail and visitors for prohibited items. Should the situation arise, they assist the responsible law enforcement authorities by helping to investigate crimes committed within their institution or by helping search for escaped inmates.

Correctional sergeants directly supervise correctional officers. They usually are responsible for maintaining security and directing the activities of a group of inmates during an assigned shift or in an assigned area.

Working Conditions

Correctional officers may work indoors or outdoors, depending on their specific duties. Some correctional institutions are well lighted, temperature controlled, and ventilated, but many others are overcrowded, hot, and noisy. Outdoors, weather conditions may be disagreeable, for example when standing watch on a guard tower in cold weather. Working in a correctional institution can be stressful and hazardous; correctional officers occasionally are injured in confrontations with inmates who may feel that they have little to lose from violent behavior.

Correctional officers usually work an eight-hour day, five days a week, on rotating shifts. Prison security must be provided around the clock, which often means that junior officers work weekends, holidays, and nights. In addition, officers may be required to work paid overtime.

Employment

Correctional officers held about 320,000 jobs in 1996. Six of every ten worked at state correctional institutions such as prisons, prison camps, and reformatories. Most of the remainder worked at city and county jails or other institutions run by local governments. About 11,000 correctional officers worked at federal correctional institutions, and about 5,100 worked in privately owned and managed prisons.

Most correctional officers work in relatively large institutions located in rural areas, although a significant number work in jails and other smaller facilities located in law enforcement agencies throughout the country.

Training, Other Qualifications, and Advancement

Most institutions require that correctional officers be at least 18 or 21 years of age, have a high school education or its equivalent, have no felony convictions, and be a United States citizen. In addition, correctional institutions increasingly seek correctional officers with postsecondary education, particularly in psychology, criminal justice, police science, criminology, and related fields.

Correctional officers must be in good health. The federal system and many states require candidates to meet formal standards of physical fitness, eyesight, and hearing. Strength, good judgment, and the ability to think and act quickly are indispensable. The federal system and some states screen applicants for drug abuse and require candidates to pass a written or oral examination, along with a background check.

Federal, state, and some local departments of corrections provide training for correctional officers based on guidelines established by the American Correctional Association, the American Jail Association, and other professional organizations. Some states have regional training academies which are available to local agencies. All states and local departments of correction provide on-the-job

training at the conclusion of formal instruction. Officer trainees receive several weeks or months of training in an actual job setting under the supervision of an experienced officer. Entry requirements and on-the-job training vary widely from agency to agency.

Academy trainees generally receive instruction on institutional policies, regulations, and operations, as well as custody and security procedures, among other subjects. New federal correctional officers must undergo 200 hours of formal training within the first year of employment. They must complete 120 hours of specialized correctional instruction at the Federal Bureau of Prisons residential training center at Glynco, Georgia, within the first 60 days after appointment. Experienced officers receive in-service training to keep abreast of new ideas and procedures.

Correctional officers have the opportunity to join prison tactical response teams, which are trained to respond to riots, hostage situations, forced cell moves, and other potentially dangerous confrontations. Team members often receive monthly training and practice with weapons, chemical agents, forced entry methods, and other tactics.

With education, experience, and training, qualified officers may advance to correctional sergeant or other supervisory or administrative positions. Many correctional institutions require experience as a correctional officer for other corrections positions. Ambitious correctional officers can be promoted all the way up to warden. Officers sometimes transfer to related areas, such as parole officer.

Job Outlook

Job opportunities for correctional officers are expected to be favorable through the year 2006. The need to replace correctional officers who transfer to other occupations or leave the labor force, coupled with rising employment demand, will generate many thousands of job openings each year. In addition, some local and a few state correctional agencies have traditionally experienced difficulty in attracting qualified applicants, largely due to relatively low salaries and the concentration of jobs in rural locations. This situation is expected to continue.

Employment of correctional officers is expected to increase faster than the average for all occupations through the year 2006 as additional officers are hired to supervise and control a growing inmate population. Increasing public concern about the spread of crime and illegal drugs—resulting in more police making more arrests and getting more convictions—and the adoption of mandatory sentencing guidelines calling for longer sentences and reduced parole for inmates will spur demand for correctional officers. Expansion and new construction of correctional facilities also are expected to create many new jobs for correctional officers, although state and local government budgetary constraints could affect the rate at which new facilities are built and staffed. Some employment opportunities also may arise in the private sector as public authorities opt to contract with private companies to provide and staff corrections facilities.

Layoffs of correctional officers are rare because security must be maintained in correctional institutions at all times.

Earnings

According to a 1996 survey in Corrections Compendium, a national journal for corrections professionals, federal and state correctional officers' annual salaries averaged about $26,100 and ranged from a low of $17,300 in South Carolina to a high of $41,700 in Rhode Island.

At the federal level, the starting salary was about $20,200 to $22,600 a year in 1996; supervisory correctional officers started at about $28,300 a year. Starting salaries were slightly higher in selected areas where prevailing local pay levels were higher. The annual average salary for correctional officers employed by the federal government was $33,540 in early 1997.

Correctional officers employed in the public sector usually are provided uniforms or a clothing allowance to purchase their own uniforms. Most are provided or can participate in hospitalization or major medical insurance plans; many officers can get disability and life insurance at group rates. They also receive vacation and sick leave and pension benefits. Officers employed by the federal government and most state governments are covered by civil service systems or merit boards. Their retirement coverage entitles them to retire at age 50 after 20 years of service or at any age with 25 years of service. In the federal system and some states, many correctional officers are represented by labor unions.

Related Occupations

A number of related careers are open to high school graduates who are interested in protective services and the field of security. Bodyguards escort people and protect them from injury or invasion of privacy. House or store detectives patrol business establishments to protect against theft and vandalism and to enforce standards of good behavior. Security guards protect government, commercial, and industrial property against theft, vandalism, illegal entry, and fire. Police officers and deputy sheriffs maintain law and order, prevent crime, and arrest offenders. Probation and parole officers monitor and counsel offenders and evaluate their progress in becoming productive members of society.

Sources of Additional Information

Information about entrance requirements, training, and career opportunities for correctional officers on the state and local levels may be obtained from state departments of corrections, or nearby correctional institutions and facilities including police department and county sheriff offices.

Information on entrance requirements, training, and career opportunities for correctional officers on the federal level may be obtained by calling the Federal Bureau of Prisons. Regional recruitment offices have toll-free telephone numbers listed in local phone directories. In addition, information on obtaining a job with the federal government may be obtained from the Office of Personnel Management through a telephone based system. Consult your telephone directory under U.S. government for a local number or call (912) 757-3000 (TDD (912) 744-2299). The number is not toll free and charges may result. Information also is available from their internet site: http:// www.usajobs.opm.gov

Cost Estimators

(D.O.T. 169.267-038; 221.362-018, and .367-014)

Significant Points

✓ *Growth of the construction industry, where over 60 percent of all cost estimators are employed, will be the driving force behind the demand for these workers.*

✓ *Job prospects in construction should be best for those workers with a degree in construction management or construction science, engineering, or architectural drafting, who have experience in various phases of construction or a specialty craft area.*

Nature of the Work

Accurately predicting the cost of future projects is vital to the survival of any business. Cost estimators develop cost information for owners or managers to use in determining resource and material quantities, making bids for contracts, determining if a new product will be profitable, or determining which products are making a profit for a firm.

Regardless of the industry in which they work, estimators compile and analyze data on all the factors that can influence costs—such as materials, labor, location, and special machinery requirements, including computer hardware and software. Job duties vary widely depending upon the type and size of the project. Those with an engineering background who apply scientific principles and methods to undertake feasibility studies, value engineering, and life-cycle costing may be referred to as cost engineers.

The methods of, and motivations for estimating costs can vary greatly, depending on the industry. On a large construction project, for example, the estimating process begins with the decision to submit a bid. After reviewing the architect's drawings and specifications, the estimator visits the site of the proposed project. The estimator needs to gather information on access to the site and availability of electricity, water, and other services, as well as surface topography and drainage. The information developed during the site visit generally is recorded in a signed report that is made part of the final project estimate.

After the site visit is completed, the estimator determines the quantity of materials and labor the firm will have to furnish. This process, called the quantity survey or "takeoff," involves completing standard estimating forms, filling in dimensions, number of units, and other information. A cost estimator working for a general contractor, for example, will estimate the costs of all items the contractor must provide. Although subcontractors will estimate their costs as part of their own bidding process, the general contractor's cost estimator often analyzes bids made by subcontractors as well. Also during the takeoff process, the estimator must make decisions concerning equipment needs, sequence of operations, and crew size. Allowances for the waste of materials, inclement weather, shipping delays, and other factors that may increase costs must also be incorporated in the takeoff.

On completion of the quantity surveys, the chief estimator prepares a total project cost summary, including the costs of labor, equipment, materials, subcontracts, overhead, taxes, insurance, markup, and any other costs that may affect the project. The chief estimator then prepares the bid proposal for submission to the developer.

Construction cost estimators may also be employed by the project's architect or owner to estimate costs or track actual costs relative to bid specifications as the project develops. In large construction companies employing more than one estimator, it is common practice for estimators to specialize. For instance, one may estimate only electrical work and another may concentrate on excavation, concrete, and forms.

In manufacturing and other firms, cost estimators generally are assigned to the engineering, cost, or pricing departments. The estimators' goal in manufacturing is to accurately estimate the costs associated with making products. The job may begin when management requests an estimate of the costs associated with a major redesign of an existing product or the development of a new product or production process. When estimating the cost of developing a new product, for example, the estimator works with engineers, first reviewing blueprints or conceptual drawings to determine the machining operations, tools, gauges, and materials that would be required for the job. The estimator then prepares a parts list and determines whether it is more efficient to produce or to purchase the parts. To do this, the estimator must initiate inquiries for price information from potential suppliers. The next step is to determine the cost of manufacturing each component of the product. Some high technology products require a tremendous amount of computer programming during the design phase. The cost of software development is one of the fastest growing and most difficult activities to estimate. Some cost estimators now specialize in only estimating computer software development and related costs.

The cost estimator then prepares time-phase charts and learning curves. Time-phase charts indicate the time required for tool design and fabrication, tool debugging—finding and correcting all problems—manufacturing of parts, assembly, and testing. Learning curves graphically represent the rate at which performance improves with practice. These curves are commonly called "cost reduction" curves because many problems—such as engineering changes, rework, parts shortages, and lack of operator skills—diminish as the number of parts produced increases, resulting in lower unit costs.

Using all of this information, the estimator then calculates the standard labor hours necessary to produce a predetermined number of units. Standard labor hours are then converted to dollar values, to which are added factors for waste, overhead, and profit to yield the unit cost in dollars. The estimator then compares the cost of purchasing parts with the firm's cost of manufacturing them to determine which is cheaper.

Computers play an integral role in cost estimating today, because estimating may involve complex mathematical calculations and require advanced mathematical techniques. For example, to undertake a parametric analysis, a process used to estimate project costs on a per unit basis subject to the specific requirements of a project, cost estimators use a computer database containing information on costs and conditions of many other similar projects. Although computers cannot be used for the entire estimating process, they can relieve estimators of much of the drudgery associated with routine, repetitive, and time-consuming calculations. Computers are also used to produce all of the necessary documentation with the help of basic word-processing and spreadsheet software. This leaves estimators with more time to study and analyze projects and can lead to more accurate estimates.

Working Conditions

Although estimators spend most of their time in an office, construction estimators must make frequent visits to project work sites that are dirty and cluttered with debris. Likewise, estimators in manufacturing must spend time on the factory floor where it also can be noisy and dirty. In some industries, frequent travel between a firm's headquarters and its subsidiaries or subcontractors also may be required.

Although estimators normally work a 40-hour week, overtime is common. Cost estimators usually operate under pressure, especially when facing deadlines. Inaccurate estimating can cause a firm to lose out on a bid or lose money on a job that proves to be unprofitable.

Employment

Cost estimators held about 188,000 jobs in 1996, over 60 percent of which were in the construction industry. Another 26 percent were employed in manufacturing industries. The remainder worked for engineering and architectural services firms, business services firms, and throughout a wide range of other industries. Operations research, production control, cost, and price analysts who work for government agencies may also do significant amounts of cost estimating in the course of their regular duties. In addition, the duties of construction managers may also include estimating costs.

Cost estimators work throughout the country, usually in or near major industrial, commercial, and government centers, and in cities and suburban areas undergoing rapid change or development.

Training, Other Qualifications, and Advancement

Entry requirements for cost estimators vary by industry. In the construction industry, employers increasingly prefer individuals with a degree in building construction, construction management, construction science, civil engineering, or architectural drafting. However, most construction estimators also have considerable construction experience. Applicants with a thorough knowledge of construction materials, costs, and procedures in areas ranging from heavy construction to electrical work, plumbing systems, or masonry work have a competitive edge.

In manufacturing industries, employers prefer to hire individuals with a degree in engineering, physical science, operations research, mathematics, or statistics, or in accounting, finance, business, economics, or a related subject. In most industries, great emphasis is placed on experience involving quantitative techniques.

Cost estimators should have an aptitude for mathematics, be able to quickly analyze, compare, and interpret detailed and sometimes poorly defined information, and be able to make sound and accurate judgments based on this knowledge. Assertiveness and self-confidence in presenting and supporting their conclusions are important, as are strong communications and interpersonal skills, because estimators may work as part of a project team alongside other managers as well as owners, engineers, and design professionals. Cost estimators also need to be at ease with computers and their application in the estimating process, including word-processing and spreadsheet packages used to produce necessary documentation. In some instances, familiarity with special estimation software or programming skills may be required.

Regardless of their background, estimators receive much training on the job; almost every company has its own way of handling estimates. Working with an experienced estimator, they become familiar with each step in the process. Those with no experience reading construction specifications or blueprints first learn that aspect of the work. They then may accompany an experienced estimator to the construction site or shop floor where they observe the work being done, take measurements, or perform other routine tasks. As they become more knowledgeable, estimators learn how to tabulate quantities and dimensions from drawings and how to select the appropriate material prices.

For most estimators, advancement takes the form of higher pay and prestige. Some move into management positions, such as project manager for a construction firm or manager of the industrial engineering department for a manufacturer. Others may go into business for themselves as consultants, providing estimating services for a fee to government or construction and manufacturing firms.

Many colleges and universities include cost estimating as part of bachelor and associate degree-level curriculums in civil engineering, industrial engineering, and construction management or construction engineering technology. In addition, cost estimating is a significant part of master's degree programs in construction science or construction management offered by many colleges and universities. Organizations representing cost estimators, such as American Association of Cost Engineers (AACE) International and the Society of Cost Estimating and Analysis, also sponsor educational and professional development programs. These programs help students, estimators-in-training, and experienced estimators stay abreast of changes affecting the profession. Specialized courses and programs in cost estimating techniques and procedures are also offered by many technical schools, community colleges, and universities.

Voluntary certification can be valuable to cost estimators, because it provides professional recognition of the estimator's competence and experience. In some instances, individual employers may even require professional certification for employment. Both AACE International and the Society of Cost Estimating and Analysis administer certification programs. To become certified, estimators generally must have between three and seven years of estimating experience and must pass both a written and an oral examination. In addition, certification requirements may include publication of at least one article or paper in the field.

Job Outlook

Overall employment of cost estimators is expected to grow about as fast as average for all occupations through the year 2006. Given the fact that no new projects in construction, manufacturing, or other industries are undertaken without careful analysis and estimation of the costs involved, job opportunities should remain favorable. Even when construction and manufacturing activity decline, there should always remain a demand for cost estimators. In addition to openings created by growth, some job openings will also arise from the need to replace workers who transfer to other occupations or leave the labor force.

Growth of the construction industry, where over 60 percent of all cost estimators are employed, will be the driving force behind the demand for these workers. The fastest growing sectors of the construction industry are expected to be special trade contractors and those associated with heavy construction and spending on the nation's infrastructure. Construction and repair of highways and streets, bridges, and construction of more subway systems, airports, water and sewage systems, and electric power plants and transmission lines will stimulate demand for many more cost estimators. Job prospects in construction should be best for those workers with a degree in construction management or construction science, engineering, or architectural drafting, who have experience in various phases of construction or a specialty craft area.

Employment of cost estimators in manufacturing should remain relatively stable as firms continue to use their services to identify and control their operating costs. Experienced estimators with degrees in engineering, science, mathematics, business administration, or economics and who have computer expertise should have the best job prospects in manufacturing.

Earnings

Salaries of cost estimators vary widely by experience, education, size of firm, and industry. According to limited available data, most starting salaries in the construction industry for cost estimators with limited training were between about $20,000 and $30,000 a year in 1996. College graduates with degrees in fields such as engineering or construction management that provide a strong background in cost estimating could start at a higher level. According to a 1997 salary survey by the National Association of Colleges and Employers, bachelor's degree candidates with degrees in construction science received offers averaging $31,949 a year. Bachelor's degree candidates with degrees in construction management received offers averaging $28,060 a year. Highly experienced cost estimators earned $75,000 a year or more. Starting salaries and annual earnings in the manufacturing sector were usually somewhat higher.

Related Occupations

Other workers who quantitatively analyze information in a similar capacity include appraisers, cost accountants, auditors, budget analysts, cost engineers, economists, financial analysts, loan officers, operations research analysts, underwriters, and value engineers. In addition, the duties of production managers and construction managers may also involve analyzing costs.

Sources of Additional Information

Information about career opportunities, certification, educational programs, and cost estimating techniques may be obtained from:

❏ AACE International, 209 Prairie Ave., Suite 100, Morgantown, WV 26505. Homepage: http://www.aacei.org
❏ Professional Construction Estimators Association of America, P.O. Box 11626, Charlotte, NC 28220-1626.
❏ Society of Cost Estimating and Analysis, 101 S. Whiting St., Suite 201, Alexandria, VA 22304. Homepage: HYPERLINK http://www.erols.com/scea/ http://www.erols.com/scea/

Counselors

(D.O.T. 045.107-010, -014, -018, -038, -042 -050, -054, -058, .117; 090.107; 094.107-010; and 169.267-026)

Significant Points

- ✓ *About six out of ten counselors have a master's degree.*
- ✓ *Rapid job growth is expected among rehabilitation and mental health counselors; however, budgetary constraints may limit growth among school counselors, and employment counselors working in government.*

Nature of the Work

Counselors assist people with personal, family, educational, mental health, and career decisions and problems. Their duties depend on the individuals they serve and the settings in which they work.

School and college counselors–who work at the elementary, middle, secondary, and postsecondary school levels–help students evaluate their abilities, interests, talents, and personality characteristics so that students can develop realistic academic and career goals. Counselors use interviews, counseling sessions, tests, or other methods when evaluating and advising students. They may operate career information centers and career education programs. High school counselors advise on college majors, admission requirements, entrance exams, and financial aid, and on trade, technical school, and apprenticeship programs. They help students develop job finding skills such as resume writing and interviewing techniques. College career planning and placement counselors assist alumni or students with career development and job hunting techniques.

Elementary school counselors observe younger children during classroom and play activities and confer with their teachers and parents to evaluate their strengths, problems, or special needs. They also help students develop good study habits. They do less vocational and academic counseling than secondary school counselors.

School counselors at all levels help students understand and deal with their social, behavioral, and personal problems. They emphasize preventive and developmental counseling to provide students with the life skills needed to deal with problems before they occur, and to enhance personal, social, and academic growth. Counselors provide special services, including alcohol and drug prevention programs, and classes that teach students to handle conflicts without resorting to violence. Counselors also try to identify cases involving domestic abuse and other family problems that can affect a student's development. Counselors work with students individually, in small groups, or with entire classes. They consult and work with parents, teachers, school administrators, school psychologists, school nurses, and social workers.

Rehabilitation counselors help people deal with the personal, social, and vocational effects of their disabilities. They may counsel people with disabilities resulting from birth defects, illness or disease, accidents, or the stress of daily life. They evaluate the strengths and limitations of individuals, provide personal and vocational counseling, and may arrange for medical care, vocational training, and job placement. Rehabilitation counselors interview individuals with disabilities and their families, evaluate school and medical reports, and confer and plan with physicians, psychologists, occupational therapists, and employers to determine the capabilities and skills of the individual. Conferring with the client, they develop a rehabilitation program, which may include training to help the person develop job skills. They also work toward increasing the client's capacity to live independently.

Employment counselors help individuals make wise career decisions. They explore and evaluate the client's education, training, work history, interests, skills, and personal traits, and may arrange for aptitude and achievement tests. They also work with individuals to develop job-seeking skills and assist clients in locating and applying for jobs.

Mental health counselors emphasize prevention and work with individuals and groups to promote optimum mental health. They help individuals deal with addictions and substance abuse, suicide, stress management, problems with self-esteem, issues associated with aging, job and career concerns, educational decisions, issues of mental and emotional health, and family, parenting, and marital problems. Mental health counselors work closely with other mental health specialists, including psychiatrists, psychologists, clinical social workers, psychiatric nurses, and school counselors.

Other counseling specialties include marriage and family, multicultural, or gerontological counseling. A gerontological counselor provides services to elderly persons who face changing lifestyles due to health problems, and helps families cope with these changes. A multicultural counselor helps employers adjust to an increasingly diverse workforce.

Working Conditions

Most school counselors work the traditional nine- to ten-month school year with a two- to three-month vacation, although an increasing number are employed on 10½- or 11-month contracts. They generally have the same hours as teachers. College career planning and placement counselors may work long and irregular hours during recruiting periods.

Rehabilitation and employment counselors generally work a standard 40-hour week. Self-employed counselors and those working in mental health and community agencies often work evenings to counsel clients who work during the day.

Counselors must possess high physical and emotional energy to handle the array of problems they address. Dealing with these day-to-day problems can cause stress and emotional burnout.

Since privacy is essential for confidential and frank discussions with clients, counselors usually have private offices.

Employment

Counselors held about 175,000 jobs in 1996. (This estimate includes only vocational and educational counselors; employment data are not available for other counselors discussed in this statement, such as rehabilitation and mental health counselors.)

In addition to elementary and secondary schools and colleges and universities, counselors work in a wide variety of public and private establishments. These include health care facilities; job training, career development, and vocational rehabilitation centers; social agencies; correctional institutions; and residential care facilities, such as halfway houses for criminal offenders and group homes for children, the aged, and the disabled. Counselors also work in organizations engaged in community improvement and social change, as well as drug and alcohol rehabilitation programs and state and local government agencies. A growing number of counselors work in health maintenance organizations, insurance companies, group practice, and private practice. This growth has been spurred by laws allowing counselors to receive payments from insurance companies, and requiring employers to provide rehabilitation and counseling services to employees.

Training, Other Qualifications, and Advancement

Recent data indicate that six out of ten counselors have a master's degree; fields of study include college student affairs, elementary or secondary school counseling, education, gerontological counseling, marriage and family counseling, substance abuse counseling, rehabilitation counseling, agency or community counseling, clinical mental health counseling, counseling psychology, career counseling, or a related field.

Graduate-level counselor education programs in colleges and universities usually are in departments of education or psychology.

Courses are grouped into eight core areas: Human growth and development; social and cultural foundations; helping relationships; groups; lifestyle and career development; appraisal; research and evaluation; and professional orientation. In an accredited program, 48 to 60 semester hours of graduate study, including a period of supervised clinical experience in counseling, are required for a master's degree. In 1996, 111 institutions offered programs in counselor education, including career, community, gerontological, mental health, school, student affairs, and marriage and family counseling, accredited by the Council for Accreditation of Counseling and Related Educational Programs (CACREP).

In 1997, 42 states and the District of Columbia had some form of counselor credentialing legislation, licensure, certification, or registry for practice outside schools. Requirements vary from state to state. In some states, credentialing is mandatory; in others, voluntary.

Many counselors elect to be nationally certified by the National Board for Certified Counselors (NBCC), which grants the general practice credential, "National Certified Counselor." To be certified, a counselor must hold a master's degree in counseling from a regionally accredited institution, have at least two years of supervised professional counseling experience, and pass NBCC's National Counselor Examination for Licensure and Certification. This national certification is voluntary and distinct from state certification. However, in some states those who pass the national exam are exempt from taking a state certification exam. NBCC also offers specialty certification in career, gerontological, school, clinical mental health, and addictions counseling. To maintain their certification, counselors must complete 100 hours of acceptable continuing education credit every five years.

All states require school counselors to hold state school counseling certification; however, certification requirements vary from state to state. Some states require public school counselors to have both counseling and teaching certificates. Depending on the state, a master's degree in counseling and two to five years of teaching experience may be required for a counseling certificate.

Vocational and related rehabilitation agencies generally require a master's degree in rehabilitation counseling, counseling and guidance, or counseling psychology for rehabilitation counselor jobs. Some, however, may accept applicants with a bachelor's degree in rehabilitation services, counseling, psychology, sociology, or related fields. A bachelor's degree may qualify a person to work as a counseling aide, rehabilitation aide, or social service worker. Experience in employment counseling, job development, psychology, education, or social work may be helpful.

The Council on Rehabilitation Education (CORE) accredits graduate programs in rehabilitation counseling. A minimum of two years of study—including 600 hours of supervised clinical internship experience—are required for the master's degree.

In most state vocational rehabilitation agencies, applicants must pass a written examination and be evaluated by a board of examiners to obtain licensure. In addition, many employers require rehabilitation counselors to be nationally certified. To become certified by the Commission on Rehabilitation Counselor Certification, counselors must graduate from an accredited educational program, complete an internship, and pass a written examination. They are then designated as "Certified Rehabilitation Counselors." To maintain their certification, counselors must complete 100 hours of acceptable continuing education credit every five years.

Some states require counselors in public employment offices to have a master's degree; others accept a bachelor's degree with appropriate counseling courses.

Clinical mental health counselors generally have a master's degree in mental health counseling, another area of counseling, or in psychology or social work. They are voluntarily certified by the National Board for Certified Counselors. Generally, to receive certification as a clinical mental health counselor, a counselor must have a master's degree in counseling, two years of post-master's experience, a period of supervised clinical experience, a taped sample of clinical work, and a passing grade on a written examination.

Some employers provide training for newly hired counselors. Many have work-study programs so that employed counselors can earn graduate degrees. Counselors must participate in graduate studies, workshops, institutes, and personal studies to maintain their certificates and licenses.

Persons interested in counseling should have a strong interest in helping others and the ability to inspire respect, trust, and confidence. They should be able to work independently or as part of a team. Counselors follow the code of ethics associated with their respective certifications and licenses.

Prospects for advancement vary by counseling field. School counselors may move to a larger school; become directors or supervisors of counseling, guidance, or pupil personnel services; or, usually with further graduate education, become counselor educators, counseling psychologists, or school administrators. Some counselors also may advance to work at the state department of education.

Rehabilitation, mental health, and employment counselors may become supervisors or administrators in their agencies. Some counselors move into research, consulting, or college teaching, or go into private or group practice.

Job Outlook

Overall employment of counselors is expected to grow about as fast as the average for all occupations through the year 2006. In addition, replacement needs should increase significantly as a large number of counselors reach retirement age.

Employment of school and vocational counselors is expected to grow as a result of increasing enrollments, particularly in secondary and postsecondary schools, state legislation requiring counselors in elementary schools, and the expanded responsibilities of counselors. Counselors are becoming more involved in crisis and preventive counseling, helping students deal with issues ranging from drug and alcohol abuse to death and suicide. Also, the growing diversity of student populations is presenting challenges to counselors in dealing with multicultural issues. Job growth among counselors, however, may be dampened by budgetary constraints. High student-to-counselor ratios in many schools could increase even more as student enrollments grow. When funding is tight, schools usually prefer to hire new teachers before adding counselors in an effort to keep classroom sizes at acceptable levels.

Rapid job growth is expected among rehabilitation and mental health counselors. Under managed care systems, insurance companies increasingly provide for reimbursement of counselors, enabling many counselors to move from schools and government agencies to private practice. Counselors are also forming group practices to receive expanded insurance coverage. The number of people who need rehabilitation services will rise as advances in medical technology continue to save lives that only a few years ago would have been lost. In addition, legislation requiring equal employment rights for people with disabilities will spur demand for counselors. Counselors not only will help individuals with disabilities with their transition into the work force, but also will help companies comply with the law. Employers are also increasingly offering employee assistance programs which provide mental health and alcohol and drug abuse services. A growing number of people are expected to use these services as the elderly population grows, and as society focuses on ways of developing mental well-being, such as controlling stress associated with job and family responsibilities.

As with other government jobs, the number of employment counselors, who work primarily for state and local government, could be limited by budgetary constraints. However, demand for government employment counseling may grow as new welfare laws require welfare recipients to find jobs. Opportunities for employment counselors working in private job training services should grow as counselors provide skill training and other services to laid-off workers, experienced workers seeking a new or second career, full-time homemakers seeking to enter or reenter the work force, and workers who want to upgrade their skills.

Earnings

Median earnings for full-time educational and vocational counselors were about $35,800 a year in 1996. The middle 50 percent earned between $25,600 and $48,500 a year. The bottom 10 percent earned less than $18,600 a year, while the top 10 percent earned over $60,100 a year.

According to the Educational Research Service, the average salary of public school counselors in the 1995-96 academic year was about $44,100. Many school counselors are compensated on the same pay scale as teachers. School counselors can earn additional income working summers in the school system or in other jobs.

Self-employed counselors who have well-established practices, as well as counselors employed in group practices, generally have the highest earnings, as do some counselors working for private firms, such as insurance companies and private rehabilitation companies.

Related Occupations

Counselors help people evaluate their interests, abilities, and disabilities, and deal with personal, social, academic, and career problems. Others who help people in similar ways include college and student affairs workers, teachers, personnel workers and managers, human services workers, social workers, psychologists, psychiatrists, psychiatric nurses, members of the clergy, occupational therapists, training and employee development specialists, and equal employment opportunity/affirmative action specialists.

Sources of Additional Information

For general information about counseling, as well as information on specialties such as school, college, mental health, rehabilitation, multicultural, career, marriage and family, and gerontological counseling, contact:

❑ American Counseling Association, 5999 Stevenson Ave., Alexandria, VA 22304.

For information on accredited counseling and related training programs, contact:

❑ Council for Accreditation of Counseling and Related Educational Programs, American Counseling Association, 5999 Stevenson Ave., Alexandria, VA 22304.

For information on national certification requirements for counselors, contact:

❑ National Board for Certified Counselors, 3 Terrace Way, Suite D, Greensboro, NC 27403. Homepage: http://www.nbcc.org/

For information on certification requirements for rehabilitation counselors and a list of accredited rehabilitation education programs, contact:

❑ Council on Rehabilitation Counselor Certification, 1835 Rohlwing Rd., Suite E, Rolling Meadows, IL 60008.

State departments of education can supply information on colleges and universities that offer approved guidance and counseling training for state certification and licensure requirements.

State employment service offices have information about job opportunities and entrance requirements for counselors.

Counter and Rental Clerks

(D.O.T. 216.482-030; 249.362-010; .366-010; 295.357-010, -014 and -018; .367-010, -014, and -026; .467; 299.367-018; 369.367-010 and -014; .467 -010; .477; and .677-010)

Significant Points

✓ *Jobs are primarily entry level and require little or no experience and little formal education.*

✓ *Part-time employment opportunities are expected to be plentiful.*

Nature of the Work

Whether renting video tapes or air compressors, dropping off clothes to be dry-cleaned or appliances to be serviced, we rely on counter and rental clerks to handle these transactions efficiently. Although specific duties vary by establishment, counter and rental clerks are responsible for answering questions involving product availability, cost, and rental provisions. Counter and rental clerks also take orders, calculate fees, receive payments, and accept returns.

Regardless of where they work, counter and rental clerks must be knowledgeable about the company's services, policies, and procedures. Depending on the type of establishment, counter and rental clerks use their special knowledge to give advice on a wide variety of products and services, which may range from hydraulic tools to shoe repair. For example, in the car rental industry, they inform customers about the features of the different types of automobiles available and daily and weekly rental costs, ensure that customers meet age and other requirements, and indicate when and in what condition cars must be returned. In dry-cleaning establishments, counter clerks inform customers when items will be ready.

When taking orders, counter and rental clerks use various types of equipment. In some establishments, they write out tickets and order forms. However, computers and bar code scanners are quickly becoming the norm. Most of these computer systems are user friendly and usually require very little data entry. Scanners "read" the product code and display a description of the item on a computer screen. Clerks must insure, however, that the data on the screen matches the actual product.

Working Conditions

Because firms employing counter and rental clerks generally operate at the convenience of customers, these workers often work night and weekend hours. However, because of this many, employers offer flexible schedules. Some counter and rental clerks work 40-hour weeks but over one-half are on part-time schedules–usually during rush periods, such as weekends, evenings, and holidays.

Working conditions are usually pleasant; most stores and service establishments are clean, well-lighted, and temperature controlled. However, clerks are on their feet much of the time and may be confined behind a small counter area. This job requires constant interaction with the public and can be taxing–especially during busy periods.

Employment

Counter and rental clerks held 374,000 jobs in 1996. About one of every four clerks worked for a video tape rental establishment. Other large employers included laundries or dry cleaners, automobile rental firms, equipment rental firms, and miscellaneous entertainment and recreation establishments.

Counter and rental clerks are employed throughout the country but are concentrated in metropolitan areas, where personal services and renting and leasing services are in greater demand.

Training, Other Qualifications, and Advancement

Counter and rental clerk jobs are primarily entry level and require little or no experience and little formal education. However, many employers prefer those with at least a high school diploma.

In most companies, counter and rental clerks are trained on the job, sometimes through the use of video tapes, brochures, and pamphlets. Clerks usually learn how to operate the equipment and become familiar with the establishment's policies and procedures, under the observation of a more experienced worker. However, some employers have formal classroom training programs, lasting from a few hours to a few weeks. Topics covered in this training usually include a description of the industry, the company and its policies

and procedures, equipment operation, sales techniques, and customer service. Counter and rental clerks must also become familiar with the different products and services rented or provided by their company in order to give customers the best possible service.

Counter and rental clerks should enjoy working with people and have the ability to deal tactfully with difficult customers. In addition, good oral and written communication skills are essential.

Advancement opportunities depend on the size and type of company. Many establishments that employ counter or rental clerks tend to be small businesses, making advancement difficult. But in larger establishments with a corporate structure, jobs as counter and rental clerks offer good opportunities for workers to learn about their company's products and business practices. These jobs can be steppingstones to more responsible positions, because it is common in many establishments to promote counter and rental clerks into assistant manager positions.

In certain industries, such as equipment repair, counter and rental jobs may be an additional or alternate source of income for workers who are unemployed or entering semi-retirement. For example, retired mechanics could prove invaluable at tool rental centers because of their relevant knowledge.

Job Outlook

Employment in this occupation is expected to increase faster than the average for all occupations through the year 2006, due to anticipated employment growth in the industries where they are concentrated– business services, automotive rentals, and amusement and recreation services. Some openings due to growth are expected to meet consumers' anticipated increased acceptance of renting items instead of buying them. Despite this, most job openings will arise from the need to replace experienced workers who transfer to other occupations or leave the labor force. Part-time employment opportunities are expected to be plentiful.

Earnings

Counter and rental clerks typically start at the minimum wage, which, in establishments covered by federal law, was $5.15 an hour in 1997. In areas where there is intense competition for workers, however, wages are often higher. In addition to wages, some counter and rental clerks receive commissions, based on the number of contracts they complete or services they sell.

Retail counter clerks earned a median weekly income of $303 in 1996. The middle 50 percent earned between $230 and $489 a week. The bottom 10 percent earned less than $184; the top 10 percent earned more than $631.

Full-time workers typically receive health and life insurance and paid vacation and sick leave. Benefits for counter and rental clerks who work part time tend to be significantly less than for those who work full time. Many companies offer discounts to both full- and part-time employees on the services they provide.

Related Occupations

Counter and rental clerks take orders and receive payment for services rendered. Other workers with similar duties include cashiers, retail sales workers, food counter clerks, postal service clerks, and bank tellers.

Sources of Additional Information

For general information on employment in the equipment rental industry contact:

❏ American Rental Association, 1900 19th St., Moline, IL 61265.

For more information about the work of counter clerks in dry cleaning and laundry establishments, contact:

❏ International Fabricare Institute, 12251 Tech Road, Silver Spring, MD 20904.

For general information on employment in the rent-to-own industry, contact:

❏ Association of Progressive Rental Organizations, 9015 Mountain Ridge Dr., Suite 220, Austin, TX 78759. Homepage: http://www.apro-rto.com

Dancers and Choreographers

(D.O.T. 151.027-010 and .047-010)

Significant Points

✓ *Due to the long hours and strenuous work, most dancers stop performing by their late thirties, but sometimes remain in the dance field as choreographers, dance teachers and coaches, or artistic directors.*

✓ *Most dancers begin their formal training between the ages of 5 to 15, and have their professional auditions by the age of 17 or 18; a college or graduate degree in dance is required to teach at the elementary/high school or college level.*

✓ *Dancers and choreographers face very keen competition for jobs; only the most talented find regular employment.*

Nature of the Work

From ancient times to the present, dancers have expressed ideas, stories, rhythm, and sound with their bodies. A variety of dance forms exist, including classical ballet and modern dance, which allows more free movement and self-expression. Others perform in dance adaptations for musical shows, in folk, ethnic, tap, and jazz dances, and in other popular kinds of dancing. In addition to being an art form for its own sake, dance also complements opera, musical comedy, television, movies, music videos, and commercials. Therefore, many dancers sing and act, as well as dance.

Dancers most often perform as a group, although a few top artists dance solo. Many dancers combine stage work with teaching or choreographing.

Choreographers create original dances. They may also create new interpretations to traditional dances like the ballet, *Nutcracker*. Few dance routines are written down. Instead, choreographers instruct performers at rehearsals to achieve the desired effect; they may also audition performers. Some choreographers use computers to develop dance routines for various productions.

Working Conditions

Dancing is strenuous. Rehearsals require very long hours and usually take place daily, including weekends and holidays. For shows on the road, weekend travel often is required. Most performances take place in the evening, while rehearsals and practice generally are scheduled during the day. Dancers must also work late hours. The work environment ranges from modern, temperature-controlled facilities to older, uncomfortable surroundings.

Due to the physical demands, most dancers stop performing by their late thirties, but they sometimes continue to work in the dance field as choreographers, dance teachers and coaches, or as artistic directors. Some celebrated dancers, however, continue performing beyond the age of 50.

Employment

Professional dancers and choreographers held an average of about 23,000 jobs at any one time in 1996. Many others were between engagements so that the total number of people employed as dancers over the course of the year was greater. Dancers work in a variety of settings, including eating and drinking establishments, theatrical and television productions, dance studios and schools, dance companies and bands, concert halls, and amusement parks.

In addition, there were many dance instructors in secondary schools, colleges and universities, and private studios. Many teachers also perform from time to time.

New York City is home to many of the major dance companies. Other cities with full-time professional dance companies include Atlanta, Boston, Chicago, Cincinnati, Cleveland, Columbus, Dallas, Houston, Miami, Milwaukee, Philadelphia, Pittsburgh, Salt Lake City, San Francisco, Seattle, and Washington, DC.

Training, Other Qualifications, and Advancement

Training depends upon the type of dance. Early ballet training for women usually begins at 5 to 8 years of age and is often given by private teachers and independent ballet schools. Serious training traditionally begins between the ages of 10 and 12. Men often begin their training between the ages of 10 and 15. Students who demonstrate potential in the early teens receive more intensive and advanced professional training at regional ballet schools or schools conducted under the auspices of the major ballet companies. Leading dance school companies often have summer training programs from which they select candidates for admission to their regular full-time training program. Most dancers have their professional auditions by age 17 or 18; however, training and practice never end. Professional ballet dancers have 60 to 90 minutes of lessons every day and spend many additional hours practicing and rehearsing.

Early and intensive training also is important for the modern dancer, but modern dance generally does not require as many years of training as ballet.

Because of the strenuous and time-consuming training required, a dancer's formal academic instruction may be minimal. However, a broad, general education including music, literature, history, and the visual arts is helpful in the interpretation of dramatic episodes, ideas, and feelings. Dancers sometimes conduct research to learn more about the part they are playing.

Many colleges and universities confer bachelor's or higher degrees in dance, generally through the departments of music, theater, or fine arts. Most programs concentrate on modern dance, but also offer courses in ballet and classical techniques, dance composition, dance history, dance criticism, and movement analysis.

A college education is not essential to obtaining employment as a professional dancer. In fact, ballet dancers who postpone their first audition until graduation may compete at a disadvantage with younger dancers. On the other hand, a college degree can help the dancer who retires at an early age, as often happens, and wishes to enter another field of work.

Completion of a college program in dance and education is essential to qualify for employment as a college or elementary/high school dance teacher. Colleges, as well as conservatories, generally require graduate degrees, but performance experience often may be substituted. However, a college background is not necessary for teaching dance or choreographing for local recreation programs. Studio schools usually require teachers to have experience as performers.

The dancer's life is one of rigorous practice and self-discipline; therefore, patience, perseverance, and a devotion to dance are essential. Good health and physical stamina are necessary in order to practice and perform and to follow the rugged schedule often required. Above all, one must have flexibility, agility, coordination, grace, a sense of rhythm, and a feeling for music, as well as a creative ability to express oneself through movement.

Dancers seldom perform unaccompanied, so they must be able to function as part of a team, highly motivated, and should be prepared to face the anxiety of intermittent employment and rejections when auditioning for work. For dancers, advancement takes the form of a growing reputation, more frequent work, bigger and better roles, and higher pay.

Choreographers typically are older dancers with years of experience in the theater. Through their performance as dancers, they develop reputations as skilled artists. Their reputation often leads to opportunities to choreograph productions.

Job Outlook

Dancers and choreographers face very keen competition for jobs. The number of applicants will continue to exceed the number of job openings, and only the most talented will find regular employment.

Employment of dancers and choreographers is expected to grow faster than the average for all occupations through the year 2006 due to the public's continued interest in this form of artistic expression. However, cuts in funding for the National Endowment for the Arts and related organizations could adversely affect employment in this field. Although jobs will arise each year due to increased demand, most job openings will occur as dancers and choreographers retire or leave the occupation for other reasons, and as dance companies search for and find outstanding talent.

National dance companies should continue to provide most jobs in this field. Opera companies and dance groups affiliated with colleges and universities and television and motion pictures will also offer some opportunities. Moreover, the growing popularity of dance in recent years has resulted in increased employment opportunities in teaching dance.

With innovations such as electronic sounds and music videos, choreography is becoming a more challenging field of endeavor, and will offer some employment opportunities for highly experienced, talented, and creative individuals.

Earnings

Earnings of many professional dancers are governed by union contracts. Dancers in the major opera ballet, classical ballet, and modern dance corps belong to the American Guild of Musical Artists, Inc., AFL-CIO; those on live or videotaped television belong to the American Federation of Television and Radio Artists; those who perform in films and on TV belong to the Screen Actors Guild; and those in musical comedies are members of the Actors' Equity Association. The unions and producers sign basic agreements specifying minimum salary rates, hours of work, benefits, and other conditions of employment. However, the contract each dancer signs with the producer of the show may be more favorable than the basic agreement.

For 1997-98, the minimum weekly salary for dancers in ballet and modern productions covered by the National Dance Basic Agreement was $693. According to the American Guild of Musical Artists, new first year dancers under the union agreement earned $543 per week. Dancers on tour received an additional allowance for room and board. The minimum performance rate for dancers in theatrical motion pictures was around $500 per day of filming. The normal workweek is 30 hours including rehearsals and matinee and evening performances, but may be longer. Extra compensation is paid for additional hours worked.

Earnings of choreographers vary greatly. Earnings from fees and performance royalties range from about $1,000 a week in small professional theaters, to over $30,000 for an eight- to ten-week rehearsal period for a Broadway production. In high budget films, choreographers make $3,400 for a five-day week; in television, $8,000 to $12,500 for up to 14 work days.

Earnings from dancing are generally low because dancers' employment is irregular. They often must supplement their income by taking temporary jobs unrelated to dancing, or teach dance to students.

Dancers covered by union contracts are entitled to some paid sick leave, paid vacations, and various health and pension benefits, including extended sick pay and child birth provisions, provided by their unions. Employers contribute toward these benefits. Most other dancers do not receive any benefits.

Related Occupations

Other occupations require the dancer's knowledge of conveying ideas through physical motion. These include ice skaters, dance critics, dance instructors, and dance therapists. Athletes in most sports also need the same strength, flexibility, agility, and body control as dancers.

Sources of Additional Information

Directories of dance study and degree programs may be purchased from:

❑ National Association of Schools of Dance, 11250 Roger Bacon Dr., Suite 21, Reston, VA 20190.

❑ The National Dance Association, 1900 Association Dr., Reston, VA 20191.

Dental Assistants

(D.O.T. 079.361-018)

Significant Points

- ✓ *Rapid employment growth and above average job turnover should result in good job opportunities.*

- ✓ *Population growth and greater retention of natural teeth by middle-aged and older people will fuel demand for dental services, and create opportunities for dental assistants.*

- ✓ *Dentists are expected to hire more assistants to perform routine tasks, so they may devote their own time to more profitable procedures.*

Nature of the Work

Dental assistants perform a variety of patient care, office, and laboratory duties. They work at chairside as dentists examine and treat patients. They make patients as comfortable as possible in the dental chair, prepare them for treatment, and obtain dental records. Assistants hand instruments and materials to dentists, and keep patients' mouths dry and clear by using suction or other devices. Assistants also sterilize and disinfect instruments and equipment; prepare tray setups for dental procedures; provide postoperative instruction; and instruct patients in oral health care. Some dental assistants prepare materials for making impressions and restorations, expose radiographs, and process dental x-ray film as directed by a dentist. They may also remove sutures, apply anesthetics and cavity preventive agents to teeth and gums, remove excess cement used in the filling process, and place rubber dams on the teeth to isolate them for individual treatment.

Those with laboratory duties make casts of the teeth and mouth from impressions taken by dentists, clean and polish removable appliances, and make temporary crowns. Dental assistants with office duties schedule and confirm appointments, receive patients, keep treatment records, send bills, receive payments, and order dental supplies and materials.

Dental assistants should not be confused with dental hygienists, who are licensed to perform different clinical tasks.

Working Conditions

Dental assistants work in a well-lighted, clean environment. Their work area is usually near the dental chair, so they can arrange instruments, materials, and medication, and hand them to the dentist when needed. Dental assistants wear gloves and masks to protect themselves from infectious diseases, such as hepatitis. Handling radiographic equipment poses dangers, but they can be minimized with safety procedures.

Most dental assistants have a 32- to 40-hour workweek, which may include work on Saturdays or evenings.

Employment

Dental assistants held about 202,000 jobs in 1996. More than one out of three worked part-time, sometimes in more than one dental office.

Almost all dental assistants work in private dental offices. Some work in dental schools, private and government hospitals, state and local public health departments, or in clinics.

Training, Other Qualifications, and Advancement

Most assistants learn their skills on the job, though many are trained in dental assisting programs offered by community and junior colleges, trade schools, and technical institutes. Some assistants are trained in Armed Forces schools. Assistants must be a dentist's "third hand"; therefore, dentists look for people who are reliable, can work well with others, and have good manual dexterity. High school students interested in careers as dental assistants should take courses in biology, chemistry, health, and office practices.

The American Dental Association's Commission on Dental Accreditation approved 240 training programs in 1996. Programs include classroom, laboratory, and preclinical instruction in dental assisting skills and related theory. In addition, students gain practical experience in dental schools, clinics, or dental offices. Most programs take one year or less to complete and lead to a certificate or diploma. Two-year programs offered in community and junior colleges lead to an associate degree. All programs require a high school diploma or its equivalent, and some require a typing or science course for admission. Some private vocational schools offer four- to six-month courses in dental assisting, but these are not accredited by the Commission on Dental Accreditation.

Certification is available through the Dental Assisting National Board. Certification is an acknowledgment of an assistant's qualifications and professional competence, but is not usually required for employment. In several states that have adopted standards for dental assistants who perform radiologic procedures, completion of the certification examination meets those standards. Candidates may qualify to take the certification examination by graduating from an accredited training program, or by having two years of full-time experience as a dental assistant. In addition, applicants must have current certification in cardiopulmonary resuscitation.

Without further education, advancement opportunities are limited. Some dental assistants working the front office become office managers. Others, working chairside, go back to school to become dental hygienists.

Job Outlook

Job prospects for dental assistants should be good. Employment is expected to grow much faster than the average for all occupations through the year 2006. Also, the proportion of workers leaving and who must be replaced is above average. Many opportunities are for entry-level positions offering on-the-job training.

Population growth and greater retention of natural teeth by middle-aged and older people will fuel demand for dental services. Also, dentists are likely to employ more assistants, for several reasons. Older dentists, who are less likely to employ assistants, will leave and be replaced by recent graduates, who are more likely to use one, or even two. In addition, as dentists' workloads increase, they are expected to hire more assistants to perform routine tasks, so they may devote their own time to more profitable procedures.

Most job openings for dental assistants will arise from the need to replace assistants leaving the occupation. For many, this entry-level occupation provides basic training and experience and serves as a stepping-stone to more highly skilled and higher paying jobs. Other assistants leave the job to take on family responsibilities, return to school, or for other reasons.

Earnings

In 1996, median weekly earnings for dental assistants working full-time were $361. The middle 50 percent earned between $284 and $452 a week. The lowest 10 percent earned less than $212; the top 10 percent, more than $516.

According to the American Dental Association, experienced dental assistants who worked 32 hours a week or more in a private practice averaged $406 a week in 1995.

Related Occupations

Workers in other occupations supporting health practitioners include medical assistants, physical therapy assistants, occupational therapy assistants, pharmacy technicians and assistants, and veterinary technicians.

Sources of Additional Information

Information about career opportunities, scholarships, accredited dental assistant programs, and requirements for certification is available from:

❑ Commission on Dental Accreditation, American Dental Association, 211 E. Chicago Ave., Suite 1814, Chicago, IL 60611. Homepage: http://www.ada.org

❑ Dental Assisting National Board, Inc., 216 E. Ontario St., Chicago, IL 60611.

For information about a career as a dental assistant and schools offering training, contact:

❑ National Association of Health Career Schools, 750 First St. NE., Suite 940, Washington, DC 20002. FAX: (202) 842-1565 E-mail: NAHCS@aol.com

Dental Hygienists

(D.O.T. 078.361-010)

Significant Points

✓ *Dental hygienists are projected to be one of the 20 fastest growing occupations.*

✓ *Job opportunities should continue to be good if graduates of dental hygiene programs do not increase greatly in number.*

✓ *Part-time work and flexible schedules are common.*

Nature of the Work

Dental hygienists clean teeth and provide other preventive dental care, as well as teach patients how to practice good oral hygiene. Hygienists examine patients' teeth and gums, recording the presence of diseases or abnormalities. They remove calculus, stains, and plaque from teeth; take and develop dental x rays; and apply cavity preventive agents such as fluorides and pit and fissure sealants. In some states, hygienists administer local anesthetics and anesthetic gas; place and carve filling materials, temporary fillings and periodontal dressings; remove sutures; and smooth and polish metal restorations.

Dental hygienists also help patients develop and maintain good oral health. For example, they may explain the relationship between diet and oral health, inform patients how to select toothbrushes, and show patients how to brush and floss their teeth.

Dental hygienists use hand and rotary instruments to clean teeth, x-ray machines to take dental pictures, syringes with needles to administer local anesthetics, and models of teeth to explain oral hygiene.

Working Conditions

Flexible scheduling is a distinctive feature of this job. Full-time, part-time, evening, and weekend work is widely available. Dentists frequently hire hygienists to work only two or three days a week, so hygienists may hold jobs in more than one dental office.

Dental hygienists work in clean, well-lighted offices. Important health safeguards include strict adherence to proper radiological procedures, and use of appropriate protective devices when administering anesthetic gas. Dental hygienists also wear safety glasses, surgical masks and gloves to protect themselves from infectious diseases, such as hepatitis.

Employment

Dental hygienists held about 133,000 jobs in 1996. Because multiple job holding is common in this field, the number of jobs greatly exceeds the number of hygienists. More than half of all dental hygienists worked part-time—less than 35 hours a week.

Almost all dental hygienists work in private dental offices. Some work in public health agencies, hospitals, and clinics.

Training, Other Qualifications, and Advancement

Dental hygienists must be licensed by the state in which they practice. To qualify for licensure, a candidate must graduate from an accredited dental hygiene school and pass both a written and clinical examination. The American Dental Association Joint Commission on National Dental Examinations administers the written examination that is accepted by all states and the District of Columbia. state or regional testing agencies administer the clinical examination. In addition, examinations on legal aspects of dental hygiene practice are required by most states. Alabama allows candidates to take its examination if they have been trained through a state-regulated on-the-job program in a dentist's office.

In 1997, 230 programs in dental hygiene were accredited by the Commission on Dental Accreditation. Although some programs lead to a bachelor's degree, most grant an associate degree. Twelve universities offer master's degree programs in dental hygiene or a related area.

An associate degree is sufficient for practice in a private dental office. A bachelor's or master's degree is usually required for research, teaching, or clinical practice in public or school health programs.

About half of the dental hygiene programs prefer applicants who have completed at least one year of college. Some of the bachelor's degree programs require applicants to have completed two years. However, requirements vary from school to school. These schools offer laboratory, clinical, and classroom instruction in subjects such as anatomy, physiology, chemistry, microbiology, pharmacology, nutrition, radiography, histology (the study of tissue structure), periodontology (the study of gum diseases), pathology, dental materials, clinical dental hygiene, and social and behavioral sciences.

Dental hygienists should work well with others and must have good manual dexterity because they use dental instruments with little room for error within a patient's mouth. Recommended high school courses for aspiring dental hygienists include biology, chemistry, and mathematics.

Job Outlook

Employment of dental hygienists is expected to grow much faster than the average for all occupations through the year 2006, in response to increasing demand for dental care and the greater substitution of hygienists for services previously performed by dentists. Job prospects are expected to remain very good unless the number of dental hygienist program graduates grows much faster than during the last decade, and results in a much larger pool of qualified applicants.

Demand will be stimulated by population growth, and greater retention of natural teeth by the larger number of middle-aged and elderly people. Also, dentists are likely to employ more hygienists for several reasons. Older dentists, who are less likely to employ dental hygienists, will leave and be replaced by recent graduates, who are more likely to do so. In addition, as dentists' workloads increase, they are expected to hire more hygienists to perform preventive dental care such as cleaning, so they may devote their own time to more profitable procedures.

Earnings

Earnings of dental hygienists are affected by geographic location, employment setting, and education and experience. Dental hygienists who work in private dental offices may be paid on an hourly, daily, salary, or commission basis.

According to the American Dental Association, experienced dental hygienists who worked 32 hours a week or more in a private practice averaged about $759 a week in 1995.

Benefits vary substantially by practice setting, and may be contingent upon full-time employment. Dental hygienists who work for school systems, public health agencies, the federal government, or state agencies usually have substantial benefits.

Related Occupations

Workers in other occupations supporting health practitioners in an office setting include dental assistants, ophthalmic medical assistants, podiatric medical assistants, office nurses, medical assistants, physician assistants, physical therapy assistants, and occupational therapy assistants.

Sources of Additional Information

For information on a career in dental hygiene and the educational requirements to enter this occupation, contact:

❑ Division of Professional Development, American Dental Hygienists' Association, 444 N. Michigan Ave., Suite 3400, Chicago, IL 60611. Homepage: http://www.adha.org

For information about accredited programs and educational requirements, contact:

❑ Commission on Dental Accreditation, American Dental Association, 211 E. Chicago Ave., Suite 1814, Chicago, IL 60611. Homepage: http://www.ada.org

The State Board of Dental Examiners in each state can supply information on licensing requirements.

Designers

(D.O.T. 141.051, .061, .067; 142 except .061-030, -054)

Significant Points

✓ *Nearly 40 percent are self-employed, almost five times the proportion in all professional occupations.*

✓ *Creativity is crucial in all design occupations; formal education requirements range from a high school diploma for floral designers to a bachelor's degree for industrial designers.*

✓ *Despite projected faster than average employment growth, keen competition is expected for most jobs because many talented individuals are attracted to careers as designers.*

Nature of the Work

Designers organize and design articles, products, and materials so they serve the purpose for which they were intended and are visually pleasing. Pleasant surroundings, beautiful clothes, and floral arrangements can boost our spirits, and products and packaging that are eye-catching are more likely to attract buyers than those that are not.

Many designers specialize in a particular area of design, such as automobiles, clothing, furniture, home appliances, industrial equipment, interiors of homes and office buildings, exhibits, movie and theater sets, packaging, or floral arrangements. Others work in more than one design field. The first step in developing a new design or altering an existing one is to determine the needs of the client. The designer then considers various factors, including the size, shape, weight, and color of the product; materials used; and the product functions. The ease of use, safety, and cost of the design are additional factors. Designers offer suggestions to their clients; some ideas are more practical, while others are more aesthetically appealing. The designer develops by hand, or with the aid of a computer, sketches of several design concepts they present for final selection to a client, an art or design director, a product development team, or producer of a play, film, or television production. The designer then makes a model, a prototype, or detailed plans drawn to scale. Designers in some specialties increasingly use computer-aided design (CAD) tools to create and better visualize a final product. Computers greatly reduce the cost and time necessary to create a model or prototype, which gives a real idea of what the product will look like. Industrial designers use computer-aided industrial design (CAID) to create designs and to communicate them to automated production tools.

Designers may supervise assistants who carry out their designs. Those who run their own businesses may also devote a considerable amount of time to developing new business contacts and to administrative tasks, such as reviewing catalogs and ordering samples.

Design encompasses a number of different fields. Industrial designers develop and design countless manufactured products including cars, home appliances, children's toys, computer equipment, and medical, office, or recreational equipment. They combine artistic talent with research on product use, marketing, materials, and production methods to create the most functional and appealing design and to make the product competitive with others in the marketplace.

Furniture designers design furniture for manufacture, according to knowledge of design trends, competitors' products, production costs, capability of production facilities, and characteristics of a company's market. They may also prepare detailed drawings of fixtures, forms, or tools required to be used in production of furniture, along with designing custom pieces or styles according to a specific period or country. They must be strongly involved with the fashion industry and aware of current trends and styles.

Interior designers plan the space and furnish the interiors of private homes, public buildings, and commercial establishments, such as offices, restaurants, hospitals, hotels, and theaters. They also may plan additions and renovations. With a client's tastes, needs, and budget in mind, they develop designs and prepare working drawings and specifications for interior construction, furnishings, lighting, and finishes. Increasingly, designers use computers to plan layouts that can be changed easily to include ideas received from the client. They also design lighting and architectural details such as crown molding, coordinate colors, and select furniture, floor coverings, and curtains. Interior designers must design space in accordance with federal, state, and local laws, including building codes. Increasingly, they plan spaces that meet accessibility standards for the disabled and elderly.

Set designers design movie, television, and theater sets. They study scripts, confer with directors, and conduct research to determine appropriate architectural styles.

Fashion designers design clothing and accessories. Some high-fashion designers are self-employed and design for individual clients. They make fashion news by establishing the "line," colors, and kinds of materials that will be worn each season. Other high-fashion designers cater to specialty stores or high-fashion department stores. They design original garments, as well as follow the established fashion trends. Most fashion designers, however, work for apparel manufacturers, adapting men's, women's, and children's fashions for the mass market.

Textile designers design fabric for garments, upholstery, rugs, and other products, using their knowledge of textile materials and fashion trends. Computers are widely used in pattern design and grading; intelligent pattern engineering (IPE) systems enable even greater automation in generating patterns.

Floral designers cut and arrange live, dried, or artificial flowers and foliage into designs to express the sentiments of the customer. They trim flowers and arrange bouquets, sprays, wreaths, dish gardens, and terrariums. They usually work from a written order indicating the occasion, customer preference for color and type of flower, price, and the date, time, and place the floral arrangement or plant is to be delivered. The variety of duties performed by a floral designer depends on the size of the shop and number of designers employed. In a small operation, the floral de-

signer may own the shop and do almost everything from growing flowers to keeping books.

Working Conditions

Working conditions and places of employment vary. Designers employed by manufacturing establishments or design firms generally work regular hours in well-lighted and comfortable settings. Self-employed designers tend to work longer hours—especially at first, when they are trying to establish themselves and cannot afford to hire assistants or clerical help.

Designers frequently adjust their workday to suit their clients, meeting with them in the evenings, or on weekends when necessary. They may transact business in their own offices, clients' homes or offices, or may travel to other locations such as showrooms or manufacturing facilities.

Industrial designers usually work regular hours but occasionally work overtime to meet deadlines. In contrast, set designers, especially those in television broadcasting, often work long and irregular hours. The pace of television production is very fast, and set designers are often under pressure to make rapid changes in the sets. Fashion designers who work in the apparel industry usually have regular hours. During production deadlines or before fashion shows, however, they may be required to put in overtime. In addition, fashion designers may be required to travel to production sites overseas and across the United States. Interior designers generally work under deadlines and often work overtime to finish a job. Floral designers usually work regular hours in a pleasant work environment, except during holidays when overtime usually is required.

All designers face frustration at times, when their designs are rejected or when they cannot be as creative as they wish. Independent consultants, who are paid by the assignment, are under pressure to please clients and to find new ones to maintain their incomes.

Employment

Designers held about 342,000 jobs in 1996. Nearly four out of ten were self-employed, compared to less than one out of ten workers in all occupations.

Salaried designers work in a number of different industries, depending on their design specialty. Most industrial designers, for example, work for consulting firms or for large corporations. Interior designers usually work for design or architectural firms, department stores and home furnishing stores, or hotel and restaurant chains. Many do freelance work—full-time, part-time, or in addition to a salaried job in another occupation.

Set designers work for theater companies and film and television production companies. Fashion designers generally work for textile, apparel, and pattern manufacturers, or for fashion salons, high-fashion department stores, and specialty shops. Some work in the entertainment industry, designing costumes for theater, dance, television, and movies. Most floral designers work for retail flower shops, but a growing number work in floral departments of grocery stores.

Training, Other Qualifications, and Advancement

Creativity is crucial in all design occupations. People in this field must have a strong sense of color, an eye for detail, a sense of balance and proportion, and sensitivity to beauty. Sketching ability is especially important for fashion designers. A good portfolio—a collection of examples of a person's best work—is often the deciding factor in getting a job. However, formal preparation in design is important in all fields with the exception of floral design.

Educational requirements for entry-level positions vary. Some design occupations, notably industrial design, require a bachelor's degree. Interior designers also generally need a college education because few clients—especially commercial clients—are willing to entrust responsibility for designing living and working space to a designer with no formal credentials. Interior designers must also be knowledgeable about federal, state, and local codes, and toxicity and flammability standards for furniture and furnishings.

Interior design is the only design field subject to government regulation. According to a 1997 survey from the American Society for Interior Designers, 22 states required interior designers to be licensed. Because licensing is not mandatory in all states, membership in a professional association is universally recognized as a mark of achievement for interior designers. Professional membership usually requires the completion of three or four years of postsecondary education in design, at least two years of practical experience in the field, and completion of the National Council for Interior Design qualification examination.

In fashion design, some formal career preparation, such as a two- or four-year degree, is usually needed to enter the field. Employers seek individuals who are knowledgeable in the areas of textiles, fabrics, and ornamentation, as well as trends in the fashion world. Similarly, furniture designers must keep abreast of trends in fashion and style, in addition to methods and tools used in furniture production. Several universities and schools of design offer degrees in furniture design.

In contrast to the other design occupations, a high school diploma ordinarily suffices for floral design jobs. Most floral designers learn their skills on the job. When they hire trainees, employers generally look for high school graduates who have a flair for color and a desire to learn. However, completion of formal training is an asset for floral designers, particularly for advancement to the chief floral designer level. Vocational and technical schools offer programs in floral design usually lasting less than a year, while two- and four-year programs in floriculture, horticulture, floral design, or ornamental horticulture are offered by community and junior colleges, and colleges and universities.

Formal training for some design professions is also available in two- and three-year professional schools which award certificates or associate degrees in design. Graduates of two-year programs generally qualify as assistants to designers. The Bachelor of Fine Arts degree is granted at four-year colleges and universities. The curriculum in these schools includes art and art history, principles of design, designing and sketching, and specialized studies for each of the individual design disciplines such as garment construction, textiles, mechanical and architectural drawing, computerized design, sculpture, architecture, and basic engineering. A liberal arts education, with courses in merchandising, business administration, marketing, and psychology, along with training in art, is also a good background for most design fields. Persons with training or experience in architecture also qualify for some design occupations, particularly interior design.

Computer-aided design (CAD) courses are very useful. CAD is used in various areas of design, and many employers expect new designers to be familiar with the use of the computer as a design tool. For example, industrial designers extensively use computers in the aerospace, automotive, and electronics industries. Interior designers are using computers to create numerous versions of space designs. Images can be inserted, edited, or replaced—making it possible for a client to see and choose among several designs. In furniture design, a chair's basic shape and structure may be duplicated and updated by applying new upholstery styles and fabrics with the use of computers.

In 1997, the National Association of Schools of Art and Design accredited about 200 postsecondary institutions with programs in art and design; most of these schools award a degree in art. Some award degrees in industrial, interior, textile, graphic, or fashion design. Many schools do not allow formal entry into a bachelor's degree program until a student has successfully finished a year of basic art and design courses. Applicants may be required to submit sketches and other examples of their artistic ability.

The Foundation for Interior Design Education Research accredits interior design programs and schools. Currently, there are over 120 accredited programs in the United States and Canada, located in schools of art, architecture, and home economics.

Individuals in the design field must be creative, imaginative, persistent, and able to communicate their ideas both visually and verbally. Because tastes in style and fashion can change quickly, designers need to be open to new ideas and influences. Problem-solving skills and the ability to work independently are important traits. People in this field need self-discipline to start projects on their own, budget their time, and meet deadlines and production schedules. Business sense and sales ability are also important for those who are freelancers or run their own businesses.

Beginning designers usually receive on-the-job training, and normally need one to three years of training before they advance to higher-level positions. Experienced designers in large firms may advance to chief designer, design department head, or other supervisory positions. Some experienced designers open their own firms.

Job Outlook

Despite projected faster than average employment growth, designers in most fields—with the exception of floral and furniture design—are expected to face competition for available positions because many talented individuals are attracted to careers as designers. Individuals with little or no formal education in design who lack creativity and perseverance will find it very difficult to establish and maintain a career in design.

Finding a job as a floral designer should be relatively easy due to the relatively low pay and limited opportunities for advancement.

Overall, the employment of designers is expected to grow faster than the average for all occupations through the year 2006. Demand for industrial designers will stem from continued emphasis on product quality and safety; design of new products that are easy and comfortable to use; high-technology products in medicine, transportation, and other fields; and increasing global competition among businesses. Rising demand for professional design of private homes, office space, restaurants and other retail establishments, and institutions that care for the rapidly growing elderly population should spur employment growth among interior designers. Floral design should experience healthy growth with the addition of floral departments in many grocery and department stores. Demand for fashion, textile, and furniture designers should rise as consumers become more concerned with fashion and style. In addition to employment growth, many job openings will result from the need to replace designers who leave the field.

Earnings

Full-time designers in all specialties combined had median weekly earnings of about $590 in 1996. The middle 50 percent earned between $380 and $890 a week. The bottom 10 percent earned less than $280, while the top 10 percent earned over $1,300.

Earnings of floral designers were lower than most types of designers. According to a survey conducted by Floral Finance, Inc., beginning floral designers had average earnings of $5.85 an hour in 1996. Designers with one to three years of experience earned $6.94, while designers with over three years of experience averaged $8.17. Managers had average earnings of $10.10 per hour in 1996.

According to the Industrial Designers Society of America, the average base salary for an entry-level industrial designer with one to two years of experience was about $27,000 in 1996. Staff designers with five years of experience earned $35,000, while senior designers with eight years of experience earned $45,000. Industrial designers in managerial or executive positions earned substantially more—up to $140,000 annually.

Related Occupations

Workers in other occupations who design or arrange objects, materials, or interiors to improve their appearance and function include visual artists, architects, landscape architects, engineers, photographers, interior decorators, and merchandise displayers. Some computer-related occupations, including Internet page designer and webmaster, require design skills.

Sources of Additional Information

For a list of accredited schools of art and design, contact:
❏ National Association of Schools of Art and Design, 11250 Roger Bacon Dr., Suite 21, Reston, VA 20190.

For information on careers and a list of academic programs in industrial design, write to:
❏ Industrial Designers Society of America, 1142-E Walker Rd., Great Falls, VA 22066. Homepage: http://www.idsa.org

For information on degree, continuing education, and licensure programs in interior design, contact:
❏ American Society for Interior Designers, 608 Massachusetts Ave. NE, Washington, DC 20002-6006.

For a list of accredited programs in interior design, contact:
❏ Foundation for Interior Design Education Research, 60 Monroe Center NW, Grand Rapids, MI 49503. Homepage: http://www.fider.org

For information about careers in floral design, contact:
❏ Society of American Florists, 1601 Duke St., Alexandria, VA 22314.

For a list of schools with accredited programs in furniture design, contact:
❏ American Society of Furniture Designers, P.O. Box 2688, High Point, NC 27261.

Dietitians and Nutritionists

(*D.O.T.* 077 except .117-010 and .124-010)

Significant Points

✓ *Employment of dietitians is expected to grow about as fast as the average for all occupations through the year 2006 due to increased emphasis on the prevention of disease by improved health habits.*

✓ *The basic educational requirement for dietitians and nutritionists is a bachelor's degree with a major in dietetics, foods and nutrition, food service systems management, or a related area.*

Nature of the Work

Dietitians and nutritionists plan nutrition programs and supervise the preparation and serving of meals. They help prevent and treat illnesses by promoting healthy eating habits, scientifically evaluating clients' diets, and suggesting diet modifications, such as less salt for those with high blood pressure or reduced fat and sugar intake for those who are overweight.

Dietitians run food service systems for institutions such as hospitals and schools, promote sound eating habits through education, and conduct research. Major areas of practice are clinical, community, management, and consultant dietetics.

Clinical dietitians provide nutritional services for patients in institutions such as hospitals and nursing homes. They assess patients' nutritional needs, develop and implement nutrition programs, and evaluate and report the results. They also confer with doctors and other health care professionals in order to coordinate medical and nutritional needs. Some clinical dietitians specialize in the management of overweight patients, care of the critically ill, or care of renal (kidney) and diabetic patients. In addition, clinical dietitians in nursing homes or small hospitals may also manage the food service department.

Community dietitians counsel individuals and groups on nutritional practices designed to prevent disease and promote good health. Working in such places as public health clinics, home health agencies, and health maintenance organizations, they evaluate individual needs, develop nutritional care plans, and instruct individuals and their families. Dietitians working in home health agencies may provide instruction on grocery shopping and food preparation to the elderly, or patients with AIDS, cancer, or diabetes.

Popular interest in nutrition has led to opportunities in food manufacturing, advertising, and marketing, in which dietitians analyze foods, prepare literature for distribution, or report on issues such as the nutritional content of recipes, dietary fiber, or vitamin supplements.

Management dietitians oversee large-scale meal planning and preparation in such places as health care facilities, company cafeterias, prisons, and schools. They hire, train, and direct other dietitians and food service workers; budget for and purchase food, equipment, and supplies; enforce sanitary and safety regulations; and prepare records and reports.

Consultant dietitians work under contract with health care facilities or in their own private practice. They perform nutrition screening for their clients, and offer advice on diet-related concerns such as weight loss or cholesterol reduction. Some work for wellness programs, sports teams, supermarkets, and other nutrition-related businesses. They may consult with food service managers, providing expertise in sanitation, safety procedures, budgeting, and planning.

Working Conditions

Most dietitians work a regular 40-hour week, although some work weekends. Many dietitians work part-time.

Dietitians and nutritionists spend much of their time in clean, well-lighted, and well-ventilated areas. However, some dietitians spend time in hot, steamy kitchens. Dietitians and nutritionists may be on their feet for most of the workday.

Employment

Dietitians and nutritionists held about 58,000 jobs in 1996. Over half were in hospitals, nursing homes, or offices and clinics of physicians.

State and local governments provided about one job in six—mostly in health departments and other public health related areas. Other jobs were in restaurants, social service agencies, residential care facilities, diet workshops, physical fitness facilities, school systems, colleges and universities, and the federal government—mostly in the Department of Veterans Affairs. Others were employed by firms that provide food services on contract to such facilities as colleges and universities, airlines, and company cafeterias.

Some dietitians were self-employed, working as consultants to facilities such as hospitals and nursing homes, and seeing individual clients.

Training, Other Qualifications, and Advancement

The basic educational requirement for dietitians and nutritionists is a bachelor's degree with a major in dietetics, foods and nutrition, food service systems management, or a related area. Students take courses in foods, nutrition, institution management, chemistry, biology, microbiology, and physiology. Other suggested courses include business, mathematics, statistics, computer science, psychology, sociology, and economics.

Of the 40 states having laws governing dietetics, 27 require licensure, 12 require certification, and one requires registration. The Commission on Dietetic Registration of the American Dietetic Association (ADA) awards the Registered Dietitian credential to those who pass a certification exam after completing their academic education and supervised experience.

As of 1997, there were 231 ADA-approved bachelor's degree programs. Supervised practice experience can be acquired in two ways. There are 49 ADA-accredited coordinated programs combining academic and supervised practice experience in a four-year program. The second option requires completion of 900 hours of supervised practice experience, either in one of the 190 ADA-accredited internships or in one of the 64 ADA-approved preprofessional practice programs. Internships and preprofessional practice programs may be full-time programs lasting 9 to 12 months, or part-time programs lasting two years. Students interested in research, advanced clinical positions, or public health should get a graduate degree.

Recommended high school courses include biology, chemistry, mathematics, health, and home economics.

Experienced dietitians may advance to assistant, associate, or director of a dietetic department, or become self-employed. Some dietitians specialize in areas such as renal or pediatric dietetics. Others may leave the occupation to become sales representatives for equipment or food manufacturers.

Job Outlook

Employment of dietitians is expected to grow about as fast as the average for all occupations through the year 2006 due to increased emphasis on the prevention of disease by improved health habits. A growing and aging population will increase demand for meals and nutritional counseling in nursing homes, schools, prisons, community health programs, and home health care agencies. Public interest in nutrition and the emphasis on health education and prudent lifestyles will also spur demand. Besides employment growth, job openings will also result from the need to replace experienced workers who leave the occupation.

Employment of dietitians in hospitals is expected to decline because of anticipated slow growth in the number of inpatients, and as hospitals contract out food service operations. On the other hand, faster than average growth in employment is expected in nursing homes as the number of elderly people rises sharply, in contract providers of food services, in residential care facilities, in offices and clinics of physicians, and in other social services.

Employment growth for dietitians and nutritionists may be somewhat constrained by some employers substituting other workers such as nurses, health educators, food service managers, and dietetic technicians. Growth would be faster but there are limitations on insurance reimbursement for dietetic services.

Earnings

According to a Hay Group survey of acute care hospitals, the median annual base salary of full-time staff dietitians was $34,400 in January 1997. The middle 50 percent earned between $31,300 and $37,200.

According to the American Dietetic Association, median annual income for registered dietitians in 1995 varied by practice area as follows: clinical nutrition, $34,131; food and nutrition management, $42,964; community nutrition, $33,902; consultation and business, $43,374; and education and research, $42,784. Salaries also vary by years in practice, educational level, geographic region, and size of community.

Related Occupations

Dietitians and nutritionists apply the principles of nutrition in a variety of situations. Workers with duties similar to those of management dietitians include home economists and food service managers. Nurses and health educators often provide services related to those of community dietitians.

Sources of Additional Information

For a list of academic programs, scholarships, and other information about dietetics, contact:

❑ The American Dietetic Association, 216 West Jackson Blvd., Suite 800, Chicago, IL 60606-6995. Homepage: HYPERLINK http://www.eatright.org

Dispensing Opticians

(D.O.T. 299.361-010 and -014)

Significant Points

✓ *Although training requirements vary by state, most dispensing opticians receive their training on-the-job or through apprenticeships lasting two to four years.*

✓ *Employment of dispensing opticians is expected to increase as fast as the average for all occupations through the year 2006 as demand grows for corrective lenses.*

Nature of the Work

Dispensing opticians fit eyeglasses and contact lenses, following prescriptions written by ophthalmologists or optometrists.

Dispensing opticians help customers select appropriate frames, order the necessary ophthalmic laboratory work, and adjust the finished eyeglasses. In some states, they fit contact lenses under the supervision of an optometrist or ophthalmologist.

Dispensing opticians examine written prescriptions to determine lens specifications. They recommend eyeglass frames, lenses, and lens coatings after considering the prescription and the customer's occupation, habits, and facial features. Dispensing opticians measure clients' eyes, including the distance between the centers of the pupils and the distance between the eye surface and the lens. For customers without prescriptions, dispensing opticians may use a lensometer to record the present eyeglass prescription. They also may obtain a customer's previous record, or verify a prescription with the examining optometrist or ophthalmologist.

Dispensing opticians prepare work orders that give ophthalmic laboratory technicians information needed to grind and insert lenses into a frame. The work order includes lens prescriptions and information on lens size, material, color, and style. Some dispensing opticians grind and insert lenses themselves. After the glasses are made, dispensing opticians verify that the lenses have been ground to specifications. Then they may reshape or bend the frame, by hand or using pliers, so that the eyeglasses fit the customer properly and comfortably. Some also fix, adjust, and refit broken frames. They instruct clients about adapting to, wearing, or caring for eyeglasses.

Some dispensing opticians specialize in fitting contacts, artificial eyes, or cosmetic shells to cover blemished eyes. To fit contact lenses, dispensing opticians measure eye shape and size, select the type of contact lens material, and prepare work orders specifying the prescription and lens size. Fitting contact lenses requires considerable skill, care, and patience. Dispensing opticians observe customers' eyes, corneas, lids, and contact lenses with special instruments and microscopes. During several visits, opticians show customers how to insert, remove, and care for their contacts, and ensure the fit is correct.

Dispensing opticians keep records on customer prescriptions, work orders, and payments; track inventory and sales; and perform other administrative duties.

Working Conditions

Dispensing opticians work indoors in attractive, well lighted, and well ventilated surroundings. They may work in medical offices or small stores where customers are served one at a time, or in large stores where several dispensing opticians serve a number of customers at once. Opticians spend a lot of time with customers, most of it on their feet. If they also prepare lenses, they need to take precautions against the hazards associated with glass cutting, chemicals, and machinery.

Most dispensing opticians work a 40-hour week, although some work longer hours. Those in retail stores may work evenings and weekends. Some work part-time.

Employment

Dispensing opticians held about 67,000 jobs in 1996. About half work for ophthalmologists or optometrists who sell glasses directly to patients. Many also work in retail optical stores that offer one-stop shopping. Customers may have their eyes examined, choose frames, and have glasses made on the spot. Some work in optical departments of drug and department stores.

Training, Other Qualifications, and Advancement

Employers generally hire individuals with no background in opticianry or those who have worked as ophthalmic laboratory technicians and then provide the required training. Training may be informal, on-the-job or formal apprenticeship. Some employers, however, seek people with postsecondary training in opticianry.

Knowledge of physics, basic anatomy, algebra, geometry, and mechanical drawing is particularly valuable because training usually includes instruction in optical mathematics, optical physics, and the use of precision measuring instruments and other machinery and tools. Because dispensing opticians deal directly with the public, they should be tactful and pleasant and communicate well.

Large employers generally offer structured apprenticeship programs, and small employers provide more informal on-the-job training. In the 21 states that license dispensing opticians, individuals without postsecondary training work from two to four years as apprentices. Apprenticeship or formal training is offered in most of the other states as well.

Apprentices receive technical training and learn office management and sales. Under the supervision of an experienced optician, optometrist, or ophthalmologist, apprentices work directly with patients, fitting eyeglasses and contact lenses. In states requiring licensure, information about apprenticeships and licensing procedures is available from the state board of occupational licensing.

Formal opticianry training is offered in community colleges and a few colleges and universities. In 1997, there were 23 programs accredited by the Commission on Opticianry Accreditation that awarded two-year associate degrees in ophthalmic dispensing or optometric technology. There are also shorter programs, including some under one year. Some states that license dispensing opticians allow graduates to take the licensure exam immediately upon graduation; others require a few months to a year of experience.

Dispensing opticians may apply to the American Board of Opticianry and the National Contact Lens Examiners for certification of their skills. Certification must be renewed every three years through continuing education.

Many experienced dispensing opticians open their own optical stores. Others become managers of optical stores or sales representatives for wholesalers or manufacturers of eyeglasses or lenses.

Job Outlook

Employment in this occupation is expected to increase as fast as the average for all occupations through the year 2006 as demand grows for corrective lenses. The number of middle-aged and elderly persons is projected to increase rapidly. Middle age is a time when many individuals use corrective lenses for the first time, and elderly persons require more vision care, on the whole, than others.

Fashion, too, influences demand. Frames come in a growing variety of styles and colors—encouraging people to buy more than one pair. Demand is also expected to grow in response to the availability of new technologies that improve the quality and look of corrective lenses, such as antireflective coatings and bifocal lenses without the line visible in old-style bifocals. Improvements in bifocal, extended wear, and disposable contact lenses will also spur demand.

Besides job openings expected due to employment growth, the need to replace those who leave the occupation will result in additional job openings. Nevertheless, the total number of job openings will be relatively small because the occupation is small. This occupation is vulnerable to changes in the business cycle because eyeglass purchases can often be deferred for a time. Employment of opticians often falls somewhat during downturns.

Earnings

According to survey results published in an April 1997 issue of Eyecare Business magazine, dispensing opticians earned an overall average salary of about $27,432. Owners, managers, and certified graduates of opticianry schools had higher earnings, as did dispensing opticians who worked in states that require licensure.

Related Occupations

Other workers who deal with customers and perform delicate work include jewelers, locksmiths, ophthalmic laboratory technicians, orthodontic technicians, dental laboratory technicians, prosthetics technicians, camera repairers, and watch repairers.

Sources of Additional Information

For general information about a career as a dispensing optician, contact:

❑ Opticians Association of America, 10341 Democracy Lane, Fairfax, VA 22030-2521.

For general information about a career as a dispensing optician and a list of accredited training programs, contact:

❑ Commission on Opticianry Accreditation, 10111 Martin Luther King, Jr. Hwy., Suite 100, Bowie, MD 20720-4299.

For general information on opticianry and a list of home-study programs, seminars, and review materials, contact:

❑ National Academy of Opticianry, 10111 Martin Luther King, Jr. Hwy., Suite 112, Bowie, MD 20720-4299.

Economists and Marketing Research Analysts

(D.O.T. 050.067)

Significant Points

✓ *Demand for qualified marketing research analysts should be strong.*

✓ *Candidates who hold a master's degree in economics have much better employment prospects than bachelor's degree holders.*

Nature of the Work

Economists. Economists study the ways society distributes scarce resources such as land, labor, raw materials, and machinery to produce goods and services. They conduct research, collect and analyze data, monitor economic trends, and develop forecasts. They research issues such as energy costs, inflation, interest rates, imports, or employment levels.

Most economists are concerned with practical applications of economic policy in a particular area. They use their understanding of economic relationships to advise businesses and other organizations, including insurance companies, banks, securities firms, industry and trade associations, labor unions, and government agencies. Economists use mathematical models to develop programs predicting answers to questions such as the nature and length of business cycles, the effects of a specific rate of inflation on the economy, or the effects of tax legislation on unemployment levels.

Economists devise methods and procedures for obtaining the data they need. For example, sampling techniques may be used to conduct a survey, and various mathematical modeling techniques may be used to develop forecasts. Preparing reports on the results of their research is an important part of the economist's job. Relevant data must be reviewed and analyzed, applicable tables and charts prepared, and the results presented in clear, concise language that can be understood by non-economists. Presenting economic and statistical concepts in a meaningful way is particularly important for economists whose research is directed toward making policies for an organization.

Economists who work for government agencies may assess economic conditions in the United States or abroad, in order to estimate the economic effects of specific changes in legislation or public policy. They may study areas such as how the dollar's fluctuation against foreign currencies affects import and export levels. The majority of government economists work in the area of agriculture, labor, or quantitative analysis; some economists work in almost every area of government. For example, some economists in the U.S. Department of Commerce study production, distribution, and consumption of commodities produced overseas, while economists employed with the Bureau of Labor Statistics analyze data on the domestic economy such as prices, wages, employment, productivity, and safety and health. An economist working in state or local government might analyze data on the growth of school-aged populations, prison growth, and employment and unemployment rates, in order to project spending needs for future years.

Marketing Research Analysts. Marketing research analysts are concerned with the potential sales of a product or service. They analyze statistical data on past sales to predict future sales. They gather data on competitors and analyze prices, sales, and methods of marketing and distribution. Like economists, marketing research analysts devise methods and procedures for obtaining the data they need. They often design telephone, personal, or mail interview surveys to assess consumer preferences. The surveys are usually conducted by trained interviewers under the marketing research analyst's direction. Once the data are compiled, marketing research analysts evaluate it. They then make recommendations to their client or employer based upon their findings. They provide a company's management with information needed to make decisions on the promotion, distribution, design, and pricing of company products or services, or to determine the advisability of adding new lines of merchandise, opening new branches, or otherwise diversifying the company's operations. Analysts may conduct opinion research to determine public attitudes on various issues. This can help political or business leaders and others assess public support for their electoral prospects or advertising policies.

Working Conditions

Economists and marketing research analysts have structured work schedules. They often work alone, writing reports, preparing statistical charts, and using computers, but they may also be an integral part of a research team. Most work under pressure of deadlines and tight schedules, and sometimes must work overtime. Their routine may be interrupted by special requests for data, as well as by the need to attend meetings or conferences; regular travel may be necessary to do this.

Employment

Economists and marketing research analysts held about 51,000 jobs in 1996. Private industry, particularly economic and marketing research firms, management consulting firms, banks, securities and commodities brokers, and computer and data processing companies, employed about three out of four salaried workers. The remainder, primarily economists, were employed by a wide range of government agencies, primarily in the state government. The Departments of Labor, Agriculture, and Commerce are the largest federal employers of economists. A number of economists and marketing research analysts combine a full-time job in government, academia, or business with part-time or consulting work in another setting.

Employment of economists and marketing research analysts is concentrated in large cities. Some economists work abroad for companies with major international operations, for U.S. government agencies, and for international organizations like the World Bank and the United Nations.

Besides the jobs described above, many economists and marketing research analysts held economics and marketing faculty positions in colleges and universities. Economics and marketing faculty have flexible work schedules, and may divide their time among teaching, research, consulting, and administration.

Training, Other Qualifications, and Advancement

Graduate training is required for most private sector economist and marketing research analyst jobs, and for advancement to more responsible positions. Economics includes many specialties at the graduate level, such as advanced economic theory, econometrics, international economics, and labor economics. Students should select graduate schools strong in specialties in which they are interested. Marketing research analysts may earn advanced degrees in economics, business administration, marketing, statistics, or some closely related discipline. Some schools help graduate students find internships or part-time employment in government agencies, economic consulting firms, financial institutions, or marketing research firms prior to graduation.

In the federal government, candidates for entry-level economist positions must have a bachelor's degree with a minimum of 21 semester hours of economics and three hours of statistics, accounting, or calculus. Competition is keen for those positions which require only a bachelor's degree, however, and additional education or superior academic performance is likely to be required to gain employment.

For a job as an instructor in many junior and some community colleges, a master's degree is the minimum requirement. In most colleges and universities, however, a Ph.D. is necessary for appointment as an instructor. A Ph.D. and extensive publications in academic journals are required for a professorship, tenure, and promotion.

Whether working in government, industry, research organizations, marketing, or consulting firms, economists and marketing research analysts who have a graduate degree usually qualify for more responsible research and administrative positions. A Ph.D. is necessary for top economist or marketing positions in many organizations. Many corporation and government executives have a strong background in economics or marketing.

A bachelor's degree with a major in economics or marketing is generally not sufficient to obtain positions as economist or marketing analyst, but is excellent preparation for many entry-level positions as a research assistant, administrative or management trainee, marketing interviewer, or any of a number of professional sales jobs.

Economics majors can choose from a variety of courses, ranging from those which are intensely mathematical such as microeconomics, macroeconomics, and econometrics, to more philosophical courses such as the history of economic thought.

In addition to courses in business, marketing, and consumer behavior, marketing majors should take other liberal arts and social science courses, including economics, psychology, English, and sociology. Because of the importance of quantitative skills to economists and marketing researchers, courses in mathematics, statistics, econometrics, sampling theory and survey design, and computer science are extremely helpful.

Aspiring economists and marketing research analysts should gain experience gathering and analyzing data, conducting interviews or surveys, and writing reports on their findings while in college. This experience can prove invaluable later in obtaining a full-time position in the field, since much of their work, in the beginning, may center around these duties. With experience, economists and marketing research analysts eventually are assigned their own research projects.

Those considering careers as economists or marketing research analysts should be able to work accurately because much time is spent on data analysis. Patience and persistence are necessary qualities since economists and marketing research analysts must spend long hours on independent study and problem solving. At the same time, they must work well with others, especially marketing research analysts, who often oversee interviews for a wide variety of individuals. Economists and marketing research analysts must be able to present their findings, both orally and in writing, in a clear, meaningful way.

Job Outlook

Employment of economists and marketing research analysts is expected to grow about as fast as the average for all occupations through the year 2006. Most job openings, however, are likely to result from the need to replace experienced workers who transfer to other occupations, retire, or leave the labor force for other reasons.

Opportunities for economists should be best in private industry, especially in research, testing, and consulting firms, as more companies contract out for economic research services. Competition, the growing complexity of the global economy, and increased reliance on quantitative methods for analyzing the current value of future funds, business trends, sales, and purchasing should spur demand for economists. The growing need for economic analyses in virtually every industry should result in additional jobs for economists. Employment of economists in the federal government should decline more slowly than the rate projected for the entire federal workforce. Average employment growth is expected among economists in state and local government.

An advanced degree coupled with a strong background in economic theory, mathematics, statistics, and econometrics provides the basis for acquiring any specialty within the field. Those skilled in quantitative techniques and their application to economic modeling and forecasting, using computers, coupled with good communications skills, should have the best job opportunities.

Those who graduate with a bachelor's degree in economics through the year 2006 will face keen competition for the limited number of economist positions for which they qualify. They will qualify for a number of other positions, however, where they can take advantage of their economic knowledge in conducting research, developing surveys, or analyzing data. Many graduates with bachelor's degrees will find good jobs in industry and business as management or sales trainees, or administrative assistants. Economists with good quantitative skills are qualified for research assistant positions in a broad range of fields. Those who meet state certification requirements may become high school economics teachers. The demand for secondary school economics teachers is expected to grow as economics becomes an increasingly important and popular course.

Candidates who hold a master's degree in economics have much better employment prospects than bachelor's degree holders. Many businesses, research and consulting firms, and government agencies seek master's degree holders who have strong computer and quantitative skills and can perform complex research, but do not command the higher salary of a Ph.D. Ph.D. holders are likely to face competition for teaching positions in colleges and universities.

Demand for qualified marketing research analysts should be strong due to an increasingly competitive economy. Marketing research provides organizations valuable feedback from purchasers, allowing companies to evaluate consumer satisfaction and more effectively plan for the future. As companies seek to expand their market and consumers become better informed, the need for marketing professionals is increasing. Opportunities for marketing research analysts with graduate degrees should be good in a wide range of employment settings, particularly in marketing research firms, as companies find it more profitable to contract out for marketing research services rather than support their own marketing department. Other organizations, including financial services organizations, health care institutions, advertising firms, manufacturing firms producing consumer goods, and insurance companies may offer job opportunities for marketing research analysts.

A strong background in marketing, mathematics, statistics, and econometrics provides the basis for acquiring any specialty within the field. Those skilled in quantitative techniques and their application to marketing research using computers should have the best job opportunities. Like economists, marketing research graduates with related work experience in a closely related business field or industry should have the best job opportunities.

Those with only a bachelor's degree but who have a strong background in mathematics, statistics, survey design, and computer science may be hired by private firms as research assistants or interviewers.

Earnings

According to a 1997 salary survey by the National Association of Colleges and Employers, persons with a bachelor's degree in economics received offers averaging $31,300 a year; for those with a bachelor's degrees in marketing, $27,900.

The median base salary of business economists in 1996 was $73,000, according to a survey by the National Association of Business Economists. The median entry-level salary was about $35,000, with most new entrants' possessing a masters degree. Ninety three percent of the respondents held advanced degrees. The highest salaries were reported by those who had a Ph.D., with a median salary of $85,000. Master's degree holders earned a median salary of $65,500, while bachelor's degree holders earned $60,000. The highest paid business economists were in the securities and investment industry, which reported a median income of $100,000, followed by banking and mining at $93,000 and the nondurable manufacturing industry at $87,000. The lowest paid were in government and nonprofit research.

The federal government recognizes education and experience in certifying applicants for entry level positions. The entrance salary for economists having a bachelor's degree was about $19,500 a year in 1997; however, those with superior academic records could begin at $24,200. Those having a master's degree could qualify for positions at an annual salary of $29,600. Those with a Ph.D. could begin at $35,800, while some individuals with experience and an advanced degree could start at $42,900. Starting salaries were slightly higher in selected areas where the prevailing local pay was higher. The average annual salary for economists employed by the federal government was $63,870 a year in early 1997.

Related Occupations

Economists are concerned with understanding and interpreting financial matters, among other subjects. Other jobs in this area include financial managers, financial analysts, underwriters, actuaries, credit analysts, loan officers, and budget officers.

Marketing research analysts do research to find out how well products or services are received by the market. This may include the planning, implementation, and analysis of surveys to determine people's needs and preferences. Other jobs using these skills include psychologists, sociologists, and urban and regional planners.

Sources of Additional Information

For information on careers in economics and business, contact:

❏ National Association of Business Economists, 1233 20th St. NW, Suite 505, Washington, DC 20036.

For information about careers and salaries in marketing research, contact:

❏ Marketing Research Association, 2189 Silas Deane Hwy., Suite 5, Rocky Hill, CT 06067.

❏ Council of American Survey Research Organizations, 3 Upper Devon, Port Jefferson, NY 11777.

Information on obtaining a job with the federal government may be obtained from the Office of Personnel Management through a telephone based system. Consult your telephone directory under U.S. government for a local number or call (912) 757-3000 (TDD 912 744-2299). That number is not toll free and charges may result. Information also is available from their internet site: http://www.usajobs.opm.gov

Education Administrators

(D.O.T. 075.117-010, -018, -030; 090.117 except -034, .167; 091.107; 092.167; 094.117-010, .167-014; 096.167; 097.167; 099.117 except -022, .167-034; 100.117-010; 169.267-022; 239.137-010)

Significant Points

✓ *Most jobs require experience in a related occupation, such as teacher or admissions counselor, and a master's or doctoral degree.*

✓ *Competition will be keen for jobs in higher education, but will be much less intense for jobs at the elementary and secondary school level.*

Nature of the Work

Smooth operation of an educational institution requires competent administrators. Education administrators provide direction, leadership, and day-to-day management of educational activities in schools, colleges and universities, businesses, correctional institutions, museums, and job training and community service organizations. Education administrators set educational standards and goals and establish the policies and procedures to carry them out. They develop academic programs; monitor students' educational progress; train and motivate teachers and other staff; manage guidance and other student services; administer recordkeeping; prepare budgets; handle relations with parents, prospective and current students, employers, and the community; and perform many other duties.

Education administrators also supervise managers, support staff, teachers, counselors, librarians, coaches, and others. In an organization such as a small daycare center, one administrator may handle all these functions. In universities or large school systems, responsibilities are divided among many administrators, each with a specific function.

Those who manage elementary and secondary schools are called principals. They set the academic tone, hire teachers and other staff, help them improve their skills, and evaluate them. Principals confer with staff—advising, explaining, or answering procedural questions. They visit classrooms, observe teaching methods, review instructional objectives, and examine learning materials. They actively work with teachers to develop and maintain high curriculum standards, develop mission statements, and set performance goals and objectives. Principals must ensure they use clear, objective guidelines for teacher appraisals, since pay is often based on performance ratings.

Principals also meet and interact with other administrators, students, parents, and representatives of community organizations. Decision-making authority has shifted from school district central offices to individual schools. Thus, parents, teachers, and other members of the community play an important role in setting school policies and goals. Principals must pay attention to the concerns of these groups when making administrative decisions.

Budgets and reports on various subjects, including finances and attendance, are prepared by principals, who also oversee the requisitioning and allocation of supplies. As school budgets become tighter, many principals are more involved in public relations and fund raising to secure financial support for their schools from local businesses and the community.

Principals must take an active role to ensure that students meet national academic standards. Many principals develop school/ business partnerships and school-to-work transition programs for students. Increasingly, principals must be sensitive to the needs of the rising number of non-English speaking and culturally diverse students. Growing enrollments, which are leading to overcrowding at many existing schools, are also a cause for concern. When addressing problems of inadequate available resources, administrators serve as advocates to build new schools or repair existing ones.

Schools continue to be involved with students' emotional welfare as well as their academic achievement. As a result, principals face responsibilities outside the academic realm. For example, in response to the growing number of dual-income and single-parent families and teenage parents, schools have established before- and after-school child-care programs or family resource centers, which also may offer parenting classes and social service referrals. With the help of community organizations, some principals have established programs to combat the increase in crime, drug and alcohol abuse, and sexually transmitted disease among students.

Assistant principals aid the principal in the overall administration of the school. Some assistant principals hold this position for several years to prepare for advancement to principal; others are career assistant principals. Depending on the number of students, the number of assistant principals a school employs may vary. They are responsible for programming student classes, ordering textbooks and supplies, and coordinating transportation, custodial, cafeteria, and other support services. They usually handle discipline, attendance, social and recreational programs, and health and safety. They also may counsel students on personal, educational, or vocational matters. With site-based management, assistant principals play a greater role in developing curriculum, evaluating teachers, and school-community relations, responsibilities previously assumed solely by the principal.

Administrators in school district central offices manage public schools under their jurisdiction. This group includes those who direct subject area programs such as English, music, vocational education, special education, and mathematics. They plan, evaluate, standardize, and improve curriculums and teaching techniques, and help teachers improve their skills and learn about new methods and materials. They oversee career counseling programs, and testing which measures students' abilities and helps place them in appropriate classes. Central office administrators also include directors of programs such as guidance, school psychology, athletics, curriculum and instruction, and professional development. With site-based management, principals and assistant principals, along with teachers and other staff, have primary responsibility for many of these programs in their individual schools.

In colleges and universities, academic deans, deans of faculty, provosts, and university deans assist presidents and develop budgets and academic policies and programs. They direct and coordinate activities of deans of individual colleges and chairpersons of academic departments.

College or university department heads or chairpersons are in charge of departments such as English, biological science, or mathematics. In addition to teaching, they coordinate schedules of classes and teaching assignments; propose budgets; recruit, interview, and hire applicants for teaching positions; evaluate faculty members; encourage faculty development; and perform other administrative duties. In overseeing their departments, chairpersons must consider and balance the concerns of faculty, administrators, and students.

Higher education administrators also provide student services. Vice presidents of student affairs or student life, deans of students, and directors of student services may direct and coordinate admissions, foreign student services, health and counseling services, career services, financial aid, and housing and residential life, as well as social, recreational, and related programs. In small colleges, they may counsel students. Registrars are custodians of students' records. They register students, prepare student transcripts, evaluate academic records, assess and collect tuition and fees, plan and implement commencement, oversee the preparation of college catalogs and schedules of classes, and analyze enrollment and demographic statistics. Directors of admissions manage the process of recruiting, evaluating, and admitting students, and work closely with financial aid directors, who oversee scholarship, fellowship, and loan programs. Registrars and admissions officers must adapt to technological innovations in student information systems. For example, for those whose institutions present information—such as college catalogs and schedules—on the Internet, knowledge of on-line resources, imaging, and other computer skills is important. Directors of student activities plan and arrange social, cultural, and recreational activities, assist student-run organizations, and may orient new students. Athletic directors plan and direct intramural and intercollegiate athletic activities, including publicity for athletic events, preparation of budgets, and supervision of coaches.

Working Conditions

Education administrators hold management positions with significant responsibility. Coordinating and interacting with faculty, parents, and students can be fast-paced and stimulating, but also stressful and demanding. Some jobs include travel. Principals and assistant principals whose main duty often is discipline may find working with difficult students frustrating, but challenging. The number of school-age children is rising, and some school systems have hired assistant principals when a school's population increased significantly. In other school systems, principals may manage larger student bodies, which can also be stressful.

Most education administrators work more than 40 hours a week, including many nights and weekends when they oversee school activities. Many administrators work 10 or 11 months a year while others work year round.

Employment

Education administrators held about 386,000 jobs in 1996. About nine out of ten were in educational services—in elementary, secondary, and technical schools and colleges and universities. The rest worked in child daycare centers, religious organizations, job training centers, state departments of education, and businesses and other organizations that provide training for their employees.

Training, Other Qualifications, and Advancement

Most education administrators begin their careers in related occupations, and prepare for a job in education administration by completing a master's or doctoral degree. Because of the diversity of duties and levels of responsibility, their educational backgrounds and experience vary considerably. Principals, assistant principals, central office administrators, and academic deans usually have held teaching positions before moving into administration. Some teachers move directly into principal positions; others first become assistant principals, or gain experience in other central office administrative jobs at either the school or district level in positions such as department head, curriculum specialist, or subject matter advisor. In some cases, administrators move up from related staff jobs such as recruiter, guidance counselor, librarian, residence hall director, or financial aid or admissions counselor.

To be considered for education administrator positions, workers must first prove themselves in their current jobs. In evaluating candidates, supervisors look for determination, confidence, innovativeness, motivation, leadership, and managerial attributes, such as ability to make sound decisions and organize and coordinate work efficiently. Since much of an administrator's job involves interacting with others, from students to parents to teachers, they must have strong interpersonal skills and be effective communicators and motivators. Knowledge of management principles and practices, gained through work experience and formal education, is important.

In most public schools, principals, assistant principals, and school administrators in central offices need a master's degree in education administration or educational supervision. Some principals and central office administrators have a doctorate or specialized degree in education administration. Most states require principals to be licensed as school administrators. Requirements for licensure vary by state. National standards for school leaders, including principals and supervisors, were recently developed by the Interstate School Leaders Licensure Consortium. States may use these national standards as guidelines for licensure requirements, or for activities such as mentoring, professional development, or accreditation of training programs. In private schools, which are not subject to state certification requirements, some principals and assistant principals hold only a bachelor's degree; however, the majority have a master's or doctoral degree.

Academic deans and chairpersons usually have a doctorate in their specialty. Most have held a professorship in their department before advancing. Admissions, student affairs, and financial aid directors and registrars sometimes start in related staff jobs with bachelor's degrees–any field usually is acceptable–and obtain advanced degrees in college student affairs or higher education administration. A Ph.D. or Ed.D. usually is necessary for top student affairs positions. Computer literacy and a background in mathematics or statistics may be assets in admissions, records, and financial work.

Advanced degrees in higher education administration, educational supervision, and college student affairs are offered in many colleges and universities. The National Council for Accreditation of Teacher Education accredits programs. Education administration degree programs include courses in school management, school law, school finance and budgeting, curriculum development and evaluation, research design and data analysis, community relations, politics in education, counseling, and leadership. Educational supervision degree programs include courses in supervision of instruction and curriculum, human relations, curriculum development, research, and advanced pedagogy courses.

Education administrators advance by moving up an administrative ladder or transferring to larger schools or systems. They also may become superintendent of a school system or president of an educational institution.

Job Outlook

Substantial competition is expected for prestigious jobs as higher education administrators. Many faculty and other staff meet the education and experience requirements for these jobs, and seek promotion. However, the number of openings is relatively small; only the most highly qualified are selected. Candidates who have the most formal education and who are willing to relocate should have the best job prospects.

On the other hand, it is becoming more difficult to attract candidates for principal, vice principal, and administration jobs at the elementary and secondary school level–competition for these jobs is declining. Many teachers no longer have an incentive to move into these positions since the pay is not significantly higher and does not compensate for the added workload and responsibility of the position. Also, site-based management has given teachers more decision-making responsibility in recent years, possibly satisfying their desire to move into administration.

Employment of education administrators is expected to grow about as fast as the average for all occupations over the 1996-2006 period. However, most job openings will result from the need to replace administrators who retire or transfer to other occupations.

School enrollments at the elementary, secondary, and postsecondary level are all expected to grow over the projection period. Rather than opening new schools, many existing school populations will expand, spurring demand for assistant principals to help with the increased workload. Employment of education administrators will also grow as more services are provided to students and as efforts to improve the quality of education continue.

However, budget constraints are expected to moderate growth in this profession. At the postsecondary level, some institutions have been reducing administrative staffs to contain costs. Some colleges are consolidating administrative jobs and contracting with other providers for some administrative functions.

Earnings

Salaries of education administrators vary according to position, level of responsibility and experience, and the size and location of the institution. Generally, principals employed in public schools earn higher salaries than those in private schools.

According to a survey of public schools, conducted by the Educational Research Service, average salaries for principals and assistant principals in the 1996-97 school year were as follows:

Principals:	
Elementary school	$62,900
Junior high/middle school	66,900
Senior high school	72,400
Assistant principals:	
Elementary school	$52,300
Junior high/middle school	56,500
Senior high school	59,700
Directors, managers, coordinators, and supervisors of instructional services	70,800

In 1995-96, according to the College and University Personnel Association, median annual salaries for selected administrators in higher education were as follows:

Academic deans:	
Medicine	$201,200
Law	141,400
Engineering	112,800
Arts and sciences	82,500
Business	81,000
Education	80,000
Social sciences	61,800
Mathematics	59,900
Student services directors:	
Admissions and registrar	$50,700
Student financial aid	45,400
Student activities	34,500

Related Occupations

Education administrators apply organizational and leadership skills to provide services to individuals. Workers in related occupations include health services administrators, social service agency administrators, recreation and park managers, museum directors, library directors, and professional and membership organization executives. Since principals and assistant principals generally have extensive teaching experience, their backgrounds are similar to those of teachers and many school counselors.

Sources of Additional Information

For information on elementary and secondary school principals, assistant principals, and central office administrators, contact:

❑ American Federation of School Administrators, 1729 21st St. NW, Washington, DC 20009.

❑ American Association of School Administrators, 1801 North Moore St., Arlington, VA 22209.

For information on elementary school principals and assistant principals, contact:

❏ The National Association of Elementary School Principals, 1615 Duke St., Alexandria, VA 22314-3483.

For information on secondary school principals and assistant principals, contact:

❏ The National Association of Secondary School Principals, 1904 Association Dr., Reston, VA 20191.

For information on college student affairs administrators, contact:

❏ National Association of Student Personnel Administrators, 1875 Connecticut Ave. NW, Suite 418, Washington, DC 20009-5728.

For information on collegiate registrars and admissions officers, contact:

❏ American Association of Collegiate Registrars and Admissions Officers, One Dupont Circle NW, Suite 330, Washington, DC 20036-1171.

Electrical and Electronics Engineers

(D.O.T. 003.061, .167 except -034 and -070, and .187)

Significant Points

✓ *A bachelor's degree in engineering is almost always required for beginning electrical and electronics engineering jobs. Good employment opportunities are expected for new graduates.*

✓ *Starting salaries are significantly higher than those of bachelor's degree graduates in other fields.*

✓ *Knowledge of technological advances must be acquired through continued study and education.*

Nature of the Work

Electrical and electronics engineers design, develop, test, and supervise the manufacture of electrical and electronic equipment. Electrical equipment includes power generating and transmission equipment used by electric utilities, and electric motors, machinery controls, and lighting and wiring in buildings, automobiles, and aircraft. Electronic equipment includes radar, computer hardware, and communications and video equipment.

The specialties of electrical and electronics engineers include several major areas—such as power generation, transmission, and distribution; communications; computer electronics; and electrical equipment manufacturing—or a subdivision of these areas—industrial robot control systems or aviation electronics, for example. Electrical and electronics engineers design new products, write performance requirements, and develop maintenance schedules. They also test equipment, solve operating problems, and estimate the time and cost of engineering projects.

Working Conditions

Most electrical and electronics engineers work in office buildings, laboratories, or industrial plants. Others spend a considerable amount of time outdoors at construction sites, where they monitor or direct operations or solve onsite problems. Some electrical and electronic engineers travel extensively to plants or worksites.

Most electrical and electronic engineers work a standard 40-hour week. At times, deadlines or design standards may bring extra pressure to a job. When this happens, engineers may work long hours and experience considerable stress.

Employment

Electrical and electronics engineers held about 367,000 jobs in 1996, making it the largest branch of engineering. Most jobs were in engineering and business consulting firms, manufacturers of electrical and electronic equipment, industrial machinery manufacturers, professional and scientific instruments, and government agencies. Communications and utilities firms, manufacturers of aircraft and guided missiles, and computer and data processing services firms accounted for most of the remaining jobs.

Training, Other Qualifications, and Advancement

A bachelor's degree in engineering is usually required for beginning engineering jobs. College graduates with a degree in a physical science or mathematics may occasionally qualify for some engineering jobs, especially in engineering specialties in high demand. Most engineering degrees are granted in electrical, mechanical, or civil engineering. However, engineers trained in one branch may work in related branches; for example, many aerospace engineers have training in mechanical engineering. This flexibility allows employers to meet staffing needs in new technologies and specialties in which engineers are in short supply. It also allows engineers to shift to fields with better employment prospects, or to ones that match their interests more closely.

In addition to the standard engineering degree, many colleges offer degrees in engineering technology, which are offered as either two- or four-year programs. These programs prepare students for practical design and production work rather than for jobs that require more theoretical, scientific and mathematical knowledge. Graduates of four-year technology programs may get jobs similar to those obtained by graduates with a bachelor's degree in engineering. Some employers regard them as having skills between those of a technician and an engineer.

Graduate training is essential for engineering faculty positions, but is not required for the majority of entry-level engineering jobs. Many engineers obtain graduate degrees in engineering or business administration to learn new technology, broaden their education, and enhance promotion opportunities. Many high-level executives in government and industry began their careers as engineers.

About 320 colleges and universities offer bachelor's degree programs in engineering that are accredited by the Accreditation Board for Engineering and Technology (ABET), and about 250 colleges offer accredited bachelor's degree programs in engineering technology. ABET accreditation is based on an examination of an engineering program's faculty, curricular content, facilities, and admissions standards. Although most institutions offer programs in the major branches of engineering, only a few offer some of the smaller specialties. Also, programs of the same title may vary in content. For example, some emphasize industrial practices, preparing students for a job in industry, while others are more theoretical and are better for students preparing to take graduate work. Therefore, students should investigate curricula and check accreditations carefully before selecting a college. Admissions requirements for undergraduate engineering schools include a solid background in mathematics (algebra, geometry, trigonometry, and calculus), sciences (biology, chemistry, and physics), and courses in English, social studies, humanities, and computers.

Bachelor's degree programs in engineering are typically designed to last four years, but many students find that it takes between four and five years to complete their studies. In a typical four-year college curriculum, the first two years are spent studying mathematics, basic sciences, introductory engineering, humanities, and social sciences. In the last two years, most courses are in engineering, usually with a concentration in one branch. For example, the last two years of an aerospace program might include courses such as fluid mechanics, heat transfer, applied aerodynamics, analytical mechanics, flight vehicle design, trajectory dynamics, and aerospace propulsion systems. Some programs offer a general engineering curriculum; students then specialize in graduate school or on the job.

Some engineering schools and two-year colleges have agreements whereby the two-year college provides the initial engineering education and the engineering school automatically admits students for their last two years. In addition, a few engineering schools have arrangements whereby a student spends three years in a liberal arts college studying pre-engineering subjects and two years in the engineering school, and receives a bachelor's degree from each. Some colleges and universities offer five-year master's degree programs. Some five- or even six-year cooperative plans combine classroom study and practical work, permitting students to gain valuable experience and finance part of their education.

All 50 states and the District of Columbia require registration for engineers whose work may affect life, health, or property, or who offer their services to the public. Registration generally requires a degree from an ABET-accredited engineering program, four years of relevant work experience, and passing a state examination. Some states will not register people with degrees in engineering technology. Engineers may be registered in several states.

Engineers should be creative, inquisitive, analytical, and detail-oriented. They should be able to work as part of a team and be able to communicate well, both orally and in writing.

Beginning engineering graduates usually work under the supervision of experienced engineers and, in larger companies, may also receive formal classroom or seminar-type training. As they gain knowledge and experience, they are assigned more difficult projects with greater independence to develop designs, solve problems, and make decisions. Engineers may advance to become technical specialists or to supervise a staff or team of engineers and technicians. Some eventually become engineering managers or enter other managerial, management support, or sales jobs.

Job Outlook

Job openings resulting from job growth and the need to replace electrical engineers who transfer to other occupations or leave the labor force should be sufficient to absorb the number of new graduates and other entrants, making for good employment opportunities through 2006. Employment of electrical and electronics engineers is expected to increase faster than the average for all occupations. The need for electronics manufacturers to invest heavily in research and development to remain competitive, will provide openings for graduates who have learned the latest technologies.

Increased demand by businesses and government for improved computers and communications equipment is expected to account for much of the projected employment growth. Consumer demand for electrical and electronic goods should create additional jobs. Job growth is expected to be fastest in non-manufacturing industries, however, because firms are increasingly getting electronic engineering expertise from consulting and service companies.

Engineers who fail to keep up with the rapid changes in technology in some specialties risk technological obsolescence, which makes them more susceptible to layoffs or, at a minimum, more likely to be passed over for advancement. Opportunities for electronics engineers in defense-related firms may improve as the trend shifts to upgrading existing aircraft and weapons systems with improved navigation, control, guidance, and targeting systems.

Earnings

Starting salaries for electrical and electronics engineers with the bachelor's degree are significantly higher than starting salaries of bachelor's degree graduates in other fields. According to the National Association of Colleges and Employers, starting salaries for those with the bachelor's degree in 1996 were about $39,513 in 1996.

The median annual salary for all electrical and electronics engineers who worked full-time in 1996 was $51,700.

The average annual salary for engineers in the federal government in nonsupervisory, supervisory, and managerial positions was $61,950 in 1997.

Related Occupations

Electrical and electronics engineers apply the principles of physical science and mathematics in their work. Other workers who use scientific and mathematical principles include engineering, science, and computer systems managers; physical, life, and computer scientists; mathematicians; engineering and science technicians; and architects.

Sources of Additional Information

High school students interested in obtaining general information on a variety of engineering disciplines should contact the Junior Engineering Technical Society by sending a self-addressed business-size envelope with six first-class stamps affixed, to:

❑ JETS-Guidance, at 1420 King St., Suite 405, Alexandria, VA 22314-2794. Homepage: http://www.asee.org/jets

High school students interested in obtaining information on ABET accredited engineering programs should contact:

❑ The Accreditation Board for Engineering and Technology, Inc., at 111 Market Place, Suite 1050, Baltimore, MD 21202-4012. Homepage: http://www.abet.ba.md.us

Non-high school students and those wanting more detailed information should contact:

❑ Institute of Electrical and Electronics Engineers, 1828 L St. NW, Suite 1202, Washington, DC 20036.

Electricians

(*D.O.T.* 729.381-018; 806.381-062; 822.361-018, -022; 824.261, .281-010, -018, .381, .681; 825.381-030, -034; 829.261-018; and 952.364 and .381)

Significant Points

- ✓ *Job opportunities are expected to be very good for qualified electricians.*
- ✓ *Most people acquire their skills by completing a formal four- or five-year apprenticeship program.*
- ✓ *In contrast to other construction trades, about a third of all electricians work in industries other than construction.*

Nature of the Work

Electricity is essential for light, power, air-conditioning, and refrigeration. Electricians install, connect, test, and maintain electrical systems for a variety of purposes, including climate control, security, and communications. They also may install and maintain the electronic controls for machines in business and industry. Although most electricians specialize in either construction or maintenance, a growing number do both.

Electricians work with blueprints when they install electrical systems in factories, office buildings, homes, and other structures. Blueprints indicate the location of circuits, outlets, load centers, panel boards, and other equipment. Electricians must follow the National Electric Code and comply with state and local building codes when they install these systems. In factories and offices, they first place conduit (pipe or tubing) inside designated partitions, walls, or other concealed areas. They also fasten to the wall small metal or plastic boxes that will house electrical switches and outlets. They then pull insulated wires or cables through the conduit to complete circuits between these boxes. In lighter construction, such as residential, plastic-covered wire usually is used rather than conduit.

Regardless of the type of wire used, electricians connect it to circuit breakers, transformers, or other components. Wires are joined by twisting ends together with pliers, and covering the ends with special plastic connectors. When stronger connections are required, electricians may use an electric "soldering gun" to melt metal onto the twisted wires, which they then cover with durable electrical tape. When the wiring is finished, they test the circuits for proper connections.

In addition to wiring a building's electrical system, electricians may install coaxial or fiber optic cable for computers and other telecommunications equipment. A growing number of electricians install telephone and computer wiring and equipment. They also may connect motors to electrical power and install electronic controls for industrial equipment.

Maintenance work varies greatly, depending on where the electrician is employed. Electricians who specialize in residential work may rewire a home and replace an old fuse box with a new circuit breaker to accommodate additional appliances. Those who work in large factories may repair motors, transformers, generators, and electronic controllers on machine tools and industrial robots. Those in office buildings and small plants may repair all types of electrical equipment.

Maintenance electricians spend much of their time in preventive maintenance. They periodically inspect equipment, and locate and correct problems before breakdowns occur. Electricians may also advise management on whether continued operation of equipment could be hazardous or not. When needed, they install new electrical equipment. When breakdowns occur, they must make the necessary repairs as quickly as possible in order to minimize inconvenience. Electricians may replace items such as circuit breakers, fuses, switches, electrical and electronic components, or wire. When working with complex electronic devices, they may work with engineers, engineering technicians, or industrial machinery repairers.

Electricians use hand tools such as screwdrivers, pliers, knives, and hacksaws. They also use power tools and testing equipment such as oscilloscopes, ammeters, and test lamps.

Working Conditions

Electricians' work is sometimes strenuous. They may stand for long periods of time and frequently work on ladders and scaffolds. They often work in awkward or cramped positions. Electricians risk injury from electrical shock, falls, and cuts; to avoid injuries, they must follow strict safety procedures. Some electricians may have to travel to job sites, which may be up to 100 miles away.

Most electricians work a standard 40-hour week, although overtime may be required. Those in maintenance work may have to work nights, on weekends, and be on call. Companies that operate 24 hours a day may employ three shifts of electricians. Generally, the first shift is primarily responsible for routine maintenance, while the other shifts perform preventive maintenance.

Employment

Electricians held about 575,000 jobs in 1996. More than half were employed in the construction industry. Others worked as maintenance electricians and were employed in virtually every industry. In addition, about one out of ten electricians was self-employed.

Because of the widespread need for electrical services, jobs for electricians are found in all parts of the country.

Training, Other Qualifications, and Advancement

Most people learn the electrical trade by completing a four- or five-year apprenticeship program. Apprenticeship gives trainees a thorough knowledge of all aspects of the trade and generally improves their ability to find a job. Although more electricians are trained through apprenticeship than workers in other construction trades, some still learn their skills informally, on the job.

Large apprenticeship programs are usually sponsored by joint training committees made up of local unions of the International Brotherhood of Electrical Workers, and local chapters of the National Electrical Contractors Association. Training may also be provided by company management committees of individual electrical contracting companies and by local chapters of the Associated Builders and Contractors and the Independent Electrical Contractors. Because of the comprehensive training received, those who complete apprenticeship programs qualify to do both maintenance and construction work.

The typical large apprenticeship program provides at least 144 hours of classroom instruction each year, and 8,000 hours of on-the-job training over the course of the apprenticeship. In the classroom, apprentices learn blueprint reading, electrical theory, electronics, mathematics, electrical code requirements, and safety and first aid practices. They also receive specialized training in welding and communications and fire alarm systems. On the job, under the supervision of experienced electricians, apprentices must demonstrate mastery of the electrician's work. At first, they drill holes, set anchors, and set up conduit. Later, they measure, fabricate, and install conduit, as well as install, connect, and test wiring, outlets, and switches. They also learn to set up and draw diagrams for entire electrical systems.

Those who do not enter a formal apprenticeship program can begin to learn the trade informally by working as helpers for experienced electricians. While learning to install conduit, connect wires, and test circuits, helpers are also taught safety practices. Many helpers supplement this training with trade school or correspondence courses.

Regardless of how one learns the trade, previous training is very helpful. High school courses in mathematics, electricity, electronics, mechanical drawing, science, and shop provide a good background. Special training offered in the Armed Forces and by postsecondary technical schools also is beneficial. All applicants should be in good health and have at least average physical strength. Agility and dexterity also are important. Good color vision is needed because workers must frequently identify electrical wires by color.

Most apprenticeship sponsors require applicants for apprentice positions to be at least 18 years old and have a high school diploma or its equivalent. For those interested in becoming maintenance electricians, a background in electronics is increasingly important because of the growing use of complex electronic controls on manufacturing equipment.

Most localities require electricians to be licensed. Although licensing requirements vary from area to area, electricians generally must pass an examination that tests their knowledge of electrical theory, the National Electrical Code, and local electric and building codes.

Electricians periodically take courses offered by their employer or union to keep abreast of changes in the National Electrical Code, materials, or methods of installation.

Experienced electricians can become supervisors and then superintendents. Those with sufficient capital and management skills may start their own contracting business, although this may require an electrical contractor's license.

Job Outlook

Job opportunities for skilled electricians are expected to be very good as the growth in demand outpaces the supply of workers trained in this craft. There is expected to be a shortage of skilled workers during the next decade because of the anticipated smaller pool of young workers entering training programs.

Employment of electricians is expected to increase more slowly than the average for all occupations through the year 2006. As the population and economy grow, more electricians will be needed to install and maintain electrical devices and wiring in homes, factories, offices, and other structures. New technologies also are expected to continue to stimulate the demand for these workers. Increasingly, buildings will be prewired during construction to accommodate use of computers and telecommunications equipment. More and more factories will be using robots and automated manufacturing systems. Installation of this equipment, which is expected to increase, should also stimulate demand for electricians. Additional jobs will be created by rehabilitation and retrofitting of existing structures.

In addition to jobs created by increased demand for electrical work, many openings will occur each year as electricians transfer to other occupations, retire, or leave the labor force for other reasons. Because of their lengthy training and relatively high earnings, a smaller proportion of electricians than other craft workers leave their occupation each year. The number of retirements is expected to rise, however, as more electricians reach retirement age.

Employment of construction electricians, like that of many other construction workers, is sensitive to changes in the economy. This results from the limited duration of construction projects and the cyclical nature of the construction industry. During economic downturns, job openings for electricians are reduced as the level of construction declines. Apprenticeship opportunities also are less plentiful during these periods.

Although employment of maintenance electricians is steadier than that of construction electricians, those working in the automotive and other manufacturing industries that are sensitive to cyclical swings in the economy may be laid off during recessions. Also, efforts to reduce operating costs and increase productivity through the increased use of contracting out for electrical services may limit opportunities for maintenance electricians in many industries. However, this should be partially offset by increased demand by electrical contracting firms.

Job opportunities for electricians also vary by geographic area. Employment opportunities follow the movement of people and businesses among states and local areas, and reflect differences in local economic conditions. The number of job opportunities in a given year may fluctuate widely from area to area. Some parts of the country may experience an oversupply of electricians, for example, while others may have a shortage.

Earnings

Median weekly earnings for full-time electricians who were not self-employed were $620 in 1996. The middle 50 percent earned between $468 and $8140 weekly. The lowest 10 percent earned less than $339, while the highest 10 percent earned more than $1,018 a week.

According to a survey of workplaces in 160 metropolitan areas, maintenance electricians had median hourly earnings of $18.78 in 1995. The middle half earned between $15.23 and $21.83 an hour. Annual earnings of electricians also tend to be higher than those of other building trades workers because electricians are less affected by the seasonal nature of construction.

Depending on experience, apprentices usually start at between 30 and 50 percent of the rate paid to experienced electricians. As they become more skilled, they receive periodic increases throughout the course of the apprenticeship program. Many employers also provide training opportunities for experienced electricians to improve their skills.

Many construction electricians are members of the International Brotherhood of Electrical Workers. Among unions organizing maintenance electricians are the International Brotherhood of Electrical Workers; the International Union of Electronic, Electrical, Salaried, Machine, and Furniture Workers; the International Association of Machinists and Aerospace Workers; the International Union, United Automobile, Aerospace and Agricultural Implement Workers of America; and the United Steelworkers of America.

Related Occupations

To install and maintain electrical systems, electricians combine manual skill and a knowledge of electrical materials and concepts. Workers in other occupations involving similar skills include air-conditioning mechanics, cable installers and repairers, electronics mechanics, and elevator constructors.

Sources of Additional Information

For details about apprenticeships or other work opportunities in this trade, contact offices of the state employment service, the state apprenticeship agency, local electrical contractors or firms that employ maintenance electricians, or local union-management electrician apprenticeship committees. This information may also be available from local chapters of the Independent Electrical Contractors, Inc.; the National Electrical Contractors Association; the Home Builders Institute; the Associated Builders and Contractors; and the International Brotherhood of Electrical Workers.

For general information about the work of electricians, contact:

❑ Independent Electrical Contractors, Inc., 507 Wythe St., Alexandria, VA 22314.

❑ National Electrical Contractors Association (NECA), 3 Metro Center, Suite 1100, Bethesda, MD 20814.

❑ International Brotherhood of Electrical Workers (IBEW), 1125 15th St. NW, Washington, DC 20005.

❑ Associated Builders and Contractors, 1300 North 17th St., Rosslyn, VA 22209.

❑ Homebuilders Institute, National Association of Home Builders, 1201 15th St. NW, Washington, DC 20005.

Electroneurodiagnostic Technologists

(D.O.T. 078.362-022 and -042)

Significant Points

✓ *Although faster than average employment growth is expected, relatively few job openings will be created because the occupation is small.*

✓ *Most technologists learn on the job, but opportunities should be best for technologists with formal postsecondary training.*

Nature of the Work

Electroneurodiagnostic technologists use instruments such as an electroencephalograph (EEG) machine, to record electrical impulses transmitted by the brain and the nervous system. They help physicians diagnose brain tumors, strokes, toxic/metabolic disorders, epilepsy and sleep disorders. They also measure the effects of infectious diseases on the brain, as well as determine whether individuals with mental or behavioral problems have an organic impairment such as Alzheimer's disease. Furthermore, they determine "cerebral" death, the absence of brain activity, and assess the probability of recovery from a coma.

Electroneurodiagnostic technologists who specialize in basic or "resting" EEGs are called EEG technologists. The range of tests performed by electroneurodiagnostic technologists is broader than, but includes, those conducted by EEG technologists. Because it provides a more accurate description of work typically performed in the field, the title electroneurodiagnostic technologists generally has replaced that of EEG technologist.

Electroneurodiagnostic technologists take patients' medical histories and help them relax, then apply electrodes to designated spots on the patient's head. They must choose the most appropriate combination of instrument controls and electrodes to correct for mechanical or electrical interferences that come from somewhere other than the brain, such as eye movement or radiation from electrical sources.

Increasingly, technologists perform EEGs in the operating room, which requires that they understand anesthesia's effect on brain waves. For special procedure EEGs, technologists may secure electrodes to the chest, arm, leg, or spinal column to record activity from both the central and peripheral nervous systems.

In ambulatory monitoring, technologists monitor the brain, and sometimes the heart, while patients carry out normal activities over a 24-hour period. They then remove the small recorder carried by the patients and obtain a readout. Technologists review the readouts, selecting sections for the physician to examine.

Using "evoked potential" testing, technologists measure sensory and physical responses to specific stimuli. After the electrodes have been attached, they set the instrument for the type and intensity of the stimulus, increase the intensity until the patient reacts, and note the sensation level. The tests may take from one to four hours.

For nerve conduction tests, used to diagnose muscle and nerve problems, technologists place electrodes on the patient's skin over a nerve and over the muscle. Then they stimulate the nerve with an electrical current and record how long it takes the nerve impulse to reach the muscle.

Technologists who specialize in and administer sleep disorder studies are called polysomnographic technologists. The sleep studies are conducted in a clinic called a "sleep center." During the procedure, technologists monitor the patient's respiration and heart activity in addition to brain wave activity and must know the dynamics of the cardiopulmonary systems during each stage of sleep. They coordinate readings from several organ systems, separating them according to the stages of sleep, and relay them to the physician. For quantitative EEGs, technologists decide which sections of the EEG should be transformed into color-coded pictures of brain wave frequency and intensity, for interpretation by a physician. They may also write technical reports summarizing test results.

Technologists also look for changes in the patient's neurologic, cardiac, and respiratory status, which may indicate an emergency, such as a heart attack, and provide emergency care until help arrives.

Electroneurodiagnostic technologists may have supervisory or administrative responsibilities. They may manage an eletroneurodiagnostic laboratory, arrange work schedules, keep records, schedule appointments, order supplies, provide instruction to less experienced technologists, and may also be responsible for the equipment's upkeep.

Working Conditions

Electroneurodiagnostic technologists usually work in clean, well-lighted surroundings, and spend about half of their time on their feet. Bending and lifting are necessary because they may work with patients who are very ill and require assistance. Technologists employed in hospitals may do all their work in a single room, or may push equipment to a patient's bedside and obtain recordings there.

Most technologists work a standard workweek, although those in hospitals may be on call evenings, weekends, and holidays. Those performing sleep studies usually work evenings and nights.

Employment

Electroneurodiagnostic technologists held more than 6,400 jobs in 1996. Most worked in neurology laboratories of hospitals, while others worked in offices and clinics of neurologists and neurosurgeons, sleep centers, and psychiatric facilities.

Training, Other Qualifications, and Advancement

Although most electroneurodiagnostic technologists currently employed learned their skills on the job, employers are beginning to favor those who have completed formal training. Some hospitals require applicants for trainee positions to have postsecondary training while others only expect a high school diploma. Recommended high school and college subjects for prospective technologists include health, biology, anatomy and mathematics. Often, on-the-job trainees are transfers from other hospital jobs, such as licensed practical nurses.

Formal postsecondary training is offered in hospitals and community colleges. In 1996, the Joint Review Committee on Education in Electroneurodiagnostic Technology had approved 11 formal programs. Programs usually last from one to two years, and include laboratory experience as well as classroom instruction in human anatomy and physiology, neurology, neuroanatomy, neurophysiology, medical terminology, computer technology, electronics, and instrumentation. Graduates receive associate degrees or certificates.

The American Board of Registration of Electroencephalographic and Evoked Potential Technologists awards the credential "Registered EEG Technologist," "Registered Evoked Potential Technologist," and "Certificate in Neurophysiologic Intraoperative Monitoring" to qualified applicants. The Association of Polysomnographic Technologists registers polysomnographic technologists. Applicants interested in taking the registration exam must have worked in a sleep center for at least one year. Although not generally required for staff level jobs, registration indicates professional competence, and is usually necessary for supervisory or teaching jobs. In addition, the American Association of Electrodiagnostic Technologists provides certification in the field of nerve conduction studies for electroneurodiagnostic technologists.

Technologists should have manual dexterity, good vision, writing skills, an aptitude for working with electronic equipment, and the ability to work with patients as well as with other health personnel.

Experienced electroneurodiagnostic technologists can advance to chief or manager of a electroneurodiagnostic laboratory. Chief technologists are generally supervised by a physician—an electroencephalographer, neurologist, or neurosurgeon. Technologists may also teach or go into research.

Job Outlook

Job prospects for qualified applicants are expected to be good. Employment of electroneurodiagnostic technologists is expected to grow faster than the average for all occupations through the year 2006, reflecting the increased numbers of neurodiagnostic tests performed. There will be more testing as new procedures are developed and as the size of the population grows. A very low number of openings each year are expected, however, because the occupation is very small. Most jobs will be found in hospitals, but growth will be fastest in offices and clinics of neurologists.

Earnings

According to a Hay Group survey of acute care hospitals, the median annual base salary of full-time EEG technologists was $26,800 in January 1997. The middle 50 percent earned between $23,200 and $30,100.

Related Occupations

Other health personnel who operate medical equipment include radiologic technologists, nuclear medicine technologists, sonographers, perfusionists, and cardiovascular technologists.

Sources of Additional Information

Local hospitals can supply information about employment opportunities.

For general information about a career in electroneurodiagnostics, as well as a list of accredited training programs, contact:

❑ Executive Office, American Society of Electroneurodiagnostic Technologists, Inc., 204 W. 7th St., Carroll, IA 51401. Homepage: http://www.aset.org/

For information on work in sleep studies, contact:

❑ Association of Polysomnographic Technology, 2025 South Washington, Suite 300, Lansing, MI 48910-0817.

Information about specific accredited training programs is also available from:

❑ Joint Review Committee on Electroneurodiagnostic Technology, Route 1, Box 63A, Genoa, WI 54632.

Information on becoming a registered Electroneurodiagnostic technologist is available from:

❑ American Board of Registration of Electroencephalgraphic and Evoked Potential Technologists, P.O. Box 916633, Longwood, FL 32791-6633.

Information on certification in the field of nerve conduction studies is available from:

❑ American Association of Electrodiagnostic Technologists, 35 Hallett Lane, Chatham, MA 02633-2408.

Electronic Equipment Repairers

(D.O.T. codes are too numerous to list.)

Significant Points

✓ *Most employers prefer to hire persons who have completed one- or two-year formal training programs in electronics.*

✓ *Although overall employment of electronic equipment repairers is projected to increase slowly, employment of computer and office machine repairers should increase rapidly while electronic home entertainment equipment repairer and telephone installer and repairer jobs should decline.*

Nature of the Work

Electronic equipment repairers, also called service technicians or field service representatives, install, maintain, and repair electronic equipment used in offices, factories, homes, hospitals, aircraft, and other places. Equipment includes televisions, radar, industrial equipment controls, computers, telephone systems, and medical diagnosing equipment. Repairers have numerous job titles, which often refer to the kind of equipment with which they work.

Electronic repairers install, test, repair, and calibrate equipment to ensure it functions properly. They keep detailed records on each piece of equipment to provide a history of tests, performance problems, and repairs.

When equipment breaks down, repairers first examine work orders, which indicate problems, or talk to equipment operators. Then they check for common causes of trouble, such as loose connections or obviously defective components. If routine checks do not locate the trouble, repairers may refer to schematics and manufacturers' specifications that show connections and provide instruction on how to locate problems. They use voltmeters, ohmmeters, signal generators, ammeters, and oscilloscopes, and run diagnostic programs to pinpoint malfunctions. It may take several hours to locate a problem, but only a few minutes to fix it. However, more equipment now has self-diagnosing features, which greatly simplifies the work. To fix equipment, repairers may replace defective components, circuit boards, or wiring, or adjust and calibrate equipment, using test equipment, small hand tools such as pliers, screwdrivers, and soldering irons.

Field repairers visit worksites in their assigned area on a regular basis to do preventive maintenance according to manufacturers' recommended schedules and whenever emergencies arise. During these calls, repairers may also advise customers on how to use equipment more efficiently and how to spot problems in their early stages. They also listen to customers' complaints and answer questions, promoting customer satisfaction and good will. Some field repairers work full-time with a lot of equipment at the clients' establishment.

Bench repairers work at repair facilities, in stores, factories, or service centers. They repair portable equipment—such as televisions and personal computers brought in by customers—or defective components and machines requiring extensive repairs that have been sent in by field repairers. They determine the source of a problem in the equipment, and may estimate whether it is wiser to buy a new part or machine, or to fix the broken one.

Working Conditions

Some electronic equipment repairers work shifts, including weekends and holidays, to service equipment in computer centers, manufacturing plants, hospitals, and telephone companies operating round the clock. Shifts are generally assigned on the basis of seniority. Repairers may also be on call at any time to handle equipment failure.

Repairers generally work in clean, well-lighted, air-conditioned surroundings—an electronic repair shop or service center, hospital, military installation, or a telephone company's central office. However, some, such as commercial and industrial electronic equipment repairers, may be exposed to heat, grease, and noise on factory floors. Some may occasionally have to work in cramped spaces. Telephone installers and repairers may work on rooftops, ladders, and telephone poles.

The work of most repairers involves lifting, reaching, stooping, crouching, and crawling. Adherence to safety precautions is essential to guard against work hazards such as minor burns and electrical shock.

Employment

Electronic equipment repairers held about 396,000 jobs in 1996. Many worked for telephone companies. Others worked for electronic and transportation equipment manufacturers, machinery and equipment wholesalers, hospitals, electronic repair shops, and firms that provide maintenance under contract (called third-party maintenance firms). The distribution of employment by occupation was as follows:

Computer and office machine repairers	141,000
Communications equipment mechanics	116,000
Commercial and industrial electronic equipment repairers	60,000
Telephone installers and repairers	37,000
Electronic home entertainment equipment repairers	33,000

Training, Other Qualifications, and Advancement

Most employers prefer applicants with formal training in electronics. Electronic training is offered by public post secondary vocational-technical schools, private vocational schools and technical institutes, junior and community colleges, and some high schools and correspondence schools. Programs take one to two years. The military services also offer formal training and work experience.

Training includes general courses in mathematics, physics, electricity, electronics, schematic reading, and troubleshooting. Students also choose courses which prepare them for a specialty, such as computers, commercial and industrial equipment, or home entertainment equipment. A few repairers complete formal apprenticeship programs sponsored jointly by employers and local chapters of the International Brotherhood of Electrical Workers.

Applicants for entry-level jobs may have to pass tests measuring mechanical aptitude, knowledge of electricity or electronics, manual dexterity, and general intelligence. Newly hired repairers, even those with formal training, usually receive some training from their employer. They may study electronics and circuit theory and math. They also get hands-on experience with equipment, doing basic maintenance and using diagnostic programs to locate malfunctions. Training may be in a classroom or it may be self-instruction, consisting of videotapes, programmed computer software, or workbooks that allow trainees to learn at their own pace.

Experienced technicians attend training sessions and read manuals to keep up with design changes and revised service procedures. Many technicians also take advanced training in a particular system or type of repair.

Good eyesight and color vision are needed to inspect and work on small, delicate parts and good hearing to detect malfunctions revealed by sound. Because field repairers usually handle jobs alone, they must be able to work without close supervision. For those who have frequent contact with customers, a pleasant personality, neat appearance, and good communications skills are important. Repairers must also be trustworthy, because they may be exposed to money and other valuables in places such as banks and securities offices, and some employers require that they be bonded. A security clearance may be required for technicians who repair equipment or service machines in areas in which people are engaged in activities related to national security.

The International Society of Certified Electronics Technicians and the Electronics Technicians Association each administer a voluntary certification program. In both, an electronics repairer with four years of experience may become a Certified Electronics Technician. Certification, which is by examination, is offered in computer, radio-TV, industrial and commercial equipment, audio, avionics, wireless communications, video distribution, satellite, and radar systems repair. An Associate Level Test, covering basic electronics, is offered for students or repairers with less than four years of experience. An A+ certification is now desired for computer technicians. This certification is awarded by the Computing Technology Industry Association (CompTIA) and requires knowledge of specific products manufactured by the vendor. The Telecommunications Act of 1996 eliminated the requirement of an FCC license for those who repair radio transmitting equipment.

Experienced repairers with advanced training may become specialists or troubleshooters who help other repairers diagnose difficult problems, or work with engineers in designing equipment and developing maintenance procedures.

Because of their familiarity with equipment, repairers are particularly well qualified to become manufacturers' sales workers. Workers with leadership ability also may become maintenance supervisors or service managers. Some experienced workers open their own repair services or shops, or become wholesalers or retailers of electronic equipment.

Job Outlook

Overall, employment of electronic equipment repairers is expected to grow slower than the average for all occupations through the year 2006. Although the amount of electronic equipment in use will grow very rapidly, improvements in product reliability and ease of service and lower equipment prices will dampen the need for repairers. The following tabulation presents the expected job change, in percent, for the various electronic equipment repairer occupations:

Computer and office machine repairers	37
Commercial and industrial electronic equipment repairers	12
Communications equipment mechanics	4
Electronic home entertainment equipment repairers	-19
Telephone installers and repairers	-74

Employment of computer equipment repairers will grow much faster the than average for all occupations through the year 2006 as the number of computers in service increases rapidly. Employment of commercial and industrial equipment repairers outside the federal government will increase faster than the average as the amount of equipment grows. Mainly because of cuts in the defense budget, their employment in the federal government will decline. Employment of those who repair electronic home entertainment equipment will decline as equipment becomes more reliable and easier to ser-

vice. Telephone installer jobs are expected to decline sharply, and communication equipment mechanics are expected to grow slower than the average because of improvements in the telephone equipment reliability, ease of maintenance, and low equipment replacement cost.

Earnings

In 1996, median weekly earnings of full-time electronic equipment repairers were $619. The middle 50 percent earned between $444 and $802. The bottom 10 percent earned less than $329, while the top 10 percent earned more than $979. Median weekly earnings varied widely by occupation and the type of equipment repaired, as follows:

Telephone installers and repairers	$717
Electronic repairers, communications and industrial equipment	602
Office machine repairers	582
Data processing equipment repairers	573

Central office installers, central office technicians, PBX installers, and telephone installers and repairers employed by AT&T and the Bell Operating Companies and represented by the Communications Workers of America and the International Brotherhood of Electrical Workers, earned between $279 and $962 a week in 1996.

According to a survey of workplaces in 160 metropolitan areas, beginning maintenance electronics technicians had median earnings of $11.50 an hour in 1995, with the middle half earning between $10.50 and $13.25 an hour. The most experienced repairers had median earnings of $20.13 an hour, with the middle half earning between $18.24 and $22.12 an hour.

Related Occupations

Workers in other occupations who repair and maintain the circuits and mechanical parts of electronic equipment include appliance and power tool repairers, automotive electricians, broadcast technicians, electronic organ technicians, and vending machine repairers. Electronics engineering technicians may also repair electronic equipment as part of their duties.

Sources of Additional Information

For career, and certification information, contact:
- ❏ The International Society of Certified Electronics Technicians, 2708 West Berry St., Fort Worth, TX 76109.

For certification, career, and placement information, contact:
- ❏ Electronics Technicians Association, 602 North Jackson, Greencastle, IN 46135.

For information on the telephone industry and career opportunities contact:
- ❏ United States Telephone Association, 1401 H St. NW, Suite 600, Washington, DC 20005-2136.
- ❏ International Brotherhood of Electrical Workers, Telecommunications Department, 1125 15th. St. NW, Room 807, Washington, DC 20005.

For information on electronic equipment repairers in the telephone industry, write to:
- ❏ Communications Workers of America, Department of Apprenticeships, Benefits, and Employment, 501 3rd St. NW, Washington, DC 20001.

Emergency Medical Technicians

(D.O.T. 079.364-026 and .374-010)

Significant Points

✓ *Employment should grow rapidly as paid emergency medical technician positions replace unpaid volunteers.*

✓ *Competition is expected for the best paying jobs with rescue squads and police and fire departments.*

✓ *Depending on state requirements, as little as 110 to 120 hours of formal training is needed to qualify for jobs.*

Nature of the Work

Automobile accident injuries, heart attacks, near drownings, unscheduled childbirths, poisonings, and gunshot wounds all demand urgent medical attention. Emergency medical technicians (EMTs) give immediate care and often transport the sick or injured to medical facilities.

Following instructions from a dispatcher, EMTs—who usually work in teams of two—drive specially equipped vehicles to the scene of emergencies. If necessary, they request additional help from police or fire department personnel. They determine the nature and extent of the patient's injuries or illness while also trying to determine whether the patient has epilepsy, diabetes, or other preexisting medical conditions. Following strict guidelines, EMTs employ procedures they are certified to use to give appropriate emergency care. All EMTs, including those with basic skills—the EMT-Basic—may open airways, restore breathing, control bleeding, treat for shock, administer oxygen, immobilize fractures, bandage wounds, assist in childbirth, manage emotionally disturbed patients, treat and assist heart attack victims, give initial care to poison and burn victims, and use automated external defibrillators to assist in the care of patients experiencing cardiac arrest.

EMT-Intermediates have more advanced training that allows them to administer intravenous fluids; use manual defibrillators to give lifesaving shocks to a stopped heart, use advanced airway techniques and equipment to assist patient's experiencing respiratory emergencies, as well as use other intensive care procedures.

EMT-Paramedics provide the most extensive pre-hospital care. In addition to the procedures already described, paramedics may administer drugs orally and intravenously, interpret eletrocardiograms (EKGs), perform endotracheal intubations, and use monitors and other complex equipment.

When victims are trapped, as in the case of an automobile accident, cave-in, or building collapse, EMTs free them or provide emergency care while others free them. Some conditions are simple enough to be handled following general rules and guidelines. More complicated problems can only be carried out under the step-by-step direction of medical personnel by radio contact.

When transporting patients to a medical facility, EMTs may use special equipment such as backboards, to immobilize them before placing them on stretchers and securing them in the ambulance. While one EMT drives, the other monitors the patient's vital signs and gives additional care as needed. Some EMTs work for hospital trauma centers or jurisdictions which use helicopters to transport critically ill or injured patients.

At a medical facility, EMTs transfer patients to the emergency department, report to the staff their observations and the care they provided, and help provide emergency treatment.

In rural areas, some EMT-Paramedics are trained to treat patients with minor injuries on the scene of an accident or at their home without transporting them to a medical facility.

After each run, EMTs replace used supplies and check equipment. If patients have had a contagious disease, EMTs decontaminate the interior of the ambulance and report cases to the proper authorities.

Working Conditions

EMTs work both indoors and outdoors, in all types of weather. Much of their time is spent standing, kneeling, bending, and lifting. They may risk noise-induced hearing loss from ambulance sirens and back injuries from lifting patients. EMTs may be exposed to diseases such as Hepatitis-B and AIDS, as well as violence from drug overdose victims or psychological emergencies. The work is not only physically strenuous, but stressful—not surprising in a job that involves life-or-death situations. Nonetheless, many people find the work exciting and challenging.

EMTs employed by fire departments often have about a 50-hour workweek. Those employed by hospitals frequently work between 45 and 60 hours a week, and those in private ambulance services, between 45 and 50 hours. Some EMTs, especially those in police and fire departments, are on call for extended periods. Because emergency services function 24 hours a day, EMTs have irregular working hours that add to job stress.

Employment

EMTs held about 150,000 jobs in 1996. About two-fifths were in private ambulance services; a third were in municipal fire, police, or rescue squad departments; and a quarter were in hospitals. In addition, there are many volunteer EMTs. Most paid EMTs work in metropolitan areas. In many smaller cities, towns, and rural areas, there are more volunteer positions than paid EMT jobs.

Training, Other Qualifications, and Advancement

Formal training is needed to become an EMT. Training is offered at three progressive levels— EMT-Basic, EMT-Intermediate, and EMT-paramedic—and fully qualified technicians complete all three programs. In some cases, First Responder training programs that provide emergency medical basics for firefighters, police officers, and others whose jobs make them likely to be the first persons to arrive at an incident scene may qualify individuals for entry-level jobs. However, continued employment requires completion of EMT training. EMT training is available in all 50 states and the District of Columbia, and is offered by police, fire, and health departments; in hospitals; and as nondegree courses in colleges and universities. In addition to EMT training, EMTs in fire and police departments must be qualified as firefighters or police officers.

The EMT-Basic is the minimum training needed to qualify for an emergency medical technician job. EMT-Basic training is 110 to 120 hours of classroom work plus ten hours of internship in a hospital emergency room. The program provides instruction and practice in dealing with bleeding, fractures, airway obstruction, cardiac arrest, and emergency childbirth. Students learn to use and care for common emergency equipment, such as backboards, suction devices, splints, oxygen delivery systems, and stretchers. Graduates of approved EMT-Basic training programs who pass a written and practical examination administered by the state certifying agency or the National Registry of Emergency Medical Technicians earn the title of Registered EMT-Basic.

EMT-Intermediate training requirements vary from state to state, but typically include 35-55 hours of additional instruction beyond EMT-Basic and cover patient assessment as well as the use of advanced airway devices, and intravenous fluids. Prerequisites for taking the EMT-Intermediate examination include registration as an EMT-Basic, required classroom work, and a specified amount of clinical experience and field internship.

Most graduates of EMT-Intermediate programs continue their education and receive the EMT-Paramedic certification. EMT-Paramedic training programs generally last between 750 and 2,000 hours. Due to this strenuous training requirement, most EMT-Paramedics are in paid positions. Refresher courses and continuing education are available for EMTs at all levels.

In most state's, registration for EMT-Paramedics by the National Registry of Emergency Medical Technicians or a state emergency medical services agency requires current registration or state certification as an EMT-Basic, completion of an EMT-Paramedic training program and required clinical and field internships, as well as passing a written and practical examination. Although not a general requirement for employment, registration acknowledges an EMT's qualifications and makes higher paying jobs easier to obtain.

All 50 states possess a certification procedure. In 38 states and the District of Columbia, registration with the National Registry is required at some or all levels of certification. Other states require their own certification examination or provide the option of taking the National Registry examination.

To maintain their certification, all EMTs must reregister, usually every two years. In order to reregister, an individual must be working as an EMT and meet a continuing education requirement.

Applicants to an EMT training course generally must be at least 18 years old and have a valid driver's license. Recommended high school subjects for prospective EMTs are driver education, health, and science. First aid training in the Armed Forces is also good preparation.

EMTs should be emotionally stable, have good dexterity, agility, and physical coordination, and be able to lift and carry heavy loads. EMTs need good eyesight (corrective lenses may be used) with accurate color vision.

Advancement beyond the EMT-Paramedic level usually means leaving fieldwork. An EMT-Paramedic can become a supervisor, operations manager, administrative director, or executive director of emergency services. Some EMTs become EMT instructors, firefighters, dispatchers, or physicians assistants, while others move into sales or marketing of emergency medical equipment. Finally, some become EMTs to assess their interest in health care and then decide to return to school and become registered nurses, physicians, or other health workers.

Job Outlook

Competition for jobs will be keen in fire, police, and rescue squad departments because of attractive pay and benefits and good job security. Opportunities for EMTs are expected to be excellent in hospitals and private ambulance services, where pay and benefits usually are low.

Employment of EMTs is expected to grow much faster than average for all occupations through the year 2006. Much of this growth will occur as positions change from volunteer to paid positions. Also driving the growth will be an expanding population, particularly in older age groups that are the greatest users of emergency medical services. Additional job openings will occur as more states begin to allow EMT-Paramedics to perform primary care on the scene without transporting the patient to a medical facility.

Many job openings will occur because of this occupation's substantial replacement needs. Turnover is quite high, reflecting this occupation's stressful working conditions, limited advancement potential, and the modest pay and benefits in the private sector.

Earnings

Earnings of EMTs depend on the employment setting and geographic location as well as the individual's training and experience. According the 1996 Journal of Emergency Medical Services salary survey, average salaries were $25,051 for EMT- Basic, and $30,407 for EMT-Paramedic. EMTs working in fire departments command the highest salaries, as the accompanying table shows.

Table 1: Average annual salaries of emergency medical technicians, by type of employer, 1996

Employer	EMT-Basic	EMT-Paramedic
All employees	$25,051	$30,407
Fire departments	29,859	32,483
Hospital based	18,686	28,373
Private ambulance services	18,617	23,995

Source: Journal of Emergency Medical Services

Those in emergency medical services who are part of fire or police departments receive the same benefits as firefighters or police officers.

Related Occupations

Other workers in occupations that require quick and level-headed reactions to life-or-death situations are police officers, firefighters, air traffic controllers, workers in other health occupations, and members of the Armed Forces.

Sources of Additional Information

Information concerning training courses, registration, and job opportunities for EMTs can be obtained by writing to the State Emergency Medical Service Director.

General information about EMTs is available from:

❑ National Association of Emergency Medical Technicians, 408 Monroe., Clinton, MS 39056.

❑ National Registry of Emergency Medical Technicians, P.O. Box 29233, Columbus, OH 43229.

Employment Interviewers

(D.O.T. 166.267-010)

Significant Points

- ✓ *Sales ability is required to succeed in personnel supply services firms, where most employment interviewers are found.*
- ✓ *Employment growth reflects expansion of personnel supply particularly temporary help firms.*

Nature of the Work

Whether you are looking for a job or trying to fill one, you could find yourself turning to an employment interviewer for help. Sometimes called personnel consultants, human resources coordinators, personnel development specialists, or employment brokers, among other job titles, these workers help job seekers find employment and help employers find qualified employees.

Working largely in private personnel supply firms or state employment security offices (also known as job or employment service centers), employment interviewers act as brokers, putting together the best combination of applicant and job. To accomplish this, they obtain information from employers as well as job seekers.

A private industry employment interviewer is a salesperson. Counselors pool together a group of qualified applicants and try to sell them to many different companies. Often a consultant will call a company that has never been a client (cold-calling) with the aim of filling their employment needs.

Employers generally pay private (but not public) agencies to recruit workers. The employer places a "job order" with the agency describing the opening and listing requirements such as education, licenses or credentials, and experience. Employment interviewers often contact the employer to determine their exact personnel needs. Job seekers are asked to fill out forms or present resumes that detail their education, experience, and other qualifications. They may be interviewed or tested and have their background, references, and credentials checked. The employment interviewer then reviews the job requirements and the job seeker qualifications to determine the best possible match of position and applicant. Although computers are increasingly used to keep records and match employers with job seekers, personal contact with an employment interviewer remains an essential part of an applicant's job search.

Maintaining good relations with employers is an important part of the employment interviewer's job because this helps assure a steady flow of job orders. Being prepared to fill an opening quickly with a qualified applicant impresses employers most and keeps them as clients.

Besides helping firms fill job openings, employment interviewers help individuals find jobs. The services they provide depend upon the company or type of agency they work for and the clientele it serves.

Employment interviewers in personnel supply firms who place permanent employees are generally called counselors. They usually place job applicants who have the right qualifications but lack knowledge of the job market for their desired position. Counselors in these firms offer tips on personal appearance, suggestions on presenting a positive image of oneself, background on the company with which an interview is scheduled, and recommendations about interviewing techniques. Many firms specialize in placing applicants in particular kinds of jobs—for example, secretarial, word processing, computer programming and computer systems analysis, engineering, accounting, law, or health. Counselors in such firms usually have three to five years of experience in the field into which they are placing applicants.

Some employment interviewers work in temporary help services companies. These companies send out their own employees to firms that need temporary help. Employment interviewers take job orders from client firms and match their requests against a list of available workers. Employment interviewers select the best qualified workers available and assign them to the firms requiring assistance. Sometimes employees placed with companies as temporaries are later hired as permanent employees.

Traditionally, firms that placed permanent employees usually dealt with highly skilled applicants, such as lawyers or accountants, and those placing temporary employees dealt with less skilled workers, such as secretaries or data entry operators. However, temporary help services increasingly place workers with a wide range of educational backgrounds and work experience; businesses are turning to temporary employees to fill all types of positions—from clerical to managerial, professional, and technical—to reduce costs of pay and benefits associated with hiring permanent employees.

Regular evaluation of employee job skills is an important part of the job for those interviewers working in temporary help services companies. Initially, interviewers evaluate or test new employees' skills to determine their abilities and weaknesses. The results, which are kept on file, are referred to when filling job orders. In some cases, the temporary help company will train employees to improve their skills. Periodically, the interviewer may reevaluate or retest employees to identify any new skills they may have developed.

The duties of employment interviewers in job service centers differ somewhat because applicants may lack marketable skills. In these centers, job seekers present resumes and fill out forms that ask about educational attainment, job history, skills, awards, certificates, and licenses. An employment interviewer reviews these forms and asks the applicant about the type of job sought and salary range desired. Applicants sometimes have exaggerated expectations. Employment interviewers must be tactful, but persuasive, if an applicant's job or salary requests are unreasonable.

Applicants may need help identifying the kind of work for which they are best suited. The employment interviewer evaluates the applicant's qualifications and either chooses an appropriate occupation or class of occupations, or refers the applicant for vocational testing.

After identifying an appropriate job type, the employment interviewer searches the file of job orders seeking a possible job match, and refers the applicant to the employer if a match is found. If no match is found, the interviewer shows the applicant how to use listings of available jobs.

Some applicants are high school dropouts or have poor English language skills, a history of drug or alcohol dependency, or a prison record, among other problems. The amount and nature of special help for such applicants vary from state to state. In some states, it is the employment interviewer's responsibility to counsel hard-to-place applicants and refer them elsewhere for literacy or language instruction, vocational training, transportation assistance, child care, and other services. In other states, specially trained counselors perform this task.

Working Conditions

Employment interviewers usually work in comfortable, well-lighted offices, often using a computer to match information about employers and job seekers. Some interviewers, however, may spend much of their time out of the office interviewing. The work can prove hectic, especially in temporary help service companies which supply clients with immediate help for short periods of time. Some overtime may be required, and temporary workers may need their own transportation to make employer visits. The private placement industry is competitive, so counselors feel pressed to give their client companies the best service.

Employment

Employment interviewers held about 87,000 jobs in 1996. About four out of five worked in the private sector for personnel supply services, generally for employment placement firms or temporary help services companies. About one out of five worked for state or local government. Others were employed by organizations that provide various services, such as job training and vocational rehabilitation.

Employees of career consulting or outplacement firms are not included in these estimates. Workers in these firms help clients market themselves; they do not act as job brokers, nor do they match individuals with particular vacancies.

Training, Other Qualifications, and Advancement

Although most public and private agencies prefer to hire college graduates for interviewer jobs, a degree is not always necessary. Hiring requirements in the private sector reflect a firm's management approach as well as the placements in which its interviewers specialize. Those that place highly trained individuals such as accountants, lawyers, engineers, physicians, or managers generally have some training or experience in the field in which they are placing workers. Thus, a bachelor's, master's, or even a doctoral degree may be a prerequisite for some interviewers. Even with the right education, however, sales ability is still required to succeed in the private sector.

Educational requirements play a lesser role for interviewers placing clerks or laborers—a high school diploma may be sufficient. In these positions, qualities such as energy level, telephone voice, and sales ability take precedence over educational attainment.

Entry-level employment interviewer positions in the public sector are generally filled by college graduates, even though the positions do not always require a bachelor's degree. Some states allow substitution of suitable work experience for college education. Suitable work experience is generally defined as public contact work or time spent at other jobs (including clerical jobs) in a job service office. In states that permit employment interviewers to engage in counseling, course work in counseling may be required.

Most states and many large city and county governments use some form of merit system for hiring interviewers. Applicants may take a written exam, undergo a preliminary interview, or submit records of their education and experience for evaluation. Those who meet the standards are placed on a list from which the top-ranked candidates are selected for later interviews and possible hiring.

Other desirable qualifications for employment interviewers include good communications skills, a desire to help people, office skills, and adaptability. A friendly, confidence-winning manner is an asset because personal interaction plays a large role in this occupation. Increasingly, employment interviewers use computers as a tool; thus, basic knowledge of computers is helpful.

Advancement as an employment interviewer in the public sector is often based on a system providing regular promotions and salary increases for those meeting established standards. Advancement to supervisory positions is highly competitive. In personnel supply firms, advancement often depends on one's success in placing workers and generally takes the form of greater responsibility and higher income. Successful individuals may form their own businesses.

Job Outlook

Employment in this occupation is expected to grow about as fast as the average for all occupations through the year 2006. The majority of new jobs will arise in personnel supply firms, especially those specializing in temporary help. Job growth is not anticipated in state job service offices because of budgetary problems and the growing use of computerized job matching and information systems, and as states increasingly contract out employment services to private firms. Other openings will stem from the need to replace experienced interviewers who transfer to other occupations, retire, or stop working for other reasons.

Rapid expansion of firms supplying temporary help will be responsible for much of the growth in this occupation. Businesses of all types are turning to temporary help services companies for additional workers for handling short-term assignments or one-time projects, for launching new programs, and to reduce costs of pay and benefits associated with hiring permanent employees.

Expansion of the personnel supply industry, in general, will also spur job growth. Job orders will increase as the economy expands and new businesses are formed; this is expected to heighten demand for employment interviewers. Firms that lack the time or resources to develop their own screening procedures will likely turn to personnel firms.

Employment opportunities should be better in private placement firms than in state job service centers. Entry to this occupation is relatively easy for college graduates, or people who have had some college courses, except in those positions specializing in placement of workers with highly specialized training, such as lawyers, doctors, and engineers.

Employment interviewers who place permanent workers may lose their jobs during recessions because employers reduce or eliminate hiring for permanent positions during downturns in the economy. State job service employment interviewers are less susceptible to layoffs than those who place permanent or temporary personnel in the private sector.

Earnings

Earnings in private firms vary, in part, because the basis for compensation varies. Workers in personnel supply firms tend to be paid on a commission basis; those in temporary help service companies receive a salary.

When workers are paid on a commission basis (or salary plus commission), total earnings depend on how much business they bring in. This is usually based on the type as well as the number of placements. Those who place more highly skilled or hard-to-find employees earn more. An interviewer or counselor working strictly on a commission basis often makes around 30 percent of what he or she bills the client, although this varies widely from firm to firm. Some work on a salary-plus-commission basis because they fill difficult or highly specialized positions requiring long periods of search. The salary, usually small by normal standards, guarantees these individuals security through slow times. The commission provides the incentive and opportunity for higher earnings.

Some personnel supply firms employ new workers for a two- to three-month probationary period during which they draw a regular salary. This gives new workers time to develop their skills and acquire some clients. At the end of the probationary period, the new employees are evaluated, and they are either let go or switched to a commission basis.

Related Occupations

Employment interviewers serve as intermediaries for job seekers and employers. Workers in several other occupations do similar jobs.

Personnel officers screen and help hire new employees, but they concern themselves mainly with the hiring needs of the firm; they never represent individual job seekers. Personnel officers may also have additional duties in areas such as payroll or benefits management.

Career counselors help students and alumni find jobs, but they primarily emphasize career counseling and decision making, not placement.

Counselors in community organizations and vocational rehabilitation facilities help clients find jobs, but they also assist with drug or alcohol dependencies, housing, transportation, child care, and other problems that stand in the way of finding and keeping a job.

Sources of Additional Information

For information on a career as an employment interviewer/counselor, contact:

❑ National Association of Personnel Services, 3133 Mt. Vernon Ave., Alexandria, VA 22305.

❑ National Association of Temporary Staffing Services, 119 S. Saint Asaph St., Alexandria, VA 22314. Homepage: http://www.natss.org

For information on a career as an employment interviewer in state employment security offices, contact offices of the state government for which you are interested in working.

Engineering Technicians

(D.O.T. 002.261-014, .262-010; 003.161, .261-010, .362; 005.261; 006.261; 007.161-026 and -030, .167-010, .181 and .267-014; 008.261; 010.261-010 and -026; 011.261-010, -014, -018, and -022, .281, .361; 012.261-014, .267; 013.161; 017.261-010; 017.684; 019.161-014, .261-018, -022, -026, and -034, .267, .281; 194.381, .382-010; 199.261-014; 726.261-010 and -014; 806.281-014; 761.281-014; 828.261-018; and 869.261-026)

Significant Points

✓ *About 43 percent of all engineering technicians employed in 1996 were electrical and electronic engineering technicians.*

✓ *Most employers prefer those with an associate degree in engineering technology.*

Nature of the Work

Engineering technicians use the principles and theories of science, engineering, and mathematics to solve technical problems in research and development, manufacturing, sales, construction, inspection, and maintenance. Their work is more limited in scope and more practically oriented than that of scientists and engineers. Many engineering technicians assist engineers and scientists, especially in research and development. Others work in quality control—inspecting products and processes, conducting tests, or collecting data. In manufacturing, they may assist in product design and development, process design, or production.

Engineering technicians who work in research and development, build or set up equipment, prepare and conduct experiments, calculate or record the results, and help engineers in other ways. Some make prototype versions of newly designed equipment. They also assist in design work, often using computer-aided design equipment.

Engineering technicians who work in manufacturing support the work of engineers. They may prepare specifications for materials, devise and run tests to ensure product quality, or study ways to improve manufacturing efficiency. They may also supervise production workers to make sure they follow prescribed procedures.

Most engineering technicians specialize in certain areas, learning skills and working in the same disciplines as engineers. Occupational titles, therefore, tend to follow the same structure as engineers. Chemical engineering technicians are usually employed in industries producing pharmaceuticals, chemicals, and petroleum products, among others. They work in laboratories as well as processing plants. They help develop new chemical products and processes, test processing equipment and instrumentation, monitor quality, and operate chemical manufacturing facilities.

Civil engineering technicians help civil engineers plan and build highways, buildings, bridges, dams, wastewater treatment systems, and other structures, and perform related surveys and studies. Some inspect water and wastewater treatment systems to ensure pollution control requirements are met. Others estimate construction costs and specify materials to be used. Some may even prepare drawings or perform land surveying duties.

Electrical and electronics engineering technicians help design, develop, test, and manufacture electrical and electronic equipment such as radios, radar, sonar, television, industrial and medical measuring or control devices, navigational equipment, and computers. They may work in product evaluation and testing, using measuring and diagnostic devices to adjust, test, and repair equipment. Workers who only repair electrical and electronic equipment are mechanics, installers, and repairers. Many of these repairers are often referred to as electronics technicians.

Electrical and electronic engineering technology is also applied to a wide variety of systems such as communications and process controls. Electromechanical engineering technicians combine fundamental principles of mechanical engineering technology with knowledge of electrical and electronic circuits to design, develop, test, and manufacture electrical and computer controlled mechanical systems.

Industrial engineering technicians study the efficient use of personnel, materials, and machines in factories, stores, repair shops, and offices. They prepare layouts of machinery and equipment, plan the flow of work, make statistical studies, and analyze production costs.

Mechanical engineering technicians help engineers design, develop, test, and manufacture industrial machinery, mechanical parts, and other equipment. They may assist in the testing of a guided missile, or in the planning and design of an electric power generation plant. They make sketches and rough layouts, record data, make computations, analyze results, and write reports. When planning production, mechanical engineering technicians prepare layouts and drawings of the assembly process and of parts to be manufactured. They estimate labor costs, equipment life, and plant space. Some test and inspect machines and equipment in manufacturing departments or work with engineers to eliminate production problems.

Working Conditions

Most engineering technicians work 40 hours a week in a laboratory, office, manufacturing or industrial plant, or on a construction site. Some may be exposed to hazards from equipment, chemicals, or toxic materials.

Employment

Engineering technicians held about 698,000 jobs in 1996. Almost 298,000 of these were electrical and electronics engineering technicians. About 33 of all engineering technicians worked in durable goods manufacturing, mainly in the electrical and electronic machinery and equipment, industrial machinery and equipment, instruments and related products, and transportation equipment industries. Another 25 percent worked in service industries, mostly in engineering or business services companies that do engineering work on contract for government, manufacturing, or other organizations.

In 1996, the federal government employed about 42,000 engineering technicians. The major employer was the Department of Defense, followed by the Departments of Transportation, Agriculture, and the Interior, the Tennessee Valley Authority, and the National Aeronautics and Space Administration. State governments employed about 37,000 and local governments about 27,000.

Training, Other Qualifications, and Advancement

Although it is possible to qualify for some engineering technician jobs with no formal training, most employers prefer to hire someone with at least a two-year degree in engineering technology. Training is available at technical institutes, junior and community colleges, extension divisions of colleges and universities, public and private vocational-technical schools, and through some technical training programs in the Armed Forces. Persons with college courses in science, engineering, and mathematics may also qualify for some positions but may need additional specialized training and experience.

Prospective engineering technicians should take as many high school science and math courses as possible to prepare for postsecondary programs in engineering technology. Most two-year associate programs accredited by the Accreditation Board for Engineering and Technology (ABET) require, at a minimum, college alge-

bra and trigonometry, and one or two basic science courses. More math or science may be required depending on the area of specialty. The type of technical courses required also varies depending on the area of specialty. For example, prospective mechanical engineering technicians may take courses in fluid mechanics, thermodynamics, and mechanical design; electrical engineering technicians may take classes in electric circuits, microprocessors, and digital electronics; and those preparing to work in environmental engineering technology need courses in environmental regulations and safe handling of hazardous materials. Because many engineering technicians may become involved in design work, creativity is desirable. Good communication skills and the ability to work well with others is also important since they are often part of a team of engineers and other technicians.

Engineering technicians usually begin by performing routine duties under the close supervision of an experienced technician, technologist, engineer, or scientist. As they gain experience, they are given more difficult assignments with only general supervision. Some engineering technicians eventually become supervisors.

Many publicly and privately operated schools provide technical training; the type and quality of programs vary considerably. Therefore, prospective students should be careful in selecting a program. They should contact prospective employers regarding their preferences and ask schools to provide information about the kinds of jobs obtained by graduates, instructional facilities and equipment, and faculty qualifications. Graduates of ABET-accredited programs are generally recognized to have achieved an acceptable level of competence in the mathematics, science, and technical courses required for this occupation.

Technical institutes offer intensive technical training, but less theory and general education than junior and community colleges. Many offer two-year associate degree programs, and are similar to or part of a community college or state university system. Other technical institutes are run by private, often for-profit, organizations, sometimes called proprietary schools. Their programs vary considerably in length and types of courses offered, although some are two-year associate degree programs.

Junior and community colleges offer curriculums similar to those in technical institutes but may include more theory and liberal arts. Often there may be little or no difference between technical institute and community college programs, as both offer associate degrees. After completing the two-year program, some graduates get jobs as engineering technicians, while others continue their education at four-year colleges. However, there is a difference between an associate degree in pre-engineering and one in engineering technology. Students who enroll in a two-year pre-engineering program may find it very difficult to find work as an engineering technician should they decide not to enter a four-year engineering program, because pre-engineering programs usually focus less on hands-on applications and more on academic preparatory work. Conversely, graduates of two-year engineering technology programs may not receive credit for many of the courses they have taken if they choose to transfer to a four-year engineering program. Colleges with these four-year programs usually do not offer engineering technician training, but college courses in science, engineering, and mathematics are useful for obtaining a job as an engineering technician. Many four-year colleges offer bachelor's degrees in engineering technology, but graduates of these programs are often hired to work as technologists or applied engineers, not technicians.

Area vocational-technical schools include postsecondary public institutions that serve local students and emphasize training needed by local employers. Most require a high school diploma or its equivalent for admission.

Other training in technical areas may be obtained in the Armed Forces. Many military technical training programs are highly regarded by employers. However, skills acquired in military programs often are narrowly focused, so they are not necessarily transferable to civilian industry, which often requires broader training. Therefore, some additional training may be needed, depending on the acquired skills and the kind of job.

The National Institute for Certification in Engineering Technologies (NICET) has established a voluntary certification program for engineering technicians. Although engineering technicians are not generally required to be certified by employers, certification may provide job seekers a competitive advantage. Certification is available at various levels, each level combining a written examination in one of over 30 specialty fields with a certain amount of job related experience.

Job Outlook

Overall, employment of engineering technicians is expected to increase as fast as the average for all occupations through the year 2006. However, the growing availability and use of advanced technologies, such as computer-aided design and drafting and computer simulation, will continue to increase productivity and impact employment growth. Opportunities should be best for individuals who have completed a two-year program in engineering technology. As technology becomes more sophisticated, employers continue to look for technicians who are skilled in new technology and require a minimum of additional job training. In addition to growth, many job openings will be created to replace technicians who retire or leave the labor force for other reasons.

As production of technical products continues to grow, competitive pressures will force companies to improve and update manufacturing facilities and product designs more rapidly than in the past. Like engineers, employment of engineering technicians is influenced by local and national economic conditions. As a result, the employment outlook varies with area of specialization and industry. Employment of some types of engineering technicians, such as civil engineering and aeronautical engineering technicians, experience greater cyclical fluctuations than others. Technicians whose jobs are defense-related may experience fewer opportunities because of recent defense cutbacks. On the other hand, employment of the largest specialty group–electrical and electronics engineering technicians–is expected to grow slightly faster than the overall rate for all engineering technicians. Increasing demand for more sophisticated electrical and electronic products, as well as the expansion of these products and systems into all areas of industry and manufacturing processes, will contribute to stronger employment growth in this specialty area.

Earnings

According to a survey of workplaces in 160 metropolitan areas, engineering technicians at the most junior level had median earn-

ings of about $20,200 in 1995, with the middle half earning between $17,700 and $22,800 a year. Engineering technicians with more experience and the ability to work with little supervision had median earnings of about $32,700, and those in supervisory or most senior level positions earned about $54,800.

In the federal government, engineering technicians started at about $15,500, $17,400, or $19,500 in early 1997, depending on their education and experience. Beginning salaries were slightly higher in selected areas of the country where the prevailing local pay level was higher. The average annual salary for engineering technicians in supervisory, nonsupervisory, and management positions in the federal government in 1997 was $42,710; for electronics technicians, $46,040; and for industrial engineering technicians, $43,510.

Related Occupations

Engineering technicians apply scientific and engineering principles usually acquired in postsecondary programs below the baccalaureate level. Similar occupations include science technicians, drafters, surveyors, broadcast technicians, and health technologists and technicians.

Sources of Additional Information

For a small fee, information on a variety of engineering technician and technology careers is available from:

❏ The Junior Engineering Technical Society (JETS), at 1420 King St., Suite 405, Alexandria, VA 22314-2794. Enclose $3.50 to obtain a full package of guidance materials and information. Brochures are available free on JETS homepage: http://www.asee.org/jets

Information on ABET-accredited engineering technology programs is available from:

❏ Accreditation Board for Engineering and Technology, Inc. 111 Market Place, Suite 1050, Baltimore, MD 21202. Homepage: htp://www.abet.ba.md.us

Engineering, Science, and Computer Systems Managers

(*D.O.T.* 002.167-018; 003.167-034 and -070; 005.167-010 and -022; 007.167-014; 008.167-010; 010.161-010, -014, and .167-018; 011.161-010; 012.167-058 and -062; 018.167-022; 019.167-014; 022.161-010; 024.167-010; 029.167-014; 162.117-030; 169.167-030 and -082; and 189.117-014)

Significant Points

✓ *The majority of growth in these managerial occupations is caused by the rapid expansion of employment in computer-related occupations.*

✓ *These managers need the specialized technical skills possessed by their staff to perform effectively.*

Nature of the Work

Engineering, science, and computer systems managers plan, coordinate, and direct research, development, design, production, and computer-related activities. They supervise a staff which may include engineers, scientists, technicians, computer specialists, and information technology workers, along with support personnel.

Engineering, science, and computer systems managers determine scientific and technical goals within broad outlines provided by top management. These goals may include the redesigning of an aircraft, improvements in manufacturing processes, the development of a large computer program, or advances in scientific research. Managers make detailed plans for the accomplishment of these goals—for example, working with their staff, they may develop the overall concepts of new products or identify problems standing in the way of project completion. They determine the cost of and equipment and personnel needed for projects and programs. They hire and assign scientists, engineers, technicians, computer specialists, information technology workers, and support personnel to carry out specific parts of the projects. The managers supervise these employees' work, and review their designs, programs, and reports. They present ideas and projects to top management for approval or when seeking additional funds for development.

Managers coordinate the activities of their unit with other units or organizations. They confer with higher levels of management; with financial, industrial production, marketing, and other managers; and with contractors and equipment and materials suppliers. They also establish working and administrative procedures and policies.

Engineering managers supervise people who design and develop machinery, products, systems, and processes; or direct and coordinate production, operations, quality assurance, testing, or maintenance in industrial plants. Many are plant engineers, who direct and coordinate the design, installation, operation, and maintenance of equipment and machinery in industrial plants. Others manage research and development teams that produce new products and processes or improve existing ones.

Science managers oversee activities in agricultural science, chemistry, biology, geology, meteorology, or physics. They manage research and development projects and direct and coordinate experimentation, testing, quality control, and production in research institutes and industrial plants. Science managers are often involved in their own research in addition to managing the work of others.

Computer systems managers direct and plan programming, computer operations, and data processing, and coordinate the development of computer hardware, systems design, and software. Top-level managers direct all computer-related activities in an organization. They analyze the computer and data information requirements of their organization and assign, schedule, and review the work of systems analysts, computer programmers, and computer operators. They determine personnel and computer hardware requirements, evaluate equipment options, and make purchasing decisions.

Some engineering, science, and computer systems managers head a section of scientists, engineers, or computer professionals and support staff. Above them are heads of divisions composed of a number of sections. A few are directors of research or of large laboratories.

Working Conditions

Engineering, science, and computer systems managers spend most of their time in an office. Some managers, however, may also work in laboratories or industrial plants, where they are normally exposed to the same conditions as research scientists and may occasionally be exposed to the same conditions as production workers.

Most managers work at least 40 hours a week and may work much longer on occasion if meeting project deadlines. Some may experience considerable pressure in meeting technical or scientific goals within a short time or a tight budget.

Employment

Engineering, science, and computer systems managers held about 343,000 jobs in 1996. Although these managers are found in almost all industries, about 38 percent are employed in manufacturing, especially in the industrial machinery and equipment, electrical and electronic equipment, instruments, chemicals, and transportation equipment industries. However, the two industries employing the greatest number of these managers were engineering and architectural services and computer and data processing services; each employed about one in ten in 1996. The majority are most likely engineering managers, often managing industrial research, development, and design projects. Others work for government agencies, research and testing services, communications and utilities companies, financial and insurance firms, and management and public relations services companies.

Training, Other Qualifications, and Advancement

It is essential that engineering, science, and computer systems managers have a base of technical knowledge that allows them to understand and guide the work of their subordinates and to explain the work in non-technical terms to senior management and potential customers. Therefore, experience as an engineer, mathematician, scientist, or computer professional is usually required to become an engineering, science, or computer systems manager. Educational requirements are consequently similar to those for scientists, engineers, and computer professionals.

Engineering managers first start as engineers. A bachelor's degree in engineering from an accredited engineering program is acceptable for beginning engineering jobs, but many engineers increase their chances for promotion to a managerial position by obtaining a master's degree in engineering, engineering management, or business administration. A degree in business administration or engineering management is especially useful for becoming a general manager, because these degree programs teach engineers about managing personnel and technical and financial resources.

Science managers usually start as a chemist, physicist, biologist, or other natural scientist. Most scientists engaged in basic research have a Ph.D. degree. Some in applied research and other activities may have lesser degrees. First-level science managers are usually specialists in the work they supervise. For example, the manager of a group of physicists doing optical research is almost always a physicist who is an expert in optics. Many scientific research firms are started and managed by scientists who obtain funding to build a staff and purchase technology to pursue their research agenda, with the goal of eventually developing a commercially successful product.

Most computer systems managers have been systems analysts, although some may have experience as computer engineers, programmers, operators, or other computer specialties. There is no universally accepted way of preparing for a job as a systems analyst. Many have degrees in computer or information science, computer information systems, or data processing and have experience as computer programmers. A bachelor's degree is usually required and a graduate degree is often preferred by employers. However, a few computer systems managers have associate degrees. A typical career advancement progression in a large organization would be from programmer to programmer/analyst, to systems analyst, and then to project leader or senior analyst. The first real managerial position might be as project manager, programming supervisor, systems supervisor, or software manager.

In addition to educational requirements, scientists, engineers, or computer specialists must demonstrate above-average technical skills to be considered for a promotion to manager. Superiors also look for leadership and communication skills, as well as managerial attributes such as the ability to make rational decisions, to manage time well, organize and coordinate work effectively, establish good working and personal relationships, and motivate others. Also, a successful manager must have the desire to perform management functions. Many scientists, engineers, and computer specialists want to be promoted but actually prefer doing technical work.

Some scientists and engineers become managers in marketing, personnel, purchasing, or other areas, or become general managers.

Job Outlook

Employment of engineering, science, and computer systems managers is expected to increase much faster than the average for all occupations through the year 2006. Underlying much of the growth of managers in science and engineering are competitive pressures and advancing technologies which force companies to update and improve products more frequently. Research and investment in plants and equipment to expand output of goods and services and to raise productivity will also add to employment requirements for science and engineering managers involved in research and development, design, and the operation and maintenance of production facilities.

Employment of computer systems managers will increase rapidly due to the fast-paced expansion of the computer and data processing services industry and the increased employment of computer systems analysts. Large computer centers are consolidating or closing as small computers become more powerful, resulting in fewer opportunities for computer systems managers at these centers. As the economy expands and as advances in technology lead to broader applications for computers, however, opportunities will increase and employment should grow rapidly.

Opportunities for those who wish to become engineering, science, and computer systems managers should be closely related to the growth of the occupations they supervise and the industries in which they are found. Because many engineers, natural scientists, and computer specialists are eligible for management and seek promotion, there may be substantial competition for these openings.

Many of the industries which employ engineers and scientists derive a large portion of their business from defense contracts. Because defense expenditures are being reduced, employment has declined and the job outlook for managers is not as favorable in these industries, compared to less defense-oriented industries.

Earnings

Earnings for engineering, science, and computer systems managers vary by specialty and level of management. According to 1996 data, science and engineering managers had average salaries that ranged from $41,000 to well over $100,000 for the most senior managers in large organizations. According to Robert Half International, computer systems managers earned salaries ranging from $33,000 to well over $100,000, depending on establishment size. Managers often earn about 15 to 25 percent more than those they directly supervise, although there are cases in which some employees are paid more than the manager who supervises them. This is especially true in research fields.

According to a survey of workplaces in 160 metropolitan areas, lower-level engineering managers had median annual earnings of $84,200 in 1995, with the middle half earning between $76,300 and $92,800. The highest-level engineering managers had median annual earnings of $117,000, with the middle half earning between $104,000 and $133,000. Beginning systems analysts managers had median annual earnings of $60,900, with the middle half earning between $55,100 and $67,000. The most senior systems analysts managers had median annual earnings of $84,200, with the middle half earning between $76,200 and $92,000.

In addition, engineering, science, and computer systems managers, especially those at higher levels, often are provided with more benefits (such as expense accounts, stock option plans, and bonuses) than non-managerial workers in their organizations.

Related Occupations

The work of engineering, science, and computer systems managers is closely related to that of engineers, natural scientists, computer personnel, and mathematicians. It is also related to the work of other managers, especially general managers and top executives.

Sources of Additional Information

For information about a career as an engineering, science, or computer systems manager, contact the sources of additional information for engineers, natural scientists, and computer occupations.

Engineers

012.061 -018, .067, .167 except -022, -026, -034, -058, and -062, and .187; 002.061 and .167; 003.061, .167 except -034 and -070, and .187; 005.061, .167-014, 026, and -018; 006.061; 007.061, .161-022, -034, and -038, and .267-010; 008.061; 010.061, .161-010, and .167-010 and -014; 011.061;; 015.061, .067, .137, and .167; 019.061-014 and 167-018

Significant Points

- ✓ *A bachelor's degree in engineering is almost always required for beginning engineering jobs. Good employment opportunities are expected for new graduates.*
- ✓ *Starting salaries are significantly higher than those of bachelor's degree graduates in other fields.*
- ✓ *Knowledge of technological advances must be acquired through continued study and education.*

Nature of the Work

Engineers apply the theories and principles of science and mathematics to research and develop economical solutions to practical technical problems. Their work is the link between scientific discoveries and commercial applications. Engineers design products, the machinery to build those products, the factories in which those products are made, and the systems that ensure the quality of the product and efficiency of the workforce and manufacturing process. They design, plan, and supervise the construction of buildings, highways, and transit systems. They develop and implement improved ways to extract, process, and use raw materials, such as petroleum and natural gas. They develop new materials that both improve the performance of products, and make implementing advances in technology possible. They harness the power of the sun, the earth, atoms, and electricity for use in supplying the nation's power needs, and create millions of products using power. Their knowledge is applied to improving many things, including the quality of health care, the safety of food products, and the efficient operation of financial systems.

Engineers consider many factors when developing a new product. For example, in developing an industrial robot, they determine precisely what function it needs to perform; design and test components; fit them together in an integrated plan; and evaluate the design's overall effectiveness, cost, reliability, and safety. This process applies to many different products, such as chemicals, computers, gas turbines, helicopters, and toys.

In addition to design and development, many engineers work in testing, production, or maintenance. They supervise production in factories, determine the causes of breakdowns, and test manufactured products to maintain quality. They also estimate the time and cost to complete projects. Some work in engineering management or in sales, where an engineering background enables them to discuss the technical aspects of a product and assist in planning its installation or use.

Most engineers specialize in a particular area. More than 25 major specialties are recognized by professional societies, and within the major branches are numerous subdivisions. Structural, environmental, and transportation engineering, for example, are subdivisions of civil engineering. Engineers may also specialize in one industry, such as motor vehicles, or in one field of technology, such as jet engines or ceramic materials.

This section, which contains an overall discussion of engineering, is followed by separate sections on ten engineering branches: Aerospace; chemical; civil; electrical and electronics; industrial; mechanical; metallurgical, ceramic, and materials; mining; nuclear; and petroleum engineering. Some branches of engineering not covered in detail here, but for which there are established college programs, include architectural engineering–the design of a building's internal support structure; biomedical engineering–the application of engineering to medical and physiological problems; environmental engineering–a growing discipline involved with identifying, solving, and alleviating environmental problems; and marine engineering–the design and installation of ship machinery and propulsion systems.

Engineers in each branch have a base of knowledge and training that can be applied in many fields. Electrical and electronics engineers, for example, work in the medical, computer, missile guidance, and power distribution fields. Because there are many separate problems to solve in a large engineering project, engineers in one field often work closely with specialists in other scientific, engineering, and business occupations.

Engineers use computers to produce and analyze designs; simulate and test how a machine, structure, or system operates; and generate blueprints for parts. Many engineers also use computers to monitor product quality and control process efficiency. They spend a great deal of time writing reports and consulting with other engineers, as complex projects often require an interdisciplinary team of engineers. Supervisory engineers are responsible for major components or entire projects.

Working Conditions

Most engineers work in office buildings, laboratories, or industrial plants. Others spend a considerable amount of time outdoors at construction sites, mines, and oil and gas exploration sites, where they monitor or direct operations or solve onsite problems. Some engineers travel extensively to plants or worksites.

Most engineers work a standard 40-hour week. At times, deadlines or design standards may bring extra pressure to a job. When this happens, engineers may work long hours and experience considerable stress.

Employment

In 1996, engineers held 1,382,000 jobs. Chart 1 shows the employment of the engineering disciplines covered in this statement. Forty-six percent of all wage and salary engineering jobs were located in manufacturing industries such as electrical and electronic equipment, industrial machinery, aircraft and parts, motor vehicles, chemicals, search and navigation equipment, fabricated metal products, and guided missiles and space vehicles. In 1996, 716,000 wage and salary jobs were in nonmanufacturing industries, primarily in engineering and architectural services, research and testing services, and business services, where firms designed construction projects or did other engineering work on a contract basis for organizations in other parts of the economy. Engineers also worked in the communications, utilities, and construction industries.

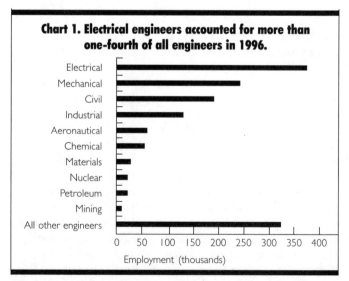

Chart 1. Electrical engineers accounted for more than one-fourth of all engineers in 1996.

Federal, state, and local governments employed about 178,000 wage and salary engineers in 1996. Over half of these were in the federal government, mainly in the Departments of Defense, Transportation, Agriculture, Interior, and Energy, and in the National Aeronautics and Space Administration. Most engineers in state and local government agencies worked in highway and public works departments. In 1996, 46,000 engineers were self-employed, many as consultants.

Engineers are employed in every state, in small and large cities, and in rural areas. Some branches of engineering are concentrated in particular industries and geographic areas, as discussed in statements later in this chapter.

Training, Other Qualifications, and Advancement

A bachelor's degree in engineering is usually required for beginning engineering jobs. College graduates with a degree in a physical science or mathematics may occasionally qualify for some engineering jobs, especially in engineering specialties in high demand. Most engineering degrees are granted in electrical, mechanical, or civil engineering. However, engineers trained in one branch may work in related branches; for example, many aerospace engineers have training in mechanical engineering. This flexibility allows employers to meet staffing needs in new technologies and specialties in which engineers are in short supply. It also allows engineers to shift to fields with better employment prospects, or to ones that match their interests more closely.

In addition to the standard engineering degree, many colleges offer degrees in engineering technology, which are offered as either two- or four-year programs. These programs prepare students for practical design and production work rather than for jobs that require more theoretical, scientific and mathematical knowledge. Graduates of four-year technology programs may get jobs similar to those obtained by graduates with a bachelor's degree in engineering. Some employers regard them as having skills between those of a technician and an engineer.

Graduate training is essential for engineering faculty positions, but is not required for the majority of entry-level engineering jobs. Many engineers obtain graduate degrees in engineering or business administration to learn new technology, broaden their education, and enhance promotion opportunities. Many high-level executives in government and industry began their careers as engineers.

About 320 colleges and universities offer bachelor's degree programs in engineering that are accredited by the Accreditation Board for Engineering and Technology (ABET), and about 250 colleges offer accredited bachelor's degree programs in engineering technology. ABET accreditation is based on an examination of an engineering program's faculty, curricular content, facilities, and admissions standards. Although most institutions offer programs in the major branches of engineering, only a few offer some of the smaller specialties. Also, programs of the same title may vary in content. For example, some emphasize industrial practices, preparing students for a job in industry, while others are more theoretical and are better for students preparing to take graduate work. Therefore, students should investigate curricula and check accreditations carefully before selecting a college. Admissions requirements for undergraduate engineering schools include a solid background in mathematics (algebra, geometry, trigonometry, and calculus), sciences (biology, chemistry, and physics), and courses in English, social studies, humanities, and computers.

Bachelor's degree programs in engineering are typically designed to last four years, but many students find that it takes between four and five years to complete their studies. In a typical four-year college curriculum, the first two years are spent studying mathematics, basic sciences, introductory engineering, humanities, and social sciences. In the last two years, most courses are in engineering, usually with a concentration in one branch. For example, the last two years of an aerospace program might include courses such as fluid mechanics, heat transfer, applied aerodynamics, analytical mechanics, flight vehicle design, trajectory dynamics, and aerospace propulsion systems. Some programs offer a general engineering curriculum; students then specialize in graduate school or on the job.

Some engineering schools and two-year colleges have agreements whereby the two-year college provides the initial engineering education and the engineering school automatically admits students for their last two years. In addition, a few engineering schools have arrangements whereby a student spends three years in a liberal arts college studying pre-engineering subjects and two years in the engineering school, and receives a bachelor's degree from each. Some colleges and universities offer five-year master's degree programs. Some five- or even six-year cooperative plans combine classroom study and practical work, permitting students to gain valuable experience and finance part of their education.

All 50 states and the District of Columbia require registration for engineers whose work may affect life, health, or property, or who offer their services to the public. Registration generally requires a degree from an ABET-accredited engineering program, four years of relevant work experience, and passing a state examination. Some states will not register people with degrees in engineering technology. Engineers may be registered in several states.

Engineers should be creative, inquisitive, analytical, and detail-oriented. They should be able to work as part of a team and be able to communicate well, both orally and in writing.

Beginning engineering graduates usually work under the supervision of experienced engineers and, in larger companies, may also receive formal classroom or seminar-type training. As they gain knowledge and experience, they are assigned more difficult projects with greater independence to develop designs, solve problems, and make decisions. Engineers may advance to become technical specialists or to supervise a staff or team of engineers and technicians. Some eventually become engineering managers or enter other managerial, management support, or sales jobs.

Job Outlook

Employment opportunities in engineering are expected to be good through the year 2006 because employment is expected to increase about as fast as the average for all occupations while the number of degrees granted in engineering may not increase as rapidly as employment.

Competitive pressures and advancing technology will force companies to improve and update product designs more frequently, and to work to optimize their manufacturing processes. Employers will rely on engineers to further increase productivity as they increase investment in plant and equipment to expand output of goods and services. New computer systems have improved the design process, enabling engineers to produce and analyze design variations much more rapidly; these systems are increasingly used to monitor and control processes. Despite this widespread application, computer technology is not expected to limit employment opportunities. Finally, more engineers will be needed to improve or build new roads, bridges, water and pollution control systems, and other public facilities.

Many of the jobs in engineering are related to developing technologies used in national defense. Because defense expenditures, particularly expenditures for the purchase of aircraft, missiles, and other weapons systems, are expected to continue at low levels (compared with the cold war years), employment growth and job outlook for engineers working for defense contractors may not be strong through 2006.

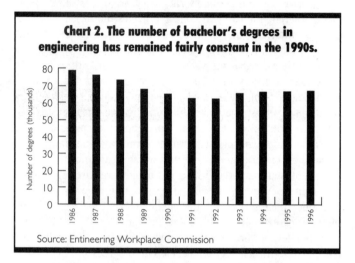

Chart 2. The number of bachelor's degrees in engineering has remained fairly constant in the 1990s.

Source: Entineering Workplace Commission

The number of bachelor's degrees awarded in engineering began declining in 1987, as shown in chart 2, and has stayed at about the same level in the 1990s. Although it is difficult to project engineering enrollments, the total number of students enrolled in colleges is expected to increase over the projection period, and it is likely that engineering enrollments and number of degrees awarded will follow. However, some engineering schools have restricted enrollments, especially in defense-related fields such as aerospace engineering, to accommodate the reduced opportunities in defense-related industries.

Only a relatively small proportion of engineers leave the profession each year. Despite this, most job openings will arise from replacement needs. A greater proportion of replacement openings is created by engineers who transfer to management, sales, or other professional specialty occupations than by those who leave the labor force.

Most industries are less likely to lay off engineers than other workers. Many engineers work on long-term research and development projects or in other activities which may continue even during recessions. In industries such as electronics and aerospace, however, large cutbacks in defense procurement expenditures, government research and development funds, and the increasing trend of contracting out engineering work to engineering services firms have resulted in significant layoffs for engineers.

It is important for engineers, like those working in other technical occupations, to continue their education throughout their careers because much of their value to their employer depends on their knowledge of the latest technology. Although the pace of technological change varies by engineering specialty and industry, advances in technology have affected every engineering discipline significantly. Engineers in high-technology areas, such as advanced electronics, may find that technical knowledge can become obsolete rapidly. Even those who continue their education are vulnerable if the particular technology or product in which they have specialized becomes obsolete. By keeping current in their field, engineers are able to deliver the best solutions and greatest value to their employers. Engineers who have not kept current in their field may find themselves passed over for promotions or vulnerable to layoffs, should they occur. On the other hand, it is often these high-technology areas that offer the greatest challenges, the most interesting work, and the highest salaries. Therefore, the choice of engineering specialty and employer involves an assessment not only of the potential rewards but also of the risk of technological obsolescence.

Earnings

Starting salaries for engineers with the bachelor's degree are significantly higher than starting salaries of bachelor's degree graduates in other fields. According to the National Association of Colleges and Employers, engineering graduates with a bachelor's degree averaged about $38,500 a year in private industry in 1997; those with a master's degree and no experience, $45,400 a year; and those with a Ph.D., $59,200. Starting salaries for those with the bachelor's degree vary by branch, as shown in the following tabulation.

Aerospace	$37,957
Chemical	42,817
Civil	33,119
Electrical	39,513
Industrial	38,026
Mechanical	38,113
Metallurgical	38,550
Mining	36,724
Nuclear	37,194
Petroleum	43,674

A survey of workplaces in 160 metropolitan areas reported that beginning engineers had median annual earnings of about $34,400 in 1995, with the middle half earning between about $30,900 and $38,116 a year. Experienced midlevel engineers with no supervisory responsibilities had median annual earnings of about $59,100, with the middle half earning between about $54,000 and $65,000 a year. Median annual earnings for engineers at senior managerial levels were about $99,200. Median annual earnings for these and other levels of engineers are shown in the following tabulation.

Engineer I	$34,400
Engineer II	41,000
Engineer III	48,500
Engineer IV	59,100
Engineer V	71,400
Engineer VI	84,200
Engineer VII	99,200
Engineer VIII	117,000

The median annual salary for all engineers who worked full-time was about $49,200 in 1996. Those with a bachelor's degree had median annual earnings of $49,800; master's degree, $56,700; and Ph.D., $64,700. Median annual salaries for some engineering specialties were:

Aerospace	$57,000
Chemical	52,600
Civil	46,000
Electrical	51,700
Industrial	43,700
Mechanical	49,700
Engineers	49,700

The average annual salary for engineers in the federal government in nonsupervisory, supervisory, and managerial positions was $61,950 in 1997.

Related Occupations

Engineers apply the principles of physical science and mathematics in their work. Other workers who use scientific and mathematical principles include engineering, science, and computer systems managers; physical, life, and computer scientists; mathematicians; engineering and science technicians; and architects.

Sources of Additional Information

High school students interested in obtaining general information on a variety of engineering disciplines should contact the Junior Engineering Technical Society by sending a self-addressed business-size envelope with six first-class stamps affixed, to:

❏ JETS-Guidance, at 1420 King St., Suite 405, Alexandria, VA 22314-2794. Homepage: http://www.asee.org/jets

High school students interested in obtaining information on ABET accredited engineering programs should contact:

❏ The Accreditation Board for Engineering and Technology, Inc., at 111 Market Place, Suite 1050, Baltimore, MD 21202-4012. Homepage: http://www.abet.ba.md.us

Non-high school students and those wanting more detailed information should contact societies representing the individual branches of engineering. Each can provide information about careers in the particular branch.

Aeronautical and Aerospace Engineering, Send $3 to:

❏ American Institute of Aeronautics and Astronautics, Inc., Suite 500, 1801 Alexander Bell Drive, Reston, VA 20191-4344.

Chemical Engineering

❏ American Institute of Chemical Engineers, 345 East 47th St., New York, NY 10017-2395.

❏ American Chemical Society, Department of Career Services, 1155 16th St. NW, Washington, DC 20036.

Civil Engineering

❏ American Society of Civil Engineers, 1801 Alexander Bell Drive, Reston, VA 20191-4400.

Electrical and Electronics Engineering

❏ Institute of Electrical and Electronics Engineers, 1828 L St. NW, Suite 1202, Washington, DC 20036.

Industrial Engineering

❏ Institute of Industrial Engineers, Inc., 25 Technology Park/ Atlanta, Norcross, GA 30092. Homepage: http://www.iienet.org

Mechanical Engineering

❏ The American Society of Mechanical Engineers, 345 E. 47th St., New York, NY 10017.

❏ American Society of Heating, Refrigerating, and Air-Conditioning Engineers, Inc., 1791 Tullie Circle NE., Atlanta, GA 30329. Homepage://www.ashrae.org

Metallurgical, Ceramic, and Materials Engineering

❏ The Minerals, Metals, & Materials Society, 420 Commonwealth Dr., Warrendale, PA 15086-7514. Homepage: http://www.tms.org

❏ ASM International, Student Outreach Program, Materials Park, OH 44073-0002.

Mining Engineering

❏ The Society for Mining, Metallurgy, and Exploration, Inc., P.O. Box 625002, Littleton, CO 80162-5002.

Nuclear Engineering

❏ American Nuclear Society, 555 North Kensington Ave., LaGrange Park, IL 60525.

Petroleum Engineering

❏ Society of Petroleum Engineers, P.O. Box 833836, Richardson, TX 75083-3836.

Financial Managers

(D.O.T. 160.167-058; 161.117-018; 169.167-086; 186.117-066, -070, -078, -086; .167-054, -086; 189.117-038)

Significant Points

✓ *A bachelor's degree in finance or a related field is the minimum academic preparation, but many employers increasingly seek graduates with a master's degree and a strong analytical background.*

✓ *The need for skilled financial management will spur average employment growth; however, the number of applicants is expected to exceed the number of openings, resulting in competition for jobs.*

Nature of the Work

Practically every firm has one or more financial managers. Among them are chief financial officers, vice presidents of finance, treasurers, controllers, credit managers, and cash managers; they prepare the financial reports required by the firm to conduct its operations and to ensure that the firm satisfies tax and regulatory requirements. Financial managers also oversee the flow of cash and financial instruments, monitor the extension of credit, assess the risk of transactions, raise capital, analyze investments, develop information to assess the present and future financial status of the firm, and communicate with stock holders and other investors.

In small firms, chief financial officers usually handle all financial management functions. In large firms, these officers oversee financial management departments and help top managers develop financial and economic policy, establish procedures, delegate authority, and oversee the implementation of these policies.

Highly trained and experienced financial managers head each financial department. Controllers direct the preparation of all financial reports—income statements, balance sheets, and special reports, such as depreciation schedules. They oversee the accounting, audit, or budget departments. Cash and credit managers monitor and control the flow of cash receipts and disbursements to meet the business and investment needs of the firm. For example, cash flow projections are needed to determine whether loans must be obtained to meet cash requirements, or whether surplus cash may be invested in interest-bearing instruments. Risk and insurance managers oversee programs to minimize risks and losses that may arise from financial transactions and business operations undertaken by the institution. Credit operations managers establish credit rating criteria, determine credit ceilings, and monitor their institution's extension of credit. Reserve officers review their institution's financial statements and direct the purchase and sale of bonds and other securities to maintain the asset-liability ratio required by law. Managers specializing in international finance develop financial and accounting systems for the banking transactions of multinational organizations. A working knowledge of the financial systems of foreign countries is essential.

Financial institutions—such as banks, savings and loan associations, credit unions, personal credit institutions, and finance companies—may serve as depositories for cash and financial instruments and offer loans, investment counseling, consumer credit, trust management, and other financial services. Some specialize in specific financial services. Financial managers in financial institutions include vice presidents, bank branch managers, savings and loan association managers, consumer credit managers, and credit union managers. These managers make decisions in accordance with policy set by the institution's board of directors and federal and state laws and regulations.

Due to changing regulations and increased government scrutiny, financial managers in financial institutions must place greater emphasis on accurate reporting of financial data. They must have detailed knowledge of industries allied to banking—such as insurance, real estate, and securities—and a broad knowledge of business and industrial activities. With growing domestic and foreign competition, financial managers must keep abreast of an expanding and increasingly complex variety of financial products and services. Besides supervising financial services, financial managers in banks and other financial institutions may advise individuals and businesses on financial planning.

Working Conditions

Financial managers are provided with comfortable offices, often close to top managers and to departments which develop the financial data these managers need. Financial managers typically work 40 hours a week, but many work longer hours. They are often required to attend meetings of financial and economic associations, and may travel to visit subsidiary firms or meet customers.

Employment

Financial managers held about 800,000 jobs in 1996. Although these managers are found in virtually every industry, more than a third were employed by services industries, including business, health, social, and management services. Nearly three out of ten were employed by financial institutions—banks, savings institutions, finance companies, credit unions, insurance companies, securities dealers, and real estate firms, for example.

Training, Other Qualifications, and Advancement

A bachelor's degree in finance, accounting, economics, or business administration is the minimum academic preparation for financial managers. However, many employers increasingly seek graduates with a master's degree, preferably in business administration, economics, finance, or risk management. These academic programs develop analytical skills, and provide knowledge of the latest financial analysis methods and information and technology management techniques, widely used in this field.

Experience may be more important than formal education for some financial manager positions—notably branch managers in banks. Banks typically fill branch manager positions by promoting experienced loan officers and other professionals who excel at their jobs.

Continuing education is vital for financial managers, reflecting the growing complexity of global trade, shifting federal and state laws and regulations, and a proliferation of new, complex financial instruments. Firms often provide opportunities for workers to broaden their knowledge and skills, and encourage employees to take graduate courses at colleges and universities or attend conferences relating to their specialty. Financial management, banking, and credit union associations, often in cooperation with colleges and universities, sponsor numerous national or local training programs. Persons enrolled prepare extensively at home, then attend sessions on subjects such as accounting management, budget management, corporate cash management, financial analysis, international banking, and information systems. Many firms pay all or part of the costs for those who successfully complete courses. Although experience, ability, and leadership are emphasized for promotion, advancement may be accelerated by this type of special study.

In some cases, financial managers may also broaden their skills and exhibit their competency in specialized fields by attaining professional certification. For example, the Association for Investment Management and Research confers the Chartered Financial Analyst designation to investment professionals who have a bachelor's degree, pass three test levels, and meet work experience requirements. The National Association of Credit Management administers a three-part certification program for business credit professionals. Through a combination of experience and examinations, these financial managers pass through the level of Credit Business Associate, to Credit Business Fellow, to Certified Credit Executive. The Treasury Management Association confers the Certified Cash Manager credential on those who have two years of relevant experience and pass an exam, and the Certified Treasury Executive designation on those more senior in treasury management who meet experience and continuing education requirements.

Persons interested in becoming financial managers should enjoy working independently, dealing with people, and analyzing detailed account information. The ability to communicate effectively, both orally and in writing, is also important. They also need tact, good judgment, and the ability to establish effective personal relationships to oversee staff.

Because financial management is critical for efficient business operations, well-trained, experienced financial managers who display a strong grasp of the operations of various departments within their organization are prime candidates for promotion to top management positions. Some financial managers transfer to closely related positions in other industries. Those with extensive experience and access to sufficient capital may start their own consulting firms.

Job Outlook

Like other managerial occupations, the number of applicants for financial management positions is expected to exceed the number of openings, resulting in competition for jobs. Those with lending experience, and familiarity with the latest lending regulations and financial products and services, should enjoy the best opportunities for branch management jobs in banks. Those with a graduate degree, a strong analytical background, and knowledge of various aspects of financial management, such as asset management and information and technology management, should enjoy the best opportunities for other financial management positions. Developing expertise in a rapidly growing industry, such as health care, could also be an advantage in the job market.

Employment of financial managers is expected to increase about as fast as the average for all occupations through the year 2006. The need for skilled financial management will increase due to the demands of global trade, the proliferation of complex financial instruments, and changing federal and state laws and regulations. Many firms have reduced the ranks of middle managers in an effort to be more efficient and competitive, but much of the downsizing and restructuring is complete. The banking industry, on the other hand, is still undergoing mergers and consolidation, and may eliminate some financial management positions as a result.

Earnings

The median annual salary of financial managers was $40,700 in 1996. The lowest 10 percent earned $21,800 or less, while the top 10 percent earned over $81,100.

According to a 1997 survey by Robert Half International, a staffing services firm specializing in accounting and finance, salaries of assistant controllers range from $41,000 in the smallest firms, to $81,000 in the largest firms; controllers, $47,000 to $138,000; and chief financial officers/treasurers, $62,000 to $307,000.

The results of the Treasury Management Association's 1997 compensation survey are presented in table 1. The earnings listed in the table represent total compensation, including bonuses. The survey also found that financial managers with a master's degree in business administration average $10,900 more than managers with a bachelor's degree.

Table 1. Annual earnings for selected financial managers, 1997

Chief financial officer	$142,900
Vice president of finance	138,000
Treasurer	122,500
Assistant treasurer	88,400
Controller	85,100
Treasury manager	66,900
Assistant controller	56,200
Senior analyst	55,600
Cash manager	51,600
Analyst	40,500
Assistant cash manager	38,800

Source: Treasury Management Association

Salary level depends upon the manager's experience and the size and location of the organization, and is likely to be higher in larger organizations and cities. Many financial managers in private industry receive additional compensation in the form of bonuses, which also vary substantially by the size of the firm.

Related Occupations

Financial managers combine formal education with experience in one or more areas of finance, such as asset management, lending, credit operations, securities investment, or insurance risk and loss control. Workers in other occupations requiring similar training and ability include accountants and auditors, budget officers, credit analysts, loan officers, insurance consultants, portfolio managers, pension consultants, real estate advisors, securities analysts and underwriters.

Sources of Additional Information

For information about financial management careers, contact:
- American Bankers Association, 1120 Connecticut Ave. NW, Washington, DC 20036.
- Financial Management Association, International, College of Business Administration, University of South Florida, Tampa, FL 33620-5500.

For information about financial careers in business credit management; the Credit Business Associate, Credit Business Fellow, and Certified Credit Executive programs; and institutions offering graduate courses in credit and financial management, contact:
- National Association of Credit Management (NACM), Credit Research Foundation, 8815 Centre Park Dr., Columbia, MD 21045-2117. E-mail address: nacm@nacm.org Homepage: http://www.nacm.org/

For information about careers in treasury management from entry level to chief financial officer, and the Certified Cash Manager and Certified Treasury Executive programs, contact:
- Treasury Management Association, 7315 Wisconsin Ave., Suite 600 West, Bethesda, MD 20814.

For information about the Chartered Financial Analyst program, contact:
- Association for Investment Management and Research, 5 Boar's Head Lane, P.O. Box 3668, Charlottesville, VA 22903. Homepage: http://www.aimr.com/

For information about financial management careers in the health care industry, contact:
- Healthcare Financial Management Association, Two Westbrook Corporate Center, Suite 700, Westchester, IL 60154.

State bankers' associations can furnish specific information about job opportunities in their respective states, or write directly to a particular bank to inquire about job openings. For the names and addresses of banks and savings and related institutions, as well as the names of their principal officers, consult the following directories.
- *The American Financial Directory* (Norcross, GA, McFadden Business Publications).
- *The U.S. Savings and Loan Directory* (Chicago, Rand McNally & Co.).
- *Rand McNally Credit Union Directory* (Chicago, Rand McNally & Co.).
- *Polk's World Bank Directory* (Nashville, R.L. Polk & Co.).

Flight Attendants

(D.O.T. 352.367-010)

Significant Points

- ✓ *Job duties are learned through extensive formal training after being are hired.*

- ✓ *The opportunity for travel attracts many to this career, but this occupation requires working nights, weekends, and holidays and frequently being away from home.*

Nature of the Work

Major airlines are required by law to provide flight attendants for the safety of the flying public. Although the primary job of the flight attendants is to ensure that safety regulations are adhered to, they also try to make flights comfortable and enjoyable for passengers.

At least one hour before each flight, flight attendants are briefed by the captain, the pilot in command, on such things as emergency evaluation procedures, crew coordination, length of flights, expected weather conditions and special passenger problems. Flight attendants check that first aid kits and other emergency equipment are aboard and in working order and that the passenger cabin is in order, with adequate supplies of food, beverages, and blankets. As passengers board the plane, flight attendants greet them, check their tickets, and instruct them on where to store coats and carry-on items.

Before the plane takes off, flight attendants instruct all passengers in the use of emergency equipment and check to see that seat belts are fastened, seat backs are forward, and all carry on items are properly stowed. In the air, helping passengers in the event of an emergency is the most important responsibility of a flight attendant. Safety-related tips may range from reassuring passengers during occasional encounters with strong turbulence to directing passengers in evacuating a plane following an emergency landing. They also may answer questions about the flight; distribute reading material, pillows, and blankets; and help small children, elderly or disabled persons, and any others needing assistance. They may administer first aid to passengers who become ill. Flight attendants may serve alcoholic beverages and other refreshments and, on many flights, heat and distribute precooked meals or snacks. After the plane has landed, flight attendants take inventory of alcoholic beverages, monies collected, and headsets and may report on medical problems of passengers, and cabin equipment conditions or incidents.

Lead or first flight attendants, sometimes known as pursers, oversee the work of the other attendants aboard the aircraft, while performing most of the same duties.

Working Conditions

Since airlines operate around the clock year round, flight attendants may work at night and on holidays and weekends. They usually fly 75 to 85 hours a month and, in addition generally spend about 75 to 85 hours a month on the ground preparing planes for flights, writing reports following completed flights, and waiting for planes to arrive. Because of variations in scheduling and limitations on flying time, many flight attendants have 11 or more days off each month. They may be away from their home base at least one-third of the time. During this period, the airlines provide assigned hotel accommodations and an allowance for meal expenses.

The combination of free time and discount air fares provides flight attendants the opportunity to travel and see new places. However, the work can be strenuous and trying. Short flights require speedy service if meals are served and a turbulent flight can make serving drinks and meals difficult. Flight attendants stand during much of the flight and must remain pleasant and efficient regardless of how tired they are or how demanding passengers may be. Flight attendants are susceptible to injuries because of the job demands in a moving aircraft. Back injuries and mishaps opening overhead compartments are common. In addition, medical problems can occur from working in a pressurized environment and breathing recycled air, irregular sleeping and eating pattens; and dealing with stressful passengers.

Employment

Flight attendants held about 132,000 jobs in 1996. Commercial airlines employed the vast majority of all flight attendants, most of whom live in major cities at the airlines' home bases. A small number of flight attendants worked for large companies that operated company aircraft for business purposes.

Training, Other Qualifications, and Advancement

Airlines prefer to hire poised, tactful, and resourceful people who can interact comfortably with strangers and remain calm under duress. Applicants usually must be at least 19 to 21 years old. Flight attendants must have excellent health and the ability to speak clearly. In addition, there are height requirements and applicants should not have visible tattoos.

Applicants must be high school graduates. Those having several years of college or experience in dealing with the public are preferred. More and more flight attendants being hired are college graduates. Highly desirable areas of concentration include such people oriented disciplines as psychology and education. Flight attendants for international airlines generally must speak an appropriate foreign language fluently. Some of the major airlines prefer candidates who can speak two major foreign languages for their international flights.

Most large airlines require that newly hired flight attendants complete four to six weeks of intensive training in the airlines' flight training centers. Airlines that do not operate training centers generally send new employees to the center of another airline. Transportation to the training centers and an allowance for board, room, and school supplies may be provided. Trainees learn emergency procedures such as evacuating an airplane, operating emergency systems and equipment, administering first aid, and water survival tactics. In addition, trainees are instructed to deal with hijacking and terrorist situations. Flight attendants also are taught flight regulations and duties, company operations and policies, and receive instruction on personal grooming and weight control. Trainees for the international routes get additional instruction in passport and customs regulations. Towards the end of their training, students go on practice flights. Additionally, flight attendants must annually receive recurrent 12 to 14 hours of training in emergency procedures and passenger relations.

After completing initial training, flight attendants are assigned to one of their airline's bases. New flight attendants are placed on "reserve status" and are called on either to staff extra flights or fill in for crew members who are sick or on vacation or rerouted. Reserve flight attendants on duty must be available on short notice, and usually remain on reserve for at least one year. However, at some cities, it may take five to ten years or longer to advance from reserve status. Flight attendants who no longer are on reserve bid monthly for regular assignments. Because assignments are based on seniority, usually only the most experienced attendants get their choices of base and flights. Advancement takes longer today than in the past because experienced flight attendants are remaining in this career for more years than they used to.

Some flight attendants transfer within the airline to become supervisors, or may take on additional duties such as recruiting and instructing.

Job Outlook

Opportunities should be favorable for persons seeking flight attendant jobs as the number of applicants is expected to be roughly in balance with the number of job openings. Those with at least two years of college and experience in dealing with the public should have the best chance of being hired.

As airline restrictions on employment have been abolished, turnover–which traditionally was very high–has declined. Therefore, the majority of job openings through the year 2006 should be due to replacement needs. Many flight attendants are attracted to the occupation by the glamour of the airline industry and the opportunity to travel, but some eventually leave in search of jobs that offer higher earnings and require fewer nights be spent away from their families. Several thousand job openings will arise each year as a result of the need to replace flight attendants who transfer to another occupation or who leave the labor force.

Employment of flight attendants is expected to grow faster than the average for all occupations through the year 2006. Growth in population and income is expected to increase the number of airline passengers. Airlines enlarge their capacity by increasing the number and size of planes in operation. Since Federal Aviation Administration safety rules require one attendant for every 50 seats, more flight attendants will be needed.

Employment of flight attendants is sensitive to cyclical swings in the economy. During recessions, when the demand for air travel declines, many flight attendants are put on part-time status or laid off. Until demand increases, few flight new attendants are hired.

Earnings

Beginning flight attendants had median earnings of about $12,800 a year in 1996, according to data from the Association of Flight Attendants. Flight attendants with six years of flying experience had median annual earnings of about $19,000, while some senior flight attendants earned as much as $40,000 a year. Flight attendants receive extra compensation for night and international flights and for increased hours. In addition, flight attendants and their immediate families are entitled to free fares on their own airline and reduced fares on most other airlines.

Many flight attendants belong to the Association of Flight Attendants. Others may be members of the Transport Workers Union of America, the International Brotherhood of Teamsters, or other unions.

Flight attendants are required to buy uniforms and wear them while on duty. Uniform replacement items are usually paid for by the company. The airlines generally provide a small allowance to cover cleaning and upkeep of the uniforms.

Related Occupations

Other jobs that involve helping people as a safety professional while requiring the ability to be pleasant even under trying circumstances include emergency medical technician, firefighter, maritime crew, and camp counselor.

Sources of Additional Information

Information about job opportunities in a particular airline and the qualifications required may be obtained by writing to the personnel manager of the company.

Food and Beverage Service Workers

(*D.O.T.* 310.137-010 and .357; 311.472, .477, .674-010, and -018, and .677; 312; 319.474, .677-014, and .687; 350.677-010, -026, -030; and 352.677-018)

Significant Points

- ✓ *Most jobs are part-time and many opportunities exist for young people–two out of three food counter and fountain workers are 16 to 19 years old.*

- ✓ *Job openings are expected to be abundant through the year 2006, reflecting substantial turnover–characteristic of occupations attractive to people seeking a short-term source of income rather than a career.*

- ✓ *Tips comprise a major portion of earnings; consequently, keen competition is expected for bartender, waiter and waitress, and other jobs in popular restaurants and fine dining establishments, where potential earnings from tips are greatest.*

Nature of the Work

Whether they work in small, informal diners or large, elegant restaurants, all food and beverage service workers deal with customers. The quality of service they deliver determines in part whether or not the patron will return.

Waiters and waitresses take customers' orders, serve food and beverages, prepare itemized checks, and sometimes accept payments. The manner in which they perform their tasks varies considerably, depending on the establishment where they work. In coffee shops, they are expected to provide fast and efficient, yet courteous, service. In fine restaurants, where gourmet meals are accompanied by attentive formal service, waiters and waitresses serve meals at a more leisurely pace and offer more personal service to patrons. For example, servers may recommend a certain wine as a complement to a particular entree, explain how various items on the menu are prepared, or complete preparations on a salad or other special dishes at table side. Additionally, waiters and waitresses may check the identification of patrons to ensure they meet the minimum age requirement for the purchase of alcohol and tobacco products.

Depending on the type of restaurant, waiters and waitresses may perform additional duties generally associated with other food and beverage service occupations. These tasks may include escorting guests to tables, serving customers seated at counters, setting up and clearing tables, or cashiering. However, formal restaurants frequently hire staff to perform these duties, allowing their waiters and waitresses to concentrate on customer service.

Bartenders fill the drink orders that waiters and waitresses take from customers seated in the restaurant or lounge, as well as orders from customers seated at the bar. They prepare standard mixed drinks and, occasionally, are asked to mix drinks to suit a customer's taste. Most bartenders know dozens of drink recipes and are able to mix drinks accurately, quickly, and without waste, even during the busiest periods. Besides mixing and serving drinks, bartenders collect payment, operate the cash register, clean up after customers leave, and, on occasion, serve food items to customers seated at the bar. Bartenders check identification of customers seated at the bar, to ensure they meet the minimum age requirement for the purchase of alcohol and tobacco products.

Bartenders at service bars have little contact with customers, as they work at small bars in restaurants, hotels, and clubs where drinks are served only by waiters and waitresses. However, the majority of bartenders who work in eating and drinking establishments directly serve patrons and interact with them.

Some establishments, especially larger ones, use automatic equipment to mix drinks of varying complexity, at the push of a button. However, bartenders still must be efficient and knowledgeable, in case the device malfunctions or a customer requests a drink not handled by the equipment. Additionally, most customers frequent drinking establishments for the friendly atmosphere and would rather have their drinks prepared by a bartender than a lifeless machine.

Bartenders usually are responsible for ordering and maintaining an inventory of liquor, mixes, and other bar supplies. They often form attractive displays out of bottles and glassware and wash the glassware and utensils after each use.

Hosts and hostesses try to evoke a good impression of the restaurant, by warmly welcoming guests. They may courteously direct patrons to where coats and other personal items may be left and indicate where patrons can wait until their table is ready. Hosts and hostesses assign guests to tables suitable for the size of their group, escort patrons to their seats, and provide menus.

Hosts and hostesses are restaurants' personal representatives. They try to insure that service is prompt and courteous and that the meal meets expectations. Hosts and hostesses schedule dining reservations, arrange parties, and organize any special services that are required. In some restaurants, they also act as cashiers.

Dining room attendants and bartender helpers assist waiters, waitresses, and bartenders by keeping serving areas stocked with supplies, cleaning tables, and removing dirty dishes to the kitchen. They replenish the supply of clean linens, dishes, silverware, and glasses in the restaurant dining room, and keep the bar stocked with glasses, liquor, ice, and drink garnishes. Bartender helpers also keep bar equipment clean and wash glasses. Dining room attendants set tables with clean tablecloths, napkins, silverware, glasses, and dishes and serve ice water, rolls, and butter. At the conclusion of meals, they remove dirty dishes and soiled linens from tables. Cafeteria attendants stock serving tables with food, trays, dishes, and silverware and may carry trays to dining tables for patrons.

Counter attendants take orders and serve food at counters. In cafeterias, they serve food displayed on counters and steam tables, as requested by patrons; carve meat; dish out vegetables; ladle sauces and soups; and fill beverage glasses. In lunchrooms and coffee shops, counter attendants take orders from customers seated at the counter, transmit the orders to the kitchen, and pick up and serve the food, when it is ready. They also fill cups with coffee, soda, and other beverages and prepare fountain specialties, such as milkshakes and ice cream sundaes. Counter attendants prepare some short-order items, such as sandwiches and salads, and wrap or place orders in containers for carry out. They also clean counters, write itemized checks, and accept payment.

Fast-food workers take orders from customers at counters or drive-through windows at fast-food restaurants. They get the ordered beverage and food items, serve them to customer, and accept payment. Many fast-food workers also cook and package food, make coffee, and fill beverage cups using drink-dispensing machines.

Working Conditions

Food and beverage service workers are on their feet most of the time and often carry heavy trays of food, dishes, and glassware. During busy dining periods, they are under pressure to serve customers quickly and efficiently. The work is relatively safe, but care must be taken to avoid slips, falls, and burns.

Part-time work is more common among food and beverage service workers than in almost any other occupation. Workers on part-time schedules include half of all bartenders, two out of three waiters and waitresses, and eight out of ten food counter and fountain workers, compared to one out of four workers throughout the economy. The wide range in dining hours creates work opportunities attractive to homemakers, students, and other individuals seeking supplemental income. For example, two out of three food counter and fountain workers are 16-19 years old. Many food and beverage service workers are expected to work evenings, weekends, and holidays. Some work split shifts—that is, they work for several hours during the middle of the day, take a few hours off in the afternoon, and then return to their jobs for the evening hours.

Employment

Food and beverage service workers held 4.8 million jobs in 1996. Waiters and waitresses held 2 million of these jobs; counter attendants and fast-food workers, 1.7 million; dining room and cafeteria attendants and bartender helpers, 439,000; bartenders, 390,000; and hosts and hostesses, 260,000.

Restaurants, coffee shops, bars, and other retail eating and drinking places employed the overwhelming majority of food and beverage service workers. Others worked in hotels and other lodging places, bowling alleys, casinos, and country clubs and other membership organizations.

Jobs are located throughout the country but are typically plentiful in large cities and tourist areas. Vacation resorts offer seasonal employment, and some workers alternate between summer and winter resorts, instead of remaining in one area the entire year.

Training, Other Qualifications, and Advancement

There are no specific educational requirements for food and beverage service jobs. Although many employers prefer to hire high school graduates for waiter and waitress, bartender, and host and hostess positions, completion of high school is generally not required for fast-food workers, counter attendants, and dining room attendants and bartender helpers. For many people, a job as a food and beverage service worker serves as a source of immediate income, rather than a career. Many entrants to these jobs are in their late teens or early twenties and have a high school education or less. Usually, they have little or no work experience. Many are full-time students or homemakers. Food and beverage service jobs are a major source of part-time employment for high school and college students.

Because maintaining a restaurant's image is important to its success, employers emphasize personal qualities. Food and beverage service workers are in close contact with the public, so these workers should be well-spoken and have a neat, clean appearance. They should enjoy dealing with all kinds of people, and possess a pleasant disposition. State laws often require that food and beverage service workers obtain health certificates showing that they are free of communicable diseases.

Waiters and waitresses need a good memory to avoid confusing customers' orders and to recall faces, names, and preferences of frequent patrons. These workers should also be good at arithmetic, so they can total bills without the assistance of a calculator or cash register if necessary. In restaurants specializing in foreign foods, knowledge of a foreign language is helpful. Prior experience waiting on tables is preferred by restaurants and hotels that have rigid table service standards. Jobs at these establishments often have higher earnings, but may also have higher educational requirements than less demanding establishments.

Generally, bartenders must be at least 21 years of age, but usually employers prefer to hire people who are 25 or older. Bartenders should be familiar with state and local laws concerning the sale of alcoholic beverages.

Most food and beverage service workers pick up their skills on the job by observing and working with more experienced workers. Some employers, particularly those in fast-food restaurants, use self-instruction programs with audiovisual presentations and instructional booklets to teach new employees food preparation and service skills. Some public and private vocational schools, restaurant associations, and large restaurant chains provide classroom training in a generalized food service curriculum.

Some bartenders acquire their skills by attending a bartending or vocational and technical school. These programs often include instruction on state and local laws and regulations, cocktail recipes, attire and conduct, and stocking a bar. Some of these schools help their graduates find jobs.

Due to the relatively small size of most food-serving establishments, opportunities for promotion are limited. After gaining some experience, some dining room and cafeteria attendants and bartender helpers are able to advance to waiter, waitress, or bartender jobs. For waiters, waitresses, and bartenders, advancement usually is limited to finding a job in a more expensive restaurant or bar where prospects for tip earnings are better. Some bartenders open their own businesses. Some hosts and hostesses and waiters and waitresses advance to supervisory jobs, such as maitre d'hotel, dining room supervisor, or restaurant manager. In larger restaurant chains, food and beverage service workers who excel at their work are often invited to enter the company's formal management training program.

Job Outlook

Job openings for food and beverage service workers are expected to be abundant through the year 2006. However, keen competition is expected for bartender, waiter and waitress, and other food and beverage service jobs in popular restaurants and fine dining establishments, where potential earnings from tips are greatest.

While employment growth will produce many new jobs, the overwhelming majority of openings will arise from the need to replace the high proportion of workers who leave this very large occupation each year. There is substantial movement into and out of the occupation because education and training requirements are minimal; and the predominance of part-time jobs is attractive to people seeking a short-term source of income rather than a career. Many of these workers move to other occupations, while others stop working to assume household responsibilities or to attend school.

Employment of food and beverage service occupations is expected to grow about as fast as the average for all occupations through the year 2006. Employment growth will stem from increases in population, personal incomes, and leisure time. Since it is common for both husband and wife to be in the work force, families may increasingly find dining out a convenience.

Growth of the different types of food and beverage service jobs will vary. As the number of families grow, and as the more affluent, 55-and-older population increases rapidly, demand will grow for restaurants that offer table service and more varied menus—spurring demand for waiters and waitresses and hosts and hostesses. Employment of fast-food workers is also expected to increase in response to growth of the 16-24 year-old population and the continuing fast-pace lifestyle of many Americans. However, little change is expected in the employment of dining room attendants as waiters and waitresses increasingly assume their duties. Employment of bartenders is expected to decline as drinking of alcoholic beverages outside the home—particularly cocktails—continues to drop.

Earnings

Food and beverage service workers derive their earnings from a combination of hourly wages and customer tips. Earnings varies greatly, depending on the type of job and establishment. For example, fast-food workers and hosts and hostesses generally do not receive tips, so their wage rates may be higher than those of waiters and waitresses and bartenders, who may earn more from tips than from wages. In some restaurants, these workers contribute a portion of their tips to a tip pool, which is distributed among the establishment's other food and beverage service workers and kitchen staff. Tip pools allow workers who normally do not receive tips, such as dining room attendants, to share in the rewards for a well-served meal.

In 1996, median weekly earnings (including reported tips) of full-time waiters and waitresses were about $270. The middle 50 percent earned between $200 and $350; the top 10 percent earned at least $470 a week. For most waiters and waitresses, higher earnings are primarily the result of receiving more in tips rather than higher hourly wages. Tips generally average between 10 and 20 percent of guests' checks, so waiters and waitresses working in busy, expensive restaurants earn the most.

Full-time bartenders had median weekly earnings (including tips) of about $310 in 1996. The middle 50 percent earned from

$230 and $400; the top 10 percent earned at least $520 a week. Like waiters and waitresses, bartenders employed in public bars may receive more than half of their earnings as tips. Service bartenders are often paid higher hourly wages, to offset their lower tip earnings.

Median weekly earnings (including tips) of full-time dining room attendants and bartender helpers were about $260 in 1996. The middle 50 percent earned between $200 and $320; the top 10 percent earned over $410 a week. Most received over half of their earnings as wages; the rest of their income was their share of the proceeds from tip pools.

Full-time counter attendants and fast-food workers had median weekly earnings (including any tips) of about $220 in 1996. The middle 50 percent earned between $190 and $270, while the highest 10 percent earned over $360 a week. Although some counter attendants receive part of their earnings as tips, fast-food workers generally do not.

In establishments covered by federal law, workers beginning at the minimum wage earn $5.15 an hour. Employers are also permitted to deduct from wages the cost, or fair value, of any meals or lodging provided. However, many employers provide free meals and furnish uniforms. Food and beverage service workers who work full-time often receive typical benefits, while part-time workers generally do not.

In some large restaurants and hotels, food and beverage service workers belong to unions—principally the Hotel Employees and Restaurant Employees International Union and the Service Employees International Union.

Related Occupations

Other workers whose jobs involve serving customers and helping them enjoy themselves include flight attendants, butlers, and tour bus drivers.

Sources of Additional Information

Information about job opportunities may be obtained from local employers and local offices of the state employment service.

A guide to careers in restaurants, a list of two- and four-year colleges that have food service programs, and information on scholarships to those programs is available from:

❑ National Restaurant Association, 1200 17th St. NW, Washington, DC 20036-3097.

For general information on hospitality careers, write to:

❑ Council on Hotel, Restaurant, and Institutional Education, 1200 17th St. NW, Washington, DC 20036-3097.

For general career information and a directory of private career colleges and schools that offer training for bartender and other food and beverage service jobs, write to:

❑ Accrediting Commission of Career Schools and Colleges of Technology, 2101 Wilson Blvd., Suite 302, Arlington, VA 22201.

Foresters and Conservation Scientists

(*D.O.T.* 040.061-030, -046, -050, -054, and -062; .167-010; 049.127)

Significant Points

✓ *About two out of three work for federal, state, or local governments.*

✓ *A bachelor's degree in forestry, range management, or a related field is generally the minimum educational requirement.*

✓ *Projected average employment growth will stem from continuing emphasis on environmental protection and responsible land management.*

Nature of the Work

Forests and rangelands serve a variety of needs" They supply wood products, livestock forage, minerals, and water; serve as sites for recreational activities; and provide habitats for wildlife. Foresters and conservation scientists manage, develop, use, and help protect these and other natural resources.

Foresters manage forested lands for a variety of purposes. Those working in private industry may procure timber from private landowners. To do this, foresters contact local forest owners and gain permission to take inventory of the type, amount, and location of all standing timber on the property, a process known as timber cruising. Foresters then appraise the timber's worth, negotiate the purchase of timber, and draw up a contract for procurement. Next, they subcontract with loggers or pulpwood cutters for tree removal, aid in road layout, and maintain close contact with the subcontractor's workers and the landowner to ensure that the work meets the landowner's requirements, as well as federal, state, and local environmental specifications. Forestry consultants often act as agents for the forest owner, performing the above duties and negotiating timber sales with industrial procurement foresters.

Throughout the process, foresters consider the economics of the purchase as well as the environmental impact on natural resources, a function which has taken on added importance in recent years. To do this, they determine how best to conserve wildlife habitats, creek beds, water quality, and soil stability and how best to comply with environmental regulations. Foresters must balance the desire to conserve forested ecosystems for future generations with the need to use forest resources for recreational or economic purposes.

Through a process called regeneration, foresters also supervise the planting and growing of new trees. They choose and prepare the site, using controlled burning, bulldozers, or herbicides to clear weeds, brush, and logging debris. They advise on the type, number, and placement of trees to be planted. Foresters then monitor the seedlings to ensure healthy growth and to determine the best time for harvesting. If they detect signs of disease or harmful insects, they decide on the best course of treatment to prevent contamination or infestation of healthy trees.

Foresters who work for state and federal governments manage public forests and parks and also work with private landowners to protect and manage forest land outside of the public domain. They may also design campgrounds and recreation areas.

Foresters use a number of tools to perform their jobs: Clinometers measure the heights, diameter tapes measure the diameter, and increment borers and bark gauges measure the growth of trees so that timber volumes can be computed and future growth estimated. Photogrammetry and remote sensing (aerial photographs and other imagery taken from airplanes and satellites) often are used for mapping large forest areas and for detecting widespread trends of forest and land use. Computers are used extensively, both in the office and in the field, for the storage, retrieval, and analysis of information required to manage the forest land and its resources.

Range managers, also called range conservationists, range ecologists, or range scientists, manage, improve, and protect rangelands to maximize their use without damaging the environment. Rangelands cover about one billion acres of the United States, mostly in the western states and Alaska. They contain many natural resources, including grass and shrubs for animal grazing, wildlife habitats, water from vast watersheds, recreation facilities, and valuable mineral and energy resources. Range managers help ranchers attain optimum livestock production by determining the number and kind of animals to graze, the grazing system to use, and the best season for grazing. At the same time, however, they maintain soil stability and vegetation for other uses such as wildlife habitats and outdoor recreation. They also plan and implement revegetation of disturbed sites.

Soil conservationists provide technical assistance to farmers, ranchers, state and local governments, and others concerned with the conservation of soil, water, and related natural resources. They develop programs designed to get the most productive use of land without damaging it. Conservationists visit areas with erosion problems, find the source of the problem, and help landowners and managers develop management practices to combat it.

Foresters and conservation scientists often specialize in one area such as forest resource management, urban forestry, wood technology, or forest economics.

Working Conditions

Working conditions vary considerably. Although some of the work is solitary, foresters and conservation scientists also deal regularly with landowners, loggers, forestry technicians and aides, farmers, ranchers, government officials, special interest groups, and the public in general. Some work regular hours in offices or labs. Others may split their time between field work and office work, while some—especially independent consultants or less experienced workers—spend the majority of their time outdoors overseeing or participating in hands-on work.

The work can be physically demanding. Foresters and conservation scientists who work outdoors do so in all kinds of weather, sometimes in isolated areas. Some foresters may need to walk long distances through densely wooded land to carry out their work. Foresters also may work long hours fighting fires. Conservation scientists often are called in to prevent erosion after a forest fire, and they provide emergency help after floods, mudslides, and tropical storms.

Employment

Foresters and conservation scientists held about 37,000 jobs in 1996. Nearly three out of ten salaried workers were in the federal government, mostly in the U.S. Department of Agriculture (USDA). Foresters were concentrated in the USDA's Forest Service; soil conservationists in the USDA's Natural Resource Conservation Service. Most range managers worked in the Department of the Interior's Bureau of Land Management or in the USDA's Natural Resource Conservation Service. Nearly another three out of ten foresters and conservation scientists worked for state governments, and nearly one out of ten worked for local governments. The remainder worked in private industry, mainly in the forestry industry, logging and lumber companies and sawmills, and research and testing services. Some were self-employed as consultants for private landowners, state and federal governments, and forestry-related businesses.

Although foresters and conservation scientists work in every state, employment of foresters is concentrated in the western and southeastern states, where many national and private forests and parks, and most of the lumber and pulpwood-producing forests, are located. Range managers work almost entirely in the western states, where most of the rangeland is located. Soil conservationists, on the other hand, are employed in almost every county in the country.

Training, Other Qualifications, and Advancement

A bachelor's degree in forestry is the minimum educational requirement for professional careers in forestry. In the federal government, a combination of experience and appropriate education occasionally may substitute for a four-year forestry degree, but job competition makes this difficult.

Fifteen states have mandatory licensing or voluntary registration requirements which a forester must meet in order to acquire the title "professional forester" and practice forestry in the state. Licensing or registration requirements vary by state, but usually entail completing a four-year degree in forestry, a minimum period of training time, and passing an exam.

Foresters who wish to perform specialized research or teach should have an advanced degree, preferably a Ph.D.

Most land-grant colleges and universities offer bachelor's or higher degrees in forestry; 48 of these programs are accredited by the Society of American Foresters. Curriculums stress science, mathematics, communications skills, and computer science, as well as technical forestry subjects. Courses in forest economics and business administration supplement the student's scientific and technical knowledge. Forestry curricula increasingly include courses on best management practices, wetlands analysis, water and soil quality, and wildlife conservation, in response to the growing focus on protecting forested lands during timber harvesting operations. Prospective foresters should have a strong grasp on policy issues and on the increasingly numerous and complex environmental regulations which affect many forestry-related activities. Many colleges require students to complete a field session either in a camp operated by the college or in a cooperative work-study program with a federal or state agency or private industry. All schools encourage students to take summer jobs that provide experience in forestry or conservation work.

A bachelor's degree in range management or range science is the usual minimum educational requirement for range managers; graduate degrees generally are required for teaching and research positions. In 1996, about 30 colleges and universities offered degrees in range management or range science or in a closely related discipline with a range management or range science option. A number of other schools offered some courses in range management or range science. Specialized range management courses combine plant, animal, and soil sciences with principles of ecology and resource management. Desirable electives include economics, forestry, hydrology, agronomy, wildlife, animal husbandry, computer science, and recreation.

Very few colleges and universities offer degrees in soil conservation. Most soil conservationists have degrees in environmental studies, agronomy, general agriculture, hydrology, or crop or soil science; a few have degrees in related fields such as wildlife biology, forestry, and range management. Programs of study generally include 30 semester hours in natural resources or agriculture, including at least three hours in soil science. The Soil and Water Conservation Society sponsors a certification program based on education, experience, and testing. Upon completion of the program, individuals are designated as Certified Professional Erosion and Sediment Control specialist.

In addition to meeting the demands of forestry and conservation research and analysis, foresters and conservation scientists generally must enjoy working outdoors, be physically hardy, and be willing to move to where the jobs are. They must also work well with people and have good communications skills.

Recent forestry and range management graduates usually work under the supervision of experienced foresters or range managers. After gaining experience, they may advance to more responsible positions. In the federal government, most entry-level foresters work in forest resource management. An experienced federal forester may supervise a ranger district, and may advance to forest supervisor, regional forester, or to a top administrative position in the national headquarters. In private industry, foresters start by learning the practical and administrative aspects of the business and acquiring comprehensive technical training. They are then introduced to contract writing, timber harvesting, and decision making. Some foresters work their way up to top managerial positions within their companies. Foresters in management usually leave the field work behind, spending more of their time in an office, working with teams to develop management plans and supervising others. After gaining several years of experience, some foresters may become consulting foresters, working alone or with one or several partners. They contract with state or local governments, private landowners, private industry, or other forestry consulting groups.

Soil conservationists usually begin working within one county or conservation district and with experience may advance to the area, state, regional, or national level. Also, soil conservationists can transfer to related occupations such as farm or ranch management advisor or land appraiser.

Job Outlook

Employment of foresters and conservation scientists is expected to grow about as fast as the average for all occupations through the year 2006. Growth should be strongest in state and local governments, where demand will be spurred by a continuing emphasis on environmental protection and responsible land management. For example, the nationwide Stewardship Incentive Program, funded by the federal government, provides money to the states to encourage landowners to practice multiple-use forest management. Foresters will continue to be needed to help landowners manage their forested property. However, job opportunities are expected to be best for soil conservationists as government regulations, such as those regarding the management of storm water and coastlines, has created demand for persons knowledgeable about erosion on farms and in cities and suburbs. Soil and water quality experts will also be needed as states attempt to improve water quality by preventing pollution by agricultural producers and industrial plants.

Fewer opportunities for foresters and conservation scientists are expected in the federal government, partly due to budgetary constraints. Also, federal land management agencies, such as the Forest Service, are deemphasizing their timber programs and increasingly focusing on wildlife, recreation, and sustaining ecosystems, thereby increasing demand for other life and social scientists relative to foresters. However, a large number of foresters is expected to retire or leave the government for other reasons, resulting in some job openings between 1996 and 2006. In addition, the need for range and soil conservationists to provide technical assistance, through the Natural Resource Conservation Service, to owners of grazing land may lead to a small number of new jobs.

The recent reductions in timber harvesting on public lands, most of which are located in the Northwest and California, also will dampen job growth for private industry foresters in these regions. Opportunities will be better for foresters in the Southeast, where much forested land is privately owned. Rising demand for timber on private lands will increase the need for forest management plans which maximize production while sustaining the environment for future growth. Salaried foresters working for private industry—such as paper companies, sawmills, and pulp wood mills—and consulting foresters will be needed to provide technical assistance and management plans to landowners.

Research and testing firms have increased their hiring of foresters and conservation scientists in recent years in response to demand for professionals to prepare environmental impact statements and erosion and sediment control plans, monitor water quality near logging sites, and advise on tree harvesting practices required by federal, state, or local regulations. Hiring in these firms should continue during the 1996-2006 period, though at a slower rate.

Earnings

In 1997, most graduates entering the federal government as foresters, range managers, or soil conservationists with a bachelor's degree started at $19,500 or $24,200 a year, depending on academic achievement. Those with a master's degree could start at $24,200 or $29,600. Holders of doctorates could start at $35,800 or, in research positions, at $42,900. Beginning salaries were slightly higher in selected areas where the prevailing local pay level was higher. In 1997, the average federal salary for foresters in nonsupervisory, supervisory, and managerial positions was $47,600; for soil conservationists, $45,200; for rangeland managers, $43,100, and for forest products technologists, $62,000.

According to the National Association of Colleges and Employers, graduates with a bachelor's degree in natural resources received an average starting salary offer of $24,800 in 1997.

In private industry, starting salaries for students with a bachelor's degree were comparable to starting salaries in the federal government, but starting salaries in state and local governments were generally lower.

Foresters and conservation scientists who work for federal, state, and local governments and large private firms generally receive more generous benefits than those working for smaller firms.

Related Occupations

Foresters and conservation scientists manage, develop, and protect natural resources. They are aided by range, soil conservation, and forestry technicians. Other workers with similar responsibilities include agricultural scientists, agricultural engineers, biological scientists, environmental scientists and engineers, farm and ranch managers, soil scientists, and wildlife managers.

Sources of Additional Information

For information about the forestry profession and lists of schools offering education in forestry, send a self-addressed, stamped business envelope to:

❑ Society of American Foresters, 5400 Grosvenor Ln., Bethesda, MD 20814. Homepage: http://www.safnet.org

For information about career opportunities in forestry in the federal government, contact:

❑ Chief, U.S. Forest Service, U.S. Department of Agriculture, P.O. Box 96090, SW, Washington, DC 20090-6090.

For information about a career in state forestry organizations, contact:

❑ National Association of State Foresters, 444 N. Capitol St. NW, Suite 540, Washington, DC 20001.

Information about a career as a range manager as well as a list of schools offering training is available from:

❑ Society for Range Management, 1839 York St., Denver, CO 80206.

Information about a career in conservation science is available from:

❑ Soil and Water Conservation Society, 7515 Northeast Ankeny Rd., RR #1, Ankeny, IA 50021-9764.

General Maintenance Mechanics

(D.O.T. 899.261-014 and .381-010)

Significant Points

✓ Job openings should be plentiful, the result of an expected average growth rate and significant turnover in this large occupation.

✓ Most workers learn their skills informally on the job; others learn by working as helpers to other repairers or construction workers such as carpenters, electricians, or machinery repairers.

Nature of the Work

Most craft workers specialize in one kind of work such as plumbing or carpentry. General maintenance mechanics, however, have skills in many different crafts. They repair and maintain machines, mechanical equipment, and buildings, and work on plumbing, electrical, and air-conditioning and heating systems. They build partitions, make plaster or drywall repairs, and fix or paint roofs, windows, doors, floors, woodwork, and other parts of building structures. They also maintain and repair specialized equipment and machinery found in cafeterias, laundries, hospitals, stores, offices, and factories. Typical duties include troubleshooting and fixing faulty electrical switches, repairing air-conditioning motors, and unclog-

ging drains. New buildings sometimes have computer-controlled systems, requiring mechanics to acquire basic computer skills. For example, new air conditioning systems often can be controlled from a central computer terminal. Additionally, light sensors can be electronically controlled to automatically turn off lights after a set amount of time.

Those in small establishments, where they are often the only maintenance worker, do all repairs except for very large or difficult jobs. In larger establishments, their duties may be limited to the general maintenance of everything in a workshop or a particular area.

General maintenance mechanics inspect and diagnose problems and determine the best way to correct them, often checking blueprints, repair manuals, and parts catalogs. They obtain supplies and repair parts from distributors or storerooms. They use common hand and power tools such as screwdrivers, saws, drills, wrenches, and hammers, as well as specialized equipment and electronic test devices. They replace or fix worn or broken parts, where necessary, or make adjustments.

These mechanics also do routine preventive maintenance and ensure that machines continue to run smoothly, building systems operate efficiently, and the physical condition of buildings does not deteriorate. Following a checklist, they may inspect drives, motors, and belts, check fluid levels, replace filters, and perform other maintenance actions. Maintenance mechanics keep records of maintenance and repair work.

Working Conditions

General maintenance mechanics often do a variety of tasks in a single day, generally at a number of different locations in a building, or in several buildings. They may have to stand for long periods, lift heavy objects, and work in uncomfortably hot or cold environments, in awkward and cramped positions, or on ladders. They are subject to electrical shock, burns, falls, and cuts and bruises. Most general maintenance workers work a 40-hour week. Some work evening, night, or weekend shifts, or are on call for emergency repairs.

Those employed in small establishments, where they may be the only maintenance worker, often operate with only limited supervision. Those working in larger establishments often work under the direct supervision of an experienced worker.

Employment

General maintenance mechanics held about 1,362,000 jobs in 1996. They were employed in almost every industry in the economy. More than one-third worked in service industries; most of these worked for elementary and secondary schools, colleges and universities, hotels, and hospitals and nursing homes. About 17 percent worked in manufacturing industries. Others worked for real estate firms that operate office and apartment buildings, wholesale and retail firms, or government agencies.

Training, Other Qualifications, and Advancement

Most general maintenance mechanics learn their skills informally on the job. They start as helpers, watching and learning from skilled maintenance workers. Helpers begin by doing simple jobs such as fixing leaky faucets and replacing light bulbs, and progress to more difficult tasks such as overhauling machinery or building walls.

Others learn their skills by working as helpers to other repair or construction workers such as carpenters, electricians, or machinery repairers. Necessary skills can also be learned in high school shop classes and postsecondary trade or vocational schools. It generally takes from one to four years of on-the-job training or school, or a combination of both, to become fully qualified, depending on the skill level required. Because a growing proportion of new buildings rely on computers to control building systems, general maintenance mechanics may need basic computer skills such as logging on to a central system and navigating through a series of menus. Usually companies that install computer-controlled equipment provide on-site training for general maintenance mechanics.

Graduation from high school is preferred for entry into this occupation. High school courses in mechanical drawing, electricity, woodworking, blueprint reading, science, and mathematics are useful. Mechanical aptitude, ability to use shop math, and manual dexterity are important. Good health is necessary because the job involves much walking, standing, reaching, and heavy lifting. Difficult jobs require problem-solving ability, and many positions require the ability to work without direct supervision.

Many general maintenance mechanics in large organizations advance to maintenance supervisor or to one of the crafts such as electrician, heating/air-conditioning mechanic, or plumber. In small organizations, promotion opportunities are limited.

Job Outlook

Job openings should be plentiful for general maintenance mechanics. Employment is related to the number of buildings—for example, office and apartment buildings, stores, schools, hospitals, hotels, and factories—and amount of equipment needing maintenance and repair. Although the pace of construction of these facilities is expected to be slower than in the past, employment growth is still expected to be about as fast as the average for all occupations through the year 2006. In addition to growth openings, this is a large occupation with a significant turnover rate, and many replacements are needed for those who transfer to other occupations or stop working for other reasons.

Earnings

Earnings vary widely by industry, geographic area, and skill level. According to a survey of workplaces in 160 metropolitan areas, general maintenance mechanics had median earnings of about $9.88 an hour in 1995, with the middle half earning between $8.36 and $11.86 an hour. Median earnings were about $9.41 an hour in service businesses, and about $9.90 an hour in manufacturing businesses. On average, workers in the Midwest and Northeast earned more than those in the West and South. Mechanics earn overtime pay for work in excess of 40 hours per week.

Some general maintenance mechanics are members of unions, including the American Federation of State, County and Municipal Employees and the United Automobile Workers.

Related Occupations

Some of the work of general maintenance mechanics is similar to that of carpenters, plumbers, industrial machinery mechanics, electricians, and air-conditioning, refrigeration, and heating mechanics.

Sources of Additional Information

Information about job opportunities may be obtained from local employers and local offices of state employment services.

General Managers and Top Executives

(*D.O.T. codes are too numerous to list.*)

Significant Points

✓ *This group is among the highest paid workers in the nation, but long hours and substantial travel often are required.*

✓ *Competition for top managerial jobs will be keen because of the large number of qualified applicants seeking jobs.*

Nature of the Work

Chief executive officer, president, executive vice president, owner, partner, brokerage office manager, school superintendent, and police chief—each is a general manager or top executive—the individual who formulates the policies and directs the operations of businesses and corporations, nonprofit institutions, and government agencies.

The fundamental objective of private for-profit companies is to make a profit for their owners, or in corporations, to increase shareholder value. Nonprofit organizations and government agencies implement programs that further their policies within budgetary constraints. General managers and top executives set strategies and try to ensure that their organizations' objectives are met.

A corporation's general goals and policies are established by the chief executive officer in collaboration with other top executives, who are overseen by a board of directors. In a large corporation, the chief executive officer meets frequently with subordinate executives to ensure that operations are being carried out in accordance with these policies. Although the chief executive officer of a corporation retains overall accountability, a chief operating officer may be delegated the authority to oversee the executives who direct the activities of various departments and are responsible for implementing the organization's policies on a day-to-day basis. In publicly-held corporations, it is the board of directors that is ultimately accountable for the success or failure of the enterprise; the chief executive officer reports to the board. In nonprofit corporations, the board of trustees or board of directors fulfills the same role.

The scope of other high level executive's responsibilities depends upon the size of the organization. In large organizations, their duties are highly specialized. Managers of cost and profit centers are responsible for the overall performance of one aspect of the organization, such as manufacturing, marketing, sales, purchasing, finance, personnel, training, administrative services, electronic data processing, property management, transportation, or the legal services department. In smaller firms, the chief executive or general manager might be responsible for all or a number of these functions.

Working Conditions

Top executives are generally provided with spacious offices and secretarial and support staff. General managers in large firms or non-profit organizations are usually provided with comfortable offices close to the top executives to whom they report. Long hours, including evenings and weekends, are the rule for most top executives and general managers, though their schedules may be flexible.

Substantial travel often is required of managers and executives, who may travel between national, regional, and local offices, or overseas, to monitor operations and meet with customers, staff, and other executives. Many managers and executives attend meetings and conferences sponsored by associations. The conferences provide an opportunity to meet with prospective donors, customers, or government officials and contractors, and allow managers and executives to keep abreast of technological and managerial innovations.

In large organizations, frequent job transfers between local offices or subsidiaries are common. General managers and top executives are under intense pressure to earn ever higher profits, provide better service, or attain fundraising and charitable goals. Executives in charge of poorly performing organizations or departments generally find their jobs in jeopardy.

Employment

General managers and top executives held over 3.2 million jobs in 1996. They are found in every industry, but wholesale, retail, and services industries employ over eight out of 10.

Training, Other Qualifications, and Advancement

The educational background of managers and top executives varies as widely as the nature of their responsibilities. Many general managers and top executives have a bachelor's degree or higher in liberal arts or business administration. Their major often is related to the departments they direct–for example, accounting for a manager of finance or computer science for a manager of information systems. Graduate and professional degrees are common. Many managers in administrative, marketing, financial, and manufacturing activities have a master's degree in business administration. Managers in highly technical manufacturing and research activities often have a master's degree in engineering or a doctoral degree in a scientific discipline. A law degree is mandatory for managers of legal departments; hospital administrators generally have a master's degree in health services administration or business administration. College presidents and school superintendents generally have an advanced degree, the former, a doctorate in the field they originally taught, and the latter, often a masters degree in education administration. On the other hand, in industries such as retail trade or transportation, it is possible for individuals without a college degree to work their way up within the company and become managers.

In the public sector, many managers have liberal arts degrees in public administration or one of the social sciences. Park superintendents, for example, often have liberal arts degrees, while police chiefs are generally graduates of law enforcement academies and hold degrees in criminal justice or a related field.

Since many general manager and top executive positions are filled by promoting experienced, lower level managers when an opening occurs, many are promoted from within the organization. Some companies prefer that their top executives have specialized backgrounds and hire individuals who are managers in other organizations. Qualities critical for success include leadership, self-confidence, motivation, decisiveness, flexibility, the ability to communicate effectively, sound business judgment, and stamina.

Advancement may be accelerated by participation in company training programs to gain a broader knowledge of company policy and operations. Through attendance at national or local training programs sponsored by various industry and trade associations and by continuing their education, normally at company expense, managers can become familiar with the latest developments in management techniques and improve their chances of promotion. Every year, thousands of senior managers, who often have experience in a particular field, such as accounting or engineering, attend executive development programs to facilitate their promotion to general managers. Participation in conferences and seminars can expand knowledge of national and international issues influencing the organization and can help develop a network of useful contacts.

General managers and top executives must have highly developed personal skills. An analytical mind able to quickly assess large amounts of information and data is very important, as is the ability to consider and evaluate the interrelationships of numerous factors; they must also be able to communicate clearly and persuasively, and need highly developed interpersonal skills.

General managers may advance to top executive positions, such as executive vice president, in their own firm or they may take a corresponding position in another firm. They may even advance to peak corporate positions such as chief operating officer or chief executive officer. Chief executive officers often become members of the board of directors of one or more firms, typically as a director of their own firm and often as chair of its board of directors. Some general managers and top executives go on to establish their own firms or become independent consultants.

Job Outlook

Employment of general managers and top executives is expected to grow about as fast as the average for all occupations through the year 2006. Because this is a large occupation, many openings will occur each year as executives transfer to other positions, start their own businesses, or retire. Nonetheless, competition for top managerial jobs will be keen. Many executives who leave their jobs transfer to other executive or managerial positions, limiting openings for new entrants.

Projected employment growth of general managers and top executives varies widely among industries. For example, employment growth is expected to be faster than average in all services industries combined, but only about as fast as average in all finance, insurance, and real estate industry subgroups. Employment of general managers and top executives is projected to decline in manufacturing industries overall.

Experienced managers whose accomplishments reflect strong leadership qualities and the ability to improve the efficiency or competitive position of an organization will have the best opportunities. In an increasingly global economy, certain types of experience, such as international economics, marketing, information systems, and knowledge of several languages, may also help.

Earnings

General managers and top executives are among the highest paid workers in the nation. However, salary levels vary substantially depending upon the level of managerial responsibility, length of service, and type, size, and location of the firm.

At the highest level, chief executive officers (CEOs) of medium and large corporations are extremely well paid. Salaries often are related to the size of the corporation–a top manager in a very large corporation can earn significantly more than a counterpart in a small firm. Total compensation often includes stock options, dividends, and other performance bonuses, in addition to salaries.

Salaries also vary substantially by type and level of responsibilities and by industry. According to a salary survey by Robert Half International, senior vice presidents/heads of lending in banks with $1 billion or more in assets earned about $200,000 to $215,000 in 1997. Executive Compensation Reports, a division of Harcourt Brace & Company, reports that the median salary for CEOs of public companies from the fiscal year 1995 Fortune 500 list was approximately $714,000, with three-quarters making less than about $900,000. In the nonprofit sector, three quarters of the CEOs make under $135,000 in 1996, according to a survey by Abbott, Langer, & Associates.

Company-paid insurance premiums and physical examinations, the use of executive dining rooms and company cars, and expense allowances are among benefits commonly enjoyed by general managers and top executives in private industry. CEOs often enjoy company-paid club memberships, a limousine with driver, and other amenities. CEOs of very large corporations may have the use of private aircraft.

Related Occupations

General managers and top executives plan, organize, direct, control, and coordinate the operations of an organization and its major departments or programs. The members of the board of directors and supervisory managers are also involved in these activities. Related occupations in government with similar functions are President, governor, mayor, commissioner, and legislator.

Sources of Additional Information

For a wide variety of information on general managers and top executives, including educational programs and job listings, contact:

❑ American Management Association, 1601 Broadway, New York, NY 10019-7420.

❑ National Management Association, 2210 Arbor Blvd., Dayton, OH 45439.

General Office Clerks

(D.O.T. 209.362-030, .562-010; 219.362-010, -022, -026; 243.362-014; 245.362-014, .367-010, -014, -018; 249.367-010, -014; 375.362-010)

Significant Points

✓ *Most general office clerk jobs are entry-level administrative support positions, although previous office or business experience may be required.*

✓ *The number of job openings is large due to the size of this occupation and high turnover.*

Nature of the Work

The duties of general office clerks are too varied and diverse for them to be classified in any specific administrative support occupation. Rather than performing a single specialized task, the duties of a general office clerk change with the needs of their employer. Some may spend their days filing or typing; others enter data at a computer terminal. They also may operate photocopiers, fax machines, or other office equipment; prepare mailings; proofread copy; and answer telephones and deliver messages.

Duties vary significantly depending upon the office in which a clerk works. A general office clerk in a doctor's office may not perform the same tasks as a clerk in a large financial institution or in the office of an auto parts wholesaler. Although they all may sort checks, keep payroll records, take inventory, or access information, they may also perform duties unique to their employer, such as organizing medications, making transparencies for a presentation, or filling orders received by fax machine.

Duties also vary by level of experience. Inexperienced employees may make photocopies, stuff envelopes, or record inquiries. Experienced clerks might maintain financial or other records, verify statistical reports for accuracy and completeness, handle and adjust customer complaints, make travel arrangements, take inventory of equipment and supplies, answer questions on departmental services and functions, or help prepare invoices or budgetary requests. In addition, senior general office clerks may be expected to oversee and direct the work of lower level clerks.

Working Conditions

For the most part, working conditions for general office clerks are the same as those for other office employees within the same company. Those on a full-time schedule usually work a standard 40-hour week. Some may work shifts or overtime during busy periods and about one in three works part-time. In addition, many general office clerks work as temporaries.

Employment

General office clerks held about 3,111,000 jobs in 1996. Most are employed in relatively small businesses. Although they work in every sector of the economy, almost 60 percent worked in the services or wholesale and retail trade industries.

Training, Other Qualifications, and Advancement

Most general office clerk jobs are entry-level administrative support positions, although previous office or business experience may be required. Employers usually require a high school diploma, and some require typing, basic computer skills, and other general office skills. Familiarity with computer word processing software and applications is becoming increasingly important.

Training for this occupation is available through business education programs offered in high schools, community and junior colleges, and postsecondary vocational schools. Courses in word-processing, computer applications, and office practices are particularly helpful.

Because general office clerks usually work with other office staff, they should be cooperative and be able to work as part of a team. They should have good communication skills and pay close attention to details. They must also be willing to change with the needs of the work environment or take on additional responsibilities.

General office clerks who exhibit strong communication, interpersonal, and analytical skills may be promoted to supervisory positions. Others may move into different, more senior clerical or administrative jobs, such as receptionist, secretary, or administrative assistant. After gaining some work experience or specialized skills, many workers often transfer to jobs with higher pay or greater advancement potential. Advancement to professional occupations within an establishment usually requires more formal education, including a college degree.

Job Outlook

Employment of general office clerks is expected to grow more slowly than the average for all occupations through the year 2006. Nonetheless, good job opportunities should continue to exist. Due to the large size and the high turnover associated with these positions, the occupation will continue to produce a large number of job openings.

Increasing use of computers and expanding office automation mean a wider variety of duties can be performed by fewer office workers. As more small businesses consolidate their clerical staffs and job responsibilities become more diverse, it is common to find a single general office clerk in charge of all clerical work. However, as duties expand, employers will seek workers with more advanced computer skills and a broader range of office experience.

Job seekers who have computer word-processing skills and other secretarial skills, and knowledge of the operation of basic office machinery, such as fax machines and copiers, should have the best opportunities. Because they must be so versatile, general office clerks find work in virtually every kind of industry. In addition, they should find many opportunities for part-time or temporary work, especially during peak business periods in industries where these jobs are concentrated.

Earnings

Median annual earnings of full-time general office clerks were about $19,300 in 1996; the middle 50 percent earned between $15,300 and $26,200 annually. Ten percent earned less than $12,400, and 10 percent more than $34,600.

According to a survey of workplaces in 160 metropolitan areas, beginning general office clerks had median annual earnings of about $14,200 in 1995, with the middle half earning about $12,500 to $16,400 a year. The most experienced general office clerks had median annual earnings of about $25,300, with the middle half earning between about $21,800 and $29,000 a year. General office clerks' salaries varied by industry.

In early 1997, the federal government paid general office clerks a starting salary of between $16,710 and $21,720 a year, depending on education and experience. General office clerks employed by the federal government earned an average annual salary of about $26,350.

Related Occupations

General office clerk usually is an entry-level office job. Since the duties of general office clerks may include a combination of bookkeeping, typing, office machine operation, and filing, a variety of other administrative support workers perform similar duties.

Entry-level jobs in other settings include cashier, medical assistant, teacher aide, and food and beverage service worker.

Sources of Additional Information

State employment service offices and agencies specializing in placing administrative support personnel can provide information about job openings for general office clerks.

Geologists and Geophysicists

(D.O.T. 024.061 except -014, and .161)

Significant Points

✓ *Work at remote field sites is common.*

✓ *A bachelor's degree in geology or geophysics is adequate for entry-level jobs; better jobs with good advancement potential usually require at least a master's degree; and a Ph.D. is required for most research positions in colleges and universities, and for some research jobs in government.*

✓ *Job opportunities are expected to be good in the petroleum and related industries, reflecting increasing demand for energy coupled with fewer degrees awarded in geology in recent years.*

Nature of the Work

Geologists and geophysicists, also known as geological scientists or geoscientists, study the physical aspects and history of the Earth. They identify and examine rocks, study information collected by remote sensing instruments in satellites, conduct geological surveys, construct field maps, and use instruments to measure the Earth's gravity and magnetic field. They also analyze information collected through seismic studies, which involves bouncing energy waves off buried rock layers. Many geologists and geophysicists search for oil, natural gas, minerals, and groundwater.

Other geological scientists play an important role in preserving and cleaning up the environment. Their activities include designing and monitoring waste disposal sites, preserving water supplies, and reclaiming contaminated land and water to comply with federal environmental regulations. They also help locate safe sites for hazardous waste facilities and landfills.

Geologists and geophysicists examine chemical and physical properties of specimens in laboratories. They study fossil remains of animal and plant life, or experiment with the flow of water and oil through rocks. Some geoscientists use two- or three-dimensional computer modeling to portray water layers and the flow of water or other fluids through rock cracks and porous materials. They use a variety of sophisticated laboratory instruments, including x-ray diffractometers, which determine the crystal structure of minerals, and petrographic microscopes, for the study of rock and sediment samples. Geoscientists also use seismographs, instruments which measure energy waves resulting from movements in the Earth's crust, to determine the locations and intensities of earthquakes.

Geoscientists working in metal mining or the oil and gas industry sometimes process and interpret the maps produced by remote sensing satellites to help identify potential new mineral, oil, or gas deposits. Seismic technology is also an important exploration tool. Seismic waves are used to develop three-dimensional computer models of underground or underwater rock formations. Seismic reflection technology may also reveal unusual underground features which sometimes indicate accumulations of natural gas or petroleum, facilitating exploration and reducing the risks associated with drilling in previously unexplored areas.

Geologists and geophysicists also apply geological knowledge to engineering problems in constructing large buildings, dams, tunnels, and highways. Some administer and manage research and exploration programs; others become general managers in petroleum and mining companies.

Geology and geophysics are closely related fields, but there are major differences. Geologists study the composition, structure, and history of the Earth's crust. They try to find out how rocks were formed and what has happened to them since formation. Geophysicists use the principles of physics, mathematics, and chemistry to study not only the Earth's surface, but its internal composition, ground and surface waters, atmosphere, oceans, and its magnetic, electrical, and gravitational forces. Both, however, commonly apply their skills and knowledge to the search for natural resources and to solve environmental problems.

There are numerous subdisciplines or specialties falling under the two major disciplines of geology and geophysics which further differentiate the type of work geoscientists do. For example, petroleum geologists explore for oil and gas deposits by studying and mapping the subsurface of the ocean or land. They use sophisticated geophysical instrumentation, well log data, and computers to collect information. Mineralogists analyze and classify minerals and precious stones according to composition and structure. Paleontologists study fossils found in geological formations to trace the evolution of plant and animal life and the geologic history of the Earth. Stratigraphers help to locate minerals by studying the distribution and arrangement of sedimentary rock layers and by examining the fossil and mineral content of such layers. Those who study marine geology are usually called oceanographers or marine geologists. They study and map the ocean floor, and collect information using remote sensing devices aboard surface ships or underwater research craft.

Geophysicists may specialize in areas such as geodesy, seismology, or marine geophysics, also known as physical oceanography. Geodesists study the size and shape of the Earth, its gravitational field, tides, polar motion, and rotation. Seismologists interpret data from seismographs and other geophysical instruments to detect earthquakes and locate earthquake-related faults. Volcanologists, geochemists, and petrologists study the chemical and physical evolution of rocks and minerals, particularly igneous and metamorphic rocks. Geomagnetists measure the Earth's magnetic field and use measurements taken over the past few centuries to devise theoretical models to explain its origin. Paleomagnetists interpret fossil magnetization in rocks and sediments from the continents and oceans, which record the spreading of the sea floor, the wandering of the continents, and the many reversals of polarity that the Earth's magnetic field has undergone through time. Physical oceanographers study the physical aspects of oceans such as currents and the interaction of the surface of the sea with the atmosphere. Other geophysicists study atmospheric sciences and space physics.

Hydrology is a discipline closely related to geology and geophysics. Hydrologists study the distribution, circulation, and physical properties of underground and surface waters. They study the form and intensity of precipitation, its rate of infiltration into the soil, movement through the Earth, and its return to the ocean and atmosphere. The work they do is particularly important in environmental preservation and remediation.

Working Conditions

Some geoscientists spend the majority of their time in an office, but many others divide their time between fieldwork and office or laboratory work. Geologists often travel to remote field sites by helicopter or four-wheel drive vehicles, and cover large areas on foot. Exploration geologists and geophysicists often work overseas or in isolated areas, leading to job relocation. Many exploration geologists travel to meet with prospective clients or investors. Marine geologists and oceanographers may spend considerable time at sea on academic research ships.

Geoscientists in positions funded by federal government agencies may be under pressure to design programs and write grant proposals in order to continue their data collection and research. Geoscientists in consulting jobs may face similar pressures to market their skills and write proposals to maintain steady work.

Employment

Geologists and geophysicists held about 47,000 jobs in 1996. Many more individuals held geology, geophysics, and oceanography faculty positions in colleges and universities, but they are considered college and university faculty.

Among salaried geologists and geophysicists, nearly four in ten were employed in engineering and management services, and two in ten worked for oil and gas extraction companies or metal mining companies. About one geoscientist in seven was self-employed; most were consultants to industry or government.

The federal government employed about 5,800 geologists, geophysicists, oceanographers, and hydrologists in 1996. Over half worked for the Department of the Interior, mostly within the U.S. Geological Survey (USGS). Others worked for the Departments of Defense, Agriculture, Commerce, and Energy, and the Environmental Protection Agency. Over 3,000 worked for state agencies such as state geological surveys and state departments of conservation.

Training, Other Qualifications, and Advancement

A bachelor's degree in geology or geophysics is adequate for entry-level jobs, but better jobs with good advancement potential usually require at least a master's degree in geology or geophysics. Persons with degrees in physics, chemistry, mathematics, or computer science may also qualify for some geophysics or geology jobs if their course work included study in geology. A Ph.D. is required for most research positions in colleges and universities, and is also important for work in federal agencies and some state geological surveys involving basic research.

Hundreds of colleges and universities offer a bachelor's degree in geology; fewer schools offer programs in geophysics, oceanography, or other geosciences. Other programs offering related training for beginning geological scientists include geophysical technology, geophysical engineering, geophysical prospecting, engineering geology, petroleum geology, hydrology, and geochemistry. In addition, several hundred more universities award advanced degrees in geology or geophysics.

Traditional geoscience courses emphasizing classical geologic methods and topics (such as mineralogy, paleontology, stratigraphy, and structural geology) are important for all geoscientists. Those students interested in working in the environmental or regulatory fields, either in environmental consulting firms or federal or state government, should take courses in hydrology, hazardous waste management, environmental legislation, chemistry, fluid mechanics, and geologic logging. An understanding of environmental regulations and government permit issues is also valuable for those planning to work in mining and oil and gas extraction. Computer skills are becoming essential for prospective geoscientists; students who have some experience with computer modeling, data analysis and integration, digital mapping, remote sensing, and geographic information systems (GIS) will be the most prepared entering the job market. A knowledge of the Global Positioning System (GPS) is very helpful. Some employers seek applicants with field experience, so a summer internship may be beneficial to prospective geoscientists.

Geologists and geophysicists must be able to work as part of a team. Strong oral and written communication skills are important, as well as the ability to think independently and creatively. Those involved in fieldwork must have physical stamina.

Geologists and geophysicists often begin their careers in field exploration or as research assistants in laboratories or offices. They are given more difficult assignments as they gain experience. Eventually, they may be promoted to project leader, program manager, or another management and research position.

Job Outlook

Many jobs for geologists and geophysicists are in or related to the petroleum industry, especially the exploration for oil and gas. This industry is subject to cyclical fluctuations. During the 1980s and the early 1990s, low oil prices, higher production costs, improvements in energy efficiency, shrinking oil reserves, and restrictions on potential drilling sites caused exploration activities to be curtailed in the United States; this limited the number of job openings for geoscientists in the petroleum and related industries. As a result of generally poor job prospects, the number of graduates in geology and geophysics, especially in petroleum geology, dropped considerably during the last decade.

Recently, a growing worldwide demand for oil and gas, and new exploration and recovery techniques, have returned stability to the petroleum industry and increased the demand for geologists and geophysicists. Growing populations, stronger economies in the United States and abroad, and continuing industrialization of developing countries are driving the need for more energy. At the same time, the oil and gas and related industries—such as petroleum engineering services—are taking advantage of new technologies that lower costs and facilitate exploration and recovery of natural gas and oil, particularly in deep water and other previously inaccessible sites. Because of the lower number of degrees awarded in geology recently and the significant number of geoscientists who left the industry during earlier periods of downsizing, job opportunities in the petroleum and related industries are expected to be good. Employment prospects will be best for job seekers who hold a master's degree and are familiar with advanced technologies, such as computer modeling and GPS, which are increasingly used to locate new oil and gas fields or pinpoint hidden deposits in existing fields. Because of the cyclical nature of the oil and gas industry, hiring on a contractual basis is common.

Employment of geologists and geophysicists is expected to grow about as fast as the average for all occupations through the year 2006, due in part to the generally improved outlook in the oil and gas industry. Geologists and geophysicists will also continue to be needed to work in areas of environmental protection and reclamation. Some will help clean up contaminated sites in the United States, and others will help private companies and government comply with numerous and complex environmental regulations. However, job opportunities in state and federal government and in environmental consulting firms are expected to be fewer in number than in the previous decade and, in some cases, may be limited to replacing retirees or those who leave geoscience jobs for other reasons. The USGS, the primary employer of geologists in the federal government, has recently faced cutbacks. Hiring should continue to be very limited in the USGS and other agencies, as the federal government attempts to balance its budget during the 1996-2006 projection period. Oceanographers, whose work is often research-oriented and dependent on grants from federal agencies, are expected to face strong competition. Budget constraints are expected to continue to limit hiring in state government as well.

Earnings

Surveys by the National Association of Colleges and Employers indicate that graduates with bachelor's degrees in geology and the geological sciences received an average starting salary offer of about $30,900 a year in 1997. However, starting salaries can vary widely depending on the employing industry. For example, according to a 1996 American Association of Petroleum Geologists survey, the average salary in the oil and gas industry for geoscientists with less than two years of experience was about $48,400.

The petroleum, mineral, and mining industries offer higher salaries, but less job security, than other industries. These industries are vulnerable to recessions and changes in oil and gas prices, among other factors, and usually release workers when exploration and drilling slow down.

In 1997, the federal government's average salary for geologists in managerial, supervisory, and nonsupervisory positions was $59,700; for geophysicists, $67,100; for hydrologists, $54,800; and for oceanographers, $62,700.

Related Occupations

Many geologists and geophysicists work in the petroleum and natural gas industry. This industry also employs many other workers in the scientific and technical aspects of petroleum and natural gas exploration and extraction, including engineering technicians, science technicians, petroleum engineers, and surveyors. Also, some life scientists, physicists, chemists, and meteorologists—as well as mathematicians, computer scientists, soil scientists, and mapping scientists—perform related work in both petroleum and natural gas exploration and extraction, and in environment-related activities.

Sources of Additional Information

Information on training and career opportunities for geologists is available from:

- ❏ American Geological Institute, 4220 King St., Alexandria, VA 22302-1502. Homepage: http://www.agiweb.org
- ❏ Geological Society of America, P.O. Box 9140, Boulder, CO 80301-9140. Homepage: http://www.geosociety.org
- ❏ American Association of Petroleum Geologists, Communications Department, P.O. Box 979, Tulsa, OK 74101.

Information on training and career opportunities for geophysicists is available from:

- ❏ American Geophysical Union, 2000 Florida Ave. NW, Washington, DC 20009.

A list of education and training programs in oceanography and related fields is available from:

- ❏ Marine Technology Society, 1828 L St. NW, Suite 906, Washington, DC 20036.

Information on acquiring a job as a geologist, geophysicist, hydrologist, or oceanographer with the federal government may be obtained from the Office of Personnel Management through a telephone-based system. Consult your telephone directory under U.S. government for a local number or call (912) 757-3000 (TDD 912 744-2299). That number is not toll-free and charges may result. Information also is available from their Internet site: http://www.usajobs.opm.gov

Guards

(D.O.T. 372.563, .567-010, .667-010, -014, -030 through -038; 376.667-010; 379.667-010)

Significant Points

- ✓ *Job opportunities are expected to be favorable through the year 2006. High turnover and this occupation's large size ranks it among those providing the greatest number of job openings in the economy.*
- ✓ *Many employers of unarmed guards do not have any specific educational requirements.*
- ✓ *Employers generally will not hire applicants that have been convicted of a serious crime.*

Nature of the Work

Guards, also called security officers, patrol and inspect property to protect against fire, theft, vandalism, and illegal entry. Their duties vary with the size, type, and location of their employer.

In office buildings, banks, hospitals, and department stores, guards protect people, records, merchandise, money, and equipment. In department stores, they often work with undercover detectives to watch for theft by customers or store employees.

At air, sea, and rail terminals, and other transportation facilities, guards protect people, merchandise being shipped, property, and equipment. They screen passengers and visitors for weapons, explosives, and other contraband, ensure nothing is stolen while being loaded or unloaded, and watch for fires and prowlers. They may direct traffic.

Guards who work in public buildings, such as museums or art galleries, protect paintings and exhibits by inspecting the people and packages entering and leaving the building. They answer routine questions from visitors and sometimes guide tours.

In factories, laboratories, government buildings, data processing centers, and military bases in which valuable property or information—such as information on new products, computer codes, or defense secrets—must be protected, guards check the credentials of persons and vehicles entering and leaving the premises. University, park, or recreation guards perform similar duties and also may issue parking permits and direct traffic. Golf course patrollers prevent unauthorized persons from using the facility and help keep play running smoothly.

At social affairs, sports events, conventions, and other public gatherings, guards provide information, assist in crowd control, and watch for persons who may cause trouble. Some guards patrol places of entertainment, such as nightclubs, to preserve order among customers and to protect property.

Armored car guards protect money and valuables during transit. Bodyguards protect individuals from bodily injury, kidnapping, or invasion of privacy.

In a large organization, a security officer is often in charge of the guard force; in a small organization, a single worker may be responsible for all security measures. Patrolling is usually done on foot, but if the property is large, guards may make their rounds by car or motor scooter. As more businesses purchase advanced electronic security systems to protect their property, more guards are being assigned to stations where they monitor perimeter security, environmental functions, communications, and other systems. In many cases, these guards maintain radio contact with other guards patrolling on foot or in motor vehicles. Some guards use computers to store information on matters relevant to security—for example, visitors or suspicious occurrences—during their hours on duty.

As they make their rounds, guards check all doors and windows, see that no unauthorized persons remain after working hours, and ensure that fire extinguishers, alarms, sprinkler systems, furnaces, and various electrical and plumbing systems are working properly.

Guards who carry weapons must be licensed by the appropriate government authority, and some receive further certification as special police officers, which allows them to make limited types of arrests while on duty. Unarmed guards may carry a flashlight, whistle, two-way radio, and a watch clock—a device that indicates the time at which they reach various checkpoints.

Working Conditions

Most guards spend considerable time on their feet patrolling buildings, industrial plants, and grounds. Indoors, they may be stationed at a guard desk to monitor electronic security and surveillance devices, or to check the credentials of persons entering or leaving the premises. They also may be stationed at a gate, or may patrol grounds in all weather.

Because some guards work alone, especially at night, there may be no one nearby to help if an accident or injury occurs. Many guards use a portable radio or telephone that allows them to be in constant contact with a central station outside the guarded area. If they fail to transmit an expected signal, the central station investigates. Guard work is usually routine, but guards must be constantly alert for threats to themselves and the property they are protecting. Guards who work during the day may have a great deal of contact with other employees and members of the public.

Many guards work alone at night; the usual shift lasts eight hours. Some employers have three shifts, and guards rotate to divide daytime, weekend, and holiday work equally. Guards usually eat on the job instead of taking a regular break away from the site.

Employment

Guards held about 955,000 jobs in 1996. Industrial security firms and guard agencies employed 59 percent of all guards. These organizations provide security services on contract, assigning their guards to buildings and other sites as needed. The remainder were in-house guards, employed in many settings including banks, building management companies, hotels, hospitals, retail stores, restaurants, bars, schools, and government.

Guard jobs are found throughout the country, mostly in metropolitan areas.

Training, Other Qualifications, and Advancement

Most states require that guards be licensed. To be licensed as a guard, individuals must generally be 18 years old, pass a background examination, and complete classroom training in such subjects as property rights, emergency procedures, and detention of suspected criminals.

Many employers of unarmed guards do not have any specific educational requirements. For armed guards, employers generally prefer individuals who are high school graduates. Some jobs require a driver's license. For positions as armed guards, employers often seek people who have had experience in the military or in law enforcement. Most persons entering guard jobs have prior work experience, although it is usually unrelated. Because of limited formal training requirements and flexible hours, this occupation attracts some persons seeking a second job.

Applicants are expected to have good character references, no serious police record, good health—especially hearing and vision—and good personal habits such as neatness and dependability. They should be mentally alert, emotionally stable, and physically fit in order to cope with emergencies. Guards who have frequent contact with the public should be friendly and personable. Some employers require applicants to take a polygraph examination or a psychological profile. Many employers require applicants and experienced workers to submit to drug screening tests as a condition of employment.

Candidates for guard jobs in the federal government must have some experience as a guard and pass a written examination in order to be certified by the General Services Administration. Armed Forces experience is an asset. For most federal guard positions, applicants must qualify in the use of firearms.

The amount of training guards receive varies. Training requirements are higher for armed guards, because their employers are legally responsible for any use of force. Armed guards receive formal training in areas such as weapons retention and laws covering the use of force.

Many employers give newly hired guards instruction before they start the job and also provide several weeks of on-the-job training. An increasing number of states are making ongoing training a legal requirement for retention of certification. Guards may receive training in protection, public relations, report writing, crisis deterrence, first aid, as well as specialized training relevant to their particular assignment.

Guards employed at establishments placing a heavy emphasis on security usually receive extensive formal training. For example, guards at nuclear power plants undergo several months of training before being placed on duty under close supervision. They are taught to use firearms, administer first aid, operate alarm systems and electronic security equipment, and spot and deal with security problems. Guards authorized to carry firearms may be periodically tested in their use. Some guards are likewise periodically tested for health, strength and endurance.

Although guards in small companies receive periodic salary increases, advancement is limited. However, most large organizations use a military type of ranking that offers the possibility of advancement in position and salary. Guards with talent and some college education may advance to jobs that involve administrative and management duties. Guards with management skills may open their own contract security guard agencies.

Job Outlook

Job opportunities for persons seeking work as guards are expected to be favorable through the year 2006. High turnover and this occupation's large size rank it among those providing the greatest number of job openings in the economy. Many opportunities are expected for persons seeking full-time employment, as well as for those seeking part-time or second jobs at night or on weekends. However, some competition is expected for higher paying, high security positions. Compared to unarmed security guards, armed guards and special police enjoy higher earnings and benefits, greater job security, more advancement potential, and are usually given more training and responsibility.

Employment of guards is expected to grow faster than the average for all occupations through the year 2006. Increased concern about crime, vandalism, and terrorism will heighten the need for security in and around homes, plants, stores, offices, and recreation areas. Demand for guards will also grow as private security firms increasingly perform duties—such as monitoring crowds at airports and providing security in courts—formerly handled by government police officers and marshals. Because engaging the services of a security guard firm is easier and less costly than assuming direct responsibility for hiring, training, and managing a security guard force, job growth is expected to be concentrated among contract security guard agencies.

Guards employed by industrial security and guard agencies are occasionally laid off when the firm at which they work does not renew its contract with their agency. Most are able to find employment with other agencies, however, and may continue to work at the same location for the firm that won the contract. Guards employed directly by the firm at which they work are seldom laid off because a plant or factory must still be protected even when economic conditions force it to close temporarily.

Earnings

Median annual earnings of guards who worked full-time in 1996 were about $17,300. The middle 50 percent earned between $10,300 and $25,100. The lowest 10 percent earned less than $10,300 and the highest tenth earned more than $35,600. Guards generally earn slightly more in urban areas.

According to a survey of workplaces in 160 metropolitan areas, guards with the least responsibility and training had median hourly earnings of $6.50 in 1995. The middle half earned between $5.50 and $7.92 an hour. Guards with more specialized training and experience had median hourly earnings of $11.73.

Depending on their experience, newly hired guards in the federal government earned $15,500 or $17,500 a year in 1997. Beginning salaries were slightly higher in selected areas where the prevailing local pay level was higher. Guards employed by the federal government averaged about $22,900 a year in 1997. These workers usually receive overtime pay as well as a wage differential for the second and third shifts.

Related Occupations

Guards protect property, maintain security, and enforce regulations for entry and conduct in the establishments at which they work. Related security and protective service occupations include bailiffs, correction officers, house or store detectives, and private investigators.

Sources of Additional Information

Further information about work opportunities for guards is available from local detective and guard firms and the nearest state employment service office.

Information about licensing requirements for guards may be obtained from the state licensing commission or the state police department. In states where local jurisdictions establish licensing requirements, contact a local government authority such as the sheriff, county executive, or city manager.

Handlers, Equipment Cleaners, Helpers, and Laborers

(*D.O.T.* codes are too numerous to list.)

Significant Points

✓ *Job openings should be numerous because the occupation is very large and turnover is relatively high.*

✓ *Most jobs require no work experience or specific training, but earnings are low.*

Nature of the Work

Employers in almost all industries hire entry-level workers to do tasks requiring little training, or to assist more skilled production, construction, operating, and maintenance workers. These workers perform a broad array of material mover, helper, or laborer jobs, ranging from moving boxes and feeding machines, to cleaning equipment and work areas. Many do tasks that are needed to make the work of more skilled employees flow smoothly. Handlers, equipment cleaners, helpers, and laborers often do routine physical work under close supervision. They generally follow oral or written instructions from supervisors or more experienced workers, and have little opportunity to make decisions. In order to perform their jobs effectively, helpers and laborers must be familiar with the duties of workers they help, as well as with the materials, tools, and machinery they use.

Freight, stock, and material hand movers move materials to and from storage and production areas, loading docks, delivery vehicles, ships' holds, and containers. They move materials either manually, or with forklifts, dollies, hand trucks, or carts. Their specific duties vary by industry and work setting. Specialized workers within this group include stevedores, who load and unload ships;

baggage and cargo handlers, who work in transportation industries; and furniture movers. In factories, they may move raw materials, components, and finished goods between loading docks, storage areas, and work areas. They receive and sort materials and supplies and prepare them according to work orders for delivery to work or storage areas.

Hand packers and packagers manually pack, package or wrap a wide variety of materials. They may inspect items for defects, label cartons, stamp information on products, keep records of items packed, and stack packages on loading docks. This group also includes order fillers, who pack materials for shipment, as well as grocery store courtesy clerks. In grocery stores, they may bag groceries, carry packages to customers' cars, and return shopping carts to designated areas.

Machine feeders and offbearers feed materials into or remove materials from automatic equipment or machines tended by other workers.

Service station attendants fill fuel tanks and wash windshields on automobiles, buses, trucks, and other vehicles. They may perform simple service and repair tasks under the direction of a mechanic, such as change oil, repair tires, and replace belts, lights, windshield wipers, and other accessories. They may also collect payment for services and supplies.

Refuse and recyclable material collectors gather trash, garbage, and recyclables from homes and businesses along a regularly scheduled route, and deposit the refuse in their truck for transport to a dump, landfill, or recycling center. They lift and empty garbage cans or recycling bins by hand, or operate a hydraulic lift truck that picks up and empties dumpsters.

Vehicle washers and equipment cleaners clean machinery, vehicles, storage tanks, pipelines, and similar equipment using water and other cleaning agents, vacuums, hoses, brushes, cloths, and other cleaning equipment.

Parking lot attendants assist customers in parking their cars in lots or storage areas and collect fees from customers.

Helpers assist skilled construction trades workers, mechanics and repairers, and workers in production and extractive occupations. They aid machine operators and tenders by moving materials, supplies, and tools to and from work areas. Some may tend machines if an operator is not available. Helpers may sort finished products, keep records of machine processes, report malfunctions to operators, and clean machinery after use. Mechanics' helpers assist mechanics and service technicians who repair motor vehicles, industrial machinery, and electrical, electronic, and other equipment. They may fetch tools, materials, and supplies; hold materials or tools; take apart defective equipment; remove rivets; prepare replacement parts; or clean work areas. Construction trades' helpers carry tools, materials, and equipment to carpenters, electricians, plasterers, masons, painters, plumbers, roofers, and other construction trades workers.

Construction craft laborers, on the other hand, are skilled workers who provide much of the physically demanding labor at building, highway, and heavy construction projects, tunnel and shaft excavations, and demolition sites. In addition to assisting other trades workers, construction craft laborers clean and prepare sites, dig trenches, set braces to support the sides of excavations, and clean up rubble and debris. They perform a variety of excavation, tunneling, and pipe work, and work on their own on highly specialized tasks. The installation of utility pipe, for example, requires the set up and operation of laser guidance equipment for precise pipe elevation and placement. Tunnel and shaft projects require workers to be trained and experienced in the use of drilling equipment and explosives. Construction craft laborers operate jackhammers, earth tampers, cement mixers, buggies, skid steer loaders, "walk-behind" ditch diggers, small mechanical hoists, laser beam equipment, and surveying and measuring equipment.

In addition to working on building and transportation projects, construction craft laborers work on other projects, such as hazardous waste cleanup and asbestos and lead abatement. In hazardous waste removal, they may operate, maintain, and read monitoring devices; perform material and atmospheric sampling; build, clean, or maintain facilities for hazardous material removal and decontamination; and package and transport hazardous or radioactive materials.

Working Conditions

Most handlers, equipment cleaners, helpers, and laborers do repetitive, physically demanding work. They may lift and carry heavy objects, and stoop, kneel, crouch, or crawl in awkward positions. Some work at great heights, or outdoors in all weather conditions. Some jobs expose workers to harmful materials or chemicals, fumes, odors, loud noise, or dangerous machinery. In order to avoid injury, these employees may need to wear safety clothing, such as gloves and hard hats, and devices to protect their eyes, mouth, or hearing.

Handlers, equipment cleaners, helpers, and laborers generally work eight-hour shifts, though 12-hour shifts are also common. In many industries, handlers, equipment cleaners, helpers, and laborers may have to work evening or "graveyard" shifts. Service station and parking lot attendants may work at night because these establishments may be open at all hours; handlers in grocery stores may stock shelves at night when stores are closed. Refuse and recyclable material collectors often work early morning shifts, starting at 5 or 6 A.M.

Employment

Handlers, equipment cleaners, helpers, and laborers held about 5 million jobs in 1996. Their employment was distributed among the following detailed occupations:

Hand packers and packagers	986,000
Freight, stock, and material movers, hand	808,000
Helpers, construction trades	546,000
Vehicle washers and equipment cleaners	274,000
Machine feeders and offbearers	265,000
Service station attendants	174,000
Refuse collectors	116,000
Parking lot attendants	68,000
All other helpers, laborers, and material movers, hand	1,737,000

Handlers, equipment cleaners, helpers, and laborers are employed throughout the country in virtually all industries, with the greatest numbers concentrated in manufacturing, construction, wholesale and retail trade, and certain services industries. Nearly one in four works part time. A growing number are employed on a temporary or contract basis, many through firms providing personnel sup-

ply services. For example, companies that only need a laborer for a few days to move materials or clean up a site, contract with temporary help agencies specializing in providing this type of worker on a short term basis.

Training, Other Qualifications, and Advancement

For most handler, equipment cleaner, helper, and laborer jobs, employers will hire people without work experience or specific training. Some require a high school diploma, others do not. Most employers, however, require workers to be at least 18 years old and physically able to perform the work. For those jobs requiring physical exertion, employers may require that applicants pass a physical exam. Some employers also require mandatory drug testing prior to employment. These workers are often younger than workers in other occupations—reflecting the limited training but significant physical requirements of many of these jobs.

For all of these jobs, employers look for people who are reliable and hard working. For those jobs that involve dealing with the public, such as grocery store helpers and service station or parking lot attendants, workers should be pleasant and courteous. Most jobs require reading and basic mathematics skills to read safety procedures and operating manuals, or billing and other records, and collect payment for services from customers.

Handlers, equipment cleaners, helpers, and laborers generally learn skills informally, on the job from more experienced workers or supervisors. However, workers who use dangerous equipment or handle toxic chemicals, for example, usually receive specialized training in safety awareness and procedures.

Formal apprenticeship programs provide more thorough preparation for jobs as construction craft laborers. Local apprenticeship programs are operated under guidelines established by the Laborers-Associated General Contractors of America (AGC) Education and Training Fund. Programs include at least 4,000 hours of on-the job training, including 144 hours of classroom training. Most union contractors and laborer unions require some training before an apprentice is placed on the job. Apprentices are instructed in the correct use of numerous tools and equipment that must be mastered before they complete the program.

Experience in many of these jobs may allow workers to qualify for, or become trainees for other skilled positions as construction trades workers, machine operators, assemblers, or other production workers; transportation, material moving equipment, or vehicle operators, or mechanics or repairers. In fact, many employers prefer to promote qualified handlers, equipment cleaners, helpers, and laborers as openings arise. Some may eventually advance to become supervisors.

Job Outlook

Employment of handlers, equipment cleaners, helpers, and laborers is expected to grow about as fast as the average for all occupations through the year 2006. Job openings should be numerous because the occupation is very large and turnover is relatively high—characteristic of occupations requiring little formal training. Many openings will arise from the need to replace workers who retire, transfer to other occupations, or who leave the labor force for other reasons.

Projected employment growth varies by detailed occupation. Among machine feeders and offbearers, for example, employment is expected to decline slightly, while employment of service station attendants is expected to experience little change. Employment of refuse collectors and other fright, stock, and material movers, on the other hand, should increase more slowly than the average, as should employment of construction trades helpers. Finally, driven largely by rapid growth in the industries in which they are most concentrated, faster than average growth is expected for vehicle washers and equipment cleaners, hand packers and packagers, and parking lot attendants.

Overall, demand for handlers, equipment cleaners, helpers, and laborers depends not only on growth in the industries employing these workers, but also on growth among the skilled workers whom they assist. Slower than average growth among helpers in construction, for example, is directly related to construction activity and the overall demand for construction trades workers. However, growth of helper and construction craft laborer employment will continue to be spurred by the Nation's emphasis on hazardous waste cleanup and other environmental projects, and on rebuilding infrastructure–roads, bridges, tunnels, and communications facilities, for example.

Employment growth will also be affected by automation. Some of these jobs are repetitive and, therefore, easily replaced by new machines and equipment that improve productivity and quality control. Some helper, handler, and hand packer and packaging jobs will be eliminated by automated material handling equipment, such as conveyor belts and computer-controlled lift mechanisms, and machines that automatically load, unload, and package materials. As more skilled jobs, such as those of assemblers, become automated, demand for these types of employees who assist them will decline.

Many employers have also begun consolidating or combining job responsibilities or contracting out labor. Job combinations may lead to displacement of handlers, equipment cleaners, helpers, and laborers because the tasks they perform may be assumed by more highly skilled workers, or they may be required to assist more than one type of worker. In addition, these types of occupations may increasingly be staffed by contingent workers as more employers turn to hiring temporary handlers, equipment cleaners, helpers, and laborers.

Earnings

Median weekly earnings for handlers, equipment cleaners, helpers, and laborers in 1996 were about $330. The middle 50 percent earned from $252 to $478 weekly. The top 10 percent earned over $648 weekly, and the bottom 10 percent earned less than $196 weekly. Median weekly earnings for the detailed occupations that comprise this group of workers are shown in the following tabulation.

Construction laborers	$372
Freight, stock, and material movers, hand	327
Helpers, construction and extractive occupations	311
Hand packers and packagers	310
Vehicle washers and equipment cleaners	292
Helpers, mechanics and repairers	283
Garage and service station related occupations	276
Parking lot attendants	272

Construction craft laborers generally have higher weekly earnings than other workers in this group. However, they may be more likely to lose work time because of bad weather and the cyclical nature of construction work. Mechanics and repairers' helpers, garage and service station related occupations, and parking lot attendants have the lowest weekly earnings among workers in this group.

About 20 percent of all handlers, equipment cleaners, helpers, construction craft, and other laborers are members of a union. Many belong to the Laborers' International Union of North America.

Related Occupations

Other entry-level workers who perform mostly physical work are roustabouts in the oil industry, certain timber cutting and logging occupations, and groundskeepers. The jobs of handlers, equipment cleaners, helpers, and laborers are often similar to those of the more experienced workers they assist, including machine operators, construction craft workers, assemblers, mechanics, and repairers.

Sources of Additional Information

For information about jobs as handlers, equipment cleaners, helpers, and laborers, contact local building or construction contractors, manufacturers, and wholesale and retail establishments, or the local office of the State employment service.

For general information about the work of construction craft laborers, contact:

❑ Laborers' International Union of North America, 905 16th St. NW, Washington, DC 20006.

Health Information Technicians

(D.O.T. 079.362-014, -018)

Significant Points

✓ *Health information technicians are projected to be one of the 20 fastest growing occupations.*

✓ *High school students can improve their chances of acceptance into a health information education program by taking courses in biology, chemistry, health, and especially computer training.*

✓ *Most technicians will be employed in hospitals, but job growth will be faster in offices and clinics of physicians, nursing homes, and home health agencies.*

Nature of the Work

Every time health care personnel treat a patient, they record what they observed, and how the patient was treated medically. This record includes information the patient provides concerning their symptoms and medical history, the results of examinations, reports of x-rays and laboratory tests, diagnoses, and treatment plans. Health information technicians organize and evaluate these records for completeness and accuracy.

When assembling patients' health information, technicians, who may also be called medical record technicians, first make sure the medical chart is complete. They ensure all forms are present and properly identified and signed, and all necessary information is on a computer file. Sometimes, they talk to physicians or others to clarify diagnoses or get additional information.

Technicians assign a code to each diagnosis and procedure. They consult a classification manual and rely, also, on their knowledge of disease processes. Technicians then use a software program to assign the patient to one of several hundred "diagnosis-related groups," or DRGs. The DRG determines the amount the hospital will be reimbursed if the patient is covered by Medicare or other insurance programs using the DRG system. Technicians who specialize in coding are called health information coders, medical record coders, coder/abstractors, or coding specialists.

Technicians also use computer programs to tabulate and analyze data to help improve patient care or control costs, for use in legal actions, or in response to surveys. Tumor registrars compile and maintain records of patients who have cancer to provide information to physicians and for research studies.

Health information technicians' duties vary with the size of the facility. In large to medium facilities, technicians may specialize in one aspect of health information, or supervise health information clerks and transcribers while a health information administrator manages the department. In small facilities, an accredited health information technician may manage the department.

Working Conditions

Health information technicians generally work a 40-hour week. Some overtime may be required. In hospitals where health information departments are open 18 to 24 hours a day, seven days a week, they may work on day, evening, and night shifts.

Health information technicians work in pleasant and comfortable offices. This is one of the few health occupations in which there is little or no physical contact with patients. Accuracy is essential, therefore concentration and close attention to detail is required. Health information technicians who work at video display terminals for prolonged periods must guard against eyestrain and muscle pain.

Employment

Health information technicians held about 87,000 jobs in 1996. Less than one half of the jobs were in hospitals. Most of the rest were in nursing homes, medical group practices, clinics, and home health agencies. Insurance, accounting, and law firms that deal in health matters employ a small number of health information technicians to tabulate and analyze health information. Public health departments also hire technicians to supervise data collection from health care institutions and to assist in research.

Training, Other Qualifications, and Advancement

Health information technicians entering the field usually have an associate degree from a community or junior college. In addition to general education, course work includes medical terminology, anatomy and physiology, legal aspects of health information, coding and abstraction of data, statistics, database management, quality assurance methods, and especially computer training. Applicants can improve their chances of admission into a program by taking biology, chemistry, health and computer courses in high school.

Technicians may also gain training through an Independent Study Program in Health Information Technology offered by the American Health Information Management Association (AHIMA). Hospitals sometimes advance promising health information clerks to jobs as health information technicians, although this practice may be less common in the future. Advancement generally requires two-4 years of job experience and completion of the hospital's in-house training program.

Most employers prefer to hire Accredited Record Technicians (ART), who must pass a written examination offered by AHIMA. To take the examination, a person must graduate from a two-year associate degree program accredited by the Commission on Accreditation of Allied Health Education Programs (CAAHEP) of the American Medical Association, or from the Independent Study Program in Health Information Technology that requires 30 semester hours of academic credit in prescribed areas. Technicians trained in non-CAAHEP accredited programs, or on the job, are not eligible to take the examination. In 1997, CAAHEP accredited 157 programs for health information technicians.

Experienced health information technicians generally advance in one of two ways—by specializing or managing. Many senior health information technicians specialize in coding, particularly Medicare coding, or in tumor registry.

In large health information departments, experienced technicians may advance to section supervisor, overseeing the work of the coding, correspondence, or discharge sections, for example. Senior technicians with ART credentials may become director or assistant director of a health information department in a small facility. However, in larger institutions, the director is a health information administrator, with a bachelor's degree in health information administration.

Job Outlook

Job prospects for formally trained technicians should be very good. Employment of health information technicians is expected to grow much faster than the average for all occupations through the year 2006, due to rapid growth in the number of medical tests, treatments, and procedures which will be increasingly scrutinized by third-party payers, regulators, courts, and consumers.

Hospitals will continue to employ the most health information technicians, but growth will not be as fast as in other areas. Increasing demand for detailed records in offices and clinics of physicians should result in fast employment growth, especially in large group practices. Rapid growth is also expected in nursing homes and home health agencies.

Earnings

According to a 1996 survey by the American Health Information Management Association, the median annual salary for accredited health information technicians was $31,200 a year. The average annual salary for health information technicians employed by the federal government was $25,570 in early 1997.

Related Occupations

Health information technicians need a strong clinical background to analyze the contents of medical records. Other occupations requiring a knowledge of medical terminology, anatomy, and physiology without directly touching the patient, are medical secretaries, medical transcribers, medical writers, and medical illustrators.

Sources of Additional Information

Information on careers in health information technology, including the Independent Study Program, and a list of CAAHEP-accredited programs is available from:

❑ American Health Information Management Association, 919 N. Michigan Ave., Suite 1400, Chicago, IL 60611-1683. Homepage: http://www.ahima.org

Health Services Managers

(D.O.T. 072.117-010; 074.167-010, 075.117-014, -022, -026, -030 and -034, .167-010 and -014; 076.117-010; 077.117-010; 078.131-010, .161-010 and -014, .162-010; 079.117-010, .131-010, .151-010, and .167-014; 187.117-010, -058, -062, and .167-034, and -090; 188.117-082

Significant Points

✓ *Earnings of health services managers are high, but long weekly work hours are common.*

✓ *Most are employed by hospitals, but the fastest employment growth will be in home health care agencies, long-term care facilities, and practitioners' offices and clinics.*

Nature of the Work

Health care is a business, albeit a special one. Like every other business, it needs good management to keep it running smoothly, especially during times of change. The term "health services manager" encompasses individuals in many different positions who plan, organize, coordinate, and supervise the delivery of health care. Health services managers include both generalists—administrators who manage or help to manage an entire facility or system—and health specialists—managers in charge of specific clinical departments or services found only in the health industry.

The structure and financing of health care is changing rapidly. Future health services managers must be prepared to deal with evolving integrated health care delivery systems, restructuring of work, technological innovations, and an increased focus on preventive care. They will be called upon to improve efficiency in all health care facilities, while continually improving quality of the health care provided. Increasingly, health services managers work in organizations in which they must optimize efficiency of a variety of interrelated services, ranging from inpatient care to outpatient follow-up care, for example.

The top administrator or chief executive officer (CEO) and the assistant administrators without specific titles are health care generalists, who set the overall direction of the organization. They concentrate on such areas as community outreach, planning, marketing, human resources, finance, and complying with government regulations. Their range of knowledge is broad, including developments in the clinical departments as well as in the business arena. They often speak before civic groups, promote public participation in health programs, and coordinate the activities of the organization with those of government or community agencies. CEOs make long-term institutional plans by assessing the need for services, personnel, facilities, and equipment and recommending changes such as opening a home health service. CEOs need leadership ability, as well as technical skills, to provide quality health care while satisfying demand for financial viability, cost containment, and public and professional accountability.

Larger facilities typically have several assistant administrators to aid the top administrator and to handle day-to-day decisions. They may direct activities in clinical areas such as nursing, surgery,

therapy, food service, and medical records; or the activities in nonhealth areas such as finance, housekeeping, human resources, and information management. (Because the nonhealth departments are not directly related to health care, these managers are not included in this statement.) In smaller facilities, top administrators may handle more of the details of day-to-day operations. For example, many nursing home administrators directly manage personnel, finance, operations, admissions, and have a larger role in resident care.

Clinical managers have more narrowly defined responsibilities than generalists, and have training and/or experience in a specific clinical area. For example, directors of physical therapy are experienced physical therapists, and most health information administrators have a bachelor's degree in health information administration. These managers establish and implement policies, objectives, and procedures for their departments; evaluate personnel and work; develop reports and budgets; and coordinate activities with other managers.

In group practices, managers work closely with the physician owners. While an office manager may handle business affairs in small medical groups, leaving policy decisions to the physicians themselves, larger groups generally employ a full-time administrator to advise on business strategies and coordinate day-to-day business.

A small group of 10 or 15 physicians might employ a single administrator to oversee personnel matters, billing and collection, budgeting, planning, equipment outlays, and patient flow. A large practice of 40 or 50 physicians may have a chief administrator and several assistants, each responsible for different areas.

Health services managers in health maintenance organizations (HMOs) and other managed care settings perform functions similar to those in large group practices, except their staffs may be larger. Also, they may do more work in the areas of community outreach and preventive care than managers of a group practice. The size of the administrative staff in HMOs varies according to the size and type of HMO.

Some health services managers oversee the activities of a number of facilities in multifacility health organizations.

Working Conditions

Most health services managers work long hours. Facilities such as nursing homes and hospitals operate around the clock, and administrators and managers may be called at all hours to deal with problems. They may also travel to attend meetings or inspect satellite facilities.

Employment

Health services managers held about 329,000 jobs in 1996. Over one-half of all jobs were in hospitals. About one in four were in nursing and personal care facilities or offices and clinics of physicians. The remainder worked in home health agencies, medical and dental laboratories, offices of dentists and other practitioners, and other health and allied services.

Training, Other Qualifications, and Advancement

Health services managers must be familiar with management principles and practices. Some learn from work experience. However, formal education is usually necessary for advancement. Most CEO positions require a graduate degree in health services administration, nursing administration, public health, or business administration. For some generalist positions, employers seek applicants with clinical experience (as nurses or therapists, for example) as well as academic preparation in business or health services administration.

Bachelor's, master's, and doctoral degree programs in health administration are offered by colleges, universities, and schools of public health, medicine, allied health, public administration, and business administration. There are also some certificate or diploma programs, generally lasting less than one year, in health services administration and in medical office management. A master's degree—in health services administration, long term care administration, health sciences, public health, public administration, or business administration—is the standard credential for most generalist positions in this field. However, a bachelor's degree is adequate for some entry-level positions in smaller operations. A bachelor's degree is required to work in some settings, such as nursing homes, and for entry level positions at the departmental level within health care organizations. Physicians' offices and some other facilities may substitute on-the-job experience for formal education. For clinical department heads, a degree in the appropriate field and work experience may be sufficient, but a master's degree in health services administration usually is required to advance.

In 1997, 67 schools had accredited programs leading to the master's degree in health services administration, according to the Accrediting Commission on Education for Health Services Administration.

Some graduate programs seek students with undergraduate degrees in business or health administration; however, many programs prefer students with a liberal arts or health professions background. Competition for entry to these programs is keen, and applicants need above-average grades to gain admission. The programs generally last between two and three years. They may include up to one year of supervised administrative experience, and course work in areas such as hospital organization and management, marketing, accounting and budgeting, human resources administration, strategic planning, health economics, and health information systems. Some programs allow students to specialize in one type of facility—hospitals; nursing homes; mental health facilities; HMOs; or outpatient care facilities, including medical groups. Other programs encourage a generalist approach to health administration education.

New graduates with master's degrees in health services administration may start as department managers or in staff positions. The level of the starting position varies with the experience of the applicant and size of the organization. Postgraduate residencies and fellowships are offered by hospitals and other health facilities; these are usually staff positions. Graduates from master's degree programs also take jobs in HMOs, large group medical practices, clinics, mental health facilities, and multifacility nursing home corporations.

Graduates with bachelor's degrees in health administration usually begin as administrative assistants or assistant department heads in larger hospitals, or as department heads or assistant administrators in small hospitals or nursing homes.

A Ph.D. degree may be required to teach, consult, or do research. Nursing service administrators are usually chosen from among supervisory registered nurses with administrative abilities and a graduate degree in nursing or health services administration.

Most states and the District of Columbia require nursing home administrators to have a bachelor's degree, pass a licensing examination, complete a state-approved training program, and pursue continuing education. A license is not required in other areas of health services management.

Health services managers are often responsible for millions of dollars of facilities and equipment and hundreds of employees. To make effective decisions, they need to be open to different opinions and good at analyzing contradictory information. They must understand finance and information systems, and be able to interpret data. Motivating others to implement their decisions requires strong leadership abilities. Tact, diplomacy, flexibility, and communication skills are essential because health services managers spend much of their time interacting with others.

Health services managers advance by moving into more responsible and higher paying positions, such as assistant or associate administrator, or by moving to larger facilities.

Job Outlook

Employment of health services managers is expected to grow faster than the average for all occupations through the year 2006 as health services continue to expand and diversify. Opportunities for health services managers should be closely related to growth in the industry in which they are employed. Opportunities will be good in home health care, long-term care and nontraditional health organizations such as managed care operations, particularly for health services managers with work experience in the health care field and strong business and management skills.

Hospitals will continue to employ the most managers, although the number of jobs will grow slowly compared to other areas. As hospitals continue to consolidate, centralize, and diversify functions, competition will increase at all job levels.

Employment will grow the fastest in home health agencies, offices of physicians and other health practitioners, and nursing and personal care facilities due to an increased number of elderly individuals who will need care. In addition, many services previously provided in hospitals will be shifted to these sectors, especially as medical technologies improve. Demand in medical group practice management will grow as medical group practices become larger and more complex. Health services managers will need to deal with the pressures of cost containment and financial accountability, as well as the increased focus on preventive and primary care. They will have more responsibility for improving the health of populations and communities.

Health services managers will also be employed by health care management companies who provide management services to hospitals and other organizations, as well as specific departments such as emergency, information management systems, managed care contract negotiations, and physician recruiting.

Earnings

Earnings of health services managers vary by type and size of the facility, as well as by level of responsibility. For example, the Medical Group Management Association reported that the median salary for administrators in small group practices—with fewer than seven physicians—was about $56,000 in 1996; for those in larger group practices—with more than seven physicians—77,000.

According to a 1997 survey by Modern Healthcare magazine, half of all hospital CEOs earned total compensation of $190,500 or more. Salaries varied according to size of facility and geographic region. Clinical department heads' salaries varied also. Median total compensation in 1997 for heads of the following clinical departments were: Respiratory therapy, $54,500; home health care, $62,000; clinical laboratory, $63,700; radiology, $64,000; physical therapy, $64,900; ambulatory/outpatient services, $68,500, rehabilitation services, $70,400; and nursing services, $97,000.

According to the Buck Survey conducted by the American Health Care Association in 1996, nursing home administrators had median annual compensation of about $49,500. The middle 50 percent earned between $42,100 and $57,300. Assistant administrators earned about $32,000, with the middle 50 percent earning between $26,200 and $40,000.

Executives often receive bonuses based on performance outcomes such as cost-containment, quality assurance, and patient satisfaction.

Related Occupations

Health services managers have training or experience in both health and management. Other occupations requiring knowledge of both fields are public health directors, social welfare administrators, directors of voluntary health agencies and health professional associations, and underwriters in health insurance companies.

Sources of Additional Information

General information about health administration is available from:

❑ American College of Healthcare Executives, One North Franklin St., Suite 1700, Chicago, IL 60606. Homepage: http://www.ache.org

Information about undergraduate and graduate academic programs in this field is available from:

❑ Association of University Programs in Health Administration, 1911 North Fort Myer Dr., Suite 503, Arlington, VA 22209. Homepage: http://www.aupha.org

For a list of accredited graduate programs in health services administration, contact:

❑ Accrediting Commission on Education for Health Services Administration, 1911 North Fort Myer Dr., Suite 503, Arlington, VA 22209.

For information about career opportunities in long term care administration, contact:

❑ American College of Health Care Administrators, 325 S. Patrick St., Alexandria, VA 22314.

For information about career opportunities in medical group practices and ambulatory care management, contact:

❑ Medical Group Management Association, 104 Inverness Terrace East, Englewood, CO 80112.

Heating, Air-Conditioning, and Refrigeration Technicians

(D.O.T. 637.261-014, -026, -030, and -034, and .381; 827.361-014; 862.281 -018, .361-010; and 869.281-010)

Significant Points

✓ *Opportunities should be very good for technicians with technical school or formal apprenticeship training.*

✓ *Technicians need a basic understanding of microelectronics because they increasingly install and service equipment with electronic controls.*

Nature of the Work

What would those living in Chicago do without heating, those in Miami do without air-conditioning, or blood banks in all parts of the country do without refrigeration? Heating and air-conditioning systems control the temperature, humidity, and the total air quality in residential, commercial, industrial, and other buildings. Refrigeration systems make it possible to store and transport food, medicine, and other perishable items. Heating, air-conditioning, and refrigeration technicians install, maintain, and repair such systems.

Heating, air-conditioning, and refrigeration systems consist of many mechanical, electrical, and electronic components, including motors, compressors, pumps, fans, ducts, pipes, thermostats, and switches. In central heating systems, for example, a furnace heats air that is distributed throughout the building via a system of metal or fiberglass ducts. Technicians must be able to maintain, diagnose, and correct problems throughout the entire system. To do this, they may adjust system controls to recommended settings and test the performance of the entire system using special tools and test equipment.

Although they are trained to do both, technicians often specialize in either installation or maintenance and repair. Some specialize in one type of equipment—for example, oil burners, solar panels, or commercial refrigerators. Technicians may work for large or small contracting companies or directly for a manufacturer or wholesaler. Those working for smaller operations tend to do both installation and servicing, and work with heating, cooling, and refrigeration equipment.

Furnace installers, also called heating equipment technicians, follow blueprints or other specifications to install oil, gas, electric, solid-fuel, and multiple-fuel heating systems. After putting the equipment in place, they install fuel and water supply lines, air ducts and vents, pumps, and other components. They may connect electrical wiring and controls and check the unit for proper operation. To ensure the proper functioning of the system, furnace installers often use combustion test equipment such as carbon dioxide and oxygen testers.

After a furnace has been installed, technicians often perform routine maintenance and repair work in order to keep the system operating efficiently. During the fall and winter, for example, when the system is used most, they service and adjust burners and blowers. If the system is not operating properly, they check the thermostat, burner nozzles, controls, or other parts in order to diagnose and then correct the problem. During the summer, when the heating system is not being used, technicians do maintenance work, such as replacing filters and vacuum-cleaning vents, ducts, and other parts of the system that may accumulate dust and impurities during the operating season.

Air-conditioning and refrigeration technicians install and service central air-conditioning systems and a variety of refrigeration equipment. Technicians follow blueprints, design specifications, and manufacturers' instructions to install motors, compressors, condensing units, evaporators, piping, and other components. They connect this equipment to the duct work, refrigerant lines, and electrical power source. After making the connections, they charge the system with refrigerant, check it for proper operation, and program control systems.

When air-conditioning and refrigeration equipment breaks down, technicians diagnose the problem and make repairs. To do this, they test parts such as compressors, relays, and thermostats. During the winter, air-conditioning technicians inspect the systems and do required maintenance, such as overhauling compressors.

When servicing equipment, heating, air-conditioning, and refrigeration technicians must use care to conserve, recover, and recycle chlorofluorocarbon (CFC) and hydrochlorofluorocarbon (HCFC) refrigerants used in air-conditioning and refrigeration systems. The release of CFCs and HCFCs contributes to the depletion of the stratospheric ozone layer, which protects plant and animal life from ultraviolet radiation. Technicians conserve the refrigerant by making sure that there are no leaks in the system; they recover it by venting the refrigerant into proper cylinders; and they recycle it for reuse with special filter-dryers.

Heating, air-conditioning, and refrigeration technicians use a variety of tools, including hammers, wrenches, metal snips, electric drills, pipe cutters and benders, measurement gauges, and acetylene torches, to work with refrigerant lines and air ducts. They use voltmeters, thermometers, pressure gauges, manometers, and other testing devices to check air flow, refrigerant pressure, electrical circuits, burners, and other components.

Cooling and heating systems sometimes are installed or repaired by other craft workers. For example, on a large air-conditioning installation job, especially where workers are covered by union contracts, duct work might be done by sheet-metal workers; electrical work by electricians; and installation of piping, condensers, and other components by plumbers and pipefitters. Room air-conditioners and household refrigerators usually are serviced by home appliance repairers.

Working Conditions

Heating, air-conditioning, and refrigeration technicians work in homes, supermarkets, hospitals, office buildings, and factories—anywhere there is climate control equipment. They may be assigned to specific job sites at the beginning of each day, or if they are making service calls, they may be dispatched to jobs by radio or telephone.

Technicians may work outside in cold or hot weather or in buildings that are uncomfortable because the air-conditioning or heating equipment is broken. In addition, technicians often work in awkward or cramped positions and sometimes are required to work in high places. Hazards include electrical shock, burns, muscle strains, and other injuries from handling heavy equipment. Appropriate safety equipment is necessary when handling refrigerants because contact can cause skin damage, frostbite, or blindness. Inhalation of refrigerants when working in confined spaces is also a possible hazard, and may cause asphyxiation.

Technicians usually work a 40-hour week, but during peak seasons they often work overtime or irregular hours. Maintenance workers, including those who provide maintenance services under contract, often work evening or weekend shifts, and are on call. Most employers try to provide a full workweek the year round by doing both installation and maintenance work and many manufacturers and contractors now provide or even require service con-

tracts. In most shops that service both heating and air-conditioning equipment, employment is very stable throughout the year.

Employment

Heating, air-conditioning, and refrigeration technicians held about 256,000 jobs in 1996, more than half of these worked for cooling and heating contractors. The remainder were employed in a wide variety of industries throughout the country, reflecting a widespread dependence on climate control systems. Some worked for fuel oil dealers, refrigeration and air-conditioning service and repair shops, and schools. Others were employed by the federal government, hospitals, office buildings, and other organizations that operate large air-conditioning, refrigeration, or heating systems. Approximately one of every seven technicians was self-employed.

Training, Other Qualifications, and Advancement

Because of the increasing sophistication of heating, air-conditioning, and refrigeration systems, employers prefer to hire those with technical school or apprenticeship training. A sizable number of technicians, however, still learn the trade informally on the job.

Many secondary and postsecondary technical and trade schools, junior and community colleges, and the Armed Forces offer six-month to two-year programs in heating, air-conditioning, and refrigeration. Students study theory, design, and equipment construction, as well as electronics. They also learn the basics of installation, maintenance, and repair.

Apprenticeship programs are frequently run by joint committees representing local chapters of the Air-Conditioning Contractors of America, the Mechanical Contractors Association of America, the National Association of Plumbing-Heating-Cooling Contractors, and locals of the Sheet Metal Workers' International Association or the United Association of Journeymen and Apprentices of the Plumbing and Pipefitting Industry of the United States and Canada. Other apprenticeship programs are sponsored by local chapters of the Associated Builders and Contractors and the National Association of Home Builders. Formal apprenticeship programs generally last three or four years and combine on-the-job training with classroom instruction. Classes include subjects such as the use and care of tools, safety practices, blueprint reading, and air-conditioning theory. Applicants for these programs must have a high school diploma or equivalent.

Those who acquire their skills on the job usually begin by assisting experienced technicians. They may begin performing simple tasks such as carrying materials, insulating refrigerant lines, or cleaning furnaces. In time, they move on to more difficult tasks, such as cutting and soldering pipes and sheet metal and checking electrical and electronic circuits.

Courses in shop math, mechanical drawing, applied physics and chemistry, electronics, blueprint reading, and computer applications provide a good background for those interested in entering this occupation. Some knowledge of plumbing or electrical work is also helpful. A basic understanding of microelectronics is becoming more important because of the increasing use of this technology in solid-state equipment controls. Because technicians frequently deal directly with the public, they should be courteous and tactful, especially when dealing with an aggravated customer. They also should be in good physical condition because they sometimes have to lift and move heavy equipment.

All technicians who purchase or work with refrigerants must be certified in their proper handling. To become certified to purchase and handle refrigerants, a technician must pass a written examination specific to the type of work in which they specialize. The three possible areas of certification are Type I–servicing small appliances, Type II–high pressure refrigerants, and Type III–low pressure refrigerants. Exams are administered by organizations approved by the Environmental Protection Agency, such as trade schools, unions, contractor associations, or building groups. Though no formal training is required for certification, training programs designed to prepare workers for the certification examination, as well as for general skills improvement training, are provided by heating and air-conditioning equipment manufacturers; the Refrigeration Service Engineers Society (RSES); the Air Conditioning Contractors of America (ACCA); the Mechanical Service Contractors of America; local chapters of the National Association of Plumbing-Heating-Cooling Contractors; and the United Association of Plumbers and Pipefitters. RSES, along with some other organizations, also offer basic self-study courses for individuals with limited experience. In addition to understanding how systems work, technicians must be knowledgeable about refrigerant products, and legislation and regulation that govern their use.

There are also two newly created certification programs for technicians. The North American Technician Excellence Program is sponsored by a coalition of associations representing all segments of the industry. The other is sponsored by the Air Conditioning Contractors of America, and Ferris State University in Big Rapids, Michigan. Both programs are voluntary measures of competency.

Advancement usually takes the form of higher wages. Some technicians, however, may advance to positions as supervisor or service manager. Others may move into areas such as sales and marketing. Those with sufficient money and managerial skill can open their own contracting business.

Job Outlook

Job prospects for highly skilled air-conditioning, heating, and refrigeration technicians are expected to be very good, particularly those with technical school or formal apprenticeship training to install, remodel, and service new and existing systems. In addition to job openings created by employment growth, thousands of openings will result from the need to replace workers who transfer to other occupations or leave the labor force.

Employment of heating, air-conditioning, and refrigeration technicians is expected to increase about as fast as the average for all occupations through the year 2006. As the population and economy grow, so does the demand for new residential, commercial, and industrial climate control systems. Technicians who specialize in installation work may experience periods of unemployment when the level of new construction activity declines, but maintenance and repair work usually remains relatively stable. People and businesses depend on their climate control systems and must keep them in good working order, regardless of economic conditions.

Concern for the environment and energy conservation should continue to prompt the development of new energy-saving heating and air-conditioning systems. An emphasis on better energy management should lead to the replacement of older systems and the installation of newer, more efficient systems in existing homes and buildings. Also, demand for maintenance and service work should increase as businesses and home owners strive to keep systems operating at peak efficiency. Regulations prohibiting the discharge of CFC and HCFC refrigerants and banning CFC production by the year 2000 also should continue to result in demand for technicians to replace many existing systems, or modify them to use new environmentally safe refrigerants. In addition, the continuing focus on improving indoor air quality should contribute to the growth of jobs for heating, air-conditioning, and refrigeration technicians. Also, certain businesses contribute to a growing need for refrigeration. For example, nearly 50 percent of products sold in convenience stores require some sort of refrigeration. Supermarkets and convenience stores have a very large inventory of refrigerated equipment. This huge inventory will also create increasing demand for service technicians in installation, maintenance, and repair.

Earnings

Median weekly earnings of air-conditioning, heating, and refrigeration technicians who worked full-time were $536 in 1996. The middle 50 percent earned between $381 and $701. The lowest 10 percent earned less than $287 a week, and the top 10 percent earned more than $887 a week.

Apprentices usually begin at about 50 percent of the wage rate paid to experienced workers. As they gain experience and improve their skills, they receive periodic increases until they reach the wage rate of experienced workers.

Heating, air-conditioning, and refrigeration technicians enjoy a variety of employer-sponsored benefits. In addition to typical benefits like health insurance and pension plans, some employers pay for work-related training and provide uniforms, company vans, and tools.

Nearly one out of every six heating, air-conditioning, and refrigeration technicians is a member of a union. The unions to which the greatest numbers of technicians belong are the Sheet Metal Workers' International Association and the United Association of Journeymen and Apprentices of the Plumbing and Pipefitting Industry of the United States and Canada.

Related Occupations

Heating, air-conditioning, and refrigeration technicians work with sheet metal and piping, and repair machinery, such as electrical motors, compressors, and burners. Other workers who have similar skills are boilermakers, electrical appliance servicers, electricians, plumbers and pipefitters, sheet-metal workers, and duct installers.

Sources of Additional Information

For more information about employment and training opportunities in this trade, contact local vocational and technical schools; local heating, air-conditioning, and refrigeration contractors; a local of the unions previously mentioned; a local joint union-management apprenticeship committee; a local chapter of the Associated Builders and Contractors; or the nearest office of the state employment service or state apprenticeship agency.

For information on career opportunities, training, and technician certification, contact:

❑ Air Conditioning Contractors of America, 1712 New Hampshire Ave. NW, Washington, DC 20009.

For information on technician certification, contact:

❏ North American Technician Excellence (NATE), P.O. Box 8127, Reston, VA 20195-2025.

❏ Air Conditioning Contractors of America, 1712 New Hampshire Ave. NW, Washington, DC 20009.

For information on career opportunities and training, write to:

❏ Associated Builders and Contractors, 1300 North 17th St., Rosslyn, VA 22209.

❏ Refrigeration Service Engineers Society, 1666 Rand Rd., Des Plaines, IL 60016-3552.

❏ Home Builders Institute, National Association of Home Builders, 1201 15th St. NW, Washington, DC 20005.

❏ National Association of Plumbing-Heating-Cooling Contractors, 180 S. Washington St., P.O. Box 6808, Falls Church, VA 22046.

❏ Mechanical Contractors Association of America, 1385 Piccard Dr., Rockville, MD 20850-4329.

❏ Air Conditioning and Refrigeration Institute, 4301 North Fairfax Dr., Suite 425, Arlington, VA 22203.

Homemaker-Home Health Aides

(D.O.T. 309.354-010 and 354.377-014)

Significant Points

✓ *Numerous job openings will result due to very fast employment growth and very high turnover.*

✓ *Education required for entry-level jobs is generally minimal, but earnings are low.*

Nature of the Work

Homemaker-home health aides help elderly, disabled, and ill persons live in their own homes instead of in a health facility. Most work with elderly or disabled clients who need more extensive care than family or friends can provide. Some homemaker-home health aides work with families in which a parent is incapacitated and small children need care. Others help discharged hospital patients who have relatively short-term needs. These workers are sometimes called home care aides and personal care attendants.

Homemaker-home health aides provide housekeeping services, personal care, and emotional support for their clients. They clean clients' houses, do laundry, and change bed linens. Aides may also plan meals (including special diets), shop for food, and cook.

Home health aides provide personal care services, also known as hands-on care, because they physically touch the patient. These aides help clients move from bed, bathe, dress, and groom. They also check pulse, temperature, and respiration; help with simple prescribed exercises; and assist with medication routines. Occasionally, they change nonsterile dressings, use special equipment such as a hydraulic lift, give massages and alcohol rubs, or assist with braces and artificial limbs. Some accompany clients outside the home, serving as guide, companion, and aide.

Homemaker-home health aides also provide instruction and psychological support. For example, they may assist in toilet training a severely mentally handicapped child, or just listen to clients talk about their problems. Aides keep records of services performed and of clients' condition and progress.

In home care agencies, homemaker-home health aides are supervised by a registered nurse, a physical therapist, or a social worker, who assigns them specific duties. Aides report changes in the client's condition to the supervisor or case manager. Homemaker-home health aides also participate in case reviews, consulting with the team caring for the client—registered nurses, therapists, and other health professionals.

Working Conditions

The homemaker-home health aide's daily routine may vary. Aides may go to the same home every day for months or even years. However, most aides work with a number of different clients, each job lasting a few hours, days, or weeks. Aides often visit four or five clients on the same day.

Surroundings differ from case to case. Some homes are neat and pleasant, while others are untidy or depressing. Some clients are angry, abusive, depressed, or otherwise difficult; others are pleasant and cooperative.

Homemaker-home health aides generally work on their own, with periodic visits by their supervisor. They receive detailed instructions explaining when to visit clients and what services to perform. Many aides work part-time, and weekend hours are common.

Most aides generally travel by public transportation, but some need a car. Either way, they are responsible for getting to the client's home. Aides may spend a good portion of the working day traveling from one client to another; motor vehicle accidents are always a danger. They are particularly susceptible to injuries resulting from all types of overexertion when assisting patients, and falls inside and outside their homes. Mechanical lifting devices that are available in institutional settings are seldom available in patients' homes.

Employment

Homemaker-home health aides held about 697,000 jobs in 1996. Most aides are employed by homemaker-home health agencies, home health agencies, visiting nurse associations, residential care facilities with home health departments, hospitals, public health and welfare departments, community volunteer agencies, and temporary help firms. Self-employed aides have no agency affiliation or supervision, and accept clients, set fees, and arrange work schedules on their own.

Training, Other Qualifications, and Advancement

In some states, this occupation is open to individuals with no formal training. On-the-job training is generally provided. Other states may require formal training, depending on federal or state law.

The federal government has enacted guidelines for home health aides whose employers receive reimbursement from Medicare. Federal law requires home health aides to pass a competency test covering twelve areas: Communication skills; observation, reporting, and documentation of patient status and the care or services furnished; reading and recording vital signs; basic infection control procedures; basic elements of body function and changes; maintenance of a clean, safe, and healthy environment; recognition of, and procedures for emergencies; the physical, emotional, and developmental characteristics of the patients served; personal hygiene and grooming; safe transfer techniques; normal range of motion and positioning; and basic nutrition.

A home health aide may also take training before taking the competency test. Federal law suggests at least 75 hours of classroom and practical training supervised by a registered nurse. Training and testing programs may be offered by the employing agency, but must meet the standards of the Health Care Financing Administration. Training programs vary depending upon state regulations.

The National Association for Home Care offers a National Homemaker-Home Health Aide certification. The certification is a voluntary demonstration that the individual has met industry standards.

Successful homemaker-home health aides like to help people and do not mind hard work. They should be responsible, compassionate, emotionally stable, and cheerful. Aides should also be tactful, honest, and discreet because they work in private homes.

Homemaker-home health aides must be in good health. A physical examination including state regulated tests such as those for tuberculosis may be required.

Advancement is limited. In some agencies, workers start out performing homemaker duties, such as cleaning. With experience and training, they may take on personal care duties. The most experienced aides assist with medical equipment such as ventilators, which help patients breathe.

Job Outlook

A large number of job openings is expected for homemaker-home health aides, due to very rapid growth and very high turnover. Homemaker-home health aides is expected to be one of the fastest growing occupations through the year 2006.

The number of people in their seventies and older is projected to rise substantially. This age group is characterized by mounting health problems requiring some assistance. Also, there will be an increasing reliance on home care for patients of all ages. This trend reflects several developments: Efforts to contain costs by moving patients out of hospitals and nursing facilities as quickly as possible, the realization that treatment can be more effective in familiar surroundings rather than clinical surroundings, and the development and improvement of medical technologies for in-home treatment.

In addition to jobs created by the increase in demand for these workers, replacement needs are expected to produce numerous openings. Turnover is high, a reflection of the relatively low skill requirements, low pay, and high emotional demands of the work. For these same reasons, many people are unwilling to perform this kind of work. Therefore, persons who are interested in this work and suited for it should have excellent job opportunities, particularly those with experience or training as homemaker-home health aides or nursing aides.

Earnings

Earnings for homemaker-home health aides vary considerably. According to a the Homecare Salary and Benefits Report, published jointly by the National Association for Home Care survey and the Hospital and Healthcare Compensation Service, the starting average hourly wage for homemakers who worked primarily in Medicare-certified agencies ranged from $5.25 to $6.95 was $6.79 in October 1996. Home health The average minimum was $5.89 and the average maximum was $7.70. The average hourly wage for home health aides' average starting hourly wage ranged from $5.96 to $8.29. was $8.34. The average minimum was $7.06 and the average

maximum was $9.63. Wages were somewhat higher in the Northeast and West and somewhat lower in the Midwest and South. Some aides are paid on a salary or per-visit basis.

Most employers give slight pay increases with experience and added responsibility. Aides are usually paid only for the time worked in the home. They normally are not paid for travel time between jobs. Most employers hire only on-call hourly workers and provide no benefits.

Related Occupations

Homemaker-home health aide is a service occupation combining duties of health workers and social service workers. Workers in related occupations that involve personal contact to help or instruct others include attendants in children's institutions, child-care attendants in schools, child monitors, companions, nursery school attendants, occupational therapy aides, nursing aides, physical therapy aides, playroom attendants, and psychiatric aides.

Sources of Additional Information

General information about training and referrals to state and local agencies about opportunities for homemaker-home health aides, a list of relevant publications, and information on national certification are available from:

❑ National Association for Home Care, 228 7th St., SE., Washington, DC 20003.

For information about a career as a home health aide and schools offering training, contact:

❑ National Association of Health Career Schools, 750 First St. NE., Suite 940, Washington, DC 20002. FAX: (202) 842-1565 E-mail: NAHCS@aol.com

Hotel and Motel Desk Clerks

(D.O.T. 238.367-038)

Significant Points

✓ *Expected faster than average employment growth and relatively high turnover should create numerous job openings for hotel and motel desk clerks.*

✓ *A high school diploma or its equivalent is the most common educational requirement for most hotel and motel desk clerk jobs.*

Nature of the Work

Hotel and motel desk clerks perform a variety of services for guests of hotels, motels, and other lodging establishments. They register arriving guests and assign them rooms, and check guests out at the end of their stay. Clerks must consider their guests' preferences while trying to maximize the establishment's revenues. They keep records of room assignments and other registration information on computers, and when guests check out, they prepare and explain the bill of charges, as well as process payments.

Front desk clerks are always in the public eye and, through their attitude and behavior, greatly influence the public's impressions of the establishment. They answer questions about services, checkout times, the local community, and other matters of public interest. Should guests report problems with their rooms, clerks contact members of the housekeeping or maintenance staff to correct them.

In some smaller hotels and motels, clerks may have a variety of additional responsibilities usually performed by specialized employees in most larger establishments. These clerks may also perform the work of a bookkeeper, advance reservation agent, cashier, laundry attendant, and telephone switchboard operator.

Working Conditions

Hotel and motel desk clerks usually work in highly visible areas, designed and furnished to make a good impression. Most work stations are clean, well-lit, and relatively quiet, and overall working conditions are usually pleasant. Hotel and motel desk clerks may be on their feet most of the time. In addition, prolonged exposure to a video display terminal may lead to eye strain.

Although most hotel and motel desk clerks work a standard 40-hour week, about three out of ten work part-time. Hotel and motel desk clerk jobs may require working evenings, late night shifts, weekends, and holidays. In many cases, employees with the least seniority are assigned the least desirable shifts.

The work of hotel and motel desk clerks can be stressful when trying to serve the needs of difficult or angry customers. When guests are dissatisfied, these clerks must act as a buffer between the establishment and its customers.

Employment

Hotel and motel desk clerks held about 144,000 jobs in 1996. This occupation is well suited to flexible work schedules, with over one in four desk clerks working part-time. Because hotels and motels are found in all parts of the country, so are these jobs.

Training, Other Qualifications, and Advancement

A high school diploma or its equivalent is the most common educational requirement. However, good interpersonal skills and familiarity or experience with computers are often more important to employers.

Because hotel and motel desk clerks deal directly with the public, good grooming habits and a pleasant personality are imperative, as are good problem-solving and interpersonal skills. A clear speaking voice and fluency in the English language are essential because hotel and motel desk clerks frequently use the telephone. Course work useful to persons wanting to enter these occupations include basic math, English, geography, U.S. history, psychology, communications, and public speaking. Good spelling, typing ability, and computer literacy are often needed, particularly because most work involves considerable computer use. It also is increasingly helpful for hotel and motel desk clerks to fluently speak a foreign language.

Orientation for hotel and motel desk clerks usually includes an explanation of the job duties and information about the establishment, such as room locations and available services. New employees learn job tasks through on-the-job training under the guidance of a supervisor or an experienced clerk. They often need additional training in how to use the computerized reservation, room assignment, and billing systems and equipment.

Advancement for hotel and motel desk clerks generally comes about either by transfer to a different, more responsible occupation or by promotion to a supervisory position. The more skills, experi-

ence, and additional training an employee possesses, the better their advancement opportunities.

In the lodging industry, hotel and motel desk clerks can improve their chances for advancement by taking home or group study courses in lodging management, such as those sponsored by the Educational Institute of the American Hotel and Motel Association. Positions such as hotel and motel desk clerk offer good opportunities for qualified workers to get started in the business. In many industries, a college degree may be required for advancement to management ranks.

Job Outlook

Employment of hotel and motel desk clerks is expected to grow faster than the average for all occupations through the year 2006 as more hotels, motels, and other lodging establishments are built, and as occupancy rates rise. Job opportunities for hotel and motel desk clerks should be good because turnover is very high. Each year, thousands of workers transfer to other occupations offering better pay and advancement opportunities, or simply leave the workforce altogether. Opportunities for part-time work should continue to be plentiful, because the front desk must be staffed 24 hours a day, seven days a week.

Employment of hotel and motel desk clerks should be favorably affected by an increase in business and leisure travel. Shifts in travel preference away from long vacations and toward long weekends and other, more frequent short trips also should increase demand. The expansion of smaller, budget hotels and less construction of larger, luxury establishments reflects a change in the composition of the hotel and motel industry. As employment shifts from luxury hotels and the broad services they provide to no-frills operations, the proportion of hotel desk clerks should increase in relation to staff such as waiters, waitresses, and recreation workers. Often the hotel desk clerk is responsible for all front office operations, information, and services in a no-frills establishment.

However, the growing effort to cut labor costs while moving towards more efficient service is expected to slow the growth somewhat of desk clerk employment. The role of the front desk is changing as some of the more traditional duties are replaced by technology. New technologies automating check-in and check-out procedures now allow guests to bypass the front desk in many larger establishments, reducing staffing needs. The expansion of automating technologies, such as interactive television and computer systems to dispense information, should further impact employment in the future as such services become more widespread.

Employment of desk clerks is also sensitive to cyclical swings in the economy. During recessions, vacation and business travel declines and hotels and motels need fewer clerks.

Earnings

In 1996, median weekly earnings of full-time hotel and motel desk clerks were about $267.

Earnings of hotel and motel desk clerks vary considerably depending on the location, size, and type of establishment in which they work. Large luxury hotels and those located in metropolitan and resort areas generally pay clerks more than less exclusive or "budget" establishments and those located in less populated areas.

In addition to their hourly wage, full-time hotel and motel desk clerks who work evenings, nights, weekends, or holidays may receive shift differential pay. Some employers offer educational assistance to their employees. Relatively few hotel and motel desk clerks belong to unions. However, some are represented by the Hotel Employees and Restaurant Employees International Union.

Related Occupations

A number of other workers deal with the public, receive and provide information, or direct people to others who can assist them. Among these are dispatchers, security guards, bank tellers, guides, telephone operators, record clerks, counter and rental clerks, survey workers, and ushers and lobby attendants.

Sources of Additional Information

Information on careers in the lodging industry, as well as information about professional development and training programs, may be obtained from:

❏ The Educational Institute of the American Hotel and Motel Association, P.O. Box 531126, Orlando, FL 32853-1126. Homepage: http://www.ei-ahma.org

Human Resources Specialists and Managers

(D.O.T. 079.127; 099.167-010; 166.067, .117, .167 except -046, .257, .267-014 through -046; 169.107, .167-062, .207; 188.117-010, -086, .217)

Significant Points

✓ *Employers generally seek college graduates for entry level jobs. Depending on the job duties, a strong background in human resources, business, technical, or liberal arts subjects is preferred.*

✓ *The job market is likely to remain competitive in view of the abundant supply of qualified college graduates and experienced workers.*

Nature of the Work

Attracting the most qualified employees available and matching them to the jobs for which they are best suited is important for the success of any organization. However, many enterprises are too large to permit close contact between top management and employees. Human resources specialists and managers provide this link. These individuals recruit and interview employees, and advise on hiring decisions in accordance with policies and requirements that have been established in conjunction with top management. In an effort to improve morale and productivity and limit job turnover, they also help their firms effectively use employees' skills, provide training opportunities to enhance those skills, and boost employees' satisfaction with their jobs and working conditions. Although some jobs in the human resources field require only limited contact with people outside the office, most involve frequent contact. Dealing with people is an essential part of the job.

In a small organization, a human resources generalist may handle many, or all, aspects of human resources work, requiring a broad range of knowledge. The responsibilities of human resources generalists can vary widely, depending on their employer's needs. In a large corporation, the top human resources executive usually develops and coordinates personnel programs and policies. These policies are usually implemented by a director or manager of human resources and, in some cases, a director of industrial relations.

The director of human resources may oversee several departments, each headed by an experienced manager, who most likely specializes in one personnel activity such as employment, compensation, benefits, training and development, or employee relations.

Employment and placement managers oversee the hiring and separation of employees and supervise various workers, including equal employment opportunity specialists and recruitment specialists.

Recruiters maintain contacts within the community and may travel extensively, often to college campuses, to search for promising job applicants. Recruiters screen, interview, and test applicants. They may also check references and extend offers of employment to qualified candidates. These workers must be thoroughly familiar with the organization and its personnel policies to discuss wages, working conditions, and promotional opportunities with prospective employees. They must also keep informed about equal employment opportunity (EEO) and affirmative action guidelines and laws, such as the Americans With Disabilities Act.

EEO representatives or affirmative action coordinators handle this area in large organizations. They investigate and resolve EEO grievances, examine corporate practices for possible violations, and compile and submit EEO statistical reports.

Employer relations representatives–who usually work in government agencies–maintain working relationships with local employers and promote the use of public employment programs and services. Similarly, employment interviewers–whose many job titles include personnel consultants, personnel development specialists, and human resources coordinators–help match job seekers with employers.

Job analysts, sometimes called position classifiers, perform very exacting work. They collect and examine detailed information about job duties to prepare job descriptions. These descriptions explain the duties, training, and skills each job requires. Whenever a large organization introduces a new job or reviews existing jobs, it calls upon the expert knowledge of the job analyst.

Occupational analysts conduct research, generally in large firms. They are concerned with occupational classification systems and study the effects of industry and occupational trends upon worker relationships. They may serve as technical liaison between the firm and industry, government, and labor unions.

Establishing and maintaining a firm's pay system is the principal job of the compensation manager. Assisted by staff specialists, compensation managers devise ways to ensure fair and equitable pay rates. They may conduct surveys to see how their rates compare with others and to see that the firm's pay scale complies with changing laws and regulations. In addition, compensation managers often oversee their firm's performance evaluation system, and they may design reward systems such as pay-for-performance plans.

Employee benefits managers handle the company's employee benefits program, notably its health insurance and pension plans. Expertise in designing and administering benefits programs continues to gain importance as employer-provided benefits account for a growing proportion of overall compensation costs, and as benefit plans increase in number and complexity. For example, pension benefits might include savings and thrift, profit-sharing, and stock ownership plans; health benefits may include long-term catastrophic illness insurance and dental insurance. Familiarity with health benefits is a top priority at present, as more firms struggle to cope with the rising cost of health care for employees and retirees. In addition to health insurance and pension coverage, some firms offer their employees life and accidental death and dismemberment insurance, disability insurance, and relatively new benefits designed to meet the needs of a changing work force, such as parental leave, child care and elder care, long-term nursing home care insurance, employee assistance and wellness programs, and flexible benefits plans. Benefits managers must keep abreast of changing federal and state regulations and legislation that may affect employee benefits.

Employee assistance plan managers—also called employee welfare managers—are responsible for a wide array of programs covering occupational safety and health standards and practices; health promotion and physical fitness, medical examinations, and minor health treatment, such as first aid; plant security; publications; food service and recreation activities; car pooling; employee suggestion systems; child care and elder care; and counseling services. Child care and elder care are increasingly important due to growth in the number of dual-income households and the elderly population. Counseling may help employees deal with emotional disorders, alcoholism, or marital, family, consumer, legal, and financial problems. Some employers offer career counseling as well. In large firms, some of these programs—such as security and safety—are in separate departments headed by other managers.

Training is supervised by training and development managers. Increasingly, management recognizes that training offers a way of developing skills, enhancing productivity and quality of work, and building loyalty to the firm. Training is widely accepted as a method of improving employee morale, but this is only one of the reasons for its growing importance. Other factors include the complexity of the work environment, the rapid pace of organizational and technological change, and the growing number of jobs in fields that constantly generate new knowledge. In addition, advances in learning theory have provided insights into how adults learn, and how training can be organized most effectively for them.

Training specialists plan, organize, and direct a wide range of training activities. Trainers conduct orientation sessions and arrange on-the-job training for new employees. They help rank-and-file workers maintain and improve their job skills, and possibly prepare for jobs requiring greater skill. They help supervisors improve their interpersonal skills in order to deal effectively with employees. They may set up individualized training plans to strengthen an employee's existing skills or to teach new ones. Training specialists in some companies set up programs to develop executive potential among employees in lower-level positions. In government-supported training programs, training specialists function as case managers. They first assess the training needs of clients, then guide them through the most appropriate training method. After training, clients may either be referred to employer relations representatives or receive job placement assistance.

Planning and program development is an important part of the training specialist's job. In order to identify and assess training needs within the firm, trainers may confer with managers and supervisors or conduct surveys. They also periodically evaluate training effectiveness.

Depending on the size, goals, and nature of the organization, trainers may differ considerably in their responsibilities and in the methods they use. Training methods include on-the-job training; schools in which shop conditions are duplicated for trainees prior to putting them on the shop floor; apprenticeship training; classroom training; programmed instruction, which may involve interactive videos, videodiscs, and other computer-aided instructional technologies; simulators; conferences; and workshops.

The director of industrial relations forms labor policy, oversees industrial labor relations, negotiates collective bargaining agreements, and coordinates grievance procedures to handle complaints resulting from disputes under the contract for firms with unionized employees. The director of industrial relations also advises and collaborates with the director of human resources, other managers, and members of their staff, because all aspects of personnel policy—such as wages, benefits, pensions, and work practices—may be involved in drawing up a new or revised contract.

Industrial labor relations programs are implemented by labor relations managers and their staff. When a collective bargaining agreement is up for negotiation, labor relations specialists prepare information for management to use during negotiation, which requires familiarity with economic and wage data as well as extensive knowledge of labor law and collective bargaining trends. The labor relations staff interprets and administers the contract with respect to grievances, wages and salaries, employee welfare, health care, pensions, union and management practices, and other contractual stipulations. As union membership is continuing to decline in most industries, industrial relations personnel are working more with employees who are not members of a labor union.

Dispute resolution—attaining tacit or contractual agreements—has become increasingly important as parties to a dispute attempt to avoid costly litigation, strikes, or other disruptions. Dispute resolution also has become more complex, involving employees, management, unions, other firms, and government agencies. Specialists involved in dispute resolution must be highly knowledgeable and experienced, and often report to the director of industrial relations. Conciliators, or mediators, advise and counsel labor and management to prevent and, when necessary, resolve disputes over labor agreements or other labor relations issues. Arbitrators, sometimes called umpires or referees, decide disputes that bind both labor and management to specific terms and conditions of labor contracts. Labor relations specialists who work for unions perform many of the same functions on behalf of the union and its members.

Other emerging specialists include international human resources managers, who handle human resources issues related to a company's foreign operations, and human resources information system specialists, who develop and apply computer programs to process personnel information, match job seekers with job openings, and handle other personnel matters.

Working Conditions

Personnel work generally takes place in clean, pleasant, and comfortable office settings. Arbitrators and mediators may work out of their homes. Many human resources specialists and managers work a standard 35- to 40-hour week. However, longer hours might be necessary for some workers—for example, labor relations specialists and managers, arbitrators, and mediators—when contract agreements are being prepared and negotiated.

Although most human resources specialists and managers work in the office, some travel extensively. For example, recruiters regularly attend professional meetings and visit college campuses to interview prospective employees; arbitrators and mediators often must travel to the site chosen for negotiations.

Employment

Human resources specialists and managers held about 544,000 jobs in 1996. They were employed in virtually every industry. Specialists accounted for three out of five positions; managers, two out of five. About 15,000 specialists were self-employed, working as consultants to public and private employers.

The private sector accounted for about 86 percent of salaried jobs. Among these salaried jobs, services industries–including business, health, social, management, and educational services–accounted for four out of ten jobs; labor organizations, the largest employer among specific industries, accounted for one out of 10. Manufacturing industries accounted for two out of ten jobs, while finance, insurance, and real estate firms accounted for about one out of ten.

Federal, state, and local governments employed about 14 percent of salaried human resources specialists and managers. They handled the recruitment, interviewing, job classification, training, salary administration, benefits, employee relations, and related matters of the nation's public employees.

Training, Other Qualifications, and Advancement

Because of the diversity of duties and level of responsibility, the educational backgrounds of human resources specialists and managers vary considerably. In filling entry-level jobs, employers generally seek college graduates. Some employers prefer applicants who have majored in human resources, personnel administration, or industrial and labor relations; others look for college graduates with a technical or business background; and still others feel that a well-rounded liberal arts education is best.

Many colleges and universities have programs leading to a degree in personnel, human resources, or labor relations. Some offer degree programs in personnel administration or human resources management, training and development, or compensation and benefits. Depending on the school, courses leading to a career in human resources management may be found in departments of business administration, education, instructional technology, organizational development, human services, communication, or public administration, or within a separate human resources institution or department.

Because an interdisciplinary background is appropriate in this field, a combination of courses in the social sciences, business, and behavioral sciences is useful. Some jobs may require a more technical or specialized background in engineering, science, finance, or law, for example. Most prospective human resources specialists should take courses in compensation, recruitment, training and development, and performance appraisal, as well as courses in principles of management, organizational structure, and industrial psychology. Other relevant courses include business administration, public administration, psychology, sociology, political science, economics, and statistics. Courses in labor law, collective bargaining, labor economics, labor history, and industrial psychology also provide a valuable background for the prospective labor relations specialist. As in many other fields, knowledge of computers and information systems is useful.

An advanced degree is increasingly important for some jobs. Many labor relations jobs require graduate study in industrial or labor relations. A strong background in industrial relations and law is highly desirable for contract negotiators, mediators, and arbitrators; in fact, many people in these specialties are lawyers. A background in law is also desirable for employee benefits managers and others who must interpret the growing number of laws and regulations. A master's degree in human resources, or labor relations, or in business administration with a concentration in human resources management is highly recommended for those seeking general and top management positions.

For many specialized jobs in the human resources field, previous experience is an asset; for more advanced positions including managers as well as arbitrators and mediators, it is essential. Many employers prefer entry-level workers who have gained some experience through an internship or work-study program while in school. Personnel administration and human resources development require the ability to work with individuals as well as a commitment to organizational goals. This field also demands other skills people may develop elsewhere–using computers, selling, teaching, supervising, and volunteering, among others. This field offers clerical workers opportunities for advancement to professional positions. Responsible positions are sometimes filled by experienced individuals from other fields, including business, government, education, social services administration, and the military.

The human resources field demands a range of personal qualities and skills. Human resources specialists and managers must speak and write effectively; work with or supervise people having various cultural backgrounds, levels of education, and experience; cope with conflicting points of view, and the unexpected and unusual; function under pressure; and demonstrate integrity, fair-mindedness, and a persuasive, congenial personality.

Entry-level workers often enter formal or on-the-job training programs in which they learn how to classify jobs, interview applicants, or administer employee benefits. They then are assigned to specific areas in the personnel department to gain experience. Later, they may advance to a managerial position, overseeing a major element of the personnel program–compensation or training, for example.

Exceptional human resources workers may be promoted to director of personnel or industrial relations, which can eventually lead to a top managerial or executive position. Others may join a consulting firm or open their own business. A Ph.D. is an asset for teaching, writing, or consulting work.

Most organizations specializing in human resources offer classes intended to enhance the marketable skills of their members. Some organizations offer certification programs, which are signs of competence and can enhance one's advancement opportunities. For example, the International Foundation of Employee Benefits Plans confers the Certified Employee Benefits Specialist certification to persons who complete a series of college-level courses and pass exams covering employee benefit plans. The Society for Human Resources Management has two levels of certification–Professional in Human Resources, and Senior Professional in Human Resources– both of which require experience and a comprehensive exam.

Job Outlook

The job market for human resources specialists and managers is likely to remain competitive through 2006, due to an abundant supply of qualified college graduates and experienced workers, despite large numbers of annual job openings that will stem from the need to replace workers who transfer to other jobs, retire, or stop working for other reasons coupled with projected average employment growth.

New jobs will stem from increasing efforts throughout industry to recruit and retain quality employees; employers are expected to devote greater resources to job-specific training programs in response to the increasing complexity of many jobs, the aging of the work force, and technological advances that can leave employees with obsolete skills. In addition, legislation and court rulings setting standards in occupational safety and health, equal employment opportunity, wages, and health, pension, family leave, and other benefits, will increase demand for experts in these areas. Rising health care costs, in particular, should spur demand for specialists to develop creative compensation and benefits packages that firms can offer prospective employees. Employment of labor relations staff, including arbitrators and mediators, should grow as firms become more involved in labor relations, and attempt to resolve potentially costly labor-management disputes out of court. Additional job growth may stem from increasing demand for specialists in international human resources management and human resources information systems.

Employment demand should be strong among firms involved in management, consulting, and personnel supply, as businesses increasingly contract out personnel functions or hire personnel specialists on a temporary basis to meet the increasing cost and complexity of training and development programs. Demand should also increase in firms that develop and administer complex employee benefits and compensation packages for other organizations.

Demand for human resources specialists and managers is also governed by the staffing needs of the firms for which they work. A rapidly expanding business is likely to hire additional human resources workers–either as permanent employees or consultants–while a business that has experienced a merger or a reduction in its work force will require fewer human resources workers. Also, as human resources management becomes increasingly important to the success of an organization, some small and medium-size businesses that do not have a human resources department may assign employees various human resources duties together with other unrelated responsibilities. In any particular firm, the size and the job duties of the human resources staff are determined by a variety of factors, including the firm's organizational philosophy and goals, the skills of its work force, the pace of technological change, government regulations, collective bargaining agreements, standards of professional practice, and labor market conditions.

Job growth could be limited by the widespread use of computerized human resources information systems that make workers more productive. Similar to other workers, employment of human resources specialists and managers, particularly in larger firms, may be adversely affected by corporate downsizing and restructuring.

Earnings

According to a salary survey conducted by the National Association of Colleges and Employers, bachelor's degree candidates majoring in human resources, including labor relations, received starting offers averaging $25,300 a year in 1996; master's degree candidates, $39,900.

According to a 1996 survey of compensation in the human resources field, conducted by Abbott, Langer, and Associates of Crete, Illinois, the median total cash compensation for selected personnel and labor relations occupations were:

Industrial/labor relations directors	$106,100
Divisional human resources directors	91,300
Compensation and benefits directors	90,500
Employee/community relations directors	87,500
Training and organizational directors	86,600
Benefits directors	80,500
Plant/location human resources managers	64,400
Recruitment and interviewing managers	63,800
Compensation supervisors	53,400
Training generalists	49,900
Employment interviewing supervisors	42,800
Safety specialists	42,500
Job evaluation specialists	39,600
Employee assistance/employee counseling specialists	39,000
Human resources information systems specialists	38,800
Benefits specialists	38,300
E.E.O./affirmative action specialists	38,200
Training material development specialists	37,200
Employee services/employee recreation specialists	35,000

According to a survey of workplaces in 160 metropolitan areas, personnel specialists with limited experience had median earnings of $25,700 a year in 1995, the middle half earned between $23,700 and $28,500 a year. Personnel supervisors/managers with limited experience had median earnings of $59,000 a year. The middle half earned between $54,000 and $65,200 a year.

In the federal government in 1997, persons with a bachelor's degree or three years' general experience in the personnel field generally started at $19,500 a year. Those with a superior academic record or an additional year of specialized experience started at $24,200 a year. Those with a master's degree may start at $29,600, and those with a doctorate in a personnel field may start at $35,800. Beginning salaries were slightly higher in areas where the prevailing local pay level was higher. There are no formal entry-level requirements for managerial positions. Applicants must possess a suitable combination of educational attainment, experience, and record of accomplishment.

Personnel specialists in the federal government averaged $52,900 a year in 1997; personnel managers, $55,400.

Related Occupations

All human resources occupations are closely related. Other workers with skills and expertise in interpersonal relations include employment, rehabilitation, and college career planning and placement counselors; lawyers; psychologists; sociologists; social workers; public relations specialists; and teachers.

Sources of Additional Information

For information about careers in employee training and devel-

opment, contact:

❑ American Society for Training and Development, 1640 King St., Box 1443, Alexandria, VA 22313.

For information about careers and certification in employee compensation and benefits, contact:

❑ American Compensation Association, 14040 Northsight Blvd., Scottsdale, AZ 85260.

Information about careers and certification in employee benefits is available from:

❑ International Foundation of Employee Benefit Plans, 18700 W. Bluemound Rd., Brookfield, WI 53045.

For information about careers in arbitration and other aspects of dispute resolution, contact:

❑ American Arbitration Association, 140 West 51st St., New York, NY 10020. Phone: (800) 778-7879

For information about academic programs in industrial relations, write to:

❑ Industrial Relations Research Association, University of Wisconsin, 7226 Social Science Bldg., 1180 Observatory Dr., Madison, WI 53706.

Information about personnel careers in the health care industry is available from:

❑ American Society for Healthcare Human Resources Administration, One North Franklin, 31st Floor, Chicago, IL 60606.

Industrial Engineers

(D.O.T. 005.167-026; 012.061 -018, .067, .167 except -022, -026, -034, -058, and -062, and .187)

Significant Points

✓ *A bachelor's degree in industrial engineering is almost always required for beginning engineering jobs. Good employment opportunities are expected for new graduates.*

✓ *Starting salaries for industrial engineers are significantly higher than those of bachelor's degree graduates in other fields.*

✓ *Knowledge of technological advances must be acquired through continued study and education.*

Nature of the Work

Industrial engineers determine the most effective ways for an organization to use the basic factors of production—people, machines, materials, information, and energy—to make or process a product or produce a service. They are the bridge between management goals and operational performance. They are more concerned with increasing productivity through the management of people, methods of business organization, and technology than are engineers in other specialties, who generally work more with products or processes.

To solve organizational, production, and related problems most efficiently, industrial engineers carefully study the product and its requirements, use mathematical methods such as operations research to meet those requirements, and design manufacturing and information systems. They develop management control systems to aid in financial planning and cost analysis, design production planning and control systems to coordinate activities and control product

quality, and design or improve systems for the physical distribution of goods and services. Industrial engineers determine which plant location has the best combination of raw materials availability, transportation, and costs. They also develop wage and salary administration systems and job evaluation programs. Many industrial engineers move into management positions because the work is closely related.

Working Conditions

Most industrial engineers work in office buildings, laboratories, or industrial plants.. Some travel extensively to plants or worksites.

Most industrial engineers work a standard 40-hour week. At times, deadlines or design standards may bring extra pressure to a job. When this happens, industrial engineers may work long hours and experience considerable stress.

Employment

Industrial engineers held about 115,000 jobs in 1996. About 73 percent of these jobs were in manufacturing industries. Because their skills can be used in almost any type of organization, industrial engineers are more widely distributed among manufacturing industries than other engineers.

Their skills can be readily applied outside manufacturing as well. Some work in engineering and management services, utilities, and business services; others work for government agencies or as independent consultants.

Training, Other Qualifications, and Advancement

A bachelor's degree in engineering is usually required for beginning engineering jobs. College graduates with a degree in a physical science or mathematics may occasionally qualify for some engineering jobs, especially in engineering specialties in high demand. Most engineering degrees are granted in electrical, mechanical, or civil engineering. However, engineers trained in one branch may work in related branches; for example, many aerospace engineers have training in mechanical engineering. This flexibility allows employers to meet staffing needs in new technologies and specialties in which engineers are in short supply. It also allows engineers to shift to fields with better employment prospects, or to ones that match their interests more closely.

In addition to the standard engineering degree, many colleges offer degrees in engineering technology, which are offered as either two- or four-year programs. These programs prepare students for practical design and production work rather than for jobs that require more theoretical, scientific and mathematical knowledge. Graduates of four-year technology programs may get jobs similar to those obtained by graduates with a bachelor's degree in engineering. Some employers regard them as having skills between those of a technician and an engineer.

Graduate training is essential for engineering faculty positions, but is not required for the majority of entry-level engineering jobs. Many engineers obtain graduate degrees in engineering or business administration to learn new technology, broaden their education, and enhance promotion opportunities. Many high-level executives in government and industry began their careers as engineers.

About 320 colleges and universities offer bachelor's degree programs in engineering that are accredited by the Accreditation Board for Engineering and Technology (ABET), and about 250 colleges offer accredited bachelor's degree programs in engineering technology. ABET accreditation is based on an examination of an engineering program's faculty, curricular content, facilities, and admissions standards. Although most institutions offer programs in the major branches of engineering, only a few offer some of the smaller specialties. Also, programs of the same title may vary in content. For example, some emphasize industrial practices, preparing students for a job in industry, while others are more theoretical and are better for students preparing to take graduate work. Therefore, students should investigate curricula and check accreditations carefully before selecting a college. Admissions requirements for undergraduate engineering schools include a solid background in mathematics (algebra, geometry, trigonometry, and calculus), sciences (biology, chemistry, and physics), and courses in English, social studies, humanities, and computers.

Bachelor's degree programs in engineering are typically designed to last four years, but many students find that it takes between four and five years to complete their studies. In a typical four-year college curriculum, the first two years are spent studying mathematics, basic sciences, introductory engineering, humanities, and social sciences. In the last two years, most courses are in engineering, usually with a concentration in one branch. For example, the last two years of an aerospace program might include courses such as fluid mechanics, heat transfer, applied aerodynamics, analytical mechanics, flight vehicle design, trajectory dynamics, and aerospace propulsion systems. Some programs offer a general engineering curriculum; students then specialize in graduate school or on the job.

Some engineering schools and two-year colleges have agreements whereby the two-year college provides the initial engineering education and the engineering school automatically admits students for their last two years. In addition, a few engineering schools have arrangements whereby a student spends three years in a liberal arts college studying pre-engineering subjects and two years in the engineering school, and receives a bachelor's degree from each. Some colleges and universities offer five-year master's degree programs. Some five- or even six-year cooperative plans combine classroom study and practical work, permitting students to gain valuable experience and finance part of their education.

All 50 states and the District of Columbia require registration for engineers whose work may affect life, health, or property, or who offer their services to the public. Registration generally requires a degree from an ABET-accredited engineering program, four years of relevant work experience, and passing a state examination. Some states will not register people with degrees in engineering technology. Engineers may be registered in several states.

Engineers should be creative, inquisitive, analytical, and detail-oriented. They should be able to work as part of a team and be able to communicate well, both orally and in writing.

Beginning engineering graduates usually work under the supervision of experienced engineers and, in larger companies, may also receive formal classroom or seminar-type training. As they gain knowledge and experience, they are assigned more difficult projects with greater independence to develop designs, solve problems, and make decisions. Engineers may advance to become technical specialists or to supervise a staff or team of engineers and technicians. Some eventually become engineering managers or enter other managerial, management support, or sales jobs.

Job Outlook

Employment of industrial engineers is expected to grow about as fast as the average for all occupations through the year 2006, making for favorable opportunities. Industrial growth, more complex business operations, and the greater use of automation in factories and in offices underlie the projected employment growth. Because the main function of an industrial engineer is to make a higher quality product as efficiently as possible, their services should be in demand in the manufacturing sector as firms seek to reduce costs and increase productivity through scientific management and safety engineering. Most job openings, however, will result from the need to replace industrial engineers who transfer to other occupations or leave the labor force.

Earnings

Starting salaries for industrial engineers with the bachelor's degree are significantly higher than starting salaries of bachelor's degree graduates in other fields. According to the National Association of Colleges and Employers, starting salaries for those with the bachelor's degree were about $38,026 in 1996.

The median annual salary for all industrial engineers who worked full-time in 1996 was $43,700.

The average annual salary for engineers in the federal government in nonsupervisory, supervisory, and managerial positions was $61,950 in 1997.

Related Occupations

Industrial engineers apply the principles of physical science and mathematics in their work. Other workers who use scientific and mathematical principles include engineering, science, and computer systems managers; physical, life, and computer scientists; mathematicians; engineering and science technicians; and architects.

Sources of Additional Information

High school students interested in obtaining general information on a variety of engineering disciplines should contact the Junior Engineering Technical Society by sending a self-addressed business-size envelope with six first-class stamps affixed, to:

❏ JETS-Guidance, at 1420 King St., Suite 405, Alexandria, VA 22314-2794. Homepage: http://www.asee.org/jets

High school students interested in obtaining information on ABET accredited engineering programs should contact:

❏ The Accreditation Board for Engineering and Technology, Inc., at 111 Market Place, Suite 1050, Baltimore, MD 21202-4012. Homepage: http://www.abet.ba.md.us

Non-high school students and those wanting more detailed information should contact:

❏ Institute of Industrial Engineers, Inc., 25 Technology Park/ Atlanta, Norcross, GA 30092. Homepage: http://www.iienet.org

Information Clerks

(*D.O.T. codes are too numerous to list.*)

Significant Points

✓ *Expected faster than average employment growth and relatively high turnover should create numerous job openings for most types of information clerks.*

✓ *A high school diploma or its equivalent is the most common educational requirement for most information clerk jobs.*

Nature of the Work

Information clerks gather information from, and provide information to the public. They are found in a variety of organizations and have many different job titles and responsibilities. Hotel and motel desk clerks are a guest's first contact for check-in, check-out, and other services within hotels, motels, and resorts. Interviewing and new account clerks, found most often in medical facilities, research firms, and financial institutions, assist the public in completing forms, applications or questionnaires. Receptionists are often a visitor's or caller's first contact within an organization, providing information and routing calls. Reservation and transportation ticket agents, as well as travel clerks, assist the public in making travel plans, reservations, and purchasing tickets for a variety of transportation services.

Although their day-to-day duties vary widely, most information clerks greet customers, guests, or other visitors. Others answer telephones or elicit information from the public. Most information clerks use general office equipment such as multiline telephones, fax machines, and personal computers. This section, which contains an overall discussion of information clerks, is followed by separate sections providing more information on the four types of clerks identified above.

Working Conditions

Information clerks who greet customers and visitors usually work in highly visible areas, designed and furnished to make a good impression. Most work stations are clean, well lighted, and relatively quiet, and overall working conditions are usually pleasant. Reservation agents and interviewing clerks who do much of their work over the telephone, generally work away from the public, often in large centralized reservation or phone centers. Because a number of agents or clerks may share the same work space, it may be crowded and noisy. Occasionally, interviewing clerks may conduct surveys on the street or in shopping malls, or go door to door. Both hotel desk clerks and ticket agents may be on their feet most of the time, and ticket agents may have to lift heavy baggage. In addition, prolonged exposure to a video display terminal may lead to eye strain.

Although most information clerks work a standard 40-hour week, about three out of ten work part-time. Some high school and college students work part-time as information clerks, after school or during vacations. Some jobs—such as those in the transportation industry, hospitals, and hotels, in particular—may require working evenings, late night shifts, weekends, and holidays. In many cases, employees with the least seniority are assigned the least desirable shifts. Interviewing clerks conducting surveys or other research may mainly work evenings or weekends.

The work performed by information clerks may be repetitious and stressful. Many receptionists spend all day answering continuously ringing telephones while performing additional clerical or secretarial tasks. Many reservation agents and travel clerks work under stringent time constraints or have quotas on the number of calls answered or reservations made. The current technology enables management to electronically monitor their use of computer systems, monitor or tape record their telephone calls, or limit the time spent on each call.

The work of hotel and motel desk clerks and transportation ticket agents also can be stressful when trying to serve the needs of difficult or angry customers. When flights are canceled, reservations mishandled, or guests are dissatisfied, these clerks must act as a buffer between the establishment and its customers.

Employment

Information clerks held almost 1.6 million jobs in 1996. The following tabulation shows 1996 employment for the individual occupations.

Receptionists	1,074,000
Interviewing and new account clerks	208,000
Reservation and transportation ticket agents and travel clerks	166,000
Hotel and motel desk clerks	144,000

Although information clerks are found in a variety of industries throughout the economy, employment is concentrated in hotels and motels, the health services industry, banks and savings institutions, the transportation industry, and firms providing business or real estate services.

Training, Other Qualifications, and Advancement

Although hiring requirements for information clerk jobs vary from industry to industry, a high school diploma or its equivalent is the most common educational requirement. However, good interpersonal skills and familiarity or experience with computers are often more important to employers. For airline reservation and ticket agent jobs, some college education may be preferred.

Because many information clerks deal directly with the public, good grooming habits and a pleasant personality are imperative, as are good problem-solving and interpersonal skills. A clear speaking voice and fluency in the English language are essential because these employees frequently use the telephone or public address systems. Course work useful to persons wanting to enter these occupations include basic math, English, geography, U.S. history, psychology, communications, and public speaking. Good spelling, typing ability, and computer literacy are often needed, particularly because most work involves considerable computer use. It also is increasingly helpful for those wishing to enter the lodging or travel industries to fluently speak a foreign language.

With the exception of airline reservation and transportation ticket agents, orientation and training for information clerks generally takes place on the job. For example, orientation for hotel and motel desk clerks usually includes an explanation of the job duties and information about the establishment, such as room locations and available services. New employees learn job tasks through on-the-job training under the guidance of a supervisor or an experienced clerk. They often need additional training in how to use the computerized reservation, room assignment, and billing systems and equipment.

Receptionists generally receive on-the-job training. However, employers often look for applicants who already possess certain skills, such as prior computer and word processing experience. Some employers may prefer previous experience, some formal education, or training with office equipment or procedures. On the job, they learn how to operate the telephone system, computers, and the proper procedures for greeting visitors, and distributing mail, fax, and parcel deliveries.

Most airline reservation and ticket agents learn their skills through formal company training programs. They spend some time in a classroom setting, learning company and industry policies, computer systems, and ticketing procedures. They learn to use the airline's computer system to obtain information on schedules, seat availability, and fares; to reserve space for passengers; and to plan passenger itineraries. They must learn airport and airline code designations, regulations, and safety procedures, and may be tested on this knowledge. After completing classroom instruction, new agents work on the job with supervisors or experienced agents for a period of time. During this period, monitoring of telephone conversations may serve as a training device to improve the quality of customer service. Agents are expected to provide good service while limiting the time spent on each call without being discourteous to customers.

In contrast, automobile clubs, bus lines, and railroads tend to train their ticket agents or travel clerks on the job, through short in-house classes that can last several days. Most information clerks continue to receive instruction on new procedures and company policies after their initial training ends.

Advancement for information clerks generally comes about either by transfer to a different, more responsible occupation or by promotion to a supervisory position. The more skills, experience, and additional training an employee possesses, the better their advancement opportunities. Receptionists, interviewers, and new accounts clerks with word processing or other clerical skills may advance to a better paying job as a secretary or administrative assistant. Within the airline industry, a ticket agent may advance to lead worker on the shift.

Additional training is helpful in preparing information clerks for promotion. In the lodging industry, clerks can improve their chances for advancement by taking home or group study courses in lodging management, such as those sponsored by the Educational Institute of the American Hotel and Motel Association. In some industries—such as lodging, banking, or the airline industry—workers commonly are promoted through the ranks. Positions such as airline reservation agent or hotel and motel desk clerk offer good opportunities for qualified workers to get started in the business. In many industries, a college degree may be required for advancement to management ranks.

Job Outlook

Overall employment of information clerks is expected to increase faster than the average for all occupations through the year 2006. In addition to the many openings occurring as businesses and organizations expand, numerous job openings for information clerks will result from the need to replace experienced workers who transfer to other occupations or leave the labor force. Replacement needs reflect the relatively high turnover among these jobs. Many young people work as information clerks for a few years before switching to other, better paying jobs. This work is well suited to flexible work schedules, and many opportunities for part-time work will continue to be available, particularly as organizations look to cut labor costs by hiring more part-time or temporary workers.

Economic growth and general business expansion are expected to stimulate faster than average growth in the large number of receptionist jobs. Hotel and motel desk clerks are also expected to grow faster than the average as the composition of the lodging industry changes and services provided by these workers expand. Employment in other information clerk jobs, however, is projected to range from a decline to average growth, reflecting the impact of new technology and trends in the industries where their employment is concentrated.

Earnings

In 1996, median weekly earnings of full-time information clerks were about $345. The middle 50 percent earned between $279 and $447. The bottom 10 percent earned less than $213, while the top 10 percent earned more than $576. Earnings vary widely by occupation and experience. Weekly earnings ranged from less than $185 for the lowest paid hotel clerks, to over $710 for the highest paid reservation agents. Salaries of reservation and ticket agents tend to be significantly higher than for other information clerks, while hotel and motel desk clerks tend to earn quite a bit less, as the following tabulation of median weekly earnings shows.

Reservation and transportation ticket agents and travel clerks	$421
Interviewing clerks	356
Receptionists	333
Hotel and motel desk clerks	267

Earnings of hotel and motel desk clerks also vary considerably depending on the location, size, and type of establishment in which they work. Large luxury hotels and those located in metropolitan and resort areas generally pay clerks more than less exclusive or "budget" establishments and those located in less populated areas.

In early 1997, the federal government commonly paid beginning receptionists with a high school diploma or six months of experience, salaries ranging from $18,980 to $19,240 a year. The average annual salary for all receptionists employed by the federal government was about $21,240 in 1997.

In addition to their hourly wage, full-time information clerks who work evenings, nights, weekends, or holidays may receive shift differential pay. Some employers offer educational assistance to their employees. Reservation and transportation ticket agents and travel clerks receive free or reduced rate travel on their company's carriers for themselves and their immediate family and, in some companies, for friends. Relatively few information clerks belong to unions. However, unions representing these workers include the Transportation Communications International Union, the Amalgamated Transit Union, and the Hotel Employees and Restaurant Employees International Union.

Related Occupations

A number of other workers deal with the public, receive and provide information, or direct people to others who can assist them. Among these are dispatchers, security guards, bank tellers, guides, telephone operators, record clerks, counter and rental clerks, survey workers, and ushers and lobby attendants.

Sources of Additional Information

For more information on information clerk jobs in your area, contact your State Employment Agency.

Insulation Workers

(D.O.T. 863.364-010 and -014, .381-010 and -014, .664-010, and .685-010)

Significant Points

✓ *Insulation worker jobs are projected to increase about as fast as the average for all occupations, but will be one of the fastest growing construction occupations.*

✓ *High turnover rate of insulation worker jobs keeps job openings plentiful.*

✓ *Workers who remove hazardous asbestos insulation from older buildings are required to be specially trained.*

Nature of the Work

Properly insulated buildings reduce energy consumption by keeping heat in during the winter and out in the summer. Refrigerated storage rooms, vats, tanks, vessels, boilers, and steam and hot water pipes also are insulated to prevent the wasteful transfer of heat. Insulation workers install this insulating material.

Insulation workers cement, staple, wire, tape, or spray insulation. When covering a steam pipe, for example, insulation workers measure and cut sections of insulation to the proper length, stretch it open along a cut that runs the length of the material, and slip it over the pipe. They fasten the insulation with adhesive, staples, tape, or wire bands. Sometimes they wrap a cover of aluminum, plastic, or canvas over it and cement or band the cover in place. Insulation workers may screw on sheet metal around insulated pipes to protect the insulation from weather conditions or physical abuse.

When covering a wall or other flat surface, workers may use a hose to spray foam insulation onto a wire mesh. The wire mesh provides a rough surface to which the foam can cling, and adds strength to the finished surface. Workers may then install drywall or apply a final coat of plaster for a finished appearance.

In attics or exterior walls of uninsulated buildings, workers blow in loose-fill insulation. A helper feeds a machine with fiberglass, cellulose, or rock wool insulation while another worker blows the insulation with a compressor hose into the space being filled.

In new construction or major renovations, insulation workers staple fiberglass or rockwool batts to exterior walls and ceilings before drywall, paneling, or plaster walls are put in place. In major renovations of old buildings or when putting new insulation around pipes and industrial machinery, insulation workers often must first remove the old insulation. In the past, asbestos—now known to cause cancer in humans—was used extensively in walls and ceilings and for covering pipes, boilers, and various industrial equipment. Because of this danger, U.S. Environmental Protection Agency regulations require that asbestos be removed before a building undergoes major renovations or is demolished. When removing asbestos, insulation workers must follow carefully prescribed asbestos removal techniques and work practices. First, they seal and depressurize the area containing the asbestos, then they remove it using hand tools and special filtered vacuum cleaners and air-filtration devices.

Insulation workers use common hand tools—trowels, brushes, knives, scissors, saws, pliers, and stapling guns. They use power saws to cut insulating materials, welding machines to join sheet metal or secure clamps, and compressors for blowing or spraying insulation.

Working Conditions

Insulation workers generally work indoors. They spend most of the workday on their feet, either standing, bending, or kneeling. Sometimes, they work from ladders or in tight spaces. However, the work is not strenuous; it requires more coordination than strength. Insulation work is often dusty and dirty. The minute particles from insulation materials, especially when blown, can irritate the eyes, skin, and respiratory system. Removing cancer-causing asbestos insulation is a hazardous task and is done by specially trained workers. To protect themselves from the dangers of asbestos and irritants, workers follow strict safety guidelines, take decontamination showers, keep work areas well-ventilated, and wear protective suits, masks, and respirators.

Employment

Insulation workers held about 65,000 jobs in 1996; most worked for insulation or other construction contractors. Others worked for the federal government, in wholesale and retail trade, in shipbuilding, and in other manufacturing industries that have extensive installations for power, heating, and cooling. Most worked in urban areas. In less populated areas, insulation work may be done by carpenters, heating and air-conditioning installers, or drywall installers.

Training, Other Qualifications, and Advancement

Most insulation workers learn their trade informally on the job, although some workers complete formal apprenticeship programs. For entry jobs, insulation contractors prefer high school graduates who are in good physical condition and are licensed to drive. High school courses in blueprint reading, shop math, sheet-metal layout, and general construction provide a helpful background. Applicants seeking apprenticeship positions must have a high school diploma or its equivalent, and be at least 18 years old.

Trainees are assigned to experienced insulation workers for instruction and supervision. They begin with simple tasks, such as carrying insulation or holding material while it is fastened in place. On-the-job training can take up to two years, depending on the work. Learning to install insulation in homes generally requires less training than insulation application in commercial and industrial settings. As they gain experience, trainees receive less supervision, more responsibility, and higher pay.

In contrast, trainees in formal apprenticeship programs receive in-depth instruction in all phases of insulation. Apprenticeship programs may be provided by a joint committee of local insulation contractors and the local union of the International Association of Heat and Frost Insulators and Asbestos Workers, to which many insulation workers belong. Programs normally consist of four years of on-the-job training coupled with classroom instruction, and trainees must pass practical and written tests to demonstrate a knowledge of the trade.

Insulation workers who work with asbestos usually have to be licensed. Although licensure requirements vary from area to area, most states require asbestos removal workers to complete a three-day training program in compliance with the 1986 Asbestos Hazard Emergency Removal Act (AHERA). The National Asbestos Council

(NAC) provides this training in over 100 locations. This program emphasizes hands-on training. Typically, students build a decontamination unit, handle a respirator and filtered vacuum cleaners, and perform simulated asbestos removal. In addition, they receive classroom instruction on a wide variety of topics, such as government regulations, health effects and worker protection, sampling for asbestos, and work practices. The NAC also offers a two-day course on compliance with Occupational Safety and Health Administration (OSHA) regulations governing industrial asbestos removal in plants and factories, and an annual AHERA recertification program.

Skilled insulation workers may advance to supervisor, shop superintendent, insulation contract estimator, or set up their own insulation or asbestos abatement business.

Job Outlook

Opportunities for insulation workers are expected to be good because is it one of the fastest growing construction occupations, and replacement needs are usually high due to the many workers who transfer to other occupations. Employment of insulation workers is expected to increase about as fast as the average for all occupations through the year 2006, reflecting the demand for insulation associated with new construction and renovation as well as the demand for asbestos removal in existing structures. Concerns about the efficient use of energy to heat and cool buildings will result in growth in demand for insulation workers in the construction of new residential, industrial, and commercial buildings. In addition, renovation and efforts to improve insulation in existing structures also will increase demand.

Asbestos removal will also provide many jobs for insulation workers, not only because insulation workers often remove asbestos, but because they replace it with another insulating material. The 1986 Asbestos Hazard Emergency Removal Act requires all public and private schools to have an asbestos management plan. Federal regulations also require that asbestos be removed from buildings that are to be demolished or undergo major renovations. In addition, many banks require that buildings be free of asbestos before a real estate loan will be granted. All of these regulatory requirements are expected to stimulate asbestos removal and employment growth. The need to maintain, remove, and replace asbestos insulation on old pipes, boilers, and a variety of equipment in chemical and refrigeration plants and petroleum refineries will also add to employment requirements.

Despite this growth in demand, replacement needs will account for most job openings. This occupation has the highest turnover of all the construction trades. Each year thousands of jobs will become available as insulation workers transfer to other occupations or leave the labor force. However there are no strict training requirements for entry, many people with limited skills work as insulation workers for a short time and then move on to other types of work, creating many job openings.

Insulation workers in the construction industry may experience periods of unemployment because of the short duration of many construction projects and the cyclical nature of construction activity. Workers employed in industrial plants generally have more stable employment because maintenance and repair must be done on a continuing basis. Most insulation is applied after buildings are enclosed.

Earnings

Median weekly earnings for insulation workers who worked full-time were $508 in 1996. The middle 50 percent earned between $351 and $758. The lowest 10 percent earned less than $267, and the top 10 percent earned more than $968.

According to the Engineering News Record, union insulation workers received an average hourly wage of $31.92 in 1997, including benefits. Wages ranged from a low of $21.68 an hour in New Orleans to a high of $47.77 in New York City. Insulation workers doing commercial and industrial work earn substantially more than those working in residential construction, which does not require as much skill.

Related Occupations

Insulation workers combine a knowledge of insulation materials with the skills of cutting, fitting, and installing materials. Workers in occupations involving similar skills include carpenters, carpet installers, drywall applicators, floor layers, roofers, and sheet-metal workers.

Sources of Additional Information

For information about training programs or other work opportunities in this trade, contact a local insulation contractor; a local chapter of the International Association of Heat and Frost Insulators and Asbestos Workers; the nearest office of the state employment service or state apprenticeship agency, or:

❑ International. Association of Heat and Frost Insulators and Asbestos Workers, 1300 Connecticut Ave. NW, Washington, DC 20005

❑ National Insulation and Abatement Contractors Association, 99 Canal Center Plaza, Suite 222, Alexandria, VA 22314.

❑ Insulation Contractors Association of America, 1321 Duke St., Suite 303, Alexandria, VA 22314.

Janitors and Cleaners and Cleaning Supervisors

(D.O.T. 321.137-010, -014; 323.137-010, .687; 350.137-026; 358.687-010; 381.137-010, .687 except -010; 382.664-010; 389.667-010, .683-010, .687-014; 739.687-198; 891.687-010 and -018; and 952.687-010)

Significant Points

✓ *Job openings should be plentiful because limited training requirements coupled with low pay and numerous part-time and temporary jobs contribute to high turnover in this very large occupation.*

Nature of the Work

Janitors and cleaners—also called building custodians, executive housekeepers, or maids—keep office buildings, hospitals, stores, apartment houses, hotels, and other types of buildings clean and in good condition. Some only do cleaning, while others have a wide range of duties. They may fix leaky faucets, empty trash cans, do painting and carpentry, replenish bathroom supplies, mow lawns, and see that heating and air-conditioning equipment works properly. On a typical day, janitors may wet- or dry-mop floors, clean bathrooms, vacuum carpets, dust furniture, make minor repairs, and exterminate insects and rodents. In hospitals, where they are mostly known as maids or housekeepers, they may also wash bed frames, brush mattresses, make beds, and disinfect and sterilize equipment and supplies using germicides and sterilizing equipment. In hotels, aside from cleaning and maintaining the premises, they may deliver ironing boards, cribs, and rollaway beds to guests' rooms.

Janitors and cleaners use various equipment, tools, and cleaning materials. For one job, they may need a mop and bucket; for another, an electric polishing machine and a special cleaning solution. Improved building materials, chemical cleaners, and power equipment have made many tasks easier and less time-consuming, but janitors must learn proper use of equipment and cleaners to avoid harming floors, fixtures, and themselves.

Cleaning supervisors coordinate, schedule, and supervise the activities of janitors and cleaners. They assign tasks and inspect building areas to see that work has been done properly, issue supplies and equipment, inventory stocks to ensure an adequate amount of supplies is present, screen and hire job applicants, and recommend promotions, transfers, or dismissals. They also train new and experienced employees. Supervisors may prepare reports concerning room occupancy, hours worked, and department expenses. Some also perform cleaning duties.

Working Conditions

Because most office buildings are cleaned while they are empty, many cleaners work evening hours. Some, however, such as school and hospital custodians, work in the daytime. When there is a need for 24-hour maintenance, janitors may be assigned to shifts. Most full-time janitors, cleaners, and cleaning supervisors work about 40 hours a week. Part-time cleaners usually work in the evenings and on weekends.

Janitors, cleaners, and cleaning supervisors in large office and residential buildings often work in teams. These teams consist of workers who specialize in vacuuming, trash pickup, and restroom cleaning, among other things. Supervisors conduct inspections to ensure the building is cleaned properly and the team is functioning efficiently.

Janitors and cleaners usually work inside heated, well-lighted buildings. However, they sometimes work outdoors sweeping walkways, mowing lawns, or shoveling snow. Working with machines can be noisy, and some tasks, such as cleaning bathrooms and trash rooms, can be dirty and unpleasant. Janitors may suffer cuts, bruises, and burns from machines, handtools, and chemicals. They spend most of their time on their feet, sometimes lifting or pushing heavy furniture or equipment. Many tasks, such as dusting or sweeping, require constant bending, stooping, and stretching. As a result, janitors may also suffer back injuries and sprains.

Employment

Janitors and cleaners, including cleaning supervisors, held over 3.2 million jobs in 1996. About a third worked part-time (more than 35 hours a week).

About 19 out of 20 jobs are held by janitors and cleaners. They worked in every type of establishment. About 24 percent worked for firms supplying building maintenance services on a contract basis; 16 percent, in educational institutions; and 14 percent, in hotels. Other employers included hospitals, restaurants, religious institutions, manufacturing firms, government agencies, and operators of apartment buildings, office buildings, and other types of real estate.

Cleaning supervisors held about 1 job in 20. About 37 percent were employed in hotels; 20 percent, in firms supplying building maintenance services on a contract basis; 15 percent, in hospitals; and 12 percent, in nursing and personal care facilities. Other employers included educational institutions, residential care establishments, and amusement and recreation facilities.

Although cleaning jobs can be found in all cities and towns, most are located in highly populated areas where there are many office buildings, schools, apartment houses, and hospitals.

Training, Other Qualifications, and Advancement

No special education is required for most cleaning jobs, but beginners should know simple arithmetic and be able to follow instructions. High school shop courses are helpful for jobs involving repair work.

Most janitors and cleaners learn their skills on the job. Usually, beginners work with an experienced cleaner, doing routine cleaning. They are given more complicated work as they gain experience.

In some cities, programs run by unions, government agencies, or employers teach janitorial skills. Students learn how to clean buildings thoroughly and efficiently, how to select and safely use various cleansing agents, and how to operate and maintain machines, such as wet and dry vacuums, buffers, and polishers. Students learn to plan their work, to follow safety and health regulations, to interact positively with people in the buildings they clean, and to work without supervision. Instruction in minor electrical, plumbing, and other repairs may also be given. Those who come in contact with the public should have good communication skills. Employers usually look for dependable, hard-working individuals who are in good health, follow directions well, and get along with other people.

Janitors and cleaners usually find work by answering newspaper advertisements, applying directly to organizations where they would like to work, contacting local labor unions, or contacting state employment service offices.

Advancement opportunities for janitorial workers are usually limited in organizations where they are the only maintenance worker. Where there is a large maintenance staff, however, janitors can be promoted to supervisor and to area supervisor or manager. A high school diploma improves the chances for advancement. Some janitors set up their own maintenance business.

Supervisors usually move up through the ranks. In many establishments, they are required to take some in-service training to perfect housekeeping techniques and procedures, and to enhance supervisory skills.

A small number of cleaning supervisors and managers are members of the International Executive Housekeepers Association (IEHA). IEHA offers two kinds of certification programs to cleaning supervisors and managers—Certified Executive Housekeeper (CEH) and Registered Executive Housekeeper (REH). The CEH designation is offered to those with a high school education, while the REH designation is offered to those who have a four-year college degree. Both designations are earned by attending courses and passing exams, and must be renewed every two years to ensure that workers keep abreast of new cleaning methods. Those with the REH designation typically oversee the cleaning services of hotels, hospitals, casinos, and other large institutions which rely on well-trained experts for their cleaning needs.

Job Outlook

Job openings should be plentiful for janitors and cleaners because limited formal education and training requirements coupled with low pay and numerous part-time and temporary jobs contribute to high turnover in this very large occupation.

While the need to replace workers who transfer to other occupations or leave the labor force will create most job openings, some opportunities will also stem from job growth. Employment of janitors, cleaners, and cleaning supervisors is expected to grow slower than the average for all occupations through the year 2006. To clean the increasing number of office complexes, apartment houses, schools, factories, hospitals, and other buildings, more workers will be assigned to specialized teams with more efficient cleaning equipment and supplies. As many firms reduce costs by hiring independent contractors, businesses providing janitorial and cleaning services on a contract basis are expected to be one of the fastest growing employers of janitors, cleaners, and cleaning supervisors.

Earnings

Median earnings for janitors and cleaners who usually worked full-time were only about $300 a week in 1996, compared to $490 for workers in all occupations combined. Among janitors and cleaners, the middle 50 percent earned between $240 and $420. Ten percent earned less than $190, and 10 percent earned more than $560. Maids and housekeepers had median earnings of $270 a week in 1996, with the middle 50 percent earning between $210 and $320. Ten percent earned less than $180 and 10 percent earned more than $410. Cleaning supervisors had median earnings of $400 a week in 1996; the middle 50 percent earned between $300 and $570. Ten percent earned less than $230 and 10 percent earned more than $760.

According to a 1997 International Executive Housekeepers Association membership survey, certified directors or managers of housekeeping who had completed some college averaged about $37,000 a year. Those who worked in industrial plants, manufacturing plants, and hospitals had higher paying jobs than those who worked in government, hotels, or as contract cleaners.

Related Occupations

Private household workers have job duties similar to janitors and cleaners. Workers who specialize in one of the many job functions of janitors and cleaners include refuse collectors, floor waxers, street sweepers, window cleaners, gardeners, boiler tenders, pest controllers, and general maintenance repairers.

Sources of Additional Information

Information about janitorial jobs may be obtained from a local state employment service office.

For information on certification in executive housekeeping, contact:

❑ International Executive Housekeepers Association, Inc., 1001 Eastwind Dr., Suite 301, Westerville, OH 43081-3361. Homepage: http://www.ieha.org

Landscape Architects

(D.O.T. 001.061-018)

Significant Points

✓ *Nearly 30 percent—over three times the proportion for all professionals—are self-employed.*

✓ *A bachelor's degree in landscape architecture is the minimum requirement for entry-level jobs; many employers prefer to hire landscape architects who have completed at least one internship.*

✓ *Because many landscape architects work for small firms or are self-employed, benefits tend to be less generous than those provided to workers in large organizations.*

Nature of the Work

Everyone enjoys attractively designed residential areas, public parks and playgrounds, college campuses, shopping centers, golf courses, parkways, and industrial parks. Landscape architects design these areas so that they are not only functional but beautiful and compatible with the natural environment as well. They may plan the location of buildings, roads, and walkways and the arrangement of flowers, shrubs, and trees. Historic preservation and natural resource conservation and reclamation are other important objectives to which landscape architects may apply their knowledge of the environment as well as their design and artistic talents.

Many types of organizations—from real estate development firms starting new projects to municipalities constructing airports or parks—hire landscape architects, who are often involved with the development of a site from its conception. Working with architects, surveyors, and engineers, landscape architects help determine the best arrangement of roads and buildings. They also collaborate with environmental scientists, foresters, and other professionals to find the best way to conserve or restore natural resources. Once these decisions are made, landscape architects create detailed plans indicating new topography, vegetation, walkways, and other landscaping details, such as fountains and decorative features.

In planning a site, landscape architects first consider the nature and purpose of the project and the funds available. They analyze the natural elements of the site, such as the climate, soil, slope of the land, drainage, and vegetation; observe where sunlight falls on the site at different times of the day and examine the site from various angles; and assess the effect of existing buildings, roads, walkways, and utilities on the project.

After studying and analyzing the site, they prepare a preliminary design. To account for the needs of the client as well as the conditions at the site, they may have to make many changes before a final design is approved. They must also take into account any local, state, or federal regulations such as those protecting wetlands or historic resources. Computer-aided design (CAD) has become an essential tool for most landscape architects in preparing designs. Many landscape architects also use video simulation to help clients envision the proposed ideas and plans. For larger scale site planning, landscape architects also use geographic information systems technology, a computer mapping system.

Throughout all phases of the planning and design, landscape architects consult with other professionals involved in the project. Once the design is complete, they prepare a proposal for the client. They produce detailed plans of the site, including written reports, sketches, models, photographs, land-use studies, and cost estimates, and submit them for approval by the client and by regulatory agencies. If the plans are approved, landscape architects prepare working drawings showing all existing and proposed features. They also outline in detail the methods of construction and draw up a list of necessary materials.

Although many landscape architects supervise the installation of their design, some are involved in the construction of the site. However, this usually is done by the developer or landscape contractor.

Some landscape architects work on a wide variety of projects. Others specialize in a particular area, such as residential development, historic landscape restoration, waterfront improvement projects, parks and playgrounds, or shopping centers. Still others work in regional planning and resource management; feasibility, environmental impact, and cost studies; or site construction.

Although most landscape architects do at least some residential work, relatively few limit their practice to landscape design for individual homeowners because most residential landscape design projects are too small to provide suitable income compared with larger commercial or multiunit residential projects. Some nurseries offer residential landscape design services, but these services often are performed by lesser qualified landscape designers or others with training and experience in related areas.

Landscape architects who work for government agencies do site and landscape design for government buildings, parks, and other public lands, as well as park and recreation planning in national parks and forests. In addition, they may prepare environmental impact statements and studies on environmental issues such as public land-use planning. Some are involved in efforts to restore degraded land, such as mines or landfills.

Working Conditions

Landscape architects spend most of their time in offices creating plans and designs, preparing models and cost estimates, doing research, or attending meetings with clients and other professionals involved in a design or planning project. The remainder of their time is spent at the site. During the design and planning stage, landscape architects visit and analyze the site to verify that the design can be incorporated into the landscape. After the plans and specifications are completed, they may spend additional time at the site observing or supervising the construction. Those who work in large firms may spend considerably more time out of the office because of travel to sites outside the local area.

Salaried employees in both government and landscape architectural firms usually work regular hours; however, they may work overtime, sometimes 60 or more hours a week, to meet a project deadline. Hours of self-employed landscape architects may vary.

Employment

Landscape architects held about 17,000 jobs in 1996. About two out of five worked for firms that provide landscape architecture services. Most of the rest were employed by architectural firms. The federal government also employs these workers, primarily in the U.S. Departments of Agriculture, Defense, and Interior. About three of every ten landscape architects was self-employed.

Employment of landscape architects is concentrated in urban and suburban areas throughout the country. Some landscape architects work in rural areas, particularly those in the federal government who plan and design parks and recreation areas.

Training, Other Qualifications, and Advancement

A bachelor's or master's degree in landscape architecture is usually necessary for entry into the profession. The bachelor's degree in landscape architecture takes four or five years to complete. There are two types of accredited master's degree programs. The master's degree as a first professional degree is a three-year program designed for students with an undergraduate degree in another discipline; this is the most common type. The master's degree as the second professional degree is a two-year program for students who have a bachelor's degree in landscape architecture and wish to teach or specialize in some aspect of landscape architecture, such as regional planning or golf course design.

In 1996, 54 colleges and universities offered 70 undergraduate and graduate programs in landscape architecture that were accredited by the Landscape Architecture Accreditation Board of the American Society of Landscape Architects.

College courses required in this field usually include technical subjects such as surveying, landscape design and construction, landscape ecology, site design, and urban and regional planning. Other courses include history of landscape architecture, plant and soil science, geology, professional practice, and general management. Many landscape architecture programs are adding courses which address environmental issues. In addition, most students at the undergraduate level take a year of prerequisite courses such as English, mathematics, and social and physical science. The design studio is an important aspect of many landscape architecture curriculums. Whenever possible, students are assigned real projects, providing them with valuable hands-on experience. While working on these projects, students may become more proficient in the use of technologies such as computer-aided design, geographic information systems, and video simulation.

In 1996, 45 states required landscape architects to be licensed or registered. Licensing is based on the Landscape Architect Registration Examination (L.A.R.E.), sponsored by the Council of Landscape Architectural Registration Boards and administered over a three-day period. Admission to the exam usually requires a degree from an accredited school plus one to four years of work experience, although standards vary from state to state. Currently, 18 states require the passage of a state examination in addition to the L.A.R.E. to satisfy registration requirements. State examinations, which are usually one hour in length and completed at the end of the L.A.R.E., focus on laws, environmental regulations, plants, soils, climate, and any other characteristics unique to the state.

Because state requirements for licensure are not uniform, landscape architects may not find it easy to transfer their registration from one state to another. However, those who meet the national standards of graduating from an accredited program, serving three years of internship under the supervision of a registered landscape architect, and passing the L.A.R.E. can satisfy requirements in most states.

In the federal government, candidates for entry positions should have a bachelor's or master's degree in landscape architecture. The federal government does not require its landscape architects to be licensed.

Persons planning a career in landscape architecture should appreciate nature and enjoy working with their hands. Creative vision and artistic talent are desirable qualities, but they are not essential to success as a landscape architect. Good oral communication skills are important, because these workers must be able to convey their ideas to other professionals and clients and to make presentations before large groups. Strong writing skills are also valuable, as is knowledge of computer applications of all kinds, including word processing, desktop publishing, and spreadsheets. Landscape architects use these tools to develop presentations, proposals, reports, and land impact studies for clients, colleagues, and superiors. The ability to draft and design using CAD software is essential. Many employers recommend that prospective landscape architects complete at least one summer internship with a landscape architecture firm in order to gain an understanding of the day-to-day operations of a small business, including how to win clients, generate fees, and work within a budget.

In states where licensure is required, new hires may be called apprentices or intern landscape architects until they become licensed. Their duties vary depending on the type and size of employing firm. They may do project research or prepare working drawings, construction documents, or base maps of the area to be landscaped. Some are allowed to participate in the actual design of a project. However, interns must perform all work under the supervision of a licensed landscape architect. Additionally, all drawings and specifications must be signed and sealed by the licensed landscape architect, who takes legal responsibility for the work. After gaining experience and becoming licensed, landscape architects usually can carry a design through all stages of development. After several years, they may become project managers, taking on the responsibility for meeting schedules and budgets, in addition to overseeing the project design; and later, associates or partners, with a proprietary interest in the business.

Many landscape architects are self-employed because start-up costs, after an initial investment in CAD software, are relatively low. Self-discipline, business acumen, and good marketing skills are important qualities for those who choose to open their own business. Even with these qualities, however, some may struggle while building a client base.

Those with landscape architecture training also qualify for jobs closely related to landscape architecture, and may, after gaining some experience, become construction supervisors, land or environmental planners, or landscape consultants.

Job Outlook

Employment of landscape architects is expected to increase faster than the average for all occupations through the year 2006. The level of new construction plays an important role in determining demand for landscape architects. Overall, anticipated growth in construction is expected to increase demand for landscape architectural services over the long run. However, opportunities will vary from year to year and by geographic region, depending on local economic conditions. During a recession, when real estate sales and construction slow down, landscape architects may face layoffs and greater competition for jobs. The need to replace landscape architects who retire or leave the labor force for other reasons is expected to produce nearly as many job openings as new openings stemming from job growth.

An increasing proportion of office and other commercial and industrial development will occur outside cities. These projects are typically located on larger sites with more surrounding land which needs to be designed, in contrast to urban development, which often includes little or no surrounding land. Also, as the cost of land rises, the importance of good site planning and landscape design grows. Increasingly, new development is contingent upon compliance with environmental regulations and land use zoning, spurring demand for landscape architects to help plan sites and integrate man-made structures with the natural environment in the least disruptive way.

Increased development of open space into recreation areas, wildlife refuges, and parks will also require the skills of landscape architects. However, budget tightening in the federal government may restrict funding for such initiatives in the Forest Service and the National Park Service, agencies which traditionally employ many landscape architects.

In addition to the work related to new development and construction, landscape architects are expected to be involved in historic preservation, land reclamation, and refurbishment of existing sites, although these activities are expected to account for only a small proportion of new jobs.

New graduates can expect to face competition for jobs in the largest and most prestigious landscape architecture firms. The number of professional degrees awarded in landscape architecture has remained steady over the years, even during times of fluctuating demand due to economic conditions. Opportunities will be best for landscape architects who develop strong technical and communication skills and a knowledge of environmental codes and regulations. Those with additional training or experience in urban planning increase their opportunities for employment in landscape architecture firms that specialize in site planning as well as landscape design. Many employers prefer to hire entry-level landscape architects who have internship experience, which significantly reduces training time.

Earnings

Median annual earnings for all architects, including landscape architects, were about $39,500 in 1996. The middle 50 percent earned between $30,200 and $53,900; 10 percent earned less than $23,900; and 10 percent earned over $65,800. In 1997, the average annual salary for all landscape architects in the federal government in nonsupervisory, supervisory, and managerial positions was about $53,300.

Because many landscape architects work for small firms or are self-employed, benefits tend to be less generous than those provided to workers in large organizations.

Related Occupations

Landscape architects use their knowledge of design, construction, land-use planning, and environmental issues to develop a landscape project. Others whose work requires similar skills are architects, surveyors, civil engineers, soil conservationists, and urban and regional planners. Landscape architects also know how to grow and use plants in the landscape. Botanists, who study plants in general, and horticulturists, who study ornamental plants as well as fruit, vegetable, greenhouse, and nursery crops, do similar work.

Sources of Additional Information

Additional information, including a list of colleges and universities offering accredited programs in landscape architecture, is available from:

❏ American Society of Landscape Architects, Career Information, 4401 Connecticut Ave. NW, Suite 500, Washington, DC 20008.

General information on registration or licensing requirements is available from:

❏ Council of Landscape Architectural Registration Boards, 12700 Fair Lakes Circle, Suite 110, Fairfax, VA 22033. FAX (703) 818-1309. E-mail address: clarb2@aol.com

Landscaping, Groundskeeping, Nursery, Greenhouse, and Lawn Service Occupations

(D.O.T. 182.167-014; 405.687-014; 406.381-010, .683-010, .684-010, -014, -018, .687-010; 408.161-010, .662-010, .684-010, -014, -018, and .687-014)

Significant Points

✓ *There usually are no minimum educational requirements for entry-level jobs; most workers learn through short-term on-the-job training.*

✓ *Applicants should find excellent job opportunities, reflecting significant turnover; however, earnings for laborer jobs are low.*

Nature of the Work

Attractively designed, healthy, and well-maintained lawns, gardens, and grounds create a positive first impression, establish a peaceful mood, and increase property values. Workers in landscaping, groundskeeping, nursery, greenhouse, and lawn service occupations are responsible for the variety of tasks necessary to achieve a pleasant and functional outdoor environment. They also care for indoor gardens and plantings in commercial and public facilities, such as malls, hotels, and botanical gardens.

Nursery and greenhouse workers help to cultivate the plants used to beautify landscapes. They prepare nursery acreage or greenhouse beds for planting; water, weed, and spray trees, shrubs, and plants; cut, roll, and stack sod; stake trees; tie, wrap, and pack flowers, plants, shrubs, and trees to fill orders; and dig up and/or move field-grown and containerized shrubs and trees. Nursery and greenhouse managers make decisions about the type and quantity of horticultural plants to be grown; select and purchase seed, fertilizers, and disease control chemicals; hire laborers and direct and coordinate their activities; manage record keeping, accounting, and marketing activities; and generally oversee operations.

Landscape contractors usually follow the designs developed by a landscape architect. They coordinate and oversee the installation of trees, flowers, shrubs, sod, benches, and other ornamental features. They also implement construction plans at the site, which may involve grading the property, installing lighting or sprinkler systems, and building walkways, terraces, patios, decks, and fountains. They must determine the type and amount of labor, equipment, and materials needed to complete a project, and inspect work at various stages of completion. Some work exclusively on large properties, such as office buildings and shopping malls, while others also provide these services to residential customers.

Landscaping laborers physically install and maintain landscaped areas. In addition to initially transporting and planting new vegetation, they also transplant, mulch, fertilize, water, and prune flowering plants, trees, and shrubs, and mow and water lawns. Supervisors generally perform the same work, but are also responsible for directing the landscaping crew's activities, adhering to schedules, and keeping track of labor costs. Some landscaping laborers, called pruners, specialize in pruning, trimming, and shaping ornamental trees and shrubs. Others, called lawn service workers, specialize in maintaining lawns and shrubs for a fee. A growing number of residential and commercial clients, such as managers of office buildings, shopping malls, multiunit residential buildings, and hotels and motels favor this full-service landscape maintenance. These workers perform a range of duties on a regular basis during the growing season, including mowing, edging, trimming, fertilizing, dethatching, and mulching. Those working for chemical lawn service firms are more specialized. They inspect lawns for problems and apply fertilizers, herbicides, pesticides, and other chemicals to stimulate growth and prevent or control weed, disease, or insect infestation, as well as practice integrated pest management techniques. Lawn service managers oversee operations, negotiate fees, schedule jobs, and hire and train new workers.

Groundskeeping laborers, also called groundskeepers or grounds maintenance personnel, maintain a variety of facilities including athletic fields, golf courses, cemeteries, university campuses, and parks. Many of their duties are similar to those of landscaping laborers. But, they also rake and mulch leaves, clear snow from walkways and parking lots, employ irrigation methods to adjust the amount of water consumption and prevent waste, and apply pesticides. They see to the proper upkeep and repair of sidewalks, parking lots, groundskeeping equipment, pools, fountains, fences, planters, and benches. Grounds managers may participate in many of the same tasks as maintenance personnel but typically have more extensive knowledge in horticulture, turf management, ornamental plants, landscape design and construction, pest management, irrigation, and erosion control. In addition, grounds managers have supervisory responsibilities and must manage and train personnel, draw up work contracts, allocate labor and financial resources efficiently, and engage in public relations activities.

Groundskeepers who care for athletic fields keep natural and artificial turf fields in top condition and mark out boundaries and paint turf with team logos and names before events. Groundskeepers must make sure the underlying soil on natural turf fields has the proper composition to allow proper drainage and support the appropriate grasses used on the field. They regularly mow, water, fertilize, and aerate the fields. In addition, groundskeepers apply chemicals and fungicides to control weeds, kill pests, and prevent diseases. Groundskeepers also vacuum and disinfect synthetic turf after use in order to prevent growth of harmful bacteria. They periodically remove the turf and replace the cushioning pad.

Workers who maintain golf courses work under the direction of golf course superintendents and are called greenskeepers. Greenskeepers do many of the same things other groundskeepers do. In addition, greenskeepers periodically relocate the holes on putting greens to eliminate uneven wear of the turf and add interest and challenge to the game. Greenskeepers also keep canopies, benches, ball washers, and tee markers repaired and freshly painted.

Some groundskeepers specialize in caring for cemetery and memorial gardens grounds. They dig graves to specified depth, generally using a back-hoe. They may place concrete slabs on the bottom and around the sides of the grave to line it for greater support. When readying a site for the burial ceremony, they position the casket-lowering device over the grave, cover the immediate area with an artificial grass carpet, erect a canopy, and arrange folding chairs to accommodate mourners. They regularly mow grass, apply fertilizers and other chemicals, prune shrubs and trees, plant flowers, and remove debris from graves. They also must periodically build the ground up around new grave sites to compensate for settling.

Groundskeepers in parks and recreation facilities care for lawns, trees, and shrubs, maintain athletic fields and playgrounds, clean buildings, and keep parking lots, picnic areas, and other public spaces free of litter. They may also remove snow and ice from roads and walkways, erect and dismantle snow fences, and maintain swimming pools. These workers inspect buildings and equipment, make needed repairs, and keep everything freshly painted.

Landscaping, groundskeeping, and lawn service workers use handtools such as shovels, rakes, pruning saws, saws, hedge and brush trimmers, and axes, as well as power lawnmowers, chain saws, snow blowers, and electric clippers. Some use equipment such as tractors and twin-axle vehicles. Park, school, cemetery, and golf course groundskeepers may use sod cutters to harvest sod that will be replanted elsewhere. Athletic turf groundskeepers use vacuums and other devices to remove water from athletic fields. In addition, some workers in large operations use spraying and dusting equipment. Landscape contractors and those in managerial positions increasingly use computers to develop plans and blueprints, to estimate and track project costs, and to maintain payroll and personnel information.

Working Conditions

Many of the jobs for landscaping, groundskeeping, and nursery workers are seasonal, mainly in the spring and summer, when most cleanup, planting, and mowing and trimming is necessary . The work, most of which is performed outdoors in all kinds of weather, can be repetitive and physically demanding, involving much bending, lifting, and shoveling. Landscaping and groundskeeping workers may be under pressure to get the job completed, especially when preparing for scheduled events, such as athletic competitions or burials.

Those who work with pesticides, fertilizers, and other chemicals, as well as potentially dangerous equipment and tools such as power lawnmowers, chain saws, and power clippers, must exercise safety precautions.

Employment

Landscaping, groundskeeping, nursery, greenhouse, and lawn service workers held about 925,000 jobs in 1996. The following tabulation shows employment by detailed occupation:

Gardening and nursery workers and landscaping and groundskeeping laborers	817,000
Lawn service managers	55,000
Pruners	26,000
Sprayers/applicators	18,000
Nursery and greenhouse managers	10,000

About 30 percent worked for lawn and garden service companies, 8 percent worked for firms operating and building real estate, 7 percent for amusement and recreation facilities such as golf courses and race tracks, 3 percent for hotels, and 2 percent for retail nurseries. Others were employed by local governments, installing and maintaining landscapes for parks, schools, hospitals, and other public facilities.

Almost one of every four landscapers, groundskeepers, and nursery workers was self-employed, providing landscape maintenance directly to customers on a contract basis. About one of every four worked part-time, many of whom were school age and most likely working their way through school.

Training, Other Qualifications, and Advancement

There usually are no minimum educational requirements for entry-level laborer positions in landscaping, groundskeeping, nursery, greenhouse, and lawn service occupations. In 1996, two in five workers did not have a high school diploma, although this diploma is necessary for some jobs. Short-term on-the-job training usually is sufficient to teach new hires how to operate equipment such as mowers, trimmers, leaf blowers, and small tractors, and follow correct safety procedures. Entry-level workers must be able to follow directions and learn proper planting procedures. If driving is an essential part of a job, employers look for applicants with a good driving record and some experience driving a truck. Workers who deal directly with customers must get along well with people. Employers also look for responsible, self-motivated individuals, since many gardeners and groundskeepers work with little supervision.

Laborers who demonstrate a willingness to work hard and quickly, have good communication skills, and take an interest in the business may advance to crew leader or other supervisory positions. Advancement or entry into positions as grounds managers or landscape contractors usually require some formal education beyond high school, and several years of progressively responsible experience. Prospective grounds managers or landscape contractors should be knowledgeable about turf care, horticulture, ornamental plants, soils, and erosion prevention and irrigation techniques. They must be familiar with all landscaping and grounds maintenance equipment, and know how and when to mix and apply fertilizers and pesticides. Some are responsible for designing and developing installation and maintenance plans for landscapes and proper grounds management. They also estimate and track project costs, and handle personnel issues. Those in managerial positions must also be aware of local or federal environmental regulations and building codes. Several years of hands-on experience plus a four-year bachelor's degree, a two-year associate degree, or a one-year vocational-technical degree in grounds management or landscape design or a closely related "green" discipline, usually provide a good background for those who wish to deal with the full range of landscaping responsibilities. Some schools offer cooperative education programs in which students work alternate semesters or quarters for a lawn care or landscape contractor.

Most states require certification for workers who apply pesticides. Certification requirements vary, but usually include passing a test on the proper and safe use and disposal of insecticides, herbicides, and fungicides. Some states require that landscape contractors be licensed.

The Professional Grounds Management Society (PGMS) offers certification to grounds managers who have a combination of eight years of experience and formal education beyond high school, and pass an examination covering subjects such as equipment management, personnel management, environmental issues, turf care, ornamentals, and circulatory systems. The PGMS also offers certification to groundskeepers who have a high school diploma or equivalent, plus two years of experience in the grounds maintenance field.

The Associated Landscape Contractors of America (ALCA) offers the designations, Certified Landscape Professional or Certified Landscape Technician, to those who meet established education and experience standards and pass an ALCA examination. The hands-on test for technicians covers areas such as maintenance equipment operation and the installation of plants by reading a plan. A written safety test is also administered.

Some workers in landscaping, groundskeeping, nursery, greenhouse, and lawn service occupations open their own business after several years of experience.

Job Outlook

Those interested in landscaping, groundskeeping, nursery, greenhouse, and lawn service occupations should find excellent job opportunities in the future. Because of high turnover, a large number of job openings are expected to result from the need to replace workers who transfer to other occupations or leave the labor force. These occupations attract many part-time workers and people who underestimate the amount of hard physical labor or are not committed to this work. Some take landscaping, groundskeeping, or nursery jobs to earn money for school or only until they find a better-paying job. Because wages for beginners are low and the work is physically demanding, many employers have difficulty attracting enough workers to fill all openings.

Employment of landscaping, groundskeeping, nursery, greenhouse, and lawn service workers is expected to grow about as fast as the average for all occupations through the year 2006 in response to increasing demand for landscaping, groundskeeping, and related services. Expected growth in the construction of commercial and industrial buildings, shopping malls, homes, highways, and recreational facilities, though slower than occurred from the early 1980s through the mid-1990s, should contribute to demand for these workers. Developers will continue to use landscaping services, both interior and exterior, to attract prospective buyers and tenants.

The upkeep and renovation of existing landscapes and grounds is a growing source of demand for landscaping, groundskeeping, and lawn service workers. Owners of many existing buildings and facilities, including colleges and universities, recognize the importance of curb appeal and are expected to use these services more extensively to maintain and upgrade their properties. In recent years, the large number of baby boomers, wishing to conserve leisure time by contracting out for basic yard services, spurred employment growth in landscaping and lawn service occupations. Homeowners are expected to continue using such services to maintain the beauty and value of their property. As the "echo" boom generation (children of baby boomers) comes of age, the demand for parks, athletic fields, and recreational facilities also can be expected to add to the demand for landscaping, groundskeeping, and lawn service workers. The need for nursery and greenhouse laborers and managers will grow due to the continued popularity of home gardening, as well as the need to cultivate and provide the vegetation used by landscaping services.

Job opportunities for nonseasonal work are more numerous in regions with temperate climates where landscaping and lawn services are required all year. However, opportunities may vary depending on local economic conditions. During economic downturns, many individuals turn to landscaping as a second source of income or a new career. At the same time, demand for landscaping services often slows as corporations, governments, and homeowners reduce spending on all nonessential expenditures, increasing the level of competition for available jobs.

Earnings

Landscapers and groundskeepers had median weekly earnings of about $300 in 1996; the middle 50 percent earned between $220 and $410; the lowest 10 percent earned less than $180, and the top 10 percent earned more than $560.

According to a salary survey conducted by Grounds Maintenance Magazine (Intertec Publishing Corporation) of its readership, institutional grounds managers had median earnings of about $38,900 in 1996; lawn-care operators, $32,500; landscape contractors, $37,300; and golf-course superintendents, $38,600.

Related Occupations

Landscaping, groundskeeping, nursery, greenhouse, and lawn service workers perform most of their work outdoors and have some knowledge of plants and soils. Others whose jobs may be performed outdoors and are otherwise related are botanists, construction workers, landscape architects, farmers, horticultural workers, tree surgeon helpers, forest conservation workers, and soil conservation technicians.

Sources of Additional Information

For career and certification information, contact:
- Associated Landscape Contractors of America, Inc., 12200 Sunrise Valley Dr., Suite 150, Reston, VA 20191.
- Professional Grounds Management Society, 120 Cockeysville Rd., Suite 104, Hunt Valley, MD 21031.

Lawyers and Judges

(D.O.T. 110; 111; 119.107, .117, .167-010, .267-014; 169.267-010)

Significant Points

✓ *Formal educational requirements usually include a four-year college degree, followed by three years in law school. After that, all states require applicants for admission to the bar to pass a written bar examination.*

✓ *Competition for admission to many law schools is intense, as the number of applicants greatly exceeds the number that may be admitted.*

✓ *Aspiring lawyers or judges should encounter keen competition for jobs.*

Nature of the Work

Lawyers. Lawyers, also called attorneys, act as both advocates and advisors in our society. As advocates, they represent one of the parties in criminal and civil trials by presenting evidence in court supporting their client. As advisors, lawyers counsel their clients as to their legal rights and obligations, and suggest particular courses of action in business and personal matters. Whether acting as advocates or advisors, all attorneys interpret the law and apply it to specific situations.

Lawyers research the purposes behind laws and judicial decisions that have been applied to circumstances similar to those faced by their client. While all lawyers continue to use law libraries to prepare cases, some supplement their search of conventional printed sources with computer sources. Software can be used to search legal literature automatically, and to identify legal texts relevant to a specific case. In litigation involving many supporting documents, lawyers may use computers to organize and index material. Tax lawyers use computers for making tax computations and exploring alternative tax strategies for clients.

Lawyers increasingly use the Internet for research and to advertise their services. Ethical standards for advertising on the Internet are still evolving. Lawyers also use electronic filing, videoconferencing, and voice-recognition technology. Electronic filing promotes the sharing of information by providing all parties in a case access to a database with all official filings, briefs, and other court documents; these technologies also save time and reduce legal costs.

Lawyers communicate the information obtained through research to others. They advise clients and draw up legal documents, such as wills and contracts. Lawyers may not disclose matters discussed in confidence with clients. They hold positions of great responsibility, and are obligated to adhere to a strict code of ethics.

The more detailed aspects of a lawyer's job depend upon his or her field of specialization and position. While all lawyers are licensed to represent parties in court, some appear in court more frequently than others; some lawyers specialize in trial work. Their ability to think quickly and speak with ease and authority as well as their familiarity with courtroom rules and strategy are particularly important in trial work. However, trial lawyers still spend most of their time outside the courtroom conducting research, interviewing clients and witnesses, and handling other details in preparation for trial.

Besides trials, lawyers may specialize in other areas, such as bankruptcy, probate, or international law. Environmental lawyers, for example, may represent public interest groups, waste disposal companies, or construction firms in their dealings with the Environmental Protection Agency (EPA) and other state and federal agencies. They help clients prepare and file for licenses and applications for approval before certain activities may occur. They also represent clients' interests in administrative adjudications.

Some lawyers concentrate in the growing field of intellectual property. These lawyers help protect clients' claims to copyrights, art work under contract, product designs, and computer programs. Still other lawyers advise insurance companies about the legality of insurance transactions. They write insurance policies to conform with the law and to protect companies from unwarranted claims. They review claims filed against insurance companies and represent the companies in court.

The majority of lawyers are in private practice, where they concentrate on criminal or civil law. In criminal law, lawyers represent individuals who have been charged with crimes and argue their cases in courts of law. In civil law, attorneys assist clients with litigation, wills, trusts, contracts, mortgages, titles, and leases. Others handle only public interest cases–civil or criminal–which may have a potential impact extending well beyond the individual client.

Lawyers are sometimes employed full-time by a single client. If the client is a corporation, the lawyer is known as "house counsel," and usually advises the company concerning legal issues related to its business activities. These issues might involve patents, government regulations, contracts with other companies, property interests, or collective bargaining agreements with unions.

A significant number of attorneys are employed at the various levels of government. Lawyers who work for state attorneys general, prosecutors, public defenders, and courts play a key role in the criminal justice system. At the federal level, attorneys investigate cases for the Department of Justice or other agencies. Government lawyers also help develop programs, draft and interpret laws and legislation, establish enforcement procedures, and argue civil and criminal cases on behalf of the government.

Other lawyers work for legal aid societies–private, nonprofit organizations established to serve disadvantaged people. These lawyers generally handle civil, rather than criminal cases.

A relatively small number of trained attorneys work in law schools. Most are faculty members who specialize in one or more subjects, and others serve as administrators. Some work full-time in nonacademic settings and teach part-time. Some lawyers become judges.

Judges. Judges apply the law and oversee the legal process in courts according to local, state, and federal statutes. They preside over cases concerning every aspect of society, from traffic offenses to disputes over management of professional sports, or from the rights of huge corporations to questions of disconnecting life support equipment for terminally ill persons. They must ensure trials and hearings are conducted fairly, and the court administers justice in a manner safeguarding the legal rights of all parties involved.

Judges preside over trials or hearings and listen as attorneys representing the parties present and argue their cases. They rule on the admissibility of evidence and methods of conducting testimony, and settle disputes between the opposing attorneys. They ensure rules and procedures are followed, and if unusual circumstances arise for which standard procedures have not been established, judges direct how the trial will proceed based on their knowledge of the law.

Judges often hold pretrial hearings for cases. They listen to allegations and, based on the evidence presented, determine whether there is enough merit for a trial to be held. In criminal cases, judges may decide that persons charged with crimes should be held in jail pending their trial, or may set conditions for release through the trial. In civil cases, judges may impose restrictions upon the parties until a trial is held.

When trials are held, juries are often selected to decide cases, including guilt or innocence in criminal cases, and the liability and the amount of compensation in civil cases. In these cases, judges instruct juries on applicable laws, direct them to deduce the facts from the evidence presented, and hear their verdict. However, judges decide cases when the law does not require a jury trial, or when the parties waive their right to a jury. In the absence of a jury, the judge determines guilt and imposes sentences in a criminal case; in civil cases, the judge rewards relief—such as compensation for damages—to the parties in the lawsuit (also called litigants).

Judges also work outside the courtroom "in chambers." In their private offices, judges read documents on pleadings and motions, research legal issues, write opinions, and oversee the court's operations. Running a court is like running a small business, and judges also manage their courts' administrative and clerical staff.

Judges' duties vary according to the extent of their jurisdictions and powers. *General trial court judges* of the federal and state court systems have jurisdiction over any case in their system. They generally try civil cases transcending the jurisdiction of lower courts, and all cases involving felony offenses. Federal and state appellate court judges, although few in number, have the power to overrule decisions made by trial court or administrative law judges if they determine that legal errors were made in a case, or if legal precedent does not support the judgment of the lower court. They rule on fewer cases and rarely have direct contacts with litigants. Instead, they usually base their decisions on lower court records and written and oral arguments by lawyers.

Many state court judges preside in courts in which jurisdiction is limited by law to certain types of cases. A variety of titles are assigned to these judges, but among the most common are *municipal court judge, county court judge, magistrate, or justice of the peace.* Traffic violations, misdemeanors, small claims cases, and pretrial hearings constitute the bulk of the work of these judges, but some states allow them to handle cases involving domestic relations, probate, contracts, and other selected areas of the law.

Administrative law judges, formerly called hearing officers, are employed by government agencies to make determinations for administrative agencies. They make decisions on a person's eligibility for various Social Security benefits or worker's compensation, protection of the environment, enforcement of health and safety regulations, employment discrimination, and compliance with economic regulatory requirements.

Working Conditions

Lawyers and judges do most of their work in offices, law libraries, and courtrooms. Lawyers sometimes meet in clients' homes or places of business and, when necessary, in hospitals or prisons. They may travel to attend meetings, gather evidence, and appear before courts, legislative bodies, and other authorities.

Salaried lawyers generally have structured work schedules. Lawyers in private practice may work irregular hours while conducting research, conferring with clients, or preparing briefs during nonoffice hours. Lawyers often work long hours, and about half regularly work 50 hours or more per week. They are under particularly heavy pressure, for example, when a case is being tried. Preparation for court includes keeping abreast of the latest laws and judicial decisions.

Although work is not generally seasonal, the work of tax lawyers and other specialists may be an exception. Because lawyers in private practice can often determine their own workload and when they will retire, many stay in practice well beyond the usual retirement age.

Many judges work a standard 40-hour week, but a third of all judges work over 50 hours per week. Some judges with limited jurisdiction are employed part-time and divide their time between their judicial responsibilities and other careers.

Employment

Lawyers held about 622,000 jobs in 1996; judges, about 78,000. About seven out of ten lawyers practiced privately, either in law firms or in solo practices. Most of the remaining lawyers held positions in government, the greatest number at the local level. In the federal government, lawyers work for many different agencies but are concentrated in the Departments of Justice, Treasury, and Defense. Other lawyers are employed as house counsel by public utilities, banks, insurance companies, real estate agencies, manufacturing firms, welfare and religious organizations, and other business firms and nonprofit organizations. Some salaried lawyers also have part-time independent practices; others work as lawyers part-time while working full-time in another occupation.

All judges, magistrates, and other judicial workers were employed by federal, state, or local governments, with about four out of ten holding positions in the federal government.

Law professors also hold law degrees, as well as other professionals such as politicians, managers, and administrators.

Training, Other Qualifications, and Advancement

Lawyers. To practice law in the courts of any state or other jurisdiction, a person must be licensed, or admitted to its bar, under rules established by the jurisdiction's highest court. All require that applicants for admission to the bar pass a written bar examination; most jurisdictions also require applicants to pass a separate written ethics examination. Lawyers who have been admitted to the bar in one jurisdiction may occasionally be admitted to the bar in another without taking an examination if they meet that jurisdiction's standards of good moral character, and have a specified period of legal experience. Federal courts and agencies set their own qualifications for those practicing before them.

To qualify for the bar examination in most states, an applicant must usually obtain a college degree and graduate from a law school accredited by the American Bar Association (ABA) or the proper state authorities. (ABA accreditation signifies that the law school—particularly its library and faculty—meets certain standards developed to promote quality legal education.) ABA currently accredits 179 law schools. Others are approved by state authorities only. With certain exceptions, graduates of schools not approved by the ABA are restricted to taking the bar examination and practicing in the state or other jurisdiction in which the school is located; most of these schools are in California. In 1997, seven states accepted the study of law in a law office or in combination with study in a law school; only California accepts the study of law by correspondence as qualifying for taking the bar examination. Several states require registration and approval of students by the state Board of Law Examiners, either before they enter law school or during the early years of legal study.

Although there is no nationwide bar examination, 47 states, the District of Columbia, Guam, the Northern Mariana Islands, and the Virgin Islands require the six-hour Multistate Bar Examination (MBE) as part of the bar examination; the MBE is not required in

Indiana, Louisiana, Washington, and Puerto Rico. The MBE covers issues of broad interest, and is sometimes given in addition to a locally prepared state bar examination. The three-hour Multistate Essay Examination (MEE) is used as part of the state bar examination in a few states. States vary in their use of MBE and MEE scores.

Performance examinations to test practical skills of beginning lawyers are required by eight states. This program has been well received and more states are expected to require performance testing in the future. Requirements vary by state, although the test usually is taken at the same time as the bar exam, and is a one-time requirement.

The required college and law school education usually takes seven years of full-time study after high school—4 years of undergraduate study followed by three years in law school. Although some law schools accept a very small number of students after three years of college, most require applicants to have a bachelor's degree. To meet the needs of students who can attend only part-time, a number of law schools have night or part-time divisions which usually require four years of study; about one in ten graduates from ABA-approved schools attends part-time.

Although there is no recommended prelaw major, prospective lawyers should develop proficiency in writing and speaking, reading, researching, analyzing, and thinking logically—skills needed to succeed both in law school and in the profession. Whatever the major, a multidisciplinary background is recommended. Courses in English, foreign language, public speaking, government, philosophy, history, economics, mathematics, and computer science, among others, are useful.

Students interested in a particular aspect of law may find related courses helpful. For example, prospective patent lawyers need a strong background in engineering or science, and future tax lawyers must have extensive knowledge of accounting.

Acceptance by most law schools depends on the applicant's ability to demonstrate an aptitude for the study of law, usually through good undergraduate grades, the Law School Admission Test (LSAT), the quality of the applicant's undergraduate school, any prior work experience, and sometimes a personal interview. However, law schools vary in the weight they place on each of these and other factors.

All law schools approved by the ABA, except for those in Puerto Rico, require applicants to take the LSAT. Nearly all law schools require applicants to have certified transcripts sent to the Law School Data Assembly Service, which then sends applicants' LSAT scores and their standardized records of college grades to the law schools of their choice. Both this service and the LSAT are administered by the Law School Admission Council.

Competition for admission to many law schools is intense. Enrollments in these schools rose very rapidly during the 1970s, with applicants far outnumbering available seats. The number of applicants decreased markedly in the 1990s, easing competition slightly; however, the number of applicants to most law schools still greatly exceeds the number that can be admitted. Competition for admission to the more prestigious law schools is always keen.

During the first year or year and a half of law school, students generally study fundamental courses such as constitutional law, contracts, property law, torts, civil procedure, and legal writing. In the remaining time, they may elect specialized courses in fields such as tax, labor, or corporation law. Law students often acquire practical experience by participation in school sponsored legal clinic activities, in the school's moot court competitions in which students conduct appellate arguments, in practice trials under the supervision of experienced lawyers and judges, and through research and writing on legal issues for the school's law journal.

In 1997, law students in 48 states were required to pass the Multistate Professional Responsibility Examination (MPRE), which tests their knowledge of the ABA codes on professional responsibility and judicial conduct. In some states, the MPRE may be taken during law school, usually after completing a course on legal ethics.

A number of law schools have clinical programs in which students gain legal experience through practice trials and law school projects under the supervision of practicing lawyers and law school faculty. Law school clinical programs might include work in legal aid clinics, for example, or on the staff of legislative committees. Part-time or summer clerkships in law firms, government agencies, and corporate legal departments also provide valuable experience. Such training can provide references or lead directly to a job after graduation, and can help students decide what kind of practice best suits them. Clerkships may also be an important source of financial aid.

Graduates receive the degree of *juris doctor* (J.D.) as the first professional degree. Advanced law degrees may be desirable for those planning to specialize, do research, or teach. Some law students pursue joint degree programs, which generally require an additional semester or year. Joint degree programs are offered in a number of areas, including law and business administration or public administration.

After graduation, lawyers must keep informed about legal and nonlegal developments that affect their practice. Currently, 37 states and jurisdictions mandate Continuing Legal Education (CLE). Many law schools and state and local bar associations provide continuing education courses that help lawyers stay abreast of recent developments. Some states allow CLE credits to be obtained through participation in seminars on the Internet.

The practice of law involves a great deal of responsibility. Individuals planning careers in law should like to work with people, and be able to win the respect and confidence of their clients, associates, and the public. Perseverance and reasoning ability are essential to analyze complex cases and reach sound conclusions. Lawyers also need creativity when handling new and unique legal problems.

Most beginning lawyers start in salaried positions. Newly hired salaried attorneys usually start as associates and work with more experienced lawyers or judges. After several years of progressively more responsible salaried employment, some lawyers are admitted to partnership in their firm, or go into practice for themselves. Some lawyers, after several years of practice, become full-time law school faculty or administrators; a growing number have advanced degrees in other fields as well.

Some attorneys use their legal training in administrative or managerial positions in various departments of large corporations. A transfer from a corporation's legal department to another department often is viewed as a way to gain administrative experience and rise in the ranks of management.

Judges. Most judges have first been lawyers. Federal and state judges are generally required to be lawyers. About 40 states allow nonlawyers to hold limited jurisdiction judgeships, but opportunities are better with law experience. Federal administrative law judges must be lawyers and pass a competitive examination administered by the U.S. Office of Personnel Management. Some state administrative law judges and other hearing officials are not required to be lawyers, but law degrees are preferred for most positions.

Federal judges are appointed for life by the President, with the consent of the Senate. Federal administrative law judges are appointed by the various federal agencies with virtually lifetime tenure. About half of all state judges are appointed, while the remainder are elected in partisan or nonpartisan state elections. Many state and local judges serve fixed renewable terms, which range from four or six years for some trial court judgeships, to as long as 14 years or life for other trial or appellate court judges. Judicial nominating commissions, composed of members of the bar and the public, are used to screen candidates for judgeships in many states, as well as for some federal judgeships.

All states have some type of orientation for newly elected or appointed judges. The Federal Judicial Center, ABA, National Judicial College, and National Center for State Courts provide judicial education and training for judges and other judicial branch personnel. General and continuing education courses usually run from a couple of days to three weeks in length. Over half of the states, including Puerto Rico, require judges to enroll in continuing education courses while serving on the bench.

Job Outlook

Individuals interested in pursuing careers as lawyers or judges should encounter keen competition through the year 2006. The number of law school graduates is expected to continue to strain the economy's capacity to absorb them. As for judges, the prestige associated with serving on the bench should insure continued, intense competition for openings.

Lawyers. Employment of lawyers grew very rapidly from the early 1970s through the early 1990s, but has started to level off in the last several years. Employment is expected to grow about as fast as the average for all occupations through the year 2006. Continuing demand for lawyers will result from growth in the population and the general level of business activities. Demand will also be spurred by growth of legal action in such areas as health care, intellectual property, international law, elder law, sexual harassment, and the environment. The wider availability and affordability of legal clinics and prepaid legal service programs should result in increased use of legal services by middle-income people.

Employment growth should be slower than in the past. In an effort to reduce the money spent on legal fees, many businesses are turning to large accounting firms to provide employee benefit counseling, process documents, and handle other services previously performed by law firms. Also, mediation and dispute resolution are increasingly used as alternatives to litigation.

Competition for job openings should continue to be keen because of the large numbers graduating from law school each year. During the 1970s, the annual number of law school graduates more than doubled, outpacing the rapid growth of jobs. Growth in the yearly number of law school graduates slowed during the early to mid-1980s, but increased again in the late 1980s to early 1990s. Although graduates with superior academic records from well-re-

garded law schools will have more job opportunities, most graduates will encounter stiff competition for jobs. As in the past, some graduates may have to accept positions in areas outside their field of interest or for which they feel overqualified. They may choose to enter jobs for which legal training is an asset, but not normally a requirement—for example, administrative, managerial, and business positions in banks, insurance firms, real estate companies, government agencies, and other organizations.

Some recent law school graduates who are unable to find permanent positions are turning to the growing number of legal temporary staffing firms, which place attorneys in short-term jobs until they are able to secure full-time positions. This service allows companies to hire lawyers on an "as needed" basis and allows beginning lawyers to develop practical skills while looking for permanent positions.

Due to the competition for jobs, a law graduate's geographic mobility and work experience assume greater importance. The willingness to relocate may be an advantage in getting a job, but to be licensed in a new state, a lawyer may have to take an additional state bar examination. In addition, employers increasingly seek graduates who have advanced law degrees and experience in a specialty such as tax, patent, or admiralty law.

Employment growth for lawyers will continue to be concentrated in salaried jobs, as businesses and all levels of government employ a growing number of staff attorneys, and as employment in the legal services industry grows in larger law firms. Most salaried positions are in urban areas where government agencies, law firms, and big corporations are concentrated. The number of self-employed lawyers is expected to increase slowly, reflecting the difficulty of establishing a profitable new practice in the face of competition from larger, established law firms. Also, the growing complexity of law, which encourages specialization, along with the cost of maintaining up-to-date legal research materials, favor larger firms.

For lawyers who wish to work independently, establishing a new practice will probably be easiest in small towns and expanding suburban areas, as long as an active market for legal services exists. In such communities, competition from larger established law firms is likely to be less than in big cities, and new lawyers may find it easier to become known to potential clients.

Some lawyers are adversely affected by cyclical swings in the economy. During recessions, the demand declines for some discretionary legal services, such as planning estates, drafting wills, and handling real estate transactions. Also, corporations are less likely to litigate cases when declining sales and profits result in budgetary restrictions. Some corporations and law firms will not hire new attorneys until business improves or may cut staff to contain costs. Several factors, however, mitigate the overall impact of recessions on lawyers. During recessions, individuals and corporations face other legal problems, such as bankruptcies, foreclosures, and divorces requiring legal action.

Judges. Employment of judges is expected to grow more slowly than the average for all occupations. Contradictory social forces affect the demand for judges. Growing public concerns about crime, safety, and efficient administration of justice should spur demand; on the other hand, tight public funding should slow job growth.

Competition for judgeships should remain keen. Most job openings will arise as judges retire. Traditionally, many judges have held their positions until late in life. Now, early retirement is becoming more common, creating more job openings. However, becoming a judge will still be difficult. Besides competing with other qualified people, judicial candidates must gain political support in order to be elected or appointed.

Earnings

Median salaries of lawyers six months after graduation from law school in 1996 varied by type of work, as indicated by table 1.

Salaries of experienced attorneys also vary widely according to the type, size, and location of their employer. The median annual salary of all lawyers was about $60,000 in 1996. General attorneys in the federal government averaged around $72,700 a year in 1997; the relatively small number of patent attorneys in the federal government averaged around $81,600.

Table 1. Median salaries of lawyers six months after graduation, 1996

All graduates	$40,000
Private practice	50,000
Business/industry	45,000
Academe	35,000
Judicial clerkship	35,000
Government	34,500
Public interest	30,000

SOURCE: National Association for Law Placement

Lawyers who practice alone usually earn less than those who are partners in law firms. Lawyers starting their own practice may need to work part-time in other occupations to supplement their income until their practice is well-established.

According to the Administrative Office of the U.S. Courts, federal district court judges had salaries of $133,600 in 1997, as did judges in the Court of Federal Claims; circuit court judges earned $141,700 a year. Federal judges with limited jurisdiction, such as magistrates and bankruptcy court judges, had salaries of $122,900. Full-time federal administrative law judges had average salaries of $94,800. The Chief Justice of the United States Supreme Court earned $171,500, and the Associate Justices earned $164,100.

According to a survey by the National Center for State Courts, annual salaries of associate justices of states' highest courts averaged $101,800 in 1997, and ranged from about $68,900 to $133,600. Salaries of state intermediate appellate court judges averaged $91,000, and ranged from $79,400 to $124,200. Salaries of state judges with limited jurisdiction vary widely; some salaries are set locally.

Most salaried lawyers and judges are provided health and life insurance, and contributions are made on their behalf to retirement plans. Lawyers who practice independently are only covered if they arrange and pay for such benefits themselves.

Related Occupations

Legal training is useful in many other occupations. Some of these are arbitrator, mediator, journalist, patent agent, title examiner, legislative assistant, lobbyist, FBI special agent, political office holder, and corporate executive.

Sources of Additional Information

Information on law schools and law as a career may be obtained from:

❑ American Bar Association, 750 North Lake Shore Dr., Chicago, IL 60611.

Information on the LSAT, the Law School Data Assembly Service, applying to law school, and financial aid for law students may be obtained from:

❑ Law School Admission Council, P.O. Box 40, Newtown, PA 18940. Homepage: http://www.lsac.org

Information on acquiring a job as a lawyer with the federal government may be obtained from the Office of Personnel Management through a telephone-based system. Consult your telephone directory under U.S. government for a local number or call (912) 757-3000 (TDD 912 744-2299). That number is not toll-free and charges may result. Information also is available from their Internet site: http://www.usajobs.opm.gov

The specific requirements for admission to the bar in a particular state or other jurisdiction may also be obtained at the state capital from the clerk of the Supreme Court or the administrator of the State Board of Bar Examiners.

Library Assistants and Bookmobile Drivers

(D.O.T. 209.387-026; 222.587-014; 249.363-010, .365-010, .367-046, .687-014)

Significant Points

✓ *Most library assistant and bookmobile driver jobs require only a high school diploma, but earnings are low.*

✓ *Turnover in this occupation will result in numerous job opportunities.*

✓ *Job growth is projected for library assistants.*

Nature of the Work

Library assistants and bookmobile drivers keep library resources in order and make them readily available to a variety of users. They work under the direction of librarians, and in some cases, library technicians.

Library assistants—sometimes referred to as *library media assistants, library aides,* or *circulation assistants*—register patrons so they can borrow materials from the library. They record the borrower's name and address from an application and then issue a library card. Most library assistants enter and update patrons' records using computer databases.

At the circulation desk, assistants lend and collect books, periodicals, video tapes, and other materials. When an item is borrowed, assistants stamp the due date on the material and record the patron's identification from his or her library card. They inspect returned materials for damage, check the due dates, and compute any fines that may be owed. They review records to compile a list of overdue materials and send out notices. They also answer patrons' questions in person and on the telephone and refer those they cannot answer to a librarian.

Throughout the library, assistants sort returned books, periodicals, and other items and return them to their designated shelves, files, or storage areas. They locate materials to be loaned, either to a patron or another library. Many card catalogues are computerized, so library assistants must be familiar with the computer system for their particular library. If any materials have been damaged, these workers repair them, if possible. For example, they use tape or paste to repair torn pages or book covers and other specialized processes to repair more valuable materials.

Some library assistants specialize in helping patrons with vision problems. Sometimes referred to as *library, talking-books,* or *Braille-and-talking-books clerks,* they review the borrower's list of desired reading material. They locate those materials or closely related substitutes from the library collection of large type or Braille volumes, tape cassettes, and open-reel talking books. They complete the necessary paperwork and give or mail them to the borrower.

To extend library services to a vast audience, many libraries operate bookmobiles. *Bookmobile drivers* drive trucks stocked with books, or drive light trucks that pull book trailers to designated sites on a regular schedule. Bookmobiles serve community organizations such as shopping centers, apartment complexes, schools, and nursing homes. They may also be used to extend library service to patrons living in remote areas. Depending on local conditions, they may drive alone or may be accompanied by a library technician.

When working alone, the drivers perform many of the same functions as a library assistant in a main or branch library. They answer patrons' questions, receive and check out books, collect fines, maintain the book collection, shelve materials, and occasionally operate audiovisual equipment to show slides or films. They participate and may assist in planning programs sponsored by the library such as reader advisory programs, used book sales, or outreach programs. Bookmobile drivers keep track of their mileage, the materials lent out, and the amount of fines collected. In some areas, they are responsible for the maintenance of the vehicle and any photocopiers or other equipment in it. They record statistics on circulation and the number of people visiting the bookmobile. Drivers may also record requests for special items from the main library and arrange for the materials to be mailed or delivered to a patron during the next scheduled visit. Many bookmobiles are equipped with personal computers and CD-ROM systems linked to the main library system; this allows bookmobile drivers to reserve or locate books immediately. Some bookmobiles now offer Internet access to users.

Because bookmobile drivers may be the only link some people have to the library, much of their work is helping the public. They may assist handicapped or elderly patrons to the bookmobile, or shovel snow to assure their safety. They may enter hospitals or nursing homes to deliver books directly to patrons who are bedridden.

The schedules of bookmobile drivers depend on the size of the area being served. Some of these workers go out on their routes every working day, while others do so only on certain days of the week. On the other days, they perform library assistant duties at the library. Some now work evenings and weekends to give patrons as much access to the library as possible.

Working Conditions

Although they do not do heavy lifting, library assistants spend a lot of time on their feet and frequently stoop, bend, and reach. Bookmobile drivers must maneuver large vehicles in all kinds of traffic and weather conditions, and may also be responsible for the maintenance of the bookmobile.

As the majority of library assistants use computers as part of their daily routine, these workers may experience eye and muscle strain, backaches, headaches, and repetitive motion injuries.

Library assistants may work evenings and weekends, but those employed in school libraries generally work only during the school year.

Employment

Library assistants and bookmobile drivers held about 125,000 jobs in 1996. Over one-half of these workers were employed by local government in public libraries; most of the remaining worked in school libraries. Opportunities for flexible schedules are abundant; over one-half of these workers were on part-time schedules.

Training, Other Qualifications, and Advancement

Most library assistant and bookmobile driver jobs are entry-level, with most employers requiring applicants to have at least a high school diploma or its equivalent. A higher level of education is usually favored over a high school diploma, but is not generally required. Most employers prefer workers who are computer-literate and who have good interpersonal skills.

Once hired, library assistants and bookmobile drivers generally receive on-the-job training. Under the guidance of a supervisor or other senior worker, new employees learn company procedures. Some formal classroom training may also be necessary, such as training in specific computer software.

Library assistants must be careful, orderly, and detail-oriented, in order to avoid making errors and to be able to recognize errors made by others. Many bookmobile drivers are now required to have a commercial driver's license.

Library assistants and bookmobile drivers usually advance by taking on more duties in the same occupation for higher pay. Others advance transferring to closely related occupations. With appropriate experience and education, some may become librarians.

Job Outlook

Opportunities should be good for persons interested in jobs as library assistants or bookmobile drivers through the year 2006. Turnover of these workers is quite high, reflecting the limited investment in training and subsequent weak attachment to this occupation. This work is attractive to retirees, students, and others who want a part-time schedule, and there is a lot of movement into and out of the occupation. Many openings will become available each year to replace workers who transfer to another occupation or leave the labor force. Some positions become available as library assistants move within the organization. Library assistants can be promoted to library technicians, and eventually supervisory positions in public service or technical service areas. Advancement opportunities are greater in larger libraries and may be more limited in smaller ones.

Employment is expected to grow about as fast as the average for all occupations through the year 2006. The vast majority of library assistants and bookmobile drivers work in public or school libraries. Efforts to contain costs in local governments and academic institutions of all types, may result in more hiring of library support staff than librarians. Because most are employed by public institutions, library assistants and bookmobile drivers are not directly affected by the ups and downs of the business cycle. Some of these workers may lose their jobs, however, if there are cuts in government budgets.

Earnings

Salaries of library assistants and bookmobile drivers vary by region of the country, size of city, and type and size of establishment. Median earnings of full-time library clerks were $19,200.

Related Occupations

Today, most library assistants enter data into a computer system and perform basic analysis of the data. Other clerical workers who enter and manipulate data include bank tellers, statistical clerks, receiving clerks, medical record clerks, hotel and motel clerks, credit clerks, and reservation and transportation ticket agents.

Sources of Additional Information

Information about a career as a library assistant can be obtained from:

❑ Council on Library/Media Technology, P.O. Box 951, Oxon Hill, MD 20750.

Public libraries and libraries in academic institutions can provide information about job openings for library assistants and bookmobile drivers.

Specific information on bookmobile drivers is available from:

❑ The State Library of Ohio, Field Operations Department, 65 South Front St., Columbus, OH 43215.

Library Technicians

(D.O.T. 100.367-018)

Significant Points

✓ *Training ranges from on-the-job training to a bachelor's degree.*

✓ *Employment is expected to grow faster than average as libraries use technicians to perform some librarian duties in an effort to stretch shrinking budgets.*

Nature of the Work

Library technicians, commonly called "paraprofessionals," help librarians acquire, prepare, and organize material, and assist users in finding materials and information. Technicians in small libraries handle a wide range of duties; those in large libraries usually specialize. As libraries increasingly use new technologies–such as CD-ROM, the Internet, virtual libraries, and automated databases–the duties of library technicians are expanding and evolving accordingly. Library technicians are assuming greater responsibilities, in some cases taking on tasks previously performed by librarians.

Depending on the employer, library technicians may have other titles, such as library technical assistants. Library technicians direct library users to standard references, organize and maintain periodicals, prepare volumes for binding, handle interlibrary loan requests, prepare invoices, perform routine cataloguing and coding of library materials, retrieve information from computer databases, and supervise other support staff.

The widespread use of computerized information storage and retrieval systems has resulted in technicians handling more technical and user services, such as entering catalogue information into the library's computer, that were once performed by librarians. Technicians may assist with customizing databases. In addition, technicians may instruct patrons how to use computer systems to access data. The increased use of automation has cut down on the amount of clerical work performed by library technicians. Many libraries now offer self-service registration and circulation with computers, decreasing the time library technicians spend manually recording and inputting records.

Some library technicians operate and maintain audiovisual equipment, such as projectors, tape recorders, and videocassette recorders, and assist library users with microfilm or microfiche readers. They may also design posters, bulletin boards, or displays.

Those in school libraries encourage and teach students to use the library and media center. They also help teachers obtain instructional materials and assist students with special assignments. Some work in special libraries maintained by government agencies, corporations, law firms, advertising agencies, museums, professional societies, medical centers, and research laboratories, where they conduct literature searches, compile bibliographies, and prepare abstracts, usually on subjects of particular interest to the organization.

Working Conditions

Technicians who work with library users answer questions and provide assistance. Those who prepare library materials sit at desks or computer terminals for long periods and may develop headaches or eyestrain from working with video display terminals. Some duties, like calculating circulation statistics, can be repetitive and boring. Others, such as performing computer searches using local and regional library networks and cooperatives, can be interesting and challenging.

Library technicians in school libraries work regular school hours. Those in public libraries and college and university (academic) libraries may work weekends, evenings and some holidays. Library technicians in special libraries usually work normal business hours, although they are often called upon to work overtime.

Library technicians usually work under the supervision of a professional librarian, although they may work independently in certain situations.

Employment

Library technicians held about 78,000 jobs in 1996. Most worked in school, academic, or public libraries. Some worked in hospitals and religious organizations. The federal government, primarily the Department of Defense and the Library of Congress, and state and local governments also employed library technicians.

Training, Other Qualifications, and Advancement

Training requirements for library technicians vary widely, ranging from a high school diploma to specialized postsecondary training. Some employers hire individuals with work experience or other training; others train inexperienced workers on the job. Other employers require that technicians have an associate or bachelor's degree. Given the rapid spread of automation in libraries, computer skills are needed for many jobs. Knowledge of databases, library automation systems, on-line library systems, on-line public access systems, and circulation systems is valuable.

Some two-year colleges offer an associate of arts degree in library technology. Programs include both liberal arts and library-related study. Students learn about library and media organization and operation, and how to order, process, catalogue, locate, and circulate library materials and work with library automation. Libraries and associations offer continuing education courses to keep technicians abreast of new developments in the field.

Library technicians usually advance by assuming added responsibilities. For example, technicians may start at the circulation desk, checking books in and out. After gaining experience, they may be responsible for storing and verifying information. As they advance, they may become involved in budget and personnel matters in their department. Some library technicians advance to supervisory positions and are in charge of the day-to-day operation of their department.

Job Outlook

Employment of library technicians is expected to grow faster than the average for all occupations through the year 2006. Many additional job openings will result from the need to replace library technicians who transfer to other fields or leave the labor force. Similar to other fields, willingness to relocate enhances an aspiring library technician's job prospects.

The increasing use of library automation may spur job growth among library technicians. Computerized information systems have simplified certain tasks, such as descriptive cataloguing, which can now be handled by technicians instead of librarians. For instance, technicians can now easily retrieve information from a central database and store it in the library's own computer. Although budgetary constraints may dampen employment growth of library technicians in school, public, and college and university libraries, libraries may use technicians to perform some librarian duties in an effort to stretch shrinking budgets. Growth in the number of professionals and other workers who use special libraries should result in relatively fast employment growth among library technicians in those settings.

Earnings

Salaries for library technicians vary widely, depending on the type of library and geographic location. According to a salary survey by Library Mosaics Magazine, library technicians employed in two-year colleges averaged $27,200 in 1996; in four-year colleges or universities, $30,200; in special libraries, $24,100; and in public libraries, $33,000. Salaries of library technicians in the federal government averaged $26,500 in 1997.

Related Occupations

Library technicians perform organizational and administrative duties. Workers in other occupations with similar duties include library clerks, information clerks, record clerks, medical record technicians, and title searchers. Library technicians also assist librarians. Other workers who assist professionals include museum technicians, teacher aides, legal assistants, and engineering and science technicians.

Sources of Additional Information

Information about a career as a library technician can be obtained from:

❑ Council on Library/Media Technology, P.O. Box 951, Oxon Hill, MD 20750.

For information on training programs for library/media technical assistants, write to:

❑ American Library Association, Office for Library Personnel Resources, 50 East Huron St., Chicago, IL 60611.

Information on acquiring a job as a library technician with the federal government may be obtained from the Office of Personnel Management through a telephone-based system. Consult your telephone directory under U.S. government for a local number or call (912) 757-3000 (TDD 912 744-2299). That number is not toll-free and charges may result. Information also is available from their Internet site: http://www.usajobs.opm.gov

Information concerning requirements and application procedures for positions in the Library of Congress may be obtained directly from:

❑ Personnel Office, Library of Congress, Washington, DC 20540.

State library agencies can furnish information on requirements for technicians, and general information about career prospects in the state. Several of these agencies maintain job hotlines reporting openings for library technicians.

State departments of education can furnish information on requirements and job opportunities for school library technicians.

Licensed Practical Nurses

(D.O.T. 079.374-014)

Significant Points

✓ *Training lasting about one year is available in about 1,100 state-approved programs, mostly in vocational or technical schools.*

✓ *Nursing homes will offer the most new jobs. Job seekers in hospitals may face competition.*

Nature of the Work

Licensed practical nurses (LPNs), or licensed vocational nurses as they are called in Texas and California, care for the sick, injured, convalescent, and disabled, under the direction of physicians and registered nurses.

Most LPNs provide basic bedside care. They take vital signs such as temperature, blood pressure, pulse, and respiration. They also treat bedsores, prepare and give injections and enemas, apply dressings, give alcohol rubs and massages, apply ice packs and hot water bottles, and insert catheters. LPNs observe patients and report adverse reactions to medications or treatments. They collect samples from patients for testing, perform routine laboratory tests, feed them and record food and liquid intake and output. They help patients with bathing, dressing, and personal hygiene, keep them comfortable, and care for their emotional needs. In states where the law allows, they may administer prescribed medicines or start intravenous fluids. Some LPNs help deliver, care for, and feed infants. Some experienced LPNs supervise nursing assistants and aides.

LPNs in nursing homes, in addition to providing routine bedside care, may also help evaluate residents' needs, develop care plans, and supervise the care provided by nursing aides. In doctors' offices and clinics, they may also make appointments, keep records, and perform other clerical duties. LPNs who work in private homes may also prepare meals and teach family members simple nursing tasks.

Working Conditions

Most licensed practical nurses in hospitals and nursing homes work a 40-hour week, but because patients need round-the-clock care, some work nights, weekends, and holidays. They often stand for long periods and help patients move in bed, stand, or walk.

LPNs may face hazards from caustic chemicals, radiation, and infectious diseases such as AIDS and hepatitis and also are subject to back injuries when moving patients and shock from electrical equipment. They often are subject to stress from heavy workloads. In addition, the patients they care for may be confused, irrational, agitated, or uncooperative.

Employment

Licensed practical nurses held about 699,000 jobs in 1996. Thirty-two percent of LPNs worked in hospitals, 27 percent worked in nursing homes, and 13 percent in doctors' offices and clinics. Others worked for temporary help agencies, home health care services, or government agencies. Almost one-third worked part-time.

Training, Other Qualifications, and Advancement

All states require LPNs to pass a licensing examination after completing a state-approved practical nursing program. A high school diploma is usually required for entry, but some programs accept people without a diploma.

In 1997, approximately 1,100 state-approved programs provided practical nursing training. Almost six out of ten students were enrolled in technical or vocational schools, while three out of ten were in community and junior colleges. Others were in high schools, hospitals, and colleges and universities.

Most practical nursing programs last about one year and include both classroom study and supervised clinical practice (patient care). Classroom study covers basic nursing concepts and patient-care related subjects, including anatomy, physiology, medical-surgical nursing, pediatrics, obstetrics, psychiatric nursing, administration of drugs, nutrition, and first aid. Clinical practice is usually in a hospital, but sometimes includes other settings.

LPNs should have a caring, sympathetic nature. They should be emotionally stable because work with the sick and injured can be stressful. As part of a health care team, they must be able to follow orders and work under close supervision.

Job Outlook

Employment of LPNs is expected to increase faster than the average for all occupations through the year 2006 in response to the long-term care needs of a rapidly growing population of very old people and to the general growth of health care. However, LPNs seeking positions in hospitals may face competition, as the number of hospital jobs for LPNs declines. The number of inpatients, with whom most LPNs work, is not expected to increase much. As in most other occupations, replacement needs will be the main source of job openings.

Employment in nursing homes is expected to grow much faster than the average. Nursing homes will offer the most new jobs for LPNs as the number of aged and disabled persons in need of long-term care rises rapidly. In addition to caring for the aged, nursing homes will be called on to care for the increasing number of patients who have been released from the hospital and have not yet recovered enough to return home.

Much faster than average growth is also expected in home health care services. This is in response to a growing number of older persons with functional disabilities, consumer preference for care in the home, and technological advances which make it possible to bring increasingly complex treatments into the home.

An increasing proportion of sophisticated procedures, which once were performed only in hospitals, are being performed in physicians' offices and clinics, including health maintenance organizations, ambulatory surgicenters, and emergency medical centers, thanks largely to advances in technology. As a result, employment is projected to grow much faster than average in these places as health care in general expands.

Earnings

Median weekly earnings of full-time salaried licensed practical nurses were $468 in 1996. The middle 50 percent earned between $388 and $563. The lowest 10 percent earned less than $318; the top 10 percent, more than $673.

According to the Buck Survey conducted by the American Health Care Association, staff LPNs in chain nursing homes had median hourly earnings of $12.00 in 1996. The middle 50 percent earned between $10.60 and $13.50.

Related Occupations

LPNs work closely with people while helping them. So do emergency medical technicians, human service workers, and teacher aides.

Sources of Additional Information

For a list of state-approved training programs and information about practical nursing, write to:

❏ Communications Department, National League for Nursing, 350 Hudson St., New York, NY 10014. FAX (212) 989-2272.

❏ National Association for Practical Nurse Education and Service, Inc., 1400 Spring St., Suite 310, Silver Spring, MD 20910. FAX (301) 588-2839 E-mail address: HYPERLINK mailto:napnes@aol.com

Line Installers and Cable Splicers

(D.O.T. 821.261-010, -014, -022, and -026, .281-010, .361-010, -018, -022, -026, -030, and -038, .684-022, .687-010; 822.381-014; 823.261-014; 829.361-010 and -014; and 959.367-010)

Significant Points

✓ *Line installers and cable splicer jobs do not require education beyond high school, but provide substantial on-the-job training that leads to relatively high earnings.*

✓ *Employment is expected to increase moderately, but competition is expected for jobs.*

✓ *Line installers and cable splicer work outdoors in all weather; when severe weather damages cables, they may be called out on short notice and work long hours until service is restored.*

Nature of the Work

Vast networks of wires and cables transmit the electric power produced in generating plants to individual customers, connect telephone central offices to customers' telephones and switchboards, and extend cable television to residential and commercial customers. These networks are constructed and maintained by line installers and cable splicers and their helpers.

To install new electric power or telephone lines, line installers or line erectors install poles and terminals, erect towers, and place wires and cables. They usually use power equipment to dig holes and set poles. Line installers climb the poles or use truck-mounted buckets (aerial work platforms) and use hand tools to attach the cables. When working with electric power lines, installers bolt or clamp insulators onto the pole before attaching the cable. They may also install transformers, circuit breakers, switches, or other equipment. To bury underground cable, they use trenchers, plows, and other power equipment.

Line installers also lay cable television lines underground or hang them on poles with telephone and utility wires. These lines transmit broadcast signals from microwave towers to customers' homes. Installers place wiring in the house, connect the customers' television sets to it, and check that the television signal is strong.

After telephone line installers place cables in position, cable splicers, also referred to as cable splicing technicians, complete the line connections. (Electric power line workers install and splice the cables simultaneously.) Splicers connect individual wires or fibers within the cable and rearrange wires when lines have to be changed. They first read and interpret service orders and circuit diagrams to determine splicing specifications. Splices are then made by joining wires and cables with small hand tools, epoxy, or mechanical equipment. At each splice, they place insulation over the conductor and seal the splice with some type of moisture proof covering. They may fill the cable sheathing on critical transmission routes with compressed air, so leaks in the sheathing can be monitored and repaired. Splicers work on poles, aerial ladders and platforms, in manholes, or in basements of large buildings.

Fiber optic cables are used to replace worn or obsolete copper cables. These tiny hair-thin strands of glass are able to carry more signals per cable because they transmit pulses of light instead of electricity. Splices of fiber optic cables are completed in a van positioned near the splice point. These vans house workshops that contain all the necessary equipment, such as machines that heat the glass fibers so they can be joined.

Line installers and cable splicers also maintain and repair telephone, power, and cable television lines. They periodically make sure lines are clear of tree limbs or other obstructions that could cause problems, and check insulation on cables and other equipment on line poles. When bad weather or earthquakes break wires or cables, knock poles down, or cause underground ducts to collapse, they make emergency repairs.

Working Conditions

Because telephone, electric, and television cables are strung from utility poles or are underground, line installers and cable splicers must climb and lift or work in stooped and cramped positions. They usually work outdoors in all kinds of weather and are subject to 24-hour calls. Most usually work a 40-hour week, but unexpected circumstances may create a need for overtime work. For example, when severe weather damages transmission and distribution lines, they may work long and irregular hours to restore service. At times, they may travel to distant locations, and occasionally stay for a lengthy period to help restore damaged facilities or build new ones.

Line installers and cable splicers face many situations in which safety procedures must be followed. They wear safety equipment when entering manholes and test for the presence of gas before going underground. They may be exposed to hazardous chemicals from the solvents and plugging compounds they use when splicing cables.

Electric power line workers have the most hazardous jobs. They typically work 20 to 40 feet above ground level because electric cable is always strung above telephone and cable television lines. In addition to this danger, the voltages in electric power lines are lethal.

Employment

Line installers and cable splicers held about 309,000 jobs in 1996. More than half were telephone and cable television line installers and repairers. Nearly all worked for telephone, cable television companies, or electric power companies, or for construction companies specializing in power line, telephone, and cable television construction.

Training, Other Qualifications, and Advancement

Line installers are often hired as helpers or ground workers. Most employers prefer high school graduates. Many employers test applicants for basic verbal, arithmetic, and abstract reasoning skills. Some employers test for physical ability such as balance, coordination, and strength and mechanical aptitude. Because the work entails a lot of climbing, applicants should have stamina and must be unafraid of heights. Knowledge of basic electricity and training in installing telephone systems obtained in the Armed Forces or vocational education programs may be helpful. The ability to distinguish colors is necessary because wires and cables are usually coded by color. Motivation, self-discipline, and the ability to work as part of a team are needed to work efficiently and safely.

Line installers and cable splicers in electric companies and construction firms specializing in cable installation generally complete a formal apprenticeship program. These are administered jointly by the employer and the union representing the workers, either the International Brotherhood of Electrical Workers or the Communications Workers of America. These programs last several years and combine formal instruction with on-the-job training. Workers in telephone companies generally receive several years of informal on-the-job training, in some cases learning other skills such as telephone installation and repair. They may also attend training provided by equipment manufacturers.

A growing number of employers are using computer-assisted instruction, video cassettes, movies, or "programmed" workbooks. Some training facilities are equipped with poles, cable-supporting clamps, and other fixtures, to simulate working conditions as closely as possible. Trainees learn to work on poles while keeping their hands free. In one exercise, for example, they play catch with a basketball while on the poles.

Formal training includes instruction in electrical codes, blueprint reading, and basic electrical theory. Afterwards, trainees learn on the job and work with a crew of experienced line installers under a line supervisor. Line installers and cable splicers receive training throughout their careers to qualify for more difficult assignments, and to keep up with technological changes.

Since deregulation of the telephone industry, many telephone companies have reduced the scope of their training programs in order to reduce their costs and to remain competitive. Increasingly, workers are responsible for their own training, which is provided by community colleges and postsecondary vocational schools.

For installers in the telephone industry, advancement may come about through promotion to splicer. Splicers can advance to engineering assistants or may move into other kinds of work, such as sales. Promotion to a supervisory position also is possible. In the electric industry, promotion is usually to a supervisory position.

Job Outlook

Job seekers are expected to face competition. Because there are few prerequisite skills, training is largely provided on the job, and earnings are above average, applicants should outnumber available job openings. Besides employment growth, many job openings will result from the need to replace the large number of older workers reaching retirement age. Job prospects will be best in telephone companies, particularly for those who combine knowledge of line installation, fiber optic and copper cable splicing, and repair of many types of equipment.

Overall employment of line installers and cable splicers is expected to grow about as fast as the average through the year 2006. Technological advances will result in divergent trends within this occupation. Technological change is expected to have little impact on electrical power line installers, and their employment is expected to grow more slowly than the average for all occupations to meet the growing demand for electricity and the need to maintain existing lines. Employment of telephone and cable television line installers and repairers, however, is projected to grow about as fast as the average, in line with the growth in telephone and cable television usage. If, as expected, telephone companies expand their services to provide cable TV, electronic publishing, and other telecommunication services, they will have to modernize their networks by laying fiber-optic cables that dramatically expand the electronic pipeline that reaches each home. Line installers and cable splicers will be needed to lay the new larger capacity cables.

Earnings

Pay rates for line installers and cable splicers vary greatly across the country and depend on length of service; specific information may be obtained from local telephone, electric power, and cable television companies. It generally takes about five years to go from the bottom to the top of the pay scale. In 1996, line installers and repairers who worked full-time earned a median weekly wage of $703. The middle 50 percent earned between $498 and $892. The bottom 10 percent earned less than $351; the top 10 percent earned more than $1,072 a week.

Line installers and cable splicers employed by AT&T and the Bell Operating Companies and represented by the Communications Workers of America earned between $279 and $962 a week in 1996.

Because of low job turnover in these occupations, many workers earn salaries near the top of the pay scale.

According to the International Brotherhood of Electrical Workers, average hourly wages in 1997 for line installers and cable splicers were between $17.81 and $19.35.

Most line installers and cable splicers belong to unions, principally the Communications Workers of America and the International Brotherhood of Electrical Workers. For these workers, union contracts set wage rates, wage increases, and the time needed to advance from one step to the next. These contracts require extra pay for overtime and all work on Sundays and holidays. Most contracts provide for additional pay for night work. Time in service determines the length of paid vacations. Depending on job locality, there are 9 to 12 holidays a year.

Related Occupations

Workers in other skilled crafts and trades who work with tools and machines include communications equipment mechanics, biomedical equipment technicians, telephone installers and repairers, electricians, and sound technicians.

Sources of Additional Information

For more details about employment opportunities, contact the telephone or electric power company in your community or local offices of the unions that represent these workers. For general information on line installer and cable splicer jobs, write to:

❑ Communications Workers of America, Department of Apprenticeships, Benefits, and Employment, 501 3rd St. NW, Washington, DC 20001.

For additional information on the telephone industry and career opportunities contact:

❑ United States Telephone Association, 1401 H St. NW, Suite 600, Washington, DC 20005-2136.

For information on employment and training contact:

❑ Utility Workers Union of America, 815 16th. St. NW, Washington, DC 20006.

❑ International Brotherhood of Electrical Workers, Telecommunications Department, 1125 15th. St. NW, Room 807, Washington, DC 20005.

Loan Officers and Counselors

(D.O.T. 186.167-078, .267-018, -022, -026)

Significant Points

✓ *Loan officer positions generally require a bachelor's degree in finance, economics, or a related field; for commercial or mortgage loan officers, training or experience in sales is advantageous.*

✓ *Faster than average employment growth will stem from increases in the number and complexity of loans and in the importance of loan officers to the success of banks and other lending institutions.*

Nature of the Work

Banks and other financial institutions need up-to-date information on companies and individuals applying for loans and credit.

Customers and clients provide this information to the financial institution's loan officers, generally the first employees to be seen by them. Loan officers prepare, analyze, and verify loan applications, make decisions regarding the extension of credit, and help borrowers fill out loan applications. Loan counselors, also called loan collection officers, contact borrowers who have delinquent accounts and help them find a method of repayment to avoid a default on the loan.

Loan officers usually specialize in commercial, consumer, or mortgage loans. Commercial or business loans help companies pay for new equipment or expand operations. Consumer loans include home equity, automobile, and personal loans. Mortgage loans are made to purchase real estate or to refinance an existing mortgage.

Consumer loan officers attempt to lower their firm's risk by receiving collateral–property pledged as security for the payment of a loan. For example, when lending money for a college education, the bank may insist that the borrower offer his or her home as collateral. If the borrower were ever unable to repay the loan, the borrower would have to sell the home to raise the necessary money.

Commercial and mortgage loan officers behave as sales people who actively seek out potential customers. Commercial loan officers contact firms that may or may not have accounts with their bank. They find out if their potential client is planning any projects for which they may need a loan; if so, loan officers try to establish a relationship with the firm so that the firm will contact them when the loan is needed. Similarly, mortgage loan officers try to develop relationships with commercial or residential real estate agencies; when an individual or firm buys a property, the real estate agent might recommend contacting that loan officer for financing.

Banks and other lenders are offering a growing variety of loans. Loan officers must keep abreast of new types of loans and other financial products and services so they can meet their customers' needs.

Loan officers meet with customers to gather basic information about the loan request, and explain the different types of loans that are available to the applicant. Often customers will not fully understand the information requested, and will call the loan officer for clarification. Once the customer completes the financial forms, the loan officer begins to process them. The loan officer verifies that the customer has correctly identified the type and purpose of the loan. The loan officer then requests a credit report from one or more of the major credit reporting agencies. This information, along with comments from the loan officer, is included in a loan file, and is compared to the lending institution's requirements. Banks and other lenders have established requirements for the maximum percentage of income that can safely go to repay loans. At this point, the loan officer, in consultation with his or her manager, decides whether or not to grant the loan. A loan that would otherwise be denied may be approved if the customer can provide the lender appropriate collateral. The loan officer also informs the borrower if the loan is approved or denied.

Loan counselors contact holders of delinquent accounts in an effort to develop a repayment plan. If a repayment plan cannot be developed, the loan counselor initiates collateral liquidation, in which case the collateral used to secure the loan–a home or car, for example–is seized by the lender and sold to repay the loan.

Working Conditions

Commercial and mortgage loan officers frequently work away from their offices, relying on laptop computers, cellular phones, and pagers to keep in contact with their offices and clients. Mortgage loan officers frequently work out of their home or car, often visiting offices or homes of clients while completing the loan application. Commercial loan officers may travel to other cities to prepare complex loan agreements. Consumer loan officers and loan counselors are likely to spend most of their time in an office.

Most loan officers and counselors work a standard 40-hour week, but may work longer, particularly mortgage loan officers who are free to take on as many customers as they choose. Loan officers usually carry a heavy caseload and sometimes cannot accept new clients until they complete current cases. They are especially busy when interest rates are low, triggering a surge in loan applications.

Employment

Loan officers and counselors held about 209,000 jobs in 1996. About three out of five are employed by commercial banks, savings institutions, and credit unions. Others are employed by nonbank financial institutions, such as mortgage brokerage firms and personal credit firms. Loan officers are concentrated in urban and suburban areas. In rural areas, the loan application process is often handled by the branch or assistant manager.

Training, Other Qualifications, and Advancement

Loan officer positions generally require a bachelor's degree in finance, economics, or a related field. Most employers also prefer applicants who are familiar with computers and their applications in banking. For commercial or mortgage loan officer jobs, training or experience in sales is highly valued by potential employers. A small number of loan officers advance through the ranks in an organization, acquiring several years of work experience in various other occupations, such as teller or customer service representative.

Persons planning a career as a loan officer or counselor should be capable of developing effective working relationships with others, confident in their abilities, and highly motivated. Loan officers must be willing to attend community events as a representative of their employer.

The American Institute of Banking, which is affiliated with the American Bankers Association, offers courses through correspondence and in some colleges and universities for students and others interested in lending, as well as for experienced loan officers. Completion of these courses and programs enhances one's employment and advancement opportunities.

Capable loan officers and counselors may advance to larger branches of the firm or to a managerial position, while less capable workers and those having inadequate academic preparation may be assigned to smaller branches and find promotion difficult. Advancement from a loan officer position usually includes becoming a supervisor over other loan officers and clerical staff.

Job Outlook

While employment in banks–where most loan officers and counselors are found–is projected to decline, employment of loan officers and counselors is expected to grow faster than the average for all occupations through the year 2006. As the population and economy grow, applications for commercial, consumer, and mortgage loans will increase, spurring demand for loan officers and counselors. Growth in the variety and complexity of loans, and the importance of loan officers to the success of banks and other lending institutions, also should assure employment growth. Although increased demand will generate many new jobs, most openings will result from the need to replace workers who leave the occupation or retire. College graduates and those with banking, lending, or sales experience should have the best job prospects.

Loan officers and counselors are less likely to lose their jobs than other workers in banks and other lending institutions during economic downturns. Because loans are the major source of income for banks, loan officers are fundamental to the success of their organizations. Also, many loan officers are compensated in part on a commission basis. Loan counselors are likely to see an increase in the number of delinquent loans during difficult economic times.

Earnings

The form of compensation for loan officers varies, depending on the lending institution. Some banks offer salary plus commission as an incentive to increase the number of loans processed, while others pay only salaries.

According to a salary survey conducted by Robert Half International, a staffing services firm specializing in accounting and finance, residential real estate mortgage loan officers earned between $30,600 and $45,000 in 1997; commercial real estate mortgage loan officers, between $45,100 and $73,000; consumer loan officers, between $28,900 and $48,000; and commercial lenders, between $37,400 and $85,000. Smaller banks generally paid 15 percent less than larger banks. Loan officers who are paid on a commission basis generally earn more than those on salary only.

Banks and other lenders sometimes offer their loan officers free checking privileges and somewhat lower interest rates on personal loans.

Related Occupations

Loan officers help the public manage financial assets and secure loans. Occupations that involve similar functions include securities and financial services sales representatives, financial aid officers, real estate agents and brokers, and insurance agents and brokers.

Sources of Additional Information

Information about a career as a loan officer or counselor may be obtained from:

❏ American Bankers Association, 1120 Connecticut Ave. NW, Washington, DC 20036.

State bankers' associations can furnish specific information about job opportunities in their state. Or, contact individual banks to inquire about job openings, and for more details about the activities, responsibilities, and preferred qualifications of their loan officers. For the names and addresses of banks and savings and related institutions, as well as the names of their principal officers, consult one of the following directories.

❏ *The American Financial Directory* (Norcross, GA, McFadden Business Publications).

❏ *Polk's World Bank Directory* (Nashville, R.L. Polk & Co.).

❏ *Rand McNally Bankers Directory* (Chicago, Rand McNally & Co.).

❏ *The U.S. Savings and Loan Directory* (Chicago, Rand McNally & Co.).

❏ *Rand McNally Credit Union Directory* (Chicago, Rand McNally & Co.).

Management Analysts and Consultants

(D.O.T. 100.117-014; 161.117-014, .167-010, -014, -018, and -022, .267 except -014 and -030; 169.167-074; 184.267; and 310.267-010)

Significant Points

✓ *About 45 percent of these workers were self-employed, almost three times the average for other executive, administrative, and managerial occupations.*

✓ *A master's degree and at least five years' specialized experience generally are required for jobs in the private sector.*

Nature of the Work

Management analysts and consultants analyze and suggest solutions to management problems. For example, a rapidly growing small company may need help in designing a better system of control over inventories and expenses and decides to engage a consultant who is an expert in just-in-time inventory management. In another case, a large company which realizes its corporate structure must be reorganized after acquiring a new division brings in management experts to restructure the company and eliminate duplicate and nonessential managerial positions. These are just some of the many organizational problems that management analysts, as they are called in government agencies, and consultants, as business firms refer to them, help solve.

The work of management analysts and consultants varies with each client or employer and from project to project. For example, some projects require a team of consultants, each specializing in one area; at other times, consultants work independently with the organization's managers. In general, analysts and consultants first collect, review, and analyze information. They then make recommendations to management and may assist in the implementation of their proposal.

Both public and private organizations use consultants for a variety of reasons. Some don't have the internal resources needed to handle a project, while others need a consultant's expertise to determine what resources will be required, and what problems may be encountered, if they pursue a particular opportunity.

Firms providing consulting services range in size from a single practitioner to large international organizations employing many thousands of consultants. Some analysts and consultants specialize in a specific industry while others specialize by type of business function, such as human resources or information systems. In government, management analysts tend to specialize by type of agency. Consulting services often are provided on a contract basis. To engage a consultant, a company first solicits proposals from a number of consulting firms specializing in the area in which it needs assistance. These proposals include the estimated cost and scope of the project, staffing requirements, references from a number of previous clients, and a completion deadline. The company then selects the best proposal for its needs.

Upon getting an assignment or contract, consultants or management analysts define the nature and extent of the problem. During this phase of the job, they analyze pertinent data such as annual revenues, employment, or expenditures and interview managers and employees while observing their operations.

The analyst or consultant develops solutions to the problem. In the course of preparing their recommendations, they take into account the nature of the organization, the relationship it has with others in that industry, and its internal organization and culture. Insight into the problem may be gained by building and solving mathematical models.

Once they have decided on a course of action, consultants report their findings and recommendations to the client, often in writing. In addition, they generally make oral presentations regarding their findings. For some projects, this is all that is required. For others, consultants assist in the implementation of their suggestions.

Management analysts in government agencies use the same skills as their private-sector colleagues to advise managers on many types of issues, most of which are similar to the problems faced by private firms. For example, if an agency is planning to purchase personal computers, it must first determine which type to buy, given its budget and data processing needs. Management analysts would assess the various types of machines available by price range and determine which best meets their department's needs.

Working Conditions

Management analysts and consultants usually divide their time between their offices and their client's site. Although much of their time is spent indoors in clean, well-lighted offices, they may experience a great deal of stress as a result of trying to meet a client's demands, often on a tight schedule.

Typically, analysts and consultants work at least 40 hours a week. Uncompensated overtime is common, especially when project deadlines are near. Since they must spend a significant portion of their time with clients, they travel frequently.

Self-employed consultants can set their workload and hours and work at home. On the other hand, their livelihood depends on their ability to maintain and expand their client base. Salaried consultants also must impress potential clients to get and keep clients for their company.

Employment

Management analysts and consultants held about 244,000 jobs in 1996. Around 45 percent of these workers were self-employed. Most of the rest worked in financial and management consulting firms and for federal, state, and local governments. The majority of those working for the federal government were found in the Department of Defense.

Management analysts and consultants are found throughout the country, but employment is concentrated in large metropolitan areas.

Training, Other Qualifications, and Advancement

Educational requirements for entry-level jobs in this field vary widely between private industry and government. Employers in private industry generally seek individuals with a master's degree in business administration or a related discipline and at least five years of experience in the field in which they hope to consult. Most government agencies hire people with a bachelor's degree and no work experience as entry-level management analysts.

Many fields of study provide a suitable educational background for this occupation because of the wide range of problem areas addressed by management analysts and consultants. These include most areas of business and management, as well as computer and information sciences and engineering.

Most entrants to this occupation have, in addition to the appropriate formal education, years of experience in management, human resources, inventory control, or other specialties . The value of this experience enables many to land consultant positions, since most prospective clients now demand experience in the area where they feel they need help.

Management analysts and consultants often work with little or no supervision, so they should be self-motivated and disciplined. Analytical skills, the ability to get along with a wide range of people, strong oral and written communication skills, good judgment, the ability to manage time well, and creativity in developing solutions to problems are other desirable qualities for prospective management analysts and consultants.

Consulting teams are becoming more common. The team is responsible for the entire project and each consultant on the team is assigned to a particular area.

As consultants gain experience, they often become solely responsible for a specific project full-time, taking on more responsibility and managing their own hours. At the senior level, consultants may supervise lower-level workers and become increasingly involved in seeking out new business. Those with exceptional skills may eventually become a partner or principal in the firm. Others with entrepreneurial ambition may open their own firm.

Analysts and consultants routinely attend conferences to keep abreast of current developments in their field.

A high percentage of management consultants are self-employed, partly because business start-up costs are low. Self-employed consultants also can share office space, administrative help, and other resources with other self-employed consultants or small consulting firms—thus reducing overhead costs. Many such firms fail, however, because of an inability to acquire and maintain a profitable client base.

The Institute of Management Consultants (a division of the Council of Consulting Organizations, Inc.) offers the Certified Management Consultant (CMC) designation to those who pass an examination and meet minimum levels of education and experience. Certification is not mandatory for management consultants to practice, but it may give a job seeker a competitive advantage.

Job Outlook

Employment of management analysts and consultants is expected to grow faster than the average for all occupations through the year 2006 as industry and government increasingly rely on outside expertise to improve the performance of their organizations. Growth is expected in very large consulting firms, but also in smaller niche consulting firms whose consultants specialize in specific areas of expertise. For example, some consultants specialize in biotechnology, pharmacy, engineering, or telecommunications. Clients increasingly demand a team approach, which enables examination of a variety of different areas within the organization; this development may hinder individual practitioners.

Increased competition has forced American industry to take a closer look at its operations. As international and domestic markets become more competitive, firms must use resources more efficiently. Management consultants are being increasingly relied upon to help reduce costs, streamline operations, and develop marketing strategies. As businesses downsize, opportunities will be created for consultants to perform duties that were previously handled internally. Businesses attempting to expand, particularly into world markets, frequently need the skills of management consultants to help with organizational, administrative, and other issues. Continuing changes in the business environment also are expected to lead the demand for consultants to incorporate new technologies, and to adapt to a changing labor force. As businesses rely more on technology, there are increasing roles for consultants with a technical background, such as engineering or biotechnology, particularly when combined with an MBA.

Federal, state, and local agencies also are expected to expand their use of management analysts. Analysts' skills at identifying problems and implementing cost reduction measures are expected to become increasingly important.

Despite projected rapid employment growth, competition for jobs as management analysts and consultants is expected to be keen. Because management consultants can come from such diverse educational backgrounds, the pool of applicants from which employers can hire is quite large. Additionally, the independent and challenging nature of the work, combined with high earnings potential, make this occupation attractive to many. Job opportunities are expected to be best for those with a graduate degree, a talent for salesmanship and public relations, and industry expertise.

Because many small consulting firms fail each year for lack of managerial expertise and clients, those interested in opening their own firm must have good organizational and marketing skills and several years of consulting experience.

Earnings

Salaries for management analysts and consultants vary widely by experience, education, and employer. In 1996, those who were full-time wage and salary workers had median annual earnings of about $39,500. The middle 50 percent earned between $30,200 and $61,300, and the top 10 percent earned more than $81,500.

In 1996, according to the Association of Management Consulting Firms, earnings–including bonuses and/or profit sharing–for research associates in member firms averaged $32,400; for entry level consultants, $35,200; for management consultants, $50,500; for senior consultants, $74,300; for junior partners, $91,100; and for senior partners, $167,100.

The average annual salary for management analysts in the federal government in nonsupervisory, supervisory, and managerial positions was $55,240 in 1997.

Typical benefits for salaried analysts and consultants include health and life insurance, a retirement plan, vacation and sick leave, profit sharing, and bonuses for outstanding work. In addition, all travel expenses usually are reimbursed by the employer. Self-employed consultants have to maintain their own office and provide their own benefits.

Related Occupations

Management analysts and consultants collect, review, and ana-lyze data; make recommendations; and assist in the implementation of their ideas. Others who use similar skills are managers, computer systems analysts, operations research analysts, economists, and financial analysts. Researchers prepare data and reports for consultants to use in their recommendations.

Sources of Additional Information

Information about career opportunities in management consulting is available from:

❑ The Association of Management Consulting Firms, 521 Fifth Ave., 35th Floor, New York, NY 10175-3598.

For information about a career as a state or local government management analyst, contact your state or local employment service.

Information on obtaining a management analyst position with the federal government may be obtained from the Office of Personnel Management through a telephone based system. Consult your telephone directory under U.S. government for a local number or call (912) 757-3000 (TDD 912 744-2299). That number is not toll free and charges may result. Information also is available from their Internet site: http:// www.usajobs.opm.gov

Manufacturers' and Wholesale Sales Representatives

(D.O.T. codes are too numerous to list.)

Significant Points

✓ *Although employers place an emphasis on a strong educational background, many individuals with previous sales experience who do not have a college degree still enter the occupation.*

✓ *Many jobs require a great deal of travel.*

✓ *Many are self-employed manufacturers' agents who work for a commission.*

Nature of the Work

For both manufacturers and wholesalers, sales representatives are an important part of their company's success. Regardless of the type of product they sell, their primary duties are to interest wholesale and retail buyers and purchasing agents in their merchandise and ensure that any questions or concerns of current clients are addressed. They market their company's products to manufacturers, wholesale and retail establishments, government agencies, and other institutions. Sales representatives also provide advice to clients on how to increase sales.

Depending on where they work, sales representatives have different job titles. Many of those working directly for manufacturers are referred to as manufacturers' representatives and those employed by wholesalers generally are called sales representatives. In addition to those employed directly by firms, manufacturers' agents are self-employed sales workers who contract their services to all types of companies. Those selling technical products, for both manufacturers and wholesalers, are usually called industrial sales workers or sales engineers. Many of these titles, however, are used interchangeably.

Manufacturers' and wholesale sales representatives spend much of their time traveling to and visiting with prospective buyers and current clients. During a sales call, they discuss the customers' needs and suggest how their merchandise or services can meet those needs. They may show samples or catalogs that describe items their company stocks and inform customers about prices, availability, and how their products can save money and improve productivity. Because of the vast number of manufacturers and wholesalers selling similar products, they also try to emphasize the unique qualities of the products and services offered by their company. They also take orders and resolve any problems or complaints with the merchandise.

Depending on the products they sell, sales representatives may have additional duties. For example, sales engineers, who are among the most highly trained sales workers, typically sell products whose installation and optimal use require a great deal of technical expertise and support—products such as material handling equipment, numerical-control machinery, and computer systems. In addition to providing information on their firm's products, these workers help prospective and current buyers with technical problems by recommending improved materials and machinery for a firm's manufacturing process, drawing up plans of proposed machinery layouts and estimating cost savings from the use of their equipment. They present this information and negotiate the sale, a process that may take several months. During their presentation, they may use a portable computer so they can have instant access to technical, sales, and other information.

Increasingly, sales representatives who lack technical expertise work as a team with a technical expert. In this arrangement, the duties of a sales representative are to make the preliminary contact with customers, introduce the company's product, and close the sale. The technical expert will attend the sales presentation to explain and answer questions and concerns. In this way, the sales representative is able to spend more time maintaining and soliciting accounts and less time acquiring technical knowledge. After the sale, sales representatives may make frequent follow-up visits to ensure the equipment is functioning properly and may even help train customers' employees to operate and maintain new equipment.

Those selling consumer goods often suggest how and where their merchandise should be displayed. Working with retailers, they may help arrange promotional programs, store displays, and advertising.

Obtaining new accounts is an important part of the job. Sales representatives follow leads suggested by other clients, from advertisements in trade journals, and from participation in trade shows and conferences. At times, they make unannounced visits to potential clients. In addition, they may spend a lot of time meeting with and entertaining prospective clients during evenings and weekends.

Sales representatives also analyze sales statistics, prepare reports, and handle administrative duties, such as filing their expense account reports, scheduling appointments, and making travel plans. They study literature about new and existing products and monitor the sales, prices, and products of their competitors.

In addition to all these duties, manufacturers' agents who operate a sales agency must also manage their business. This requires organizational skills as well as knowledge of accounting, marketing, and administration.

Working Conditions

Some manufacturers' and wholesale sales representatives have large territories and do considerable traveling. Because a sales region may cover several states, they may be away from home for several days or weeks at a time. Others work near their "home base" and do most of their traveling by automobile. Due to the nature of the work and the amount of travel, sales representatives typically work more than 40 hours per week.

Although the hours are long and often irregular, most sales representatives have the freedom to determine their own schedule. As a result, they may be able to arrange their appointments so they can have time off when they want it.

Dealing with different types of people can be demanding but stimulating. In addition, sales representatives often face competition from representatives of other companies as well as from fellow workers. Companies may set goals or quotas that representatives are expected to meet. Because their earnings depend upon commissions, manufacturers' agents are also under the added pressure to maintain and expand their clientele.

Employment

Manufacturers' and wholesale sales representatives held about 1,557,000 jobs in 1996. Three of every four worked in wholesale trade—mostly for distributors of machinery and equipment, groceries and related products, and motor vehicles and parts. Others were employed in manufacturing and mining. Due to the diversity of products and services sold, employment opportunities are available in every part of the country.

In addition to those working directly for a firm, many sales representatives are self-employed manufacturers' agents who work for a straight commission based on the value of their sales. However, these workers generally gain experience and recognition with a manufacturer or wholesaler prior to going into business for themselves.

Training, Other Qualifications, and Advancement

The background needed for sales jobs varies by product line and market. As the number of college graduates has increased and the job requirements have become more technical and analytical, most firms have placed a greater emphasis on a strong educational background. Nevertheless, many employers still hire individuals with previous sales experience who do not have a college degree. In fact, for some consumer products, sales ability, personality, and familiarity with brands are as important as a degree. On the other hand, firms selling industrial products often require a degree in science or engineering in addition to some sales experience. In general, companies are looking for the best and brightest individuals who display the personality and desire necessary to sell.

Many companies have formal training programs for beginning sales representatives lasting up to two years. However, most businesses are accelerating these programs to reduce costs and expedite the return from training. In some programs, trainees rotate among jobs in plants and offices to learn all phases of production, installation, and distribution of the product. In others, trainees take formal classroom instruction at the plant, followed by on-the-job training under the supervision of a field sales manager.

In some firms, new workers are trained by accompanying more

experienced workers on their sales calls. As these workers gain familiarity with the firm's products and clients, they are given increasing responsibility until they are eventually assigned their own territory. As businesses experience greater competition, increased pressure is placed upon sales representatives to produce faster.

These workers must stay abreast of new merchandise and the changing needs of their customers. They may attend trade shows where new products are displayed or conferences and conventions where they meet with other sales representatives and clients to discuss new product developments. In addition, many companies sponsor meetings of their entire sales force where presentations are made on sales performance, product development, and profitability.

Manufacturers' and wholesale sales representatives should be goal oriented, persuasive, and able to work both as part of a team and independently. A pleasant personality and appearance, the ability to communicate well with people, and problem-solving skills are important as well. In addition, patience and perseverance are needed because completing a sale can take several months. Because these workers may be on their feet for long periods and may have to carry heavy sample cases, some physical stamina is necessary. Sales representatives should also enjoy traveling because much of their time is spent visiting current and prospective clients.

Frequently, promotion takes the form of an assignment to a larger account or territory where commissions are likely to be greater. Experienced sales representatives may move into jobs as sales trainers—workers who train new employees on selling techniques and company policies and procedures. Those who have good sales records and leadership ability may advance to sales supervisor or district manager.

In addition to advancement opportunities within a firm, some go into business for themselves as manufacturers' agents. Others find opportunities in buying, purchasing, advertising, or marketing research.

Job Outlook

Overall, employment of manufacturers' and wholesale sales representatives is expected to grow about as fast as the average for all occupations through the year 2006 due to continued growth in the amount of goods provided that need to be sold. Many job openings will also result from the need to replace workers who transfer to other occupations or leave the labor force.

Unlike many other occupations, technology is not expected to have a dramatic effect on the demand for these workers because sales workers will still be needed to go to the prospective customer in order to demonstrate or illustrate the particulars about the good or service. Technology is expected, however, to make them more effective and productive because it allows them to provide accurate and current information to customers during sales presentations.

Within manufacturing, job opportunities as manufacturers' agents should be a little better than those for sales representatives. Manufacturers are expected to continue outsourcing their sales duties to these workers rather than using in-house or direct selling personnel because agents are more likely to work in a sales area or territory longer than representatives, creating a better working relationship and understanding how customers operate their businesses. Also, by using agents who usually lend their services to more than one company, companies can share costs with the other companies involved with that agent.

Those interested in this occupation should keep in mind that direct selling opportunities in manufacturing are likely to be best for products with strong demand. Furthermore, jobs will be most plentiful in small wholesale and manufacturing firms because a growing number of these companies will rely on wholesalers and manufacturers' agents to market their products as a way to control their costs and expand their customer base.

Employment opportunities and earnings may fluctuate from year to year because sales are affected by changing economic conditions, legislative issues, and consumer preferences. Prospects will be best for those with the appropriate knowledge or technical expertise as well as the personal traits necessary for successful selling.

Earnings

Compensation methods vary significantly by the type of firm and product sold. However, most employers use a combination of salary and commission or salary plus bonus. Commissions are usually based on the amount of sales, whereas bonuses may depend on individual performance, on the performance of all sales workers in the group or district, or on the company's performance.

Median annual earnings of full-time manufacturers' and wholesale sales representatives were about $36,100 in 1996. The middle 50 percent earned between $24,900 and $51,900 per year. The bottom 10 percent earned less than $16,700; the top 10 percent earned more than $75,000 per year. Earnings vary by experience and the type of goods or services sold.

In addition to their earnings, sales representatives are usually reimbursed for expenses such as transportation costs, meals, hotels, and entertaining customers. They often receive benefits such as health and life insurance, a pension plan, vacation and sick leave, personal use of a company car, and "frequent flyer" mileage. Some companies offer incentives such as free vacation trips or gifts for outstanding sales workers.

Unlike those working directly for a manufacturer or wholesaler, manufacturers' agents get paid strictly on commission. Depending on the type of product they are selling, their experience in the field, and the number of clients, their earnings can be significantly higher or lower than those working in direct sales. In addition, because manufacturers' agents are self-employed, they must pay their own travel and entertainment expenses as well as provide for their own benefits, which can be a significant cost.

Related Occupations

Manufacturers' and wholesale sales representatives must have sales ability and knowledge of the products they sell. Other occupations that require similar skills are retail, services, real estate, insurance, and securities sales workers, as well as wholesale and retail buyers.

Sources of Additional Information

Information on manufacturers' agents is available from:
- ❏ Manufacturers' Agents National Association, P.O. Box 3467, Laguna Hills, CA 92654-3467.

Career and certification information is available from:
- ❏ Sales and Marketing Executives International, Statler Office Tower, Suite 977, 1127 Euclid Ave., Cleveland OH, 44115. Homepage: http://www.smei.org

❑ Manufacturers' Representatives Educational Research Foundation, P.O. Box 247, Geneva, IL 60134.

Marketing, Advertising, and Public Relations Managers

(D.O.T. 096.161-010; 141.137-010; 159.167-022; 163.117-014, -018, -022, -026, .167-010, -014, -018, -022, .267-010; 164.117-010, -014, -018, .167-010; 165.117-010, -014; 185.157-014, .167-042; 187.167-162, -170; 189.117-018)

Significant Points

✓ *Employment is projected to increase rapidly, but competition is expected to be intense.*

✓ *Marketing, advertising, and public relations managers have high earnings, but substantial travel and long hours, including evenings and weekends, are common.*

✓ *A college degree with almost any major is suitable for entering this occupation, but most people enter these jobs after acquiring experience in related, less responsible positions.*

Nature of the Work

The objective of any firm is to market its products or services profitably. In small firms, all marketing responsibilities may be assumed by the owner or chief executive officer. In large firms, which may offer numerous products and services nationally or even worldwide, experienced marketing, advertising, and public relations managers coordinate these and related activities.

In large firms an executive vice president directs the overall marketing policy–including market research, marketing strategy, sales, advertising, promotion, pricing, product development, and public relations activities. Middle and supervisory managers oversee and supervise staffs of professionals and technicians.

Marketing managers develop the firm's detailed marketing strategy. With the help of subordinates, including product development managers and market research managers, they determine the demand for products and services offered by the firm and its competitors and identify potential consumers–for example, business firms, wholesalers, retailers, government, or the general public. Mass markets are further categorized according to various factors such as region, age, income, and lifestyle. Marketing managers develop pricing strategy with an eye towards maximizing the firm's share of the market and its profits while ensuring that the firm's customers are satisfied. In collaboration with sales, product development, and other managers, they monitor trends that indicate the need for new products and services and oversee product development. Marketing managers work with advertising and promotion managers to best promote the firm's products and services and to attract potential users.

Sales managers direct the firm's sales program. They assign sales territories and goals and establish training programs for their sales representatives. Managers advise their sales representatives on ways to improve their sales performance. In large, multiproduct firms, they oversee regional and local sales managers and their staffs. Sales managers maintain contact with dealers and distributors. They analyze sales statistics gathered by their staffs to determine sales potential and inventory requirements and monitor the preferences of customers. Such information is vital to develop products and maximize profits.

Except in the largest firms, advertising and promotion staffs generally are small and serve as a liaison between the firm and the advertising or promotion agency to which many advertising or promotional functions are contracted out. Advertising managers oversee the account services, creative services, and media services departments. The account services department is managed by account executives, who assess the need for advertising and, in advertising agencies, maintain the accounts of clients. The creative services department develops the subject matter and presentation of advertising. This department is supervised by a creative director, who oversees the copy chief and art director and their staffs. The media services department is supervised by the media director, who oversees planning groups that select the communication media–for example, radio, television, newspapers, magazines, or outdoor signs–to disseminate the advertising.

Promotion managers supervise staffs of promotion specialists. They direct promotion programs combining advertising with purchase incentives to increase sales. In an effort to establish closer contact with purchasers–dealers, distributors, or consumers–promotion programs may involve direct mail, telemarketing, television or radio advertising, catalogs, exhibits, inserts in newspapers, in-store displays and product endorsements, and special events. Purchase incentives may include discounts, samples, gifts, rebates, coupons, sweepstakes, and contests.

Public relations managers supervise public relations specialists. These managers direct publicity programs to a targeted public. They use any necessary communication media in their effort to maintain the support of the specific group upon whom their organization's success depends, such as consumers, stockholders, or the general public. For example, public relations managers may clarify or justify the firm's point of view on health or environmental issues to community or special interest groups. They evaluate advertising and promotion programs for compatibility with public relations efforts, and, in effect, serve as the eyes and ears of top management. They observe social, economic, and political trends that might ultimately have an effect upon the firm, and make recommendations to enhance the firm's image based on those trends. Public relations managers may confer with labor relations managers to produce internal company communications–such as news about employee-management relations–and with financial managers to produce company reports. They assist company executives in drafting speeches, arranging interviews, and other forms of public contact; oversee company archives; and respond to information requests. In addition, some handle special events such as sponsorship of races, parties introducing new products, or other activities the firm supports in order to gain public attention through the press without advertising directly.

Working Conditions

Marketing, advertising, and public relations managers are provided with offices close to top managers. Long hours, including evenings and weekends, are common. Almost 45 percent of marketing, advertising, and public relations managers worked 50 hours or more a week, compared to 20 percent for all occupations. Working under pressure is unavoidable as schedules change, problems arise, and deadlines and goals must be met. Marketing, advertising, and public relations managers meet frequently with other managers; some meet with the public and government officials.

Substantial travel may be involved. For example, attendance at meetings sponsored by associations or industries is often mandatory. Sales managers travel to national, regional, and local offices and to various dealers and distributors. Advertising and promotion managers may travel to meet with clients or representatives of communications media. At times, public relations managers travel to meet with special interest groups or government officials. Job transfers between headquarters and regional offices are common—particularly among sales managers—and can disrupt family life.

Employment

Marketing, advertising, and public relations managers held about 482,000 jobs in 1996. They are found in virtually every industry. Industries employing them in significant numbers include motor vehicle dealers, printing and publishing, advertising, department stores, computer and data processing services, and management and public relations.

Training, Other Qualifications, and Advancement

A wide range of educational backgrounds are suitable for entry into marketing, advertising, and public relations managerial jobs, but many employers prefer a broad liberal arts background. A bachelor's degree in sociology, psychology, literature, or philosophy, among other subjects, is acceptable. However, requirements vary depending upon the particular job.

For marketing, sales, and promotion management positions, some employers prefer a bachelor's or master's degree in business administration with an emphasis on marketing. Courses in business law, economics, accounting, finance, mathematics, and statistics are also highly recommended. In highly technical industries, such as computer and electronics manufacturing, a bachelor's degree in engineering or science combined with a master's degree in business administration is preferred. For advertising management positions, some employers prefer a bachelor's degree in advertising or journalism. A course of study should include courses in marketing, consumer behavior, market research, sales, communications methods and technology, and visual arts—for example, art history and photography. For public relations management positions, some employers prefer a bachelor's or master's degree in public relations or journalism. The individual's curriculum should include courses in advertising, business administration, public affairs, political science, and creative and technical writing. For all these specialties, courses in management and completion of an internship while in school are highly recommended. Familiarity with word processing and data base applications also are important for many marketing, advertising, and public relations management positions. Today interactive marketing, product promotion, and advertising experience are increasingly important, and computer skills are very important.

Most marketing, advertising, and public relations management positions are filled by promoting experienced staff or related professional or technical personnel, for example, sales representatives, purchasing agents, buyers, product or brand specialists, advertising specialists, promotion specialists, and public relations specialists. In small firms, where the number of positions is limited, advancement to a management position generally comes slowly. In large firms, promotion may occur more quickly.

Although experience, ability, and leadership are emphasized for promotion, advancement can be accelerated by participation in management training programs conducted by many large firms. Many firms also provide their employees with continuing education opportunities, either in-house or at local colleges and universities, and encourage employee participation in seminars and conferences, often provided by professional societies. Often in collaboration with colleges and universities, numerous marketing and related associations sponsor national or local management training programs. Courses include brand and product management, international marketing, sales management evaluation, telemarketing and direct sales, promotion, marketing communication, market research, organizational communication, and data processing systems procedures and management. Many firms pay all or part of the cost for those who successfully complete courses.

Some associations (listed under Sources of Additional Information) offer certification programs for marketing, advertising, and public relations managers. Certification is a sign of competence and achievement in this field that is particularly important in a competitive job market. While relatively few marketing, advertising, and public relations managers currently are certified, the number of managers who seek certification is expected to grow. For example, Sales and Marketing Executives International offers a management certification program based on education and job performance. The Public Relations Society of America offers an accreditation program for public relations practitioners based on years of experience and an examination. The International Association of Business Communicators offers an accreditation program for the manager or the person ready to move into communication management. The American Marketing Association is developing a certification program for marketing managers.

Persons interested in becoming marketing, advertising, and public relations managers should be mature, creative, highly motivated, resistant to stress, and flexible, yet decisive. The ability to communicate persuasively, both orally and in writing, with other managers, staff, and the public is vital. Marketing, advertising, and public relations managers also need tact, good judgment, and exceptional ability to establish and maintain effective personal relationships with supervisory and professional staff members and client firms.

Because of the importance and high visibility of their jobs, marketing, advertising, and public relations managers often are prime candidates for advancement. Well-trained, experienced, successful managers may be promoted to higher positions in their own or other firms. Some become top executives. Managers with extensive experience and sufficient capital may open their own businesses.

Job Outlook

Marketing, advertising, and public relations manager jobs are highly coveted and will be sought by other managers or highly experienced professional and technical personnel, resulting in substantial job competition. College graduates with extensive experience, a high level of creativity, and strong communication skills should have the best job opportunities. Those who have new media and interactive marketing skills will be particularly sought after.

Employment of marketing, advertising, and public relations managers is expected to increase faster than the average for all occupations through the year 2006. Increasingly intense domestic and global competition in products and services offered to consumers should require greater marketing, promotional, and public relations efforts by managers. Management and public relations firms may experience particularly rapid growth as businesses increasingly hire contractors for these services rather than support additional full-time staff.

Projected employment growth varies by industry. For example, employment of marketing, advertising, and public relations managers is expected to grow much faster than average in most business services industries, such as computer and data processing, and management and public relations firms, while average growth is projected in manufacturing industries overall. Many companies that eliminated in-house marketing and advertising departments during downsizing in recent years are now relying on firms which specialize in promotion, marketing, and advertising activities to provide these services.

Earnings

According to a National Association of Colleges and Employers survey, starting salaries for marketing majors graduating in 1997 averaged about $29,000; advertising majors, about $27,000.

The median annual salary of marketing, advertising, and public relations managers was $46,000 in 1996. The lowest 10 percent earned $23,000 or less, while the top 10 percent earned $97,000 or more. Many earn bonuses equal to 10 percent or more of their salaries. Surveys show that salary levels vary substantially depending upon the level of managerial responsibility, length of service, education, and the employer's size, location, and industry. For example, manufacturing firms generally pay marketing, advertising, and public relations managers higher salaries than nonmanufacturing firms. For sales managers, the size of their sales territory is another important determinant of salary.

According to a 1996 survey by *Advertising Age Magazine*, the average annual salary of a vice president brand manager was $79,000; vice president product manager, $105,000; vice president advertising, $130,000; and vice president marketing, $133,000.

According to a 1996 survey by the Public Relations Society of America, senior public relations managers earned an average of $76,790.

Related Occupations

Marketing, advertising, and public relations managers direct the sale of products and services offered by their firms and the communication of information about their firms' activities. Other personnel involved with marketing, advertising, and public relations include art directors, commercial and graphic artists, copy chiefs, copywriters, editors, lobbyists, marketing research analysts, public relations specialists, promotion specialists, sales representatives, and technical writers.

Sources of Additional Information

For information about careers in sales and marketing management, contact:
- ❑ American Marketing Association, 250 S. Wacker Dr., Chicago, IL 60606.
- ❑ Sales and Marketing Executives International, 458 Statler Office Tower, Cleveland, OH 44115.

For information about careers in advertising management, contact:
- ❑ American Advertising Federation, Education Services Department, 1101 Vermont Ave. NW, Suite 500, Washington, DC 20005.

Information about careers in promotion management is available from:
- ❑ Association of Promotion and Marketing Agencies Worldwide (APMA), 750 Summer St., Stamford, CT 06901.
- ❑ Promotion Marketing Association of America, Inc., 322 Eighth Ave., Suite 1201, New York, NY 10001.

Information about careers in public relations management is available from:
- ❑ Public Relations Society of America, 33 Irving Place, New York, NY 10003-2376.

Information on accreditation for business communicators is available from:
- ❑ International Association of Business Communicators, One Hallidie Plaza, Suite 600, San Francisco, CA 94102.

Material Moving Equipment Operators

(*D.O.T. codes are too numerous to list.*)

Significant Points

✓ *Most acquire their skills on the job, but some construction equipment operators complete formal apprenticeship programs.*

✓ *Employment is expected to grow slowly because jobs are concentrated in the manufacturing and construction industries.*

✓ *Workers in these occupations often have high pay rates, but many cannot work in inclement weather, thus reducing earnings.*

Nature of the Work

Material moving equipment operators use machinery to move construction materials, earth, petroleum products, coal, grain, manufactured goods, and other heavy materials. Generally, they move materials over short distances—around a construction site; factory; warehouse; or on or off trucks and ships. Operators control equipment by moving levers or foot pedals, operating switches, or turning dials. They may also set up and inspect equipment, make adjustments, and perform minor repairs.

Material moving equipment operators are classified by the type of equipment they operate. Each piece of equipment requires different skills to move the different types of loads.

Crane and tower operators lift materials, machinery, or other heavy objects from the ground. They extend or retract a horizontally mounted boom to lower, or raise a hook attached to the loadline, often in response to hand signals and radioed instructions. Operators position the loads from the on-board console or from a remote console at the site. While crane and tower operators are conspicuous at office building and other construction sites, the biggest group works in primary metal, metal fabrication, and transportation equipment manufacturing industries that use heavy, bulky materials as inputs.

Excavation and loading machine operators dig and load sand, gravel, earth, or similar materials into trucks or onto conveyors using machinery equipped with scoops, shovels, or buckets. Construction and mining industries employ virtually all excavation and loading machine operators.

Grader, dozer, and scraper operators gouge out, distribute, level, and grade earth with vehicles equipped with a concave blade attached across the front. In addition to the familiar bulldozers, they operate trench excavators, road graders, and similar equipment. Operators maneuver the equipment in successive passes to raise or lower terrain to a specific grade. They may uproot trees and move large rocks while preparing the surface. Although most work in the mining and construction industries, a significant number of grader, dozer, and scraper operators work for state and local governments.

Hoist and winch operators control movement of cables, cages and platforms to move workers and materials for construction, manufacturing, logging and other industrial operations. They also lube and maintain the drum and cables and make other minor repairs.

Industrial truck and tractor operators drive and control industrial trucks or tractors equipped with lifting devices, such as a forklift or boom, and trailer hitches. A typical industrial truck, often called a forklift or lift truck, has a hydraulic lifting mechanism and forks. Industrial truck operators use these to carry loads on a skid, or pallet, around a factory or warehouse. They also pull trailers loaded with materials, goods, or equipment within factories and warehouses, or around outdoor storage areas.

Operating engineers are unique in that they use several types of moving equipment discussed above. They also may operate and maintain compressors, pumps, and other power equipment at the worksite.

Other material moving equipment operators only tend air compressors or pumps at construction sites, or operate oil or natural gas pumps and compressors at wells and on pipelines. Still, some others operate ship loading and unloading equipment, conveyors, hoists, and other kinds of various specialized material handling equipment such as mine or railroad tank car unloading equipment.

Material moving equipment operators may keep records of materials moved, and do some manual loading and unloading. They also may clean, fuel, and service their equipment.

Working Conditions

Many material moving equipment operators work outdoors, in nearly every type of climate and weather condition. Industrial truck and tractor operators work mainly indoors, in warehouses or manufacturing plants. Some machines, particularly bulldozers and scrapers, are noisy and shake or jolt the operator. These jobs have become much safer with the adoption of overhead guards on forklift trucks and roll bars on construction machinery. As with most machinery, most accidents can be avoided when observing proper operating procedures and safety practices.

Employment

Material moving equipment operators held about 1,097,000 jobs in 1996. They were distributed among the detailed occupation groups as follows:

Industrial truck and tractor operators	479,000
Operating engineers	157,000
Grader, dozer, and scraper operators	107,000
Excavation and loading machine operators	97,000
Crane and tower operators	45,000
Hoist and winch operators	9,000
All other material moving equipment operators	202,000

The largest proportion–30 percent–of material moving equipment operators worked in manufacturing. Most of these were industrial truck and tractor operators or crane and tower operators; a little over 50 percent of both worked for manufacturing companies. Over 25 percent of all material moving equipment operators worked in mining and construction; these operators were mostly in the remaining occupations, nearly half of whom worked in these two industries. Significant numbers of industrial truck and tractor operators also worked in state and local governments and in the trucking and warehousing, and wholesale trade industries. State and local governments also employed a large proportion of grader, dozer, and scraper operators, and operating engineers. A few material moving equipment operators were self-employed.

Material moving equipment operators work in every section of the country. Some work in remote locations on large construction projects, such as highways and dams, or in factory or mining operations.

Training, Other Qualifications, and Advancement

Material moving equipment operators usually learn their skills on the job. Operators need a good sense of balance, the ability to judge distance, and good eye-hand-foot coordination. Employers of material moving equipment operators prefer high school graduates, although, some equipment may require less education to operate. Mechanical aptitude and high school training in automobile mechanics are helpful because workers may perform some maintenance on their machines. Experience operating mobile equipment, such as farm tractors or heavy equipment in the Armed Forces, is an asset.

Beginning material moving equipment operators handle light equipment under the guidance of an experienced operator. Later, they may operate heavier equipment such as bulldozers and cranes. Some construction equipment operators, however, train in formal three-year apprenticeship programs administered by union-management committees of the International Union of Operating Engineers and the Associated General Contractors of America. Because apprentices learn to operate a wider variety of machines than other beginners, they usually have better job opportunities. Apprenticeship programs consist of at least three years, or 6,000 hours of on-the-job training and 144 hours a year of related classroom instruction.

Private vocational schools offer instruction in the operation of certain types of construction equipment. Completion of such a program may help a person get a job as a trainee or apprentice. However, persons considering such training should check the reputation of the school among employers in the area.

Job Outlook

Employment of material moving equipment operators will increase about as fast as the average for all occupations through the year 2006. The expected growth stems from increased spending on improving the nation's infrastructure of highways, bridges, and dams. However, equipment improvements, including the growing automation of material handling in factories and warehouses, continue to raise productivity and moderate for demand skilled operators. In addition to employment growth in this large occupation, many jobs will open up because of the need to replace experienced workers who transfer to other occupations or leave the labor force.

Growth of employment among material moving equipment operators largely depends on the growth of the various industries that employ them. Construction and manufacturing employ the majority of these workers. Total employment in construction will grow more slowly than the average for all occupations, but employment of construction material moving equipment operators will grow as fast as the average. Employment of operators in manufacturing should decline in tandem with overall industry employment. However, very rapid employment growth of material moving operators is expected in temporary help organizations and companies that lease equipment

Growth of industrial truck and tractor operators, the largest occupation in this group, will be about as fast as the average for all occupations due to increased demand for operators who can maneuver multiple pieces of equipment. In addition, more operator jobs will result as large factories and warehouses consolidate material handling systems and require more operators. However, growth of industrial truck and tractor operators will be constrained by technological improvements. Some systems use computerized dispatching or onboard data communication devices to enable industrial truck and tractor operators to move goods more efficiently. In other handling systems, industrial trucks and tractors may be replaced by computer-controlled conveyor systems, overhead handling systems, or automated vehicles that do not require operators.

Precision computerized controls and robotics will automate crane and tower operator and hoist and winch operator positions, slowing employment growth. Slow employment growth in construction and declines in manufacturing should cause all other material moving equipment operating occupations to grow more slowly than the average for all occupations. In addition, both construction and manufacturing are very sensitive to changes in economic conditions, so the number of job openings for operators in these industries may fluctuate from year to year.

Earnings

Earnings for material moving equipment operators vary considerably. In 1996, median earnings of all material moving equipment operators were $456 a week; the middle 50 percent earned between $329 and $606. The lowest ten percent earn an average $264 a week and the highest ten percent averaged $806 a week. The following shows 1996 median weekly earnings among the detailed occupation groups:

Crane and tower operators	$551
Operating engineers	508
Grader, dozer, and scraper operators	490
Hoist and winch operators	490
Excavation and loading machine operators	485
Industrial truck and tractor operators	415
All other material moving equipment operators	451

Pay scales generally are higher in metropolitan areas. Annual earnings of some workers may be lower than weekly rates would indicate, because the amount of time they work may be limited by bad weather.

Related Occupations

Other workers who operate mechanical equipment include truck and bus drivers, manufacturing equipment operators, and farmers.

Sources of Additional Information

For further information about apprenticeships or work opportunities for construction equipment operators, contact a local of the International Union of Operating Engineers; a local apprenticeship committee; or the nearest office of the state apprenticeship agency. In addition, the local office of the state employment service may provide information about apprenticeship and other training programs.

For general information about the work of construction equipment operators, contact:

- ❑ National Center for Construction Education and Research, University of Florida, P.O. Box 141104, Gainsville, FL 32614-1104.
- ❑ Associated General Contractors of America, Inc., 1957 E St. NW, Washington, DC 20006.
- ❑ International Union of Operating Engineers, 1125 17th St. NW, Washington, DC 20036.
- ❑ Specialized Carriers and Rigging Association, 2750 Prosperity Ave., Suite 620, Fairfax, VA 22301.

Information on industrial truck and tractor operators is available from:

- ❑ Industrial Truck Association, 1750 K St. NW, Suite 460, Washington, DC 20006.

Material Recording, Scheduling, Dispatching, and Distributing Occupations

(*D.O.T. codes are too numerous to list.*)

Significant Points

- ✓ *Slower than average growth is expected as additional automation increases worker productivity.*
- ✓ *Many of the occupations in this group are entry-level and do not require more than a high school degree.*

Nature of the Work

Workers in this group are responsible for a variety of communications, record keeping, and scheduling operations in business and government. Typically, they coordinate, expedite, and track orders for personnel, materials, and equipment.

Dispatchers receive requests for service and initiate action to provide that service. Duties vary, depending on the needs of the employer. Police, fire, and ambulance dispatchers, also called public safety dispatchers, handle calls from people reporting crimes, fires, and medical emergencies; truck, bus, and train dispatchers schedule and coordinate the movement of these vehicles to ensure they arrive on schedule; taxicab dispatchers relay requests for cabs to individual drivers; tow truck dispatchers take calls for emergency road service; and utility company dispatchers handle calls related to utility and telephone service.

Stock clerks receive, unpack, and store materials and equipment, and issue and maintain inventories. Inventories may be merchandise in wholesale and retail establishments, or equipment, supplies, or materials in other kinds of organizations. In small firms, they may perform all of the above tasks, as well as those usually handled by shipping and receiving clerks. In large establishments, they may be responsible only for one task.

Traffic, shipping, and receiving clerks track all incoming and outgoing shipments of goods transferred between businesses, suppliers, and customers. Traffic clerks record destination, weight, and charge of all incoming and outgoing shipments. Shipping clerks assemble, address, stamp, and ship merchandise or materials. Receiving clerks unpack, verify, and record incoming merchandise. In a small company, one clerk may perform all of these tasks. More detail on these occupations is available in the following statements.

Other administrative support occupations in this group include production, planning, and expediting clerks—who coordinate and expedite the flow of work and material according to production schedules; procurement clerks—who draw up purchase orders to obtain merchandise or material; weighers, measurers, checkers, and samplers—who weigh, measure, and check materials; and utility meter readers—who read electric, gas, water, or steam meters and record the quantity used.

Working Conditions

Working conditions vary considerably by occupation and employment setting. Meter readers, for example, spend a good portion of their workday traveling around communities and neighborhoods taking readings, either directly or with remote reading equipment. The work of dispatchers can be very hectic when a large number of calls come in at the same time. The job of public safety dispatcher is particularly stressful, because slow or improper response to a call can result in serious injury or further harm. Also, callers who are anxious or afraid may become excited and be unable to provide needed information; some may become abusive. Despite provocations, dispatchers must remain calm, objective, and in control of the situation.

Dispatchers work in surroundings that are typical of office jobs. They sit for long periods, using telephones, computers, and two-way radios. Much of their time is spent at video display terminals, viewing monitors and observing traffic patterns. As a result of working for long stretches with computers and other electronic equipment, dispatchers can experience significant eyestrain and back discomfort. Generally, dispatchers work a 40-hour week; however, rotating shifts and compressed work schedules are common. Alternative work schedules are necessary to accommodate evening, weekend, and holiday work, as well as 24-hours-per-day, seven-days-per-week operations.

Traffic, shipping, receiving, and stock clerks work in a wide variety of businesses, institutions, and industries. Some work in warehouses, stock rooms, or in shipping and receiving rooms that may not be temperature controlled. Others may spend time in cold storage rooms or outside on loading platforms, where they are exposed to the weather. Most jobs involve frequent standing, bending, walking, and stretching. Some lifting and carrying of smaller items may be involved. Although automation, robotics, and pneumatic devices have lessened the physical demands in this occupation, their use remains somewhat limited. Work still can be strenuous, even though mechanical material-handling equipment is employed to move heavy items. The typical workweek is Monday through Friday; however, evening and weekend hours are standard for some jobs, such as stock clerks who work in retail trade, and may be required in others when large shipments are involved or when inventory is taken.

Employment

In 1996, material recording, scheduling, dispatching, and distributing workers held about 3,633,000 jobs. Employment was distributed among the occupations in this group as follows:

Total	3,633,000
Stock clerks	1,844,000
Traffic, shipping, and receiving clerks	759,000
Production, planning, and expediting clerks	239,000
Dispatchers	234,000
Order fillers, wholesale and retail sales	227,000
Procurement clerks	56,000
Meter readers, utilities	55,000
Weighers, measurers, checkers, and samplers	47,000
All other	170,000

Almost three out of four material recording, scheduling, dispatching, and distributing jobs were in manufacturing or wholesale and retail trade. Although these workers are found throughout the country, most work near population centers where retail stores, warehouses, factories, and large communications centers are concentrated.

Training, Other Qualifications, and Advancement

Many of the occupations in this group are entry-level, and do not require more than a high school degree. Employers, however, increasingly prefer to hire those with some familiarity with computers and other high technology office and business equipment. Those who have taken business courses or have previous business, dispatching, or specific job-related experience may be preferred. Also, good oral and written communications skills are becoming essential. This is true, in part, because the nature of the work is to communicate effectively with other people. Typing, filing, record keeping, and other clerical skills are important functions of these occupations. In larger, more automated facilities, these tasks may be accomplished electronically.

Traffic, shipping, and receiving clerks and stock clerks who handle jewelry, liquor, or drugs may be bonded. Police, fire, and ambulance dispatching jobs generally are governed by state or local government civil service regulations. Candidates for these positions may have to pass written, oral, and performance tests. Also, they may be asked to attend certification training classes and attain the proper certification in order to qualify for advancement.

Trainees usually develop the necessary skills on the job. This informal training lasts from several days to a few months, depending on the complexity of the job. Dispatchers usually require the most extensive training. Working with an experienced dispatcher, they monitor calls and learn how to operate a variety of communications equipment, including telephones, radios, and wireless appliances. As trainees gain confidence, they begin to handle calls themselves. Many public safety dispatchers also participate in structured training programs sponsored by their employer. Some employers offer a course designed by the Associated Public Safety Communications Officers (APCO). This course covers topics such as interpersonal communications; overview of the police, fire, and rescue functions; modern public safety telecommunications systems; basic radio broadcasting; local, state, and national crime information computer systems; and telephone complaint/report processing procedures. Other employers develop in-house programs based on their own needs. Emergency medical dispatchers often receive special training or have special skills. Increasingly, public safety dispatchers receive training in stress and crisis management, as well as family counseling. Employers are recognizing the toll this work has on daily living and the potential impact stress has on the job, on the work environment, and in the home.

Although there are no mandatory licensing or certification requirements, some states require that public safety dispatchers possess a certificate to work on a state network, such as the Police Information Network. Certification programs are offered by both APCO and the International Municipal Signal Association. Many dispatchers participate in these programs in order to improve their prospects for career advancement.

Stock clerks and traffic, shipping, and receiving clerks usually learn the job by doing simple tasks under close supervision. They learn how to count and mark stock, and then start keeping records and taking inventory. Stock clerks whose sole responsibility is to bring merchandise to the sales floor and stock shelves and racks need little or no training. Traffic, shipping, and receiving clerks start out by checking items to be shipped and then attaching labels and making sure the addresses are correct. Training in the use of automated equipment is usually done informally, on the job. As these occupations become more automated, however, workers in these jobs may need longer training in order to master the use of the equipment.

Communications skills and the ability to work under pressure are important personal qualities for dispatchers. Residency in the city or county of employment frequently is required for public safety dispatchers. Dispatchers in transportation industries must be able to deal with sudden influxes of shipments and disruptions of shipping schedules caused by bad weather, road construction, or accidents. Strength, stamina, good eyesight, and an ability to work at repetitive tasks, sometimes under pressure, are important characteristics for stock clerks and traffic, shipping, and receiving clerks.

Advancement opportunities vary with the place of employment. Dispatchers who work for private firms, which are usually small, will find few opportunities for advancement. Public safety dispatchers, on the other hand, may become a shift or divisional supervisor or chief of communications, or move to higher paying administrative jobs. Some go on to become police officers or firefighters. In large firms, stock clerks can advance to invoice clerk, stock control clerk, or procurement clerk. Traffic, shipping, and receiving clerks are promoted to head clerk, and those with a broad understanding of shipping and receiving may enter a related field such as industrial traffic management. With additional training, some stock clerks and traffic, shipping, and receiving clerks advance to jobs as warehouse manager or purchasing agent.

Job Outlook

Overall employment of material recording, scheduling, dispatching, and distributing workers is expected to grow more slowly than the average for all occupations through the year 2006. However, employment growth among the individual occupations in this group is expected to vary. Employment of stock clerks, for example, will be affected by increased automation. New technologies will enable clerks to handle more stock, thus holding down employment growth. The effect of automation also will tend to restrict potential employment

growth of employment of traffic, shipping, and receiving clerks. Automation in warehouses and stockrooms plus other productivity improvements will enable these clerks to handle materials more efficiently and more accurately than before. Employment of public safety dispatchers is expected to grow more slowly than the average as governments endeavor to combine dispatching services across governmental units and across governmental jurisdictions.

Because employment in material recording, scheduling, dispatching, and distributing occupations is substantial, workers who leave the labor force or transfer to other occupations are expected to create many job openings each year.

Earnings

Median weekly earnings of workers in all material recording, scheduling, dispatching, and distributing occupations were $412 in 1996. The middle 50 percent earned between $303 and $567. The lowest 10 percent earned $241 or less; the top 10 percent earned over $746.

Earnings vary somewhat by occupation and industry. Dispatchers earn slightly more than the average for these occupations, and stock clerks and traffic, shipping, and receiving clerks generally earn less. Median weekly earnings of dispatchers were $471 in 1996, whereas the median weekly earnings of traffic, shipping, and receiving clerks and stock clerks were $367 and $429, respectively, in 1996.

Workers in material recording, scheduling, dispatching, and distributing occupations usually receive the same benefits as most other workers. If uniforms are required, employers usually either provide the uniforms, or an allowance to purchase them.

Related Occupations

Other occupations that involve directing and controlling the movement of vehicles, freight, and personnel, as well as information and message distribution, are airline dispatchers, air traffic controllers, radio and television transmitter operators, telephone operators, customer service representatives, and transportation agents.

Sources of Additional Information

For further information on training for police, fire, and emergency dispatchers contact:

❑ National Academy of Emergency Medical Dispatch, 139 East South Temple, Suite 530, Salt Lake City, UT 84111.

❑ Associated Public Safety Communications Officers, 2040 S. Ridgewood, South Daytona, FL 32119-2257.

❑ International Municipal Signal Association, 165 East Union St., P.O. Box 539, Newark, NY 14513-1526.

❑ American Society for Testing and Materials, 100 Barr Harbor Drive, West Conshohocken, PA 19428.

For general information on dispatchers contact:

❑ Service Employees International Union, AFL-CIO; CLC, 1313 L St. NW, Washington, DC 20005-4100.

❑ American Train Dispatchers Association, 1370 Ontario St., Cleveland, OH 44113.

Information on job opportunities for police, fire, and emergency dispatchers is available from the personnel offices of state and local governments or police departments. Information about work opportunities for other types of dispatchers is available from local employers and state employment service offices.

Mechanical Engineers

(*D.O.T.* 007.061, .161-022, -034, and -038, and .267-010)

Significant Points

✓ *A bachelor's degree in mechanical engineering is almost always required for beginning jobs. Good employment opportunities are expected for new graduates.*

✓ *Starting salaries for mechanical engineers are significantly higher than those of bachelor's degree graduates in other fields.*

✓ *Knowledge of technological advances must be acquired through continued study and education.*

Nature of the Work

Mechanical engineers plan and design tools, engines, machines, and other mechanical equipment. They design and develop power-producing machines such as internal combustion engines, steam and gas turbines, and jet and rocket engines. They also design and develop power-using machines such as refrigeration and air-conditioning equipment, robots, machine tools, materials handling systems, and industrial production equipment.

The work of mechanical engineers varies by industry and function. Specialties include, among others, applied mechanics, design, energy systems, pressure vessels and piping, and heating, refrigeration, and air conditioning systems. Mechanical engineers design tools needed by other engineers for their work.

Mechanical engineering is the broadest engineering discipline, extending across many interdependent specialties. Mechanical engineers may work in production operations, maintenance, or technical sales; many are administrators or managers.

Working Conditions

Most mechanical engineers work in office buildings, laboratories, or industrial plants. engineers travel extensively to plants or worksites.

Most mechanical engineers work a standard 40-hour week. At times, deadlines or design standards may bring extra pressure to a job. When this happens, engineers may work long hours and experience considerable stress.

Employment

Mechanical engineers held about 228,000 jobs in 1996. Almost six out of ten jobs were in manufacturing–of these, most were in the machinery, transportation equipment, electrical equipment, instruments, and fabricated metal products industries. Business and engineering consulting services and federal government agencies provided most of the remaining jobs.

Training, Other Qualifications, and Advancement

A bachelor's degree in engineering is usually required for beginning engineering jobs. College graduates with a degree in a physical science or mathematics may occasionally qualify for some engineering jobs, especially in engineering specialties in high demand. Most engineering degrees are granted in electrical, mechanical, or civil engineering. However, engineers trained in one branch may work in related branches; for example, many aerospace engineers have training in mechanical engineering. This flexibility allows employers to meet staffing needs in new technologies and specialties in which engineers are in short supply. It also allows engineers to shift to fields with better employment prospects, or to ones that match their interests more closely.

In addition to the standard engineering degree, many colleges offer degrees in engineering technology, which are offered as either two- or four-year programs. These programs prepare students for practical design and production work rather than for jobs that require more theoretical, scientific and mathematical knowledge. Graduates of four-year technology programs may get jobs similar to those obtained by graduates with a bachelor's degree in engineering. Some employers regard them as having skills between those of a technician and an engineer.

Graduate training is essential for engineering faculty positions, but is not required for the majority of entry-level engineering jobs. Many engineers obtain graduate degrees in engineering or business administration to learn new technology, broaden their education, and enhance promotion opportunities. Many high-level executives in government and industry began their careers as engineers.

About 320 colleges and universities offer bachelor's degree programs in engineering that are accredited by the Accreditation Board for Engineering and Technology (ABET), and about 250 colleges offer accredited bachelor's degree programs in engineering technology. ABET accreditation is based on an examination of an engineering program's faculty, curricular content, facilities, and admissions standards. Although most institutions offer programs in the major branches of engineering, only a few offer some of the smaller specialties. Also, programs of the same title may vary in content. For example, some emphasize industrial practices, preparing students for a job in industry, while others are more theoretical and are better for students preparing to take graduate work. Therefore, students should investigate curricula and check accreditations carefully before selecting a college. Admissions requirements for undergraduate engineering schools include a solid background in mathematics (algebra, geometry, trigonometry, and calculus), sciences (biology, chemistry, and physics), and courses in English, social studies, humanities, and computers.

Bachelor's degree programs in engineering are typically designed to last four years, but many students find that it takes between four and five years to complete their studies. In a typical four-year college curriculum, the first two years are spent studying mathematics, basic sciences, introductory engineering, humanities, and social sciences. In the last two years, most courses are in engineering, usually with a concentration in one branch. For example, the last two years of an aerospace program might include courses such as fluid mechanics, heat transfer, applied aerodynamics, analytical mechanics, flight vehicle design, trajectory dynamics, and aerospace propulsion systems. Some programs offer a general engineering curriculum; students then specialize in graduate school or on the job.

Some engineering schools and two-year colleges have agreements whereby the two-year college provides the initial engineering education and the engineering school automatically admits students for their last two years. In addition, a few engineering schools have arrangements whereby a student spends three years in a liberal arts college studying pre-engineering subjects and two years in the engineering school, and receives a bachelor's degree from each. Some colleges and universities offer five-year master's degree programs. Some five- or even six-year cooperative plans combine classroom study and practical work, permitting students to gain valuable experience and finance part of their education.

All 50 states and the District of Columbia require registration for engineers whose work may affect life, health, or property, or who offer their services to the public. Registration generally requires a degree from an ABET-accredited engineering program, four years of relevant work experience, and passing a state examination. Some states will not register people with degrees in engineering technology. Engineers may be registered in several states.

Engineers should be creative, inquisitive, analytical, and detail-oriented. They should be able to work as part of a team and be able to communicate well, both orally and in writing.

Beginning engineering graduates usually work under the supervision of experienced engineers and, in larger companies, may also receive formal classroom or seminar-type training. As they gain knowledge and experience, they are assigned more difficult projects with greater independence to develop designs, solve problems, and make decisions. Engineers may advance to become technical specialists or to supervise a staff or team of engineers and technicians. Some eventually become engineering managers or enter other managerial, management support, or sales jobs.

Job Outlook

Employment of mechanical engineers is expected to grow about as fast as the average for all occupations through the year 2006. Graduates of mechanical engineering programs should have favorable job opportunities. Most of the expected job openings, resulting from both employment growth and the need to replace those who will leave the occupation, should be sufficient to absorb the supply of new graduates and other entrants.

Although overall employment in manufacturing is expected to decline, employment of mechanical engineers in manufacturing should increase as the demand for improved machinery and machine tools grows and industrial machinery and processes become increasingly complex. Employment of mechanical engineers in business and engineering services firms is expected to grow faster than average as other industries in the economy increasingly contract out to these firms to solve engineering problems.

Earnings

Starting salaries for mechanical engineers with the bachelor's degree are significantly higher than starting salaries of bachelor's degree graduates in other fields. According to the National Association of Colleges and Employers, starting salaries for those with the bachelor's degree were about $38,113 in 1996.

The median annual salary for all mechanical engineers who worked full-time was in 1996 was $49,700.

The average annual salary for engineers in the federal government in nonsupervisory, supervisory, and managerial positions was $61,950 in 1997.

Related Occupations

Mechanical engineers apply the principles of physical science and mathematics in their work. Other workers who use scientific and mathematical principles include engineering, science, and computer systems managers; physical, life, and computer scientists; mathematicians; engineering and science technicians; and architects.

Sources of Additional Information

High school students interested in obtaining general information on a variety of engineering disciplines should contact the Junior Engineering Technical Society by sending a self-addressed business-size envelope with six first-class stamps affixed, to:

❑ JETS-Guidance, at 1420 King St., Suite 405, Alexandria, VA 22314-2794. Homepage: http://www.asee.org/jets

High school students interested in obtaining information on ABET accredited engineering programs should contact:

❑ The Accreditation Board for Engineering and Technology, Inc., at 111 Market Place, Suite 1050, Baltimore, MD 21202-4012. Homepage: http://www.abet.ba.md.us

Non-high school students and those wanting more detailed information should contact:

❑ The American Society of Mechanical Engineers, 345 E. 47th St., New York, NY 10017.

❑ American Society of Heating, Refrigerating, and Air-Conditioning Engineers, Inc., 1791 Tullie Circle NE., Atlanta, GA 30329. Homepage://www.ashrae.org

Medical Assistants

(*D.O.T.* 078.361-038; 079.362-010, .364-010 and -014, and .374-018; and 355.667-010)

Significant Points

✓ *Medical assistants is expected to be one of the ten fastest growing occupations through the year 2006.*

✓ *Job prospects should be best for medical assistants with formal training or experience.*

Nature of the Work

Medical assistants perform routine administrative and clinical tasks to keep the offices and clinics of physicians, podiatrists, chiropractors, and optometrists running smoothly. Medical assistants should not be confused with physician assistants who examine, diagnose, and treat patients, under the direct supervision of a physician.

The duties of medical assistants vary from office to office, depending on office location, size, and specialty. In small practices, medical assistants are usually "generalists," handling both administrative and clinical duties and reporting directly to an office manager, physician, or other health practitioner. Those in large practices tend to specialize in a particular area under the supervision of department administrators.

Medical assistants perform many administrative duties. They answer telephones, greet patients, update and file patient medical records, fill out insurance forms, handle correspondence, schedule appointments, arrange for hospital admission and laboratory services, and handle billing and bookkeeping.

Clinical duties vary according to state law and include taking medical histories and recording vital signs, explaining treatment procedures to patients, preparing patients for examination, and assisting the physician during the examination. Medical assistants collect and prepare laboratory specimens or perform basic laboratory tests on the premises, dispose of contaminated supplies, and sterilize medical instruments. They instruct patients about medication and special diets, prepare and administer medications as directed by a physician, authorize drug refills as directed, telephone prescriptions to a pharmacy, draw blood, prepare patients for x rays, take electrocardiograms, remove sutures, and change dressings.

Medical assistants may also arrange examining room instruments and equipment, purchase and maintain supplies and equipment, and keep waiting and examining rooms neat and clean.

Assistants who specialize have additional duties. Podiatric medical assistants make castings of feet, expose and develop x rays, and assist podiatrists in surgery. Ophthalmic medical assistants help ophthalmologists provide medical eye care. They administer diagnostic tests, measure and record vision, and test the functioning of eyes and eye muscles. They also show patients how to use eye dressings, protective shields, and safety glasses, and how to insert, remove, and care for contact lenses. Under the direction of the physician, they may administer medications, including eye drops. They also maintain optical and surgical instruments and assist the ophthalmologist in surgery.

Working Conditions

Medical assistants work in well-lighted, clean environments. They constantly interact with other people, and may have to handle several responsibilities at once.

Most full-time medical assistants work a regular 40-hour week. Some work part-time, evenings or weekends.

Employment

Medical assistants held about 225,000 jobs in 1996. Seven in ten jobs were in physicians' offices, and over one in ten were in offices of other health practitioners such as chiropractors, optometrists, and podiatrists. The rest were in hospitals, nursing homes, and other health care facilities.

Training, Other Qualifications, and Advancement

Most employers prefer to hire graduates of formal programs in medical assisting. Formal programs in medical assisting are offered in vocational-technical high schools, postsecondary vocational schools, community and junior colleges, and in colleges and universities. Postsecondary programs usually last either one year, resulting in a certificate or diploma, or two years, resulting in an associate degree. Courses cover anatomy, physiology, and medical terminology as well as typing, transcription, record keeping, accounting, and insurance processing. Students learn laboratory techniques, clinical and diagnostic procedures, pharmaceutical principles, medication administration, and first aid. They study office practices, patient relations, medical law, and ethics. Accredited programs include an internship that provides practical experience in physicians' offices, hospitals, or other health care facilities.

Although formal training in medical assisting is available, such training(while generally preferred(is not always required. Some medical assistants are trained on the job, although this is less common than in the past. Applicants usually need a high school diploma or the equivalent. Recommended high school courses include mathematics, health, biology, typing, bookkeeping, computers, and office skills. Volunteer experience in the health care field is also helpful.

Two agencies recognized by the U.S. Department of Education accredit programs in medical assisting: the Commission on Accreditation of Allied Health Education Programs (CAAHEP) and the Accrediting Bureau of Health Education Schools (ABHES). In 1997, there were about 350 medical assisting programs accredited by CAAHEP and over 150 accredited by ABHES. The Committee on Accreditation for Ophthalmic Medical Personnel accredited 18 programs in ophthalmic medical assisting.

Although there is no licensing for medical assistants, some states require them to take a test or a short course before they can take x rays or perform other specific clinical tasks. Employers prefer to hire experienced workers or certified applicants who have passed a national examination, indicating that the medical assistant meets certain standards of competence. The American Association of Medical Assistants awards the Certified Medical Assistant credential; the American Medical Technologists awards the Registered Medical Assistant credential; the American Society of Podiatric Medical Assistants awards the Podiatric Medical Assistant Certified credential; and the Joint Commission on Allied Health Personnel in Ophthalmology awards the Ophthalmic Medical Assistant credential at three levels: Certified Ophthalmic Assistant, Certified Ophthalmic Technician, and Certified Ophthalmic Medical Technologist.

Because medical assistants deal with the public, they must be neat and well-groomed and have a courteous, pleasant manner. Medical assistants must be able to put patients at ease and explain physicians' instructions. They must respect the confidential nature of medical information. Clinical duties require a reasonable level of manual dexterity and visual acuity.

Medical assistants may be able to advance to office manager. They may qualify for a wide variety of administrative support occupations, or may teach medical assisting. Some, with additional education, enter other health occupations such as nursing and medical technology.

Job Outlook

Employment of medical assistants is expected to grow much faster than the average for all occupations through the year 2006 as the health services industry expands due to technological advances in medicine, and a growing and aging population. It is one of the fastest growing occupations.

Employment growth will be driven by the increase in the number of group practices, clinics, and other health care facilities that need a high proportion of support personnel, particularly the flexible medical assistant who can handle both administrative and clinical duties. Medical assistants primarily work in outpatient settings, where much faster than average growth is expected.

In view of the preference of many health care employers for trained personnel, job prospects should be best for medical assistants with formal training or experience, particularly those with certification.

Earnings

The earnings of medical assistants vary widely, depending on experience, skill level, and location. According to the 1997 Staff Salary Survey published by the Health Care Group(, average hourly wages for medical assistants with less than two years of experience ranged from $8.07 to $10.90 in 1996. Average hourly wages for medical assistants with more than five years of experience ranged from $10.38 to $13.46. Wages were higher in the Northeast and West and lower in the Midwest and South.

Related Occupations

Workers in other medical support occupations include medical secretaries, hospital admitting clerks, pharmacy helpers, medical record clerks, dental assistants, occupational therapy aides, and physical therapy aides.

Sources of Additional Information

Information about career opportunities, CAAHEP-accredited educational programs in medical assisting, and the Certified Medical Assistant exam is available from:

❑ The American Association of Medical Assistants, 20 North Wacker Dr., Suite 1575, Chicago, IL 60606-2903.

Information about career opportunities and the Registered Medical Assistant certification exam is available from:

❑ Registered Medical Assistants of American Medical Technologists, 710 Higgins Rd., Park Ridge, IL 60068-5765.

For a list of ABHES-accredited educational programs in medical assisting, write:

❑ Accrediting Bureau of Health Education Schools, 2700 South Quincy St., Suite 210, Arlington, VA 22206.

For information about a career as a medical assistant and schools offering training, contact:

❑ National Association of Health Career Schools, 750 First St. NE, Suite 940, Washington, DC 20002. FAX: (202) 842-1565 E-mail: NAHCS@aol.com

Information about career opportunities, training programs, and the Certified Ophthalmic Assistant exam is available from:

❑ Joint Commission on Allied Health Personnel in Ophthalmology, 2025 Woodlane Dr., St. Paul, MN 55125-2995.

Information about careers for podiatric assistants is available from:

❑ American Society of Podiatric Medical Assistants, 2124 S. Austin Blvd., Cicero, IL 60650.

Metalworking and Plastics-Working Machine Operators

(D.O.T. codes are too numerous to list.)

Significant Points

✓ *A few weeks of on-the-job training is sufficient for most workers to learn basic machine operations, but several years are required to become a skilled operator.*

✓ *Projected employment change in the occupation varies. Employment of most manual cutting and forming machine tool operators, and sheet metal workers, is expected to decline. Operators of automated machines will grow.*

Nature of the Work

Consider the parts of a toaster, such as the metal or plastic housing or the lever that lowers the toast. These parts, and many other metal and plastic products, are produced by metalworking and plastics-working machine operators. In fact, machine tool operators in the metalworking and plastics industries play a major part in producing most of the consumer products on which we rely daily.

In general, these workers can be separated into two groups—those who set up machines for operation and those who tend the machines during production. Set-up workers prepare the machines prior to production and may adjust the machinery during operation. Operators and tenders, on the other hand, primarily monitor the machinery during operation, sometimes loading or unloading the machine or making minor adjustments to the controls. Many workers do both—set up and operate the equipment. Because the set-up process requires an understanding of the entire production process, setters usually have more training and are more highly skilled than those who simply operate or tend machinery. As new automation simplifies the setup process, however, less skilled workers are also increasingly able to set up machines for operation.

Setters, operators, tenders, and set-up operators are usually identified by the type of machine with which they work. Some examples of specific titles are screw machine operator, plastics-molding machine set-up operator, punch press operator, and lathe tender. Although some workers specialize in one or two types of machinery, many are trained to set up or operate a variety of machines. Job duties usually vary based on the size of the firm and on the type of machine being operated.

Metalworking machine setters and operators set up and tend machines that cut and form all types of metal parts. Traditionally, set-up workers plan and set up the sequence of operations according to blueprints, layouts, or other instructions. They adjust speed, feed, and other controls, choose the proper coolants and lubricants, and select the instruments or tools for each operation. Using micrometers, gauges, and other precision measuring instruments, they may also compare the completed work with the tolerance limits stated in the specifications.

Although there are many different types of metalworking machine tools that require specific knowledge and skills, most operators perform similar tasks. Whether tending grinding machines that remove excess material from the surface of machined products or presses that extrude metal through a die to form wire, operators usually perform simple, repetitive operations that can be learned quickly. Typically, these workers place metal stock in a machine on which the operating specifications have already been set. They may watch one or more machines and make minor adjustments according to their instructions. Regardless of the type of machine they operate, machine tenders usually depend on skilled set-up workers for major adjustments when the machines are not functioning properly.

Plastics-working machine operators set up and tend machines that transform plastic compounds—chemical-based products that can be produced in powder, pellet, or syrup form—into a wide variety of consumer goods such as toys, tubing, and auto parts. These products are produced by various methods, of which injection molding is the most common. The injection molding machine heats a plastic compound and forces it into a mold. After the part has cooled and hardened, the mold opens and the part is released. Many common kitchen products are produced using this method. To produce long parts such as pipes or window frames, an extruding machine is usually employed. These machines force a plastic compound through a die that contains an opening of the desired shape of the final product. Yet another type of plastics working technique is blow molding. Blow-molding machines force hot air into a mold which contains a plastic tube. As the air moves into the mold, the plastic tube is inflated to the shape of the mold and a plastic container is formed. The familiar two-liter soft drink bottles are produced using this method.

Regardless of the process used, plastics-working machine operators check the materials feed, the temperature and pressure of the machine, and the rate at which the product hardens. Depending on the type of equipment in use, they may also load material into the machine, make minor adjustments to the machinery, or unload and inspect the finished products. Plastics-working machine operators also remove clogged material from molds or dies. Because molds and dies are quite costly, operators must exercise care to avoid damaging them.

Metalworking and plastics-working machine operators are increasingly being called upon to work with numerically controlled (NC) equipment. These machine tools have two major components—an electronic controller and a machine tool. Today, most NC machines are computer numerically controlled (CNC), which means that the controllers are computers. The controller directs the mechanisms of the machine tool through the positioning and machining described in the program or instructions for the job. A program could contain, for example, commands that cause the controller to move a drill bit to certain spots on a workpiece and drill a hole at each spot.

Each type of CNC machine tool, such as a milling machine, a lathe, or a punch press, performs a specific task. A part may be worked on by several machines before it is finished. CNC machines are often used in computer-integrated manufacturing systems. In these systems, automated material handling equipment moves workpieces through a series of work stations where machining processes are computer numerically controlled. In some cases, the workpiece is stationary and the tools change automatically. Although the machining is done automatically, numerically controlled machine tools must be set up and used properly in order to obtain the maximum benefit from their use. These tasks are the responsibility of NC machine-tool operators or, in some instances, machinists.

Like the duties of manual metal and plastics machine operators, the duties of numerical-control machine-tool operators vary. In some shops, operators tend just one machine. More likely, however, they tend a number of machines or do some programming. As a result, the skill requirements of these workers vary from job to job. Although there are many variations in operators' duties, they generally involve many of the tasks described below.

Working from given instructions, operators load programs that are usually stored on disks into the controller. They also securely position the workpiece, attach the necessary tools, and check the coolants and lubricants. Many NC machines are equipped with automatic tool changers, so operators may also load several tools in the proper sequence. This entire process may require a few minutes or several hours, depending on the size of the workpiece and the complexity of the job.

A new program often must be adjusted to obtain the desired results. If the tool moves to the wrong position or makes a cut that is too deep, the program must be changed so the job is done properly. A machinist or tool programmer usually performs this function, occasionally with the assistance of a computer automated design program that simulates the operation of machine tools. However, a new generation of machine tool technology, known as direct numerical control, allows operators to make changes to the program and enter new specifications using minicomputers on the shop floor.

Because NC machine tools are very expensive, an important duty of operators is to monitor the machinery to prevent situations that could result in costly damage to the cutting tools or other parts. The extent to which the operator performs this function depends on the type of job as well as the type of equipment being used. Some NC machine tools automatically monitor and adjust machining operations. When the job has been properly set up and the program has been checked, the operator may only need to monitor the machine as it operates. These operators often set up and monitor more than one machine. Other jobs require frequent loading and unloading, tool changing, or programming. Operators may check the finished part using micrometers, gauges, or other precision inspection equipment to ensure that it meets specifications. Increasingly, however, this function is being performed by NC machine tools that are able to inspect products as they are produced.

CNC machines are changing the nature of the work that machine setters and operators perform. Computer-controlled machines simplify setups by using formerly tested computer programs for new workpieces. If a workpiece is similar to one previously produced, small adjustments can be made to the old program instead of developing a new program from scratch. Also, operators of this equipment have less physical interaction with the machinery or materials. They primarily act as troubleshooters, monitoring machines on which the loading, forming, and unloading processes are often controlled by computers.

Working Conditions

Most metalworking and plastics-working machine operators work in areas that are clean, well lit, and well ventilated. Regardless of setting, all of these workers operate powerful, high-speed machines that can be dangerous if strict safety rules are not observed. Most operators wear protective equipment, such as safety glasses and earplugs to protect against flying particles of metal or plastic and noise from the machines. Other required equipment varies by work setting and machine. For example, workers in the plastics industry who work near materials that emit dangerous fumes or dust must wear face masks or self-contained breathing apparatuses.

Most metal and plastics-working machine operators work a 40-hour week, but overtime is common during periods of increased production. Because many metalworking and plastics-working shops operate more than one shift daily, some operators work nights and weekends.

The work requires stamina because operators are on their feet much of the day and may do moderately heavy lifting. Approximately one-third of these workers are union members; the metalworking industries have a higher rate of unionization than the plastics industry.

Employment

Metalworking and plastics-working machine operators held about 1,512,000 jobs in 1996. Of these, 1,420,000 were manual machine operators, and 92,000 were NC machine operators. About eight out of every ten metalworking and plastics-working machine operators are found in five manufacturing industries—fabricated metal products, industrial machinery and equipment, miscellaneous plastic products, transportation equipment, and primary metals. The following tabulation shows the distribution of employment of metalworking and plastics-working machine operators by detailed occupation.

Cutting and forming machine tool setters and operators	723,000
Molding machine setters and operators	228,000
Sheet metal workers and duct installers	120,000
Combination machine tool setters and operators	96,000
Numerical control machine operators	92,000
Metal fabricators, structural metal products	46,000
Plating machine setters and operators	42,000
Heat treating machine setters and operators	21,000
All other metal and plastics-working machine operators	144,000

Training, Other Qualifications, and Advancement

Metalworking and plastics-working machine operators learn their skills on the job. Trainees begin by observing and assisting experienced workers, often in formal training programs. Under supervision they may supply material, start and stop the machine, or remove finished products from the machine. As part of their training they advance to more difficult tasks like adjusting feed speeds, changing cutting tools, or inspecting a finished product for defects. Eventually they become responsible for their own machines.

The complexity of equipment largely determines the time required to become an operator. Most operators learn the basic machine operations and functions in a few weeks, but they may need several years to become a skilled operator or to advance to the more highly skilled job of set-up operator.

Set-up operators often need a thorough knowledge of the machinery and of the products being produced. They may study blueprints, plan the sequence of work, make the first production run, and determine which adjustments need to be made. Strong analytical abilities are particularly important to perform this job. Some companies have formal training programs for set-up operators that combine classroom instruction with on-the-job training.

CNC machine tool operators undergo similar training. Working under a supervisor or an experienced operator, trainees learn to set up and run one or more types of numerically controlled machine tools. They usually learn the basics of their jobs within a few months. However, the length of the training period varies with the number and complexity of the machine tools the operator will run and with the individual's ability. If the employer expects operators to write programs, trainees may attend programming courses offered by machine tool manufacturers or technical schools.

Although no special education is required for most operating jobs, employers prefer to hire applicants with good basic skills. Many require employees to have a high school education and to read, write, and speak English. This is especially true for NC machine operators, who may need to be retrained often in order to learn to operate new equipment. Because machinery is becoming more complex and shop floor organization is changing, employers increasingly look for persons with good communication and interpersonal skills. Mechanical aptitude, manual dexterity, and experience working with machinery are also helpful. Those interested in becoming metalworking or plastics-working machine operators can improve their employment opportunities by completing high school courses in shop, mathematics, and blueprint reading and by gaining a working knowledge of the properties of metals and plastics.

Advancement for operators usually takes the form of higher pay, although there are some limited opportunities for operators to advance to new positions as well. For example, they can become multiple machine operators, set-up operators, or trainees for the more highly skilled positions of machinist or tool and die maker. Manual machine operators can move on to CNC equipment when it is introduced in their establishments. Some set-up workers and CNC operators may advance to supervisory positions. CNC operators who have substantial training in NC programming may advance to the higher-paying job of tool programmer.

Job Outlook

Divergent employment trends are expected over the 1996-2006 period among the various metalworking and plastics-working machine operators. In general, employment of these workers will be affected by the rate of technological implementation, the demand for the goods they produce, the effects of trade, and the reorganization of production processes. These trends are expected to spur employment growth among NC machine operators, combination machine tool operators, plastics molding machine operators, and a number of miscellaneous operating positions. On the other hand, employment is projected to decline in some of the more traditional operator occupations, such as manual cutting and forming machine tool operators, and sheet metal workers. Despite differing rates of employment change, a large number of metalworking and plastics-working machine operator jobs will become available as workers transfer to other occupations or leave the labor force.

One of the most important factors influencing employment change in this occupation is the implementation of labor-saving machinery. In order to remain competitive, many firms are adopting new technologies, such as computer-controlled machine tools, to improve quality and lower production costs. Computer-controlled equipment allows operators to simultaneously tend a greater number of machines and often makes setup easier, thereby reducing the amount of time set-up workers spend on each machine. For these reasons, the lower-skilled positions of manual machine tool operators and tenders are more likely to be eliminated by this new technology because the functions they perform are more easily automated. The spread of new automation will lead to rising employment, however, for NC machine tool operators.

The demand for metalworking and plastics-working machine operators largely mirrors the demand for the parts they produce. Recent growth in the domestic economy, for example, has led to rebounding employment in a number of machine tool operating occupations. In addition, the consumption of plastic products has grown as they have been substituted for metal goods in many consumer and manufacturing products in recent years. Although the rate of substitution may slow in the future, this process is likely to continue and should result in stronger demand for machine operators in plastics than in metalworking. Both industries, however, face stiff foreign competition that is limiting the demand for domestically-produced parts. One way that larger U.S. producers have responded to this competition is by moving production operations to other countries where labor costs are lower. These moves are likely to continue and will further reduce employment opportunities for many metalworking and plastics-working machine tool operators in the United States.

Workers with a thorough background in machine operations, exposure to a variety of machines, and a good working knowledge of the properties of metals and plastics will be best able to adjust to this changing environment. In addition, new shop floor arrangements will reward workers with good basic mathematics and reading skills, good communication skills, and the ability and willingness to learn new tasks. As workers are called upon to adapt to new production methods and to operate more machines, the number of combination machine tool operators will continue to rise.

Earnings

Median weekly earnings for most metalworking and plastics-working machine operators were about $440 in 1996. The middle 50 percent earned between $320 and $600. The top 10 percent earned over $770 and the bottom 10 percent earned less than $250. Metal and plastics molding, plating, heat-treating, and other processing machine operators earned somewhat less, about $400 a week. NC machine operators had median weekly earnings of about $520, more than either of these groups.

Earnings of production workers vary considerably by industry. The following tabulation shows 1996 average weekly wages for production workers in manufacturing industries where employment of metalworking and plastics-working machine operators is concentrated.

Transportation equipment	$760
Primary metals industries	660
Industrial machinery and equipment	590
Fabricated metal products	530
Rubber and miscellaneous plastics products	470

Related Occupations

Workers in occupations closely related to metalworking and plastics-working machine occupations include machinists, tool and die makers, extruding and forming machine operators producing synthetic fibers, woodworking machine operators, and metal patternmakers. Numerical-control machine-tool operators may program CNC machines or alter existing programs, which are functions closely related to those performed by NC machine tool programmers.

Sources of Additional Information

For general information about the metalworking trades, contact:

- ❑ The National Tooling and Machining Association, 9300 Livingston Rd., Fort Washington, MD 20744.
- ❑ The Precision Machined Products Association, 6700 West Snowville Rd., Brecksville, OH 44141.

Musicians

(*D.O.T.* 152 except .021)

Significant Points

- ✓ *Musicians often must supplement their income with earnings from other sources because they can find only part-time or sporadic engagements.*
- ✓ *Aspiring musicians begin studying an instrument or training their voices at an early age; a bachelor's or higher degree in music or music education is required to teach at the elementary/secondary school or college level.*
- ✓ *Competition for jobs is keen because the glamour and potentially high earnings in this occupation attract many talented individuals.*

Nature of the Work

Musicians may play musical instruments, sing, compose, arrange, or conduct groups in instrumental or vocal performances. Musicians may perform alone or as part of a group, before live audiences or on radio, or in recording studios, television, or movie productions. While most musicians play for live audiences, some prepare music exclusively for studios or computers.

Some specialize in a particular kind of music or performance. Instrumental musicians play a musical instrument in an orchestra, band, rock group, or jazz group. Some play any of a wide variety of string, brass, woodwind, or percussion instruments or electronic synthesizers; others learn several related instruments, such as the flute and clarinet, often improving their employment opportunities.

Singers interpret music using their knowledge of voice production, melody, and harmony. They sing character parts or perform in their own individual style. Singers are often classified according to their voice range–soprano, contralto, tenor, baritone, or bass–or by the type of music they sing, such as opera, rock, reggae, folk, rap, or country and western.

Composers create original music such as symphonies, operas, sonatas, or popular songs. They transcribe ideas into musical notation using harmony, rhythm, melody, and tonal structure. Many songwriters now compose and edit music using computers. Also, they may play the composition into the computer, which can record and play it back.

Arrangers transcribe and adapt musical composition to a particular style for orchestras, bands, choral groups, or individuals. Components of music–including tempo, volume, and the mix of instruments needed–are arranged to express the composer's message. While some arrangers write directly into a musical composition, others use computer software to make changes. Compositions created with computer software can also be mailed electronically or placed on an Internet site.

Conductors lead instrumental music groups, such as orchestras, dance bands, and various popular ensembles. Conductors audition and select musicians, choose the music to accommodate the talents and abilities of the musicians, and direct rehearsals and performances, applying conducting techniques to achieve desired musical effects.

Choral directors lead choirs and glee clubs, sometimes working with a band or orchestra conductor. Directors audition and select singers and direct them at rehearsals and performances to achieve harmony, rhythm, tempo, shading, and other desired musical effects.

All musicians spend a considerable amount of time practicing, individually and with their band, orchestra, or other musical group.

Working Conditions

Musicians often perform at night and on weekends and spend considerable time in practice and rehearsal. Performances frequently require travel. Because many musicians find only part-time work or experience unemployment between engagements, they often supplement their income with other types of jobs. In fact, many decide they cannot support themselves as musicians and take permanent, full-time jobs in other occupations, while working only part-time as musicians.

Most instrumental musicians come into contact with a variety of other people, including their colleagues, agents, employers, sponsors, and audiences. They usually work indoors, although some may perform outdoors for parades, concerts, and dances. Certain performances create noise and vibration. In some taverns and restaurants, smoke and odors may be present, and lighting and ventilation may be inadequate.

Employment

An average of about 274,000 musicians held jobs in 1996. Many were between engagements, so that the total number of people employed as musicians during the course of the year might have been greater. Many musicians were self-employed, and nearly three out of five musicians employed in 1996 worked part-time.

Many work in cities in which entertainment and recording activities are concentrated, such as New York, Los Angeles, and Nashville. Classical musicians may perform with professional orchestras or in small chamber music groups like quartets or trios. Musicians may work in opera, musical comedy, and ballet productions. Many are organists who play in churches and synagogues—two out of three musicians who are paid a wage or salary work in religious organizations. Musicians also perform in clubs and restaurants, and for weddings and other events. Well-known musicians and groups give their own concerts, appear live on radio and television, make recordings and music videos, or go on concert tours. The Armed Forces, too, offer careers in their bands and smaller musical groups.

Training, Other Qualifications, and Advancement

Aspiring musicians begin studying an instrument at an early age. They may gain valuable experience playing in a school or community band or orchestra, or with a group of friends. Singers usually start training when their voices mature. Participation in school musicals or in a choir often provides good early training and experience. Musicians need extensive and prolonged training to acquire the necessary skill, knowledge, and ability to interpret music. This training may be obtained through private study with an accomplished musician, in a college or university music program, in a music conservatory, or through practice with a group. For study in an institution, an audition frequently is necessary. Formal courses include musical theory, music interpretation, composition, conducting, and instrumental and voice instruction. Composers, conductors, and arrangers need advanced training in these subjects as well.

Many colleges, universities, and music conservatories grant bachelor's or higher degrees in music. A master's or doctoral degree is usually required to teach advanced courses in music in colleges and universities; a bachelor's degree may be sufficient to teach basic courses. A degree in music education qualifies graduates for a state certificate to teach music in an elementary or secondary school.

Those who perform popular music must have an understanding of and feeling for the style of music that interests them, but classical training can expand their employment opportunities, as well as their musical abilities. Although voice training is an asset for singers of popular music, many with untrained voices have successful careers. As a rule, musicians take lessons with private teachers when young, and seize every opportunity to make amateur or professional appearances.

Young persons who are considering careers in music should have musical talent, versatility, creative ability, and poise and stage presence to face large audiences. Since quality performance requires constant study and practice, self-discipline is vital. Moreover, musicians who play concert and nightclub engagements must have physical stamina because frequent travel and night performances are required. They must also be prepared to face the anxiety of intermittent employment and rejections when auditioning for work.

Advancement for musicians generally means becoming better known and performing for greater earnings with better known bands and orchestras. Successful musicians often rely on agents or managers to find them performing engagements, negotiate contracts, and plan their careers.

Job Outlook

Competition for musician jobs is keen, and talent alone is no guarantee of success. The glamour and potentially high earnings in this occupation attract many talented individuals. The ability to play several instruments and types of music enhances a musician's employment prospects.

Overall employment of musicians is expected to grow faster than the average for all occupations through the year 2006, reflecting the growing popularity of this form of entertainment. Almost all new wage and salary jobs for musicians will arise in religious organizations, bands, orchestras, and other entertainment groups. A decline in employment is projected for salaried musicians in restaurants and bars, although they comprise a very small proportion of all wage and salary musicians. Bars, which regularly employ musicians, are expected to grow more slowly than eating establishments, where live entertainment is unusual, because consumption of alcoholic beverages outside the home is expected to continue to decline. Overall, most job openings for musicians will arise from the need to replace those who leave the field each year because they are unable to make a living solely as musicians.

Earnings

Earnings often depend on a performer's professional reputation, place of employment, and on the number of hours worked. The most successful musicians can earn far more than the minimum salaries indicated below.

According to the American Federation of Musicians, minimum salaries in major orchestras ranged from about $22,000 to $90,000 per year during the 1996-97 performing season. Each orchestra works out a separate contract with its local union. Top orchestras have a season ranging from 29 to 52 weeks, with most major orchestras working 52 weeks. In regional orchestras, minimum salaries are between $8,000 and $22,000 per year; the season lasts 7 to 48 weeks, with an average of 35 weeks. In contrast, community orchestras have more limited levels of funding and offer salaries that are much lower for seasons of shorter duration.

Musicians employed in motion picture or television recording and those employed by recording companies were paid a minimum ranging from about $120 to $250 per service (three hours of work) in 1996.

Musicians employed by some symphony orchestras work under master wage agreements, which guarantee a season's work up to 52 weeks. Many other musicians may face relatively long periods of unemployment between jobs. Even when employed, however, many work part-time. Thus, their earnings generally are lower than those in many other occupations. Moreover, since they may not work steadily for one employer, some performers cannot qualify for unemployment compensation, and few have typical benefits such as sick leave or vacations with pay. For these reasons, many musicians give private lessons or take jobs unrelated to music to supplement their earnings as performers.

Many musicians belong to a local of the American Federation of Musicians. Professional singers usually belong to a branch of the American Guild of Musical Artists.

Related Occupations

There are many music-related occupations. These include librettists, songwriters, and music therapists. A large number of music teachers work in elementary and secondary schools, music conservatories, and colleges and universities, or are self-employed. Many who teach music also perform.

Technical knowledge of musical instruments is required by instrument repairers, tuners, and copyists. In addition, there are a number of occupations in the business side of music such as booking agents, concert managers, music publishers, and music store owners and managers, as well as salespersons of records, sheet music, and musical instruments. Others whose work involves music include disc jockeys, music critics, sound and audio technicians, music librarians, and radio and television announcers.

Sources of Additional Information

For a directory of schools, colleges, and universities that offer accredited programs in music and music teacher education, contact:

❏ National Association of Schools of Music, 11250 Roger Bacon Dr., Suite 21, Reston, VA 22091.

Information on careers and employment opportunities for organists is available from:

❏ American Guild of Organists, 475 Riverside Dr., Suite 1260, New York, NY 10115.

For information on careers for bluegrass musicians, contact:

❏ International Bluegrass Music Association, 207 East 2nd St., Owensboro, KY 42303.

Nursing Aides and Psychiatric Aides

(D.O.T. 354.374-010, .377-010, and .677-010; 355.377-014 and -018, .674-014 and -018, and .677-014)

Significant Points

✓ *Job prospects for nursing aides will be good because of fast growth and high turnover in this large occupation.*

✓ *Minimum education or training is generally required for entry level jobs, but earnings are low.*

Nature of the Work

Nursing aides and psychiatric aides help care for physically or mentally ill, injured, disabled, or infirm individuals confined to hospitals, nursing or residential care facilities, and mental health settings.

Nursing aides, also known as nursing assistants, geriatric aides, unlicensed assistive personnel, or hospital attendants, perform routine tasks under the supervision of nursing and medical staff. They answer patients' call bells, deliver messages, serve meals, make beds, and help patients eat, dress, and bathe. Aides may also provide skin care to patients, take temperatures, pulse, respiration, and blood pressure, and help patients get in and out of bed and walk. They may also escort patients to operating and examining rooms, keep patients' rooms neat, set up equipment, or store and move supplies. Aides observe patients' physical, mental, and emotional conditions and report any change to the nursing or medical staff.

Nursing aides employed in nursing homes are often the principal caregivers, having far more contact with residents than other members of the staff. Since some residents may stay in a nursing home for months or even years, aides develop ongoing relationships with them and interact with them in a positive, caring way.

Psychiatric aides are also known as mental health assistants and psychiatric nursing assistants. They care for mentally impaired or emotionally disturbed individuals. They work under a team that may include psychiatrists, psychologists, psychiatric nurses, social workers, and therapists. In addition to helping patients dress, bathe, groom, and eat, psychiatric aides socialize with them and lead them in educational and recreational activities. Psychiatric aides may play games such as cards with the patients, watch television with them, or participate in group activities such as sports or field trips. They observe patients and report any physical or behavioral signs which might be important for the professional staff to know. They accompany patients to and from wards for examination and treatment. Because they have the closest contact with patients, psychiatric aides have a great deal of influence on patients' outlook and treatment.

Working Conditions

Most full-time aides work about 40 hours a week, but because patients need care 24 hours a day, some aides work evenings, nights, weekends, and holidays. Many work part-time. Aides spend many hours standing and walking, and they often face heavy workloads. Because they may have to move patients in and out of bed or help them stand or walk, aides must guard against back injury. Nursing aides may also face hazards from minor infections and major diseases such as AIDS and hepatitis, but can avoid infections by following proper procedures.

Nursing aides often have unpleasant duties; they empty bed pans and change soiled bed linens. The patients they care for may be disoriented, irritable, or uncooperative. Psychiatric aides must be prepared to care for patients whose illness may cause violent behavior. While their work can be emotionally demanding, many aides gain satisfaction from assisting those in need.

Employment

Nursing aides held about 1,312,000 jobs in 1996, and psychiatric aides held about 103,000 jobs. About one-half of all nursing aides worked in nursing homes, and about one-fourth worked in hospitals. Others worked in residential care facilities, such as halfway houses and homes for the aged or disabled, or in private households. Most psychiatric aides worked in psychiatric units of general hospitals, psychiatric hospitals, state and county mental institutions, homes for mentally retarded and psychiatric patients, and community mental health centers.

Training, Other Qualifications, and Advancement

In many cases, neither a high school diploma nor previous work experience is necessary for a job as a nursing or psychiatric aide. A few employers, however, require some training or experience. Hospitals may require experience as a nursing aide or home health aide. Nursing homes often hire inexperienced workers who must complete a minimum of 75 hours of mandatory training and pass a competency evaluation program within four months of employment. Aides who complete the program are placed on the state registry of nursing aides. Some states require psychiatric aides to complete a formal training program.

These occupations can offer individuals an entry into the world of work. The flexibility of night and weekend hours also provides high school and college students a chance to work during the school year.

Nursing aide training is offered in high schools, vocational-technical centers, some nursing homes, and community colleges. Courses cover body mechanics, nutrition, anatomy and physiology, infection control, communication skills, and resident rights. Personal care skills such as how to help patients bathe, eat, and groom are also taught.

Some facilities, other than nursing homes, provide classroom instruction for newly hired aides, while others rely exclusively on informal on-the-job instruction from a licensed nurse or an experienced aide. Such training may last several days to a few months. From time to time, aides may also attend lectures, workshops, and in-service training.

Applicants should be healthy, tactful, patient, understanding, emotionally stable, dependable, and have a desire to help people. They should also be able to work as part of a team, have good communication skills, and be willing to perform repetitive, routine tasks.

Opportunities for advancement within these occupations are limited. To enter other health occupations, aides generally need additional formal training. Some employers and unions provide opportunities by simplifying the educational paths to advancement. Experience as an aide can also help individuals decide whether to pursue a career in the health care field.

Job Outlook

Job prospects for nursing aides should be good through the year 2006. Numerous openings will arise from a combination of fast growth and high turnover for this large occupation. Employment of nursing aides is expected to grow faster than the average for all occupations in response to an emphasis on rehabilitation and the long-term care needs of a rapidly aging population. Employment will increase as a result of the expansion of nursing homes and other long-term care facilities for people with chronic illnesses and disabling conditions, many of whom are elderly. Financial pressure on hospitals to release patients as soon as possible should produce more nursing home admissions. Modern medical technology will also increase the employment of nursing aides. This technology, while saving and extending more lives, increases the need for long-term care provided by aides. As a result, nursing and personal care facilities are expected to grow very rapidly and to provide most of the new jobs for nursing aides.

Employment of psychiatric aides is expected to grow slower than the average for all occupations. Employment will rise in response to the sharp increase in the number of older persons–many of whom will require mental health services. Employment of aides in outpatient community mental health centers is likely to grow because of increasing public acceptance of formal treatment for drug abuse and alcoholism, and a lessening of the stigma attached to those receiving mental health care. However, employment in hospitals (where one-half of psychiatric aides work (is likely to decline due to attempts to contain costs by limiting inpatient psychiatric treatment.

Replacement needs will constitute the major source of openings for aides. Turnover is high, a reflection of modest entry requirements, low pay, and lack of advancement opportunities.

Earnings

Median weekly earnings of full-time salaried nursing aides and psychiatric aides were $292 in 1996. The middle 50 percent earned between $233 and $372. The lowest 10 percent earned less than $189; the top 10 percent, more than $507.

According to the Buck Survey conducted by the American Health Care Association, nursing aides in chain nursing homes had median hourly earnings of about $6.60 in 1996. The middle 50 percent earned between $5.95 and $7.50.

Aides in hospitals generally receive at least one week's paid vacation after one year of service. Paid holidays and sick leave, hospital and medical benefits, extra pay for late-shift work, and pension plans also are available to many hospital and some nursing home employees.

Related Occupations

Nursing aides and psychiatric aides help people who need routine care or treatment. So do homemaker-home health aides, childcare workers, companions, occupational therapy aides, and physical therapy aides.

Sources of Additional Information

For information about a career as a nursing aide and schools offering training, contact:

❑ National Association of Health Career Schools, 750 First St. NE., Suite 940, Washington, DC 20002. FAX: (202) 842-1565 E-mail: NAHCS@aol.com

Information about employment opportunities may be obtained from local hospitals, nursing homes, psychiatric facilities, state boards of nursing and local offices of the state employment service.

Occupational Therapists

(D.O.T. 076.121-010 and 076.167-010)

Significant Points

- ✓ *Occupational therapy offers good job opportunities and high pay.*
- ✓ *Occupational therapists will be among the fastest growing occupations, as rapid growth in the number of middle-aged and elderly individuals increases the demand for therapeutic services.*
- ✓ *Additional demand will result from medical advances that allow more patients with critical problems to survive and require rehabilitation.*

Nature of the Work

Occupational therapists work with individuals who have conditions that are mentally, physically, developmentally, or emotionally disabling, and help them to develop, recover, or maintain daily living and work skills. They not only help clients improve basic motor functions and reasoning abilities, but also compensate for permanent loss of function. Their goal is to help clients have independent, productive, and satisfying lives.

Occupational therapists assist clients in performing activities of all types, ranging from using a computer, to caring for daily needs such as dressing, cooking, and eating. Physical exercises may be used to increase strength and dexterity, while paper and pencil exercises may be chosen to improve visual acuity and the ability to discern patterns. A client with short-term memory loss, for instance, might be encouraged to make lists to aid recall. One with coordination problems might be assigned exercises to improve hand-eye coordination. Occupational therapists also use computer programs to help clients improve decision making, abstract reasoning, problem solving, and perceptual skills, as well as memory, sequencing, and coordination—all of which are important for independent living.

For those with permanent functional disabilities, such as spinal cord injuries, cerebral palsy, or muscular dystrophy, therapists instruct in the use of adaptive equipment such as wheelchairs, splints, and aids for eating and dressing. They also design or make special equipment needed at home or at work. Therapists develop and teach clients with severe limitations to operate computer-aided adaptive equipment that helps them to communicate, and control other aspects of their environment.

Some occupational therapists, called industrial therapists, treat individuals whose ability to function in a work environment has been impaired. They arrange employment, plan work activities and evaluate the client's progress.

Occupational therapists may work exclusively with individuals in a particular age group, or with particular disabilities. In schools, for example, they evaluate children's abilities, recommend and provide therapy, modify classroom equipment, and in general, help children participate as fully as possible in school programs and activities.

Occupational therapists in mental health settings treat individuals who are mentally ill, mentally retarded, or emotionally disturbed. To treat these problems, therapists choose activities that help people learn to cope with daily life. Activities include time management skills, budgeting, shopping, homemaking, and use of public transportation. They may also work with individuals who are dealing with alcoholism, drug abuse, depression, eating disorders, or stress related disorders.

Recording a client's activities and progress is an important part of an occupational therapist's job. Accurate records are essential for evaluating clients, billing, and reporting to physicians and others.

Working Conditions

Occupational therapists in hospitals and other health care and community settings generally work a 40-hour week. Those in schools may also participate in meetings and other activities, during and after the school day. Almost one-third of occupational therapists work part-time. In large rehabilitation centers, therapists may work in spacious rooms equipped with machines, tools, and other devices generating noise. The job can be tiring, because therapists are on their feet much of the time. Those providing home health care may spend several hours a day driving from appointment to appointment. Therapists also face hazards, such as backstrain from lifting and moving clients and equipment.

Therapists are increasingly taking on supervisory roles. Due to rising health care costs, third party payers are beginning to encourage occupational therapy assistants and aides to take more hands-on responsibility. By having assistants and aides work more closely with clients under the guidance of a therapist, the cost of therapy should be more modest.

Employment

Occupational therapists held about 57,000 jobs in 1996. The largest number of jobs was in hospitals, including many in rehabilitation and psychiatric hospitals. Other major employers include offices and clinics of occupational therapists and other health practitioners, school systems, home health care services, nursing homes, community mental health centers, adult daycare programs, job training services, and residential care facilities.

A small number of occupational therapists are in private practice. Some are solo practitioners, while others are in group practices. They see clients referred by physicians or other health professionals, or provide contract or consulting services to nursing homes, schools, adult daycare programs, and home health agencies.

Training, Other Qualifications, and Advancement

A bachelor's degree in occupational therapy is the minimal requirement for entry into this field. All states, Puerto Rico, and the District of Columbia regulate occupational therapy. To obtain a license, applicants must graduate from an accredited educational program, and pass a national certification examination. Those who pass the test are awarded the title of registered occupational therapist.

In 1996, entry-level education was offered in 84 bachelor's degree programs; 15 post-bachelor's certificate programs for students with a degree other than occupational therapy; and 29 entry-level master's degree programs. Ten programs offered a combined bachelor's and master's degree. Most schools have full-time programs, although a growing number also offer weekend or part-time programs.

Occupational therapy course work includes physical, biological, and behavioral sciences, and the application of occupational therapy theory and skills. Completion of six months of supervised fieldwork is also required.

Persons considering this profession should take high school courses in biology, chemistry, physics, health, art, and the social sciences. College admissions offices also look with favor on paid or volunteer experience in the health care field.

Occupational therapists need patience and strong interpersonal skills to inspire trust and respect in their clients. Ingenuity and imagination in adapting activities to individual needs are assets. Those working in home health care must be able to successfully adapt to a variety of settings.

Job Outlook

Job opportunities for occupational therapists are expected to continue to be good. Employment of occupational therapists is expected to increase much faster than the average for all occupations through the year 2006, due to anticipated growth in demand for rehabilitation and long-term care services. The baby-boom generation's move into middle age, a period during which the incidence of heart attack and stroke increases, will increase the demand for therapeutic services. Additional services will also be demanded by the population 75 years of age and above, a rapidly growing age group that suffers from a very high incidence of disabling conditions.

Medical advances are now making it possible for more patients with critical problems to survive. These patients, however, may need extensive therapy. Finally, additional therapists will be needed to help children with disabilities prepare to enter special education programs, as required by federal legislation.

Due to industry growth and more intensive care, hospitals will continue to employ a large number of occupational therapists. Hospitals will also need occupational therapists to staff their growing home health-care and outpatient rehabilitation programs.

Fast employment growth in schools will result from expansion of the school-age population and extended services for disabled students. Employment of occupational therapists in the home health field is also expected to grow very fast. The rapidly growing number of people age 75 and older who are more likely to need home health care, and the greater use of at-home follow-up care, will encourage this growth.

Earnings

Median weekly earnings of full-time salaried occupational therapists were $780 in 1996. The middle 50 percent earned between $622 and $982. The lowest 10 percent earned less than $479; the top 10 percent earned more than $1,116.

According to a Hay Group survey of acute care hospitals, the median annual base salary of full-time occupational therapists was $42,700 in January 1997. The middle 50 percent earned between $39,100 and $46,100.

Related Occupations

Occupational therapists use specialized knowledge to help individuals perform daily living skills and achieve maximum independence. Other workers performing similar duties include orthotists, prosthetists, physical therapists, chiropractors, speech pathologists, audiologists, rehabilitation counselors, and recreational therapists.

Sources of Additional Information

For more information on occupational therapy as a career and a list of education programs, send a self-addressed label and $5.00 to:

❑ The American Occupational Therapy Association, 4720 Montgomery Ln., P.O. Box 31220, Bethesda, MD 20824-1220. Homepage: HYPERLINK http://www.aota.org

Occupational Therapy Assistants and Aides

(*D.O.T.* 076.364-010 and 355.377-010)

Significant Points

✓ *Occupational therapy assistants and aides are projected to be among the ten fastest growing occupations, but only a small number of job openings will result, because the occupation is small.*

✓ *Occupational therapy assistants need an associate degree or certificate from an accredited community college or technical school; occupational therapy aides usually receive most of their training on the job.*

Nature of the Work

Occupational therapy assistants and aides work under the direction of occupational therapists to provide rehabilitative services to persons with mental, physical, emotional, or developmental impairments. The ultimate goal is to improve clients' quality of life by helping them compensate for limitations. For example, they help injured workers re-enter the labor force by improving their motor skills, or help persons with learning disabilities increase their independence by teaching them to prepare meals or use public transportation.

Occupational therapy assistants help clients with rehabilitative activities and exercises outlined in a treatment plan developed in collaboration with the occupational therapist. The activities range from teaching the proper method of moving from a bed into a wheelchair, to the best way to stretch and limber the muscles of the hand. Assistants monitor the individual to ensure activities are performed correctly and to provide encouragement. They also record their observations of client's progress for use by the occupational therapist. If the treatment is not having the intended effect, or the client is not improving as expected, the treatment program may be altered to obtain better results. They also document billing of the client's health insurance provider.

Occupational therapy aides typically prepare materials and assemble equipment used during treatment, and are responsible for a range of clerical tasks. Their duties may include scheduling appointments, answering the telephone, restocking or ordering depleted supplies, and filling out insurance forms or other paperwork. Aides are not licensed, so by law they are not allowed to perform as wide a range of tasks as occupational therapy assistants.

Working Conditions

Occupational therapy assistants and aides usually work during the day, but may occasionally work evenings or weekends in order to accommodate the client's schedule. They should be in good physical shape because they are on their feet for long periods of time and may be asked to help lift and move clients or equipment.

Employment

Occupational therapy assistants and aides held 16,000 jobs in 1996. Over one-third worked in hospitals, and about one-fourth worked in nursing and personal care facilities. The rest primarily worked in offices and clinics of occupational therapists and other health practitioners. A small number of assistants and aides worked in residential care facilities, outpatient rehabilitation centers, and home health care services.

Training, Other Qualifications, and Advancement

Occupational therapy assistants need an associate degree or certificate from an accredited community college or technical school. There were 117 accredited occupational therapy assistant programs in the United States in 1996. The first year of study typically involves an introduction to healthcare, basic medical terminology, anatomy, and physiology. In the second year, courses are more rigorous and usually include occupational therapy courses in areas such as mental health, gerontology, and pediatrics. Students must also complete supervised fieldwork in a clinic or community setting. Applicants to occupational therapy assistant programs can improve their chances of admission by taking high school courses in biology and health, and by performing volunteer work in nursing homes, occupational or physical therapist's offices, or elsewhere in the healthcare field.

Occupational therapy assistants are regulated in most states, and must pass a national certification examination after they graduate. Those who pass the test are awarded the title of certified occupational therapy assistant.

Occupational therapy aides usually receive most of their training on the job. Qualified applicants must have a high school diploma, strong interpersonal skills, and a desire to help people in need. Applicants may increase their chances of getting a job by volunteering their services, thus displaying initiative and their aptitude to the employer.

Assistants and aides must be responsible, patient, and willing to take directions and work as part of a team. Furthermore, they should be caring and want to help people who are not able to help themselves.

Job Outlook

Opportunities for job seekers should be favorable. Employment of occupational therapy assistants and aides is expected to grow much faster than the average for all occupations through 2006. Although the occupation is expected to be one of the fastest growing in the economy, only a small number of job openings will result, because the occupation is small.

Growth will result from an aging population, including the baby-boom cohort, which will need more occupational therapy services. Demand will also result from advances in medicine that allow more people with critical problems to survive, who then need rehabilitative therapy. Furthermore, employers seeking to reduce health care costs are expected to hire more occupational therapy assistants and aides for tasks currently performed by more highly paid occupational therapists.

Earnings

According to a membership survey of the American Occupational Therapy Association, mean annual income for new full-time occupational therapy assistants was about $27,442 in 1995. Based on limited information, occupational therapy aides usually start between $6.50 and $7.50 an hour.

Related Occupations

Occupational therapy assistants and aides work under the direction of occupational therapists. Other occupations in the healthcare field that work under the supervision of professionals include dental assistants, medical assistants, optometric assistants, pharmacy assistants, and physical therapy assistants and aides.

Sources of Additional Information

Information on a career as an occupational therapy assistant and a list of accredited programs can be obtained by sending a self-addressed label and $5.00 to:

❑ The American Occupational Therapy Association, 4720 Montgomery Lane., P.O. Box 31220, Bethesda, MD 20824-1220. Homepage: http://www.aota.org

Painters and Paperhangers

(D.O.T. 840.381, .681, and .684; 841.381)

Significant Points

- ✓ Painters and paperhangers are one of the larger construction occupations.
- ✓ Most painters and paperhangers learn their craft informally, on the job as helpers to experienced painters.
- ✓ Opportunities for jobs should be good due to high job turnover rates in the occupation.

Nature of the Work

Paint and wall coverings make surfaces clean, attractive and bright. In addition, paints and other sealers protect outside walls from wear caused by exposure to the weather. Although some people do both painting and paperhanging, each requires different skills.

Painters apply paint, stain, varnish, and other finishes to buildings and other structures. They choose the right paint or finish for the surface to be covered, taking into account customers' wishes, durability, ease of handling, and method of application. They first prepare the surfaces to be covered so the paint will adhere properly. This may require removing the old coat by stripping, sanding, wire brushing, burning, or water and abrasive blasting. Painters also wash walls and trim to remove dirt and grease, fill nail holes and cracks, sandpaper rough spots, and brush off dust. On new surfaces, they apply a primer or sealer to prepare them for the finish coat. Painters also mix paints and match colors, relying on knowledge of paint composition and color harmony.

There are several ways to apply paint and similar coverings. Painters must be able to choose the right paint applicator for each job, depending on the surface to be covered, the characteristics of the finish, and other factors. Some jobs only need a good bristle brush with a soft, tapered edge; others require a dip or fountain pressure roller; still others can best be done using a paint sprayer. Many jobs need several types of applicators. The right tools for each job not only expedite the painter's work but also produce the most attractive surface.

When working on tall buildings, painters erect scaffolding, including "swing stages," scaffolds suspended by ropes, or cables attached to roof hooks. When painting steeples and other conical structures, they use a "bosun chair," a swinglike device.

Paperhangers cover walls and ceilings with decorative wall coverings made of paper, vinyl, or fabric. They first prepare the surface to be covered by applying sizing, which seals the surface and makes the covering stick better. When redecorating, they may first remove the old covering by soaking, steaming, or applying solvents. When necessary, they patch holes and take care of other imperfections before hanging the new wall covering.

After the surface has been prepared, paperhangers must prepare the paste or other adhesive. Then they measure the area to be covered, check the covering for flaws, cut the covering into strips of the proper size, and closely examine the pattern to match it when the strips are hung.

The next step is to brush or roll the adhesive onto the back of the covering, then to place the strips on the wall or ceiling, making sure the pattern is matched, the strips are hung straight, and the edges butted together to make tight, closed seams. Finally, paperhangers smooth the strips to remove bubbles and wrinkles, trim the top and bottom with a razor knife, and wipe off any excess adhesive.

Working Conditions

Most painters and paperhangers work 40 hours a week or less; about one out of six works part-time. Painters and paperhangers must stand for long periods. Their jobs also require a considerable amount of climbing and bending. These workers must have stamina because much of the work is done with their arms raised overhead. Painters often work outdoors, but seldom in wet, cold, or inclement weather.

Painters and paperhangers risk injury from slips or falls off ladders and scaffolds. They may sometimes work with materials that can be hazardous if masks are not worn or if ventilation is poor. Some painting jobs can leave a worker covered with paint.

Employment

Painters and paperhangers held about 4449,000 jobs in 1996; most were painters. The majority of painters and paperhangers work for contractors engaged in new construction, repair, restoration, or remodeling work. In addition, organizations that own or manage large buildings, such as apartment complexes, employ maintenance painters, as do some schools, hospitals, and factories.

Self-employed independent painting contractors accounted for over 40 percent of all painters and paperhangers, significantly greater than the proportion of building trades workers in general.

Training, Other Qualifications, and Advancement

Painting and paperhanging are learned through apprenticeship or informal, on-the-job instruction. Although training authorities recommend completion of an apprenticeship program as the best way to become a painter or paperhanger, most painters learn the trade informally on the job as a helper to an experienced painter. Few opportunities for informal training exist for paperhangers because few paperhangers have a need for helpers.

The apprenticeship for painters and paperhangers consists of three to four years of on-the-job training, in addition to 144 hours of related classroom instruction each year. Apprentices receive instruction in color harmony, use and care of tools and equipment, surface preparation, application techniques, paint mixing and matching, characteristics of different finishes, blueprint reading, wood finishing, and safety.

Whether a painter learns the trade through a formal apprenticeship or informally as a helper, on-the-job instruction covers similar skill areas. Under the direction of experienced workers, trainees carry supplies, erect scaffolds, and do simple painting and surface preparation tasks while they learn about paint and painting equipment. Within two or three years, trainees learn to prepare surfaces for painting and paperhanging, to mix paints, and to apply paint and wall coverings efficiently and neatly. Near the end of their training, they may learn decorating concepts, color coordination, and cost-estimating techniques. In addition to learning craft skills, painters must become familiar with safety and health regulations so their work is in compliance with the law.

Apprentices or helpers generally must be at least 16 years old and in good physical condition. A high school education or its equivalent that includes courses in mathematics is generally required to enter an apprenticeship program. Applicants should have good manual dexterity and good color sense.

Painters and paperhangers may advance to supervisory or estimating jobs with painting and decorating contractors. Many establish their own painting and decorating businesses.

Job Outlook

Employment of painters and paperhangers is expected to grow about as fast as the average for all occupations through the year 2006, as the level of new construction increases and the stock of buildings and other structures that require maintenance and renovation grows. Painting is very labor intensive and not suitable to technological gains which might make workers more productive and restrict employment growth. In addition to job openings created by rising demand for the services of these workers, thousands of jobs will become available each year as painters and paperhangers transfer to other occupations or leave the labor force. There are no strict training requirements for entry, so many people with limited skills work as painters or paperhangers for a short time and then move on to other types of work, creating many job openings. Many fewer openings will occur for paperhangers because the number of these jobs is comparatively small.

Prospects for jobs as painters or paperhangers should be favorable since there are no strict training requirements and many individuals are able to enter the field. However, job seekers considering these occupations should expect some periods of unemployment, especially until they become fully skilled. Many construction projects are of the short duration and construction activity is cyclical and seasonal in nature. Remodeling, restoration, and maintenance projects, however, often provide many jobs for painters and paperhangers even when new construction activity declines. The most versatile painters and skilled paperhangers generally are most able to keep working steadily during downturns in the economy.

Earnings

Median weekly earnings for painters who were not self-employed were about $381 in 1996. Most earned between $285 and $517 weekly. The top 10 percent earned over $688 and the bottom 10 percent earned less than $2150 a week. In general, paperhangers earn more than painters. Earnings for painters may be reduced on occasion because of bad weather and the short-term nature of many construction jobs.

Hourly wage rates for apprentices usually start at 40 to 50 percent of the rate for experienced workers and increase periodically.

Some painters and paperhangers are members of the International Brotherhood of Painters and Allied Trades. Some maintenance painters are members of other unions.

Related Occupations

Painters and paperhangers apply various coverings to decorate and protect wood, drywall, metal, and other surfaces. Other occupations in which workers apply paints and similar finishes include billboard posterers, metal sprayers, undercoaters, and transportation equipment painters.

Sources of Additional Information

For details about painting and paperhanging apprenticeships or work opportunities, contact local painting and decorating contractors; a local of the International Brotherhood of Painters and Allied Trades; a local joint union-management apprenticeship committee; or an office of the state apprenticeship agency or state employment service.

For general information about the work of painters and paperhangers, contact:

- ❑ Associated Builders and Contractors, 1300 North 17th St., Rosslyn, VA 22209.
- ❑ International Brotherhood of Painters and Allied Trades, 1750 New York Ave. NW, Washington, DC 20006.
- ❑ Home Builders Institute, National Association of Home Builders, 1201 15th St. NW, Washington, DC 20005.

Paralegals

(D.O.T. 119.267-022 and -026)

Significant Points

- ✓ *Paralegals are expected to rank among the 20 fastest growing occupations in the economy as employers recognize that paralegals perform many legal tasks for lower salaries than lawyers.*
- ✓ *Competition for jobs should continue as the growing number of graduates from paralegal education programs keeps pace with employment growth.*

Nature of the Work

Not all legal work requires a law degree. Lawyers are often assisted in their work by paralegals or legal assistants. Paralegals perform many of the same tasks as lawyers, except for those considered to be the practice of law.

Paralegals work for lawyers. Although the lawyers assume responsibility for the legal work, they often delegate many of their tasks to paralegals. Paralegals are prohibited from setting legal fees, giving legal advice, and presenting cases in court.

Paralegals generally do the preparatory work for lawyers involved in closings, hearings, trials, and corporate meetings. Paralegals investigate the facts of cases, ensuring all relevant information is uncovered. They conduct legal research to identify the appropriate laws, judicial decisions, legal articles, and other materials that are relevant to assigned cases. After organizing and analyzing the information, paralegals may prepare written reports that attorneys use in determining how cases should be handled. Should attorneys decide to file lawsuits on behalf of clients, paralegals may help prepare the legal arguments, draft pleadings and motions to be filed with the court, obtain affidavits, and assist attorneys during trials. Paralegals also organize and track files of all documents and correspondence important to cases, and make them available to attorneys.

Paralegals may work in all areas of the law, including litigation, bankruptcy, corporate law, criminal law, employee benefits, patent and copyright law, and real estate. They help draft contracts, mortgages, separation agreements, and trust instruments. They may also help prepare tax returns and plan estates. Some paralegals coordinate the activities of other law office employees, and keep the financial records for the office.

Paralegals who work for corporations help attorneys with employee contracts, shareholder agreements, stock option plans, and employee benefit plans. They may help prepare and file annual financial reports, maintain corporate minute books and resolutions, and help secure loans for the corporation. Paralegals may also review government regulations to ensure the corporation operates within the law.

The duties of paralegals who work in government vary depending on the agency in which they are employed. Generally, paralegals in government analyze legal material for internal use, maintain reference files, conduct research for attorneys, collect and analyze evidence for agency hearings, and prepare informative or explanatory material on the law, agency regulations, and agency policy for general use by the agency and the public.

Paralegals employed in community legal service projects help the poor, the aged, and others in need of legal assistance. They file forms, conduct research, and prepare documents. When authorized by law, they may represent clients at administrative hearings.

Some paralegals, usually those in small and medium-sized law firms, perform a variety of duties that require a general knowledge of the law. For example, they may research judicial decisions on improper police arrests or help prepare a mortgage contract.

Some paralegals employed by large law firms, government agencies, and corporations specialize in one aspect of the law, including real estate, estate planning, family law, labor law, litigation, and corporate law. Within specialties, functions often are broken down further so paralegals may deal with a specific area. For example, paralegals specializing in labor law may deal exclusively with employee benefits.

A growing number of paralegals use computers in their work. Computer software packages and on-line legal research are increasingly used to search legal literature stored in computer databases and on CD-ROM. The Internet is also used extensively for legal research. In litigation involving many supporting documents, paralegals may use computer databases to organize, index, and retrieve the material. Imaging software allows paralegals to scan documents directly into a database. Paralegals sometimes use billing programs to track hours billed to clients. They may also use computer software packages to perform tax computations and explore the consequences of possible tax strategies for clients.

Working Conditions

Paralegals do most of their work at desks in offices and law libraries. Occasionally, they travel to gather information and perform other duties.

Paralegals employed by corporations and government usually work a standard 40-hour week. Although most paralegals work year round, some are temporarily employed during busy times of the year, then released when the workload diminishes. Paralegals who work for law firms sometimes work very long hours when they are under pressure to meet deadlines. Some law firms reward such loyalty with bonuses and additional time off.

Paralegals handle many routine assignments, particularly when they are inexperienced. Paralegals usually assume more responsible and varied tasks as they gain experience. Furthermore, as new laws and judicial interpretations emerge, paralegals are exposed to new legal problems that make their work more interesting and challenging.

Employment

Paralegals held about 113,000 jobs in 1996. Private law firms employed the vast majority; most of the remainder worked for the various levels of government. Within the federal government, the Department of Justice is the largest employer, followed by the Departments of Treasury and Defense, and the Federal Deposit Insurance Corporation. Other employers include state and local governments, publicly funded legal service projects, banks, real estate development companies, and insurance companies. A small number of paralegals own their own businesses; as freelance legal assistants, they contract their services to attorneys or corporate legal departments.

Training, Other Qualifications, and Advancement

There are several ways to become a paralegal. Employers generally require formal paralegal training obtained through associate or bachelor's degree programs, or certificate programs. Increasingly employers prefer graduates of four-year paralegal programs, or college graduates who have completed short-term paralegal certificate programs. However, the majority of paralegals hold associate degrees. Some employers prefer to train paralegals on the job, promoting experienced legal secretaries or hiring college graduates with no legal experience. Other entrants have experience in a technical field that is useful to law firms, such as a background in tax preparation for tax and estate practice or nursing or health administration for personal injury practice.

Over 800 formal paralegal training programs are offered by four-year colleges and universities, law schools, community and junior colleges, business schools, and proprietary schools. There are currently 214 programs approved by the American Bar Association (ABA). Although this approval is neither required nor sought by many programs, graduation from an ABA-approved program can enhance one's employment opportunities. The requirements for admission to formal training programs vary widely. Some require some college courses or a bachelor's degree; others accept high school graduates or those with legal experience; and a few schools require standardized tests and personal interviews.

Paralegal programs include two-year associate degree programs, four-year bachelor's degree programs, or certificate programs that take only a few months to complete. Many certificate programs only require a high school diploma or GED for admission. Programs typically include general courses on the law and legal research techniques, in addition to courses covering specialized areas of the law, such as real estate, estate planning and probate, litigation, family law, contracts, and criminal law. Many employers prefer applicants with specialized training. Programs increasingly include courses introducing students to the legal applications of computers. Many paralegal training programs include an internship in which students gain practical experience by working for several months in a law office, corporate legal department, or government agency. Experience gained in internships is an asset when seeking a job after graduation.

The quality of paralegal training programs varies; the better programs generally emphasize job placement. Prospective students should examine the experiences of recent graduates of programs in which they are considering enrolling.

Paralegals need not be certified, but the National Association of Legal Assistants has established standards for voluntary certification requiring various combinations of education and experience. Paralegals who meet these standards are eligible to take a two-day examination, given three times each year at several regional testing centers. Those who pass this examination may use the designation Certified Legal Assistant (CLA). This designation is a sign of competence in the field and may enhance employment and advancement opportunities. The Paralegal Advanced Competency Exam, established in 1996 and administered through the National Federation of Paralegal Associations, offers professional recognition to paralegals with a bachelor's degree and at least two years of experience. Those who pass this examination may use the designation Registered Paralegal (RP).

Paralegals must be able to handle legal problems logically and communicate, both orally and in writing, their findings and opinions to their supervising attorney. They must understand legal terminology and have good research and investigative skills. Familiarity with the operation and applications of computers in legal research and litigation support is increasingly important. Paralegals must always stay abreast of new developments in the law that affect their area of practice. Paralegals can participate in continuing legal education seminars to maintain their legal knowledge.

Because paralegals often deal with the public, they must be courteous and uphold the high ethical standards of the legal profession. The National Association of Legal Assistants, the National Federation of Paralegal Associations, and a few states have established ethical guidelines paralegals must follow.

Paralegals are usually given more responsibilities and less supervision as they gain more work experience. In large law firms, corporate legal departments, and government agencies, experienced paralegals may supervise other paralegals and clerical staff, and delegate work assigned by the attorneys. Advancement opportunities include promotion to managerial and other law-related positions within the firm or corporate legal department. However, some paralegals find it easier to move to another law firm when seeking increased responsibility or advancement.

Job Outlook

Competition for jobs should continue as the growing number

of graduates from paralegal education programs keeps pace with employment growth. Employment of paralegals is expected to grow much faster than average–ranking among the fastest growing occupations in the economy through the year 2006–as law firms and other employers with legal staffs increasingly hire paralegals to lower the cost, and increase the availability and efficiency, of legal services. While new jobs created by rapid employment growth will create most of the job openings for paralegals in the future, other job openings will arise as people leave the occupation.

Private law firms will continue to be the largest employers of paralegals as a growing population requires additional legal services, especially in areas such as intellectual property, health care law, international law, elder law, sexual harassment, and the environment. The growth of prepaid legal plans should also contribute to the demand for the services of law firms. A growing array of other organizations, such as corporate legal departments, insurance companies, real estate and title insurance firms, and banks will also hire paralegals.

Job opportunities for paralegals will expand even in the public sector. Community legal service programs–which provide assistance to the poor, aged, minorities, and middle-income families–operate on limited budgets. They will seek to employ additional paralegals in order to minimize expenses and serve the most people. Federal, state, and local government agencies, consumer organizations, and the courts should continue to hire paralegals in increasing numbers.

To a limited extent, paralegal jobs are affected by the business cycle. During recessions, demand declines for some discretionary legal services, such as planning estates, drafting wills, and handling real estate transactions. Corporations are less inclined to initiate litigation when falling sales and profits lead to fiscal belt tightening. As a result, full-time paralegals employed in offices adversely affected by a recession may be laid off or have their work hours reduced. On the other hand, during recessions, corporations and individuals are more likely to face other legal problems, such as bankruptcies, foreclosures, and divorces, that require legal assistance. Paralegals, who provide many of the same legal services at a lower cost, may fare better than lawyers.

Earnings

Earnings of paralegals vary greatly. Salaries depend on education, training, experience, the type and size of employer, and the geographic location of the job. Generally, paralegals who work for large law firms or in large metropolitan areas earn more than those who work for smaller firms or in less populated regions.

According to the National Federation of Paralegal Associations, paralegals had an average annual salary of $32,900 in 1995. Starting salaries of paralegals with one year or less experience averaged $29,300. In addition to a salary, many paralegals received an annual bonus, which averaged about $1,900 in 1995.

The average annual salary of paralegal specialists who work for the federal government was about $44,400 in 1997.

Related Occupations

Several other occupations call for a specialized understanding of the law and the legal system, but do not require the extensive training of a lawyer. Some of these are abstractors, claim examiners, compliance and enforcement inspectors, occupational safety and health workers, patent agents, police officers, and title examiners.

Sources of Additional Information

General information on a career as a paralegal can be obtained from:

❑ Standing Committee on Legal Assistants, American Bar Association, 750 North Lake Shore Dr., Chicago, IL 60611.

For information on certification of paralegals, schools that offer training programs in a specific state, and standards and guidelines for paralegals, contact:

❑ National Association of Legal Assistants, Inc., 1516 South Boston St., Suite 200, Tulsa, OK 74119. Homepage: http://www.nala.org

Information on a career as a paralegal, schools that offer training programs, the Paralegal Advanced Competency Exam, and local paralegal associations can be obtained from:

❑ National Federation of Paralegal Associations, P.O. Box 33108, Kansas City, MO 64114.

Information on careers, training programs, and job postings for paralegals are available at the following Internet site: http://www.paralegals.org

Information on paralegal training programs, including the pamphlet "How to Choose a Paralegal Education Program," may be obtained from:

❑ American Association for Paralegal Education, P.O. Box 40244, Overland Park, KS 66204.

Information on acquiring a job as a paralegal specialist with the federal government may be obtained from the Office of Personnel Management through a telephone-based system. Consult your telephone directory under U.S. government for a local number or call (912) 757-3000 (TDD 912 744-2299). That number is not toll-free and charges may result. Information also is available from their Internet site: HYPERLINK http://www.usajobs.opm.gov http://www.usajobs.opm.gov

Photographers and Camera Operators

(D.O.T. 143)

Significant Points

✓ *Good business sense, imagination, creativity are essential.*

✓ *Only the most skilled, and those with the best business ability, can maintain a long-term career.*

✓ *A much higher proportion than average are self-employed.*

Nature of the Work

By creatively using lighting, lenses, film, filters, and camera settings, photographers and camera operators produce pictures that record and event, capture a mood, or tell a story. Making commercial quality photographs and movies requires technical expertise and creativity. Producing a successful picture includes choosing and presenting a subject to achieve a particular effect and selecting equipment to accomplish the desired goal. For example, photographers and camera operators may enhance the subject's appearance with lighting or draw attention to a particular aspect of the subject by blurring the background.

Today, many cameras adjust settings like shutter speed and aperture automatically and also let the photographer to adjust these settings manually, thus allowing greater creative and technical control over the picture-taking process. In addition to automatic and manual cameras, photographers and camera operators use an array of film, lenses, and equipment—from filters, tripods, and flash attachments to specially constructed motorized vehicles and lighting equipment.

Photography increasingly involves the use of computer technology. A photographer using a traditional silver-halide film camera can take a picture and, once the film is processed and prints are made, use a scanner to transfer the images into digital form. Some photographers prefer to use digital cameras, which use electronic memory rather than a film negative to record an image. The electronic image can be transmitted instantly via a computer modem and telephone line or otherwise downloaded onto a personal computer. Then, using the computer and specialized software, the photographer can manipulate and enhance the scanned or digital image to create a desired effect. The images can be stored on a compact disk (CD) the same way as music. There are some photographers who use this technology to create electronic portfolios, as well.

Some photographers prefer to develop and print their own photographs, especially those who use black and white film or require special effects, but this requires a fully-equipped darkroom and the technical skill to operate it. Other photographers send their film to laboratories for processing. Color film, especially, requires expensive equipment and exacting conditions for correct processing and printing.

Most photographers specialize in portrait, commercial, or news photography. Others specialize in areas such as aerial, police, medical, or scientific photography, which typically involves further specialization in fields like engineering, medicine, biology, or chemistry.

Portrait photographers take pictures of individuals or groups of people and often work in their own studios. Some specialize in weddings or school photographs. Portrait photographers who are business owners arrange for advertising; schedule appointments; set and adjust equipment; develop and retouch negatives; and mount and frame pictures. They also purchase supplies, keep records, bill customers, and may hire and train employees.

Commercial and industrial photographers take pictures of various subjects, such as manufactured articles, models, buildings, merchandise, landscapes, and groups of people. This photography is used in a wide variety of mediums, including reports, advertisements, and catalogs. Industrial photographers often take still or motion pictures of equipment and machinery, products, workers, and company officials. The pictures are then used for analyzing engineering projects, publicity, or as records of equipment development or deployment, such as the placement of an off-shore oil rig. Companies also use these photographs in publications to report to stockholders or to advertise company products or services. This photography frequently is done on location.

News photographers, also called photojournalists, photograph newsworthy people and places, as well as sporting, political, and community events, for newspapers, journals, magazines, or television. Some photojournalists are salaried staff, while others are work independently and are known as freelance photographers.

Self-employed photographers may license the use of their photographs through stock photo agencies. These agencies grant magazines and other customers the right to purchase the use of a photograph, and, in turn, pay the photographer on a commission basis. Stock photo agencies require an application from the photographer and a sizable portfolio. Once accepted, a large number of new submissions are generally required from a photographer each year. Photographers frequently have their photos placed on CDs for this purpose.

Photography also is a fine art medium, and a small portion of photographers sell their photographs as artwork. In addition to technical proficiency, artistic photography requires an even greater emphasis on self expression and creativity.

Like photographers, camera operators work in a variety of settings. They generally use motion picture or video cameras to film a wide range of subjects, including commercial motion pictures, documentaries, music videos, news events, and training sessions. Some film private ceremonies and special events.

Many video camera operators are employed by independent television stations, local affiliates, or large cable and television networks. They often work in a broadcast studio or cover news events as part of a reporting team. Camera operators employed in the entertainment field use motion picture cameras to film movies, television programs, and commercials. Some camera operators specialize in filming cartoons or special effects for television and movies. Camera operators who work in the entertainment field often meet with directors, actors, and camera assistants to discuss ways of filming and improving scenes.

Working Conditions

Working conditions for photographers and camera operators vary considerably. Photographers employed in government, commercial studios, and advertising agencies usually work a five-day, 40-hour week. News photographers and camera operators often work long, irregular hours and must be available to work on short notice.

Self-employment allows for greater autonomy, freedom of expression, and flexible scheduling. However, income can be uncertain and necessitates a continuous, time-consuming, and sometimes stressful search for new clients. Some self-employed photographers hire an assistant solely for the purpose of seeking additional business.

Portrait photographers often work in their own studios but may also travel to take photographs at schools and other places, as well as at weddings and other events. Press and commercial photographers and camera operators frequently travel locally, can stay overnight on an assignment, or may travel to distant places for long periods of time. Their work may put them in uncomfortable, or even dangerous, surroundings. This is especially true for photojournalists covering natural disasters, civil unrest, or military conflicts.

Some photographers and camera operators must wait long hours in all kinds of weather for an event to take place and stand or walk for long periods while carrying heavy equipment. Photographers often work under severe time restrictions to meet deadlines and satisfy customers. While working on a motion picture production, camera operators are often required to work long and irregular hours. It may also be necessary for camera operators to work in helicopters or on the back of specially equipped vehicles in order to capture a scene or cover a news event.

Employment

Photographers and camera operators held about 154,000 jobs in 1996. About four out of ten were self-employed, a much higher proportion than the average for all occupations. Some self-employed photographers contracted with advertising agencies, magazines, or others to do individual projects at a predetermined fee, while others operated portrait studios or provided photographs to stock photo agencies.

Most salaried photographers worked in portrait or commercial photography studios. Others were employed by newspapers, magazines, advertising agencies, and government agencies. Most camera operators were employed in television broadcasting or at motion picture studios; relatively few were self-employed. Most photographers and camera operators worked in metropolitan areas.

Training, Other Qualifications, and Advancement

Employers usually seek applicants with a good technical understanding of photography who are also imaginative and creative. Entry level positions in photojournalism, as well as in industrial, scientific, or technical photography, are likely to require a college degree in photography, with courses in the specific field being photographed, such as industrial products or botany. Camera operators generally acquire their skills through formal post-secondary training at colleges, photographic institutes, universities, or through on-the-job training. Those in entry-level jobs, including photography and cinematography assistants, learn to set up lights, cameras, and other equipment, and learn to load and unload film. They may receive routine assignments requiring camera adjustments or decisions on what subject matter to capture. With increased experience, they may advance to more demanding assignments. Photography assistants often learn to mix chemicals, develop film, print photographs, and the various other skills necessary to run a photography business.

Individuals interested in photography should subscribe to photographic newsletters and magazines, join camera clubs, and seek employment in camera stores or photo studios. Individuals also should decide on an area of interest and specialize in it. Completing a course of study at a private photographic institute, university, or community college provides many of the necessary skills to be a successful photographer. Summer or part-time work for a photographer, cable or television network, newspaper, or magazine is an excellent way to gain experience and eventual entry into this field.

Courses in photography are offered in many places, including universities, community and junior colleges, vocational-technical institutes, and private trade and technical schools. Courses in cinematography are most often offered by photography institutes and universities. Many photographers enhance their technical expertise by attending seminars.

Basic courses in photography cover equipment, processes, and techniques. Bachelors degree programs, especially those including business courses, provide a well-rounded education. Art schools offer useful training in design and composition, but may be weak in the commercial aspects of photography.

Photographers who wish to operate their own businesses need business skills as well as talent. These individuals must know how to submit bids; write contracts; hire models, if needed; get permission to take on-site photographs at locations normally not open to the public; obtain releases to use photographs of people; price photographs; know about copyright protection for their work; and keep financial records. Self-employed photographers should also develop individual styles of photography to differentiate themselves from the competition. Some photographers enter the field by submitting unsolicited photographs to magazines and art directors at advertising agencies.

Both photographers and camera operators need good eyesight, artistic ability, and manual dexterity. They should be patient, accurate, and enjoy working with details. In addition, photographers should be able to work alone or with others, as they frequently deal with clients, graphic designers, and advertising and publishing specialists. Camera operators should have good hand-eye coordination, communication skills, and, if needed, the ability to handhold a camera for extended periods of time.

Commercial photographers must be imaginative and original. Portrait photographers also need the ability to help people relax in front of the camera. Photojournalists must not only be good with a camera, but must also understand the story behind an event, so their pictures match the story. They must be decisive in recognizing a potentially good photograph and act quickly to capture it. This requires journalistic skills and explains why such employers increasingly look for individuals with a four-year degree in photojournalism or journalism with an emphasis on photography.

Different types of filming environments require camera operators to have different strengths. For example, camera operators who want to work on music videos need a good sense of music and rhythm, while those who want to work in news teams must be able to set up quickly and capture the image on the first take whenever possible.

Camera operators are usually hired for a project based on recommendations from individuals such as producers, directors of photography, and camera assistants from previous projects, or through interviews with the producer.

As for career advancement, camera operators can become directors of photography for movie studios, advertising agencies, or television programs. Magazine and news photographers may become photography editors. A few photographers and camera operators become teachers and provide instruction in their own particular area of expertise.

Job Outlook

Photography, particularly commercial photography and photojournalism, is a highly competitive field, because there are more people who want to be photographers than there is employment to support them. Only the most skilled, those with the best business ability, and those who have developed the best reputations in the industry are able to find salaried positions or attract enough work to support themselves as self-employed photographers. Many persons have full-time jobs in other fields and take photographs or videos of weddings and other events on weekends.

Employment of photographers is expected to increase as fast as the average for all occupations through the year 2006. The growing demand for visual images in education, communication, entertainment, marketing, research and development, and other areas should spur demand for photographers. Demand for portrait photographers should increase as the population grows. Also, as advances in telecommunications create new markets and products—electronic newspapers and magazines, for example, which rely heavily on images—the demand for pictures and images is expected to increase over the projection period.

Employment of camera operators is expected to grow as fast as the average for all occupations through the year 2006. Despite businesses making greater use of videos for training films, business meetings, sales campaigns, and public relations work, the growth in employment of camera operators will be restrained as their work and duties in motion pictures and film are expected to be slowly taken over by directors of photography or cinematographers. Expansion of the entertainment industry will create some additional openings, but competition for these jobs will be keen for what generally is regarded as an exciting career field.

Earnings

The median annual earnings for salaried photographers and camera operators who worked full-time were about $30,600 in 1996. The middle 50 percent earned between $21,000 and $46,500. The top 10 percent earned more than $75,100, while the lowest 10 percent earned less than $14,500.

Most salaried photographers work full-time and earn more than the majority of self-employed photographers, many of whom work part-time, but some self-employed photographers have high earnings. Earnings are affected by the number of hours worked, skills, marketing ability, and general business conditions. Because many camera operators who work in film or video do so as freelancers, earnings tend to fluctuate from year to year.

Unlike photojournalists and commercial photographers, very few artistic photographers are successful enough to support themselves solely through this specialty.

Related Occupations

Other jobs requiring visual arts talents include illustrators, visual artists, designers, painters, sculptors, and photo editors.

Sources of Additional Information

Career information on photography is available from:
- ❑ Professional Photographers of America, Inc., 57 Forsyth St., Suite 1600, Atlanta, GA 30303.
- ❑ Advertising Photographers of America, 7201 Melrose Ave., Los Angeles, CA 90046.
- ❑ American Society of Media Photographers, 14 Washington Rd., Suite 502, Princeton Junction, NJ 08550-1033.

General information on news photography careers is available from:
- ❑ National Press Photographers Association, 3200 Croasdaile Dr., Suite 306, Durham, NC 27705.

Physical Therapy Assistants and Aides

(*D.O.T.* 076.224-010 and 355.354-010)

Significant Points

✓ *Physical therapist assistants and aides are projected to be among the fastest growing occupations in the economy, as growth in the number of individuals with disabilities or limited function increases the demand for support personnel for physical therapy services.*

✓ *Most licensed physical therapist assistants have an associate degree, but aides usually learn skills on the job.*

Nature of the Work

Physical therapist assistants and aides perform physical therapy procedures and related tasks selected and delegated by a supervising physical therapist. They assist the physical therapist in providing services that help improve mobility, relieve pain, and prevent or limit permanent physical disabilities of patients suffering from injuries or disease. Their patients include accident victims and individuals with disabling conditions such as low back pain, arthritis, heart disease, fractures, head injuries, and cerebral palsy.

Physical therapist assistants perform a wide variety of tasks. Treatment procedures delegated to physical therapist assistants may involve exercises, massages, electrical stimulation, paraffin baths, hot/cold packs, traction, and ultrasound. Assistants record the patient's progress during treatment and report the outcome of each treatment to the physical therapist.

Physical therapist aides help make therapy sessions productive, under the direct supervision of a physical therapist or physical therapist assistant. They are usually responsible for keeping the treatment area clean and organized, and preparing for each patient's therapy. When patients need assistance to, or from the treatment area, aides may push them in a wheelchair, or provide them with a shoulder to lean on. Aides may inform the therapist or assistant if patients are experiencing difficulty with the treatment. Because they are not licensed, aides perform a smaller range of tasks than physical therapist assistants.

The duties of assistants and aides include some clerical tasks, such as ordering depleted supplies, maintaining patient records, answering the phones, and filling out insurance forms and other paperwork. Records kept by the assistant or aide keep the therapist informed about patients' progress and any problems that may develop during treatment. The extent to which an aide, or even an assistant, performs clerical tasks depends on the size and location of the facility.

Working Conditions

The hours and days that physical therapist assistants and aides work vary depending on the facility, and whether they are full or part-time employees. Many outpatient physical therapy offices and clinics have evening and weekend hours to help coincide with patients' personal schedules.

Physical therapist assistants and aides need to have a moderate degree of strength due to the physical exertion required in assisting patients with their treatment. For example, constant kneeling, stooping and standing for long periods of time are all part of the job. In some cases, assistants and aides may need to help lift patients.

Employment

Physical therapist assistants and aides held 84,000 jobs in 1996. They work alongside physical therapists in a variety of settings. Two-thirds of all assistants and aides work in hospitals or offices of physical therapists. Others work in outpatient rehabilitation centers, nursing homes, offices and clinics of physicians, and in patients' homes. In sports physical therapy, they may work part of the time on the sidelines of sporting events.

Training, Other Qualifications, and Advancement

Physical therapist assistants typically have earned an associate degree from an accredited physical therapist assistant program. As of January 1997, 44 states and Puerto Rico regulated assistants. Other requirements include certification in CPR and First Aid, and a minimum number of hours of clinical experience.

According to the American Physical Therapy Association, there were 225 accredited physical therapist assistant programs in the United States as of July, 1997. Accredited physical therapist assistant programs are designed to last two years, or four semesters, and culminate in an associate degree. Admission into physical therapist assistant programs is competitive and it is not unusual for colleges to have long waiting lists of prospective candidates. The programs are divided into academic study and hands-on clinical experience. Academic course work includes algebra, anatomy and physiology, biology, chemistry, and psychology. Before students begin their clinical field experience, many programs require that they complete a semester of anatomy and physiology and have certifications in CPR and First Aid. Both educators and prospective employers view clinical experience as an integral part of ensuring that students understand the responsibilities of a physical therapist assistant.

Employers typically require physical therapist aides to have a high school diploma, strong interpersonal skills, and a desire to assist people in need. Most employers provide clinical on-the-job training.

Job Outlook

Physical therapist assistants and aides are expected to be among the fastest growing occupations through the year 2006. Demand for physical therapist assistants and aides will continue to rise with growth in the number of individuals with disabilities or limited function. The rapidly growing elderly population is particularly vulnerable to chronic and debilitating conditions that require therapeutic services. Also, the baby-boom generation is entering the prime age for heart attacks and strokes, increasing the demand for cardiac and physical rehabilitation. Older patients often need more assistance in their treatment, making the roles of assistants and aides vital.

Licensed physical therapist assistants can enhance the cost-effective provision of physical therapy services. After a patient is evaluated and a treatment plan is designed by the physical therapist, the physical therapist assistant can provide many aspects of treatment, as prescribed by the therapist.

Earnings

According to the limited information available, starting salaries for physical therapist assistants average about $24,000 a year in 1996. Starting salaries of assistants working in hospitals tended to be lower than those in private practice. The American Physical Therapy Association reports that experienced assistants working in private practice earned an average of about $30,000 in 1996.

In 1996, median annual earnings of full-time salaried health aides, including physical therapist aides, were $16,000. The middle 50 percent earned between $13,000 and $21,000. The top 10 percent earned at least $28,000, and the bottom 10 percent earned less than $10,000.

Related Occupations

Physical therapist assistants and aides work under the supervision of physical therapists. Other occupations in the healthcare field that work under the supervision of professionals include dental, medical, occupational therapy, optometric, recreational therapy, and pharmacy assistants.

Sources of Additional Information

Information on a career as a physical therapist assistant or aide, and a list of schools offering accredited programs can be obtained from:

❑ The American Physical Therapy Association, 1111 North Fairfax Street, Alexandria, VA 22314-1488. Homepage: http://www.apta.org

Physical Therapists

(*D.O.T.* 076.121-014)

Significant Points

✓ *Physical therapy offers very good job opportunities and high pay.*

✓ *Physical therapists will be among the fastest growing occupations, as growth in the number of individuals with disabilities or limited function increases the demand for physical therapy services.*

Nature of the Work

Physical therapists provide services that help restore function, improve mobility, relieve pain, and prevent or limit permanent physical disabilities of patients suffering from injuries or disease. They restore, maintain, and promote overall fitness and health. Their patients include accident victims and individuals with disabling conditions such as low back pain, arthritis, heart disease, fractures, head injuries, and cerebral palsy.

Therapists examine patients' medical histories, then test and measure their strength, range of motion, balance and coordination, posture, muscle performance, respiration, and motor function. They also determine patients' ability to be independent and reintegrate into the community or workplace after injury or illness. Next, they develop treatment plans describing the treatment strategy, its purpose, and the anticipated outcome. After devising a treatment strategy, physical therapists often delegate specific procedures to physical therapist assistants and aides. Therapists are increasingly taking on supervisory roles.

Treatment often includes exercise for patients who have been immobilized and lack flexibility, strength, or endurance. They encourage patients to use their own muscles to further increase flexibility and range of motion before finally advancing to other exercises improving strength, balance, coordination, and endurance. Their goal is to improve how an individual functions at work and home.

Physical therapists also use electrical stimulation, hot packs or cold compresses, and ultrasound to relieve pain and reduce swelling. They may use traction or deep-tissue massage to relieve pain. Therapists also teach patients to use assisting and adaptive devices such as crutches, prostheses, and wheelchairs. They may show patients exercises to do at home to expedite their recovery.

As treatment continues, physical therapists document progress, conduct periodic examinations, and modify treatments when necessary. Such documentation is used to track the patient's progress, and identify areas requiring more or less attention.

Physical therapists often consult and practice with a variety of other professionals, such as physicians, dentists, nurses, educators, social workers, occupational therapists, speech-language pathologists, and audiologists.

Some physical therapists treat a wide range of ailments; others specialize in areas such as pediatrics, geriatrics, orthopedics, sports medicine, neurology, and cardiopulmonary physical therapy.

Working Conditions

Physical therapists practice in hospitals, clinics, and private offices that have specially equipped facilities or they treat patients in hospital rooms, homes, or schools.

Most physical therapists work a 40-hour week, which may include some evenings and weekends. The job can be physically demanding because therapists often have to stoop, kneel, crouch, lift, and stand for long periods of time. In addition, physical therapists move heavy equipment and lift patients or help them turn, stand, or walk.

Employment

Physical therapists held about 115,000 jobs in 1996; about one in four worked part-time. Almost two-thirds were employed in either hospitals or offices of physical therapists. Other jobs were in home health agencies, outpatient rehabilitation centers, offices and clinics of physicians, and nursing homes. Some physical therapists are self-employed in private practices. They may provide services to individual patients or contract to provide services in hospitals, rehabilitation centers, nursing homes, home health agencies, adult daycare programs, and schools. They may be in solo practice or be part of a consulting group. Physical therapists also teach in academic institutions and conduct research.

Training, Other Qualifications, and Advancement

All states require physical therapists to pass a licensure exam after graduating from an accredited physical therapist educational program before they can practice.

According to the American Physical Therapy Association , there were 173 accredited physical therapist programs as of July, 1997. Of the accredited programs, 46 offered bachelor's degrees and 116 were master's degree programs. By the year 2001, all accredited physical therapy programs will be at the master's degree level and above. Currently, the bachelor's degree curriculum starts with basic science courses such as biology, chemistry, and physics, and then introduces specialized courses such as biomechanics, neuroanatomy, human growth and development, manifestations of disease, examination techniques, and therapeutic procedures. Besides classroom and laboratory instruction, students receive supervised clinical experience. Individuals who have a four-year degree in another field and want to be a physical therapist, should enroll in a master's or a doctoral level physical therapist educational program.

Competition for entrance into physical therapist educational programs is very intense, so interested students should attain superior grades in high school and college, especially in science courses. Courses useful when applying to physical therapist educational programs include anatomy, biology, chemistry, social science, mathematics, and physics. Before granting admission, many professional education programs require experience as a volunteer in a physical therapy department of a hospital or clinic.

Physical therapists should have strong interpersonal skills to successfully educate patients about their physical therapy treatments. They should also be compassionate and posses a desire to help patients. Similar traits are also needed to interact with the patient's family.

Physical therapists are expected to continue professional development by participating in continuing education courses and workshops. A number of states require continuing education to maintain licensure.

Job Outlook

Anecdotal reports about shortages of physical therapists that existed in recent years are no longer common. The number of physical therapist educational programs has increased and more graduates have moved into the labor force. Nevertheless, job prospects are expected to continue to be very good.

Physical therapists are expected to be among the fastest growing occupations through the year 2006 as the demand for physical therapy services grows. The rapidly growing elderly population is particularly vulnerable to chronic and debilitating conditions that require therapeutic services. Also, the baby-boom generation is entering the prime age for heart attacks and strokes, increasing the demand for cardiac and physical rehabilitation. More young people will need physical therapy as technological advances save the lives of a larger proportion of newborns with severe birth defects. Future medical developments will also permit a higher percentage of trauma victims to survive, creating additional demand for rehabilitative care. Growth may also result from advances in medical technology which permit treatment of more disabling conditions.

Widespread interest in health promotion should also increase demand for physical therapy services. A growing number of employers are using physical therapists to evaluate worksites, develop exercise programs, and teach safe work habits to employees in the hope of reducing injuries.

Employment of physical therapists would grow even faster were it not for continued emphasis on controlling health care costs by limiting the use of therapeutic services in some instances.

Earnings

In 1996, median weekly earnings of salaried physical therapists who usually work full-time were $757. The middle 50 percent earned between $577 and $1,055. The top 10 percent earned at least $1,294 and the bottom 10 percent earned less than $400.

According to the American Physical Therapy Association's survey of physical therapists practicing in hospital settings, the median annual base salary of full-time physical therapists was $48,000 in 1996. The middle 50 percent earned $42,000 and $57,000.

Related Occupations

Physical therapists rehabilitate persons with physical disabilities. Others who work in the rehabilitation field include occupational therapists, speech pathologists, audiologists, orthotists, prosthetists, and respiratory therapists.

Sources of Additional Information

Additional information on a career as a physical therapist and a list of accredited educational programs in physical therapy are available from:

❏ American Physical Therapy Association, 1111 North Fairfax St., Alexandria, VA 22314-1488. Homepage: http://www.apta.org/

Physician Assistants

(D.O.T. 079.364-018)

Significant Points

✓ *The typical physician assistant program lasts about two years and generally requires at least two years of college and some health care experience for admission.*

✓ *Earnings are high and job opportunities are expected to be excellent.*

Nature of the Work

Physician assistants (PAs) provide health care services with supervision by physicians. They should not be confused with medical assistants, who perform routine clinical and clerical tasks. PAs are formally trained to provide diagnostic, therapeutic, and preventive health care services under the direction of a physician. Working as members of the health care team, they take medical histories, examine patients, order and interpret laboratory tests and x rays, and make diagnoses. They also treat minor injuries by suturing, splinting, and casting. PAs record progress notes, instruct and counsel patients, and order or carry out therapy. In 39 states and the District of Columbia, physician assistants may prescribe medications. PAs may also have managerial duties. Some order medical and laboratory supplies and equipment, while others supervise technicians and assistants.

Physician assistants always work under the supervision of a physician. The extent of supervision, however, depends upon state law. For example, a PA may provide care in rural or inner city clinics where a physician is present for only one or two days each week, conferring with the supervising physician and other medical professionals as needed or required by law. PAs may also make house calls or go to hospitals and nursing homes to check on patients and report back to the physician.

In some states, the duties of a physician assistant are determined by the supervising physician; in others, they are determined by the state's regulatory agency. Aspiring PAs should investigate the laws and regulations in the states where they wish to practice.

Many PAs work in primary care areas such as general internal medicine, pediatrics, and family practice. Others work in specialty areas, such as general and thoracic surgery, emergency medicine, orthopedics, and geriatrics. PAs specializing in surgery provide pre- and post-operative care and may work as first or second assistants during major surgery.

Working Conditions

Although PAs generally work in a comfortable, well-lighted environment, those in surgery often stand for long periods, and others do considerable walking. Schedules vary according to practice setting and often depend on the hours of the supervising physician. The workweek of PAs in physicians' offices may include weekends, night hours, or early morning hospital rounds to visit patients. They may also be on-call. PAs in clinics usually work a five-day, 40-hour week.

Employment

Physician assistants held about 64,000 jobs in 1996. Sixty-six percent were in the offices and clinics of physicians, dentists, or other health practitioners. Almost 20 percent were in hospitals. The rest were mostly in public health clinics, nursing homes, prisons, home health care agencies, and the Department of Veterans Affairs.

According to the American Academy of Physician Assistants, about one-third of all PAs provide health care to communities having fewer than 50,000 residents where physicians may be in limited supply.

Training, Other Qualifications, and Advancement

Almost all states require that new PAs complete an accredited, formal education program. In 1997, there were 96 such educational programs for physician assistants; 53 of these programs offered a baccalaureate degree or a degree option. The rest offered either a certificate, an associate degree, or a master's degree. Most PA graduates have at least a bachelor's degree.

Admission requirements vary, but many programs require two years of college and some work experience in the health care field. Students should take courses in biology, English, chemistry, math, psychology, and social sciences. More than half of all applicants hold a bachelor's or master's degree. Many applicants are former emergency medical technicians, other allied health professionals, or nurses.

PA programs generally last two years. Most programs are in schools of allied health, academic health centers, medical schools, or four-year colleges; a few are in community colleges, the military, or hospitals. Many accredited PA programs have clinical teaching affiliations with medical schools.

PA education includes classroom instruction in biochemistry, nutrition, human anatomy, physiology, microbiology, clinical pharmacology, clinical medicine, geriatric and home health care, disease prevention, and medical ethics. Students obtain supervised clinical training in several areas, including primary care medicine, inpatient medicine, surgery, obstetrics and gynecology, geriatrics, emergency medicine, psychiatry, and pediatrics. Sometimes, PA students serve one or more of these rotations under the supervision of a physician who is seeking to hire a PA. These rotations often lead to permanent employment.

As of 1997, 49 states and the District of Columbia had legislation governing the qualifications or practice of physician assistants. Mississippi did not. Forty-nine states required physician assistants to pass the Physician Assistants National Certifying Examination that is only open to graduates of an accredited educational program. Only those successfully completing the examination may use the credential "Physician Assistant-Certified (PA-C)." In order to remain certified, PAs must complete 100 hours of continuing medical education every two years. Every six years, they must pass a recertification examination or complete an alternate program combining learning experiences and a take-home examination.

Although they are not accredited, PA postgraduate residency training programs are available in gynecology, geriatrics, surgery, pediatrics, neonatology, and occupational medicine. Candidates must be graduates of an accredited program and be certified by the National Commission on Certification of Physician Assistants.

Physician assistants need leadership skills, self-confidence, and emotional stability. They must be willing to continue studying throughout their career to keep up with medical advances.

Some PAs pursue additional education in order to practice in a specialty area such as surgery, neonatology, or emergency medicine. Others, as they attain greater clinical knowledge and experience, advance to added responsibilities and higher earnings. However, by the very nature of the profession, individual PAs are usually supervised by physicians.

Job Outlook

Employment opportunities are expected to be excellent for physician assistants, particularly in areas or settings that have difficulty attracting physicians, such as rural and inner city clinics. Employment of PAs is expected to grow much faster than the average for all occupations through the year 2006 due to anticipated expansion of the health services industry and an emphasis on cost containment. Physicians and institutions are expected to employ more PAs to provide primary care and assist with medical and surgical procedures, because PAs are cost-effective and productive members of the health care team. Physician assistants can relieve physicians of routine duties and procedures. Telemedicine(using technology to facilitate interactive consultations between physicians and physician assistants(will also expand the use of physician assistants. Besides the traditional office-based setting, PAs should find a growing number of jobs in institutional settings such as hospitals, academic medical centers, public clinics, and prisons. Additional PAs may be needed to augment medical staffing in inpatient teaching hospital settings if the number of physician residents is reduced. In addition, state-imposed legal limitations on the numbers of hours worked by physician residents are increasingly common and encourage hospitals to use PAs to supply some physician resident services. Opportunities will be best in states that allow PAs a wider scope of practice, such as the ability to prescribe medication.

Earnings

According to the American Academy of Physician Assistants, the median income for physician assistants in full-time clinical practice in 1996 was $60,687; median income for first year graduates was $52,116. Income varies by specialty, practice setting, geographical location, and years of experience.

According to a Hay Group survey of HMOs, group practices, and hospital-based clinics, the median annual base salary of full-time physician assistants was $54,100 in May 1996. The middle 50 percent earned between $49,100 and $60,000.

The average annual salary for physician assistants employed by the federal government was $48,670 in early 1997.

Related Occupations

Other health workers who provide direct patient care that requires a similar level of skill and training include nurse practitioners, physical therapists, occupational therapists, clinical psychologists, speech-language pathologists, and audiologists.

Sources of Additional Information

For information on a career as a physician assistant, contact:
❑ American Academy of Physician Assistants Information Center, 950 North Washington St., Alexandria, VA 22314-1552. Homepage: http://www.aapa.org

For a list of accredited programs and a catalog of individual PA training programs, contact:
❑ Association of Physician Assistant Programs, 950 North Washington St., Alexandria, VA 22314-1552.

For eligibility requirements and a description of the Physician Assistant National Certifying Examination, write to:
❑ National Commission on Certification of Physician Assistants, Inc., 6849-B2 Peachtree Dunwoody Rd., Atlanta, GA 30328.

Physicians

(D.O.T. 070 and 071)

Significant Points

✓ *Amid reports of an oversupply of physicians, opportunities will be best in primary care fields of general and family medicine, internal medicine, and general pediatrics.*

✓ *Physicians are much more likely to work as salaried employees of group medical practices, clinics, or health care networks than in the past.*

✓ *It takes many years of education and training to become a physician, but earnings are among the highest of any occupation.*

Nature of the Work

Physicians serve a fundamental role in our society and have an effect upon all our lives. They diagnose illnesses and prescribe and administer treatment for people suffering from injury or disease. Physicians examine patients, obtain medical histories, and order, perform, and interpret diagnostic tests. They counsel patients on diet, hygiene, and preventive health care.

There are two types of physicians: MD–Doctor of Medicine–and the DO–Doctor of Osteopathic Medicine. MDs are also known as allopathic physicians. While MDs and DOs may use all accepted methods of treatment, including drugs and surgery, DOs place special emphasis on the body's musculoskeletal system, preventive medicine, and holistic patient care.

About one third of MDs are primary care physicians. They practice general and family medicine, general internal medicine, or general pediatrics and are usually the first health professionals patients consult. Primary care physicians tend to see the same patients on a regular basis for preventive care and to treat a variety of ailments. General and family practitioners emphasize comprehensive health care for patients of all ages and for the family as a group. Those in general internal medicine provide care mainly for adults who have a wide range of problems associated with the body's organs. General pediatricians focus on children's health. When appropriate, primary care physicians refer patients to specialists, who are experts in medical fields such as obstetrics and gynecology, cardiology, psychiatry, or surgery (see table 1). DOs are more likely to be primary care providers than allopathic physicians, although they can be found in all specialties.

Table 1. Percentage distribution of MDs by specialty, 1995

Percentage

Total	100.0
Primary care	
General internal medicine	16.0
General and family medicine	10.5
General pediatrics	7.0
Medical specialties	
Allergy	.5
Cardiovascular diseases	2.6
Dermatology	1.2
Gastroenterology	1.3
Obstetrics and gynecology	5.2
Pediatric cardiology	.2
Pulmonary diseases	1.0
Surgical specialties	
Colon and rectal surgery	.1
General surgery	5.2
Neurological surgery	.7
Ophthalmology	2.4
Orthopedic surgery	3.1
Otalaryngology	1.3
Plastic surgery	.8
Thoracic surgery	.3
Urological surgery	1.4
Other specialties	
Aerospace medicine	.1
Anesthesiology	4.6
Child psychiatry	.8
Diagnostic radiology	2.7
Emergency medicine	2.7
Forensic pathology	.1
General preventive medicine	.2
Neurology	1.6
Nuclear medicine	.2
Occupational medicine	.4
Pathology	2.5
Physical medicine and rehabilitation	.8
Psychiatry	5.3
Public health	.2
Radiology	1.1
Radiation oncology	.5
Other specialty	1.0
Unspecified/unknown/inactive	14.4

SOURCE: American Medical Association

Working Conditions

Many physicians work long, irregular hours. About one-third of all full-time physicians worked 60 hours or more a week in 1996. They must travel frequently between office and hospital to care for their patients. Increasingly, physicians practice in groups or health care organizations that provide back-up coverage and allow for more time off. These physicians work as part of a team that coordinates care for a population of patients; they are less independent than solo practitioners of the past. Physicians who are on-call deal with many patients' concerns over the phone, and may make emergency visits to hospitals.

Employment

Physicians (MDs and DOs) held about 560,000 jobs in 1996. About seven out of ten were in office-based practice, including clinics and HMOs; about two out of ten were employed by hospitals. Others practiced in the federal government, most in Department of Veterans Affairs hospitals and clinics or in the Public Health Service of the Department of Health and Human Services.

A growing number of physicians are partners or salaried employees of group practices. Organized as clinics or as groups of physicians, medical groups can afford expensive medical equipment and realize other business advantages. Also, hospitals are integrating physician practices into health care networks that provide a continuum of care both inside and outside of the hospital setting.

The northeastern and western states have the highest ratio of physicians to population; the southcentral states, the lowest. DOs are more likely than MDs to practice in small cities and towns and in rural areas. MDs tend to locate in urban areas, close to hospital and educational centers.

Osteopathic physicians locate chiefly in states that have osteopathic schools and hospitals. In 1997, about one-half of active DOs practiced in six states: Pennsylvania, Michigan, Ohio, Florida, New Jersey, and Texas.

Training, Other Qualifications, and Advancement

It takes many years of education and training to become a physician: four years of undergraduate school, four years of medical school, and three to eight years of internship and residency, depending on the specialty selected. A few medical schools offer a combined undergraduate and medical school program that lasts six years instead of the customary eight years.

Premedical students must complete undergraduate work in physics, biology, mathematics, English, and inorganic and organic chemistry. Students also take courses in the humanities and the social sciences. Some students also volunteer at local hospitals or clinics to gain practical experience in the health professions.

The minimum educational requirement for entry to a medical or osteopathic school is three years of college; most applicants, however, have at least a bachelor's degree, and many have advanced degrees. There are 142 medical schools in the United States—125 teach allopathic medicine and award a Doctor of Medicine (MD); 17 teach osteopathic medicine and award the Doctor of Osteopathy (DO). Acceptance to medical school is very competitive. Applicants must submit transcripts, scores from the Medical College Admission Test, and letters of recommendation. Schools also consider character, personality, leadership qualities, and participation in extracurricular activities. Most schools require an interview with members of the admissions committee.

Students spend most of the first two years of medical school in laboratories and classrooms taking courses such as anatomy, biochemistry, physiology, pharmacology, psychology, microbiology, pathology, medical ethics, and laws governing medicine. They also learn to take medical histories, examine patients, and diagnose illness. During the last two years, students work with patients under the supervision of experienced physicians in hospitals and clinics to learn acute, chronic, preventive, and rehabilitative care. Through rotations in internal medicine, family practice, obstetrics and gynecology, pediatrics, psychiatry, and surgery, they gain experience in the diagnosis and treatment of illness.

Following medical school, almost all MDs enter a residency—graduate medical education in a specialty that takes the form of paid on-the-job training, usually in a hospital. Most DOs serve a 12-month rotating internship after graduation before entering a residency which may last two to six years. Physicians may benefit from residencies in managed care settings by gaining experience with this increasingly common type of medical practice.

All states, the District of Columbia, and U.S. territories license physicians. To be licensed, physicians must graduate from an accredited medical school, pass a licensing examination, and complete one to seven years of graduate medical education. Although physicians licensed in one state can usually get a license to practice in another without further examination, some states limit reciprocity. Graduates of foreign medical schools can qualify for licensure after passing an examination and completing a U.S. residency.

MDs and DOs seeking board certification in a specialty may spend up to seven years—depending on the specialty—in residency training. A final examination immediately after residency, or after one or two years of practice, is also necessary for board certification by the American Board of Medical Specialists (ABMS) or the American Osteopathic Association (AOA). There are 24 specialty boards, ranging from allergy and immunology to urology. For certification in a subspecialty, physicians usually need another one to two years of residency.

A physician's training is costly. While education costs have increased, student financial assistance has not. Over 80 percent of medical students borrow money to cover their expenses.

People who wish to become physicians must have a desire to serve patients, be self-motivated, and be able to survive the pressures and long hours of medical education and practice. Physicians must also have a good bedside manner, emotional stability, and the ability to make decisions in emergencies. Prospective physicians must be willing to study throughout their career to keep up with medical advances. They will also need to be flexible to respond to the changing demands of a rapidly evolving health care system.

Job Outlook

Employment of physicians will grow faster than the average for all occupations through the year 2006 due to continued expansion of the health care industries. The growing and aging population will drive overall growth in the number of physicians. In addition, new technologies permit more intensive care: Physicians can do more tests, perform more procedures, and treat conditions previously regarded as untreatable. Job prospects will be best for primary care physicians such as general and family practitioners, general pediatricians, and general internists; and for geriatric and preventive care specialists.

Because of efforts to control health care costs and increased reliance on utilization guidelines that often limit the use of specialty services, a lower percentage of specialists will be in demand. At the same time, the number of specialists continues to grow. Competition for jobs among specialists will be especially keen in large urban and suburban areas, and for those who work directly for hospitals, such as anesthesiologists and radiologists.

A number of prestigious organizations, including the National

Academy of Sciences Institute of Medicine and the Pew Health Professions Commission, have found a current oversupply of physicians. They suggest that measures should be taken to reduce the number being trained through such means as a reduction in the number of residency slots. If successful, a reduction in the number of new physicians entering the workforce will help to alleviate the effects of any physician oversupply.

A physician oversupply may not substantially limit the ability of physicians to find employment. However, it could result in physicians working fewer hours, having lower earnings, and having to practice in underserved areas. Opportunities should be good in some rural and low income areas, because some physicians find these areas unattractive due to lower earnings potential, isolation from medical colleagues, or other reasons. It is also possible that physicians trained in specialties will provide primary care services as well as specialty care.

Unlike their predecessors, newly trained physicians face radically different choices of where and how to practice. New physicians are much less likely to enter solo practice and more likely to take salaried jobs in group medical practices, clinics, and health care networks.

Earnings

Physicians have among the highest earnings of any occupation. According to the American Medical Association, median income, after expenses, for allopathic physicians was about $160,000 in 1995. The middle 50 percent earned between $115,000 and $238,000. Self-employed physicians—those who own or are part owners of their medical practice—had higher median incomes than salaried physicians. Earnings vary according to number of years in practice; geographic region; hours worked; and skill, personality, and professional reputation. As shown in table 2, median income of allopathic physicians, after expenses, also varies by specialty.

Average salaries of medical residents ranged from $32,789 in 1996-97 for those in their first year of residency to $40,849 for those in their sixth year, according to the Association of American Medical Colleges.

Table 2. Median net income of MDs after expenses, 1995

All physicians	$160,000
Radiology	230,000
Surgery	225,000
Anesthesiology	203,000
Obstetrics/gynecology	200,000
Pathology	185,000
Emergency medicine	170,000
General internal medicine	138,000
Pediatrics	129,000
Psychiatry	124,000
General/Family practice	124,000

SOURCE: American Medical Association

Related Occupations

Physicians work to prevent, diagnose, and treat diseases, disorders, and injuries. Professionals in other occupations that require similar kinds of skill and critical judgment include acupuncturists, audiologists, chiropractors, dentists, nurse practitioners, optometrists, physician assistants, podiatrists, speech pathologists, and veterinarians.

Sources of Additional Information

For a list of allopathic medical schools and residency programs, as well as general information on premedical education, financial aid, and medicine as a career, contact:

❑ American Medical Association, 515 N. State St., Chicago, IL 60610.

❑ Association of American Medical Colleges, Section for Student Services, 2450 N St. NW, Washington, DC 20037-1131. Homepage: http://www.aamc.org

For general information on osteopathic medicine as a career, contact:

❑ American Osteopathic Association, Department of Public Relations, 142 East Ontario St., Chicago, IL 60611. Homepage: http://www.am-osteo-assn.org

❑ American Association of Colleges of Osteopathic Medicine, 5550 Friendship Blvd., Suite 310, Chevy Chase, MD 20815-7321. Homepage: http://www.aacom.org

Information on federal scholarships and loans is available from the directors of student financial aid at schools of allopathic and osteopathic medicine.

Information on licensing is available from state boards of examiners.

Police, Detectives, and Special Agents

(D.O.T. 168.167-010; 372.167-018, .267, .363 and .367-010; 375.133, .137 except -022 and -038, .163, .167 except -018, -026, and -054, .263, .264, .267, .363 through .384; 376.167 and .667-018; 377; and 379.167 and .263-014)

Significant Points

✓ *Police work can be dangerous and stressful.*

✓ *The number of qualified candidates exceeds the number of job openings in federal law enforcement agencies and in most state, local, and special police departments.*

✓ *Opportunities will be best in those urban communities whose departments offer relatively low salaries and where the crime rate is relatively high.*

Nature of the Work

The safety and well being of our nation's citizens greatly depends on the police officers, detectives, and special agents responsible for enforcing statutes, laws, and regulations. Duties vary widely by the size and type of organization but in most jurisdictions, whether on or off duty, law enforcement officers are expected to exercise their authority whenever necessary. And, regardless of where they work or what they do, police, detectives, and special agents must spend considerable time writing reports and maintaining records that are needed when legal actions require them to testify in court.

Police officers who work in small communities and rural areas have general law enforcement duties. In the course of a day's work, they may direct traffic at the scene of a fire, investigate a burglary, or give first aid to an accident victim. In large police departments, by contrast, officers usually are assigned to a specific type of duty. Most officers are detailed to patrol a designated area to prevent crime. Patrols generally cover an area such as business districts or outlying residential neighborhoods. Officers may work alone, but in large agencies they usually patrol with a partner. They attempt to become thoroughly familiar with conditions throughout their patrol area and, while on patrol, remain alert for anything unusual. Suspicious circumstances, such as open windows or lights in vacant buildings, as well as hazards to public safety are noted. They identify, pursue, and arrest suspected criminals, resolve problems within the community, and enforce traffic laws. Officers are becoming more involved in community policing–building partnerships with the citizens of local neighborhoods and mobilizing the public to help the police fight crime.

Some police officers specialize and become experts in chemical and microscopic analysis, firearms identification, handwriting and fingerprint identification. Others may work with special units such as mounted and motorcycle patrol, harbor patrol, canine corps, special weapons and tactics or emergency response teams, or task forces formed to combat specific types of crime.

Detectives and special agents are plainclothes investigators who gather facts and collect evidence for criminal cases. They conduct interviews, examine records, observe the activities of suspects, and participate in raids or arrests.

Some local departments provide security officers, sometimes called bailiffs, to maintain order in courtrooms.

Sheriffs and deputy sheriffs enforce the law on the county level. In metropolitan areas where there are also regular police departments, the sheriffs' department may perform specialized duties such as serving legal documents or operating the jail. A sheriffs' duties resemble those of a local or county police chief, but the department is generally on a smaller scale. Most sheriffs' departments employ fewer than 25 sworn officers, and many employ fewer than 10.

State police officers (sometimes called state troopers or highway patrol officers) patrol highways and enforce motor vehicle laws and regulations. They issue traffic citations to motorists who violate the law. At the scene of an accident, they may direct traffic, give first aid, and call for emergency equipment. They also write reports that may be used to determine the cause of the accident. In addition, state police officers may provide services to motorists on the highways, such as calling for road service for drivers with mechanical trouble.

State police also enforce criminal laws. They are frequently called upon to render assistance to officers of other law enforcement agencies. In rural areas that do not have a police force or a local deputy from the sheriff's department, the state police are the primary law enforcement agency, investigating any crimes that occur, such as burglary or assault.

The federal government maintains a high profile in many areas of law enforcement. Federal Bureau of Investigation (FBI) special agents are the government's principal investigators, responsible for investigating violations of more than 260 statutes. Agents may conduct surveillance, monitor court-authorized wiretaps, examine business records to investigate white-collar crime, track the interstate movement of stolen property, collect evidence of espionage activities, or participate in sensitive undercover assignments. Drug Enforcement Administration (DEA) special agents specialize in enforcement of drug laws and regulations. Agents may conduct complex criminal investigations, carry out surveillance of criminals, and infiltrate illicit drug organizations using undercover techniques. U.S. marshals and deputy marshals provide security for federal courts, including judges, witnesses, and prisoners, and apprehend fugitives. U.S. Border Patrol special agents are responsible for protecting more than 8,000 miles of international land and water boundaries. Their primary mission is to detect and prevent the smuggling and unlawful entry of undocumented aliens into the United States and to apprehend those persons found in violation of the immigration laws. Immigration and Naturalization Service (INS) agents facilitate the entry of legal visitors and immigrants to the United States and detain and deport those arriving illegally.

Special agents employed by the U.S. Department of the Treasury work for the Bureau of Alcohol, Tobacco, and Firearms, the U.S. Customs Service, the Internal Revenue Service, and U.S. Secret Service. Bureau of Alcohol, Tobacco, and Firearms special agents investigate violations of federal firearms and explosives laws, as well as federal alcohol and tobacco regulations. Customs agents inspect cargo, collect appropriate duties or fees, and intercept contraband while ensuring that all goods entering the United States comply with United States laws and regulations. Internal Revenue Service special agents collect evidence against individuals and companies that are evading the payment of federal taxes. U.S. Secret Service special agents protect the President, Vice President, and their immediate families, Presidential candidates, ex-Presidents, and foreign dignitaries visiting the United States. Secret Service agents also investigate counterfeiting, the forgery of government checks or bonds, and the fraudulent use of credit cards.

Various other federal agencies employ police and special agents with sworn arrest powers and the authority to carry firearms. These agencies include the U.S. Forest Service under the Department of Agriculture, the National Park Service under the Department of the Interior, and Federal Air Marshals under the Department of Transportation. Other police agencies generally evolved from the need for security for the agency's property and personnel. The largest such agency is the General Services Administration's Federal Protective Service, which provides security for federal buildings and property nationwide.

Working Conditions

Police work can be very dangerous and stressful. In addition to the obvious dangers of confrontations with criminals, the need to be constantly alert and ready to deal appropriately with any situation can be very stressful. Police, detectives, and special agents usually work a 40-hour week, but paid overtime work is common. Shift work is necessary because police protection must be provided around the clock. Junior officers frequently must work weekends, holidays, and nights. Police officers, detectives, and special agents are subject to call at any time their services are needed and may work long hours during investigations. All law enforcement officers are required to file reports of their activities, often involving long hours of paperwork. In most jurisdictions, whether on or off duty, officers are expected to be armed and to exercise their arrest authority whenever necessary.

The jobs of some federal agents such as U.S. Secret Service and DEA special agents require extensive travel, often on very short notice. They frequently relocate a number of times over the course of their career. Some police, detectives, and special agents with agencies such as the U.S. Border Patrol must work outdoors for long periods in all kinds of weather.

Employment

Police, detectives, and special agents held about 704,000 jobs in 1996. About 63 percent of police detectives and investigators were employed by local governments, primarily in cities with more than 25,000 inhabitants. Some cities have very large police forces, while hundreds of small communities employ fewer than 25 officers each. State police agencies employed about 10 percent of all police, detectives, and investigators; various federal agencies employed the other 27 percent.

Training, Other Qualifications, and Advancement

Civil service regulations govern the appointment of police and detectives in practically all state and large city agencies and in many smaller ones. Candidates must be U.S. citizens, usually at least 20 years of age, and must meet rigorous physical and personal qualifications. Eligibility for appointment generally depends on performance in competitive written examinations as well as on education and experience. Physical examinations often include tests of vision, hearing, strength, and agility.

Because personal characteristics such as honesty, judgment, integrity, and a sense of responsibility are especially important in law enforcement work, candidates are interviewed by senior officers, and their character traits and background are investigated. In some agencies, candidates are interviewed by a psychiatrist or a psychologist, or given a personality test. Most applicants are subjected to lie detector examinations or drug testing. Some agencies subject sworn personnel to random drug testing as a condition of continuing employment. Although police, detectives, and special agents work independently, they must perform their duties in accordance with the law and departmental rules. They should enjoy working with people and meeting the public.

In larger police departments, where the majority of law enforcement jobs are found, applicants usually must have at least a high school education. Federal agencies generally require a college degree. A few police departments accept applicants as recruits who have less than a high school education, but the number is declining.

The federal agency with the largest number of special agents is the FBI. To be considered for appointment as an FBI special agent, an applicant either must be a graduate of an accredited law school; be a college graduate with a major in accounting; or be a college graduate with either fluency in a foreign language or three years of full-time work experience. All new agents undergo 16 weeks of training at the FBI academy on the U.S. Marine Corps base in Quantico, Virginia.

Applicants for special agent jobs with the U.S. Department of Treasury's Secret Service and the Bureau of Alcohol, Tobacco, and Firearms must have a bachelor's degree or a minimum of three years' work experience which demonstrates the ability to deal effectively with individuals or groups, among other things. Prospective special agents undergo eight weeks of training at the Federal Law Enforcement Training Center in Glynco, Georgia, and another 8 to 11 weeks of specialized training with their particular agencies.

Applicants for special agent jobs with the U.S. Drug Enforcement Administration (DEA) must have a college degree and either one year of experience conducting criminal investigations, one year of graduate school, or have achieved at least a 2.95 grade point average while in college. DEA special agents undergo 14 weeks of specialized training at the FBI Academy in Quantico, Virginia.

Police departments are encouraging applicants to take postsecondary school training in law enforcement. Many entry level applicants to police jobs have completed some formal postsecondary education and a significant number are college graduates. In 1993, the most recent year for which data are available, 12 percent of local police departments required new officer recruits to have at least some college education. Many junior colleges, colleges, and universities offer programs in law enforcement or administration of justice. Other courses helpful in preparing for a career in law enforcement include accounting, finance, electrical engineering or computer science, and foreign languages. Physical education and sports are helpful in developing the courage, competitiveness, stamina, and agility needed for law enforcement work. Knowledge of a foreign language is an asset in many agencies.

Some large cities hire high school graduates who are still in their teens as police cadets or trainees. They do clerical work and attend classes, and can be appointed to the regular force at the conclusion of their training, usually in one to two years, upon reaching the minimum age requirement.

Before their first assignments, officers usually go through a period of training. In state and large local departments, recruits get training in their agency's police academy, often for 12 to 14 weeks. In small agencies, recruits often attend a regional or state academy. Training includes classroom instruction in constitutional law and civil rights, state laws and local ordinances, and accident investigation. Recruits also receive training and supervised experience in patrol, traffic control, use of firearms, self-defense, first aid, and handling emergencies.

Police officers usually become eligible for promotion after a probationary period ranging from six months to three years. In a large department, promotion may enable an officer to become a detective or specialize in one type of police work such as laboratory analysis of evidence or working with juveniles. Promotions to corporal, sergeant, lieutenant, and captain usually are made according to a candidate's position on a promotion list, as determined by scores on a written examination and on-the-job performance.

Continuing training helps police officers, detectives, and special agents improve their job performance. Through police department academies, regional centers for public safety employees established by the states, and federal agency training centers, instructors provide annual training in defensive tactics, firearms, use-of-force policies, sensitivity and communications skills, crowd-control techniques, legal developments that affect their work, and advances in law enforcement equipment. Many agencies pay all or part of the tuition for officers to work toward degrees in criminal justice, police science, administration of justice, or public administration, and pay higher salaries to those who earn such a degree.

Job Outlook

The opportunity for public service through law enforcement work is attractive to many. The job is challenging and involves much personal responsibility. Furthermore, in many agencies, law enforcement officers may retire with a pension after 20 or 25 years of service, allowing them to pursue a second career while still in their 40s. Because of relatively attractive salaries and benefits, the number of qualified candidates exceeds the number of job openings in federal law enforcement agencies and in most state, local, and special police departments–resulting in increased hiring standards and selectivity by employers. Competition is expected to remain keen for the higher paying jobs with state and federal agencies and police departments in more affluent areas. Persons having college training in police science, military experience, or both should have the best opportunities. Opportunities will be best in those urban communities whose departments offer relatively low salaries and where the crime rate is relatively high.

Employment of police officers, detectives, and special agents is expected to increase about as fast as the average for all occupations through the year 2006. A more security-conscious society and concern about drug-related crimes should contribute to the increasing demand for police services. At the local and state levels, growth is likely to continue as long as crime remains a serious concern. However, employment growth at the federal level will be tempered by continuing budgetary constraints faced by law enforcement agencies. Turnover in police, detective, and special agent positions is among the lowest of all occupations; nevertheless, the need to replace workers who retire, transfer to other occupations, or stop working for other reasons will be the source of most job openings.

The level of government spending determines the level of employment for police officers, detectives, and special agents. The number of job opportunities, therefore, can vary from year to year and from place to place. Layoffs, on the other hand, are rare because retirements enable most staffing cuts to be handled through attrition. Trained law enforcement officers who lose their jobs because of budget cuts usually have little difficulty finding jobs with other agencies.

Earnings

In 1996, the median salary of nonsupervisory police officers and detectives was about $34,700 a year. The middle 50 percent earned between about $25,700 and $45,300; the lowest 10 percent were paid less than $19,200, while the highest 10 percent earned over $58,500 a year.

Police officers and detectives in supervisory positions had a median salary of about $41,200 a year, also in 1996. The middle 50 percent earned between about $29,200 and $38,400; the lowest 10 percent were paid less than $22,500, while the highest 10 percent earned over $64,500 annually.

Sheriffs and other law enforcement officers had a median annual salary of about $26,700 in 1996. The middle 50 percent earned between about $20,300 and $37,800; the lowest 10 percent were paid less than $15,900, while the highest 10 percent earned over $48,400.

Federal law provides special salary rates to federal employees who serve in law enforcement. Additionally, federal special agents receive availability pay or administratively uncontrolled overtime (AUO)–equal to 25 percent of the agent's grade and step–awarded because of the large amount of overtime that these agents are expected to work. For example, in 1996 FBI agents started at a base salary of $33,800 a year, earning $42,250 a year with availability pay. Other Justice and Treasury Department special agents started at about $25,000 or $30,700 a year, earning $31,300 or $38,400 per year including availability pay, depending on their qualifications. Salaries of federal special agents progress to $55,600 including availability pay, while supervisory agents started at $66,100 including availability pay. Salaries were slightly higher in selected areas where the prevailing local pay level was higher. Because federal agents may be eligible for a special law enforcement benefits package, applicants should ask their recruiter for more information.

Total earnings for local, state, and special police and detectives frequently exceed the stated salary due to payments for overtime, which can be significant. In addition to the common benefits—paid vacation, sick leave, and medical and life insurance—most police and sheriffs' departments provide officers with special allowances for uniforms. In addition, because police officers generally are covered by liberal pension plans, many retire at half-pay after 20 or 25 years of service.

Related Occupations

Police, detectives, and special agents maintain law and order. Workers in related occupations include correctional officers, guards, fire marshals, and inspectors.

Sources of Additional Information

Information about entrance requirements may be obtained from federal, state, and local law enforcement agencies.

Further information about qualifications for employment as an FBI Special Agent is available from the nearest state FBI office; the address and phone number are listed in the local telephone directory.

Further information about qualifications for employment as a DEA Special Agent is available from the nearest DEA office, or call 1-800 DEA-4288.

Information about career opportunities, qualifications, and training to become a deputy marshal is available from:

❏ United States Marshals Service, Employment and Compensation Division, Field Staffing Branch, 600 Army Navy Dr., Arlington, VA 22202.

An overview of career opportunities, qualifications, and training for U.S. Secret Service Special Agents is available from:

❏ U.S. Secret Service, Personnel Division, Room 912, 1800 G St. NW, Washington, DC 20223.

Postal Clerks and Mail Carriers

(*D.O.T.* 209.687-014; 222.387-050; .587-018 and -034; and .687-022; 230.363-010, .367-010; 239.367-018; and 243.367-014)

Significant Points

- ✓ *Those seeking a job in the Postal Service can expect to encounter keen competition because of the large number of qualified applicants.*
- ✓ *Jobs as postal clerks and mail carriers offer attractive salaries, a good pension plan, and job security.*
- ✓ *Few people under the age of 25 are hired as career postal clerks or mail carriers.*

Nature of the Work

Each day, the U.S. Postal Service receives, sorts, and delivers millions of letters, bills, advertisements, and packages. To do this, it employs about 856,000 workers. Almost three out of four of these workers are either mail handlers or clerks, who sort mail and serve customers in post offices, or mail carriers, who deliver the mail.

Clerks and carriers are distinguished by the type of work they do. Clerks are usually classified by the mail processing function they perform, whereas carriers are classified by their type of route—city or rural.

Postal clerks at local post offices—sometimes called window or counter clerks—sort local mail for delivery to individual customers; sell stamps, money orders, postal stationary, and mailing envelopes and boxes; weigh packages to determine postage; and check that packages are in satisfactory condition for mailing. These clerks also register, certify, and insure mail and answer questions about postage rates, post office boxes, mailing restrictions, and other postal matters. They also may help customers file claims for damaged packages.

About 350 mail processing centers throughout the country service post offices in surrounding areas and are staffed primarily by clerks and mail handlers. Mail handlers unload the sacks of incoming mail; separate letters, parcel post, magazines, and newspapers; and transport these to the proper sorting and processing area. In addition, they may load mail into automated letter sorting machines, perform postage canceling operations, and rewrap packages damaged in processing.

After letters have been put through stamp-canceling machines, they are taken to other workrooms to be sorted according to destination. A growing proportion of clerks operate optical character readers (OCRs) and bar code sorters. Optical character readers "read" the ZIP code and spray a bar code onto the mail. Bar code sorters then scan the code and sort the mail. Because this is significantly faster than older sorting methods, it is becoming the standard sorting technology in mail processing centers.

Other clerks, who operate older electronic letter-sorting machines, push keys corresponding to the ZIP code of the local post office to which each letter will be delivered; the machine then drops the letters into the proper slots. This older, less automated method of letter sorting is being phased out. Still other clerks sort odd-sized letters, magazines, and newspapers by hand. Finally, the mail is sent to local post offices for sorting according to delivery route and delivered.

Once the mail has been processed and sorted, it is ready to be delivered by mail carriers. Duties of city and rural carriers are very similar. Most travel established routes delivering and collecting mail. Mail carriers start work at the post office early in the morning, where they spend a few hours arranging their mail in delivery sequence and taking care of other details. Recently, automated equipment has reduced the time needed to sort the mail, allowing mail carriers to spend more time delivering mail.

Carriers cover their routes on foot, by vehicle, or a combination of both. On foot, they carry a heavy load of mail in a satchel or push it in a cart. In some urban and most rural areas, they use a car or small truck. Although the Postal Service may provide vehicles to city carriers, most rural carriers use their own automobiles. Deliveries are made house-to-house, to roadside mailboxes, and to large buildings, such as offices or apartments, which generally have all the mailboxes on the first floor.

Besides delivering and collecting mail, carriers collect money for postage-due and c.o.d. (cash on delivery) fees and obtain signed receipts for registered, certified, and insured mail. If a customer is not home, the carrier leaves a notice that tells where special mail is being held.

After completing their routes, carriers return to the post office with mail gathered from street collection boxes, homes, and businesses. They turn in the mail receipts and money collected during the day and may separate letters and parcels for further processing by clerks.

The duties of some city carriers may be very specialized; some deliver only parcel post while others collect mail from street boxes and receiving boxes in office buildings. In contrast, rural carriers provide a wider range of postal services—in addition to delivering and picking up mail, they sell stamps and money orders and accept parcels, letters, and items to be registered, certified, or insured.

All carriers answer customers' questions about postal regulations and services and provide change-of-address cards and other postal forms when requested. In addition to their regularly scheduled duties, carriers often participate in neighborhood service programs in which they check on elderly or shut-in patrons or notify the police of any suspicious activities along their routes.

Postal clerks and mail carriers are classified as casual, part-time flexible, part-time regular, or full-time. Casual workers, hired for 90 days at a time, help process and deliver mail during peak mailing or vacation periods. Part-time flexible workers do not have a regular work schedule or weekly guarantee of hours; they replace absent workers and help with extra work as the need arises. Part-time regulars have a set work schedule of fewer than 40 hours per week. Full-time postal employees work a 40-hour week over a five-day period.

Working Conditions

Window clerks usually work in clean, well ventilated, and well lit buildings. They have a wide variety of duties, frequent contact with the public, and rarely work at night. However, they may have to deal with upset customers and stand for long periods of time, and they are held accountable for the assigned stock of stamps and postal funds. Depending on the size of the post office in which they work, they may also be required to perform some sorting as well.

The working conditions of other postal clerks can vary. In small post offices, mail handlers use handtrucks to move heavy mail sacks from one part of the building to another and clerks may sort mail by hand. In large post offices and mail processing centers, chutes and conveyors move the mail, and much of the sorting is done by machines. Despite the use of automated equipment, the work of mail handlers and postal clerks can be physically demanding. These workers are usually on their feet, reaching for sacks and trays of mail or placing packages and bundles into sacks and trays.

Mail handlers and distribution clerks may become wearied with the routine of moving and sorting mail. Many work at night or on weekends because most large post offices process mail around the clock, and the largest volume of mail is sorted during the evening and night shifts. Workers may experience stress as they process and deliver ever larger quantities of mail under tight production deadlines and quotas.

Most carriers begin work early in the morning, in some cases as early as 4 A.M., if they have routes in a business district. A carrier's schedule has its advantages, however. Carriers who begin work early in the morning are through by early afternoon, and they spend most of the day on their own, relatively free from direct supervision. Overtime hours may be required during peak delivery times, such as before holidays.

Carriers spend most of their time outdoors, and deliver mail in all kinds of weather. Even those who drive often must walk when making deliveries and must lift heavy sacks of parcel post items when loading their vehicles. In addition, carriers always must be cautious of potential hazards on their routes. Wet roads and sidewalks can be treacherous, and each year numerous carriers are bitten by dogs.

Employment

The U.S. Postal Service employed 297,000 clerks and mail handlers and 332,000 mail carriers in 1996. About 90 percent of them worked full-time. Most postal clerks provided window service and sorted mail at local post offices, although some worked at mail processing centers. Although most mail carriers worked in cities and suburban communities, 48,000 were rural carriers.

Training, Other Qualifications, and Advancement

Postal clerks and mail carriers must be U.S. citizens or have been granted permanent resident-alien status in the United States. They must be at least 18 years old (or 16, if they have a high school diploma). Qualification is based on a written examination that measures speed and accuracy at checking names and numbers and the ability to memorize mail distribution procedures. Applicants must pass a physical examination and drug test as well, and may be asked to show that they can lift and handle mail sacks weighing up to 70 pounds. Applicants for jobs as postal clerks operating electronic sorting machines must pass a special examination that includes a machine aptitude test. Applicants for mail carrier positions must have a driver's license, a good driving record, and receive a passing grade on a road test.

Applicants should apply at the post office or mail processing center where they wish to work in order to determine when an exam will be given. Applicants' names are listed in order of their examination scores. Five points are added to the score of an honorably discharged veteran, and ten points to the score of a veteran wounded in combat or disabled. When a vacancy occurs, the appointing officer chooses one of the top three applicants; the rest of the names remain on the list to be considered for future openings until their eligibility expires, usually two years from the examination date.

Relatively few people under the age of 25 are hired as career postal clerks or mail carriers, a result of keen competition for these jobs and the customary waiting period of one to two years or more after passing the examination. It is not surprising, therefore, that most entrants transfer from other occupations.

New postal clerks and mail carriers are trained on the job by experienced workers. Many post offices offer classroom instruction. Workers receive additional instruction when new equipment or procedures are introduced. They usually are trained by another postal employee or, sometimes, a training specialist hired under contract by the Postal Service.

Window clerks and mail carriers must be courteous and tactful when dealing with the public, especially when answering questions or receiving complaints. A good memory, good coordination, and the ability to read rapidly and accurately are also important. Mail handlers and distribution clerks work closely with other clerks, frequently under the tension and strain of meeting dispatch transportation deadlines.

Postal clerks and mail carriers often begin on a part-time flexible basis and become regular or full-time in order of seniority as vacancies occur. Full-time clerks may bid for preferred assignments such as the day shift or a higher level nonsupervisory position as expediter or window service technician. Carriers can look forward to obtaining preferred routes as their seniority increases, or to higher level jobs such as carrier technician. Both clerks and carriers can advance to supervisory positions.

Job Outlook

Those seeking a job in the Postal Service can expect to encounter keen competition—the number of applicants for postal clerk and mail carrier positions is expected to continue to far exceed the number of openings. Job opportunities will vary by occupation and duties performed.

Overall employment of postal clerks is expected to increase more slowly than the average through the year 2006. Despite efforts by the U.S. Postal Service to provide higher levels of customer service at their window and counter operations, the demand for window clerks will be moderated by the increased sales of stamps and other postal products by grocery stores and other retail outlets, as well as the use of electronic communications technologies and private delivery companies. As for other postal clerks, more mail will be moved using automated materials handling equipment and sorted using optical character readers, bar code sorters, and other automated sorting equipment. Despite the increase in the use of productivity increasing machinery, the expected increase in mail volume will require some additional clerks.

Conflicting factors also are expected to influence demand for mail carriers. Despite competition from alternative delivery systems and new forms of electronic communication, the volume of mail handled by the U.S. Postal Service is expected to continue to grow. Population growth and the formation of new households will stimulate demand for mail delivery. However, increased use of the "ZIP + 4" system, which sorts mail to the carrier route, and other automated sorting equipment should decrease the amount of time carriers spend sorting their mail, allowing them more time to handle longer routes. In addition, the Postal Service is moving toward more centralized mail delivery, such as the use of more cluster boxes, to cut down on the number of door-to-door deliveries. These trends are expected to increase carrier productivity. Employment of mail carriers is expected to increase about as fast as average for all occupations through the year 2006.

Jobs will become available because of the need to replace postal clerks and mail carriers who retire or stop working for other reasons. However, the factors that make entry to these occupations highly competitive—attractive salaries, a good pension plan, job security, and modest educational requirements—contribute to a high degree of job attachment. Accordingly, replacement needs produce relatively fewer job openings than in other occupations of this size. In contrast to the typical pattern, postal workers generally remain in their jobs until they retire; relatively few transfer to other occupations.

Although the volume of mail to be processed and delivered rises and falls with the level of business activity, as well as with the season of the year, full-time postal clerks and mail carriers have never been laid off. When mail volume is high, full-time clerks and carriers work overtime, part-time clerks and carriers work additional hours, and casual clerks and carriers may be hired. When mail volume is low, overtime is curtailed, part-timers work fewer hours, and casual workers are discharged.

Earnings

In 1996, base pay for beginning full-time postal clerks who operate scanning and sorting machines was $24,599 a year, rising to a maximum of $35,683 after 14 years of service. Entry-level pay for window clerks and clerks in retail outlets was $26,063 a year in 1996 whereas those with 14 years of service earned $36,551 a year. Entry-level pay for full-time regular mail handling clerks ranged from $21,676 to $22,944 a year in 1996.

Experienced, full-time, city delivery mail carriers earn, on average, $34,135 a year. Postal clerks and carriers working part-time flexible schedules begin at $12.82 an hour and, based on the number of years of service, increase to a maximum of $18.07 an hour. Rural delivery carriers had average base salaries of $35,000 in 1996. Their earnings are determined through an evaluation of the amount of work required to service their routes. Carriers with heavier workloads generally earn more than those with lighter workloads. Rural carriers also receive an equipment maintenance allowance when required to use their own vehicles. In 1996, this was approximately 36.5 cents per mile.

Postal workers enjoy a variety of employer-provided benefits. These include health and life insurance, vacation and sick leave, and a pension plan.

In addition to their hourly wage and benefits package, some postal workers receive a uniform allowance. This group includes those workers who are in the public view for four or more hours each day and various maintenance workers. The amount of the allowance depends on the job performed—some workers are only required to wear a partial uniform, and their allowance is lower. In 1996, for example, the allowance for a letter carrier was $277 per year, compared to $119 for a window clerk.

Most of these workers belong to one of four unions: American Postal Workers Union, AFL-CIO; National Association of Letter Carriers, AFL-CIO; National Postal Mail Handlers Union, AFL-CIO; and National Rural Letter Carriers Association.

Related Occupations

Other workers whose duties are related to those of postal clerks include mail clerks, file clerks, routing clerks, sorters, material moving equipment operators, clerk typists, cashiers, data entry operators, and ticket sellers. Others with duties related to those of mail carriers include messengers, merchandise deliverers, and delivery-route truck drivers.

Sources of Additional Information

Local post offices and state employment service offices can supply details about entrance examinations and specific employment opportunities for postal clerks and mail carriers.

Preschool Teachers and Child-Care Workers

(*D.O.T.* 092.227-018; 355.674-010; 359.677-010, -018, -026)

Significant Points

- ✓ *About 40 percent of preschool teachers and child-care workers—four times the proportion for all workers—are self-employed; most are family daycare providers.*
- ✓ *Turnover is high due to stressful conditions and low pay and benefits.*
- ✓ *While training requirements vary from a high school diploma to a college degree, a high school diploma and little or no experience is usually adequate.*

Nature of the Work

Preschool teachers and child-care workers nurture and teach preschool children—age 5 or younger—in child-care centers, nursery schools, preschools, public schools, and family child-care homes. These workers play an important role in a child's development by caring for the child when the parents are at work or away for other reasons. Some parents enroll their children in nursery schools or child-care centers primarily to provide them with the opportunity to interact with other children. In addition to attending to children's basic needs, these workers organize activities that stimulate the children's physical, emotional, intellectual, and social growth. They help children explore their interests, develop their talents and independence, build self-esteem, and learn how to behave with others.

Preschool teachers and child-care workers spend most of their day working with children. However, they do maintain contact with parents or guardians, through daily informal meetings or scheduled conferences, to discuss each child's progress and needs. Many preschool teachers and child-care workers keep records of each child's progress and suggest ways parents can increase their child's learning and development at home. Some preschools and child-care centers actively recruit parent volunteers to work with the children and participate in administrative decisions and program planning.

Most preschool teachers and child-care workers perform a combination of basic care and teaching duties. Through many basic care activities, preschool teachers and child-care workers provide opportunities for children to learn. For example, a worker who shows a child how to tie a shoe teaches the child and also provides for that child's basic care needs. Through their experiences in preschool and child-care programs, children learn about trust and gain a sense of security.

Children at this age learn mainly through play. Recognizing the importance of play, preschool teachers and child-care workers build their program around it. They capitalize on children's play to further language development (storytelling and acting games), improve social skills (working together to build a neighborhood in a sandbox), and introduce scientific and mathematical concepts (balancing and counting blocks when building a bridge or mixing colors when painting).

Thus, a less structured approach is used to teach preschool children, including small group lessons, one-on-one instruction, and learning through creative activities, such as art, dance, and music.

Interaction with peers is an important part of a child's early development. Preschool children are given an opportunity to engage in conversation and discussions, and learn to play and work cooperatively with their classmates. Preschool teachers and child-care workers play a vital role in preparing children to build the skills they will need in elementary school.

Preschool teachers and child-care workers greet children as they arrive, help them remove outer garments, and select an activity of interest. When caring for infants, they feed and change them. To ensure a well-balanced program, preschool teachers and child-care workers prepare daily and long-term schedules of activities. Each day's activities balance individual and group play and quiet and active time. Children are given some freedom to participate in activities in which they are interested.

Helping to keep children healthy is an important part of the job. Preschool teachers and child-care workers serve nutritious meals and snacks and teach good eating habits and personal hygiene. They see to it that children have proper rest periods. They spot children who may not feel well or show signs of emotional or developmental problems and discuss these matters with their supervisor and the child's parents. In some cases, preschool teachers and child-care workers help parents identify programs that will provide basic health services.

Early identification of children with special needs, such as those with behavioral, emotional, physical, or learning disabilities, is important to improve their future learning ability. Special education teachers often work with these preschool children to provide the individual attention they need.

Working Conditions

Preschool facilities include private homes, schools, religious institutions, workplaces where employers provide care for employees' children, or private buildings. Individuals who provide care in their own homes are generally called family child-care providers.

Watching children grow, enjoy learning, and gain new skills can be very rewarding. While working with children, preschool teachers and child-care workers often improve the child's communication, learning, and other personal skills. Also, the work is never routine; each day is marked by new activities and challenges. However, child-care can be physically and emotionally taxing, as workers constantly stand, walk, bend, stoop, and lift to attend to each child's interests and problems.

To ensure that children receive proper supervision, state regulations require certain ratios of workers to children. The ratio varies with the age of the children. Child development experts generally recommend that a single caregiver be responsible for no more than three or four infants (less than 1 year old), five or six toddlers (1 to 2 years old), or ten preschool-age children (between 2 and 5 years old).

The working hours of preschool teachers and child-care workers vary widely. Child-care centers are generally open year round with long hours so that parents can drop off and pick up their children before and after work. Some centers employ full-time and part-time staff with staggered shifts to cover the entire day. Some workers are unable to take regular breaks during the day due to limited staffing. Public and many private preschool programs operate during the typical nine- or ten-month school year, employing both full-time and part-time workers. Many preschool teachers may work extra unpaid hours each week on curriculum planning, parent meetings, and occasional fundraising activities. Family daycare providers have flexible hours and daily routines, but may work long or unusual hours to fit parents' work schedules.

Turnover in this occupation is high. Many preschool teachers and child-care workers suffer burnout due to long hours, low pay and benefits, and stressful conditions.

Employment

Preschool teachers and child-care workers held about 1.2 million jobs in 1996. Many worked part-time. About four out of ten preschool teachers and child-care workers are self-employed, most of whom are family daycare providers.

Over 50 percent of all salaried preschool teachers and child-care workers are found in child-care centers and preschools, and more than 15 percent work for a religious institution. The rest work in other community organizations and in government. Some child-care programs are for-profit centers; some are affiliated with a local or national chain. Religious institutions, community agencies, school systems, and state and local governments operate nonprofit programs. A growing number of business firms operate on-site child-care centers for the children of their employees.

Training, Other Qualifications, and Advancement

The training and qualifications required of preschool teachers and child-care workers vary widely. Each state has its own licensing requirements that regulate caregiver training, ranging from a high school diploma, to community college courses, to a college degree in child development or early childhood education. Some states require continuing education for workers in this field. However, most state requirements are minimal. Formal education requirements in some private preschools and child-care centers are often lower than in public programs since they are not bound by state requirements. Often, child-care workers can obtain employment with a high school diploma and little or no experience.

Some states prefer preschool teachers and child-care workers to have a Child Development Associate (CDA) credential, which is offered by the Council for Early Childhood Professional Recognition. The CDA credential is recognized as a qualification for teachers and directors in 46 states and the District of Columbia. To be eligible, applicants must have 120 hours of training, a high school diploma, and 480 hours of experience. If applicants lack the required experience, they may participate in a one-year child development training program. Those who meet eligibility requirements must also demonstrate their knowledge and skills to a team of child-care professionals from the Council for Early Childhood Professional Recognition. Applicants whose skills meet certain nationally recognized standards receive the CDA credential.

Some employers may not require a CDA credential, but may require secondary or postsecondary courses in child development and early childhood education, and possibly work experience in a child-care setting. Other schools require their own specialized training. For example, Montessori preschool teachers must complete an additional year of training after receiving their bachelor's degree in early childhood education or a related field. Public schools typically require a bachelor's degree and state teacher certification. Teacher training programs include a variety of liberal arts courses, courses in child development, student teaching, and prescribed professional courses, including instruction in teaching gifted, disadvantaged, and other children with special needs.

Preschool teachers and child-care workers must be enthusiastic and constantly alert, anticipate and prevent problems, deal with disruptive children, and provide fair but firm discipline. They must communicate effectively with the children and their parents, as well as other teachers and child-care workers. Workers should be mature, patient, understanding, and articulate, and have energy and physical stamina. Skills in music, art, drama, and storytelling are also important. Those who work for themselves must have business sense and management abilities.

Opportunities for advancement are limited in this occupation. However, as preschool teachers and child-care workers gain experience, some may advance to supervisory or administrative positions in large child-care centers or preschools. Often these positions require additional training, such as a bachelor's or master's degree. Other workers move on to work in resource and referral agencies, consulting with parents on available child services. Some workers become involved in policy or advocacy work related to child-care and early childhood education. With a bachelor's degree, preschool teachers may become certified to teach in public schools at the kindergarten, elementary, and secondary school levels. Some workers set up their own child-care businesses.

Job Outlook

Employment of preschool teachers and child-care workers is projected to increase faster than the average for all occupations through the year 2006. In addition, many preschool teachers and child-care workers leave the occupation each year for other—often better paying—jobs, family responsibilities, or other reasons. High turnover, combined with rapid job growth, is expected to create many openings for preschool teachers and child-care workers. Qualified persons who are interested in this work should have little trouble finding and keeping a job.

Although the number of children under 5 years of age is expected to decline slightly through the year 2006, the proportion of youngsters in child-care and preschool should increase, keeping demand high for preschool teachers and child-care workers. Women between the ages of 20 and 44 have been joining the labor force in growing numbers. Moreover, women are returning to work sooner after childbirth. As more mothers of preschool and school-age children enter the work force, the need for child-care will grow. Many parents will continue to turn to formal child-care arrangements because they find it too difficult to set up a satisfactory arrangement with a relative, baby-sitter, or live-in worker, or because they prefer a more structured learning and social environment. Additionally, many employers are increasing child-care benefits to their employees in the form of direct child-care assistance—such as vouchers and subsidies for community child-care centers—more flexible work schedules, and on-site child-care facilities, thus making child-care more affordable and convenient for many parents.

Recently enacted welfare reform legislation requiring more mothers of young children to work may also spur demand for child-care workers as parents seek suitable child-care for children previously cared for at home. These women may turn to lower-cost child-care, such as family child-care homes, rather than child-care centers or nursery schools.

Earnings

Pay depends on the employer and educational attainment of the worker. Although the pay is generally very low, more education means higher earnings in some cases.

In 1996, median weekly earnings of full-time, salaried child-care workers were $250. The middle 50 percent of child-care workers earned between $190 and $310. The top 10 percent earned at least $390; the bottom 10 percent earned less than $140.

Preschool teachers in public schools who have state teacher certification generally have salaries and benefits comparable to kindergarten and elementary school teachers. According to the National Education Association, public elementary school teachers earned an estimated average salary of $37,300 in the 1995-96 school year. Preschool teachers in privately funded child-care centers generally earn much lower salaries than other comparably educated workers.

Earnings of self-employed child-care workers vary depending on the hours worked, number and ages of the children, and the location.

Benefits vary, but are minimal for most preschool and child-care workers. Many employers offer free or discounted child-care to employees. Some offer a full benefits package, including health insurance and paid vacations, but others offer no benefits at all. Some employers offer seminars and workshops to help workers improve upon or learn new skills. A few are willing to cover the cost of courses taken at community colleges or technical schools. Nonprofit and religiously-affiliated centers often pay higher wages and offer more generous benefits than independent for-profit centers.

Related Occupations

Child-care work requires patience; creativity; an ability to nurture, motivate, teach, and influence children; and leadership, organizational, and administrative abilities. Others who work with children and need these aptitudes include teacher aides, children's tutors, kindergarten and elementary school teachers, early childhood program directors, and child psychologists.

Sources of Additional Information

For information on careers in educating children and issues affecting preschool teachers and child-care workers, contact:

❑ National Association for the Education of Young Children, 1509 16th St. NW, Washington, DC 20036.

❑ Association for Childhood Education International, 11501 Georgia Ave., Suite 315, Wheaton, MD 20902-1924.

For eligibility requirements and a description of the Child Development Associate credential, write to:

❑ Council for Early Childhood Professional Recognition, 2460 16th St. NW, Washington, DC 20009.

For information on salaries and efforts to improve compensation in child-care, contact:

❑ National Center for the Early Childhood Work Force, 733 15th St. NW, Suite 1037, Washington, DC 20005.

State Departments of Human Services or Social Services can supply state regulations and training requirements for child-care workers.

Private Detectives and Investigators

(*D.O.T.* 189.167-054; 343.367-014; 376.137, .267; 367; and .667-014)

Significant Points

✓ *Work hours are often irregular.*

✓ *No formal education requirements exist for applicants, although almost all have experience in other occupations, often law enforcement or the military.*

✓ *A license is required in most areas.*

Nature of the Work

Private detectives and investigators assist attorneys, businesses, and the public with a variety of problems. Their services include protecting businesses and their employees, customers, and guests from theft, vandalism, and disorder as well as gathering evidence for a trials, tracing debtors, or conducting background investigations. While detectives concentrate on providing protection and investigators specialize in gathering information, many do some of each.

Private detectives and investigators' duties range from locating missing persons to exposing fraudulent workers' compensation claims. Some specialize in one field, such as finance, where they might use accounting skills to investigate the financial standing of a company or locate funds stolen by an embezzler. Others specialize in locating missing persons, investigating infidelity, or conducting background investigations, including financial profiles and asset searches; others do executive protection and bodyguard work.

Most detectives and investigators are trained to perform physical surveillance, often for long periods of time, in a car or van. They may observe a site, such as the home of a subject, from an inconspicuous location. The surveillance continues using still and video cameras, binoculars, and a citizen's band radio or a car phone, until the desired evidence is obtained. They perform on-line computer database searches, or work with someone who does. Computers allow detectives and investigators to obtain massive amounts of information in a short period of time from the dozens of on-line data bases containing probate records, motor-vehicle registrations, credit reports, association membership lists, and other information.

Private detectives and investigators obtain information by interviewing witnesses and assembling evidence and reports for litigation or criminal trials. They get cases from clients or are assigned to cases by the manager of the firm they work for. Many spend considerable time conducting surveillance, seeking to observe inconsistencies in a subject's behavior. For example, a person who has recently filed a workers' compensation claim stating that an injury has made walking difficult should not be able to jog or mow the lawn. If such behavior is observed, the investigator takes video or still photographs to document the activity and reports back to the supervisor or client.

Some investigations involve verification of facts, such as an individual's place of employment or income. This might involve a phone call or a visit to the workplace. In other investigations, especially in missing persons cases and background checks, the investigator interviews people to gather as much information as possible about an individual.

Legal investigators specialize in cases involving the courts and are normally employed by law firms or lawyers. They frequently assist in preparing criminal defenses, locate witnesses, interview police, gather and review evidence, take photographs, and testify in court. To assist attorneys in the preparation of civil litigation, they interview prospective witnesses, collect information on the parties to the litigation, and search out testimonial, documentary, or physical evidence.

Corporate investigators work for companies other than investigative firms—often large corporations. They conduct internal or external investigations. External investigations may consist of undercover operations aimed at preventing criminal schemes, thefts of company assets, or fraudulent deliveries of products by suppliers. In internal investigations, they may investigate drug use in the workplace, insure that expense accounts are not abused, and determine if employees are stealing merchandise or information.

Detectives and investigators who specialize in finance may be hired to develop confidential financial profiles of individuals or companies who may be parties to large financial transactions and often work with investment bankers and accountants. They also may search for assets after fraud or theft, to recover damages awarded by a court.

Private detectives and investigators who work for retail stores or malls are responsible for loss control and asset protection. Store detectives safeguard the assets of retail stores by apprehending anyone attempting to steal merchandise or destroy store property. They detect theft by shoplifters, vendor representatives, delivery personnel, and even store employees. Store detectives also conduct periodic inspections of stock areas, dressing rooms, and rest rooms, and sometimes assist in the opening and closing of the store. They may prepare loss prevention and security reports for management and testify in court against persons they apprehend.

Working Conditions

Private detectives and investigators often work irregular hours because of the need to conduct surveillance and contact people who may not be available during normal working hours. Early morning, evening, weekend, and holiday work is common.

Many detectives and investigators spend much time away from their offices conducting interviews or doing surveillance, but some work in their office most of the day conducting computer searches and making phone calls. Some split their time between office and field. Those who have their own agencies and employ other investigators may work primarily in an office and have normal business hours.

When working a case away from the office, the environment might range from plush boardrooms to seedy bars. Store and hotel detectives work mostly in the businesses that they protect. Investigators generally work alone, but sometimes work with others during surveillance or when following a subject.

Much of the work detectives and investigators do can be confrontational because the person being observed or interviewed may not want to be. As a result, the job can be stressful and sometimes dangerous. Some detectives and investigators carry handguns. In most cases, a weapon is not necessary because the purpose of their work is the gathering of information and not law enforcement or

apprehension of criminals. Owners of investigative agencies have the added stress of having to deal with demanding and sometimes distraught clients.

Employment

Private detectives and investigators held about 58,000 jobs in 1996. About 17 percent were self-employed. About 36 percent of wage and salary workers worked for detective agencies and about 42 percent were employed as store detectives in department or clothing and accessories stores. Others worked for hotels and other lodging places, legal services firms, and in other industries.

Training, Other Qualifications, and Advancement

There are no formal education requirements for most private detective and investigator jobs, although most employers prefer high school graduates; many private detectives have college degrees. Almost all private detectives and investigators have previous experience in other occupations. Some work initially for insurance or collections companies or in the security industry. Many investigators enter the field after serving in military or law enforcement jobs.

Retired law enforcement officers, military investigators, and government agents frequently become private detectives and investigators as a second career. Others enter from such diverse fields as finance, accounting, investigative reporting, insurance, and law. These individuals often can apply their prior work experience in a related investigation specialty. A few enter the occupation directly after graduation from college, generally with majors in such fields as criminal justice or police science.

The majority of the states and the District of Colombia require private detectives and investigators be licensed by the state or local authorities. Licensing requirements vary widely. Some states have very liberal requirements, or none at all, while others have stringent regulations. For example, the California Department of Consumer Affairs Bureau of Security and Investigative Services requires 6,000 hours of investigative experience, a background check, and a qualifying score on a written examination. A growing number of states are enacting mandatory training programs for private detectives and investigators. In most states, convicted felons may not be licensed.

In most investigations firms, the screening process for potential employees includes a background check, to confirm education and work experience, to inquire about criminal history, and to interview references and others who know the applicant.

For private detective and investigator jobs, most employers look for individuals with ingenuity who are curious, aggressive, persistent, and assertive. A candidate must not be afraid of being confrontational, should communicate well, and should be able to think on his or her feet. The courts are often the ultimate judge of a properly conducted investigation, so the investigator must be able to present the facts in a manner a jury will believe.

Training in subjects such as criminal justice are helpful to the aspiring private detective and investigator. Most corporate investigators must have a bachelor's degree, preferably in a business-related field. Some corporate investigators have masters of business administration or law degrees, while others are certified public accountants.

Corporate investigators hired by larger companies may receive formal training from their employers on business practices, management structure, and various finance-related topics. Good interviewing and interrogation skills are important and are usually acquired in earlier careers in law enforcement or other fields.

Most investigations firms are small, with little room for advancement. Usually there are no defined ranks or steps, so advancement is in terms of salary and assignment status. Many detectives and investigators work for various investigations firms at the beginning of their careers and after a few years try to start their own firms. Corporate and legal investigators may rise to supervisor or manager of the security or investigations department.

Job Outlook

Employment of private detectives and investigators is expected to grow about as fast as the average for all occupations through the year 2006. In addition, job turnover should create many additional job openings, particularly among wage and salary workers. Nevertheless, competition is expected for the available openings because private detective and investigator careers are attractive to many, and there are many individuals who retire from law enforcement and military careers at a relatively young age who are qualified to enter the field.

Increased demand for private detectives and investigators is expected to be generated by fear of crime, increased litigation, and the need to protect confidential information and property of all kinds. Additional private investigators will be needed by law firms to meet the needs for criminal defense and civil litigation among companies and individuals. Greater corporate financial activity worldwide will increase the demand for investigators to control internal and external financial losses, as well as to find out what competitors are doing and to prevent industrial spying.

Opportunities should be best for entry-level jobs as store detectives or with detective agencies on a part-time basis. Those seeking store detective jobs may find the best opportunities with private guard and security firms since some retail businesses are replacing their own workers with outside contract workers.

Earnings

Earnings of private detectives and investigators vary greatly depending on their employer, specialty, and the geographic area in which they work. According to a study by Abbott, Langer & Associates, security/loss prevention directors and vice presidents earned an average $67,700 a year in 1996, investigators about $37,800 a year, and store detectives about $19,100.

Most private investigators bill their clients between $50 and $150 per hour to conduct investigations. Except for those working for large corporations, most private investigators do not receive paid vacation or sick days, health or life insurance, retirement packages, or other benefits. Investigators are usually reimbursed for expenses and generally receive a car allowance.

Most corporate investigators received health insurance, pension plans, profit-sharing plans, and paid vacation.

Related Occupations

Private detectives and investigators often collect information and protect property and assets of companies. Others with related concerns include security guards, insurance claims examiners, inspectors, collectors, and law enforcement officers. Investigators who specialize in conducting financial profiles and asset searches do work closely related to that of accountants and financial analysts.

Sources of Additional Information

For information on local licensing requirements, contact your State Department of Public Safety, state division of licensing, or your local or state police headquarters.

Property Managers

(D.O.T. 186.117-042, -046, -058, and -062, .167-018, -030, -038, -042, -046, -062, -066, and -090; 187.167-190; 191.117-046 and -050)

Significant Points

✓ *Most persons enter the occupation as an on-site manager of an apartment complex, condominium, or community association, or as an assistant manager at a large property management company. Opportunities should be best for persons with college degrees in business administration and related fields.*

✓ *About 40 percent were self-employed, over twice the average for other executive, administrative, and managerial occupations.*

Nature of the Work

Many people own real estate in the form of a home. To businesses and investors, however, properly managed real estate is a potential source of income and profits rather than simply a place for shelter. For this reason, property managers perform an important function in increasing and maintaining the value of real estate investments for investors. In general, property managers oversee the performance of income-producing commercial and residential properties or manage the communal property and services of condominium and community associations.

Most property managers work in the field of property management. When owners of apartments, office buildings, retail, or industrial properties lack the time or expertise needed for the day-to-day management of their real estate investments, they often hire a property manager, either directly or by contracting with a property management company.

Property managers handle the financial operations of the property, seeing to it that mortgages, taxes, insurance premiums, payroll, and maintenance bills are paid on time. They also supervise the preparation of financial statements and periodically report to the owners on the status of the property, occupancy rates, dates of lease expirations, and other matters.

If necessary, property managers negotiate contracts for janitorial, security, groundskeeping, trash removal, and other services. When contracts are awarded competitively, managers must solicit bids from several contractors and recommend to the owners which bid to accept. They monitor the performance of the contractors, and investigate and resolve complaints from residents and tenants when services are not properly provided. Managers also purchase supplies and equipment needed for the property, and make arrangements with specialists for any repairs that cannot be handled by the regular property maintenance staff.

On top of these duties, property managers must understand the provisions of legislation, such as the Americans With Disabilities Act and the Federal Fair Housing Amendment Act, as well as local fair housing laws, to be sure their renting and advertising practices are not discriminatory.

On-site property managers are responsible for the day-to-day operations for one piece of property, such as an office building, shopping center, or apartment complex. To insure the property is safe and being maintained properly, on-site managers routinely inspect the grounds, facilities, and equipment to determine what repairs are needed. They meet not only with current residents (when handling requests for repairs or trying to resolve complaints, for example), but also show vacant apartments or office space to prospective residents or tenants and explain the occupancy terms. On-site managers are also responsible for enforcing the terms of the rental or lease agreement, such as rent collection, parking and pet restrictions, and termination-of-lease procedures.

Other important duties of on-site managers include keeping accurate, up-to-date records of income and expenditures from property operations and the submission of regular expense reports to the property manager or owners.

The work of property managers who do not work on-site is similar to that of on-site managers, except that most of these managers are responsible for multiple properties and supervise on-site personnel. They act as a liaison between the on-site manager and the owner. They also market vacant space to prospective tenants through the use of a leasing agent, advertising, or by other means, and establish rental rates in accordance with prevailing local conditions.

Some property managers, termed real estate asset managers, act as the property owners' agent and adviser for the property. They plan and direct the purchase, development, and disposition of real estate on behalf of businesses and investors. These managers are involved in long-term strategic financial planning rather than the day-to-day operations of the property.

When looking to acquire property, real estate asset managers take several factors into consideration, such as property values, taxes, zoning, population growth, and traffic volume and patterns. Once a site is selected, they negotiate contracts for the purchase or lease of the property, securing the most beneficial terms.

Real estate asset managers periodically review their company's real estate holdings, identifying properties that are no longer commercially attractive. They then negotiate the sale or termination of the lease of properties selected for disposal.

The work of property managers employed by condominium and homeowner associations, often known as community association managers, is different than that of other property managers. Instead of renters, they interact on a daily basis with homeowners—members of the community association that employs the manager. Hired by the volunteer board of directors of the association, the community association manager administers daily affairs and oversees the maintenance of property and facilities that the homeowners own and use jointly through the association. Smaller community associations usually cannot afford professional management, but managers of larger condominiums or homeowner associations have many of the same responsibilities as the managers of large apartment complexes. Some homeowner associations encompass thousands of homes, and, in addition to administering the associations' financial records and budget, their managers are responsible for the operation of community pools, golf courses, community centers, and the maintenance of landscaping, parking areas, and streets. Other responsibilities usually include meeting with the elected boards of directors to discuss and solve legal and environmental issues and aiding in resolving disputes between neighbors.

Property managers who work for land development companies acquire land and plan the construction of shopping centers, houses and apartments, office buildings, or industrial parks. They negotiate with representatives of local government, other businesses, community and public interest groups, and public utilities to eliminate obstacles to the development of the land and gain support for the planned project. It sometimes takes years to win approval for a project, and in the process managers may have to modify the plans for the project many times. Once they are free to proceed with a project, managers negotiate short-term loans to finance the construction of the project, and later negotiate long-term permanent mortgage loans. They then contract with architectural firms to draw up detailed plans, and with construction companies to build the project.

Working Conditions

Offices of most property managers are clean, modern, and well-lighted. Many spend a major portion of their time away from their desks, however. On-site managers in particular may spend a large portion of their workday away from their office visiting the building engineer in the boiler room, showcasing apartments, checking on the janitorial and maintenance staff, or investigating problems reported by tenants. Property managers frequently visit the properties they oversee, sometimes on a daily basis when contractors are doing major repair or renovation work. Real estate asset managers may spend time away from home while traveling to company real estate holdings or searching for properties that might be acquired.

Property managers often must attend meetings in the evening with residents, property owners, community association boards of directors, or civic groups. Not surprisingly, many property managers put in long work weeks. Some apartment managers are required to live in the apartment complexes where they work so they are available to handle any emergency that occurs while they are off duty. They usually receive compensatory time off, however, for working at night or on weekends. Many apartment managers receive time off during the week so that they are available on weekends to show apartments to prospective residents.

Employment

Property managers held about 271,000 jobs in 1996. Most worked for real estate operators and lessors or for property management firms. Others worked for real estate development companies, government agencies that manage public buildings, and corporations with extensive holdings of commercial properties. About four out of ten property managers were self-employed, and over a quarter worked part time.

Training, Other Qualifications, and Advancement

Most employers prefer to hire college graduates for property management positions. Degrees in business administration, finance, real estate, public administration, or related fields are preferred, but persons with degrees in the liberal arts are often accepted. Good speaking, writing, and financial skills, as well as an ability to deal tactfully with people, are essential in all areas of property management.

Most persons enter property management as an on-site manager of an apartment complex, condominium, or community association, or as an assistant manager at a large property management company. As they acquire experience working under the direction of a property manager, they may advance to positions with greater responsibility at larger properties. Persons who excel as on-site managers often transfer to assistant property manager positions where they can acquire experience handling a broader range of property management responsibilities.

Previous employment as a real estate agent may be an asset to on-site managers because it provides experience useful in showing apartments or office space and dealing with people, as well as an understanding that an attractive, well-maintained property can command higher rental rates and result in lower turnover among tenants. In the past, many persons with backgrounds in building maintenance have advanced to on-site manager positions on the strength of their knowledge of building mechanical systems, but this is becoming less common as employers are placing greater emphasis on administrative, financial, and communication abilities for managerial jobs.

Although most persons who enter jobs as assistant property managers do so on the strength of on-site management experience, employers are increasingly hiring inexperienced college graduates with bachelor's or master's degrees in business administration, finance, or real estate for these jobs. Assistants work closely with a property manager and acquire experience performing a variety of management tasks, such as preparing the budget, analyzing insurance coverage and risk options, marketing the property to prospective tenants, and collecting overdue rent payments. In time, many assistants advance to property manager positions.

The responsibilities and compensation of property managers increase as they manage larger properties. Most property managers are responsible for several properties at a time, and as their careers advance they are gradually entrusted with properties that are larger or whose management is more complex. Many specialize in the management of one type of property, such as apartments, office buildings, condominiums, cooperatives, homeowner associations, or retail properties. Managers who excel at marketing properties to tenants may specialize in managing new properties, while those who are particularly knowledgeable about buildings and their mechanical systems might specialize in the management of older properties that require renovation or more frequent repairs. Some experienced property managers open their own property management firms.

Persons most commonly enter real estate asset manager jobs by transferring from positions as property managers or real estate brokers. Real estate asset managers must be good negotiators, adept at persuading and handling people, and good at analyzing data to assess the fair market value of property or its development potential. Resourcefulness and creativity in arranging financing are essential for managers who specialize in land development.

Attendance at short-term formal training programs conducted by various professional and trade associations active in the real estate field is often encouraged. Employers send managers to these programs to improve their management skills and expand their knowledge of specialized subjects, such as the operation and maintenance of building mechanical systems, enhancing property values, insurance and risk management, personnel management, business and real estate law, resident/tenant relations, communications, and accounting and financial concepts. Managers also participate in these programs to prepare themselves for positions of greater responsibility in property management. Completion of these programs, together with meeting job experience standards and achieving a satisfactory score on a written examination, leads to certification, or the formal award of a professional designation, by the sponsoring association. In addition to these qualifications, some associations require their members to adhere to a specific code of ethics. Some of the organizations that offer such programs are listed at the end of this statement.

Managers of public housing subsidized by the federal government are required to be certified, but many property managers who work with all types of property choose to earn a professional designation voluntarily because it represents formal industry recognition of their achievements and status in the occupation.

Job Outlook

Employment of property managers is projected to increase as fast as the average for all occupations through the year 2006. In addition to rising demand for these workers, many job openings are expected to occur as property managers transfer to other occupations or leave the labor force. Opportunities should be best for persons with college degrees in business administration, real estate, and related fields, as well as those who attain professional designations.

Growth in the demand for property managers will be evident in several areas. In commercial real estate, the demand for managers is expected to coincide with the projected expansion in wholesale and retail trade; finance, insurance, and real estate; and services. Some additional employment growth will come from adding on to existing buildings.

An increase in the nation's stock of apartments and houses also should require more property managers. Developments of new homes are increasingly being organized with community or homeowner associations that provide community services and oversee jointly owned common areas, requiring professional management. To help properties become more profitable, more commercial and multi-unit residential property owners are expected to place their investments in the hands of professional managers.

Growth in demand should also arise as a result of the changing demographic composition of the population. The number of older people will increase during the projection period, creating a need for various types of suitable housing, such as assisted living arrangements and retirement communities. Accordingly, there will be a need for property managers to operate these facilities, especially those who have a background in the operation and administrative aspects of running a health unit.

Earnings

Median annual earnings of all property managers were $28,500 in 1996. The middle 50 percent earned between $19,000 and $39,800. Ten percent earned less than $12,000 and 10 percent earned more than $60,700 annually.

Community association managers received compensation comparable to on-site and property managers employed by other types of properties. Many resident apartment managers receive the use of an apartment as part of their compensation package. Property managers often are given the use of a company automobile, and managers employed in land development often receive a small percentage of ownership in projects they develop.

Related Occupations

Property managers plan, organize, staff, and manage the real estate operations of businesses. Workers who perform similar functions in other fields include restaurant and food service managers, hotel and resort managers, facilities managers, health services managers, education administrators, and city managers.

Sources of Additional Information

General information about careers in property management and programs leading to the award of a professional designation in the field is available from:

❏ Institute of Real Estate Management, 430 N. Michigan Ave., Chicago, IL 60611. Homepage: http://www.irem.org

For information on careers and certification programs in commercial property management, contact:

❏ Building Owners and Managers Association International, 1201 New York Ave. NW, Suite 300, Washington, DC 20005. Homepage: http://www.boma.org

❏ Building Owners and Managers Institute (BOMI) International, 1521 Ritchie Hwy., Arnold, MD 21012. Homepage: http://www.bomi-edu.org

For information on careers and certification programs in residential property management, contact:

❏ Community Associations Institute, 1630 Duke St., Alexandria, VA 22314. Homepage: http://www.caionline.org

❏ National Apartment Association, Education Department, 201 N. Union St., Suite 200, Alexandria, VA 22314.

❏ National Association of Home Builders, 1201 15th St. NW, Washington, DC 20005. Homepage: http://www.nahb.com/multi.html

❏ National Association of Residential Property Managers, 35 E. Wacker Dr., Suite 500, Chicago, IL 60601.

Public Relations Specialists

(*D.O.T.* 165.017 and .167)

Significant Points

✓ *Employment of public relations specialists is expected to increase rapidly, while keen competition is expected for entry-level jobs.*

✓ *Opportunities should be best for college graduates with degrees in journalism, public relations, advertising, or other communications-related fields.*

✓ *Public relations work experience in gained as an intern is an asset in competing for entry-level jobs.*

Nature of the Work

An organization's reputation, profitability, and even its continued existence can depend on the degree to which its goals and policies are supported by its targeted "publics." Public relations specialists serve as advocates for businesses, governments, universities, hospitals, schools, and other organizations, and strive to build and maintain positive relationships with the public. As managers recognize the growing importance of good public relations to the success of their organizations, they increasingly rely on public relations specialists for advice on strategy and policy of such programs.

Public relations specialists handle such organizational functions as media, community, consumer, and governmental relations; political campaigns; interest-group representation; conflict mediation; or employee and investor relations. However, public relations is not only "telling the organization's story." Understanding the attitudes and concerns of consumers, employees, and various other groups is also a vital part of the job. To improve communications, public relations specialists establish and maintain cooperative relationships with representatives of community, consumer, employee, and public interest groups and those in print and broadcast journalism.

Public relations specialists put together information that keeps the general public, interest groups, and stockholders aware of an organization's policies, activities, and accomplishments. Their work keeps management aware of public attitudes and concerns of the many groups and organizations with which it must deal.

Public relations specialists prepare press releases and contact people in the media who might print or broadcast their material. Many radio or television special reports, newspaper stories, and magazine articles start at the desks of public relations specialists. Sometimes the subject is an organization and its policies toward its employees or its role in the community. Often the subject is a public issue, such as health, nutrition, energy, or the environment.

Public relations specialists also arrange and conduct programs for contact between organization representatives and the public. For example, they set up speaking engagements and often prepare the speeches for company officials. These specialists represent employers at community projects; make film, slide, or other visual presentations at meetings and school assemblies; and plan conventions. In addition, they are responsible for preparing annual reports and writing proposals for various projects.

In government, public relations specialists—who may be called press secretaries, information officers, public affairs specialists, or communications specialists—keep the public informed about the activities of government agencies and officials. For example, public affairs specialists in the Department of Energy keep the public informed about the proposed lease of offshore land for oil exploration. A press secretary for a member of Congress keeps constituents aware of their elected representative's accomplishments.

In large organizations, the key public relations executive, who is often a vice president, may develop overall plans and policies with other executives. In addition, public relations departments employ public relations specialists to write, do research, prepare materials, maintain contacts, and respond to inquiries.

People who handle publicity for an individual or who direct public relations for a small organization may deal with all aspects of the job. They contact people, plan and do research, and prepare material for distribution. They may also handle advertising or sales promotion work to support marketing.

Working Conditions

Some public relations specialists work a standard 35- to 40-hour week, but unpaid overtime is common. In addition, schedules often have to be rearranged to meet deadlines, deliver speeches, attend meetings and community activities, and travel out of town. Occasionally they have to be at the job or on call around the clock, especially if there is an emergency or crisis.

Employment

Public relations specialists held about 110,000 jobs in 1996. About two-thirds worked in services industries–management and public relations firms, educational institutions, membership organizations, health care organizations, social service agencies, and advertising agencies, for example. Others worked for a wide range of employers, including manufacturing firms, financial institutions, and government agencies. A few were self-employed.

Public relations specialists are concentrated in large cities in which press services and other communications facilities are readily available, and many businesses and trade associations have their headquarters. Many public relations consulting firms, for example, are in New York, Los Angeles, Chicago, and Washington, DC. There is a trend, however, for public relations jobs to be dispersed throughout the nation.

Training, Other Qualifications, and Advancement

Although there are no defined standards for entry into a public relations career, a college degree combined with public relations experience, usually gained through an internship, is considered excellent preparation for public relations work. The ability to write and speak well is essential. Many beginners have a college major in public relations, journalism, advertising, or communications. Some firms seek college graduates who have worked in electronic or print journalism. Other employers seek applicants with demonstrated communications skills and training or experience in a field related to the firm's business–science, engineering, sales, or finance, for example.

In 1996, well over 200 colleges and about 100 graduate schools offered degree programs or special curricula in public relations, usually in a journalism or communications department. In addition, many other colleges offered at least one course in this field. The Accrediting Council on Education in Journalism and Mass Communications is the only agency authorized to accredit schools or department in public relations. A commonly used public relations sequence includes the following courses: Public relations principles and techniques; public relations management and administration, including organizational development; writing, emphasizing news releases, proposals, annual reports, scripts, speeches, and related items; visual communications, including desktop publishing and computer graphics; and research, emphasizing social science research and survey design and implementation. Courses in advertising, journalism, business administration, political science, psychology, sociology, and creative writing also are helpful, as is familiarity with word processing and other computer applications. Specialties are offered in public relations for business, government, or nonprofit organizations.

Many colleges help students gain part-time internships in public relations that provide valuable experience and training. The Armed Forces can also be an excellent place to gain training and experience. Membership in local chapters of the Public Relations Student Society of America or the International Association of Business Communicators provides an opportunity for students to exchange views with public relations specialists and to make professional contacts who may help them find a full-time job in the field. A portfolio of published articles, television or radio programs, slide presentations, and other work is an asset in finding a job. Writing for a school publication or television or radio station provides valuable experience and material for one's portfolio.

Creativity, initiative, good judgment, and the ability to express thoughts clearly and simply are essential. Decision making, problem solving, and research skills are also important.

People who choose public relations as a career need an outgoing personality, self-confidence, an understanding of human psychology, and an enthusiasm for motivating people. They should be competitive, yet flexible and able to function as part of a team.

Some organizations, particularly those with large public relations staffs, have formal training programs for new employees. In smaller organizations, new employees work under the guidance of experienced staff members. Beginners often maintain files of material about company activities, scan newspapers and magazines for appropriate articles to clip, and assemble information for speeches and pamphlets. After gaining experience, they write news releases, speeches, and articles for publication, or design and carry out public relations programs. Public relations specialists in smaller firms generally get all-around experience, whereas those in larger firms tend to be more specialized.

The Public Relations Society of America accredits public relations specialists who have at least five years of experience in the field and have passed a comprehensive six-hour examination (five hours written, one hour oral). The International Association of Business Communicators also has an accreditation program for professionals in the communications field, including public relations specialists. Those who meet all the requirements of the program earn the designation, Accredited Business Communicator. Candidates must have at least five years of experience in a communication field and pass a written and oral examination. They also must submit a portfolio of work samples demonstrating involvement in a range of communication projects and a thorough understanding of communication planning. Employers consider professional recognition through accreditation a sign of competence in this field, and it may be especially helpful in a competitive job market.

Promotion to supervisory jobs may come as public relations specialists show they can handle more demanding managerial assignments. In public relations firms, a beginner may be hired as a research assistant or account assistant and be promoted to account executive, account supervisor, vice president, and eventually senior vice president. A similar career path is followed in corporate public relations, although the titles may differ. Some experienced public relations specialists start their own consulting firms.

Job Outlook

Keen competition for public relations jobs will likely continue among recent college graduates with a degree in communications–journalism, public relations, advertising, or a related field–as the number of applicants is expected to exceed the number of job openings. People without the appropriate educational background or work experience will face the toughest obstacles in finding a public relations job.

Employment of public relations specialists is expected to increase faster than the average for all occupations through the year 2006. Recognition of the need for good public relations in an increasingly competitive business environment should spur demand for public relations specialists in organizations of all sizes. Employment in public relations firms should grow as firms hire contractors to provide public relations services rather than support full-time staff. The vast majority of job opportunities should result from the need to replace public relations specialists who leave the occupation to take another job, retire, or for other reasons.

Earnings

Median annual earnings for salaried public relations specialists who usually worked full-time were about $34,000 in 1996. The middle 50 percent earned between $25,000 and $54,000 annually; the lowest 10 percent earned less than $16,000, and the top 10 percent earned more than $75,000.

According to a 1995 salary survey conducted for the Public Relations Society of America, the overall median salary in public relations was $49,070. Salaries in public relations ranged from less than $15,000 to more than $150,000. There was little difference between the median salaries in public relations firms and corporations, $51,340 and $50,770, respectively. However, practitioners working for government, health-care, or non-profit organizations had a considerably lower median salary of $43,260.

Public affairs specialists in the federal government in nonsupervisory, supervisory, and managerial positions averaged about $52,540 a year in 1996.

Related Occupations

Public relations specialists create favorable attitudes among various organizations, special interest groups, and the public through effective communication. Other workers with similar jobs include fund raisers, lobbyists, promotion managers, advertising managers, and police officers involved in community relations.

Sources of Additional Information

A comprehensive directory of schools offering degree programs or a sequence of study in public relations, a brochure on careers in public relations, and a $5 brochure entitled Where Shall I go to Study Advertising and Public Relations are available from:

❑ Public Relations Society of America, Inc., 33 Irving Place, New York, NY 10003-2376.

Career information on public relations in hospitals and other health care settings is available from:

❑ The Society for Health Care Strategy and Market Development , One North Franklin St., Suite 3100S, Chicago, IL 60606.

For a list of schools with accredited programs in public relations in their journalism departments, send a stamped self-addressed envelope to:

❑ Accrediting Council on Education in Journalism and Mass Communications, University of Kansas School of Journalism, Stauffer Flint Hall, Lawrence, KS 66045.

For information on accreditation for public relations specialists contact:

❑ International Association of Business Communicators, One Hallidie Plaza, Suite 600, San Francisco, CA 94102.

Purchasers and Buyers

(D.O.T. 162.117-014 and -018, .157-018, -022, -030, -034, and -038, .167-022, and -030; 163.117-010; 169.167-054; 184.117-078; and 185.167-034)

Significant Points

✓ *Computerization has reduced the demand for lower-level buyers.*

✓ *About one-half were employed in wholesale or retail trade.*

Nature of the Work

Purchasers and buyers seek to obtain the highest quality merchandise at the lowest possible purchase cost for their employers. (In general, purchasers buy goods and services for the use of their company or organization whereas buyers buy items for resale.) They determine which commodities or services are best, choose the suppliers of the product or service, negotiate the lowest price, and award contracts that ensure the correct amount of the product or service is received at the appropriate time. In order to accomplish these tasks successfully, purchasers and buyers study sales records and inventory levels of current stock, identify foreign and domestic suppliers, and keep abreast of changes affecting both the supply of and demand for products and materials for which they are responsible.

Purchasers and buyers evaluate suppliers based upon price, quality, service support, availability, reliability, and selection. To assist them in their search, they review listings in catalogs, industry periodicals, directories, and trade journals, research the reputation and history of the suppliers, and advertise anticipated purchase actions in order to solicit bids. Also, meetings, trade shows, conferences, and visits to suppliers' plants and distribution centers provide opportunities for purchasers and buyers to examine products, assess a supplier's production and distribution capabilities, as well as discuss other technical and business considerations that influence the purchasing decision. Once all the necessary information on suppliers is gathered, orders are placed and contracts are awarded to those suppliers who meet the purchasers' needs. Other specific job duties and responsibilities vary by employer and by the type of commodities or services to be purchased.

Purchasing professionals employed by government agencies or manufacturing firms are usually called purchasing directors, managers, or agents; buyers or industrial buyers; or contract specialists. These workers acquire product materials, intermediate goods, machines, supplies, services, and other materials used in the production of a final product. Some purchasing managers specialize in negotiating and supervising supply contracts and are called contract or supply managers. Purchasing agents and managers obtain items ranging from raw materials, fabricated parts, machinery, and office supplies to construction services and airline tickets. The flow of work—or even the entire production process—can be slowed or halted if the right materials, supplies, or equipment are not on hand when needed. In order to be effective, purchasers and buyers must have a working technical knowledge of the goods or services to be purchased.

In large industrial organizations, a distinction often is drawn between the work of a buyer or purchasing agent and that of a purchasing manager. Purchasing agents and buyers typically focus on routine purchasing tasks, often specializing in a commodity or group of related commodities–for example, steel, lumber, cotton, fabricated metal products, or petroleum products. This usually requires the purchaser to track such things as market conditions, price trends, or futures markets. Purchasing managers usually handle the more complex or critical purchases and may supervise a group of purchasing agents handling other goods and services. Whether a person is titled purchasing agent, buyer, or manager depends more on specific industry and employer practices than on specific job duties.

Changing business practices have altered the traditional roles of purchasing professionals in many industries. For example, manufacturing companies increasingly involve purchasing professionals at most stages of product development because of their ability to forecast a part's or material's cost, availability, and suitability for its intended purpose. Furthermore, potential problems with the supply of materials may be avoided by consulting the purchasing department in the early stages of product design.

Another new practice is for businesses to enter into integrated supply contracts. These contracts increase the importance of supplier selection because agreements are larger in scope and longer in duration. A major responsibility of most purchasers is to work out problems that may occur with a supplier because the success of the relationship directly affects the buying firm's performance.

Purchasing professionals often work closely with other employees in their own organization when deciding on purchases, an arrangement sometimes called team buying. For example, they may discuss the design of custom-made products with company design engineers, quality problems in purchased goods with quality assurance engineers and production supervisors, or shipment problems with managers in the receiving department before submitting an order.

Contract specialists and managers in various levels of government award contracts for an array of items, including office and building supplies, services for the public, and construction projects. They typically use sealed bids, but sometimes use negotiated agreements for complex items. Increasingly, purchasing professionals in government are placing solicitations for and accepting bids through the Internet. Government purchasing agents and managers must follow strict laws and regulations in their work. These legal requirements occasionally are changed, so agents and contract specialists must stay informed about the latest regulations and their applications.

Other professionals, who buy finished goods for resale, are employed by wholesale and retail establishments where they commonly are referred to as "buyers" or "merchandise managers." Wholesale and retail buyers are an integral part of a complex system of distribution and merchandising that caters to the vast array of consumer needs and desires. Wholesale buyers purchase goods directly from manufacturers or from other wholesale firms for resale to retail firms, commercial establishments, institutions, and other organizations. In retail firms, buyers purchase goods from wholesale firms or directly from manufacturers for resale to the public. Buyers largely determine which products their establishment will sell. Therefore,

it is essential that they have the ability to accurately predict what will appeal to consumers. They must constantly stay informed of the latest trends because failure to do so could jeopardize profits and the reputation of their company. Buyers also follow ads in newspapers and other media to check competitors' sales activities and watch general economic conditions to anticipate consumer buying patterns. Buyers working for large and medium-sized firms usually specialize in acquiring one or two lines of merchandise, whereas buyers working for small stores may purchase their complete inventory.

The use of private-label merchandise and the consolidation of buying departments have increased the responsibilities of retail buyers. Private-label merchandise, produced for a particular retailer, requires buyers to work closely with vendors to develop and obtain the desired product. The downsizing and consolidation of buying departments is also increasing the demands placed on buyers because, although the amount of work remains unchanged, there are fewer people needed to accomplish it. The result is an increase in the workloads and levels of responsibility.

Many merchandise managers assist in the planning and implementation of sales promotion programs. Working with merchandising executives, they determine the nature of the sale and purchase accordingly. They also work with advertising personnel to create the ad campaign. For example, they may determine the media in which the advertisement will be placed–newspapers, direct mail, television, or some combination of these. In addition, merchandising managers often visit the selling floor to ensure that the goods are properly displayed. Often, assistant buyers are responsible for placing orders and checking shipments.

Computers are having a major effect on the jobs of purchasers and buyers. In manufacturing and service industries, computers handle most of the more routine tasks–enabling purchasing professionals to concentrate mainly on the analytical aspects of the job. Computers are used to obtain up-to-date product and price listings, to track inventory levels, process routine orders, and help determine when to make purchases. Computers also maintain bidders' lists, record the history of supplier performance, and issue purchase orders.

Computerized systems have dramatically simplified many of the routine buying functions and improved the efficiency of determining which products are selling. For example, cash registers connected to computers, known as point-of-sale terminals, allow organizations to maintain centralized, up-to-date sales and inventory records. This information can then be used to produce weekly sales reports that reflect the types of products in demand. Buyers also use computers to gain instant access to the specifications for thousands of commodities, inventory records, and their customers' purchase records. Some firms are linked with manufacturers or wholesalers by electronic purchasing systems. These systems speed selection and ordering and provide information on availability and shipment, allowing buyers to better concentrate on the selection of goods and suppliers.

Working Conditions

Most purchasers and buyers work in comfortable, well-lighted offices at stores, corporate headquarters, or production or service facilities. They frequently work more than a 40-hour week because of special sales, conferences, or production deadlines. Evening and weekend work is common. For those working in retail trade, this is especially true prior to holiday seasons. Consequently, many retail firms discourage the use of vacation time from late November until early January.

Buyers and merchandise managers often work under great pressure because wholesale and retail stores are so competitive; buyers need physical stamina to keep up with the fast-paced nature of their work.

Many purchasers and buyers spend at least several days a month traveling. Purchasers for worldwide manufacturing companies and large retailers, and buyers of high fashion, may travel outside the United States.

Employment

Purchasers and buyers held about 639,000 jobs in 1996. Purchasing agents and purchasing managers each accounted for slightly more than one-third of the total, while buyers accounted for the remainder.

About one-half of all purchasers and buyers worked in wholesale and retail trade establishments such as grocery or department stores, and another one-fourth worked in manufacturing. The remainder worked mostly in service establishments or different levels of government.

Training, Other Qualifications, and Advancement.

Qualified persons usually begin as trainees, purchasing clerks, expediters, junior buyers, or assistant buyers. Retail and wholesale firms prefer to hire applicants who are familiar with the merchandise they sell as well as with wholesaling and retailing practices. Some retail firms promote qualified employees to assistant buyer positions; others recruit and train college graduates as assistant buyers. Most employers use a combination of methods.

Educational requirements tend to vary with the size of the organization. Large stores and distributors, especially those in wholesale and retail trade, prefer applicants who have completed a bachelor's degree program with a business emphasis. Many manufacturing firms prefer applicants with a bachelor's or master's degree in business, economics, or technical training such as engineering or one of the applied sciences and tend to put a greater emphasis on formal training.

Regardless of academic preparation, new employees must learn the specifics of their employers' business. Training periods vary in length, with most lasting one to five years. In wholesale and retail establishments, most trainees begin by selling merchandise, supervising sales workers, checking invoices on material received, and keeping track of stock on hand, although widespread use of computers has simplified some of these tasks. As they progress, retail trainees are given more buying-related responsibilities. In manufacturing, new purchasing employees often are enrolled in company training programs and spend a considerable amount of time learning about company operations and purchasing practices. They work with experienced purchasers to learn about commodities, prices, suppliers, and markets. In addition, they may be assigned to the production planning department to learn about the material requirements system and the inventory system the company uses to keep production and replenishment functions working smoothly.

Because the procurement process is becoming more automated, it is extremely important for purchasers and buyers to be computer literate, including knowing how to use word processing and spread-sheet software. Other important qualities include the ability to analyze technical data in suppliers' proposals, good communicating, negotiating, and math skills, knowledge of supply chain management, and the ability to perform financial analyses.

Persons who wish to become wholesale or retail buyers should be good at planning and decision making and have an interest in merchandising. Anticipating consumer preferences and ensuring that goods are in stock when they are needed require resourcefulness, good judgment, and self-confidence. Buyers must be able to make decisions quickly and take risks. Marketing skills and the ability to identify products that will sell are also very important. Employers often look for leadership ability because buyers spend a large portion of their time supervising assistant buyers and dealing with manufacturers' representatives and store executives.

Experienced buyers may advance by moving to a department that manages a larger volume or by becoming a merchandise manager. Others may go to work in sales for a manufacturer or wholesaler.

An experienced purchasing agent or buyer may become an assistant purchasing manager in charge of a group of purchasing professionals before advancing to purchasing manager, supply manager, or director of materials management. At the top levels, duties may overlap into other management functions such as production, planning, and marketing.

Regardless of industry, continuing education is essential for advancement. Many purchasers participate in seminars offered by professional societies and take college courses in purchasing. Although no national standard exists, professional certification is becoming increasingly important.

In private industry, the recognized marks of experience and professional competence are the designations Accredited Purchasing Practitioner (APP) and Certified Purchasing Manager (CPM), conferred by the National Association of Purchasing Management, and Certified Purchasing Professional (CPP), conferred by the American Purchasing Society. In federal, state, and local government, the indications of professional competence are the designations Certified Professional Public Buyer (CPPB) and Certified Public Purchasing Officer (CPPO), conferred by the National Institute of Governmental Purchasing.

As more materials purchasing is conducted on a long-term basis, both private and public purchasing professionals are specializing in the contractual aspects of purchasing. The National Contract Management Association confers the designations Simplified Acquisition Specialists (SAS), Certified Associate Contract Manager (CACM), and Certified Professional Contract Manager (CPCM). These designations primarily apply to contract managers in the federal government and its suppliers.

Most designations are awarded only after work-related experience and education requirements are met, and written or oral exams are completed successfully.

Job Outlook

Employment of purchasers and buyers is expected to increase more slowly than the average for all occupations through the year 2006. Demand for these workers will not keep pace with the rising level of economic activity because the increasing use of computers has allowed much of the paperwork typically involved in ordering and procuring supplies to be eliminated, reducing the demand for lower-level buyers who traditionally performed these duties. Also, limited sourcing and long-term contracting have allowed companies to negotiate with fewer suppliers less frequently. Consequently, most job openings will result from the need to replace workers who transfer to other occupations or leave the labor force.

In retail trade, mergers and acquisitions have forced the consolidation of buying departments, eliminating jobs. In addition, larger retail stores are removing their buying departments from geographic markets and centralizing them at their headquarters, eliminating more jobs.

The increased use of credit cards by some employees to purchase supplies without using the services of the procurement or purchasing office, combined with the growing number of buys being made electronically, will restrict demand of purchasing agents within governments and many manufacturing firms.

Persons who have a bachelor's degree in business should have the best chance of obtaining a buyer job in wholesale or retail trade or within government. A bachelor's degree, combined with industry experience and/or knowledge of a technical field, will be an advantage for those interested in working for a manufacturing or industrial company. A master's degree in business or public administration is usually required by government agencies and larger companies for top-level purchasing positions.

Earnings

Median annual earnings of purchasers and buyers were $33,200 in 1996. The middle 50 percent earned between $23,300 and $45,900. The lowest 10 percent earned less than $18,400 while the top 10 percent earned more than $63,000. Merchandise managers and purchasing managers generally earned higher salaries than buyers or agents. As a general rule, those with the most education in their field have the highest incomes.

The average annual salaries for purchasing agents and contract specialists in the federal government in early 1997 were about $28,700 and $51,110, respectively.

Purchasers and buyers receive the same benefits package as their coworkers, frequently including vacations, sick leave, life and health insurance, and pension plans. In addition to standard benefits, retail buyers often earn cash bonuses based on their performance and may receive discounts on merchandise bought from the employer.

Related Occupations

Workers in other occupations who need a knowledge of marketing and the ability to assess demand are retail sales workers, sales managers, marketing and advertising managers, manufacturers' and wholesale sales representatives, insurance sales agents, services sales representatives, and procurement services, materials, and traffic managers.

Sources of Additional Information

Further information about education, training, and/or certification for purchasing careers is available from:

❑ American Purchasing Society, 30 W. Downer Pl., Aurora, IL 60506. Homepage: http://www.american-purchasing.com
❑ National Association of Purchasing Management, Customer Service, 2055 East Centennial Circle, P.O. Box 22160, Tempe, AZ 85285. Homepage: http://www.napm.org

❑ National Institute of Governmental Purchasing, Inc., 11800 Sunrise Valley Dr., Suite 1050, Reston, VA 20191-5302. Homepage: http://www.nigp.org
❑ National Contract Management Association, 1912 Woodford Rd., Vienna, VA 22182. Homepage: http://www.ncmahq.org
❑ Federal Acquisition Institute (MVI), Office of Acquisition Policy, General Services Administration, 18th & F Streets NW, Room 4019, Washington, DC 20405. Homepage: http://www.gsa.gov/staff/v/mvi/key.htm

General information on buying careers in retail establishments is available from:

❑ National Retail Federation, 325 7th St. NW, Suite 1000, Washington, DC 20004. Homepage: HYPERLINK http://www.nrf.com http://www.nrf.com

Radiologic Technologists

(*D.O.T.* 078.361-034, .362-026, -046, -054, -058, .364-010)

Significant Points

Job seekers may face competition for jobs as hospitals merge radiologic and nuclear medicine departments in an effort to cut costs; radiographers with cross training in nuclear medicine technology will have the best prospects.

Sonographers should experience somewhat better job opportunities than other radiologic technologists, as ultrasound becomes an increasingly attractive alternative to radiologic procedures.

Nature of the Work

Perhaps the most familiar use of the x ray is the diagnosis of broken bones. However, medical uses of radiation go far beyond that. Radiation is used not only to produce images of the interior of the body, but to treat cancer as well. At the same time, the use of imaging techniques that do not involve x rays, such as ultrasound and magnetic resonance scans, is growing rapidly. The term "diagnostic imaging" embraces these procedures as well as the familiar x ray.

Radiographers produce x-ray films (radiographs) of parts of the human body for use in diagnosing medical problems. They prepare patients for radiologic examinations by explaining the procedure, removing articles such as jewelry, through which x rays cannot pass, and positioning patients so that the correct parts of the body can be radiographed. To prevent unnecessary radiation exposure, technologists surround the exposed area with radiation protection devices, such as lead shields, or limit the size of the x-ray beam. Radiographers position radiographic equipment at the correct angle and height over the appropriate area of a patient's body. Using instruments similar to a measuring tape, technologists may measure the thickness of the section to be radiographed and set controls on the machine to produce radiographs of the appropriate density, detail, and contrast. They place the x-ray film under the part of the patient's body to be examined and make the exposure. They then remove the film and develop it.

Experienced radiographers may perform more complex imaging tests. For fluoroscopies, radiographers prepare a solution of contrast medium for the patient to drink, allowing the radiologist, a physician who interprets x rays, to see soft tissues in the body. Some radiographers who operate computerized tomography scanners to produce cross sectional views of patients are called CT tech-nologists. Others operate machines that use giant magnets and radiowaves rather than radiation to create an image and are called magnetic resonance imaging (MRI) technologists.

Radiation therapy technologists, also known as radiation thera-pists, prepare cancer patients for treatment and administer prescribed doses of ionizing radiation to specific body parts. They operate many kinds of equipment, including high-energy linear accelerators with electron capabilities. They position patients under the equipment with absolute accuracy in order to expose affected body parts to treatment while protecting the rest of the body from radiation.

They also check the patient's reactions for radiation side effects such as nausea, hair loss, and skin irritation. They give instructions and explanations to patients who are likely to be very ill. Radiation therapists, in contrast to other radiologic technologists, are likely to see the same patient a number of times during the course of treat-ment.

Sonographers, also known as ultrasound technologists, direct nonionizing, high frequency sound waves into areas of the patient's body; the equipment then collects reflected echoes to form an im-age. The image is viewed on a screen and may be recorded on vid-eotape or photographed for interpretation and diagnosis by physicians. Sonographers explain the procedure, record additional medical history, and then position the patient for testing. Viewing the screen as the scan takes place, sonographers look for subtle differences between healthy and pathological areas, decide which images to include, and judge if the images are satisfactory for diag-nostic purposes. Sonographers may specialize in neurosonography (the brain), vascular (blood flows), echocardiography (the heart), abdominal (the liver, kidneys, spleen, and pancreas), obstetrics/gy-necology (the female reproductive system), and ophthalmology (the eye).

Radiologic technologists must follow physicians' instructions precisely and conform with regulations concerning use of radiation to ensure that they, patients, and coworkers are protected from over exposure.

In addition to preparing patients and operating equipment, radiologic technologists keep patient records and adjust and main-tain equipment. They may also prepare work schedules, evaluate equipment purchases, or manage a radiology department.

Working Conditions

Most full-time radiologic technologists work about 40 hours a week; they may have evening, weekend, or on-call hours.

Technologists are on their feet for long periods and may lift or turn disabled patients. They work at radiologic machines but may also do some procedures at patients' bedsides. Some radiologic tech-nologists travel to patients in large vans equipped with sophisti-cated diagnostic equipment.

Radiation therapists are prone to emotional "burn out" because they treat extremely ill and dying patients on a daily basis. Although potential radiation hazards exist in this occupation, they have been minimized by the use of lead aprons, gloves, and other shielding devices, as well as by instruments that monitor radiation exposure. Technologists wear badges that measure radiation levels in the ra-diation area, and detailed records are kept on their cumulative life-time dose.

Employment

Radiologic technologists held about 174,000 jobs in 1996. Most technologists were radiographers. Some were sonographers and ra-diation therapists. About one radiologic technologist in four worked part-time. More than half of jobs for technologists are in hospitals. Most of the rest are in physicians' offices and clinics, including diagnostic imaging centers.

Training, Other Qualifications, and Advancement

Preparation for this profession is offered in hospitals, colleges and universities, vocational-technical institutes, and the Armed Forces. Hospitals, which employ most radiologic technologists, prefer to hire those with formal training.

Formal training is offered in radiography, radiation therapy, and diagnostic medical sonography (ultrasound). Programs range in length from one to four years and lead to a certificate, associate degree, or bachelor's degree. Two-year programs are most preva-lent.

Some one-year certificate programs are for individuals from other health occupations, such as medical technologists and regis-tered nurses, who want to change fields or experienced radiographers who want to specialize in radiation therapy technology or sonography. A bachelor's or master's degree in one of the radiologic technolo-gies is desirable for supervisory, administrative, or teaching posi-tions.

The Joint Review Committee on Education in Radiologic Tech-nology accredits most formal training programs for this field. They accredited 629 radiography programs and 97 radiation therapy pro-grams in 1997. The Joint Review Committee on Education in Diag-nostic Medical Sonography accredited 74 programs in sonography in 1997.

Radiography programs require, at a minimum, a high school diploma or the equivalent. High school courses in mathematics, phys-ics, chemistry, and biology are helpful. The programs provide both classroom and clinical instruction in anatomy and physiology, pa-tient care procedures, radiation physics, radiation protection, prin-ciples of imaging, medical terminology, positioning of patients, medical ethics, radiobiology, and pathology.

For training programs in radiation therapy and diagnostic medi-cal sonography, applicants with a background in science, or experi-ence in one of the health professions, generally are preferred. Some programs consider applicants with liberal arts backgrounds, how-ever, as well as high school graduates with courses in math and science.

Radiographers and radiation therapists are covered by provi-sions of the Consumer-Patient Radiation Health and Safety Act of 1981, which aims to protect the public from the hazards of unneces-sary exposure to medical and dental radiation by ensuring opera-tors of radiologic equipment are properly trained. The act requires the federal government to set standards that the states, in turn, may use for accrediting training programs and certifying individuals who engage in medical or dental radiography. Because ultrasound does not use ionizing radiation, sonographers are excluded from this act.

In 1997, 36 states and Puerto Rico licensed radiologic tech-nologists. No state requires that sonographers be licensed. Volun-tary registration is offered by the American Registry of Radiologic Technologists (ARRT) in both radiography and radiation therapy.

The American Registry of Diagnostic Medical Sonographers (ARDMS) certifies the competence of sonographers. To become registered, technologists must be graduates of an accredited program or meet other prerequisites and have passed an examination. Many employers prefer to hire registered technologists.

With experience and additional training, staff technologists may become specialists, performing CT scanning, ultrasound, angiography, and magnetic resonance imaging. Experienced technologists may also be promoted to supervisor, chief radiologic technologist, and—ultimately—department administrator or director. Depending on the institution, courses or a master's degree in business or health administration may be necessary for the director's position. Some technologists progress by becoming instructors or directors in radiologic technology programs; others take jobs as sales representatives or instructors with equipment manufacturers.

With additional education, available at major cancer centers, radiation therapy technologists can specialize as medical radiation dosimetrists. Dosimetrists work with health physicists and oncologists (physicians who specialize in the study and treatment of tumors) to develop treatment plans.

Radiographers and radiation therapists are required to fulfill 24 hours of continuing education every other year and provide documentation to prove that they are complying with these requirements. Sonographers must complete 30 hours of continuing education every three years.

Job Outlook

Job seekers are likely to face competition from many other qualified applicants for most job openings through the year 2006. In an attempt to employ fewer technologists and lower labor costs, hospitals have begun to merge radiologic with nuclear medicine technology departments. Consequently, technologists who can perform both radiologic and nuclear medicine procedures will have the best job opportunities. The streamlining of these departments has led to slower job growth in hospitals at the same time that the number of qualified applicants entering the field has increased. The imbalance between job openings and job seekers has caused competition for jobs to become intense. Though it is unclear how severe the imbalance will remain, it is expected to persist at some level through the year 2006.

Sonographers should experience somewhat better job opportunities than other radiologic technologist occupations. Ultrasound is becoming an increasingly attractive alternative to radiologic procedures. Ultrasound technology is expected to continue to evolve rapidly and spawn many new ultrasound procedures. Furthermore, because radiation is absent from ultrasound procedures, there are no known side effects to patients.

Employment of radiologic technologists is expected to grow faster than the average for all occupations through 2006, as the population grows and ages, increasing the demand for diagnostic imaging and therapeutic technology. For example, radiation therapy will continue to be used—alone or in combination with surgery or chemotherapy—to treat cancer. Although physicians are enthusiastic about the clinical benefits of new technologies, the extent to which they are adopted depends largely on cost and reimbursement considerations. Some promising new technologies may not come into widespread use because they are too expensive and third-party payers may not be willing to pay for their use.

Hospitals will remain the principal employer of radiologic technologists. However, employment is expected to grow most rapidly in offices and clinics of physicians, including diagnostic imaging centers. Health facilities such as these are expected to grow very rapidly through 2006 due to the strong shift toward outpatient care, encouraged by third-party payers and made possible by technological advances that permit more procedures to be performed outside the hospital. Some jobs will also come from the need to replace technologists who leave the occupation.

Earnings

In 1996, median weekly earnings for full-time salaried radiologic technologists were $559. Half earned between $478 and $672; 10 percent earned less than $317; and 10 percent earned more than $849.

According to a Hay Group Survey of acute care hospitals, the median annual base salary of full-time radiologic technologists was $28,800 in January 1997. The middle 50 percent earned between $26,600 and $31,800. Full-time radiation therapy technologists earned a median annual base salary of $37,300; and ultrasound technologists, $36,100.

Related Occupations

Radiologic technologists operate sophisticated equipment to help physicians, dentists, and other health practitioners diagnose and treat patients. Workers in related occupations include radiation dosimetrists, nuclear medicine technologists, cardiovascular technologists and technicians, perfusionists, respiratory therapists, clinical laboratory technologists, and electroneurodiagnostic technologists.

Sources of Additional Information

For career information, enclose a stamped, self-addressed business size envelope with your request to:

❏ American Society of Radiologic Technologists, 15000 Central Ave. SE., Albuquerque, NM 87123-3917.

❏ Society of Diagnostic Medical Sonographers, 12770 Coit Rd., Suite 708, Dallas, TX 75251.

❏ American Healthcare Radiology Administrators, 111 Boston Post Rd., Suite 105, P.O. Box 334, Sudbury, MA 01776.

For the current list of accredited education programs in radiography and radiation therapy technology, write to:

❏ Joint Review Committee on Education in Radiologic Technology, 20 N. Wacker Dr., Suite 600, Chicago, IL 60606-2901.

For a current list of accredited education programs in diagnostic medical sonography, write to:

❏ The Joint Review Committee on Education in Diagnostic Medical Sonography, 7108 S. Alton Way, Building C., Englewood, CO 80112.

Real Estate Agents, Brokers, and Appraisers

(*D.O.T.* 191.267-010 and 250.157-010, .357-010, -014, and -018)

Significant Points

✓ *Real estate sales positions should continue to be relatively easy to obtain due to the thousands of people who leave this occupation each year.*

✓ *Real estate agents and brokers must be licensed in every state and in the District of Columbia.*

Nature of the Work

The purchase or sale of a home or investment property is not only one of the most important financial events in peoples' lives, but one of the most complex transactions as well. As a result, people generally seek the help of real estate agents, brokers, and appraisers when trying to buy, sell, or establish a price for real estate.

Real estate agents and brokers have a thorough knowledge of the real estate market in their community. They know which neighborhoods will best fit their clients' needs and budgets. They are familiar with local zoning and tax laws, and know where to obtain financing. Agents and brokers also act as an intermediary in price negotiations between buyers and sellers. Real estate agents are generally independent sales workers who provide their services to a licensed broker on a contract basis. In return, the broker pays the agent a portion of the commission earned from property sold through the firm, by the agent.

Brokers are independent business people who, for a fee, sell real estate owned by others and rent and manage properties. In closing sales, brokers often provide buyers with information on loans to finance their purchase. They also arrange for title searches and for meetings between buyers and sellers when details of the transactions are agreed upon and the new owners take possession. A broker's knowledge, resourcefulness, and creativity in arranging financing that is most favorable to the prospective buyer often mean the difference between success and failure in closing a sale. In some cases, agents assume the responsibilities in closing sales, but in many areas, this is done by lawyers or lenders. Brokers also manage their own offices, advertise properties, and handle other business matters. Some combine other types of work, such as selling insurance or practicing law, with their real estate business.

Before showing properties to potential buyers, the broker or agent has an initial meeting with them to get a feeling for the type of home they would like and can afford. Often, an agent or broker uses a computer to generate lists of properties for sale, their location and description, and to identify available sources of financing. Traditionally, they then take the clients to see a number of homes that are likely to meet their needs and income. Increasingly, however, agents and brokers are able to use computers in their office to give clients a "virtual" tour of properties in which they are interested, allowing them to look at various types of images of the property, including interior and exterior images and floor plans.

Because buying real estate is such an important decision of a person's life, agents may have to meet several times with prospective buyers to discuss available properties. In answering questions, agents emphasize selling points likely to be most important to the buyer. To a young family looking at a house, for example, they may point out the convenient floor plan and the fact that quality schools and shopping centers are close by. To a potential investor seeking the tax advantages of owning a rental property, they may point out the proximity to the city and the ease of finding a renter. If bargaining over price becomes necessary, agents must carefully follow their client's instructions and may have to present counteroffers in order to get the best possible price.

Once the contract has been signed by both parties, the real estate broker or agent must see to it that all special terms of the contract are met before the closing date. For example, if the seller has agreed to a home inspection or a termite and radon inspection, the agent must make sure this is done. Also, if the seller has agreed to any repairs, the broker or agent must see they are made. Increasingly, brokers and agents handle environmental problems by making sure the property they are selling meets environmental regulations. For example, they may be responsible for dealing with problems such as lead paint on the walls. While many details are handled by loan officers, attorneys, or other persons, the agent must check to make sure that they also are completed.

There is more to an agent's and broker's job, however, than just making sales. Because they must have properties to sell, they may spend a significant amount of time obtaining "listings" (owner agreements to place properties for sale with the firm). When listing property for sale, agents and brokers compare the listed property with similar properties that have been sold recently to determine its competitive market price.

Most real estate agents and brokers sell residential property. A few, usually in large firms or small specialized firms, sell commercial, industrial, agricultural, or other types of real estate. Each specialty requires knowledge of that particular type of property and clientele. Selling or leasing business property, for example, requires an understanding of leasing practices, business trends, and location needs. Agents who sell or lease industrial properties must know about transportation, utilities, and labor supply. To sell residential properties, the agent or broker must know the location of schools, religious institutions, shopping facilities, and public transportation, and be familiar with tax rates and insurance coverage.

Because real estate transactions involve substantial financial commitments, parties to the transactions may seek the advice of real estate appraisers, who are objective experts and do not have a vested interest in the property. An appraisal is an unbiased estimate of the quality, value, and best use of a specific property. Appraisals may be used by prospective sellers to set a competitive price, by a lending institution to estimate the market value of a property as a condition for a mortgage loan, or by local governments to determine the assessed value of a property for tax purposes. Many real estate appraisers are independent fee appraisers or work for real estate appraisal firms, while others are employees of banks, savings and loan associations, mortgage companies, government agencies, or multiservice real estate companies.

During a property inspection, real estate appraisers investigate the quality of the construction, the overall condition of the property, and its functional design. They gather information on properties by taking measurements, interviewing persons familiar with the properties' history, and searching public records of sales, leases, assessments, and other transactions. Appraisers compare the subject property with similar properties for which recent sale prices or rental data are available, to arrive at an estimate of value. They may also estimate the current cost of reproducing any structures on the properties and how much the value of existing structures may have depreciated over time. Appraisers must consider the influence of the location of the properties, potential income, current market conditions, and real estate trends or impending changes that could influence the present and future value of the property. Depending on the purpose of the appraisal, they may estimate the market value of the property, the insurable value, the investment value, or other kinds of value. Appraisers must prepare formal written reports of their findings that meet the standards of The Appraisal Foundation.

Real estate appraisers often specialize in certain types of properties. Most appraise only homes, but others specialize in appraising apartment or office buildings, shopping centers, or a variety of other types of commercial, industrial, or agricultural properties. The amount of time necessary to do an appraisal varies by the type of property—for a residential property it may take a week, whereas for a commercial property, several months may be needed to complete the appraisal.

Working Conditions

Because of advances in telecommunications and the ability to retrieve data on properties over the Internet, a growing number of real estate agents, brokers, and appraisers work out of their homes instead of offices. Even with this convenience, much of their time is spent away from their desk—showing properties to customers, analyzing properties for sale, meeting with prospective clients, researching the state of the market, inspecting properties for appraisal, and performing a wide range of other duties.

Agents, brokers, and appraisers often work more than a standard 40-hour week; nearly one of every four worked 50 hours or more a week in 1996. They often work evenings and weekends to suit the needs of their clients.

Employment

Real estate agents, brokers, and appraisers held about 408,000 jobs in 1996. Many worked part time, combining their real estate activities with other careers. Most real estate agents and brokers were self-employed, working on a commission basis.

Most real estate and appraisal firms are relatively small; indeed, some are a one-person business. Some large real estate firms have several hundred real estate agents operating out of many branch offices. Many brokers have franchise agreements with national or regional real estate organizations. Under this type of arrangement, the broker pays a fee in exchange for the privilege of using the more widely known name of the parent organization. Although franchised brokers often receive help in training salespeople and in running their offices, they bear the ultimate responsibility for the success or failure of the firm.

Persons who are real estate agents, brokers, and appraisers are older, on average, than those in most other occupations. Historically, many homemakers and retired persons were attracted to real estate sales by the flexible and part-time work schedules characteristic of this field and may enter, leave, and later reenter the occupation, depending on the strength of the real estate market, family responsibilities, or other personal circumstances. Recently, however, the high startup costs associated with becoming an agent have made some look elsewhere when looking for part-time work. In addition to those entering or reentering the labor force, some transfer into real estate jobs from a wide range of occupations, including clerical and other sales jobs.

Real estate is sold and appraised in all areas, but employment is concentrated in large urban areas and in smaller, but rapidly growing communities.

Training, Other Qualifications, and Advancement

In every state and in the District of Columbia, real estate agents and brokers must be licensed. All states require prospective agents to be a high school graduate, be at least 18 years old, and pass a written test. The examination—more comprehensive for brokers than for agents—includes questions on basic real estate transactions and laws affecting the sale of property. Most states require candidates for the general sales license to complete between 30 and 90 hours of classroom instruction, whereas those seeking the broker's license are required to complete between 60 and 90 hours of formal training in addition to a specified amount of experience in selling real estate (generally one to three years). Some states waive the experience requirements for the broker's license for applicants who have a bachelor's degree in real estate. State licenses generally must be renewed every one or two years, usually without reexamination. Many states, however, require continuing education for license renewal. Prospective agents and brokers should contact the real estate licensing commission of the state(s) in which they wish to work to verify exact licensing requirements.

Federal law requires appraisers of most types of real estate (all property being financed by a federally regulated lender) to be state licensed or certified. In some states, appraisers who are not involved with federally regulated institutions do not have to be certified. State certification requirements for appraisers must meet federal standards, but states are free to set more stringent requirements. Formal courses, appraisal experience, and a satisfactory score on an examination are needed to be certified. Requirements for licensure vary by state, but are somewhat less stringent than for certification. In some states, college education may be substituted for a portion of the experience requirement for licensure.

Individuals enter real estate appraisal from a variety of backgrounds. Traditionally, persons enter from real estate sales, management, and finance positions. However, as real estate transactions have become more complex, involving complicated legal requirements, many firms have turned to college graduates to fill positions. A large number of agents, brokers, and appraisers have some college training, and the number of college graduates selling real estate has risen substantially in recent years. College courses in real estate, finance and business administration, statistics, computer science, economics, and English are helpful. Because many workers start their own company, business courses such as marketing and accounting may be as important as those in real estate or finance.

However, personality traits are equally as important as academic background. Brokers look for applicants who possess a pleasant personality, honesty, and a neat appearance. Maturity, tact, and enthusiasm for the job are required in order to motivate prospective customers in this highly competitive field. Agents should also be well organized and detail oriented, as well as have a good memory for names, faces, and business details, such as taxes, zoning codes, and local land-use regulations. Appraisers should have good judgment, writing, and math skills.

Persons interested in beginning jobs as real estate agents often apply in their own communities, where their knowledge of local neighborhoods is an advantage. A beginner usually learns the practical aspects of the job, including the use of computers to locate or list available properties or identify sources of financing, under the direction of an experienced agent.

Many firms offer formal training programs for both beginners and experienced agents. Larger firms generally offer more extensive programs than smaller firms. Over 1,000 universities, colleges, and junior colleges offer courses in real estate. At some, a student can earn an associate or bachelor's degree with a major in real estate; several offer advanced degrees. Many local real estate associations that are members of the National Association of Realtors, sponsor courses covering the fundamentals and legal aspects of the field. Advanced courses in appraisal, mortgage financing, property development and management, and other subjects are also available through various affiliates of the National Association of Realtors.

Many real estate appraisers voluntarily earn professional designations, representing formal recognition of their professional competence and achievements. A number of appraisal organizations have programs that, through a combination of experience, professional education, and examinations, lead to the award of such designations. These professional designations are desirable because requirements for them are more stringent than state standards.

Advancement opportunities for agents often take the form of higher commission rates and more and bigger sales, both of which increase earnings. This occurs as agents gain knowledge and expertise and become more efficient in closing a greater number of transactions. Experienced agents can advance in many large firms to sales or general manager. Persons who have received their broker's license may open their own offices. Others with experience and training in estimating property value may become real estate appraisers, and people familiar with operating and maintaining rental properties may become property managers. Agents, brokers, and appraisers who gain general experience in real estate and a thorough knowledge of business conditions and property values in their localities, may enter mortgage financing or real estate investment counseling.

Job Outlook

Employment of real estate agents, brokers, and appraisers is expected to grow more slowly than the average for all occupations through the year 2006. However, a large number of job openings will arise due to replacement needs. Each year, thousands of jobs will become available as workers transfer to other occupations or leave the labor force. Because turnover is high, real estate sales positions should continue to be relatively easy to obtain. Not everyone is successful in this highly competitive field; many beginners become discouraged by their inability to get listings and to close a sufficient number of sales. Lacking financial sustenance and motivation, they subsequently leave the occupation. Well-trained, ambitious people who enjoy selling should have the best chance for success.

Increasing use of electronic information technology may increase the productivity of agents, brokers, and appraisers as the use of computers, faxes, modems, and databases becomes more commonplace. Some real estate companies are using computer generated images to show houses to customers without even leaving the office. These devices enable one agent to serve a greater number of customers. Use of this technology may eliminate some of the more marginal agents such as those practicing real estate part time or between jobs. These workers will not be able to compete as easily with full-time agents who have invested in this technology.

Another factor expected to impact the need for agents and brokers is the ability for prospective customers to search for properties that meet their criteria themselves by accessing certain real estate sites on the Internet. While they won't be able to conduct the entire real estate transaction on-line, it does allow the prospective homebuyer the convenience of looking at properties, as well as the ability to find out about issues such as financing, from their own home.

Computer technology has also impacted the need for appraisers. For example, the length of time needed to do a residential appraisal has declined as access to electronic databases has increased, streamlining their work process. Furthermore, specialized computer software programs have allowed lending institutions to derive property values without as much input from appraisers.

Employment growth in this field will stem primarily from increased demand for home purchases and rental units. Shifts in the age distribution of the population over the next decade will result in a growing number of persons in the prime working ages (25 to 54 years old) with careers and family responsibilities. This is the most geographically mobile group in our society, and the one that traditionally makes most of the home purchases. As their incomes rise, they also may be expected to invest in additional real estate.

Employment of real estate agents, brokers, and appraisers is sensitive to swings in the economy. During periods of declining economic activity and tight credit, the volume of sales and the resulting demand for sales workers may decline. During these periods, the earnings of agents, brokers, and appraisers decline, and many work fewer hours or leave the occupation.

Earnings

Commissions on sales are the main source of earnings of real estate agents and brokers–few receive a salary. The rate of commission varies according to the type of property and its value; the percentage paid on the sale of farm and commercial properties or unimproved land usually is higher than that paid for selling a home. Appraisers typically receive a flat fee.

Commissions may be divided among several agents and brokers. The broker and the agent in the firm who obtained the listing generally share their part of the commission when the property is sold; the broker and the agent in the firm who made the sale also generally share their part of the commission. Although an agent's share varies greatly from one firm to another, often it is about half of the total amount received by the firm. The agent who both lists and sells the property, maximizes his or her commission.

Real estate agents, brokers, and appraisers who usually worked full time had median annual earnings of $31,500 in 1996. The middle 50 percent earned between $20,500 and $49,700. The top 10 percent earned more than $75,400 and the lowest 10 percent earned less than $12,600.

Income usually increases as an agent gains experience, but individual ability, economic conditions, and the type and location of the property also affect earnings. Sales workers who are active in community organizations and local real estate associations can broaden their contacts and increase their earnings. A beginner's earnings are often irregular because a few weeks or even months may go by without a sale. Although some brokers allow an agent a drawing account against future earnings, this practice is not usual with new employees. The beginner, therefore, should have enough money to live on for about six months or until commissions increase.

Related Occupations

Selling expensive items such as homes requires maturity, tact, and a sense of responsibility. Other sales workers who find these character traits important in their work include motor vehicle sales workers, securities and financial services sales workers, insurance agents and brokers, and manufacturers' representatives. Other appraisers specialize in performing many types of appraisals besides real estate, including aircraft, antiques and fine arts, and business valuations.

Sources of Additional Information

Details on licensing requirements for real estate agents, brokers, and appraisers are available from most local real estate and appraiser organizations or from the state real estate commission or board.

For more information about opportunities in real estate, contact:

❑ National Association of Realtors, Realtor Information Center, 430 North Michigan Ave., Chicago, IL 60611.

Information on careers, and licensing and certification requirements, in real estate appraising is available from:

❑ The Appraisal Foundation, 1029 Vermont Avenue NW, Suite 900, Washington, DC 20005-3517.

Receptionists

(*D.O.T.* 203.362-014; 205.367-038; 237.267, .367-010, -018, -022, -026, -038, -042, -046, and -050; 238.367-022 and -034; 249.262 and .367-082)

Significant Points

Expected faster than average employment growth and relatively high turnover should create numerous job openings for receptionists.

A high school diploma or its equivalent is the most common educational requirement for most receptionist jobs.

Nature of the Work

All organizations want to make a good first impression, and this is often the responsibility of the receptionist, who may be the first representative of the organization a visitor encounters. Receptionists answer questions from the public and provide information about the organization. In addition to traditional duties such as answering telephones, routing calls, and greeting visitors, a receptionist may serve a security function within an organization, such as monitoring the access of visitors.

The day-to-day duties of a receptionist can vary depending upon the type of establishment in which they work. Receptionists in hospitals and doctors' offices may obtain personal and financial information and direct patients to the proper waiting rooms. At beauty or hair salons, they arrange appointments, direct customers to the hair stylist, and also may serve as cashier. In factories, large corporations, and government offices, they may provide identification cards and arrange for escorts to take visitors to the proper office.

Those working for bus and train companies respond to inquiries about departures, arrivals, stops, and related matters.

Increasingly, receptionists use multi-line telephone systems, personal computers, and fax machines. Despite the widespread use of automated answering systems or voice mail, many receptionists take messages and inform other employees of a visitors' arrival or cancellation of an appointment. When they are not busy with callers, most are expected to perform a variety of secretarial duties including opening and sorting mail, collecting and distributing parcels, making fax transmittals and deliveries, updating appointment calendars, preparing travel vouchers, and doing simple bookkeeping, word processing, and filing.

Working Conditions

Receptionists greet customers and visitors in highly visible areas, designed and furnished to make a good impression. Most work stations are clean, well lighted, and relatively quiet, and overall working conditions are usually pleasant.

Although most receptionists work a standard 40-hour week, about three out of ten work part-time. Some high school and college students work part-time as receptionists, after school or during vacations.

The work performed by receptionists may be repetitious and stressful. Many spend all day answering continuously ringing telephones while performing additional clerical or secretarial tasks.

Employment

Receptionists held about 1,074,000 jobs in 1996, accounting for over two-thirds of all information clerk jobs. More than two-thirds of all receptionists worked in services industries, and almost half of these were located in the health services industry—doctors' and dentists' offices, hospitals, nursing homes, urgent care centers, surgical centers, and clinics. Manufacturing, wholesale and retail trade, government, and real estate industries also employed large numbers of receptionists. About three of every ten receptionists worked part-time.

Training, Other Qualifications, and Advancement

A high school diploma or its equivalent is the most common educational requirement. However, good interpersonal skills and familiarity or experience with computers are often more important to employers.

Because receptionists deal directly with the public, good grooming habits and a pleasant personality are imperative, as are good problem-solving and interpersonal skills. A clear speaking voice and fluency in the English language are essential because receptionists frequently use the telephone or public address systems. Good spelling, typing ability, and computer literacy are often needed, particularly because most work involves considerable computer use.

Receptionists generally receive on-the-job training. However, employers often look for applicants who already possess certain skills, such as prior computer and word processing experience. Some employers may prefer previous experience, some formal education, or training with office equipment or procedures. On the job, they learn how to operate the telephone system, computers, and the proper procedures for greeting visitors, and distributing mail, fax, and parcel deliveries.

Advancement for receptionists generally comes about either by transfer to a different, more responsible occupation or by promotion to a supervisory position. The more skills, experience, and additional training an employee possesses, the better their advancement opportunities. Receptionists with word processing or other clerical skills may advance to a better paying job as a secretary or administrative assistant.

Job Outlook

Employment of receptionists is expected to grow faster than the average for all occupations through the year 2006, because so many receptionists work for firms in services industries—including physician's offices, law firms, temporary help agencies, and consulting firms—that are expected to experience significant growth. Job openings should be plentiful due to the large size and high rate of turnover associated with this occupation. In addition to openings from growth, thousands of openings are expected each year from the need to replace receptionists who transfer to other occupations, seeking better pay or career advancement, or who leave the labor force altogether. Opportunities should be best for persons with a wide range of clerical skills and experience.

The demand for receptionists may be tempered somewhat by the increasing use of voice mail and other telephone automation. Where several receptionists may have been required to answer the company's telephones in the past, voice mail now makes it possible for one person to do the job of many. However, many receptionists also perform secretarial duties and often employers look to hire receptionists with good word processing and computer skills, coupled with strong interpersonal and communications skills. Because establishments need someone to perform their duties even during economic downturns, receptionists are less subject to layoffs during recessions than other clerical workers.

Earnings

In 1996, median weekly earnings of full-time receptionists were about $333.

In early 1997, the federal government commonly paid beginning receptionists with a high school diploma or six months of experience, salaries ranging from $18,980 to $19,240 a year. The average annual salary for all receptionists employed by the federal government was about $21,240 in 1997.

Related Occupations

A number of other workers deal with the public, receive and provide information, or direct people to others who can assist them. Among these are dispatchers, security guards, bank tellers, guides, telephone operators, record clerks, counter and rental clerks, survey workers, and ushers and lobby attendants.

Sources of Additional Information

State employment offices can provide information on job openings for receptionists.

Recreation Workers

(*D.O.T.* 153.137-010; 159.124-010; 187.167-238; 195.227-010, -014; 352.167-010)

Significant Points

✓ *The recreation field has an unusually large number of part-time, seasonal, and volunteer jobs.*

✓ *Educational requirements range from a high school diploma, or sometimes less for many summer jobs, to a graduate degree in parks and recreation or leisure studies for some administrative positions.*

✓ *Competition will remain keen for full-time career positions; persons with experience gained in part-time or seasonal recreation jobs, together with formal recreation training, should have the best opportunities.*

Nature of the Work

Many people spend much of their leisure time participating in a wide variety of organized recreation activities, such as aerobics, arts and crafts, water sports, tennis, camping and softball. Recreation programs, as diverse as the people they serve, are offered at local playgrounds and recreation areas, parks, community centers, health clubs, religious organizations, camps, theme parks, and most tourist attractions. Recreation workers plan, organize, and direct these activities.

Recreation workers organize and lead programs and watch over recreational facilities and equipment. They help people pursue their interest in crafts, art, or sports by leading activities. These activities enable people to share common interests in physical and mental activities for entertainment, physical fitness, and self-improvement. Recreation workers organize teams and leagues, and also teach the correct use of equipment and facilities.

In the workplace, recreation workers organize and direct leisure activities and athletic programs for all ages, such as bowling and softball leagues, social functions, travel programs, discount services, and, to an increasing extent, exercise and fitness programs. These activities are generally for adults.

Recreation workers hold a variety of positions at many different levels of responsibility. Recreation leaders are responsible for a recreation program's daily operation, and organize and direct participants. They may lead and give instruction in dance, drama, crafts, games, and sports; schedule use of facilities and keep records of equipment use; and ensure recreation facilities and equipment are used properly. Workers who provide instruction in specialties such as art, music, drama, swimming, or tennis may be called activity specialists. They conduct classes and coach teams in the activity in which they specialize.

Recreation supervisors plan, organize, and manage recreation activities to meet the needs of the population they serve, and supervise recreation leaders. A recreation supervisor serves as a liaison between the director of the park or recreation center and the recreation leaders. A recreation supervisor who has more specialized responsibilities may also direct special activities or events, and oversee a major activity, such as aquatics, gymnastics, or performing arts.

Directors of recreation and parks develop and manage comprehensive recreation programs in parks, playgrounds, and other settings. Directors usually serve as a technical advisor to state and local recreation and park commissions, and may be responsible for recreation and park budgets.

Camp counselors lead and instruct children and teenagers in outdoor-oriented forms of recreation, such as swimming, hiking, horseback riding, and camping. Activities are often intended to enhance campers' appreciation of nature and responsible use of the environment. In addition, counselors provide campers with specialized instruction in activities such as archery, boating, music, drama, gymnastics, tennis, and computers. In resident camps, counselors also provide guidance and supervise daily living and general socialization.

In a related occupation, recreational therapists help individuals recover or adjust to illness, disability, or specific social problems.

Working Conditions

Recreation workers must work while others engage in leisure time activities. While most recreation workers put in about 40 hours a week, people entering this field, especially camp counselors, should expect some night and weekend work and irregular hours. About three out of ten work part-time, and many jobs are seasonal. The work setting for recreation workers may be anywhere from a cruise ship, to a woodland recreational park, to a playground in the center of a large urban community. Recreation workers often spend much of their time outdoors and may work under a variety of weather conditions. Recreation directors and supervisors may spend most of their time in an office planning programs and special events. Because full-time recreation workers spend more time acting as managers than hands-on activities leaders, they engage in less physical activity. However, as is the case for anyone engaged in physical activity, recreation workers risk suffering an injury, and the work can be physically challenging.

Employment

Recreation workers held about 233,000 jobs in 1996, and many additional workers held summer jobs in this occupation. Of those who held year-round jobs as recreation workers, about half worked in park and recreation departments of municipal and county governments. Nearly two out of ten worked in membership organizations with a civic, social, fraternal, or religious orientation—the Boy Scouts, the YWCA, and Red Cross, for example. About one out of ten were in programs run by social service organizations—senior centers and adult daycare programs, or residential care facilities such as halfway houses, group homes, and institutions for delinquent youth. Another one out ten worked for nursing and other personal care facilities.

Other employers included commercial recreation establishments, amusement parks, sports and entertainment centers, wilderness and survival enterprises, tourist attractions, vacation excursion companies, hotels and resorts, summer camps, health and athletic clubs, and apartment complexes.

The recreation field has an unusually large number of part-time, seasonal, and volunteer jobs. These jobs include summer camp counselors, lifeguards, craft specialists, and after-school and weekend recreation program leaders. Teachers and college students take many jobs as recreation workers when school is not in session.

Many unpaid volunteers assist paid recreation workers. The vast majority of volunteers serve as activity leaders at local daycamp programs, or in youth organizations, camps, nursing homes, hospitals, senior centers, YMCAs, and other settings. Some volunteers serve on local park and recreation boards and commissions. Volunteer experience, part-time work during school, or a summer job can lead to a full-time career as a recreation worker.

Training, Other Qualifications, and Advancement

Education needed for recreation worker jobs ranges from a high school diploma, or sometimes less for many summer jobs, to graduate education for some administrative positions in large public recreation systems. Full-time career professional positions usually require a college degree with a major in parks and recreation or leisure studies, but a bachelor's degree in any liberal arts field may be sufficient for some jobs in the private sector. In industrial recreation, or "employee services" as it is more commonly called, companies prefer to hire those with a bachelor's degree in recreation or leisure studies and a background in business administration.

Specialized training or experience in a particular field, such as art, music, drama, or athletics, is an asset for many jobs. Some jobs also require a certification. For example, when teaching or coaching water-related activities, a lifesaving certificate is a prerequisite. Graduates of associate degree programs in parks and recreation, social work, and other human services disciplines also enter some career recreation positions. Occasionally high school graduates are able to enter career positions, but this is not common. Some college students work part-time as recreation workers while earning degrees.

A bachelor's degree and experience are preferred for most recreation supervisor jobs and required for most higher-level administrator jobs. However, increasing numbers of recreation workers who aspire to administrator positions are obtaining master's degrees in parks and recreation or related disciplines Also, many persons in other disciplines, including social work, forestry, and resource management, pursue graduate degrees in recreation.

Programs leading to an associate or bachelor's degree in parks and recreation, leisure studies, or related fields are offered at several hundred colleges and universities. Many also offer master's or doctoral degrees in this field.

In 1997, 93 bachelor's degree programs in parks and recreation were accredited by the National Recreation and Park Association (NRPA). Accredited programs provide broad exposure to the history, theory, and philosophy of park and recreation management. Courses offered include community organization, supervision and administration, recreational needs of special populations, such as older adults or the disabled, and supervised fieldwork. Students may specialize in areas such as therapeutic recreation, park management, outdoor recreation, industrial or commercial recreation, and camp management.

The American Camping Association offers workshops and courses for experienced camp directors at different times and locations throughout the year. Some national youth associations offer training courses for camp directors at the local and regional levels.

Persons planning recreation careers should be outgoing, good at motivating people, and sensitive to the needs of others. Good health and physical fitness are required. Activity planning calls for creativity and resourcefulness. Willingness to accept responsibility and the ability to exercise good judgment are important qualities since recreation personnel often work without close supervision. Part-time or summer recreation work experience while in high school or college may help students decide whether their interests really point to a human services career. Such experience also may increase their leadership skills and understanding of people.

Individuals contemplating careers in recreation at the supervisory or administrative level should develop managerial skills. College courses in management, business administration, accounting, and personnel management are likely to be useful.

Certification for this field is offered by the NRPA National Certification Board. The National Recreation and Parks Association, along with its state chapters, offers certification as a Certified Leisure Professional (CLP) for those with a college degree in recreation, and as a Certified Leisure Technician (CLT) for those with less than four years of college. Other NRPA certifications include Certified Leisure Provisional Professional (CLPP), Certified Playground Inspector (CPI), and Aquatic Facility Operations (AFO) Certification. Continuing education is necessary to remain certified.

Certification is not usually required for employment or advancement in this field, but it is an asset. Employers choosing among qualified job applicants may opt to hire the person with a demonstrated record of professional achievement represented by certification.

Job Outlook

Competition will remain keen for full-time career positions in recreation. All college graduates are eligible for recreation jobs, regardless of major. Also, many high school and junior college graduates are eligible, so the number of full-time career job seekers often greatly exceed the number of job openings. Opportunities for staff positions should be best for persons with experience gained in part-time or seasonal recreation jobs, together with formal recreation training. Those with graduate degrees should have the best opportunities for supervisory or administrative positions.

Prospects are better for the large number of temporary seasonal jobs. These positions, typically filled by high school or college students, do not generally have formal education requirements and are open to anyone with the desired personal qualities. Employers compete for a share of the vacationing student labor force, and, while salaries in recreation are often lower than those in other fields, the nature of the work and the opportunity to work outdoors is attractive to many. Seasonal employment prospects should be good for applicants with specialized training and certification in an activity like swimming. These workers may obtain jobs as program directors.

Employment of recreation workers is expected to grow faster than the average for all occupations through the year 2006 as growing numbers of people possess both the time and the money to enjoy leisure services. Growth in these jobs will also stem from increased interest in fitness and health and the rising demand for recreational opportunities for older adults in senior centers and retirement communities. However, overall employment in local government—where half of all recreation workers are employed—is expected to grow more slowly than in other industries due to budget constraints, and some local park and recreation departments are expected to do less hiring for permanent, full-time positions than in the past. As a result, this sector's share of recreation worker employment will vary widely by region, since resources as well as priorities for public services differ from one community to another. Thus,

hiring prospects for recreation workers will be much better in some park and recreation departments, but worse in others.

Recreation worker jobs should also increase in social services—more recreation workers will be needed to develop and lead activity programs in senior centers, halfway houses, children's homes, and daycare programs for the mentally retarded or developmentally disabled. Similarly, the increasing elderly population will spur job growth in nursing homes and other personal care facilities where recreation activities are becoming more important.

Recreation worker jobs in employee services and recreation will continue to increase as more businesses recognize the benefits to their employees of recreation programs and other services such as wellness programs and elder care. Job growth will also occur in the commercial recreation industry, composed of amusement parks, athletic clubs, camps, sports clinics, and swimming pools, for example.

Earnings

Median annual earnings of recreation workers who worked full-time in 1996 were about $18,700, significantly lower than the median of $25,600 for workers in all occupations. The middle 50 percent earned between about $12,900 and $28,900, while the top 10 percent earned $37,500 or more. However, earnings of recreation directors and others in supervisory or managerial positions can be substantially higher.

Most public and private recreation agencies provide full-time recreation workers with typical benefits; part-time workers receive few, if any, benefits.

Related Occupations

Recreation workers must exhibit leadership and sensitivity in dealing with people. Other occupations that require similar personal qualities include recreational therapists, social workers, parole officers, human relations counselors, school counselors, clinical and counseling psychologists, and teachers.

Sources of Additional Information

For information on jobs in recreation, contact employers such as local government departments of parks and recreation, nursing and personal care facilities, and YMCAs.

Ordering information for materials describing careers and academic programs in recreation is available from:

❑ National Recreation and Park Association, Division of Professional Services, 2775 South Quincy St., Suite 300, Arlington, VA 22206. Homepage: http://www.nrpa.org

For information on careers in employee services and corporate recreation, contact:

❑ National Employee Services and Recreation Association, 2211 York Rd., Suite 207, Oakbrook, IL 60521.

For information on careers in camping and summer counselor opportunities, contact:

❑ American Camping Association, 5000 State Rd. 67 North, Martinsville, IN 46151.

Recreational Therapists

(D.O.T. 076.124-014)

Significant Points

- ✓ *Employment of recreational therapists is expected to increase rapidly as demand grows for physical and psychiatric rehabilitative services and for services for people with disabilities.*
- ✓ *Opportunities should generally be good for persons with a bachelor's degree in therapeutic recreation or in recreation with an option in therapeutic recreation.*

Nature of the Work

Recreational therapists provide treatment services and recreation activities to individuals with illnesses or disabling conditions. They use a variety of techniques to treat or maintain the physical, mental, and emotional well-being of clients. Treatments may include the use of arts and crafts, animals, sports, games, dance and movement, drama, music, and community outings. Therapists help individuals reduce depression, stress, and anxiety. They help individuals recover their basic motor functioning and reasoning abilities, build confidence, and socialize more effectively to allow them to be more independent, as well as reduce or eliminate the effects of illness or disability. Their focus is to help integrate people with disabilities into the community by helping them use community resources and recreational activities. Recreational therapists should not be confused with recreation workers, who organize recreational activities primarily for enjoyment.

In acute health care settings, such as hospitals and rehabilitation centers, recreational therapists treat and rehabilitate individuals with specific health conditions, usually in conjunction or collaboration with physicians, nurses, psychologists, social workers, and physical and occupational therapists. In long-term care facilities and residential facilities, they use leisure activities–especially structured group programs–to maintain general health and well-being. They may also treat clients and provide interventions to prevent further medical problems and secondary complications related to illness and disabilities. In these settings they may be called activity directors or therapeutic recreation specialists.

Recreational therapists assess clients based on information from standardized assessments, observations, medical records, medical staff, family, and clients themselves. They then develop and carry out therapeutic interventions consistent with patient needs and interests. For instance, clients isolated from others may be encouraged to play games with others, a right-handed person with a right-side paralysis may be instructed in adaptation and compensatory strategies to use his or her non-affected left side to throw a ball or swing a racket. Recreational therapists may instruct patients in relaxation techniques to reduce stress and tension, in correct stretching and limbering exercises, in proper body mechanics for participation in recreation activities, in pacing and energy conservation techniques, and in individual as well as team activities.

Community based recreational therapists work in park and recreation departments, special education programs for school districts, or programs for older adults and people with disabilities. In these programs, therapists help clients develop leisure activities and provide them with opportunities for exercise, mental stimulation, creativity, and fun.

In schools, recreational therapists help counselors, parents, and special education teachers address the special needs of students. They are especially important in helping to ease the transition phase into adult life for the disabled. The transition phase extends from age 14 until high school graduation. Recreational therapists provide assistance in teaching the student about recreational activities and how to use community resources. The primary responsibility for these therapists is to integrate students into the community.

Recreational therapists observe and record patients' participation, reactions, and progress. These records are used by the medical staff and others, to monitor progress, to justify changes or end treatment, and for billing.

Working Conditions

Recreational therapists provide services in special activity rooms, but also must plan events and keep records in offices. When working with clients during community integration programs, they may travel locally to instruct clients on the accessibility of public transportation and other public areas, such as parks, playgrounds, swimming pools, restaurants, and theaters.

Therapists often lift and carry equipment as well as lead recreational activities. Recreational therapists generally work a 40-hour week, which may include some evenings, weekends, and holidays.

Employment

Recreational therapists held about 38,000 jobs in 1996. About 42 percent of salaried jobs for therapists were in hospitals and 38 percent were in nursing homes. Others worked in residential facilities, community mental health centers, adult day care programs, correctional facilities, community programs for people with disabilities, and substance abuse centers. About one out of four therapists was self-employed, generally contracting with long-term care facilities or community agencies to develop and oversee programs.

Training, Other Qualifications, and Advancement

A bachelor's degree in therapeutic recreation (or in recreation with an option in therapeutic recreation) is the usual requirement for entry-level positions. Persons may qualify for paraprofessional positions with an associate degree in recreational therapy or a health care related field. An associates degree in recreational therapy; training in art, drama, or music therapy; or qualifying work experience may also be sufficient for activity director positions in nursing homes.

Most employers prefer to hire candidates who are certified therapeutic recreation specialists (CTRS). The National Council for Therapeutic Recreation Certification (NCTRC) certifies therapeutic recreation specialists. To become certified, specialists must have a bachelor's degree, pass a written certification examination, and complete an internship of at least 360 hours under the supervision of a certified therapeutic recreation specialist. A few colleges or agencies may require 600 hours of internship.

There are about 130 programs that prepare recreational therapists. Most offer bachelors degrees, although some offer associates, masters, or doctoral degrees. As of 1996, there were fewer than 50 recreation programs with options in therapeutic recreation that were accredited by the National Council on Accreditation.

In addition to therapeutic recreation course work in assessment, treatment and program planning, and intervention design and evaluation, students study human anatomy, physiology, abnormal psychology, medical and psychiatric terminology, characteristics of illnesses and disabilities, and the concepts of inclusion and normalization. Courses cover professional ethics, assessment and referral procedures, interdisciplinary teamwork, management, and the use of assistive devices and technology.

Recreational therapists should be comfortable working with persons who are ill or have disabilities. Therapists must be patient, tactful, and persuasive when working with people who have a variety of special needs. Ingenuity, a good sense of humor, and a strong imagination are needed to adapt activities to individual needs, and good physical coordination is necessary to demonstrate or participate in recreational events.

Therapists can advance to supervisory or administrative positions. Some teach, conduct research, or perform contract consulting work.

Job Outlook

Employment of recreational therapists is expected to grow faster than the average for all occupations through the year 2006, because of anticipated expansion in long-term care, physical and psychiatric rehabilitation, and services for people with disabilities. Job prospects are expected to be favorable for those with a strong health care background.

Health care facilities will provide a large number of recreational therapy jobs through the year 2006. A growing number of these will be in hospital-based adult day care and outpatient programs, or in units offering short-term mental health and alcohol or drug abuse services. Long-term rehabilitation, home-health care, transitional programs, and psychiatric facilities will provide additional jobs.

The rapidly growing number of older adults is expected to spur job growth for activity directors and recreational therapy paraprofessionals in nursing homes, assisted living facilities, adult day care programs, and social service agencies. Continued growth is expected in community residential facilities as well as day care programs for individuals with disabilities.

Earnings

According to a survey by the American Therapeutic Recreation Association, the average salary for recreational therapists was about $33,000 in 1996. The average annual salary for consultants, supervisors, administrators, and educators was about $42,000 in 1996. The average for all recreational therapists in the federal government in non-supervisory, supervisory, and managerial positions was about $39,400 in 1997.

Related Occupations

Recreational therapists design activities to help people with disabilities lead more fulfilling and independent lives. Other workers who have similar jobs are recreational therapy paraprofessionals, orientation therapists for persons who are blind or have visual impairments, art therapists, drama therapists, dance therapists, music therapists, occupational therapists, physical therapists, and rehabilitation counselors.

Sources of Additional Information

For information on how to order materials describing careers and academic programs in recreational therapy, write to:

❑ American Therapeutic Recreation Association, P.O. Box 15215, Hattiesburg, MS 39402-5215. Homepage: http://www.atra-tr.org.

❑ National Therapeutic Recreation Society, 22377 Belmont Ridge Rd., Ashburn, VA 20148 or by e-mail: NTRSNRPA@aol.com.

Certification information may be obtained from:

❑ National Council for Therapeutic Recreation Certification, P.O. Box 479, Thiells, NY 10984-0479.

Registered Nurses

(D.O.T. 075.124-010 and -014, .127-014, -026, -030 and -034, .137-010 and -014, .264-010 and -014, .364-010, .371-010, .374-014, -018, and -022)

Significant Points

✓ *The largest health care occupation, with over 1.9 million jobs.*

✓ *One of the five occupations projected to have the largest numbers of new jobs.*

✓ *Earnings are above average, particularly for advanced practice nurses who have additional education or training.*

Nature of the Work

Registered nurses (RNs) work to promote health, prevent disease, and help patients cope with illness. They are advocates and health educators for patients, families, and communities. When providing direct patient care, they observe, assess, and record symptoms, reactions, and progress; assist physicians during treatments and examinations; administer medications; and assist in convalescence and rehabilitation. RNs also develop and manage nursing care plans; instruct patients and their families in proper care; and help individuals and groups take steps to improve or maintain their health. While state laws govern the tasks RNs may perform, it is usually the work setting which determines their day-to-day job duties.

Hospital nurses form the largest group of nurses. Most are staff nurses, who provide bedside nursing care and carry out medical regimens. They may also supervise licensed practical nurses and aides. Hospital nurses usually are assigned to one area such as surgery, maternity, pediatrics, emergency room, intensive care, or treatment of cancer patients or may rotate among departments.

Office nurses assist physicians in private practice, clinics, surgicenters, emergency medical centers, and health maintenance organizations (HMOs). They prepare patients for and assist with examinations, administer injections and medications, dress wounds and incisions, assist with minor surgery, and maintain records. Some also perform routine laboratory and office work.

Home health nurses provide periodic services, prescribed by a physician, to patients at home. After assessing patients' home environments, they care for and instruct patients and their families. Home health nurses care for a broad range of patients, such as those recovering from illnesses and accidents, cancer, and child birth. They must be able to work independently and may supervise home health aides.

Nursing home nurses manage nursing care for residents with conditions ranging from a fracture to Alzheimer's disease. Although they generally spend most of their time on administrative and supervisory tasks, RNs also assess residents' medical condition, develop treatment plans, supervise licensed practical nurses and nursing aides, and perform difficult procedures such as starting intravenous fluids. They also work in specialty-care departments, such as long-term rehabilitation units for strokes and head-injuries.

Public health nurses work in government and private agencies and clinics, schools, retirement communities and other community settings. They focus on populations, working with individuals, groups, and families to improve the overall health of communities. They also work as partners with communities to plan and implement programs. Public health nurses instruct individuals, families, and other groups in health education, disease prevention, nutrition, and child care. They arrange for immunizations, blood pressure testing, and other health screening. These nurses also work with community leaders, teachers, parents, and physicians in community health education.

Occupational health or industrial nurses provide nursing care at worksites to employees, customers, and others with minor injuries and illnesses. They provide emergency care, prepare accident reports, and arrange for further care if necessary. They also offer health counseling, assist with health examinations and inoculations, and assess work environments to identify potential health or safety problems.

Head nurses or nurse supervisors direct nursing activities. They plan work schedules and assign duties to nurses and aides, provide or arrange for training, and visit patients to observe nurses and to insure that care is proper. They may also insure that records are maintained and that equipment and supplies are ordered.

At the advanced level, nurse practitioners provide basic primary health care. They diagnose and treat common acute illnesses and injuries. Nurse practitioners can prescribe medications in most states. Other advanced practice nurses include clinical nurse specialists, certified registered nurse anesthetists, and certified nurse-midwives. Advanced practice nurses have met higher educational and clinical practice requirements beyond the basic nursing education and licensing required of all RNs.

Working Conditions

Most nurses work in well-lighted, comfortable health care facilities. Home health and public health nurses travel to patients' homes and to schools, community centers, and other sites. Nurses may spend considerable time walking and standing. They need emotional stability to cope with human suffering, emergencies, and other stresses. Because patients in hospitals and nursing homes require 24-hour care, nurses in these institutions may work nights, weekends, and holidays. They may also be on-call. Office, occupational health, and public health nurses are more likely to work regular business hours. Almost one in ten RNs held more than one job in 1996.

Nursing has its hazards, especially in hospitals, nursing homes, and clinics where nurses may care for individuals with infectious diseases such as hepatitis and AIDS. Nurses must observe rigid guidelines to guard against these and other dangers such as radiation, chemicals used for sterilization of instruments, and anesthetics. In addition, they face back injury when moving patients, shocks from electrical equipment, and hazards posed by compressed gases.

Employment

As the largest health care occupation, registered nurses held about 1,971,000 jobs in 1996. About two out of three jobs were in hospitals, in both inpatient and outpatient departments. Others were in offices and clinics of physicians, home health care agencies, nurs-

ing homes, temporary help agencies, schools, and government agencies. About three out of ten RNs worked part-time.

Training, Other Qualifications, and Advancement

In all states, students must graduate from a nursing program and pass a national licensing examination to obtain a nursing license. Nurses may be licensed in more than one state, either by examination or endorsement of a license issued by another state. Licenses must be periodically renewed. Some states require continuing education for licensure renewal.

In 1996, there were over 1,500 entry level RN programs. There are three major educational paths to nursing: associate degree (ADN), diploma, and bachelor of science degree in nursing (BSN). ADN programs, offered by community and junior colleges, take about two years. About two-thirds of all RN graduates in 1995 were from ADN programs. BSN programs, offered by colleges and universities, take four or five years. Nearly one-third of all graduates in 1995 were from these programs. Diploma programs, given in hospitals, last two to three years. Only a small number of graduates come from these programs. Generally, licensed graduates of any of the three program types qualify for entry level positions as staff nurses.

There have been attempts to raise the educational requirements for an RN license to a bachelor's degree and, possibly, create new job titles. These changes, should they occur, will probably be made state by state, through legislation or regulation. Changes in licensure requirements would not affect currently licensed RNs, who would be "grandfathered" in, no matter what their educational preparation. However, individuals considering nursing should carefully weigh the pros and cons of enrolling in a BSN program, since their advancement opportunities are broader. In fact, some career paths are open only to nurses with bachelor's or advanced degrees. A bachelor's degree is generally necessary for administrative positions and is a prerequisite for admission to graduate nursing programs in research, consulting, teaching, or a clinical specialization.

Many ADN and diploma-trained nurses enter bachelor's programs to prepare for a broader scope of nursing practice. They can often find a hospital position and then take advantage of tuition reimbursement programs to work toward a BSN in their spare time.

Nursing education includes classroom instruction and supervised clinical experience in hospitals and other health facilities. Students take courses in anatomy, physiology, microbiology, chemistry, nutrition, psychology and other behavioral sciences, and nursing. Course work also includes liberal arts classes.

Supervised clinical experience is provided in hospital departments such as pediatrics, psychiatry, maternity, and surgery. A growing number of programs include clinical experience in nursing homes, public health departments, home health agencies, and ambulatory clinics.

Nurses should be caring and sympathetic. They must be able to accept responsibility, direct or supervise others, follow orders precisely, and determine when consultation is required.

Experience and good performance can lead to promotion to more responsible positions. Nurses can advance, in management, to assistant head nurse or head nurse. From there, they can advance to assistant director, director, and vice president. Increasingly, management level nursing positions require a graduate degree in nursing or health services administration. They also require leadership, negotiation skills, and good judgment. Graduate programs preparing executive level nurses usually last one to two years.

Within patient care, nurses can advance to clinical nurse specialist, nurse practitioner, certified nurse-midwife, or certified registered nurse anesthetist. These positions require one or two years of graduate education, leading in most instances to a master's degree, or to a certificate.

Some nurses move into the business side of health care. Their nursing expertise and experience on a health care team equip them to manage ambulatory, acute, home health, and chronic care services. Some are employed by health care corporations in health planning and development, marketing, and quality assurance.

Job Outlook

Employment of registered nurses is expected to grow faster than the average for all occupations through the year 2006 and, because the occupation is large, many new jobs will result. As nursing school enrollments level off or decline, as they have on a cyclical basis in the past, the number of qualified applicants will fall, reducing reported competition for jobs. There will always be a need for traditional hospital nurses, but a large number of new nurses will be employed in home health, long-term, and ambulatory care.

Faster than average growth will be driven by technological advances in patient care, which permit a greater number of medical problems to be treated, and increasing emphasis on primary care. In addition, the number of older people, who are much more likely than younger people to need medical care, is projected to grow very rapidly. Many job openings also will result from the need to replace experienced nurses who leave the occupation, especially as the average age of the registered nurse population continues to rise.

Employment in hospitals, the largest sector, is expected to grow more slowly than in other health-care sectors. While the intensity of nursing care is likely to increase, requiring more nurses per patient, the number of inpatients (those who remain overnight) is not likely to increase much. Also, patients are being released earlier and more procedures are being done on an outpatient basis, both in and outside hospitals. Most rapid growth is expected in hospitals' outpatient facilities, such as same-day surgery, rehabilitation, and chemotherapy.

Employment in home health care is expected to grow the fastest. This is in response to a growing number of older persons with functional disabilities, consumer preference for care in the home, and technological advances which make it possible to bring increasingly complex treatments into the home. The type of care demanded will require nurses who are able to perform complex procedures.

Employment in nursing homes is expected to grow much faster than average due to increases in the number of people in their eighties and nineties, many of whom will require long-term care. In addition, the financial pressure on hospitals to release patients as soon as possible should produce more nursing home admissions. Growth in units to provide specialized long-term rehabilitation for stroke and head injury patients or to treat Alzheimer's victims will also increase employment.

An increasing proportion of sophisticated procedures, which once were performed only in hospitals, are being performed in physicians' offices and clinics, including HMOs, ambulatory surgicenters, and emergency medical centers. Accordingly, employment is expected to grow faster than average in these places as health care in general expands.

In evolving integrated health care networks, nurses may rotate among employment settings. Since jobs in traditional hospital nursing positions are no longer the only option, RNs will need to be flexible. Opportunities will be best for nurses with advanced education and training, such as nurse practitioners.

Earnings

Median weekly earnings of full-time salaried registered nurses were $697 in 1996. The middle 50 percent earned between $571and $868. The lowest 10 percent earned less than $415; the top 10 percent, more than $1,039.

According to a Hay Group survey of HMOs, group practices, and hospital-based clinics, the median annual base salary of full-time nurse practitioners was $66,800 in May 1996. The middle 50 percent earned between $54,200 and $69,200. Nurse midwives earned about $70,100, and the middle 50 percent earned between $59,300 and $75,700. According to the Hay Group's survey of acute care hospitals, the median annual base salary of full-time nurse anesthetists was $82,000 in January 1997. The middle 50 percent earned between $74,700 and $90,300.

According to the Buck Survey conducted by the American Health Care Association, staff RNs in chain nursing homes had median hourly earnings of $15.85 in 1996. The middle 50 percent earned between $14.03 and $17.73.

Many employers offer flexible work schedules, child care, educational benefits, and bonuses.

Related Occupations

Workers in other health care occupations with responsibilities and duties related to those of registered nurses are occupational therapists, emergency medical technicians, physical therapists, physician assistants, and respiratory therapists.

Sources of Additional Information

The National League for Nursing (NLN) publishes a variety of nursing and nursing education materials, including a list of nursing programs and information on student financial aid. For a complete list of NLN publications, write for a career information brochure. Send your request to:

❏ Communications Department, National League for Nursing, 350 Hudson St., New York, NY 10014. FAX: (212) 989-2272.

For a list of BSN and graduate programs, write to:

❏ American Association of Colleges of Nursing, 1 Dupont Circle NW, Suite 530, Washington, DC 20036. FAX: (202) 785-8320.

Information on registered nurses is also available from:

❏ American Nurses Association, 600 Maryland Ave. SW., Washington, DC 20024-2571.

Respiratory Therapists

(D.O.T. 076.361-014)

Significant Points

✓ *Hospitals will continue to employ more than nine out of ten respiratory therapists, but a growing number will work outside of hospitals under contract to home health agencies and nursing homes.*

✓ *Job opportunities will be best for therapists who work with newborns and infants.*

Nature of the Work

You can live without water for a few days and without food for a few weeks. But without oxygen, you will suffer brain damage within a few minutes and die after about nine minutes. Respiratory therapists, also known as respiratory care practitioners, evaluate, treat, and care for patients with breathing disorders.

In evaluating patients, therapists test the capacity of the lungs and analyze the oxygen and carbon dioxide concentration as well as the potential of hydrogen (pH), a measure of the acidity or alkalinity level of the blood. To measure lung capacity, therapists have patients breathe into an instrument that measures the volume and flow of oxygen during inhalation and exhalation. By comparing the reading with the norm for the patient's age, height, weight, and sex, respiratory therapists can determine whether lung deficiencies exist. To analyze oxygen, carbon dioxide, and pH levels, therapists draw an arterial blood sample, place it in a blood gas analyzer, and relay the results to a physician.

Respiratory therapists treat all types of patients, ranging from premature infants whose lungs are not fully developed, to elderly people whose lungs are diseased. They provide temporary relief to patients with chronic asthma or emphysema and emergency care for patients who suffered heart failure or a stroke, or are victims of drowning or shock. Respiratory therapists most commonly use oxygen or oxygen mixtures, chest physiotherapy, and aerosol medications. Therapists may place an oxygen mask or nasal cannula on a patient and set the oxygen flow at the level prescribed by a physician to increase a patient's concentration of oxygen. Therapists also connect patients who cannot breathe on their own to ventilators, which deliver pressurized oxygen into the lungs. They insert a tube into a patient's trachea, or windpipe; connect the tube to the ventilator; and set the rate, volume, and oxygen concentration of the oxygen mixture entering the patient's lungs.

Therapists regularly check on patients and equipment. If the patient appears to be having difficulty or if the oxygen, carbon dioxide, or pH level of the blood is abnormal, they change the ventilator setting according to the doctor's order or check equipment for mechanical problems. In home care, therapists teach patients and their families to use ventilators and other life support systems. They visit several times a month to inspect and clean equipment and ensure its proper use and make emergency visits if equipment problems arise.

Respiratory therapists perform chest physiotherapy on patients to remove mucus from their lungs to make it easier for them to breathe. For example, during surgery, anesthesia depresses respiration, so this treatment may be prescribed to help get the patient's lungs back to normal and prevent congestion. Chest physiotherapy also is used on patients suffering from lung diseases that cause mucus to collect in the lungs, such as cystic fibrosis. Therapists place patients in positions to help drain mucus, thump and vibrate patients' rib cages, and instruct them to cough.

Respiratory therapists also administer aerosols—generally liquid medications suspended in a gas that forms a mist which is inhaled—and teach patients how to inhale the aerosol properly to assure its effectiveness.

Therapists are increasingly working under the supervision of nurses and are being asked to perform tasks that fall outside of their traditional role. They are expanding into cardiopulmonary procedures like electrocardiograms and stress testing, but also perform other tasks like drawing blood samples from patients. They also keep records of the materials used and charges to patients. Some therapists teach or supervise other respiratory therapy personnel.

Working Conditions

Respiratory therapists generally work between 35 and 40 hours a week. Because hospitals operate around the clock, therapists may work evenings, nights, or weekends. They spend long periods standing and walking between patients' rooms. In an emergency, they work under a great deal of stress. Gases used by respiratory therapists are potentially hazardous because they are used and stored under pressure. However, adherence to safety precautions and regular maintenance and testing of equipment minimize the risk of injury. As with many health occupations, respiratory therapists run a risk of catching infectious diseases, but careful adherence to proper procedures minimizes this risk, as well.

Employment

Respiratory therapists held about 82,000 jobs in 1996. About nine out of ten jobs were in hospital departments of respiratory care, anesthesiology, or pulmonary medicine. Home health agencies, respiratory therapy clinics, and nursing homes accounted for most of the remaining jobs.

Training, Other Qualifications, and Advancement

Formal training is necessary for entry to this field. Training is offered at the postsecondary level by hospitals, medical schools, colleges and universities, trade schools, vocational-technical institutes, and the Armed Forces. Some programs prepare graduates for jobs as respiratory therapists; other, shorter programs lead to jobs as respiratory therapy technicians. In 1996, 210 programs for respiratory therapists were accredited by the Commission on Accreditation of Allied Health Education Programs (CAAHEP) of the American Medical Association (AMA). Another 158 programs offered CAAHEP-accredited preparation for respiratory therapy technicians.

Formal training programs vary in length and in the credential or degree awarded. Most of the CAAHEP-accredited therapist programs last two years and lead to an associate degree. Some, however, are four-year bachelor's degree programs. Technician programs last about one year and award certificates. Areas of study for respiratory therapy programs include human anatomy and physiology, chemistry, physics, microbiology, and mathematics. Technical courses deal with procedures, equipment, and clinical tests.

More and more therapists receive on-the-job training, allowing them to administer electrocardiograms and stress tests, as well as draw blood samples from patients.

Therapists should be sensitive to patients' physical and psychological needs. Respiratory care workers must pay attention to detail, follow instructions, and work as part of a team. Operating complicated respiratory therapy equipment requires mechanical ability and manual dexterity.

High school students interested in a career in respiratory care should take courses in health, biology, mathematics, chemistry, and physics. Respiratory care involves basic mathematical problem-solving and an understanding of chemical and physical principles. For example, respiratory care workers must be able to compute medication dosages and calculate gas concentrations.

Forty-seven states license respiratory care personnel. Only Nevada, Delaware, and Washington do not require licensure. The National Board for Respiratory Care offers voluntary certification and registration to graduates of CAAHEP-accredited programs. Two credentials are awarded to respiratory care practitioners who satisfy the requirements: Certified Respiratory Therapy Technician (CRTT) and Registered Respiratory Therapist (RRT). All graduates—those from two- and four-year programs in respiratory therapy, as well as those from one-year technician programs—may take the CRTT examination first. CRTTs who meet education and experience requirements can take a separate examination, leading to the award of the RRT.

Individuals who have completed a four-year program in a nonrespiratory field, but have college level courses in anatomy, physiology, chemistry, biology, microbiology, physics, and mathematics, can become a CRTT after graduating from an AMA accredited one- or two-year program. After they receive two years of clinical experience, they are eligible to take the registry exam to become an RRT.

Most employers require that applicants for entry-level or generalist positions hold the CRTT or are eligible to take the certification examination. Supervisory positions and those in intensive care specialties, usually require the RRT (or RRT eligibility).

Respiratory therapists advance in clinical practice by moving from care of "general" to "critical" patients, who have significant problems in other organ systems such as the heart or kidneys. Respiratory therapists, especially those with four-year degrees, may also advance to supervisory or managerial positions in a respiratory therapy department. Respiratory therapists in home care and equipment rental firms may become branch manager.

Job Outlook

Job opportunities are expected to remain good. Employment of respiratory therapists is expected to increase much faster than the average for all occupations through the year 2006 because of substantial growth of the middle-aged and elderly population, a development that will heighten the incidence of cardiopulmonary disease.

Older Americans suffer most from respiratory ailments and cardiopulmonary diseases such as pneumonia, chronic bronchitis, emphysema, and heart disease. As their numbers increase, the need for respiratory therapists will increase as well. In addition, advances in treating victims of heart attacks, accident victims, and premature infants (many of who may be dependent on a ventilator during part of their treatment) will increase the demand for the services of respiratory care practitioners.

Opportunities are expected to be highly favorable for respiratory therapists with cardiopulmonary care skills and experience in working with infants.

Although hospitals will continue to employ the vast majority of therapists, a growing number of therapists can expect to work outside of hospitals under contract to home health agencies and nursing homes.

Earnings

Median weekly earnings for full-time salaried respiratory therapists were $636 in 1996. The middle 50 percent earned between $506 and $767. The lowest 10 percent earned less than $367; the top 10 percent earned more than $978.

According to a Hay Group survey of acute care hospitals, the median annual base salary of full-time respiratory therapists was $32,500 in January 1997. The middle 50 percent earned between $29,300 and $35,000.

Related Occupations

Respiratory therapists, under the supervision of a physician, administer respiratory care and life support to patients with heart and lung difficulties. Other workers who care for, treat, or train people to improve their physical condition include dialysis technicians, registered nurses, occupational therapists, physical therapists, and radiation therapy technologists.

Sources of Additional Information

Information concerning a career in respiratory care is available from:

❑ American Association for Respiratory Care, 11030 Ables Ln., Dallas, TX 75229.

Information on gaining credentials as a respiratory therapy practitioner can be obtained from:

❑ The National Board for Respiratory Care, Inc., 8310 Nieman Rd., Lenexa, KS 66214.

For the current list of CAAHEP-accredited educational programs for respiratory therapy occupations, write to:

❑ Joint Review Committee for Respiratory Therapy Education, 1701 W. Euless Blvd., Suite 300, Euless, TX 76040.

Restaurant and Food Service Managers

(D.O.T. 185.137; 187.161-010 and .167-026, -106, -126, -206, and -210; 319.137-014, -018, and -030)

Significant Points

✓ *While many jobs are filled by promoting experienced food and beverage preparation and service workers, job opportunities are expected to be best for those with bachelor's or associate degrees in restaurant and institutional food service management.*

✓ *Employment of wage and salary managers is expected to increase more rapidly than self-employed managers, as restaurants increasingly affiliate with national chains rather than being independently owned.*

Nature of the Work

Food is consumed outside the home in a variety of settings. Eating places range from institutional cafeterias and fast food to elegant dining establishments. The cuisine, price, and setting where the meals are consumed vary, but managers of these dining facilities share many of the same responsibilities. Efficient and profitable operation of restaurants and institutional food service facilities requires managers and assistant managers to select and appropriately price menu items, use food and other supplies efficiently, and achieve consistent quality in food preparation and service. They also must attend to the various administrative aspects of the business, which includes recruiting, training, and supervising an adequate number of workers.

In most restaurants and institutional food service facilities, the manager is assisted by one or more assistant managers, depending on the size and operating hours of the establishment. In large establishments, as well as in many smaller ones, the management team consists of a general manager, one or more assistant managers, and an executive chef. The executive chef is responsible for the operation of the kitchen, while the assistant managers oversee service in the dining room and other areas of the operation. In smaller restaurants, the executive chef may be the general manager, and sometimes an owner. In fast-food restaurants and other food service facilities open for long hours, often seven days a week, the manager is aided by several assistant managers, each of whom supervises a shift of workers.

Many restaurants rarely change their menu, while others make frequent alterations. Institutional food service facilities and some restaurants offer a new menu every day. Managers or executive chefs select menu items, taking into account the likely number of customers, and the past popularity of dishes. Other issues taken into consideration when planning a menu include unserved food left over from prior meals that should not be wasted, the need for variety, and the availability of foods due to seasonality and other factors. Managers or executive chefs analyze the recipes of the dishes to determine food, labor, overhead costs and to assign prices to the various dishes. Menus must be developed far enough in advance that supplies can be ordered and received in time.

On a daily basis, managers estimate food consumption, place orders with suppliers, and schedule the delivery of fresh food and beverages. They receive and check the content of deliveries, evaluating the quality of meats, poultry, fish, fruits, vegetables, and baked goods. Managers meet with the sales representatives from restaurant suppliers to place orders replenishing stocks of tableware, linens, paper, cleaning supplies, cooking utensils, and furniture and fixtures. They also arrange for equipment maintenance and repairs, and for a variety of services such as waste removal and pest control.

Managers interview, hire, and, when necessary, fire employees. Many managers report difficulty in hiring experienced food and beverage preparation and service workers. Managers may attend career fairs or arrange for newspaper advertising to expand their pool of applicants. Managers explain the establishment's policies and practices to newly hired workers and oversee their training. Managers schedule the work hours of employees, making sure there are enough workers present to cover peak dining periods. If employees are unable to work, managers may have to fill in for them. Some managers regularly help with cooking, clearing of tables, or other tasks.

Restaurant and food service managers supervise the kitchen and the dining room. They oversee food preparation and cooking, examining the quality and portion sizes to ensure that dishes are prepared and garnished correctly and in a timely manner. They also investigate and resolve customers' complaints about food quality or service. They direct the cleaning of the kitchen and dining areas and the washing of tableware, kitchen utensils, and equipment to maintain company and government sanitation standards. They monitor the actions of their employees and patrons on a continual basis to ensure the health and safety standards and local liquor regulations are obeyed.

Managers have a variety of administrative responsibilities. In larger establishments, much of this work is delegated to a bookkeeper; in smaller establishments, including most fast-food restaurants, managers must keep records of the hours and wages of employees, prepare the payroll, and do paperwork to comply with licensing laws and reporting requirements of tax, wage and hour, unemployment compensation, and Social Security laws. They also maintain the records of supplies and equipment purchased, and ensure that accounts with suppliers are paid on a regular basis. In addition, some managers record the number, type, and cost of items sold to exclude dishes that are unpopular or less profitable.

Many managers are able to ease the burden of recordkeeping and paperwork through the use of computers. Point-of-service (POS) systems are used in many restaurants to increase employee productivity and allow managers to track the sales of specific menu items. Using a POS system, a server keys in the customer's order and the computer immediately sends the order to the kitchen so preparation can begin. The same system totals checks, acts as a cash register and credit card authorizer, and tracks daily sales. To minimize food costs and spoilage, many managers use inventory tracking software to compare the record of daily sales from the POS with a record of present inventory. In some establishments, when supplies needed for the preparation of popular menu items run low, additional inventory can be ordered directly from the supplier using the computer. Computers also allow restaurant and food service managers to more efficiently keep track of employee schedules and pay.

Managers are among the first to arrive and the last to leave. At the conclusion of each day, or sometimes each shift, managers tally the cash and charge receipts received and balance them against the record of sales. They are responsible for depositing the day's receipts at the bank, or securing it in a safe place. Managers are also responsible for locking up, checking that ovens, grills, and lights are off, and switching on alarm systems.

Working Conditions

Evenings and weekends are popular dining periods, making night and weekend work common. Many managers of institutional food service facilities work more conventional hours because factory and office cafeterias are generally open only on weekdays for breakfast and lunch. However, hours are unpredictable, as managers may have to fill in for absent workers on short notice. It is common for restaurant and food service managers to work 50 to 60 hours or more per week.

Managers often experience the pressure of simultaneously coordinating a wide range of activities. When problems occur, it is the responsibility of the manager to resolve them with minimal disruption to customers. The job can be hectic during peak dining hours, and dealing with irate customers or uncooperative employees can be stressful.

Employment

Restaurant and food service managers held about 493,000 jobs in 1996. Most managers were salaried workers, but many others were self-employed. Most worked in restaurants or for contract institutional food service companies, while a smaller number were employed by educational institutions, hospitals, nursing and personal care facilities, and civic, social, and fraternal organizations. Jobs are located throughout the country, with large cities and tourist areas providing more opportunities for more formal dining positions.

Training, Other Qualifications, and Advancement

Many restaurant and food service manager positions are filled by promoting experienced food and beverage preparation and service workers. Waiters, waitresses, chefs, and fast-food workers demonstrating potential for handling increased responsibility sometimes advance to assistant manager or management trainee jobs when openings occur. Executive chefs need extensive experience working as a chef, and general managers need experience working as assistant manager. However, most food service management companies and national or regional restaurant chains also recruit management trainees from two- and four-year college hospitality management programs. Food service and restaurant chains prefer to hire people with degrees in restaurant and institutional food service management, but they often hire graduates with degrees in other fields who have demonstrated interest and aptitude.

A bachelor's degree in restaurant and food service management provides a particularly strong preparation for a career in this occupation. In 1996, more than 160 colleges and universities offered four-year programs in restaurant and hotel management or institutional food service management. For people not interested in pursing a four-year degree, a good alternative are the more than 800 community and junior colleges, technical institutes, and other institutions that offer programs in these fields leading to an associate degree or other formal certification. Both two- and four-year programs provide instruction in subjects such as nutrition and food planning and preparation, as well as accounting, business law and management, and computer science. Some programs combine classroom and laboratory study with internships that provide on-the-job experience. In addition, many educational institutions offer culinary programs that provide food preparation training which can lead to a career as a cook or chef and provide a foundation for advancement to an executive chef position.

Most employers emphasize personal qualities. Restaurant and food service management can be demanding, so good health and stamina are important. Self-discipline, initiative, and leadership ability are essential. Managers must be able to solve problems and concentrate on details. They need good communication skills to deal with customers and suppliers, as well as to motivate and direct their subordinates. A neat and clean appearance is a must because they often are in close personal contact with the public.

Most restaurant chains and food service management companies have rigorous training programs for their management positions. Through a combination of classroom and on-the-job training, trainees receive instruction and gain work experience in all aspects of the operations of a restaurant or institutional food service facility—food preparation, nutrition, sanitation, security, company policies and procedures, personnel management, recordkeeping, and preparation of reports. Training on use of the restaurant's computer system is increasingly important as well. Often, supplies are ordered electronically and many restaurants use computers to track the popularity of menu items. Usually after six months or a year,

trainees receive their first permanent assignment as an assistant manager.

A measure of professional achievement for restaurant and food service managers is to earn the designation of certified Foodservice Management Professional (FMP). Although not a requirement for employment or advancement in the occupation, voluntary certification provides recognition of professional competence, particularly for managers who acquired their skills largely on the job. The Educational Foundation of the National Restaurant Association awards the FMP designation to managers who achieve a qualifying score on a written examination, complete a series of courses that cover a range of food service management topics, and who meet standards of work experience in the field.

Willingness to relocate, usually to a big city, often is essential for advancement to positions with greater responsibility. Managers advance to larger establishments, or regional management positions within restaurant chains. Some eventually open their own eating and drinking establishments. Others transfer to hotel management positions, because their restaurant management experience provides a good background for food and beverage manager jobs at hotels and resorts.

Job Outlook

Job opportunities are expected to be best for those with a bachelor's or associate degree in restaurant and institutional food service management. Employment of restaurant and food service managers is expected to increase faster than the average for all occupations through the year 2006. In addition to employment growth, the need to replace managers who transfer to other occupations or stop working will create many job openings.

Projected employment growth varies by industry. Eating and drinking places will provide the most new jobs as the number of eating and drinking establishments increases and other industries continue to contract out their food services. Increases in population, personal incomes, and leisure time will continue to produce growth in the number of meals consumed outside the home. To meet the demand for prepared food, more restaurants will be built, and more managers will be employed to supervise them. In addition, the number of manager jobs will increase in eating and drinking places as schools, hospitals, and other businesses contract out more of their food services to institutional food service companies within the eating and drinking industry.

Employment of wage and salary managers in eating and drinking places is expected to increase more rapidly than self-employed managers. New restaurants are increasingly affiliated with national chains rather than being independently owned and operated. As this trend continues, fewer owners will manage restaurants themselves, and more restaurant managers will be employed to run the establishments.

Food service manager jobs are expected to increase in other industries, but growth will be slowed as contracting out becomes more common. Growth in the elderly population should result in more food service manager jobs in nursing homes and other healthcare institutions, and residential-care and assisted-living facilities.

Employment in eating and drinking establishments is not very sensitive to changes in economic conditions, so restaurant and food service managers are rarely laid off during hard times. However, competition among restaurants is always intense, and many restaurants do not survive.

Earnings

Median earnings for restaurant and food service managers were about $460 a week in 1996. The middle 50 percent earned between about $320 and $630 a week. The lowest paid 10 percent earned $240 a week or less, while the highest paid 10 percent earned over $900 a week.

Earnings of restaurant and food service managers vary greatly according to their responsibilities and the type and size of establishment. Based on a survey conducted by the National Restaurant Association, the median base salary of restaurant managers was about $30,000 in 1995; managers of the largest restaurants and institutional food service facilities often had annual salaries in excess of $50,000. Besides a salary, most managers received an annual bonus or incentive payment based on their performance. In 1995, most bonuses ranged between $2,000 and $10,000.

Executive chefs had a median base salary of $38,000 in 1995. Annual bonus or incentive payments for most executive chefs averaged $3,000.

The median base salary of assistant managers was $23,000 in 1995, but ranged from $21,000 in fast-food restaurants to $27,000 in some of the largest restaurants and food service facilities. Annual bonus or incentive payments for most assistant managers ranged from $1,000 to $4,000.

Manager trainees had a median base salary of $21,000 in 1995, but earned $30,000 in some of the largest restaurants and food service facilities. Annual bonus or incentive payments of most trainees averaged $900.

In addition to typical benefits, most salaried restaurant and food service managers receive free meals and the opportunity for additional training depending on their length of service.

Related Occupations

Restaurant and food service managers direct the activities of businesses which provide a service to customers. Other managers in service-oriented businesses include hotel managers and assistants, health services administrators, retail store managers, and bank managers.

Sources of Additional Information

Information about job opportunities may be obtained from local employers and local offices of the state employment service.

Information about a career as a restaurant and food service manager, two- and four-year college programs in restaurant and food service management, and certification as a Foodservice Management Professional is available from:

❏ The Educational Foundation of the National Restaurant Association, Suite 1400, 250 South Wacker Dr., Chicago, IL 60606.

General information on hospitality careers may be obtained from:

❏ Council on Hotel, Restaurant, and Institutional Education, 1200 17th St. NW, Washington, DC 20036-3097.

For general career information and a directory of accredited private trade and technical schools offering programs in restaurant and food service management, write to:

❏ Accrediting Commission of Career Schools and Colleges of Technology, 2101 Wilson Blvd., Suite 302, Arlington, VA 22201.

Retail Sales Worker Managers and Supervisors

(D.O.T. 185.167-030, -038, and -046; 187.167-158; 291.157; 299.137-010 and -026)

Significant Points

✓ *Candidates who have experience as a retail sales worker, cashier, or customer service worker should have the best opportunities.*

✓ *Work schedules may be irregular and often include evening and weekend work.*

✓ *Increasingly, a postsecondary degree is needed for advancement into upper management positions.*

Nature of the Work

In every one of the thousands of retail stores across the country, there is at least one retail sales worker supervisor or manager. Because the retail trade industry provides goods and services directly to customers, the retail supervisor or manager is responsible for ensuring that customers receive satisfactory service and quality goods. They also answer customers' inquiries and handle complaints.

Retail supervisors and managers oversee the work of sales associates and cashiers, and customer service, stock, inventory, and grocery clerks. They are responsible for interviewing, hiring, and training employees, as well as preparing work schedules and assigning workers to specific duties.

The responsibilities of retail sales worker supervisors and managers vary, depending on the size and type of establishment, as well as the level of management. As the size of retail stores and the types of goods and services increase, these workers increasingly specialize in one department or one aspect of merchandising. Larger organizations tend to have many layers of management. As in other industries, supervisory-level retail managers usually report to their mid-level counterparts who, in turn, report to top-level managers. Small stores, and stores that carry specialized merchandise, typically have fewer levels of management.

Supervisory-level retail managers, often referred to as department managers, provide day-to-day oversight of individual departments, such as shoes, cosmetics, or housewares in large department stores; produce and meat in grocery stores; and sales in automotive dealerships. Department managers commonly are found in large retail stores. These managers establish and implement policies, goals, objectives, and procedures for their specific departments; coordinate activities with other department heads; and strive for smooth operations within their departments. They supervise employees who price and ticket goods and place them on display; clean and organize shelves, displays, and inventory in stockrooms; and inspect merchandise to ensure that none is outdated. Department managers also review inventory and sales records, develop merchandising techniques, coordinate sales promotions, and may greet and assist customers and promote sales and good public relations.

In small or independent retail stores, retail sales worker supervisors and managers not only directly supervise sales associates, but are also responsible for the operation of the entire store. In these instances, they may be called store managers. Some are also store owners.

Working Conditions

Most retail sales worker supervisors and managers have offices within the stores. Although some time is spent in the office completing merchandise orders or arranging work schedules, a large portion of a their workday is spent on the sales floor.

Work hours of supervisors and managers vary greatly among retail establishments, with work schedules usually depending on consumers' needs. Most managers and supervisors work 40 hours or more a week. This is especially true during holidays, busy shopping hours and seasons, sales, and when inventory is taken. They are expected to work evenings and weekends but usually are compensated by getting a weekday off. Hours can change weekly, and managers sometimes may have to report to work on short notice, especially when employees are absent. Independent owners can often set their own schedules, but hours usually must be convenient to customers.

Employment

Retail sales worker supervisors and managers who work in retail trade held about 929,000 wage and salary jobs in 1996. In addition, there were thousands of self-employed retail sales managers, mainly store owners. Although managers are found throughout the retail trade industry, establishments that employ the most are grocery, department, and clothing and accessory stores.

Training, Other Qualifications, and Advancement

Knowledge of management principles and practices, often an essential requirement for a management position in retail trade, is usually acquired through work experience. Many supervisors and managers begin their careers on the sales floor as sales clerks, cashiers, or customer service workers. In these positions, they learn merchandising, customer service, and the basic policies and procedures of the store.

The educational background of retail sales worker supervisors and managers varies widely. Regardless of the education received, business courses, including accounting; administration; marketing; management; and sales; as well as courses in psychology; sociology; and communication; are helpful. Supervisors and managers increasingly must be computer literate since cash registers and inventory control systems have become computerized.

Most supervisors and managers who have postsecondary education hold associate or bachelor's degrees in liberal arts, social science, business, or management. To gain experience, many postsecondary students participate in internship programs that are usually planned between individual schools and retail firms.

Once on the job, the type and amount of training available for supervisors and managers varies from store to store. Many national chains have formal training programs for management trainees, that include both classroom and in-store training. Training may last from one week to one year or more, as many retail organizations require their trainees to gain experience during all shopping seasons. Other retail organizations may not have formal training programs.

Ordinarily, classroom training includes such topics as interviewing and customer service skills, employee and inventory management, and scheduling. Management trainees may be placed in one specific department while training on the job, or they may be rotated through several departments to gain a well-rounded knowledge of the store's operation. Training programs for franchises are generally extensive, covering all functions of the company's operation, including promotion, marketing, management, finance, purchasing, product preparation, human resource management, and compensation. College graduates can usually enter management training programs directly.

Retail sales worker supervisors and managers must get along with all types of people. They need initiative, self-discipline, good judgment, and decisiveness. Patience and a mild temperament are necessary when dealing with demanding customers. They must also be able to motivate, organize, and direct the work of subordinates and communicate clearly and persuasively with customers and other managers.

Individuals who display leadership and team building skills, self-confidence, motivation, and decisiveness become candidates for promotion to assistant store manager or store manager. Increasingly, a postsecondary degree is needed for advancement, because it is viewed by employers as a sign of motivation and maturity—qualities deemed important for promotion to more responsible positions. In many retail establishments, managers are promoted from within the company. In small retail establishments, where the number of positions is limited, advancement to a higher management position may come slowly. Large establishments most often have extensive career ladder programs and may offer managers the opportunity to transfer to another store in the chain or to the central office if an opening occurs. Promotions may occur more quickly in large establishments, but relocation every several years may also be necessary for advancement. Within a central office, sales supervisors and managers can become marketing, advertising, or public relations managers. These managers coordinate marketing plans, monitor sales, and propose advertisements and promotions. Supervisors and managers can also become and purchasers or buyers, who purchase goods and supplies for their organization or for resale.

Some supervisors and managers, who have worked in the retail industry for a long time, decide to open their own stores. However, retail trade is highly competitive, and although many independent retail owners succeed, some fail to cover expenses and eventually go out of business. To prosper, retail owners usually need good business sense and strong customer service and public relations skills.

Job Outlook

Because most jobs for retail sales worker supervisors and managers do not require postsecondary education, competition is expected for jobs with the most attractive earnings and working conditions. Candidates who have retail experience will have the best opportunities.

Employment of wage and salary retail sales worker supervisors and managers is expected to grow more slowly than the average for all occupations through the year 2006. Growth in this occupation will be restrained as retail companies place more emphasis on sales staff employment levels and increase the number of responsibilities their retail sales worker supervisors and managers have. Furthermore, some companies have begun requiring their sales staff to report directly to upper management personnel, bypassing the department-level manager. However, many job openings are expected to occur as experienced supervisors and managers move into higher levels of management, transfer to other occupations, or leave the labor force.

Projected employment growth of retail managers will mirror, in part, the patterns of employment growth in the industries in which they are concentrated. For example, faster than average growth is expected in grocery stores as they expand their selection of merchandise to accommodate customers' desires for one-stop shopping.

Unlike middle- and upper-level management positions, store-level retail supervisors and managers generally will not be affected by the restructuring and consolidating that is taking place at the corporate and headquarters level of many retail chain companies.

Earnings

Salaries of retail managers vary substantially, depending upon the level of responsibility; length of service; and type, size, and location of the firm.

Supervisors or managers of sales workers in the retail trade industry who usually worked full time had median annual earnings of $24,400 in 1996. The middle 50 percent earned between $16,900 and $34,400. The top 10 percent earned more than $50,400, and the lowest 10 percent earned less than $12,900.

According to a survey sponsored by the National Association of Convenience Stores, the average total compensation for assistant store managers in the U.S. and Canada ranged between $12,400 and $15,800 a year in 1996, depending on where the organization is located. Store managers received between $24,400 and $31,200 on average.

Compensation systems vary by type of establishment and merchandise sold. Many managers receive a commission, or a combination of salary and commission. Under a commission system, retail managers receive a percentage of department or store sales. These systems offer managers the opportunity to significantly increase their earnings, but they may find that their earnings depend on their ability to sell their product and the condition of the economy. Those managers who sell large amounts of merchandise often are rewarded with bonuses and awards and receive recognition throughout the store or chain.

Retail managers receive typical benefits and, in some cases, stock options. In addition, retail managers generally are able to buy their store's merchandise at a discount.

Related Occupations

Retail supervisors and managers serve customers, supervise workers, and direct and coordinate the operations of an establishment. Others with similar responsibilities include managers in wholesale trade, hotels, banks, and hospitals.

Sources of Additional Information

Information on employment opportunities for retail managers may be obtained from the employment offices of various retail establishments or state employment service offices.

General information on management careers in retail establishments is available from:

- ❏ National Retail Federation, 325 7th St. NW, Suite 1000, Washington, DC 20004. Homepage: http://www.nrf.com

- ❏ International Mass Retail Association, 1700 N. Moore St., Suite 2250, Arlington, VA 22209-1998. Homepage: http://www.imra.org

Information on management careers in grocery stores, and schools offering related programs, is available from:

- ❏ Food Marketing Institute, 800 Connecticut Ave. NW, Publications Dept., Washington, DC 20006-2701.

Information about management careers and training programs in the motor vehicle dealers industry is available from:

- ❏ National Automobile Dealers Association, Communications/Public Relations Dept., 8400 Westpark Dr., McLean, VA 22102-3591.

Information about management careers in convenience stores is available from:

- ❏ National Association of Convenience Stores, 1605 King St., Alexandria, VA 22314-2792.

Information about management careers in service stations is available from:

- ❏ Service Station Dealers of America, 9420 Annapolis Rd., Suite 307, Lanham, MD 20706.

Retail Sales Workers

(D.O.T. codes are too numerous to list.)

Significant Points

- ✓ *Good employment opportunities are expected due to the need to replace the large number who leave the occupation each year.*

- ✓ *Most salespersons can expect to work some evening and weekend hours, and longer than normal hours may be scheduled during Christmas and other peak retail periods. Plentiful opportunities for part time work exist.*

Nature of the Work

Whether selling shoes, computer equipment, or automobiles, retail sales workers assist customers in finding what they are looking for and try to interest them in the merchandise. This may be done by describing a product's features, demonstrating its use, or showing various models and colors. For some sales jobs, particularly those selling expensive and complex items, special knowledge or skills are needed. For example, workers who sell automobiles must be able to explain to customers the features of various models, the meaning of manufacturers' specifications, and the types of options and financing that are available.

Consumers, who spend millions of dollars a day on merchandise, often form their impressions of a store by evaluating its sales force. Therefore, retailers are increasingly stressing the importance of providing courteous and efficient service, in order to remain competitive. When a customer wants an item that is not on the sales floor, for example, the sales worker may check the stockroom or place a special order or call another store to locate the item.

In addition to selling, most retail sales workers, especially those who work in department and apparel stores, make out sales checks; receive cash, check, and charge payments; bag or package purchases; and give change and receipts. Depending on the hours they work, retail sales workers may have to open or close cash registers. This may include counting the money; separating charge slips, coupons, and exchange vouchers; and making deposits at the cash office. Sales workers are often held responsible for the contents of their registers, and repeated shortages are cause for dismissal in many organizations.

Sales workers may also handle returns and exchanges of merchandise, perform gift wrapping services, and keep their work areas neat. In addition, they may help stock shelves or racks, arrange for mailing or delivery of purchases, mark price tags, take inventory, and prepare displays.

Frequently, sales workers must be aware of, not only the promotions their store is sponsoring, but also those that are being sponsored by competitors. Also, salespersons must often recognize possible security risks and know how to handle such situations.

Although most sales workers have many duties and responsibilities, in jobs selling standardized articles, such hardware, linens, and housewares, they often do little more than take payments and wrap purchases.

Working Conditions

Most sales workers in retail trade work in clean, comfortable, well-lighted stores. However, they often stand for long periods and may need supervisory approval to leave the sales floor.

The Monday-through-Friday, 9-to-5 work week is the exception, rather than the rule, in retail trade. Most salespersons can expect to work some evening and weekend hours, and longer than normal hours may be scheduled during Christmas and other peak retail periods. In addition, most retailers restrict the use of vacation time from Thanksgiving until early January.

This job can be rewarding for those who enjoy working with people. Patience is required, however, when the work is repetitious and the customers demanding.

Employment

Retail sales workers held about 4,522,000 jobs in 1996. They worked in stores ranging from small specialty shops employing several workers, to giant department stores with hundreds of salespersons. In addition, some were self-employed representatives of direct sales companies and mail-order houses. The largest employers of retail sales workers, however, are department stores, clothing and accessories stores, furniture and home furnishing stores, and motor vehicle dealers.

This occupation offers many opportunities for part-time work and is especially appealing to students, retirees, and others looking to supplement their income. However, most of those selling "big ticket" items, such as cars, furniture, and electronic equipment, work full time and have substantial experience.

Because retail stores are found in every city and town, employment is distributed geographically in much the same way as the population.

Training, Other Qualifications, and Advancement

There usually are no formal education requirements for this type of work, although a high school diploma or equivalent is increasingly preferred. Employers look for persons who enjoy working with people and have the tact and patience to deal with difficult customers. Among other desirable characteristics are an interest in sales work, a neat appearance, and the ability to communicate clearly

and effectively. The ability to speak more than one language may be helpful for employment in stores in communities where people from various cultures tend to live and shop. Before hiring a sales worker, some employers may conduct a background check, especially for a job selling high-priced items.

In most small stores, an experienced employee, or the proprietor, instructs newly-hired sales personnel in making out sales checks and operating cash registers. In large stores, training programs are more formal and usually conducted over several days. Topics usually discussed are customer service, security, the store's policies and procedures, and how to work a cash register. Depending on the type of product they are selling, they may be given additional specialized training by manufacturers' representatives. For example, those working in cosmetics receive instruction on the types of products available and for whom the cosmetics would be most beneficial. Likewise, sales workers employed by motor vehicle dealers may be required to participate in training programs, designed to provide information on the technical details of standard and optional equipment available on new models. Because providing the best service to customers is a high priority for many employers, employees are often given periodic training to update and refine their skills.

As salespersons gain experience and seniority, they usually move to positions of greater responsibility and may be given their choice of departments. This often means moving to areas with potentially higher earnings and commissions. The highest earnings potential is usually found in selling big-ticket items. This type of position often requires the most knowledge of the product and the greatest talent for persuasion.

Traditionally, capable sales workers without college degrees could advance to management positions; but today, large retail businesses generally prefer to hire college graduates as management trainees, making a college education increasingly important. Despite this trend, capable employees without college degrees should still be able to advance to administrative or supervisory positions in large establishments.

Opportunities for advancement vary in small stores. In some establishments, advancement is limited, because one person, often the owner, does most of the managerial work. In others, however, some sales workers are promoted to assistant managers.

Retail selling experience may be an asset when applying for sales positions with larger retailers or in other industries, such as financial services, wholesale trade, or manufacturing.

Job Outlook

As in the past, employment opportunities for retail sales workers are expected to continue to be good because of the many job openings created each year due to the need to replace the large number of workers who transfer to other occupations or leave the labor force. Additional openings will be created by growth in employment of retail sales workers, which is expected to increase about as fast as the average for all occupations through the year 2006 due to anticipated growth in retail sales created by a growing population. There will continue to be many opportunities for part-time workers, and demand will be strong for temporary workers during peak selling periods, such as the Christmas season.

During economic downturns, sales volumes and the resulting demand for sales workers generally decline. Purchases of costly items, such as cars, appliances, and furniture, tend to be postponed during difficult economic times. In areas of high unemployment, sales of many types of goods decline. However, because turnover of sales workers is usually very high, employers often can control employment simply by not replacing all those who leave.

Earnings

The starting wage for many retail sales positions is the federal minimum wage, which was $5.15 an hour in 1997. In some areas where employers are having difficulty attracting and retaining workers, wages are higher than the established minimum. The following tabulation shows 1996 median weekly earnings by class of sales worker:

Motor vehicle and boats	$593
Radio, television, hi-fi, and appliances	423
Parts	409
Furniture and home furnishings	403
Hardware and building supplies	372
Street and door-to-door sales workers	372
Shoes	328
Apparel	265

Compensation systems vary by type of establishment and merchandise sold. Sales workers receive either hourly wages, commissions, or a combination of wages and commissions. Under a commission system, salespersons receive a percentage of the sales that they make. This system offers sales workers the opportunity to significantly increase their earnings, but they may find their earnings depend on their ability to sell their product and the ups and downs of the economy. Employers may use incentive programs such as awards, banquets, and profit-sharing plans to promote teamwork among the sales staff.

Benefits may be limited in smaller stores, but in large establishments benefits are usually comparable to those offered by other employers. In addition, nearly all sales workers are able to buy their store's merchandise at a discount, with the savings depending upon on the type of merchandise.

Related Occupations

Sales workers use sales techniques, coupled with their knowledge of merchandise, to assist customers and encourage purchases. These skills are used by people in a number of other occupations, including manufacturers' and wholesale trade sales representatives, service sales representatives, securities and financial services sales representatives, counter and rental clerks, real estate sales agents, purchasers and buyers, insurance agents and brokers, and cashiers.

Sources of Additional Information

Information on careers in retail sales may be obtained from the personnel offices of local stores, or from state merchants' associations.

General information about retailing is available from:

❏ National Retail Federation, 325 7th St. NW, Suite 1000, Washington, DC 20004. Homepage: http://www.nrf.com

❏ International Mass Retail Association, 1700 N. Moore St., Suite 2250, Arlington, VA 22209-1998.

Information about retail sales employment opportunities is available from:

❏ United Food and Commercial Workers International Union, Education Office, 1775 K St. NW, Washington, DC 20006-1502.

Information about training for a career in automobile sales is available from:

❏ National Automobile Dealers Association, Communications/ Public Relations Dept., 8400 Westpark Dr., McLean, VA 22102-3591.

School Teachers—Kindergarten, Elementary, and Secondary

(D.O.T. 091.221, .227; 092.227-010, -014; 099.224-010, .227-022)

Significant Points

✓ *Public school teachers must have a bachelor's degree, complete an approved teacher education program, and be licensed; some states require a master's degree.*

✓ *Many states offer alternative licensure programs to attract people into teaching and to fill certain jobs.*

✓ *Employment growth for secondary school teachers will be more rapid than for kindergarten and elementary school teachers due to student enrollments, but job outlook will vary by geographic area and by subject specialty.*

Nature of the Work

Teachers act as facilitators or coaches, using interactive discussions and hands-on learning to help students learn and apply concepts in subjects such as science, mathematics, or English. As teachers move away from the traditional repetitive drill approaches and rote memorization, they are using more "props" or "manipulatives" to help children understand abstract concepts, solve problems, and develop critical thought processes. For example, they teach the concepts of numbers or adding and subtracting by playing board games. As children get older, they use more sophisticated materials such as tape recorders, science apparatus, cameras, or computers.

Many classes are becoming less structured, with students working in groups to discuss and solve problems together. Preparing students for the future workforce is the major stimulus generating the changes in education. To be prepared, students must be able to interact with others, adapt to new technology, and logically think through problems. Teachers provide the tools and environment for their students to develop these skills.

Kindergarten and elementary school teachers play a vital role in the development of children. What children learn and experience during their early years can shape their views of themselves and the world, and affect later success or failure in school, work, and their personal lives. Kindergarten and elementary school teachers introduce children to numbers, language, science, and social studies. They use games, music, artwork, films, slides, computers, and other tools to teach basic skills.

Most elementary school teachers instruct one class of children in several subjects. In some schools, two or more teachers work as a team and are jointly responsible for a group of students in at least one subject. In other schools, a teacher may teach one special subject—usually music, art, reading, science, arithmetic, or physical education—to a number of classes. A small but growing number of teachers instruct multilevel classrooms, with students at several different learning levels.

Secondary school teachers help students delve more deeply into subjects introduced in elementary school and expose them to more information about the world and themselves. Secondary school teachers specialize in a specific subject, such as English, Spanish, mathematics, history, or biology. They teach a variety of related courses—for example, American history, contemporary American problems, and world geography.

Special education teachers—who instruct elementary and secondary school students who have a variety of disabilities—are discussed separately.

Teachers may use films, slides, overhead projectors, and the latest technology in teaching, including computers, telecommunication systems, and video discs. Use of computer resources, such as educational software and the Internet, exposes students to a vast range of experiences and promotes interactive learning. Through the Internet, American students can communicate with students in other countries to share personal experiences. Students also use the Internet for individual research projects and information gathering. Computers are used in other classroom activities as well, from helping students solve math problems to learning English as a second language. Teachers may also use computers to record grades and for other administrative and clerical duties. Teachers must continually update their skills to use the latest technology in the classroom.

Teachers often work with students from varied ethnic, racial, and religious backgrounds. With growing minority populations in many parts of the country, it is important for teachers to establish rapport with a diverse student population. Accordingly, some schools offer training to help teachers enhance their awareness and understanding of different cultures. Teachers may also include multicultural programming in their lesson plans to address the needs of all students, regardless of their cultural background.

Classroom presentations are designed by teachers to meet student needs and abilities. They also work with students individually. Teachers plan, evaluate, and assign lessons; prepare, administer, and grade tests; listen to oral presentations; and maintain classroom discipline. They observe and evaluate a student's performance and potential, and increasingly use new assessment methods. For example, teachers may examine a portfolio of a student's artwork or writing at the end of a learning period to judge the student's overall progress. They then provide additional assistance in areas where a student needs help. Teachers also grade papers, prepare report cards, and meet with parents and school staff to discuss a student's academic progress or personal problems.

In addition to classroom activities, teachers oversee study halls and homerooms and supervise extracurricular activities. They identify physical or mental problems and refer students to the proper resource or agency for diagnosis and treatment. Secondary school teachers occasionally assist students in choosing courses, colleges, and careers. Teachers also participate in education conferences and workshops.

In recent years, site-based management, which allows teachers and parents to participate actively in management decisions, has gained popularity. In many schools, teachers are increasingly involved in making decisions regarding the budget, personnel, text-book choices, curriculum design, and teaching methods.

Working Conditions

Seeing students develop new skills and gain an appreciation of knowledge and learning can be very rewarding. However, teaching may be frustrating when dealing with unmotivated and disrespectful students. Teachers may also experience stress when dealing with large classes, students from disadvantaged or multicultural backgrounds, and heavy workloads.

Teachers face isolation from their colleagues since they often work alone in a classroom of students. However, this autonomy provides teachers considerable freedom to choose their own teaching styles and methods.

Including school duties performed outside the classroom, many teachers work more than 40 hours a week. Most teachers work the traditional ten-month school year with a two-month vacation during the summer. Those on the ten-month schedule may teach in summer sessions, take other jobs, travel, or pursue other personal interests. Many enroll in college courses or workshops to continue their education. Teachers in districts with a year-round schedule typically work eight weeks, are on vacation for one week, and have a five-week midwinter break.

Most states have tenure laws that prevent teachers from being fired without just cause and due process. Teachers may obtain tenure after they have satisfactorily completed a probationary period of teaching, normally three years. Tenure does not absolutely guarantee a job, but it does provide some security.

Employment

Teachers held about 3.1 million jobs in 1996. Of those, about 1.7 million were kindergarten and elementary school teachers, and 1.4 million were secondary school teachers. Employment is distributed geographically, much the same as the population.

Training, Other Qualifications, and Advancement

All 50 states and the District of Columbia require public school teachers to be licensed. Licensure is not required for teachers in private schools. Usually licensure is granted by the state board of education or a licensure advisory committee. Teachers may be licensed to teach the early childhood grades (usually nursery school through grade 3); the elementary grades (grades 1 through 6 or 8); the middle grades (grades 5 through 8); a secondary education subject area (usually grades 7 through 12); or a special subject, such as reading or music (usually grades K through 12).

Requirements for regular licenses vary by state. However, all states require a bachelor's degree and completion of an approved teacher training program with a prescribed number of subject and education credits and supervised practice teaching. Some states require specific minimum grade point averages for teacher licensure. Some states require teachers to obtain a master's degree in education, which involves at least one year of additional course work beyond the bachelor's degree with a specialization in a particular subject.

Almost all states require applicants for teacher licensure to be tested for competency in basic skills such as reading and writing, teaching skills, or subject matter proficiency. Most states require continuing education for renewal of the teacher's license. Many states have reciprocity agreements that make it easier for teachers licensed in one state to become licensed in another.

Increasingly, many states are moving toward implementing performance-based standards for licensure, which require passing a rigorous comprehensive teaching examination to obtain provisional licensure, and then demonstrating satisfactory teaching performance over an extended period of time to obtain full licensure.

Many states offer alternative teacher licensure programs for people who have bachelor's degrees in the subject they will teach, but lack the necessary education courses required for a regular license. Alternative licensure programs were originally designed to ease teacher shortages in certain subjects, such as mathematics and science. The programs have expanded to attract other people into teaching, including recent college graduates and midcareer changers. In some programs, individuals begin teaching quickly under provisional licensure. After working under the close supervision of experienced educators for one or two years while taking education courses outside school hours, they receive regular licensure if they have progressed satisfactorily. Under other programs, college graduates who do not meet licensure requirements take only those courses that they lack, and then become licensed. This may take one or two semesters of full-time study. States may issue emergency licenses to individuals who do not meet requirements for a regular license when schools cannot attract enough qualified teachers to fill positions. Teachers who need licensure may enter programs that grant a master's degree in education, as well as licensure.

In recent years, the National Board for Professional Teaching Standards began offering voluntary national certification for teachers. To become nationally certified, teachers must prove their aptitude by compiling a portfolio showing their work in the classroom, and by passing a written assessment and evaluation of their teaching knowledge. A teacher who is nationally certified may find it easier to obtain employment in another state. Certified teachers may also earn higher salaries, have more senior titles, and be eligible for more bonuses than noncertified teachers. While all states recognize national certification, however, many states have not established policies on specific benefits of holding national certification, such as salary differentials or reimbursement of certification fees.

The National Council for Accreditation of Teacher Education currently accredits over 500 teacher education programs across the United States. Generally, four-year colleges require students to wait until their sophomore year before applying for admission to teacher education programs. Traditional education programs for kindergarten and elementary school teachers include courses—designed specifically for those preparing to teach—in mathematics, physical science, social science, music, art, and literature, as well as prescribed professional education courses, such as philosophy of education, psychology of learning, and teaching methods. Aspiring secondary school teachers either major in the subject they plan to teach while also taking education courses, or major in education and take subject courses. Teacher education programs are now required to include classes in the use of computers and other technologies to maintain accreditation. Most programs require students to perform student teaching.

Many states now offer professional development schools, which are partnerships between universities and elementary or secondary schools. Students enter these one-year programs after completion of their bachelor's degree. Professional development schools merge theory with practice and allow the student to experience a year of teaching first-hand, with professional guidance.

In addition to being knowledgeable in their subject, the ability to communicate, inspire trust and confidence, and motivate students, as well as understand their educational and emotional needs, is essential for teachers. Teachers must be able to recognize and respond to individual differences in students, and employ different teaching methods that will result in high student achievement. They also should be organized, dependable, patient, and creative. Teachers must also be able to work cooperatively and communicate effectively with other teaching staff, support staff, parents, and other members of the community.

With additional preparation, teachers may move into positions as school librarians, reading specialists, curriculum specialists, or guidance counselors. Teachers may become administrators or supervisors, although the number of these positions is limited and competition for these desirable positions can be intense. In some systems, highly qualified, experienced teachers can become senior or mentor teachers, with higher pay and additional responsibilities. They guide and assist less experienced teachers while keeping most of their teaching responsibilities.

Job Outlook

The job market for teachers varies widely by geographic area and by subject specialty. Many inner cities—characterized by high crime rates, high poverty rates, and overcrowded conditions—and rural areas—characterized by their remote location and relatively low salaries—have difficulty attracting enough teachers, so job prospects should continue to be better in these areas than in suburban districts. Currently, many school districts have difficulty hiring qualified teachers in some subjects—mathematics, science (especially chemistry and physics), bilingual education, and computer science. Specialties that currently have an abundance of qualified teachers include general elementary education, English, art, physical education, and social studies. Teachers who are geographically mobile and who obtain licensure in more than one subject should have a distinct advantage in finding a job. With enrollments of minorities increasing, coupled with a shortage of minority teachers, efforts to recruit minority teachers should intensify. Also, the number of non-English speaking students has grown dramatically, especially in California and Florida which have large Spanish-speaking student populations, creating demand for bilingual teachers and those who speak English as a second language (ESL).

Overall employment of kindergarten, elementary, and secondary school teachers is expected to increase about as fast as the average for all occupations through the year 2006. The expected retirement of a large number of teachers currently in their 40s and 50s should open up many additional jobs. However, projected employment growth varies among individual teaching occupations.

Employment of secondary school teachers is expected to grow faster than the average for all occupations through the year 2006, while average employment growth is projected for kindergarten and elementary school teachers. Assuming relatively little change in average class size, employment growth of teachers depends on population growth rates and corresponding student enrollments. Enrollment of 14- to 17-year-olds is expected to grow through the year 2006. Enrollment of 5- to 13-year-olds also is projected to increase, but at a slower rate, through the year 2002, and then decline.

The number of teachers employed is also dependent on state and local expenditures for education. Pressures from taxpayers to limit spending could result in fewer teachers than projected; pressures to spend more to improve the quality of education could increase the teacher workforce.

The supply of teachers also is expected to increase in response to reports of improved job prospects, more teacher involvement in school policy, and greater public interest in education. In recent years, the total number of bachelor's and master's degrees granted in education has steadily increased. In addition, more teachers will be drawn from a reserve pool of career changers, substitute teachers, and teachers completing alternative certification programs, relocating to different schools, and reentering the workforce.

Earnings

According to the National Education Association, the estimated average salary of all public elementary and secondary school teachers in the 1995-96 school year was $37,900. Public secondary school teachers averaged about $38,600 a year, while public elementary school teachers averaged $37,300. Private school teachers generally earn less than public school teachers.

In 1996, over half of all public school teachers belonged to unions–mainly the American Federation of Teachers and the National Education Association–that bargain with school systems over wages, hours, and the terms and conditions of employment.

In some schools, teachers receive extra pay for coaching sports and working with students in extracurricular activities. Some teachers earn extra income during the summer working in the school system or in other jobs.

Related Occupations

Kindergarten, elementary, and secondary school teaching requires a wide variety of skills and aptitudes, including a talent for working with children; organizational, administrative, and record keeping abilities; research and communication skills; the power to influence, motivate, and train others; patience; and creativity. Workers in other occupations requiring some of these aptitudes include college and university faculty, counselors, education administrators, employment interviewers, librarians, preschool teachers, public relations specialists, sales representatives, social workers, and trainers and employee development specialists.

Sources of Additional Information

Information on licensure or certification requirements and approved teacher training institutions is available from local school systems and state departments of education.

Information on teachers' unions and education-related issues may be obtained from:

❑ American Federation of Teachers, 555 New Jersey Ave. NW, Washington, DC 20001.

❑ National Education Association, 1201 16th St. NW, Washington, DC 20036.

A list of institutions with accredited teacher education programs can be obtained from:

❑ National Council for Accreditation of Teacher Education, 2010 Massachusetts Ave. NW, Suite 500, Washington, DC 20036.

For information on voluntary national teacher certification requirements, contact:

❑ National Board for Professional Teaching Standards, 26555 Evergreen Rd., Suite 400, Southfield, MI 48076.

Securities and Financial Services Sales Representatives

(D.O.T. 162.167-034 and -038; 250.257-014, -018, and -022.)

Significant Points

✓ *A college degree and sales ability are among the most important qualifications.*

✓ *Employment is expected to grow much faster than average as investment increases.*

✓ *Many beginning securities sales representatives leave the occupation because they are unable to establish a sufficient clientele; once established, however, these workers have a very strong attachment to their occupation because of high earnings and the considerable investment in training.*

Nature of the Work

Most investors, whether they are individuals with a few hundred dollars to invest or large institutions with millions, use securities sales representatives when buying or selling stocks, bonds, shares in mutual funds, insurance annuities, or other financial products. Securities sales representatives often are called stock brokers, registered representatives, or account executives.

When an investor wishes to buy or sell securities, sales representatives may relay the order through their firms' offices to the floor of a securities exchange, such as the New York Stock Exchange. There, securities sales representatives known as brokers' floor representatives buy and sell securities. If a security is not traded on an exchange, the sales representative sends the order to the firm's trading department, where it is traded directly with a dealer in an over-the-counter market, such as the NASDAQ computerized trading system. After the transaction has been completed, the sales representative notifies the customer of the final price.

Securities sales representatives also provide many related services for their customers. They may explain the meaning of stock market terms and trading practices; offer financial counseling; devise an individual client financial portfolio, including securities, life insurance, corporate and municipal bonds, mutual funds, certificates of deposit, annuities, and other investments; and offer advice on the purchase or sale of particular securities.

Not all customers have the same investment goals. Some individuals prefer long-term investments for capital growth or to provide income over the years; others might want to invest in speculative securities that they hope will rise in price quickly. Securities sales representatives furnish information about advantages and disadvantages of an investment based on each person's objectives. They also supply the latest price quotations on any security in which an investor is interested, as well as information on the activities and financial positions of the corporations issuing these securities.

Most securities sales representatives serve individual investors, but others specialize in institutional investors. In institutional investing, most sales representatives concentrate on a specific financial product, such as stocks, bonds, options, annuities, or commodity futures. Some handle the sale of new issues, such as corporate securities issued to finance plant expansion.

The most important part of a sales representative's job is finding clients and building a customer base. Thus, beginning securities sales representatives spend much of their time searching for customers—relying heavily on telephone solicitation. They may meet some clients through business and social contacts. Many sales representatives find it useful to get additional exposure by teaching adult education investment courses or by giving lectures at libraries or social clubs. Brokerage firms may give sales representatives lists of people with whom the firm has done business in the past. Sometimes sales representatives inherit the clients of representatives who have retired.

Financial services sales representatives sell banking and related services. They contact potential customers to explain their services and to ascertain customers' banking and other financial needs. They may discuss services such as deposit accounts, lines of credit, sales or inventory financing, certificates of deposit, cash management, or investment services. They may solicit businesses to participate in consumer credit card programs. At most small and medium-size banks, branch managers and commercial loan officers are responsible for marketing the bank's financial services. As banks offer more and increasingly complex financial services—for example, securities brokerage and financial planning—the job of financial services sales representative is assuming greater importance.

Financial planners, using their knowledge of tax and investment strategies, securities, insurance, pension plans, and real estate, develop and implement financial plans for individuals and businesses. They interview clients to determine their assets, liabilities, cash flow, insurance coverage, tax status, and financial objectives. Then they analyze this information and develop a financial plan tailored to each client's needs.

Working Conditions

Securities sales representatives usually work in offices, where there is much activity. They have access to "quote boards" or computer terminals that continually provide information on the prices of securities. When sales activity increases, due perhaps to unanticipated changes in the economy, the pace can become very hectic.

Established securities sales representatives usually work the same hours as others in the business community. Beginners who are seeking customers may work much longer hours, however. Most securities sales representatives accommodate customers by meeting with them in the evenings or on weekends.

Financial services sales representatives normally work in a comfortable, less stressful office environment. They generally work 40 hours a week. They may spend considerable time outside the office meeting with present and prospective clients, attending civic functions, and participating in trade association meetings. Some financial services sales representatives work exclusively inside banks, providing service to "walk-in" customers.

Employment

Securities and financial services sales representatives held 263,000 jobs in 1996; securities sales representatives accounted for eight out of 10. In addition, a substantial number of people in other occupations sold securities. These include partners and branch office managers in securities firms, as well as insurance agents and brokers offering securities to their customers.

Securities sales representatives are employed by brokerage and investment firms in all parts of the country. Many of these firms are very small. Most sales representatives, however, work for a small number of large firms with main offices in large cities, especially New York.

Financial services sales representatives are employed by banks, savings and loan associations, and other credit institutions.

Training, Other Qualifications, and Advancement

Because securities sales representatives must be well informed about economic conditions and trends, a college education is increasingly important, especially in the larger securities firms. In fact, the overwhelming majority of workers in this occupation are college graduates. Although employers seldom require specialized academic training, courses in business administration, economics, and finance are helpful.

Many employers consider personal qualities and skills more important than academic training. Employers seek applicants who have good sales ability and communication skills, are well groomed, and have a strong desire to succeed. Self-confidence and an ability to handle frequent rejections also are important ingredients for success.

Because maturity and the ability to work independently also are important, many employers prefer to hire those who have achieved success in other jobs. Some firms prefer candidates with sales experience, particularly those who have worked on commission in areas such as real estate or insurance. Therefore, most entrants to this occupation transfer from other jobs. Some begin working as securities sales representatives following retirement from other fields.

Securities sales representatives must meet state licensing requirements, which generally include passing an examination and, in some cases, furnishing a personal bond. In addition, sales representatives must register as representatives of their firm, according to regulations of the securities exchanges where they do business or the National Association of Securities Dealers, Inc. (NASD). Before beginners can qualify as registered representatives, they must pass the General Securities Registered Representative Examination, administered by the NASD, and be an employee of a registered firm for at least four months. Most states require a second examination—the Uniform Securities Agents State Law Examination. These tests measure the prospective representative's knowledge of the securities business, customer protection requirements, and recordkeeping procedures. Many take correspondence courses in preparation for the securities examinations.

Most employers provide on-the-job training to help securities sales representatives meet the requirements for registration. In most firms, this training period takes about four months. Trainees in large firms may receive classroom instruction in securities analysis, effective speaking, and the finer points of selling; take courses offered by business schools and associations; and undergo a period of on-the-job training lasting up to two years. Many firms like to rotate their trainees among various departments in the firm, to give them a broad perspective of the securities business. In small firms, sales representatives often receive training in outside institutions and on the job.

Securities sales representatives must understand the basic characteristics of a wide variety of financial products offered by brokerage firms. Representatives periodically take training, through their firms or outside institutions, to keep abreast of new financial products as they are introduced on the market and to improve their sales techniques. Training in the use of computers is important, as the securities sales business is highly automated.

The principal form of advancement for securities sales representatives is an increase in the number and size of the accounts they handle. Although beginners usually service the accounts of individual investors, eventually they may handle very large institutional accounts, such as those of banks and pension funds. Some experienced sales representatives become branch office managers and supervise other sales representatives while continuing to provide services for their own customers. A few representatives advance to top management positions or become partners in their firms.

Banks and other credit institutions prefer to hire college graduates for financial services sales jobs. A business administration degree with a specialization in finance or a liberal arts degree including courses in accounting, economics, and marketing serves as excellent preparation for this job.

Financial services sales representatives learn through on-the-job training under the supervision of bank officers. Outstanding performance can lead to promotion to managerial positions.

Job Outlook

Due to the highly competitive nature of securities sales work, many beginners leave the occupation because they are unable to establish a sufficient clientele. Once established, however, securities sales representatives have a very strong attachment to their occupation because of high earnings and the considerable investment in training.

The demand for securities sales representatives fluctuates, as the economy expands and contracts. Thus, in an economic downturn, the number of persons seeking jobs usually exceeds the number of openings—sometimes by a great deal. Even during periods of rapid economic expansion, competition for securities sales training positions—particularly in larger firms—is keen, because of potentially high earnings.

Job opportunities for both securities and financial services sales representatives should be best for mature individuals with successful work experience. Opportunities for inexperienced sales representatives should be best in smaller firms.

Employment of securities sales representatives is expected to grow much faster than the average for all occupations through the year 2006, as economic growth, rising personal incomes, and greater inherited wealth increase the funds available for investment. As banks offer increasingly complex financial services, employment of financial services sales representatives should grow rapidly, even as overall employment in banking declines and more people conduct their banking from home via personal computer.

More individual investors are expected to purchase common stocks, mutual funds, and other financial products after seeking advice from securities sales representatives regarding the increasing array of investment alternatives. Deregulation has enabled brokerage firms to sell certificates of deposit, offer checking and deposit services through cash management accounts, and sell insurance products, such as annuities and life insurance. Growth in the number and size of institutional investors will be strong, as more people enroll in pension plans, set up individual retirement accounts, establish trust funds, and contribute to the endowment funds of colleges and other nonprofit institutions. Additional representatives also will be needed to sell securities issued by new and expanding corporations, by state and local governments financing public improvements, and by foreign governments, whose securities have become attractive to U.S. investors, as international trade expands.

Investors increasingly rely on the growing number of financial planners to assist them in selecting the proper options among a wide variety of financial alternatives. In addition, demand should increase as banks and credit institutions expand the range of financial services they offer and issue more loans for personal and commercial use.

Earnings

In 1996, median annual earnings of securities and financial services sales representatives were $38,800; the middle 50 percent earned between $24,300 and $73,500. Ten percent earned less than $18,100 and 10 percent earned more than $98,400. On average, financial services sales representatives earn considerably less than securities sales representatives.

Trainees usually are paid an hourly wage or salary, until they meet licensing and registration requirements. After candidates are licensed and registered, their earnings depend on commissions from the sale or purchase of stocks and bonds, life insurance, or other securities for customers. Commission earnings are likely to be high when there is much buying and selling and low when there is a slump in market activity. Most firms provide sales representatives with a steady income by paying a "draw against commission"—a minimum salary based on commissions which they can be expected to earn. Securities sales representatives who can provide their clients with the most complete financial services should enjoy the greatest income stability.

Financial services sales representatives usually are paid a salary; some receive a bonus, if they meet certain established goals.

Related Occupations

Similar sales jobs requiring specialized knowledge include insurance agents and real estate agents.

Sources of Additional Information

Information about job opportunities as a securities sales representative may be obtained from the personnel departments of individual securities firms.

For information about job opportunities for financial services sales representatives in various states, contact state bankers' associations or write directly to a particular bank.

Services Sales Representatives

(D.O.T. 165.157; 236.252; 250.357-022; 251.157, .257, .357; 252.257, .357; 253; 254; 259 except .257-014; 269.357-018; 273.357-014; 279.357-042; and 293 except .137-010 and .357-018)

Significant Points

✓ *A significant part of earnings may be in the form of commissions, which can vary considerably depending on performance.*

✓ *Considerable travel may be required.*

Nature of the Work

Services sales representatives sell a wide variety of services. For example, sales representatives for data processing services firms sell complex services such as inventory control, payroll processing, sales analysis, and financial reporting systems. Hotel sales representatives contact government, business, and social groups to solicit convention and conference business. Sales representatives for temporary help services firms locate and acquire clients who will hire the firm's employees. Telephone services sales representatives visit commercial customers to review their telephone systems, analyze their communications needs, and recommend services, such as installation of additional equipment. Other representatives sell automotive leasing, public utility, burial, shipping, protective, and management consulting services.

Services sales representatives act as industry experts, consultants, and problem solvers when selling their firm's services. The sales representative, in some cases, creates demand for his or her firm's services. A prospective client who is asked to consider buying a particular service may never have used, or even been aware of a need for, that service. For example, wholesalers might be persuaded to order a list of credit ratings for checking their customers' credit prior to making sales, because the list could be used to solicit new business.

There are several different categories of services sales jobs. Outside sales representatives call on clients and prospects at their homes or offices. They may have an appointment, or they may practice "cold calling," arriving without an appointment. Inside sales representatives work on their employer's premises, assisting individuals interested in the company's services. Telemarketing sales representatives sell over the telephone. They make large numbers of calls to prospects, attempting to sell the company's service themselves, or to arrange an appointment between the prospect and an outside sales representative. Some sales representatives deal exclusively with one, or a few, major clients.

Despite the diversity of services sold, the jobs of all services sales representatives have much in common. All sales representatives follow similar procedures and must fully understand and be able to discuss the services their company offers. Many sales representatives develop lists of prospective clients through telephone and business directories, asking business associates and customers for leads, and calling on new businesses as they cover their assigned territory. Some services sales representatives acquire clients through inquiries about their company's services.

Regardless of how they first meet the client, all services sales representatives must explain how the offered services meet the client's needs. This often involves demonstrations of the company's services. They answer questions about the nature and cost of the services and try to overcome objections in order to persuade potential customers to purchase the services. If they fail to make a sale on the first visit, they may follow up with more visits, letters, or phone calls. After closing a sale, services sales representatives generally follow up to see that the purchase meets the customer's needs, and to determine if additional services can be sold. Good customer service is becoming increasingly important and can give a company a competitive advantage.

Because services sales representatives obtain many of their new accounts through referrals, their success hinges on developing a satisfied clientele who will continue to use the services and recommend them to other potential customers. Like other types of sales jobs, a services sales representative's reputation is crucial to his or her success.

Services sales work varies with the kind of service sold. Selling highly technical services, such as communications systems or computer consulting services, involves complex and lengthy sales negotiations. In addition, sales of such complex services may require extensive after-sale support. In these situations, sales representatives may operate as part of a team of sales representatives and experts from other departments. Sales representatives receive valuable technical assistance from these experts. For example, those who sell data processing services might work with a systems engineer or computer scientist, and those who sell telephone services might receive technical assistance from a communications consultant. Teams enhance customer service and build strong long-term relationships with customers, resulting in increased sales.

Because of the length of time between the initial contact with a customer and the actual sale, representatives who sell complex technical services generally work with several customers simultaneously. Sales representatives must be well organized and efficient in managing their work. Selling less complex services, such as linen supply or pest control services, generally involves simpler and shorter sales negotiations.

A sales representative's job may also vary with the size of the employer. Those working for large companies are generally more specialized and are assigned a specific territory, a specific line of services, and their own accounts. In smaller companies, sales representatives may have broader responsibilities—administrative, marketing, or public relations, for example—in addition to their sales duties.

A sales representative often services a specific territory. A representative for a company offering services widely used by the general public, such as lawn care, generally has numerous clients in a relatively small territory. On the other hand, a sales representative for a more specialized organization, such as a standardized testing service, may need to service several states to acquire an adequate customer base.

Working Conditions

Working conditions for sales representatives vary. Outside sales representatives responsible for a large territory may spend a great deal of time traveling, sometimes for weeks at a time. Representatives with smaller territories may seldom, or never, travel overnight.

Outside sales representatives may spend part of their time in an office keeping records, preparing various documents, and setting up appointments with customers. Increasingly, sales representatives may share office space with others rather than have their own permanently assigned space. Inside sales representatives and telemarketers spend all their time in their offices, which can range from bright and cheerful customer showrooms to cramped and noisy rooms. Many outside sales representatives have the flexibility to set their own schedules as long as they meet their company's goals.

Selling is stressful work. Companies generally set sales quotas and have contests with prizes for those who make the most sales. There often is considerable pressure on the sales representative to meet monthly sales quotas. Many sales representatives work more than 40 hours per week.

Employment

Services sales representatives held over 694,000 wage and salary jobs in 1996. Over half were in firms providing business services, including computer and data processing; personnel supply; advertising; mailing, reproduction, and stenographic services; and equipment rental and leasing. Other sales representatives worked for firms offering a wide range of other services, as the following tabulation shows.

Total	100%
Business services	59
Computer and data processing	10
Personnel supply	10
Advertising	7
Mailing, reproduction, and stenographic	3
Miscellaneous equipment rental and leasing	3
Miscellaneous business services	26
Engineering and management services	11
Personal services	5
Amusement and recreation services	5
Automotive repair services	4
Membership organizations	3
Hotels and other lodging places	2
Motion pictures	2
Health services	2
Social services	2
All other services	5

Training, Other Qualifications, and Advancement

Some employers require services sales representatives to have a college degree, but requirements vary depending on the industry a company represents. Employers who market advertising services seek individuals with a college degree in advertising, marketing or business administration. Companies marketing educational services prefer individuals with a degree in education, marketing or a related field. Many hotels seek graduates from college hotel or tourism administration programs. Companies selling computer, communications, engineering and other highly technical services generally require a bachelor's degree appropriate to their field. Certification and licensing is also becoming more common for technical sales representatives.

Employers may hire sales representatives with only a high school diploma if they have a proven sales record. This is particularly true for those who sell nontechnical services, such as linen supply, pest control, cleaning services, or funeral services. Applicants enhance their chances of being hired into these positions if they have taken some college courses.

Many firms conduct intensive training programs for their sales representatives, including the history of the business, origin, development, and uses of the service, effective prospecting methods, presentation of the service, answering customer objections, creating customer demand, closing a sale, using the company's computer system, entering an order, company policies, communications technology, and the use of technical support personnel. Sales representatives may also attend seminars on a wide range of subjects given by outside or in-house training institutions. These sessions acquaint them with new services and products, and help them maintain and update their sales techniques, and may include motivational or sensitivity training to make sales representatives more effective in dealing with people.

Large companies often hire sales representatives directly out of college and closely monitor their progress while training them. In general, smaller companies prefer to hire individuals with a proven sales record because they cannot afford the expense of providing formal training programs.

In order to be successful, sales representatives should be persuasive and have a pleasant, outgoing, and enthusiastic disposition. Sales representatives must be highly motivated, energetic, well organized, and efficient. Good grooming and a neat appearance are essential, as are self-confidence, reliability, and the ability to communicate effectively both orally, and in writing. Sales representatives should be self-starters who have the ability to work under pressure to meet sales goals. They must also have a thorough knowledge of the service they are selling, and be able to anticipate and respond to their clients' questions and objections in a professional manner.

Sales representatives with good sales records and leadership ability may advance to supervisory and managerial positions. Frequent contact with business people in other firms provides sales workers with leads about job openings, enhancing advancement opportunities.

Job Outlook

Employment of services sales representatives, as a group, is expected to grow much faster than the average for all occupations through the year 2006, in response to growth of the services industries employing them. However, the projected growth of particular services industries varies. For example, the continued growth in factory and office automation should lead to much faster than average employment growth for computer and data processing services sales representatives. Growth will be tempered in some industries by the expanded use of various technologies, such as voice and electronic mail, cellular telephones, and laptop computers that increase sales workers' productivity.

In addition to the jobs generated by this growth, openings will occur each year because of the need to replace sales workers who transfer to other occupations or leave the labor force. Each year, many sales representatives discover they are unable to earn enough money and leave the occupation. Turnover is generally higher among representatives who sell nontechnical services, because they have invested less time and effort in specialized training. As a result of this turnover, job opportunities should be good, especially for those with a college degree or a proven sales record.

With improved technology, companies are finding it harder to justify the expense of travel, on-site presentations, waiting, and the preparation that supports those activities. Therefore, many companies are putting more emphasis on in-house sales by phone and other methods, and less emphasis on the use of outside sales staff. In addition, temporary or contract sales people are used more frequently for outside sales.

Earnings

In 1996, the median annual income for full-time advertising sales representatives was $26,000, while representatives selling other business services earned $30,264. Earnings of representatives who sold technical services were generally higher than earnings of those who sold nontechnical services.

Earnings of experienced sales representatives depend on performance. Successful sales representatives who establish a strong customer base can earn more than managers in their firm. According to Dartnell Corporation's 1996 Sales Compensation Survey, entry-level sales representatives received $36,000 in average total cash compensation, intermediate-level sales representatives earned $46,000, and senior sales representatives received $63,000.

Sales representatives are paid in a variety of ways. Some receive a straight salary; others are paid solely on a commission basis–a percentage of the dollar value of their sales. Most firms use a combination of salary and commissions. Some services sales representatives receive a base salary, plus incentive pay that can add 25 to 75 percent to the sales representative's base salary. In addition to the same benefits package received by other employees of the firm, outside sales representatives have expense accounts to cover meals and travel, and some drive a company car. Many employers offer bonuses, including vacation trips and prizes, for sales that exceed company quotas.

Because sales are affected by changing economic conditions and consumer and business expectations, earnings may vary greatly from year to year.

Related Occupations

Services sales representatives must have sales ability and knowledge of the service they sell. Workers in other occupations requiring these skills include real estate agents, insurance agents, securities and financial services sales representatives, retail sales workers, manufacturers' and wholesale sales representatives, and travel agents.

Sources of Additional Information

For details about employment opportunities for services sales representatives, contact:

❑ Sales and Marketing Executives International, 6600 Hidden Lake Trail, Brecksville, OH 44141.

Social and Human Service Assistants

(*D.O.T.* 195.367 except -026 and -030)

Significant Points

✓ *Social and human service assistants rank among the top ten fastest growing occupations.*

✓ *Job opportunities should be excellent, particularly for applicants with appropriate postsecondary education, but pay is low.*

Nature of the Work

Social and human service assistants is a generic term for people with various job titles, including social service assistant, case management aide, social work assistant, residential counselor, community support worker, alcohol or drug abuse counselor, mental health technician, child-care worker, community outreach worker, life skill counselor, and gerontology aide. They generally work under the direction of professionals from a wide variety of fields, such as nursing, psychiatry, psychology, rehabilitation, or social work. The amount of responsibility and supervision they are given varies a great deal. Some are on their own most of the time and have little direct supervision; others work under close direction.

Social and human service assistants provide direct and indirect client services. They assess clients' needs, establish their eligibility for benefits and services, and help clients obtain them. They examine financial documents such as rent receipts and tax returns to determine whether the client is eligible for food stamps, Medicaid, welfare, and other human service programs. They also arrange for transportation and escorts, if necessary, and provide emotional support. Social and human service assistants monitor and keep case records on clients and report progress to supervisors. Social and human service assistants also may transport or accompany clients to group meal sites, adult daycare programs, or doctors' offices; telephone or visit clients' homes to make sure services are being received; or help resolve disagreements, such as those between tenants and landlords. They may also help clients complete applications for financial assistance or assist with daily living needs.

Social and human service assistants play a variety of roles in community settings. They may organize and lead group activities, assist clients in need of counseling or crisis intervention, or administer a food bank or emergency fuel program. In halfway houses, group homes, and government-supported housing programs, they assist adult residents who need supervision in personal hygiene and daily living skills. They review clients' records, ensure they take correct doses of medication, talk with their families, and confer with medical personnel to gain better insight into clients' backgrounds and needs. They also provide emotional support and help clients become involved in community recreation programs and other activities.

In psychiatric hospitals, rehabilitation programs, and outpatient clinics, they may help clients master everyday living skills and teach them how to communicate more effectively and get along better with others. They support the client's participation in the treatment plan, such as individual or group counseling and occupational therapy.

Working Conditions

Working conditions of social and human service assistants vary. They work in offices, group homes, shelters, day programs, sheltered workshops, hospitals, clinics, and in the field visiting clients. Most work a regular 40-hour week, although some work may be in the evening and on weekends. Social and human service assistants in residential settings generally work in shifts because residents need supervision around the clock.

The work, while satisfying, can be emotionally draining. Understaffing and relatively low pay may add to the pressure. Turnover is reported to be high, especially among workers without academic preparation for this field.

Employment

Social and human service assistants held about 178,000 jobs in 1996. About one in three were employed by state and local governments, primarily in public welfare agencies and facilities for mentally disabled and developmentally delayed individuals. Another third worked in private social or human services agencies, offering a variety of services, including adult daycare, group meals, crisis intervention, counseling, and job training. Many social and human service assistants supervised residents of group homes and halfway houses. Social and human service assistants also held jobs in clinics, detoxification units, community mental health centers, psychiatric hospitals, day treatment programs, and sheltered workshops.

Training, Other Qualifications, and Advancement

While some employers hire high school graduates, most prefer applicants with some college preparation in human services, social work, or one of the social or behavioral sciences. Some prefer to hire persons with a four-year college degree. The educational attainment of social and human service assistants often influences the kind of work they are assigned and the amount of responsibility entrusted to them. Workers with no more than a high school education are likely to receive on-the-job training to work in direct care services, while those with a college degree might be assigned to do supportive counseling, coordinate program activities, or manage a group home. Employers may also look for experience in other occupations, leadership experience in an organization, or human service volunteer exposure. Some enter the field on the basis of courses in human services, psychology, rehabilitation, social work, sociology, or special education. Most employers provide in-service training such as seminars and workshops.

Because so many human services jobs involve direct contact with people who are vulnerable to exploitation or mistreatment, employers try to select applicants with appropriate personal qualifications. Relevant academic preparation is generally required, and volunteer or work experience is preferred. A strong desire to help others, patience, and understanding are highly valued characteristics. Other important personal traits include communication skills, a strong sense of responsibility, and the ability to manage time effectively. Hiring requirements in group homes tend to be more stringent than in other settings. In some settings, applicants may need a valid driver's license and must meet the Criminal Offense Record Investigation (CORI) requirement. Special licensure or state certifications may also apply.

In 1996, about 380 certificate and associate degree programs in human services or mental health were offered at community and junior colleges, vocational-technical institutes, and other postsecondary institutions. In addition, approximately 400 programs offered a bachelor's degree in human services. Master's degree programs in human services administration are offered as well.

Generally, academic programs in this field educate students for specialized roles. Human services programs have a core curriculum that trains students in observation and recording, interviewing, communication techniques, behavior management, group dynamics, counseling, crisis intervention, case management, and referral. General education courses in liberal arts, sciences, and the humanities are also part of the curriculum. Many degree programs require completion of an internship.

Formal education is almost always necessary for advancement. In general, advancement requires a bachelor's or master's degree in counseling, rehabilitation, social work, or a related field.

Job Outlook

Opportunities for social and human service assistants are expected to be excellent, particularly for applicants with appropriate postsecondary education. The number of social and human service assistants is projected to grow much faster than the average for all occupations between 1996 and the year 2006–ranking among the most rapidly growing occupations. The need to replace workers who retire or stop working for other reasons will create additional job opportunities. These jobs are not attractive to everyone due to the emotionally draining work and relatively low pay, so qualified applicants should have little difficulty finding employment.

Opportunities are expected to be best in job training programs, residential settings, and private social service agencies, which include such services as adult daycare and meal delivery programs. Demand for these services will expand with the growing number of older people, who are more likely to need services. In addition, social and human service assistants will continue to be needed to provide services to the mentally disabled and developmentally delayed, those with substance-abuse problems, the homeless, and pregnant teenagers. Faced with rapid growth in the demand for services, but slower growth in resources to provide the services, employers are expected to rely increasingly on social and human service assistants rather than more highly trained workers, such as social workers, who command higher pay.

Job training programs are expected to require additional social and human service assistants as the economy grows and businesses change their mode of production, requiring workers to be retrained. Social and human service assistants help determine workers' eligibility for public assistance programs and help them obtain services while unemployed.

Residential settings should expand also as pressures to respond to the needs of the chronically mentally ill persist. For many years, chronic mental patients have been deinstitutionalized and left to their own devices. Now, more community-based programs, supported independent living sites, and group residences are expected to be established to house and assist the homeless and chronically mentally ill, and demand for social and human service assistants will increase accordingly.

The number of jobs for social and human service assistants will grow more rapidly than overall employment in state and local governments. State and local governments employ most of their social and human service assistants in corrections and public assistance departments. Corrections departments are growing faster than other areas of government, so social and human service assistants should find that their job opportunities increase along with other corrections jobs. Public assistance programs have been employing more social and human service assistants in an attempt to employ fewer social workers, who are more educated and higher paid.

Earnings

Based on limited information, starting salaries for social and human service assistants ranged from about $15,000 to $24,000 a year in 1997. Experienced workers generally earned between $20,000 and $30,000 annually, depending on their education, experience, and employer.

Related Occupations

Workers in other occupations that require skills similar to those of social and human service assistants include social workers, religious workers, occupational therapy assistants, physical therapy assistants, psychiatric aides, and activity leaders.

Sources of Additional Information

Information on academic programs in human services may be found in most directories of two- and four-year colleges, available at libraries or career counseling centers.

For information on programs and careers in human services, contact:

- ❑ National Organization for Human Service Education, Brookdale Community College, Lyncroft, NJ 07738.
- ❑ Council for Standards in Human Service Education, Northern Essex Community College, Haverhill, MA 01830.

Information on job openings may be available from state employment service offices or directly from city, county, or state departments of health, mental health and mental retardation, and human resources.

Social Workers

(D.O.T. 189.267-010; 195.107, .137, .164, .167-010, -014, .267-018, -022, and .367-026)

Significant Points

- ✓ *A bachelor's degree is the minimum requirement for many entry-level jobs; however, a master's degree in social work (MSW) is generally required for advancement.*
- ✓ *Employment is projected to grow faster than average.*
- ✓ *Competition for jobs is stronger in cities where training programs for social workers are prevalent; rural areas often find it difficult to attract and retain qualified staff.*

Nature of the Work

Social work is a profession for those with a strong desire to help people. Social workers help people deal with their relationships with others; solve their personal, family, and community problems; and grow and develop as they learn to cope with or shape the social and environmental forces affecting daily life. Social workers often encounter clients facing a life-threatening disease or a social problem requiring a quick solution. These situations may include inadequate housing, unemployment, lack of job skills, financial distress, serious illness or disability, substance abuse, unwanted pregnancy, or antisocial behavior. They also assist families that have serious conflicts, including those involving child or spousal abuse.

Social workers practice in a variety of settings, including hospitals, from the obstetrics unit to the intensive care unit; in schools, helping children, teachers, and parents cope with problems; in mental health clinics and psychiatric hospitals; and in public agencies, from the employment office to the public welfare department. Through direct counseling, social workers help clients identify their concerns, consider solutions, and find resources. Often, they refer clients to specialists in various areas, including debt counseling, child care or elder care, public assistance or other benefits, or alcohol or drug rehabilitation programs. Social workers typically arrange for services in consultation with clients, following through to assure the services are helpful. They may review eligibility requirements, fill out forms and applications, arrange for services, visit clients on a regular basis, and provide support during crises.

Most social workers specialize—for example, in child welfare and family services, mental health, or school social work. Clinical social workers offer psychotherapy or counseling and a range of services in public agencies and clinics, and in private practice. Other social workers are employed in community organization, administration, or research.

Those specializing in child welfare or family services may counsel children and youths who have difficulty adjusting socially, advise parents on how to care for disabled children, or arrange for homemaker services during a parent's illness. If children have serious problems in school, child welfare workers may consult with parents, teachers, and counselors to identify underlying causes and develop plans for treatment. Some social workers assist single parents, arrange adoptions, and help find foster homes for neglected, abandoned, or abused children. Child welfare workers also work in residential institutions for children and adolescents.

Social workers in child or adult protective services investigate reports of abuse and neglect and intervene if necessary. They may institute legal action to remove children from homes and place them temporarily in an emergency shelter or with a foster family.

Mental health social workers provide services for persons with mental or emotional problems, such as individual and group therapy, outreach, crisis intervention, social rehabilitation, and training in skills of everyday living. They may also help plan for supportive services to ease patients' return to the community. (Counselors and psychologists may provide similar services.)

Health care social workers help patients and their families cope with chronic, acute, or terminal illnesses and handle problems that may stand in the way of recovery or rehabilitation. They may organize support groups for families of patients suffering from cancer, AIDS, Alzheimer's disease, or other illnesses. They also advise family caregivers, counsel patients, and help plan for their needs after discharge by arranging for at-home services—from meals-on-wheels to oxygen equipment. Some work on interdisciplinary teams that evaluate certain kinds of patients—geriatric or organ transplant patients, for example.

School social workers diagnose students' problems and arrange needed services, counsel children in trouble, and help integrate disabled students into the general school population. School social workers deal with problems such as student pregnancy, misbehavior in class, and excessive absences. They also advise teachers on how to deal with problem students.

Criminal justice social workers make recommendations to courts, prepare pre-sentencing assessments, and provide services for prison inmates and their families. Probation and parole officers provide similar services to individuals sentenced by a court to parole or probation.

Occupational social workers generally work in a corporation's personnel department or health unit. Through employee assistance programs, they help workers cope with job-related pressures or personal problems that affect the quality of their work. They often offer direct counseling to employees whose performance is hindered by emotional or family problems or substance abuse. They also develop education programs and refer workers to specialized community programs.

Some social workers specialize in gerontological services. They run support groups for family caregivers or for the adult children of aging parents; advise elderly people or family members about the choices in such areas as housing, transportation, and long-term care; and coordinate and monitor services.

Social workers also focus on policy and planning. They help develop programs to address such issues as child abuse, homelessness, substance abuse, poverty, and violence. These workers research and analyze policies, programs, and regulations. They identify social problems and suggest legislative and other solutions. They may help raise funds or write grants to support these programs.

Working Conditions

Although some social workers work a standard 40-hour week, many work some evenings and weekends to meet with clients, attend community meetings, and handle emergencies. Some, particularly in voluntary nonprofit agencies, work part-time. They may spend most of their time in an office or residential facility, but may also travel locally to visit clients or meet with service providers. Some have several offices within a local area.

The work, while satisfying, can be emotionally draining. Understaffing and large caseloads add to the pressure in some agencies.

Employment

Social workers held about 585,000 jobs in 1996. About four out of ten jobs were in state, county, or municipal government agencies, primarily in departments of health and human resources, mental health, social services, child welfare, housing, education, and corrections. As government increasingly contracts out social services, many jobs are likely to shift from government to private organizations in the future. Most jobs in the private sector were in social service agencies, community and religious organizations, hospitals, nursing homes, or home health agencies.

Although most social workers are employed in cities or suburbs, some work in rural areas.

Training, Other Qualifications, and Advancement

A bachelor's degree is the minimum requirement for many entry-level jobs. Besides the bachelor's in social work (BSW), undergraduate majors in psychology, sociology, and related fields satisfy hiring requirements in some agencies, especially small community agencies. A master's degree in social work (MSW) is generally necessary for positions in health and mental health settings. Jobs in public agencies may also require an MSW. Supervisory, administrative, and staff training positions usually require at least an MSW. College

and university teaching positions and most research appointments normally require a doctorate in social work.

In 1996, the Council on Social Work Education accredited over 430 BSW programs and over 130 MSW programs. There were 55 doctoral programs for Ph.D.s in social work and DSWs (Doctor of Social Work). BSW programs prepare graduates for direct service positions such as case worker or group worker. They include courses in social work practice, social welfare policies, human behavior and the social environment, and social research methods. Accredited BSW programs require at least 400 hours of supervised field experience.

An MSW degree prepares graduates to perform assessments, manage cases, and supervise other workers. Master's programs usually last two years and include 900 hours of supervised field instruction, or internship. Entry into an MSW program does not require a bachelor's in social work, but courses in psychology, biology, sociology, economics, political science, history, social anthropology, urban studies, and social work are recommended. In addition, a second language can be very helpful. Some schools offer an accelerated MSW program for those with a BSW.

Since 1993, all states and the District of Columbia have had licensing, certification, or registration laws regarding social work practice and the use of professional titles. Standards for licensing vary by state. In addition, voluntary certification is offered by the National Association of Social Workers (NASW), which grants the title ACSW (Academy of Certified Social Worker) or ACBSW (Academy of Certified Baccalaureate Social Worker) to those who qualify. For clinical social workers, who are granted the title QCSW (Qualified Clinical Social Worker), professional credentials include listing in the NASW Register of Clinical Social Workers. Advanced credentials include the NASW Diplomate in Clinical Social Work, and School Social Work Specialist. An advanced credential is also offered by the Directory of American Board of Examiners in Clinical Social Work. Credentials are particularly important for those in private practice; some health insurance providers require them for reimbursement.

Social workers should be emotionally mature, objective, and sensitive to people and their problems. They must be able to handle responsibility, work independently, and maintain good working relationships with clients and coworkers. Volunteer or paid jobs as a social work aide offer ways of testing one's interest in this field.

Advancement to supervisor, program manager, assistant director, or executive director of a social service agency or department is possible but generally requires an MSW degree and related work experience. Although some social workers with a BSW may be promoted to these positions after gaining experience, some employers choose to hire managers directly from MSW programs that focus specifically on management. These graduates often have little work experience but have an understanding of management through their education and training. Other career options for social workers include teaching, research, and consulting. Some help formulate government policies by analyzing and advocating policy positions in government agencies, in research institutions, and on legislators' staffs.

Some social workers go into private practice. Most private practitioners are clinical social workers who provide psychotherapy, usually paid through health insurance. Private practitioners must have an MSW and a period of supervised work experience. A network of contacts for referrals is also essential.

Job Outlook

Employment of social workers is expected to increase faster than the average for all occupations through the year 2006. The number of older people, who are more likely to need social services, is increasing rapidly. In addition, growing concern about crime, juvenile delinquency, and services for the mentally ill, the mentally retarded, AIDS patients, and individuals and families in crisis will spur demand for social workers. Many job openings will also stem from the need to replace social workers who leave the occupation.

As hospitals increasingly emphasize early discharge of patients in an effort to control costs, more social workers will be needed to ensure that the necessary medical and social services are in place when individuals leave the hospital. Social worker employment in home health care services is growing, not only because hospitals are releasing patients earlier, but because a large and growing number of people have impairments or disabilities that make it difficult to live at home without some form of assistance.

Employment of social workers in private social service agencies will grow, but not as rapidly as demand for their services. Agencies will increasingly restructure services and hire more lower-paid human services workers instead of social workers. Employment in government may grow in response to increasing needs for public welfare and family services; however, many of these jobs will be contracted out to private agencies. Additionally, employment levels will depend on government funding for various social service programs.

Employment of school social workers is expected to grow, due to expanded efforts to respond to rising rates of teen pregnancy and to the adjustment problems of immigrants and children from single-parent families. Moreover, continued emphasis on integrating disabled children into the general school population will lead to more jobs. Availability of state and local funding will dictate the actual job growth in schools, however.

Opportunities for social workers in private practice will expand because of the anticipated availability of funding from health insurance and public-sector contracts. Also, with increasing affluence, people will be better able to pay for professional help to deal with personal problems. The growing popularity of employee assistance programs is also expected to spur demand for private practitioners, some of whom provide social work services to corporations on a contractual basis.

Competition for social worker jobs is stronger in cities where training programs for social workers are prevalent; rural areas often find it difficult to attract and retain qualified staff.

Earnings

Based on limited information, social workers with an MSW had median earnings of about $35,000 in 1997, while social workers with a BSW earned about $25,000.

According to a Hay Group survey of acute care hospitals, the median annual salary of full-time social workers with a master's degree was $35,000 in 1997. The middle 50 percent earned between $32,300 and $38,700.

The average annual salary for all social workers in the federal government in nonsupervisory, supervisory, and managerial positions was about $46,900 in 1997.

Related Occupations

Through direct counseling or referral to other services, social workers help people solve a range of personal problems. Workers in occupations with similar duties include the clergy, mental health counselors, counseling psychologists, and human services workers.

Sources of Additional Information

For information about career opportunities in social work, contact:

❏ National Association of Social Workers, Career Information, 750 First St. NE., Suite 700, Washington, DC 20002-4241.

❏ National Network For Social Work Managers, Inc., 1316 New Hampshire Ave. NW, Suite 602, Washington, DC 20036.

An annual Directory of Accredited BSW and MSW Programs is available for a nominal charge from:

❏ Council on Social Work Education, 1600 Duke St., Alexandria, VA 22314-3421.

Special Education Teachers

(D.O.T. 094.107, .224, .227, .267; 099.227-042; 195.227-018)

Significant Points

✓ *A bachelor's degree, completion of an approved teacher preparation program, and a license are required; many states require a master's degree.*

✓ *Many states offer alternative licensure programs to attract people into special education teaching jobs.*

✓ *Job openings arising from rapid employment growth and job turnover, coupled with a declining number of graduates from special education teaching programs, mean excellent job prospects; many school districts report shortages of qualified teachers.*

Nature of the Work

Special education teachers work with children and youth who have a variety of disabilities. Most special education teachers instruct students at the elementary, middle, and secondary school level, although some teachers work with infants and toddlers. Special education teachers design and modify instruction to meet a student's special needs. Teachers also work with students who have other special instructional needs, including those who are gifted and talented.

The various types of disabilities delineated in government special education programs include specific learning disabilities, mental retardation, speech or language impairment, serious emotional disturbance, visual and hearing impairment, orthopedic impairment, autism, traumatic brain injury, and multiple disabilities. Students are classified under one of the categories, and special education teachers are prepared to work with specific groups.

Special education teachers use various techniques to promote learning. Depending on the disability, teaching methods can include individualized instruction, problem-solving assignments, and group or individual work. Special education teachers are legally required to help develop an Individualized Education Program (IEP) for each special education student. The IEP sets personalized goals for each student and is tailored to a student's individual learning style and ability. This program includes a transition plan outlining specific steps to prepare special education students for middle school or high school, or in the case of older students, a job or postsecondary study. Teachers review the IEP with the student's parents, school administrators, and often the student's general education teacher. Teachers work closely with parents to inform them of their child's progress and suggest techniques to promote learning at home.

Teachers design curricula, assign work geared toward each student's ability, and grade papers and homework assignments. Special education teachers are involved in a student's behavioral as well as academic development. They help special education students develop emotionally, be comfortable in social situations, and be aware of socially acceptable behavior. Preparing special education students for daily life after graduation is an important aspect of the job. Teachers may help students with routine skills, such as balancing a check book, or provide them with career counseling.

As schools have become more inclusive, special education teachers and general education teachers increasingly work together in general education classrooms. Special education teachers help general educators adapt curriculum materials and teaching techniques to meet the needs of students with disabilities.

Special education teachers work in a variety of settings. Some have their own classrooms and teach classes comprised entirely of special education students; others work as special education resource teachers and offer individualized help to students in general education classrooms; and others teach along with general education teachers in classes composed of both general and special education students. Some teachers work in a resource room, where special education students work several hours a day, separate from their general education classroom. A significantly smaller proportion of special education teachers work in residential facilities or tutor students in homebound or hospital environments. Special education teachers who work with infants usually travel to the child's home to work with the child and his or her parents.

A large part of a special education teacher's job involves interacting with others. They communicate frequently with parents, social workers, school psychologists, occupational and physical therapists, school administrators, and other teachers.

Early identification of a child with special needs is another important part of a special education teacher's job. Early intervention is essential in educating these children.

Technology is playing an increasingly important role in special education. Special education teachers use specialized equipment such as computers with synthesized speech, interactive educational software programs, and audio tapes.

Working Conditions

Helping students with disabilities achieve goals, and making a difference in their lives can be highly rewarding. Special education teachers enjoy the challenge of working with these students and the opportunity to establish meaningful relationships. However, the work can also be emotionally and physically draining. Special education teachers are under considerable stress due to heavy workloads and tedious administrative tasks. They must produce a substantial amount of paperwork documenting each student's progress. Exacerbating this stress is the threat of litigation by students' parents if correct

procedures are not followed, or if the parent feels their child is not receiving an adequate education. Some special educators feel they are not adequately supported by school administrators, and feel isolated from general education teachers. The physical and emotional demands of the job result in a high "burnout" rate.

Many schools offer year-round education for special education students, but most special education teachers work the traditional ten-month school year with a two-month vacation during the summer.

Employment

Special education teachers held about 407,000 jobs in 1996. The majority of special education teachers were employed in elementary, middle, and secondary public schools. The rest worked in separate educational facilities–public or private–residential facilities, or in homebound or hospital environments.

Training, Other Qualifications, and Advancement

All 50 states and the District of Columbia require special education teachers to be licensed. Special education licensure varies by state. In many states, special education teachers receive a general education credential to teach kindergarten through grade 12. These teachers train in a specialty, such as learning disabilities or behavioral disorders. Some states offer general special education licensure, others license several different specialties within special education, while others require teachers to first obtain general education licensure and then additional licensure in special education. Usually licensure is granted by the state board of education or a licensure advisory committee.

All states require a bachelor's degree and completion of an approved teacher preparation program with a prescribed number of subject and education credits and supervised practice teaching. Many states require special education teachers to obtain a master's degree in special education, involving at least one year of additional course work, including a specialization, beyond the bachelor's degree.

Some states have reciprocity agreements allowing special education teachers to transfer their licensure from one state to another, but many still require special education teachers to pass licensure requirements for that state. National certification standards for special education teachers are currently being developed by the National Board for Professional Teaching Standards.

About 700 colleges and universities across the United States offer programs in special education, including undergraduate, master's, and doctoral programs. Special education teachers usually undergo longer periods of training than general education teachers. Most bachelor's degree programs are four-year programs including general and specialized courses in special education. However, an increasing number of institutions require a fifth year or other postbaccalaureate preparation. Courses include educational psychology, legal issues of special education, child growth and development, and knowledge and skills needed for teaching students with disabilities. Some programs require a specialization. Others offer generalized special education degrees, or study in several specialized areas. The last year of the program is usually spent student teaching in a classroom supervised by a certified teacher.

Alternative and emergency licensure is available in many states, due to the need to fill special education teaching positions. Alternative licensure is designed to bring college graduates and those changing careers into teaching more quickly. Requirements for alternative licensure may be less stringent than for regular licensure and vary by state. In some programs, individuals begin teaching quickly under provisional licensure. They can obtain regular licensure by teaching under the supervision of licensed teachers for a period of one to two years while taking education courses. Emergency licensure is enacted when states are having difficulty finding licensed special education teachers to fill positions.

Special education teachers must be patient, able to motivate students, understanding of their students' special needs, and accepting of differences in others. Teachers must be creative and apply different types of teaching methods to reach students who are having difficulty. Communication and cooperation are essential traits because special education teachers spend a great deal of time interacting with others, including students, parents, and school faculty and administrators.

Special education teachers can advance to become supervisors or administrators. They may also earn advanced degrees and become instructors in colleges that prepare others for special education teaching. In some school systems, highly experienced teachers can become mentor teachers to less experienced ones; they provide guidance to these teachers while maintaining a light teaching load.

Job Outlook

Special education teachers have excellent job prospects, as many school districts report shortages of qualified teachers. Job outlook varies by geographic area and specialty. Positions in rural areas and inner cities are more plentiful than job openings in suburban or wealthy urban areas. Also, job opportunities may be better in certain specialties—such as speech or language impairments, and learning disabilities—due to the considerable shortages of teachers in these fields. Recent legislation encouraging early intervention and special education for infants, toddlers, and preschoolers has created a need for early childhood special education teachers. Special education teachers who are bilingual or have multicultural experience are also needed to work with an increasingly diverse student population.

Employment of special education teachers is expected to increase much faster than the average for all occupations through the year 2006, spurred by continued growth in the number of special education students needing services, legislation emphasizing training and employment for individuals with disabilities, growing public interest in individuals with special needs, and educational reform. The high burnout rate will lead to many additional job openings as special education teachers switch to general education or change careers altogether. Rapid employment growth and job turnover, coupled with a declining number of graduates from special education teaching programs, should result in a very favorable job market.

The number of students requiring special education services has been steadily increasing, as indicated by the accompanying chart. This trend is expected to continue due to legislation which expanded the age range of children receiving special education services to include those from birth to age 21; medical advances resulting in more survivors of accidents and illness; the postponement of childbirth by more women, resulting in a greater number of premature births and children born with birth defects; and growth in the general population.

The growing use of inclusive school settings, which integrate special education students into general education settings, will also lead to more reliance on special education teachers. The role of these teachers is expanding to include acting as a consultant to general education teachers, in addition to teaching special education students in resource rooms, general education classrooms, and separate classrooms made up entirely of special education students.

Earnings

Salaries of special education teachers follow the same scale as those for general education teachers. According to the National Education Association, the estimated average salary of all public elementary and secondary school teachers in the 1995-96 school year was $37,900. Public secondary school teachers averaged about $38,600 a year, while public elementary school teachers averaged $37,300. Private school teachers generally earn less than public school teachers.

In 1996, over half of all public school teachers belonged to unions—mainly the American Federation of Teachers and the National Education Association—that bargain with school systems over wages, hours, and the terms and conditions of employment.

In some schools, teachers receive extra pay for coaching sports and working with students in extracurricular activities. Some teachers earn extra income during the summer, working in the school system or in other jobs.

Related Occupations

Special education teachers work with students who have disabilities and special needs. Other occupations involved with the identification, evaluation, and development of students with disabilities include school psychologists, social workers, speech pathologists, rehabilitation counselors, adapted physical education teachers, special education technology specialists, and occupational, physical, creative arts, and recreational therapists.

Sources of Additional Information

For information on a career as a special education teacher, a list of accredited schools, financial aid information, and general information on special education-related personnel issues, contact:

❏ National Clearinghouse for Professions in Special Education, Council for Exceptional Children, 1920 Association Dr., Reston, VA 20191. Homepage: http://www.cec.sped.org

To learn more about the special education teacher certification and licensing requirements in your state, contact your state's department of education.

Speech-Language Pathologists and Audiologists

(D.O.T. 076.101-010, .104-010, and .107-010)

Significant Points

✓ *About half work in schools, and most others are employed by healthcare facilities.*

✓ *A master's degree in speech-language pathology or audiology is the standard credential.*

✓ *Projected much-faster-than-average employment growth reflects the increasing number of people who will need speech-language pathology and audiology services.*

Nature of the Work

Speech-language pathologists assess, treat, and help to prevent speech, language, cognitive communication, voice, swallowing, fluency, and other related disorders; audiologists identify, assess, and manage auditory, balance, and other neural systems.

Speech-language pathologists work with people who cannot make speech sounds, or cannot make them clearly; those with speech rhythm and fluency problems, such as stuttering; people with voice quality problems, such as inappropriate pitch or harsh voice; those with problems understanding and producing language; and those with cognitive communication impairments, such as attention, memory, and problem solving disorders. They may also work with people who have oral motor problems causing eating and swallowing difficulties.

Speech and language problems can result from hearing loss, brain injury or deterioration, cerebral palsy, stroke, cleft palate, voice pathology, mental retardation, or emotional problems. Problems can be congenital, developmental, or acquired. Speech-language pathologists use written and oral tests, as well as special instruments, to diagnose the nature and extent of impairment and to record and analyze speech, language, and swallowing irregularities. Speech-language pathologists develop an individualized plan of care, tailored to each patient's needs. For individuals with little or no speech capability, speech-language pathologists select augmentative alternative communication methods, including automated devices and sign language, and teach their use. They teach these individuals how to make sounds, improve their voices, or increase their language skills to communicate more effectively. Speech-language pathologists help patients develop, or recover, reliable communication skills so patients can fulfill their educational, vocational, and social roles.

Most speech-language pathologists provide direct clinical services to individuals with communication disorders. In speech and language clinics, they may independently develop and carry out treatment programs. In medical facilities, they may work with physicians, social workers, psychologists, and other therapists to develop and execute treatment plans. Speech-language pathologists in schools develop individual or group programs, counsel parents, and may assist teachers with classroom activities.

Speech-language pathologists keep records on the initial evaluation, progress, and discharge of clients. This helps pinpoint problems, tracks client progress, and justifies the cost of treatment when applying for reimbursement. They counsel individuals and their families concerning communication disorders and how to cope with the stress and misunderstanding that often accompany them. They also work with family members to recognize and change behavior patterns that impede communication and treatment and show them communication-enhancing techniques to use at home.

Some speech-language pathologists conduct research on how people communicate. Others design and develop equipment or techniques for diagnosing and treating speech problems.

Audiologists work with people who have hearing, balance, and related problems. They use audiometers and other testing devices to measure the loudness at which a person begins to hear sounds, the ability to distinguish between sounds, and the nature and extent of hearing loss. Audiologists interpret these results and may coordinate them with medical, educational, and psychological information to make a diagnosis and determine a course of treatment.

Hearing disorders can result from trauma at birth, viral infections, genetic disorders, or exposure to loud noise. Treatment may include examining and cleaning the ear canal, fitting and dispensing a hearing aid or other assistive device, and audiologic rehabilitation (including auditory training or instruction in speech or lip reading). Audiologists may recommend, fit, and dispense personal or large area amplification systems, such as hearing aids and alerting devices. Audiologists provide fitting and tuning of cochlear implants and provide the necessary rehabilitation for adjustment to listening with implant amplification systems. They also test noise levels in workplaces and conduct hearing protection programs in industry, as well as in schools and communities.

Audiologists provide direct clinical services to individuals with hearing or balance disorders. In audiology (hearing) clinics, they may independently develop and carry out treatment programs. Audiologists, in a variety of settings, work as members of interdisciplinary professional teams in planning and implementing service delivery for children and adults, from birth to old age. Similar to speech-language pathologists, audiologists keep records on the initial evaluation, progress, and discharge of clients. These records help pinpoint problems, track client progress, and justify the cost of treatment, when applying for reimbursement.

Audiologists may conduct research on types of, and treatment for, hearing, balance, and related disorders. Others design and develop equipment or techniques for diagnosing and treating these disorders.

Working Conditions

Speech-language pathologists and audiologists usually work at a desk or table in clean comfortable surroundings. The job is not physically demanding but does require attention to detail and intense concentration. The emotional needs of clients and their families may be demanding. Most full-time speech-language pathologists and audiologists work about 40 hours per week; some work part-time. Those who work on a contract basis may spend a substantial amount of time traveling between facilities.

Employment

Speech-language pathologists and audiologists held about 87,000 jobs in 1996. About one-half provided services in preschools, elementary and secondary schools, or colleges and universities. More than one in ten were in hospitals. Others were in offices of physicians; offices of speech-language pathologists and audiologists; speech, language, and hearing centers; home health care agencies; or other facilities. Some were in private practice, working either as solo practitioners or in a group practice. Some speech-language pathologists and audiologists contract to provide services in schools, hospitals, or nursing homes, or work as consultants to industry. Audiologists are more likely to be employed in independent healthcare offices, while speech-language pathologists are more likely to work in school settings.

Training, Other Qualifications, and Advancement

Of the states that regulate licensing (44 for speech-language pathologists and 47 for audiologists), almost all require a master's degree or equivalent. Other requirements are 300 to 375 hours of supervised clinical experience, a passing score on a national examination, and nine months of postgraduate professional clinical experience. Thirty-four states have continuing education requirements for licensure renewal. Medicaid, Medicare, and private health insurers generally require a practitioner to be licensed to qualify for reimbursement.

About 230 colleges and universities offer graduate programs in speech-language pathology. Courses cover anatomy and physiology of the areas of the body involved in speech, language, and hearing; the development of normal speech, language, and hearing; the nature of disorders; acoustics; and psychological aspects of communication. Graduate students also learn to evaluate and treat speech, language, and hearing disorders and receive supervised clinical training in communication disorders.

About 120 colleges and universities offer graduate programs in audiology in the United States. Course work includes anatomy; physiology; basic science; math; physics; genetics; normal and abnormal communication development; auditory, balance and neural systems assessment and treatment; audiologic rehabilitation; and ethics.

Speech-language pathologists can acquire the Certificate of Clinical Competence in Speech-Language Pathology (CCC-SLP) offered by the American Speech-Language-Hearing Association, and audiologists can earn the Certificate of Clinical Competence in Audiology (CCC-A). To earn a CCC, a person must have a graduate degree and 375 hours of supervised clinical experience, complete a 36-week postgraduate clinical fellowship, and pass a written examination.

Speech-language pathologists and audiologists should be able to effectively communicate diagnostic test results, diagnoses, and proposed treatment in a manner easily understood by their clients. They must be able to approach problems objectively and provide support to clients and their families. Because a client's progress may be slow, patience, compassion, and good listening skills are necessary.

Speech-language pathologists and audiologists may work in a variety of settings, including schools, hospitals, health departments, clinics, and private practices. Some members of these professions also serve as clinical supervisors for student clinicians, professors in universities and colleges, or conduct research.

Job Outlook

Employment of speech-language pathologists and audiologists is expected to increase much faster than the average for all occupations through the year 2006. Employment in health and rehabilitation services will increase as a result of advances in medical technology and growth in the elderly population. Because hearing loss is strongly associated with aging, rapid growth in the population age 55 and over will cause the number of persons with hearing impairment to increase markedly. In addition, baby boomers are now entering middle age, when the possibility of neurological disorders and associated speech, language, and hearing impairments increases. Medical advances are also improving the survival rate of premature infants and trauma and stroke victims, who then need assessment and possible treatment.

Employment in schools will increase along with growth in elementary and secondary school enrollments, including enrollment of special education students. Federal law guarantees special education and related services to all eligible children with disabilities. Greater awareness of the importance of early identification and diagnosis of speech, language, and hearing disorders will also increase employment.

The number of speech-language pathologists and audiologists in private practice, though small, is likely to rise sharply due to the increasing use of contract services by managed care, hospitals, schools, and nursing homes. In addition to job openings stemming from rapid job growth over the 1996-2006 period, some openings for speech-language pathologists and audiologists will arise from the need to replace those who leave the occupation.

Earnings

Median weekly earnings of full-time salaried speech-language pathologists and audiologists were about $690 in 1996. The middle 50 percent earned between $560 and $880. The lowest 10 percent earned less than $440 and the top 10 percent more than $1,160.

According to a 1997 survey by the American Speech-Language-Hearing Association, the median annual salary for full-time certified speech-language pathologists was $44,000; for audiologists, $43,000. Certified speech-language pathologists with one to three years of experience earned a median annual salary of $38,000; licensed audiologists with one to three years of experience earned $32,000. Speech-language pathologists with 22 years' experience earned a median annual salary of $52,000, while audiologists with comparable experience earned about $55,000. Salaries also vary according to geographic location and type of employment facility.

Related Occupations

Speech-language pathologists specialize in the prevention, diagnosis, and treatment of speech and language problems. Workers in related occupations include occupational therapists, optometrists, physical therapists, psychologists, recreational therapists, and rehabilitation counselors.

Audiologists specialize in the prevention, diagnosis, and treatment of hearing problems. Workers in related occupations include neurologists, neonatologists, acoustical engineers, industrial hygienists, and other rehabilitation professionals.

Sources of Additional Information

State licensing boards in each state can provide information on licensure requirements. State departments of education can supply information on certification requirements for those who wish to work in public schools.

General information on careers in speech-language pathology and audiology is available from:

❑ American Speech-Language-Hearing Association, 10801 Rockville Pike, Rockville, MD 20852. Homepage: http://www.asha.org

Information on a career in audiology is also available from:

❑ American Academy of Audiology, 8201 Greensboro Dr., Suite 300, McLean, VA 22102.

Stock Clerks

(*D.O.T.* 219.367-018, .387-026 and -030; 221.587-018 and -022; 222.167, .367-014, -026, -038, -042, -050, and -062, .387-018, -026, -030, -034, -042, -058, and -062, .487, .587-022 and -054, .684, .687-038 and -046; 229.367, .587-014; 249.367-058; 299.367-014, .677-014; 339.687; 381.687-010; and 969.367)

Significant Points

✓ *Slower than average growth is expected as additional automation increases worker productivity.*

✓ *Many stock clerk positions are entry-level and do not require more than a high school degree.*

Nature of the Work

Stock clerks receive, unpack, check, store, and track merchandise or materials. They keep records of items entering or leaving the stock room and inspect damaged or spoiled goods. They sort, organize, and mark items with identifying codes, such as prices or stock or inventory control codes, so that inventories can be located quickly and easily. In many firms, stock clerks use hand-held scanners connected to computers to keep inventories up to date. In retail stores, stock clerks bring merchandise to the sales floor and stock shelves and racks. In stockrooms and warehouses, they store materials in bins, on floors, or on shelves. In larger establishments, where they may be responsible for only one specific task, they may be known as inventory clerk, stock-control clerk, merchandise distributor, order filler, property custodian, or storekeeper. In smaller firms, they may also be responsible for tasks usually handled by shipping and receiving clerks.

Working Conditions

Stock clerks work in a wide variety of businesses, institutions, and industries. Some work in warehouses, stock rooms, or in shipping and receiving rooms that may not be temperature controlled. Others may spend time in cold storage rooms or outside on loading platforms, where they are exposed to the weather. Most jobs involve frequent standing, bending, walking, and stretching. Some lifting and carrying of smaller items may be involved. Although automation, robotics, and pneumatic devices have lessened the physical demands in this occupation, their use remains somewhat limited. Work still can be strenuous, even though mechanical material-handling equipment is employed to move heavy items. The typical workweek is Monday through Friday; however, evening and weekend hours are standard for some jobs, such as stock clerks who work in retail trade, and may be required in others when large shipments are involved or when inventory is taken.

Employment

Stock clerks held about 1,844,000 jobs in 1996, with almost 80 percent working in wholesale or retail trade. The greatest numbers were employed in grocery and department stores, respectively. Jobs for stock clerks are found in all parts of the country, but most work in large urban areas that have many large suburban shopping centers, warehouses, and factories.

Training, Other Qualifications, and Advancement

Many stock clerk jobs are entry-level and do not require more than a high school degree. Employers, however, increasingly prefer to hire those with some familiarity with computers and other high technology office and business equipment. Those who have taken business courses or have previous business or specific job-related experience may be preferred. Also, good oral and written communications skills are becoming essential. Typing, filing, record keeping, and other clerical skills are important functions of these occupations. In larger, more automated facilities, these tasks may be accomplished electronically.

Stock clerks who handle jewelry, liquor, or drugs may be bonded. Trainees usually develop the necessary skills on the job. This informal training lasts from several days to a few months, depending on the complexity of the job.

Stock clerks usually learn the job by doing simple tasks under close supervision. They learn how to count and mark stock, and then start keeping records and taking inventory. Stock clerks whose sole responsibility is to bring merchandise to the sales floor and stock shelves and racks need little or no training. Training in the use of automated equipment is usually done informally, on the job. As these occupations become more automated, however, workers in these jobs may need longer training in order to master the use of the equipment.

Strength, stamina, good eyesight, and an ability to work at repetitive tasks, sometimes under pressure, are important characteristics for stock clerks.

Advancement opportunities vary with the place of employment. In large firms, stock clerks can advance to invoice clerk, stock control clerk, or procurement clerk. With additional training, some stock clerks advance to jobs as warehouse manager or purchasing agent.

Job Outlook

Job prospects for stock clerks should be favorable even though employment is expected to grow more slowly than the average for all occupations through the year 2006. This occupation is very large, and many job openings will occur each year to replace those who transfer to other jobs or leave the labor force. Many jobs are entry-level, and many vacancies tend to occur naturally through normal career progression.

The growing use of computers for inventory control and the installation of new, automated equipment are expected to slow growth in demand for stock clerks somewhat. This is especially true in manufacturing and wholesale trade, industries whose operations are automated most easily. In addition to computerized inventory control systems, firms in these industries are expected to rely more on sophisticated conveyor belts and automatic high stackers to store and retrieve goods. Also, expanded use of battery-powered, driverless automatically guided vehicles can be expected.

Employment of stock clerks who work in grocery, general merchandise, department, apparel, and accessories stores is expected to be somewhat less affected by automation because much of their work is done manually on the sales floor and is difficult to automate. In addition, the ever-increasing role of large retail outlets and warehouses, as well as catalogue, mail, telephone, and Internet shopping services in the nation's economy should bolster employment of stock clerks in these sectors of retail trade.

Earnings

Median weekly earnings of stock clerks were $429 in 1996.

Stock clerks usually receive the same benefits as most other workers. If uniforms are required, employers usually either provide the uniforms, or an allowance to purchase them.

Related Occupations

Other workers who handle, move, organize, and store materials include shipping and receiving clerks, distributing clerks, routing clerks, stock supervisors, and cargo checkers.

Sources of Additional Information

State employment service offices can provide information about job openings for stock clerks. Also, see clerical and sales occupations for sources of additional information.

General information about stock clerks can be obtained by contacting:

❑ National Retail Federation, 325 Seventh Street, NW, Suite 1000, Washington, DC 20004. Homepage: http://, owww.nrf.com

Surgical Technologists

(D.O.T. 079.374-022)

Significant Points

✓ *Most educational programs for surgical technologists last approximately one year and result in a certificate.*

✓ *Increased demand for surgical technologists is expected as the number of surgical procedures grows.*

Nature of the Work

Surgical technologists, also called surgical or operating room technicians, assist in operations under the supervision of surgeons, registered nurses, or other surgical personnel. Before an operation, surgical technologists help set up the operating room with surgical instruments and equipment, sterile linens, and sterile solutions. They assemble, adjust, and check nonsterile equipment to ensure that it is working properly. Technologists also prepare patients for surgery by washing, shaving, and disinfecting incision sites. They transport patients to the operating room, help position them on the operating table, and cover them with sterile surgical "drapes." Technologists also observe patients' vital signs, check charts, and help the surgical team scrub and put on gloves, gowns, and masks.

During surgery, technologists pass instruments and other sterile supplies to surgeons and surgeon assistants. They may hold retractors, cut sutures, and help count sponges, needles, supplies, and instruments. Surgical technologists help prepare, care for, and dispose of specimens taken for laboratory analysis and may help apply dressings. They may operate sterilizers, lights, or suction machines, and help operate diagnostic equipment. Technologists may also maintain supplies of fluids, such as plasma and blood.

After an operation, surgical technologists may help transfer patients to the recovery room and clean and restock the operating room.

Working Conditions

Surgical technologists work in clean, well-lighted, cool environments. They must stand for long periods and remain alert during operations. At times they may be exposed to communicable diseases and unpleasant sights, odors, and materials.

Most surgical technologists work a regular 40-hour week, although they may be on call or work nights, weekends and holidays on a rotating basis.

Employment

Surgical technologists held about 49,000 jobs in 1996. Most are employed by hospitals, mainly in operating and delivery rooms. Others are employed in clinics and surgical centers, and in the offices of physicians and dentists who perform outpatient surgery. A few, known as private scrubs, are employed directly by surgeons who have special surgical teams like those for liver transplants.

Training, Other Qualifications, and Advancement

Surgical technologists receive their training in formal programs offered by community and junior colleges, vocational schools, universities, hospitals, and the military. In 1997, the Commission on Accreditation of Allied Health Education Programs (CAAHEP) recognized 145 accredited programs. High school graduation normally is required for admission. Programs last 9 to 24 months and lead to a certificate, diploma, or associate degree. Shorter programs are designed for students who are already licensed practical nurses or military personnel.

Programs provide classroom education and supervised clinical experience. Students take courses in anatomy, physiology, microbiology, pharmacology, professional ethics, and medical terminology. Other studies cover the care and safety of patients during surgery, aseptic techniques, and surgical procedures. Students also learn to sterilize instruments; prevent and control infection; and handle special drugs, solutions, supplies, and equipment.

Technologists may obtain voluntary professional certification from the Liaison Council on Certification for the Surgical Technologist by graduating from a formal program and passing a national certification examination. They may then use the designation Certified Surgical Technologist, or CST. Continuing education or reexamination is required to maintain certification, which must be renewed every six years. Graduation from a CAAHEP-accredited program will be a prerequisite for certification by March 2000. Most employers prefer to hire certified technologists.

Surgical technologists need manual dexterity to handle instruments quickly. They also must be conscientious, orderly, and emotionally stable to handle the demands of the operating room environment. Technologists must respond quickly and know procedures well so that they may have instruments ready for surgeons without having to be told. They are expected to keep abreast of new developments in the field. Recommended high school courses include health, biology, chemistry, and mathematics.

Technologists advance by specializing in a particular area of surgery, such as neurosurgery or open heart surgery. They may also work as circulating technologists. A circulating technologist is the "unsterile" member of the surgical team who prepares patients; helps with anesthesia; gets, opens, and holds packages for the "sterile" persons during the procedure; interviews the patient before surgery; keeps a written account of the surgical procedure; and answers the surgeon's questions about the patient during the surgery. With additional training, some technologists advance to first assistants, who help with retracting, sponging, suturing, cauterizing bleeders, and closing and treating wounds. Some surgical technologists manage central supply departments in hospitals, or take positions with insurance companies, sterile supply services, and operating equipment firms.

Job Outlook

Employment of surgical technologists is expected to grow faster than the average for all occupations through the year 2006 as the volume of surgery increases. The number of surgical procedures is expected to rise as the population grows and ages. Older people require more surgical procedures. Technological advances, such as fiber optics and laser technology, will also permit new surgical procedures.

Hospitals will continue to be the primary employer of surgical technologists, although much faster employment growth is expected in offices and clinics of physicians, including ambulatory surgical centers.

Earnings

According to a 1996 membership survey conducted by the Association of Surgical Technologists, the average annual salary for surgical technologists, excluding overtime or on-call pay, was about $25,000. Beginning technologists earned about $20,900 a year, while the most experienced technologists earned about $28,000 a year.

Related Occupations

Other health occupations requiring approximately one year of training after high school include licensed practical nurses, respiratory therapy technicians, medical laboratory assistants, medical assistants, dental assistants, optometric assistants, and physical therapy aides.

Sources of Additional Information

For additional information on a career as a surgical technologist and a list of CAAHEP-accredited programs, contact:
- ❏ Association of Surgical Technologists, 7108-C South Alton Way, Englewood, CO 80112. Homepage: http://www.ast.org/

For information on certification, contact:
- ❏ Liaison Council on Certification for the Surgical Technologist, 7790 East Arapahoe Rd., Suite 240, Englewood, CO 80112-1274.

Teacher Aides

(*D.O.T.* 099.327; 219.467; 249.367-074, -086)

Significant Points

- ✓ *Half of all teacher aides work part-time.*
- ✓ *Educational requirements range from a high school diploma to some college training.*
- ✓ *Strong demand for aides to assist and monitor students, to provide teachers with clerical assistance, and to help teachers meet the education needs of a growing special education population will contribute to much faster than average employment growth.*

Nature of the Work

Teacher aides, also called instructional aides or paraeducators, provide instructional and clerical support for classroom teachers, allowing teachers more time for lesson planning and teaching. Teacher aides tutor and assist children in learning class material using the teacher's lesson plans, providing students with individualized attention. Aides also assist and supervise students in the cafeteria, schoolyard, school discipline center, or on field trips. They record grades, set up equipment, and help prepare materials for instruction.

In large school districts, some teacher aides are hired to perform exclusively noninstructional or clerical tasks, such as monitoring nonacademic settings. Playground and lunchroom attendants are examples of such aides. Most teacher aides, however, perform a combination of instructional and clerical duties. They generally instruct children, under the direction and guidance of teachers. They work with students individually or in small groups—listening while students read, reviewing or reinforcing class work, or helping them find information for reports. At the secondary school level, teacher aides often specialize in a certain subject, such as math or science. Aides often take charge of special projects and prepare equipment or exhibits, such as for a science demonstration. Some aides work in computer laboratories, assisting students using computers and educational software programs.

In addition to instructing, assisting, and supervising students, teacher aides grade tests and papers, check homework, keep health and attendance records, type, file, and duplicate materials. They also may stock supplies, operate audiovisual equipment, and keep classroom equipment in order.

Many teacher aides work extensively with special education students. Schools are becoming more inclusive, integrating special education students into general education classrooms. As a result, teacher aides in general education and special education classrooms increasingly assist students with disabilities. Aides may attend to a student's physical needs, including feeding, teaching good grooming habits, or assisting students riding the school bus. They also may provide personal attention to students with other special needs, such as those whose families live in poverty, or students who speak English as a second language or need remedial education. Aides help assess a student's progress by observing performance and recording relevant data.

Working Conditions

Half of all teacher aides work part-time. Most aides who provide educational instruction work the traditional nine- to ten-month school year, usually in a classroom setting. Aides also may work outdoors supervising recess when weather allows, and spend much of their time standing, walking, or kneeling.

Seeing students develop and gain appreciation of the joy of learning can be very rewarding. However, working closely with students can be both physically and emotionally tiring. Teacher aides who work with special education students may perform more strenuous tasks, including lifting, as they help students with their daily routine. Those who perform clerical work may feel overwhelmed by tedious administrative duties, such as making copies or typing.

Employment

Teacher aides held about 981,000 jobs in 1996. About nine out of ten worked in elementary and secondary schools, mostly in the lower grades. A significant number assisted special education teachers in working with children who have disabilities. Most of the others worked in child daycare centers and religious organizations.

Training, Other Qualifications, and Advancement

Educational requirements for teacher aides range from a high school diploma to some college training. Aides with instructional responsibilities usually require more training than those who don't perform teaching tasks. Increasingly, employers prefer aides who have some college training. Some teacher aides are aspiring teachers who are working towards their degree while gaining experience. Many schools require previous experience in working with children. Schools may also require a valid driver's license, and perform a background check on applicants.

A number of two-year and community colleges offer associate degree programs that prepare graduates to work as teacher aides. However, most teacher aides receive on-the-job training. Those who tutor and review lessons with students must have a thorough understanding of class materials and instructional methods, and should be familiar with the organization and operation of a school. Aides also must know how to operate audiovisual equipment, keep records, and prepare instructional materials, as well as have adequate computer skills.

Teacher aides should enjoy working with children from a wide range of cultural backgrounds, and be able to handle classroom situations with fairness and patience. Aides also must demonstrate initiative and a willingness to follow a teacher's directions. They must have good oral and writing skills and be able to communicate effectively with students and teachers. Teacher aides who speak a second language, especially Spanish, are in great demand to communicate with growing numbers of students and parents whose primary language is not English.

About half of all states have established guidelines or minimum educational standards for the hiring and training of teacher aides, and an increasing number of states are in the process of implementing them. Although requirements vary by state, most require an individual to have at least a high school diploma or general equivalency degree (GED), or some college training.

Advancement for teacher aides, usually in the form of higher earnings or increased responsibility, comes primarily with experience or additional education. Some school districts provide time away from the job or tuition reimbursement so that teacher aides can earn their bachelor's degrees and pursue licensed teaching positions. In return for tuition reimbursement, aides are often required to commit to teaching a certain length of time for the school district.

Job Outlook

Employment of teacher aides is expected to grow much faster than the average for all occupations through the year 2006. Student enrollments at the elementary and secondary level are expected to rise, spurring strong demand for teacher aides to assist and monitor students and provide teachers with clerical assistance. Teacher aides will also be required to help teachers meet the educational needs of a growing special education population, particularly as these students are increasingly assimilated into general education classrooms. Education reform and the rising number of students who speak English as a second language will continue to contribute to the demand for teacher aides. In addition to jobs stemming from employment growth, numerous job openings will arise as workers transfer to other occupations, leave the labor force to assume family responsibilities, return to school, or leave for other reasons—characteristic of occupations that require limited formal education and offer relatively low pay.

The number of special education programs is growing in response to increasing enrollments of students with disabilities. Federal legislation mandates appropriate education for all children, and emphasizes placing disabled children into regular school settings, when possible. Children with special needs require much personal attention, and special education teachers, as well as general education teachers with special education students, rely heavily on teacher aides. At the secondary school level, teacher aides work with special education students as job coaches, and help students make the transition from school to work.

School reforms which call for more individual instruction should further enhance employment opportunities for teacher aides. Schools are hiring more teacher aides to provide students with the personal instruction and remedial education they need.

Teacher aide employment is sensitive to changes in state and local expenditures for education. Pressures on education budgets are greater in some states and localities than in others. A number of teacher aide positions, such as those in Head Start classrooms, are financed through federal government programs, which also may be affected by budget constraints.

Earnings

According to a survey of salaries in public schools, conducted by the Educational Research Service, aides involved in teaching activities averaged $9.04 an hour in 1995-96; those performing only nonteaching activities averaged $8.52 an hour. Earnings varied by region, work experience, and academic qualifications. About three out of ten teacher aides belonged to unions in 1996—mainly the American Federation of Teachers and the National Education Association—which bargain with school systems over wages, hours, and the terms and conditions of employment.

Related Occupations

Teacher aides who instruct children have duties similar to those of preschool, elementary, and secondary school teachers and school librarians. However, teacher aides do not have the same level of responsibility or training. The support activities of teacher aides and their educational backgrounds are similar to those of child-care workers, family daycare providers, library technicians, and library assistants.

Sources of Additional Information

For information on teacher aides, including training and unionization, and on a wide range of education-related subjects, contact:

❑ American Federation of Teachers, Organizing Department, 555 New Jersey Ave. NW, Washington, DC 20001.

For information on a career as a teacher aide, contact:

❑ National Resource Center for Paraprofessionals in Education and Related Services, 25 West 43rd St., Room 620, New York, NY 10036.

School superintendents and state departments of education can provide details about employment requirements.

Traffic, Shipping, and Receiving Clerks

(D.O.T. 209.367-042; 214.587-014; 219.367-022 and -030; 221.367-022; 222.367-066, .387-014, -022, -050, and -054, .485, .567-010 and -014, .587-018, -034, and -058, .687-022 and -030; 248.362-010, .367-014 and -022; 919.687-010; and 976.687-018)

Significant Points

✓ *Slower than average growth is expected as additional automation increases worker productivity.*

✓ *Many traffic, shipping, and receiving clerk jobs are entry-level and do not require more than a high school degree.*

Nature of the Work

Traffic, shipping, and receiving clerks keep records of all goods shipped and received. Their duties depend on the size of the establishment and the level of automation employed. Larger companies typically are better able to finance the purchase of computers and other equipment to handle some or all of a clerk's responsibilities. In smaller companies, an individual clerk may be responsible for maintaining records, preparing shipments, and accepting deliveries.

Traffic clerks maintain records on the destination, weight, and charges on all incoming and outgoing freight. They verify rate charges by comparing the classification of materials with rate charts. In many companies, this work may be automated. Information either is scanned, or is hand-entered into a computer for use by accounting or other departments within the company. Also, they keep a file of claims for overcharges and for damage to goods in transit.

Shipping clerks are record keepers responsible for all outgoing shipments. They prepare shipping documents and mailing labels, and make sure orders have been filled correctly. Also, they record items taken from inventory and note when orders were filled. Sometimes they fill the order themselves, obtaining merchandise from the stockroom, noting when inventories run low, and wrapping it or packing it in shipping containers. They also address and label packages, look up and compute freight or postal rates, and record the weight and cost of each shipment. Shipping clerks also may prepare invoices and furnish information about shipments to other parts of the company, such as the accounting department. Once a shipment is checked and ready to go, shipping clerks may move the goods from the plant—sometimes by forklift truck—to the shipping dock and direct its loading.

Receiving clerks perform tasks similar to those of shipping clerks. They determine whether orders have been filled correctly by verifying incoming shipments against the original order and the accompanying bill of lading or invoice. They make a record of the shipment and the condition of its contents. In many firms, receiving clerks record the information by using hand-held scanners to read bar codes on incoming products or by hand-entering this information into computers. These data then can be transferred to the appropriate departments. The shipment is checked for any discrepancies in quantity, price, and discounts. Receiving clerks may route or move shipments to the proper department, warehouse section, or stockroom. They may also arrange for adjustments with shippers whenever merchandise is lost or damaged. Receiving clerks in small businesses also may perform some stock clerk duties. In larger establishments, receiving clerks may control all receiving-platform operations, such as truck scheduling, recording of shipments, and handling of damaged goods.

Working Conditions

Traffic, shipping, and receiving clerks work in a wide variety of businesses, institutions, and industries. Some work in warehouses, stock rooms, or in shipping and receiving rooms that may not be temperature controlled. Others may spend time in cold storage rooms or outside on loading platforms, where they are exposed to the weather. Most jobs involve frequent standing, bending, walking, and stretching. Some lifting and carrying of smaller items may be involved. Although automation, robotics, and pneumatic devices have lessened the physical demands in this occupation, their use remains somewhat limited. Work still can be strenuous, even though mechanical material-handling equipment is employed to move heavy items. The typical workweek is Monday through Friday; however, evening and weekend hours are standard for some jobs, and may be required in others when large shipments are involved or when inventory is taken.

Employment

Traffic, shipping, and receiving clerks held about 759,000 jobs in 1996. Nearly seven out of eight were employed in manufacturing or by wholesale or retail establishments. Although jobs for traffic, shipping, and receiving clerks are found throughout the country, most clerks work in urban areas, where shipping depots in factories and wholesale establishments generally are located. Many traffic, shipping, and receiving clerks work for the U.S. Postal Service.

Training, Other Qualifications, and Advancement

Most traffic, shipping, and receiving clerk jobs are entry-level, and do not require more than a high school degree. Employers, however, increasingly prefer to hire those with some familiarity with computers and other high technology office and business equipment. Those who have taken business courses or have previous business, dispatching, or specific job-related experience may be preferred. Also, good oral and written communications skills are becoming essential. Typing, filing, record keeping, and other clerical skills are important functions of these occupations. In larger, more automated facilities, these tasks may be accomplished electronically.

Traffic, shipping, and receiving clerks who handle jewelry, liquor, or drugs may be bonded.

Traffic, shipping, and receiving clerks usually learn the job by doing simple tasks under close supervision. They learn how to count and mark stock, and then start keeping records and taking inventory. Traffic, shipping, and receiving clerks start out by checking items to be shipped and then attaching labels and making sure the addresses are correct. Training in the use of automated equipment is usually done informally, on the job. As these occupations become more automated, however, workers in these jobs may need longer training in order to master the use of the equipment.

Strength, stamina, good eyesight, and an ability to work at repetitive tasks, sometimes under pressure, are important characteristics for traffic, shipping, and receiving clerks.

Advancement opportunities vary with the place of employment.

Traffic, shipping, and receiving clerks are promoted to head clerk, and those with a broad understanding of shipping and receiving may enter a related field such as industrial traffic management. With additional training, some traffic, shipping, and receiving clerks advance to jobs as warehouse manager or purchasing agent.

Job Outlook

Employment of traffic, shipping, and receiving clerks is expected to increase about as fast as the average for all occupations through the year 2006. Employment growth will continue to be affected by automation, as all but the smallest firms move to hold down labor costs by using computers to store and retrieve shipping and receiving records.

Methods of material handling have changed significantly in recent years. Large warehouses are increasingly automated, using equipment such as computerized conveyor systems, robots, computer-directed trucks, and automatic data storage and retrieval systems. Automation, coupled with the growing use of hand-held scanners and personal computers in shipping and receiving departments, has increased the productivity of these workers.

Despite automation, job openings will continue to arise due to increasing economic and trade activity, and because certain tasks cannot be automated. For example, someone needs to check shipments before they go out and when they arrive to ensure everything is in order. However, most job openings will occur because of the need to replace traffic, shipping, and receiving clerks who leave the occupation. Because this is an entry-level occupation, many vacancies are created by normal career progression.

Earnings

Median weekly earnings of traffic, shipping, and receiving clerks were $367 in 1996.

Workers in material recording, scheduling, dispatching, and distributing occupations usually receive the same benefits as most other workers. If uniforms are required, employers usually either provide the uniforms, or an allowance to purchase them.

Related Occupations

Traffic, shipping, and receiving clerks record, check, and often store the materials that a company receives. They also process and pack goods for shipment. Other workers who perform similar duties are stock clerks, material clerks, distributing clerks, routing clerks, express clerks, expediters, and order fillers.

Sources of Additional Information

General information about traffic, shipping, and receiving clerks can be obtained by contacting:

❑ National Retail Federation, 325 Seventh St. NW, Suite 1000, Washington, DC 20004. Homepage: http://www.nrf.com

Travel Agents

(D.O.T. 252.152-010)

Significant Points

✓ *Training at a postsecondary vocational school or college or university is increasingly important for getting a job.*

✓ *Projected faster-than-average employment growth reflects expected increases in spending on pleasure and business travel.*

Nature of the Work

Constantly changing air fares and schedules, thousands of available vacation packages and business/pleasure trips, and the vast amount of travel information advertised on the Internet, makes travel planning frustrating and time-consuming. Many people who travel turn to travel agents, who assess their needs and make the best possible travel arrangements for them. Also, many major cruise lines, resorts, and specialty travel groups use travel agents to promote travel packages to the millions of people who travel every year.

Depending on the needs of the client, travel agents give advice on destinations, make arrangements for transportation, hotel accommodations, car rentals, tours, and recreation, or plan the right vacation package or business/pleasure trip. They may also advise on weather conditions, restaurants, and tourist attractions and recreation. For international travel, agents also provide information on customs regulations, required papers (passports, visas, and certificates of vaccination), and currency exchange rates.

Travel agents consult a variety of published and computer-based sources for information on departure and arrival times, fares, and hotel ratings and accommodations. They may visit hotels, resorts, and restaurants to judge, firsthand, their comfort, cleanliness, and quality of food and service so they can base recommendations on their own travel experiences or those of colleagues or clients.

Travel agents also promote their services, using telemarketing, direct mail, and the Internet. They make presentations to social and special interest groups, arrange advertising displays, and suggest company-sponsored trips to business managers.

Depending on the size of the travel agency, an agent may specialize by type of travel, such as leisure or business, or destination, such as Europe or Africa.

Working Conditions

Travel agents spend most of their time behind a desk conferring with clients, completing paperwork, contacting airlines and hotels for travel arrangements, and promoting group tours. They may be under a great deal of pressure at times, such as during vacation seasons. Many agents, especially those who are self-employed, frequently work long hours. With advanced computer systems and telecommunication networks, some travel agents are able to work at home. These agents make travel arrangements for their clients, and promote travel offered by the travel agency and organizations they represent.

Employment

Travel agents held about 142,000 jobs in 1996 and are found in every part of the country. More than nine out of ten salaried agents worked for travel agencies; some worked for membership organizations.

Training, Other Qualifications, and Advancement

The minimum requirement for those interested in becoming a travel agent is a high school diploma or equivalent. With technology and computerization having a profound effect on the work of travel agents, formal or specialized training is becoming increasingly important. Many vocational schools offer 6- to 12-week full-time travel agent programs, as well as evening and weekend programs. Travel courses are also offered in public adult education programs and in community and four-year colleges. A few colleges offer bachelor's or master's degrees in travel and tourism. Although few college courses relate directly to the travel industry, a college education is sometimes desired by employers to establish a background in areas such as computer science, geography, communication, foreign languages, and world history. Courses in accounting and business management also are important, especially for those who expect to manage or start their own travel agencies. Travel agents must be well-organized, accurate, and meticulous to compile information from various sources, and plan and organize their clients' travel itineraries. Other desirable qualifications include good writing, computer, and sales skills.

The American Society of Travel Agents (ASTA) offers a correspondence course that provides a basic understanding of the travel industry. Travel agencies also provide on-the-job training for their employees, a significant part of which consists of computer instruction. Computer skills are required by all employers to operate airline and centralized reservation systems.

Experienced travel agents can take advanced self or group study courses from the Institute of Certified Travel Agents (ICTA), that lead to the designation of Certified Travel Counselor (CTC). The ICTA also offers marketing and sales skills development programs and destination specialist programs, which provide a detailed knowledge of the geographic areas of North America, Western Europe, the Caribbean, and the Pacific Rim.

Travel experience is an asset since personal knowledge about a city or foreign country often helps to influence clients' travel plans, as is experience as an airline reservation agent. Patience and the ability to gain the confidence of clients are also useful qualities.

Some employees start as reservation clerks or receptionists in travel agencies. With experience and some formal training, they can take on greater responsibilities and eventually assume travel agent duties. In agencies with many offices, travel agents may advance to office manager or to other managerial positions.

Those who start their own agencies generally have experience in an established agency. They must generally gain formal supplier or corporation approval before they can receive commissions. Suppliers or corporations are organizations of airlines, ship lines, or rail lines. The Airlines Reporting Corporation and the International Airlines Travel Agency Network, for example, are the approving bodies for airlines. To gain approval, an agency must be financially sound and employ at least one experienced manager/travel agent.

There are no federal licensing requirements for travel agents. However, nine states require some form of registration or certification of retail sellers of travel services: California, Florida, Hawaii, Illinois, Iowa, Ohio, Oregon, Rhode Island, and Washington. More information may be obtained by contacting the Office of the Attorney General or Department of Commerce for each state.

Job Outlook

Employment of travel agents is expected to grow faster than the average for all occupations through the year 2006. Many job openings will arise as new agencies open and existing agencies expand, but most openings will occur as experienced agents transfer to other occupations or leave the labor force.

Spending on travel is expected to increase significantly over the next decade. With rising household incomes, smaller families, and an increasing number of older people who are more likely to travel, more people are expected to travel on vacation—and to do so more frequently—than in the past. In fact, many people take more than one vacation a year. Business-related travel should also grow as business activity expands. Employment of managerial, professional, and sales workers—those who do most business travel—is projected to grow at least as fast as the average for all occupations.

Charter flights and larger, more efficient planes have brought air transportation within the budgets of more people. The easing of government regulation of air fares and routes has fostered greater competition among airlines, resulting in more affordable service. In addition, American travel agents organize tours for the growing number of foreign visitors. Also, travel agents are often able to offer various travel packages at a substantial discount. Although most travel agencies now have automated reservation systems, this has not weakened demand for travel agents.

Some developments, however, may reduce job opportunities for travel agents in the future. The Internet allows people to access travel information from their personal computers and make their own travel arrangements. Suppliers of travel services are increasingly able to make their services available through other means, such as electronic ticketing machines and remote ticket printers. Also, airline companies have put a cap on the amount of commissions they will pay to travel agencies. The full effect of these practices, though, has yet to be determined as many consumers prefer to use a professional travel agent to ensure reliability and save time and, in some cases, money.

The travel industry generally is sensitive to economic downturns and international political crises, when travel plans are likely to be deferred. Therefore, the number of job opportunities fluctuates.

Earnings

Experience, sales ability, and the size and location of the agency determine the salary of a travel agent. According to a Louis Harris survey, conducted for Travel Weekly, 1996 median annual earnings of travel agents on straight salary with less than one year experience were $16,400; from one to three years, $20,400; from three to five years, $22,300; from five to ten years, $26,300; and more than ten years, $32,600. Salaried agents usually have standard benefits, such as medical insurance coverage and paid vacations, that self-employed agents must provide for themselves. Among agencies, those focusing on corporate sales pay higher salaries and provide more extensive benefits, on average, than those who focus on leisure sales.

Earnings of travel agents who own their agencies depend mainly on commissions from airlines and other carriers, cruise lines, tour operators, and lodging places. Commissions for domestic travel arrangements, cruises, hotels, sightseeing tours, and car rentals are about 7 to 10 percent of the total sale; and for international travel, about 10 percent. They may also charge clients a service fee for the time and expense involved in planning a trip.

During the first year of business or while awaiting corporation approval, self-employed travel agents generally have low earnings. Their income usually is limited to commissions from hotels, cruises, and tour operators and to nominal fees for making complicated arrangements. Even established agents have lower profits during economic downturns.

When they travel for personal reasons, agents usually get reduced rates for transportation and accommodations.

Related Occupations

Travel agents organize and schedule business, educational, or recreational travel or activities. Other workers with similar responsibilities include tour guides, meeting planners, airline reservation agents, rental car agents, and travel counselors.

Sources of Additional Information

For further information on training opportunities, contact:
❑ American Society of Travel Agents, Education Department, 1101 King St., Alexandria, VA 22314. Homepage: http://www.astanet.com/www/astanet/whatis/becomeag.html

For information on certification qualifications, contact:
❑ The Institute of Certified Travel Agents, 148 Linden St., P.O. Box 812059, Wellesley, MA 02181-0012. Phone: (800) 542-4282.

Truck Drivers

(D.O.T. 292.353, .363, .463, .483, and .667; 900 through 904; 905.483, .663, and .683; 906; 909.663; 919.663-018, -022, -026 and .683-022 and -030; and 953.583)

Significant Points

✓ *Opportunities in truck driving should be good because this occupation has among the greatest number of job openings each year.*

✓ *Competition is expected for jobs offering the highest earnings or most favorable work schedules.*

✓ *A commercial drivers' license is required to operate most larger trucks.*

Nature of the Work

Throughout the day and night, trucks transport everything from milk to automobiles. Due to a trucks ability to link with rail, sea, or air transportation facilities, truck drivers usually make the initial pickup from factories, consolidate cargo at terminals for inter-city shipment, and deliver goods from terminals to stores and homes. Indeed, trucks move nearly all goods at some point in their journey from producers to consumers

Before leaving the terminal or warehouse, truck drivers check their trucks for fuel and oil. They also inspect the trucks to make sure the brakes, windshield wipers, and lights are working and that a fire extinguisher, flares, and other safety equipment are aboard and in working order. Drivers adjust mirrors so that both sides of the truck are visible from the driver's seat, and make sure cargo will not shift during the trip. Drivers report to the dispatcher any equipment that does not work or is missing, or cargo that is not loaded properly.

Once underway, drivers must be alert to prevent accidents. Because drivers of large tractor-trailers sit higher than cars, pickups, and vans, they can see farther down the road. They seek traffic lanes that allow them to move at a steady speed, while keeping sight of varying road conditions.

The length of deliveries varies according to the merchandise being transported and the goods final destination. Local drivers provide daily service for a specific route while other drivers provide inter-city and interstate services that may vary from job to job. The drivers responsibilities and assignments reflect the time spent on the road and the type of payloads they transport.

On short turnarounds, truck drivers deliver a shipment to a nearby city, pick up another loaded trailer, and drive it back to their home base the same day; other runs take an entire day and keep drivers on the road overnight. On longer runs, drivers may haul loads from city to city for a week or more before returning home. Some companies use two drivers on very long runs. One drives while the other sleeps in a berth behind the cab. "Sleeper" runs may last for days, or even weeks, usually with the truck stopping only for fuel, food, loading, and unloading.

Some long-distance drivers who have regular runs transport freight to the same city on a regular basis. Many drivers perform unscheduled runs because shippers request varying service to different cities every day. Dispatchers tell these drivers when to report for work and where to haul the freight.

After long-distance truck drivers reach their destination or complete their operating shift, the U.S. Department of Transportation requires they complete reports detailing the trip, the condition of the truck, and the circumstances of any accidents. In addition, federal regulations require employers to subject drivers to random alcohol and drug tests while on duty.

Long-distance truck drivers spend most of their working time behind the wheel but may load or unload their cargo after arriving at the final destination. This is especially common when drivers haul specialty cargo, because they may be the only one at the destination familiar with this procedure or certified to handle the materials. Auto-transport drivers, for example, drive and position cars on the trailers and head ramps and remove them at the dealerships. When picking up or delivering furniture, drivers of long-distance moving vans hire local workers to help them load or unload.

When local truck drivers receive assignments from the dispatcher to make deliveries, pickups, or both, they also get delivery forms. Before the drivers arrive for work, material handlers generally have loaded the trucks and arranged the items in order of delivery to minimize handling of the merchandise.

Local truck drivers usually load or unload the merchandise at the customer's place of business. Drivers may have helpers if there are many deliveries to make during the day or if the load requires heavy moving. Customers must sign receipts for goods and pay the drivers the balance due on the merchandise if there is a cash-on-delivery arrangement. At the end of the day, drivers turn in receipts, money, records of deliveries made, and report any mechanical problems on their trucks.

The work of local truck drivers varies depending on the product they transport. Produce truckers usually pick up a loaded truck early in the morning and spend the rest of the day delivering produce to many different grocery stores. Lumber truck drivers, on the other hand, make several trips from the lumber yard to one or more construction sites. Gasoline tank truck drivers attach the hoses and operate the pumps on their trucks to transfer the gasoline to gas stations' storage tanks.

Some local truck drivers have sales and customer relations responsibilities. The primary responsibility of *driver-sales workers*, or *route drivers*, is to deliver their firm's products and represent the company in a positive manner. Their reaction to customer complaints and requests for special services makes the difference between a large order and a lost customer. Route drivers also use their selling ability to increase sales and gain additional customers.

The duties of driver-sales workers vary according to their industry, the policies of their particular company, and the emphasis placed on their sales responsibility. Most have wholesale routes that deliver to businesses and stores rather than homes. For example, wholesale bakery driver-sales workers deliver and arrange bread, cakes, rolls, and other baked goods on display racks in grocery stores. They estimate the amount and variety of baked goods to stock by paying close attention to the items that sell well, and those sitting on the shelves. They may recommend changes in a store's order or may encourage the manager to stock new bakery products. Driver-sales workers employed by laundries that rent linens, towels, work clothes, and other items visit businesses regularly to replace soiled laundry. From time to time, they solicit new orders from businesses along their route.

Vending machine driver-sales workers service machines in factories, schools, and other buildings. They check items remaining in the machines, replace stock, and remove money deposited in the cash boxes. They also examine each vending machine to make minor repairs, clean machines, and to see merchandise and change are dispensed properly.

After completing their route, driver-sales workers order items for the next delivery based on what products have been selling well, the weather, time of year, and any customer feedback.

Working Conditions

Truck driving has become less physically demanding because most trucks now have more comfortable seats, better ventilation, and improved ergonomically designed cabs. However, driving for many hours at a stretch, unloading cargo, and making many deliveries can be tiring. Local truck drivers, unlike long-distance drivers, usually return home in the evening. Some self-employed long-distance truck drivers who own and operate their trucks spend over 240 days a year away from home.

Design improvements in newer trucks are reducing stress and increasing the efficiency of long-distance drivers. Many are a virtual mini-apartment on wheels, equipped with refrigerators, televisions, and bunks. Satellites and tracking systems link many of these state-of-the-art vehicles with company headquarters. Troubleshooting, directions, weather reports, and other important communications can be delivered to the truck anywhere in the country in a matter of seconds. Drivers can easily communicate with the dispatcher to discuss delivery schedules and courses of action, should there be mechanical problems. The satellite link-up also allows the dispatcher to track the truck's location, fuel consumption, and engine performance.

Local truck drivers frequently work 48 or more hours a week. Many who handle food for chain grocery stores, produce markets, or bakeries drive at night or early morning. Although most drivers have a regular route, some have different routes each day. Many local truck drivers, particularly driver-sales workers, load and un-

load their own trucks. This requires considerable lifting, carrying, and walking each day.

The U.S. Department of Transportation governs work hours and other matters of trucking companies engaged in interstate commerce. For example, a long-distance driver cannot work more than 60 hours in any seven-day period. Federal regulations also require that truckers rest eight hours for every ten hours of driving. Many drivers, particularly on long runs, work close to the maximum time permitted because they are typically compensated by the number of miles or hours they drive. Drivers on long runs may face boredom, loneliness, and fatigue. Drivers frequently travel at night, on holidays, and weekends to avoid traffic delays and deliver cargo on time.

Employment

Truck drivers held about 3,050,000 jobs in 1996. Most truck drivers find employment in large metropolitan areas where major trucking, retail, and wholesale companies have their distribution outlets. Some drivers work in rural areas where they provide specialized services, such as delivering milk to dairies or coal to a railhead.

Trucking companies employed about a third of all truck drivers in the U.S. Another 30 percent worked for companies engaged in wholesale or retail trade, such as auto parts stores, oil companies, lumber yards, or distributors of food and grocery products. The remaining truck drivers were distributed across many industries including, construction, manufacturing, and services.

Fewer than one in ten truck drivers is self-employed. Of these, a significant number are owner-operators who either serve a variety of businesses independently or lease their services and trucks to a trucking company.

Training, Other Qualifications, and Advancement

State and federal regulations govern the qualifications and standards for truck drivers. All drivers must comply with federal regulations and any state regulations exceeding federal requirements. Truck drivers must have a driver's license issued by the state in which they live, and most employers require a clean driving record. Drivers of trucks designed to carry at least 26,000 pounds—including most tractor-trailers as well as bigger straight trucks—must obtain a commercial driver's license (CDL) from the state in which they live. All truck drivers who operate trucks transporting hazardous materials must obtain a CDL regardless of truck size. Federal regulations governing the CDL exempt certain groups including farmers, emergency medical technicians, firefighters, some military drivers, and snow and ice removers. In many states, a regular driver's license is sufficient for driving light trucks and vans.

To qualify for a commercial driver's license, applicants must pass a written test on rules and regulations, and then demonstrate they can operate a commercial truck safely. A national data bank permanently records all driving violations incurred by persons who hold commercial licenses. A state will check these records and not issue a commercial driver's license to a driver who already has a license suspended or revoked in another state. Licensed drivers must accompany trainees until they get their own CDL. Information on how to apply for a commercial driver's license may be obtained from state motor vehicle administrations.

While many states allow those who are 18 years and older to

drive trucks within state borders, the U.S. Department of Transportation establishes minimum qualifications for truck drivers engaged in interstate commerce. Federal Motor Carrier Safety Regulations require that drivers must be at least 21 years old and pass a physical examination once every two years. The main physical requirements include good hearing, 20/40 vision with or without glasses or corrective lenses, and a 70-degree field of vision in each eye. Drivers can not be color blind. Drivers must be able to hear a forced whisper in one ear at not less than five feet, with or without a hearing aide. Drivers must have normal use of arms and legs and normal blood pressure. Drivers cannot use any controlled substances, unless prescribed by a licensed physician. Persons with epilepsy or diabetes controlled by insulin are not permitted to be interstate truck drivers. Federal regulations also require employers to test their drivers for alcohol and drug use as a condition of employment, and require periodic random tests while on duty. In addition, a driver must not have been convicted of a felony involving the use of a motor vehicle; a crime using drugs; driving under the influence of drugs or alcohol; or hit-and-run driving which resulted in injury or death. All drivers must be able to read and speak English well enough to read road signs, prepare reports, and communicate with law enforcement officers and the public. Also, drivers must take a written examination on the Motor Carrier Safety Regulations of the U.S. Department of Transportation.

Many trucking operations have higher standards than those described. Many firms require that drivers be at least 25 years old, be able to lift heavy objects, and have driven trucks for three to five years. Many prefer to hire high school graduates and require annual physical examinations.

Because drivers often deal directly with the company's customers, they must get along well with people. For jobs as driver-sales workers, employers emphasize the ability to speak well, a neat appearance, self-confidence, initiative, and tact. Employers also look for responsible, self-motivated individuals able to work with little supervision.

Driver-training courses are a desirable method of preparing for truck driving jobs and for obtaining a commercial driver's license. High school courses in driver-training and automotive mechanics may also be helpful. Many private and public technical-vocational schools offer tractor-trailer driver training programs. Students learn to inspect the trucks and freight for compliance with federal, state, and local regulations. They also learn to maneuver large vehicles on crowded streets and in highway traffic. Some programs provide only a limited amount of actual driving experience, and completion of a program does not assure a job. Persons interested in attending one of these schools should check with local trucking companies to make sure the school's training is acceptable. It is also a good idea to seek a school certified by the Professional Truck Driver Institute of America as providing training that meets Federal Highway Administration guidelines for training tractor-trailer drivers.

Training given to new drivers by employers is usually informal, and may consist of only a few hours of instruction from an experienced driver, sometimes on the new employee's own time. New drivers may also ride with, and observe experienced drivers before assignment of their own runs. Drivers receive additional training for driving a special type of truck or for handling hazardous materials. Some companies give one to two days of classroom instruction covering general duties, the operation and loading of a truck, company policies, and the preparation of delivery forms and company records. Driver-sales workers also receive training on the various types of products they carry so they will be more effective sales workers and better able to handle customer requests.

Very few people enter truck driving professions directly out of school; most truck drivers previously held jobs in other occupations. Driving experience in the Armed Forces can be an asset. In some instances, a person may also start as a truck driver's helper, driving part of the day and helping to load and unload freight. Senior helpers receive promotion when driving vacancies occur.

New drivers sometimes start on panel, or other small "straight" trucks. As they gain experience and show competent driving skills, they may advance to larger and heavier trucks, and finally to tractor-trailers.

Although most new truck drivers are assigned immediately to regular driving jobs, some start as extra drivers, substituting for regular drivers who are ill or on vacation. They receive a regular assignment when an opening occurs.

Advancement of truck drivers is generally limited to driving runs that provide increased earnings or preferred schedules and working conditions. For the most part, a local truck driver may advance to driving heavy or special types of trucks, or transfer to long-distance truck driving. Working for companies that also employ long-distance drivers is the best way to advance to these positions. A few truck drivers may advance to dispatcher, manager, or traffic work—for example, planning delivery schedules.

Some long-distance truck drivers purchase a truck and go into business for themselves. Although many of these owner-operators are successful, some fail to cover expenses and eventually go out of business. Owner-operators should have good business sense as well as truck driving experience. Courses in accounting, business, and business arithmetic are helpful, and knowledge of truck mechanics can enable owner-operators to perform their own routine maintenance and minor repairs.

Job Outlook

Opportunities should be favorable for persons interested in truck driving. This occupation has among the largest number of job openings each year. Although growth in demand for truck drivers will create thousands of openings, the majority will occur as experienced drivers transfer to other fields of work, retire, or leave the labor force for other reasons. Jobs vary greatly in terms of earnings, weekly work hours, number of nights spent on the road, and in the quality of equipment operated. Because truck driving does not require education beyond high school, competition is expected for jobs with the most attractive earnings and working conditions.

Employment of truck drivers is expected to increase about as fast as the average for all occupations through the year 2006 as the economy grows and the amount of freight carried by trucks increases. The increased use of rail, air, and ship transportation requires truck drivers to pick up and deliver shipments. Growth of long-distance drivers may slow as rail cars increasingly ship loaded trailers across country, but long-distance truck drivers will continue to haul perishable goods.

Average growth of local and long-distance truck driver employment should outweigh the slow growth in driver-sales worker jobs.

The number of truck drivers with sales responsibilities is expected to increase slowly because companies are increasingly splitting their responsibilities among other workers. They will shift sales, ordering, and customer service tasks to sales and office staffs, and use regular truck drivers to make deliveries to customers.

Job opportunities may vary from year to year, because the strength of the economy dictates the amount of freight moved by trucks. Companies tend to hire more drivers when the economy is strong and deliveries are in high demand. Consequently, when the economy slows, employers hire fewer drivers or even lay off drivers. Independent owner-operators are particularly vulnerable to slowdowns. Industries least likely to be affected by economic fluctuation tend to be the most stable places for employment.

Earnings

As a general rule, local truck drivers receive an hourly wage and extra pay for working overtime, usually after 40 hours. Employers pay long-distance drivers primarily by the mile. Their rate per mile can vary greatly from employer to employer and may even depend on type of the cargo. Typically, earnings increase with mileage driven, seniority, and the size and type of truck driven. Most driver-sales workers receive a commission, based on their sales in addition to an hourly wage.

In 1995, truck drivers had average straight-time hourly earnings of $13.39. Depending on the size of the truck, average hourly earnings were as follows:

Medium trucks	$14.64
Tractor-trailers	14.07
Heavy straight trucks	13.17
Light trucks	8.56

Typically, the size of the trucking establishment influenced the relative size of drivers' earnings. Drivers employed by large establishments—those with 2,500 or more employees—had the highest earnings, averaging about $11.17 to $19.23 an hour in 1995. Smaller establishments—those with fewer than 500 employees—had average earnings that ranged from $8.31 to $16.11 an hour in 1995. Truck drivers in the Northeast and West had the highest earnings; those in the South had the lowest.

Most long-distance truck drivers operate tractor-trailers, and their earnings vary widely, from as little as $20,000 to over $40,000 annually. Most self-employed truck drivers are primarily engaged in long-distance hauling. After deducting their living expenses and the costs associated with operating their trucks, earnings of $20,000 to $25,000 a year are common.

Many truck drivers are members of the International Brotherhood of Teamsters. Some truck drivers employed by companies outside the trucking industry are members of unions representing the plant workers of the companies for which they work.

Related Occupations

Other driving occupations include ambulance driver, bus driver, chauffeur, and taxi driver.

Sources of Additional Information

Information on truck driver employment opportunities is available from local trucking companies and local offices of the state employment service.

Information on career opportunities in truck driving may be obtained from:

American Trucking Associations, Inc., 2200 Mill Rd., Alexandria, VA 22314.

American Trucking Association Foundation, 660 Roosevelt Ave., Pawtucket, RI 02860.

The Professional Truck Driver Institute of America, a nonprofit organization established by the trucking industry, manufacturers, and others, certifies truck driver training programs meeting industry standards. A free list of certified tractor-trailer driver training programs may be obtained from:

❑ Professional Truck Driver Institute of America, 2200 Mill Rd., Alexandria, VA 22314, or by calling (703) 838-8842.

Veterinarians

(*D.O.T. 073.*)

Significant Points

✓ *Graduation from an accredited college of veterinary medicine and a license to practice are required.*

✓ *Competition for admission to veterinary school is keen.*

✓ *Job prospects may be better for those who specialize in farm animals than for small animal practitioners because fewer graduates have a desire to work in rural and isolated areas.*

Nature of the Work

Veterinarians play a major role in the health care of pets, livestock, and zoo, sporting, and laboratory animals. Veterinarians also use their skills to protect humans against diseases carried by animals, and conduct clinical research on human and animal health problems.

Most veterinarians perform clinical work in private practices. About one-half of these veterinarians predominately or exclusively treat small animals. Small animal practitioners usually care for companion animals, such as dogs and cats, but also treat birds, reptiles, rabbits, and other animals that may be kept as pets. Some veterinarians work in mixed animal practices, where they see pigs, goats, sheep, and some nondomestic animals, in addition to companion animals. Veterinarians in clinical practice diagnose animal health problems, vaccinate against diseases such as distemper and rabies, medicate animals with infections or illnesses, treat and dress wounds, set fractures, perform surgery, and advise owners about feeding, behavior, and breeding.

A smaller number of private practice veterinarians work exclusively with large animals, focusing mostly on horses or cows, but may care for all kinds of food animals. These veterinarians usually drive to farms or ranches to provide veterinary services for herds or individual animals. Much of their work involves preventive care in order to maintain the health of food animals. They test for and vaccinate against diseases, and consult with farm or ranch owners and managers on production, feeding, and housing issues. They also treat and dress wounds, set fractures, perform surgery—including cesarean sections on birthing animals—and do artificial insemination. Veterinarians also euthanize animals when necessary.

Veterinarians who treat animals use surgical instruments; medical equipment, such as stethoscopes; and diagnostic equipment, such as radiology machines.

Veterinarians contribute to human as well as animal health. A number of veterinarians work with physicians and scientists as they research better ways to prevent and treat human health problems such as cancer, AIDS, and alcohol or drug abuse. Some test the effects of drug therapies, antibiotics, or new surgical techniques on animals. Veterinarians who are livestock inspectors check animals for transmissible diseases, advise owners on treatment, and may quarantine animals. Veterinarians who are meat, poultry, or egg product inspectors examine slaughtering and processing plants, check live animals and carcasses for disease, and enforce government regulations regarding food purity and sanitation. Some veterinarians care for zoo or aquarium animals, or for laboratory animals.

Working Conditions

Veterinarians often work long hours, with nearly half spending 50 or more hours on the job. Those in group practices may take turns being on call for evening, night, or weekend work, and solo practitioners may work extended and weekend hours responding to emergencies and squeezing in unexpected appointments.

Veterinarians in large animal practice also spend time driving between office and farm or ranch. They work outdoors in all kinds of weather, and may have to treat animals or perform surgery under less-than-sanitary conditions. When working with animals that are frightened or in pain, veterinarians risk being bitten, kicked, or scratched.

Employment

Veterinarians held about 58,000 jobs in 1996. About a third were self-employed, in solo or group practices. Most others were employees of a practice. The federal government employed about 2,000 civilian veterinarians, chiefly in the U.S. Department of Agriculture, and about 500 military veterinarians in the U.S. Army and U.S. Air Force. Other employers of veterinarians are state and local governments, colleges of veterinary medicine, medical schools, research laboratories, animal food companies, and pharmaceutical companies. A few veterinarians work for zoos. Most veterinarians caring for zoo animals are private practitioners who contract with zoos to provide services, usually on a part-time basis.

Although veterinarians are located in every state, in 1996 about three out of ten establishments providing veterinary services were located in just four states: California, Florida, New York, and Texas.

Training, Other Qualifications, and Advancement

Prospective veterinarians must graduate from a four-year program at an accredited college of veterinary medicine with a Doctor of Veterinary Medicine (DVM or VMD) degree and obtain a license to practice. There are 27 colleges in 26 states that meet accreditation standards set by the Council on Education of the American Veterinary Medical Association. The prerequisites for admission vary by veterinary medical college. Many do not actually require a bachelor's degree for entrance, but all require a significant number of credit hours at the undergraduate level, ranging from 45 to 90 semester hours. Preveterinary courses emphasize the sciences, and veterinary medical colleges typically require classes in organic and

inorganic chemistry, physics, biochemistry, general biology, animal biology, animal nutrition, genetics, vertebrate embryology, cell or microbiology, zoology, and systemic physiology. Some programs require calculus; some require only statistics, college algebra and trigonometry, or precalculus; and others require no math at all. Most veterinary medical colleges also require some core courses, including English or literature, social science, and the humanities. Although a bachelor's degree is generally not required for entry to veterinary medical school, most of the students admitted have completed an undergraduate program.

Most veterinary medical colleges will only consider applicants who have a minimum grade point average (GPA). The required GPA varies by school from a low of 2.5 to a high of 3.2, based on a maximum GPA of 4.0. However, the average GPA of candidates at most schools is higher than these minimums. Those who receive offers of admission usually have a GPA of 3.0 or better.

In addition to satisfying preveterinary course requirements, applicants must also submit test scores from the Graduate Record Examination (GRE), the Veterinary College Admission Test (VCAT), or the Medical College Admission Test (MCAT), depending on the preference of each college.

Veterinary medical colleges also weigh heavily a candidate's veterinary and animal experience in the admissions process. Formal experience, such as work with veterinarians or scientists in clinics, agribusiness, research, or in some area of health science, is particularly advantageous. Less formal experience, such as working with animals on a farm, ranch, stable, or animal shelter, is also helpful. Students must demonstrate ambition and eagerness to work with animals.

Competition for admission to veterinary school is keen. The number of accredited veterinary colleges has remained at 27 since 1983, while the number of applicants has risen. About one in three applicants was accepted in 1996. Most veterinary medical colleges are public, state-supported institutions, and reserve the majority of their openings for in-state residents. Twenty states that do not have a veterinary medical college agree to pay a fee or subsidy to help cover the cost of veterinary education for a limited number of their residents at one or more out-of-state colleges. Nonresident students who are admitted under such a contract arrangement may have to pay out-of-state tuition, or they may have to repay their state of residency all or part of the subsidy that was provided to the contracting college. Residents of the remaining four states and the District of Columbia may apply to any of the 27 veterinary medical colleges as an at-large applicant. The number of positions available to at-large applicants is very limited at most schools, making admission difficult.

While in veterinary medical college, students receive additional academic instruction and are exposed to clinical procedures such as diagnosing and treating animal diseases and performing surgery. They also do laboratory work in anatomy, biochemistry, and other scientific and medical subjects. At most veterinary medical colleges, students who plan a career in research can earn both a DVM and a Doctor of Philosophy (Ph.D.) degree at the same time.

Veterinary graduates who plan to work with specific types of animals or specialize in a clinical area, such as pathology, surgery, radiology, or laboratory animal medicine, usually complete a one-year internship. Interns receive only a small salary, but usually find that their internship experience leads to higher starting salaries relative to other starting veterinarians. Veterinarians who seek board certification in a specialty must also complete a two- to three-year residency program which provides intensive training in one of the following areas: Internal medicine, oncology, radiology, surgery, dermatology, anesthesiology, neurology, cardiology, ophthalmology, or exotic small animal medicine.

All states and the District of Columbia require that veterinarians be licensed before they can practice. The only exemptions are for veterinarians working for some federal agencies and some state governments. Licensing is controlled by the states and is not strictly uniform, although all states require successful completion of the D.V.M. degree—or equivalent education—and passage of a national board examination. The Educational Commission for Foreign Veterinary Graduates (ECFVG) grants certification to individuals trained outside the U.S. who demonstrate that they meet specified English language and clinical proficiency requirements. ECFVG certification fulfills the educational requirement for licensure in all states except Nebraska.

Applicants for licensure satisfy the examination requirement by passing the National Board Examination (NBE) and the Clinical Competency Test (CCT). The NBE comprises 400 multiple choice questions covering all aspects of veterinary medicine and takes one day to complete. The CCT is a half-day examination consisting of 14 problems covering real-life situations in which the candidate is given a set of facts and must choose the correct course of action for the patient. Many states permit candidates to take the NBE in their third year of veterinary school, but those who pass must still graduate with the D.V.M. before they can be licensed.

The majority of states also require candidates to pass a state jurisprudence examination, covering state laws and regulations. Some states also do additional testing on clinical competency. There are very few reciprocal agreements between states, making it difficult for a veterinarian to practice in a new state without first taking another state examination.

Thirty-nine states have continuing education requirements for licensed veterinarians. Requirements differ by state, and may involve attending a class or otherwise demonstrating knowledge of recent medical and veterinary advances.

Most veterinarians begin as employees or partners in established practices. Despite the substantial financial investment in equipment, office space, and staff, many veterinarians with experience set up their own practice or purchase an established one.

Newly trained veterinarians may become U.S. government meat and poultry inspectors, disease-control workers, epidemiologists, research assistants, or commissioned officers in the U.S. Public Health Service, U.S. Army, or U.S. Air Force. A state license may be required.

Prospective veterinarians must have good manual dexterity. They should have an affinity for animals and the ability to get along with animal owners. They must also be able to make decisions in emergencies.

Job Outlook

Employment of veterinarians is expected to grow faster than the average for all occupations through the year 2006. Job openings stemming from the need to replace veterinarians who retire or oth-

erwise leave the labor force will be almost as numerous as new jobs resulting from employment growth over the 1996-2006 period.

Most veterinarians practice in animal hospitals or clinics, many of whom care primarily for companion animals. The number of pets is expected to increase more slowly during the projection period than in the previous decade, partly because the large baby-boom generation is aging and will acquire fewer dogs and cats. Slower pet population growth may curtail the demand for veterinarians who specialize in small animals. Nevertheless, new technologies and medical advancements will permit veterinarians to offer more and better care to animals. Pet owners are becoming more aware of the availability of advanced care. They may increasingly take advantage of nontraditional veterinary services such as preventive dental care, and more willingly pay for intensive care than in the past. Veterinarians who enter small animal practice may face competition. Large numbers of new graduates continue to be attracted to small animal medicine because they prefer to deal with pets, and live and work near or in populated areas. However, an oversupply does not necessarily limit the ability of veterinarians to find employment or set up and maintain a practice. It could result in more veterinarians taking positions requiring much evening or weekend work to accommodate the extended hours of operation which more practices are offering. Others could take salaried positions in retail stores offering limited veterinary services. Self-employed veterinarians may have to work harder and longer to build a sufficient clientele.

The number of jobs for large animal veterinarians is expected to grow slowly because productivity gains in the agricultural production industry mean demand for fewer veterinarians to treat food animals. Nevertheless, job prospects may be better for veterinarians who specialize in farm animals than for small animal practitioners because fewer veterinary medical college graduates have the desire to work in rural or isolated areas.

Continued support for public health and food safety, disease control programs, and biomedical research on human health problems will contribute to the demand for veterinarians, although such positions are relatively few in number. Also, anticipated budget tightening in the federal government may lead to lower funding levels for some programs, limiting job growth. Veterinarians with training in public health and epidemiology should have the best opportunities for a career in the federal government.

Earnings

Average starting salaries of 1995 veterinary medical college graduates varied by type of practice or employing industry, as indicated by Table 1.

Table 1. Average starting salaries of veterinary medical college graduates, 1995

All graduates $29,900

Type of practice:

Large animal, exclusive	39,500
Large animal, predominate	34,300
Mixed animal	31,900
Small animal, exclusive	31,900
Small animal, predominate	31,000
Equine	27,500

Industry:

Industry/commercial	44,500
Uniformed services	41,100
State/local government	40,000
Not-for-profit	36,000
Federal government	32,800
University	19,700
Other public or corporate	34,000

SOURCE: American Veterinary Medical Association

The average income of veterinarians in private practice was $57,500 in 1995. New veterinary medical college graduates who enter the federal government usually start at $35,800. Beginning salaries were slightly higher in selected areas where the prevailing local pay level was higher. The average annual salary for veterinarians in the federal government in nonsupervisory, supervisory, and managerial positions was $57,600 in 1997.

Related Occupations

Veterinarians prevent, diagnose, and treat diseases, disorders, and injuries in animals. Those who do similar work for humans include chiropractors, dentists, optometrists, physicians, and podiatrists. Veterinarians also have extensive training in physical and life sciences, and some do scientific and medical research, closely paralleling occupations such as biological, medical, and animal scientists.

Animal trainers, animal breeders, and veterinary technicians work extensively with animals. Like veterinarians, they must have patience and feel comfortable with animals. However, the level of training required for these occupations is substantially less than that needed by veterinarians.

Sources of Additional Information

For more information on careers in veterinary medicine and a list of U.S. schools and colleges of veterinary medicine, send a letter-size, self-addressed, stamped envelope to:

❏ American Veterinary Medical Association, 1931 N. Meacham Rd., Suite 100, Schaumburg, IL 60173-4360.

For information on scholarships, grants, and loans, contact the financial aid officer at the veterinary schools to which you wish to apply.

For information on veterinary education, write to:

❏ Association of American Veterinary Medical Colleges, 1101 Vermont Ave. NW, Suite 710, Washington, DC 20005.

For information on the federal agencies that employ veterinarians and a list of addresses for each agency, write to:

❏ National Association of Federal Veterinarians, 1101 Vermont Ave. NW, Suite 710, Washington, DC 20005.

Veterinary Assistants and Nonfarm Animal Caretakers

(D.O.T. 410.674-010, -022; 412.674-010, -014; 418.381-010, .674-010, 677-010; and 449.674-010)

Significant Points

✓ *People who love animals get satisfaction in this occupation, but the work can be unpleasant and physically and emotionally demanding.*

✓ *Most animal caretakers are trained on the job, but advancement depends on experience and/or formal training.*

✓ *Job outlook is generally good; however, competition will be keen for animal caretaker jobs in zoos.*

Nature of the Work

Many people like animals. But, as pet owners can attest, taking care of them is hard work. Animal caretakers, sometimes called animal attendants or animal keepers, feed, water, groom, bathe, and exercise animals and clean, disinfect, and repair their cages. They also play with the animals, provide companionship, and observe behavioral changes that could indicate illness or injury.

Kennels, animal shelters, animal hospitals and clinics, stables, laboratories, aquariums, and zoological parks all house animals and employ caretakers. Job titles and duties vary by employment setting.

Kennel staff usually care for small companion animals like dogs and cats while their owners are working or traveling out of town. Beginning attendants perform basic tasks, such as cleaning cages and dog runs, filling food and water dishes, and exercising animals. Experienced attendants may provide basic animal health care, bathe and groom animals, and clean their ears. Caretakers who work in kennels also sell pet food and supplies, assist in obedience training, help with breeding, or prepare animals for shipping.

Animal caretakers who specialize in grooming, or maintaining a pet's—usually a dog's or cat's—appearance are called groomers. Some groomers work in kennels and others operate their own grooming business. Groomers answer telephones, schedule appointments, discuss with clients how they want their pets to look, and collect information on the pet's disposition and veterinarian. Grooming the pet involves several steps: An initial brush-out is followed by a first clipping of hair or fur using electric clippers, combs, and grooming shears; the groomer then cuts the nails, cleans the ears, bathes, and blow-dries the animal, and ends with a final clipping and styling.

Animal caretakers in animal shelters perform a variety of duties and work with a wide variety of animals. In addition to attending to the basic needs of the animals, caretakers must also keep records of the animals received and discharged and any tests or treatments done. Some vaccinate newly admitted animals under the direction of a veterinarian, and euthanize (put to death) seriously ill, severely injured, or unwanted animals. Caretakers in animal shelters also interact with the public, answering telephone inquiries, screening applicants for animal adoption, or educating visitors on neutering and other animal health issues.

Workers in stables saddle and unsaddle horses, give them rubdowns, and walk them through a cool-off after a ride. They also feed, groom, and exercise the horses, clean out stalls and replenish bedding, polish saddles, clean and organize the tack (harness, saddle, and bridle) room, and store supplies and feed. Experienced staff may help train horses.

Animal caretakers in animal hospitals or clinics are called veterinary assistants. Veterinarians rely on caretakers to keep a constant eye on the condition of animals under their charge. Caretakers watch as animals recover from surgery, check whether dressings are still on correctly, observe the animals' overall attitude, and notify a doctor if anything seems out of the ordinary. While among the animals, caretakers clean constantly to maintain sanitary conditions in the hospital.

Laboratory animal caretakers work in research facilities and assist with the care of a wide variety of animals, including mice, rats, sheep, pigs, cattle, dogs, cats, monkeys, birds, fish, and frogs. They feed and water the animals, clean cages and change bedding, and examine the animals for signs of illness, disease, or injury. They may administer medications orally or topically according to instructions, prepare samples for laboratory examination, sterilize laboratory equipment, and record information regarding genealogy, diet, weight, medications, and food intake. They work with scientists, physicians, veterinarians, and laboratory technicians.

In zoos, caretakers called keepers prepare the diets and clean the enclosures of animals, and sometimes assist in raising their wards. They watch for any signs of illness or injury, monitor eating patterns or any changes in behavior, and record their observations. Keepers also may answer questions and assure that the visiting public behaves responsibly toward the exhibited animals. Depending on the zoo, keepers may be assigned to work with a broad group of animals such as mammals, birds, or reptiles, or they may work with a limited collection of animals such as primates, large cats, or small mammals.

Working Conditions

People who love animals get satisfaction from working with and helping animals. However, some of the work may be unpleasant and physically and emotionally demanding. Caretakers have to clean animal cages and lift, hold, or restrain animals, risking exposure to bites or scratches. Their work often involves kneeling, crawling, repeated bending, and lifting heavy supplies like bales of hay or bags of feed. Animal caretakers must take precautions when treating animals with germicides or insecticides. The work setting can be noisy. Animal caretakers who witness abused animals or assist in the euthanizing of unwanted, aged, or hopelessly injured animals may experience emotional stress.

Caretakers may work outdoors in all kinds of weather. Hours are irregular. Animals have to be fed every day, so caretakers must work weekend and holiday shifts. In some animal hospitals, research facilities, and animal shelters an attendant is on duty 24 hours a day, which means night shifts. Most full-time caretakers work about 40 hours a week; some work 50 hours a week or more. Caretakers of show and sports animals travel to competitions.

Employment

Animal caretakers held about 163,000 jobs in 1996. About 33,000 of the total worked as veterinary assistants in veterinary services. The remainder worked primarily in boarding kennels, but also in animal shelters, stables, grooming shops, zoos, and local, state, and federal agencies. In 1996, two out of every ten caretakers was self-employed, and four in ten worked part-time.

Training, Other Qualifications, and Advancement

Most animal caretakers are trained on the job. Employers generally prefer to hire people with some experience with animals. Some training programs are available for specific types of animal caretakers, but formal training is usually not necessary for entry-level positions.

Most pet groomers learn their trade by completing an informal apprenticeship, usually lasting six to ten weeks, under the guidance of an experienced groomer. Prospective groomers may also attend one of the 50 state-licensed grooming schools throughout the country, with programs varying in length from 4 to 18 weeks. The National Dog Groomers Association of America certifies groomers who pass a written and practical skills examination. Beginning groomers often start by taking on one duty, such as bathing and drying the pet. They eventually assume responsibility for the entire grooming process, from the initial brush-out to the final clipping. Groomers who work in large retail establishments or kennels may, with experience, move into supervisory or managerial positions. Experienced groomers often choose to open their own shops.

Beginning animal caretakers in kennels learn on the job, and usually start by cleaning cages and feeding and watering animals. Kennel caretakers may be promoted to kennel supervisor, assistant manager, and manager, and those with enough capital and experience may open up their own kennels. The American Boarding Kennels Association (ABKA) offers a three-stage, home-study program for individuals interested in pet care. The first two study programs address basic and advanced principles of animal care, while the third program focuses on in-depth animal care and good business procedures. Those who complete the third program and pass oral and written examinations administered by the ABKA become Certified Kennel Operators (CKO).

There are no formal educational requirements for animal caretakers in veterinary facilities. They are trained on the job, usually under the guidance of a veterinarian or veterinary technician. They start by performing tasks related to basic animal health care, such as keeping cages and examination areas sanitary. They also help veterinarians prepare for surgery, sterilize surgical equipment, observe recovering animals, and give medications and basic medical treatment under the directions of a veterinarian or veterinary technician. Highly motivated veterinary assistants may become veterinary technicians, with additional training from one of approximately 65 accredited veterinary technology programs.

Employers of entry-level laboratory animal caretakers generally require a high school diploma or General Educational Development (GED) test. A few colleges and vocational schools offer programs in laboratory animal science which provide training for technician positions, but such training is not strictly necessary. New animal caretakers working in laboratories begin by providing basic care to laboratory animals. With additional training and experience, they may advance to more technical positions in laboratory animal care, such as research assistant, mid-level technician, or senior-level technologist. The American Association for Laboratory Animal Science (AALAS) offers certification for three levels of technician competence. Those who wish to become certified as Assistant Laboratory Animal Technicians (ALAT) must satisfy education and experience requirements before taking an examination administered by AALAS.

Some zoological parks may require their caretakers to have a bachelor's degree in biology, animal science, or a related field. Most require experience with animals, preferably as a volunteer or paid keeper in a zoo. Zoo keepers may advance to senior keeper, assistant head keeper, head keeper, and assistant curator, but few openings occur, especially for the higher-level positions.

Animal caretakers in animal shelters are not required to have any specialized training, but training programs and workshops are increasingly available through the Humane Society of the United States and the National Animal Control Association. Workshop topics include cruelty investigations, appropriate methods of euthanasia for shelter animals, and techniques for preventing problems with wildlife. With experience and additional training, caretakers in animal shelters may become an adoption coordinator, animal control officer, emergency rescue driver, assistant shelter manager, or shelter director.

Job Outlook

Employment opportunities for animal caretakers generally are expected to be good. The outlook for caretakers in zoos, however, is not favorable; job seekers will face keen competition because of expected slow growth in zoo capacity, low turnover, and the fact that the occupation attracts many candidates.

Employment is expected to grow faster than the average for all occupations through the year 2006. The growth of the pet population, which drives employment of animal caretakers in kennels, grooming shops, animal shelters, and veterinary clinics and hospitals, is expected to slow. Nevertheless, pets remain popular and pet owners—including a large number of baby boomers whose disposable income is expected to increase as they age—may increasingly take advantage of grooming services, daily and overnight boarding services, and veterinary services, spurring employment growth for animal caretakers and veterinary assistants. Demand for animal caretakers in animal shelters is expected to remain steady. Communities are increasingly recognizing the connection between animal abuse and abuse toward humans, and should continue to commit funds to animal shelters, many of which are working hand-in-hand with social service agencies and law enforcement teams.

Despite growth in demand for animal caretakers, the overwhelming majority of jobs will result from the need to replace workers leaving the field. Many animal caretaker jobs that require little or no training have work schedules which tend to be flexible; therefore, it is ideal for people seeking their first job and for students and others looking for temporary or part-time work. Because turnover is quite high, largely due to the hard physical labor, the overall availability of jobs should be very good. Much of the work of animal caretakers is seasonal, particularly during vacation periods.

Earnings

Animal caretakers who worked full-time earned a median weekly salary of $290 in 1996. The middle 50 percent earned between $220 and $380. The bottom 10 percent earned less than $170; the top 10 percent earned more than $500 a week. According to a salary survey by the National Animal Control Association, nonsupervisory animal caretakers working in animal care and control agencies earned a yearly average of about $17,100 in 1996.

Related Occupations

Others who work extensively with animals include animal breeders, animal trainers, livestock farm workers, ranchers, veterinarians, veterinary technicians and technologists, and wildlife biologists and zoologists.

Sources of Additional Information

For more information on jobs in animal caretaking and control, and the animal shelter and control personnel training program, write to:

❑ The Humane Society of the United States, 2100 L St. NW, Washington, DC 20037-1598.

❑ National Animal Control Association, P.O. Box 480851, Kansas City, MO 64148-0851.

To obtain a listing of state-licensed grooming schools, send a stamped, self-addressed envelope to:

❑ National Dog Groomers Association of America, Box 101, Clark, PA 16113.

For information on training and certification of kennel staff and owners, contact:

❑ American Boarding Kennels Association, 4575 Galley Rd., Suite 400A, Colorado Springs, CO 80915. Homepage: http://www.abka.com

For information on laboratory animal technicians and certification, contact:

❑ American Association for Laboratory Animal Science, 70 Timber Creek Dr., Cordova, TN 38018-4233. FAX (901) 753-0046 E-mail address: info@aalas.org

Visual Artists

(D.O.T. 102.261-014; 141.031-010, .061-010, -014, -018, -022, -026, -030, -034, .081-010; 142.061-030, -054; 144; 149.041, .051, .261; 970.131-014, .281-014, .361-018)

Significant Points

✓ *Nearly 60 percent are self-employed—about seven times the proportion in all professional occupations.*

✓ *Artists usually develop their skills through a bachelor's degree program or other postsecondary training in art or design.*

✓ *Keen competition is expected for both salaried jobs and freelance work because the glamorous and exciting image of the graphic and fine arts fields attracts many talented people.*

Nature of the Work

Visual artists communicate ideas, thoughts, and feelings through various methods and materials—including computers, oils, watercolors, acrylics, pastels, magic markers, pencils, pen and ink, silkscreen, plaster, or clay—or other media, such as photographs and sound. They create realistic and abstract works or images of objects, people, nature, topography, or events.

Visual artists generally fall into one of two categories—graphic artists or graphic designers, and fine artists—depending not so much on the medium, but on the artist's purpose in creating a work of art. Graphic artists, many of who own their own studios, put their artistic skills and vision at the service of commercial clients, such as major corporations, retail stores, and advertising, design, or publishing firms. Fine artists, on the other hand, often create art to satisfy their own need for self-expression, and may display their work in museums, corporate collections, art galleries, and private homes. Some of their work may be done on request from clients, but not as exclusively as graphic artists.

Graphic artists, whether freelancers or employed by a firm, use a variety of print, electronic, and film media to create art that meets a client's needs. Most graphic artists use computer software to design new images; some of this work appears on the Internet and CD-ROM. As computer software becomes increasingly sophisticated, more artists are likely to become involved with this medium. Graphic artists may create promotional displays and marketing brochures for new products, visual designs of annual reports and other corporate literature, or distinctive logos for products or businesses. Artists may be responsible for the overall layout and design of magazines, newspapers, journals, and other publications, and may create graphics for television and computer-generated media. For example, many magazines and newspapers have a homepage on the Internet.

Fine artists may sell their works to stores, commercial art galleries, and museums, or directly to collectors. Commercial galleries may sell artists' works on consignment. The gallery and artist predetermine how much each earns from a sale. Only the most successful fine artists are able to support themselves solely through sale of their works; however, most fine artists hold other jobs as well. Those with teaching certification may teach art in elementary or secondary schools, while those with a master's or Ph.D. degree may teach in colleges or universities. Some fine artists work in arts administration in city, state, or federal arts programs. Others may work as art critics, art consultants, or as directors or representatives in fine art galleries; give private art lessons; or work as curators setting up art exhibits in museums. Sometimes fine artists work in an unrelated field in order to support their careers.

Fine artists usually work independently, choosing whatever subject matter and medium suits them. Usually, they specialize in one or two forms of art. Painters generally work with two-dimensional art forms. Using techniques of shading, perspective, and color mixing, painters produce works depicting realistic scenes or may evoke different moods and emotions, depending on the artist's goals. Artists may combine mediums and include sound and motion in their works.

Sculptors design three-dimensional art works—either molding and joining materials such as clay, glass, wire, plastic, or metal, or cutting and carving forms from a block of plaster, wood, or stone. Some sculptors combine various materials such as concrete, metal, wood, plastic, and paper.

Printmakers create printed images from designs cut into wood, stone, or metal, or from computer-driven data. The designs may be engraved, as in the case of woodblocking; etched, as in the production of etchings; or derived from computers using advanced color printers.

Painting restorers preserve and restore damaged and faded paintings. They apply solvents and cleaning agents to clean the surfaces, reconstruct or retouch damaged areas, and apply preservatives to protect the paintings. This is very detailed work and is usually reserved for experts in the field.

Illustrators paint or draw pictures for books, magazines, and other publications; films; and paper products, including greeting cards, calendars, wrapping paper, and stationery. Many do a variety of illustrations, while others specialize in a particular style. Some illustrators draw "story boards" for television commercials, movies, and animated features. Storyboards present television commercials in a series of scenes similar to a comic strip, so an advertising agency and client (the company doing the advertising) can evaluate proposed commercials. Story boards may also serve as guides to placement of actors and cameras and to other details during the production of commercials. Some work is done electronically, using advanced computer software. This allows ideas to be electronically mailed between clients, or presented on the Internet.

Medical and scientific illustrators combine artistic skills with knowledge of the biological sciences. Medical illustrators draw illustrations of human anatomy and surgical procedures. Scientific illustrators draw illustrations of animals and plants. These illustrations are used in medical and scientific publications, and in audiovisual presentations for teaching purposes. Medical illustrators also work for lawyers, producing exhibits for court cases and doctors. Fashion artists draw illustrations of women's, men's, and children's clothing and accessories for newspapers, magazines, and other media.

Cartoonists draw political, advertising, social, and sports cartoons. Some cartoonists work with others who create the idea or story and write the captions. Most cartoonists, however, have humorous, critical, or dramatic talents in addition to drawing skills.

Animators work in the motion picture and television industries. They draw by hand and use computers to create the large series of pictures which, when transferred to film or tape, form the animated cartoons seen in movies and on television.

Art directors, also called visual journalists, read the material to be printed in periodicals, newspapers, and other printed media, and decide how to best present visually the information in an eye-catching and organized manner. They make decisions about which photographs or art work to use, and oversee production of the printed material. Art directors may also review graphics that will be shown on the Internet.

Working Conditions

Graphic and fine artists generally work in art and design studios located in office buildings or their own studios. While their surroundings are usually well lighted and ventilated, odors from glues, paint, ink, or other materials may be present. They may use computers for extended periods of time.

Graphic artists employed by publishing companies and art and design studios generally work a standard 40-hour week. During busy periods, they may work overtime to meet deadlines. Self-employed graphic artists can set their own hours, but may spend much time and effort selling their services to potential customers or clients and establishing a reputation.

Employment

Visual artists held about 276,000 jobs in 1996. Nearly six out of ten were self-employed. Self-employed artists are either graphic artists who freelance, offering their services to advertising agencies, publishing firms, and other businesses, or fine artists who earn income when they sell a painting or other art work.

Of the artists who were not self-employed, many were graphic artists who worked for advertising agencies, design firms, commercial art and reproduction firms, or printing and publishing firms. Other artists were employed by the motion picture and television industries, wholesale and retail trade establishments, and public relations firms.

Training, Other Qualifications, and Advancement

In the fine arts field, formal training requirements do not exist, but it is very difficult to become skilled enough to make a living, without training. Many colleges and universities offer bachelor's and master's degree programs in fine arts; specialized art schools also offer postsecondary training in this field. In the graphic arts field, demonstrated artistic ability, appropriate training, or other qualifications are needed for success. Evidence of appropriate talent and skill, displayed in an artist's "portfolio," is an important factor used by art and design directors and others in deciding whether to hire or contract out work to an artist. The portfolio is a collection of hand-made, computer-generated, or printed examples of the artist's best work. Assembling a successful portfolio requires skills usually developed in a bachelor's degree program or other postsecondary training in art, design, or visual communications. Internships also provide excellent opportunities for artists to develop and enhance their portfolios. Formal educational programs in art and design also provide training in computer design techniques; computers are widely used in art and design, and knowledge and training in computer techniques are critical for many jobs in these fields.

Recent data from The American Institute of Graphic Arts indicate that over nine out of ten artists have a college degree; among this group, over six out of ten majored in graphic design and nearly two out of ten majored in fine arts. Nearly two out of ten have a master's degree.

The appropriate training and education for prospective medical illustrators is more specific. Medical illustrators must not only demonstrate artistic ability, but must also have a detailed knowledge of living organisms, surgical and medical procedures, and human and sometimes animal anatomy. A four-year bachelor's degree combining art and premedical courses is usually required, followed by a master's degree in medical illustration. This degree is offered in only a few accredited schools in the United States.

Persons hired in advertising agencies or graphic design studios often start with relatively routine work. While doing this work, however, they may observe and practice their skills on the side. Many graphic artists work part-time as freelancers while continuing to hold a full-time job until they get established. Others have enough talent, perseverance, and confidence in their ability to start out freelancing full-time immediately after graduating from art school. Many freelance part-time while still in school in order to develop experience and a portfolio of published work.

The freelance artist develops a set of clients who regularly contract for work. Some successful freelancers are widely recognized for their skill in specialties, such as children's book illustration, design, or magazine illustration. These artists may earn high incomes and can pick and choose the type of work they do.

Fine artists and illustrators advance as their work circulates, and as they establish a reputation for a particular style. The best artists and illustrators continually develop new ideas, and their work constantly evolves over time. Graphic artists may advance to assistant art director, art director, design director, and in some companies, creative director of an art or design department. Some artists may gain enough skill to succeed as a freelancer or may prefer to specialize in a particular area. Some graphic artists become webmasters, maintaining their company's Internet site. Others decide to open their own businesses.

Job Outlook

The glamorous and exciting image of graphic and fine arts fields attracts many talented people with a love for drawing and creative ability. As a result, the supply of aspiring artists will continue to exceed the number of job openings, resulting in keen competition for both salaried jobs and freelance work. Freelance work may be particularly hard to come by, especially at first, and many freelancers earn very little until they acquire experience and establish a good reputation. Fine artists, in particular, may find it difficult to earn a living solely by selling their art work. Nonetheless, graphic arts studios, galleries, and individual clients are always on the lookout for artists who display outstanding talent, creativity, and style. Talented artists who have developed a mastery of artistic techniques and skills, including computer skills, will have the best job prospects.

Employment of visual artists is expected to grow faster than the average for all occupations through the year 2006. Demand for graphic artists should remain strong as producers of information, goods, and services put increasing emphasis on visual appeal in product design, advertising, marketing, and television. The explosive growth of the Internet is expected to provide many additional opportunities for graphic artists. Employment growth for graphic artists, however, may be limited because some firms are turning to employees without formal artistic or design training to operate computer-aided design systems. Employment of fine artists is expected to grow because of population growth, rising incomes, and growth in the number of people who appreciate fine arts.

Demand for artists may also depend on the level of government funding for certain programs. For example, the National Endowment for the Arts offers a variety of grants to artists; however, competition is intense for most awards.

Earnings

Median earnings for salaried visual artists who usually work full-time were about $27,100 a year in 1996. The middle 50 percent earned between $20,000 and $36,400 a year. The top 10 percent earned more than $43,000, and the bottom 10 percent earned less than $15,000.

The Society of Publication Designers estimates that entry-level graphic designers earned between $23,000 and $27,000 annually in 1997.

Earnings for self-employed visual artists vary widely. Those struggling to gain experience and a reputation may be forced to charge close to the minimum wage for their work. Well-established freelancers and fine artists may earn much more than salaried artists. Like other workers, self-employed artists must provide their own benefits.

Related Occupations

Many occupations in the advertising industry, such as account executive or creative director, are related to commercial and graphic art and design. Other workers who apply visual art skills include architects, display workers, landscape architects, photographers, and floral, industrial, and interior designers. Various printing occupations are also related to graphic art, as is the work of art and design teachers. In addition, several occupational options associated with the Internet have emerged—for example, webmaster and Internet

page designer. These jobs often require artistic talent as well as computer skills.

Sources of Additional Information

Students interested in careers as illustrators should contact:

❑ The National Association of Schools of Art and Design, 11250 Roger Bacon Dr., Suite 21, Reston, VA 20190.

For information on careers in medical illustration, contact:

❑ The Association of Medical Illustrators, 1819 Peachtree St. NE., Suite 712, Atlanta, GA 30309-1848.

For a list of schools offering degree programs in graphic design, contact:

❑ The American Institute of Graphic Arts, 164 Fifth Ave., New York, NY 10010.

For information on magazine art and design occupations, contact:

❑ The Society of Publication Designers, 60 East 42nd St., Suite 721, New York, NY 10165-1416.

Water and Wastewater Treatment Plant Operators

(D.O.T. 954.382-010, -014; 955.362-010, .382, and .585)

Significant Points

✓ *Employment is concentrated in local government and private water supply and sanitary services companies.*

✓ *In 49 states, operators must pass exams certifying that they are capable of overseeing various treatment processes.*

✓ *Educational requirements are increasing as treatment plants become more complex to meet new water pollution control regulations.*

Nature of the Work

Clean water is essential for good health, recreation, fish and wildlife, and industry. Water treatment plant operators treat water so that it is safe to drink. Wastewater treatment plant operators remove harmful pollutants from domestic and industrial wastewater so that it is safe to return to the environment.

Water is pumped from wells, rivers, and streams to water treatment plants where it is treated and distributed to customers. Wastewater is collected from customers, traveling through sewer pipes to wastewater treatment plants where it is treated and returned to streams, rivers, and oceans, or reused for irrigation and landscaping. Operators in both types of plants control processes and equipment to remove solid materials, chemical compounds, and micro-organisms from the water or to render them harmless. They also control pumps, valves, and other processing equipment to move the water or wastewater through the various treatment processes, and dispose of the waste materials removed from the water.

Operators read and interpret meters and gauges to make sure plant equipment and processes are working properly and adjust controls as needed. They operate chemical-feeding devices, take samples of the water or wastewater, perform chemical and biological laboratory analyses, and test and adjust the amount of chemicals such as chlorine in the water. Operators also make minor repairs to valves, pumps, and other equipment. They use a variety of instruments to sample and measure water quality, gauges, and common hand and power tools to make repairs.

Water and wastewater treatment plant operators increasingly rely on computers to help monitor equipment, store sampling results, make process control decisions, schedule and record maintenance activities, and produce reports. When problems occur, operators may use their computers to determine the cause of and solution to the malfunction.

Occasionally operators must work under emergency conditions. A heavy rainstorm, for example, may cause large amounts of wastewater to flow into sewers, exceeding a plant's treatment capacity. Emergencies also can be caused by conditions inside a plant, such as chlorine gas leaks or oxygen deficiencies. To handle these conditions, operators are trained in emergency management response using special safety equipment and procedures to protect public health and the facility. During these periods, operators may work under extreme pressure to correct problems as quickly as possible. These periods may create dangerous working conditions and operators must be extremely cautious.

The specific duties of plant operators depend on the type and size of plant. In smaller plants, one operator may control all machinery, perform tests, keep records, handle complaints, and do repairs and maintenance. A few operators may handle both a water treatment and a wastewater treatment plant. In larger plants with many employees, operators may be more specialized and only monitor one process. The staff may also include chemists, engineers, laboratory technicians, mechanics, helpers, supervisors, and a superintendent.

Water pollution standards have become increasingly stringent since adoption of two major federal environmental statutes: the Clean Water Act of 1972, which implemented a national system of regulation on the discharge of pollutants, and the Safe Drinking Water Act of 1974, which established standards for drinking water. Industrial facilities that send their wastes to municipal treatment plants must meet certain minimum standards and ensure that these wastes have been adequately pretreated so that they do not damage municipal treatment facilities. Municipal water treatment plants also must meet stringent drinking water standards. The list of contaminants regulated by these statutes has grown over time. For example, the 1996 Safe Drinking Water Act Amendments includes standards for the monitoring of cryptosporidium and giardia, two biological organisms that have caused health problems recently. Operators must be familiar with the guidelines established by federal regulations and how they affect their plant. In addition to federal regulations, operators also must be aware of any guidelines imposed by the state or locality in which the plant operates.

Working Conditions

Water and wastewater treatment plant operators work both indoors and outdoors and may be exposed to noise from machinery and some unpleasant odors, although chemicals may be used to minimize these. Operators have to stoop, reach, and climb and sometimes get their clothes dirty. They must pay close attention to safety procedures for they may be confronted with hazardous conditions, such as slippery walkways, dangerous gases, and malfunctioning equipment. Because plants operate 24 hours a day, seven days a week, operators work one of three eight-hour shifts and weekends and holidays on a rotational basis. Whenever emergencies arise, operators may be required to work overtime.

Employment

Water and wastewater treatment plant operators held about 98,000 jobs in 1996. The vast majority worked for local governments. Some worked for private water supply and sanitary services companies, which increasingly provide operation and management services to local governments on a contract basis. About half worked as water treatment plant operators and half worked as wastewater treatment plant operators.

Water and wastewater treatment plant operators are employed throughout the country, with most jobs in larger towns and cities. Although nearly all work full-time, those who work in small towns may only work part-time at the water or wastewater treatment plant—the remainder of their time may be spent handling other municipal duties.

Training, Other Qualifications, and Advancement

Trainees usually start as attendants or operators-in-training and learn their skills on the job under the direction of an experienced operator. They learn by observing the processes and equipment in operation and by doing routine tasks such as recording meter readings; taking samples of wastewater and sludge; and doing simple maintenance and repair work on pumps, electric motors, valves, and other plant equipment. Larger treatment plants generally combine this on-the-job training with formal classroom or self-paced study programs.

Operators need mechanical aptitude and should be competent in basic mathematics, as they need to apply data to formulas of treatment requirements, flow levels, and concentration levels. Because of the introduction of computer-controlled equipment and more sophisticated instrumentation, a high school diploma generally is required. In addition, employers prefer those who have had high school courses in chemistry, biology, and mathematics.

Some positions, particularly in larger cities and towns, are covered by civil service regulations, and applicants may be required to pass written examinations testing elementary mathematics skills, mechanical aptitude, and general intelligence.

Some two-year programs leading to an associate degree in water and/or wastewater technology and one-year programs leading to a certificate are available. These provide a good general knowledge of water and wastewater treatment processes as well as basic preparation for becoming an operator. Because plants are becoming more complex, completion of such courses increases an applicant's chances for employment and promotion.

Most state drinking water and water pollution control agencies offer training courses to improve operators' skills and knowledge. These courses cover principles of treatment processes and process control, laboratory procedures, maintenance, management skills, collection systems, safety, chlorination, sedimentation, biological treatment, sludge treatment and disposal, and flow measurements. Some operators take correspondence courses on subjects related to water and wastewater treatment, and some employers pay part of the tuition for related college courses in science or engineering.

As operators are promoted, they become responsible for more complex treatment processes. Some operators are promoted to plant supervisor or superintendent, while others advance by transferring to a larger facility. Some postsecondary training in water and wastewater treatment coupled with increasingly responsible experience as an operator may be sufficient to qualify for superintendent of a small plant, since at many small plants the superintendent also serves as an operator. However, educational requirements are rising as larger, more complex treatment plants are built to meet new drinking water and water pollution control standards. With each promotion, the operator must have greater knowledge of federal, state, and local regulations. Superintendents of large plants generally need an engineering or science degree. A few operators get jobs with state drinking water or water pollution control agencies as technicians, who monitor and provide technical assistance to plants throughout the state. Vocational-technical school or community college training generally is preferred for technician jobs. Experienced operators may transfer to related jobs with industrial wastewater treatment plants, companies selling water or wastewater treatment equipment and chemicals, engineering consulting firms, or vocational-technical schools.

In 49 states, operators must pass an examination to certify that they are capable of overseeing wastewater treatment plant operations. A voluntary certification program is in effect in the remaining state. Typically, there are different levels of certification depending on the operator's experience and training. Higher certification levels qualify the operator for a wider variety of treatment processes. Certification requirements vary by state, and by size of treatment plants. While relocation may mean having to become certified in a new location, many states accept other states' certifications.

There is presently no nationally mandated certification program for operators. However, the Safe Drinking Water Act Amendments of 1996 require that within two years the Environmental Protection Agency specify minimum standards for drinking water operator certification, and that states implement those standards within another two years.

Job Outlook

Those who wish to become water and wastewater treatment plant operators should have good opportunities through the year 2006. Despite job growth that is expected to be faster than average, the number of applicants in this field is normally low, making for good job prospects for qualified applicants.

The increasing population and growth of the economy are expected to increase demand for water and wastewater treatment services. As new plants are constructed to meet this demand, employment of water and wastewater treatment plant operators should increase. In addition, some job openings will occur as experienced operators transfer to other occupations or leave the labor force.

Although local government is the largest employer of water and wastewater treatment plant operators, increased reliance on private firms specializing in the operation and management of water and wastewater treatment facilities should shift some employment demand to these companies. Increased pretreatment activity by manufacturing firms should also create new job opportunities.

Water and wastewater treatment plant operators generally have steady employment because the services they provide are essential and required by law.

Earnings

Water and wastewater treatment plant operators had median weekly earnings of $551 in 1996; the lowest paid 10 percent of the occupation earned about $313 a week, the middle 50 percent of the occupation earned between $392 and $703 a week, and the top 10 percent earned about $808 a week. According to information from union surveys, wages for water and wastewater treatment plant operators ranged from $335 to $1,034 weekly, averaging $668 in 1995. Salaries depend, among other things, on the size and location of the plant, the complexity of the operator's job, and the operator's level of certification.

In addition to their annual salaries, water and wastewater treatment plant operators generally receive benefits that include health and life insurance, a retirement plan, and educational reimbursement for job-related courses.

Related Occupations

Other workers whose main activity consists of operating a system of machinery to process or produce materials include boiler operators, gas-compressor operators, power plant operators, power reactor operators, stationary engineers, turbine operators, chemical plant operators, and petroleum refinery operators.

Sources of Additional Information

For information on certification, contact:
- ❏ Association of Boards of Certification, 208 Fifth St., Ames, IA 50010-6259.

For educational information on careers as a water treatment plant operator, contact:
- ❏ American Water Works Association, 6666 West Quincy Ave., Denver, CO 80235.
- ❏ Water Environment Federation, 601 Wythe St., Alexandria, VA 22314.

For information on jobs, contact state or local water pollution control agencies, state water and waste water operator associations, state environmental training centers, or local offices of the state employment service.

Welders, Cutters, and Welding Machine Operators

(D.O.T. 613.667-010; 614.684-010; 709.684-086; 727.662, .684-022; 810; 811; 812; 814; 815; 816 except .482 and .682; 819.281-010, -014, -022, .361, .381, .384, .684, and .685)

Significant Points

✓ *Training for welders can range from a few weeks of school or on-the-job training for low skilled positions to several years of combined school and on-the-job training for highly skilled jobs.*

✓ *Although much of the welding done in manufacturing settings is increasingly being automated, there still will be a significant demand for welders in other areas, making for good employment opportunities.*

Nature of the Work

Welding is the most common way of permanently joining metal parts. Heat is applied to the pieces to be joined, melting and fusing them to form a permanent bond. Because of its strength, welding is used to construct and repair ships, automobiles, spacecraft, and thousands of other manufactured products. Welding is used to join beams when constructing buildings, bridges, and other structures, and pipes in pipelines, nuclear power plants and refineries.

Welders use all types of welding equipment in a variety of positions, such as flat, vertical, horizontal, and overhead. They may perform manual welding, in which the work is entirely controlled by the welder, or semi-automatic welding, in which the welder uses machinery, such as a wire feeder, to help perform welding tasks. They generally plan work from drawings or specifications, or by analyzing damaged metal parts, using their knowledge of welding and metals. They select and set up welding equipment and examine welds to insure they meet standards or specifications. Some welders have more limited duties. They perform routine production work that has already been planned and laid out. These jobs do not require knowledge of all welding techniques.

In some production processes—in which the work is repetitive and the items to be welded are relatively uniform—automated welding is used. In this process, a machine performs the welding tasks while monitored by a welding machine operator. Welding machine operators set up and operate welding machines as specified by layouts, work orders, or blueprints. Operators must constantly monitor the machine to ensure that it produces the desired weld.

The work of arc, plasma, and flame cutters is closely related to that of welders. However, instead of joining metals, cutters use the heat from burning gases or an electric arc to cut and trim metal objects to specific dimensions. Cutters also dismantle large objects, such as ships, railroad cars, automobiles or aircraft. Some operate and monitor cutting machines similar to those used by welding machine operators.

Working Conditions

Welders and cutters are often exposed to potential hazards. They wear protective clothing, safety shoes, goggles, hoods with protective lenses, and other devices to prevent burns and eye injuries, and to protect them from falling objects. Automated welding machine operators are not exposed to as many hazards. A face shield or goggles generally provide adequate protection. Because some metals may give off toxic gases and fumes as they melt, federal regulations require ventilation to meet strict guidelines to minimize these hazards. Occasionally, some workers are in contact with rust, grease, and dirt on metal surfaces. Some welders are isolated for short intervals while they work in booths constructed to contain sparks and glare. Welders often work in a variety of awkward positions, having to make welds while bending, stooping, or working overhead. In some settings, however, working conditions are much better and there are few hazards or discomforts. Overtime is sometimes necessary to complete special projects.

Employment

Welders, cutters, and welding machine operators held about 453,000 jobs in 1996. About nine out of ten welders and cutters were employed in manufacturing, services, construction, or wholesale trade. The majority of those in manufacturing were employed in transportation equipment, industrial machinery and equipment, or fabricated metal products. All welding machine operators were employed in manufacturing industries, primarily fabricated metal products, machinery, and motor vehicles. Almost two of five welders are employed in six states: Texas, California, Ohio, Pennsylvania, Michigan, and Illinois—states heavily dominated by automobile and fabricated metal products manufacturing, and by the petroleum and chemical industry.

Training, Other Qualifications, and Advancement

Training for welders can range from a few weeks of school or on-the-job training for low skilled positions to several years of combined school and on-the-job training for highly skilled jobs. Formal training is available in high schools, vocational schools, and post-secondary institutions such as vocational-technical institutes, community colleges, and private welding schools. The Armed Forces operate welding schools as well. Some employers provide training to help welders improve their skills. Courses in blueprint reading, shop mathematics, mechanical drawing, physics, chemistry, and metallurgy are helpful. A knowledge of computers is gaining importance, especially for welding machine operators, as some welders are becoming responsible for the programming of computer-controlled welding machines, including robots.

Some welders become certified, a process whereby the employer sends a worker to an institution, such as an independent testing lab or technical school, to weld a test specimen to specific codes and standards required by the employer. The testing procedures are based on the standards and codes set by one of several industry associations with which the employer may be affiliated. If the welding inspector at the examining institution determines that the worker has performed according to the employer's guidelines, he or she then certifies that the welder being tested is able to work with a particular welding procedure.

Welders and cutters need good eyesight, good hand-eye coordination, and manual dexterity. They should be able to concentrate on detailed work for long periods and be able to bend, stoop, and work in awkward positions. In addition, welders need to be adaptable, as it is becoming increasingly common for welders and cutters to receive cross-training for other production jobs.

Welders can advance to more skilled welding jobs with additional training and experience. They may be promoted to welding technicians, supervisors, inspectors, or instructors. Some experienced welders open their own repair shops.

Job Outlook

Opportunities for those who wish to become welders, cutters, and welding machine operators differ by occupational specialty. Employment of welders and cutters is expected to increase slowly, while that of welding machine operators should remain unchanged through the year 2006. Most job openings will result from the need to replace experienced workers who transfer to other occupations or leave the labor force. Certified welders, especially those certified in more than one process, will have much better employment opportunities than non-certified welders.

As research in welding technology expands, an increase in the use of automated and robotic welding techniques in manufacturing will result in the employment of welding machine operators staying about level, despite an expected increase in production. Manual welders, however, especially those with a wide variety of skills, will increasingly be needed for sophisticated fabrication tasks and re-

pair work that do not lend themselves to automation. Also, the aging of the nation's infrastructure is adding to the number of metal products needing repairs and will provide additional opportunities. Welders can expect to find more jobs in the business services industry as companies increasingly contract out repair and maintenance functions.

Welders, cutters, and welding machine operators in construction and manufacturing are vulnerable to periodic layoffs due to economic downturns.

Earnings

Median earnings for welders and cutters were about $478 a week in 1996. The middle 50 percent earned between $346 and $605. The top 10 percent earned more than $807, and the lowest 10 percent earned less than $278.

More than one-fourth of welders belong to unions. Among these are the International Association of Machinists and Aerospace Workers; the International Brotherhood of Boilermakers, Iron Ship Builders, Blacksmiths, Forgers and Helpers; the International Union, United Automobile, Aerospace and Agricultural Implement Workers of America; the United Association of Journeymen and Apprentices of the Plumbing and Pipe Fitting Industry of the United States and Canada; and the United Electrical, Radio, and Machine Workers of America.

Related Occupations

Welders and cutters are skilled metal workers. Other metal workers include blacksmiths, forge shop workers, all-round machinists, machine-tool operators, tool and die makers, millwrights, sheet-metal workers, boilermakers, and metal sculptors.

Welding machine operators run machines that weld metal parts. Others who run metalworking machines include lathe and turning, milling and planing, punching and stamping press, and rolling machine operators.

Sources of Additional Information

For information on training opportunities and jobs for welders, cutters, and welding machine operators, contact local employers, the local office of the state employment service, or schools providing welding training.

Information on careers in welding is available from:

❑ American Welding Society, 550 NW Lejeune Rd., Miami, FL 33126-5699.

For a list of accredited schools that offer training in welding, contact:

❑ Career College Association, 750 1st Street NE, Suite 900, Washington, DC 20002.

Writers and Editors

(D.O.T. 052.067-010; 131 except .262-010 and -018; 132; and 203.362-026)

Significant Points

✓ *Most jobs require a college degree in the liberal arts—communications, journalism, and English are preferred—or a technical subject for technical writing positions.*

✓ *Less competition is expected for lower paying jobs at small daily and weekly newspapers, trade publication, and radio and television broadcasting stations in small communities.*

✓ *Persons who fail to gain better paying jobs or earn enough as independent writers, are usually able to readily transfer to communications-related jobs in other occupations.*

Nature of the Work

Writers and editors communicate through the written word. Writers develop original fiction and nonfiction for books, magazines and trade journals, newspapers, technical reports, company newsletters, radio and television broadcasts, movies, and advertisements. Editors select and prepare material for publication or broadcasting and supervise writers.

Writers first select a topic or are assigned one by an editor. They then gather information through personal observation, library research, and interviews. Writers select and organize the material and put it into words, effectively conveying it to the reader, and often revise or rewrite sections, searching for the best organization of the material or the right phrasing.

News writers prepare news items for newspapers or news broadcasts, based on information supplied by reporters or wire services. Columnists analyze news and write commentaries, based on personal knowledge and experience. Editorial writers write comments to stimulate or mold public opinion, in accordance with their publication's viewpoint. Columnists and editorial writers are able to take sides on issues, be subjective, and express their opinions while other news writers must be objective and neutral in their coverage.

Technical writers make scientific and technical information easily understandable to a nontechnical audience. They prepare operating and maintenance manuals, catalogs, parts lists, assembly instructions, sales promotion materials, and project proposals. They also plan and edit technical reports and oversee preparation of illustrations, photographs, diagrams, and charts.

Copy writers write advertising copy for use by publication or broadcast media, to promote the sale of goods and services.

Established writers may work on a freelance basis; they sell their work to publishers or publication units, manufacturing firms, and public relations and advertising departments or agencies. They sometimes contract to complete specific assignments such as writing about a new product or technique.

Editors frequently write and almost always review, rewrite, and edit the work of writers. However, their primary duties are to plan the contents of books, magazines, or newspapers and to supervise their preparation. They decide what will appeal to readers, assign topics to reporters and writers, and oversee the production of the publications. In small organizations, a single editor may do everything. In larger ones, an executive editor oversees associate or assistant editors who have responsibility for particular subjects, such as fiction, local news, international news, or sports, or who edit one or a few publications. Editors hire writers, reporters, or other employees; plan budgets; and negotiate contracts with freelance writers. In broadcasting companies, program directors have similar responsibilities.

Editors and program directors often have assistants, with the title of assistant editor, editorial assistant, copy editor, or production assistant. Many assistants hold entry-level jobs. They review copy for errors in grammar, punctuation, and spelling. They check manuscripts for readability, style, and agreement with editorial policy. They add and rearrange sentences to improve clarity or delete incorrect and unnecessary material. Editorial assistants do research for writers and verify facts, dates, and statistics. Assistants may also arrange page layouts of articles, photographs, and advertising. They may compose headlines, prepare copy for printing, and proofread printer's galleys. Some editorial assistants read and evaluate manuscripts submitted by freelance writers or answer letters about published or broadcast material. Production assistants on small papers or in radio stations clip stories that come over the wire services' printers, answer phones, and make photocopies. Most writers and editors use personal computers or word processors; many use desktop or electronic publishing systems.

Working Conditions

Some writers and editors work in comfortable, private offices; others work in noisy rooms filled with the sound of keyboards and computer printers as well as the voices of other writers tracking down information over the telephone. The search for information sometimes requires travel and visits to diverse workplaces, such as factories, offices, laboratories, the ballpark, or the theater, but many have to be content with telephone interviews and the library.

The workweek usually runs 35 to 40 hours. Those who prepare morning or weekend publications and broadcasts, work nights and/or weekends. Writers may work overtime to meet deadlines or to cover late-developing stories. They often face pressure to meet deadlines. On some jobs, deadlines are part of the daily routine.

Employment

Writers and editors held about 286,000 jobs in 1996. Nearly a third of salaried writers and editors work for newspapers, magazines, and book publishers. Substantial numbers also work in advertising agencies, in radio and television broadcasting, in public relations firms, and on journals and newsletters published by business and nonprofit organizations, such as professional associations, labor unions, and religious organizations. Others develop publications for government agencies or write for motion picture companies.

Many technical writers work for computer software firms or manufacturers of aircraft, chemicals, pharmaceuticals, and computers and other electronic equipment.

Jobs with major book publishers, magazines, broadcasting companies, advertising agencies and public relations firms, and the federal government are concentrated in New York, Chicago, Los Angeles, Boston, Philadelphia, San Francisco, and Washington, DC. Jobs with newspapers; and professional, religious, business, technical, and trade union magazines or journals are more widely dispersed throughout the country. Technical writers are employed throughout the country, but the largest concentrations are in the Northeast, Texas, and California.

Thousands of other individuals work as freelancers, earning some income from their articles, books, and less commonly, television and movie scripts. Most support themselves primarily with income derived from other sources.

Training, Other Qualifications, and Advancement

A college degree generally is required for a position as a writer or editor. Although some employers look for a broad liberal arts background, most prefer to hire people with degrees in communications, journalism, or English.

Technical writing requires a degree in, or some knowledge about a specialized field–engineering, business, or one of the sciences, for example. In many cases, people with good writing skills can learn specialized knowledge on the job. Some transfer from jobs as technicians, scientists, or engineers. Others begin as research assistants, editorial assistants, or trainees in a technical information department, develop technical communication skills, and then assume writing duties.

Writers and editors must be able to express ideas clearly and logically and should love to write. Creativity, curiosity, a broad range of knowledge, self-motivation, and perseverance are also valuable. For some jobs, the ability to concentrate amid confusion, and to work under pressure is essential. Familiarity with electronic publishing, graphics, and video production equipment is increasingly needed. Online newspapers and magazines require knowledge of computer software used to combine online text with graphics, audio, video, and 3-D animation. Editors must have good judgment in deciding what material to accept and what to reject. They need tact and the ability to guide and encourage others in their work.

High school and college newspapers, literary magazines, and community newspapers and radio and television stations all provide valuable, but sometimes unpaid, practical writing experience. Many magazines, newspapers, and broadcast stations have internships for students. Interns write short pieces, conduct research and interviews, and learn about the publishing or broadcasting business.

In small firms, beginning writers and editors may not only work as editorial or production assistants, but also write or edit material right away. They often advance by moving to other firms. In larger firms, jobs usually are more formally structured. Beginners generally do research, fact checking, or copy editing. They take on full-scale writing or editing duties less rapidly than do the employees of small companies. Advancement comes as they are assigned more important articles.

Job Outlook

Through the year 2006, the outlook for most writing and editing jobs is expected to continue to be competitive, because so many people are attracted to the field. However, opportunities will be good for technical writers because of the more limited number of writers who can handle technical material. Online publications and services, which are relatively new, will continue to grow and require an increased number of writers and editors. Opportunities should be better on small daily and weekly newspapers, and in small radio and television stations, where the pay is low. Some small publications are hiring freelance copy editors as back-up for their staff editors, or for additional help with special projects. Persons preparing to be writers and editors should also have academic preparation in another field as well, either to qualify them as writers specializing in that field, or to enter that field if they are unable to get a job in writing.

Employment of writers and editors is expected to increase faster than the average for all occupations through the year 2006. Employment of salaried writers and editors by newspapers, periodicals, book publishers, and nonprofit organizations is expected to increase with growing demand for their publications. Growth of advertising and public relations agencies should also be a source of new jobs. Demand for technical writers is expected to increase because of the continuing expansion of scientific and technical information, and the continued need to communicate it. Many job openings will also occur as experienced workers transfer to other occupations or leave the labor force. Turnover is relatively high in this occupation–many freelancers leave because they cannot earn enough money.

Earnings

In 1996, beginning salaries for writers and editorial assistants averaged $21,000 annually, according to the Dow Jones Newspaper Fund. According to the Newspaper Guild those who had at least five years experience averaged more than $30,000 and senior editors at the largest newspapers earned over $67,000 a year.

According to the 1996 Technical Communicator's Salary Survey, the median annual salary for technical writers was $44,000 annually.

The average annual salary for technical writers and editors in the federal government in nonsupervisory, supervisory, and managerial positions was about $47,440 in 1996; other writers and editors averaged about $46,590.

Related Occupations

Writers and editors communicate ideas and information. Other communications occupations include newspaper reporters and correspondents, radio and television announcers, advertising and public relations workers, and teachers.

Sources of Additional Information

For a guide to journalism careers and scholarships, contact:
❑ The Dow Jones Newspaper Fund, P.O. Box 300, Princeton, NJ 08540.

For information on college internships in magazine editing, contact:
❑ American Society of Magazine Editors, 919 3rd. Ave., New York, NY 10022.

For information on careers in technical writing, contact:
❑ Society for Technical Communication, Inc., 901 N. Stuart St., Suite 904, Arlington, VA 22203.

For information on union wage rates for newspaper and magazine editors, contact:
❑ The Newspaper Guild, Research and Information Department, 8611 Second Ave., Silver Spring, MD 20910.

For career information and a pamphlet entitled Newspaper Careers and Challenges for the Next Century contact:
❑ National Newspaper Association, 1525 Wilson Blvd., Suite 550, Arlington, VA 22209.

Section Two

CAREER PLANNING
AND JOB SEARCH ADVICE

THE QUICK JOB SEARCH
A RESULTS-ORIENTED CAREER PLANNING
AND JOB SEARCH MINIBOOK

by Mike Farr

While *The Quick Job Search* is short, it covers **all** the major topics needed to explore career options and to conduct an effective job search. The techniques it presents have been proven to reduce the time it takes to find a job and are widely used by job search programs throughout North America.

Major Topics Include

- **Skills Identification:** Includes checklists and activities to help you identify your key skills—essential for career planning, interviewing, and writing resumes.

- **Career Planning:** Provides activities to help define your ideal job and a list of the top 250 jobs (85 percent of us work in one of these jobs)—and tips on getting more information on each one.

- **Results-Oriented Job Seeking Skills:** Research-based advice on traditional and nontraditional job search methods, with an emphasis on the two most effective techniques: networking and cold contacts.

- **Interview Skills, Resumes, Time Management, and More:** Specific techniques on answering problem interview questions, writing a superior resume, setting a daily schedule, getting two interviews a day, and many other innovative and useful techniques.

- **Dealing with Job Loss:** Practical and upbeat advice on coping with the stress and discouragement of being unemployed.

- **Handling Your Finances While out of Work:** Brief but helpful tips on conserving cash and stretching your resources.

- **Sources of Other Information:** Books and other sources of information on occupations, employers, resumes, interviewing skills, industries, and a range of job search topics.

Introduction

I've spent much of the past 20 years of my professional life learning more about career planning and job search methods. My original interest was in helping people find jobs in less time, and in helping them find better jobs. In a broad sense, that is—or should be—the real task of career counseling and job seeking skills. While there is a lot of complexity to these tasks, I have also found some elements of simplicity:

1. If you are going to work, you might as well define what it is you really want to do and are good at.

2. If you are looking for a job, you might as well use techniques that will reduce the time it takes to find one—and that helps you get a better job than otherwise.

This section covers these topics, along with a few others. While I have written much more detailed works on career planning and job seeking, I present the basics of career planning and job seeking in this section. I think that there is enough information here to make a difference for most people, and I hope that it gives you some things to think about, as well as some techniques you have not considered.

About ten years ago, I decided to write something very short but that would cover the most important ele-

While this book will teach you techniques to find a better job in less time, job seeking requires you to act, not just learn. So, in going through this book, consider what you can do to put the techniques to work for you. Do the activities. Create a daily plan. Get more interviews. Today, not tomorrow. You see, the sooner and harder you get to work on your job search, the shorter it is likely to be.

ments of effective career planning and job seeking. Writing short things is harder for me than writing longer things, since every word has to count. I began by asking myself, "If I only had 30 or so pages, what were the most important things to tell someone?"

The Quick Job Search was the result. While it is a section in this book, it has also been published separately and, in an expanded form, as a book titled *How to Get a Job Now!* It has sold about 300,000 copies in its various forms. I hope you can make good use of it.

Avoid the Temptation; Do the Activities

I already know that you will resist doing the activities included in *The Quick Job Search*. But trust me, doing them is worth while. Those who do them will have a better sense of what they are good at, what they want to do, and how to go about doing it. They are more likely to get more interviews and to present themselves better in those interviews. Is this worth giving up a night of TV? Yes, I think so.

Interestingly enough, you will—after reading *The Quick Job Search* and doing its activities—have spent more time on planning your career than most people. And you will know far more than the average job seeker about how to go about finding a job. While you may want to know more, I hope that this is enough to get you started.

Changing Jobs and Careers Is Often Healthy

Most of us were told from an early age that each career move must be up—involving more money, responsibility, and prestige. Yet research indicates people change careers for many other reasons as well.

In a survey conducted by the Gallup Organization for the National Occupational Information Coordinating Committee, 44 percent of the working adults surveyed expected to be in a different job within three years. This is a very high turnover rate, yet only 41 percent had a definite plan to follow in mapping out their careers.

Logical, ordered careers are found more often with increasing levels of education. For example, while 25 percent of the high school dropouts took the only job available, this was true for only 8 percent of those with at least some college. But you should not assume this means that such occupational stability is healthy. Many adult developmental psychologists believe occupational change is not only normal but may even be necessary for sound adult growth and development. It is common, even normal, to reconsider occupational roles during your twenties, thirties, and forties—even in the absence of economic pressure to do so.

One viewpoint is that a healthy occupational change is one that allows some previously undeveloped aspect of yourself to emerge. The change may be as natural as from clerk to supervisor; or as drastic as from professional musician to airline pilot. Although risk is always a factor when change is involved, reasonable risks are healthy and can raise self-esteem.

But Not Just Any Job Should Do— Nor Any Job Search

Whether you are seeking similar work in another setting or changing careers, you need a workable plan to find the right job. This section will give you the information you need to help you find a good job quickly.

While the techniques are presented here briefly, they are based on my years of experience in helping people find good jobs (not just any job) and to find jobs in less time. The career decision-making section will help you consider the major issues you need to make a good decision about the job you want. The job-seeking skills are ones that have been proven to reduce the amount of time required to find a good job.

Of course, more thorough books have been written on job-seeking techniques, and you may want to look into buying one or more of the better ones to obtain additional information. (A list of such books is included in the Bibliography of this book.) But, short as this section is, it DOES present the basic skills to find a good job in less time. The techniques work.

The Six Steps for a Quick and Successful Job Search

You can't just read about getting a job. The best way to get a job is to go out and get interviews! And the best way to get interviews is to make a job out of getting a job.

After many years of experience, I have identified just six basic things you need to do that make a big difference in your job search. Each will be covered in this section.

The Six Steps for a Quick Job Search

1. Know your skills.

2. Have a clear job objective.

3. Know where and how to look for job leads.

4. Spend at least 25 hours a week looking.

5. Get two interviews a day.

6. Follow up on all contacts.

Identify Your Key Skills

One survey of employers found that 90 percent of the people they interviewed did not present the skills they had to do the job they sought. They could not answer the basic question, "Why should I hire you?"

Knowing your skills is essential to do well in an interview. This same knowledge is important in deciding what type of job you will enjoy and do well. For these reasons, I consider identifying your skills an essential part of a successful career plan or job search.

The Three Types of Skills

Most people think of "skills" as job-related skills such as using a computer. But we all have other types of skills that are also important for success on a job—and that are very important to employers. The triangle below presents skills in three groups, and I think that this is a very useful way to consider skills for our purposes.

The Skills Triad

Let's review these three types of skills and identify those that are most important to you.

Self-Management Skills

Write down three things about yourself that you think make you a good worker.

Your "Good Worker" Traits

1. _____

2. _____

3. _____

The things you just wrote down are among the most important things for an employer to know about you! They have to do with your basic personality—your ability to adapt to a new environment. They are some of the most important things to emphasize in an interview, yet most job seekers don't realize their importance—and don't mention them.

Review the Self-Management Skills Checklist and put a checkmark beside any skills you have. The Key Self-Management Skills are skills that employers find particularly important. If one or more of the Key Self-Management Skills apply to you, mentioning them in an interview can help you greatly.

Self-Management Skills Checklist

Key Self-Management Skills

___ accept supervision	___ hard worker
___ get along with coworkers	___ honest
___ get things done on time	___ productive
___ good attendance	___ punctual

Other Self-Management Skills

___ able to coordinate	___ friendly
___ ambitious	___ good-natured
___ assertive	___ helpful
___ capable	___ humble
___ cheerful	___ imaginative
___ competent	___ independent
___ complete assignments	___ industrious
___ conscientious	___ informal
___ creative	___ intelligent
___ dependable	___ intuitive
___ discreet	___ learn quickly
___ eager	___ loyal
___ efficient	___ mature
___ energetic	___ methodical
___ enthusiastic	___ modest
___ expressive	___ motivated
___ flexible	___ natural
___ formal	___ sense of humor

___ open-minded
___ optimistic
___ original
___ patient
___ persistent
___ physically strong
___ practice new skills
___ reliable
___ resourceful
___ responsible
___ self-confident

___ sincere
___ solve problems
___ spontaneous
___ steady
___ tactful
___ take pride in work
___ tenacious
___ thrifty
___ trustworthy
___ versatile
___ well-organized

Other Self-Management Skills You Have:

_____

_____

_____

After you are done with the list, circle the five skills you feel are most important and list them in the box that follows.

Note: Some people find it helpful to complete now the "Essential Job Search Data Worksheet" provided later in this book. It organizes skills and accomplishments from previous jobs and other life experiences.

Your Top 5 Self-Management Skills

1. _____

2. _____

3. _____

4. _____

5. _____

Transferable Skills

We all have skills that can transfer from one job or career to another. For example, the ability to organize events could be used in a variety of jobs and may be essential for success in certain occupations. Your mission should be to find a job that requires the skills you have and enjoy using.

In the following list, put a check mark beside the skills you have. You may have used them in a previous job or in some nonwork setting.

Transferable Skills Checklist

Key Transferable Skills

___ instruct others
___ manage money, budget
___ manage people
___ meet deadlines
___ meet the public

___ negotiate
___ organize/manage projects
___ public speaking
___ written communication skills

Skills Working with Things

___ assemble things
___ build things
___ construct/repair
___ drive, operate vehicles
___ good with hands

___ observe/inspect
___ operate tools, machines
___ repair things
___ use complex equipment

Skills Working with Data

___ analyze data
___ audit records
___ budget
___ calculate/compute
___ check for accuracy
___ classify things
___ compare
___ compile
___ count
___ detail-oriented

___ evaluate
___ investigate
___ keep financial records
___ locate information
___ manage money
___ observe/inspect
___ record facts
___ research
___ synthesize
___ take inventory

Skills Working with People

___ administer
___ advise
___ care for
___ coach
___ confront others
___ counsel people
___ demonstrate
___ diplomatic
___ help others
___ instruct
___ interview people
___ kind
___ listen
___ negotiate

___ outgoing
___ patient
___ perceptive
___ persuade
___ pleasant
___ sensitive
___ sociable
___ supervise
___ tactful
___ tolerant
___ tough
___ trusting
___ understanding

Skills Working with Words, Ideas

___ articulate
___ communicate verbally
___ correspond with others
___ create new ideas
___ design
___ edit
___ ingenious

___ inventive
___ library research
___ logical
___ public speaking
___ remember information
___ write clearly

© Copyright, 1998 · J. Michael Farr · JIST Works, Inc. · Indianapolis, IN

Leadership Skills

___ arrange social functions	___ mediate problems
___ competitive	___ motivate people
___ decisive	___ negotiate agreements
___ delegate	___ plan events
___ direct others	___ results-oriented
___ explain things to others	___ risk-taker
___ influence others	___ run meetings
___ initiate new tasks	___ self-confident
___ make decisions	___ self-motivate
___ manage or direct others	___ solve problems

Creative/Artistic Skills

___ artistic	___ expressive
___ dance, body movement	___ perform, act
___ drawing, art	___ present artistic ideas

Other Similar Skills You Have:

_____

_____

_____

_____

_____

_____

_____

When you are finished, identify the five transferable skills you feel are most important for you to use in your next job and list them in the box below.

Your Top 5 Transferable Skills ✓

1. _____

2. _____

3. _____

4. _____

5. _____

Job-Related Skills

Job content or job-related skills are those you need to do a particular job. A carpenter, for example, needs to know how to use various tools and be familiar with a variety of tasks related to that job.

You may already have a good idea of the type of job that you want. If so, it may be fairly simple for you to identify your job-related skills to emphasize in an interview. But I recommend that you complete at least two other things in this book first:

1. Complete the material that helps you define your job objective more clearly. Doing so will help you clarify just what sort of a job you want and allow you to better select those skills that best support it.

2. Complete the Essential Job Search Data Worksheet that appears later in this book (pages 343-345). It will give you lots of specific skills and accomplishments to consider.

Once you have done these two things, come back and complete the box below. Include the job-related skills you have that you would most like to use in your next job.

Your Top 5 Job-Related Skills ✓

1. _____

2. _____

3. _____

4. _____

5. _____

Begin by Defining Your Ideal Job (You Can Compromise Later)

Too many people look for a job without having a good idea of exactly what they are looking for. Before you go out looking for "a" job, I suggest that you first define exactly what it is you really want– "the" job. Most people think a job objective is the same as a job title, but it isn't. You need to consider other elements of what makes a job satisfying for you. Then, later, you can decide what that job is called and what industry it might be in.

The Eight Factors to Consider in Defining the Ideal Job for You

Following are eight factors to consider when you define your ideal job. Once you know what you want, your task then becomes finding a job that is as close to your ideal job as you can find.

1. What Skills Do You Want to Use?

From the previous skills lists, select the top five skills that you enjoy using and most want to use in your next job.

1. _____

2. _____

3. _____

4. _____

5. _____

2. What Type of Special Knowledge Do You Have?

Perhaps you know how to fix radios, keep accounting records, or cook food. Write down the things you know about from schooling, training, hobbies, family experiences, and other sources. One or more of them could make you a very special applicant in the right setting.

_____

_____

_____

_____

_____

3. With What Type of People Do You Prefer to Work?

Do you like to work with aggressive hardworking folks, creative types, or what?

_____

_____

_____

_____

4. What Type of Work Environment Do You Prefer?

Do you want to work inside, outside, in a quiet place, a busy place, a clean place, have a window with a nice view, or what? List those things that are important to you.

_____

_____

_____

_____

_____

5. Where Do You Want Your Next Job to Be Located— In What City or Region?

Near a bus line? Close to a child care center? If you are open to live or work anywhere, what would your ideal community be like?

_____

_____

_____

_____

6. How Much Money Do You Hope to Make in Your Next Job?

Many people will take less money if the job is great in other ways—or to survive. Think about the minimum you would take as well as what you would eventually like to earn. Your next job will probably be somewhere between.

_____

_____

_____

_____

_____

7. How Much Responsibility Are You Willing to Accept?

Usually, the more money you want to make, the more responsibility you must accept. Do you want to work by yourself, be part of a group, or be in charge? If so, at what level?

_____

_____

_____

_____

_____

8. What Things Are Important or Have Meaning to You?

Do you have values that you would prefer to include as a basis of the work you do? For example, some people want to work to help others, clean up our environment, build things, make machines work, gain power or prestige, or care for animals or plants. Think about what is important to you and how you might include this in your next job.

_____

_____

_____

_____

_____

Your Ideal Job

Use the points at left and on previous pages to help you define your ideal job. Think about each one and select the points that are most important to you. Don't worry about a job title yet; just focus on the most important things to include from the previous questions to define your ideal job.

My Ideal Job Objective:

_____

_____

_____

_____

_____

_____

_____

_____

_____

_____

Setting a Specific Job Objective

Whether or not you have a good idea of the type of job you want, it is important to know more about various job options. About 85 percent of all workers work in one of the 250 jobs in the list that follows.

A very simple but effective way for exploring job alternatives is to go through this list and check those about which you want to learn more. Descriptions for many of them can be found in this book. I encourage you to learn more about the jobs that interest you.

If you need help figuring out what type of job to look for, remember that most areas have free or low-cost career counseling and testing services. Contact local government agencies and schools for referrals.

The Top 250 Jobs in Our Workforce

EXECUTIVE, ADMINISTRATIVE, AND MANAGERIAL OCCUPATIONS

Accountants and auditors[1]

Administrative services managers

Budget analysts

Construction and building inspectors

Construction managers

Cost estimators

Education administrators

Employment interviewers

Engineering, science, and computer systems managers

Farmers and farm managers

Financial managers

Funeral directors

General managers and top executives

Government chief executives and legislators

Health services managers

Hotel managers and assistants

Human resources specialists and managers

Industrial production managers

Inspectors and compliance officers, except construction

Insurance underwriters

Loan officers and counselors

Management analysts and consultants

Marketing, advertising, and public relations managers

Property managers

Purchasers and buyers

Restaurant and food service managers

PROFESSIONAL AND TECHNICAL OCCUPATIONS

AIR TRANSPORTATION-RELATED OCCUPATIONS

Aircraft pilots

Air traffic controllers

ENGINEERS AND ENGINEERING TECHNICIANS

ENGINEERS

Aerospace engineers

Chemical engineers

Civil engineers

Electrical and electronics engineers

Industrial engineers

Mechanical engineers

Metallurgical, ceramic, and materials engineers

Mining engineers

Nuclear engineers

Petroleum engineers

ENGINEERING TECHNICIANS

ARCHITECTS, SURVEYORS, AND DRAFTERS

Architects

Drafters

Landscape architects

Surveyors and mapping scientists

COMPUTER, MATHEMATICAL, AND OPERATIONS RESEARCH OCCUPATIONS

Actuaries

Computer programmers

Computer scientists, computer engineers, and systems analysts

Mathematicians

Operations research analysts

Statisticians

SCIENTISTS AND SCIENCE TECHNICIANS

LIFE SCIENTISTS

Agricultural scientists

Biological and medical scientists

Foresters and conservation scientists

PHYSICAL SCIENTISTS

Chemists

Geologists and geophysicists

Meteorologists

Physicists and astronomers

SCIENCE TECHNICIANS

LEGAL OCCUPATIONS

Lawyers and judges

Paralegals

SOCIAL SCIENTISTS

Economists and marketing research analysts

Psychologists

Urban and regional planners

SOCIAL AND RECREATION WORKERS

Recreation workers

Social and human service assistants

Social workers

CLERGY

Protestant ministers

Rabbis

Roman Catholic priests

TEACHERS, COUNSELORS, AND LIBRARY OCCUPATIONS

Adult education teachers

Archivists and curators

College and university faculty

Counselors

Librarians

Library technicians

School teachers–kindergarten, elementary, and secondary

Special education teachers

HEALTH DIAGNOSING PRACTITIONERS

Chiropractors

Dentists

Optometrists

Physicians

Podiatrists

Veterinarians

HEALTH ASSESSMENT AND TREATING OCCUPATIONS

Dietitians and nutritionists

Occupational therapists

Pharmacists

Physical therapists

Physician assistants

Recreational therapists

Registered nurses

Respiratory therapists

Speech-language pathologists and audiologists

HEALTH TECHNOLOGISTS AND TECHNICIANS

Cardiovascular technologists and technicians

Clinical laboratory technologists and technicians

Dental hygienists

Dispensing opticians

Electroneurodiagnostic technologists

Emergency medical technicians

Health information technicians

Licensed practical nurses

Nuclear medicine technologists

Radiologic technologists

Surgical technicians

COMMUNICATIONS-RELATED OCCUPATIONS

Broadcast technicians

Public relations specialists

Radio and television announcers and newscasters

Reporters and correspondents

Writers and editors

VISUAL ARTS OCCUPATIONS

Designers

Photographers and camera operators

Visual artists

PERFORMING ARTS OCCUPATIONS

Actors, directors, and producers

Dancers and choreographers

Musicians

MARKETING AND SALES OCCUPATIONS

Cashiers

Counter and rental clerks

Insurance agents and brokers

Manufacturers' and wholesale sales representatives

Real estate agents, brokers, and appraisers

Retail sales worker supervisors and managers

Retail sales workers

Securities and financial services sales representatives

Services sales representatives

Travel agents

ADMINISTRATIVE SUPPORT OCCUPATIONS, INCLUDING CLERICAL

Adjusters, investigators, and collectors

Bank tellers

Clerical supervisors and managers

Computer operators

Court reporters, medical transcriptionists, and stenographers

General office clerks

Information clerks

    Hotel and motel desk clerks

    Interviewing and new accounts clerks

    Receptionists

    Reservation and transportation ticket agents and travel clerks

Loan clerks and credit authorizers, checkers, and clerks

Mail clerks and messengers

Material recording, scheduling, dispatching, and distributing occupations

    Dispatchers

    Stock clerks

    Traffic, shipping, and receiving clerks

Postal clerks and mail carriers

Record clerks

    Billing clerks and billing machine operators

    Bookkeeping, accounting, and auditing clerks

    Brokerage clerks and statement clerks

    File clerks

    Library assistants and bookmobile drivers

    Order clerks

    Payroll and timekeeping clerks

    Personnel clerks

Secretaries

Teacher aides

Telephone operators

Typists, word processors, and data entry keyers

SERVICE OCCUPATIONS

FOOD PREPARATION AND BEVERAGE SERVICE OCCUPATIONS

Chefs, cooks, and other kitchen workers

Food and beverage service occupations

HEALTH SERVICE OCCUPATIONS

Dental assistants

Medical assistants

Nursing aides and psychiatric aides

Occupational therapy assistants and aides

Physical and corrective therapy assistants and aides

PERSONAL, BUILDINGS, AND GROUNDS SERVICE OCCUPATIONS

Barbers and cosmetologists

Flight attendants

Homemaker-home health aides

Janitors and cleaners and cleaning supervisors

Landscaping, groundskeeping, nursery, greenhouse, and lawn service occupations

Preschool teachers and child-care workers

Private household workers

Veterinary assistants and nonfarm animal caretakers

Protective service occupations

Correctional officers

Firefighting occupations

Guards

Police, detectives, and special agents

Private detectives and investigators

Mechanics, Installers, and Repairers

Aircraft mechanics, including engine specialists

Automotive body repairers

Automotive mechanics

Diesel mechanics

Electronic equipment repairers

Commercial and industrial electronic equipment repairers

Communications equipment mechanics

Computer and office machine repairers

Electronic home entertainment equipment repairers

Telephone installers and repairers

Elevator installers and repairers

Farm equipment mechanics

General maintenance mechanics

Heating, air-conditioning, and refrigeration technicians

Home appliance and power tool repairers

Industrial machinery repairers

Line installers and cable splicers

Millwrights

Mobile heavy equipment mechanics

Motorcycle, boat, and small-engine mechanics

Musical instrument repairers and tuners

Vending machine servicers and repairers

Construction Trades Occupations

Bricklayers and stonemasons

Carpet installers

Concrete masons and terrazzo workers

Drywall workers and lathers

Electricians

Glaziers

Insulation workers

Painters and paperhangers

Plasterers

Plumbers and pipefitters

Roofers

Sheetmetal workers

Structural and reinforcing ironworkers

Tilesetters

Production Occupations

Assemblers

Precision assemblers

Blue-collar worker supervisors

Fishing, hunting, and forestry occupations

Fishers, hunters, and trappers

Forestry and logging workers

Food processing occupations

Butchers and meat, poultry, and fish cutters

Inspectors, testers, and graders

Metalworking and plastic-working occupations

Boilermakers

Jewelers

Machinists and tool programmers

Metalworking and plastics-working machine operators

Tool and die makers

Welders, cutters, and welding machine operators

Plant and systems operators

Electric power generating plant operators and power distributors and dispatchers

Stationary engineers

Water and wastewater treatment plant operators

Printing occupations

Bindery workers

Prepress workers

Printing press operators

Textile, apparel, and furnishings occupations

Apparel workers

Shoe and leather workers and repairers

Textile machinery operators

Upholsterers

Woodworking occupations

Miscellaneous production occupations

Dental laboratory technicians

Ophthalmic laboratory technicians

Painting and coating machine operators

Photographic process workers

Transportation and Material Moving Occupations

Busdrivers

Material moving equipment operators

Rail transportation occupation

Taxi drivers and chauffeurs

Truckdrivers

Water transportation occupations

Handlers, Equipment Cleaners, Helpers, and Laborers

Job Opportunities in the Armed Forces

Job Search Methods That Help You Get a Better Job in Less Time

One survey found that 85 percent of all employers don't advertise at all. They hire people they already know, people who find out about the jobs through word of mouth, or people who simply happen to be in the right place at the right time. This is sometimes just luck, but this book will teach you ways to increase your "luck" in finding job openings.

Traditional Job Search Methods Are Not Very Effective

Most job seekers don't know how ineffective some traditional job hunting techniques tend to be.

How People Find Jobs

35%
30%
14%
6%
5%
2%
8%

Heard about opening from someone 35%
Contacted employer directly 30%
Answered want ad 14%
Referred by private employment agency 6%
Referred by state employment agency 5%
Took civil service (government) tests 2%

Other methods (referred by school, union referral, placed ads in journals, etc.) 8%

The chart above shows that fewer than 15 percent of all job seekers get jobs from reading the want ads. Let's take a quick look at want ads and other traditional job search methods.

Help Wanted Ads: As you should remember, only about 15 percent of all people get their jobs through the want ads. Everyone who reads the paper knows about these job openings, so competition for advertised jobs is fierce. Still, some people do get jobs this way, so go ahead and apply. Just be sure to spend most of your time using more effective methods.

The State Employment Service: Each state has a network of local offices to administer unemployment compensation and provide job leads and other services. These services are provided without charge to you or employers. Names vary by state, so it may be called "Job Service," "Department of Labor," "Unemployment Office," or another name.

Nationally, only about 5 percent of all job seekers get their jobs here, and these organizations typically know of only one-tenth (or fewer) of the actual job openings in a region. Still, it is worth a weekly visit. If you ask for the same counselor, you might impress the person enough to remember you and refer you for the better openings.

You should also realize that some of the state employment services provide substantial help in the form of job search workshops and other resources. Look into it; the price is right.

Private Employment Agencies: Recent studies have found that private agencies work reasonably well for those who use them. But there are cautions to consider. For one thing, these agencies work best for entry-level positions or for those with specialized skills that are in demand. Most people who use a private agency usually find their jobs using some other source and their success record is quite modest.

Private agencies also charge a fee either to you (as high as 20 percent of your annual salary!) or to the employer. Most of them call employers asking if they have any openings, something you could do yourself. Unless you have skills that are in high demand, you may do better on your own–and save money. At the least, you should rely on a private agency as only one of the techniques you use and not depend on them too heavily.

Temporary Agencies: These can be a source of quick but temporary jobs to bring in some income as well as give you experience in a variety of settings–something that can help you land full-time jobs later. More and more employers are also using them as a way to evaluate workers for permanent jobs. So consider using these agencies if it makes sense to do so, but make certain that you continue an active search for a full-time job as you do.

Sending Out Resumes: *One survey found that you would have to mail more than 500 unsolicited resumes to get one interview!* A much better approach is to contact the person who might hire you by phone to set up an interview directly; then send a resume. If you insist on sending out unsolicited resumes, do this on weekends–save your "prime time" for more effective job search techniques.

Filling Out Applications: Most applications are used to screen you out. Larger organizations may require them, but remember that your task is to get an interview, not fill out an application. If you do complete them, make them neat and error-free, and do not include anything that could get you screened out. If necessary, leave a problematic section blank. It can always be explained after you get an interview.

Personnel Departments: Hardly anyone gets hired by interviewers in a personnel department. Their job is to screen you and refer the "best" applicants to the person who would actually supervise you. You may need to cooperate with them, but it is often better to go directly to the person who is most likely to supervise you–even if no job opening exists at the moment. And remember that most organizations don't even have a personnel office, only the larger ones do!

The Two Job Search Methods That Work Best

Two-thirds of all people get their jobs using informal methods. These jobs are often not advertised and are part of the "hidden" job market. How do **you** find them?

There are two basic informal job search methods: networking with people you know (which I call warm contacts), and making direct contacts with an employer (which I call cold contacts). They are both based on the most important job search rule of all.

▼

The Most Important Job Search Rule: Don't wait until the job is open before contacting the employer!

Most jobs are filled by someone the employer meets before the job is formally "open." So the trick is to meet people who can hire you before a job is available! Instead of saying, "Do you have any jobs open?" say, "I realize you may not have any openings now, but I would still like to talk to you about the possibility of future openings."

Develop a Network of Contacts in Five Easy Steps

One study found that 40 percent of all people found their jobs through a lead provided by a friend, a relative, or an acquaintance. Developing new contacts is called "networking," and here's how it works:

1. **Make lists of people you know.** Develop a list of anyone with whom you are friendly; then make a separate list of all your relatives. These two lists alone often add up to 25-100 people or more. Next, think of other groups of people with whom you have something in common, such as former co-workers or classmates; members of your social or sports groups; members of your professional association; former employers; and members of your religious group. You may not know many of these people personally, but most will help you if you ask them.

2. **Contact them in a systematic way.** Each of these people is a contact for you. Obviously, some lists and some people on those lists will be more helpful than others, but almost any one of them could help you find a job lead.

3. **Present yourself well.** Begin with your friends and relatives. Call them and tell them you are looking for a job and need their help. Be as clear as possible about what you are looking for and what skills and qualifications you have. Look at the sample JIST Card and phone script later in this book for presentation ideas.

4. **Ask them for leads.** It is possible that they will know of a job opening just right for you. If so, get the details and get right on it! More likely, however, they will not, so here are three questions you should ask.

▼

The Three Magic Networking Questions

1. *Do you know of any openings for a person with my skills?* If the answer is no (which it usually is), then ask:

2. *Do you know of someone else who might know of such an opening?* If your contact does, get that name and ask for another one. If he or she doesn't, ask:

3. *Do you know of anyone who might know of someone else who might?* Another good way to ask this is, "Do you know someone who knows lots of people?" If all else fails, this will usually get you a name.

5. **Contact these referrals and ask them the same questions.** For each original contact, you can extend your network of acquaintances by hundreds of people. Eventually, one of these people will hire you or refer you to someone who will! This process is called networking, and it does work if you are persistent.

Contact Employers Directly

It takes more courage, but contacting an employer directly is a very effective job search technique. I call these cold contacts because you don't have an existing connection with these contacts. Following are two basic techniques for making cold contacts.

Use the *Yellow Pages* to Find Potential Employers

One effective cold contact technique uses the *Yellow Pages*. You can begin by looking at the index and asking for each entry, "Would an organization of this kind need a person with my skills?" If the answer is "yes," then that type of organization or business is a possible target. You can also rate "yes," entries based on your interest, giving an A to those that seem very interesting, a B to those you are not sure of, and a C to those that don't seem interesting at all.

Next, select a type of organization that got a "yes" response (such as "hotels") and turn to the section of the *Yellow Pages* where they are listed. Then call the organizations listed and ask to speak to the person who is most likely to hire or supervise you. A sample telephone script is included later in this section to give you ideas about what to say.

Drop In Without an Appointment

You can also simply walk in to many potential employers' organizations and ask to speak to the person in charge. This is particularly effective in small businesses, but it works surprisingly well in larger ones too. Remember, you want an interview even if there are no openings now. If your timing is inconvenient, ask for a better time to come back for an interview.

Use the Internet

If you have computer access to the Internet and the World Wide Web, you'll find many useful job search, career planning, and other resources there. As with other job search techniques, you can also waste a lot of time. I've included some information on using the Internet in your job search at the end of this section, so check it out if you are interested.

Most Jobs Are with Small Employers

About 70 percent of all people now work in small businesses—those with 250 or fewer employees. While the largest corporations have reduced the number of employees, small businesses have been creating as many as 80 percent of the new jobs. There are many opportunities to obtain training and promotions in smaller organizations, too. Many do not even have a personnel department, so nontraditional job search techniques are particularly effective with them.

JIST Cards—an Effective "Mini Resume"

JIST Cards are a job search tool that gets results. Typed, printed, or even neatly written on a 3-by-5-inch card, a JIST Card contains the essential information most employers want to know. Look at the sample cards that follow.

JIST Cards are an effective job search tool! Give them to friends and to each of your network contacts. Attach one to your resume. Enclose one in your thank-you notes before or after an interview.

Leave one with employers as a "business card." Use them in many creative ways. Even though they can be typed or even handwritten, it is best to have 100 or more printed so you can put lots of them in circulation. Thousands of job seekers have used them, and they get results!

Use the Phone to Get Job Leads

Once you have created your JIST Card, it is easy to create a telephone contact "script" based on it. Adapt the basic script to call people you know or your *Yellow Pages* leads. Select *Yellow Pages* index categories that might use a person with your skills and get the numbers of specific organizations in that category. Then ask for the person who is most likely to supervise you and present your phone script.

While it doesn't work every time, most people, with practice, can get one or more interviews in an hour by making these "cold" calls. Here is a phone script based on a JIST Card:

"Hello, my name is Pam Nykanen. I am interested in a position in hotel management. I have four years' experience in sales, catering, and accounting with a 300-room hotel. I also have an associate degree in Hotel Management plus one year of experience with the Bradey Culinary Institute. During my employment, I helped double revenues from meetings and conferences and increased bar revenues by 46 percent. I have good problem-solving skills and am good with people. I am also well-organized, hardworking, and detail-oriented. When may I come in for an interview?"

While this example assumes you are calling someone you don't know, the script can be easily modified for presentation to warm contacts, including referrals. Using the script for making cold calls takes courage, but it does work for most people.

Sandy Zaremba

Home: (219) 232-7608   **Message:** (219) 234-7465

Position: General Office/Clerical

Over two years' work experience, plus one year of training in office practices. Type 55 wpm, trained in word processing operations, post general ledger, handle payables, receivables, and most accounting tasks. Responsible for daily deposits averaging $5,000. Good interpersonal skills. Can meet strict deadlines and handle pressure well.

Willing to work any hours.

Organized, honest, reliable, and hardworking.

Chris Vorhees

Home: (602) 253-9678

Leave Message: (602) 257-6643

OBJECTIVE: Electronics—installation, maintenance, and sales

SKILLS: Four years' work experience, plus two years advanced training in electronics. A.S. degree in Electronics Engineering Technology. Managed a $300,000/yr. business while going to school full time, with grades in the top 25%. Familiar with all major electronic diagnostic and repair equipment. Hands-on experience with medical, consumer, communications, and industrial electronics equipment and applications. Good problem-solving and communication skills. Customer service oriented.

Willing to do what it takes to get the job done.

Make Your Job Search a Full-Time Job

On the average, job seekers spend fewer than 15 hours a week actually looking for work. The average length of unemployment varies from three or more months, with some being out of work far longer (older workers and higher earners are two groups who take longer). I believe there is a connection.

Based on many years of experience, I can say that the more time you spend on your job search each week, the less time you are likely to remain unemployed. Of course, using more effective job search methods also helps. Those who follow my advice have proven, over and over, that they get jobs in less than half the average time and they often get better jobs, too. Time management is the key.

Spend at Least 25 Hours a Week Looking for a Job

If you are unemployed and looking for a full-time job, you should look for a job on a full-time basis. It just makes sense to do so, although many do not because of discouragement, lack of good techniques, and lack of structure. Most job seekers have no idea what they are going to do next Thursday—they don't have a plan. The most important thing is to decide how many hours you can commit to your job search, and stay with it. You should spend a minimum of 25 hours a week on hard-core job search activities with no goofing around. Let me walk you through a simple but effective process to help you organize your job search schedule.

Write here how many hours you are willing to spend each week looking for a job: _____

Decide on Which Days You Will Look for Work

Answering the questions below requires you to have a schedule and a plan, just as you had when you were working, right?

Which days of the week will you spend looking for a job?

_____

How many hours will you look each day? _____

At what time will you begin and end your job search on each of these days? _____

_____

Create a Specific Daily Schedule

Having a specific daily job search schedule is very important because most job seekers find it hard to stay productive each day. You already know which job search methods are most effective, and you should plan on spending most of your time using those methods. The sample daily schedule that follows has been very effective for people who have used it, and it will give you ideas for your own. Although you are welcome to create your own daily schedule, I urge you to consider one similar to this one. Why? Because it works.

A Daily Schedule That Works

7:00 - 8:00 a.m.	Get up, shower, dress, eat breakfast.
8:00 - 8:15 a.m.	Organize work space; review schedule for interviews or follow-ups; update schedule.
8:15 - 9:00 a.m.	Review old leads for follow-up; develop new leads (want ads, *Yellow Pages*, networking lists, etc.).
9:00 - 10:00 a.m.	Make phone calls, set up interviews.
10:00 - 10:15 a.m.	Take a break!
10:15 - 11:00 a.m.	Make more calls.
11:00 - 12:00 p.m.	Make follow-up calls as needed.
12:00 - 1:00 p.m.	Lunch break.
1:00 - 5:00 p.m.	Go on interviews; call cold contacts in the field; research for upcoming interviews at the library.

Do It Now: Get a Schedule Book and Write Down Your Job Search Schedule

This is important: If you are not accustomed to using a daily schedule book or planner, promise yourself that you will get a good one tomorrow. Choose one that allows plenty of space for each day's plan on an hourly basis, plus room for daily "to do" listings. Write in your daily schedule in advance; then add interviews as they come. Get used to carrying it with you and use it!

Redefine What "Counts" as an Interview; Then Get Two a Day

The average job seeker gets about five interviews a month—fewer than two interviews a week. Yet many job seekers using the techniques I suggest get routinely two interviews a day. But to accomplish this, you must redefine what an interview is.

The New Definition of an Interview

An interview is any face-to-face contact with someone who has the authority to hire or supervise a person with your skills—even if the person doesn't have an opening at the time you interview.

With this definition, it is *much* easier to get interviews. You can now interview with all kinds of potential employers, not only those who have a job opening. Many job seekers use the *Yellow Pages* to get two interviews with just one hour of calls by using the telephone contact script discussed earlier. Others simply drop in on potential employers and ask for an unscheduled interview–and they get them. And getting names of others to contact from those you know–networking–is quite effective if you persist.

Getting two interviews a day equals 10 a week and 40 a month. That's 800 percent more interviews than the average job seeker gets. Who do you think will get a job offer quicker? So set out each day to get at least two interviews. It's quite possible to do, now that you know how.

How to Answer Tough Interview Questions

Interviews are where the job search action happens. You have to get them; then you have to do well in them. If you have done your homework, you are getting interviews for jobs that will maximize your skills. That is a good start, but your ability to communicate your skills in the interview makes an enormous difference. This is where, according to employer surveys, most job seekers have problems. They don't effectively communicate the skills they have to do the job, and they answer one or more problem questions poorly.

While thousands of problem interview questions are possible, I have listed just 10 that, if you can answer them well, will prepare you for most interviews.

The Top 10 Problem Questions

1. Why don't you tell me about yourself?

2. Why should I hire you?

3. What are your major strengths?

4. What are your major weaknesses?

5. What sort of pay do you expect to receive?

6. How does your previous experience relate to the jobs we have here?

7. What are your plans for the future?

8. What will your former employer (or references) say about you?

9. Why are you looking for this type of position, and why here?

10. Why don't you tell me about your personal situation?

I don't have the space here to give thorough answers to all of these questions, and there are potentially hundreds more. Instead, let me suggest several techniques that I have developed which you can use to answer almost any interview question.

A Traditional Interview Is Not a Friendly Exchange

Before I present the techniques for answering interview questions, it is important to understand what is going on. In a traditional interview situation, there is a job opening, and you are one of several (or one of a hundred) applicants. In this setting, the employer's task is to eliminate all but one applicant.

Assuming that you got as far as an interview, the interviewer's questions are designed to elicit information that can be used to screen you out. If you are wise, you know that your task is to avoid getting screened out. It's not an open and honest interaction, is it?

This illustrates yet another advantage of nontraditional job search techniques: the ability to talk to an employer before an opening exists. This eliminates the stress of a traditional interview. Employers are not trying to screen you out, and you are not trying to keep them from finding out stuff about you.

Having said that, knowing a technique for answering questions that might be asked in a traditional interview is good preparation for whatever you might run into during your job search.

The Three-Step Process for Answering Interview Questions

I know this might seem too simple, but the Three-Step Process is easy to remember. Its simplicity allows you to evaluate a question and create a good answer. The technique is based on sound principles and has worked for thousands of people, so consider trying it.

Step 1. Understand what is really being asked.

Most questions are really designed to find out about your self-management skills and personality. While they are rarely this blunt, the employer's *real* question is often:

✓ Can I depend on you?

✓ Are you easy to get along with?

✓ Are you a good worker?

✓ Do you have the experience and training to do the job if we hire you?

✓ Are you likely to stay on the job for a reasonable period of time and be productive?

Ultimately, if the employer is not convinced that you will stay and be a good worker, it won't matter if you have the best credentials–he or she won't hire you.

Step 2. Answer the question briefly.

Acknowledge the facts, but . . .

✓ Present them as an advantage, not a disadvantage.

There are lots of examples in which a specific interview question will encourage you to provide negative information. The classic is the "What are your major weaknesses?" question that I included in my top 10 problem questions list. Obviously, this is a trick question, and many people are just not prepared for it. A good response might be to mention something that is not all that damaging, such as "I have been told that I am a perfectionist, sometimes not delegating as effectively as I might." But your answer is not complete until you continue.

Step 3. Answer the real concern by presenting your related skills.

✓ Base your answer on the key skills that you have identified and that are needed in this job.

✓ Give examples to support your skills statements.

For example, an employer might say to a recent graduate, "We were looking for someone with more experience in this field. Why should we consider you?" Here is one possible answer: "I'm sure there are people who have more experience, but I *do* have more than six years of work experience including three years of advanced training and hands-on experience using the latest methods and techniques. Because my training is recent, I am open to new ideas and am used to working hard and learning quickly."

In the example I presented in Step 2 (about your need to delegate), a good skills statement might be, "I have been working on this problem and have learned to be more willing to let my staff do things, making sure that they have good training and supervision. I've found that their performance improves, and it frees me up to do other things."

Whatever your situation, learn to use it to your advantage. It is essential to communicate your skills during an interview, and the Three-Step Process gives you a technique that can dramatically improve your responses. It works!

Interview Dress and Grooming Rule

If you make a negative first impression, you won't get a second chance to make a good one. So do everything possible to make a good impression.

A Good Rule for Dressing for an Interview

Dress as you think
the boss will dress—*only neater.*

Dress for success! If necessary, get help selecting an interview outfit from someone who dresses well. Pay close attention to your grooming too. Written things like correspondence and resumes must be neat and errorless because they create an impression as well.

Follow Up on All Contacts

People who follow up with potential employers and with others in their network get jobs faster than those who do not.

Four Rules for Effective Follow-Up

1. Send a thank-you note to every person who helps you in your job search.

2. Send the thank-you note within 24 hours after you speak with the person.

3. Enclose JIST Cards with thank-you notes and all other correspondence.

4. Develop a system to keep following up with "good" contacts.

Thank-You Notes Make a Difference

Thank-you notes can be handwritten or typed on quality paper and matching envelopes. Keep them simple, neat, and errorless. Following is a sample:

April 16, 19XX

2234 Riverwood Ave.
Philadelphia, PA 17963

Ms. Sandra Kijek
Henderson & Associates, Inc.
1801 Washington Blvd., Suite 1201
Philadelphia, PA 17963

Dear Ms. Kijek:

Thank you for sharing your time with me so generously today. I really appreciated seeing your state-of-the-art computer equipment.

Your advice has already proved helpful. I have an appointment to meet with Mr. Robert Hopper on Friday as you anticipated.

Please consider referring me to others if you think of someone else who might need a person with my skills.

Sincerely,

William Richardson

William Richardson

Use Job Lead Cards to Organize Your Contacts

Use a simple 3-by-5-inch card to keep essential information on each person in your network. Buy a 3-by-5-inch card file box and tabs for each day of the month. File the cards under the date you want to contact the person, and the rest is easy. I've found that staying in touch with a good contact every other week can pay off big. Here's a sample card to give you ideas to create your own:

ORGANIZATION:	*Mutual Health Insurance*
CONTACT PERSON:	*Anna Tomey* PHONE: *317-355-0216*
SOURCE OF LEAD:	*Aunt Ruth*
NOTES:	*4/10 Called. Anna on vacation. Call back 4/15. 4/15 Interview set 4/20 at 1:30. 4/20 Anna showed me around. They use the same computers we used in school! (Friendly people) Sent thank-you note and JIST Card, call back 5/1. 5/1 Second interview 5/8 at 9 a.m.!*

Resumes: Write a Simple One Now, and a "Better" One Later

You have already learned that sending out resumes and waiting for responses is not an effective job seeking technique. However, many employers *will* ask you for them, and they are a useful tool in your job search. If you feel that you need a resume, I suggest that you begin with a simple one that you can complete quickly. I've seen too many people spend weeks working on their resume while they could have been out getting interviews instead. If you want a "better" resume, you can work on it on weekends and evenings. So let's begin with the basics.

Basic Tips to Create a Superior Resume

The following tips make sense for any resume format.

Write it yourself. It's OK to look at other resumes for ideas, but write yours yourself. It will force you to organize your thoughts and background.

Make it errorless. One spelling or grammar error will create a negative impressionist (see what I mean?). Get someone else to review your final draft for any errors. Then review it again because these rascals have a way of slipping in.

Make it look good. Poor copy quality, cheap paper, bad type quality, or anything else that creates a poor physical appearance will turn off employers to even the best resume content. Get professional help with design and printing if necessary. Many resume writers and print shops have desktop publishing services and can do it all for you.

Be brief, be relevant. Many good resumes fit on one page and few justify more than two. Include only the most important points. Use short sentences and action words. If it doesn't relate to and support the job objective, cut it!

Be honest. Don't overstate your qualifications. If you end up getting a job you can't handle, it will not be to your advantage. Most employers will see right through it and not hire you.

Be positive. Emphasize your accomplishments and results. This is no place to be too humble or to display your faults.

Be specific. Instead of saying "I am good with people," say "I supervised four people in the warehouse and increased productivity by 30 percent." Use numbers whenever possible, such as the number of people served, percent of sales increase, or dollars saved.

You should also know that everyone feels he or she is a resume expert. Whatever you do, someone will tell you it is wrong. For this reason, it is important to understand that a resume is a job search tool. You should never delay or slow down your job search because your resume is not "good enough." The best approach is to create a simple and acceptable resume as soon as possible, then use it. As time permits, create a better one if you feel you must.

Chronological Resumes

Most resumes use the chronological format. It is a simple format where the most recent experience is listed first, followed by each previous job. This arrangement works fine for someone with work experience in several similar jobs, but not as well for those with limited experience or for career changers.

Look at the two Judith Jones resumes. Both use the chronological approach, but notice that the second one includes some improvements over her first. The improved resume is clearly better, but either would be acceptable to most employers.

Tips for Writing a Simple Chronological Resume

Here are some tips for writing a basic chronological resume.

Name. Use your formal name rather than a nickname if the formal name sounds more professional.

Address. Be complete. Include your zip code and avoid abbreviations. If moving is a possibility, use the address of a friend or relative or be certain to include a forwarding address.

Telephone Number. Employers are most likely to try to reach you by phone, so having a reliable way to be reached is very important. Always include your area code because you never know where your resume might travel. If you don't have an answering machine, get one and make sure you leave it on whenever you are not home. Listen to your message to be sure it presents you in a professional way. Also available are a variety of communication systems: voice

© Copyright, 1998 · J. Michael Farr · JIST Works, Inc. · Indianapolis, IN

[Sample of a simple chronological resume.]

Judith J. Jones

115 South Hawthorne Avenue
Chicago, Illinois 46204
(312) 653-9217 (home)
(312) 272-7608 (message)

JOB OBJECTIVE

Desire a position in the office management, secretarial, or clerical area. Prefer a position requiring responsibility and a variety of tasks.

EDUCATION AND TRAINING

Acme Business College, Chicago, Illinois
Graduate of a one-year business/secretarial program, 1996

John Adams High School, South Bend, Indiana
Diploma: Business Education

U.S. Army

Financial procedures, accounting functions. Other: Continuing education classes and workshops in Business Communication, Scheduling Systems, and Customer Relations.

EXPERIENCE

1995-1996 — Returned to school to complete and update my business skills. Learned word processing and other new office techniques.

1992-1995 — Claims Processor, Blue Spear Insurance Co., Chicago, Illinois. Handled customer medical claims, filed, miscellaneous clerical duties.

1990-1992 — Sales Clerk, Judy's Boutique, Chicago, Illinois. Responsible for counter sales, display design, and selected tasks.

1988-1990 — Specialist, U.S. Army. Assigned to various stations as a specialist in finance operations. Promoted prior to honorable discharge.

Previous Jobs — Held part-time and summer jobs throughout high school.

PERSONAL

I am reliable, hardworking, and good with people.

Previous Experience. The standard approach is to list employer, job title, dates employed, and responsibilities. But there are better ways of presenting your experience. Look over the "Improved Chronological Resume" for ideas. The improved version emphasizes results, accomplishments, and performance.

Personal Data. Neither of the sample resumes has the standard height, weight, or marital status included on so many resumes. That information is simply not relevant! If you do include some personal information, put it at the bottom and keep it related to the job you want.

References. There is no need to list references. If employers want them, they will ask. If your references are particularly good, it's okay to say so.

Tips for an Improved Chronological Resume

Once you have a simple, errorless, and eye-pleasing resume, get on with your job search. There is no reason to delay! But you may want to create a better one in your spare time (evenings or weekends). If you do, here are some additional tips.

Job Objective. Job objectives often limit the type of jobs for which you will be considered. Instead, think of the type of work you want to do and can do well and describe it in more general terms. Instead of writing "Restaurant Manager," write "Managing a small to mid-sized business" if that is what you are qualified to do.

Education and Training. New graduates should emphasize their recent training and education more than those with five years or so of recent and related work experience. Think about any special accomplishments while in school and include these if they relate to the job. Did you work full time while in school? Did you do particularly well in work-related classes, get an award, or participate in sports?

Skills and Accomplishments. Employers are interested in what you accomplished and did well. Include those things that relate to doing well in the job you seek now. Even "small" things count. Maybe your attendance was perfect, you met a tight deadline, did the work of others during vacations, etc. Be specific and include numbers—even if you have to estimate them.

mail, professional answering services, beepers, mobile phones, online e-mail programs, etc. If you do provide an alternative phone number or another way to reach you, just make it clear to the caller what to expect.

Job Objective. This is optional for a very basic resume but is still important to include. Notice that Judy is keeping her options open with her objective. Writing "Secretary" or "Clerical" might limit her to lower-paying jobs or even prevent her from being considered for jobs she might take.

Education and Training. Include any formal training you've had, plus any training that supports the job you seek. If you did not finish a formal degree or program, list what you did complete. Include any special accomplishments.

[Sample of an improved chronological resume.]

Judith J. Jones

115 South Hawthorne Avenue
Chicago, Illinois 46204
(312) 653-9217 (home)
(312) 272-7608 (message)

JOB OBJECTIVE

Seeking position requiring excellent management and secretarial skills in an office environment. Position should require a variety of tasks including typing, word processing, accounting/bookkeeping functions, and customer contact.

EDUCATION AND TRAINING

Acme Business College, Chicago, Illinois.
Completed one-year program in Professional Secretarial and Office Management. Grades in top 30 percent of my class. Courses: word processing, accounting theory and systems, time management, basic supervision, and others.

John Adams High School, South Bend, Indiana.
Graduated with emphasis on business and secretarial courses. Won shorthand contest.

Other: Continuing education at my own expense (Business Communications, Customer Relations, Computer Applications, other courses).

EXPERIENCE

1995-1996 — Returned to business school to update skills. Advanced course work in accounting and office management. Learned to operate word processing and PC-based accounting and spreadsheet software. Gained operating knowledge of computers.

1992-1995 — Claims Processor, Blue Spear Insurance Company, Chicago, Illinois. Handled 50 complex medical insurance claims per day—18 percent above department average. Received two merit raises for performance.

1990-1992 — Assistant Manager, Judy's Boutique, Chicago, Illinois. Managed sales, financial records, inventory, purchasing, correspondence, and related tasks during owner's absence. Supervised four employees. Sales increased 15 percent during my tenure.

1988-1990 — Finance Specialist (E4), U.S. Army. Responsible for the systematic processing of 500 invoices per day from commercial vendors. Trained and supervised eight employees. Devised internal system allowing 15 percent increase in invoices processed with a decrease in personnel.

1984-1988 — Various part-time and summer jobs through high school. Learned to deal with customers, meet deadlines, work hard, and other skills.

SPECIAL SKILLS AND ABILITIES

Type 80 words per minute and can operate most office equipment. Good communication and math skills. Accept supervision, able to supervise others. Excellent attendance record.

Problem Areas. Employers look for any sign of instability or lack of reliability. It is very expensive to hire and train someone who won't stay or who won't work out. Gaps in employment, jobs held for short periods of time, or a lack of direction in the jobs you've held are all things that employers are concerned about. If you have any legitimate explanation, use it. For example:

"1994–Continued my education at . . ."

"1995–Traveled extensively throughout the United States."

"1995 to present–Self-employed barn painter and widget maker."

"1995–Had first child, took year off before returning to work."

Use entire years or even seasons of years to avoid displaying a shorter gap you can't explain easily: "Spring 1994–Fall 1995" will not show you as unemployed from October to November, 1995, for example.

Remember that a resume can get you screened out, but it is up to you to get the interview and the job. So, cut out *anything* that is negative in your resume!

Job Titles. Many job titles don't accurately reflect the job you did. For example, your job title may have been "Cashier" but you also opened the store, trained new staff, and covered for the boss on vacations. Perhaps "Head Cashier and Assistant Manager" would be more accurate. Check with your previous employer if you are not sure.

Promotions. If you were promoted or got good evaluations, say so. A promotion to a more responsible job can be handled as a separate job if this makes sense.

[Sample of a simple skills resume.]

ALAN ATWOOD
3231 East Harbor Road
Woodland Hills, California 91367
Home: (818) 447-2111   Message (818) 547-8201

Objective: A responsible position in retail sales

Areas of Accomplishment:

Customer Service
- Communicate well with all age groups.
- Able to interpret customer concerns to help them find the items they want.
- Received 6 Employee of the Month awards in 3 years.

Merchandise Display
- Developed display skills via in-house training and experience.
- Received Outstanding Trainee Award for Christmas toy display.
- Dress mannequins, arrange table displays, and organize sale merchandise.

Stock Control and Marketing
- Maintained and marked stock during department manager's 6-week illness.
- Developed more efficient record-keeping procedures.

Additional Skills
- Operate cash register, IBM-compatible hardware, calculators, and electronic typewriters.
- Punctual, honest, reliable, and a hard-working self-starter.

Experience:
Harper's Department Store
Woodland Hills, California
1995 to Present

Education:
Central High School
Woodland Hills, California
3.6/4.0 Grade Point Average
Honor Graduate in Distributive Education

Two years retail sales training in Distributive Education. Also courses in Business Writing, Accounting, Typing, and Word Processing.

Skills and Combination Resumes

The functional or "skills" resume emphasizes your most important *skills,* supported by specific examples of how you have used them. This approach allows you to use any part of your life history to support your ability to do the job you seek.

While the skills resume can be very effective, it does require more work to create. And some employers don't like them because they can hide a job seeker's faults (such as job gaps, lack of formal education, or no related work experience) better than a chronological resume.

Still, a skills resume may make sense for you. Look over the sample resumes for ideas. Notice that one resume includes elements of a skills *and* a chronological resume. This is called a "combination" resume–an approach that makes sense if your previous job history or education and training are positive.

[Sample skills resume for someone with substantial experience—but using only one page. Note that no dates are included.]

Ann McLaughlin

Career Objective

Challenging position in programming or related areas that would best utilize expertise in the business environment. This position should have many opportunities for an aggressive, dedicated individual with leadership abilities to advance.

Programming Skills

Include functional program design relating to business issues including payroll, inventory and database management, sales, marketing, accounting, and loan amortization reports. In conjunction with design would be coding, implementation, debugging, and file maintenance. Familiar with distributed network systems including PCs and Macs and working knowledge of DOS, UNIX, COBOL, BASIC, RPG, and FORTRAN. Also familiar with mainframe environments including DEC, Prime, and IBM, including tape and disk file access, organization, and maintenance.

Areas of Expertise

Interpersonal communication strengths, public relations capabilities, plus innovative problem-solving and analytical talents.

Sales

A total of nine years of experience in sales and sales management. Sold security products to distributors and burglar alarm dealers. Increased company's sales from $16,000 to over $70,000 per month. Creatively organized sales programs and marketing concepts. Trained sales personnel in prospecting techniques while training also service personnel in proper installation of burglar alarms. Result: 90 percent of all new business was generated through referrals from existing customers.

Management

Managed burglar alarm company for four years while increasing profits yearly. Supervised office, sales, and installation personnel. Supervised and delegated work to assistants in accounting functions and inventory control. Worked as assistant credit manager, responsible for over $2 million per month in sales. Handled semiannual inventory of five branch stores totaling millions of dollars and supervised 120 people.

Accounting

Balanced all books and prepared tax forms for burglar alarm company. Eight years of experience in credit and collections, with emphasis on collections. Collection rates were over 98% each year; was able to collect a bad debt in excess of $250,000 deemed "uncollectible" by company.

Education

School of Computer Technology, Pittsburgh, PA
Business Applications Programming/TECH EXEC- 3.97 GPA

Robert Morris College, Pittsburgh, PA
Associate degree in Accounting, Minor in Management

2306 Cincinnati Street, Kingsford, PA 15171 (412) 437-6217
Message: (412) 464-1273

[Sample combination resume emphasizing skills and accomplishments within jobs. Note that each position within a company is listed.]

THOMAS P. MARRIN
80 Harrison Avenue
Baldwin L.I., New York 11563
Answering Service: (716) 223-4705

OBJECTIVE:

A middle/upper-level management position with responsibilities including problem solving, planning, organizing, and budget management.

EDUCATION:

University of Notre Dame, B.S. in Business Administration. Course emphasis on accounting, supervision, and marketing. Upper 25% of class. Additional training: Advanced training in time management, organization behavior, and cost control.

MILITARY:

U.S. Army — 2nd Infantry Division, 1985 to 1989, 1st Lieutenant and platoon leader — stationed in Korea and Ft. Knox, Kentucky. Supervised an annual budget of nearly $4 million and equipment valued at over $40 million. Responsible for training, scheduling, and activities of as many as 40 people. Received several commendations. Honorable discharge.

BUSINESS EXPERIENCE:

Wills Express Transit Co., Inc. — Mineola, New York

Promoted to Vice President, Corporate Equipment — 1994 to Present
Controlled purchase, maintenance, and disposal of 1100 trailers and 65 company cars with $6.7 million operating and $8.0 million capital expense responsibilities.

- Scheduled trailer purchases, six divisions.
- Operated 2.3% under planned maintenance budget in company's second best profit year while operating revenues declined 2.5%.
- Originated schedule to correlate drivers' needs with available trailers.
- Developed systematic Purchase and Disposal Plan for company car fleet.
- Restructured Company Car Policy, saving 15% on per car cost.

Promoted to Asst. Vice President, Corporate Operations — 1993 to 1994
Coordinated activities of six sections of Corporate Operations with an operating budget over $10 million.

- Directed implementation of zero-base budgeting.
- Developed and prepared Executive Officer Analyses detailing achievable cost-reduction measures. Resulted in cost reduction of over $600,000 in first two years.
- Designed policy and procedure for special equipment leasing program during peak seasons. Cut capital purchases by over $1 million.

Manager of Communications — 1991 to 1993
Directed and managed $1.4 million communication network involving 650 phones, 150 WATS lines, 3 switchboards, 1 teletype machine, 5 employees.

- Installed computerized WATS Control System. Optimized utilization of WATS lines and pinpointed personal abuse. Achieved payback earlier than originally projected.
- Devised procedures that allowed simultaneous 20% increase in WATS calls and a $75,000/year savings.

Hayfield Publishing Company, Hempstead, New York

Communications Administrator — 1989 to 1991

Managed daily operations of a large Communications Center. Reduced costs and improved services.

The Quick Job Search Review

There are a few thoughts I want to emphasize in closing my brief review of job seeking skills:

1. Approach your job search as if it were a job itself.

2. Get organized and spend at least 25 hours per week actively looking.

3. Follow up on all the leads you generate and send out lots of thank-you notes and JIST Cards.

4. If you want to get a good job quickly, you must get lots of interviews!

5. Pay attention to all the details; then be yourself in the interview. Remember that employers are people, too. They will hire someone who they feel will do the job well, be reliable, and fit easily into the work environment.

6. When you want the job, tell the employer that you want the job and why. You need to have a good answer to the question "Why should I hire you?" It's that simple.

Essential Job Search Data Worksheet

Completing this worksheet will help you create your resume, fill out applications, and answer interview questions. Take it with you as a reference as you look for a job. Use an erasable pen or pencil so you can make changes. In all sections, emphasize skills and accomplishments that best support your ability to do the job you want. Use extra sheets as needed.

Key Accomplishments

List three accomplishments that best prove your ability to do well in the kind of job you want.

1. _____
   _____

2. _____
   _____

3. _____
   _____

Education/Training

Name of high school(s)/Years attended: _____
_____
_____
_____

Subjects related to job objective: _____
_____
_____
_____

Extracurricular activities/Hobbies/Leisure activities:
_____
_____
_____
_____

Accomplishments/Things you did well: _____
_____
_____
_____

Schools you attended after high school, years attended, degrees/certificates earned: _____
_____
_____
_____

Courses related to job objective: _____
_____
_____
_____

Extracurricular activities/Hobbies/Leisure activities:
_____
_____
_____
_____

Accomplishments/Things you did well: _____

_____

_____

_____

_____

Military training, on-the-job, or informal training, such as from a hobby; dates of training; type of certificate earned: _____

_____

_____

_____

_____

Specific things you can do as a result: _____

_____

_____

_____

Work and Volunteer History

List your most recent job first, followed by each previous job. Include military experience and unpaid work here too, if it makes sense to do so. Use additional sheets to cover *all* your significant jobs or unpaid experiences.

Whenever possible, provide numbers to support what you did: number of people served over one or more years, number of transactions processed, percentage of sales increase, total inventory value you were responsible for, payroll of the staff you supervised, total budget you were responsible for, etc. As much as possible, mention results using numbers because they can be impressive when mentioned in an interview or resume.

Job #1 _____

Name of organization: _____

_____

_____

Address: _____

_____

_____

Phone number: _____

_____

Dates employed: _____

Job title(s): _____

_____

_____

Supervisor's name: _____

_____

Details of any raises or promotions: _____

_____

_____

_____

Machinery or equipment you handled: _____

_____

_____

_____

Special skills this job required: _____

_____

_____

_____

List what you accomplished or did well: _____

_____

_____

_____

Job #2 _____

Name of organization: _____

_____

_____

Address: _____

_____

_____

Phone number: _____

_____

Dates employed: _____

Job title(s): _____

_____

Supervisor's name: _____

_____

Details of any raises or promotions: _____

_____

_____

_____

Machinery or equipment you handled: _____

_____

_____

_____

Special skills this job required: _____

_____

_____

_____

List what you accomplished or did well: _____

_____

_____

_____

Job #3 _____

Name of organization: _____

_____

_____

Address: _____

_____

_____

Phone number: _____

_____

Dates employed: _____

Job title(s): _____

_____

_____

Supervisor's name: _____

_____

Details of any raises or promotions: _____

_____

_____

_____

Machinery or equipment you handled: _____

_____

_____

_____

Special skills this job required: _____

_____

_____

_____

List what you accomplished or did well: _____

_____

_____

_____

References

Contact your references and let them know what type of job you want and why you are qualified. Be sure to review what they will say about you. Because some employers will not give out references by phone or in person, have previous employers write a letter of reference for you in advance. If you worry about a bad reference from a previous employer, negotiate what the employer will say about you or get written references from other people you worked with there. When creating your list of references, be sure to include your reference's name and job title, where he or she works, a business address and phone number, how that person knows you, and what your reference will say about you.

The following material is based on content from a book titled Job Strategies for Professionals *written by a team of authors from the U.S. Employment Service for use by the unemployed. (published by JIST)*

Some Tips for Coping with Job Loss

Being out of work is not fun for most people and is devastating to some. It may help you to know that you are not alone in this experience, and I've included some information here on what to expect and some suggestions for getting through it.

Some Problems You May Experience

Here are some feelings and experiences that you may have after losing your job.

Loss of professional identity: Most of us identify strongly with our careers, and unemployment can often lead to a loss of self-esteem. Being employed garners respect in the community and in the family. When a job is lost, part of your sense of self may be lost as well.

Loss of a network: The loss may be worse when your social life has been strongly linked to the job. Many ongoing "work friendships" are suddenly halted. Old friends and colleagues often don't call because they feel awkward or don't know what to say. Many don't want to be reminded of what could happen to them.

Emotional unpreparedness: If you have never before been unemployed, you may not be emotionally prepared for it and devastated when it happens. It is natural and appropriate to feel this way. You might notice that some people you know don't take their job loss as hard as you have taken it. Studies show that those who change jobs frequently, or who are in occupations prone to cyclic unemployment, suffer far less emotional impact after job loss than those who have been steadily employed and who are unprepared for cutbacks.

Adjusting

You can often adjust to job loss by understanding its psychology. There have been a lot of studies done on how to deal with loss. Psychologists have found that people often have an easier time dealing with loss if they know what feelings they might experience during the "grieving process." Grief doesn't usually overwhelm us all at once; it usually is experienced in stages. The stages of loss or grief may include

Shock–you may not be fully aware of what has happened.

Denial–usually comes next; you cannot believe that the loss is true.

Relief–you may feel a burden has lifted and opportunity awaits.

Anger–often follows; you blame (often without cause) those you think might be responsible, including yourself.

Depression–may set in some time later, when you realize the reality of the loss.

Acceptance–the final stage of the process; you come to terms with the loss and get the energy and desire to move beyond it. The "acceptance" stage is the best place to be when starting a job search, but you might not have the luxury of waiting until this point to begin your search.

Knowing that a normal person will experience some predictable "grieving" reactions can help you deal with your loss in a constructive way. The faster you can begin an active search for a new job, the better off you will be.

Keeping Healthy

Unemployment is a stressful time for most people, and it is important to keep healthy and fit. Try to

✓ **Eat properly.** How you look and your sense of self-esteem can be affected by your eating habits. It is very easy to snack on junk food when you're home all day. Take time to plan your meals and snacks so they are well-balanced and nutritious. Eating properly will help you maintain the good attitude you need during your job search.

✓ **Exercise.** Include some form of exercise as part of your daily activities. Regular exercise reduces stress and depression and can help you get through those tough days.

✓ **Allow time for fun.** When you're planning your time, be sure to build fun and relaxation into your plans. You are allowed to enjoy life even if you are unemployed. Keep a list of activities or tasks that you want to accomplish such as volunteer work, repairs around the house, or hobbies. When free time occurs, you can refer to the list and have lots of things to do.

Family Issues

Unemployment is a stressful time for the entire family. For them, your unemployment means the loss of income and the fear of an uncertain future, and they are also worried about your happiness. Here are some ways you can interact with your family to get through this tough time.

✓ **Do not attempt to "shoulder" your problems alone.** Be open with family members even though it may be hard. Discussions about your job search and the feelings you have allow your family to work as a group and support one another.

✓ **Talk to your family.** Let them know your plans and activities. Share with them how you will be spending your time.

✓ **Listen to your family.** Find out their concerns and suggestions. Maybe there are ways they can assist you.

✓ **Build family spirit.** You will need a great deal of support from your family in the months ahead, but they will also need yours.

✓ **Seek outside help.** Join a family support group. Many community centers, mental health agencies, and colleges have support groups for the unemployed and their families. These groups can provide a place to let off steam and share frustrations. They can also be a place to get ideas on how to survive this difficult period. More information about support groups is presented later in this chapter.

Helping Children

If you have children, realize that they can be deeply affected by a parent's unemployment. It is important for them to know what has happened and how it will affect the family. However, try not to overburden them with the responsibility of too many emotional or financial details.

✓ **Keep an open dialogue with your children.** Letting them know what is really going on is vital. Children have a way of imagining the worst, so the facts can actually be far less devastating than what they envision.

✓ **Make sure your children know it's not anyone's fault.** Children may not understand about job loss and may think that *you* did something wrong to cause it. Or they may feel that somehow *they* are responsible or financially burdensome. They need reassurance in these matters, regardless of their age.

✓ **Children need to feel they are helping.** They want to help, and having them do something like taking a cut in allowance, deferring expensive purchases, or getting an after-school job can make them feel as if they are part of the team.

Some experts suggest that it can be useful to alert school counselors to your unemployment so that they can watch the children for problems at school before they become serious.

Coping with Stress

Here are some coping mechanisms that can help you deal with the stress of being unemployed.

✓ **Write down what seems to be causing the stress.** Identify the "stressors"; then think of possible ways to handle each one. Can some demands be altered, lessened, or postponed? Can you live with any of them just as they are? Are there some that you might be able to deal with more effectively?

✓ **Set priorities.** Deal with the most pressing needs or changes first. You cannot handle everything at once.

✓ **Establish a workable schedule.** When you set a schedule for yourself, make sure it is one that can be achieved. As you perform your tasks, you will feel a sense of control and accomplishment.

✓ **Reduce stress.** Learn relaxation techniques or other stress-reduction techniques. This can be as simple as sitting in a chair, closing your eyes, taking a deep breath and breathing out slowly while imagining all the tension going out with your breath. There are a number of other methods, including listening to relaxation tapes, which may help you cope with stress more effectively. Check the additional source material books that offer instruction on these techniques—many of these are available at your public library.

✓ **Avoid isolation.** Keep in touch with your friends, even former coworkers, if you can do that comfortably. Unemployed people often feel a sense of isolation and loneliness. See your friends, talk with them, socialize with them. You are the same person you were before unemployment. The same goes for the activities that you have enjoyed in the past. Evaluate them. Which can you afford to continue? If you find that your old hobbies or activities can't be part of your new budget, maybe you can substitute new activities that are less costly.

✓ **Join a support group.** No matter how understanding or caring your family or friends might be, they may not be able to understand all that you're going through, and you might be able to find help and understanding at a job seeking support group.

These groups consist of people who are going through the same experiences and emotions as you. Many groups also share tips on job opportunities, as well as feedback on ways to deal more effectively in the job search process. *The National Business Employment Weekly,* available at major newsstands, lists support groups throughout the country. Local churches, YMCAs, YWCAs, and libraries often list or facilitate support groups. A list of self-help organizations—some of which cover the unemployed—is available from the National Self-Help Clearinghouse, 25 West 43rd St., Room 620, New York, NY 10036. The cost is $3, plus a self-addressed, stamped envelope.

Forty Plus is a national nonprofit organization and an excellent source of information about clubs around the country and on issues concerning older employees and the job search process. The address is 15 Park Row, New York, NY 10038. The telephone number is (212) 233-6086.

Keeping Your Spirits Up

Here are some ways you can build your self-esteem and avoid depression.

✓ **List your positives.** Make a list of your positive qualities and your successes. This list is always easier to make when you are feeling good about yourself. Perhaps you can enlist the assistance of a close friend or caring relative, or wait for a sunnier moment.

✓ **Replay your positives.** Once you have made this list, replay the positives in your mind frequently. Associate the replay with an activity you do often; for example, you might review the list in your mind every time you go to the refrigerator!

✓ **Use the list before performing difficult tasks.** Review the list when you are feeling down or to give you energy before you attempt some difficult task.

✓ **Recall successes.** Take time every day to recall a success.

✓ **Use realistic standards.** Avoid the trap of evaluating yourself using impossible standards that come from others. You are in a particular phase of your life; don't dwell on what you think society regards as success. Remind yourself that success will again be yours.

✓ **Know your strengths and weaknesses.** What things do you do well? What skills do you have? Do you need to learn new skills? Everyone has limitations. What are yours? Are there certain job duties that are just not right for you and that you might want to avoid? Balance your limitations against your strong skills so that you don't let the negatives eat at your self-esteem. Incorporate this knowledge into your planning.

✓ **Picture success.** Practice visualizing positive results or outcomes and view them in your mind before the event. Play out the scene in your imagination and picture yourself as successful in whatever you're about to attempt.

✓ **Build success.** Make a "to do" list. Include small, achievable tasks. Divide the tasks on your list and make a list for every day so you will have some "successes" daily.

✓ **Surround yourself with positive people.** Socialize with family and friends who are supportive. You want to be around people who will "pick you up," not "knock you down." You know who your fans are. Try to find time to be around them. It can really make you feel good.

✓ **Volunteer.** Give something of yourself to others through volunteer work. Volunteering will help you feel more worth while and may actually give you new skills.

Overcoming Depression

Are you depressed? As hard as it is to be out of work, it also can be a new beginning. A new direction may emerge that will change your life in positive ways. This may be a good time to reevaluate your attitudes and outlook.

✓ **Live in the present.** The past is over and you cannot change it. Learn from your mistakes and use that knowledge to plan for the future; then let the past go. Don't dwell on it or relive it over and over. Don't be overpowered by guilt.

✓ **Take responsibility for yourself.** Try not to complain or blame others. Save your energy for activities that result in positive experiences.

✓ **Learn to accept what you cannot change.** However, realize that in most situations, you do have some control. Your reactions and your behavior are in your control and will often influence the outcome of events.

✓ **Keep the job search under your own command.** This will give you a sense of control and prevent you from giving up and waiting for something to happen. Enlist everyone's aid in your job search, but make sure you do most of the work.

✓ **Talk things out with people you trust.** Admit how you feel. For example, if you realize you're angry, find a positive way to vent it, perhaps through exercise.

✓ **Face your fears.** Try to pinpoint them. "Naming the enemy" is the best strategy for relieving the vague feeling of anxiety. By facing what you actually fear, you can see if your fears are realistic or not.

✓ **Think creatively.** Stay flexible, take risks, and don't be afraid of failure. Try not to take rejection personally. Think of it as information that will help you later in your search. Take criticism as a way to learn more about yourself. Keep plugging away at the job search despite those inevitable setbacks. Most importantly, forget magic. What lies ahead is hard work!

Sources of Professional Help

If your depression won't go away or leads you to self-destructive behaviors such as abuse of alcohol or drugs, you may consider asking a professional for help. Many people who have never sought professional assistance before find that in a time of crisis it really helps to have someone listen and give needed aid. Consult your local mental health clinics, social services agencies, religious organizations, or professional counselors for help for yourself and family members who are affected by your unemployment. Your health insurance may cover some assistance, or, if you do not have insurance, counseling is often available on a "sliding scale" fee, based on income.

Managing Your Finances While Out of Work

As you already know, being unemployed has financial consequences. While the best solution to this is to get a good job in as short a time as possible, you do need to manage your money differently during the time between jobs. Following are some things to think about.

Apply for Benefits Without Delay

Don't be embarrassed to apply for unemployment benefits as soon as possible, even if you're not sure you are eligible. This program is to help you make a transition between jobs, and you helped pay for it by your previous employment. Depending on how long you have worked, you can collect benefits for up to 26 weeks and sometimes even longer. Contact your state labor department or employment security agency for further information. Their addresses and telephone numbers are listed in your phone book.

Prepare Now to Stretch Your Money

Being out of work means lower income and the need to control your expenses. Don't avoid doing this, because the more you plan, the better you can control your finances.

Examine Your Income and Expenses

Create a budget and look for ways to cut expenses. The Monthly Income and Expense Worksheet can help you isolate income and expense categories, but your own budget may be considerably more detailed. I've included two columns for each expense category. Enter in the "Normal" column what you have been spending in that category during the time you were employed. Enter in the "Could Reduce To" column a lower number that you will spend by cutting expenses in that category.

Tips on Conserving Your Cash

While you are unemployed, it is likely that your expenses will exceed your income, and it is essential that you be aggressive in managing your money. Your objective here is very clear: you want to conserve as much cash as possible early on so you can have some for essentials later. Here are some suggestions.

✓ **Begin cutting all nonessential expenses right away.** Don't put this off! There is no way to know how long you will be out of work, and the faster you deal with the financial issues, the better.

✓ **Discuss the situation with other family members.** Ask them to get involved by helping you identify expenses they can cut.

✓ **Look for sources of additional income.** Can you paint houses on weekends? Pick up a temporary job or consulting assignment? Deliver newspapers in the early morning? Can a family member get a job to help out? Any new income will help, and the sooner the better.

✓ **Contact your creditors.** Even if you can make full payments for a while, work out interest-only or reduced-amount payments as soon as possible. When I was unemployed, I went to my creditors right away and asked them to help. They were very cooperative, and most are if you are reasonable with them.

✓ **Register with your local consumer credit counseling organization.** Many areas have free consumer credit counseling organizations that can help you get a handle on your finances and encourage your creditors to cooperate.

✓ **Review your assets.** Make a list of all your assets and their current value. Money in checking, savings, and other accounts is the most available, but you may have additional assets in pension programs, life insurance, and stocks that could be converted to cash if needed. You may also have an extra car that could be sold, equity in your home that could be borrowed against, and other assets that could be sold or used if needed.

✓ **Reduce credit card purchases.** Try to pay for things in cash to save on interest charges and prevent overspending. Be disciplined; you can always use your credit cards later if you are getting desperate for food and other basics.

✓ **Consider cashing in some "luxury" assets.** For example, sell a car or boat you rarely use to generate cash and to save on insurance and maintenance costs.

✓ **Comparison shop** for home/auto/life insurance and other expenses to lower costs.

✓ **Deduct job hunting expenses from your taxes.** Some job hunting expenses may be tax deductible as a "miscellaneous deduction" on your federal income tax return. Keep receipts for employment agency fees, resume expenses, and transportation expenses. If you find work in another city and you must relocate, some moving expenses are tax deductible. Contact an accountant or the IRS for more information.

Monthly Income and Expense Worksheet

Income

Unemployment benefits	_____	Interest/Dividends	_____
Spouse's income	_____	Other income	_____
Severance pay	_____	**TOTALS**	_____

Expenses

	Normal	Could Reduce To		Normal	Could Reduce To
Mortgage/rent:	_____	_____	_____	_____	_____
maintenance/repairs	_____	_____	_____	_____	_____
			Health insurance:	_____	_____
Utilities:			other medical/	_____	_____
electric	_____	_____	dental expenses	_____	_____
gas/oil heat	_____	_____	**Tuition:**	_____	_____
water/sewer	_____	_____	other school costs	_____	_____
telephone	_____	_____	**Clothing:**	_____	_____
Food:	_____	_____	**Entertainment:**	_____	_____
restaurants	_____	_____	**Taxes:**	_____	_____
Car payment:	_____	_____	**Job hunting costs:**	_____	_____
fuel	_____	_____	**Other expenses:**	_____	_____
maintenance/repairs	_____	_____		_____	_____
insurance	_____	_____		_____	_____
Other loan payments:				_____	_____
_____	_____		**TOTALS**	_____	_____

Review Your Health Coverage

You already know that it is dangerous to go without health insurance, so there is no need to lecture you on this, but here are some tips.

- ✓ **You can probably maintain coverage at your own expense.** Under the COBRA law, if you worked for an employer that provided medical coverage and had 20 or more employees, you may continue your health coverage. However, you must tell your former employer within 60 days of leaving the job.

- ✓ **Contact professional organizations to which you belong.** They may provide group coverage for their members at low rates.

- ✓ **Speak to an insurance broker.** If necessary, arrange for health coverage on your own or join a local health maintenance organization (HMO).

- ✓ **Practice preventive medicine.** The best way to save money on medical bills is to stay healthy. Try not to ignore minor ills. If they persist, phone or visit your doctor.

- ✓ **Investigate local clinics.** Many local clinics provide services based on a sliding scale. These clinics often provide quality health care at affordable prices. In an emergency, most hospitals will provide you with services on a sliding scale, and most areas usually have one or more hospitals funded locally to provide services to those who can't afford them.

Using the Internet for Career Planning and Job Seeking

This brief review assumes you know how to use the Internet, so I won't get into how it works here. If the Internet and World Wide Web are new to you, I recommend a book titled *Using the Internet and the World Wide Web in Your Job Search* by Fred Jandt and Mary Nemnich. This book covers the basics about how the Internet works, how to get connected, plus a great deal of information on using it for career planning and job seeking.

Some Cautionary Comments

Let me begin by saying that the Internet has its problems as a tool for collecting information or for getting job leads. While the Internet has worked for many in finding job leads, far more users have been disappointed in the results they obtained. The problem is that many users assume that they can simply put their resume in resume databases and that employers will line up to hire them. It sometimes happens, but not often. That is the very same negative experience of people sending out lots of unsolicited resumes to personnel offices, a hopeful approach that has been around since long before computers.

There are two points that I made earlier about job seeking methods which also apply to using the Internet:

1. It is unwise to rely on just one or two job search methods in conducting your job search.
2. It is essential that you conduct an active rather than a passive approach in your job search.

Just as with sending out lots of unsolicited resumes, simply listing your resume on the Internet is a passive approach that is unlikely to work well for you. Use the Internet in your job search, but plan to use other techniques, including direct contacts with employers.

A Success Story

Having now cautioned you regarding its limitations, the Internet does work very well for some people. To illustrate this, let me share with you a real situation I recently uncovered.

I was doing a series of interviews on jobs for a TV station in a rural area and asked the staff how they got their jobs there. They were all young, and the news anchor had told me that she had only been on the job a few months. It turned out that many of the previous employees had left the station about six months earlier to go to larger markets. That left a remaining recent graduate and new hire in charge but with few staff–and something of an emergency. He had obtained his job by responding to a job posting on a Web site used by broadcasters, so he went ahead and listed on that site all the jobs that were open at his station.

In a few days, new broadcasting graduates from all over the country saw the Internet postings and responded. E-mail went back and forth, and the relatively few willing to come to the station at their expense were invited to interview. Within a few weeks, most of the open positions were filled by young people who had responded on the Internet.

The crises for the TV station ended, and many of those hired told me that they were getting a great opportunity that they did not expect to obtain in any other way. I have to agree. More traditional recruiting methods would have created long delays for the employer and the job seekers. Traditional recruiting would also probably have screened out those with less experience and credentials. These job seekers got these jobs because of their using the Internet. While there were surely people with better credentials, they did not know about or get these jobs.

But note that the ones who got the jobs were those willing to take the chance and travel to the employer at their own expense. They had to be active and take some chances. And they had to be able to make a quick decision to move–something that a young person can more easily do. And they did not simply post their resumes in a resume database somewhere. The winning applicants were proactive in using the Internet to make direct contact with this employer, and then they followed up agressively.

Specific Tips to Increase Your Internet Effectiveness

Here are some things you can do to increase the effectiveness of using the Internet in your job search.

1. **Be as specific as possible in the job you seek**–This is important in using any job search method and even more so in using the Internet. I say this because the Internet is so enormous in its reach that looking for a nonspecific job is simply not an appropriate task. So do your career planning homework and be specific in what you are looking for.

2. **Keep your expectations reasonable**–The people who have the most success on the Internet are those who best understand its limitations. For example, those with technical skills that are in short supply–such as network engineers–will have more employers looking for these skills and more success on the Internet. Keep in mind that many of the advertised jobs are already filled by the time you see them and that thousands of people may apply to those that sound particularly attractive. People do get job leads on the Internet, but be reasonable in your expectations and use a variety of job search methods in addition to the Internet

3. **Consider your willingness to move**–If you don't want to move, or are willing only to move to certain locations, you should restrict your job search to geographic areas that meet your criteria. Many of the Internet databases allow you to view only those jobs that meet your criteria.

4. **Create a resume that is appropriate for use on the Internet**–With some exceptions, most of the resumes submitted on the Internet end up as simple text files with no graphic elements. Employers can then search a database of resumes for key words or use other searchable criteria. This is why your Internet resume should include a list of key words likely to be used by an employer as search criteria. Additional information on resumes and the Internet can be found in books listed in the bibliography.

5. **Get your resume into the major resume databases used by employers**–Many of the major resume databases allow job seekers to list their resumes for free. Employers are typically charged for advertising their openings or sorting the database for candidates that meet their criteria. Most of these sites are easy to understand and use, and they often provide all sorts of useful information for job seekers. Major sites are listed in the bibliography.

6. **Seek out relevant sites**–Simply getting your resume listed on several Internet sites is often not enough. Many employers do not use these sites, or they use one but not another. Remember the example, that I used earlier–those people found out about TV-related jobs from an Internet site that was run by a trade publication for broadcasters. Many professional associations post job openings on their sites or list other sites that would be of interest to that profession. Check out the resources that are available to people in the industries or occupations that interest you, since many of these resources also have Internet sites.

7. **Find specific employer sites**–Some employers have their own Internet sites that list job openings, allow you to apply online, and even provide access to staff who can answer your questions. While this is mostly used by larger technology-oriented companies, many smaller employers and government agencies have set up their own sites to attract candidates.

8. **Use informal chat rooms or request help**–Many Internet sites have interactive chat rooms or allow you to post a message for others to respond to. If you are not familiar with a chat room, it is a way for you to type responses to what someone else types as you are both online. Many sites also have a place for you to leave a message for others to respond to by sending you e-mail messages. Both of these methods allow you to meet potential employers or others in your field who can provide you with the advice or leads you seek.

9. **Use the listings of large Internet browsers or service providers**–While there are thousands of career-related Internet sites, some are better than others. Many sites I list in the bibliography provide links to other sites they recommend. Large service providers such as America Online (www.aol.com) and the Microsoft Network (www.msn.com) provide career-related information and job listings on their sites as well as links to other sites. Most of the larger "search engines" provide links to recommended career-related sites and can be quite useful. Some of the larger such sites include Alta Vista (www.altavista.com), Lycos (www.lycos.com), and Yahoo (www.Yahoo.com)

10. **Don't get ripped off**–Since the Internet has few regulations, many crooks use it as a way to take money from trusting souls. Remember that anyone can set up a site, even if the person does not provide a legitimate service, so be careful before you pay money for anything on the Internet. A general rule is that if it sounds too good to be true, it probably is. For example, if a site "guarantees" that it will find you a job or charges high fees. I recommend you look elsewhere.

Some Useful Internet Sites

There are hundreds and even thousands of Internet sites that provide information on careers or education, list job openings, or provide other career-related information. I've listed just a few of the many in the Bibliography at the end of this book. Since most of these sites will list other useful sites, there is enough information in that section of the Bibliography to get started.

In Closing

Few people will get a job offer because someone knocks on their door and offers one. The craft of job seeking does involve some luck, but you are far more likely to get lucky if you are out getting interviews. Structure your job search as if it were a full-time job and try not to get discouraged. There are lots of jobs out there, and someone needs what you can do—your job is to find them.

I hope this book helps, though you should consider learning more. Career planning and job seeking skills are, I believe, adult survival skills for our new economy. Good luck!

Mike Farr

Appendix A

ARTICLES OF INTEREST

The articles in this appendix were written by staff of the U.S. Department of Labor and published in one of its publications. The first article appeared in the introduction to the 1998-99 edition of the *Occupational Outlook Handbook*. It provides an excellent review of important trends in the labor market, including occupations and industries that are growing and declining, the fastest growing jobs, the importance of education, fast-growth jobs with high pay, and many other useful details. The other articles give information on high-paying jobs that do not require a four-year college degree, plus advice on training and education options.

Making informed career decisions requires reliable information about opportunities in the future. Opportunities result from the relationships between the population, labor force, and the demand for goods and services.

Population ultimately limits the size of the labor force—individuals working or looking for work—which constrains how much can be produced. Demand for various goods and services determines employment in the industries providing them. Occupational employment opportunities, in turn, result from skills needed within

specific industries. Opportunities for registered nurses and other health-related specialists, for example, have surged in response to the rapid growth in demand for health services.

Examining the past and anticipating changes in these relationships are the foundation of the Occupational Outlook Program. This appendix presents highlights of Bureau of Labor Statistics projections of the labor force and occupational and industry employment that can help guide your career plans.

The labor force will grow more slowly.

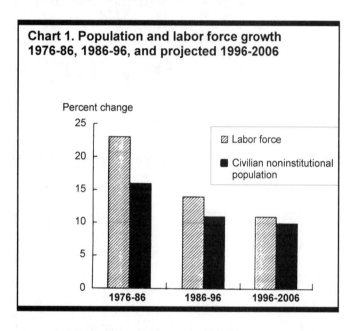

Chart 1. Population and labor force growth 1976-86, 1986-96, and projected 1996-2006

The labor force will become increasingly diverse.

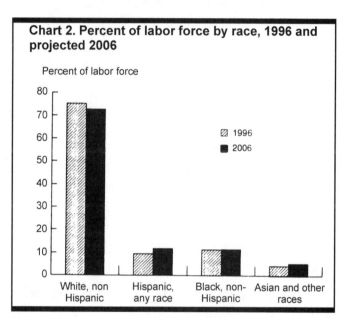

Chart 2. Percent of labor force by race, 1996 and projected 2006

- The Bureau of Labor Statistics (BLS) projects that the labor force will grow to 14.9 million between 1996 and 2006. This is 1.2 million less than the previous 10 years reflecting a slower growth in the civilian noninstitutional population 16 years of age and older. Growth was much faster from 1976 to 1986, when the baby boomers were entering the labor force.

- The labor force will grow 11 percent between 1996 and 2006, slightly slower than during the 1986-96 period but only half the rate of growth during the 1976-86 period.

- As a result of an increase in the percentage of the population working or looking for work, the labor force will continue to grow faster than the population rate.

- Between 1996 and 2006, employment will increase by 18.6 million or 14 percent. This is slower than during the 1986-96 period, when the economy added 21 million jobs.

- Wage and salary worker employment will account for 94 percent of this increase. In addition, the number of self-employed workers is expected to increase to 11.6 million in 2006, while the number of unpaid family workers will decline.

- The labor force growth of Hispanics, Asians and other races, will be faster than for blacks and white non-Hispanics. The projected labor force growth of these ethnic groups stems primarily from immigration.

- Despite relatively slow growth, white non-Hispanics will have the largest numerical growth between 1996 and 2006.

- Between 1996 and 2006, women's share of the labor force is projected to slowly increase from 46 to 47 percent, continuing a pattern since 1976. The participation rate for women will continue to increase for those 20- to 65-years old.

- The number of men in the labor force will grow at a slower rate than in the past, in part reflecting declining employment in well-paid production jobs in manufacturing, and a continued shift in demand for workers from the goods-producing sector to the service-producing sector. Participation rates for men will decline for all age groups below age 45 except for 16-19; the rates for those 16-19 will remain steady at 53 percent. Rates for age groups 45 and above will increase.

The labor force will become older.

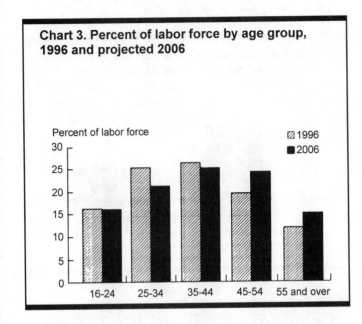

Chart 3. Percent of labor force by age group, 1996 and projected 2006

Percent of labor force

☑ 1996
■ 2006

- Workers over age 45 will account for a larger share of the labor force as the baby-boom generation ages.
- Two age groups with large numbers of baby boomers will grow by more than 30 percent—people 45 to 54 and those 55 to 64. Only the trailing edge of the baby boomers, those born from 1962 to 1964, will be younger than 45 in 2006.
- The very large group of workers aged 35 to 44, which is about one-fourth of the labor force, will change hardly at all during the period. The 25- to 34-year old group will decline by 3.0 million, a result of falling birth rates in the late 1960's. Those 16 to 24 will increase by more than 3.0 million, making this group the largest it has been in 25 years.

Industry employment growth is projected to be highly concentrated in service-producing industries.

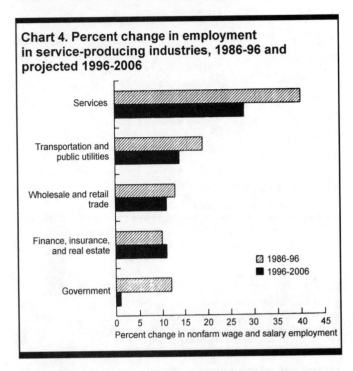

Chart 4. Percent change in employment in service-producing industries, 1986-96 and projected 1996-2006

☑ 1986-96
■ 1996-2006

Percent change in nonfarm wage and salary employment

- Employment in service-producing industries will increase faster than average, with growth near 30 percent. Service and retail trade industries will account for 14.8 million out of a total projected growth of 17.5 million wage and salary jobs.
- Business, health, and education services will account for 70 percent of the growth within the service industry.
- Health care services will increase 30 percent and account for 3.1 million new jobs, the largest numerical increase of any industry from 1996-2006. Factors contributing to continued growth in this industry include the aging population, which will continue to require more services, and the increased use of innovative medical technology for intensive diagnosis and treatment. Patients will increasingly be shifted out of hospitals and into outpatient facilities, nursing homes, and home health care in an attempt to contain costs.
- Educational services are projected to increase by 1.8 million jobs between 1996 and 2006. Most jobs will be for teachers, who are projected to account for 1.3 million jobs.
- Computer and data processing services will add over 1.3 million jobs from 1996-2006. The 108 percent increase is due to technological advancements and the need for higher skilled workers. The high percent increase makes this the fastest growing industry over the projection period.

Growth in goods-producing industries will be restrained by declines in manufacturing and mining.

Replacement needs will account for three-fifths of the 50.6 million projected job openings between 1996 and 2006.

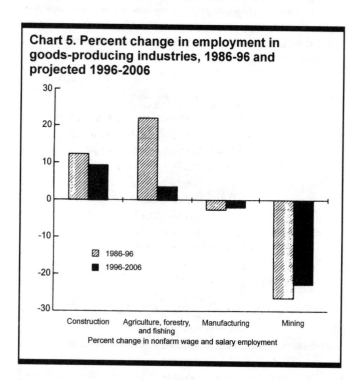

Chart 5. Percent change in employment in goods-producing industries, 1986-96 and projected 1996-2006

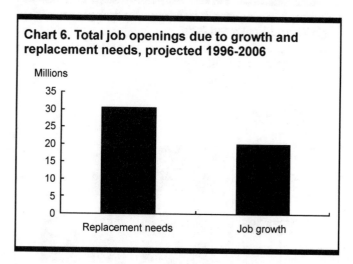

Chart 6. Total job openings due to growth and replacement needs, projected 1996-2006

- Projected employment growth in the construction and agriculture industries will be offset by a decline in manufacturing and mining jobs. Manufacturing will account for 13 percent of total wage and salary worker employment in 2006, compared to 15 percent in 1996.
- Construction employment will grow one-fourth slower than during the previous 10-year period.
- Within the agriculture, forestry, and fishing industry, growth in agriculture services and forestry will more than offset the projected declines in crops, livestock, and livestock related products, and fishing, hunting, and trapping.

- Job growth can be measured by percent change and numerical change. The fastest growing occupations do not necessarily provide the largest number of jobs. A larger occupation with slower growth may produce more openings than a smaller occupation with faster growth.
- Job opportunities are enhanced by additional openings resulting from the need to replace workers who leave the occupation. Some workers leave the occupation as they are promoted or change careers; others stop working to return to school, to assume household responsibilities, or retire.
- Replacement needs are greater in occupations with low pay and low training requirements with a high proportion of young and part-time workers.

Service and professional specialty occupations will provide about 2 out of every 5 job openings—primarily due to high replacement needs.

Of the 25 occupations with fast growth, high pay, and low unemployment that have the largest numerical growth, 18 require at least a bachelor's degree.

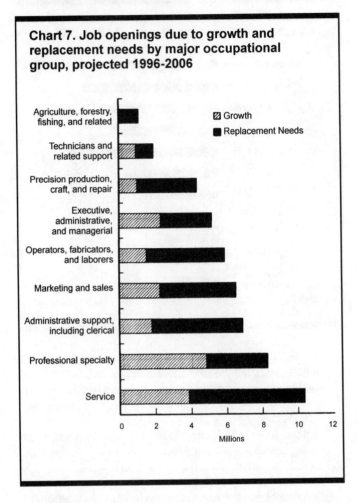

Chart 7. Job openings due to growth and replacement needs by major occupational group, projected 1996-2006

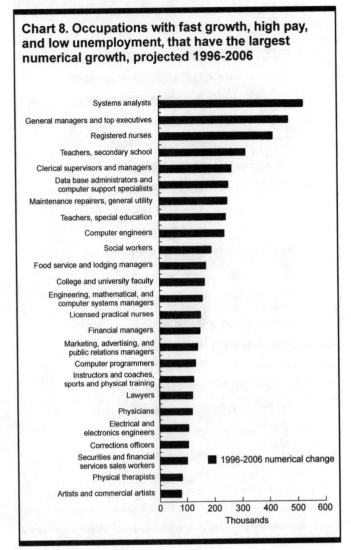

Chart 8. Occupations with fast growth, high pay, and low unemployment, that have the largest numerical growth, projected 1996-2006

- Employment in professional specialty occupations is projected to increase at a faster rate and have more job growth than any major occupational group.
- Within professional specialty occupations, computer related occupations and teachers will add 2.3 million new jobs, accounting for 15 percent of all new jobs from 1996 to 2006. Professional specialty occupations comprise the only group that will have a majority of job openings stemming from growth.
- Little or no change is expected in employment in agriculture, forestry, fishing, and related occupations. All job openings in this cluster will stem from replacement needs.
- Office automation will significantly affect many individual administrative and clerical support occupations. Overall, these occupations will increase more slowly than average, though some are projected to decline.
- Precision production, craft, and repair occupations and operators, fabricators, and laborers are projected to grow slower than average due to continuing advances in technology, changes in production methods. and overall decline in manufacturing jobs.

- These 25 occupations are somewhat concentrated, with 5 occupations in computer technology, 4 in health care, and 5 in education.
- The 25 occupations with fast growth, higher than average pay, and lower than average unemployment that have the largest numerical growth, will account for 5 million new jobs, or 27 percent of all job growth.

The fastest growing occupations reflect growth in computer technology and health care services.

Job growth varies widely by education and training requirements.

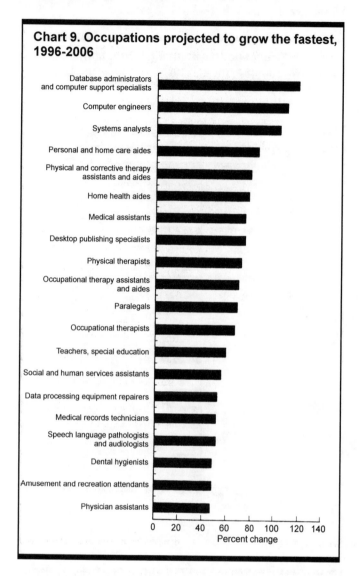

Chart 9. Occupations projected to grow the fastest, 1996-2006

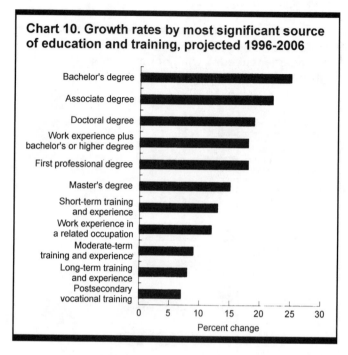

Chart 10. Growth rates by most significant source of education and training, projected 1996-2006

- Computer engineers and systems analysts jobs are expected to grow rapidly in order to satisfy expanding needs of scientific research and applications of computer technology. The three fastest growing occupations are in computer related fields.
- Many of the fastest growing occupations are concentrated in health services, which are expected to increase more than twice as fast as the whole economy. Personal and home care aides, and home health aides, will be in great demand to provide personal care for an increasing number of elderly people and for persons who are recovering from surgery and other serious health conditions. This is occurring, as hospitals and insurance companies require shorter stays for recovery to reduce costs.

- Five out of the 6 education and training categories projected to have the fastest growth require at least a bachelor's degree, and the sixth requires an associate's degree. All categories that do not require a college degree are projected to grow slower than average.
- Table 1 presents the fastest growing occupations and those having the largest numerical increase in employment over the 1996-2006 period, categorized by the level of education and training.
- Occupations usually requiring short-term on-the-job training accounted for 53.5 million jobs in 1996, more than any other education and training category. Occupations requiring a bachelor's degree or more education accounted for 22 percent of all jobs. Occupations in the four education categories not requiring postsecondary education accounted for about 70 percent of all jobs.
- Occupations that require a bachelor's degree are projected to grow the fastest, nearly twice as fast as the average for all occupations. All of the 20 occupations with the highest earnings require at least a bachelor's degree. Engineering and health occupations dominate this list.
- Education is essential in getting a high paying job. However, many occupations—for example, registered nurses, blue-collar worker supervisors, electrical and electronic technicians/technologists, automotive mechanics, and carpenters—do not require a college degree, yet offer higher than average earnings.
- Labor force groups with lower than average educational attainment in 1996, including Hispanics and blacks, will continue to have difficulty obtaining a share of the high paying jobs unless they raise their educational attainment. Although high paying jobs will be available without college training, most jobs that pay above average wages will require a college degree.

Jobs will be available for job seekers from every education and training background.

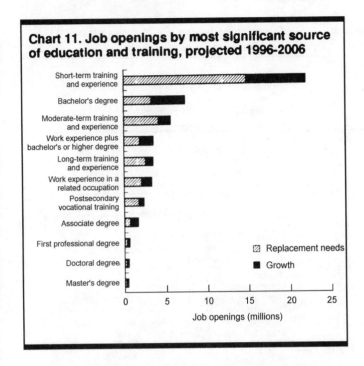

Chart 11. Job openings by most significant source of education and training, projected 1996-2006

- Almost two-thirds of the projected growth will be in occupations that require less than a college degree. However, these positions generally offer the lowest pay and benefits.
- Jobs requiring the least education and training–those that can be learned on the job–will provide 2 of every 3 openings due to growth and replacement needs; 3 of every 4 openings will be in occupations that generally require less than a bachelor's degree.

Declining occupational employment stems from declining industry employment and technological advancement.

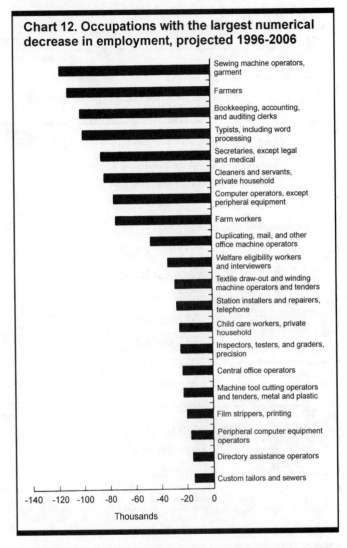

Chart 12. Occupations with the largest numerical decrease in employment, projected 1996-2006

- Manufacturing and agricultural related jobs, such as sewing machine operators and farmers, are examples of occupations that will lose employment due to declining employment in some goods-producing industries.
- Many declining occupations are affected by structural changes, as a result of factors including technological advances and organizational changes. For example, the use of typists and word processors will decline dramatically because of productivity improvements in office automation, and the increased use of word processing equipment by professional and managerial employees.

Table 1. Fastest growing occupations and occupations having the largest numerical increase in employment, projected 1996-2006, by level of education and training

Fastest growing occupations	Education/training category	Occupations having the largest numerical increase in employment
	First professional degree	
Chiropractors Veterinarians and veterinary inspectors Physicians Lawyers Clergy		Lawyers Physicians Clergy Veterinarians and veterinary inspectors Dentists
	Doctoral degree	
Biological scientists Medical scientists College and university faculty Mathematicians and all other mathematical scientists		College and university faculty Biological scientists Medical scientists Mathematicians and all other mathematical scientists
	Master's degree	
Speech-language pathologists and audiologists Counselors Curators, archivists, museum technicians Psychologists Operations research analysts		Speech-language pathologists and audiologists Counselors Psychologists Librarians, professional Operations research analysts
	Work experience plus bachelor's or higher degree	
Engineering, science, and computer systems managers Marketing, advertising, and public relations managers Artists and commercial artists Management Analysts Financial managers		General managers and top executives Engineering, science, and computer systems managers Finance managers Marketing, advertising, and public relations manager Artists and commercial artists
	Bachelor's degree	
Data base administrators and computer support specialists Computer engineers Systems analysts Physical therapists Occupational therapists		Systems analysts Teachers, secondary school Data base administrators and computer support specialists Teachers, special education Computer engineers
	Associate degree	
Paralegals Health information technicians Dental hygienists Respiratory therapists Cardiology technologists		Registered nurses Paralegals Dental hygienists Radiologic technologists and technicians Health information technicians
	Postsecondary vocational training	
Data processing equipment repairers Emergency medical technicians Manicurists Surgical technologists Medical secretaries		Licensed practical nurses Automotive mechanics Medical secretaries Emergency medical technicians Hairdressers, hairstylists, and cosmetologists
	Work experience	
Food service and lodging managers Teachers and instructors, vocational education and training Lawn service managers Instructors, adult education Nursery and greenhouse managers		Clerical supervisors and managers Marketing and sales worker supervisors Food service and lodging managers Teachers and instructors, vocational education and training Instructors, adult (nonvocational) education
	Long-term training and experience (more than 12 months of on-the-job training)	
Desktop publishing specialists Flight attendants Musicians Correction officers Producers, directors, actors, and entertainers		Cooks, restaurant Correction officers Musicians Police patrol officers Carpenters
	Moderate-term training and experience (I to 12 months of combined on-the-job experience and informal training)	
Physical and corrective therapy assistants and aides Medical assistants Occupational therapy assistants and aides Social and human services assistants Instructors and coaches, sports and physical training		Medical assistants Instructors and coaches, sports and physical training Social and human services assistants Dental assistants Physical and corrective therapy assistants
	Short-term training and experience (up to 1 month of on-the-job experience)	
Personal and home care aides Home health aides Amusement and recreation attendants Adjustment clerks Bill and account collectors		Cashiers Salespersons, retail Truck drivers, light and heavy Home health aides Teacher aides and educational assistants

High-Earning Workers Who Don't Have a Bachelor's Degree

By Theresa Cosca

What makes a job good? To many people, it's earnings. For them, the good news is that over 9 million, or one in every six, full-time salaried workers age 25 and older who didn't have a bachelor's degree in 1993 earned $700 or more a week. That's close to the median for college graduates. However, it is necessary to go beyond wages in determining whether a position is the right one for you. Job characteristics, such as the nature of the work and working conditions, are also important.

Still, everyone agrees that high earnings are better than low earnings. Furthermore, earnings can be measured, but many other factors cannot. The following pages discuss occupations in which many highly paid workers do not have a college degree and point out other factors that make for a good job.

Many people are concerned that high-paid jobs are no longer available for those without a bachelor's degree. Employment has declined in manufacturing, telephone communications, and some other industries that traditionally provided high-paying jobs. For men without a four-year degree, earnings adjusted for inflation have fallen over the past 15 years, due at least in part to these declines. Rising entry requirements for some professional, managerial, and other jobs have made entry without a degree more difficult. Despite these trends, many people without college degrees, including many people under 35, still have high earnings. In fact, 1 of these workers in 20 earns $1,000 or more a week.

What the Numbers Say

There is no accepted definition of high earnings. Among the more objective measures available is the median earnings of all workers, the median being the point at which half the workers earned more and half earned less. The median earnings of workers with a bachelor's degree is another possible yardstick.

In 1993, the median for all workers was about $500 a week. More precisely, median weekly earnings for all full-time, year-round workers age 25 and older were $493, or about $25,600 annually. The median for those with at least a bachelor's degree was $716, or about $37,200 annually. The low figure is almost three times higher than the minimum wage ($4.25 an hour) and the high figure is more than four times higher.

Number of Workers, by Usual Weekly Earnings and Education, 1993 (numbers in millions)		
	Less than a bachelor's degree	Bachelor's degree or higher
Less than $500	32.7	4.7
$500-699	12.1	5.2
$700-999	6.6	5.5
$1000 or more	2.7	5.8

In 1993, 21.4 million workers without four-year degrees earned $500 or more a week, and 9.3 million earned $700 or more. In other words, two of five workers without a college degree earned more than the median for all workers.

Percentage of Workers, by Usual Weekly Earnings and Education, 1993 (numbers in millions)		
	Less than a bachelor's degree	Bachelor's degree or higher
Less than $500	61%	23%
$500-699	22	25
$700-999	12	26
$1000 or more	5	27

As these charts show, earnings were even higher, at $1,000 or more a week, for many workers. In a few occupations, more than 10 percent of the workers without college degrees earned over $1,000 a week. Consider the top earners–the most motivated, best prepared, or most fortunate workers–in these occupations:

Occupation	Minimum weekly earnings of the top 10%, 1993
Mining, manufacturing, and wholesale sales representatives	$1,051
Production occupation supervisors	1,000
Registered nurses	961
Police and detectives	889
Administrative support occupations, supervisors	888
Engineering and related technologists and technicians	856
Carpenters	801
Truck drivers	800

To some extent, earnings reflect the innate skill and talent of the worker. Other factors, such as geographic region, urban or rural environment, industry, size of the facility, and unionization also affect earnings. And men, on average, earn more than women. Three other factors significantly affect the proportion of workers who have high earnings:

- Occupation
- Age
- Education and training

Occupation

Tables 1 and 2 list all occupations that have more than 50,000 full-time wage and salary workers age 25 and older who usually earn $700 a week or more. Some small occupations in which workers have high earnings are not listed; among these are elevator installer and air traffic controller. Table 1 lists the occupations and the number and percentage of workers who do not have a bachelor's degree. Table 2 lists the occupations by the percentage who usually earn $700 a week or more. Tables for all workers would show somewhat lower earnings, because part-timers and workers under 25 typically make less. Also, in seasonal occupations, annual earnings may be lower than implied by weekly earnings.

Age

Generally speaking, earnings increase with age, as workers gain experience and seniority. This progression usually peaks between the ages of 45 to 54. For the same reasons, the number of high-wage earners is concentrated in the 35-to-44 and 45-to-54 age groups. Some may argue from this that highly paid workers without bachelors'degrees entered the job market years ago, when entry standards were lower and more high-wage manufacturing jobs were available. However, some workers without a bachelor's degree achieve high earnings at a relatively young age, and obviously did so since "the good old days." For example, 2.2 million workers without a degree, age 25 to 29, earned $500 or more a week; and 725,000, $700 or more.

Percentage of Workers Without College Degrees Earning $500 or More a Week, by Age, 1993		
Age group	$500 or more a week	$700 or more a week
25-29	25.7%	8.4%
30-34	36.1	14.7
35-44	43.6	19.3
45-54	46.5	22.4
55 and over	39.3	17.2

Education

Lack of a four-year degree doesn't mean one has no postsecondary education or training. In fact, research done for the *Occupational Outlook Handbook* indicates that training other than a bachelor's degree is the most appropriate preparation for some high-paying jobs. In general, workers with more training are more likely to have high earnings. Some high-wage occupations are difficult to enter without training, and within occupations, workers with the most training tend to have the highest paid and supervisory jobs. A 1991 study of job training also found that workers who said they needed some kind of training for their jobs earned substantially more than those who said they didn't.

High-wage earners develop the skills they need in many ways: associate degree programs, college courses, postsecondary vocational schools and technical institutes, apprenticeships or other formal employer training, informal on-the-job training, and Armed Forces experience. Earnings data are not available for all these types of training, but the chart below shows that earnings increase steadily with education.

Percentage of Workers Without College Degrees Earning $500 or More a Week, by Education, 1993		
Education level	$500 or more	$700 or more
Less than high school	19.4%	6.8%
High school	37	14.5
Some college, no degree	48.4	23.1
Associate degree	55.6	27.8

What's Good Besides Earnings?

As I said above, many people equate high earnings with good jobs. But jobs with relatively low wages in certain areas of the country may be better than the salary indicates because living costs are also likely to be lower. And there is more to work than wages. Other important concerns when evaluating an occupation include the following:

- Benefits
- Projected growth and openings
- Unemployment rate
- Advancement potential
- Nature of the work and working conditions.

Depending on the importance you give each of these factors, a good job might be one with lower than average earnings.

Benefits

Employee benefits, once a minor addition to wages and salaries, are an increasingly important factor in defining a good job. In 1993, benefits averaged about 29 percent of total compensation costs. Some benefits, such as health and life insurance or subsidized child care, are virtually the same as cash, because they would otherwise have to be paid for out of earnings. Paid holidays and vacation leave improve the recipients' quality of life. Most employers also provide other benefits that add to the quality of a job, such as sick leave. Some employers, like airlines, provide free or subsidized travel, while retailers may provide discounts on merchandise.

Projected Growth and Openings

The projected growth rate and number of job openings serve to gauge how easy or difficult it will be to find a job in an occupation and, perhaps, also to be promoted. Section One of this book provides projections for the jobs described there, and the appendices provide additional growth projections for many other jobs. In some cases, information on competition for jobs is also given. Some high-wage occupations available without a college degree, such as the precision production occupations, are not expected to grow. Others are expected to grow about as fast as the average for all workers, including engineering and science technicians; construction workers; and mechanics, installers, and repairers. Registered nurse and most health technician and technologist occupations are projected to grow much faster than average.

More job openings result from the need to replace workers who transfer to different occupations, retire, or stop working for some other reason than from growth. For example, employment of secretaries is projected to increase by 386,000 jobs by 2005, but net replacement needs are expected to provide more than twice as many openings. Even occupations with little or no projected job growth have some openings. For example, precision production occupations are expected to have 68,000 job openings annually due to net replacement needs.

Unemployment Rate

Some occupations have high unemployment rates. This does not necessarily disqualify them as high-paying jobs. Those that provide high hourly earnings and unemployment compensation can still yield a high annual income. Furthermore, many workers in these occupations do have steady year-round jobs. High unemployment rates are common in many construction occupations, such as carpenter and electrician, as well as manufacturing jobs, such as assembler and machine operator.

Unemployment rates actually reflect two kinds of unemployment: cyclical and long-term. Recessions and seasonal changes in production create cyclical unemployment in many occupations. During slack periods, workers may face temporary layoffs but can expect to be re-employed when conditions improve. On the other hand, long-term unemployment or even permanent job loss may be caused by restructuring or plant closings. Jobs in organizations or industries with good long-term prospects are obviously more desirable. Even if you lose your job, you are more likely to find another one in such an industry.

Advancement Potential

Some occupations offer a natural progression of career advancement, such as from electrician apprentice to journey-level electrician to electrician supervisor or contractor. Workers in other occupations may need to carve their own paths to success, following less orthodox routes. Still other occupations or jobs offer few if any chances for advancement.

Often, promotion potential varies from employer to employer. In general, fast-growing occupations and organizations offer better promotion prospects. Large employers offer better prospects, at least without the need to change employers, but small organizations may offer broader responsibilities and opportunities to learn a wider range of skills. In any job, it is important to be ready to act on opportunities as they arise.

Nature of the Work

For most people, a good job is one that they find interesting, that fully uses their skills, or that satisfies their needs in other ways. Almost everybody appreciates a job in which they can see the results of their work and feel a sense of accomplishment. Others seek a job related to an interest, such as cars, music, or children. Helping others is often the central satisfaction for those in health, teaching, or social work occupations. Satisfying aspects of a job may include analyzing data or information, coordinating events and activities, teaching or mentoring, selling to or persuading others, operating or fixing machinery, or designing or creating new ideas, concepts, or works of art.

Other characteristics that define a good job include the level of physical exertion necessary, cleanliness and safety of the workplace, level of contact with people, ability to decide how work is to be done, and the level of stress. For some, no amount of money is worth the grueling hours and stress that many physicians live with, or the physical exertion, danger, or dirt faced by coal miners and some construction workers, or the boredom of assembly line work. Others find job pressures exciting, don't mind the danger or dirt, or welcome the stress.

For many, working with people they like and respect and having a good supervisor are essential elements of a good job. They may also want an employer whose goals and policies they agree with. Likewise, some workers seek the security of a salaried job with a well-established, stable organization, but others find stimulation in risk taking—running their own business, working for a fledgling organization, or selling on commission.

Where a job is located may also be important. Some people do not want a long commute or a geographic relocation. For them, a good job is one that is available where they live.

Finally, the steady hours that high pay demands may be just the opposite of what a worker wants. Some only want part-time work, due to family responsibilities, school, or other pursuits.

Despite the public's perception that the economy is creating mostly lower-skill, low-wage jobs, examination of the data reveals that there are many good jobs for those who do not have a bachelor's degree—not only jobs with high wages but also jobs that are good for other, less tangible reasons.

Any job is a complicated medley of positives and negatives. One factor seldom makes a job good or bad. Get to know all you can about occupations you are considering. It is extremely important to research the entry requirements and other characteristics, so that you will know what to expect out of the job. Above all, remember that it is important to make a career choice that is good for you. The demand for skilled workers will remain strong. Will you be ready?

Table 1. Occupations of workers with less than a bachelor's degree, 1993

Occupation[1]	Number (thousands)[2]	Percentage
Total all workers	54,095	71
Accountants and auditors	313	28
Administrators and officials, public administration	215	42
Assemblers	845	96
Automobile mechanics	480	96
Bus, truck, and stationary engine mechanics	274	98
Carpenters	606	93
Computer operators	367	82
Computer programmers	197	40
Computer system analysts and scientists	190	31
Correctional institution officers	261	91
Designers	154	53
Electrical and electronic engineers	121	26
Electrical and electronic equipment repairers, except telephone	271	87
Electrical and electronic technicians	212	83
Electrical power installers and repairers	101	96
Electricians	475	95
Financial managers	203	42
Fire-fighting occupations	155	90
Health technologists and technicians	808	79
Industrial, mechanical, and all other engineers	274	27
Industrial machinery repairers	487	96
Insurance sales occupations	200	55
Investigators and adjusters, insurance and other	673	75
Machine operators and tenders, except precision	3,667	96
Machinists and precision metalworking occupations	669	96
Mail carriers and postal clerks	513	89
Managers, marketing, advertising, and public relations	181	41
Managers, properties and real estate	201	65
Managers, food service and lodging establishments	469	78
Managers and administrators not elsewhere classified	2,065	57
Other financial officers	249	43
Personnel, training, and labor relations specialists	164	47
Plumbers, pipefitters, and steamfitters	287	96
Police and detectives	353	75
Purchasing agents and buyers	260	66
Rail transportation occupations	95	94
Real estate sales occupations	168	54
Registered nurses	656	51
Sales occupations, other business services	190	53
Sales representatives, mining and manufacturing and wholesale	635	56
Science and engineering technicians	287	75
Secretaries	2,326	90
Stationary engineers and other plant and system operators	230	91
Supervisors, police and fire fighting	92	71
Supervisors, mechanics and repairers	181	89
Supervisors, construction occupations	419	88
Supervisors, production occupations	1,010	87
Supervisors, administrative support occupations	519	73
Supervisors and proprietors, sales occupations	1,658	72
Telephone and telephone line installers and repairers	211	95
Truck drivers	2,000	96
Welders and cutters	438	98
All other occupations	26,021	70

[1]Includes only occupations with at least 50,000 workers with less than a bachelor's degree whose usual weekly earnings are $700 or more.
[2]Employed wage and salary workers.

Source: Current Population Survey.

Table 2. Workers with less than a bachelor's degree and usual weekly earnings of $700 or more, by occupation, 1993

Occupation[1]	Number (thousands)[3]	Percentage
Total	9,269	17
Electrical and electronic engineers [2]	81	67
Industrial, mechanical, and all other engineers [2]	165	60
Rail transportation occupations	56	59
Computer system analysts and scientists [2]	108	56
Supervisors, police and fire fighting	50	54
Electrical power installers and repairers	55	54
Computer programmers	107	54
Managers, marketing, advertising, and public relations [1]	91	50
Supervisors, mechanics and repairers	81	45
Fire-fighting occupations	69	44
Telephone and telephone line installers and repairers	92	44
Financial managers [2]	87	43
Managers and administrators not elsewhere classified	874	42
Supervisors, construction occupations	177	42
Registered nurses	269	41
Real estate sales occupations	65	39
Police and detectives	135	38
Electrical and electronic technicians	75	35
Designers	52	34
Sales representatives, mining and manufacturing and wholesale	212	33
Stationary engineers and other plant and system operators	75	33
Supervisors, production occupations	326	32
Sales occupations, other business services	61	32
Personnel, training, and labor relations specialists [2]	52	32
Other financial officers	79	32
Electricians	149	31
Administrators and officials, public administration	66	30
Electrical and electronic equipment repairers, except telephone	82	30
Plumbers, pipefitters, and steamfitters	78	27
Insurance sales occupations	52	26
Supervisors, administrative support occupations	134	26
Managers, properties and real estate [1]	51	25
Machinists and precision metalworking occupations	165	25
Science and engineering technicians	69	24
Industrial machinery repairers	116	24
Supervisors and proprietors, sales occupations	378	23
Accountants and auditors [2]	68	22
Mail carriers and postal clerks	109	21
Purchasing agents and buyers	5	20
Bus, truck, and stationary engine mechanics	53	19
Truck drivers	382	19
Correctional institution officers	5	19
Managers, food service and lodging establishments	83	18
Carpenters	107	18
Automobile mechanics	81	17
Welders and cutters	64	15
Computer operators	50	14
Health technologists and technicians	106	13
Assemblers	96	11
Investigators and adjusters, insurance and other	73	11
Machine operators and tenders, except precision	255	7
Secretaries	117	5
All other occupations	2,687	10

[1]Includes only occupations with at least 50,000 workers with less than a bachelor's degree.
[2]A bachelor's degree is usually required for entry. Those without a degree may have entered the occupation when requirements were lower or may be in the limited number of positions that do not require a degree.

[3]Employed wage and salary workers.
Source: Current Population Survey.

College, No; Training, Yes: A Guide for High School Graduates

By Rachel Moskowitz

High school diploma in hand, you want a good-paying job without going to college. What are your choices? You could go fight to work in an occupation that does not require any training. Or you could take some additional training either from an employer or at a school. What's the difference? More than $150 a week, on average. That's how much more money high school graduates make when they have jobs that require training compared to when they have jobs that don't (see Table 1). Training that takes less time and costs less than four years of college can prepare you for a better paying, more highly skilled job with advancement opportunities.

Most jobs require some form of qualifying training, which provides the skills and knowledge people need to begin working. In 1991, more than 21 million employed high school graduates, or 46 percent of the total, said they needed specific training to obtain their current job, according to the Current Population Survey for January of that year. They got this training in many different ways, such as the following:

- Postsecondary school courses
- Formal and informal on-the-job training, including the Armed Forces
- Other sources of training, such as informal training from a friend or relative

Often, the different kinds of training are associated with specific occupations.

Postsecondary School Courses

Several different kinds of schools offer training to prepare high school graduates for specific occupations. These include postsecondary vocational programs, junior or community colleges, and technical institutes. See "What to Look for in a Vocational or Technical Program" for some pointers on choosing a program that's right for you.

Postsecondary Vocational Programs

These programs are designed to teach a specialized skill or trade in a relatively short period of time. They stress hands-on training. Programs are flexible, offering both day and evening classes, and range from several months to a couple of years. Good programs use modern, state-of-the-art equipment, employ qualified instructors who have related work experience, and provide job placement assistance. Postsecondary vocational programs do not award degrees or college credit upon completion.

The cost of attending a postsecondary vocational program varies widely, depending on the occupation, length of the program, and type of institution. Private, for-profit institutions generally are more expensive than public institutions, which receive government assistance. Students at accredited private or public postsecondary vocational programs may qualify for federal or state financial aid.

In 1991, hairdresser and cosmetologist, registered nurse, nursing aide, orderly, licensed practical nurse, bookkeeper, accounting clerk, and barber were among the occupations in which many workers said they needed post-high school vocational training in order to qualify for their jobs.

Table 1. Median Weekly Earnings of Full-Time Workers Who are High School Graduates and Need Qualifying Training for Their Jobs Compared with Those Who Did Not, 1991

	Training needed	No training needed
All workers	$491	$322
Professional specialty	581	390
Precision production, craft, and repair	551	428
Transportation and material moving	540	365
Executive, administrative, and managerial	533	437
Technicians and related support	511	495
Machine operators, assemblers, and inspectors	502	311
Sales	497	280
Farming, forestry, and fishing	470	251
Service, except private household	465	250
Handlers, equipment cleaners, helpers, and laborers	398	311
Administrative support, including clerical	375	340

Junior and Community Colleges and Technical Institutes

In addition to awarding associate degrees and offering courses that transfer with credit to other colleges and universities, junior and community colleges also offer a wide variety of technical and vocational training programs. Technical institutes award an associate degree or a certificate of completion to graduates of their programs, which range from one to three years in length. Similar to technical programs in junior and community colleges, technical institute programs are designed to teach students marketable skills.

Junior and community colleges offer a wide variety of technical programs, such as accounting, advertising, tourism, and zoology. Graduates are awarded a general degree, such as associate in applied science (AAS) or associate in occupational studies (AOS), or an occupation-specific degree, such as associate of science in business (ASB).

Technical institutes teach many of the same subjects as postsecondary vocational programs, but training is more intense and advanced mathematics and science courses may be included in the curriculum. Graduates of technical institutes may be qualified for more responsible jobs than graduates of postsecondary vocational programs.

Technical institutes often have contacts in various fields that may lead to job opportunities for their graduates. Many businesses donate equipment and supplies and take a personal interest in students, who are prospective employees. Like some four-year colleges, technical institutes may offer co-op programs that give students an opportunity for additional hands-on training and provide exposure to on-the-job situations that may not occur in a classroom setting. Co-op students alternate periods of work and study. Some students who successfully complete these programs are hired by the company upon graduation.

Junior and community colleges and technical institutes offer many advantages for some students. The schools generally practice a liberal admissions policy and offer day and evening classes. Convenient locations mean an easy commute to classes, which keeps living expenses down. Tuition is relatively inexpensive but can vary, depending on the length of the program and the type of equipment used. For example, programs in aircraft mechanics and maintenance and computer-aided drafting are likely to cost more than programs in accounting, and two-year programs cost more than those that last only one year.

Among the occupations in which many workers said that junior college or technical institutes were important sources of training were registered nurse, licensed practical nurse, hairdresser and cosmetologist, real estate sales, computer programmer, drafter, and designer.

Correspondence Courses

All types of schools offer correspondence courses. They allow people to study independently in their own homes. Subjects range from English and basic mathematics to electronics and automotive engine repair. Students take the courses through the mail or by means of specially designed computer software that links students to instructors. Using a computer, a telephone, and a modem, students "attend" lectures, take tests, and submit homework. Some schools offer such courses at off-campus sites, where students have use of the necessary computers, videotapes, and two-way television broadcasts. Correspondence courses often use television to broadcast lectures. Students taking such courses also study print material and may communicate with instructors and other students by telephone.

Correspondence courses were an important source of training for insurance sales workers, electronic equipment repairers, industrial machinery repairers, electrical and electronic technicians, securities and financial services sales workers, and aircraft engine mechanics, according to the 1991 survey.

On-the-Job Training

Almost all employers provide new workers with some kind of training, even if it is just a quick introduction to the office's equipment and procedures. In many cases, however, the training is more extensive, especially in the Armed Forces. Training that is given from time to time as the worker needs to learn a new task is called informal on-the-job training. Janitors and cleaners, fast-food cooks, stock clerks, and waiters and waitresses, to name a few, generally learn their jobs this way. Formal company training is much more structured.

Formal Company Training

Any structured classroom or on-the-job training held during the workday is formal company training. It is always paid for by the employer. It is often taught by a supervisor or a trainer the firm employs for just this purpose; in other cases, companies pay for courses held outside of work. Electricians, insurance sales workers, police officers and detectives, insurance adjusters, and securities and financial services sales workers were among those who said that formal company training was an important source of qualifying training for their positions in 1991.

One of the best-known and most beneficial forms of formal company training is the apprenticeship. An apprentice is paid by the company and follows a specified course of on-the-job and classroom training. Often, the apprenticeship is managed by a union. By the end of the apprenticeship, which often lasts about four years, the worker reaches journey worker status. Apprenticeships are most common in the construction trades, such as carpenter, plumber, and electrician; but they are also offered to laboratory technicians, horse trainers, and a wide range of other occupations.

Competition for apprenticeships is often fierce. The availability of apprenticeships in any area depends on economic conditions, the willingness of employers to train employees as skilled craft workers, and new technology.

At least one employer provides formal training for everyone it hires: the Armed Forces. The first responsibility of military personnel is to defend the United States. But since the defense of our nation is so encompassing, there are a wide variety of jobs available. All branches of the uniformed services-Army, Navy, Air Force, and Coast Guard-offer education and career training.

All new members of the Armed Forces receive basic training to prepare them for military life. Most then go on to advanced training for specific occupations. Although many of these occupations, such as infantryman, exist only in the military, most have a civilian counterpart, such as electronics specialist or pilot. The job training may also count toward academic credit in a civilian college. Occupations for which Armed Forces training is important, according to the 1991 survey, include electrician, police officer and detective, aircraft engine mechanic, electrical and electronic engineer, airplane pilot and navigator, electronic repairer, telephone installer and repairer, and data processing equipment repairer.

Other Sources of Training

Besides receiving training from schools and employers, people learn job skills in many other ways, such as from friends and relatives. Private lessons can also be important, as is the case with musicians. Other sources of training include conventions, seminars, conferences, trade shows, and workshops—often sponsored by various associations, societies, or unions.

One or another of these sources of training is important in a great variety of occupations, such as actor, athlete, barber, bookkeeper and accounting clerk, camera instrument repairer, computer science teacher, farmer, hairdresser and cosmetologist, heavy truck driver, pattern maker, real estate sales worker, and secretary.

What to Look for in a Vocational or Technical Program

When investigating postsecondary technical programs and schools, there are several things you'll want to look into:
- Accreditation
- State license
- Certification
- Tuition policy
- Job placement
- The campus and faculty

Accreditation may be very important. Accreditation certifies that the school and its programs offer high-quality training. Some employers, especially those in technical fields such as computers or electronics, will only hire graduates of accredited institutions. And only students enrolled in an accredited institution or program usually qualify for government financial aid.

Schools and programs are accredited by agencies recognized by the US. Department of Education. Accreditation may be awarded through a regional accrediting commission or through a national association such as the Commission on Recognition of Postsecondary Accreditation. Specialized programs, such as dietetics, interior design, and auto repair, are accredited by their professional trade organizations. A list of recognized accrediting agencies is available from the U.S. Department of Education, Accreditation and State Liaison Division, Room 3036, 400 Maryland Ave. SW, Washington, DC 20202.

In order to operate, many states require that schools be licensed; to verify if a school is licensed, contact the Department of Education in your state.

If you are interested in a career that requires a state certificate to practice, such as real estate or cosmetology, verify that you will be prepared for the state examination upon graduation. Find out the proportion of students who pass the examination. You should also inquire about the student dropout rate and instructor turnover. A high dropout rate may mean student dissatisfaction and inadequate education, and high instructor turnover may signify problems within the school's programs and administration.

Make sure the school's tuition and refund policy are in writing. Find out if tuition is refundable, in full or in part, if an unexpected emergency occurs or if your career plans change.

Find out about the job placement services provided. Quality schools generally offer these services, which can be helpful in finding your first job. A competent and successful job placement service will help you write your resume, strengthen your interview skills, and host employer visits and interviews. Ask what proportion of students find jobs upon graduations high placement rate is a good sign. Before applying to a school, you should also tour the school and attend some classes. Talk to students already enrolled and meet the teachers and instructors.

Cooperative Education: Learn More, Earn More, Prepare for the Workplace

I hear.
I remember.
I do and I understand.
    —Confucius

By Matthew Mariani

Studies show that few people learn to drive a car without getting behind the wheel. Imagine a nonmotorist just reading a book about driving and then zooming off to Albuquerque. That would be hitting the highway the hard way.

As it happens, clever college students also learn by doing, and, in the United States, about a quarter of a million of them choose cooperative education. Co-op jump starts classroom study by alternating it with periods of work. Students gain hands-on experience related to their major field of study and career goals by following a school-approved plan.

Co-oping has many benefits. It helps students map out a career path. The money they earn as co-op employees pays some of their academic tolls along that path. After graduation, their work experience revs up a résumé and may lead them to permanent employment.

The road ahead offers a view of cooperative education starting at orientation and moving through graduation and finding employment afterwards. A section called "Transfers and Career Changers" looks at co-op students who transfer from a 2-year to a 4-year school and those who change careers. Along the way, you'll see real-life experiences of co-op students, past and present, from around the U.S.A. For them, co-op was the trip of a lifetime, and it might be for you.

Orientation

To get things rolling, co-op coordinators often orient students to the program in one session. Like cars, co-op programs have their own custom features, so coordinators cover the particulars about their school, as well as the basics.

Students first learn the magic number for cooperative education. It's the number three, because co-op depends on a partnership between three players: Student, college (represented by the coordinator), and co-op employers who hire students for work lasting from 2 to 6 months.

The scheduling of this work varies at the 900 or so U.S. colleges offering coop. Not all schools alternate between separate periods of work and study. Some have students go to class in the morning and work in the afternoon. Community colleges most often do this. Certain colleges mix the two modes of scheduling.

Programs leading to an associate's degree take at least 2 years. For a bachelor's degree, schools offer 4- or 5-year co-op programs. The total time spent on co-op work ranges from 6 months to 2 years, depending on the degree and the school. Some colleges grant academic credit for the work experience.

Get Ready, Get Set

Co-op gives students a head start on learning job search skills. Students write résumés and then interview with employers to compete for available co-op positions. Luckily, they have help from coordinators like Rubye Guest at Mississippi State University. "Most of these students have never done résumé or had a formal interview," says Guest. "We try to work with them in group sessions and with each student individually whenever we possibly can."

The timing and mode of job search training differs from one program to another. Students can't wait too long to polish their résumés and interviewing skills, though, because they need to start work quickly. Two-year schools may allow students to go to work after only one term of study. In bachelor's programs, co-op work may begin after a year or two in the classroom and sometimes sooner.

At Mississippi State, Guest does brief seminars on interviewing tips. Students might sign up before or after scheduling a job interview. After the seminar, Guest refers students to a mock interview for practice, if they're interested.

At other schools, such as LaGuardia Community College in Queens, New York, students take a one-credit course that blends

> *"[Co-op] helped me present myself as a good candidate. . .it prepared me to compete."*
>   —M. Rafiqul Alam

orientation with tips on resume writing and interviewing. M. Rafiqul Alam, a LaGuardia graduate now working for IBM, thinks the course helped him zip into the fast lane. "It helped me present myself as a good candidate," he says. "I never had a job interview, so it prepared me to compete."

Once students learn how to interview, they need jobs to interview for. Even if they've already chosen a major, they might not know what sort of job they want at first. Coordinators usually maintain a listing of available co-op positions and files telling what previous holders of the positions said about their experience. Using these aids, students explore their options. They also meet with their coordinators, who help them define what they want to learn at work. Students do this to match themselves with jobs that would foster the desired learning. In some programs, students may hunt for jobs not on the official list or even attempt to convince an employer to create a suitable job. The coordinator helps steer the student here, too.

After students identify jobs they might want, the real interviewing begins. Once again, the process varies by school. At some, coordinators forward students' résumés to the employers. Then it's up to each employer to contact individual applicants to arrange an interview. Other schools take an all-at-once approach. Mississippi State, for example, invites co-op employers to campus twice a year to conduct most of the interviews over a 3-day period. Students submit their preferences, which Guest and the other coordinators use to assign all interview slots.

After years on the job, Guest still marvels over her students' performance at interviews. "It's just amazing," she says. "You can just tell they're nervous wrecks at the first interview. But by the third day, they come in like they're old pros. It really builds their confidence."

Some co-op students receive offers from more than one employer, so they have a choice of jobs. However, co-op programs never guarantee employment, and not all students find jobs they like. A lot depends on the economy and the local job market.

Some students accept positions far from their residence and must find a place to live, negotiate the rent, set up housekeeping, and learn to schedule their time. Like most coordinators, Guest sees this as part of the learning experience.

Go to Work: The Co-op Job

Before co-op employees report to work their first day, they know they'll be driving on a two-way street. They will benefit from the experience, but their employer expects to benefit as well.

"Co-op," says Leo Peters, president of Weston & Sampson Engineers, "allows us to get people who we know are dependable to do pre-professional work. We get a very productive workforce that can hit the ground running." All co-op employers share this expectation, whether they're mom-and-pop shops, Fortune 500 companies, nonprofits, or government agencies. For students, the co-op tour brings multiple benefits. As employees, they learn technical skills, develop people skills, and earn some green while they're at it.

Getting experience. Students of every major learn technical skills. Those studying very technical subjects-like engineering or computer science-go further in this direction. Still, those in the liberal arts, social sciences, and business glean practical know-how from the experience, too.

Emily Waggel, a student at Cincinnati State Technical and Community College, worked for a company that makes conveyor belts. In class, she was studying motors, encoders, capacitors, and much else relating to electromechanical engineering technology. At work, she applied her knowledge, using computer aided drafting to design the circuits for control panels. "If I had just been in class," she says, "it would have been just numbers and words. But when I was out in the field looking at how everything fit together, it made more sense."

Monica Posey thinks Waggel's experience is the norm for co-op students. Posey serves as Assistant Dean for the Engineering Technologies Division at Cincinnati State. She says co-op students learn more by going beyond theory to application on the job. "When they go out to the worksite," she says, "it's sort of like they have another set of teachers. Now, they have teachers in the industry who can help them see how what they've learned in class is used in troubleshooting and problem solving."

Civil engineer Cynthia Lee agrees wholeheartedly. "You're going to have tons of questions," she says, recalling her days as a co-op employee. "There's always someone there who will answer your

question for you." Lee learned much from the answers she received from colleagues at Weston & Sampson Engineers. When she finished her bachelor's degree at Northeastern University in 1995,

> *"If I had just been in class, it would have been just numbers and words. But when I was out in the field looking At how everything fit together, it made More sense."*
>
> –Emily Waggel

she left with technical savvy she could not have gained just by attending classes.

Amy Killoran recently graduated from Antioch College with a psychology major and some technical savvy of her own. Located in Yellow Springs, Ohio, Antioch became the first liberal arts school in America to offer co-op in 1921. One term, Killoran worked in Antioch's Office of Institutional Research. "I did a lot of number crunching," she says, "and I was also put in charge of a research project on campus." One of her goals was to learn to use spreadsheet software and overcome her "computer phobia." She achieved it. "Immediately after that job," she says, "I got an e-mail account and started surfing the Net and everything."

She toots co-op's horn for people skills, too. Through experience, she learned to express herself well. On her fourth job, she chaired a conference in England with 160 attendees. Preparing for this gave her much practice dealing with people. She had to consult with workshop presenters, caterers, building and maintenance officials, hotel staff, and the researchers employing her.

Robert Krinsky thinks the co-op experience does even more to improve people skills than it does to teach practical know-how. After graduating from Antioch in 1957 as a math major, he went to work as an actuary for The Segal Company in New York. "I remember," he says, reflecting on his early coop work, "the first time I had to call a rather low-level person at one of our client firms to check on some data. My palms were sweaty, and I prepared for about 15 minutes for that phone call." By the end of his senior year, however, he could palaver with mid-level officials without overheating. Today, he does his talking at the top. Still at The Segal Company, he's now the guy heading the table in the corporate board room.

Mark Morgan, one of Guest's students at Mississippi State University, is just starting out in the business world. Like many co-op employees, he played a customer service role. Morgan worked in an IBM call center, aiding laptop computer users with hardware problems. "I'd have to talk to customers day in and day out," he says, "so I learned to communicate better that way." Lane McKinney, another of Guest's business students, did similar work. Employed by Fidelity Investments in Irving, Texas, she processed requests to transfer mutual fund accounts by phone in cases of marriage, divorce, or death.

Table 1

Median Monthly Salaries of Co-op Employees at the Associate's Degree Level in the Midwest by Major, 1993[1]

Major	Median monthly salary Starting	Ending
Business		
All business	$1,183	$1,320
Accounting	1,204	1,364
Banking and finance	1,360	1,440
Secretarial sciences	1,126	1,216
Business, management, agribusiness	1,161	1,320
Data processing	1,204	1,290
Hospitality and hotel and food management	1,226	1,469
Sales, marketing, and merchandising	1,161	1,400
Engineering and related		
All engineering and related	1,275	1,429
Automotive services	1,060	1,188
Civil and construction	1,204	1,420
Drafting and design	1,202	1,256
Electrical and electronic	1,440	1,591
Mechanical and mechanics	1,371	1,548
Other		
Graphics and commercial an	1,161	1,292
Medical, nursing and related	1,393	1,613
Criminal justice and law enforcement	1,591	2,000

[1]The survey included schools in Illinois, Indiana, Iowa, Kentucky, Michigan, Minnesota, Missouri, Ohio, and Wisconsin.

Source: 1993 Cooperative Education Student Employee Salary & Benefits Survey (Midwest Region), Wayne State University.

Both Morgan and McKinney received training from their employers at the start. Morgan learned how the company's products worked. McKinney was taught procedures for making account transfers. Some initial monitoring and coaching from experienced employees helped both students as they began speaking with customers.

The two of them agree that their experience gave them more than skills and knowledge. "I feel like I grew up a lot," says McKinney. "It gave me maturity," echoes Morgan. "In a co-op job, you learn how to be on your own."

Earnings. Going on your own takes money, though. Back when Americans drove Studebakers to work, colleges boasted that co-op earnings could finance an entire education. But that was over 25 years ago. Today, students find that their paychecks cover some college costs, but, usually, the money pays only part of the sticker price on a diploma.

Earnings vary by major. Technical majors, like computer science, command more money than nontechnical ones in liberal arts, social sciences, or humanities. Some jobs pay only a small stipend or nothing at all. These positions are typically in less technical areas, like human services.

In some cases, students do earn enough to pay their own way. Those who attend a community college with low tuition or opt for a very technical major like engineering technology might manage fine. Someone pursuing a bachelor's degree in sociology at a costly liberal arts school, however, might afford to buy little more with co-op earnings than books and a few days worth of tuition. Most students will find themselves someplace in between these two examples.

National data on co-op earnings are not available, but a Wayne State University survey sent to co-op schools in nine Midwestern States offers a useful measure. The accompanying tables show initial and final earnings for co-op employees by major. The survey also shows that 25 percent or more of the employers provided benefits such as medical insurance, retirement credit, and paid holidays, vacation, and sick days.

Reflect, Ask, Seek a Career

Half the fun of any trip happens after returning home, when the travelers fondly recall all the things they saw and did. The value of the co-op experience is like that, too. Half the benefits come to students by thinking purposefully about the work they did. Reflecting on their experience helps students learn more. It also guides them in exploring, altering, and confirming career options and plans.

For nearly 40 years, James Wilson has thought about the way this reflection profits co-op students. A professor of cooperative

> *"In a co-op job, you learn how to be on your own."*
>
> —Mark Morgan

education now retired from Northeastern University, he stresses that good co-op programs find methods of encouraging students to mull things over. He notes that reflecting on experience is not just silent self-study. It often involves social activity, and it actually begins during a term of work.

At Lane Community College in Eugene, Oregon, students do weekly reports during their work experience. Each week, the students describe their on-the-job learning, how it ties in with their classroom studies, and any problems they run into. The coordinators read these reports and make worksite visits two or three times per quarter, according to Bob Way, the director of co-op at Lane. Once in a while, instructors drop by to see students at work, as well.

At some colleges, like Lane and LaGuardia, students attend weekly seminars during their work terms. They chat about how they interact with supervisors or coworkers, adapt to employer expectations, and deal with way, they benefit from each other's experiences. Seminars like these are more common at community colleges, because their students usually work nearby. For the same reason, worksite visits might also occur more often at these schools. Students at all types of colleges may have to write a final report when the job is done.

After the work ends, students return to classes but now attend the lectures and read the books in a brighter light. Experience increases learning by revealing new questions, ideas, and views. Lori Mingus studied computer networking at Lane, and for her co-op job, she helped install a wide area network linking the computers in an entire school district. Instead of alternating terms of work and study, she shuttled between work and class daily. On the job, she thought about what she had learned in class; this helped her ask questions of coworkers and learn more. In the class, she pondered what she had learned at work. Again, this increased her grasp of the subject, proving for her that work and study reinforce each other.

All co-op students may experience what Mingus did in some way. The insight she gained on the job, however, affected her course work more than it does for the average student. "Because of my co-op work experience," she says, "I decided that a couple of the classes required for my degree weren't as appropriate for computer networking as some electronics classes would be." Enlightened with the knowledge only experience can teach, she convinced the college to let her swap classes.

When students come back to campus after a work term, they may talk to their coordinator. Some schools require this. Wilson thinks coordinators—and faculty—should have a strong role helping students reflect on their experience. Talking it over helps students understand what it means, so they can let that experience guide them towards future learning and the right career.

Why do career explorers benefit from the experience? As Way puts it, "You really don't know what you want to do until you've done it." Co-op lets students take a career out for a test drive to see if it suits them.

Tom Davila, a sociology major at Cincinnati State, works with kids at the Emanuel Community Center. Many come from troubled homes. Davila organizes activities for them and acts as a big brother they can talk to. He says this experience confirmed his desire for a career in social work. Similarly, Killoran has decided she will pursue graduate study in clinical psychology, in part because of her co-op assignment in a shelter for battered women.

Chris Allgier had a slightly different experience at Cincinnati State. He majored in chef technology. On his first co-op job, he discovered that he actually wanted to be a dietetic technician. He changed his major and did work relating to dietetics during the rest of his co-op days. Since graduating in the spring of 1996, he has worked happily in the career he chose.

"One of the greatest benefits of co-op," says Guest, "is not the work experience but the fact that the student finally has that feeling, 'This is what I really want to do.'" She thinks the work usually confirms students' career plans, but she does recall a student who made a much sharper turn than Allgier. "He loved his employer," she says, "but he hated accounting, and he didn't realize that until he went to work."

After discussing the matter with Guest, the student decided he liked working with computers much more than keeping books. Soon after, he switched his major to business management information systems. Students like him save a lot of time and money. Less lucky students would finish an entire degree before starting their first job and learning that they hate their field.

More fortunate co-op students let their own carefully considered experiences direct them. When they return to work, the learning process starts over. What they learn in the next work experiences, however, depends partly on who they work for, and each co-op program influences this somewhat. Some programs encourage students to stick with the same employer all through school. Others suggest staying with an employer for at least two terms of work. Yet others invite students to seek a variety of experience.

Graduate and Find the Job

Co-op creates a rich mixture by blending academic degrees with work experiences, but does it really fuel success in the labor market after college? There's some reason to think so. Co-op may help recent graduates obtain their first job because their co-op employers sometimes offer them permanent positions after college. If this does not happen, the grads still have solid work experience on their resumes, something all employers look for. Furthermore, some research supports claims about the economic benefits of co-op.

Like many of the approximately 50,000 participating U.S. employers, Weston & Sampson Engineers relies on co-op as part of its recruiting strategy. That's how Lee landed her job there after graduating from Northeastern. Having spent a year and a half as a co-op employee, Lee had plenty of chances to prove her abilities on the job. Some employers actually think of a student's work term as a paid job interview which lasts a few months. It enables employers to make more informed hiring decisions. As Peters says of Lee, "Her evaluations were exceptionally good, so there wasn't much doubt in our minds as to whether we were going to hire her."

All types of employers use co-op to recruit. In the private sector, 85 of the Fortune 100 companies (the top companies in the better known Fortune 500) employ co-op students, according to a survey recently done for the *Directory of College Cooperative Education Programs.* Many do so partly as a way of meeting long-term personnel needs, though sometimes companies just want temporary help.

In some cases, smaller companies depend on co-op for recruiting more than the corporate giants. Peters describes Weston & Sampson as a medium-sized firm, with 150 permanent employees and 3 or 4 co-op employees. He notes that larger firms can afford to do more training of new recruits. "The importance of co-op," he adds, "may be a little greater to a smaller firm. If it can get a co-op student who has some experience, it doesn't have to do as much training or teaching."

In the Federal Government, agencies employing co-op students can hire them upon graduation without the competition usually required for civil service. In the past, this made co-op a popular recruiting source, but Government downsizing and a rule change by the Office of Management and Budget have sharply curtailed co-op employment in recent years. According to the Office of Personnel Management (OPM), the Federal Government still employed 14,826 co-op students as of September 1994. After that, OPM merged cooperative education with other student work programs, so no more recent statistics are obtainable. For those who find co-op jobs in Federal agencies, it's still an inroad to permanent Federal employment.

Table 2

Median Monthly Salaries of Co-op Employees at the Bachelor's Degree Level in the Midwest by Major, 1993[1]

Major	Median monthly salary Starting	Ending
Business		
All business	$1,337	$1,621
Accounting	1,360	1,640
Banking and finance	1,380	1,562
Management	1,238	1,548
Management information systems	1,396	1,793
Marketing	1,290	1,548
Humanities and social sciences		
All humanities and social sciences	1,069	1,443
Humanities	1,079	1,548
Social sciences	1,061	1,364
Sciences		
All sciences	1,321	1,633
Agriculture	1,336	1,290
Biological	1,413	1,800
Computer science	1,406	1,832
Chemistry	1,462	2,040
Mathematics	1,400	1,829
Physics	1,400	1,850
Engineering		
All engineering	1,562	1,988
Chemical	1,664	2,193
Civil	1,400	1,672
Electrical, electronic, and computer	1,624	2,064
Industrial	1,575	2,000
Mechanical	1,585	2,039
Engineering technology (all types)	1,396	1,735
Other		
Architecture	1,119	1,473
Economics	1,400	1,470
Nursing and allied health	1,400	1,708
Criminal justice	1,400	1,500

[1]The survey included schools in Illinois, Indiana, Iowa, Kentucky, Michigan, Minnesota, Missouri, Ohio, and Wisconsin.

Source: 1993 Cooperative Education Student Employee Salary & Benefits Survey (Midwest Region), Wayne State University.

The percent of graduating students not receiving job offers from former co-op employers varies among schools. Luckily, the many grads not snapped up by their co-op employers still benefit. Mingus did, and she knows why. "Not only did I have a 2-year degree to go look for work with," she says, "I had a year's worth of work experience in the field." That experience fortified her resume and gave her professional references. It also gave her confidence at job interviews. "Having proof about what you can do puts you at ease," she explains. Mingus easily found a job doing technical support for a small software maker.

Morgan did not receive an offer from his former co-op employer, either. IBM didn't turn him down, however. He declined to interview. Even though Morgan had a very positive co-op experience with the company, he decided to pursue programming work in a client-server environment instead of the technical support work he had done at IBM. By the time he earned his bachelor's degree in business management information systems, he had interviewed with

10 companies, received 2 firm job offers, and cultivated additional prospects as well.

All the co-op graduates portrayed here have tested co-op through their own personal experience. They're just a few people, but researchers have also put co-op to the test, studying outcomes for thousands of co-op graduates. The results are mixed. Some studies find that co-op grads have shorter job search times, receive slightly higher starting salaries, and advance more quickly compared to their nonco-op counterparts. Other studies fail to confirm such findings. On balance, though, the research lends modest support for these economic benefits.

Wilson views these findings in a broad context. Once a researcher and now the editor of *The Journal of Cooperative Education,* he speaks often of the less tangible benefits of co-op. He sees it as much more than a method of jacking up starting salary or finding a job a few weeks sooner than the average graduate. It's an avenue wide open for learning, and it fosters independence, maturity, and the ability to adapt. Co-op graduates don't always finish first in the workplace, but they've learned how to drive, they know where they're going, and they know how to get there.

Transfers and Career Changers

Cooperative education serves as a bridge between college and

> *"Having proof about what you can do put you at ease [at a job interview]."*
>
> –Lori Mingus

the workplace for the typical co-op student. But it can also serve as a bridge for people in other situations.

Some students, like Alam and Davila, use it as a link from an associate's to a bachelor's degree. Others, like Mingus, use it to cross to a new career.

Alam emigrated from Bangladesh to the United States at age 20. He wanted a bachelor's degree but knew that a degree did not guarantee a good job. Some of his friends had bachelor's or even master's degrees but no work experience, and they had trouble finding work. As a result, Alam decided to try co-op at LaGuardia in 1985.

He studied computer science in class during the day and worked for IBM as a computer operator on the evening shift. He also did a 3-month tour with Chemical Bank, where he did COBOL programming. After that, he returned to IBM, which offered him a permanent job after he graduated. He took it.

While working at IBM, he attended evening classes at Teikyo Post University in Waterbury, Connecticut. He finished his bachelor's degree in management information systems in 1993. Now a systems analyst, Alam concludes that his 2 years in a co-op program gave him the best start toward a bachelor's he could have had. For him, the co-op experience led to a job that enabled him to earn enough to finish his journey.

It's not just engineers or computer pros like Alam who find co-op a bridge to further education. Davila is counting on that. He wants a master's in social work but knows he can't do it all at once, so he adopted a plan similar to the one Alam used. The community center

Davila worked for as a co-op student hired him as a permanent employee before graduation. After completing his Associate of Arts program, he expects the job to carry him toward the next degree down the road.

Cooperative education suits some career changers because their previous employment experience inclines them toward hands-on learning. Maintaining an income while crossing from one career to another is also vital for many students, such as unemployed workers with families. Co-op bridges offer options for career changers, even those in unusual or extreme situations. Lane, for example, offers individualized co-op for injured workers to prepare them for something new.

Mingus suffered no physical injury, but when her husband abandoned her and their four children, she felt the sting of change. At first, she went on welfare and worked as a bartender to support the children. After graduating from high school in 1975, she had performed many jobs. She had assembled and packaged products, operated machines, sold jewelry, and even run a small business, among other things. Now, she needed a new career that could pay the bills-and fast.

"I decided I needed a degree to prove my abilities," she says. "I was talented and skilled, but nobody believed me." She concluded that a degree from a co-op program might do the convincing. It would at least let her continue earning money while she was earning her degree. At the beginning of 1996, Mingus finished her associate's in computer networking after 2-1/2 years of co-op work and study. Shortly after obtaining her current job, she helped install a new local area network for her firm. Her employer made her network administrator after seeing what co-op had taught her.

An Executive's Summary

Besides being chairman of the board of directors at The Segal Company, Krinsky also chairs the board of trustees at Antioch University. As someone who has scanned through the resumes of graduates and made hiring decisions, Krinsky stresses the need for students to gain some experience at work. "Cooperative education isn't the only way of getting this kind of experience," he says, "but it's sort of an automatic way. If you go to a college that doesn't have cooperative education, you probably have to work harder at finding those experiences, but if you do, that's also good."

Onward to Information

If traveling the workways of cooperative education appeals to you, find out more from the nearest career counselor. The organizations listed next also provide information.

Cooperative Education Division
　(American Society for Engineering Education)
　c/o Ms. Mary Jo Fairbanks
Director of Cooperative Education
Syracuse University, 367 Link Hall
Syracuse, NY 13244-1240
(315) 443-4345; fax (315) 443-4655
E-mail: encscoop@summon.syr.edu

Cooperative Education Association (CEA)
8640 Guilford Rd., Suite 215
Columbia, MD 21046
Phone (410) 290-3666
Fax (410) 290-7084

CEA offers the following services:
- Database searches to identify co-op schools meeting the criteria specified by an individual student at no charge.
- Fax-on-demand service: Receive by fax a 2-page article entitled, "Secure Your Place Through Cooperative Education." Call (503) 402-1307 from a touchtone phone and select item 300. Have your fax number handy when you call.
- *Community College Resource Guide.* Brief descriptions of 65 co-op programs at 2-year and community colleges. 53 pp.

National Commission for Cooperative Education (NCCE)
360 Huntington Ave., 384CP
Boston, MA 02115-5096
Phone: (617) 373-3770
Fax: (617) 373-3463
E-mail: ncce@iynx.neu.edu
Web page: http://www.co-op.edu/

NCCE offers these publications:
- *Student/Patient Guide to Cooperative Education.* Booklet describing the benefits and operation of cooperative education which includes a roster of more than 300 colleges offering co-op. Free, 21 pp.
- Free brochures describing the advantages of co-op.
- *Directory of College Cooperative Education Programs.* Profiles 461 co-op colleges listed by State and indexed by institution name and degree programs offering co-op. May be available in libraries or high school guidance offices. Cost is $49.95. To order, call Oryx Press at 1 (800) 279-6799.

Appendix B

DETAILS ON THE TOP 500 JOBS

EARNINGS, PROJECTED GROWTH, EDUCATION REQUIRED, UNEMPLOYMENT RATES, AND OTHER DETAILS

Selected Occupational Data, 1996 and Projected 2006

This appendix presents data on current and projected employment, employment change, self-employment, and annual average job openings for all national industry-occupation matrix occupations. For most of the preceding, and some additional, categories of occupational information, rankings are presented designating the relative magnitude of data for each detailed occupation. In addition, Table 1 identifies the category of education and training most workers took to become proficient in each detailed occupation.

Data Sources

Table 1 presents information from three sources: 1) the national industry-occupation matrix, 2) the Occupational Employment Statistics (OES) survey, and 3) the Current Population Survey (CPS). The industry-occupation matrix is predominantly based on wage and salary occupational employment data collected from establishments as part of the OES survey. This survey counts jobs. Individuals who hold more than one job are counted at each place they work. The CPS is a monthly survey of about 50,000 households that obtains demographic and labor force information about individuals. Employment information from the CPS counts individuals, not jobs. Data on self-employed and unpaid family workers are derived from the CPS and combined with OES data on wage and salary employment in order to develop total employment estimates.

Occupational data in the industry-occupation matrix are not entirely comparable with those in the CPS because of differences in occupational classification systems, and differences in concepts and methods used in the surveys. Information about worker characteristics that is based on CPS data is applied to industry-occupation matrix occupations based on judgments identifying the most comparable CPS occupations. Comparisons based on CPS occupations with fewer than 50,000 workers in 1996 and some other occupations for which the data appeared unreliable were excluded; data for CPS proxy occupations were substituted. Where possible, larger, closely related CPS occupations were chosen as proxies. For example, data for purchasing agents and buyers, n.e.c., were used to represent purchasing agents and buyers, farm products. When no detailed occupation could be identified, a summary occupation group was used. For example, data about all therapists were substituted for that of inhalation therapists.

Data Presented

The source of the data for each variable and a brief discussion of its potential use are presented below. Rankings for most data categories identify the relative magnitude of variables in terms of the distribution of employment. For example, 1996 employment and projected 1996-2006 percent change in employment data were assembled for each occupation. Each occupation's employment as a percent of 1996 total employment was calculated. The occupations were sorted by employment change in descending order, and the cumulative percent of 1996 employment for each was determined. Occupations within the group comprising less than 25 percent of total employment are designated VH for a Very High growth rate. Similarly, occupations sorted by descending order of employment change comprising 25-50 percent of employment receive H for High; 50-75 percent, L for Low; and 75-100 percent, VL for Very Low. Occupations were sorted by other data elements and rankings were determined in the same manner.

Employment, 1996 and 2006

(Source: Bureau of Labor Statistics, national industry-occupation matrices for 1996 and 2006.) Employment information is a useful starting point for assessing opportunities because large occupations usually have more openings than small ones regardless of growth or replacement rates.

Employment Change, 1996-2006, Numeric

(Source: Bureau of Labor Statistics, national industry-occupation matrices for 1996 and 2006.) Information on numerical change provides an absolute measure of projected job gains or losses.

Employment Change, 1996-2006, Percent

(Source: Bureau of Labor Statistics, national industry-occupation matrices for 1996 and 2006.) The percent change

in employment measures the rate of change. When an occupation grows rapidly, this usually indicates favorable prospects for employment. Moreover, the high demand for workers in a rapidly growing occupation improves chances for advancement and mobility. A modest percentage increase in employment growth can result in many more job openings in a large occupation than in a small occupation that is growing rapidly.

Percent Self-employed, 1996

(Source: Bureau of Labor Statistics, national industry-occupation matrices for 1996 and 2006.) Individuals who are interested in creating and managing their own business may find it important to know the percentage of self-employed workers. This percentage is calculated from CPS data about unincorporated self-employed persons included in industry-occupation matrix employment data. Unincorporated self-employed persons work for earnings or fees in their own business and, unlike self-employed persons in businesses that are incorporated, do not receive a wage or salary.

Job Openings Due to Growth Plus Total Replacement Needs, 1996-2006

(Source: Bureau of Labor Statistics, this publication.) These data provide the broadest measure of opportunities and identify the total number of employees needed annually to enter an occupation. Growth is calculated using data on increases in occupational employment from national industry-occupation matrices for 1996-2006. If employment declines, job openings due growth are zero. Total replacement needs are calculated from 1995-96 CPS data. Data from CPS proxy occupations are used to estimate replacement needs for some matrix occupations. (See Table 2.)

Job Openings Due to Growth Plus Net Replacement Needs, 1996-2006

(Source: Bureau of Labor Statistics, this publication.) These data estimate the number of new workers needed annually for an occupation and, if training is required, measure minimum training needs. Growth is calculated using data on increases in occupational employment from national industry-occupation matrices for 1996-2006. If employment declines, job openings due growth are zero. Net replacement needs are calculated from CPS data. Data from CPS proxy occupations estimate replacement needs for some matrix occupations (see Table 2).

Median Hourly Earnings

(Source: 1996 Occupational Employment Statistics survey with some exceptions. These exceptions are that OES data are not available for Government chief executives and legislators, and Producers, directors, actors, and entertainers. OES data also arc not available for Private household workers; Farm operators and managers; Captains and other officers, fishing vessels; and Fishers, hunters, and trappers. Hourly 1996 Current Population Survey annual average data for wage and salary employees provide information for the latter group.) Table 1 uses median hourly earnings of workers to compare earnings among different occupations.

Unemployment Rate

(Source: Average of 1994-96 Current Population Survey annual average data.) Some occupations are more susceptible to factors that result in unemployment: Seasonality, fluctuations in economic conditions, and individual business failures. A high unemployment rate indicates that individuals in that occupation are more likely to become unemployed than those in one with a low rate. Data from CPS proxy occupations are used to estimate unemployment rates for some matrix occupations. (See Table 2.)

Percent Part-Time

(Source: Average of 1994-96 Current Population Survey annual average data.) It may be important to those persons who prefer part-time work to know the proportion of employees who work fewer than 35 hours per week. Data from CPS proxy occupations are used to estimate the proportion of part-time workers for some matrix occupations. (See Table 2.)

Most Significant Source of Training

(Source: Bureau of Labor Statistics.) Occupations are classified into 1 of 11 categories that describe the education and training needed by most workers to become fully qualified. The categories are first professional degree; doctoral degree; master's degree; work experience in an occupation requiring a bachelor's or higher degree; bachelor's degree; associate degree; postsecondary vocational training; work experience in a related occupation; long-term, on-the-job training; moderate-term, on-the-job training; and short-term, on-the-job training. The following are definitions of these categories.

Occupations that require a first professional degree. The first professional degree is the minimum preparation required for entry into several professions, including law, medicine, dentistry, and the clergy. Completion of this academic program usually requires at least 2 years of full-time academic study beyond a bachelor's degree.

Occupations that generally require a doctoral degree. The doctoral degree can also be easily related to specific occupations. It normally requires at least 3 years of full-time academic work beyond the bachelor's degree.

Occupations that generally require a master's degree. Completion of a master's degree program mostly requires 1 or 2 years of full-time study beyond the bachelor's degree.

Occupations that generally require work experience in an occupation requiring a bachelor's or higher degree. Most occupations in this category are managerial occupations that require experience in a related nonmanagerial occupation. Jobs in these occupations usually are filled with experienced staff who are promoted into a managerial position, such as engineers who advance to engineering manager. It is very difficult to become a judge without first working as a lawyer, or to become a personnel, training, or labor relations manager without first gaining experience as a specialist in one of these fields.

Occupations that generally require a bachelor's degree. This is a degree program requiring at least 4 but not more than 5 years of full-time academic work after high school. The bachelor's degree is considered the minimum training requirement for most professional occupations, such as mechanical engineer, pharmacist, recreational therapist, and landscape architect.

Occupations that generally require an associate degree. Completion of this degree program usually requires at least 2 years of full-time academic work after high school. Most occupations in this training category are health related, such as registered nurse, respiratory therapist, and radiologic technologist. Also included are science and mathematics technicians and paralegals.

Occupations that generally require completion of vocational training provided in postsecondary vocational schools. Workers normally qualify for jobs by completing vocational training programs or by taking job-related college courses that do not result in a degree. Some programs take less than a year to complete and lead to a certificate or diploma. Others last longer than a year but less than 4 years. Occupations in this category include some that require only completion of a training program, such as a travel agent, and those that require passing a licensing exam after completion of the program, such as a barber and cosmetologist.

Occupations that generally require skills developed through work experience in a related occupation. Jobs in this category require skills and experience gained in another occupation; this category also includes occupations in which skills may be developed from hobbies or other activities besides current or past employment or from service in the Armed Forces. Among the occupations are cost estimators, who generally need prior work experience in one of the construction trades; police detectives, who are selected based on their experience as police patrol officers; and lawn service managers, who may be hired based on their experience as groundskeepers.

Long-term, on-the-job training. This category includes occupations that usually require more than 12 months of on-the-job training or combined work experience and formal classroom instruction before workers develop the skills needed for average job performance. This category includes occupations such as electrician, bricklayer, and machinist that normally require formal or informal apprenticeships lasting up to 4 years. Also included in this type of training are intensive occupation-specific, employer-sponsored programs that workers must successfully complete before they can begin work. These include fire and police academies and schools for air traffic controllers and flight attendants. In other occupations—insurance sales and securities sales, for example—trainees take formal courses, often provided at the job site, to prepare for the required licensing exams. Individuals undergoing training are usually considered employed in the occupation. This group of occupations also includes musicians, athletes, actors, and other entertainers, occupations that require natural ability that must be developed over several years.

Moderate-term, on-the-job training. Workers can achieve average job performance after 1 to 12 months of combined job experience and informal training, which can include observing experienced workers. Individuals undergoing training are normally considered employed in the occupation. This type of training is found among occupations such as dental assistants, drywall installers and finishers, operating engineers, and machine operators. This training relies on trainees watching experienced workers and asking questions. Trainees are given progressively more difficult assignments as they demonstrate their mastery of lower level skills.

Short-term, on-the-job training. Included are occupations like cashier, bank teller, messenger, highway maintenance worker, and veterinary assistant. In these occupations, workers usually can achieve average job performance in just a few days or weeks by working with and observing experienced employees and by asking questions.

Using Ranked Information

Table 1 consolidates 1996 and 2006 projected employment data. Table 1 also provides comparisons of occupational data. It contains rankings of information about current and projected employment, projected job openings, earnings, unemployment rates, and the proportion of part-time workers. Except for the unemployment and part-time categories, a high rating indicates a favorable assessment. A high rating for the unemployment rate is considered undesirable. Unemployment rates in construction occupations, however, are inflated by the nature of the industry and distort comparisons. Workers in these occupations typically incur periods of unemployment after completing a project and before starting work at a new job site.

The rating for the part-time category also should not be used routinely in assessing the desirability of employment because the assessment depends on the perspective of the user. For example, high school students may consider a large proportion of part-time workers desirable because they normally prefer not to work full time. A recent college graduate or anyone seeking full-time employment may reach the opposite conclusion.

The data in Table 1 has many potential uses. At times, users may want to know how a particular occupation, cashiers, for example, compares with others. The "VH" (Very High) rankings in Table 1 for the increase in the number of jobs and for both categories of job openings, point out that many jobs are available, certainly a favorable rating. The "VL" (Very Low) ranking for earnings and "VH" (Very High) for unemployment, however, are unfavorable in comparison with other occupations, and these characteristics detract from the desirability of employment in the occupation. Table 1 also shows that cashiers require only short-term, on-the-job training.

Readers may wish to identify occupations with favorable characteristics that job seekers can pursue through a specific type of training. For example, a student may be interested in a scientific or engineering occupation but not care to obtain a 4-year college degree. In another instance a planner may wish to ensure that training programs provided by junior colleges in the area are consistent with the needs of the national labor market. For example, the planner could examine information for occupations placed in the associate degree educational and training category.

Although Table 1 contains a great deal of information useful for career guidance, information about occupational comparisons should be used as an aid, not a sole source. After using the table to identify occupations with favorable prospects, additional information should be obtained from other sources such as the *Occupational Outlook Handbook* and local sources, if available. Consideration should be given to individual aptitudes and preferences, and alternative sources of training available in the local area should be investigated.

The appendix identifies sources of state and local area information.

An electronic version of Table 1 is available on request–call the Chief, Division of Occupational Outlook at (202) 606-5703. The data in Table 1 also are available from the Internet. For access, select the "Employment, Training, & Earnings" button of the "Employment Projections Home Page" (http://stats.bls.gov/emphome.htm) at the BLS site.

Table 1. Occupational employment and job openings data, 1996-2006, and worker characteristics, 1996
(Numbers in thousands)

1996 Matrix Occupation	Employment 1996	Employment 2006	Employment change, 1996-2006 Numeric Number	Rank	Percent Number	Rank	Percent self-employed, 1996	Annual average job openings due to growth and total replacement needs, 1996-2006 Number	Rank
Total, all occupations	132,353	150,927	18,574	–	14.0	–	7.9	26,666	–
Executive, administrative, and managerial occupations	13,542	15,866	2,324	–	17.2	–	13.2	1,960	–
Managerial and administrative occupations	9,539	11,262	1,723	–	18.1	–	15.4	1,344	–
Administrative services managers	291	324	33	L	11.3	L	0.0	34	VL
Communication, transportation, and utilities operations managers	156	179	23	L	14.5	H	0.0	19	VL
Construction managers	249	294	45	L	18.0	H	16.1	32	VL
Education administrators	386	430	45	L	11.6	L	7.7	51	L
Engineering, science, and computer systems managers	343	498	155	H	45.2	VH	0.0	58	L
Financial managers	800	946	146	H	18.3	H	1.2	95	L
Food service and lodging managers[1]	589	757	168	H	28.5	VH	35.0	152	L
Funeral directors and morticians[1]	33	33	1	VL	2.0	VL	24.8	4	VL
General managers and top executives	3,210	3,677	467	VH	14.6	H	0.0	393	VH
Government chief executives and legislators[1]	93	95	2	VL	2.2	VL	0.0	7	VL
Industrial production managers	207	202	−5	VL	-2.5	VL	0.0	21	VL
Marketing, advertising, and public relations managers	482	620	138	H	28.5	VH	2.5	93	L
Personnel, training, and labor relations managers	216	254	38	L	17.8	H	0.0	30	VL
Property and real estate managers[1]	271	315	44	L	16.4	H	41.7	42	VL
Purchasing managers	232	251	18	VL	7.8	L	0.0	33	VL
All other managers and administrators[1]	1,981	2,387	406	VH	20.5	H	52.8	281	H
Management support occupations	4,003	4,604	601	–	15.0	–	7.9	615	–
Accountants and auditors	1,002	1,127	125	H	12.4		10.8	122	L
Budget analysts	66	73	8	VL	11.7	L	0.0	10	VL
Claims examiners, property and casualty insurance	57	69	13	VL	22.2	VH	0.0	5	VL
Construction and building inspectors	66	76	10	VL	14.5	H	1.9	3	VL
Cost estimators	188	217	29	L	15.5	H	0.0	35	VL
Credit analysts	40	46	6	VL	15.8	H	0.0	7	VL
Employment interviewers, private or public employment service	87	101	14	VL	16.3	H	0.0	19	VL
Inspectors and compliance officers, except construction	163	172	8	VL	5.2	VL	2.3	17	VL
Loan officers and counselors	209	268	59	L	28.1	VH	0.0	39	VL
Management analysts[1]	244	296	52	L	21.2	VH	45.5	15	VL
Personnel, training, and labor relations specialists	328	387	59	L	17.9	H	4.6	74	L
Purchasing agents, except wholesale, retail, and farm products ..	224	238	14	VL	6.4	L	1.4	41	VL
Tax examiners, collectors, and revenue agents	64	66	1	VL	2.3	VL	0.0	5	VL
Underwriters	95	100	6	VL	6.1	L	0.0	4	VL
Wholesale and retail buyers, except farm products	183	183	0	VL	-0.1	VL	6.4	48	L
All other management support workers[1]	988	1,185	198	H	20.0	H	6.4	171	H
Professional specialty occupations	18,173	22,998	4,826	–	26.6	–	8.3	2,539	–
Engineers	1,382	1,632	250	–	18.1	–	3.3	119	–
Aeronautical and astronautical engineers	53	57	4	VL	7.8	L	0.0	2	VL
Chemical engineers[1]	49	57	7	VL	15.0	H	2.2	4	VL
Civil engineers, including traffic engineers	196	231	35	L	17.9	H	6.6	20	VL
Electrical and electronics engineers	367	472	105	H	28.5	VH	3.6	32	VL
Industrial engineers, except safety engineers	115	131	16	VL	13.6	L	3.3	12	VL
Mechanical engineers	228	264	36	L	15.8	H	1.8	10	VL
Metallurgists and metallurgical, ceramic, and materials engineers[1]	18	20	1	VL	6.8	L	0.0	1	VL
Mining engineers, including mine safety engineers[1]	3	3	0	VL	−12.6	VL	0.0	0	VL
Nuclear engineers[1]	14	14	1	VL	5.2	VL	0.0	1	VL
Petroleum engineers[1]	13	11	−2	VL	−14.3	VL	5.4	1	VL
All other engineers[1]	326	373	47	L	14.4	H	3.1	36	VL
Architects and surveyors	212	232	20	–	9.7	–	18.5	27	–
Architects, except landscape and marine	94	113	18	VL	19.6	H	28.1	7	VL
Landscape architects	17	20	3	VL	20.7	H	30.7	1	VL
Surveyors[1]	101	99	−1	VL	-1.4	VL	7.5	18	VL
Life scientists	180	221	41	–	22.6	–	4.6	18	–

[1] One or more Current Population Survey (CPS) based occupations may be used to estimate CPS based data. See Table 2.
NOTE: Rankings are based on employment in all detailed occupations in the National Industry-Occupation Matrix. For details, see "Data presented" section of text. Codes for describing the ranked variables are: VH = Very high, H = High, L = Low, VL = Very low, n. a. = Data not available. A dash indicates data are not applicable.

Table 1. Occupational employment and job openings data, 1996-2006, and worker characterisitcs, 1996
(Numbers in thousands)

Number	Rank	Median hourly earnings	Unemployment rate	Percent part-time	Most significant source of training	1996 Matrix Occupation
5,056	–	–	–	–	–	**Total, all occupations**
517	–	–	–	–	–	**Executive, administrative, and managerial occupations**
374	–	–	–	–	–	Managerial and administrative occupations
9	VL	VH	VL	VL	Work experience plus degree	Administrative services managers
6	VL	VH	VL	VL	Work experience plus degree	Communication, transportation, and utilities operations managers
10	VL	VH	VL	VL	Bachelor's degree	Construction managers
15	L	VH	VL	L	Work experience plus degree	Education administrators
23	L	VH	VL	VL	Work experience plus degree	Engineering, science, and computer systems managers
30	L	VH	VL	VL	Work experience plus degree	Financial managers
29	L	H	L	L	Work experience in a related occupation	Food service and lodging managers[1]
1	VL	VH	VL	L	Long-term on-the-job-training	Funeral directors and morticians
115	VH	VH	VL	VL	Work experience plus degree	General managers and top executives
2	VL	n. a.	VL	VL	Work experience plus degree	Government chief executives and legislators[1]
4	VL	VH	VL	VL	Bachelor's degree	Industrial production managers
23	L	VH	L	VL	Work experience plus degree	Marketing, advertising, and public relations managers
10	VL	VH	L	VL	Work experience plus degree	Personnel, training, and labor relations managers
9	VL	H	L	H	Bachelor's degree	Property and real estate managers[1]
7	VL	VH	VL	VL	Work experience plus degree	Purchasing managers
83	VH	VH	VL	L	Work experience plus degree	All other managers and administrators[1]
143	–	–	–	–	–	Management support occupations
33	H	VH	VL	VL	Bachelor's degree	Accountants and auditors
2	VL	VH	VL	VL	Bachelor's degree	Budget analysts
2	VL	VH	VL	VL	Bachelor's degree	Claims examiners, property and casualty insurance
3	VL	VH	L	VL	Work experience in a related occupation	Construction and building inspectors
5	VL	VH	L	VL	Bachelor's degree	Cost estimators
1	VL	VH	VL	VL	Bachelor's degree	Credit analysts
4	VL	H	L	VL	Bachelor's degree	Employment interviewers, private or public employment service
4	VL	VH	L	VL	Work experience in a related occupation	Inspectors and compliance officers, except construction
10	VL	VH	VL	VL	Bachelor's degree	Loan officers and counselors
8	VL	VH	L	H	Work experience plus degree	Management analysts[1]
15	L	VH	L	VL	Bachelor's degree	Personnel, training, and labor relations specialists
8	VL	VH	L	VL	Bachelor's degree	Purchasing agents, except wholesale, retail, and farm products
1	VL	VH	VL	VL	Bachelor's degree	Tax examiners, collectors, and revenue agents
3	VL	VH	L	VL	Bachelor's degree	Underwriters
5	VL	H	L	H	Bachelor's degree	Wholesale and retail buyers, except farm products
40	H	VH	VL	VL	Bachelor's degree	All other management support workers[1]
829	–	–	–	–	–	**Professional specialty occupations**
58	–	–	–	–	–	Engineers
1	VL	VH	L	VL	Bachelor's degree	Aeronautical and astronautical engineers
2	VL	VH	VL	VL	Bachelor's degree	Chemical engineers[1]
8	VL	VH	VL	VL	Bachelor's degree	Civil engineers, including traffic engineers
20	L	VH	L	VL	Bachelors degree	Electrical and electronics engineers
4	VL	VH	VL	VL	Bachelor's degree	Industrial engineers, except safety engineers
8	VL	VH	VL	VL	Bachelor's degree	Mechanical engineers
1	VL	VH	VL	VL	Bachelor's degree	Metallurgists and metallurgical, ceramic, and materials engineers[1]
0	VL	VH	VL	VL	Bachelor's degree	Mining engineers, including mine safety engineers[1]
0	VL	VH	VL	VL	Bachelor's degree	Nuclear engineers[1]
0	VL	VH	VL	VL	Bachelor's degree	Petroleum engineers[1]
13	L	VH	L	VL	Bachelor's degree	All other engineers[1]
7	–	–	–	–	–	Architects and surveyors
4	VL	VH	L	L	Bachelor's degree	Architects, except landscape and marine
1	VL	VH	L	L	Bachelor's degree	Landscape architects
2	VL	H	L	VL	Postsecondary vocational training	Surveyors[1]
6	–	–	–	–	–	Life scientists

[1]One or more Current Population Survey (CPS) based occupations may be used to estimate CPS based data. See Table 2.
NOTE: Rankings are based on employment in all detailed occupations In the National Industry-Occupation Matrix. For details, see "Data presented" section of text. Codes for describing the ranked variables are: VH = Very high, H = High, L = Low, VL = Very low, n. a. = Data not available. A dash indicates data are not applicable.

Table 1. Occupational employment and job openings data, 1996-2006, and worker characteristics, 1996—Continued
(Numbers in thousands)

1996 Matrix Occupation	Employment		Employment change, 1996-2006				Percent self-employed, 1996	Annual average job openings due to growth and total replacement needs, 1996-2006	
			Numeric		Percent				
	1996	2006	Number	Rank	Number	Rank		Number	Rank
Agricultural and food scientists[1]	24	29	5	VL	19.6	H	8.2	2	VL
Biological scientists	83	103	21	L	25.1	VH	4.7	9	VL
Foresters and conservation scientists[1]	37	43	6	VL	17.4	H	4.9	3	VL
Medical scientists	35	44	9	VL	25.1	VH	1.8	4	VL
All other life scientists	1	1	0	VL	–3.0	VL	0.0	0	VL
Computer, mathematical, and operations research occupations	1,028	2,038	1,010	–	98.2	–	6.0	261	–
Actuaries[1]	16	16	0	VL	1.9	VL	0.0	2	VL
Computer systems analysts, engineers, and scientists	933	1,937	1,004	–	107.6	–	6.3	253	–
Computer engineers and scientists	427	912	485	–	113.4	–	4.8	119	–
Computer engineers	216	451	235	H	109.1	VH	7.0	59	L
Database administrators, computer support specialists, and all other computer scientists	212	461	249	VH	117.8	VH	2.5	60	L
Systems analysts	506	1,025	520	VH	102.8	VH	7.5	133	L
Statisticians[1]	14	14	0	VL	0.7	VL	0.0	1	VL
Mathematicians and all other mathematical scientists[1]	16	17	1	VL	9.1	L	8.1	2	VL
Operations research analysts	50	54	4	VL	7.8	L	3.3	3	VL
Physical scientists	207	242	36	–	17.3	–	5.0	18	–
Chemists	91	108	17	VL	18.3	H	0.0	8	VL
Geologists, geophysicists, and oceanographers[1]	47	54	7	VL	14.6	H	15.0	4	VL
Meteorologists[1]	7	8	1	VL	8.2	L	0.0	1	VL
Physicists and astronomers[1]	18	17	0	VL	–1.6	VL	0.0	1	VL
All other physical scientists[1]	43	55	12	VL	27.5	VH	7.2	4	VL
Social scientists	263	288	24	–	9.2	–	27.6	35	–
Economists	51	60	9	VL	18.6	H	21.7	8	VL
Psychologists	143	154	11	VL	8.0	L	41.0	18	VL
Urban and regional planners[1]	29	31	1	VL	4.7	VL	3.2	4	VL
All other social scientists[1]	41	43	2	VL	5.1	VL	5.5	5	VL
Social, recreational, and religious workers	1,469	1,939	470	–	32.0	–	1.1	257	–
Clergy	208	236	28	L	13.2	L	0.0	20	VL
Directors, religious activities and education[1]	85	115	30	L	35.5	VH	0.0	11	VL
Human services workers[1]	178	276	98	L	55.4	VH	0.0	62	L
Recreation workers	233	285	52	L	22.3	VH	0.0	44	–
Residential counselors	180	254	74	L	41.2	VH	0.0	25	VL
Social workers	585	772	188	H	32.1	VH	2.8	96	L
Lawyers and judicial workers	699	820	120	–	17.2	–	28.0	39	–
Judges, magistrates, and other judicial workers[1]	78	79	2	VL	2.2	VL	0.0	3	VL
Lawyers	622	740	118	H	19.0	H	31.5	36	VL
Teachers, librarians, and counselors	6,565	7,914	1,349	–	20.6	–	2.6	1,000	–
Teachers, preschool and kindergarten	499	596	98	L	19.6	H	1.1	56	L
Teachers, elementary	1,491	1,644	153	H	10.3	L	0.0	170	H
Teachers, secondary school	1,406	1,718	312	VH	22.2	VH	0.0	131	L
Teachers, special education	407	648	241	H	59.1	VH	0.0	49	L
College and university faculty[1]	864	1,026	162	H	18.8	H	0.0	134	L
Other teachers and instructors	878	1,118	240	–	27.3	–	10.6	254	–
Farm and home management advisors	16	10	–6	VL	–38.3	VL	10.0	3	VL
Instructors and coaches, sports and physical training	303	427	123	H	40.7	VH	0.0	96	L
Adult and vocational education teachers	559	682	123	–	21.9	–	16.3	155	–
Instructors, adult (nonvocational) education	248	299	51	L	20.6	H	36.8	68	L
Teachers and instructors, vocational education and training	311	383	72	L	23.0	VH	0.0	87	L
All other teachers and instructors[1]	671	770	99	H	14.8	H	10.0	158	L
Librarians, archivists, curators, and related workers	174	185	10	–	5.9	–	0.0	29	–
Curators, archivists, museum technicians, and restorers[1]	20	23	3	VL	14.7	H	0.0	4	VL
Librarians, professional	154	162	7	VL	4.8	VL	0.0	25	VL
Counselors	175	209	33	L	19.1	H	2.5	19	VL
Health diagnosing occupations	877	1,039	162	–	18.4	–	26.0	43	–
Chiropractors[1]	44	55	12	VL	27.1	VH	56.1	3	VL
Dentists	162	175	13	VL	8.1	L	44.8	3	VL
Optometrists[1]	41	46	5	VL	11.7	L	38.2	2	VL
Physicians	560	678	118	H	21.0	VH	16.2	321	VL

[1]One or more Current Population Survey (CPS) based occupations may be used to estimate CPS based data. See Table 2.
NOTE: Rankings are based on employment in all detailed occupations in the National Industry-Occupation Matrix. For details, see "Data presented" section of text. Codes for describing the ranked variables are: VH = Very high, H = High, L = Low, VL = Very low. n. a. = Data not available. A dash indicates data are not applicable.

Table 1. Occupational employment and job openings data, 1996-2006, and worker characteristics, 1996—Continued
(Numbers in thousands)

Annual average job openings due to growth and total replacement needs, 1996-2006		Median hourly earnings	Unemployment rate	Percent part-time	Most significant source of training	1996 Matrix Occupation
Number	Rank					
1	VL	VH	VL	VL	Bachelor's degree	Agricultural and food scientists[1]
3	VL	VH	L	VL	Doctoral degree	Biological scientists
1	VL	VH	VL	VL	Bachelor's degree	Foresters and conservation scientists[1]
1	VL	VH	L	VL	Doctoral degree	Medical scientists
0	VL	VH	L	VL	Doctoral degree	All other life scientists
110	–	–	–	–	–	Computer, mathematical, and operations research occupations
0	VL	VH	VL	VL	Bachelor's degree	Actuaries[1]
107	–	–	–	–	–	Computer systems analysis, engineers, and scientists
52	–	–	–	–	–	Computer engineers and scientists
25	L	VH	VL	VL	Bachelor's degree	Computer engineers
27	L	VH	VL	VL	Bachelor's degree	Database administrators, computer support specialists, and all other computer scientists
55	H	VH	VL	VL	Bachelor's degree	Systems analysts
0	VL	VH	VL	VL	Bachelor's degree	Statisticians[1]
0	VL	VH	VL	VL	Doctoral degree	Mathematicians and all other mathematical scientists[1]
2	VL	VH	VL	VL	Master's degree	Operations research analysts
8	–	–	–	–	–	Physical scientists
4	VL	VH	VL	VL	Bachelor's degree	Chemists
2	VL	VH	VL	VL	Bachelor's degree	Geologists, geophysicists, and oceanographers[1]
0	VL	VH	VL	VL	Bachelor's degree	Meteorologists[1]
0	VL	VH	VL	VL	Doctoral degree	Physicists and astronomers
2	VL	VH	VL	VL	Bachelor's degree	All other physical scientists
6	–	–	–	–	–	Social scientists
2	VL	VH	L	VL	Bachelor's degree	Economists
3	VL	VH	VL	H	Master's degree	Psychologists
1	VL	VH	VL	H	Master's degree	Urban and regional planners[1]
1	VL	VH	VL	H	Master's degree	All other social scientists[1]
79	–	–	–	H	–	Social, recreational, and religious workers
7	VL	H	VL	H	First professional degree	Clergy
5	VL	L	VL	VH	Bachelor's degree	Directors, religious activities and education[1]
13	L	L	H	VH	Moderate-term on-the-job-training	Human services workers[1]
15	L	VL	VH	H	Bachelor's degree	Recreation workers
12	L	L	VL	L	Bachelor's degree	Residential counselors
28	L	H	VL	L	Bachelor's degree	Social workers
22	–	–	–	–	–	Lawyers and judicial workers
1	VL	H	VL	L	Work experience plus degree	Judges, magistrates, and other judicial workers[1]
21	L	VH	VL	L	First professional degree	Lawyers
271	–	–	–	–	–	Teachers, librarians, and counselors
19	L	L	L	H	Bachelor's degree	Teachers, preschool and kindergarten
44	H	VH	VL	L	Bachelor's degree	Teachers, elementary
73	VH	VH	VL	L	Bachelor's degree	Teachers, secondary school
30	L	VH	VL	L	Bachelor's degree	Teachers, special education
41	H	VH	L	VH	Doctoral degree	College and university faculty[1]
33	–	–	–	–	–	Other teachers and instructors
0	VL	VH	L	VH	Bachelor's degree	Farm and home management advisors
15	L	L	L	VH	Moderate-term on-the-job-training	Instructors and coaches, sports and physical training
17	–	–	–	–	–	Adult and vocational education teachers
7	VL	H	L	VH	Work experience in a related occupation	Instructors, adult (nonvocational) education
10	VL	VH	L	VH	Work experience in a related occupation	Teachers and instructors, vocational education and training
19	L	VH	L	VH	Master's degree	All other teachers and instructors[1]
5	–	–	–	–	–	Librarians, archivists, curators, and related workers
1	VL	H	VL	H	Master's degree	Curators, archivists, museum technicians, and restorers[1]
5	VL	VH	VL	H	Master's degree	Librarians, professional
7	VL	VH	VL	L	Master's degree	Counselors
30	–	–	–	–	–	Health diagnosing occupations
2	VL	VH	VL	L	First professional degree	Chiropractors[1]
5	VL	VH	VL	H	First professional degree	Dentists
1	VL	VH	VL	L	First professional degree	Optometrists[1]
20	L	VH	VL	L	First professional degree	Physicians

[1]One or more Current Population Survey (CPS) based occupations may be used to estimate CPS based data. See Table 2.

NOTE: Rankings are based on employment in all detailed occupations in the National Industry-Occupation Matrix. For details, see "Data presented" section of text. Codes for describing the ranked variables are: VH = Very high, H = High, L = Low, VL = Very low, n. a. = Data not available. A dash indicates data are not applicable.

Table 1. Occupational employment and job openings data, 1996-2006, and worker characteristics, 1996—Continued
(Numbers in thousands)

1996 Matrix Occupation	Employment		Employment change, 1996-2006				Percent self-em-ployed,	Annual average job openings due to growth and total replacement	
			Numeric		Percent				
	1996	2006	Number	Rank	Number	Rank		Number	Rank
Podiatrists[1]	11	12	1	VL	10.1	L	33.6	0	VL
Veterinarians and veterinary inspectors[1]	58	71	13	VL	22.7	VH	35.1	3	VL
Health assessment and treating occupations	2,684	3,393	709	–	26.4	–	2.2	253	–
Dietitians and nutritionists	58	69	11	VL	18.2	H	16.4	9	VL
Pharmacists	172	194	22.	L	12.6	L	4.7	7	VL
Physician assistants[1]	64	93	30	L	46.6	VH	1.2	6	VL
Registered nurses	1,971	2,382	411	VH	20.8	VH	0.7	183	H
Therapists	419	655	236	–	56.3	–	6.7	49	–
Occupational therapists[1]	57	95	38	L	66.1	VH	4.9	7	VL
Physical therapists[1]	115	196	81	L	70.8	VH	7.0	15	VL
Recreational therapists[1]	38	46	8	VL	21.3	VH	26.2	3	VL
Respiratory therapists[1]	82	119	37	L	45.8	VH	0.0	8	VL
Speech-language pathologists and audiologists[1]	87	131	44	L	50.6	VH	6.8	10	VL
All other therapists[1]	40	67	27	L	67.4	VH	3.1	5	VL
Writers, artists, and entertainers	2,606	3,242	636	–	24.4	–	22.0	470	–
Artists and commercial artists	276	354	78	L	28.3	VH	57.3	54	L
Athletes, coaches, umpires, and related workers	42	49	7	VL	15.5	H	31.6	15	VL
Dancers and choreographers[1]	23	30	7	VL	28.0	VH	30.2	5	VL
Designers	342	431	89	–	26.1	–	37.3	58	–
Designers, except interior designers	279	351	72	L	25.7	VH	36.4	48	L
Interior designers	63	80	17	VL	27.5	VH	41.5	11	VL
Musicians	274	366	92	L	33.4	VH	26.8	54	L
Photographers and camera operators	154	180	26	–	16.9	–	41.6	23	–
Camera operators, television, motion picture, video	20	23	3	VL	14.5	H	7.4	3	VL
Photographers	134	157	23	L	17.3	H	46.7	20	VL
Producers, directors, actors, and entertainers[1]	105	130	25	L	23.6	VH	27.3	21	VL
Public relations specialists and publicity writers	110	140	30	L	27.2	VH	4.4	23	VL
Radio and TV announcers and newscasters	52	52	0	VL	–0.6	VL	0.0	11	VL
Reporters and correspondents	60	58	–2	VL	–3.1	VL	8.6	6	VL
Writers and editors, including technical writers	286	347	61	L	21.2	VH	31.6	43	VL
All other professional workers[1]	880	1,104	224	H	25.5	VH	2.2	158	L
Technicians and related support occupations	4,618	5,558	940		20.4		1.5	512	–
Health technicians and technologists	2,301	2,872	571	–	24.8	–	1.1	236	–
Cardiology technologists[1]	17	23	6	VL	34.9	VH	0.0	3	VL
Clinical laboratory technologists and technicians	285	328	42	L	14.9	H	1.8	18	VL
Dental hygienists	133	197	64	L	48.2	VH	0.5	16	VL
Electroneurodiagnostic technologists[1]	6	8	2	VL	24.0	VH	0.0	1	VL
EKG technicians[1]	15	11	–4	VL	–24.2	VL	0.0	1	VL
Emergency medical technicians[1]	150	217	67	L	45.1	VH	0.0	26	VL
Licensed practical nurses	699	848	148	H	21.2	VH	0.4	45	L
Medical records technicians[1]	87	132	44	L	50.9	VH	0.0	12	VL
Nuclear medicine technologists	13	15	2	VL	13.3	L	0.0	1	VL
Opticians, dispensing and measuring	67	76	9	VL	14.1	L	4.0	5	VL
Pharmacy technicians[1]	83	92	9	VL	11.1	L	0.0	10	VL
Psychiatric technicians	66	72	6	VL	9.1	L	0.0	15	VL
Radiologic technologists and technicians	174	224	50	L	28.9	VH	0.4	14	VL
Surgical technologists[1]	49	64	15	VL	31.9	VH	0.0	8	VL
Veterinary technicians and technologists[1]	26	34	7	VL	27.4	VH	0.0	3	VL
All other health professionals and paraprofessionals	430	531	101	H	23.5	VH	3.0	59	L
Engineering and science technicians and technologists	1,236	1,342	106	–	8.6	–	1.0	146	–
Engineering technicians	698	767	70	–	10.0	–	0.7	96	–
Electrical and electronic technicians and technologists	297	341	43	L	14.5	H	0.6	37	VL
All other engineering technicians and technologists[1]	400	427	26	L	6.6	L	0.8	60	L
Drafters	310	317	7	VL	2.3	VL	1.5	30	VL
Science and mathematics technicians[1]	228	258	29	L	12.9	L	1.0	19	VL
Technicians, except health and engineering and science	1,082	1,345	263	–	24.3	–	3.0	130	–
Air,craft pilots and flight engineers	110	125	151	VL	13.8	L	1.4	6	VL

[1]One or more Current Population survey (CPS) based occupations may be used to estimate CPS based data. See Table 2.
NOTE: Rankings are based on employment In all detailed occupations in the National Industry-Occupation Matrix. For details, see "Data presented" section of text. Codes for describing the ranked variables are: VH = Very high, H = High, L = Low, VL = Very low, n. a. = Data not available. A dash indicates data are not applicable.

Table 1. Occupational employment and job openings data, 1996-2006, and worker characteristics, 1996—Continued
(Numbers in thousands)

Annual average job openings due to growth and total replacement needs, 1996-2006		Median hourly earnings	Unem- ployment rate	Per- cent part- time	Most significant source of training	1996 Matrix Occupation
Number	Rank					
0	VL	VH	VL	L	First professional degree	Podiatrists[1]
2	VL	VH	VL	L	First professional degree	Veterinarians and Veterinary inspectors[1]
109	–	–	–	–	–	Health assessment and treating occupations
2	VL	VH	L	H	Bachelor's degree	Dietitians and nutritionists
6	VL	VH	VL	L	Bachelor's degree	Pharmacists
4	VL	VH	VL	H	Bachelor's degree	Physician assistant[1]
68	H	VH	VL	H	Associate degree	Registered nurses
28	–	–	–	–	–	Therapists
4	VL	VH	VL	H	Bachelor's degree	Occupational therapists[1]
9	VL	VH	VL	H	Bachelor's degree	Physical therapists[1]
1	VL	H	VL	H	Bachelor's degree	Recreational therapists[1]
5	VL	VH	VL	L	Associate degree	Respiratory therapists[1]
5	VL	VH	VL	H	Master's degree	Speech-language pathologists and audiologists[1]
3	VL	H	VL	H	Bachelor's degree	All other therapists[1]
102	–	–	–	–	–	Writers, artists, and entertainers
14	L	H	L	H	Work experience plus degree	Artists and commercial artists
2	VL	L	H	VH	Long-term on-the-job-training	Athletes, coaches, umpires, and related workers
1	VL	H	L	H	Postsecondary vocational training	Dancers and choreographers[1]
15	–	–	–	–	–	Designers
12	L	H	L	H	Bachelor's degree	Designers, except interior designers
3	VL	H	L	H	Bachelor's degree	Interior designers
13	L	H	H	VH	Long-term on-the-job-training	Musicians
5	–	–	–	–	–	Photographers and camera operators
1	VL	L	L	VH	Moderate-term on-the-job-training	Camera operators, television, motion picture, video
4	VL	L	L	VH	Moderate-term on-the-job-training	Photographers
5	VL	n. a.	VH	VH	Long term on-the-job-training	Producers, directors, actors, and entertainers[1]
7	VL	H	L	L	Bachelor's degree	Public relations specialists and publicity writers
2	VL	L	H	VH	Long-term on-the-job-training	Radio and TV announcers and newscasters
2	VL	H	VL	L	Bachelor's degree	Reporters and correspondents
12	L	VH	VL	H	Bachelor's degree	Writers and editors, including technical writers
44	H	H	L	H	Bachelor's degree	All other professional workers[1]
193	–	–	–	–	–	**Technicians and related support occupations**
101	–	–	–	–	–	Health technicians and technologists
1	VL	VH	L	H	Associate degree	Cardiology technologists[1]
7	VL	H	VL	L	Bachelor's degree	Clinical laboratory technologists and technicians
10	L	VH	VL	VH	Associate degree	Dental hygienists
0	VL	H	L	H	Moderate-term on-the-job-training	Electroneurodiagnostic technologists[1]
0	VL	H	L	H	Moderate-term on-the-job-training	EKG techniciansl
10	VL	L	L	H	Postsecondary vocational training	Emergency medical technicians[1]
30	L	H	L	H	Postsecondary vocational training	Licensed practical nurses
6	VL	L	VL	H	Associate degree	Medical records technicians[1]
0	VL	VH	VL	L	Associate degree	Nuclear medicine technologists
2	VL	L	L	L	Long-term on-the-job-training	Opticians, dispensing and measuring
3	VL	L	L	H	Moderate-term on-the-job-training	Pharmacy technicians[1]
1	VL	L	H	H	Associate degree	Psychiatric technicians
8	VL	H	VL	L	Associate degree	Radiologic technologists and technicians
2	VL	H	L	H	Postsecondary vocational training	Surgical technologists[1]
1	VL	L	H	L	Associate degree	Veterinary technicians and technologists[1]
18	L	H	VL	H	Associate degree	All other health professionals and paraprofessionals[1]
38	–	–	–	–	–	Engineering and science technicians and technologists
23	–	–	–	–	–	Engineering technicians
12	L	VH	L	VL	Associate degree	Electrical and electronic technicians and technologists
11	L	VH	L	VL	Associate degree	All other engineering technicians and technologists[1]
7	VL	H	L	VL	Postsecondary vocational training	Drafters
8	VL	H	L	L	Associate degree	Science and mathematics technicians[1]
54	–	–	–	–	–	Technicians, except health and engineering and science
4	VL	VH	VL	VH	Bachelor's degree	Aircraft pilots and flight engineers

[1]One or more Current Population Survey (CPS) based occupations may be used to estimate CPS based data. See Table 2.
NOTE: Rankings are based on employment in all detailed occupations in the National Industry-Occupation Matrix. For details, see "Data presented" section of text. Codes for describing the ranked variables are: VH = Very high, H = High, L = Low, VL = Very low, n. a. = Data not available. A dash indicates data are not applicable.

Table 1. Occupational employment and job openings data, 1996-2006, and worker characteristics, 1996—Continued
(Numbers in thousands)

1996 Matrix Occupation	Employment		Employment change, 1996-2006				Percent self-em-ployed, 1996	Annual average job openings due to growth and total replacement needs, 1996-2006	
			Numeric		Percent				
	1996	2006	Number	Rank	Number	Rank		Number	Rank
Air traffic controllers and airplane dispatchers[1]	29	29	0	VL	−0.3	VL	0.0	2	VL
Broadcast technicians[1]	46	53	7	VL	15.1	H	3.8	4	VL
Computer programmers	568	697	129	H	22.8	VH	3.5	60	L
Legal assistants and technicians, except clerical	221	310	90	–	40.7	–	4.1	42	–
Paralegals	113	189	76	L	67.7	VH	2.1	29	VL
Title examiners and searchers	26	29	3	VL	13.4	L	18.3	4	VL
All other legal assistants, including law clerks	82	92	10	VL	12.1	L	2.4	9	VL
Programmers, numerical, tool, and process control[1]	7	7	0	VL	5.7	L	0.0	1	VL
Technical assistants, library[1]	78	100	22	L	28.0	VH	0.0	11	VL
All other technicians[1]	24	23	0	VL	−2.0	VL	0.0	2	VL
Marketing and sales occupations	**14,633**	**16,897**	**2,264**	**–**	**15.5**	**–**	**12.4**	**4,070**	**–**
Cashiers	3,146	3,677	530	VH	16.8	H	0.5	1,265	VH
Counter and rental clerks	374	458	84	L	22.5	VH	1.9	158	L
Insurance sales workers	409	426	18	VL	4.3	VL	30.1	43	VL
Marketing and sales worker supervisors	2,316	2,562	246	VH	10.6	L	34.3	370	VH
Real estate agents, brokers, and appraisers	408	441	32	–	7.9	–	64.8	52	–
Brokers, real estate	78	89	11	VL	14.1	L	64.8	11	VL
Real estate appraisers	48	54	6	VL	12.1	L	23.5	7	VL
Sales agents, real estate	282	298	16	VL	5.5	VL	71.9	35	VL
Salespersons, retail	4,072	4,481	408	VH	10.0	L	4.5	1,272	VH
Securities and financial services sales workers	263	363	100	H	37.8	VH	24.3	52	L
Travel agents[1]	142	176	34	L	24.0	VH	15.8	19	VL
All other sales and related workers[1]	3,503	4,314	811	VH	23.2	VH	9.5	840	VH
Administrative support occupations, including clerical	**24,019**	**25,825**	**1,806**	**–**	**7.5**	**–**	**1.8**	**4,844**	**–**
Adjusters, investigators, and collectors	1,283	1,605	322	–	25.1	–	0.9	292	–
Adjustment clerks	401	584	183	H	45.5	VH	0.0	129	L
Bill and account collectors	269	381	112	H	41.8	VH	1.1	96	L
Insurance claims and policy processing occupations	466	526	60	–	12.9	–	1.8	58	·
Insurance adjusters, examiners, and Investigators	165	203	38	L	23.1	VH	5.1	15	VL
Insurance claims clerks	121	153	31	L	25.7	VH	0.0	12	VL
Insurance policy processing clerks	179	171	−9	VL	−5.0	VL	0.0	31	VL
Welfare eligibility workers and interviewers	109	76	−34	VL	−30.8	VL	0.0	2	VL
All other adjusters and investigators	38	39	0	VL	1.3	VL	0.0	7	VL
Communications equipment operators	328	295	−33	–	−9.9	–	0.0	74	–
Telephone operators	319	289	−30	–	−9.3	–	0.0	73	–
Central off ice operators	48	26	−23	VL	−47.0	VL	0.0	9	VL
Directory assistance operators	33	18	−16	VL	−47.1	VL	0.0	6	VL
Switchboard operators	237	246	9	VL	3.7	VL	0.0	58	L
All other communications equipment operators[1]	9	6	−3	VL	−33.7	VL	0.0	2	VL
Computer operators	291	198	−94	–	−32.1	–	2.0	36	–
Computer operators, except peripheral equipment	258	181	−77	VL	−29.8	VL	2.3	32	VL
Peripheral computer equipment operators[1]	33	17	−17	VL	−50.0	VL	0.0	4	VL
Information clerks	1,591	1,958	366	–	23.0	–	1.1	475	–
Hotel desk clerks	144	174	30	L	21.0	VH	0.7	58	L
Interviewing clerks, except personnel and social welfare	98	115	17	VL	17.7	H	1.8	33	VL
New accounts clerks, banking	110	115	5	VL	4.5	VL	0.0	33	VL
Receptionists and Information clerks	1,074	1,392	318	VH	29.7	VH	1.4	336	H
Reservation and transportation ticket agents and travel clerks[1]	166	162	−4	VL	−2.7	VL	0.0	16	VL
Mail clerks and messengers	268	291	23	–	8.6	–	4.1	67	–
Mail clerks, except mail machine operators and postal service	130	137	7	VL	5.7	L	0.0	26	VL
Messengers	138	154	16	VL	11.3	L	7.9	41	VL
Postal clerks and mail carriers	403	443	40	–	9.9	–	0.0	13	–
Postal mail carriers	332	369	37	L	11.2	L	0.0	9	VL
Postal service clerks	71	74	3	VL	3.8	VL	0.0	4	VL
Material recording, scheduling, dispatching, and distributing occupations	3,859	4,084	225	–	5.8	–	0.2	822	–
Dispatchers	234	258	24	–	10.1	–	0.9	44	–

[1]One or more Current Population Survey (CPS) based occupations may be used to estimate CPS based data. See Table 2.
NOTE: Rankings are based on employment in all detailed occupations in the National Industry-Occupation Matrix. For details, see "Data presented" section of text. Codes for describing the ranked variables are: VH = Very high, H = High, L = Low, VL = Very low, n. a. = Data not available. A dash indicates data are not applicable.

Table 1. Occupational employment and job openings data, 1996-2006, and worker characteristics, 1996—Continued
(Numbers in thousands)

Annual average job openings due to growth and total replacement needs, 1996-2006		Median hourly earnings	Unem-ployment rate	Per-cent part-time	Most significant source of training	1996 Matrix Occupation
Number	Rank					
1	VL	VH	VL	L	Long-term on-the-job-training	Air traffic controllers and airplane dispatchers[1]
2	VL	H	VL	L	Postsecondary vocational training	Broadcast technicians[1]
31	L	VH	VL	VL	Bachelor's degree	Computer programmers
11	–	–	–	–		Legal assistants and technicians, except clerical
9	VL	H	L	L	Associate degree	Paralegals
1	VL	H	L	L	Moderate-term on-the-job-training	Title examiners and searchers
2	VL	H	VL	L	Associate degree	All other legal assistants, including law clerks
0	VL	VH	VL	L	Work experience in a related occupation	Programmers, numerical, tool, and process control[1]
4	VL	L	L	H	Short-term on-the-job-training	Technical assistants, library[1]
1	VL	H	L	H	Moderate-term on-the-job-training	All other technicians[1]
652	–	–	–	–	–	**Marketing and sales occupations**
190	VH	VL	VH	VH	Short-term on-the-job-training	Cashiers
22	L	VL	H	VH	Short-term on-the-job-training	Counter and rental clerks
9	VL	VH	VL	L	Bachelor's degree	Insurance sales workers
62	H	H	VL	L	Work experience in a related occupation	Marketing and sales worker supervisors
10						Real estate agents, brokers, and appraisers
2	VL	VH	VL	H	Work experience in a related occupation	Brokers, real estate
1	VL	VH	VL	H	Bachelor's degree	Real estate appraisers
6	VL	H	VL	H	Postsecondary vocational training	Sales agents, real estate
170	VH	VL	H	VH	Short-term on-the-job-training	Salespersons, retail
12	L	VH	L	L	Bachelor's degree	Securities and financial services sales workers
7	VL	L	L	L	Postsecondary vocational training	Travel agents[1]
170	VH	H	H	H	Moderate-term on-the-job-training	All other sales and related workers[1]
691	–	–	–	–	–	**Administrative support occupations, including clerical**
52	–	–	–	–		Adjusters, investigators, and collectors
21	L	L	L	L	Short-term on-the-job-training	Adjustment clerks
17	L	L	L	L	Short-term on-the-job-training	Bill and account collectors
13						Insurance claims and policy processing occupations
6	VL	VH	VL	VL	Long-term on-the-job-training	Insurance adjusters, examiners, and investigators
5	VL	H	VL	VL	Moderate-term on-the-job-training	Insurance claims clerks
2	VL	H	L	L	Moderate-term on-the-job-training	Insurance policy processing clerks
2	VL	H	L	VL	Moderate-term on-the-job-training	Welfare eligibility workers and interviewers
1	VL	H	L	L	Moderate-term on-the-job-training	All other adjusters and investigators
7	–	–	–	–		Communications equipment operators
7	–	–	–	–		Telephone operators
1	VL	H	H	H	Moderate-term on-the-job-training	Central office operators
1	VL	H	H	H	Moderate-term on-the-job-training	Directory assistance operators
5	VL	L	H	H	Short-term on-the-job-training	Switchboard operators
0	VL	H	H	H	Moderate-term on-the-job-training	All other communications equipment operators[1]
5						Computer operators
4	VL	H	L	L	Moderate-term on-the-job-training	Computer operators, except peripheral equipment
1	VL	L	L	L	Moderate-term on-the-job-training	Peripheral computer equipment operators[1]
73	–	–	–	–	–	Information clerks
9	VL	VL	H	H	Short-term on-the-job-training	Hotel desk clerks
5	VL	L	VH	H	Short-term on-the-job-training	Interviewing clerks, except personnel and social welfare
4	VL	L	VH	H	Work experience in a related occupation	New accounts clerks, banking
52	H	L	H	VH	Short-term on-the-job-training	Receptionists and information clerks
4	VL	H	L	L	Short-term on-the-job-training	Reservation and transportation ticket agents and travel clerks[1]
9	–	–	–	–	–	Mail clerks and messengers
4	VL	L	H	H	Short-term on-the-job-training	Mail clerks, except mail machine operators and postal service
5	VL	L	H	VH	Short-term on-the-job-training	Messengers
13						Postal clerks and mail carriers
12	L	H	VL	VL	Short-term on-the-job-training	Postal mail carriers
2	VL	H	L	VL	Short-term on-the-job-training	Postal service clerks
83	–	–	–	–	–	Material recording, scheduling, dispatching, and distributing occupations
6	–	–	–	–	–	Dispatchers

[1]One or more Current Population Survey (CPS) based occupations may be used to estimate CPS based data. See Table 2.
NOTE: Rankings are based on employment in all detailed occupations in the National Industry-Occupation Matrix. For details, see "Data presented" section of text. Codes for describing the ranked variables are: VH = Very high, H = High, L = Low, VL = Very low, n. a. = Data not available. A dash indicates data are not applicable.

Table 1. Occupational employment and job openings data, 1996-2006, and worker characteristics, 1996—Continued
(Numbers in thousands)

1996 Matrix Occupation	Employment		Employment change, 1996-2006				Percent self-employed, 1996	Annual average job openings due to growth and total replacement needs, 1996-2006	
			Numeric		Percent				
	1996	2006	Number	Rank	Number	Rank		Number	Rank
Dispatchers, except police, fire, and ambulance	148	165	17	VL	11.4	L	1.5	29	VL
Dispatchers, police, fire, and ambulance	86	93	7	VL	7.7	L	0.0	16	VL
Meter readers, utilities[1]	55	56	1	VL	2.2	VL	0.0	13	VL
Order fillers, wholesale and retail sales	227	255	28	L	12.1	L	0.0	39	VL
Procurement clerks	56	55	−1	VL	−1.9	VL	0.0	10	VL
Production, planning, and expediting clerks	239	254	15	VL	6.3	L	0.4	63	L
Stock clerks	1,844	1,898	54	L	2.9	VL	0.2	346	H
Traffic, shipping, and receiving clerks	985	1,070	85	L	8.6	L	0.1	251	H
Weighers, measurers, checkers, and samplers, recordkeeping[1]	47	50	3	VL	6.1	L	0.0	11	VL
All other material recording, scheduling, and distribution workers[1]	170	188	17	VL	10.3	L	0.0	45	L
Records processing occupations	3,870	3,887	16	–	0.4	–	5.9	699	–
Advertising clerks[1]	18	18	0	VL	−1.3	VL	0.0	3	VL
Brokerage clerks	76	91	15	VL	19.1	H	0.0	17	VL
Correspondence clerks[1]	31	41	10	VL	30.8	VH	0.0	6	VL
File clerks	293	315	22	L	7.4	L	1.1	125	L
Financial records processing occupations	2,848	2,790	−58	–	−2.0	–	7.7	439	–
Billing, cost, and rate clerks	335	391	55	L	16.5	H	0.6	63	L
Billing, posting, and calculating machine operators[1]	102	100	−1	VL	−1.4	VL	1.3	10	VL
Bookkeeping, accounting, and auditing clerks	2,250	2,147	−102	VL	−4.5	VL	9.5	351	H
Payroll and timekeeping clerks	161	151	−10	VL	−5.9	VL	1.5	14	VL
Library assistants and bookmobile drivers	125	145	19	VL	15.4	H	0.0	35	VL
Order clerks, materials, merchandise, and service	329	338	8	VL	2.6	VL	1.2	51	L
Personnel clerks, except payroll and timekeeping[1]	124	126	2	VL	1.4	VL	0.0	19	VL
Statement clerks	25	25	−1	VL	−2.8	VL	4.1	5	VL
Secretaries, stenographers, and typists	4,153	4,081	−72	–	−1.7	–	2.4	574	–
Secretaries	3,403	3,427	25		0.7		1.6	466	–
Legal secretaries	284	319	35	L	12.5	L	0.6	44	–
Medical secretaries	239	314	76	L	31.7	VH	0.3	44	L
Secretaries, except legal and medical	2,881	2,794	−87	VL	−3.0	VL	1.9	378	VH
Stenographers and/or court reporters[1]	98	101	4	VL	3.7	VL	27.2	13	VL
Typists, including word processing	653	552	−100	VL	−15.4	VL	2.9	95	L
Other clerical and administrative support workers	7,972	8,983	1,011	–	12.7	–	0.6	1,792	–
Bank tellers	545	550	5	VL	0.8	VL	0.3	108	L
Clerical supervisors and managers	1,369	1,630	262	VH	19.1	H	0.2	202	H
Court clerks	53	57	5	VL	8.7	L	0.0	14	VL
Credit authorizers, credit checkers, and loan and credit clerks	252	256	3	–	1.3	–	0.0	61	–
Credit authorizers	16	10	−6	VL	−38.5	VL	0.0	3	VL
Credit checkers	42	33	−9	VL	−22.2	VL	0.0	8	VL
Loan and credit clerks	181	200	19	VL	10.2	L	0.0	46	L
Loan interviewers	12	13	1	VL	4.5	VL	0.0	3	VL
Customer service representatives, utilities	151	206	55	L	36.3	VH	0.0	32	VL
Data entry keyers, except composing	418	453	35	L	8.3	L	1.3	103	L
Data entry keyers, composing	18	10	−8	VL	−44.6	VL	0.0	3	VL
Duplicating, mail, and other office machine operators[1]	196	149	−47	VL	−24.1	VL	0.0	37	VL
General office clerks	3,111	3,326	215	H	6.9	L	0.5	713	VH
Municipal clerks	22	24	2	VL	9.3	L	0.0	6	VL
Proofreaders and copy markers[1]	26	16	−10	VL	−38.5	VL	7.7	5	VL
Real estate clerks	24	25	2	VL	6.4	L	0.0	5	VL
Statistical clerks	78	65	−13	VL	−17.3	VL	0.0	5	VL
Teacher aides and educational assistants	981	1,352	370	VH	37.7	VH	0.0	296	H
All other clerical and administrative support workers	727	864	137	H	18.8	H	2.5	203	H
Service occupations	21,294	25,147	3,853	–	18.1	–	5.7	6,373	–
Cleaning and building service occupations, except private household	3,545	3,713	168	–	4.7	–	4.6	755	–
Institutional cleaning supervisors	108	115	6	VL	5.7	L	1.8	10	VL

[1]One or more Current Population Survey (CPS) based occupations may be used to estimate CPS based data. See Table 2.
NOTE: Rankings are based on employment in all detailed occupations in the National Industry-Occupation Matrix. For details, see "Data presented" section of text. Codes for describing the ranked variables are: VH = Very high, H = High, L = Low, VL = Very low, n. a. = Data not available. A dash indicates data are not applicable.

Table 1. Occupational employment and job openings data, 1996-2006, and worker characteristics, 1996—Continued
(Numbers in thousands)

Annual average job openings due to growth and total replacement needs, 1996-2006		Median hourly earnings	Unemployment rate	Percent part-time	Most significant source of training	1996 Matrix Occupation
Number	Rank					
4	VL	H	L	VL	Moderate-term on-the-job-training	Dispatchers, except police, fire, and ambulance
2	VL	L	L	VL	Moderate-term on-the-job-training	Dispatchers, police, fire, and ambulance
1	VL	H	H	L	Short-term on-the-job-training	Meter readers, utilities[1]
7	VL	L	L	L	Short-term on-the-job-training	Order fillers, wholesale and retail sales
1	VL	L	H	L	Short-term on-the-job-training	Procurement clerks
5	VL	H	L	H	Short-term on-the-job-training	Production, planning, and expediting clerks
33	H	VL	H	L	Short-term on-the-job-training	Stock clerks
23	L	L	H	VL	Short-term on-the-job-training	Traffic, shipping, and receiving clerks
1	VL	L	H	L	Short-term on-the-job-training	Weighers, measurers, checkers, and samplers, recordkeeping[1]
5	VL	L	H	L	Short-term on-the-job-training	All other material recording, scheduling, and distribution workers[1]
89	–	–	–	–	–	Records processing occupations
0	VL	L	L	L	Short-term on-the-job-training	Advertising clerks[1]
2	VL	H	L	L	Moderate-term on-the-job-training	Brokerage clerks
2	VL	L	L	L	Short-term on-the-job-training	Correspondence clerks[1]
13	L	VL	VH	VH	Short-term on-the-job-training	File clerks
54	–	–	–	–	–	Financial records processing occupations
12	L	L	L	L	Short-term on-the-job-training	Billing, cost, and rate clerks
2	VL	L	L	L	Short-term on-the-job-training	Billing, posting, and calculating machine operators[1]
38	H	L	L	VH	Moderate-term on-the-job-training	Bookkeeping, accounting, and auditing clerks
3	VL	H	L	L	Short-term on-the-job-training	Payroll and timekeeping clerks
7	VL	L	H	VH	Short-term on-the-job-training	Library assistants and bookmobile drivers
7	VL	L	L	L	Short-term on-the-job-training	Order clerks, materials, merchandise, and service
3	VL	H	L	VL	Short-term on-the-job-training	Personnel clerks, except payroll and timekeeping[1]
0	VL	L	L	L	Short-term on-the-job-training	Statement clerks
83	–	–	–	–	–	Secretaries, stenographers, and typists
70	–	–	–	–	–	Secretaries
8	VL	H	L	H	Postsecondary vocational training	Legal secretaries
12	L	L	L	H	Postsecondary vocational training	Medical secretaries
50	H	H	L	H	Postsecondary vocational training	Secretaries, except legal and medical
2	VL	H	VL	H	Postsecondary vocational training	Stenographers and/or court reporters[1]
11	L	L	H	H	Moderate-term on-the-job-training	Typists, including word processing
276	–	–	–	–	–	Other clerical and administrative support workers
23	L	L	L	VH	Short-term on-the-job-training	Bank tellers
58	H	H	VL	VL	Work experience in a related occupation	Clerical supervisors and managers
1	VL	L	L	L	Short-term on-the-job-training	Court clerks
4	–	–	–	–	–	Credit authorizers, credit checkers, and loan and credit clerks
0	VL	L	L	L	Short-term on-the-job-training	Credit authorizers
0	VL	L	L	L	Short-term on-the-job-training	Credit checkers
4	VL	L	L	L	Short-term on-the-job-training	Loan and credit clerks
0	VL	H	L	L	Short-term on-the-job-training	Loan interviewers
9	VL	H	L	L	Short-term on-the-job-training	Customer service representatives, utilities
5	VL	L	H	L	Postsecondary vocational training	Data entry keyers, except composing
0	VL	L	H	L	Postsecondary vocational training	Data entry keyers, composing
8	VL	L	H	H	Short-term on-the-job-training	Duplicating, mail, and other office machine operators[1]
92	VH	L	H	H	Short-term on-the-job-training	General office clerks
0	VL	L	L	L	Short-term on-the-job-training	Municipal clerks
1	VL	L	L	H	Short-term on-the-job-training	Proofreaders and copy markers[1]
1	VL	L	H	H	Short-term on-the-job-training	Real estate clerks
1	VL	L	VL	VL	Moderate-term on-the-job-training	Statistical clerks
50	H	VL	L	VH	Short-term on-the-job-training	Teacher aides and educational assistants
22	L	L	L	L	Short-term on-the-job-training	All other clerical and administrative support workers
1,037	–	–	–	–	–	**Service occupations**
87	–	–	–	–	–	Cleaning and building service occupations, except private household
3	VL	L	L	VL	Work experience in a related occupation	Institutional cleaning supervisors

[1]One or more Current Population Survey (CPS) based occupations may be used to estimate CPS based data. See Table 2.
NOTE: Rankings are based on employment in all detailed occupations in the National Industry-Occupation Matrix. For details, see "Data presented" section of text. Codes for describing the ranked variables are: VH = Very high, H = High, L = Low, VL = Very low, n. a. = Data not available. A dash indicates data are not applicable.

Table 1. Occupational employment and job openings data, 1996-2006, and worker characteristics, 1996—Continued
(Numbers in thousands)

1996 Matrix Occupation	Employment 1996	Employment 2006	Numeric Number	Numeric Rank	Percent Number	Percent Rank	Percent self-employed, 1996	Annual average job openings due to growth and total replacement needs, 1996-2006 Number	Rank
Janitors and cleaners, including maids and housekeeping cleaners	3,134	3,262	128	H	4.1	VL	4.4	679	VH
Pest controllers and assistants[1]	60	73	13	VL	22.2	VH	10.0	9	VL
All other cleaning and building service workers[1]	3	263	20	L	8.3	L	7.8	56	L
Food preparation and service occupations	6	9,571	1,175	–	14.0	–	0.9	3,301	–
Chefs, cooks, and other kitchen workers	3,402	3,984	583	–	17.1	–	1.6	1,266	–
Cooks, except short order	1,344	1,519	175	–	13.0	–	3.2	432	–
Bakers, bread and pastry	182	231	48	L	26.4	VH	9.1	65	L
Cooks, institution or cafeteria	435	455	21	L	4.7	VL	0.0	131	L
Cooks, restaurant	727	833	106	H	14.6	H	3.7	236	H
Cooks, short order and fast food	804	978	174	H	21.6	VH	1.0	275	H
Food preparation workers[1]	1,253	1,487	234	H	18.7	H	0.1	559	VH
Food and beverage service occupations	4,766	5,296	530	–	11.1	–	0.4	1,934	–
Bartenders	390	392	2	VL	0.4	VL	1.8	82	L
Dining room and cafeteria attendants and bar helpers	439	501	62	L	14.1	L	0.0	211	H
Food counter, fountain, and related workers[1]	1,720	1,963	243	H	14.1	H	0.1	841	VH
Hosts and hostesses, restaurant, lounge, or coffee shop	260	278	18	VL	6.7	L	1.2	89	L
Waiters and waitresses	1,957	2,163	206	H	10.5	L	0.4	711	VH
All other food preparation and service workers	228	290	62	L	27.1	VH	1.3	101	L
Health service occupations	2,167	2,874	706	–	32.6	–	1.6	530	–
Ambulance drivers and attendants, except EMTs	18	25	7	VL	36.5	VH	0.0	4	VL
Dental assistants	202	278	77	L	38.1	VH	0.0	48	L
Medical assistants[1]	225	391	166	H	74.0	VH	0.0	49	L
Nursing aides and psychiatric aides	1,415	1,757	342	–	24.2	–	2.4	363	–
Nursing aides, orderlies, and attendants	1,312	1,645	333	VH	25.4	VH	2.6	340	H
Psychiatric aides	103	112	9	VL	8.6	L	0.0	23	VL
Occupational therapy assistants and aides[1]	16	26	11	VL	68.7	VH	0.0	4	VL
Pharmacy assistants[1]	47	52	5	VL	10.7	L	0.0	7	VL
Physical and corrective therapy assistants and aides	84	151	66	L	78.6	VH	0.0	25	VL
All other health service workers	160	192	33	L	20.4	H	0.0	31	VL
Personal service occupations	2,750	3,875	1,126	–	40.9	–	29.6	837	–
Amusement and recreation attendants	288	426	138	H	47.9	VH	1.1	135	L
Baggage porters and bellhops[1]	38	40	2	VL	5.4	VL	0.0	9	VL
Barbers	59	54	-6	VL	-9.6	VL	74.0	2	VL
Child care workers	830	1,129	299	VH	36.1	VH	57.5	322	H
Cosmetologists and related workers	641	720	78	–	12.2	–	42.0	79	–
Hairdressers, hairstylists, and cosmetologists	586	644	58	L	9.9	L	42.8	71	L
Manicurists	43	62	19	VL	44.7	VH	43.3	7	VL
Shampooers	13	13	1	VL	7.1	L	0.0	1	VL
Flight attendants	132	178	46	L	35.1	VH	0.0	8	VL
Homemaker-home health aides	697	1,247	5501	–	78.8	–	3.0	263	–
Home health aides	495	873	3781	VH	76.5	VH	4.2	180	H
Personal and home care aides[1]	202	374	171	H	84.7	VH	0.0	83	L
Ushers, lobby attendants, and ticket takers[1]	64	82	18	VL	28.4	VH	0.0	19	VL
Private household workers	802	681	-121	–	-15.1	–	0.1	250	–
Child care workers, private households[2]	275	250	-25	VL	-9.0	VL	0.0	117	L
Cleaners and servants, private household[1,2]	505	421	-84	VL	-16.7	VL	0.2	129	L
Cooks, private household[1,2]	8	3	-5	VL	-62.1	VL	0.0	2	VL
Housekeepers and butlers[1,2]	14	7	-7	VL	-50.7	VL	0.0	3	VL
Protective service occupations	2,523	2,980	457	–	18.1	–	0.4	398	–
Firefighting occupations	293	308	16	–	5.3	–	0.0	18	–
Fire fighters	225	238	14	VL	6.1	L	0.0	10	VL
Fire fighting and prevention supervisors[1]	54	54	1	VL	1.1	VL	0.0	7	VL
Fire inspection occupations[1]	14	16	1	VL	9.2	L	0.0	1	VL
Law enforcement occupations	1,024	1,217	193	–	18.9	–	0.0	110	–
Correction officers	320	423	103	H	32.3	VH	0.0	51	L
Police and detectives	704	793	90	–	12.7	–	0.0	59	–
Police and detective supervisors	90	89	-1	VL	-0.7	VL	0.0	10	VL

[1]One or more Current Population Survey (CPS) based occupations may be used to estimate CPS based data. See Table 2.

[2]Current Population Survey data used to determine median weekly earnings ranking.

NOTE: Rankings are based on employment in all detailed occupations in the National Industry-Occupation Matrix, For details, see "Data presented" section of text. Codes for describing the ranked variables are: H = Very high, H = High, L = Low, VL = Very low, n. a. = Data not available. A dash indicates data are not applicable.

Table 1. Occupational employment and job openings data, 1996-2006, and worker characteristics, 1996—Continued
(Numbers in thousands)

Number	Rank	Median hourly earnings	Unemployment rate	Percent part-time	Most significant source of training	1996 Matrix Occupation
74	VH	VL	VH	H	Short-term on-the-job-training	Janitors and cleaners, Including maids and housekeeping cleaners
2	VL	L	H	L	Moderate-term on-the-job-training	Pest controllers and assistants[1]
7	VL	L	VH	H	Short-term on-the-job-training	All other cleaning and building service workers[1]
479	–	–	–	–	–	Food preparation and service occupations
173	–	–	–	–	–	Chefs, cooks, and other kitchen workers
49	–	–	–	–	–	Cooks, except short order
9	VL	L	VH	VH	Moderate-term on-the-job-training	Bakers, bread and pastry
12	L	VL	VH	VH	Long-term on-the-job-training	Cooks, institution or cafeteria
28	L	VL	VH	VH	Long-term on-the-job-training	Cooks, restaurant
37	H	VL	VH	VH	Short-term on-the-job-training	Cooks, short order and fast food
87	VH	VL	VH	VH	Short-term on-the-job-training	Food preparation workers[1]
290						Food and beverage service occupations
15	L	VL	VH	VH	Short-term on-the-job-training	Bartenders
20	L	VL	VH	VH	Short-term on-the-job-training	Dining room and cafeteria attendants and bar helpers
125	VH	VL	VH	VH	Short-term on-the-job-training	Food counter, fountain, and related workers[1]
9	VL	VL	H	VH	Short-term on-the-job-training	Hosts and hostesses, restaurant, lounge, or coffee shop
120	VH	VL	VH	VH	Short-term on-the-job-training	Waiters and waitresses
15	L	VL	VH	VH	Short-term on-the-job-training	All other food preparation and service worker's
106	–	–	–	–	–	Health service occupations
1	VL	VL	L	H	Short-term on-the-job-training	Ambulance drivers and attendants, except EMTs
13	L	L	L	VH	Moderate-term on-the-job-training	Dental assistants
21	L	L	L	H	Moderate-term on-the-job-training	Medical assistants[1]
53	–	–	–	–	–	Nursing aides and psychiatric aides
51	H	VL	H	H	Short-term on-the-job-training	Nursing aides, orderlies, and attendants
2	VL	L	H	H	Short-term on-the-job-training	Psychiatric aides
1	VL	H	L	H	Moderate-term on-the-job-training	Occupational therapy assistants and aides[1]
1	VL	L	L	H	Short-term on-the-job-training	Pharmacy assistants[1]
9	VL	L	L	H	Moderate-term on-the-job-training	Physical and corrective therapy assistants and aides
7	VL	L	L	H	Short-term on-the-job-training	All other health service workers
162	–	–	–	–	–	Personal service occupations
19	L	VL	VH	VH	Short-term on-the-job-training	Amusement and recreation attendants
1	VL	VL	VH	VH	Short-term on-the-job-training	Baggage porters and bellhops[1]
2	VL	L	VL	H	Postsecondary vocational training	Barbers
39	H	VL	H	VH	Short-term on-the-job-training	Child care workers
25	–	–	–	–	–	Cosmetologists and related workers
21	L	VL	VL	VH	Postsecondary vocational training	Hairdressers, hairstylists, and cosmetologists
3	VL	VL	VL	VH	Postsecondary vocational training	Manicurists
0	VL	VL	VL	VH	Short-term on-the-job-training	Shampooers
8	VL	VH	VL	VH	Long-term on-the-job-training	Flight attendants
65	–	–	–	–	–	Homemaker-home health aides
44	H	L	H	H	Short-term on-the-job-training	Home health aides
21	L	VL	H	VH	Short-term on-the-job-training	Personal and home care aides[1]
3	VL	VL	VH	VH	Short-term on-the-job-training	Ushers, lobby attendants, and ticket takers[1]
25	–	–	–	–	–	Private household workers
14	L	VL	VH	VH	Short-term on-the-job-training	Child care workers, private households[2]
11	L	VL	VH	VH	Short-term on-the-job-training	Cleaners and servants, private household[1,2]
0	VL	VL	VH	VH	Moderate-term on-the-job-training	Cooks, private household[1,2]
0	VL	VL	VH	VH	Moderate-term on-the-job-training	Housekeepers and butlers[1,2]
116	–	–	–	–	–	Protective service occupations
13	–	–	–	–	–	Firefighting occupations
10	VL	H	VL	VL	Long-term on-the-job-training	Fire fighters
2	VL	VH	VL	VL	Work experience in a related occupation	Fire fighting and prevention supervisors[1]
1	VL	VH	VL	VL	Work experience in a related occupation	Fire inspection occupations[1]
46	–	–	–	–	–	Law enforcement occupations
15	L	H	VL	VL	Long-term on-the-job-training	Correction officers
31	–	–	–	–	–	Police and detectives
3	VL	VH	VL	VL	Work experience in a related occupation	Police and detective supervisors

[1]One or more Current Population Survey (CPS) based occupations may be used to estimate CPS based data. See Table 2.

[2]Current Population Survey data used to determine median weekly earnings ranking.

NOTE: Rankings are based on employment in all detailed occupations in the National Industry-Occupation Matrix. For details, see "Data presented" section of text. Codes for describing the ranked variables are: VH = Very high, H = High, L = Low, VL = Very low, n. a. = Data not available. A dash indicates data are not applicable.

Table 1. Occupational employment and job openings data, 1996-2006, and worker characteristics, 1996—Continued
(Numbers in thousands)

1996 Matrix Occupation	Employment		Employment change, 1996-2006				Percent self-employed, 1996	Annual average job openings due to growth and total replacement needs, 1996-2006	
			Numeric		Percent				
	1996	2006	Number	Rank	Number	Rank		Number	Rank
Police detectives and investigators	70	75	5	VL	7.8	L	0.0	6	VL
Police patrol officers	413	486	73	L	17.8	H	0.0	40	VL
Sheriffs and deputy sheriffs	88	96	8	VL	9.3	L	0.0	1	VL
Other law enforcement occupations	43	47	3	VL	7.7	L	0.0	2	VL
Other protective service workers	1,206	1,455	249	–	20.6	–	0.9	270	–
Detectives and investigators, except public................	58	69	1.1	VL	18.5	H	17.3	13	VL
Guards	955	1,175	221	H	23.1	VH	0.1	228	H
Crossing guards[1]	61	55	–6	VL	–9.2	VL	0.0	10	VL
All other protective service workers	133	156	23	L	17.2	H	0.0	18	VL
All other service workers[1]	1,112	1,453	341	VH	30.7	VH	9.9	302	H
Agriculture, forestry, fishing, and related occupations	3,785	3,823	37	–	1.0	–	39.0	660	–
Animal caretakers, except farm	130	158	28	L	21.4	VH	26.1	41	VL
Farm operator's and managers	1,292	1,175	–118	–	–9.1	–	86.0	126	–
Farmers[2]	1,109	997	–112	VL	–10.1	VL	99.8	115	L
Farm managers[2]	184	178	–6	VL	–3.2	VL	3.2	12	VL
Farm workers	873	798	–75	VL	–8.6	VL	4.2	160	L
Fishers, hunters, and trappers	47	37	–10	–	–20.7	–	72.1	10	–
Captains and other officers, fishing vessels[1,2]	8	7	0	VL	–4.4	VL	47.8	2	VL
Fishers, hunters, and trappers[1,2]	39	30	–9	VL	–23.9	VL	76.9	8	VL
Forestry and logging occupations	122	123	1	–	1.0	–	23.6	19	–
Forest and conservation workers[1]	40	41	1	VL	2.5	VL	3.1	7	VL
Timber cutting and fogging occupations	82	82	0	–	0.3	–	33.5	13	–
Fallers and buckers	17	16	–1	VL	–3.5	VL	36.8	2	VL
Logging tractor operators	21	22	1	VL	4.4	VL	6.2	4	VL
Log handling equipment operators	33	34	1	VL	3.1	VL	60.2	5	VL
All other timber cuffing and related logging workers	11	10	–1	VL	–10.3	VL	0.0	1	VL
Gardening, nursery, and greenhouse and lawn service occupations	925	1,105	180	–	19.5	–	23.6	225	–
Gardeners, nursery workers and laborers, landscaping and groundskeeping	817	975	158	H	19.4	H	21.5	206	H
Lawn service managers[1]	55	67	12	VL	22.2	VH	64.3	7	VL
Nursery and greenhouse managers[1]	10	12	2	VL	19.1	H	73.6	1	VL
Pruners	26	30	4	VL	16.2	H	0.0	6	VL
Sprayers/applicators	18	21	4	VL	21.2	VH	0.0	5	VL
Supervisors, farming, forestry, and agricultural related occupations[1]	88	92	4	VL	4.2	VL	9.0	10	VL
Veterinary assistants	33	42	9	VL	28.0	VH	0.0	11	VL
All other agricultural, forestry, fishing, and related workers[1]	275	293	18	VL	6.5	L	1.7	57	L
Precision production, craft, and repair occupations	14,446	15,448	1,002	–	6.9	–	11.0	1,960	–
Blue collar worker supervisors[1]	1,899	1,947	48	L	2.5	VL	9.9	169	H
Construction trades	3,710	4,014	304	–	8.2	–	22.7	640	–
Bricklayers and stone masons[1]	142	162	19	VL	13.6	L	22.3	27	VL
Carpenters	979	1,038	59	L	6.0	L	31.7	214	H
Carpet installers	64	72	8	VL	12.2	L	60.6	9	VL
Ceiling tile installers and acoustical carpenters	16	18	1	VL	8.7	L	0.0	4	VL
Concrete and terrazzo finishers	137	147	10	VL	7.4	L	8.0	14	VL
Drywall installers and finishers	133	140	7	VL	4.9	VL	29.4	26	VL
Electricians	575	627	52	L	9.1	L	10.6	80	L
Glaziers[1]	36	38	2	VL	5.3	VL	11.6	6	VL
Hard tile setters[1]	29	30	1	VL	4.1	VL	45.1	5	VL
Highway maintenance workers	171	158	–14	VL	–7.9	VL	0.0	19	VL
Insulation workers	65	78	13	VL	19.3	H	1.5	8	VL
Painters and paperhangers, construction and maintenance	444	509	66	L	14.8	H	41.6	86	L
Paving, surfacing, and tamping equipment operators[1]	79	103	24	L	29.9	VH	1.5	18	VL
Pipelayers and pipelaying fitters	62	66	4	VL	5.7	L	10.9	8	VL

[1]One or more Current Population Survey (CPS) based occupations may be used to estimate CPS based data. See Table 2.

[2]Current Population Survey data used to determine median weekly earnings ranking.

NOTE: Rankings are based on employment in all detailed occupations in the National Industry-Occupation Matrix. For details, see "Data presented" section of text. Codes for describing the ranked variables are: VH = Very high, H = High, L = Low, VL = Very low, n. a. = Data not available. A dash indicates data are not applicable.

Table 1. Occupational employment and job openings data, 1996-2006, and worker characteristics, 1996—Continued
(Numbers in thousands)

Annual average job openings due to growth and total replacement needs, 1996-2006		Median hourly earnings	Unemployment rate	Percent part-time	Most significant source of training	1996 Matrix Occupation
Number	Rank					
3	VL	VH	VL	VL	Work experience In a related occupation	Police detectives and investigators
22	L	VH	VL	VL	Long-term on-the-job-training	Police patrol officers
2	VL	H	VL	VL	Long-term on-the-job-training	Sheriffs and deputy sheriffs
1	VL	H	VL	VL	Moderate-term on-the-job-training	Other law enforcement occupations
57	–	–	–	–	–	Other protective service workers
2	VL	L	VH	H	Moderate-term on-the-job-training	Detectives and investigators, except public
42	H	VL	VH	H	Short-term on-the-job-training	Guards
2	VL	VL	VH	H	Short-term on-the-job-training	Crossing guards[1]
11	L	L	VH	VH	Short-term on-the-job-training	All other protective service workers
62	H	L	H	H	Work experience in a related occupation	All other service workers[1]
112	–	–	–	–	–	**Agriculture, forestry, fishing, and related occupations**
6	VL	VL	L	VH	Short-term on-the-job-training	Animal caretakers, except farm
25	–	–	–	–	–	Farm operators and managers
21	L	VL	VL	VH	Long-term on-the-job-training	Farmers[2]
4	VL	L	VL	H	Work experience plus degree	Farm managers[2]
24	L	VL	VH	VH	Short-term on-the-job-training	Farm workers
1	–	–	–	–	–	Fishers, hunters, and trappers
0	VL	L	VH	VH	Work experience in a related occupation	Captains and other officers, fishing vessels[1,2]
1	VL	VL	VH	VH	Short-term on-the-job-training	Fishers, hunters, and trappers[1,2]
4	–	–	–	–	–	Forestry and logging occupations
1	VL	L	VH	H	Short-term on-the-job-training	Forest and conservation workers[1]
2	–	–	–	–	–	Timber cutting and logging occupations
1	VL	H	VH	H	Short-term on-the-job-training	Fallers and buckers
1	VL	L	H	VL	Short-term on-the-job-training	Logging tractor operators
1	VL	H	VH	H	Short-term on-the-job-training	Log handling equipment operators
0	VL	H	VH	H	Short-term on-the-job-training	All other timber cutting and related logging workers
40	–	–	–	–	–	Gardening, nursery, and greenhouse and lawn service occupations
36	H	L	VH	VH	Short-term on-the-job-training	Gardeners, nursery workers and laborers. landscaping and groundskeeping
2	VL	H	L	L	Work experience in a related occupation	Lawn service managers[1]
0	VL	L	L	L	Work experience in a related occupation	Nursery and greenhouse managers[1]
1	VL	L	VH	VH	Short-term on-the-job-training	Pruners
1	VL	L	VH	VH	Moderate-term on-the-job-training	Sprayers/applicators
2	VL	H	H	H	Work experience in a related occupation	Supervisors, farming, forestry, and agricultural related occupations[1]
2	VL	VL	L	VH	Short-term on-the-job-training	Veterinary assistants
9	VL	VL	VH	H	Short-term on-the-job-training	All other agricultural, forestry, fishing, and related workers[1]
435	–	–	–	–	–	**Precision production, craft, and repair occupations**
47	H	VH	L	VL	Work experience in a related occupation	Blue collar worker supervisors[1]
113	–	–	–	–	–	Construction trades
4	VL	VH	VH	L	Long-term on-the-job-training	Bricklayers and stone masons[1]
23	L	H	VH	L	Long-term on-the-job-training	Carpenters
3	VL	H	H	H	Moderate-term on-the-job-training	Carpet installers
0	VL	H	VH	L	Moderate-term on-the-job-training	Ceiling tile installers and acoustical carpenters
4	VL	H	VH	L	Long-term on-the-job-training	Concrete and terrazzo finishers
5	VL	H	VH	L	Moderate-term on-the-job-training	Drywall installers and finishers
17	L	VH	H	VL	Long-term on-the-job-training	Electricians
1	VL	H	VH	L	Long-term on-the-job-training	Glaziers[1]
1	VL	VH	VH	H	Long-term on-the-job-training	Hard tile setters[1]
5	VL	H	VH	L	Short-term on-the-job-training	Highway maintenance workers
3	VL	H	VH	VL	Moderate-term on-the-job-training	Insulation workers
16	L	H	VH	L	Moderate-term on-the-job-training	Painters and paperhangers, construction and maintenance
4	VL	H	VH	L	Moderate-term on-the-job-training	Paving, surfacing, and tamping equipment operators[1]
2	VL	H	VH	L	Moderate-term on-the-job-training	Pipelayers and pipelaying fitters

[1]One or more Current Population Survey (CPS) based occupations may be used to estimate CPS based data. See Table 2.

[2]Current Population Survey data used to determine median weekly earnings ranking.

NOTE: Rankings are based on employment in all detailed occupations in the National Industry-Occupation Matrix. For details, see "Data presented" section of text. Codes for describing the ranked variables are: VH = Very high, H = High, L = Low, VL = Very low, n. a. = Data not available. A dash indicates data are not applicable.

Table 1. Occupational employment and job openings data, 1996-2006, and worker characteristics, 1996—Continued
(Numbers in thousands)

1996 Matrix Occupation	Employment		Employment change, 1996-2006				Percent self-em-ployed, 1996	Annual average job openings due to growth and total replacement needs, 1996-2006	
			Numeric		Percent				
	1996	2006	Number	Rank	Number	Rank		Number	Rank
Plasterers[1]	32	36	4	VL	13.3	L	22.0	6	VL
Plumbers, pipefitters, and steamfitters	389	406	18	VL	4.5	VL	18.2	53	L
Roofers	138	144	6	VL	4.3	VL	29.5	23	VL
Structural and reinforcing metal workers	67	73	6	VL	9.0	L	2.9	12	VL
All other construction trades workers[1]	150	169	19	VL	12.5	L	13.6	21	VL
Extractive and related workers, including blasters	220	220	0	–	–0.1	–	1.6	16	–
Oil and gas extraction occupations	65	53	–13	–	–19.2	–	0.0	3	–
Roustabouts[1]	28	18	–9	VL	–33.7	VL	0.0	1	VL
All other oil and gas extraction occupations[1]	37	34	–3	VL	–8.4	VL	0.0	2	VL
Mining, quarrying, and tunneling occupations[1]	16	12	–4	VL	–25.8	VL	0.0	1	VL
All other extraction and related workers[1]	138	155	17	VL	12.0	L	2.6	12	VL
Mechanics, installers, and repairers	5,233	5,889	656	–	12.5	–	7.7	717	–
Communications equipment mechanics, installers, and repairers	116	121	5	–	4.3	–	2.7	9	–
Central office and PBX installers and repairers[1]	81	85	4	VL	5.2	VL	3.8	6	VL
Radio mechanics	8	7	–1	VL	–7.2	VL	0.0	1	VL
All other communications equipment mechanics, installers, and repairers[1]	27	28	1	VL	5.1	VL	0.0	3	VL
Electrical and electronic equipment mechanics, installers, and repairers	562	627	66	–	11.7	–	3.2	62	–
Data processing equipment repairers	80	121	42	L	52.3	VH	4.6	21	VL
Electrical powerline installers and repairers	108	111	3	VL	3.0	VL	1.5	6	VL
Electronic home entertainment equipment repairers	33	27	–6	VL	–19.0	VL	14.5	3	VL
Electronics repairers, commercial and industrial equipment	60	67	7	VL	11.8	L	10.6	8	VL
Station installers and repairers, telephone[1]	37	10	–27	VL	–73.5	VL	0.0	1	VL
Telephone and cable TV line installers and repairers[1]	201	242	41	L	20.5	H	0.0	18	VL
All other electrical and electronic equipment mechanics, installers, and repairers[1]	44	50	6	VL	13.0	L	3.5	4	VL
Machinery and related mechanics, installers, and repairers	1,899	2,173	274	–	14.4	–	3.1	261	–
Industrial machinery mechanics[1]	459	489	30	L	6.6	L	2.9	33	VL
Maintenance repairers, general utility	1,362	1,608	246	H	18.0	H	3.2	223	H
Millwrights	78	76	–2	VL	–2.2	VL	0.9	5	VL
Vehicle and mobile equipment mechanics and repairers	1,597	1,764	168	–	10.5	–	15.1	209	–
Aircraft mechanics, including engine specialists	137	155	18	–	13.2	–	1.9	12	–
Aircraft engine specialists[1]	25	27	2	VL	8.9	L	6.3	2	VL
Aircraft mechanics[1]	112	128	16	VL	14.2	H	0.9	10	VL
Automotive body and related repairers	225	254	29	L	12.8	L	19.1	32	VL
Automotive mechanics[1]	775	871	96	L	12.4	L	20.4	112	L
Bus and truck mechanics and diesel engine specialists	266	288	22	L	8.2	L	6.8	22	VL
Farm equipment mechanics[1]	44	37	–7	VL	–15.9	VL	7.1	6	VL
Mobile heavy equipment mechanics	104	111	7	VL	6.5	L	4.8	18	VL
Motorcycle, boat, and small engine mechanics	45	49	3	–	7.1	–	25.8	7	–
Motorcycle repairers[1]	12	13	1	VL	5.7	L	22.1	2	VL
Small engine specialists[1]	34	36	3	VL	7.6	L	27.1	5	VL
Other mechanics, installers, and repairers	1,695	1,814	119	–	7.0	–	4.7	266	–
Bicycle repairers	13	17	4	VL	33.5	VH	0.0	2	VL
Camera and photographic equipment repairers[1]	14	18	3	VL	24.0	VH	53.1	3	VL
Coin and vending machine servicers and repairers	21	19	–1	VL	–6.5	VL	0.0	3	VL
Electric meter installers and repairers[1]	12	8	–4	VL	–33.7	VL	0.0	1	VL
Electromedical and biomedical equipment repairers	10	11	1	VL	11.7	L	0.0	1	VL
Elevator installers and repairers[1]	25	27	2	VL	8.0	L	0.0	4	VL
Heat, air conditioning, and refrigeration mechanics and installers	256	300	44	L	17.0	H	14.9	27	VL
Home appliance and power tool repairers[1]	71	73	2	VL	3.5	VL	8.7	10	VL
Locksmiths and safe repairers[1]	25	29	4	VL	15.0	H	39.0	4	VL
Musical instrument repairers and tuners[1]	9	10	1	VL	7.4	L	51.5	1	VL
Office machine and cash register servicers	62	73	11	VL	17.8	H	4.8	3	VL
Precision instrument repairers[1]	38	38	–1	VL	–2.2	VL	0.0	6	VL
Riggers	9	8	–2	VL	–18.3	VL	0.0	1	VL
Tire repairers and changers	94	101	7	VL	7.0	L	1.7	29	VL

[1]One or more Current Population Survey (CPS) based occupations may be used to estimate CPS based data. See Table 2.
NOTE: Rankings are based on employment in all detailed occupations in the National Industry-Occupation Matrix. For details, see "Data presented" section of text. Codes for describing the ranked variables are: VH = Very high, H = High, L = Low, VL = Very low, n. a. = Data not available. A dash indicates data are not applicable.

Table 1. Occupational employment and job openings data, 1996-2006, and worker characteristics, 1996—Continued
(Numbers in thousands)

Annual average job openings due to growth and total replacement needs, 1996-2006		Median hourly earnings	Unemployment rate	Percent part-time	Most significant source of training	1996 Matrix Occupation
Number	Rank					
1	VL	H	VH	L	Long-term on-the-job-training	Plasterers[1]
10	L	VH	H	VL	Long-term on-the-job-training	Plumbers, pipefitters, and steamfitters
5	VL	H	VH	H	Moderate-term on-the-job-training	Roofers
2	VL	VH	VH	VL	Long-term on-the-job-training	Structural and reinforcing metal workers
6	VL	H	VH	L	Moderate-term on-the-job-training	All other construction trades workers[1]
6	–	–	–	–	–	Extractive and related workers, including blasters
1	–	–	–	–	–	Oil and gas extraction occupations
1	VL	L	H	L	Short-term on-the-job-training	Roustabouts[1]
1	VL	L	H	L	Moderate-term on-the-job-training	All other oil and gas extraction occupations[1]
0	VL	H	H	L	Long-term on-the-job-training	Mining, quarrying, and tunneling occupations[1]
4	VL	H	VH	L	Moderate-term on-the-job-training	All other extraction and related workers[1]
190	–	–	–	–	–	Mechanics, installers, and repairers
3	–	–	–	–	–	Communications equipment mechanics, installers, and repairers
2	VL	VH	VL	VL	Postsecondary vocational training	Central office and PBX installers and repairers[1]
0	VL	H	L	VL	Postsecondary vocational training	Radio mechanics
1	VL	VH	L	VL	Postsecondary vocational training	All other communications equipment mechanics, installers, and repairers[1]
22	–	–	–	–	–	Electrical and electronic equipment mechanics, installers, and repairers
7	VL	H	L	VL	Postsecondary vocational training	Data processing equipment repairers
3	VL	VH	VL	VL	Long-term on-the-job-training	Electrical powerline installers and repairers
1	VL	H	L	VL	Postsecondary vocational training	Electronic home entertainment equipment repairers
2	VL	VH	L	VL	Postsecondary vocational training	Electronics repairers, commercial and industrial equipment
1	VL	VH	VL	VL	Postsecondary vocational training	Station Installers and repairers, telephone[1]
8	VL	H	VL	VL	Long-term on-the-job-training	Telephone and cable TV line installers and repairers[1]
2	VL	H	L	VL	Postsecondary vocational training	All other electrical and electronic equipment mechanics, installers, and repairers
67	–	–	–	–	–	Machinery and related mechanics, installers, and repairers
13	L	H	L	VL	Long-term on-the-job-training	Industrial machinery mechanics[1]
52	H	L	L	L	Long-term on-the-job-training	Maintenance repairers, general utility
2	VL	VH	H	VL	Long-term on-the-job-training	Millwrights
58	–	–	–	–	–	Vehicle and mobile equipment mechanics and repairers
5	–	–	–	–	–	Aircraft mechanics, including engine specialists
1	VL	H	L	VL	Postsecondary vocational training	Aircraft engine specialists[1]
4	VL	VH	L	VL	Postsecondary vocational training	Aircraft mechanics[1]
10	VL	H	L	L	Long-term on-the-job-training	Automotive body and related repairers
30	L	H	H	L	Postsecondary vocational training	Automotive mechanics[1]
8	VL	H	L	VL	Long-term on-the-job-training	Bus and truck mechanics and diesel engine specialists
1	VL	L	L	VL	Long-term on-the-job-training	Farm equipment mechanics[1]
3	VL	H	L	VL	Long-term on-the-job-training	Mobile heavy equipment mechanics
1	–	–	–	–	–	Motorcycle, boat, and small engine mechanics
0	VL	H	L	L	Long-term on-the-job-training	Motorcycle repairers[1]
1	VL	L	L	L	Long-term on-the-job-training	Small engine specialists[1]
38	–	–	–	–	–	Other mechanics, installers, and repairers
1	VL	VL	L	L	Moderate-term on-the-job-training	Bicycle repairers[1]
1	VL	H	L	VL	Moderate-term on-the-job-training	Camera and photographic equipment repairers[1]
0	VL	L	L	L	Long-term on-the-job-training	Coin and vending machine servicers and repairers
0	VL	VH	L	VL	Long-term on-the-job-training	Electric meter installers and repairers[1]
0	VL	H	L	L	Long-term on-the-job-training	Electromedical and biomedical equipment repairers
1	VL	VH	L	VL	Long-term on-the-job-training	Elevator installers and repairers[1]
10	L	H	L	VL	Long-term on-the-job-training	Heat, air conditioning, and refrigeration mechanics and installers
2	VL	H	L	VL	Long-term on-the-job-training	Home appliance and power tool repairers[1]
1	VL	H	L	VL	Moderate-term on-the-job-training	Locksmiths and safe repairers[1]
0	VL	L	L	VL	Long-term on-the-job-training	Musical instrument repairers and tuners[1]
3	VL	H	VL	VL	Long-term on-the-job-training	Office machine and cash register servicers
1	VL	VH	L	VL	Long-term on-the-job-training	Precision instrument repairers[1]
0	VL	H	L	L	Long-term on-the-job-training	Riggers
4	VL	VL	VH	H	Short-term on-the-job-training	Tire repairers and changers

[1]One or more Current Population Survey (CPS) based occupations may be used to estimate CPS based data. See Table 2.
NOTE: Rankings are based on employment in all detailed occupations in the National Industry-Occupation Matrix. For details, see "Data presented" section of text. Codes for describing the ranked variables are: VH = Very high, H = High, L = Low, VL = Very low, n. a. = Data not available. A dash indicates data are not applicable.

Table 1. Occupational employment and job openings data, 1996-2006, and worker characteristics, 1996—Continued
(Numbers in thousands)

1996 Matrix Occupation	Employment 1996	Employment 2006	Numeric Number	Numeric Rank	Percent Number	Percent Rank	Percent self-employed, 1996	Annual average job openings Number	Annual average job openings Rank
Watchmakers[1]	7	7	0	VL	−5.1	VL	53.5	1	VL
All other mechanics, installers, and repairers[1]	394	467	73	L	18.4	H	1.4	78	L
Production occupations, precision	3,054	3,016	−38	–	−1.2	–	5.2	387	–
Assemblers, precision	380	383	3	–	0.7	–	0.0	61	–
Aircraft assemblers, precision[1]	25	27	2	VL	9.9	L	0.0	3	VL
Electrical and electronic equipment assemblers, precision	194	193	−1	VL	−0.6	VL	0.0	35	VL
Electromechanical equipment assemblers, precision	51	51	0	VL	0.6	VL	0.0	9	VL
Fitters, structural metal, precision[1]	15	12	−3	VL	−18.3	VL	0.0	2	VL
Machine builders and other precision machine assemblers[1]	57	58	1	VL	1.6	VL	0.0	7	VL
All other precision assemblers[1]	38	41	3	VL	8.2	L	0.0	5	VL
Food workers, precision	299	301	2	–	0.6	–	2.3	36	–
Bakers, manufacturing	44	47	3	VL	7.0	L	7.3	9	VL
Butchers and meatcutters	217	205	−12	VL	−5.7	VL	1.2	18	VL
All other precision food and tobacco workers[1]	38	49	1.1	VL	29.3	VH	2.7	8	VL
Inspectors, testers, and graders, precision	634	610	−24	VL	−3.8	VL	0.7	90	L
Metal workers, precision[1]	934	924	−10	–	−1.1	–	3.9	88	–
Boilermakers[1]	18	18	−1	VL	−3.2	VL	5.5	2	VL
Jewelers and silversmiths[1]	32	31	−1	VL	−1.7	VL	36.3	4	VL
Machinists	386	384	−2	VL	−0.5	VL	1.6	35	VL
Sheet metal workers and duct installers[1]	237	236	−1	VL	−0.4	VL	2.9	19	VL
Shipfitters[1]	9	9	0	VL	−0.6	VL	0.0	1	VL
Tool and die makers	134	124	−9	VL	−7.0	VL	0.9	14	VL
All other precision metal workers[1]	117	120	3	VL	2.9	VL	8.6	13	VL
Printing workers, precision	141	124	−17	–	−12.1	–	0.0	24	–
Bookbinders[1]	4	4	−1	VL	−15.0	VL	0.0	1	VL
Prepress printing workers, precision	123	106	−16	–	−13.4	–	0.0	21	–
Compositors and typesetters, precision[1]	6	3	−3	VL	−50.3	VL	0.0	1	VL
Job printers	15	15	1	VL	4.9	VL	0.0	2	VL
Paste-up workers[1]	15	4	−11	VL	−75.0	VL	0.0	2	VL
Desktop publishing specialists[1]	30	53	22	L	73.5	VH	0.0	9	VL
Photoengravers[1]	5	3	−2	VL	−35.8	VL	0.0	1	VL
Camera operators[1]	11	10	−2	VL	−14.9	VL	0.0	2	VL
Film strippers, printing[1]	26	7	−20	VL	−75.0	VL	0.0	3	VL
Platemakers[1]	14	12	−2	VL	−15.1	VL	0.0	2	VL
All other printing workers, precision[1]	13	14	0	VL	1.1	VL	0.0	2	VL
Textile, apparel, and furnishings workers, precision	230	212	−18	–	−7.7	–	30.1	22	–
Custom tailors and sewers	87	73	−15	VL	−16.7	VL	51.5	7	VL
Patternmakers and layout workers, fabric and apparel[1]	14	14	0	VL	−3.3	VL	0.0	1	VL
Shoe and leather workers and repairers, precision[1]	21	17	−4	VL	−20.1	VL	28.5	2	VL
Upholsterers[1]	57	57	0	VL	0.4	VL	28.1	5	VL
All other precision textile, apparel, and furnishings workers[1]	50	51	1	VL	2.8	VL	4.4	8	VL
Woodworkers, precision	229	249	19	–	8.4	–	11.3	37	–
Cabinetmakers and bench carpenters	121	128	7	VL	6.1	L	16.5	20	VL
Furniture finishers[1]	30	33	3	VL	11.5	L	20.2	5	VL
Wood machinists	45	51	6	VL	13.9	L	0.0	8	VL
All other precision woodworkers[1]	33	36	2	VL	6.8	L	0.0	5	VL
Other precision workers	206	213	7	–	3.3	–	7.1	30	–
Dental laboratory technicians, precision	47	48	0	VL	0.7	VL	14.4	4	VL
Optical goods workers, precision	19	19	0	VL	0.4	VL	0.0	1	VL
Photographic process workers, precision	14	14	0	VL	−2.7	VL	28.4	3	VL
All other precision workers	126	133	7	VL	5.4	VL	3.0	22	VL
Plant and system occupations	330	362	32	–	9.9	–	0.0	31	–
Chemical plant and system operators[1]	36	36	0	VL	−0.8	VL	0.0	2	VL
Electric power generating plant operators, distributors, and dispatchers	47	49	2	–	4.3	–	0.0	3	–
Power distributors and dispatchers[1]	15	15	−1	VL	−3.7	VL	0.0	1	VL
Power generating and reactor plant operators[1]	31	34	3	VL	8.3	L	0.0	2	VL
Gas and petroleum plant and system occupations[1]	33	29	−3	VL	−10.5	VL	0.0	2	VL
Stationary engineers	27	26	−2	VL	−5.9	VL	0.0	2	VL

[1]One or more Current Population Survey (CPS) based occupations may be used to estimate CPS based data. See Table 2.
NOTE: Rankings are based on employment in all detailed occupations In the National Industry-Occupation Matrix. For details, see "Data presented" section of text. Codes for describing the ranked variables are: VH = Very high, H = High, L = Low, VL = Very low, n. a. = Data not available, A dash indicates data are not applicable.

Table 1. Occupational employment and job openings data, 1996-2006, and worker characteristics, 1996—Continued
(Numbers in thousands)

Annual average job openings due to growth and total replacement needs, 1996-2006		Median hourly earnings	Unemployment rate	Percent part-time	Most significant source of training	1996 Matrix Occupation
Number	Rank					
0	VL	H	L	VL	Long-term on-the-job-training	Watchmakers[1]
15	L	H	L	VL	Long-term on-the-job-training	All other mechanics, installers, and repairers[1]
68	–	–	–	–	–	Production occupations, precision
9	–	–	–	–		Assemblers, precision
1	VL	VH	L	VL	Work experience in a related occupation	Aircraft assemblers, precision[1]
5	VL	L	H	VL	Work experience in a related occupation	Electrical and electronic equipment assemblers, precision
1	VL	L	H	VL	Work experience in a related occupation	Electromechanical equipment assemblers, precision
0	VL	H	L	VL	Work experience in a related occupation	Fitters, structural metal, precision[1]
1	VL	H	L	VL	Work experience in a related occupation	Machine builders and other precision machine assemblers[1]
1	VL	L	L	VL	Work experience in a related occupation	All other precision assemblers[1]
9	–	–	–	–		Food workers, precision
1	VL	L	H	H	Moderate-term on-the-job-training	Bakers, manufacturing
6	VL	L	H	VL	Long-term on-the-job-training	Butchers and meatcutters
2	VL	H	H	L	Long-term on-the-job-training	All other precision food and tobacco workers[1]
12	L	L	H	VL	Work experience in a related occupation	Inspectors, testers, and graders, precision
20	–	–	–	–	–	Metal workers, precision[1]
0	VL	VH	L	VL	Long-term on-the-job-training	Boilermakers[1]
1	VL	L	H	H	Postsecondary vocational training	Jewelers and silversmiths[1]
9	VL	H	L	VL	Long-term on-the-job-training	Machinists
5	VL	H	VH	VL	Moderate-term on-the-job-training	Sheet metal workers and duct installers[1]
0	VL	H	L	VL	Long-term on-the-job-training	Shipfitters[1]
2	VL	VH	VL	VL	Long-term on-the-job-training	Tool and die makers
3	VL	H	L	VL	Long-term on-the-job-training	All other precision metal workers[1]
4	–	–	–	–	–	Printing workers, precision
0	VL	H	H	VL	Moderate-term on-the-job-training	Bookbinders[1]
4	–	–	–	–		Prepress printing workers, precision
0	VL	L	H	VL	Long-term on-the-job-training	Compositors and typesetters, precision[1]
0	VL	H	L	VL	Long-term on-the-job-training	Job printers
0	VL	L	H	VL	Long-term on-the-job-training	Paste-up workers[1]
3	VL	H	H	VL	Long-term on-the-job-training	Desktop publishing specialists[1]
0	VL	H	H	VL	Long-term on-the-job-training	Photoengravers[1]
0	VL	H	H	VL	Long-term on-the-job-training	Camera operators[1]
0	VL	H	H	VL	Long-term on-the-job-training	Film strippers, printing[1]
0	VL	H	H	VL	Long-term on-the-job-training	Platemakers[1]
0	VL	H	H	VL	Long-term on-the-job-training	All other printing workers, precision[1]
3	–	–	–	–		Textile, apparel, and furnishings workers, precision
1	VL	L	H	VH	Work experience in a related occupation	Custom tailors and sewers
0	VL	L	H	H	Long-term on-the-job-training	Patternmakers and layout workers, fabric and apparel[1]
0	VL	L	H	H	Long-term on-the-job-training	Shoe and leather workers and repairers, precision[1]
1	VL	L	L	H	Long-term on-the-job-training	Upholsterers[1]
1	VL	VL	VH	H	Long-term on-the-job-training	All other precision textile, apparel, and furnishings workers[1]
5	–	–	–	–	–	Woodworkers, precision
2	VL	L	L	L	Long-term on-the-job-training	Cabinetmakers and bench carpenters
1	VL	L	L	L	Long-term on-the-job-training	Furniture finishers[1]
1	VL	L	L	L	Long-term on-the-job-training	Wood machinists
1	VL	H	L	L	Long-term on-the-job-training	All other precision woodworkers[1]
6	–	–	–	–	–	Other precision workers
1	VL	H	VL	H	Long-term on-the-job-training	Dental laboratory technicians, precision
0	VL	L	L	L	Long-term on-the-job-training	Optical goods workers, precision
0	VL	L	H	H	Moderate-term on-the-job-training	Photographic process workers, precision
4	VL	L	H	VL	Long-term on-the-job-training	All other precision workers
11	–	–	–	–	–	Plant and system occupations
1	VL	VH	VL	VL	Long-term on-the-job-training	Chemical plant and system operators[1]
1	–	–	–	–	–	Electric power generating plant operators, distributors, and dispatchers
0	VL	VH	VL	VL	Long-term on-the-job-training	Power distributors and dispatchers[1]
1	VL	VH	VL	VL	Long-term on-the-job-training	Power generating and reactor plant operators[1]
1	VL	VH	VL	VL	Long-term on-the-job-training	Gas and petroleum plant and system occupations[1]
1	VL	VH	VL	VL	Long-term on-the-job-training	Stationary engineers

[1]One or more Current Population Survey (CPS) based occupations may be used to estimate CPS based data. See Table 2.
NOTE: Rankings are based on employment in all detailed occupations in the National Industry-Occupation Matrix. For details, see "Data presented" section of text. Codes for describing the ranked variables are: VH = Very high, H = High, L = Low, VL = Very low, n. a. = Data not available. A dash indicates data are not applicable.

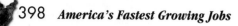

Table 1. Occupational employment and job openings data, 1996-2006, and worker characteristics, 1996—Continued
(Numbers in thousands)

1996 Matrix Occupation	Employment		Employment change, 1996-2006				Percent self-em-ployed, 1996	Annual average job openings due to growth and total replacement needs, 1996-2006	
			Numeric		Percent				
	1996	2006	Number	Rank	Number	Rank		Number	Rank
Water and liquid waste treatment plant and system operators	98	121	23	L	23.2	VH	0.0	14	VL
All other plant and system operators[1]	88	101	13	VL	14.8	H	0.0	8	VL
Operators, fabricators, and laborers	17,843	19,365	1,522	–	8.5	–	3,5	3,748	–
Machine setters, set-up operators, operators, and tenders	4,898	4,956	58	–	1.2	–	2.0	773	–
Numerical control machine tool operators and tenders, metal and plastic[1]	92	117	25	L	27.4	VH	0.0	21	VL
Combination machine tool setters, set-up operators, operators, and tenders[1]	96	113	17	VL	17.8	H	0.0	20	VL
Machine tool cut and form setters, operators, and tenders, metal and plastic	723	677	−46	–	−6.4	–	0.3	81	–
Drilling and boring machine tool setters and set-up operators, metal and plastic[1]	46	36	−10	VL	−22.0	VL	0.0	7	VL
Grinding machine setters and set-up operators, metal and plastic	63	56	−7	VL	−11.4	VL	3.2	3	VL
Lathe and turning machine tool setters and set-up operators, metal and plastic[1]	71	61	−10	VL	−13.7	VL	0.0	11	VL
Machine forming operators and tenders, metal and plastic	174	168	−6	VL	−3.2	VL	0,0	17	VL
Machine tool cutting operators and tenders, metal and plastic ...	127	105	−22	VL	−17.4	VL	0.0	7	VL
Punching machine setters and set-up operators, metal and plastic	51	47	−4	VL	−8.3	VL	0.0	6	VL
All other machine tool setters, set-up operators, metal and plastic[1]	191	204	13	VL	6.7	L	0.0	29	VL
Metal fabricating machine setters, operators, and related workers	157	162	5	–	3.3	–	0.0	20	–
Metal fabricators, structural metal products[1]	46	50	5	VL	10.6	L	0.0	9	VL
Soldering and brazing machine operators and tenders[1]	11	11	0	VL	0.6	VL	0.0	2	VL
Welding machine setters, operators, and tenders	100	101	0	VL	0.3	VL	0.0	9	VL
Metal and plastic processing machine setters, operators, and related workers	466	528	62	–	13.4	–	0.0	56	–
Electrolytic plating machine operators and tenders, setters and set-up operators, metal and plastic[1]	42	46	4	VL	10.4	L	0.0	5	VL
Foundry mold assembly and shakeout workers	10	10	0	VL	−4.0	VL	0.0	1	VL
Furnace operators and tenders[1]	21	20	−1	VL	−4.6	VL	0.0	2	VL
Heat treating machine operators and tenders, metal and plastic[1]	21	20	−1	VL	−3.7	VL	0.0	2	VL
Metal molding machine operators and tenders, setters and set-up operators	45	49	4	VL	9.1	L	0.0	5	VL
Plastic molding machine operators and tenders, setters and set-up operators	183	216	34	L	18.3	H	0.0	23	VL
All other metal and plastic machine setters, operators, and related workers[1]	144	167	23	L	15.6	H	0.0	18	VL
Printing, binding, and related workers	383	394	11	–	2.9	–	2.8	61	–
Bindery machine operators and set-up operators[1]	81	85	4	VL	4.9	VL	0.0	14	VL
Prepress printing workers, production	19	8	−11	–	−56.2	–	0.0	2	–
Photoengraving and lithographic machine operators and tenders[1]	6	5	−1	VL	−9.5	VL	0.0	1	VL
Typesetting and composing machine operators and tenders[1] ..	14	3	−10	VL	−75.1	VL	0.0	1	VL
Printing press operators	215	226	11	–	5.0	–	5.0	33	–
Letterpress operators	14	9	−5	VL	−34.8	VL	0.0	2	VL
Offset lithographic press operators	76	80	4	VL	5.9	L	6.0	12	VL
Printing press machine setters, operators and tenders	119	129	10	VL	8.6	L	5.1	19	VL
All other printing press setters and set-up operators	6	7	1	VL	14.4	H	0.0	1	VL
Screen printing machine setters and set-up operators	29	31	2	VL	6.1	L	0.0	4	VL
All other printing, binding, and related workers[1]	38	44	5	VL	14.0	L	0.0	7	VL
Textile and related setters, operators, and related workers	933	777	−156	–	−16.7	–	2.8	120	–
Extruding and forming machine operators and tenders, synthetic or glass fibers[1]	22	24	2	VL	9.7	L	0.0	4	VL
Pressing machine operators and tenders, textile, garment, and related materials	78	80	3	VL	3.5	VL	0.0	12	VL

[1]One or more Current Population Survey (CPS) based occupations may be used to estimate CPS based data. See Table 2.
NOTE: Rankings are based on employment in all detailed occupations in the National Industry-Occupation Matrix. For details, see "Data presented" section of text. Codes for describing the ranked variables are: VH = Very high, H = High, L = Low, VL = Very low, n. a. = Data not available. A dash indicates data are not applicable.

Table 1. Occupational employment and job openings data, 1996-2006. and worker characteristics, 1996—Continued
(Numbers in thousands)

Annual average job openings due to growth and total replacement needs, 1996-2006		Median hourly earnings	Unem- ployment rate	Per- cent part- time	Most significant source of training	1996 Matrix Occupation
Number	Rank					
4	VL	H	VL	VL	Long-term on-the-job-training	Water and liquid waste treatment plant and system operators
4	VL	L	VL	VL	Long-term on-the-job-training	All other plant and system operators[1]
590	–	–	–	–	–	**Operators, fabricators, and laborers**
138	–	–	–	–	–	Machine setters, set-up operators, operators, and tenders
						Numerical control machine tool operators and tenders, metal
4	VL	H	H	VL	Moderate-term on-the-job-training	and plastic[1]
						Combination machine tool setters, set-up operators, operators,
3	VL	L	H	VL	Moderate-term on-the-job-training	and tenders[1]
						Machine tool cut and form setters, operators, and tenders,
17	–	–	–	–	–	metal and plastic
						Drilling and boring machine tool setters and set-up operators,
1	VL	H	H	VL	Moderate-term on-the-job-training	metal and plastic[1]
						Grinding machine setters and set-up operators, metal and
1	VL	H	H	VL	Moderate-term on-the-job-training	plastic
						Lathe and turning machine tool setters and set-up operators,
1	VL	H	H	VL	Moderate-term on-the-job-training	metal and plastic[1]
5	VL	L	H	VL	Moderate-term on-the-job-training	Machine forming operators and tenders, metal and plastic[1]
3	VL	L	L	VL	Moderate-term on-the-job-training	Machine tool cutting operator's and tenders, metal and plastic
						Punching machine setters and set-up operators, metal and
1	VL	L	H	VL	Moderate-term on-the-job-training	plastic
						All other machine tool setters, set-up operators, metal and
5	VL	H	H	VL	Moderate-term on-the-job-training	plastic[1]
						Metal fabricating machine setters, operators, and related
4	–	–	–	–	–	workers
1	VL	L	H	VL	Moderate-term on-the-job-training	Metal fabricators, structural metal products[1]
0	VL	L	VL	VL	Moderate-term on-the-job-training	Soldering and brazing machine operators and tenders[1]
3	VL	H	H	VL	Moderate-term on-the-job-training	Welding machine setters, operators, and tenders
						Metal and plastic processing machine setters, operators, and
20	–	–	–	–	–	related workers
						Electrolytic plating machine operator's and tenders, setters
2	VL	L	H	VL	Moderate-term on-the-job-training	and set-up operators, metal and plastic[1]
0	VL	L	H	VL	Moderate-term on-the-job-training	Foundry mold assembly and shakeout workers
0	VL	H	H	VL	Moderate-term on-the-job-training	Furnace operators and tenders[1]
						Heat treating machine operators and tenders, metal and
1	VL	H	H	VL	Moderate-term on-the-job-training	plastic[1]
						Metal molding machine operators and tenders, setters and
2	VL	H	H	VL	Moderate-term on-the-job-training	set-up operators
						Plastic molding machine operators and tenders, setters and
9	VL	L	H	VL	Moderate-term on-the-job-training	set-up operators
						All other metal and plastic machine setters, operators. and
6	VL	L	H	VL	Moderate-term on-the-job-training	related workers[1]
8	–	–	–	–	–	Printing, binding, and related workers
2	VL	L	H	VL	Moderate-term on-the-job-training	Bindery machine operators and set-up operators[1]
0	–	–	–	–	–	Prepress printing workers, production
						Photoengraving and lithographic machine operators and
0	VL	L	H	VL	Moderate-term on-the-job-training	tenders[1]
0	VL	L	H	VL	Moderate-term on-the-job-training	Typesetting and composing machine operators and tenders[1]
5	–	–	–	–	–	Printing press operators
0	VL	H	L	VL	Moderate-term on-the-job-training	Letterpress operators
1	VL	H	L	VL	Moderate-term on-the-job-training	Offset lithographic press operators
3	VL	H	L	VL	Moderate-term on-the-job-training	Printing press machine setters, operators and tenders
0	VL	H	L	VL	Moderate-term on-the-job-training	All other printing press setters and set-up operators
1	VL	L	L	VL	Moderate-term on-the-job-training	Screen printing machine setters and set-up operators
1	VL	L	L	VL	Moderate-term on-the-job-training	All other printing, binding, and related workers[1]
16	–	–	–	–	–	Textile and related setters, operators, and related workers
						Extruding and forming machine operators and tenders,
1	VL	H	VH	L	Moderate-term on-the-job-training	synthetic or glass fibers[1]
						Pressing machine operators and tenders, textile, garment,
2	VL	VL	VH	H	Moderate-term on-the-job-training	and related materials

[1]One or more Current Population Survey (CPS) based occupations may be used to estimate CPS based data. See Table 2.
NOTE: Rankings are based on employment in all detailed occupations in the National Industry-Occupation Matrix. For details, see "Data presented" section of text. Codes for describing the ranked variables are: VH = Very high, H = High, L = Low, VL = Very low, n. a. = Data not available. A dash indicates data are not applicable.

Table 1. Occupational employment and job openings data, 1996-2006, and worker characteristics, 1996—Continued
(Numbers in thousands)

1996 Matrix Occupation	Employment		Employment change, 1996-2006				Percent self-employed, 1996	Annual average job openings due to growth and total replacement needs, 1996-2006	
			Numeric		Percent				
	1996	2006	Number	Rank	Number	Rank		Number	Rank
Sewing machine operators, garment	453	334	−118	VL	−26.1	VL	4.7	53	L
Sewing machine operators, non-garment	130	128	−2	VL	−1.9	VL	1.0	17	VL
Textile bleaching and dyeing machine operators and tenders[1]	26	28	3	VL	10.0	L	0.0	5	VL
Textile draw-out and winding machine operators and tenders[1]	183	155	−28	VL	−15.4	VL	2.2	23	VL
Textile machine setters and set-up operators	41	27	−14	VL	−34.4	VL	0.0	5	VL
Woodworking machine setters, operators, and other related workers	130	118	−12	–	−9.0	–	6.7	41	–
Head sawyers and sawing machine operators and tenders, setters and set-up operators	66	59	−6	VL	−9.7	VL	4.6	23	VL
Woodworking machine operators and tenders, setters and set-up operators[1]	64	59	−5	VL	−8.3	VL	8.9	18	VL
Other machine setters, set-up operators, operators, and tenders	1,919	2,070	151	–	7.9	–	2.6	354	–
Boiler operators and tenders, low pressure	17	14	−4	VL	−20.7	VL	0.0	1	VL
Cement and gluing machine operators and tenders[1]	35	30	−5	VL	−15.5	VL	0.0	6	VL
Chemical equipment controllers, operator's and tenders[1]	79	82	3	VL	4.4	VL	0.0	14	VL
Cooling and roasting machine operators and tenders, food and tobacco[1]	30	32	2	VL	7.7	L	0.0	4	VL
Crushing and mixing machine operators and tenders	145	144	0	VL	−0.3	VL	0.0	25	VL
Cuffing and slicing machine setters, operators and tenders	95	103	8	VL	8.3	L	6.9	19	VL
Dairy processing equipment operators, including setters[1]	13	12	−2	VL	−13.0	VL	0.0	2	VL
Electronic semiconductor processors	58	65	7	VL	12.3	L	0.0	7	VL
Extruding and forming machine setters, operators and tenders[1]	107	106	−1	VL	−1.3	VL	0.0	19	VL
Furnace, kiln, or kettle operators and tenders[1]	28	25	−3	VL	−9.3	VL	2.6	3	VL
Laundry and dry-cleaning machine operators and tenders, except pressing	180	219	39	L	21.9	VH	12.0	45	L
Motion picture projectionists[1]	8	5	−4	VL	−45.1	VL	0.0	1	VL
Packaging and filling machine operators and tenders	354	410	56	L	15.8	H	0.0	85	L
Painting and coating machine operators	171	185	14	–	8.4	–	6.1	35	–
Coating, painting, and spraying machine operators, tenders, setters, and set-up operators	122	127	5	VL	4.1	VL	1.0	24	VL
Painters, transportation equipment	49	58	9	VL	18.9	H	18.7	11	VL
Paper goods machine setters and set-up operators[1]	51	44	−7	VL	−14.5	VL	0.0	7	VL
Photographic processing machine operators and tenders	49	53	4	VL	8.0	L	0.0	12	VL
Separating and still machine operator's and tenders[1]	19	17	−1	VL	−6.0	VL	0.0	3	VL
Shoe sewing machine operators and tenders[1]	11	6	−5	VL	−41.7	VL	0.0	1	VL
Tire building machine operators	14	12	−2	VL	−15.0	VL	0.0	1	VL
All other machine operators, tenders, setters, and set-up operators[1]	454	504	51	L	11.1	L	2.5	63	L
Hand workers, including assemblers and fabricators	2,813	2,898	85	–	3.0	–	3.3	546	–
Cannery workers	66	62	−5	VL	−6.8	VL	0.0	13	VL
Coil winders, tapers, and finishers	22	21	−1	VL	−3.2	VL	0.0	5	VL
Cutters and trimmers, hand[1]	46	48	2	VL	3.9	VL	2.1	9	VL
Electrical and electronic assemblers	229	226	−3	VL	−1.5	VL	0.0	51	L
Grinders and polishers, hand	74	72	−1	VL	−2.0	VL	0.0	12	VL
Machine assemblers	59	57	−2	VL	−3.6	VL	0.0	13	VL
Meat, poultry, and fish cutters and trimmers, hand[1]	151	186	35	L	23.0	VH	0.0	35	VL
Painting, coating, and decorating workers, hand[1]	31	34	3	VL	10.3	L	8.8	6	VL
Pressers, hand	14	13	−2	VL	−12.4	VL	0.0	2	VL
Sewers, hand	13	13	0	VL	0.9	VL	0.0	1	VL
Solderers and brazers[1]	26	32	5	VL	20.7	H	0.0	6	VL
Welders and cutters	352	384	32	L	9.0	L	7.6	37	VL
All other assemblers, fabricators, and hand workers[1]	1,729	1,751	22	L	1.3	VL	3.6	357	H
Transportation and material moving machine and vehicle operators	5,157	5,857	699	–	13.6	–	7.2	837	–
Motor vehicle operators	3,775	4,344	569	–	15.1	–	8.7	624	–
Bus drivers	592	710	117	–	19.8	–	0.3	91	–
Bus drivers, except school	167	192	24	L	14.6	H	1.1	24	VL
Bus drivers, school	425	518	93	L	21.8	VH	0.0	67	L

[1]One or more Current Population Survey (CPS) based occupations may be used to estimate CPS based data. See Table 2.
NOTE: Rankings are based on employment in all detailed occupations in the National Indus"-Occupation Matrix. For details, see "Data presented" section of text. Codes for describing the ranked variables are: VH = Very high, H = High, L = Low, VL = Verv low. n. a. = Data not available. A dash indicates data are not applicable.

Table 1. Occupational employment and job openings data, 1996-2006, and worker characteristics, 1996—Continued
(Numbers in thousands)

Annual average job openings due to growth and total replacement needs, 1996-2006		Median hourly earnings	Unemployment rate	Percent part-time	Most significant source of training	1996 Matrix Occupation
Number	Rank					
7	VL	VL	VH	VL	Moderate-term on-the-job-training	Sewing machine operators, garment
2	VL	VL	VH	VL	Moderate-term on-the-job-training	Sewing machine operators, non-garment
1	VL	L	VH	L	Moderate-term on-the-job-training	Textile bleaching and dyeing machine operators and tenders[1]
3	VL	L	VH	L	Moderate-term on-the-job-training	Textile draw-out and winding machine operators and tenders[1]
1	VL	L	VH	L	Moderate-term on-the-job-training	Textile machine setters and set-up operators
3	–	–	–	–	–	Woodworking machine setters, operators, and other related workers
2	VL	L	VH	VL	Moderate-term on-the-job-training	Head sawers and sawing machine operators and tenders, setters and set-up operators
1	VL	L	VH	VL	Moderate-term on-the-job-training	Woodworking machine operators and tenders, setters and set-up operators[1]
61	–	–	–	–	–	Other machine setters, set-up operators, operators, and tenders
0	VL	H	VL	VL	Moderate-term on-the-job-training	Boiler operators and lenders, low pressure
1	VL	L	H	VL	Moderate-term on-the-job-training	Cement and gluing machine operators and tenders[1]
2	VL	VH	L	VL	Moderate-term on-the-job-training	Chemical equipment controllers, operators and tenders[1]
1	VL	L	H	VL	Moderate-term on-the-job-training	Cooking and roasting machine operators and tenders, food and tobacco[1]
4	VL	L	H	VL	Moderate-term on-the-job-training	Crushing and mixing machine operators and tenders
3	VL	L	H	VL	Moderate-term on-the-job-training	Cutting and slicing machine sellers, operators and tenders
0	VL	L	L	VL	Moderate-term on-the-job-training	Dairy processing equipment operators, including setters[1]
2	VL	H	H	VL	Moderate-term on-the-job-training	Electronic semiconductor processors
3	VL	L	H	VL	Moderate-term on-the-job-training	Extruding and forming machine setters, operators and tenders[1]
0	VL	H	H	VL	Moderate-term on-the-job-training	Furnace, kiln, or kettle operators and tenders[1]
8	VL	VL	VH	H	Moderate-term on-the-job-training	Laundry and dry-cleaning machine operators and tenders, except pressing
0	VL	VL	H	VL	Short-term on-the-job-training	Motion picture protectionists[1]
12	L	L	VH	VL	Moderate-term on-the-job-training	Packaging and filling machine operators and tenders
6	–	–	–	–	–	Painting and coating machine operators
3	VL	L	H	VL	Moderate-term on-the-job-training	Coating, painting, and spraying machine operators, tenders, setters, and set-up operators
2	VL	H	H	VL	Moderate-term on-the-job-training	Painters, transportation equipment
1	VL	H	H	VL	Moderate-term on-the-job-training	Paper goods machine setters and set-up operators[1]
2	VL	L	H	H	Short-term on-the-job-training	Photographic processing machine operators and tenders
0	VL	H	L	VL	Moderate-term on-the-job-training	Separating and still machine operators and tenders[1]
0	VL	L	VH	VL	Moderate-term on-the-job-training	Shoe sewing machine operators and tenders[1]
0	VL	VH	H	VL	Moderate-term on-the-job-training	Tire building machine operators
14	L	L	H	VL	Moderate-term on-the-job-training	All other machine operators, tenders, setters, and set-up operators[1]
67	–	–	–	–	–	Hand workers, including assemblers and fabricators
1	VL	VL	VH	VL	Short-term on-the-job-training	Cannery workers
0	VL	L	VH	VL	Short-term on-the-job-training	Coil winders, tapers, and finishers
1	VL	L	VH	VL	Short-term on-the-job-training	Cutters and trimmers, hand[1]
5	VL	L	VH	VL	Short-term on-the-job-training	Electrical and electronic assemblers
1	VL	L	H	VH	Short-term on-the-job-training	Grinders and polishers, hand
1	VL	L	VH	VL	Short-term on-the-job-training	Machine assemblers
7	VL	VL	VH	VL	Short-term on-the-job-training	Meat, poultry, and fish cutters and trimmers, hand[1]
1	VL	L	VH	VL	Short-term on-the-job-training	Painting, coating, and decorating workers, hand[1]
0	VL	VL	H	VH	Short-term on-the-job-training	Pressers, hand
0	VL	VL	H	VH	Short-term on-the-job-training	Sewers, hand
1	VL	L	VH	VL	Short-term on-the-job-training	Solderers and brazers[1]
12	L	H	H	VL	Postsecondary vocational training	Welders and cutters
35	H	L	VH	L	Short-term on-the-job-training	All other assemblers, fabricators, and hand workers[1]
156	–	–	–	–	–	Transportation and material moving machine and vehicle operators
113	–	–	–	–	–	Motor vehicle operators
20	–	–	–	–	–	Bus drivers
5	VL	H	L	VH	Moderate-term on-the-job-training	Bus drivers, except school
151	L	L	L	VH	Short-term on-the-job-training	Bus drivers, school

[1]One or more Current Population Survey (CPS) based occupations may be used to estimate CPS based data. See Table 2.
NOTE: Rankings are based on employment in all detailed occupations In the National Industry-Occupation Matrix. For details, see "Data presented" section of text. Codes for describing the ranked variables are: VH = Very high, H = High, L = Low, VL = Very low, n. a. = Data not available. A dash indicates data are not applicable.

Table 1. Occupational employment and job openings data, 1996-2006, and worker characteristics, 1996—Continued
(Numbers in thousands)

1996 Matrix Occupation	Employment		Employment change, 1996-2006				Percent self-em-ployed, 1996	Annual average job openings due to growth and total replacement needs, 1996-2006	
			Numeric		Percent				
	1996	2006	Number	Rank	Number	Rank		Number	Rank
Taxi drivers and chauffeurs	106	114	8	VL	7.6	L	32.0	19	VL
Truck drivers	3,050	3,492	442	–	14.5	–	9.6	510	–
Driver/sales workers	331	370	39	L	11.6	L	2.8	28	VL
Truck drivers light and heavy	2,719	3,123	404	VH	14.9	H	10.4	482	VH
All other motor vehicle operators[1]	27	28	1	VL	3.3	VL	0.0	4	VL
Rail transportation workers	83	79	–4	–4.7	–	0.0	6	–	–
Locomotive engineers[1]	27	28	1	VL	3.3	VL	0.0	4	VL
Railroad brake, signal, and switch operators[1]	18	13	–5	VL	–28.2	VL	0.0	1	VL
Railroad conductors and yardmasters[1]	25	25	0	VL	–1.8	VL	0.0	2	VL
Rail yard engineers, dinkey operators, and hostlers[1]	5	4	–1	VL	–19.6	VL	0.0	0	VL
Subway and street car operators[1]	13	14	1	VL	9.2	L	0.0	1	VL
Water transportation and related workers	51	49	–2	–	–3.8	–	7.5	9	–
Able seamen, ordinary seamen, and marine oilers[1]	22	20	–1	VL	–6.2	VL	5.4	4	VL
Captains and pilots, ship[1]	14	13	0	VL	–1.6	VL	10.5	3	VL
Mates, ship, boat, and barge[1]	7	7	0	VL	2.4	VL	0.0	1	VL
Ship engineers[1]	9	8	–1	VL	–6.6	VL	14.4	2	VL
Material moving equipment operators	1,097	1,212	114	–	10.4	–	3.7	171	–
Crane and tower operators	45	45	0	VL	–1.1	VL	0.0	6	VL
Excavation and loading machine operators[1]	97	107	10	VL	10.5	L	18.5	5	VL
Grader, bulldozer, and sewer operators	107	111	5	VL	4.3	VL	5.3	5	VL
Hoist and winch operators[1]	9	10	0	VL	4.8	VL	0.0	1	VL
Industrial truck and tractor operators	479	536	57	L	11.9	L	0.3	96	L
Operating engineers	157	180	23	L	14.4	H	8.9	26	VL
All other material moving equipment operators[1]	202	222	20	L	9.7	L	0.9	32	VL
All other transportation and material moving equipment operators[1]	151	173	22	L	14.5	H	0.0	27	VL
Helpers, laborers, and material movers, hand	4,975	5,654	679	–	13.7	–	1.1	1,591	–
Freight, stock, and material movers, hand[1]	808	849	41	L	5.1	VL	1.8	310	H
Hand packers and packagers	986	1,208	222	H	22.5	VH	0.0	252	H
Helpers, construction trades	546	596	49	L	9.0	L	0.3	161	H
Machine feeders and offbearers	265	263	–2	VL	–0.8	VL	0.0	50	L
Parking lot attendants[1]	68	86	18	VL	26.2	VH	0.0	13	VL
Refuse collectors[1]	116	123	7	VL	6.0	L	0.0	46	L
Service station attendants	174	174	0	VL	0.1	VL	1.7	50	L
Vehicle washers and equipment cleaners	274	343	69	L	25.2	VH	6.6	111	L
All other helpers, laborers, and material movers, hand[1]	1,737	2,012	275	VH	15.8	H	1.1	598	VH

[1]One or more Current Population Survey (CPS) based occupations may be used to estimate CPS based data. See Table 2.
NOTE: Rankings are based on employment in all detailed occupations in the National Industry-Occupation Matrix. For details, see "Data presented" section of text. Codes for describing the ranked variables are: VH = Very high, H = High, L = Low, VL = Very low, n. a. = Data not available. A dash indicates data are not applicable.

Table 1. Occupational employment and job openings data, 1996-2006, and worker characteristics, 1996—Continued
(Numbers in thousands)

Annual average job openings due to growth and total replacement needs, 1996-2006		Median hourly earnings	Unemployment rate	Percent part-time	Most significant source of training	1996 Matrix Occupation
Number	Rank					
2	VL	VL	H	H	Short-term on-the-job-training	Taxi drivers and chauffeurs
90	–	–	–	–	–	Truck drivers
12	L	L	L	L	Short-term on-the-job-training	Driver/sales workers
78	VH	H	H	L	Short-term on-the-job-training	Truck drivers light and heavy
1	VL	L	H	H	Short-term on-the-job-training	All other motor vehicle operators[1]
2	–	–	–	–		Rail transportation workers
1	VL	H	VL	L	Work experience in a related occupation	Locomotive engineers[1]
0	VL	H	VL	L	Work experience in a related occupation	Railroad brake, signal, and switch operators[1]
1	VL	H	VL	L	Work experience in a related occupation	Railroad conductors and yardmasters[1]
0	VL	VH	VL	L	Work experience in a related occupation	Rail yard engineers, dinkey operators, and hostlers[1]
0	VL	VH	VL	L	Moderate-term on-the-job-training	Subway and streetcar operators[1]
2	–	–	–	–		Water transportation and related workers
1	VL	L	VH	H	Short-term on-the-job-training	Able seamen, ordinary seamen, and marine oilers[1]
1	VL	VH	VH	H	Work experience in a related occupation	Captains and pilots, ship[1]
0	VL	H	VH	H	Work experience in a related occupation	Mates, ship, boat, and barge[1]
0	VL	VH	VH	H	Work experience in a related occupation	Ship engineers[1]
34	–	–	–	VL		Material moving equipment operators
1	VL	H	H	VL	Moderate-term on-the-job-training	Crane and tower operators
3	VL	H	VH	L	Moderate-term on-the-job-training	Excavation and loading machine operators[1]
1	VL	H	VH	L	Moderate-term on-the-job-training	Grader, bulldozer, and scraper operators
0	VL	H	VH	VL	Moderate-term on-the-job-training	Hoist and winch operators[1]
16	L	H	H	VL	Short-term on-the-job-training	Industrial truck and tractor operators
6	VL	VH	VH	VL	Moderate-term on-the-job-training	Operating engineers
7	VL	H	VH	VL	Moderate-term on-the-job-training	All other material moving equipment operators[1]
5	VL	H	H	H	Moderate-term on-the-job-training	All other transportation and material moving equipment operators[1]
229	–	–	–	–		Helpers, laborers, and material movers, hand
33	H	L	VH	VH	Short-term on-the-job-training	Freight, stock, and material movers, hand[1]
48	H	VL	VH	L	Short-term on-the-job-training	Hand packers and packagers
24	L	L	VH	H	Short-term on-the-job-training	Helpers, construction trades
7	VL	L	VH	L	Short-term on-the-job-training	Machine feeders and offbearers
3	VL	VL	H	H	Short-term on-the-job-training	Parking lot attendants[1]
5	VL	H	VH	VH	Short-term on-the-job-training	Refuse collectors[1]
7	VL	VL	VH	H	Short-term on-the-job-training	Service station attendants
15	L	VL	VH	H	Short-term on-the-job-training	Vehicle washers and equipment cleaners
86	VH	L	VH	H	Short-term on-the-job-training	All other helpers, laborers, and material movers, hand[1]

[1]One or more Current Population Survey (CPS) based occupations may be used to estimate CPS based data. See Table 2.
NOTE: Rankings are based on employment in all detailed occupations in the National Industry-Occupation Matrix. For details, see "Data presented" section of text. Codes for describing the ranked variables are: VH = Very high, H = High, L = Low, VL = Very low, n. a. = Data not available. A dash indicates data are not applicable.

Table 2. 1996 National industry-occupation matrix occupations which use Current Population Survey proxy occupation data to estimate one or more data elements

1996 Matrix Occupation	Percent part-time and unemployment rate	Replacement needs	
		Total	Net
Executive, administrative, and managerial occupations			
Food service and lodging managers			●
Funeral directors and morticians	●	●	●
Government chief executives and legislators	●	●	●
Property and real estate managers	●		
All other managers and administrators	●	●	●
Management analysts		●	
All other management support workers	●	●	●
Professional specialty occupations			
Chemical engineers		●	
Metallurgists and metallurgical, ceramic, and materials engineers	●	●	●
Mining engineers, including mine safety engineers	●	●	●
Nuclear engineers	●	●	●
Petroleum engineers	●	●	●
All other engineers	●	●	●
Surveyors	●	●	●
Agricultural and food scientists	●	●	●
Foresters and conservation scientists	●	●	●
Actuaries	●	●	●
Statisticians	●	●	●
Mathematicians and all other mathematical scientists	●	●	●
Geologists, geophysicists, and oceanographers	●	●	●
Meteorologists	●	●	●
Physicists and astronomers	●	●	●
All other physical scientists	●	●	●
Urban and regional planners		●	●
All other social scientists	●	●	●
Directors, religious activities and education		●	
Human services workers		●	
Judges, magistrates, and other judicial workers		●	●
College and university faculty	●	●	●
All other teachers and instructors	●	●	●
Curators, archivists, museum technicians, and restorers	●	●	●
Chiropractors	●	●	●
Optometrists	●	●	●
Podiatrists	●	●	●
Veterinarians and veterinary inspectors		●	●
Physician assistants			●
Occupational therapists		●	●
Physical therapists		●	●
Recreational therapists		●	●
Respiratory therapists		●	●
Speech-language pathologists and audiologists		●	●
All other therapists		●	●
Dancers and choreographers	●	●	●
Producers, directors, actors, and entertainers		●	●
All other professional workers		●	●
Technicians and related support occupations			
Cardiology technologists			●
Electroneurodiagnostic technologists			●
EKG technicians			●
Emergency medical technicians			●
Medical records technicians	●		●
Pharmacy technicians			●
Surgical technologists			●
Veterinary technicians and technologists			●
All other health professionals and paraprofessionals	●	●	●
All other engineering technicians and technologists	●	●	●

1996 Matrix Occupation	Percent part-time and unemployment rate	Replacement needs	
		Total	Net
Science and mathematics technicians		●	●
Air traffic controllers and airplane dispatchers	●	●	●
Broadcast technicians	●	●	●
Programmers, numerical, tool, and process control	●	●	●
Technical assistants, library	●	●	●
All other technicians	●	●	●
Marketing and sales occupations			
Travel agents			●
All other sales and related workers			●
Administrative support occupations, including clerical			
All other communications equipment operators	●	●	●
Peripheral computer equipment operators	●	●	●
Reservation and transportation ticket agents and travel clerks			●
Meter readers, utilities	●	●	●
Weighers, measurers, checkers, and samplers, recordkeeping		●	●
All other material recording, scheduling, and distribution workers	●	●	●
Advertising clerks	●	●	●
Correspondence clerks	●	●	●
Billing, posting, and calculating machine operators			●
Personnel clerks, except payroll and timekeeping		●	
Stenographers and/or court reporters			●
Duplicating, mail, and other office machine operators			
Proofreaders and copy markers	●	●	●
Service occupations			
Pest controllers and assistants			●
All other cleaning and building service workers	●	●	●
Food preparation workers			●
Food counter, fountain, and related workers			●
Medical assistants			●
Occupational therapy assistants and aides			●
Pharmacy assistants			●
Baggage porters and bellhops	●	●	●
Personal and home care aides		●	●
Ushers, lobby attendants, and ticket takers	●	●	●
Cleaners and servants, private household	●	●	●
Cooks, private household	●	●	●
Housekeepers and butlers	●	●	●
Fire fighting and prevention supervisors	●	●	●
Fire inspection occupations	●	●	●
Crossing guards	●	●	●
All other service workers		●	●
Agriculture, forestry, fishing, and related occupations			
Captains and other officers, fishing vessels	●	●	●
Fishers, hunters, and trappers	●	●	●
Forest and conservation workers	●	●	●
Lawn service managers	●	●	●
Nursery and greenhouse managers	●	●	
Supervisors, farming, forestry, and agricultural related occupations	●	●	●
All other agricultural, forestry, fishing, and related workers	●	●	●
Precision production, craft, and repair occupations			
Blue collar worker supervisors	●	●	●

Table 2. 1996 National industry-occupation matrix occupations which use Current Population Survey proxy occupation data to estimate one or more data elements—Continued

1996 Matrix Occupation	Percent part-time and unemployment rate	Replacement needs	
		Total	Net
Bricklayers and stone masons		●	
Glaziers	●	●	●
Hard tile setters			●
Paving, surfacing, and tamping equipment operators	●	●	●
Plasterers	●	●	●
All other construction trades workers			●
Roustabouts		●	●
All other oil and gas extraction occupations	●	●	●
Mining, quarrying, and tunneling occupations	●	●	●
All other extraction and related workers	●	●	●
Central office and PBX installers and repairers		●	
All other communications equipment mechanics, installers, and repairers		●	
Station installers and repairers, telephone		●	
Telephone and cable TV line installers and repairers	●	●	●
Industrial machinery mechanics	●	●	●
Aircraft engine specialists	●	●	●
Aircraft mechanics	●	●	●
Automotive mechanics	●		
Farm equipment mechanics	●	●	●
Motorcycle repairers			●
Small engine specialists			●
Camera and photographic equipment repairers	●	●	●
Electric meter installers and repairers	●	●	●
Elevator installers and repairers	●	●	●
Home appliance and power tool repairers	●	●	●
Locksmiths and safe repairers	●	●	●
Musical instrument repairers and tuners	●	●	●
Precision instrument repairers	●	●	●
Watchmakers	●	●	●
All other mechanics, installers, and repairers	●	●	●
Aircraft assemblers, precision	●	●	●
Fitters, structural metal, precision	●	●	●
Machine builders and other precision machine assemblers	●	●	●
All other precision assemblers	●	●	●
All other precision food and tobacco workers	●	●	●
Metal workers, precision		●	●
Boilermakers	●	●	●
Jewelers and silversmiths		●	●
Sheet metal workers and duct installers	●	●	●
Shipfitters	●	●	●
All other precision metal workers	●	●	●
Bookbinders	●	●	●
Compositors and typesetters, precision	●	●	●
Paste-up workers	●	●	●
Desktop publishing specialists	●	●	●
Photoengravers	●	●	●
Camera operators	●	●	●
Film strippers, printing	●	●	●
Platemakers	●	●	●
All other printing workers, precision	●	●	●
Patternmakers and layout workers, fabric and apparel		●	●
Shoe and leather workers and repairers, precision	●	●	●
Upholsterers		●	
All other precision textile, apparel, and furnishings workers		●	●
Furniture finishers	●	●	●
All other precision woodworkers	●	●	●
Chemical plant and system operators	●	●	●
Power distributors and dispatchers	●	●	●
Power generating and reactor plant operators	●	●	●
Gas and petroleum plant and system occupations	●	●	●

1996 Matrix Occupation	Percent part-time and unemployment rate	Replacement needs	
		Total	Net
All other plant and system operators	●	●	●
Operators, fabricators, and laborers			
Numerical control machine tool operators and tenders, metal and plastic	●	●	●
Combination machine tool setters, set-up operators, operators, and tenders	●	●	●
Drilling and boring machine tool setters and set-up operators, metal and plastic	●	●	●
Lathe and turning machine tool setters and set-up operators, metal and plastic	●	●	●
All other machine tool setters, set-up operators, metal and plastic	●	●	●
Metal fabricators, structural metal products	●	●	●
Soldering and brazing machine operators and tenders	●	●	●
Electrolytic plating machine operators and tenders, setters and set-up operators, metal and plastic	●	●	●
Furnace operators and tenders		●	
Heat treating machine operators and tenders, metal and plastic	●	●	●
All other metal and plastic machine setters, operators, and related workers	●	●	●
Bindery machine operator's and set-up operators	●	●	●
Photoengraving and lithographic machine operators and tenders	●	●	●
Typesetting and composing machine operators and tenders	●	●	●
All other printing, binding, and related workers	●	●	●
Extruding and forming machine operators and tenders, synthetic or glass fibers	●	●	●
Textile bleaching and dyeing machine operators and tenders	●	●	●
Textile draw-out and winding machine operators and tenders	●	●	●
Woodworking machine operators and tenders, setters and set-up operators	●	●	●
Cement and gluing machine operators and tenders	●	●	●
Chemical equipment controllers, operators and tenders		●	●
Cooking and roasting machine operators and tenders, food and tobacco	●	●	●
Dairy processing equipment operators, including setters		●	●
Extruding and forming machine setters, operators and tenders	●	●	●
Furnace, kiln, or kettle operators and tenders	●	●	●
Motion picture protectionists	●	●	
Paper goods machine setters and set-up operators	●	●	●
Separating and still machine operators and tenders		●	●
Shoe sewing machine operators and tenders		●	
All other machine operators, tenders, setters, and set-up operators	●	●	●
Cutters and trimmers, hand	●	●	●
Meat, poultry, and fish cutters and trimmers, hand	●	●	●
Painting, coating, and decorating workers, hand	●	●	●
Solderers and brazers	●	●	●
All other assemblers, fabricators, and hand workers	●	●	●
All other motor vehicle operators	●	●	●
Locomotive engineers	●	●	●
Railroad brake, signal, and switch operators	●	●	●
Railroad conductors and yardmasters	●	●	●
Rail yard engineers, dinkey operators, and hostlers	●	●	●

1996 Matrix Occupation	Percent part-time and unemployment rate	Replacement needs	
		Total	Net
Subway and streetcar Operators			
Able seamen, ordinary seamen, and marine .... oilers	●	●	●
Captains and pilots, ship	●	●	●
Mates, ship, boat, and barge	●	●	●
Ship engineers	●	●	●
Excavation and loading machine operators	●	●	●
Hoist and winch operators	●	●	●

1996 Matrix Occupation	Percent part-time and unemployment rate	Replacement needs	
		Total	Net
All other Material moving equipment operators	●	●	●
All other transportation and material moving equipment operators	●	●	●
Freight, stock, and material movers, hand	●	●	●
Parking lot attendants	●	●	●
Refuse collectors	●	●	●
All other helpers, laborers, and material movers, hand	●	●	●

Appendix C

EMPLOYMENT TRENDS WITHIN MAJOR INDUSTRIES

Introduction

While there are many hundreds of specialized industries, more than 70 percent of all workers are employed in just 40 major ones. While space limitations do not allow me to list detailed information on each of these industries, the article that follows provides a good overview of trends within industry types.

The article comes, with minor changes, from the introduction to a book published by the U.S. Department of Labor titled the *Career Guide to Industries*. It includes important information you should consider in making your career plans.

While you may not have thought much about it, the industry you work in is often as important as the career you choose. For example, some industries pay significantly higher wages than others for similar jobs. So, read this article over carefully and consider the possibilities—it can make a big difference.

If you want more information on a specific industry, look for the *Career Guide to Industries* in your library. A more widely available version of the same book, titled *Career Guide to America's Top Industries,* may be available in your library or bookstore. This book is published by JIST.

Here are the industries covered in these books:

Goods-Producing Industries

Agriculture, Mining, and Construction
  Agricultural services
  Construction
  Mining and quarrying
  Oil and gas extraction

Manufacturing
  Aerospace manufacturing
  Apparel and other textile products
  Chemicals manufacturing, except drugs
  Drug manufacturing
  Electronic equipment manufacturing
  Food processing
  Motor vehicle and equipment manufacturing
  Printing and publishing
  Steel manufacturing
  Textile mill products

Service-Producing Industries

Transportation, Communications, and Public Utilities
  Air transportation
  Public utilities
  Radio and television communications
  Telephone communications
  Trucking and warehousing

Wholesale and Retail Trade
  Department, clothing, and accessory stores
  Eating and drinking places
  Grocery stores
  Motor vehicle dealers
  Wholesale trade

Finance and Insurance
  Banking
  Insurance
  Securities and commodities

Services
  Advertising
  Amusement and recreation services
  Child-care services
  Computer and data processing services
  Educational services
  Health services
  Hotels and lodging places
  Management and public relations services
  Motion picture production and distribution
  Personnel supply services
  Social services, except child care

Government
  Federal government
  State and local government

Industry Characteristics: An Overview

The U.S. economy contains industries with increasingly diverse characteristics. For each industry covered in the *Career Guide*, detailed information is provided about specific characteristics: Nature of the industry, working conditions, employment, occupational composition, training and advancement requirements, earnings, and job outlook. This chapter provides an overview of these characteristics for the economy as a whole.

Nature of the Industry

Industries are defined by the goods and services an industry provides. Because workers in the United States produce such a wide variety of products and services, industries in the U.S. economy vary widely, from steel manufacturers to grocery stores. Although many of these industries are related, each industry contains a unique combination of occupations, production techniques, and business characteristics. Understanding the nature of the industry is important, because it is this unique combination that determines working conditions, educational requirements, and the job outlook for each of the industries discussed in the *Career Guide*.

Industries are comprised of many different places of work, *called establishments*, which range from large factories and office complexes, employing thousands of workers, to small businesses employing only a few workers. Establishments that produce similar goods or services are grouped together into *industries*. Industries that produce related types of goods or services are, in turn, grouped together into *major industry divisions*, which are further categorized as the *goods-producing sector* (agriculture, forestry, and fishing; mining; construction; and manufacturing) or the *service-producing sector* (transportation, communications, and public utilities; wholesale and retail trade; finance and insurance; services; and government).

Distinctions within industries are also varied. Each industry comprises a number of subdivisions that are determined largely by the production processes unique to each industry. An easily recognized example of these subdivisions is in the food processing industry, which is made up of segments that produce meat products, preserved fruits and vegetables, bakery items, beverages, and dairy products-among others. Each of these segments require workers with varying skills and employs unique production techniques. Another example of these subdivisions is in public utilities, which employs workers in establishments that provide electricity, sanitary services, water, and natural gas. Working conditions and establishment characteristics differ widely in each of these subdivisions.

Currently, there are nearly 7 million business establishments in the United States. The average size of these establishments varies widely across industries. Among industry divisions, manufacturing included many industries having among the highest employment per establishment in 1994. For example, industries manufacturing tobacco, transportation equipment, and primary metals each averaged 100 or more employees per establishment. Nonmanufacturing industries with relatively high employment per establishment included general merchandise stores and metal mining, each with 50 or more workers per establishment.

Most small establishments are in the retail trade and services industries. Other industries that tend to have relatively few employees per establishment included auto repair and parking services, agricultural services, insurance agents and brokers, and real estate; each averaged 6 or fewer workers per establishment in 1994. On the other hand, educational services had nearly 50 employees per establishment.

Establishments in the United States are predominantly small; 55 percent of all establishments employed fewer than five workers in 1994. Medium to large establishments, however, employ a greater proportion of all workers. For example, establishments that employed 50 or more workers accounted for only 5 percent of all establishments, yet employed 57 percent of all workers. Large establishments—those with more than 500 workers—accounted for only 0.3 percent of all establishments but employed 20 percent of all workers. Percent distribution of employment according to establishment size is shown in Table 1.

Establishment size can play a role in the characteristics of each job. Large establishments offer workers greater occupational mobility and advancement potential, whereas small establishments may provide their employees with broader experience, by requiring them to assume a wider range of responsibilities. Also, small establishments are distributed throughout the nation; every locality has a few small businesses. Large establishments, in contrast, are less common, yet hire more workers.

Table 1. Percent distribution of establishments and employment in all industries by establishment size, 1994

Establishment Size (Number of Workers)	Establishments	Employment
Total	100.0	100.0
1-4	54.9	6.3
5-9	19.8	8.8
10-19	12.2	11.1
20-49	8.1	16.4
50-99	2.7	12.6
100-249	1.6	15.8
250-499	0.4	9.1
500-999	2	6.9
1,000 or more	1	13.0

SOURCE: Department of Commerce, *County Business Patterns*, 1994

Working Conditions

Just as the goods and services of each industry are different, working conditions in industries vary significantly. In some industries, the work setting is quiet, temperature-controlled, and virtually hazard free. Other industries are characterized by noisy, uncomfortable, and sometimes dangerous work environments. Some industries require long workweeks and shift work; in many industries, standard 35-to 40-hour workweeks are common. Still other industries can be seasonal, requiring long hours during busy periods and abbreviated schedules during slower months. These varying conditions usually are determined by production processes, establishment size, and the physical location of work.

One of the most telling indicators of working conditions is an industry's injury and illness rate. Overexertion, contact with dangerous equipment, falls, repetitive motion, and fires are among the most common causes of injury and illness. In 1995, approximately 6.6 million nonfatal injuries and illnesses were reported throughout private industry. Among major industry divisions, manufacturing had the highest rate of injury and illness—11.6 cases for every 100 full-time workers—while finance, insurance, and real estate had the lowest rate—2.6. About 6,000 work-related fatalities were reported in 1995; transportation accidents, violent acts, contact with objects and equipment, falls, and exposure to harmful substances or environments were among the most common causes. Industries with the highest and lowest rates of nonfatal injury and illness are shown in Table 2.

Table 2. Nonfatal injury and Illness rates of selected Industries, 1994

Industry	Cases per 100 Full-Time Employees
All Industries	8.1
High rates	
Motor vehicle manufacturing	23.2
Nursing and personal care facilities	18.2
Food processing	16.3
Sanitary services	14.0
Trucking and warehousing	13.8
Low rates	
Telephone communications	2.4
Insurance	2.3
Banking	2.2
Amusement and recreation services	2.2
Radio and TV broadcasting	1.9

Work schedules are another important reflection of working conditions, and the operational requirements of each industry lead to large differences in hours worked and part-time versus full-time status. The contrast in an average workweek was notable between retail trade and manufacturing—28.8 hours and 41.6 hours, respectively, in 1996. More than 40 percent of workers in retail trade work part time (1 to 34 hours per week), compared to only 10 percent in manufacturing. Industries having relatively high and low percentages of part-time workers are shown in Table 3.

The low proportion of part-time workers in some manufacturing industries often reflects the continuity of the production processes and the specificity of skills. Once begun, it is costly to halt such processes, since machinery and materials must be tended and moved continuously. For example, the chemical manufacturing industry produces many different chemical products through controlled chemical reactions. These chemical processes require chemical operators to monitor and adjust the flow of materials into and out of the line of production. Production may continue 24 hours a day, 7 days a week, under the watchful eyes of chemical operators working in shifts.

Table 3. Percent of part-time workers in selected industries, 1996

Industry	Percent Part-Time
All Industries	25.4
Many part-time workers	
Eating and drinking places	51.5
Apparel and accessory stores	48.0
Department stores	40.8
Child day care services	40.2
Personnel supply services	28.9
Few part-time workers	
Chemicals and allied products	8.2
Drug manufacturing	6.5
Motor vehicle manufacturing	6.1
Aircraft and parts	4.6
Guided missiles, space vehicles, and parts	3.5

Retail trade and service industries, on the other hand, have seasonal cycles marked by various events, such as school openings or important holidays, that affect hours worked. During busy times of the year, longer hours are common, whereas slack periods lead to cutbacks and shorter workweeks. Jobs in these industries are generally appealing to students and others who desire flexible, part-time schedules.

Employment

The number of wage and salary worker jobs in the United States totaled nearly 122 million in 1996 and is projected to reach almost 140 million by 2006. (See Table 4.) In addition to these workers, the U.S. economy also provided employment for nearly 11 million self-employed workers and about 180,000 unpaid family workers.

Employment is not evenly divided among various industries, as shown in Table 4. The services industry is the largest source of employment, with over 44 million workers, followed by wholesale and retail trade and manufacturing. Among the industries covered in the *Career Guide,* wage and salary employment ranged from 240,000 in steel manufacturing to 10.7 million in educational services. Three industries—educational services, health services, and eating and drinking places—together accounted for about 29 million jobs, or nearly a quarter of the Nation's employment.

Although workers of all ages are employed in each industry, certain industries tend to possess workers of distinct age groups. For the reason mentioned above, retail trade employs a relatively high proportion of young workers to fill part-time and temporary positions. The manufacturing sector, on the other hand, has a relatively high median age, because many jobs in this sector require a number of years to learn and also rely on skills that do not easily transfer to other firms. Additionally, manufacturing employment has been declining, providing fewer opportunities for young workers to get jobs. As a result, almost one-third of the workers in retail trade were 24 years of age or younger, whereas only 10 percent of workers in manufacturing were 24 or younger. The age distribution of workers in all industries is contrasted with the distributions in retail trade and manufacturing in Table 5.

Table 4. Wage and salary employment in selected industries, 1996 and projected change, 1996 to 2006 (Employment in thousands)

Industry	1996		2006	1996-2006	
	Employment	Percent Distribution	Employment	Employment Change	Percent Change
All Industries	121,685	100.0	139,192	17,507	14.4
Goods-producing	26,547	21.8	26,550	3	0.0
Agriculture, forestry, and fishing	2,026	1.7	2,099	234	3.6
Agricultural services	928	0.8	1,118	190	20.5
Mining	574	.5	443	-69	-22.7
Oil and gas extraction	318	.3	248	-70	-22.1
Mining and quarrying	256	.2	196	-61	-23.6
Construction	5,400	4.4	5,900	500	9.3
Manufacturing	18,457	15.2	18,108	-518	-1.9
Food processing	1,693	1.4	1,713	-21	-1.2
Printing and publishing	1,538	1.3	1,501	-37	-2.4
Electronics manufacturing	1,486	1.2	1,451	-35	-2.3
Motor vehicle and equipment manufacturing	963	.8	929	-33	-3.5
Apparel and other textile products manufacturing	864	.7	714	-150	-17.3
Chemicals manufacturing, except drugs	773	.6	751	-22	-2.9
Textile mill products manufacturing	624	.5	588	-36	-5.7
Aerospace manufacturing	550	.5	596	46	8.4
Drug manufacturing	259	.2	319	61	23.5
Steel manufacturing	240	.2	197	-44	-18.2
Service-producing	95,228	78.3	112,643	17,415	18.3
Transportation, communications, and public utilities	6,260	5.1	7,111	789	13.6
Trucking and warehousing	1,641	1.3	1,860	219	13.4
Air transportation	1,122	.9	1,401	279	24.9
Telephone communications	924	.8	940	17	1.8
Public utilities	885	.7	976	91	10.3
Radio and television broadcasting	414	.3	420	6	1.5
Wholesale and retail trade	28,108	23.1	31,103	5,576	10.7
Eating and drinking places	7,499	6.2	8,884	1,384	18.5
Wholesale retail	6,483	5.3	7,228	745	11.5
Department, clothing, and variety stores	3,827	3.1	3,717	-110	-2.9
Grocery stores	3,030	2.5	3,390	360	11.9
Motor vehicle dealers	1,117	.9	1,148	31	2.8
Finance, insurance, and real estate	6,899	5.7	7,561	1,398	10.9
Insurance	2,217	1.8	2,471	254	11.5
Banking	2,024	1.7	1,950	-74	-3.6
Securities and commodities	551	.5	740	189	34.3
Services	44,223	36.3	56,647	15,506	28.1
Educational services	10,692	8.8	12,480	1,789	16.7
Health services	10,507	8.6	13,638	3,131	29.8
Personnel supply services	2,646	2.2	4,039	1,393	52.7
Social services	1,834	1.5	2,727	894	48.7
Hotels and other lodging places	1,716	1.4	1,978	262	15.3
Amusement and recreation services	1,466	1.2	1,998	531	36.3
Computer and data processing services	1,208	1.0	2,509	1,301	107.7
Management and public relations services	874	.7	1,400	527	60.3
Child-care services	569	.5	734	164	28.8
Motion picture production and distribution	247	.2	328	81	32.7
Advertising	242	.2	270	28	11.4
Government	9,738	8.0	10,131	913	4.0
State and local government	6,981	5.7	7,461	480	6.9
Federal Government	1,901	1.6	1,790	-111	-5.8

Table 5. Percent distribution of industry sector employment by age group, 1996

Age Group	All Industries	Retail Trade	Manufacturing
Total	100.0	100.0	100.0
16-24	14.7	32.2	9.9
24-54	73.1	77.7	78.4
55 and older	12.2	10.1	11.6

Because employment in some industries is concentrated in one region of the country, job opportunities in these industries should be best in the States in which these establishments are located. Such industries are often located near a source of raw materials upon which the industries rely. For example, oil and gas extraction jobs are concentrated in Texas, Louisiana, and Oklahoma; many textile mill products manufacturing jobs are found in North Carolina, Georgia, and South Carolina; and a significant proportion of motor vehicle and equipment manufacturing jobs are located in Michigan. On the other hand, some industries–such as grocery stores and educational services–have jobs distributed throughout the Nation, reflecting population density in different areas.

Occupations in the industry

As mentioned above, the occupations found in each industry depend on the types of services provided or goods produced. For example, manufacturing companies use machinery and other industrial equipment to fabricate goods, so these companies employ a large number of machine operators and industrial machinery repairers. Other occupations common to the manufacturing sector include assemblers, inspectors, machine setters, and material movers. Retail trade, on the other hand, displays and sells manufactured goods to consumers, so this sector hires numerous sales clerks and other workers, including nearly 5 out of 6 cashiers. Major industry divisions and the occupational groups which predominate in each division are shown in Table 6.

The Nation's occupational distribution clearly is influenced by its industrial structure, yet there are many occupations (such as general manager or secretary) that are found in all industries. In fact, some of the largest occupations in the U.S. economy are dispersed across many industries. Because nearly every industry relies on administrative support, for example, the executive, administrative, and managerial occupational group is the largest in the Nation. (See Table 7.) Other large occupational groups include services; professional specialty; and operators, fabricators, and laborers.

Training and advancement

Workers prepare for employment in myriad ways, but the most fundamental form of job training in the United States is a high school education. Fully 87 percent of the Nation's workforce possessed a high school diploma, or its equivalent, in 1996. As the premium placed on education in today's economy increases, workers are responding by pursuing additional training. In 1996, the Nation's workforce that had some college or an associate's degree totaled 29 percent, while an additional 26 percent had continued in their studies and had attained a bachelor's degree, or higher. In addition to these types of formal education, other sources of qualifying training include formal company training; informal on-the-job training; correspondence courses; the Armed Forces; and friends, relatives, and other non-work-related training.

Table 6. Industry divisions and largest occupational concentration, 1996

Industry Division	Largest Occupational Group	Percent of Wage and Salary Jobs
Agriculture, forestry, and fishing	Agriculture and related	70.6
Mining	Precision production	37.2
Construction	Precision production	53.7
Manufacturing	Operators, fabricators and laborers	45.4
Transportation, communications, and public utilities	Operators, fabricators and laborers	31.3
Wholesale and retail trade	Marketing and sales	33.3
Finance, insurance, and real estate	Administrative support	49.9
Services	Professional specialty	28.7
Government	Administrative support	27.0

Table 7. Total employment in broad occupational groups, 1996 and projected change, 1996-2006

(Employment in thousands)

Occupational Group	1996 Employment	1996-2006 Percent Change
Total, all occupations	132,353	14.0
Executive, administrative, and managerial	13,542	17.2
Professional specialty	18,173	26.6
Technicians and related support	4,618	20.4
Marketing and sales	14,633	15.5
Administrative support, including clerical	24,019	7.5
Services	21,294	18.1
Agriculture, forestry, fishing, and related	3,785	1.0
Precision production, craft, and repair	14,446	6.9
Operators, fabricators, and laborers	17,843	8.5

Table 8. Percent distribution of highest grade completed or degree received by industry division, 1996

Industry Division	Bachelor's Degree or Higher	Some College or Associate Degree	High School Graduate or Equivalent	Less than 12 Years or No Diploma
Agriculture, forestry, and fishing	14	21	35	31
Mining	20	23	42	15
Construction	10	25	44	21
Manufacturing	20	25	40	15
Transportation, communications, and public utilities	20	34	39	8
Wholesale and retail trade	14	30	37	19
Finance, insurance, and real estate	36	33	25	4
Services	39	28	24	9
Government, public administration	36	36	25	3

The unique combination of training required to succeed in each industry is determined largely by the industry's occupational composition. For example, machine operators in manufacturing generally need little formal education after high school but sometimes complete considerable on-the-job training. Requirements by major industry division are demonstrated in Table 8. About 66 percent of workers in agriculture, forestry, and fishing; 65 percent in construction; 62 percent in manufacturing; and 56 percent in wholesale and retail trade had a high school diploma or less. On the other hand, 72 percent of workers in government; 69 percent in finance, insurance, and real estate; and 67 percent in services had acquired at least some training at the college level. A more detailed illustration of the variety of training requirements is given in Tables 9 and 10, which show industries having the highest percentages of college graduates and those with workers who have less than 12 years of schooling, or no high school diploma.

Table 9. Industries with the highest percentage of workers who have a bachelor's degree or higher, 1996

Industry	Percent
Offices and clinics of health practitioners, not elsewhere classified	77.7
Management and public relations services	71.1
Miscellaneous professional and related services	64.7
Elementary and secondary schools	63.7
Security, commodity brokerage, and investment companies	62.7

Table 10. Industries with the highest percentage of workers who have 12 years or less of schooling, or no diploma, 1996

Industry	Percent
Dairy products stores	40.3
Private households	40.2
Agricultural production, crops	39.8
Meat products	36.4
Apparel and accessories, except knit	35.8

Education and training are also important factors in the various advancement paths found in different industries. In general, workers who attain additional on-the-job training or education help their chances of promotion. In much of the manufacturing sector, for example, production workers who receive. training in management and computer skills are often more likely to be promoted to supervisors. Other factors which figure prominently in the industries covered in the *Career Guide* include the size of the company or establishment, institutionalized career tracks, and the skills and aptitude of each worker. Advancement paths are unique to each industry, so jobseekers should become familiar with the most common paths in the industries in which they are interested.

Earnings

Like other characteristics, earnings differ from industry to industry. These differences are the result of a highly complicated process that relies on a number of factors. For example, wages may vary due to the occupations in the industry, average hours worked, geographical location, industry profits, union affiliation, and educational requirements. In general, to compensate for the higher cost of living, wages are highest in metropolitan areas. And, as would be expected, industries that employ relatively few minimum-wage or part-time workers tend to offer higher earnings.

A good illustration of difference in earnings is shown by comparing earnings of production and nonsupervisory workers in coal mining, averaging $857 a week in 1996, and those of eating and drinking places, where the weekly average was $146. This difference is so large because the coal mining industry employs a relatively highly skilled, highly unionized workforce. On the other hand, eating and drinking places hire many lower-skilled, part-time workers who rely largely on tips, which are not included in the industry earnings data. More differences in industry earnings are highlighted in Table 11. In general, these data understate average earnings for all workers in a given industry, because supervisors are excluded.

Table 11. Average weekly earnings of nongovernment production or nonsupervisory workers in selected industries, 1996

Industry	Earnings
All Industries	$407
Industries with high earnings	
Coal mining	857
Computer programming services	822
Crude petroleum and natural gas	810
Motor vehicle production	801
Aerospace manufacturing	800
Steel manufacturing	794
Public utilities	768
Metal mining	764
Motion picture production and services	762
Search and navigation equipment	718
Industries with low earnings	
Individual and family services	282
Residential care	278
Job training and related services	255
Grocery stores	253
Hotels and other lodging places	251
Social services	244
General merchandise stores	231
Child care services	218
Apparel and accessory stores	203
Eating and drinking places	146

Employee benefits, once a minor addition to wages and salaries, continue to grow in diversity and cost. Along with traditional benefits—paid vacations, life and health insurance, and pensions—many employers now offer various benefits to accommodate the needs of a changing labor force—for example, child care; employee assistance programs that provide counseling for personal problems; and wellness programs that encourage exercise, stress management, and self-improvement. Benefits vary among occupational groups, full- and part-time workers, public and private sector workers, regions, unionized and nonunionized workers, and small and large establishments. Data indicate that full-time workers and those in medium-size and large establishments (100 or more workers) receive better benefits than part-time workers and those in small establishments.

Union affiliation may also play a role in earnings and benefits. In 1996, about 16 percent of workers throughout the Nation were union members or covered by union contracts. As Table 12 demonstrates, unionization of workers varies widely by industry. Over a third of the workers in government and transportation, communications, and public utilities are union members or are covered by union contracts. This compares with about 4 percent in finance, insurance, and real estate and under 3 percent in agriculture, forestry, and fishing.

Outlook

Total employment in the United States is projected to increase about 14 percent over the 1996-2006 period. Employment growth, however, is only one source of job openings; the total number of openings provided by any industry depends on its current employment level, its growth rate, and its need to replace workers who leave their jobs. Throughout the economy, in fact, replacement needs will create more job openings than employment growth. Employment size is a major determinant of job openings—large industries generally provide more openings than small ones. The occupational composition of an industry is another factor. Industries with a high concentration of professional, technical, and other jobs that require more formal education generally have fewer openings resulting from replacement needs, because these workers tend to leave their occupations less frequently. On the other hand, industries with a high concentration of service, laborer, and other jobs that require little formal education generally have more replacement openings, because these workers are more likely to leave their occupations.

Table 12. Percent of workers who are union members or covered by union contracts by Industry division, 1996

Industry Division	Union Members or Covered by Union Contracts
Total, all industries	16.2
Agriculture, forestry, and fishing	2.5
Mining	14.9
Construction	20.7
Manufacturing	18.4
Transportation, communications, and public utilities	35.3
Wholesale and retail trade	6.3
Finance, insurance, and real estate	0.1
Services	16.2
Government, public administration	37.2

Employment growth is determined largely by changes in worker productivity and the demand for the goods and services produced by an industry. Each industry is affected by a different set of variables that impacts the number and composition of jobs that will be available. Even within an industry, employment in different occupations may grow at different rates. For example, changes in technology, production methods, and business practices in an industry might eliminate some jobs, while creating others. Some industries may be growing rapidly overall, yet opportunities for workers in occupations that are adversely affected by technological change could be stagnant. Similarly, the rate of growth of some occupations may be declining in the economy as a whole, yet may be increasing in a rapidly growing industry.

Employment growth rates will vary widely among industries shown in Table 4. Employment in goods-producing industries is expected to remain constant, as growth in construction and agriculture, forestry, and fishing is expected to be offset by declining employment in mining and manufacturing. Growth in construction employment will be driven by new factory construction, as existing facilities are modernized; by new school construction, reflecting growth in the school-age population; and by infrastructure improvements, such as road and bridge construction. Overall employment in agriculture, forestry, and fishing will grow more slowly than average, with almost all new jobs occurring in the rapidly growing agricultural services industry, which includes landscaping, farm management, veterinary, soil preparation, and crop services.

Employment in mining is expected to decline, due to the spread of labor-saving technology and increased reliance on foreign sources of energy. Manufacturing employment also will decline, as improvements in production technology and rising imports eliminate many production occupations. Due primarily to increasing imports, apparel manufacturing is projected to lose about 150,000 jobs over the 1996-2006 period—more than any other manufacturing industry. Some manufacturing industries with strong domestic markets and export potential, however, are expected to experience increases in employment. Projected growth in drug manufacturing, for example, is based on the increasing domestic demand of an expanding elderly population and continued strong export growth.

Over the 1996-2006 period, growth in overall employment will result primarily from growth in service-producing industries, almost all of which are expected to witness increasing employment. Rising employment in these industries will be driven by service industries—the largest and fastest growing major industry sector—which is projected to provide more than 3 out of 5 new jobs across the Nation. Health, education, and business services will account for almost 6.5 million of these new jobs. In addition, employment in the Nation's fastest growing industry—computer and data processing services—is expected to more than double, adding another 1.3 million jobs. Overall population growth, the rise in the elderly and school age population, and the trend toward contracting out for computer, personnel, and other business services will stimulate job growth in the services sector.

Wholesale and retail trade is expected to add an additional 5.6 million jobs over the coming decade. Nearly 750,000 of these jobs will arise in wholesale trade, driven mostly by growth in trade and the overall economy. Retail trade is expected to add 4.8 million jobs over the 1996-2006 period, resulting largely from increased personal income levels. Eating and drinking places will account for more than 1.3 million of these openings. In contrast to most other industries in the major industry division, employment in department, clothing, and variety stores is expected to decline, as jobs in relatively labor-intensive clothing and accessory stores are displaced by the growth of "mega-retailers" and discount stores.

By 2006, employment in transportation, communications, and public utilities will likely increase by nearly 800,000 new jobs. Trucking and air transportation are expected to add more than half of these jobs, as these industries combined will generate about 500,000 jobs. Trucking industry growth will be fueled by growth in the volume of goods that need to be shipped as the economy expands. Air transportation will expand, a consumer demand increases, reflecting rising personal income and relatively inexpensive fares resulting from increasing corn petition. Despite strong growth in demand for telephone services, employment in the telephone communications industry will increase by only about 20,000 jobs, due to labor-saving technology and increased competition. Broadcasting industry employment will not sustain the rapid growth of the past, as the cable television market approaches saturation.

Overall employment growth in finance and insurance is expected to be around 11 percent, adding 1.4 million jobs by 2006. In spite of this growth, employment in banking will decline, as services traditionally offered by commercial banks are increasingly offered by a range of other institutions. Nondepository institutions—including personal and business credit institutions, as well as mortgage banks—are expected to grow at a rapid rate, at the expense of commercial banks. Insurance is expected to add the most jobs—more than 250,000—within this major industry sector.

All 913,000 new government jobs will likely occur in state and local government, reflecting growth in the population and its demand for non-Federal public services. The Federal government is expected to lose more than 100,000 jobs over the 1996-2006 period, as attempts to balance the Federal budget and contract out services to private establishments are felt.

In sum, recent changes in the economy are having far-reaching and complex effects on employment in each of the industries covered in the *Career Guide*. Jobseekers would be well-advised to follow these changes closely, keeping track of developments in industries and the variety of occupations which are found in each industry. For more information on specific occupations within industries, consult the *Career Guide's* companion publication, the 1998-1999 *Occupational Outlook Handbook*, which provides detailed information on 250 occupations.

Bibliography

USEFUL CAREER RESOURCES AND INTERNET SITES

Compiled by Mike Farr

This is not a conventional bibliography. My comments are informal and admittedly biased, and I include only materials I like in some way. I developed this bibliography for a book I wrote titled *The Very Quick Job Search*. Because the bibliography was so well received there, I made a few changes and include it here for your information.

I've been looking at career materials for over 20 years, and it still amazes me how much junk is out there. A good example are resume books that still suggest that sending out many good-looking resumes is the way to get a job. While the advice on creating a resume may be good, the advice on *using* it is–too often–not. I tried to sort the wheat from the chaff, so materials that I do not consider good or useful are not listed.

I emphasize books you are most likely to find in a bookstore or good library. Materials published or distributed by JIST are among those listed, as are some that I have written. Of course, I tend to be enthusiastic about materials I have been involved in, although I try to be objective.

I organize the materials into categories and provide comments on many titles. Within categories, books are not presented in a particular order, although titles published by JIST are listed first. For brevity, I only mention a publisher if it is JIST. I don't provide publication dates, because materials are often updated regularly.

A good bookstore or library should be able to locate a book by its title and author. Most bookstores have a computer that allows them to find any book you want. Ask them to look up a desired title in *Books in Print*. Some materials are rather obscure and not easy to obtain. Others are out of print (it's difficult to keep up with all this), although you may find them though an interlibrary loan program. Ask your librarian to help you locate something you *really* want.

So browse the descriptions that follow. Remember that this an informal list rather than a formal bibliography, but I hope you find it helpful.

General Advice on Finding Career and Job Search Information

As mentioned, many resource materials I mention in this bibliography can be found in a good library. Libraries have more information than I can list, including journals, newspapers, books, CD-ROM databases, access to the Internet, and other resources. So here are some tips for using the library as your job search friend.

The librarian: Your friendly librarian can be one of your best sources of specific information during your job search. If you can ask the question, he or she can probably give you some ideas on where to find an answer.

Finding Facts Fast: Todd. Perhaps the best book on finding out about anything at the library or elsewhere. Great research aid.

Trade magazines and journals: Most libraries will have one or more professional journals related to a variety of major career areas. Staying current on the publications in your field will help you in the interviewing process. These publications sometimes have job listings.

You Can Get Anything You Want: Dawson.

Develop a Network of Contacts, Including Networking with Members of Professional and Trade Associations

You already know hundreds of people, and networking to meet more is covered in many job search books I recommend. Consider joining professional associations related to the job you want. Your membership gives you access to meetings, newsletters, and other information sources. But the biggest benefit is that other members are an excellent source of networking opportunities. They often hire or supervise people with similar skills—or know those who do. You can get access to membership lists and use the contact information to call members in your area or in any part of the country. Make lots of phone contacts, send JIST Cards, resumes, and thank-you notes—and get lots of interviews!

Directories

People who work in the careers that interest you can tell you which organizations to join. A good library will often have one or more helpful directories including the following:

Career Guide to Professional Associations: Garrett Park Press. Describes more than 2,500 professional associations. The information is more oriented to the job seeker than is the *Encyclopedia of Associations,* but some information may not be current.

Encyclopedia of Associations: Gale Research Company. A listing of more than 22,000 professional, trade, and other nonprofit organizations in the United States, representing more issues than you can imagine. It cross-references them in various helpful ways.

Encyclopedia of Associations—International Organizations: Gale Research. A listing of more than 11,000 organizations in 180 countries. Includes trade, business, and commercial associations, and associations of labor unions.

Professional & Trade Association Job Finder: By career category, details over 1,000 sources of information, referrals and more.

Newspapers and Professional Journals

While the want ads in newspapers represent relatively few of the available job openings—and allow almost everyone to apply for them—some people do get jobs from want ads. Newspapers also contain other useful employment information. Look for tips on new or expanding businesses and leads for unadvertised job openings. Articles about new or expanding companies can be valuable leads for new job possibilities.

If relocating is a possibility, look at newspapers from other areas. They can serve as a source of job leads as well as indicate some idea of the job market. The major out-of-town newspapers are sold in most large cities and are available in many public libraries.

Some newspapers such as *The New York Times, The Chicago Tribune,* and *The Financial Times* are national in scope. *The National Business Employment Weekly,* published by *The Wall Street Journal,* contains much information of interest to professional job seekers. But remember that competition for jobs advertised in these sources is fierce and don't rely on them too heavily.

Review these sources for articles mentioning your target companies. Look for information on new products, expansions, consolidations, relocations, promotions, articles by executives in the companies, annual company earnings, and current problems.

Check back issues of newspapers for old want ads. They can provide important information on job duties, salary, and benefits. There may even be a want ad for a job in which you are interested. Perhaps the job was never filled or the person previously hired has already moved on.

Specialty newspapers such as *The National Business Employment Weekly* have a compilation of the previous week's want ads from the regional editions of *The Wall Street Journal,* plus its own want ads. *National Ad Search* is a weekly tabloid that has a compilation of want ads from 75 key newspapers across the U.S. Expect major competition for jobs listed this widely.

Back issues of major newspapers can be accessed on the Internet, allowing you to sort by key words or for specific geographic areas.

Business Newsbank, Newsbank, Inc.: This service provides the narrative of articles from newspapers and business journals from 400 cities. It cross-references information by company name, individual's name, industry, or product category.

New York Times Index: A thorough index of all stories that appear in the *Times.*

Wall Street Journal Index: This is an important source of information on larger business and business trends.

Where the Jobs Are: 1200 Journals with Job/Career Openings: Feingold and Winkler. A unique resource providing tips on responding to journal ads and a cross-reference to specific journals by job type.

Where to Find Business Information: Brownstone and Curruth. Lists and describes the many newsletters, journals, computer databases, books, and other sources of business information.

I provide additional details on using the newspapers in the section titled "Getting Information on Specific Employers."

Job Search and Career Planning Books by Yours Truly

I've worked on many job search, career planning, and occupational information books, assessment tests, videos, and software over the years. Some are readily available in bookstores and libraries, while others are used by schools, institutions, and instructors. Most of my materials are published by JIST and many are included in the various sections of this bibliography, along with brief descriptions.

I feel strongly that only two main issues in the career planning and job search field really matter. The first is that it is essential to select a career that will satisfy you. This involves knowing yourself well enough to select *the* job rather than *a* job. The second issue is, if you need to find a job, you might as well find a good one and do it in as little time as possible. All of my books incorporate these simple principles and tend to be practical and results-oriented. Here is a partial list, should this be of interest to you:

Books You Are Most Likely to Find in Bookstores and Libraries

The Very Quick Job Search—Get a Good Job in Less Time

How to Get a Job Now!—Six Easy Steps to Getting a Better Job

The Quick Resume and Cover Letter Book

The Quick Interview and Salary Negotiations Book

America's Top Resumes for America's Top Jobs

America's Fastest Growing Jobs

America's Top Jobs for College Graduates

America's Top Jobs for People Without a Four-Year Degree

America's Top Medical, Education, and Human Services Jobs

America's Top Office, Management Sales, & Professional Jobs

Best Jobs for the 21st Century (coauthored with LaVerne Ludden)

Occupational Reference Books

My name appears on several occupational reference books that can be found in libraries. These books are mostly based on information obtained from government sources. I was part of a team that made the information useful. Calling anyone an author of these books is a bit of a stretch, although I spent many hours working on them. These titles include the following:

*The O*NET Dictionary of Occupational Titles*

The Enhanced Occupational Outlook Handbook

The Complete Guide to Occupational Exploration

Materials Used in Schools and Other Programs

One of my life's missions has been to improve the information and training that students and job seekers receive in career and job search programs. Here are some materials I have authored for this use —most are *not* available in bookstores but can be obtained from JIST.

The Quick Job Search: A 36-page book covering the essentials needed for a successful job search. Very short but covers the basics.

The JIST Career Planning and Job Search Course: For instructors, a complete curriculum I wrote to support the use of *The Very Quick Job Search*. It includes lesson plans, over 50 overhead transparencies, and reproducible handout masters.

The JIST Course: The Young Person's Guide to Getting and Keeping a Good Job: Coauthored by Marie Pavlicko for use by high school students. It was field tested with thousands of students. Good graphics and easy-to-follow narrative. Accompanying instructor's guide and transparency set.

The Right Job for You: A thorough career planning book that includes lots of information and worksheets.

The Guide for Occupational Exploration Inventory: This is an interest "test" to help with career exploration.

The Work Book: Getting the Job You Want: This is my first job search book. Originally published in 1981, it has been revised several times and has sold over 300,000 copies. It remains popular in postsecondary schools and programs. An instructor's guide is available. Published by McGraw-Hill, Glencoe Division.

Job Finding Fast: A thorough book that includes sections on career decision making as well as job seeking. It was written to support a full course or program at the postsecondary or college level. An instructor's guide is available. Also published by McGraw-Hill, Glencoe Division.

Videos and software: I've written content scripts for numerous job search and career-related videos and have worked on a variety of career-related software.

Etcetera: I've worked on many workbooks and other projects over the years, including several series for youth coauthored with Susan Christophersen (The Living Skills Series and The Career and Life Skills Series). I have edited or helped to develop many others. It's been work and it's been fun.

Career Materials Published by JIST

I formerly listed career-related books published by JIST in a separate section, but the list became too long. Besides, I only included those JIST books that were likely to be found in a bookstore or library and excluded many videos, assessment tests, instructional materials, and books used in schools and institutions. The JIST books you are most likely to find in a bookstore or library are now included in the various subsections of this bibliography. If you want a more thorough list, contact JIST for a catalog. JIST's Internet site (www.JIST.com) provides free chapters of many books and links to other career-related sites.

Information on Occupations and Industries

Hundreds of books provide information on jobs, and most libraries have a basic selection. I suggest you begin with the general career references, and then look for more specific information on jobs that interest you most.

While most people focus their career-planning time on choosing an occupation, I suggest you also consider the industry where you want to work. For example, if you have experience in accounting (a career) and an interest in airplanes (an industry), perhaps accounting-oriented jobs in a flight-related industry such as airports, airplane manufacturing, or air-transportation regulation would be your best fit. I include industry references for this reason and recommend you browse some of them.

Best Sources of Information on Industries

Career Guide to America's Top Industries: Based on information from the U.S. Department of Labor, provides details on over 40 major industries. Easy-to-read and loaded with helpful information, it was written specifically to assist in career planning and job seeking. If you are going to use one book on industries, this is the one I recommend. JIST.

U.S. Industrial Outlook: Based on information from the U.S. Department of Commerce, it provides business forecasts for over 300 industries. Good source of information to review prior to interviews.

Standard Industrial Classification Manual (SIC): A standard reference developed by the U.S. Department of Commerce that lists all industries in an organized way. Accountants, banks, the IRS, and many others use it as a way to codify business. While I would not recommend this as light reading, it is useful for identifying more specialized industries for a job search or career exploration. Available from JIST.

North American Industrial Classification System (NAICS): A new system to replace the SIC Manual was introduced in 1998 and will be used in Mexico, the United States, and Canada. This book has similar uses to the older SIC manual. Available from JIST.

Best Sources of Information on Occupations

The Occupational Outlook Handbook: Highly recommended. Published by the U.S. Department of Labor and updated every other year, provides descriptions for 250 major jobs covering 87 percent of the workforce. The descriptions are well written and provide information on pay, working conditions, related jobs, projected growth, and more. A very helpful book for exploring career options or for job seeking. Available from JIST.

America's Top 300 Jobs: This is a "bookstore" version of the *Occupational Outlook Handbook* that includes descriptions for all 250 jobs plus additional information. JIST.

The Enhanced Occupational Outlook Handbook: Includes all the descriptions in the *Occupational Outlook Handbook* plus 3,000 descriptions of more specialized jobs and 5,000 additional titles. Easy to use. JIST.

The O*NET Dictionary of Occupational Titles: This is the first book to provide information on the new O*NET jobs. A new database of occupations called the Occupational Information Network (O*NET) will replace the *Dictionary of Occupational Titles.* This new book provides descriptions for the approximately 1,200 new O*NET jobs plus details on related skills, earnings, abilities, education, and other requirements for each. JIST.

America's Top Jobs Series. Each book in this series includes about 100 job descriptions plus a review of job market trends, career planning and job search advice, summary information on hundreds of additional jobs, and useful appendices. The job descriptions are based on those used in the *Occupational Outlook Hand-*

book and include details on pay, education required, working conditions, and more. All are published by JIST.

America's Fastest Growing Jobs: J. Michael Farr.

America's Top Jobs for College Graduates: J. Michael Farr.

America's Top Jobs for People Without a Four-Year Degree: J. Michael Farr.

America's Top Medical, Education, and Human Services Jobs: J. Michael Farr.

America's Top Office, Management, Sales & Professional Jobs: J. Michael Farr.

America's Federal Jobs

America's Top Military Careers

Best Jobs for the 21st Century: J. Michael Farr and LaVerne Ludden. Lists of jobs for best paying, highest earning at different education levels and other criteria, plus hundreds of job descriptions. JIST.

Complete Guide For Occupational Exploration: The U.S. Department of Labor developed the GOE to help people explore careers based on interests. The CGOE narrows broad interests to the many specific jobs within each major category. It lists over 12,000 jobs by occupational cluster, interests, abilities, and traits required for successful performance. You can look up jobs by industry, types of skills or abilities required, values, related home/leisure activities, military experience, education required, or related jobs you have had. JIST.

Enhanced Guide For Occupational Exploration: Similar to the CGOE, but also provides descriptions for 2,500 jobs. These jobs cover 95 percent of the workforce, and few people will miss those that are not listed. JIST.

Dictionary Of Occupational Titles: Published by the U.S. Department of Labor, the DOT provides brief descriptions for 12,741 jobs—more than any other reference. It is a large book, over 1,400 pages, and not particularly easy-to-use. But it is a standard reference that many other books cross-reference. Available from JIST.

More Career Information Books

Hundreds of books provide information on specific careers. I've selected representative titles, but you will find many others in a good library.

American Almanac of Jobs and Salaries: Wright. Useful data on pay and opportunities for hundreds of jobs.

Career Connection for College Education—A Guide to College Education and Related Career Opportunities, revised edition: Fred Rowe. Provides information on over 100 college majors and 1,000 occupations that are related to them. Includes information on salaries, course requirements, related high school courses, and other details useful in planning a college major. JIST.

Career Connection for Technical Education—A Guide to Technical Training and Related Career Opportunities: Fred Rowe. Similar to the above but providing information on 70 technical training majors and 450 related occupations. JIST

Career Finder—Pathways to Over 1,500 Entry-Level Jobs: Schwartz and Breckner.

Careers without College Series: A series of 11 books for those not planning on a four-year college degree. Topics on health care, fashion, cars, office, sports, and others.

Choosing an Airline Career: March.

Discover the Best Jobs for You!: Krannich and Krannich. Explores skills and interests and explores specific jobs.

Encyclopedia of Careers: Ferguson Publishing. A series of books providing useful information on all major occupations.

Great Careers: The 4th of July Guide to Careers, Internships, and Volunteer Opportunities in the Non-Profit Sector: An enormous reference of books and programs covering jobs with a social cause.

High Paying Jobs in 6 Months or Less: For jobs requiring brief training.

High Tech Jobs for Non High Tech Grads: O'Brien. Good ideas for those without technical training.

Jobs Rated Almanac: Krantz. Ranks 250 jobs by pay, benefits, stress, and other criteria.

Occu-facts: Provides one-page descriptions for over 500 jobs in an easy-to-read format. Jobs are arranged into groups of similar occupations, which encourages its use as a career exploration tool.

Opportunities in... Series: A series of books published by VGM Career Horizons. Each covers related jobs in that field, skills required, working conditions, pay, education required, jargon. Some of the careers covered are Secretarial; Health and Medical Careers; Office Occupations; Data Processing; Computer Science; Travel Careers; Hotel and Motel Management; Cable Television; Accounting.

Outdoor Careers: Shenk.

Peterson's Engineering, Science and Computer Jobs: An annual update of 900 employers, types of jobs, more.

Professional Careers Series: Another series of books on a variety of professional jobs including finance, medicine, law, computers, accounting, business, and others.

Real Estate Careers: Jamic and Rejnis.

Revised Handbook for Analyzing Jobs: A technical book describing various coding systems used to quantify and categorize jobs. Available from JIST.

The Worker Traits Data Book: Donald Mayall. A technical book that provides coded information on over 12,000 jobs in the Dictionary of Occupational Titles. Much of this information is not available elsewhere. JIST.

Worker Trait Group Guide: A simpler version of the *Guide for Occupational Exploration* providing information on clusters of similar jobs. Available from JIST.

Career Planning and Job Search Books

There are innumerable job search and career planning books, and more are published all the time. Most are written by corporate recruiters, headhunters, social workers, academics, and personnel experts who are well intentioned but have little practical experience in determining whether the job search methods they recommend actually work. Many books provide advice that would, if followed, actually slow down the job search process.

Generally, I discard books that suggest sending out resumes or answering want ads as good job search methods—or that do not include methods appropriate for approaching smaller businesses. The research clearly indicates the importance of these issues, and anyone who is not aware of this should not be considered an expert. So, in my humble opinion, here are some of the better books.

Highly Recommended Career Planning and Job Search Books

This is a short list that includes a few of my own books, a few books published by JIST, and a few books published by others that I like and are widely regarded as among the best books on their topics.

The Very Quick Job Search—Get a Good Job in Less Time: J. Michael Farr. This is my most thorough job search book, and it includes lots of information on career planning and, of course, job seeking. This is the book I would recommend to a friend who was out of work, if I had to recommend just one book. While written as a "bookstore" book, it is widely used in schools and colleges. There is an accompanying activities book, curriculum, and transparency set. This book has won a variety of awards including best career book of the year. JIST.

How to Get a Job Now!—Six Easy Steps for Getting a Better Job: J. Michael Farr. This is a short book that covers the basics in an interactive format. I included those things I believe most important to know if you want to get a better job in less time. JIST.

Using the Internet and the World Wide Web in Your Job Search: Fred Jandt and Mary Nemnich. For new or more experienced Internet users, it is full of information on getting career information, finding job listings, creating electronic resumes, networking with user groups, and other interesting techniques. Reviews all major career sites. JIST.

The PIE Method for Career Success—A New Job Search Strategy: Daniel Porot. The PIE method (Pleasure, Information, and Employment) uses a visual and creative format to present career planning and job search techniques. The author is one of Europe's major career consultants, and this book presents his powerful career planning and job seeking concepts in a memorable way. JIST.

Inside Secrets of Finding a Teaching Job: Jack and Diane Warner and Clyde Bryan. Practical advice for new and experienced teachers looking for a new job. JIST.

What Color Is Your Parachute?: Richard N. Bolles. This is the best selling career-changing book ever. Well written and entertaining, it is updated each year and includes a useful self assessment section, "The Quick Job Hunting Map." Bolles is fun to read, and the book is highly recommended.

The Complete Job Search Handbook: All the Skills You Need to Get Any Job, and Have a Good Time Doing It: Howard Figler. A solid book with lots of exercises to assess skills, values, and needs. Procedures for exploring careers and developing a job objective. An excellent book that is loaded with innovative ideas.

Other Career and Job Search Books for a General Audience

Getting the Job You Really Want: J. Michael Farr. Covers career planning and job seeking topics in a workbook format with lots of activities. Very popular in schools and job search programs and available in bookstores. An instructor's guide is also available. JIST.

Job Search 101—Getting Started on Your Career Path: Pat Morton and Marcia Fox. For college seniors and recent graduates seeking entry-level jobs. JIST.

Job Finding Fast: J. Michael Farr. A thorough career planning and job search workbook used in colleges. An instructor's guide is available. Available from JIST.

Job Strategies for Professionals: Based on advice provided by the U.S. Department of Labor, it provides job search advice for professionals and managers who have lost their jobs. JIST.

Job Rights and Survival Strategies–A Handbook for Terminated Employees: Paul Tobias and Susan Sauter. Covers the legal rights and benefits as well as how to handle these traumatic situations with dignity. Distributed by JIST.

900,000 Plus Jobs Annually: Feingold and Winkler. Reviews 900+ periodicals that list openings and positions wanted in hundreds of fields.

Big Splash in a Small Pond–Finding a Great Job in a Small Company: Resnick and Pechter.

Change Your Job, Change Your Life: Krannich. Reviews jobs trends and job search methods.

Do What You Are–Discover the Perfect Career for You Through the Secrets of Personality Type: Tieger and Barron-Tieger.

Go Hire Yourself An Employer: Richard Irish. Lots of good stuff in this new revision. Covers skills identification, job search, resumes, interviews, the unemployment "blahs," succeeding on the next job, and other topics.

Guerrilla Tactics in the New Job Market: Tom Jackson.

Professional Careers Sourcebook, an Informational Guide for Career Planning: K. Savage and C. Dorgan

Hardball Job Hunting Tactics: Dick Wright. From a trainer with lots of experience with the hard to employ. Excellent sections on completing applications (a topic not often covered well) and resumes. Brief but good section on job search. Tips for people with various "problems" on how to overcome them.

How to Get Interviews from Classified Job Ads: Elderkin.

Information Interviewing: What It Is and How to Use It in Your Career: Martha Stoodley.

Job & Career Building: Richard Germann and Peter Arnold. A good choice for laid-off professionals, managers, and others with more experience and training.

Job Hunters Sourcebook: Where to Find Employment Leads and Other Job Search Sources: Michelle LeCompte.

Marketing Yourself: The Ultimate Job Seeker's Guide: Dorothy Leeds.

New Network Your Way to Job and Career Success: Ron and Carol Krannich.

Re-Careering in Turbulent Times: Ronald Krannich. Lots of good material including employment trends, selecting a career, getting training and education, communication skills, sources of job leads, interviewing, resumes, relocation, public employment opportunities, and career advancement.

Robert Half On Hiring: Robert Half. Written to help employers select better employees. Most of the advice is based on a series of employer surveys providing unique insight into how employers make hiring decisions.

Selling On The Phone: Porterfield. Self-teaching guide for telemarketing and other sales approaches. Good ideas for reinforcing effective phone skills in the job search.

Starting Over: You in the New Workplace: Jo Danna.

The Complete Job Search Book: Richard Beatty.

The Job Bank Guide to Employment Services: Bob Adams.

The Only Job Hunting Guide You'll Ever Need: Kathryn Ross Petras.

Three Boxes Life and How to Get Out of Them: Richard Bolles. Introduces the concepts of "life/work planning." Very thorough.

Where Do I Go From Here With the Rest of My Life?: John Crystal and Richard Bolles. John Crystal has died, but his techniques and insights into the career planning process helped to start an important movement that came to be called "Life/Work Planning."

Who's Hiring Who: Richard Lathrop. Solid, practical information for job seekers. Good self-assessment sections and excellent resume advice (he calls them "qualifications briefs"). I particularly like this book and respect Lathrop's work.

Specialized Career and Job Search Books

Many books have been written on specialized career and job search topics. For example, there are books to help various segments of our population gain a competitive edge; books on specialized job search methods (such as using the telephone); and books on getting certain types of jobs (such as those with small business or overseas jobs). Some of these materials are not easily categorized into one group, so look through the entire list for things related to your situation–there is probably something in here that "fits."

Internet Job Search Books

The Internet is a growing source of information on all topics, but you can also waste a lot of time there unless you know where to look. Here are a few helpful guides to get you started.

Using the Internet and the World Wide Web in Your Job Search: Fred Jandt and Mary Nemnich. A good book for both new and more experienced Internet users. Lists all major career sites and, more importantly, tells you how to use the Internet in effective ways. JIST.

The Quick Internet Guide to Career and College Information: Anne Wolfinger. A time-saving and brief guide for educators, counselors, and employment professionals to the best sites and how to use them. JIST.

Electronic Job Search Revolution: Kennedy and Morrow. Tips on using your computer and online services to get jobs.

Resources for Youth and Parents

An enormous number of materials are available for young people to help them explore career alternatives. I present only a few here. Most are not available in bookstores and are available only from the publishers. If you help youth, I suggest you contact JIST and ask for their institutional catalog; it presents materials from a variety of publishers. I also include a few good books for parents to help their kids in their quest for a career (and, of course, to get them out of the house).

Helping Your Child Choose a Career: Luthor Otto. One of the most helpful books available on the topic for parents, teachers, and even kids. Comprehensive and sensible advice. JIST.

Young Person's OOH: For grades 6-10. Provides information on 250 jobs listed in the ***Occupational Outlook Handbook,*** plus career exploration advice. JIST.

Young Person's Guide to Getting & Keeping a Good Job: J. Michael Farr and Marie Pavilicko. A practical workbook for high school students. A separate instructor's guide and overhead transparencies are also available. JIST.

Creating Your Life's Work Portfolio for High School Students: Good activities and content. JIST.

Career and Life Skills Series: J. Michael Farr and Susan Christophersen. Four books for grades 7-12 on career preparation. JIST.

HIRE Learning Series: Patricia Duffy and T. Walter Wannie. Three books for high school students on career planning, job seeking, and job success. JIST.

Dream Catchers: Norene Lindsay. A career exploration workbook for grades 5 to 8. JIST.

Pathfinder–Exploring Career and Educational Paths: Norene Lindsay. A workbook for high school students with a separate instructor's guide. JIST.

Secrets to Getting Better Grades: Brian Marshall and Wendy Ford. Teaches students to study smart, with lots of practical tips for notes, tests, papers, memory, and other techniques. JIST.

Exploring Careers–A Young Person's Guide to Over 300 Careers, revised edition: A revision of the original, published by the U.S. Department of Labor. An excellent resource for young people, providing details on over 300 jobs in an interesting format. JIST.

Career Coaching Your Kids: Montross et al. Tips on helping your children explore career options.

Career Discovery Encyclopedia: This is a six-volume set for grades 4 and up with reading level at about the 7th grade, appropriate through high school. Excellent, with over 1,000 pages and helpful ways to look up jobs. A school or other good library may have this set. Excellent.

Children's Dictionary of Occupations. For elementary and middle school students, covers 300 occupations.

Directory of American Youth Organizations: Erickson. Lists more than 500 organizations.

Job Power: The Young People's Job Finding Guide: Haldane and Martin. One of our favorite books for group process ideas on skills identification and selecting a job objective. Simple, direct, useful for any age.

Joyce Lain Kennedy's Career Book: Kennedy and Laramore. A very thorough book, covering just about everything that a young person (or parent) would need to know about career and life decisions. Highly recommended.

Parents With Careers Workbook: Good worksheets and advice on getting organized, child care, home management, single parents, dual careers, time use, and so on.

Summer Jobs for Students: Reviews sources for 20,000 summer jobs and explains how to use the Internet for additional information.

Books for Working Parents and Couples

Home but Not Alone–The Parents' Work-at-Home Handbook: Katherine Murray. A very good book that won an award for being one of the top three business books of the year. Lots of solid tips. JIST.

The Working Parents' Handbook–How to Succeed at Work, Raise Your Kids, Maintain a Home, and Still Have Time for You: Katherine Murray. An entertaining and helpful book

providing advice on handling the multiple roles of working parents. Excellent. JIST.

Surviving Your Partner's Job Loss: Jukes and Rosenberg.

The Three Career Couple: Byalick and Saslow. On handling two jobs plus a family.

Books to Help Get Jobs in the Government, Education, and Nonprofit Sector

The Unauthorized Teacher's Survival Guide: Jack Warner, Clyde Bryan with Diane Warner. Great advice for new and experienced teachers, telling you the things you do not learn in teacher's college. JIST.

Inside Secrets of Finding a Teaching Job: Jack Warner, Clyde Bryan with Diane Warner. Helpful techniques for finding a job in teaching, based on years of experience and interviews with many educators. JIST.

Alternative Careers for Teachers: Pollack and Beard. Good ideas on getting a job in another field using transferable skills.

Careers in Local and State Government: Zehring. Where they are, how to apply, take tests, internships, and summer jobs. Job search tips.

Complete Guide to Public Employment: Krannich. Reviews opportunities with federal and local governments, associations, nonprofits, foundations, research, international, and many other institutions. Well done.

Doing Well by Doing Good–The First Complete Guide to Careers in the Non-Profit Sector: McAdam.

Moving Out Of Education: A Guide To Career Management & Change: Krannich and Banis. Good tips for this special situation from an ex-educator who moved out.

Take Charge of Your Own Career–A Guide to Federal Employment: Moore and Vanderwey.

Minorities and Immigrants

Best Companies for Minorities: Graham. Profiles of 85 companies.

Career Opportunities for Bilinguals and Multiculturals –A Directory of Resources in Education, Employment and Business: Wertsman. Over 3,500 listings.

Directory of Special Programs for Minority Group Members: Willis L. Johnson. Over 2,800 sources of training, jobs, scholarships, programs.

Finding a Job in the United States: Friedenberg and Bradley.

Minority Career Guide: Kastre, Kastre, and Edwards.

Minority Organizations–The Directory of Special Programs for Minority Group Members: Oakes. The largest source of information available covering over 5,800 professional organizations and resources.

Stepping Up: Placing Minority Women Into Managerial and Professional Jobs: Tips to replicate results of a program that increased the pay, advancement, and retention of minority women.

The Big Book of Minority Opportunities–Directory of Special Programs for Minority Group Members: Oakes. 4,000 source of scholarships, financial aid, and special programs.

The Black Woman's Career Guide: Nivens. Good advice on over 50 good jobs, dress and grooming, skills ID, job search, and more.

The Colorblind Career: Stenson. Tips for African-American, Hispanic, and Asian-Americans to succeed.

Workers Over 40, Displaced Workers, Retirement Issues

Arthur Young's Pre-Retirement Planning Book: Very well done book. Lots of worksheets.

Cracking the Over 50 Job Market: Conner. Good job search advice.

Getting a Job After 50: John S. Morgan.

Getting a Job After 50: Morgan. Age discrimination is real and people over 50 need better-than-average job seeking skills to overcome this.

Helping the Dislocated Worker: Ashley and Zahniser. Reviews suggested services and programs—helpful for program planners.

Job Hunting After 50: Strategies for Success: Samuel Ray.

Job Hunting for the 40+ Executive: Birsner. Good advice on the personal and job search needs of middle-aged executives.

Mid Career Job Hunting: Official Handbook of the 40+ Club: E. Patricia Birsner. Solid advice on getting back on track and getting a job.

Retirement Careers: Marsh.

Second Careers—New Ways to Work After 50: Bird. Analyzes career changes of over 6,000 people and how it worked out.

The Over 40 Job Guide: Petras.

People with Disabilities, Disadvantaged Groups, The Homeless

Know-How is the Key: Dixie Lee Wright. A job search program (student workbook and instructor's guide) for high school through young adult "special needs" students with learning and other disabilities. JIST.

Americans with Disabilities Handbook—and Technical Assistance Manual: Government publication providing comprehensive information on the Americans With Disabilities Act (ADA) and how it is interpreted. Available from JIST.

A Helping Hand, A Guide to Customized Support Services for Special Populations: Thorough guide for program operators who emphasize employment—JTPA, older workers, ex-offenders, others.

Bouncing Back from Injury: How to Take Charge of Your Recuperation: Karen Klein and Carla Derrick Hope.

Career Success for People with Physical Disabilities: Kissane. Good advice for job seekers. Lots of exercises.

Complete Guide to Employing Persons with Disabilities: Henry McCarthy. From the National Rehabilitation Information Center; phone (800) 346-2742.

Job Hunting for the Disabled: Adele Lewis and Edith Marks. Interest surveys, programs, job descriptions, and job search tips.

Job Strategies for People With Disabilities: Witt. Good advice as well as lists of resource materials and programs.

Job-Hunting Tips for the So-Called Handicapped or People Who Have Disabilities: Richard N. Bolles.

No One is Unemployable: Angel and Harney. A good resource for welfare-to-work, ex-offender programs, and other "difficult" populations.

Recovery from Alcohol and Substance Abuse, Coping with Job Loss

Career Knockouts: How to Battle Back: Joyce Lain Kennedy. Avoiding, learning, and even benefiting from job failures.

Clean, Sober and Unemployed: Elliot. Good advice for recovering substance abusers.

Coping with Unemployment: Jud. Dealing with long-term unemployment.

Sacked! Why Good People Get Fired and How to Avoid It: Gould.

Termination Trap: Best Strategies for a Job Going Sour: Cohen. Excellent insights on avoiding or dealing with job loss.

The Career Seekers: Tannenbaum. For anyone recovering from codependency or in a recovery program.

People with Four-Year College, Advanced Degrees, and Technical Training

Finding a Job in Your Field: A Handbook for Ph.D.'s & M.A.'s

Jobs for English Majors and Other Smart People: Good tips for liberal arts grads.

The MBA's Guide to Career Planning: Ed Holton

The High-Tech Career Book: Collard.

Job Search for the Technical Professional: Moore. For programmers and engineers.

Military/Veterans

Many good materials are available to help vets transition to "civilian" employment. Following are some of the specific ones, but many of the career and job search books (such as *America's Top Resumes*) include veterans among their examples.

America's Top Military Careers: Based on Dept. of Defense information, provides details on 200 enlisted and officer occupations including civilian counterparts. JIST.

Complete Guide for Occupational Exploration: Among other things, this comprehensive career reference book cross references military occupations to over 12,000 civilian job titles. JIST.

Jobs and the Military Spouse—Married, Mobile, and Motivated for the New Job Market: Farley.

Resume and Job Hunting Guide for Present and Future Veterans: DePrez. Helpful book with some good techniques.

Veteran's Survival Guide to Good Jobs in Bad Times: Grant's Guides.

You and the Armed Forces: Marrs. Better understand career options and what to expect from military life.

Young Person's Guide to Military Service: Bradley. Covers pros and cons of going into the services. Good sections for minorities and women.

Your Career in the Military: Gordan. Reviews advantages of education and money. Enlistment options and procedures.

Women

More women are in the workforce more than ever, and they tend to be better educated than average. But women without advanced educations and who are single heads of households are not doing as well. Special advice and resources are clearly needed; here are just a few.

Congratulations! You've Been Fired: Sound Advice for Women Who've Been Terminated, Pink Slipped, Downsized or Otherwise Unemployed: Emily Koltnow and Lynne S. Dumas.

Developing New Horizons for Women: Ruth Helm Osborn. Very good text to improve self-esteem, identify strengths, and develop long-range life and career plans.

Directory of Special Opportunities for Women: Over 1,000 resources for women entering and reentering the workforce. Recommended.

Good Enough for Mothers: Marshall. Balancing work and family.

Homemaker's Complete Guide to Entering the Job Market: Lussier. Useful techniques to transfer homemaking skills to work world and find a job.

Resume Guide for Women of the '90s: Marino.

The Extra Edge: Mitchell. Success strategies for women, based on data from women grads of Harvard Business School.

The Woman's Job Search Handbook: Bloomburg and Holden. Well-done career planning and job search techniques.

Time for a Change: A Woman's Guide to Non-Traditional Occupations: For women considering nontraditional jobs: exercises and narrative, plus a review of 10 growth-oriented jobs.

Winning the Salary Game: Salary Negotiations for Women: Sherry Chastain.

Yes to Career Success!: Hennekins.

International Jobs

If you want to work in another country, you had better do your homework in advance. For example, you should carefully consider personal and family issues that might impede a full adjustment to your host country. Here are some resources to help you consider this option.

Directory of European Industrial and Trade Associations: CBD Research, Kent, England. Lists the industrial and trade associations of Europe.

Directory of European Professional and Learned Societies: CBD Research, Kent, England. Similar in format but deals strictly with learned and professional societies.

Foreign Jobs: The Most Popular Countries: Casewit. Profiles desirable countries and how to get jobs there.

How to Get a Job in Europe—The Insider's Guide: Surrey Books. Gives country-by-country listings of newspapers, business directories, regulations, organizations, and other useful information.

How to Get a Job in the Pacific Rim: Surrey Books. Information similar to above, but for countries bordering the Pacific Ocean.

International Agencies: These agencies maintain lists of people available to work as consultants, and you might want to register with one or more: World Bank; U.S. Aid for International Development (USAID); United Nations Development Program; United National Industrial Development Organization.

International Careers: Bob Adams, Inc. Information on finding government, corporate, and nonprofit jobs.

International Employment Hotline: Names and addresses of government and nongovernment hiring organizations.

International Jobs: Where They Are, How to Get Them: A Handbook for Over 500 Career Opportunities Around the World: Kocher.

Key British Enterprises: Dun and Bradstreet. Detailed information on the 50,000 British companies that together employ more than a third of the British workforce.

Passport to Overseas Employment—100,000 Job Opportunities Abroad: Information on overseas careers, study, and volunteer programs.

Principal International Businesses: Dun and Bradstreet. While not aimed at the job seeker, it provides details on more than 55,000 companies in 143 countries.

Teaching English Abroad: Griffith.

The Complete Guide to International Jobs and Careers: Your Passport to a World of Exciting and Exotic Employment: Ron and Carol Krannich

The Peace Corps: Wages are low and living conditions basic, but if you are interested in helping people, the Peace Corps is a possibility.

The U.S. government: Don't overlook government jobs; there are many foreign assignments. A larger library may have the publications *Federal Career Opportunities* or **the** *Federal News Digest,* which list openings. Federal jobs are listed on the Internet and available through most state employment service offices.

Books on Interviewing and Salary Negotiations

The two most important parts of a job search are getting interviews and doing well in them. I suggest that *the* most important interview question to answer well is "Why should I hire you over someone else?" It takes considerable self-analysis to answer this well. Curling up with a good job search book will help you know that you *do* have good things to say about yourself. Then there is the interview issue of pay, which is where many people lose more money in 30 seconds than at any other time in their lives. Or, worse, they get a job they hate. So here are some good resources on interviewing and salary negotiations, in hopes that they are of help to you.

The Quick Interview and Salary Negotiation Book—Dramatically Improve Your Interviewing Skills and Pay in a Matter of Hours: Mike Farr. A substantial book, but I arranged it so that you can read the first section and do better in interviews later that day. Also covers career planning, job seeking, resumes, pay rates, and other topics of importance for a job seeker. JIST.

101 Dynamite Questions to Ask at Your Job Interview: Fein.

50 Winning Answers to Interview Questions: Albrecht.

American Almanac of Jobs and Salaries: Wright. Covers hundreds of careers in the public and private sector.

American Salaries and Wages Survey: Gale Research. Detailed information on salaries and wages for thousands of jobs, by region. Also gives cost-of-living data, which is helpful in determining what the salary differences really mean.

AMS Office, Professional and Data Processing Salaries Report: Administrative Management Society. Salary distributions for 40 occupations by company size, type of business, and geographic region.

Dynamite Answers to Interview Questions: Ron and Carol Krannich.

Getting To Yes: Negotiating Agreements Without Giving In: Fisher and Ury. Good negotiating tips for anything.

How To Have A Winning Job Interview: Bloch. Good advice in a readable format, with lots of activities.

How to Make $1000 a Minute–Negotiating Your Salaries and Raises: Jack Chapman. Tips on getting more money and benefits during the critical part of a job offer.

Interviewing for Success: Ron and Carol Krannich.

Interviews That Get Results: Vik. Good tips for job seekers.

Knock'em Dead: With Great Answers to Tough Interview Questions: Martin John Yate.

Make Your Job Interview A Success: Biegeleisen. Good checklists, interview answers, grooming tips, and other content.

Out Interviewing the Interviewer: Merman and McLaughlin. Good exercises, case studies and tips for experienced and not-so-experienced job seekers.

Perks and Parachutes: Tarrant.

Power Interviewing: Job Winning Tactics from Fortune 500 Recruiters: Yeager and Hough.

Ready, Aim, You're Hired!: How to Job-Interview Successfully Anytime, Anywhere with Anyone: Hellman.

State and Metropolitan Area Data Book: Helpful details from the U.S. Department of Commerce providing unemployment rates, average income, employment and population growth, and other details for all major regions–important for those considering a move.

Sweaty Palms–The Neglected Art of Being Interviewed: Anthony Medley. Fun factual tips on illegal questions, problem interviews, appropriate dress and behaviors.

The Evaluation Interview: Richard Fear. Considered a classic for anyone who is, or wants to be, a professional interviewer.

The Five Minute Interview: Richard H. Beatty.

The Ultimate Interview: How to Get It, Get Ready, and Get the Job You Want: Caple.

When Do I Start?: Clearly written, good content.

White Collar Pay: Private Goods-Producing Industries: U.S. Department of Labor's Bureau of Labor Statistics. Good source of salary information for white collar jobs.

Winning The Salary Game: Salary Negotiations for Women: Chastain. Good Strategies for men, too.

Books on Resumes and Cover Letters

There are hundreds (thousands?) of resume books, and most offer bad advice. They often suggest that a good/better/best/perfect resume, sent out to lots of people, will get interviews, but the research clearly indicates that this is not the case. In addition to bad job search advice, many resume books offer unnecessarily rigid advice about the resume itself (that their way is the one enlightened way to do a resume).

In contrast, I believe that resumes are an important tool in the job search but that active job search methods (such as contacting employers by phone) are more effective than passive ones (like sending unsolicited resumes). And I do not believe that one formula exists for a good resume. Like people, resumes can be different. Of course, JIST's resume books are included here; I think they are among the best available.

America's Top Resumes for America's Top Jobs: J. Michael Farr. This is a big book, with 381 sample resumes covering over 200 major jobs. Resumes were selected from submissions by professional resume writers from all over North America. I took this approach to provide a rich array of writing styles, designs, and approaches to solving resume problems. From entry-level to very experienced, there are good examples here for everyone. JIST.

The Quick Resume and Cover Letter Book–Write and Use an Effective Resume in Only One Day: J. Michael Farr. Starting with an "instant" resume worksheet and basic formats you can complete in an hour or so, this book then takes you on a tour of everything you need to know about resumes and, more importantly, how to use them in your job search. Lots of good examples plus advice on cover letters, the job search, and related matters. JIST.

The Resume Solution–How to Write (and Use) a Resume That Gets Results: David Swanson. Lots of good advice and examples for creating superior resumes. Very strong on resume design and layout and provides a step-by-step approach that is very easy to follow. JIST.

Gallery of Best Resumes: David Noble. Advice and over 200 examples from professional resume writers. Lots of variety in content and design; an excellent resource. I consider it to be the best resume library, because the resumes are organized into useful categories and are all different. JIST.

The Edge Resume & Job Search Strategy: Bill Corbin and Shelbi Wright. The only book I know of that includes sample resumes using special papers and die-cut shapes. Unique. Distributed by JIST.

Gallery of Best Resumes for Two-Year Degree Graduates: David Noble. An excellent selection of 229 sample resumes submitted by professional resume writers. Good advice and lots of excellent samples. A very good resource book that organizes resumes by occupational category. JIST.

Professional Resumes for Executives, Managers, and Other Administrators: A New Gallery of Best Resumes by Professional Resume Writers: David Noble. Includes more than 340 resumes, organized by occupation. JIST.

The Federal Resume Guidebook: Kathryn Troutman. A thorough book covering the new procedures for applying for jobs with the federal government. JIST.

Using WordPerfect in Your Job Search: David Noble. A unique and thorough book that reviews how to use WordPerfect to create effective resumes, correspondence, and other job search documents including scannable and hypertext resumes. JIST.

100 Winning Resumes for $100,000+ Jobs: Enelow.

College Student's Resume Guide: Marino.

Complete Resume Guide: Faux. Some good ideas and examples.

Damn Good Resume Guide: Yana Parker. An irreverent title, but it has many good examples and an easy-to-follow process for creating resumes.

Developing a Professional Vita or Resume: McDaniels. Special resume advice for professionals with advanced education or experience.

Don't Use a Resume: Richard Lathrop. A booklet providing good examples and advice on a special resume that emphasizes skills.

Dynamic Cover Letters: Hanson. A very focused book, just on cover letters.

Dynamite Cover Letters: Ron and Carol Krannich. Good content.

Dynamite Resumes: Ron and Carol Krannich. Lots of good examples and advice.

Encyclopedia of Job Winning Resumes: Fournier and Spin. Lots of examples in a wide variety of jobs.

High Impact Resumes & Letters: Krannich and Banis. Good job search advice and lots of sample resumes and letters.

How to Write a Winning Resume: Bloch. Good examples for college grads, more experienced job seekers, and professionals.

Job Search Letters That Get Results: Ron and Carol Krannich. Good advice and over 200 sample letters.

Liberal Arts Power: Nadler. *How to sell it on your resume.*

Ready, Aim, Hired: Developing Your Brand Name Resume: Karson.

Resume Kit: Beatty. Better-than-average advice on putting together effective resumes and cover letters.

Resume Pro: The Professional Guide: Yana Parker. A how-to guide for those who help others write resumes.

Resumes for Computer Professionals: Shanahan. Many examples.

Resumes for Executives and Professionals: Shy and Kind.

Resumes for High School Graduates: VGM editors. An unusual but useful focus.

Resumes for Mid-Career Job Changes: VGM *editors.*

Resumes for Technicians: Shanahan. Examples, tips for use, and so on.

The No Pain Resume Workbook: Hiyaguha Cohen.

The Perfect Resume: Tom Jackson. Uses a workbook format, making it easy to identify job objective, skills, interests, and achievements. Good examples.

The Resume Catalog—200 Damn Good Resumes: Yana Parker. Organized by job objective. Good.

Writing a Job Winning Resume: John McLaughlin and Stephen Merman. A good book with examples showing how the resume covered a weakness.

Dress and Grooming Advice

One survey of employers I read found that about 40 percent of job seekers who made it through initial screening and got an interview then created a negative first impression based on dress and grooming. Another study found that candidates who made a negative impression within five minutes had virtually no chance of getting a job offer. So, put the two studies together, and you can see that a big problem exists with first impressions. How you dress and groom is only one issue, of course, but it is one that most people can easily change. So here are some books on that topic.

Always in Style with Color Me Beautiful: Pooser. By a noted color consultant, clothing styles, colors, and makeup for women. Many photos.

Big and Beautiful: Olds. Larger women can be gorgeous, too.

Color Me Beautiful: Jackson. Discover your "seasonal" colors and coordinate your look. Color photos. Well done.

Dress for Success: John Molloy. Some of the advice is dated, but this still gives good research-based advice on business attire.

Professional Image: Bixler. One of few on dress, grooming, body language, and details for both men and women.

Red Socks Don't Work: Karpinski. Dressing tips for men in formal corporate environments.

Women's Dress for Success: Molloy. Same thorough approach as for men.

Personal and Career Success and Advancement

There are thousands of personal and career success books and tapes. Some are very good, some are not. I include a selection of the better ones here.

Beat Stress with Strength—A Survival Guide for Work and Life: Stephanie Spera and Sandra Lanto. Includes a personal stress test and many tips for handling stress and achieving balance. JIST.

Career Satisfaction and Success—How to Know and Manage Your Strengths: Bernard Haldane. A complete revision of a classic by one of the founders of the modern career planning movement. It presents techniques for succeeding on the job and concepts that have changed many lives for the better, including defining your "motivated skills" and using them as a basis for career planning. JIST.

Dare to Change Your Job and Your Life: Carole Kanchier. Based on interviews with more than 5,000 adults, provides a proven self-help approach to developing a more meaningful career and more fulfilling life. JIST.

Job Savvy—How to Be a Success at Work: LaVerne Ludden. A workbook covering work-appropriate behaviors. JIST.

Jobscape—Career Survival in the New Global Economy: Colin Campbell. A well-written and fascinating book that presents the essential trends shaping the future workforce and how we can best prepare to benefit. JIST.

Networking for Everyone!: Michelle Tullier. More than for the job search, covers creating a network to help you through life—lots of motivational and practical tips. JIST.

Ready, Set, Organize!: Pipi Peterson. Time management strategies for your personal and work lives. Good advice and a fun read. JIST.

SuccessAbilities!—1,001 Practical Ways to Keep Up, Stand Out, and Move Ahead at Work: Paula Ancona. Short and motivational tips from Ancona's nationally syndicated column. JIST.

The Customer Is Usually Wrong!: Fred Jandt. Great tips for handling customers and doing the right thing. JIST.

The Perfect Memo!—Write Your Way to Career Success!: Patricia Westheimer. Good tips and activities for more effective business writing. JIST.

We've Got to Start Meeting Like This!: Roger Mosvick and Robert Nelson. An essential book for getting the most out of meeting time. JIST.

Brushing Up Your Clerical Skills: Steinberg. For new and returning office workers. Exercise on spelling, punctuation, typing, business letters, filing, and more.

Business Protocol: Yager. On-the-job manners.

Do What You Love, The Money Will Follow: Sinetar. For those who seek meaning as our first priority, there is hope that we can also make a living doing the things we really want to do.

Getting Things Done When You Are Not in Charge: Bellman.

How to Jump Start a Stalled Career: Prugh.

How to Make a Habit of Success: Bernard Haldane. Originally published many years ago, it was a best-seller and is still available. Many consider Haldane one of the founders of the career planning movement that began in the 1950s. This is an important book that has much good advice.

Improve Your Writing for Work: Chesla. Includes lots of samples and activities.

Love Your Work and Success Will Follow: Hirsch. For those who are not happy with their current career.

Moving Up—How To Get High Salaried Jobs: Djeddah. Techniques to get promoted or move out to a new job.

Not Just a Secretary: Morrow and Lebov. Techniques for doing well and getting ahead.

Secretary Today, Manager Tomorrow: How to Turn a Secretarial Job into a Managerial Position: Marrs.

Skills for Success: Scheele. Good advice on getting ahead in all sorts of careers.

Wish Craft: Barbara Sher. An upbeat book that provides activities and advice on setting goals and reaching your full potential.

Working Smart: Zehring. Advice on getting ahead, organizing time, dealing with people, developing leadership skills.

Would You Put That in Writing?: Booher. Good primer for improving your business communications.

Future Trends/Labor Market Information

Jobscape—Career Survival in the New Global Economy: Colin Campbell. A well-written and fascinating book that presents the essential trends shaping the future workforce and how we can best prepare to benefit. JIST.

Work in the New Economy: Robert Wegmann, Robert Chapman, and Miriam Johnson. A very well-researched book on where our economy is going and how we should adapt our career planning and job search methods to get better results. While this is now an older book, I consider Wegman's work to be among the best on the topic and much of the advice remains current. JIST.

Emerging Careers: New Occupations for the Year 2000 & Beyond: Based on years of research; details hundreds of new careers. Very good.

Megatrends: Nesbitt. A best-seller that provides a review of where the economy is heading.

The Work Revolution: Schwartz and Neikirk. Thorough and well done. Predicts retraining, education, and other needs of rapid change.

Work Force 2020—Work and Workers in the 21st Century: Richard Judy and Carol D'Amico of the Hudson Institute. A well-researched book predicting likely trends in the workforce.

Work in the 21st Century: Isaac Asimov and others. Anthology of well-done articles on work trends for the future. Stimulating.

Self-Employment, Starting Your Own Business, Temporary, Part-Time, and Volunteer Jobs

More people are working for themselves; starting small businesses; or working in part-time, temporary, or volunteer jobs. There are hundreds of books on these topics, and a good library will have more resources than I can list. Here are a few suggestions.

Self-Employment: From Dream to Reality—An Interactive Workbook for Starting Your Small Business: Linda Gilkerson and Theresia Paauwe. A workbook to encourage "microenterprises," very small business started by those with little money or experience. Unique. JIST.

Mind Your Own Business—Getting Started as an Entrepreneur: LaVerne Ludden and Bonnie Maitlen. A good book for those considering their own business, with lots of good advice. JIST.

Be your Own Business—The Definitive Guide to Entrepreneurial Success: Marsha Fox and LaVerne Ludden. JIST.

Franchise Opportunities Handbook: LaVerne Ludden. Lists over a thousand franchise companies and provides tips on selecting one that makes sense for a business.

America's New Breed of Entrepreneurs: Presents collective experiences of 48 successful entrepreneurs and how they achieved their goals.

Beginning Entrepreneur: Matthews.

Best Home Businesses for the '90s: Edwards and Edwards.

Directory of Microenterprise Programs: Lists loans and programs for low-income entrepreneurs.

Getting Business to Come to You: Edwards and Edwards. Low-cost marketing tips.

Home Sweet Office: Meade. Telecommunicating from home to a regular job.

How to Build a Successful One Person Business: Bautista.

How to Run Your Own Home Business: Kern and Wolfgram.

How to Start, Run, and Stay in Business: Kishel. Good primer for the school of hard knocks.

Inc. Yourself: How to Profit from Setting Up your Own Corporation: Shows financial and other advantages, plus how to set up.

Job Sharing Handbook: Smith. Provides guidelines for setting up a shared job, case histories, and so on. Good.

Making It on Your Own—What to Know Before Starting Your Own Business: Feingold.

Opportunities in Your Own Service Business: McKay.

Part-Time Professional: Good information on finding part time jobs, benefits, negotiating with employers, converting full-time to part-time jobs, and other tips.

Running a One Person Business: Whitmeyer, Rasberry, Phillips. Practical.

Side by Side: Cuozzo and Graham.

Starting on a Shoe String: Building a Business Without a Bankroll: Goldstein.

Ten Best Opportunities for Starting a Home Business Today: Reed Glenn.

The Mid-Career Entrepreneur: Mancuso.

The Small Business Administration: The U.S. Small Business Administration (SBA) offers loans, training, and planning, and many useful publications. Its toll-free number is 1-800-U ASK SBA. In addition, its Service Corps of Retired Executives (SCORE) provides free help on how to set up and run a small business.

The Temp Track: Justice. *Reviews the many opportunities for temporary jobs.*

Volunteer America: Kipps. Lists over 1,400 organizations for training, service, and work experience.

Working from Home: Edwards and Edwards.

Places to Live or Move to

Some people will be unhappy wherever they live, but living in a place you like does make life more enjoyable. Here are a few books that provide details.

Best Towns In America: Bayless. 50 of the U.S.'s most desirable places, plus ways to evaluate all communities.

Country Careers–Successful Ways to Live and Work in the Country: Rojak.

Finding Your Best Place To Live In America: Bowman and Guiliani. Another good book providing information on good places to live.

Greener Pastures Relocation Guide: Finding the Best State in the U.S. for You!

Places Rated Almanac: Richard Boyer and David Savagean. A thorough review of over 270 metropolitan areas with information on housing, education, climate, health services, recreation, arts, transportation, crime, and income.

Getting Information on Specific Employers

There are two basic reasons for you to be interested in specific employers. The first has to do with identifying potential job search targets, and the second is to get more information on an employer prior to an interview.

Some books and businesses "sell" the idea of sending your resume to potential employers as a good thing. Some even sell lists in print or computer form so you can mount a big mail campaign. And some sell the idea of having special lists of employers that you can buy from them. I do not think that sending unsolicited resumes to any list is a good idea. While any technique works for some people, you will be better off if your job search is more targeted and involves more direct contact.

You have to begin with knowing the type of job you want and the industries where you will find them. Then and only then can you intelligently begin your search for specific employers.

Free Resources

The *Yellow Pages:* The best resource you can get is probably free: it's the *Yellow Pages* of the phone book. Think about it: it lists all the organizations by type and gives you what you need to contact them. All of my job search books tell you how to use the *Yellow Pages* as an effective tool in your job search. The *Yellow Pages* for regions throughout the country is also now available on the Internet, as are many other sources of information on organizations.

Networking: Another free resource of information is networking. If you want to know more about a particular job or place of employment, ask the people who do that kind of work or who work in that place. This is often the only source of information for small organizations not listed in the directories. A good book on networking is *Networking for Everyone–Connecting with People for Career and Job Success* by Michelle Tullier. It provides lots of practical advice for personal and business success and is published by JIST.

Chambers of commerce: Most are not staffed to provide specific information to job seekers, but many do provide information such as new businesses in the area, larger employers, and other details.

Contact the organization directly: For large organizations, contact the human resources or public relations departments. In smaller ones the receptionist or manager may be able to help. Get brochures, an annual report, description of relevant jobs, and anything else that describes the organization.

Annual reports: All publicly owned and many smaller organizations provide annual reports detailing earnings, trends, strategies, and other information. If one is available, it is an excellent source of information.

A good bookstore or library has many sources of information on specific businesses and other organizations. While many of these resources were not specifically developed for use by job seekers, they can work just fine.

You can use resource materials in several ways. The first is to get information on a specific organization as background for an interview. You can also get names of organizations as well as background information to use in making direct contact lists. With so many potential sources of information, ask a librarian to help you once you have a good idea of what you are looking for.

Following are just a few of the many books and other resources for obtaining information on employers. Some are organized by industry or region or in other ways that may be of help to you. If you use the Internet, more and more information is now available there. I suggest you read one of the Internet job search books published by JIST for the most useful sites.

100 Best Companies to Work for in America: Levering and Moscowitz.

America's Corporate Families, The Billion Dollar Directory: Describes 2,500 large corporate "families" and their 28,000 subsidiaries; provides information on each; and cross references by location, business or product type, and other methods.

America's Fastest Growing Employers: Bob Adams. Lists more than 700 of the fastest-growing companies in the country.

American Business Information Inc. of Omaha Nebraska: Publishes business directories for many different industries. Phone (402) 593-4600.

Bay Area 500: Hoover. An example of a regional listing, this one providing profiles of the largest companies in the San Francisco area.

Business Newsbank: Newsbank, Inc. This service provides the narrative of articles from newspapers and business journals from 400 cities. Cross-references by company name, individual's name, industry, or product category.

Business Organizations and Agencies Directory: Gale Research Company. Provides useful information to look up by business name and types of activity. Provides contact information.

Business Periodicals Index: Cross-references business articles from over 300 periodicals by subject and company name.

Career Guide–Dun's Employment Opportunities Directory: Aimed specifically at the professional job seeker, lists more than 5,000 major U.S. companies and their personnel directors, career opportunities, and benefits packages.

Chamber of Commerce and local business associations: These often publish directories of local companies, available in libraries or by writing to the individual associations.

Contacts Influential: A series of directories providing information on smaller businesses. Allows look up by organization name or type to learn details of its operations and size.

Directory of Executive Recruiters: Joyce Lain Kennedy.

Directory of Executive Search Firms: Lists and cross-references 100s of these businesses, should they be appropriate for you.

Dun & Bradstreet Million Dollar Directory: Provides information on 180,000 of the largest companies in the country. Gives the type of business, number of employees, and sales volume for each. It also lists the company's top executives.

Hidden Job Market: A Guide to America's 2000 Little-Known Fastest Growing High-Tech Companies: Peterson's Guides. Concentrates on high-tech companies with good growth potential.

Hoover's Handbook of American Business: Profiles more than 750 larger companies.

Hoover's Handbook of Emerging Companies: Spain, Campbell, Talbot. Profiles of 250 entrepreneurial companies.

Job Bank Series: Bob Adams Inc. Series of books for job-seeking professionals, each covering a different large city or metropolitan area with details on economic outlook for the covered area, list of major companies, and positions within the company.

Job Hunter's Guide to 100 Great American Cities: Brattle Communications. Lists major employers for 100 of America's largest cities.

Little Known, Fastest Growing High-Tech Companies: Peterson's Guides.

Macrae's State Industrial Directories: Published for northeastern states, but similar volumes are produced for other parts of the country by other publishers. Each book lists thousands of companies, concentrating on those that produce products, rather than services. They include a large number of small firms, in addition to the larger ones listed in many other guides.

Million Dollar Directory: Dun's Marketing Services. Provides general information on over 115,000 businesses.

Moody's Industrial Manual: Provides detailed information on over 3,000 larger organizations.

Moody's Industrial News Reports: Provides articles related to each of the businesses listed in the related directory.

National Business Telephone Directory: Gale Research. An alphabetical listing of companies across the United States, with their addresses and phone numbers. It includes many smaller firms (20 employees minimum).

Peterson's Business and Management Jobs: An annual listing of 100s of employers plus essential background information on each.

Polk's Directories: R. L. Polk & Co. Each major city has its own Polk Directory created by door-to-door canvass of individuals and businesses in the area. Cross-references by name, address, type of business.

Reference Book of Corporate Management: Dun's Marketing Services. Provides information on the executives and officers of the 6,000 largest U.S. corporations.

Standard & Poor's Register of Corporations, Directors and Executives: Brief information on over 40,000 corporations and their key people cross-referenced by names, types of businesses, and other methods. Lists parent companies with subsidiaries and the interlocking affiliations of directors.

Thomas Register: Lists more than 100,000 companies across the country by name, type of product made, and brand name of product produced.

Yellow Pages *(the phone book):* As I mentioned earlier, your best source is often the *Yellow Pages* of the phone book, because it lists virtually all business, government, and not-for-profit organizations in a given area–and even organizes them by type of business! And this book is free.

Many directories give information about firms in a particular industry. Here are just a few.

The Blue Book of Building and Construction
Directory of Advertising Agencies
Directory of Computer Dealers
McFadden American Bank Directory

School and Training Admissions, Financing, and Survival

Education pays. People with more education and training tend to earn substantially more. Most of the rapidly growing jobs require technical training beyond high school or a four-year college degree. While a four-year college degree makes sense for a lot of people, many occupations with high pay and rapid growth can be learned in two years or less.

More adults are going back to school to upgrade their career skills, and any young person should consider getting as much education and training as possible. Knowledge of computers is now important in most jobs, and, if you have not kept up with the new developments in your field, it is important to do so as soon as possible. There are a wide variety of training options including technical schools, adult-education classes, workshops, formal college courses, and even classes you can take on the Internet.

You can finance postsecondary training or education in many ways, so don't let a lack of money be a barrier to getting what you need. If you want to do it, seek, and ye shall find a way. Here are some resources.

Back to School: A College Guide for Adults: LaVerne Ludden. A comprehensive guide that includes self-assessment activities and good advice on setting goals, considering various degrees, selecting a college, juggling priorities, and much more. Includes a directory of 1,000 adult friendly degree programs. JIST.

Ludden's Adult Guide to Colleges and Universities: LaVerne and Marsha Ludden. Good advice for adults going back to school, plus information on more than 1,500 degree programs. Includes many nontraditional programs that can be used to reduce the time required to get a degree. JIST.

Career Connection for College Education—A Guide to College Education and Related Career Opportunities: Fred Rowe. Information on over 100 college majors and 1,000 related occupations. Includes details on salaries, course requirements, related high school courses, and other details useful in planning a college major. JIST.

Career Connection for Technical Education—A Guide to Technical Training and Related Career Opportunities: Fred Rowe. Similar to the above, describes over 60 technical education majors and the careers they lead to. JIST.

Bear's Guide to Finding Money For College: John Bear. Well written, readable, helpful.

But What if I Don't Want to Go to College?: Ungar. Reviews alternative education or training needed for hundreds of jobs.

College 101: Farrar. Primer for getting along in college.

College Admissions Data Handbook: Orchard House. The most thorough and up-to-date source of information on colleges available, four volumes cover different sections of the country.

College Degrees by Mail: John Bear. Brief descriptions for 100 nonresident schools.

College Degrees You Can Earn from Home: Frey.

College Guide for Students with Learning Disabilities: Sciafini and Lynch. Covers over 500 programs.

College Majors and Careers: A Resource Guide for Effective Life Planning: Phifer. Good information on college majors, skills, related leisure activities, personal attributes, and additional resource materials for major occupational interests.

College Survival Guide: Mayer. Well-done, new student orientation to basics of making it.

Earn College Credit for What You Know: Simosko. On nontraditional college credit programs: types, application procedures, and so on.

Electronic University: A Guide to Distance Learning Programs: Peterson's Guides.

Free Dollars From the Federal Government: Blum.

Free Money for College: A Guide to More Than 1,000 Grants and Scholarships: Blum.

Guide to Non-Traditional College Degrees: John Bear. Fun to read, well done, thorough.

Guide to Technical, Trade, and Business Schools: A four-volume set with thorough profiles of 2,200 accredited schools.

Historically Black Colleges and Universities: Details on all 91 such schools.

How to Apply to American Colleges and Universities: Brennan and Briggs.

Internships: 50,000 On-The-Job Training Opportunities for Students and Adults: Rushing.

Liberal Education and Careers Today: Howard Figler. "I dropped out of pre-med in my junior year of college (a long story) and got a degree in liberal arts–and I turned out OK." Figler makes a case for a liberal arts education with research and advice on how liberal arts is a good way to go.

Major Decisions–A Guide to College Majors: Orchard House. Provides brief descriptions for all college majors.

Minority Student Enrollments in Higher Education: Provides information on 500 schools with the highest minority enrollments.

New Horizons–Education and Career Guide for Adults: Haponski. Methods of seeking and using education to get ahead.

Paying Less for College: Peterson's College Money Handbook: Provides costs, types of aid, and other details from over 1,700 schools.

Person's College Money Handbook.

Peterson's Colleges and Programs for Students with Learning Disabilities: Mangrum and Strichart. Lists over 1,000 colleges with these programs.

Peterson's Internships. Lists 40,000 positions to get experience as interns.

Peterson's Scholarships, Grants, and Prizes.

Peterson's Competitive Colleges: Tips on getting into the top 300 schools.

Peterson's Guide to College Admissions: Student workbook on preparing and competing. Well done.

Peterson's Guide to Four-Year Colleges: 1,900 schools and 400 majors. Organized to select by many criteria, plus tips on applying.

Peterson's Guide to Two-Year Colleges: Details on over 1,400 schools with associate degrees.

Peterson's Independent Study Catalog: Guide to over 12,000 correspondence and Internet courses.

Peterson's National College Databank: Data in over 350 categories, a major source of data for colleges of all descriptions.

Tech Prep Guide: Technical, Trade, & Business School Data Handbook: Orchard House. The most thorough reference of its kind, providing thorough information on over 1,600 schools, plus summary information on another 3,000 schools. Four volumes cover different parts of the country.

Time for College–The Adult Student's Guide to Survival and Success: Siebert and Gilpin.

Who Offers Part-Time Degree Programs?: Peterson's Guides. Data on over 2500 institutions.

Winning Money for College: High school student's guide to scholarship contests.

You Can Make It Without a College Degree: Roesch.

Instructor and Trainer Resources

While you should be able to find books on public speaking in most bookstores and libraries, more specific materials, such as instructor's guides for a job search workshop, are very hard to find. JIST publishes or distributes a variety of these more specialized materials, should you be interested.

Career Exploration Groups: A Facilitator's Guide: Garfield and Nelson. Includes group activities and exercises to aid in self-knowledge, career information, and decision making.

Career Information Service: Norris. One of the few texts for university-level career counseling and development courses. Thorough book for career counselors.

Career Planning Workshop Manual: Instructor's guide for life/work planning workshops. Includes group exercises, worksheets.

Developing Vocational Instruction: Mager and Beach. Easy to understand, step-by-step guidelines to developing good curriculum.

How to Organize and Manage a Seminar: What to Do and How to Do It: Murray. Budgets, plans, staffing, promotion, and more. Very good.

Louder & Funnier: A Practical Guide for Overcoming Stage Fright: Nelson. Getting over fear of groups is a major obstacle to success as a trainer or presenter. Excellent.

Making Successful Presentations: Smith. Good for the new or moderately experienced trainer.

Making Vocational Choices: A Theory of Careers: John Holland: There are few career theory books, and this is one of the most influential. In plain and readable English, it presents the research, rationale, and practical uses of his theory of six personality types.

The Business of Public Speaking: Good tips on business aspects of doing presentations.

Where To Start: An Annotated Career Planning Bibliography: Thorough, helpful. Organized by topic.

Work in the New Economy: Robert Wegmann, Robert Chapman, and Miriam Johnson. Well-researched and written review of the research on labor market trends and how a job seeker is affected. Though written some time ago, I consider this the best book of its kind. JIST.

Career Interest Tests and Books on Test-Taking

Too many people think a magical solution exists to their career planning problems that does not require effort. Tests are only tools to provide you with information and can't tell you what to do. I prefer assessment instruments that are self-scored and encourage you to participate in the career decision-making process.

If you have access to a career counselor, ask about taking a career interest test. But remember that it can only provide you food for thought, not an answer to what you should do. Following are a few of the self-administered and self-scored interest inventories that I like. Most are available from JIST but in packages. Individuals must get them through a counselor, though several inventories are available as a package for individuals on JIST's Internet site at JIST.com. Test-related books are listed after the tests themselves.

Career Exploration Inventory (CEI): John Liptak. Uses a unique past/present and future orientation and results in scores that cross-reference to major occupational interest areas. Includes a large chart of occupational information and an action plan, and recommends sources of additional information. Spanish version available. JIST.

The Guide for Occupational Exploration Inventory (GOEI): J. Michael Farr. Uses an intuitive process to lead to one or more of the 12 career interest areas from the *Guide for Occupational Exploration.* A related information chart then provides substantial information on the jobs in each area, related courses, and leisure activities. Includes an action plan and suggests additional sources of information. JIST.

Leisure/Work Search Inventory (LSI): John Liptak. Ties leisure activities to related jobs, making this a good test for young people with limited work experience or adults looking for more interesting career options. Includes substantial chart of career information, an action plan, and other useful elements. JIST.

Occupational Clues—A Career Interest Survey. A thorough book that includes checklists for values, interests, activities, school subjects. and work experience—all cross-referenced to related job clusters. JIST.

Barriers to Employment Success Inventory (BESI): John Liptak. Self-scored inventory that helps identify barriers to employment—very helpful for programs. JIST.

The Job Search Attitude Inventory: John Liptak. A self-scored that identifies potential problem areas for success in the job search. JIST.

Career Decision-Making System (CDM): Thomas Harrington and Arthur J. O'Shea. A popular interest test that is easy to use, self-scoring and interpreted. Records occupational preferences, school subjects, job values, abilities, plans for future education, and training.

College Majors Finder: Cross-references Holland codes (which can be obtained from the *SDS* and *CDM* described in this section as well as from other devices) to over 900 college majors.

Self-Directed Search (SDS): John L. Holland. Widely used, responses result in recommended jobs in six major clusters. A separate booklet cross-references over 1,100 jobs in a logical manner.

American College Testing Program (ACT): Over 450 pages of skills, reviews, sample questions, study tips, and tips to raise ACT scores.

Book of U.S. Postal Exams: Bautista. Sample exams for 44 job categories.

Career Aptitude Tests: Klein and Outerman. Series of self-scored tests measuring aptitudes against over 250 jobs.

Career Finder: The Pathways to Over 1500 Entry-Level Jobs: Schwartz and Breckner. Checklists result in recommended jobs for more exploration. List salary, openings, and more.

Civil Service Test Tutor: Practice drills and samples for government tests for beginning office jobs such as accounting, file clerk, telephone operator.

Counselor's Guide to Vocational Guidance Instruments: Kappes and Mastie. Reviews of many tests.

Fairness in Employment Testing: National Academy of Sciences.

Guide to 75 Tests for Special Education: Up-to-date guide covering major tests and how to select, interpret, and use them.

How to Get a Clerical Job in Government: Hundreds of sample questions and answers covering major topics on federal, state, and local exams.

How to Pass Employment Tests: How to do well in tests you may encounter in your job search, plus tests given to evaluate advancement potential.

Making the Grade: Study habits and techniques for getting good grades by doing well on all sorts of tests.

Practice for Clerical, Typing, Steno Tests: Sample questions, drills, exercises to improve scores on most clerical tests.

Practice For The Armed Forces Tests: Drills, sample questions, test-taking tips, general review for all service tests.

Preparation for the GED: Thorough preparation to increase scores.

Preparation for the SAT: Thorough preparation to increase scores.

Career-Oriented Software

I formerly listed software that you could find for reasonable prices in a retail software store, but changes occur so rapidly that any list is quickly out-of-date. A number of good resume preparation programs are quite helpful in preparing basic resumes, though you won't need them if you have access to a good word processing program and a good resume book. Two good resume programs that have been consistently available are ***WinWay Resume on CD-ROM*** and ***PFS Resume Pro***—both are popular and widely available.

The major word processing programs include resume formats, but they force you to use formats that may not be the best for your situation. David Noble's book ***Using WordPerfect in Your Job Search*** shows you the many tricks you can do with a powerful word-processing program.

Another category of software that is very helpful in the job search is that of contact management programs such as ACT! or GoldMine. These are designed for individuals like sales people to follow up on their contacts and are well suited for any follow-up tasks including letters, schedules, and phone calls.

A growing number of career planning, occupational exploration, and related programs are becoming available. Some are poorly done while others seem helpful, so buyer beware.

JIST publishes a variety of software, but the software is priced for multiple users such as in schools or programs, and it is too expensive for individuals. JIST has a free job search program on its Internet site at www.JIST.com if you want to check it out.

To give you an idea of the types of information becoming available, here are some JIST-published programs followed by a few of the many available from other sources:

JIST's Career Explorer on CD-ROM: Answering a series of questions about your interests and other factors results in a list of the 20 jobs that best match your responses. The program then allows you to get information on each of these jobs. Takes about 15 minutes.

JIST's Multimedia Occupational Outlook Handbook: Very easy to use, includes descriptions for the 250 major jobs in the OOH, powerful search features, and color images and sounds.

Mike Farr's Get a Job Workshop on CD-ROM: Includes activities, text, video clips, and sound in an interactive format covering setting a job objective, details on all major jobs, identifying skills, job search methods, resumes, job survival, and related topics. JIST.

The Electronic Enhanced Dictionary of Occupational Titles: This is a sophisticated CD-ROM program that includes the complete content of the ***Dictionary of Occupational Titles***, the ***Occupational Outlook Handbook***, the ***Complete Guide for Occupational Exploration,*** and over additional details on over 12,000 jobs. While it is easy to use, it provides access to detailed technical information on over 12,000 jobs that has not been readily available in the past. JIST.

Young Person's Electronic Occupational Outlook Handbook: A lively and simple-to-use format provides basic information on 250 major jobs.

Free Phone CD-ROM: Toll-free numbers for over 1,000 business categories covering the entire country. Allows lookup by region and other criteria.

Information USA: Provides substantial information on federal jobs, government resources, agencies, grants, loans, scholarships, statistics.

Lovejoy's College Counselor CD-ROM: Provides details on thousands of colleges and technical schools, 2,500 scholarships, and video clips of many schools. Excellent.

Scholarships 101: Information on over 5,000 scholarship sources. Sorts by various criteria and helps write letters asking for additional information.

Select Phone CD-ROM: Includes all listings in the white and yellow pages directories for the entire U.S. Search by name, region, business heading, and so on.

Recommended Internet and World Wide Web Sites for Information on Career Planning, Job Seeking, Education, and Related Topics

The information available on the Internet and World Wide Web is amazing, and the sites keep getting better. I still prefer old-fashioned books for many uses, but the Internet is clearly superior for certain tasks. If you have not already read Section 2, you should do so now, before you waste lots of hours on the Internet. That section gives you good advice on career planning and job seeking that will help you decide what, precisely, you want to look for before you dive into the cold deep waters of the Internet. At the end of that section, are a few brief cautions regarding the use of the Internet as well as tips for getting the most from it. Do use caution, as the Internet is addictive to some people. Remember, your objective is to get things done, not to play with your computer. Enough said.

The selection of Internet sites that follows is based on recommendations in a book by Anne Wolfinger titled *The Quick Internet Guide to Career and College Information*, published by JIST and used here with permission. I shortened comments and deleted sites that were primarily for professional counselors, educators, and the like. JIST's Internet site provides free access to the complete list, including many categories and sites that are not presented here. Anne's book has more detailed comments and many more entries, so you may want to buy the book as well.

Sites Providing Good Information on Careers, Job Search, Industries, and Related Subjects

These sites do a variety of useful things. Most provide good information as well as links to other career-related sites. Some have job listings or will accept your resume in a database for employers to search. You can start with almost any one of them and eventually get to what you want through links to other sites. With a few exceptions, I've arranged them in alphabetical order.

JIST Works

http://www.jist.com

JIST, the publisher of this book, maintains a site offering a variety of free information including career planning and job search advice, downloadable chapters from several books, an interactive job search workshop, (based on content provided by yours truly), and direct links to recommended career, education, and job search sites. They also have an online bookstore that includes many good books, assessment tests, and other products.

Careers On-Line

http://www.disserv.stu.umn.edu/TC/Grants/COL

This site has job search and employment information for people with disabilities.

Career Resource Center

http://www.careers.org

You'll find more than 11,000 links here to jobs, employers, business, education, and career services on the Web. This site also includes links to bibliographies, software lists, publications, resource evaluations, event calendars, and resources for small businesses and self-employed people. It even lists career resources by geographic location.

Career Resource Homepage, Rensselaer Polytechnic Institute

http://www.rpi.edu/dept/cdc/homepage.html

This lists commercial job databases and resume banks and employers who post job openings on their own Web sites. There are also links to professional associations, college career services, human resource management resources, alumni services, and various USENET newsgroups.

Career Toolbox

http://www.careertoolbox.com

Sponsored by Chevas Regal, this site features multimedia information on career planning, job search, entrepreneurship, professional development, and money management. While produced for recent college grads, it has useful information for anyone.

Catapult on JobWeb

http://www.jobweb.org/catapult/catapult.htm

From the National Association of Colleges and Employers, this site is aimed at career services professionals working with college students and alumni. It provides links to employment centers, colleges and universities, job search vehicles, industry information, relocation resources, and professional associations.

Definitive Guide to Internet Career Resources

http://phoenix.placement.oakland.edu/

From the Oakland University Career Services Office, this site boasts a thorough listing of career resources.

The Riley Guide: Employment Opportunities and Job Resources on the Internet

http://www.dbm.com/jobguide

One of the best career and job information clearinghouses, this site provides extensive information on using the Internet in your job search. Resources are organized into categories such as arts and humanities, computing and technology, and government jobs, with additional links for state, national, and international resources.

Emory Colossal List of Career Links

http://www.emory.edu/CAREER/Main/Links.html

From the placement office of Emory University, this site is oriented toward its student audience but contains links to and rates career and job search sites.

HomeFair

http://www.homefair.com

If you are relocating, you'll find here useful information on homes and cost of living in hundreds of U.S. and international cities. The site includes a salary calculator and many other resources.

Hoover's Online

http://www.hoovers.com

With information on more than 10,000 companies and a list of 4,000 specific corporate websites, this is a very useful site.

Job Search and Employment Opportunities: Best Bets

http://asa.ugl.lib.umich.edu/chdocs/employment

Best Bets includes only sites that meet the clearinghouse's standards and provides a lengthy description and evaluation of each. Links are organized by field, with additional information for beginners on the Web.

JobHunt

http://www.job-hunt.org

This is a comprehensive list of sites with descriptions and recommendations, plus job listings and other job resources.

JobSmart

http://jobsmart.org/index.htm

From the Bay Area Library System, this site has links to job banks, job hotlines, career centers, and libraries—plus information on salary surveys, resume writing, the hidden job market, high tech, and career guides.

Military Career Guide Online

http://www.militarycareers.com

From the Department of Defense, this provides information on 152 enlisted and officer occupations, education, and other benefits. Browse the occupations by category or search occupations that meet your criteria.

National Occupational Information Coordinating Committee (NOICC)

http://www.noicc.gov

A federal agency addressing the needs of vocational education and the career development needs of youth and adults, NOICC provides links to job search assistance sites, career information, education and financial aid sites, and sources of occupational labor market information and educational statistics.

Peace Corps

http://www.peacecorps.gov

This site has comprehensive information on volunteering for the Peace Corps, including application information for agriculture, education, forestry, health, engineering, skilled trades, business, environmental, urban planning, youth development, and more. About 6,500 volunteers now serve in over 90 countries.

Public Register's Annual Report Service (PRARS)

http://www.prars.com

PRARS provides company financials, including annual reports, on more than 3,200 public companies. Listings are organized alphabetically or by industry.

Purdue University Placement Service

http://www.ups.purdue.edu/student/jobsites.htm

You'll find here well-organized links to job search sites, federal government and international job listings, classifieds, newsgroups, resume services, and professional recruiters. The *Reference and Resource Material* category links to helpful information on career planning, job search, resume writing, interviewing, and more.

What Color Is Your Parachute? Job Hunting Online

http://www.washingtonpost.com/parachute

This site provides an online version of Richard Bolles's *Parachute* book, plus his comments on Internet sites organized in useful groupings.

Sites with Online Listings of Job Openings, Want Ads, and Resume Banks

In addition to listing job openings, most of these sites provide substantial resources for job seekers. For example, some have interactive resume-writing software, and others offer tips for job seeking or a bookstore offering recommended books. Most allow free posting of your resume to their resume databanks for employers, who pay to view the resumes. They all make it easy to use their services and provide links to other sites that provide specialized information or services.

E-Span

http://www.espan.com

This is one of the largest resume banks and listings of job openings. Search for job openings by keyword or preferences; they will even e-mail you updates about openings that fit your needs. The site also offers well-organized links to additional resources on career assessment, job fairs, business indexes, education, relocation, and local, national and world newspaper want ads.

JIST maintains E-span's bookstore and free resource library of online career materials.

America's Job Bank

http://www.ajb.dni.us

Run by the U.S. Employment Service, this site lists all the job openings posted at the 1,800 state employment service offices throughout the country, searchable in a variety of ways. Free listings to employers and job seekers.

Best Jobs in the USA Today

http://www.bestjobsusa.com

Best Jobs lists want ads from *USA Today* and from thousands of companies across the nation. Search by state, category, job title, or company name, or enter your own resume. There is no fee for job seekers. The site also features corporate profiles, lists of career fairs, and recent issues of *Employment Review*.

Career City

http://www.careercity.com

Career City features a no-fee resume and job bank and informative articles on resumes and interviewing. Sponsored by Adams Media, the site sells their job search and career information books and software.

Career Magazine

http://www.careermag.com

This is an online career resource magazine with articles, job updates, employer profiles, discussion groups, a resume bank, and classified ads. It combines job postings from USENET newsgroups into a database searchable by preferred job locations, skills, and title, with a list ranked by best fit or most recent job postings.

CareerPath

http://www.careerpath.com

CareerPath allows a quick search of want ads from 25 major newspapers across the country. Search by specific newspaper, job category, keyword, or other criteria.

CareerSite

http://www.careersite.com

This unique site lets job seekers and employers create profiles of their credentials or job opportunities. You can search and respond to openings online or wait for them to e-mail you jobs that match your preferences. They only send your resume with your permission and only to employers with matching job needs.

CareerWeb

http://www.cweb.com

CareerWeb features a database of job openings, employer profiles, online career fairs, online bookstore, and links to other career sites. For a fee, they will e-mail you openings that meet your preferences.

Federal Jobs Digest

http://www.jobsfed.com

This site claims to list more federal job vacancies than any other source. Organizes job openings by categories such as engineering, science and math, and trade and postal. For a fee, the matching service will analyze which kinds of federal jobs you may be eligible for.

Internet Career Connection

http://www.iccweb.com

This site offers both a job bank and a resume/talent bank. Free to job seekers looking for openings, they do charge for posting your resume. The site also provides a computerized personality assessment and a list of career resources.

JobBank USA

http://www.jobbankusa.com

JobBank lets you search its own and other job databases for openings, making this a quick way to sort openings from a variety of sites. There is no fee for posting your resume.

JOBTRAK
http://www.jobtrak.com

A job and resume bank with access limited to students and alumni of the more than 400 colleges and universities, JOBTRAK includes employer profiles and full-time and part-time job listings. There is no charge to job seekers.

JobWeb
http://www.jobweb.com

JobWeb contains both job and employer databases with more than 450 employer links you can browse or search.

Online Career Center
http://www.occ.com

This large database of jobs is searchable by type, location, and other criteria, with no charge to job seekers to search the database or post their resumes. Also includes lots of career information.

Monster Board
http://www.monster.com

One of the largest, Monster Board allows you to search more than 50,000 job openings by location, discipline, or keywords, and delivers results to your personal in-box each time you log in to see your matches. Includes more than 4,000 employer profiles and lots of useful features.

Sites for Choosing a College or Training and for Getting Financial Aid

Many schools have their own Internet sites offering detailed information on their programs, student body, activities, admissions requirements, and more. Some of the sites listed here will help you sort through and then link to these schools, while others will help you select programs that meet your criteria or provide other information.

Adventures in Education
http://www.tgslc.org

This site covers financial aid resources with links to educational institutions, financial institutions, scholarship information, government agencies, standardized tests/admissions, and other resources.

Center for All Collegiate Information
http://www.collegiate.net

A clearinghouse for information on postsecondary education, this site links to almost all major college-related sites in a variety of useful ways.

College and University Home Pages
http://www.mit.edu:8001/people/
cdemello/univ.html

This links to more than 3,000 college and university home pages worldwide, this site is sorted alphabetically and geographically. Also links to other school information Web sites around the world.

College Board Online
http://www.collegeboard.org

Run by an association of 3,000 two- and four-year colleges, universities, and education associations, this site offers many services for educators plus good searches for colleges, career searches, and scholarships.

CollegeNET
http://www.collegenet.com

CollegeNet lets you search for two-year and four-year schools and offers links to school home pages, scholarship searches, and education and financial aid resources.

CollegeView
http://www.collegeview.com

Here you can search colleges by criteria including field of study, state, student body size, athletics, and cost. The site also offers multimedia profiles of more than 3,500 colleges, e-mail connections to college admissions offices, and links to college home pages.

fastWEB
http://www.fastweb.com

This is a database of more than 180,000 private sector scholarships, fellowships, grants, and loans. There is no fee for matching with your profile of skills and abilities.

FinAid: The Financial Aid Information Page
http://www.finaid.org

With links to online scholarship databases and to many other financial aid resources, such as aid for students over 30 and other special groups, this is a good site.

Mapping Your Future
http://www.mapping-your-future.org

The main focus of this site is selecting a postsecondary school and applying for financial aid.

Peterson's Education and Career Center
http://www.petersons.com

You'll find substantial information here on K-12 schools, colleges and universities, graduate study, studying abroad, summer programs, language study, distance learning, financial aid, and other topics. Search colleges alphabetically, geographically, by major, or by keyword.

Project EASI (Easy Access for Students and Institutions)
http://easi.ed.gov/index.html

Run by the U.S. Department of Education to help parents and students get financial aid, this site covers planning for your education, applying, receiving financial aid, and repaying your loan, with links to related Web sites. Free download or online view of *Preparing Your Child For College: A Resource Book for Parents.*

The Princeton Review
http://www.review.com/index.cfm

Search databases for colleges, business schools, law schools, and medical schools; then link to the schools' home pages. This site offers information on admissions, testing, financial aid, and programs. Experts moderate discussion groups on related topics such as the SAT, the GRE, and the Bar Exam.

National Association of Colleges and Employers (NACE)
http://www.jobweb.org

NACE serves colleges, employer organizations, students, and alumni. The site includes employer/college surveys, salary surveys of newly hired college graduates, a quarterly journal, and a biweekly newsletter.

U.S. News & World Report Colleges & Careers Center
http://www.usnews.com/usnews/edu/home.htm

From *U.S. News & World Report*, this site features college rankings, admissions, articles on careers and self-employment, links to financial aid sites, online discussion forums, a parents' guide, and campus culture stuff.

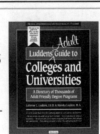

Networking for Everyone!

Connecting With People for Career and Job Success

By L. Michelle Tullier, Ph.D.

Networking is the key to business and professional success. And it's all here in this lively, entertaining book by a seasoned business professional, with many practical worksheets.

ISBN: 1-56370-440-4 ■ **$16.95**
Order Code: J4404

Cyberspace Resume Kit

How to Make a Snazzy Online Resume!

By Fred E. Jandt & Mary B. Nemnich

More than 80% of today's college graduates expect to use online resources to find jobs. This hands-on, how-to guide increases success rates with expert insight and information.

ISBN: 1-56370-484-6 ■ **$16.95**
Order Code: J4846

Job Search 101

Getting Started on Your Career Path

Edited by Pat Morton and Marcia R. Fox, Ph.D.

This book, edited by two long-time career guidance professionals, is filled with information and advice for first-time job seekers. Detailed sections on choosing the right career.

ISBN: 1-56370-314-9 ■ **$12.95**
Order Code: J3149

SuccessAbilities!

1,003 Practical Ways to Keep Up, Stand Out, and Move Ahead at Work

By Paula Ancona

With this book you can find more time in your busy day, handle conflicts like an old pro, balance work and family life, network, negotiate, and take charge of your career. A wonderful new book for the millions of people who want to succeed and get ahead.

ISBN: 1-56370-444-7 ■ **$14.95**
Order Code: J4447

Using the Internet & the World Wide Web in Your Job Search, 2nd Edition

The Complete Guide to Online Job Seeking and Career Information

By Fred E. Jandt & Mary B. Nemnich

There are thousands of job opportunities online, and this book shows you how to find them, with expert advice on everything from getting connected to getting the job.

ISBN: 1-56370-292-4 ■ **$16.95**
Order Code: J2924

Franchise Opportunities Handbook,

Revised Edition

A Complete Guide for People Who Want to Start Their Own Franchise

By LaVerne L. Ludden, Ed.D.

This reference book provides expert advice on selecting the right franchise—more than 1,500 listings by industry, with an alphabetical index for franchising participants.

ISBN: 1-57112-091-2 ■ **$16.95**
Order Code: P0912

JIST Ordering Information

JIST specializes in publishing the very best results-oriented career and self-directed job search material. Since 1981 we have been a leading publisher in career assessment devices, books, videos, and software. We continue to strive to make our materials the best there are so that people can stay abreast of what's happening in the labor market, and so they can clarify and articulate their skills and experiences for themselves as well as for prospective employers. **Our products are widely available through your local bookstores, wholesalers, and distributors.**

The World Wide Web

For more occupational or book information, get online and see our Web site at **www.jist.com**. Advance information about new products, services, and training events is continually updated.

Quantity Discounts Available!

Quantity discounts are available for businesses, schools, and other organizations.

The JIST Guarantee

We want you to be happy with everything you buy from JIST. If you aren't satisfied with a product, return it to us within 30 days of purchase along with the reason for the return. Please include a copy of the packing list or invoice to guarantee quick credit to your order.

How to Order

For your convenience, the last page of this book contains an order form.

24-Hour Consumer Order Line:
Call toll free 1-800-JIST-USA
Please have your credit card (VISA, MC, or AMEX) information ready!

Mail: Mail your order to:

JIST Works, Inc.
720 North Park Avenue
Indianapolis, IN 46202-3490
Fax: Toll free 1-800-JIST-FAX

JIST Order Form

Please copy this form if you need more lines for your order.

Purchase Order #: _____

Billing Information

Organization Name: _____

Accounting Contact: _____

Street Address: _____

_____

_____

City, State, Zip: _____

Phone Number: ( ) _____

Shipping Information (if different from above)

Organization Name: _____

Contact: _____

Street Address: (we *cannot* ship to P.O. boxes) _____

_____

_____

City, State, Zip: _____

Phone Number: ( ) _____

```
┌ ─ ─ ─ ─ ─ ─ ─ ─ ─ ─ ─ ─ ─ ─ ┐
          Phone:
|    1-800-JIST-USA         |
     Fax: 1-800-JIST-FAX
└ ─ ─ ─ ─ ─ ─ ─ ─ ─ ─ ─ ─ ─ ─ ┘
```

Credit Card Purchases: VISA_____ MC_____ AMEX_____

Card Number: _____

Exp. date: _____

Name as on card: _____

Signature: _____

Quantity	Order Code	Product Title	Unit Price	Total
			Subtotal	
			+Sales Tax *Indiana Residents add 5% sales tax.*	
			+Shipping / Handling *Add $3.00 for the first item and an additional $.50 for each item thereafter.*	
			TOTAL	

JiSt Works, Inc.
720 North Park Avenue
Indianapolis, IN 46202

JIST thanks you for your order!